Tat Tvam Asi

The Universal Message in The Bhagavad-gītā

SAM. DVACA

BLESSINGS

DR NATH SAMAVAYH

2/2/20

To

All the Arjunas of the world

Tat Tvam Asi

The Universal Message
in
The Bhagawadgita

DR. PATHIRONDA VISWAMBARA NATH
M.B.E.

Part 1

(Chapter 1-6)

MOTILAL BANARSIDASS
SINCE 1903 IN INDOLOGY

MOTILAL BANARSIDASS
INTERNATIONAL • DELHI

Second Revised and Enlarged Edition : Delhi, 2019
First Edition : Delhi, 1998

ISBN : 978-81-208-1584-1
(Set of 3 Parts) HB

Also available at

MOTILAL BANARSIDASS
41 U.A. Bungalow Road, Jawahar Nagar, Delhi 110 007
1 B, J S Compound, Kennedy Bridge, Nana Chowk, Mumbai 400 007
203 Royapettah High Road, Mylapore, Chennai 600 004
49, 8th F Main III Block, Jayanagar, Bengaluru 560 011
9, Panchanan Ghosh Lane, 1st Floor, Kolkata 700 009
Ashok Rajpath, Patna 800 004
Chowk, Varanasi 221 001

Published by
MOTILAL BANARSIDASS INTERNATIONAL
www.mlbdbook.com • mlbdbook@gmail.com
Printed by Nice Printing Press

Avadhoota Datta Peethadhipati
Jagadguru Paramapujya
Sri Sri Sri Ganapathy Sachchidananda Swamiji's
Karakamala Sanjata
Datta Peetha Uttaradhipati
Paramahamsa Parivrajakacharyavarya
SRI DATTA VIJAYANANDA TEERTHA SWAMIJI'S

***Blessings for the second edition of* Tat Tvam Asi**

Bhagavad Gita carries the essence of all sacred Scriptures. The study of Bhagavad Gita resolves all spiritual conflicts.

sarvōpaniṣadō gāvō dōgdhā gōpālanandanaḥ |
pārthō vatsaḥ sudhīrbhōktā dugdhaṁ gītāmr̥tam mahat ||

The collection of all Upanishads is the cow. He,who milks the cow is Krishna. Arjuna is the calf. The wise are the consumers of the milk, which is immortal nectar.

Bhagavad Gita is not the exclusive property of any one nation or any one group of people. It belongs to all humanity. Sastra is that which makes a decree. 'It should be so', it states categorically to benefit everyone. Like a scalpel it slices away sorrow and ignorance.

It is wrong to think that the study of Bhagavad Gita is suited only for the elderly. This science equally benefits both the young and the old.

In this world, there are only two paths; the Path of Action, and the Path of Knowledge. Bhagavad Gita clearly elucidates both these paths.

Bhagavad Gita awakens those who lie in a stupor of laziness. Bhagavad Gita gets tasks accomplished. Bhagavad Gita exhorts one to ever remain dedicated to duty.

'Personality Development Management Courses' are a norm these days. It can be proudly declared that there is no greater authority on the subject than the Bhagavad Gita.

Many renowned authors have based their works on the Bhagavad Gita. This work serves as the source material for all. It may be inferred that the chief intent of Sage Vyasa in composing the Mahabharata was to gift the Bhagavad Gita to the world.

Dr. P.V. Nath has dedicated his entire life for the spreading of the message of Bhagavad Gita. He is an individual who has faced many trials and tribulations in life. He stands as a model for others to follow. He is rendering great service both socially and spiritually. The support given to him by his wife Satyavati is certainly commendable.

In the vehicle called marriage, the husband and wife serve as the two wheels. This couple has amply proven that. Because of his wife's unstinting cooperation, Dr. Nath has been able to render great spiritual service.

SRI DATTA NARAYANA SMARANAM
SRI DATTA VIJAYANANDA TEERTHA SWAMIJI
MYSORE

FOREWORD

It is pure pleasure to subscribe a 'Foreword' to Dr. Nath's recorded reflections on the Bhagavad Gita. Dr. Nath started his illustrious career as a practitioner of the art and science of healing human ailments, but his long spiritual quest and the purity of his personal life, his dedication to the study of Bhagavad Gita and a life of total surrender to Lord Krishna have made him a healer of the soul. All those who have the benefit of his association are involved in the celebration of Gita Jnana Yagna. He now has the spiritual wealth and worth of a doctor, who has been spreading the lambent light of Bhagavad Gita across continents. He recorded in this precious book the foundational essentials of the philosophy of The Bhagavad Gita.

The scientist's explanation of the origin of life on earth and its evolution takes the mechanizing stand. That stand does not support the theological interpretation that there is a consciousness or purpose in evolution, is the advent of human life on this planet the result an accident? Many conditions needed to happen in a particular sequence before life could emerge on the planet. Statisticians tell us that if you put in your pocket ten coins numbered one to ten, give them a shuffle, take out one, put it back, give a shuffle and take out the second and so on the chances of your getting out the coins in a serial order of one to ten is one in ten thousand million. Therefore the odds are clearly against origin of life being the result of an accident. The earth is supposed to move around the sun in its elliptical orbit at a speed of 1000mph.

If the speed is less or more, the seasons will drastically change. The earth during its movement spins on its own axis. If the speed of the spin is a little more or little less the duration of days and nights change. If the moon was a little nearer to the earth than what it is. The oceans would rise and inundate the earth. If the bottom of the sea was one fathom deeper, all the oxygen would be absorbed. It is an arcane and mysteriously ordered beauty of creation. Is this all accidental and without any purpose?

The purpose of pursuit of spiritual knowledge is not to solve any problem but to transcend the plenary non–dual experience so that there is no longer any problem to be solved at all. As a scholar explains how the one non–dual Consciousness, that is the 'self', appears split into Cogniser, Cognition and object cognized, it is not possible to explain. To say that this apparent splitting is the work of Maya is to admit that it is in explicable. The purpose for which a study of the problem of knowledge is under–taken is not to solve the problem but to go beyond it. Western philosophers have readily accepted that 'mind' is the product of neurological frame work of the brain. Prof.John Searle, a Professor of Philosophy in California, says there is nothing much to explain and consciousness is an emergent property of the Brain. It is the first person phenomenal experience that we understand as consciousness.The concept of consciousness in the west is used by neurologists to describe our contemporary sense of the self. There is an answer to this dilemma in the Vedanta concept of consciousness. According to Vedanta, 'mind' is a subtle 'Antahkarana' illuminated by the 'self'. It is not the cogniser but only an instrumentof cognition. The appropriate mental mode is the window of consciousness manifesting as knowledge.

Swami Satprakashananda says:

"Vedanta stresses the cognitive mind and takes into account its four states or function (vrtti): deliberations (manas), determination (buddhi), egoism (ahamkara), and recollection (citta). In every external perception, these four are involved".

Dharmaraja Adhvarindra in his "Vedanta Paribhasha" speaks of the primary and secondary aims of Vedanta and the nature of liberation. Liberation is achieved only through 'Jnana' alone. Jnana alone brings about cessation of ignorance. The object of

'Jnana' is the identity of the individual self with the 'Brahman' 'Nitya' 'Anithya' 'Viveka' are the basis. Different systems of philosophy emphasize different means and methods for that 'knowledge'. While Vaishesikas rely on perception and inference, the Sankhya emphasizes perception, inference and 'Shabda'. The Vedantins believe in all the six means of knowledge like perception, inference, comparison, verbal testimony, presumption and non–apprehension. Vedanta holds knowledge as eternal pure consciousness manifested through mental states. The purpose of the pursuit of Vedanta is essentially the study of the Self– Athmanam Vidhi.

Swami Krishnananda of revered memory says that the proclamation of Yagnavalkya "Idam brahma, idam kshatram, ime lokah, ime devah, imani bhutani, idam sarvam yad ayam atma" is like a Brahmastra the sage is discharging against every kind of attachment. He says:

"Now, here, a thunderbolt is discharged by Sage Yajnavalkya when he says the Self also is everywhere. Imani bhutani, idam sarvam yad ayam atma. All the fourteen worlds are the Self. Here we will not find it so easy to accept it, because we cannot spatialise the concept of Self. Our Self cannot be somewhere else; it must be within us only. But, what does one mean by saying:

"all the worlds, all the gods, all this is the Self".

What is this that the Sage is telling us? What exactly is the Self? Can anyone tell us what the Self is? What meaning can we attach to this word?

There is myself, yourself, this self, that self! The self is something which cannot be externalized, objectified or spatialised in any way. The Self is the utter subjectivity of Universality. Whoever knows this possesses the whole world. He himself is the world".

In Indian philosophical thought Bhagavad Gita occupies a primordial position commanding great admiration. The two main characters Lord Krishna and Arjuna were the most fascinating. In its teachings the Bhagavad Gita:

"Breathes throughout a spirit of toleration which is an outstanding characteristic of Hindu thought. Whoever with true devotion worships any deity, in him I deepen that devotion;

and through it he fulfills his desire. Those that devotedly worship other gods, they also worship me though only imperfectly. The thought here is not, as it sometimes unfortunately is, that 'one man's God is another's devil, but that every conception of God, however crude or defective in itself, still has its own divine side and that it is not so much the nature of the object worshipped as the spirit in which the worshipper turns to it that counts.

In the Bhagavad Gita, the Lord himself assures that his bhakta shall not perish and the egalitarian definition of the bhakta in Lord's own words include four types of Bhakatas, including the one who seeks from the Lord worldly goods.

"Another fine reconciliation is to discover to golden mean between the two ideals of pravrtti and nivritti or of action and contemplation, as we might term the, preserving the excellence of both. Karma–yoga is such a mean. While it does not abandon activity, it preserves the spirit of renunciation. It commends a strenuous life, and yet gives no room for the play of selfish impulses. Thus it discards neither ideal, by combining them refines and ennobles both. That particular attitude of the soul which renunciation signifies still remains; only it ceases to look askance at action. In other words the Gita teaching stands not for renunciation of action, but for renunciation in action".

The Bhagavad Gita is both Moksha–shastra and psycho–therapy. It is the art and science of living too. Dr. Nath has brought out those precious nuggets from the Bhagavad Gita and has presented to us in simple and sincere style. In a sense Dr.Nath's reflection on the Bhagavad Gita hold a mirror to the purity of his own truth and surrender to the Lord's words are constant companions.

M.N.VENKATACHALIAH
(FORMER CHIEF JUSTICE OFINDIA)

NO.5A, SIR M.N.KRISHNA RAO
ROAD, BANGALORE–4-INDIA

CONTENTS

कृष्णाय वासुदेवाय नमः

Om Kṛṣnāya Vasudevaya namaḥ

I asked for strength and God gave me difficulties to make me strong,
I asked for wisdom and God gave me problems to solve,
I asked for prosperity and God gave me brawn and brain to work,
I asked for courage and God gave me dangers to overcome,
I asked for love and God gave me troubled people to help,
I asked for favours and God gave me opportunities,
I received nothing I wanted but I received everything I needed.

Om asato mā sad gamaya,tamaso mā jyotir gamaya,mṛtyor mā amṛtaṃ gamaya

Om śāntiḥ śāntiḥ śāntiḥ

Om Vasudeva-sutaṁ devaṁ kaṁsa- cāṇūra- mardanam Devaki paramānandaṁ Kṛṣṇaṁ vande' jagad-gurum

Ātmano mokṣārtham jagat hitāya ca
(The physical body with the Atman/The Soul within is to strive for Moksha/Liberation and for Universal welfare.)

O Lord Krishna,
Please make me blind for the pleasures of
the world from this mortal body,
Open my eyes of wisdom,
To realize Your immortal Divine nature;
Let my bodily organs express Your Divinity,
Light the lamp of antaratma,
Be a guide and sarathi in my path to attain salvation.
Please bless me to understand this
Adhyatma vidya.

Tat Tvam Asi - (That Pure Existence You Are)

PREFACE

At the outset I would like to make it clear that the commentary in this book on the slokas from the sacred text "Sreemad Bhagawadgita" is from what I have learnt from reading the commentaries on the subject and listening to the various discourses on the subject of spirituality from so many spiritual masters and great scholars. From the study of the sacred text one can find so many answers for the various problems faced in one's life.

I consider myself to be a farmer collecting the seeds of spirituality for the garden called "Tat Tvam Asi" to make it a beautiful garden of intellectual flowers. It is from so many sources and my presentation is only a compilation of my collection with an intellectual analysis of what I have read, what I have heard and what I have discussed with those who were interested in the philosophy. This has given me an insight into the intricate meaning of the important words in the sacred text. I hope that it attracts the attention of many and gives them answers to their problems in life and guides them in the right path to progress in life so that they could continue to contribute for the "Peace and Prosperity" of the beautiful universe we live in.

Having moved to UK in 1968, facing many problems in the new land, I was privileged to come across so many I could share and discuss on the Bhagawadgita.

The year 1998 is a very special year in my life. It was the year when the first edition of Tat Tvam Asi was released. It is also the year when I received the commendations from H.M. The Queen of England who awarded me with the prestigious award of M.B.E for services to the community.

I would like to offer my humble salutations to:

To my parents and my dear wife Satyavathi's parents,

The late .H.H.Sri TAPASWIJI MAHARAJ, a great soul who blessed us by visiting our house at Hospet several times between 1940–1954 and blessed me personally,

The late H. H. Sri MALLIGI MAHARAJ, another great soul who also visited our house frequently in 40's and 50's and blessed the family,

The late H. H. Sri HARI HARJI MAHARAJ who prevailed upon me to write the commentary when he visited UK for the 10th International Gita Conference in 1994 at Harrow and gave me his blessings,

H.H. Sri GANAPATI SACHCHIDANANDA SWAMIJI, Avadhoota Datta Peetham, Mysore who blessed me by giving opportunities to translate his life history into English, give discourses at Geseke (Germany) and Trinidad and continued to give His blessings so that the International Gita Foundation Trust (which was formed in 2002 for promoting the message from the sacred text) could continue to conduct annual Global Gita Conferences (16 so far) across the globe.

The late H.H. Sri VIDYAPRAKASHANANDA SWAMIJI of Sukha Brahma ashrama at Kalahasti, whose book Gita Makarandam was the first book on the Gita which clarified so many of my doubts,

The late H. H. Sri SWAMY CHINMAYANANDA whose commentaries on the Gita and the Upanisads are so wonderful to read and understand,

The late H. H. Sri. PRANAVANANDA SWAMIJI of Omkara Ashrama, the guru for Satya's family and with whom I have spent several pleasant and useful hours discussing various philosophical points,

H.H. Sri SUKHABODHANANDA SWAMIJI, Bangalore whose masterly presentations inspire so many across the globe,

H.H. Sri JAPANANDA SWAMIJI, Pavagada who carries the baton of Swamy Vivekananda and has put Karma Yoga, Bhakti

Yoga into practice and thereby assisting a large number of needy in the region,

The late Prof. NANJUNDA SASTRY, (retired English Professor) who corrected my first edition of Tat Tvam Asi. His knowledge of the shastras was immense and he guided me on various aspects of presentation of the first edition.

My sincere thanks to the trustees of the Hindu Mandir, Baxter Avenue, Newcastle Upon Tyne who allowed me to conduct Gita Classes at the temple every Thursday evening since 1990 and for the full co-operation extended by all the priests since 1990 and especially to Panditji Balakishan who has been the present priest for a number of years.

There are many more who I would like to salute and thank. But it is going to be difficult to name so many and here are the acknowledgements to some of them:

My dear wife Satya who sat for hours while writing this, gave valuable suggestions and helped in correcting this manuscript. Many of the commentaries I would say express her view and it is no exaggeration if I say she is the co–author of this book.

My two dear darling daughters Uma and Chandrika, who gave immense support and love to their father and put up with his fanatism on the Gita,

My dear grand–son Kiran, who has developed a keen interest in philosophy and has been discussing the philosophy of Gita on several occasions,

My dear sister–in–law, Hon'ble Justice Manjula Chellur, former Chief Justice of Mumbai High Court who took a lot of initiative in getting the book reach the publishers. During the period when I was otherwise engaged with family commitments and commitments of profession as a General medical practitioner she took the trouble in arranging the publication of the first edition of this book,

Hon'ble Justice Sri M. N. VENKATACHALIAH, Former Chief Justice of India who spent hours with me discussing the Hindu philosophy before publishing the first edition and gave a beautiful preface to the first edition of this book. He also has given the foreword for this edition.

My special thanks to Sri. G. M. RAO, Chairman, G.M.R group, Bangalore in supporting so many of the activities in promoting the message from the sacred text over the years.

Hundreds of friends including young children that are part of the regular Gita discussion group in our region, members of the monthly Gita satsang group have spent several hours discussing the commentary on the sacred text.

Discussing with them has helped to put forward many intricate points in a way that can be grasped by the modern mind.

I cannot forget the input from our guide dog Lindsay. Lindsay came into our life as a guide dog to help Satya. She was nearly 13yr old when Poojya HARI HARJ Swamiji suggested that I write the commentary on the Gita. The task needed work during Brahmi Mahurta (about 4am) period of the day. I was not used to get up that early. For some unknown reason (after the advice by Hari Har Ji Maharaj Swamiji), she started coming near the bed and nudging me to get her out to the toilet. It was not easy especially in winter months to do so. I had no choice than to take her out for few mins at that time of the day. She persisted with this for nearly 4 weeks. It was not easy to go back to bed after being woken up and I started my reading and writing. After 4 weeks, surprisingly she stopped nudging me but I had developed the habit of getting up at 4am and carry on the task of writing the book. I sincerely believe that it was a divine act that made Lindsay disturb my sleep and do the study. May Lord Krishna and Gita Maata bless her.

I will be failing in my duty if I do not thank Mr. N. P.Jain of Motilal Banarasidas, Publishers for agreeing to publish both the editions of this book. They are considered as the highly respected publishers in India on any texts concerning the Hindu philosophy. My grateful thanks to them for accepting the book for publication of the second edition.

The first person who introduced to the Gita was the swamiji from the Gita Mandir at Hospet. My mother used to take me to the mandir once a week. When I was about 7yr old, swamiji arranged for Gita recitation by the young. He wanted the children to recite the Gita. There were prizes on offer. Tempted by the prizes I memorized all the slokas from the first two chapters. This was my introduction to the Gita. My mother insisted that I should not let go of the practice and recite the entire two chapters at least once a day and when I am on any long distance journeys. I have not forgotten her advice and practice recitation of the Gita regularly every day even today.

My real learning of the sacred texts is from reading the various texts on Hindu philosophy and the Gita in general from the age of about 30yrs onwards. I dare say that as and when the life started showing the ugly side of it to me, mother Gita gave me the answers to the problems I faced and encouraged me to continue discharging my ordained duties. On several occasions when faced with difficulties in life, it is no exaggeration that I did slam the book and put it away. But it would be that way for only a day or two. The habit of reading and reciting the Gita which my mother introduced me at an early age helped me a lot in persevering with the task ahead.

As the days rolled into years, my faith in the sacred text has multiplied so many times.

I say that one should learn to analyse the In–depth meaning of the words in the sacred text and find not only the word meaning (vakyartha) but also,

Lakshyartha: directed to the aim of study,

Tatvartha: the spiritual essence in the word.

This is the way to progress in the spiritual path in one's life.

As I discussed with so many individuals and groups in my stay in UK since 1969 and with my frequent visits to India and other parts of the world, I found that there was need to present the contents of the sacred text in a format that suits the present generation. My efforts are directed to that group of people who want to know but who cannot understand and who want the same in a language they can understand and make it applicable to the life they have led in this so called modern world. My commentary is based on this line and I hope the second edition/Tat Tvam Asi reflects on this need to present the philosophy in a language which is easy and interesting to understand.

I will be failing in my duty if I do not acknowledge the immense help/support from:

My. Nephew, Mr. Phalgun Polepalli and

Mr.Terry Rann.

Who helped me in formatting the text to the requirements specified by the publishers and got it ready for publishing. My ignorance of the workings of the modern gadgets/computer was a major handicap and without these two, I could not have finished the work. Sincere thanks also to Mr.Watchaspati Pandey, Editor, Motilal Banarasidas.

I would like to acknowledge the technical support given to me by Prof. Dr. Sree Bahulkar, Honorary Secretary of Bhandarkar Oriental Research Institute, Pune, India who worked at putting diacritical marks on all the verses which was the condition put by the publishers. I am ever greatful to him for the time spent on this work.

HARI OM TAT SAT

Dr. P.V.Nath, MBE
Tapaswi
21 Beamish View,
Stanley
DH90XB, UK
snath@btinternet.com
00447779178430

INTRODUCTION

Life teaches us so many lessons. Sometime or other in their life some feel that they need to study and understand those texts that will assist in bringing about changes in their life for the better.

Gita is that text which was narrated to Arjuna by Lord Krishna that will help us not only to change our direction in life but with proper understanding assist us to reach that Supreme destination which is the abode of "Eternal Peace".

The first step forward is to make constant and regular efforts to learn the text. This is "abhyasa".

But, past habits take a long time to die. We need to learn to be patient. One cannot transform overnight. We need to bring slow, steady and subtle changes in our life. All along we should be prepared to accept the results of our own past actions/inactions conducted/not conducted without the basis of true knowledge:

What is needed is:

Willingness to learn

Take the decision to learn

Start walking in the new path chosen Develop the habit to practice (abhyasa)

Be patient, (nothing in life comes by the touch of a magic wand).

And learn to accept gracefully what is offered by the Lord (which includes the results of past actions).

The study of the sacred text, the Sreemad Bhagawadgita for success in the endeavour should follow this path.

"Sastra"

"Shasanaat Trayate its Satraha": that which protects by command is shastras.

The Gita is considered as a "Sastra" because it is an authoritative source of knowledge.

Sree Krishna like a loving parent gives commands several times in the Gita so that by following them we are protected from harm by our actions/inactions to us, our family, our loved ones and our universe.

"OMKARA":

It is also known as "Pranava akshara".

It is the first word used by our great spiritual masters of the past to express "Nirakara Nirguna Brahman. (pure fundamental energy with no form and no specific qualities attributed to it)" It is a "mantra" in its own merit and also it enhances the power of all other mantras when prefixed to them.

It is to be looked upon as a way of expressing the "Divine Energy" which is responsible for "Creation, sustenance and dissolution" and we should show our reverence to the same.

It is the first expression of the "Sound" of this energy which one can appreciate as emanating from the inner depths of the earth, the ocean, the sound of the expression of the fire, the sound of the force of the wind and the sound in the silence of the space. These are the five natural great elements and the energy in them is expressed as the sound "Om".

This sound has been given a form using the figure of number "3". The figure of number three is prominent in the depiction. The number "3" can be read in so many different ways and here is an attempt to bring those ideas out.

It is important not just to repeat the sacred word "Om" but to understand the concept behind it, the concept being "Divinity."

When one sees closely the representation of the syllable OM, three salient features can be noticed.

They are: number 3

A curvy line projecting from the middle of the number 3

A circular spot (bindu) over a saucer like representation at the top. We should understand the significance of the number 3 in it.

The "Bindu" at the top represents the primordial energy: "The Parabrahman". Sri Krishna: sloka 33, chapter 13:

O Bharata just as the one sun illumines the whole world, so also the Lord of the field illumines the whole field.

Understanding the significance of the number "3" with reference to this sloka will help us to understand the significance of the sacred syllable.

There are several sets of three in relation to our body and life.

The word "Krutsnam" from the sloka refers to all of these.

They are:

The Trinity as "Brahma, the creator, Vishnu, the protector and Shiva, the destroyer,

The three "Shaktis" (powers) needed to achieve success: Itcha Shakti, Medha Shakti and Kriya Shakti,

Representation of "Time" as "Past, Present and Future",

The three states of existence: Jagrata, Swapna and Sushupta states: wakeful, dream and deep sleep states,

The three gunas: Satvic, Rajasic and Tamasic (Pure, Passionate and Indolent),

The three bodies: Gross, subtle and causal (sthoola, sukshma and karana sharira),

The three spheres of existence: The earth, the regions above the earth and the regions below the earth (bhooloka, Swarga loka and Patala loka).

The senses, mind and the intellect

The three aspects of life on earth: shrishti, sthithi, pralaya – creation, sustenance and dissolution. –(only nitya/constant factor is Parabrahman)

Beyond the knowledge of the three Vedas Rig,Yajur, Sama Veda.

Beyond the three sections of the Vedas: Karma, Upasana and Jnana kandas.

Trivikrama –Vamana—covered the earth, space and nether worlds with his three steps.

The three states of sufferings (tapatraya) --Adhiboutika, Adhyatmika and Adhi Daivika.

Beyond the three times in a day-trikala—morning, noon and sandhya.(meaning, "He" is Eternal)

To unite with: Father, Mother, Guru

The three duties: Yajna, Dana, Tapas.

The number "3" in "Om" refers to all of the above.

The tail projecting from the number 3 should be understood as: "Beyond all these three".

Beyond the Trinity of Gods—Supreme Parabrahman without a name and form and without any qualities,

Beyond the confines of "Time" (Kalatita), Beyond the three states of experiences –"Turiya", Beyond the three gunas –"Gunatita",

Beyond the three bodies –gross, subtle and causal, "Supreme Parabrahman",

Beyond the Vedas,

The one sun illumines the whole world, so also the Lord of the field (Parabrahman) illumines the whole field, says the Lord .

The Bindu" (dot at the top of the syllable) represents the "Light of Parabrahman illuming all".

This is the message to understand by the number 3, the curve and the dot above the number "3"

The bindu/dot:

The entire universe we know of and what is beyond what we know of is sheltered under the sky which is in the shape of an upside down saucer.

The Supreme Parabrahman, with no form and qualities envelopes the entire universe and is beyond its boundaries. "He" represented as the "Dot" at the top which is placed just above the saucer shaped mark.

One can say that the saucer shaped drawing is an inverted sky representation. The Parabrahman is beyond the sky, one can interpret.

Overall, one can say that the Parabrahman as "The Dot" (nirakara, nirguna) is enveloping the entire universe, is the light of it and He is beyond it also.

This is described in the hymn "Poornamadhah Poornamidam"-

It is the invocatory Shanti (Peace) mantra from the Isa Upanisad which is part of Shukla Yajurveda.

Auṃ pūrṇamadaḥ pūrṇamidam pūrṇāt pūrṇamudacyate
pūrṇasya pūrṇamādāya pūrṇamevāvaśiṣyate
oṃ śāntiḥ śāntiḥ śāntiḥ

That (Brahman) is whole,
This (creation) is also whole,
From that whole (Brahman) this whole(Creation) came out
But, even though this whole has come out of that whole,
Yet, that whole remains whole/completely only.

Poornam: whole; complete. Adam: That; Poornam Idam: This whole; Poornaat: from that whole, Poornam udachyate: this whole comes out; Poornasya: if from that whole; Poornam adaya: this whole is taken out; Poornam eva; whole only; Avashishyate: remains. That (Brahman) is whole:

The "Dot" on top of the syllable OM, represents "Poornam" meaning "Whole." He pervades the entire universe we know of and what we do not know off and beyond it also.

"He" is beyond all and above all and so is inserted on the top. This (Creation) is also whole:

The number three, what it represents and what is beyond that it represents is the "Entire universe". This is also "whole" but within "that whole" which is "Parabrahman."

From that whole, (Supreme Brahman),

This whole (entire creation) has come out.

If from that (adam) whole (Parabrahman), This (idam) whole is taken out (the universe), "That" whole only still remains.

We can understand this by looking at the human body:

The entire human body is enveloped by the Parabrahman and inside the body is the divine energy of Parabrahman that gives it the life.

This is to be looked as "Viswa Roopa" (Vision of the Universal form of Parabrahman/macrocosm). This is "Whole" and remains "whole" at all times. It is not dependent upon the individual cells. The Parabrahman is not dependent upon the creation.

Every individual cell/microcosm inside the body is a living entity on its own and is said to be complete (whole) on its own. It has a limited independent existence.

The death of the individual cell does not affect the body.

But, the death of the physical body means death of the cell too.

The Supreme, (the Dot, bindu) is beyond time and is present at all times,

We come out of that Supreme energy and are inside (enveloped by) the Supreme energy,

The Supreme energy is constant and is there at all times.

"He" is beyond "Time, Space and Causation".

We are limited by "Time, Space and Causation."

What is Bhagawadgita ?

The sacred text Sreemad Bhagawadgita as it is popularly known is a dialogue between Lord Krishna, the Divine incarnate and Arjuna. With reference to the Bhagawadgita, the Gita is that through the medium of which Sri Krishna has narrated the nuances of Brahma Vidya. Hence it is also known as Krishna Geeta. Bhagawadgita is the nectar of immortality given to the mankind by Lord Krishna, the incarnate of Parabrahman in Dwapara Yuga presented in the form of a dialogue between Krishna and Arjuna during the battle of Kurukshetra between the Pandavas and the evil Kauravas. It dates back to 3067 BCE approximately 5085 yrs and its philosophy still holds true for the mankind.

It consists of a total of 701 slokas divided into 18 chapters with each chapter given a specific title which ends with the word "Yoga".

It was upadesha (instruction/teaching) of the summary of the Upanisads from Sri Krishna to Arjuna and it is the "adesha" (command) to mankind on how to live and be a useful member of the society.

It was narrated by Sri Krishna to Arjuna.

Sanjaya had the blessings of Sage Veda Vyasa to visualize the battle and narrate to his Emperor Dhritarashtra.

It was incorporated by Bhagawan Veda Vyasa who compiled the epic Mahabharata in its section titled "Bheeshma Parva."

The Gita is an approved and tested tool by the masters whose only wish was "Universal Welfare." It is the tool for uplifting each one of us spiritually and for destroying our ego.

It is a navigational tool that helps one to negotiate the obstacles in the spiritual journey in quest of "The Eternal Bliss."

It is for reorganization of the mind and brings about "Renaissance."

It is for reorganization of lives and brings about "Transformation."

It is Moksha Sastra for rare few who look for "Moksha."(Liberation)

It is Dharma Sastra for those who want to lead the life of "Righteousness." with minimal pains and sorrows.

It is Jivana Sastra (life of living) for those who want to live the life full of peace.

It is considered to be the summary of 108 Upanisads.

The Upanisads in turn are the summary of the four Vedas.

The Vedas are the "Revealed Sacred Texts" for the Hindus and are the most ancient texts on philosophy.

It incorporates the "Sanatana dharma" (the most ancient and accepted path of righteousness by the learned scholars/rishis of the past)

To understand the true meaning incorporated in the sacred text, it will be useful for the reader to have the knowledge of the epic "Mahabharata." Understanding the story of Mahabharata helps greatly to follow the Gita.

Upanisad, Brahma Vidya, Yoga Sastra.

Amongst all forms of life on this earth man is the only one who has got the fully developed reasoning capacity known as "Buddhi." Unfortunately this can get perverted with what is known as "Ego"/ selfishness.

Man needs that knowledge which releases him from the clutches of the ego. Upanisads, Yoga sastras and Brahma Vidya are the tools to get the release. We need these texts and the guru who helps us to understand them.

How to make use of the birth as human?

Buddhi/intelligence will help us to plan and build our life. We, the humans are blessed with this capacity.

We, because of the sense organs which relate with the world around have built a so called cage around ourselves. This is fortified by the ego.

We need to break this cage and come out of it.

Yoga Sastras, Upanisads and Brahma Vidya are the tools to break open the cage and get release.

Unfortunately till we realize who we really are (Atma swaroopa) and manage to reach our inner Self (Atman) we have to undergo several births and deaths. In this journey we need the buddhi that does not get perverted and ruin us.

Sri Krishna, the Lord incarnate has summarized the Upanisads, Brahma Vidya and Yoga sastras into one in the form of the Bhagawadgita and given it to us through the medium of Arjuna. This is the sacred text which is the best manual for our life's journey.

For this we need the blessings of the guru.

The true definition for a guru is "He who gives tatva jnanopadesha" (Teaches us all about The Truth).

Mantras are given by mahatmas (great souls) to bless us but guru does not give mantropadesha but imparts the light of knowledge of the sastras.

Jagadguru Krishna has given us this light of knowledge in the form of the Gita. We have to use it to open up the "Eye of Knowledge" and thereby see where we are going, what obstacles are in the way and how to overcome the obstacles.

Each chapter in the Gita ends with a statement asserting that the sacred text is: Upanisad, Brhamavidya and Yoga Sastra

And it is a dialogue between Sri Krishna and Arjuna.

Upanisad: (sitting down near): sitting down near the guru/ teacher to receive spiritual instructions to expel the ignorance.

Upa: near; ni: down; sad: to sit.

Deeper significance of the word "Upa ni sad".

"Sad" (pronounced as "shad"): that to get release from the cycle of births and deaths and that which confers Liberation.

"ni": "Nischala Tatva": Know that Truth which undergoes no change. (Ni— changeless). That which has no change is "Atma Tatva". (Eternal Truth – which is Atman)

Upa: near.

To sit near that which is changeless, which is eternal knowledge to get released from the cycle of births and deaths and which confers "Moksha" is "Upanisad."

That by which the body has life in it,

That, in the absence of which the body has no life in it, is the "Life Force –Atman" and to sit near "that" is "Upa."

Sadguru is the personification of the Parabrahman and The Vedas are the form of Brahman. These are that which the seeker sits near to listen/study, understand, and clarify doubts so that he/she can change the outlook in their life, drop the body identification and thereby achieve Liberation.

These two are the mediums for reaching the life's destination (moksha).

Upanisads are considered to be the last portion of the Vedas and are popularly known as "Vedanta".

Our sacred ancient seers dwelled on some basic questions concerning the life.

What is the origin of existence?

Where does one go after death?

Where can one get happiness which does not end in sorrow?

Who am I? and similar questions relating to the life and its experiences on this earth.

They sat in deep contemplation trying to get an answer to these dilemmas.

They came to a unanimous conclusion that the entire universe was created by the will of "Supreme Divine Energy" (primordial energy) which they called as "Parabrahman".

They considered that this was un–manifest with no form (Nirakara) and with no attributes/ qualities (Nirguna). From it arose the "First Primordial Sound" that reverberated and enveloped the entire universe known and unknown to the mankind. They called this "Primordial Sound" as "OM".

They heard and visualized a number of sacred words during the state of deep contemplation and felt that they were instructions from an unknown divine source.

The masters contemplated deeply on what they heard during deep meditation, analyzed them to the best of their capacity and developed deep reverence to the same.

There were no written texts in the earlier days. The only method of instruction was "oral" and passed on from the teacher (guru) to the student (shishya).

These mantras which were heard and then passed on came to be designated as "Vedas".

The Veda mantras are those mantras which the teachers had heard and which was taught to the students and passed down to subsequent generations. The subject was kept alive by this method.

As they arose from a source which had no known form and qualities they said it was "apourusheyam" meaning "that which came without the effort on the part of human".

As they were heard only and not taught they came to be known as "sravanas". (sravana: to hear).

It is believed that the mantras heard were far too many and were not in any order (unfortunately what we have of Vedas now is only a small portion of the original). Credit to Bhagawan Veda Vyasa who undertook the task of collecting the Veda mantras from all available sources and compiling them into four Vedas.

These are: Rig Veda, Sama Veda, Yajur Veda and Atharva Veda:

Each one of these Vedas was divided into three sections:

Karma Kanda dealing with mantras and rituals and sacrifices to worship the Supreme,

Upasana Kanda: Personal teaching of the spiritual content of the Vedas. The seekers came to the master, sat very near to the master (meaning with their minds sitting near and getting totally absorbed in what was taught),

Jnana Kanda: Deep contemplation on what was taught, developing total knowledge of the Supreme, annihilation of ego and uniting with the Supreme and thus experiencing the total unalloyed bliss (Ananda).

The subject matter of Jnana Kanda is the essence of the Vedas. It is known as Vedanta which is the culmination in quest of "spiritual knowledge" by the seeker. These are the Upanisads that deal with the subject matter of Vedanta.

There are more than 108 Upanisads. Even these are not easy to understand. Sri Krishna, out of compassion to mankind has summarized the contents of the Upanisads into the sacred text: The Sreemad Bhagawadgita.

It is considered to be the simplest form of the Vedas for the mankind in general.

The experts agree that the contents of the Bhagawadgita fit in with the Maha Vakya

"Tat Tvam Asi" (Thou Art That) from Sama Veda.

The first six chapters deal with "Tvam" (Thou) aspect of the mantra, The second six chapters deal with "Tat" (tat) aspect of the mantra and the last six chapters deal with "Asi" (art) aspect of the mantra.

On this basis, the title of this book is "Tat Tvam Asi."

Origin of life:

The rishis in their meditation came to the conclusion that the life existed because of energy. In the absence of "the energy" the physical body is considered to be "Dead". While alive the energy was enveloped by the five elements of nature known collectively as Pancha Maha Bhutas". These are: "The earth (bhoomi); water (apo); fire (anila); air (vayu) and space (antarikshaha).

This is true of all forms of life on the earth. Each form is given a name. The body with the energy within gets a form (roopa) and a name (nama). The conclusions by the masters were:

The energy pervades the universe at all times and is constant. (the physicists of the day say that the "co–efficient" of energy is constant at all time).

The same energy is inside all forms of life.

The energy was the same yesterday, same today and will be same tomorrow but its manifestation may vary.

The energy is not partial to any one single individual. It gives results in proportion to the efforts one puts in. (like the farmer sowing the seeds. Results for the farmer will be dependent on the type of seeds put in, the soil, and the environment and the maintenance during the period of growth. The energy does not favour any particular farmer. Even a murderer/most wicked one will get the results if he/she follows the rules.)

The energy sustains life.

In its primordial form the energy is not seen by anybody.

It is all powerful.

It is beyond comprehension at physical, mental levels of perception (one has to transcend these levels of perception to comprehend it).

The rishis gave this primordial energy with no form and no qualities a name and said it was "Nirakara, Nirguna Brahman."

For the purpose of meditation and thanksgiving to the benefits one got out of this energy they gave it a form and called it as "OM." This became the "Pranava Akshara."

They further postulated that the "Parabrahman" decided to have a play (Leela) and create life in the universe. This energized the five great elements first.

Brahma with four heads came forth from this energy during the leela. This was "Saguna Sakara Brahma" and was given the command to create life.

Brahma out of his mind created life. These were the four mind born sons of Brahma (manasa putras). They were: Sanaka, Sanandana, Sanatkumara, and Sanatsujata.

As the leela progressed men, women and other forms of life were created by Brahma.

On an individual basis:

The spark of energy from the Supreme Energy of Parabrahman during the leela, the Atman, got united with the five gross elements of nature which formed the physical body over the Atman. The physical body developed the intellect and the mind along with the sense organs and organs of action. With all these the Atman associated and developed unity with the world around.

There are three constituents in a living entity, with the Atman within.

They are:

Subtle body: the intellect and the mind,

Gross physical body.

The five pranas (Prana, apana, vyana, samana and udana),

The Atman developing the association with the subtle body forgets its true nature and develops "I" ness (individuality) and this leads to "ego" (ahamkara).

The ego in turn because of false identification with the body suffers pains, experiences pleasures; happiness and sorrow; feels victory/gain as the case may be by developing likes and dislikes with the objects of the world.

The rishis came to the conclusion that the only way to come out the misery of life is by realizing one's true identity as the Atman and to withdraw the association of the body to its surroundings. This was the only way to experience the "unalloyed happiness" and they said it was "Moksha" (Liberation") from bondage with the physical world.

The masters concluded that:

OM is Truth of eternal/Absolute existence –Sat,

The total/complete knowledge/Absolute knowledge –Chit and

The Happiness –Ananda.

With the association of the nature, it gets a name and form (nama, roopa).

The purpose of human life they said was to realize the true identity as the spark of Parabrahman, try to be released from shackles of worldly life and experience the eternal happiness of unity with Parabrahman. But, they said, that each individual has to fulfil the role as humans on earth, behave humanely and live the life of human as long as the body is alive. Expressing the divinity through thought, speech and action was the way to live, they said.

Sri Krishna through the medium of the Gita has emphasised the same and put the same into an easy format to understand.

Yoga Sastra:

Yoga – to unite

Sastra: authoritative scriptures concerning "Parabrahman" and the creation of life on this universe. They are for the moral and spiritual welfare of life.

The union of the ego, its merging with the Atman is Yoga,

Union of the Atman with Paramatman is Yoga.

The method to achieve this unity is also Yoga.

He who practices yoga is considered to be a Yogi.

The Yoga that brings this union which results in the experience of "Ananda" (bliss) that does not end in sorrow is Yoga Sastra.

The Gita specifically deals with such union and is a Yoga Sastra.

Brahma Vidya:

The primordial energy which is un–manifest energy is "nirakara" (no form) and "nirguna" (no qualities). It is also known as "Nirguna Nirakara Brahman."

This manifests in various ways (forms of energy) each one with forms and properties of its own. This is the "Saguna Sakara Brahman" (with qualities and form).

The knowledge of "Omkara" (OM is Brahman) is Brahma Vidya,

The knowledge of individual and universal existence is Brahma Vidya,

The knowledge of the welfare of the individual and the universe is Brahma Vidya,

That knowledge which teaches the lesson that the individual is not a single entity but only a part of the universe is Brahma Vidya.

The ancient seers with the welfare of life on this universe (sarve jana sukhino bhavantu) gave us this Brahma Vidya.

Sri Krishna through the medium of the Gita has given us this Brahma Vidya in a simplified format easier to understand and follow.

TAT TVAM ASI

(An explanation to the title of this book)

"Tat Tvam Asi" (Thou art that) is one of the four great proclamations known as "Maha Vakyas", each one of the four from one of the four Vedas asserting the "Truth" about Parabrahman.

"Tat: that"—"The Truth (The Supreme Consciousness) to be apprehended through sravana (listening), manana (recollecting) and nidhi dhyasa (concentrating)." This denotes the Parabrahman with no name and form and attributes.

"Tvam: you"

"Asi: are".

The Bhagawadgita is considered to fit in with the Mahavakya "Tat Tvam Asi".

The spiritual seeker in search of the answer to the question of "who am I" (his true identity) approaches the guru (with total faith and devotion) and puts forward his question:

The master starts by defining what Brahman (essential Knowledge/nature about oneself) is:

He starts off with the proclamation "Prajnanam Brahma". (knowledge is Brahman) Next, the master turns towards the seeker and roars the truth—Tat Tvam Asi. (Thou art that)

This is the upadesha vakya (teaching/advice) from the master to the disciple, who then goes into the detailed study on the subject and lets the student meditate on the statement.

The seeker meditating on "The Truth", examines himself analytically and comes to the conclusion "Ayam Atma Brahma". (This Atman is Brahman. considered as anubhava vakya--that comes from practical experience)

This comes from anubhava. (experience)

The seeker comes back to the master. The master enquires on what he has learnt? The seeker after having experienced the Truth and living constantly aware of the Truth happily pronounces:

"Aham Brahmasmi" (I am Brahman).

These four statements are from the four Vedas and are collectively known as "Maha Vakyas" (great proclamations).

Prajñānam Brahma – " from Aitareya Upanisad, Rig Veda.

Ayam Atmā Brahma - "This Self (Atman) is Brahman", Mandukya Upanisad, Atharva Veda,

Tat Tvam Asi- "Thou art That", Chandogya Upanisad, Sama Veda,

Aham Brahmāsmi - "I am Brahman", or "I am Divine", Brihadaranyaka Upanisad, Yajur Veda.

The essence of Advaita Vedanta has been brought out so beautifully by Jagadguru Shankaracharya in Manisha Panchakam. It consists of 5 verses out of which four verses are asserting the essence of the Maha Vakyas. (it is recommended that those who are interested should make an attempt to get and read this text).

There are a total of 18 chapters in the Gita.

The first six chapters deal with "Tvam" (Thou) aspect of the mantra,

The second six chapters deal with "Tat" (tat) aspect of the mantra and

The last six chapters deal with "Asi" (art) aspect of the mantra.

There is another school of thought which says that:

The first six chapters deal with "Karma",

Second six chapters deal with "Bhakti" and

The last six chapters deal with "Jnana".

On this basis they say that:

The contents of the first six chapters constitute "Karma Shatka",

The second six chapters, "The Bhakti Shatka" and

The last six chapters constitute "Jnana Shatka"

(Shatka—meaning "section consisting of six chapters".)

Let us now briefly look into the three words of the mahavakya "Tat Tvam Asi."

Tat: That,

Tvam: thou,
Asi: Are
You are really that Parabrahman.

Tvam: Thou, You.

The sastras say that the "Parabrahman" is subtler than the subtlest, all pervading, within and without all and beyond the comprehension by the senses, the mind and the intellect. If it is so, how can one find out about "That Force"?

It is by the process by way of negation, known as "Ne'ti, Ne'ti" meaning "Not this, not this." The teacher in his explanation about the Parabrahman uses the day to day examples of what is known, seen, understood by the student about the world he is living in and keeps on negating that and says "That is not, that is not" and finally leads him into the inner world of the student himself. It is "Tvam".

"You" are "that" which you are searching

Tat Tvam Asi-

On this line of thought: the first six chapters of the sacred text deal with "Tvam" aspect of Tat Tvam Asi.

The first chapter is "Arjuna Vishada Yoga".

Despondency makes the seeker/ individual turn towards the idea of God for help.

The second chapter: Samkhya Yoga. It gives the summary of the complete knowledge for the spiritual seeker for union with the Supreme.

Third chapter: Karma Yoga. The seeker is introduced to the basics of how to conduct actions.

Fourth chapter: Jnana Yoga. The seeker is given basic introduction to the knowledge concerning the identity of the Atman/Parabrahman.

Fifth chapter: Karma Sanyasa Yoga. The seeker is told that desire–less actions and surrendering the fruits of action is the means to unite with the Supreme.

Sixth chapter: Dhyana Yoga/Atma Samyama Yoga. The seeker is given the technique of meditation on "Union with the Atman within."

Tat: "That".

Chapters 7–12 conform to the "Tat", the Parabrahman.

7th Chapter: Jnana Vijnana Yoga. The seeker is asked to convert the knowledge into wisdom and unite with the Parabrahman.

8th chapter: Akshara Parabrahma yoga. "Who/what is Tat", the Parabrahman is discussed in this chapter.

9th chapter: Rajavidya, Rajaguhya Yoga: It gives information on the most secret knowledge concerning the most secret of all secrets (Parabrahman).

10th chapter: Vibhuti Yoga. The various manifestations of Parabrahman are described in this chapter.

11th chapter: Viswaroopa Sandarshana Yoga. The physical description of the Universal form of the Parabrahman is given in this chapter.

12th chapter: Bhakti Yoga. The devotional practice to unite with the Supreme is given in this chapter.

Asi: "Art". (asserting the Truth of who you are)

13th chapter: Kshetra Kshetrajna Vibhaga Yoga. This chapter gives a description of the field (individual mind) and the knower of the field (Atman within).

14th chapter: Gunatraya Vibhaga Yoga: This chapter deals with the three inherent basic qualities in the mind of the individual.

15th chapter: Purushottama Prapti Yoga. This chapter gives means of uniting with the Supreme.

16th chapter. Daivasura sampat vibhaga yoga. This chapter is about the divine and demonical qualities inside the mind of the seeker.

17th chapter: Sraddhatraya Vibhaga Yoga: This chapter is about the three types of faiths (in the life) one may have.

18th chapter: Moksha Sanyasa Yoga. The final chapter gives advice to the seeker to sincerely drop the idea of "Moksha" (Liberation) and to bring out the total divinity from within in all actions and to attain Peace and prosperity not just for him but for the entire life in this universe.

ISAVASYA UPANISAD

This Upanisad is one of the ten main Upanisads (out of nearly over 108) and is from Yajur Veda.

It has only 18 mantras and is also known as "Mantropanisad."

Two great rishis Kanva and Madhyandina have been given the honor of being its authors.

The 1st sloka:
Om îshâ vâsyamidam sarvam yat kiñca jagatyâm jagat, tena tyaktena bhuñjîthâ mâ gridhah kasya sviddhanam.

All things whatsoever move in this universe and the universe itself is clothed by the Lord. Thou should enjoy by abandonment, covet not anybody's wealth.

Isavasyam idam: indwelling or clothed by the Lord (Isha)

Yat kincha jagatyaan jagat: whatever in this universe, the moving world.

Tena tyaktena bhunjitha: therefore by Him, by abandonment (by that which is left) may enjoy,

Ma grdhah kasya svid dhanam: do not covet anybody's wealth.

Idam Sarvam vasyam: all this clothing (enveloping, pervading). What is "all this"?

It is the "Loka" (world, sphere) we perceive.

The total of impulses received from the five sense organs,

The interpretation of the impulses by the mind,

The analysis by the intellect, together constitute our world/loka.

The general consensus of the majority on what the world perceived is "all this" referred to in this sloka.

As the physical body consisting of the sense organs, mind and the intellect are alive because of the life principle "Atman" within,

"The Atman" is considered to be its master and "The Paramatman" as the master of this universe.

We need special knowledge to recognize this and this knowledge comes from the Vedas. Sri Krishna has given this knowledge in His maha/great upadesha, "The Gita."

Isavasyam idam: this, which is enveloped. "This" refers to that which is moving in this universe including the universe which is constantly in motion. ("moving" is not moving from "a" to "b" but moving in course of time and so includes plants, animals, birds and all other forms of life in this universe.

Yat kincha: "whatever is in this universe." It is not just man but whatever that has a spark of life in them due to the presence of the life's energy within.

All are enveloped by Him.

"May enjoy" by abandonment: enjoy the presence of Lord within by realizing Him. The enjoyments one experiences with the objects from the world around are momentary and sooner or later end in sorrow. The total happiness is when one cognises the Lord within. It simply means developing the sense of detachment (abandonment) to this world and learning the art of associating with the Lord within.

We should not misunderstand and consider that we must run away from this world. Many consider "sanyasa" as abandoning the possessions/attachments in life. This is not true and one does not get enjoyment from such so called act of renunciation.

Sri Madhvacharya has given a beautiful explanation to the words:

"Tena Tyaktena Bhunjitha". He says enjoy whatever is given away to you by the Lord.

What is given away to us by the Lord?

This is discussed in detail in sloka 31, chapter 4, the Gita— yajna shishtamruta bhujo):

After contributing to the welfare of the society and the nature and supporting the spiritual institutions/temples what is left is for personal and family needs. This is what the Acharya means with this statement: "enjoy whatever is given away to you by the Lord."

Do not covet anybody's wealth: it simply means "earn by righteous means". Whatever earned by unrighteous means is considered to be stolen property.

"Renounce the fleeting world and the fleeting objects, renounce the pleasures you get from them, recognize that the "Lord is all this". See the Self in you and in all and then you will experience the "Bliss".

This is the summary of this sloka and also the message from the Gita.

Sanatana Dharma:

The four paths towards "self–perfection" constitute the "Sanatana Dharma". The Hindu philosophy advocates four paths depending on the temperament of individuals to experience the "Bliss" of union with the Parabrahman.

The Bhagawadgita encompasses these four paths for "Self–Realization".

These are:

Karma----- actions;

Jnana—-----------------knowledge;

Bhakti—---------------- devotion;

Dhyana—-------------- meditation.

Self–realization is the result of realizing one's own true nature of "Sat Chit Ananda" which is nothing but a spark of "The Parabrahman". To unite with this "Truth" and experience the "Bliss" is "Self-Realization". This is "Moksha" "Liberation". Swami Vivekananda proclaims loudly that it is the "Birth Right" of every individual and not just for selected few.

The three Shaktis:

To achieve/gain something one needs "Strength" and this in Sanskrit is "Shakti". It is the inherent power in each one of us but due to accumulation of impurities in the journey of life this power gets masked.

There are basically three types of "Shakti" the masters say.

They are:

Itcha Shakti—power of the will/desire,

Medha Shakti – power of intelligence/knowledge and

Kriya Shakti— – power in actions.

One needs the strength of desire, use the strength of intelligence and put into action the power to get what is desired.

Dhyana Yoga: yoga of meditation. It is to unite with the "Power" within which is "The Atman" and with the Supreme Parabrahman. This is achieved by perfect "Itcha Shakti".

Jnana Yoga: it is Yoga of knowledge. Making use of the "Itcha" and using the intelligence/Medha Shakti inherent in each one of us and taught to us by the learned masters we can unite with the Supreme Parabrahman".

Karma Yoga: it is yoga of action. The actions that assist one to wipe off the impurities in the mind and unite with "Parabrahman" is "Karma Yoga", it is the "Kriya Shakti" and needs Itcha and Jnana Shakti".

This brings us to Bhakti Yoga". We will discuss this topic in detail in chapter 12.

What is Bhakti?

"Bhava Shakti" is Bhakti. It is Bhavana. What is "Bhavana"?

It is– "conception, imagination, thought, idea."

The power/Shakti that imagines a Super Power/Divinity and dedicates totally to that power with Supreme Love is "Bhavana Shakti".

Another appropriate word for Bhakti is "Prema". "Prema" is "Love". That act which offers total dedicated love to the loved one without any expectation of returns/reward is true "Prema". In Sanskrit it is described as an act without "Pratiphala Apeksha" (actions towards the Supreme without expectations).

Bhakti Yoga is Yoga of devotion. That which is truly "Prema Bhakti" which is triggered by the thought/bhavana of "Love for Supreme" is Bhakti Yoga.

Let me stress one more point at this juncture.

There are three ways one can approach to get what they want/ achieve in life. As we are in the topic of "Divinity" let us take it as:

a) I want God

b) I want God also

c) I Want God alone.

Those who with Bhavana Shakti pursue the path "I want God alone" will be able to experience the Bliss.

True bhakti starts off as two different entities –the God and the devotee. The aim is the union of the devotee with the God. This results in experience of "Total unalloyed Bliss" which is union with the Supreme". Sri Krishna says in the 12th chapter that the Bhakta and He (Krishna) are one and the same.

Contrary to this is "Kama" which is "desire." The desire also starts with two entities– the object of desire and the individual with the desire. The happiness one gets on achieving the desired object, we will learn in the Gita is short lived and is followed by pain and sorrow in course of time.

The Santana Dharma to attain Liberation/experience the "Bliss" can be achieved by any one of the four paths enumerated.

One must be clear that the four paths are not separate entities. As a matter of fact they intermingle with each other and towards the end it is a combination of these four paths that leads one to self–perfection.

The Gita says:

All paths mingle with each other, Real karma gives one jnana,

Real jnana makes one perform proper karma, Real dhyana assists one to unite with knowledge and perform actions as prescribed in the sastras.

We will discuss the four paths in detail as we go through the 18 chapters in the sacred text.

Moksha and Samsara

What is Moksha?

General consensus is "Liberation".

"Liberation from what" is the burning question?

Liberation from cycles of birth and death is considered as "Moksha". "Mukti/Total freedom" is another word used to describe Moksha.

"Mukti" is free and unaffected by the "Panchakosas" (the five sheaths: annamaya, pranamaya, manomaya, jnanamaya and anandamaya) or free and unaffected by the mind, body and the intellect.

Moksha can also be said to be freedom from "Jeevabrahnti" (Identification with the Ego).

What is Samsara?

"Samsara" is the chain of cycles of births and deaths.

The Hindu philosophy is based on the subject matter of "The Atman and Paramatman".

The Paramatman is the all–pervading Primordial energy that is responsible for expression of life with the five great elements of nature (Space, Air, Fire, Water and Earth) and using it as the medium for creation, sustenance and dissolution of life on this earth.

The Atman is the life force within each form of life. It is also known as "The Soul".

The subtle body consisting of the five pranas (prana, apana, vyana, samana and udana), mind and the intellect and the gross physical body gets a form and acts as the suit for the individual soul. It is given a name.

Each one of us are born into this world, (Birth) and are given a name, live in this world (Growth) and leave this world (Death) at some point (lose name and form).

From birth to death we get associated with various forms of life and objects in this world.

The body undergoes gross and subtle changes during its stay. The gross changes bring in the stages of:

Toddler, Young child, Teenager, Adult and Old age.

The subtle changes are the changes in the mental makeup as one grows. Illnesses, injury affect the physical body sometime or other during its life.

The association with other forms of life and objects of the world does bring in a feeling of happiness or sorrow.

The happiness is a pleasurable feeling and one would like to have more and more of the happiness; also, one would like the feeling of happiness to be permanent.

The law of nature being what it is, no one can get the permanent feeling of happiness with the objects of the world. Either we have to part with the objects of the world or the objects of the world have to part with us.

The parting of the objects or parting with the objects of love brings in an experience of sorrow.

Also when one does not get what they want there is a feeling of sorrow. Finally when one loses the object of love there is a feeling of sorrow.

Whatever it may be, one thing is for certain that there is no feeling of happiness that remains permanent.

The Hindu philosophy also believes that the soul after the death of the physical body at some point in the future gets a new body and the new body gets a new name (has no memory of the previous state of life) and goes through the cycles of association with the world and states of happiness and sorrow.

This repeated cycles of birth and death is "Samsara" and Total freedom from this life of samsara is "Moksha". : mokṣa ; liberation) or Mukti : release is the liberation from samsara . Unfortunately, whether we like it or not, the world we live in is a place of happiness and sorrow.

No one on this earth is said to be free from these two experiences.

The feeling of happiness is a state of mind, it is like addiction. When the mind experiences the happiness it would like to have that feeling with it at all times but the happiness is the result of actions and has a time span.

Experience of happiness has a birth, growth, decline and death.

The quest for experiencing the happiness that will not fade or end in sorrow has brought in the thcory of "Moksha".

The ancient seers graded the experience of happiness and sorrow into 14 levels. Including the earth we live in, they say that there are 14 "Lokas".

Each Loka is a field of experience for all.

Starting from the earth, tracing it above, there are 7 Lokas of happiness. They are:

Bhuloka (earth);

Bhuvarloka (Pitru loka-antariksha. the realm of semi-divine beings- celestials-Gandharvas);

Suvarloka (abode of the illumined ones/also known as Indra Loka. its celestail garden is the famous Nandana vana);

Maharloka: abode of great sages);

Janaloka (abode of great men/women highly spiritually evolved);

Tapoloka (abode of great sage in states of deep Samadhi);

Brahma loka or Satya Loka (abode of Lord Brahma).

There are 7 Lokas of sorrow below the earth.

Atala, Vitala, Sutala, Talatala, Mahatala, Rasatala and Patala.

The sensation and the period of happiness increases as one climbs up to higher Lokas.

The sensation and the period of sorrow increases as one traces downwards from the sphere of earth.

Entry into the spheres either above or below the earth can come only from the results of action conducted on the earth.

The stay in any one sphere is also limited to the amount of credit or debit accumulated by results of actions (good or bad) conducted on the earth.

None of the spheres are the abode of permanent happiness. Entry into any of the 7 higher loka is not Moksha.

Many look at moksha as an escape from the pains and sorrows on this earth. It comes therefore from developing an attitude of mind that does not get elated on experiencing happiness or looks forward for experiencing happiness and does not get depressed on experiencing sorrow (also accepts sorrow as a result of one's past actions and takes full responsibility for the same).

This state comes for the rare few who are known as "Jivanmuktas" (Liberated souls living on this earth waiting for the period of departure from this earth and continuing to discharge their ordained duties while alive).

For the rest it is a process of learning at every stage of life and coming to the stage where they do not crave for any happiness and do not sit back and cry on experiencing sorrow. Developing equanimity to the pairs of opposites of happiness and sorrow eventually takes one to Moksha (Krama Mukti—gradual Liberation).

Entering into the abodes of named Gods (Vishnu, Shiva etc.) is not the same as "Moksha".

We can attain the state of "Moksha" only when the mind is absolutely/totally pure. This depends upon the thoughts imprints/ vasanas on the mind.

Vasanas and Gunas:

Vasanas: the thought imprints stored in the mind are called as "Vasanas".

Each one of us has organs of knowledge/Jnanedriyas:
the eyes, ears, nose, tongue and the skin.
The eyes are for vision,

The ears for hearing the sounds,
The nose is for smell,
The tongue is for taste and
The skin is for touch.
We have five organs of action/karmendriyas:
The hands, the feet, the tongue, the excretory organs and genital organs.

The sense organs bring in the impulses from the world around to the centre of action: the Mind.

The mind analyses the impulses received,

When it likes what is received it gets attached to such feeling of happiness experienced. It stores such imprints on the mind,

When the thought is converted into action, the imprint gets wiped out, When it is not converted into action it remains as an imprint on the mind, When it does not like what is received it develops the feeling of hatred. Feelings of happiness and hate are imprinted on the mind.

Such stored imprints of what it likes does not like are called as "Vasanas".

The process of build–up of vasana imprints is a life–long process. The life is a cycle of converting some thoughts into actions and accumulating some more thoughts which get converted into actions later.

The total clearance of all the vasanas is "Vasana Kshaya". Vasana kshaya is absolute purity of the mind which is essential requisite for "Moksha.

This is not possible for many. Even at the time of physical death most people will have a number of vasanas on their mind.

Repeated births and deaths are the opportunities given to clear all the vasanas and attain Moksha.

The thought imprints on the mind can be of three kinds or combination of the three kinds.

These are:
Good/pure thoughts –Satvic,
Passionate – Rajasic,
Lazy/indolent –Tamas.

These are the "Gunas."(quality of thoughts):

Chapter 14 is dedicated totally to the gunas. The entire text dwells on the subject of desires and hatreds and the consequences of actions conducted accordingly.

Birth and Death

Birth is when a new body is born with "Life Power" in it and is alive.

Physical death is when the body which is alive loses its "Life Power" and is no more alive.

The Hindu philosophy gives explanations for these two events "Birth and Death." The first entry into this world is the entry into this world of the Paramatma as individual Atman projecting and taking up the five great elements and giving life to it. It has a totally pure mind on entry into the new world.

From that day, "Atman" gets a name and form and a family to it. He/she goes through the various stages of growth (childhood to old age), gets involved and attached with the objects of the world (likes and dislikes), suffers victory and loss, experiences happiness or sorrow and gains and losses. Most importantly the mind gets a number of imprints of vasanas, some get fulfilled and some remain dormant.

He/she reaches the point of death with the mind (subtle body) filled with a number of dormant vasanas.

On death, the subtle body (mind, intellect and the Atman encased in them, with no name and form to it) enters the land of "Hiranyagarbha/Moola Prakriti (technically depicted as the 1000 hooded serpent "Adishehsha" which acts as a bed wherein rests Lord Narayana.)

The Lord is said to decide on when, where and what surroundings and what form of life the subtle body has to get and work at clearing the vasanas accumulated.

Most people do not achieve this end result of totally pure mind at the time of death.

The day it happens, the encased Atman merges back with the Paramatman and this is "Moksha" with no re–entry into this world.

The philosophy of the Gita is to assist the individuals (who can analyze their thoughts) and guide them towards conduct of proper duties, to stay away from duties contrary to the sastras, get the full knowledge of "Kshetra and Kshetrajna" (chapter 13) and many more tools to achieve "Liberation". In the process it is also a tool for "Universal peace and Prosperity".

Those who achieve total purity of the mind in the present life are "Jivanmuktas" (Liberated souls).

Gunatita

(beyond the sway of the Gunas).

In continuation of the theme of births and deaths, each one of us has to climb up from:

Tamasic (laziness) to Rajas (passionate), Rajasic to Satva (pure),

Satvic to Shuddha Satva (totally pure) state of mind.

The stone man has to move from
Stone man to animal man
Animal man to man–man and
finally Man–man to God–man on earth.
It is transcending from Tamas to Shuddha Satva.

Gunatita is he who is free from the sway of the gunas and reached a totally pure state of mind. He is also a "Jivanmukta."

Such an individual experiences absolute bliss in himself (Ananda). It is a state that is to be experienced and is beyond the influence of words to explain it.

This theme is taken up in chapter 14, slokas 22–25.

The Soul, body and the Ego.

The life principle inside each form of life on this earth is "The Soul". It is a spark of Paramatma (the Supreme Soul) who in his "Leela" (sport) associated Himself with the nature and got a suit (body) over it. This is the "Life Energy" which acts like the petrol to the car and propels the body into action.

It remains with the body in all the three planes of existence (awake, dream and deep sleep states) and is said to remain as a

"Neutral witness" and observes, takes note of all thoughts, actions and speech undertaken by the individual.

The physical body is the active body propelled by the "Life Force". It is said to be made up of:

The Earth The Water The Fire The Air and The Space.

These five are the five gross elements of nature and are known as "Pancha Maha Bhootas" (five gross elements).

All forms of life, all men, women and children, whether small or big, minute or gross are constituted of these five elements.

In the absence of "Life Principle" the five elements go back to the five elements of nature and the body is considered to be dead.

Ego:

When the body gets life to it, the mind develops the feeling of individuality to it. It gets attached to those objects of the world it likes and develops the sense of hatred to what it does not like. It develops a strong sense of "me and mine". This attitude is the expression of "ego" (I–ness, my–ness).

The Soul within is "The Self" with the capital "S". The body kept alive by the soul is "self" with little "s".

Prana:

The life force, the energy which keeps us alive is "Prana".

Sadhaka, Sadhana and Sadhya.

Sadhana is to realize "The Eternal Truth" which is Parabrahman without name and qualities. (Nirakara, Nirguna Brahman).

Just believing in the "Eternal Truth" is not true sadhana. The seeker who works at achieving this union has to attempt to purify the mind totally (clear all vasanas). He has to develop absolute purity of "Thought, speech and action".

He who works for absolute purity to realize the "Parabrahman" is real sadhaka. The effort he puts in to achieve this is "Sadhana".

With the effort put in it is possible to achieve the end result which is "Sadhya".

Knowledge and Ignorance

The entire text is all about knowledge and ignorance.

We are all ignorant when we first come into this world as babies and are totally dependent.

In course of time we acquire knowledge and it gives us the means for independence.

This in turn gets us bound to the world of births, deaths and re–births into this world.

Spiritual knowledge which we can get from the sacred text is to detach ourselves from attachment to "the ego" and gives us the chance to unite back with the "Supreme" and experience the "Eternal Bliss" (Moksha).

We will learn the following facts by studying/understanding the text:

What is "Ignorance"?

Selfish, egotistic behaviour in one's actions influenced by thoughts generated in the mind is "Ignorance."

Not realizing that what we have today is from yesterday's actions is "Ignorance."

Not realizing that what we get tomorrow will be only the result of actions of yesterday and today is "Ignorance."

Wanting to enjoy and get benefits beyond one's means is "Ignorance."

Enjoying the benefits which come from bringing sorrow to others is "Ignorance." Wanting to fulfil all worldly desires and forget the spiritual existence of "The Parabrahman" is "Ignorance."

Harming nature is "Ignorance."

Cruelty to any other forms of life is "Ignorance."

Neglecting one's responsibility to the, disabled, old and young ones in the society is "Ignorance."

What is "Knowledge"?

Contrary to what constitutes ignorance is "Knowledge."

Living in peace with what one has which is acquired by righteous means is "Knowledge."

Thanking the power that created us, sustaining us and takes us away at the end is "Knowledge."

Wanting to unite back with the force that created us is "Knowledge."

To practice sincerely that what we can offer from what we get by righteous means is "Knowledge."

To realize and remember at all times the summary of the last sloka in the Gita:

Wherever there is Krishna, the Yogeshwara and Arjuna, the archer. There are: prosperity, victory, happiness, expansion and sound policy, Is "True Knowledge."

Yoga

He, who had yoked his mind to the intellect is a Yogi.

He who is striving to unite with the Supreme by sraddha, bhakti, jnana and dhyana, is a Yogi.

Tuning the mind towards the concept of the higher reality, lifting it from the world of objects is yoga. It is detachment with the outer world through attachment to the Supreme.

He who has succeeded in spiritual sadhana and has united with the Supreme is a Yogi.

Sraddha is the power to understand and assimilate new ideas (given by the scriptures. Gurus, elders) so that one can spiritually evolve from the stage of stone man to that of God–man on earth. It is the power for self–education and is the function of the intellect.

The background

Sage poet Sri Veda Vyasa dictated the entire Mahabharata to Lord Ganesha. Lord Ganesha acted as short hand typist and wrote down the dictation. The Gita is incorporated in the Mahabharata and forms part of the great mythological epic.

The great epic Mahabharata is considered as the "Panchama Veda" (The fifth Veda.). The four Vedas being: Rig, Yajur, Sama and Atharva Veda. It is the epic which tells us the historical story of the two families. Along with it the epic has the following philosophical topics which actually justify the title "Panchama Veda". These topics are:

Sree Vishnu Sahasranama.
Sree Shiva sahasranama
Yaksha prashna between Yaksha and Dharmaraya
Vidura neeti

The Pandavas, (Five brothers, sons of King Pandu:–Yudhistira, Bhima, Arjuna, Nakula and Sahadeva) and the Kauravas (100 brothers, sons of the blind king Dhritarashtra; Duryodhana being the eldest of the Kaurava brothers,) are the two forces assembled with their respective armies on the battlefield of Kurukshetra, (North India).

This epic battle that lasted a total of 18 days led to the death of the evil Kaurava brothers. 18 battalion of soldiers laid their lives down in this battle. This epic battle is considered as the battle of righteousness (Dharma yuddha).

Dhritarashtra was acting as a caretaker king in the absence of his younger brother, king Pandu who had retreated to the forest for austerities. Unfortunately, Pandu died in the forest and Dhritarashtra had to take over the rule as a caretaker King while the heirs apparent, the Pandavas were still not old enough to ascend the throne.

Yudhishtira, the eldest of the Panadavas, on coming of age was expected to be crowned as the king. This was not carried out. Duryodhana, son of Dhritarashtra made sure by using all the tricks in the world to persuade his father not to give up the throne. As the story unfolds, he cheats the cousins in the game of dice, robs them of all their wealth and possessions and sends them to the forest for 13years. On completion of the 13 years of life in exile, he refuses to give them their due share of the kingdom. Lord Krishna, the well–wisher of the Pandavas tries his best to mediate on behalf of the Pandavas but fails to make Duryodhana see justice.

This led to the decision to fight to death by the two groups of cousins and their followers.

Arjuna requests Krishna to act as the charioteer on the battlefield and Krishna gladly agrees to be so.

On the first day of the battle Arjuna requests Krishna to place the chariot wherein he could see the leaders he had to fight against. Krishna takes the chariot as requested and lets Arjuna see Bheeshma (beloved grandfather of Arjuna), Drona (who taught the art of war to both the Pandavas and the Kauravas) and Kripacharya (the family priest) standing in the opposite camp ready to fight.

Suddenly Arjuna loses heart. The horror that would ensue with the inevitable slaying of so many warriors including the family and friends makes him drop the bow and arrow and fall down near the feet of Krishna. He requests Krishna to guide him in the right path of action to take.

Sri Krishna brings out the philosophy of action in the battle of life, which is “The Sreemad Bhagawadgita”

Gitopadesham

The scene of the picture of Krishna preaching to Arjuna the sacred philosophy on the battlefield is “The Picture of Gitopadesham” and is the most popular picture for the Hindus.

(please look for the pictures depicting the Gitopadesam and look for the characters depicted in it.)

This is a description of the explanations for the characters in the pictures.

We should pause a second and analyze the meaning of this most beautiful scene which has the entire philosophy hidden in it.

Sri Krishna represents “the Intellect” (reasoning capacity),

Arjuna represents: the Mind.

The four white horses represent the four qualities “Desire, Anger, Greed and Delusion.” (Kama,Krodha,Lobha, Moha.)

Krishna holding on to the reins which represent: the senses.

Bow (Gandiva) represents: weapon of action.

The two armies: the good and bad forces in life (also within the mind of each individual).

Picture of Hanuman on the top of chariot signifies Devotion.

The warrior in the chariot has to move forward, face the enemies and defeat them.

In the battle of life, we must learn to be on the move and conduct our normal duties. The enemies we have to face are our own bad thought imprints and our friends are our own good thought imprints on our mind.

The guide for us who will lead us, destroy our bad thought imprints and help us to reach the destination (Moksha) is our inner voice of wisdom from the Lord himself (Atman, the spiritual voice of inner conscience).

The end of spiritual quest for a seeker is when the enemy (bad qualities) is totally destroyed. Only then there is "Peace."

Each one of us symbolically travels with a tool of trade in our hands. (Like the doctor with a stethoscope) We must carry that tool of action and use it. (unlike Arjuna on the scene, we must not drop the tool down at times of despair or dejection).

We must let our intellectual capacity of reasoning (Krishna as the Atman within) hold on to our senses.

The mind (Arjuna) should be dictated to by the intellect (Krishna). It should carry out the ordained duties. (Arjuna must take up the Gandiva and be ready to fight.)

The four qualities of desire, anger, greed and delusion need to be under total control.

This is represented by Krishna holding on to the reins of the four horses. The white colour of the horses depict "Satva guna/ Pure quality. (Pure desire for liberation, pure anger at those who block our journey, pure greed to attain Liberation and pure delusion with total bhakti/devotion to the Lord).

The four horses have blinkers on them. This is to stop them from looking sideways in their journey and avoid distraction and injury to the passengers on the chariot. We must similarly, control the four qualities and keep a tight rein on them.

On the battlefield of life, we must kill the enemy within, which is "Evil qualities" inside us.

Five Pandavas represent five good qualities and 100 Kauravas represent 100 evil qualities.

In life, against each good quality, there is said to be 20 bad qualities.

Like Hanuman we must follow the path of devotion in our actions and not let the ego dominate our lives.

With the guidance of Krishna, by taking shelter under Him, we can be victorious in the battle of life and attain "Liberation."

Statistics

There are in total 701 slokas in the sacred text. Some consider there are 700 verses only.

(This is because, in chapter 13, the first sloka by Arjuna (prakrutim purusham chaiva — is not present in all the versions of the Gita.)

Dhritarashtra	001	
Sanjaya	041	just under 06%
Arjuna	084	under 12%
Krishna	576	82%
Total	701	

The Gita we are familiar with is this format of 700–701 slokas divided into 18 chapters, each chapter with a named title to it.

Really speaking it is not the actual dialogue between the Krishna and Arjuna. On the battlefield Arjuna raised his doubt on the validity of fighting respected elders. Krishna then gave him the knowledge in the form of the Gita. There was no gap between chapters, no title to the chapters. One could not expect any room for this in the battlefield. What went on was simply questions by Arjuna (84) and answers or explanations by Krishna (575). This is the true Bhagawadgita.

The format we are familiar with has narration by Sanjaya in return to the command by Dhritarashtra about the events on the battlefield. This is in 18 chapters, totalling 701 slokas and divided into 18 chapters with a title for each. Also, this format has as an end at the end of each chapter with the statement : iti srimadbahgawadgitastu.......

These statements are additions from the great masters who have come along in the course of history after the Kurukshetra war of righteousness.

Dhritarashtra starts it with a question to Sanjaya about the impending war. He has no more involvement in the entire text.

It is a dialogue between Krishna and Arjuna which consists of 659 slokas (94% of the modified text).

Of these Arjuna's contribution is 84 and Krishna's contribution is 575. (12% and 82% respectively).

Out of 84 slokas from Arjuna 34 slokas are in chapter 1 and 33 in chapter 11.

To narrate his state of mind to Krishna, Arjuna used 34 slokas out of 47 slokas in the first chapter. It is the true sincere student needing help opening his heart entirely to the master teacher.

The next major contribution from Arjuna is in chapter 11, where his contribution is 33 slokas. This is taken up to describe his state of mind on seeing the "Universal Form" of the Lord which is not a sight even the greatest of the rishis could see in their life time.

In the rest of the chapters his contribution is very little. He is just a listener/student putting forward a few pertinent important questions to clear his doubts.

He has contributed only 2 slokas out of 78 in the last chapter. A good student need not say any more when the master completes his superb talk to express his wonder at the excellent narration.

In the last six chapters of the text, his contribution is only 5 slokas. A student who is in his post graduate course has very few questions to his tutor. Arjuna was a post–graduate student and Krishna was his tutor.

It is all a lesson for those students (who want help from the guru/master) to remember not to be a chatter box when the master is giving the most important message and to keep their contribution to the discussion to bare minimum and at the same time not to forget to express grateful thanks to the guru for a superb discourse to open his eyes of knowledge.

Sanjaya's contribution is 41 slokas making it to just less than 6%. Of these 25 slokas are in the first chapter. This is mainly to update his master on the organization of the battlefield by the two opposite forces assembled. Rest of the time his contribution is almost nil. Only towards the end his contribution is 5 slokas expressing his wonder at the masterly dialogue he had just heard.

The Hindus have a strong un-flinching faith that the Gita is the word of God, Lord Krishna, the divine incarnation of Vishnu on earth.

It is narrated to Arjuna, one of the five Pandava brothers during the battle of Kurukshetra, the great war of righteousness between the cousins, the Pandavas and the Kauravas.

Arjuna is the embodiment of so many good virtues that make him fit to receive the sacred philosophy directly from the Lord Himself.

Emperor Dhritarashtra, blind by birth was given an opportunity to listen to a graphic description of the events on the battlefield by his most devoted and trusted counsellor Sanjaya.

Sage poet Veda Vyasa blessed Sanjaya with the power of seeing the events on the battlefield and narrating live commentary of the same to Dhritarashtra. Unlike the present day war reporters with sophisticated instruments for communication but with the spiritual instrument of "Grace" (of Veda Vyasa) Sanjaya did a most wonderful job of narration.

The beauty of it is: this is the first battle line report in the world where there were no sophisticated instruments, like we know of in the present day and worked evidently on the "Grace of a great seer", Veda Vyasa.

Sreemad Bhagawadgita is one scripture which has "Universal Message" to all irrespective of religion, nationality, sex, creed, caste or age.

It is for "Universal Peace and Harmony".

Let us all pray Lord that there are no obstacles in our learning and let us put our small efforts in making the world a safer place for our future generations to come.

The sacred text is divided into 18 chapters. Every chapter has a special title name that ends with the word "Yoga".

The word "Yoga" is derived from the word "Yuj" which means "Unite." Every chapter is a guide for the sincere seeker to unite with the Supreme.

The seeker is he/she who is looking for attaining the union with the "Parabrahman" and experience the "Eternal Bliss." In

Sanskrit the name for the word "seeker" is "Sadhaka". The efforts put forward by the seeker is known as "Sadhana".

To undertake the task, the seeker must have "Faith" and "Devotion" in the text, the teacher and "Parabrahman."

Despite the great scientific progress which has unravelled a number of mysteries over the last two centuries or so which our ancestors could not find answer to, we are still living the life which has become a constant threat to ourselves, the society and the nature.

Our ancestors took shelter under the name of divinity for answers to their problems and we are taking shelter under the name of "ego" to overcome our problems.

We are becoming more and more selfish. Instead of working hard, we want all the pleasures to come to us at the touch of a button.

We want all the pleasures to ourselves and forget the masses that are in need of help and support.

We want to enjoy all the comforts whether we have the means to possess it or not. We have a devilish pride in us that says, "We can do it, we can get it, we can acquire it" and words to that effect.

We are already seeing the results of having taken this path which has resulted in massive loss of life all over the world. We had two world wars within a period of 40 years in the last century. We are desperately trying to avoid a third world war and the prediction is, if it does take place, it almost amounts to the end of the world we know of.

Is it the scientific advancement we are proud of?

Which is the better of the two?

Give in to the selfishness (in an individual, in a family, in a society, in a country) and fight against the rest of the life on earth?

Or

Take the life of prayer to the unknown requesting "It" to give us the moral strength to stick to truthfulness, conduct selfless work, share the fruits of work with those in need, work with universal love and affection and most importantly to destroy the demon "ego" in us?

Instead of being grateful to "Him" (to that divine force) and continuing to discharge our ordained duties to the society, the majority of us have taken to the life of "Armchair luxuries." We are becoming too egotistic and forget to show respect to elders and divinity.

Humanity is really speaking going through a period of crisis. If we want avoid total destruction, we must take recourse back to the scriptures and follow the advice within.

Bhagawadgita is a unique philosophical book where there are directions/guidance to work on the principle of:

I am a small part of the big society, I am limited by "space, time and causation", I owe an obligation to the society, I owe a debt to the society and the entire universe is "Vasudaivika kutumbam" (family of Vasudeva) where there are no bars because of religion, nationality, sex, creed, age etc.

With this introduction let us now enter into the subject matter of the different chapters in the sacred text.

CHAPTER 1

ARJUNA–VIṢĀDA–YOGA

Despondency of Arjuna/Mental agony of Arjuna.

INTRODUCTION:

The main characters that we get introduced in the Gita by the sage poet Veda Vyasa, the composer of the Gita are:
The blind king Dhritarashtra,
Sanjaya, the trusted minister for the king, Arjuna and finally,
Sri Krishna the Lord incarnate.

Satva, Rajas and Tamas are the three qualities inherent in each of us with one quality predominating at any one time. (We will learn more about this in chapter 14)

There is another quality, Shuddha Satva which is the purest of the pure.

Dhritarashtra belonged to the warrior class and as such comes under "Rajas". But, he was physically blind and therefore can be placed under lowest ladder of rajas almost becoming one with the Tamas.

A blind tamasic natured person's understanding of the scriptures is limited. Dhritarashtra, even though he heard the entire text did not get spiritually evolved.

Arjuna also belonged to the warrior class and like Dhritarashtra comes under "Rajas". He is not physically blind but is spiritually blind. He comes under higher rajas in the spiritual ladder for evolution.

If we study the Mahabharata we will understand that Sanjaya was a gentle, obedient, trusted minister for Dhritarashtra and always advised his king to follow the path of truth and righteousness. He had mastered over the emotions and did not act passionately or lazily at any time. He therefore can be placed under "Satva".

Lord Krishna, divine incarnate is the one and the only master and controller over the gunas.

Vyasa is the guru who composed the Mahabharata and incorporated the Gita in it. He is considered as Bhagawan and is popularly known as "Bhagawan Veda Vyasa." The Lord Krishna in the form of Vyasa composed the Gita.

The message in the Gita was understood by Arjuna and helped to clear his ignorance.

The same message was not understood by Dhritarashtra and his ignorance did not get cleared.

The sincere spiritual seeker trying to study the text has to evolve from tamasic nature to rajasic nature and climb up to the higher levels of Rajas like Arjuna. Only then his spiritual blindness is cured, the ignorance is cleared and its message can be understood.

With this understanding we have to enter into the first chapter.

The first chapter is about the despondency of Arjuna on encountering the armed forces arrayed in the battlefield. Arjuna as such was a great and well respected warrior who had won many laurels. The thought of the deaths of beloved family and friends and of so many soldiers and heroes in the battle and his own role in that made him loose heart. He was in a severe state of mental agony thinking of the consequences of the great war. He lost the will to fight and was prepared to let wicked cousin Duryodhana and his brothers rule the kingdom. He forgot he was fighting for his brothers in the battle of "righteousness." He was confused and unclear of the right course of action. Instead of turning his back and leaving the battlefield, he decided to take the guidance of Sri Krishna, the charioteer, on the right path of action to take.

His grief/mental agony and surrender to the Lord brought out the "Sreemad Bhagawadgita" to the mankind. The Gita as the "Light of Knowledge" has given a great number of people including Arjuna himself, the first recipient of the teaching, the opportunity to attain union with the "Parabrahman."

In life, at times, we go through extreme phases of both grief and happiness. The state of happiness unfortunately makes the "ego" strong and we feel proud of achieving the success. We forget to remember/thank the Lord who blessed us in experiencing the happiness.

Grief can at times make an individual utterly despondent and many a time we tend to blame the God for the miseries in our lives.

Why then call this chapter as "yoga"?

Grief takes us nearer to God than happiness. When we encounter grief, we find that whatever wealth we may possess is not going to be useful to overcome the grief, we tend to turn to God as the final resort for help, as a pillar of support.

Arjuna's despondency on thinking of the grave calamity that was going to befall the community after the war, made him turn to his counsellor who was none other than Lord Krishna. As a result we are blessed with the "Jewel of Crown", the Sreemad Bhagawadgita.

We, through the medium of Arjuna are taken into the 18 chapters that culminate in the experience of "Ananda" which is simply clearance of the ignorance and lighting the "Light of Knowledge".

It helped Arjuna to pick up his weapon of action Gandiva and undertake the duties of the Kshatriya and conduct his ordained duty in the spirit of "Nishkama karma and Karma Phala Tyaga". At the same time he became an instrument of Lord Krishna upholding dharma and bringing peace and prosperity to the citizens of the land.

Let us pray that the sacred text makes us instruments of the Lord and that we conduct our duties on this stage of life, of which we are one of the actors selected by the director Lord Krishna.

धृतराष्ट्र उवाच
धर्मक्षेत्रे कुरुक्षेत्रे समवेता युयुत्सवः।
मामकाः पाण्डवाश्चैव किमकुर्वत सञ्जय ॥1॥

dhṛtarāṣṭra uvāca
dharmakṣetre kurukṣetre samavetā yuyutsavaḥ |
māmakāḥ pāṇḍavāś caiva kim akurvata saṃjaya ||1||

Dhritarashtra said
Having assembled together on the holy plain of Kurukshetra, desirous of fighting the battle, O Sanjaya, what did the sons of Pandu and also my people do? ||1||

Sanjaya: O Sanjaya; Dharma kshetre: on the holy plain; Kurukhsetre: in Kurukshetra; Samaveta: assembled; Yuyutsavaha: desirous to fight; Mamakaha: my people; Pandavas: the sons of Pandu; Chaiva: and also; Kim: what; Akurvata: did do?

Dharma Kshetre: on the field of righteousness.

Kuru Kshetre: the place where the battle took place: i.e.: Kurukshetra (historically it is about 150miles north west of New Delhi).

On the face of it the sloka sounds like a straight forward command from Dhritarashtra to Sanjaya asking him to narrate the events on the battlefield.

It is important to get the correct meaning and understand it clearly.

In this instance, it is the field of Kurukshetra where the battle took place.

As we move along, when we come to the 13th chapter, we will realize that the field referred to was the battlefield in our own mind and that the battlefield of Kurukshetra in the epic Mahabharata is only an example to understand the significance.

Emperor Dhritarashtra, blind father of Kauravas is eager to know what was happening on the battlefield and receive the live commentary by Sanjaya of the events in the battlefield.

Sanjaya was given the special powers to actually visualize the events on the battlefield by sage poet Bhagawan Veda Vyasa.

We can look upon Sanjaya as the battlefield reporter giving "the breaking news" to his king.

Few salient points to note:

Dhritarashtra The word "Dhritarashtra" means "He who holds on to the kingdom which is not his".

He was only caretaker ruler of the kingdom. He was visually handicapped. The law of the land at that period, it is said specifically barred handicapped people holding on to the reigns of the throne.

We are not here to argue rights and wrongs of the law prevailing 5000yrs ago.

How can a totally visually impaired person provide justice in his administration and fight the enemies that attack the kingdom?

The story of Mahabharata tells us that Dhritarashtra did not realize or was blind to the atrocities committed by his son Duryodhana against Pandavas. The Pandavas were his own brother's sons. If he could not give justice and protect his nephews how could he protect the subjects in his kingdom?

Because of blind love to his son, he decided to hold on to the kingdom that was not rightfully his.

We, the beings on earth have developed a strong hold on to our physical bodies.

The blind king was a Dhritarashtra who was holding on to the kingdom which was not his own.

Each one of us is made up of: the "Soul", the "Energy" within and the "Physical body" that envelops the "Soul within."

We cannot live even for a second without the energy which is the "Life Principle." We all have got attached to the physical body and it is the "Ego" that conducts all the various activities..

"Kshetra", the field referred to (dharma kshetre) is the "Physical body." We should look upon this body as the "kingdom" ruled by the "King within" which is the "Atman. The Atman being the "Soul" which is a spark of the Parabrahman.

Instead of letting the "King" rule, we are letting "Ego" hold on to the body and dictate terms.

We are holding on to the field, because of the "Ego" and something which is not rightfully ours.

In this sense, we are all "Dhritarashtras" and we are getting the narration from Sanjaya.

Dharma: it is the "Law of the being." There are a number of explanations/meanings to this word. As we go through the Gita, we will take up the different meanings.

"Dharma is that principle without which, the being has no existence." (quote: Swami Chinmayananda)

The fire has so many qualities. The essential quality of it is "Burn." It burns. We can draw a beautiful picture of the fire. When we touch the picture, we do not feel the heat and it does not burn us.

Live fire, on the contrary is hot and it burns. In the absence of the heat, the fire is "dead." It is said to be alive, when it exhibits the property of "heat."

We, the humans, are alive because of the "Energy" within. In its absence the physical body is certified "Dead" by the experts.

So, our dharma has to be the dharma of the soul and not dharma of the ego.

What is dharma of the soul?

We all attribute so many qualities to God and look for Him to help us in distress. We tend to say:

"God, why don't you come down and help me out of this distress."

If, the power inside us is the God, our dharma has to be dharma of the "Soul." We should be showing divinity in all our actions. Our true dharma is therefore "Universal welfare."

Dharma should be looked upon as "acts of righteousness" at the three levels of:

Moral, Social and spiritual planes of existence.

Moral dharma: irrespective of where we live in this world we have to live the life of moral values.

Oxford dictionary meaning of "Moral":

a) standard of conduct expected by good men independently of position, law and religion.
b) practicing virtue.
c) Justifiable to conscience if not law
d) faculty that distinguishes between right and wrong.

Being truthful, honest and not harming others are some of the examples of moral living.

Social Dharma is actions that need to be conducted according to the law of the land. We must obey the laws of any place where we live. We must follow the law of our own home we live in, the law of the town/city we reside and law of the country we either take as our residence or visit. We must be prepared to face the consequences of breaking the law.

Spiritual dharma: It is the law of the Lord. Acts according to the scriptures for the welfare of life on this universe is dharma, undertaking the prescribed rituals and worship of the Lord according to the sastras, following the rules at various stages of one's life all come under spiritual dharma.

Few points to ponder over:

Dhritarashtra was the uncle of the Pandavas (who had lost their father) and father of the Kauravas.

On the death of Pandu, father of the Pandavas, he had a moral duty, social duty and spiritual duty to care for the Pandavas.

Unfortunately, he did not consider the Pandavas as his own. He deprived them of their rightful inheritance to the throne.

In this sloka, he uses the word "Mamakaha" - "My People." Referring to his 100 sons.

He refers to the Pandavas, as "children of Pandu."

He asks the question: "What did Pandavas do and what did "my people" do?"

As a matter of fact, it is said that every king has to look upon his subjects as his own children and protect them.

Sri Shankaracharya compares the attitude of Dhritarashtra to that of a stone in the water. The stone remains in the water but the water does not enter into the stone.

Sanjaya offered and gave advice to Dhritarashtra on spiritual and moral dharma.

Vidura, his own brother offered guidance but the message did not sink in. The words of advice did not sink in.

He heard the narration by Sanjaya but the message did not sink in. He was like a stone in the ocean referred to by Sree Shankaracharya. Few other points to ponder over:

Dharma kshetre kuru kshetre:

If we juggle the four words we can come up with Kshetre kshetre dharmam kuru.

It would then mean:

Every single kshetra, conduct righteous actions.

Accordingly each one of us has a duty to be righteous at all the three planes of existence.

The first word in the first chapter is "Dharma" and the last word together in the last chapter is "Mama". Putting the first and the last word would make it: "Mama Dharma" meaning: My Dharma.

The entire sacred text is "mama dharma" to be followed by each one of us.

Kurukshetra: It is the place where the famous war between the Pandavas and Kauravas took place about 5300 yrs ago.

In Sanskrit "Kuru" means: "To do".

We should use this meaning to understand the meaning of the word "Kurukshetra". It means: "The place to conduct actions".

This meaning comes into prominence in the 13th chapter where the scene is shifted from the war field of the historic Kurukshetra, to the war field called "The Mind".

सञ्जय उवाच
दृष्ट्वा तु पाण्डवानीकं व्यूढं दुर्योधनस्तदा।
आचार्यमुपसङ्गम्य राजा वचनमब्रवीत् ||2||

saṃjaya uvāca
dṛṣṭvā tu pāṇḍavānīkaṃ vyūḍhaṃ duryodhanas tadā |
ācāryam upasaṃgamya rājā vacanam abravīt ||2||

Sanjaya said,
Having seen the Pandava army arranged in a battle order, King Duryodhana then approaching the teacher Dronacarya spoke these words. ||2||

Drushtvatu: having seen well; Pandavanikam: the Pandava army; Vyudham: marshalled/arranged in battle order; Duryodhanaha: Duryodhana; Tada: then; Acharyam: the teacher (Dronacharya);

Upasangamya: approaching; Raja: to the king; Vachanam: words; Abravit: spoke.

Sanjaya starts his narration with Duryodhana's activities on the battlefield on the first day of the battle. After all Duryodhana was the beloved son of Dhritarashtra and Sanjaya himself was an employee of the emperor.

He says that Duryodhana went first to the teacher Dronacharya and spoke to him.

We need to analyze the psychology behind Duryodhana's approach to his guru first. One may wonder why he did not go first to Bheeshma who was the commander–in–chief but went first to Dronacharya.

Duryodhana was frightened of Bheeshma. He dare not speak to him. He knew that he would only get rebuke from Bheeshma.

Bheeshma was the eldest of the family and a master warrior. It was not easy to defeat him even by the great archer Arjuna.

He was the recipient of a rare boon from his father Shantanu. The boon was that he could decide on the time to depart from this physical world and no one on earth could kill him in battle. The timing of his departure from this world would be under his control. The Sanskrit word for it is "Itcha Marana"

Bheeshma loved the Pandavas and Arjuna was his favorite great grand–son. But, he had taken a solemn oath in front of his father that he would protect the throne of Hastinapura. As per the oath, emperor Dhritarashtra was on the throne at the time of the battle and it was his duty therefore to be on the side of Kauravas and fight the Pandavas.

Duryodhana was frightened to approach Bheeshma. So, instead of going to his commander– in–chief Bheeshma he went first to the guru Dronacharya.

Why he went to Dronacharya?

He went to Dronacharya as he was eager to get reassurance from his teacher, who would not be soft–hearted towards the Pandavas.

Dronacharya was the teacher who taught the art of warfare for both Kauravas and the Pandavas. Arjuna was his favorite student. Still, as he was under the employment of Dhritarashtra he had no option but to fight against the Pandavas. It was easy for Duryodhana to build up the courage and approach his teacher because he was literally speaking, an employee of the Kauravas. He wanted to remind his teacher that partiality towards the Pandavas would not be correct.

पश्यैतां पाण्डुपुत्राणामाचार्य महतीं चमूम्।
व्यूढां द्रुपदपुत्रेण तव शिष्येण धीमता ||3||

paśyaitāṃ pāṇḍuputrāṇām ācārya mahatīṃ camūm |
vyūḍhāṃ drupadaputreṇa tava śiṣyeṇa dhīmatā ||3||

O teacher, behold the great Pandava army, formed in the battle order by the son of Drupada, your wise disciple. ||3||

Paschya: behold; Etaam: this; Pandu putranaam: of the sons of Pandu; Acharya: O' master; Mahateem: great; Chamoom: army; Vyoodham: arranged in battle order; Drupada Putrena: by the son of Drupada; Tava: your; Shishyena: disciple; Dheemata: wise (in the art of war).

Duryodhana starts his conversation by naming the commander–in–chief of the Pandava army first.

Drushtadyumna, son of king Drupada was the commander–in–chief of the Pandava army.

Droupadi was the daughter of Drupada and the wife of the Pandava brothers.

Drona had a personal feud with Drupada. By pointing out the enemy armed forces were arranged skillfully on the battlefield by Drushtadyumna (son of Drupada). Duryodhana is trying his best to rouse the anger in his teacher Drona, which he holds due to his animosity to king Drupada.

Here it is essential that the reader should know the background for the feud between Dronacharya and Drupada.

Drona and Drupada both learnt under the same teacher in their younger days and were good friends.

Drupada was in–line to become the king (on return from the gurukula ashrama). Drona, a poor brahmin had to go back to his little hut.

On the day of parting from the gurukula ashrama, Drupada gives an open invitation for Drona to come for help/assistance at any time in future.

Few years later, Drona's wife (Kripi), unable to live the life of poverty, reminds Drona of the promise by his friend Drupada. Drona makes a trip to the court of Drupada hoping to get some help.

Unfortunately, Drupada chooses not to recognize his old friend and insults him in the open court. Unable to bear the insult, Drona returns home empty handed.

Circumstances changed for the better in the latter years and Drona became the teacher for the Pandavas and Kauravas. Arjuna becomes the best and favorite pupil of his teacher.

One day, Drona commands Arjuna to catch Drupada and fetch him to his hut. Arjuna, a great warrior by that time fulfills the command by his teacher. He defeats Drupada, ties him to a rope and brings him to the presence of Drona.

This time, it was the turn of Drupada to beg of mercy from Drona. Instead of being merciful, Drona reminds Drupada of the insult at the court by kicking him and setting him free afterwards.

Unable to bear this insult, Drupada takes a vow to get a son who will avenge this insult to his father. Conducting special penances he manages to get a son and that son was Drushtadyumna, the commander–in–chief of the Pandava army.

Drushtadyumna, surprisingly was also a student in his early days of Drona. (in days gone by, the brahmin teacher followed a code of practice. They would not refuse to accept any student who wanted to learn.)

Duryodhana who knew this side of Drona's past life history, used this opportunity to name Drupada and Drushtadyumna and increase the flow of adrenaline in his teacher Drona. This way, he hoped that the despite the presence of the favorite pupil Arjuna in the opposite camp, Drona would use all his skills to defeat the Pandavas.

अत्र शूरा महेष्वासा भीमार्जुनसमा युधि।
युयुधानो विराटश्च द्रुपदश्च महारथः ॥4॥

atra śūrā maheṣvāsā bhīmārjunasamā yudhi |
yuyudhāno virāṭaś ca drupadaś ca mahārathaḥ ||4||

In the Pandava army, there are heroes and mighty archers equal to Bhima and Arjuna. They are Yuyudhana, Virata, Drupada, of the first order of warriors. ||**4**||

Atra: here; Shoora: heroes; Maheshwasa: mighty archers; Sama yudhi: equal in battle; Veeryavaan: the valiant; Sarva eva: all these; Maharathaha: great car– warriors.

धृष्टकेतुश्चेकितानः काशिराजश्च वीर्यवान्|
पुरुजित्कुन्तिभोजश्च शैब्यश्च नरपुङ्गवः ||5||

dhṛṣṭaketuś cekitānaḥ kāśirājaś ca vīryavān |
purujit kuntibhojaś ca śaibyaś ca narapuṃgavaḥ ||5||

युधामन्युश्च विक्रान्त उत्तमौजाश्च वीर्यवान्|
सौभद्रो द्रौपदेयाश्च सर्व एव महारथाः ||6||

yudhāmanyuś ca vikrānta uttamaujāś ca vīryavān |
saubhadro draupadeyāś ca sarva eva mahārathāḥ ||6||

Drushtakethu, Cekitana, the valiant king of Kasi, Purujit, Kuntibhoja,Saibya, the best men, the strong Yudhamanyu (Satyaki), valiant Utatmauja, Abhimanyu, the son of Subhadra and Arjuna, and the sons of Droupadi, all of them, divisional commanders. ||**5-6**||

Herein are the names of the warriors of repute in the Pandava army.

Duryodhana is giving those names to his teacher Drona. He puts some adjectives like valiant, best of men, strong, in front of the names of some warriors.

In the Pandava army, Cekitana, the valiant king of Kasi, Purujit, Kuntibhoja, Saibya, the best of men, the strong Yudhamanyu, (Satyaki), valiant Uttamouja, Abhimanyu, the son of Subhadra and Arjuna, and the sons of Droupadi, all of them divisional commanders.

All these were given the title of "Maharati." "Maharati" is he who can fight single handed with 10000 archers and is also a master in the use of various weapons of warfare.

अस्माकं तु विशिष्टा ये तान्निबोध द्विजोत्तम|
नायका मम सैन्यस्य संज्ञार्थं तान्ब्रवीमि ते ||7||

asmākaṃ tu viśiṣṭā ye tān nibodha dvijottama |
nāyakā mama sainyasya saṃjñārthaṃ tān bravīmi te ||7||

O best of twice born, now, I will recall to you, for your information, the names of those who are most distinguished amongst ourselves, the leaders of our army. ||7||

Asmakam tu: ours also; vishishta: distinguished chiefs; nibhoda: know; dwijottama: best among twice born; nayaka: leaders; samjnartha: for information; braveemi: I will tell; Te: to you.

Duryodhana continues his discussion with his teacher Drona and reiterates the names of the great warriors on the side of his Kaurava army.

He addresses Drona as "best among twice born." Drona was a Brahmin by birth.

The Brahmins, the Kshatriyas (and in some families the Vysyas too) among the Hindus undertake a traditional ritual known as "Sacred thread ceremony." This is carried out between the ages of 7–11yrs. After the child passes through the infancy and early childhood (6–10yrs of life) where he/she learns the alphabets and comes out of playful moods, it is time for initiating them into the spiritual studies.

The Hindu philosophy stresses that every individual is ignorant at birth irrespective of the caste he/she is born into. To let the individual into society to act according to the dharma needs initiation into the spiritual education.

The first common entry for all is "birth and entry into the material world" and this is considered as birth into the ignorance.

The entry after the ceremony is "entry into the world of knowledge."

This initiation into spiritual education is considered to be "second birth" for the child.

Drona who had undergone this ritual is therefore addressed as "best among the twice born."

There is another subtle hint Duryodhana is throwing at his master. Even though Drona was a great warrior, he was a Brahmin by birth. Brahmins generally are not warriors and not physically strong to take part in the battle. Duryodhana was a tactical warrior. He knew how to get the adrenaline flowing in his master. By stressing that Drona was a Brahmin (timid) and by giving names of great warriors on his side, Duryodhana is making Drona get angry.

भवान्भीष्मश्च कर्णश्च कृपश्च समितिञ्जयः।
अश्वत्थामा विकर्णश्च सौमदत्तिस्तथैव च ||8||

bhavān bhīṣmaś ca karṇaś ca kṛpaś ca samitiṃjayaḥ |
aśvatthāmā vikarṇaś ca saumadattis tathaiava ca ||8||

अन्ये च बहवः शूरा मदर्थे त्यक्तजीविताः।
नानाशस्त्रप्रहरणाः सर्वे युद्धविशारदाः||9||

anye ca bahavaḥ śūrā madarthe tyaktajīvitāḥ |
nānāśastrapraharaṇāḥ sarve yuddhaviśāradāḥ ||9||

Yourself, Bheeshma and Karna, also Kripa the victorious in war, Ashwathama, Vikarna and also the son of Somadatta, as also many other heroes who are prepared to give up their lives for my sake, armed with various weapons and missiles, all well-skilled in the battle. ||8-9||

Bhavan: yourself; Anye cha: and others; Bahavaha: many; Shooraha: heroes; Mad arthe: for my sake; Tyakta jeevitaha: who have given up their lives; Nana shastra praharanah: armed with various weapons of war; Sarve Yuddha visharadaha: all well skilled in battle.

This is the list of main warriors on the side of Kauravas. It is not as though Drona did not know any of these warriors. If we read the Mahabharata we will know more about these great skilled warriors.

While naming the warriors it is interesting to note that Duryodhana places the name of Drona first, ahead of Bheeshma the commander–in–chief. It is possible that Duryodhana realized that he had gone too far and used the word "Brahmana" by addressing Drona as "twice born."

अपर्याप्तं तदस्माकं बलं भीष्माभिरक्षितम्।
पर्याप्तं त्विदमेतेषां बलं भीमाभिरक्षितम् ||10||

aparyāptaṃ tad asmākaṃ balaṃ bhīṣmābhirakṣitam |
paryāptaṃ tv idam eteṣāṃ balaṃ bhīmābhirakṣitam ||10||

This army of ours defended by Bheeshma, is inadequate. Whereas, that army of our enemies well-defended by Bhima is quite adequate. ||10||

Aparyaptam: unlimited; Ta: that; Asmakam: our; Balam: army; Bheeshmabhi: by Bheeshma; Rakshitam: protected; Paryaptam: limited; Tu idam (tvidam): this is; Yetesham: of the Pandavas; Abhirakshitam: well–defended by.

The two words "Aparyptam and Paryaptam" have two different meanings given by the masters and according to the version taken, there are two different explanations for this verse.

The first meaning is: aparyaptam: unlimited Paryaptam: limited Accordingly, the verse reads as follows:

This army of ours defended by Bheeshma is unlimited and the army of theirs defended by Bhima is limited.

The Kaurava army had 11 battalions and the Pandava army had 7 battalions. It is therefore natural to gloat about the large size of the army and Duryodhana is doing the same.

Second meaning:

Aparyaptam: incomplete, inefficient, Paryaptam: complete, efficient, sufficient.

This army of ours defended by Bheeshma is inefficient and the army of theirs defended by Bhima is efficient.

Mahatma Gandhi has given this second explanation to this sloka.

It is interesting to note that Duryodhana says "Army defended by Bhima" instead of Drushtadyumna the Commander–in–chief for the Pandavas.

Why?

The most important person Duryodhana was frightened of was Bhima. Bhima was his sworn enemy.

During the game of dice that was played which decided the fate of the Pandavas, Duryodhana with the help of the cunning Shakuni cheats Dharmaraya. Dharmaraya loses all his empire along with his brothers in the game. Finally he even loses Droupadi.

Duryodhana orders his brother Dushasana to bring Droupadi to the court and commands him to de–robe her in front of the full assembly.

Bhima who was bound by the laws of the game to be subservient to Duryodhana could not bear the insult any longer. In front of the large assembly, he takes a solemn oath to kill all the brothers of Duryodhana and drink the blood of Dushasana.

Duryodhana was well aware of the strength of Bhima and could imagine what havoc he would cause to keep up to his promise.

Imagining Bheema to fulfill his promise, Duryodhana must have got really frightened and hence says "Pandava army well protected by Bheema."

अयनेषु च सर्वेषु यथाभागमवस्थिताः।
भीष्ममेवाभिरक्षन्तु भवन्तः सर्व एव हि॥11॥

ayaneṣu ca sarveṣu yathābhāgam avasthitāḥ |
bhīṣmam evābhirakṣantu bhavantaḥ sarva eva hi ||11||

Therefore, do you all, standing firmly in your respective positions, in the divisions, guard Bheeshma alone. ||11||

Ayaneshu: divisions of the army; Cha: and; Sarveshu: all; Yatha bhagam: respective positions; Avasthitaaha: stationed/standing;

Bheeshmam eva: Bheeshma alone; Rakshantu: protect/guard; Bhavantu: you; Abhirakshantu hi: protect indeed; Sarva: all; Eva: even; Hi: indeed.

One can see the tone of the command from Duryodhana to his guru. True, Duryodhana, the heir apparent to the throne had everybody at his command including his own guru. During the battle, he, as the future emperor has the highest authority.

Having said that, there is what is called as "humility." He did not show "humility and reverence" to his elder statesman and guru. The fact that Drona was fighting for the Kauravas should have been sufficient for him.

Why is he asking everyone to guard Bheeshma alone?

We should recollect the life of Bheeshma in his younger days.

Bhishma's father Shantanu had fallen madly in love with Satyavati, the fisherwoman. Satyavati's father, a clever person, had realized that Bheeshma would be the heir to the throne after Shantanu. The children born out of wedlock of Satyavati to Shantanu would not inherit the throne. He therefore objects to his daughter marrying the king. Shantanu was torn between the duty to Bheeshma, the son of his first wife Ganga and his infatuation towards the fisherwoman.

He showed signs of depression for a long time.

Bheeshma came to know of the dilemma his father was facing. He therefore brings Satyavati to his father and takes a solemn oath in front of both of them that he would not demand the right to the throne as long he was alive. Instead he would let Satyavati's child ascend to the throne. He promises that on his part he would protect the kingdom/throne at any cost. He swears to be a bachelor for life and be subservient to the occupant of the throne.

For the sacrifice he made, father Shantanu blesses his son and bestows on him a rare boon. The boon was that death will not approach Bheeshma and he could choose the time of his departure from this world.

The war of righteousness was to be fought to the bitter end. By cleverly making Bheeshma, the commander–in–chief Duryodhana had already won the tactical battle. Bheeshma would not die in the war and so Pandavas could not win.

Even though Bheeshma could not be killed, it was possible that he could be mortally wounded and may have to retire from the war. As long as Bheeshma was holding the fort, the Pandavas had no chance to win.

It was therefore imperative that Bheeshma was not going to be injured. Hence the command, "Guard Bheeshma alone."

तस्य संजनयन्हर्षं कुरुवृद्धः पितामहः।
सिंहनादं विनद्योच्चैः शङ्खं दध्मौ प्रतापवान् ॥12॥

tasya saṃjanayan harṣaṃ kuruvṛddhaḥ pitāmahaḥ | siṃhanādaṃ vinadyoccaiḥ śaṅkhaṃ dadhmau pratāpavān ||12||

In order to embolden Duryodhana, Bheeshma, the mighty grandsire, the oldest of the Kurus, now raised a lions roar and blew his conch. ||12||

Tasya: to him (Duryodhana); Sanjanayan: causing; Harsham: joy; Kuruvruddha: senior–most of the Kurus; Pitamaha: grandsire; Simhanadam: mighty lion's roar; Vinadya: having sounded; Uchai: loudly; Shankam: the conch; Dadmou: blew; Pratapavan: mighty.

It was a tradition in the days–gone–bye to let the senior most states–man have the honor of announcing the start of the war by letting them blow their conch first. In this war, Bheeshma being the eldest states–man for both the armies was given the honor.

It was also the policy to let the eldest states–man blow his conch and signal the end of the fight for the day.

It is interesting to note that Dronacharya did not give any reply to Duryodhana. He just went on his duty to fight for the Kauravas.

Why did he do so?

He considered that Duryodhana was a spoilt prince and took the option of not replying to the prince.

Drona was on the side of Kauravas not by choice but because of sense of duty to the employer.

ततः शङ्खाश्च भेर्यश्च पणवानकगोमुखाः।
सहसैवाभ्यहन्यन्त स शब्दस्तुमुलोऽभवत् ||13||

tataḥ śaṅkhāś ca bheryaś ca paṇavānakagomukhā
sahasaivābhyahanyanta sa śabdas tumulo 'bhavat ||13||

(When Bheeshma blew the conch) all the other warriors quiet suddenly blew their conches, trumpets, drums and horns. The sound filled all sides and was tremendous. ||13||

Tataha: then; Shankhascha: conches and; Bheryascha: kettle drums (war drums); Panavanaka: trumpets and drums; Gomukhah: horns; Sahasaiva: and suddenly; Abhya hanyanta: blared forth; Sa shabhdaha: that sound; Tumulo: filled all sides; abhavat: was.

As was the custom in those days, all the leaders of various sections in the vast army carried their conchs with them and blew them after eldest state–man did the honours first.

There were others who carried the trumpets and horns instead of the conchs. The two armies together had 18 great divisions and the sound by the war drums, trumpets and conchs filled the air on all the sides. This, the poet describes as "tremendous."

ततः श्वेतैर्हयैर्युक्ते महति स्यन्दने स्थितौ।
माधवः पाण्डवश्चैव दिव्यौ शङ्खौ प्रदध्मतुः ||14||

tataḥ śvetair hayair yukte mahati syandane sthitau |
mādhavaḥ pāṇḍavaś caiva divyau śaṅkhau pradadhmatuḥ ||14||

Then, seated in the magnificent chariot, yoked with white horses, Krishna and Arjuna blew their divine conches. ||14||

Tataha: then; Svetaih: with white; Hayair: horses; Yukta: yoked; Mahati: magnificent; Syandane: in the chariot; Sthitou: seated; Madhavaha: Krishna; Pandavaschaiva: and also Arjuna; Divyou: celestial; Shankou: conches; Pradadmatuhu: blew.

One has to imagine the majesty of Lord Krishna, taking up the role of the charioteer, bringing the chariot with Arjuna on to the center of the battlefield. Any chariot with the Lord will be majestic to look at and be divine.

In this instance, divinity was enhanced as the chariot belonged to the Lord of Fire and the horses were the property of Chitraratha, the king of Gandharvas. (celestial divinities.). The chariot was a gift to Arjuna from the Lord of Fire.

Arjuna, during the period of exile in the forest with his brothers, had assisted the Lord of Fire in destroying the Khandava forest and the gift was in return for the services rendered. The chariot and the horses gifted were possessed with special magical powers. They could move from one position in the battlefield to another by flying over any obstacle and reach the selected spot within seconds. Arjuna could therefore be in any position within seconds.

The horses, the poet describes as "white horses." One can interpret the color white as representing "Dharma" symbolizing "Purity." As the Lord himself was the charioteer whatever that is under His control has to represent "Purity."

Madhava:

One of the names given to Lord Krishna is Madhava. (Each of the number of names given to the Hindu deities does carry a special meaning and represent a divine quality.)

Madhava is one of the names of Lord Vishnu and Sri Krishna is an incarnation of Lord Vishnu.

Madhava means "husband of wealth." Goddess Lakshmi, symbolizing the wealth is the consort of Lord Vishnu. Poet Vyasa, by using the word Madhava is letting us know that the Goddess of wealth, Lakshmi had showered her grace on the Pandavas. There was no way the Pandavas could be defeated. By their victory over the Kauravas, they would rule over the kingdom. ("Rajya" in Sanskrit means "Kingdom." "Rajya Lakshmi", one of the eight names of Goddess Lakshmi is appropriate in this context.)

The word "Vijaya" in Sanskrit means "Victory." Another name given to Goddess Lakshmi is "Vijaya Lakshmi." (The Goddess of victory.)

By using the word "Madhava" the poet is assuring that the Pandavas will achieve victory and regain the kingdom.

Lord Krishna was given the honor to blow this conch first for the Pandavas. Arjuna was the next in line to blow his conch and others followed later.

पाञ्चजन्यं हृषीकेशो देवदत्तं धनंजयः।
पौण्ड्रं दध्मौ महाशङ्खं भीमकर्मा वृकोदरः॥15॥

pāñcajanyaṃ hṛṣīkeśo devadattaṃ dhanaṃjayaḥ |
pauṇḍraṃ dadhmau mahāśaṅkhaṃ bhīmakarmā vṛkodaraḥ ||15||

Hrishikesha blew the Panchajanya, and Dhananjaya blew Devadatta, and Vrikodhara the doer of terrible deeds, blew the great conch Paundra ||15||

अनन्तविजयं राजा कुन्तीपुत्रो युधिष्ठिरः।
नकुलः सहदेवश्च सुघोषमणिपुष्पकौ ॥16॥

anantavijayaṃ rājā kuntīputro yudhiṣṭhiraḥ |
nakulaḥ sahadevaś ca sughoṣamaṇipuṣpakau ||16||

King Yudhistira, son of Kunti blew Anantavijayaṃ, Nakula and Sahadeva blew Sughosha and Manipushpaka; ||16||

काश्यश्च परमेष्वासः शिखण्डी च महारथः।
धृष्टद्युम्नो विराटश्च सात्यकिश्चापराजितः ॥17॥

kāśyaś ca parameṣvāsaḥ śikhaṇḍī ca mahārathaḥ |
dhṛṣṭadyumno virāṭaś ca sātyakiś cāparājitaḥ ||17||

द्रुपदो द्रौपदेयाश्च सर्वशः पृथिवीपते।
सौभद्रश्च महाबाहुः शङ्खान्दध्मुः पृथक्पृथक् ॥18॥

drupado draupadeyāś ca sarvaśaḥ pṛthivīpate |
saubhadraś ca mahābāhuḥ śaṅkhān dadhmuḥ pṛthak pṛthak ||18||

The King of Kasi, an excellent archer; Sikhandi, the mighty commander Drushtadyumna, Virata and the unconquered Satyakai; Drupada, the sons of Droupadi, Abhimanyu, the mighty armed, all blew their respective conchs. ||17-18||

Prithiveepate: O King Dhritarashtra; Hrishikesha: Krishna; Panchajanyam: the conch Panchajanyam; Devadattam: conch named Devadatta; Bheema karma: doer of terrible deed; Vrukodharaha: Bheema; Maha shankam: great conch; Dadhmou: blew; Kuntee putra: son of Kunti; Parameshwasaha: an excellent archer; Kashyascha: the king of Kasi; Maharataha: mighty leader; Aparajitaha: the unconquered; Droupadeyascha: and the sons of Droupadi; Saubhadrascha: and the son of Subhadra; Prithak prithak: separately; Dadhmou: blew.

The main warriors from the Pandava army who were given the honor of blowing their respective conch are mentioned in the four verses.

Let us analyze a few words in these slokas.

Hrishikesha: another name for Lord Krishna. It means "he who is the ruler over the mind and the senses."

Dhananjaya: it is another name for Arjuna and it means "conqueror of wealth." Arjuna went round the country and won over many rulers and amassed a number of regions for his brother Yudhistira. By his battle skills, he expanded his brother's kingdom.

Vrikodhara: this word refers to Bheema. It is said that he carried fire in his stomach and could consume anything. Duryodhana once drowned Bhima (when he was very young) in the river and a number of snakes bit him. None of the poison from the bites affected him and he came back alive and strong. Duryodhana, at another time gave poison in disguise but it did not kill Bhima. Hence, he is called "Vrikodhara."

Panchajanyam: it is the name of Krishna's conch. Krishna was taught by the Guru "Sandipani." The guru's son was abducted once by a demon Panchajanya and hid him under deep waters. The guru as a gurudakshina asked Krishna to get his son back. The story goes on to say that in this task, Krishna had to kill the demon Panchajanya. The conch was made by the bones of the demon.

स घोषो धार्तराष्ट्राणां हृदयानि व्यदारयत्।
नभश्च पृथिवीं चैव तुमुलो व्यनुनादयन् ||19||

sa ghoṣo dhārtarāṣṭrāṇāṃ hṛdayāni vyadārayat |
nabhaś ca pṛthivīṃ caiva tumulo vyanunādayan ||19||

The tumultuous sounds of the Pandava army filling all sides reverberated through the earth and sky and rent the hearts of the Kauravas. ||19||

Sa: that; Ghosho: sound; Dhartarashtranam: of the Kauravas; Hridayaan: hearts;Vyadarayat: rent/frightened; Nabhahscha: the sky and; Prithiveem: the earth; Chaiva: and also; Tumulo: tumultuous; Vyanunadayan: made to reverberate.

The Pandavas army consisted of seven massive battalions of soldiers. Lord Krishna and the great warriors from their side sounded their instruments. This sound was too loud and frightening to hear. Apart from a handful, the Kauravas army, though fighting for Dhritarashtra, respected the Pandavas. They were aware of the powers of Krishna and the Pandava brothers. To hear the sound that signaled the beginning of the great war, brought a feeling of terror for them.

अथ व्यवस्थितान् दृष्ट्वा धार्तराष्ट्रान्कपिध्वजः।
प्रवृत्ते शस्त्रसंपाते धनुरुद्यम्य पाण्डवः ||20||
हृषीकेशं तदा वाक्यमिदमाह महीपते।

atha vyavasthitān dṛṣṭvā dhārtarāṣṭrān kapidhvajaḥ |
pravṛtte śastrasaṃpāte dhanur udyamya pāṇḍavaḥ ||20||

hṛṣīkeśaṃ tadā vākyam idam āha mahīpate |

Then, O ruler of the Earth, seeing Dhritarashtra's sons being Positioned (positioned in the battlefield) and the fighting about to commence, Pandava, whose ensign badge is Hanuman, lifting his bow spoke the following words to Krishna. ||20||

Atha: now; Vyavasthitaan: standing/assembled/positioned; Drishtva: seeing; Dhartra rashtraan: Kauravas; Kapidwajaha: ensign of monkey on the flag; Pravrutte: about to begin; Shastra sampate: discharge of weapons/fighting ; Dhanur udyamya: lifting bow; Pandavaha: Pandava (Arjuna); Hrishikesham: to Hrishikesha; Idam: this; Tada: then; Vakyam: words; Aha: spoke; Maheepate: O King (Dhritarashtra)

Dhartra rashtraan: army of the Emperor Dhritarashtra with Bheeshma as the Commander–in–chief and the rest of their army of 11 battalions.

Bheeshma had arranged a strategic formation of his army and the warriors had taken up their respective positions.

The chariot of Arjuna was driven to the spot by Sri Krishna wherein Arjuna could see those with whom he had to fight. He was eager to take up the final task of regaining the lost kingdom.

The ensign badge (on the flag flying on top of their chariot) had the picture of Hanuman. This has some significance and we should learn about the same.

Hanuman represents the path of "Bhakti." His bhakti was only to Lord Rama.

During the period of exile of the Pandavas for 13yrs, one fine day Bhima had taken a journey into the forest to fulfill Droupadi's wish. Droupadi had accidentally come across a lovely fragrance from a special flower (Saugandhika) in the forest and fell in love with it. She pleads with Bhima to get her the flower from which the beautiful fragrance had sprung forth.

Bhima went on a mission to find the source of that fragrance. On the way, in the narrow path, there sat an old monkey which obstructed the path. Bhima arrogantly orders the monkey to move out of his way. The monkey replies that he is old and week and has no physical strength to move even an inch. He pleads Bhima to shift him physically to the side of the path (and thereby free the path for Bhima to proceed). Bhima who was physically very strong, could not even lift the tail of the monkey an inch off the ground.

Realizing that the monkey was someone special, he begs pardon for the arrogant behavior. The monkey in turn reveals his true identity as Hanuman.

(Hanuman is considered to be the son of the Lord of the Wind. Bhima is also considered to be the son of the Lord of the Wind. Thus, the two were really brothers.)

Hanuman blesses Bhima and gives him directions to find the flower whose fragrance had reached the site where Droupadi was. He also promises to help the Pandavas during the forthcoming war with the Kauravas. He says that he would station himself on the flag that carried the insignia of the Pandava prince Arjuna.

Hanuman is considered to be the eternal servant of Lord Rama. For him there exists only one God and he is no other than Lord Rama.

He knew that Sri Krishna was none other than his beloved Lord Rama.

This confirms that Sri Krishna is the "Avatara" of Vishnu. Lord Rama from Treta Yuga, had reincarnated as Krishna in Dwapara Yuga.

Hanuman represents Bhakti. The Pandavas led by Arjuna, had the flag with Hanuman as their insignia.

It signifies that the Pandavas engaged in war had followed the path of Bhakti.

Also it is interesting to note that apart from Sanjaya, Dhritarashtra and Arjuna who heard the sacred Gita narrated by Lord Krishna, Hanuman was another special person, a silent witness to the conversation.

Hrishikesha is another name of Sri Krishna. (Refer sloka 18).

अर्जुन उवाच
सेनयोरुभयोर्मध्ये रथं स्थापय मेऽच्युत ||21||

arjuna uvāca
senayor ubhayor madhye ratham sthāpaya me 'cyuta ||21||

यावदेतान्निरीक्षेऽहं योद्धुकामानवस्थितान्|
कैर्मया सह योद्धव्यमस्मिन्रणसमुद्यमे ||22||

yāvad etān nirīkṣe 'haṃ yoddhukāmān avasthitān |
kair mayā saha yoddhavyam asmin raṇasamudyame ||22||

Arjuna said:
Place my chariot, O Achyuta, between the two armies so that I may behold the war-minded that stand here, with whom I must wage this war. ||21-22||

Senayor: armies; Ubhayor madhye: in the middle of both; Ratham: the chariot; Sthapaya: place; Achyuta: Krishna; Yavat: from hence; Etam: them; Nireeksheham: I behold; Yoddhukamaan: desirous to fight; Avasthitaam: standing here; Kair: with; Maya: by me; Saha: them; Yoddhavyam: the battle to be fought (I must wage the war); Rana samudyame: commencement of battle.

Achyuta refers to Krishna: "The one who does not fall." Also means He, who is free from the cycle of the process of birth, growth, decay and death.

The seekers have to lift themselves in the spiritual evolution from the lower state of "Tamas to Rajas, Rajas to Satva and from "Satva to Shuddha Satva."

The only ones who can climb up even further than "Satva" are those who manage to drop the "Ego" and merge with the "Supreme." This state is called "Shuddha Satva."

Having become one with the "Supreme", there is no further drop from the spiritual heights reached. This can happen only when the seeker loses his own identity (ego).

The Lord/Achyuta never falls down from the state of "Supreme Purusha". One can also see that from this sloka onwards, Arjuna uses the word "my", "I" many number of times. This demonstrates the power of "Ego" in him.

योत्स्यमानानवेक्षेऽहं य एतेऽत्र समागताः।
धार्तराष्ट्रस्य दुर्बुद्धेर्युद्धे प्रियचिकीर्षवः ||23||

yotsyamānān avekṣe 'haṃ ya ete 'tra samāgatāḥ |
dhārtarāṣṭrasya durbuddher yuddhe priyacikīrṣavaḥ ||23||

I will see these warriors assembled here for the fight, wishing to please the evil minded Duryodhana. ||23||

Yotsyamanaan: ready to fight; Avekseham: I will see; Yete: these (warriors); Atra: here; Samagataha: assembled; dhartarashtrasya: of Duryodhana; Durbuddhe: evil minded; Yuddhe: in the battle; Priyachikeershavaha: wishing to please.

The Pandavas were fighting for the rightful share of the kingdom. On the other hand Duryodhana was not willing to part even a small portion of the kingdom to his cousins. He was evil minded and was guided and supported in his evil plans to fight the Pandavas by his maternal uncle Shakuni and friend Karna. The blind love for his son Duryodhana made the blind emperor Dhritarashtra agree to declare war against the Pandavas.

Those were the days, 5000yrs ago, when each kingdom had its allies and vassals. In case of war, the allies and the vassals pledged their army to their superior, the king. On that basis, the Pandavas had a total army that equaled seven battalions and the Kauravas, 11 battalions. The leaders of the various sections in the battalions were ready fight to win or die for their king.

Arjuna states that he wanted to see the warriors assembled to fight for the enemy Duryodhana. He uses the adjunctive "evil minded" with reference to Duryodhana. He devised so many evil plans to kill the Pandava brothers. When the attempts failed, he devised plans to snatch their kingdom by unjust means. He stooped down to the level of insulting Droupadi in the open assembly. Arjuna's blood was boiling and he could not wait for the war to begin.

Those who were on the side of Kauravas could be divided into respected elders like the grandsire Bheeshma, guru Dronacharya, family priest Kripacharya and others. Bheeshma fought for the Kauravas because of the solemn promise he had given to his father.

Dronacharya and Kripacharya were the employees of Dhritarashtra and had solemn duty to fight for their employer.

All these could not be called "evil minded". The fact is though, they fought for unrighteousness, and so did not deserve any mercy from the Pandavas. The Pandava brothers and their allies were roaring to face the enemy and kill them.

Arjuna had the entered the battle scene with this frame of mind and hence the request for placing the chariot at the most suitable spot so that he could see the assembled enemy forces and get the adrenaline flowing.

सञ्जय उवाच
एवमुक्तो हृषीकेशो गुडाकेशेन भारत।
सेनयोरुभयोर्मध्ये स्थापयित्वा रथोत्तमम् ||24||

sañjaya uvāca
evam ukto hṛṣīkeśo guḍākeśena bhārata |
senayor ubhayor madhye sthāpayitvā rathottamam ||24||

भीष्मद्रोणप्रमुखतः सर्वेषां च महीक्षिताम्।
उवाच पार्थ पश्यैतान्समवेतान्कुरूनिति ||25||

bhīṣmadroṇapramukhataḥ sarveṣāṃ ca mahīkṣitām |
uvāca pārtha paśyaitān samavetān kurūn iti ||25||

Sanjaya said:
Thus addressed by Arjuna, Lord Krishna placed the noble chariot in the middle of the armies, and in front of Bheeshma, Drona and all other prominent kings. He said, O Arjuna, behold the Kauravas gathered together. ||24-25||

Evam: thus; Hrishikesha: Lord Krishna; Gudakeshena: by Arjuna; Bharata: descendant of Bharata; Senayor ubhayor madhye: in the middle of the two armies; Stapayitva: having placed; Rathottamam: the noble chariot; Pramukathaha: prominent; Sarvesham cha: and all; Mahekeshitaam: kings; Uvacha: spoke (said); Paschaitan: behold these; Samavetaan: assembled; Kurun: Kauravas; Iti: thus.

Note that Sanjaya uses the words "thus addressed" and not "thus commanded". After all, the charioteer of Arjuna was not ordinary employee but the Lord himself. Arjuna could never command Krishna, his charioteer. He fulfilled the request by Arjuna and placed the chariot at a suitable spot which would provide Arjuna with a good view of all the senior warriors on the side of the Kauravas.

There are three words to note from these slokas: "Hrishikesha", "Gudakesha." and "Partha." Let us look at the meaning of these words:

"Hrishikesha": "Hrishika" means "senses" and "Esa" means Lord. "Lord over the senses" is "The Lord Himself". In this context it refers to Lord Krishna.

"Gudakesha" means "Conqueror over sleep." As we know sleep is a tamasic quality. Arjuna is receiving the "Great spiritual lesson", his mind needs to be constantly awake and alert to every word spoken. Krishna imparted the Gita to Arjuna because he had this special quality in listening to the highest spiritual teaching.

Also, Arjuna was a passionate rajasic warrior and not lazy by nature.

"Partha": it is another name for "Arjuna." Arjuna was the son of "Pritha" and hence he got the name. "Pritha" is another name for his mother Kunti.

Sura was a Yadava king and he had a daughter by name Pritha. He had a cousin Kuntibhoja who was childless and requested to adopt Pritha. Sura obliged with the request and gave Pritha to Kuntibhoja. As she was adopted by Kuntibhoja, Pritha got the name "Kunti." Kunti, as a maiden was given the job of looking after the guests who visited the country. One of the guests she looked after once for a full year was the sage "Durvasa."

Pleased by her services, the sage gave her a special boon. He gave her six special mantras. Recitation of each of the mantra would bring the deity of the mantra to her and he would bless her with a child. Using the mantra she begot the five Pandava brothers and Karna.

There is a Sanskrit word "Parthiva" which means "made of clay." The word "Pritha" relates to this word "Parthiva." Clay is perishable and our body made of the five gross elements is perishable. Our body is therefore "mortal" which means "perishable."

The sacred text is from the "Imperishable Lord Krishna" to " Arjuna who is a mortal." Arjuna is the representative for all of us, the passionate mortals.

तत्रापश्यत्स्थितान्पार्थः पितृनथ पितामहान्।
आचार्यान्मातुलान्भ्रातृन्पुत्रान्पौत्रान्सखींस्तथा ||26||
श्वशुरान्सुहृदश्चैव सेनयोरुभयोरपि।

tatrāpaśyat sthitān pārthaḥ pitṝn atha pitāmahān |
ācāryān mātulān bhrātṝn putrān pautrān sakhīṃs tathā ||26||

śvaśurān suhṛdaś caiva senayor ubhayor api |

There, Arjuna saw fathers, grandfathers, teachers, maternal uncles, brothers, sons, grandsons, companions, fathers-in-law and friends in both the armies. ||26||

तान्समीक्ष्य स कौन्तेयः सर्वान्बन्धूनवस्थितान् ||27||
कृपया परयाऽऽविष्टो विषीदन्निदमब्रवीत्।

tān samīkṣya sa kaunteyaḥ sarvān bandhūn avasthitān |
kṛpayā parayāviṣṭo viṣīdann idam abravīt ||27||

Seeing all those relations, standing arrayed in the battle, Arjuna thus spoke sorrowfully, filled with deep pity. ||27||

Tatra: there; Pashyat: saw; Sthitan: stationed/standing; Pitrun: fathers; Atha: and; Pitamahaan: grandfathers; Acharyaan: teachers; Matulaan: maternal uncles; Bhratran: brothers; Putran: sons; Poutran: grandchildren; Sakheen: companions/comrades; Tatha: also; Shvashuran: fathers–in–law; Suhrud: friends; chaiva: and also; Senayor ubhayorapi: in both the armies also. Taan: these; Saha: he; Sameekshya: having seen; Kounteya: son of Kunti (Arjuna);Sarvaan: all; Bandhoon: relations; Avasthitaam: assembled/arrayed; Krupaya: by pity; Paraya: deep; Avishta: filled; Visheedan: sorrowfully; Idam: this; Abraveet: said.

We should remember that the great war was a consequence of acts of "adharma" by Duryodhana. Sri Krishna, the Divine Incarnate, sided with the Pandavas. To prevent the bloodshed in the battle, He took personally the responsibility of reconciliation. When all the efforts at the peaceful negotiations failed, the war was declared by the Lord Himself.

Those were the days of rule by the royalty who kept a tight rein over their territory. War with the ruler over the adjoining territory to expand the kingdom was not considered wrong. Democracy as we know now (with leaders elected by the public) was not in vogue.

The Kshatriya race were born warriors. Taking part in a righteous war was considered as heroic. They believed that winning the war would give control over new territory and dying in the battle would confer entry into heaven.

Unfortunately, Arjuna who entered with a positive frame of mind to win back the territory (which belonged to his brother rightfully) is seen to be entering into a state of mental crisis. Change of attitude can be seen in the following verses. Instead of being a stout lion hearted Kshatriya, he becomes a soft hearted, week individual. He entered the battle as a well acclaimed hero. His attitude is that of a kinsman looking at the arrayed army in terms of personal relationship.

It was not really an act of discrimination but an act of ignorance on his part. This unfortunately, is the downfall of an individual from spiritual heights achieved by gaining knowledge. It is the gateway to the fall and degradation.

He pitied all the relations who had entered the battlefield on either side. He experienced severe mental agony that is reflected in the way he spoke to Krishna.

The word to note is "Kripa". It means "Pity."

"Pity" as such is a noble quality in the spiritual path. Expressing pity and forgetting "Dharma" cannot be termed as "noble quality." Arjuna was exactly in this frame of mind. It was "mental weakness" born out of "ignorance."

Just like we go to the physician to get cured of the bodily illness, we need to go the "Spiritual physician" to cleanse the mind of the "ignorance."

After letting Arjuna express his sorrow, Sri Krishna gives the "Spiritual medicine" which is the sacred text "Sreemad Bhagawadgita", courtesy of Sage Poet Veda Vyasa.

अर्जुन उवाच
दृष्ट्वेमं स्वजनं कृष्ण युयुत्सुं समुपस्थितम् ||28||
सीदन्ति मम गात्राणि मुखं च परिशुष्यति|

Arjuna Uvāca
dṛṣṭvemāṃ svajanāṃ kṛṣṇa yuyutsuṃ samupasthitam| ||28||
sīdanti mama gātrāṇi mukhaṃ ca pariśuṣyati |

वेपथुश्च शरीरे मे रोमहर्षश्च जायते ||29||
गाण्डीवं स्रंसते हस्तात्त्वक्चैव परिदह्यते|
न च शक्नोम्यवस्थातुं भ्रमतीव च मे मनः ||30||

vepathuś ca śarīre me romaharṣaś ca jāyate ||29||

gāṇḍīvaṃ sraṃsate hastāt tvak caiva paridahyate |
na ca śaknomy avasthātuṃ bhramatīva ca me manaḥ ||30||

Arjuna said
O Krishna, seeing these my own kinsmen gathered, eager to fight, my limbs fail, my tongue is dried up, my body trembles, my skin is burning all over and my hair stands on end and even my mind is whirling. My Gandiva is slipping from my hand. I cannot stand up. ||28 29 30||

Drishtva: having seen; Mam: my; Swajanam: kinsmen; Yuyutsum: eager to fight; Samupasthitam: arrayed; Seedanti: fail; Mama: my; Gatrani: limbs; Mukham: mouth; Cha: and; Paritushyati: is parching; Vepatuscha: and trembling; Shareera: in the body; Me': in my body; Romaharsha: horrification; Jayate: arise; Gandeevam: Gandeeva; bow of Arjuna; Sramsate: slips; Hastaat: from my hands; Tvak chaiva: and also skin; Paridakshate: burns all over; Na: not; Cha: and; Shaknosi: able; Avasthatum: to stand;Bhramateeva: seems whirling; Me': my; Manaha: mind.

Note that Arjuna has used the word "my" nine times in these three slokas.

From medical point of view, as a man of depression approaches his psychologist/psychoanalyst, the words used by Arjuna express his "weakness, despair and sorrowful state" (mental agony).The psychoanalyst would say that the patient is showing symptoms of "Anxiety Neurosis."

Arjuna is showing signs of "self pity."

Arjuna's weapon of action was "Gandeeva." It was the magical bow presented to him by the Gandharvas. (Gandeeva was the bow said to be created by Brahma to protect Dharma.) It had the power of a thousand bows and came with two inexhaustible quivers. No other weapon could damage it. (After the departure of Krishna from the physical world at the end of His Avatara, it is said that the bow lost its magical powers)

Symbolically, "Gandiva slipping from the hand" means that Arjuna lost the power to hold the weapon. This was the result of "mental weakness". Whatever the strength of the individual may be, during moments of mental weakness like depression, the body suddenly loses all the physical strength. We lose the strength to hold on to the tool of action in our life and fail to conduct the ordained duties.

Why did a great warrior like Arjuna suddenly develop this symptom, especially on the battlefield, the first day of the most important battle of his life?

One can say that Arjuna developed the symptoms of depression because he saw his "personal relationship" of the warriors assembled. This made him lose the "knowledge of right action." As we have discussed before, he had given his full support to brother Yudhistira to fight the "war of righteousness". As a Kshatriya warrior of repute, he had only one duty to perform and it was "to assist his brother in uprooting the evil." Towards this he had the support and blessings of the Lord Himself.

What he said to Krishna shows his "Ignorance."

The remedy for the ignorance is "Atma Jnana". Arjuna had to realise the true identity of all individuals including himself. The knowledge of the "Self" clears the veil of "Maya" and the spiritual seeker can get the mental strength to fight the "ignorance".

Sage poet, Bhagawan Veda Vyasa is referring to all the "Arjuna's of the world" and helping them to clear the "spiritual ignorance." What we are going to get in the chapters to come is the "Knowledge of the true Self" in each of us.

Let us offer our prayers to the Lord and request Him to lead us in the spiritual journey in search of the "Eternal Bliss".

निमित्तानि च पश्यामि विपरीतानि केशव|
न च श्रेयोऽनुपश्यामि हत्वा स्वजनमाहवे ||31||

nimittāni ca paśyāmi viparītāni keśava |
na ca śreyo 'nupaśyāmi hatvā svajanam āhave ||31||

O Krishna, I see many ill omens. I do not understand what good could come in killing my kinsmen in the battle. ||31||

Nimittani: omens; Cha: and; Pashyani: I see; Vipareetani: adverse/ ill; Shreyon: good;Anupashyani: I see; Hatva: killing; Svajanam: own people/kinsmen; Ahave: in battle.

In states of hysteria, instead of the reasoning capacity ruling over the thoughts arising in the mind, the mind neglects the advice given by the reasoning capacity (intellect). Arjuna's mind, (because of his family relationship of the warriors assembled) was looking at each leader assembled in terms of personal relationship. His intellect would be telling the mind that the leading warriors assembled on the opposite camp were siding with adharma.

But, Arjuna's mind became stronger and intellect got weaker (the junior worker in an office, second in command decides to neglect his senior officer, first-in-command). Because of this mental state, Arjuna starts seeing ill omens. (It is interesting to note that even in those days, 5000yrs ago, people believed in ill omens)

The junior (mind) who took charge neglected the senior's (intellect) advice. He took a wrong decision and interpreted the dharma wrongly.

The feelings felt by Arjuna were subjective and not objective. His intellect got clouded.

It is like the brilliant light of the sun hidden by the dark clouds. Because the mind got weaker the organs of action lost their strength and the Gandeeva slipped from his hands. He could not even remain standing. Mental weakness got reflected as physical weakness.

न काङ्क्षे विजयं कृष्ण न च राज्यं सुखानि च|
किं नो राज्येन गोविन्द किं भोगैर्जीवितेन वा ||32||

na kāṅkṣe vijayaṃ kṛṣṇa na ca rājyaṃ sukhāni ca |
kiṃ no rājyena govinda kiṃ bhogair jīvitena vā ||32||

O Krishna, I do not desire victory or kingdom, or pleasures. Of what avail is this kingdom to us? Of what avail is the enjoyment or even life itself to us? ||32||

येषामर्थे काङ्क्षितं नो राज्यं भोगाः सुखानि च|
त इमेऽवस्थिता युद्धे प्राणांस्त्यक्त्वा धनानि च||33||

yeṣām arthe kāṅkṣitaṃ no rājyaṃ bhogāḥ sukhāni ca|
ta ime 'vasthitā yuddhe prāṇāṃs tyaktvā dhanāni ca ||33||

Those for whose sake we desire kingdom, enjoyment and pleasures stand here ready for the battle, having renounced their wealth and life. ||33||

आचार्याः पितरः पुत्रास्तथैव च पितामहाः|
मातुलाः श्वशुराः पौत्राः श्यालाः सम्बन्धिनस्तथा ||34||

ācāryāḥ pitaraḥ putrās tathaiva ca pitāmahāḥ |
mātulāḥ śvaśurāḥ pautrāḥ śyālāḥ saṃbandhinas tathā ||34||

Teachers, fathers, sons, grandfathers, maternal uncles, fathers-in-law, grandsons, brothers-in-law and other relatives. ||34||

Na: not; Kankche: desire; Vijayam: victory; Rajyam: kingdom; Sukhani: pleasures; Kim: what then; No': to us; Govinda: Krishna; Bhogair: by enjoyments; Jeevitena: life itself; Eshamarthe: for what sake; Kankshitam: is desired; Naha: by us; Rajyam: kingdom; Bhogaha: enjoyments; Sukhani: pleasures/ happiness; Te: these; Ime: people; Avasthitaha: standing; Yuddhe: in battle; Pranaan: life; Tyaktva: having abandoned; Dhanani: wealth; Acharyaha: teachers; Pitaraha: fathers; Putraha: sons; Tathaiva: others also; Pitamahaha: grandparents; Matulaha: maternal uncles; Shvashuraha: fathers in law; Poutraha: grandchildren; Shyalaha: brothers in law; Sambandhim: relations; tatha: thus.

Note the words "desires, enjoyments, pleasures," used by Arjuna. "For whose sake we desire kingdom and enjoyment" he says. Duryodhana, his cousin on the opposite side was definitely fighting to keep his kingdom, not share it with cousins and desirous of enjoying the bounties from the war.

It is common knowledge that most of us would like to share and enjoy the benefits of our action with our close family and friends. In the beginning, the royal family of king Dhritarashtra was beaming with sounds of merriment from the Pandavas and the Kauravas. As children they were playing together in and around the palace. As they grew Duryodhana showed jealousy towards Pandavas as he did not want them to rule the kingdom. He came to the battlefield to win the kingdom or die in the battlefield.

The thought of losing so many family members in the war had not occurred to Arjuna so far. Suddenly, it dawned on him that the palace would be like "crematorium grounds" with no sounds of happiness shared by the family members.

Certainly Arjuna was on a higher pedestal. He wanted to enjoy the results with all the various members of the family and other relatives. The war was between the two cousins who lived together but fighting to get rid of the other side.

The fault, as far as we can see at this juncture is "Arjuna's desire for the fruits of actions." The idea of sharing it with family is laudable. As we proceed with the rest of the Gita we will come to understand that we have to fight the battle of life as a sacred duty and not be looking for the results of the actions.

Arjuna is showing signs of renunciation. It is not enough. Single pointed concentration during discharge of duties is essential to get the best results. The aim of the Pandavas was to accept the guidance from the Lord Himself, fight the injustice and protect the citizens of the kingdom from those who ruled against the injunctions of the scriptures. Arjuna, the highly trained warrior should have showed signs of "concentration" on the task ahead.

By using the words expressing renunciation of enjoying the pleasures to be accrued by winning the war, Arjuna can be seen actually ready to receive the most precious knowledge from Sri Krishna. The Lord is going to impart the "Atma Jnana", the knowledge of ones' true Self.

एतान्न हन्तुमिच्छामि घ्नतोऽपि मधुसूदन।
अपि त्रैलोक्यराज्यस्य हेतोः किं नु महीकृते ||35||

etān na hantum icchāmi ghnato 'pi madhusūdana |
api trailokyarājyasya hetoḥ kiṃ nu mahīkṛte ||35||

O Madhusudhana, I do not wish to kill them, though they may kill me, even for the sake of dominion over all the three worlds, much less for a fragment of this earth. ||35||

Etan: these/them; Na: not; Hantum: to kill; Itchami: wish; Ghnato'pi: even if killed by them; Madhusudhana: Krishna; Api: even; Trailokya Rajyosya hetoho: for the sake of dominion over the three worlds; Kim tu: how then; Maheekrute: for the sake of fragment of the earth.

Madhusudhana: destroyer of the demon Madhu. It is another name referring to Krishna, the incarnation of Vishnu. In Puranas and mythology, Brahma is represented as Light and Madhu as Darkness. Madhu seeks continually to destroy Brahma, the Light and was finally destroyed by Krishna/Vishnu.

By using the words "I" and "me" Arjuna is still referring to his physical body. As a Kshatriya he had the right to fight for his kingdom. The Kshatriya was brought up from childhood to realize that it was the duty of every member of his race to be prepared to fight when needed. Killing the enemy in the battle was not considered to be an act of sin.

In the present situation, his mental disposition makes him say that he is ready to disarm and not bothered if the enemy kills him. He was ready to let Duryodhana take over the kingdom and rule the land.

The philosophy says that our actions are due to our thought imprints of the past. In this instance, Arjuna had a strong bank of thought imprint in his mind to kill the wicked cousin Duryodhana and his brothers. If he decided not to fight, the past thought imprints would not disappear by magic. They would still be stored in his memory bank. They would have to manifest at a later date. In other words, by not fighting Arjuna would only be postponing the inevitable and has to be born again to clear those thought imprints.

Arjuna was ignorant of the "vasanas and the art to extinguish them from the mind." As we go through the Gita we will find an answer to the question of "how to get rid of the vasanas." Even a learned gentleman and a great warrior like Arjuna succumbed to the weakness of the mind. Luckily he had Krishna, the Lord Himself to guide him in the right path.

We are lucky and blessed to have the philosophy of the Gita in front of us to help us to overcome the ignorance in our lives.

निहत्य धार्तराष्ट्रान्नः का प्रीतिः स्याज्जनार्दन|
पापमेवाश्रयेदस्मान्हत्वैतानाततायिनः ||36||

nihatya dhārtarāṣṭrān naḥ kā prītiḥ syāj janārdana |
pāpam evāśrayed asmān hatvaitān ātatāyinaḥ ||36||

What pleasure can be ours, O Janardana, by killing these sons of Dhritarashtra. Sin alone will be our gain by killing these felons. ||36||

Nihatya: having killed; dhartarashtran: sons of Dhritarashtra; nah: to us; ka: what; preetihi: pleasure; syat: may be; janardhana: Krishna; papam: sin; eva: only; asrayet: will take hold; asman: to us; hatva: having killed; etan: these; atatayinaha: felons.

Arjuna evidently is aware of "results of actions conducted". In the present situation he is faced with the actions involving killing the soldiers including some members of one's own family. Analyzing from the "mental plane" he is concluding that by killing his own cousins he would have committed an act of sin. He would not feel happy by conduct of such action. So he puts in a question: "what pleasure can be ours"?

His next statement is "Sin alone will be our gain by killing these felons." He feels that killing the beloved ones in the war is an act of sin.

If we can understand the true meaning of the word "felon" we can see that his statement is wrong. As a member of the ruling caste, he has to know the law of the land. In those days "Manu Dharma Sastra" was the basis for ruling the land. Let us look at who is a "felon" according to Manu.

A felon is he who has committed one of the following five heinous crimes:

Sets fire to another person's house with an intention of killing the inmates.

Poisons an individual with an intention to kill.

Falls on an individual with a sword to kill.

Steals unlawfully the wealth of another person.

Steals the wife of another person.

Manu categorically states in his "Dharma Sastra" that the penalty for a felon is "Death." Irrespective of who the felon is, he should have to be killed.

Arjuna accepts that the Kauravas had committed not one but all the above five crimes. The verdict of the jury should be anonymous: "they are the felons."

"Having said that, he should then pass the verdict of "death." When one has followed the law of the land in the conduct of an action, then he is said to have not committed a sinful act.

Here, Arjuna says that by killing the "felons", the Kauravas, he would have committed a sin and so should be punished. He is confused and his verdict is wrong.

"Janardhana". This is another of the name for Lord Krishna.

The word means "giver of rewards." Janardhana is considered as one of the 24 Avataras of Lord Vishnu. As Janardhana, Vishnu takes the form of planets and gives fruits of consequences for actions of men/women on the earth.

From the point of view of mankind, the planets are divinities and spiritual element predominates in them. They bestow benefits to the life on the earth by their configuration. They are considered as "celestial wanderers."

On the contrary, we, part of life on this earth have predominance of "life element" in us.

The position of the planets at the time of birth of an individual is taken into considering when writing the horoscope by experts on the subject.

तस्मान्नार्हा वयं हन्तुं धार्तराष्ट्रान्स्वबान्धवान्।
स्वजनं हि कथं हत्वा सुखिनः स्याम माधव ||37||

tasmān nārhā vayaṃ hantuṃ dhārtarāṣṭrān svabāndhavān |
svajanaṃ hi kathaṃ hatvā sukhinaḥ syāma mādhava ||37||

O Madhava, therefore we should not kill the sons of Dhritarashtra who are our relations. How can we be happy by killing our own people? ||37||

Tasmat: therefore; narha: not justified; vayam: we; hantum: to kill; dhartarashtran: the sons of Dhritarashtra; svabandhavan: our relatives; swajanam: kinsmen; hi: indeed; hatva: having killed; katham: how; sukhinaha: happy; syam: may be; madhava: Krishna.

Arjuna on his part has so far expressed his distress. Here, he is giving his final opinion. "Therefore we should not kill the sons of Dhritarashtra", he says.

Like a scholar he proceeds and puts forward the question: "How can we be happy killing our own people?"

It shows his ignorance about the Vedas and his duty to the society. He did not learn the Vedas completely and is passing judgment on the subject even though he is not qualified. He has not understood the principle of "Karma." Through the medium of Arjuna, we are going to be taught in the subsequent chapters the fine arts of conducting our actions.

If we conduct work as "duty" most of the misconceptions will disappear and the results will be beneficial for us and the society.

We have a duty to the "God outside our body" and to the "God inside our body". The "God outside" is the society and the various forms of life in the universe.

The "God inside" is the "Atman" within us.

We cannot live for a second without the presence of the Atman inside and without the society and the various forms of life. We live a life of co–operation for mutual benefit.

In the present context of the battle of righteousness, there is no question of "killing our own people" and experiencing "happiness/ sorrow" by such acts. Arjuna should be looking at what is beneficial to the subjects in their land. He is already confident of success in the battle but is of the opinion that the happiness of victory is not worth the sorrow in losing the kith and kin. These are the words of a confused man. He needs treatment that can clear the ignorance.

यद्यप्येते न पश्यन्ति लोभोपहतचेतसः।
कुलक्षयकृतं दोषं मित्रद्रोहे च पातकम् ||38||

yady apy ete na paśyanti lobhopahatacetasaḥ |
kulakṣayakṛtaṃ doṣaṃ mitradrohe ca pātakaṃ ||38||

कथं न ज्ञेयमस्माभिः पापादस्मान्निवर्तितुम्।
कुलक्षयकृतं दोषं प्रपश्यद्भिर्जनार्दन ||39||

kathaṃ na jñeyam asmābhiḥ pāpād asmān nivartitum |
kulakṣayakṛtaṃ doṣaṃ prapaśyadbhir janārdana ||39||

O Krishna, though these men whose minds are overpowered by greed, see no evil in their destruction of families and the sin in hostility to friend, why do not we realize the evil of self-destruction and turn away from the path of sin? ||38-39||

Yad api: though; Ete: these; Na: not; Pashyanti: see; Lobhopahatachetasaha: with intelligence overpowered by greed;

Kula kshaya krutam: in the destruction of families; Dosham: evil; Mitradrohe: in hostility to friends; Cha: and; Patakam: sin.

Katham: why; Na: not; Jneyam: should be learnt; Asmabhihi: by us; Paapaan: from sin; Asmaat: this; Nivartitum: to turn away; Kulakshaya krutam: in the destruction of family; Dosham: evil; Prapashyadbhihi: clearly seeing; Janardhana: Krishna. Kula kshaya: destruction of family.

Arjuna is now talking about the "Destruction of the family" What is "family?"

In childhood, the parents are the family. The parents have a duty to look after their children and to see that the children become useful members of the society. In some instances it is not just useful member of the society but also a respected member of the society.

As the child grows into an adult, the roles gradually change and the child as an adult has a duty to look after the parents.

As one climbs up the ladder, the responsibility also increases.

The responsibility as a teacher is to all the children in the class. For the head master it is for the entire school.

Department of education is for all the children/students. One can say that the family gets wider and bigger.

Arjuna held a higher position and he could not just look at his immediate family and cousins as his. The entire subjects in the kingdom should be looked upon as his family. Really speaking his responsibility is first to the subjects in his brother's kingdom. Not fulfilling responsibilities to the subjects would then become an act of sin.

Arjuna has to change his idea of the family.

If he fails in his role, he will be causing destruction of the subjects in their kingdom.

Sin in hostility to a friend:

In the war of righteousness the matter of friendship does not arise. Those friends who have taken the side of Kauravas would not be friends anymore. Arjuna had to be 100% hostile to the soldiers in the opposite camp.

कुलक्षये प्रणश्यन्ति कुलधर्माः सनातनाः|
धर्मे नष्टे कुलं कृत्स्नमधर्मोऽभिभवत्युत ||40||

kulakṣaye praṇaśyanti kuladharmāḥ sanātanāḥ |
dharme naṣṭe kulaṃ kṛtsnam adharmo 'bhibhavaty uta ||40||

अधर्माभिभवात्कृष्ण प्रदुष्यन्ति कुलस्त्रियः|
स्त्रीषु दुष्टासु वार्ष्णेय जायते वर्णसङ्करः||41||

adharmābhibhavāt kṛṣṇa praduṣyanti kulastriyaḥ |
strīṣu duṣṭāsu vārṣṇeya jāyate varṇasaṃkaraḥ ||41||

सङ्करो नरकायैव कुलघ्नानां कुलस्य च|
पतन्ति पितरो ह्येषां लुप्तपिण्डोदकक्रियाः||42||

saṃkaro narakāyaiva kulaghnānāṃ kulasya ca |
patanti pitaro hy eṣāṃ luptapiṇḍodakakriyāḥ ||42||

O Krishna, when the family is destroyed, immemorial religious rites and rituals perish. When these perish, they fall into a state of impiety. By impiety the women of the family become corrupt, when women become corrupt, the purity of the caste is polluted by confusion and admixture. Caste pollution leads to hell for both the family and the slayers of the family, the dead forefathers fall form the higher realms of existence, being deprived of the rites of sraddha and tarpana. ||40-41-42||

Kulskshaye: in the destruction of a family; Pranashyanti: perish; Kuladharmaha: family religious rites; Santanaha: ancient/ immemorial; Dharme': spirituality/dharma; Nashte: being destroyed; Kulam: the family; Krutsnam: the entire; Adharmaha: impiety/adharma; Abhivandati: overcomes; Uta: indeed.

Adharm abhivaat: from the prevalence of adharma; Pradushyanti: become corrupt; Kulastriyaha: women of the family; Streeshu: the women; Drushtvasu: being corrupt; Varshneya: Krishna; Jayate': arises; Varnasankaraha: caste admixture.

Sankaro: confusion; Narakaya: for the hell; Kulaghnanaam: of the slayers of the family; Kulasya: of the family; Cha: and; Patanti: fall; Pitaraha: the forefathers; Hi: verily; Eshaam: their; Lupta pindodaka kriyaha: deprived of the offerings of the rice–ball and water.

Through the medium of Arjuna sage Veda Vyasa has indirectly given us some information on the family system of the days gone by. We have to understand that the family was the unit and families together formed the society. The elders in the family conducted various religious rites and rituals. These were passed on from generation to generation. The entire family took part in the rituals conducted with family and friends.

The children as they grow up continue the same tradition. If not for the traditions, the religion would be dead by now. (We need to understand the intellectual meaning and significance of many of the rituals conducted. If not they become actions of blind faith and the present generation of youngsters lose interest and sometimes turn against the religion itself.)

When the family is destroyed:

the men in the olden days were the breadwinners and the women were responsible for bringing up the children. There were no universities and teaching institutions like what we have now. The Brahmin and Kshatriya children went to the Gurukula ashrama to learn the Vedas and Upanisads. The children from the Vysya (business) community learnt the trade by observing and assisting their father. The art was passed from generation to generation and kept alive by this method.

In those days there were wars frequently between the adjoining kingdoms. The men went as soldiers to protect their country. War as we know leads to a number of catastrophes.

Death of the soldiers in the war is unavoidable. The death of the soldier would mean death of the breadwinner for that family. This means destruction of the families' infrastructure. Hence the statement "when the family is destroyed." Without the men, the religious rites come to a halt.

The children would have no one to control their actions. They would take part in acts of crime and sin.

The women in the family become corrupt:

There are mainly two reasons for this to happen.

The women not having the financial support would become prey to unscrupulous men who take advantage of the situation.

The invading soldiers would conduct sinful acts on the helpless women.

This brings about the pollution of the caste. The method of transmitting the skills from father to son comes to a halt. There ensues a major confusion in the society. The assault from foreign soldiers brings about admixture of various castes.

As this destroys the society the learned elders use strong words like: "Caste pollution leads to hell for both the family and the slayers of the family." In the name of hell and suffering in hell, they wanted to prevent the men and women from undertaking sinful acts that bring destruction of the infrastructure of the entire society.

One of the Hindu customs is conduct of religious rites (sraddha) to the departed forefathers of the family. Sraddha and tarpana are supplementary rites to the funeral ceremony performed in honor of the deceased elder/elders. It includes offering a cake of rice to the immediate three generations of the deceased. The subtle bodies of the forefathers would come down and partake the cake offered. Through the medium of the cake, the merits collected by the living family members are passed on the deceased elders. This would assist them in their final union with "Brahman".

Failure to conduct the sraddha would prevent the deceased from attaining the moksha. They would fall down from the heights of spiritual progress achieved.

दोषैरेतैः कुलघ्नानां वर्णसङ्करकारकैः।
उत्साद्यन्ते जातिधर्माः कुलधर्माश्च शाश्वताः॥43॥

doṣair etaiḥ kulaghnānāṃ varṇasaṃkarakārakaiḥ |
utsādyante jātidharmāḥ kuladharmāś ca śāśvatāḥ ||43||

O Krishna, by these evil deeds of the destroyers of the family who can cause caste pollution, the eternal laws of race and family perish. ||43||

उत्सन्नकुलधर्माणां मनुष्याणां जनार्दन।
नरकेऽनियतं वासो भवतीत्यनुशुश्रुम ||44||

utsannakuladharmāṇāṃ manuṣyāṇāṃ janārdana |
narake niyataṃ vāso bhavatīty anuśuśruma ||44||

Men whose sacred rites and rituals are destroyed are compelled to inherit hell for an unknown period.
Thus have we heard, O Janardhana. ||44||

अहो बत महत्पापं कर्तुं व्यवसिता वयम्।
यद्राज्यसुखलोभेन हन्तुं स्वजनमुद्यताः ||45||

aho bata mahat pāpaṃ kartuṃ vyavasitā vayam |
yad rājyasukhalobhena hantuṃ svajanam udyatāḥ ||45||

Oh, see, we have engaged in committing a heinous sin, as we are ready to kill our own kinsmen just for the sake of the pleasures of the sovereignty. ||45||

Doshai: by evil deeds; Etaihai: these; Kulaghnanaam: of the family destroyers; Varna sankara karakaihi: causing intermingling of castes; Utsadyante: are destroyed; Jati dharma: religious rites of the caste; Kula dharma: family religious rites; Cha: and; Shaswataha: eternal.

Utsanna kuladharmanaam: whose family religious practices are destroyed; Manushyanaam: of the men; Narake: in hell; Aniyatam: for unknown period; Vasaha: dwelling; Bhavati: is; Iti: thus; Anushushruma: we have heard.

Aho bata: alas; Mahat: great; Papam: sin; Kartum: to do; Vyavasitaha: prepared; Vayam: we; Yat: that; Rajya sukha lobhena: by the greed of pleasure of kingdom; Hantum: to kill; Swajanam: kinsmen; Udyayataha: prepared.

One can see that the caste system of "Brahmana, Kshatriya, Vysya and Shudra" was in vogue in those days. We can also imply that roles and duties were allotted to men of different castes. The society lived in harmony when each individual family unit carried on its duties.

As a consequence of war, (which we discussed in the previous slokas) several men, the bread–winners of family lose their lives. This causes havoc to the remaining family members of that unit. Arjuna refers to his cousins Kauravas who would have destroyed the family and cause caste pollution. By taking part in the war, the Pandavas would also be responsible for the problems the society would face "post– war."

The routine religious rites in a number of families would come to a halt. With this the eternal laws of family perish. When a large number of families are destroyed, the race would soon perish.

To stop this catastrophe, the learned elders brought out the idea of "heaven and hell." Those that caused destruction of family and thereby destroy the religion, they said, would end up in hell. They also said that it would be a very long period in hell. Hell is to be considered as a place of suffering.

Arjuna was taught this in his gurukula ashrama and by the elders in their family.

He expresses the fact to Krishna that by taking part in the war, the Pandavas would suffer the same fate as the Kauravas.

According to him, there is no difference between Pandavas and Kauravas in the aim of the war. Both were fighting to get sovereignty of the land. Whoever wins the war would still have to face life in hell for the sin committed. "Family dharma" in this context means "code of conduct" as prescribed by the sastras and which is beneficial to the family and the society by the members of each family unit.

यदि मामप्रतीकारमशस्त्रं शस्त्रपाणयः।
धार्तराष्ट्रा रणे हन्युस्तन्मे क्षेमतरं भवेत् ||46||

yadi mām apratīkāram aśastraṃ śastrapāṇayaḥ |
dhārtarāṣṭrā raṇe hanyus tan me kṣemataraṃ bhavet ||46||

If the sons of Dhritarashtra, weapons in hand, slay me in the battle, unresisting and unarmed, that would be better (beneficial) for me. ||46||

Yadi: if; Maam: me; Aprateekaram: unresisting; Ashastram: unarmed; Sastra panayaha: weapons in hand; Dhartarashtra: the sons of Dhritarashtra; Rane: in the battle; hanyuhu: should slay; tat: that; me': of me; kshema taram: better; bhavet: would be.

Having decided not to fight, Arjuna is trying to justify the decision. He is looking at the end result of his decision not to fight. He is misreading the word "Kshema" (welfare) which is the ensuing result and thereby is to be looked upon as fruits of action.

By running away from the battle and not killing the respected elders and teachers he thought there would be merit points for him. It shows his ignorance of the sastras.

He is wrong also to think of the "fruits of action." The rest of the Gita is about actions and the spirit of conducting the same.

Through the medium of Arjuna, the Lord is going to correct our mistakes in the understanding of the sacred philosophy.

सञ्जय उवाच
एवमुक्त्वाऽर्जुनः संख्ये रथोपस्थ उपाविशत्।
विसृज्य सशरं चापं शोकसंविग्नमानसः||47||

sanjaya uvaca
evam uktvārjunaḥ saṃkhye rathopastha upāviśat |
visṛjya saśaraṃ cāpaṃ śokasaṃvignamānasaḥ ||47||

Sanjaya said
Having spoken in this manner, Arjuna, distressed with sorrow in the battle field, dropped his bow and arrows and sat on the seat of his chariot. ||47||

Evam: thus; Uktva: having said; Sankhye: in the battle; Rathopasta: on the seat of the chariot; Upavishat: sat down; Visrujya: having cast away; Sasharam: arrow; Chapam: bow; Shoka samvighna manasa: with the mind distressed with sorrow.

What has Arjuna done so far and why did he do what he did?

Arjuna expressed the symptoms of depression in greater detail. He was fortunate and blessed with the presence of the greatest teacher in the form of Lord Krishna. Lord Krishna was the charioteer. It was not coincidence that Krishna was Arjuna's charioteer. He was aware of this situation developing and he knew that for the welfare of humanity in general there was a dire need to make the philosophy of "Karma, Jnana, Bhakti and Dhyana" clear to those who were desirous to know. The war between the cousins was the most appropriate moment for lighting the knowledge of wisdom.

Arjuna as a patient, who suddenly felt extremely depressed just before undertaking the major battle in his life, decided that he needed the help of a psychoanalyst. Sri Krishna, we can say is the world's first "Psychoanalyst" we know of. True to the profession, He listened to all the symptoms the patient came up with and did not interrupt him in the middle with probing questions.

The dropping of the bow and arrows expresses his mental weakness. The body of the great warrior lost its physical strength due to "grief." The grief was due to the ignorance of the shastras. Shastras are meant for the welfare of the mankind and the universe.

Each one of us has a God ordained duty to conduct in this world and has the presence of the God inside to guide us in the discharge of our duties to God and the society. We must not let the "ego" make us blind us to this reality.

God is there constantly to bestow His Grace and we must know how to approach Him and receive the Grace.

iti srīmadbhagavadgītasūpaniṣatsu brahmavidyāyāṃ yogaśāstre śrīkṛṣṇārjunasaṃvāde arjunaviṣādayogo nāma prathamo'dhyāyaḥ ||

CHAPTER 2

SĀṂKHYA–YOGA

Comments from Swami Japananda on Bhagavad-Gita & Swami Vivekananda

The objective of religion is to make a person fit enough to survive.

Swami Vivekananda was very much fond of Bhagavad-Gita. He never missed opportunity to teach this subject to his monastic members as well as to his western followers. Even though he has not written any commentary on Bhagavad-Gita he has delivered wonderful lectures on the subject, the Bhagavad-Gita the song celestial, Bhagavad-Gita sweet to the ear, heart and mind too.

Swami Sharadananda a great thinker and brother monk of Swami Vivekananda explains Bhagavad-Gita in this manner.

If we are not able to understand any teaching in the Gita, we can study the life of Sri Krishna and through that we will understand the correct meaning.

Swami Ranganathanandaji explains in his lecture on Gita: the Upanishads are like the pure science and the Gita teaches us how to convert these messages in to applied science.

Sri Ramakrishna Paramahamsa said that one has to renounce everything and surrender at the Holy Lotus feet of Lord. Bhagavad-Gita gives this message to the Sadhaka who wants to realize the Self.

Swami Sharadanandaji continues: Some may say that the Gita was taught only to Arjuna. What significance can it have for us? None of us are going to take part in any war. Nor do we ordinary people have anything in common with the great warrior Arjuna.

How can the teaching given to such a great student be of any benefit to us?

In answer Swami Sharadanandaji says: Although Arjuna was much superior to us, he was also a human being. We too are human beings. Just as he was deluded at times, we too are deluded often. Like him, we too are called upon to face many obstacles and calamities in our quest for truth. Like him again, we too are in the midst of both inner and outer warfare.

The study of the Gita holds a message for us, gives us peace of mind, and offers solution to the problems of life. Thanks to the study of the Gita, those who had lost their way have shed tears of repentance and have changed their entire life-course, directing it toward high ideals.

Swami Vivekananda's view about Gita: Practical Spirituality.

Even though you are handling all the responsibilities of your worldly life still you will become steady and you will advance towards the goal. You yourself can find a way to the highest realization.

Sri Krishna profoundly announces a new philosophy of life and new philosophy of work. By work you will gain a double result. External human welfare in society, human development etc. and inwardly you will advance towards the infinite spiritual world.

This is the double efficiency you gain by adopting yoga in your day-to-day life. This is the central message of Bhagavad-Gita.

We can achieve this double efficiency by following Sri Krishna's teachings in Bhagavad-Gita i.e. Yoga

In the second chapter Sri Krishna expounds this central theme of the philosophy and in the succeeding chapters he enriches it. What we get in the Bhagavad-Gita is all-round human fulfillment, individual as well as collective, that is the Yoga of Bhagavad-Gita.

INTRODUCTION

"Samkhya" is one of the six Hindu schools of philosophy and its author is said to be Sage Kapila. "Darshana" is "to view".

The views of the scholars on the Hindu philosophy are represented in the six schools. These are considered to represent six orthodox Hindu priestly schools.

The schools authors

Vaisheshika	Kanada
Samkhya	Kapila Vasudeva
Nyaya	Gowtama
Yoga	Patanjali
Purva Mimamsa	Jaimini
Uttara mimamsa	Badarayana

In addition there are three more darshanas. They are called as "Nastika darshanas". These are not a break from the traditional views but are considered to be a modification and an addition to the six schools.

These are:

Caravaka
Jainism
Buddhism

It is believed that most of the original "Sankhya"by sage Kapila Vasudeva has been lost in course of time.

"The Samkhya yoga" in the Bhagawadgita is not considered to be a repetition of the Samkhya philosophy.

Swamy Chinmayananda defines Samkhya as: "The logic of thought in a philosophy." Originally Samkhya was said to be atheistic philosophy, (Niriswara –no Iswara). Its purpose was to analyze the phenomenal world. It distinguishes two fundamental constituents of existence.

They are:

Spirit – also known as "Purusha" which is the "Intelligence" behind creation and is considered to be "The Life principle". This is the "Parabrahman/Paramatman." (also addressed as "Supreme Consciousness).

Nature – also known as "Prakriti" which has no life to it on its own and so said to be "Jada" (no life).

The Prakriti is composed of three gunas (qualities):

Satva (pure), Rajas (passionate) and Tamas (lazy/indolence).

"Samyoga" (union) of the un- manifest prakriti with the life principle Purusha leads to the manifestation of life as we know of. The universe, they say is the evolution/ manifestation of the prakriti by association with the Purusha.

Samkhya philosophy believes that every effect is inherant in a primary cause. Purusha is the cause and Prakriti is the effect.

On an individual basis, the Life Principle is "The Atman/The Soul" and the Prakriti is the "The physical body, the mind, the senses and the ego".

The Gita teaches us that realization of our true identity as the "Life Principle/Soul" leads to union with our Parabrahman which is "Moksha" (Liberation from bondage to the physical world).

Maya or illusion makes the individual forget his identification as "The Soul" and gets strongly bound to the physical body. The lack of discrimination between the Self (Atman) and the non-self (body), leads to bondage and the consequence experience of pains and pleasures of the mundane worldly existence. "Viveka" (true knowledge) removes this bondage and lets the experience of "Bliss" (Ananda) come to the seeker. Dawn of Viveka in this life makes one a "Liberated Soul" while living in this universe. It is the state of "Jivanmukta" (liberated Soul).

Samkhya: "Sam" – union, completeness

"Khya" – to be known, knowledge

Samkhya is "union with the knowledge (ultimate knowledge/the highest Truth)" or can also mean "to have complete knowledge."

In our day to day life, on encountering problems, difficulties, catastrophes etc. we tend to get lost without our knowledge and fail to do what we are supposed to do. To get back to do what is expected of us by the divine and the society we need to have

"Complete Knowledge" of ourselves. Incomplete knowledge is the cause for the experience of happiness and sorrow. "Samkhya yoga" is the information in brief about the summary of the entire Gita and paves the way to understand the rest of the sacred text.

Samkhya yoga is to teach us the practical application of the principles by which the spirit becomes the matter and about the means by which the matter can be diverted towards the union with the Soul/Spirit. It believes/ propagates 24 tatvas of the evolutionary process by which the spirit becomes the matter and the matter finally unites with the Spirit. That which is connected to a number (samkhya) is Samkhya. The numbers associated with all the elements is samkhya. To know the 24 phenomenal modifications and reject them as non- eternal and find out the single eternal factor is the knowledge of Samkhya which is Samkhya yoga.

These are:

Prakriti the basic creative power in the field,
Mahat: the cosmic intelligence/Citta, and for the individual being the buddhi (ahamkara)
Manas: the mind
5 Jnanendriyas: the eyes, ears, nose, tongue and the skin.
5 Karmendriyas: Organs of action: the hands, feet, tongue, excretory organs and reproductory organs (Karmendriyas),
5 Tanmatras: the subtle qualities of gross elements (sound, touch, form, taste and smell –or shabdha, sparsha, roopa, rasa and gandha),
5 Pancha maha bhootas - the space, air, fire, water and the earth (the five gross elements)

The samkhya postulates that from the five subtle qualities of the Tanmatras, arise the five gross matter/Pancha maha bhootas in solid, liquid or/and gaseous forms. From the union of the Prakriti with the Purusha evolves the "chitta". Inherent in the "citta" are the ahamkara, buddhi and the manas. The chitta polarized by the manas (mind) and the buddhi gives rise to the Pancha maha bhootas. With the help of the gunas/qualities these manifest as the jnanedriyas, karmendriyas, and the five pranas (prana, apana, vyana, samana and udana).

Yoga is the union of the soul with the Spirit by withdrawal from the gross to the fine/subtle. It involves dropping/discarding the ego to enter into the realm of "Citta", from "Citta to Om" and from "Om to Parabrahman". This comes initially by the process of reason and in the later stages of progress by intuition and self-realization.

The process of creation: (As in Bhagawata Purana)

Vishnu, personification of the Parabrahman first created the four headed Brahma (as a play/leela) who arose via the stalk of a Lotus flower from His naval. He commanded Brahma to create life on earth (a ground and characters to play).

Brahma from His mind created first the four eternal youths "Sanaka, Sanandana, Sanatana and santkumara" and commanded them to create. They refused to obey the command and begged to be excused from taking up the task of creation.

Then arose Shiva (Rudra) from the anger (out of his eyebrows) pent up inside by the refusal to obey His command.

Brahma then created ten sons – "Attri, Angirasa, Pulastya, Pulaha, Kratu, Bhrigu, Daksha, Marichi, Vasishta and Narada". He also created "Dharma and Adharma". Out of his heart arose "Desire".

From His shadow, Brahma took a form and he becomes the first son "Kardama". He then developed from His four heads the Four Vedas.

From His mind and body was created the entire world.

He divided His body into two: The male part became Swayambhu Manu and female counterpart became Shatarupa. These two produced five children, three daughters and two sons.

Akuti, Prasuti and Devahuti were the daughters.

Priyavrata and Uttanapada were the sons.

Akuti married the rishi Ruchi,

Devahuti married Kardama and Prasuti married Daksha.

The children of these with their descendants have populated the world.

Brahma asked Kardama to create life.

Kardama meditated on Narayana. Lord Narayana gave him a boon. Kardama asked for a perfect woman to help in the task of creation and also asked for "Moksha". Narayana asked him to marry Devahuti. The couple begot nine daughters who married the nine rishis. Lord Narayana was born as their son who is Kapila Vasudeva, the author of Sankhya philosophy.

The Sankhya philosophy is considered to be "Brahmavidya". This was taught by Kapila to his own mother who asks him for means to Liberation.

Kapila preaches to his mother Devahuti how the mind becomes the cause of bondage and at the same time how the mind can be the tool for Liberation.

Slokas 11-46 of this chapter expound the samkhya philosophy of knowledge (Jnana yoga),

Slokas 47-60 expound the path of action (Karma yoga),

Slokas 61 -70 give an insight into path of devotion (Bhakti yoga) and

Slokas 71-72 indicate the path of renunciation (Sanyasa yoga).

We learnt from the first chapter how Arjuna (the sincere student) approached the guru Krishna when he was in a state of utter despair and did not know what was the correct action to take:

to fight to win by killing the enemy (consisted of his respected elders) or

to renounce all and go to the forest (let the evil rule).

Krishna then takes up the task of imparting the knowledge to dispel the ignorance. As a preliminary step He briefly enumerated the entire summary of the Gita in this chapter and gave a form of introduction to what was going to come in the class. He starts by explaining about the Atman first.

Arjuna really wanted Krishna to tell him what to do: to fight or abandon the wish to fight and retreat to the forest. Krishna could have given the command and told Arjuna what exactly he had to do. Instead, He gave Arjuna the knowledge to decide on the correct action to take. Carrying on any task after analyzing the pros and cons and then doing what the intellect (reasoning capacity) guides is the best option at any time for anybody.

सञ्जय उवाच
तं तथा कृपयाऽविष्टमश्रुपूर्णाकुलेक्षणम्।
विषीदन्तमिदं वाक्यमुवाच मधुसूदनः॥1॥

saṃjaya uvāca
taṃ tathā kṛpayāviṣṭam aśrupūrṇākulekṣaṇam |
viṣīdantam idaṃ vākyam uvāca madhusūdanaḥ ||1||

Sanjaya said
To him who was thus overwhelmed with compassion and was grieving, his eyes full of tears, Madhusudhana spoke these words. ||1||

tam: to him; tatha: thus; krupaya: with pity; avishtam: overcome; ashrupoorna akula eekshanam: with the eyed filled with tears and agitated; visheedantam: despondent; idam: this; vakyam: speech; uvacha: said/spoke; madhusudhana: Madhusudhana.

Sanjaya has in one simple line given us the picture of Arjuna on the battlefield in a state of utter despondency. Arjuna after all had decided to fight the battle and win it so that he could get justice for his brother. But, alas, the mind succumbed to the thought of consequences of the action about to be undertaken. So instead of a determined warrior eager for the fight to begin, we see a weak warrior in grief not at the consequences but at the thought of consequences. He was in grief on thinking of the fruits of action. Also, we should note the word "Krupaya" meaning "with pity/compassion." Sanjaya has used a wrong word in this instance and it just shows that he is not an advanced spiritual seeker.

"Krupa" or compassion is a divine quality and has an important place in daily life. One needs to be compassionate to the needy and those in distress. In this instance Arjuna himself was in distress and there is no sign of him attending to the needs of the distressed. What Arjuna told Krishna in chapter 1 was all about what could happen to his family and friends in the battle. There was no question of pity for Bheeshma, Drona etc. but fear of having to kill the respected and learned elders in the family. It is true that he mentioned about the possible fate of the dependent citizens of the land when the bread winners/soldiers died in the battle. He was a Kshatriya and faced many battles before and many soldiers had been killed before. There was no pity then and on this score the pity to the family of those soldiers is not the compassion the word "Krupa" implies.

Lord Krishna is also known as Madhusudhana for having killed the demon Madhu. (sloka 35, chapter 1)

He heard the lamentations of the patient in depression and as a great psychoanalyst is ready to give his opinion and offer a remedy for the illness.

श्री भगवानुवाच
कुतस्त्वा कश्मलमिदं विषमे समुपस्थितम्।
अनार्यजुष्टमस्वर्ग्यमकीर्तिकरमर्जुन॥2॥

śrī-bhagavān uvāca
kutas tvā kaśmalam idaṃ viṣame samupasthitam |
anārya-juṣṭam asvargyam akīrti-karam arjuna ||2||

The Lord said
O Arjuna, whence is this perilous state, mental dejection has come upon thee? This un-aryan, shameful and heaven excluding. ||2||

kutah: whence; tva: upon thee; kashmalam: dejection; idam: this; vishame: in perilous state; samupasthitam: comes; anarya jushtam: un-aryan like, unworthy; asvargyam: heaven excluding; akeertikaram: disgraceful.

Sri Krishna finds faults in Arjuna's statement on three counts.

a) It is un-aryan. b) It is heaven excluding. c) It is shameful.

Un-aryan: the word "Arya", let me say that contrary to belief, does not refer to any race or stock of people.

Quotation from Manu Smriti, the highest authority:

"Performing one's duty as per the shastras and at the same time avoiding forbidden acts is the way of an Arya.

Only such highly evolved, cultural men are entitled to be called Aryans." Those who follow the path of dharma seek for the light and purity, who are bold and active are true Aryans, not just of India but of the world. Contrary to this are those who live the life of ignorance of dharma, subject to passions like kama, krodha (desire, anger) and follow the demonical way of living. These groups of men are un-aryan."

It also states that children born of parents who act with self-control and follow the shastras are Aryans. It is not a title one can inherit but only a title that comes from the right conduct.

The Vedas tell us how to be and remain as Aryans. If one becomes and stays Aryan, he is said to have understood Vedanta and lives the life of Vedanta.

So the word "Aryan" is not meant for a particular race of people. Krishna is making an observation only. He states that what you are intending to do is "unaryan" and He did not say "You are not an Arya."

Heaven excluding:

As we discussed before, Arjuna was a Kshatriya warrior. In the olden days Kshatriyas were taught that fighting in war was not a wrong act. Death in the war would guarantee entry into heaven.

With the decision not to fight/uncertainty to fight, Arjuna would be excluded from entry into heaven.

It is shameful: Arjuna was a well-respected warrior. He was a competent warrior who could fight with 10000 soldiers at a time. (hence the title "Maharathi") It would have been a topic for ridicule from the friends, family and the future generation to come if he did not fight the war of righteousness.

Sri Krishna is simply informing Arjuna that his decision not to fight was wrong.

क्लैब्यं मा स्म गमः पार्थ नैतत्त्वय्युपपद्यते|
क्षुद्रं हृदयदौर्बल्यं त्यक्त्वोत्तिष्ठ परन्तप||3||

klaibyaṃ mā sma gamaḥ pārtha naitat tvayy upapadyate |
kṣudraṃ hṛdaya-daurbalyaṃ tyaktvottiṣṭha paraṃtapa ||3||

O Partha, do not yield to this wretchedness. It does not befit you. Cast off this wretched weakness of the heart. Arise, O scorcher of enemies. ||3||

klaibyam: wretchedness; maa sma gamaha: do not get/yield; etat: this; tvayi: in you; upapadyate: is befitting; na: not; kshudram: wretched/mean; hrudaya dourbalya: weakness of heart; tyaktva: having abandoned; uttishta: stand up; parantapa: scorcher of enemies.

This is one of the most often quoted verses in the Gita by the experts. Swami Vivekananda who spread the message of Hindu philosophy across the globe and in whose name a number of institutions have blossomed all over, says that the two most important words in this sloka are:

Klaibyam and Utthishta.

He considers that the two words summarize the essence of the Gita.

It is therefore necessary for us to analyze these words in greater detail.

Klaibyam - wretchedness

Arjuna as we know was a highly competent and well-respected soldier holding the highest rank. He was a physically strong warrior and well-versed in archery. Unfortunately, the grief he got himself into considering the consequences of the war, made him mentally weak.

Any well respected individual who does not fit in with the expectation of the society in relation to his duty will be labeled as "wretched." Arjuna was expected to lead the Pandava army and help in defeating the famous warriors like Bheeshma, Drona, Karna and others in the opposite camp. There was no one else in the Pandava army who could take up the mammoth task of defeating the great soldiers in the Kaurava army.

Sri Krishna is reprimanding Arjuna for thinking of surrendering to the Kauravas. For a Kshatriya, in the olden days, it was the worst form of criticism.

This state of mental weakness made Arjuna drop his weapon of action and slump to the floor. What a sorry state to see of a great warrior!

So, Sri. Krishna uses the next word: Uttishta. It means "get up."

It is not physically getting up from the state of slumping down to the floor.

It is getting the mental strength back and determination to take up the task of fighting for righteousness.

In our life, each one of us is expected to fulfill certain duties by the members of our own family and the society in general. We are after all prone to states of grief for some reason or other.

During such times, we must remember this sloka which is a "Mantra" and the words "Klaibyam and Uttishta." We must with determination bounce back and take up our ordained duties for the acts of welfare.

We must awaken, arise, stand up and fulfill our duties till the goal is reached.

The most important goal for a spiritual seeker is to achieve "Liberation." No matter what happens in our life, we must not stop proceeding in the spiritual path.

Another word used in this sloka is the title of "Parantapa". Arjuna was given this title because he was a "scorcher of enemies."

All our enemies in the spiritual battle are within us. They are "Kama (desire), Krodha (anger), Lobha (greed), Moha (delusion), Mada (pride) and Matsarya (enmity)." When they dominate, the consequence of their predominance is "grief." We should learn to scorch these enemies out and not let grief dominate our life. There is a famous Upanisad statement: "Nayam Atma Balaheenena Labhyate."

It means "This Atman cannot be attained by the weak."

We, in the process of realizing our true identity with the "Atman" within, should not succumb to grief and develop any weakness.

The entire philosophical text is meant to give us the mental strength to overcome "grief."

अर्जुन उवाच
कथं भीष्ममहं संख्ये द्रोणं च मधुसूदन।
इषुभिः प्रतियोत्स्यामि पूजार्हावरिसूदन॥4॥

arjuna uvāca
kathaṃ bhīṣmam ahaṃ saṃkhye droṇaṃ ca madhusūdana |
iṣubhiḥ pratiyotsyāmi pūjārhāv arisūdana ||4||

Arjuna said:
O Krishna, Bheeshma and Drona are fit to be worshipped.
How can I with the arrows fight them in the battle? ||4||

Katham: how? Bheeshmam: Bheeshma; Aham: I; Sankhye: in the battle; Dronam: Drona; Madhsudhana: Krishna; Ishubhihi: with arrows; Pratiyotsaami: shall fight; Poojarhau: worthy to be worshipped; Arishudhana: O' destroyer of enemies.

Arjuna continues to justify his decision not to fight.

Bheeshma and Drona, the two senior most members in the opposite camp had declared their allegiance to Emperor Dhritarashtra. After having decided to fight, having taken the advice of Lord Krishna, the Pandavas had entered the battlefield. Arjuna knew that only by killing Bheeshma and Drona the Pandavas could regain the lost kingdom.

Before the war, these two were fit to be worshipped with reverence but certainly not in the war. This was the fundamental flaw in his thinking.

When the cause is glorious, when one follows the path of dharma, the names and relations in the enemy rank should not carry any meaning.

गुरूनहत्वा हि महानुभावान्
श्रेयो भोक्तुं भैक्ष्यमपीह लोके|
हत्वार्थकामांस्तु गुरूनिहैव
भुञ्जीय भोगान् रुधिरप्रदिग्धान्||5||

gurūn ahatvā hi mahānubhāvāñ
śreyo bhoktuṃ bhaikṣyam apīha loke |
hatvārtha-kāmāṃs tu gurūn ihaiva
bhuñjīya bhogān rudhira-pradigdhān ||5||

Better is in this world to eat and live on food of beggars than to kill the most noble of the teachers. But if I kill them, I could enjoy only such pleasures as are stained with blood. || 5||

Guroon: the gurus; Ahatva: instead of slaying; Hi: indeed; Mahanubahvaan: most noble; Shreyo: better; Bhoktum: to eat; Bhaikshyam: alms; Apeeha (api iha): even here; Loke': in the world; Hatvaa: having slain; Artha: wealth; Kamaan: desires; Tu: indeed; Gurun: the gurus; Iha eva: here also; Bhunjeeya: enjoy; Bhogān: pleasures; Rudhira pradigdhaan: stained with blood.

With the incomplete knowledge (half educated) of the shastras Arjuna continues his arguments supporting the decision he has taken. His main case is about killing the gurus and great men like Drona, Kripa and Bheeshma. By withdrawing from the fighting even at the 11th hour, which he thinks unnecessary and sinful, bloodshed could be avoided. The price for taking such decision is to forego the right to climb the throne by his brother Dharmaraja and to go back to the forest. He felt that he would rather take the second option.

He was sure that in order to win, the senior most elders in the opposite camp had to be killed. As long as they lived, Pandavas had no chance of winning the battle. He feels that the pleasures of ruling the kingdom on achieving victory would be tainted with the blood of the gurus and respected elders.

न चैतद्विद्मः कतरन्नो गरीयो
यद्वा जयेम यदि वा नो जयेयुः।
यानेव हत्वा न जिजीविषाम
स्तेऽवस्थिताः प्रमुखे धार्तराष्ट्राः॥6॥

na caitad vidmaḥ kataran no garīyo
yad vā jayema yadi vā no jayeyuḥ |
yān eva hatvā na jijīviṣāmas
te 'vasthitāḥ pramukhe dhārtarāṣṭrāḥ ||6||

I can hardly say which will be better for us, whether we should conquer them or whether they should conquer us. Those very people, sons of Dhritarashtra, slaying whom we do not wish to live, stand facing us. ||6||

Na: not; Chaitat (cha etat): and this; Vidmaha: know; Kataran: which; Gareeyo: better; Yadya(yat ya): that or; Jayena: we should conquer; Yadi: if; Vaa: or; Naha: us; Jayeyuhu: they should conquer; Yan: whom; Eva: even; Hatva: having slain; Na: not; Jejeevishamaha: we wish; Te': those; Avastitaha: standing; Pramukhe: in face; Dhartarashtraha: sons of Dhritarashtra.

Arjuna's mind which was tuned perfectly to the war against their cousins had suddenly gone out of tune. Having decided and prepared for the war, he keeps on expressing his feelings about the outcome of the war.

The scriptures clearly state that there should be no thinking of the fruits of action, either good or bad, once a decision has been taken to undertake the task. We will learn as we proceed that we should understand the shastras and conduct actions that are according to the dharma. Arjuna has come out of the hysterical state but is still trying to argue in his own way of thinking and finding reasons to support his way of thinking.

He is looking at the problems from the mental plane. He needs to elevate himself and learn to look at the problem from the intellectual plane of proper reasoning. His senses needed to be tuned to the channel of discrimination and understanding. There would be a definite change for the better if this would be carried out.

Krishna now has to respond to Arjuna's lamentations. He has to retune his disciple's mind to the right channel of understanding. He needs to bring Arjuna's personality to a higher intellectual level.(the reception and broadcast from the radio will be good if it is tuned to the right channel)

कार्पण्यदोषोपहतस्वभावः
पृच्छामि त्वां धर्मसंमूढचेताः।
यच्छ्रेयः स्यान्निश्चितं ब्रूहि तन्मे
शिष्यस्तेऽहं शाधि मां त्वां प्रपन्नम्॥7॥

kārpaṇya-doṣopahata-svabhāvaḥ
pṛcchāmi tvāṃ dharma-saṃmūḍha-cetāḥ |
yac chreyaḥ syān niścitaṃ brūhi tan me
śiṣyas te ‹haṃ śādhi māṃ tvāṃ prapannam ||7||

O Krishna, my mind is overpowered by taint of pity.
I am ignorant of the right action. I am confused.
I ask you to teach me decisively what is good for me.
I am your disciple, I take refuge in you. ||7||

Karpanya dosha upahata swabhavam: overpowered by taint of pity; Prucchami: I ask; Tvam: you; Dharma sammodha cheta: ignorant of the right action; Sreyaha: good; Syaat: may be; Nischitam: decisively; Broohi: say; Tan me': tat: that; Me': for me; Shishyasteham: thy disciple I am; Shadhi: teach; Maam: me; Tvam: you; Prapannam: refuge.

Usually when there are no physical symptoms it is difficult for patients to recognize their mental symptoms. Once the condition is accepted, it is easy for the specialist to discuss the line of treatment needed to help his patient.

Arjuna, though a strong warrior and a great leader in his own right has realized now that there is something wrong with him. His problem was depression due to ignorance of the right action in the present battle he was facing which made him feel sorry for the teachers, elders and family members in the battlefield.

The words "teach what is good for me" are extremely important. It is therefore important to note that the sacred text is aimed at helping those who are trained in a particular field of work, have achieved competency but are unable to continue the work in which they are trained. One can realize that the resources that are put in to train the individual would go to waste.

Gita is the manual and guide for men of rajasic temperament who are men of passion and want to achieve something higher in life. In the case of Arjuna, it was the feeling of "pity" that stopped him from facing the elders in the battle.

The word "Karpanya" means "pity". According to the Upanisads, if we do not strive for spiritual enlightenment, we are bound, like Arjuna, to grieve when we come across problems in our lives. We will become Krpanas.

Arjuna was feeling as though he was in the dark (ignorance of the shastras) and did not know what would be righteous action. He also realized that what he studied in gurukula ashrama was not sufficient and he needed a guru who could guide him correctly.

He approached Krishna for both the clearance of his ignorance and to guide him in the right path.

The other word to note in this sloka is "Sreyas." Arjuna requests for guidance to help him in the journey of life. There are two words to note in this context. One is "sreyas" and the other is "preyas."

Sreyas is what is good for the spiritual upliftment.

Preyas is what is pleasant for the life in the material world.

He who pursues the path of "good" is on the path to become holy and he who pursues the path for "pleasant" falls from the spiritual goal.

Sadhaka/spiritual seekers should be looking for sreyas rather than preyas.

Arjuna, a true sadhaka is asking for "sreyas." Not only that, he has come to accept that he is ignorant of the scriptures and needs guidance. Further, he has decided to take refuge in the Lord Himself to clear his ignorance.

The sadhaka needs a guru for guidance. As we go through the Gita we will find slokas that give the qualities to look for in the guru and the qualities needed to be accepted by the guru. The Vedas clearly advocate total surrender to the guru by the disciple striving for Moksha. Arjuna has fulfilled all the criteria for a true and sincere disciple and hence he was blessed by the Lord who took upon Himself the task of giving the guidance.

Our thanks to Arjuna and salutations to Lord Krishna.

न हि प्रपश्यामि ममापनुद्या
यच्छोकमुच्छोषणमिन्द्रियाणाम्।
अवाप्य भूमावसपत्नमृद्धम्
राज्यं सुराणामपि चाधिपत्यम्॥8॥

na hi prapaśyāmi mamāpanudyād
yac chokam ucchoṣaṇam indriyāṇām |
avāpya bhūmāv asapatnam ṛddhaṃ
rājyaṃ surāṇām api cādhipatyam ||8||

Even though possessing a prosperous kingdom free from rivals and holding even lordship over the Gods I do not see that which would remove the sorrow of mine which burns up my senses. ||8||

Na hi: not; Prapashyami: I see; Mama: my; Apnudyat: would remove; Yat: which/that; Shokam: grief; Ucchoshanam: dries up; Indriyanaam: of my senses; Avapya: having obtained; Bhoomou: in the earth; Asapatnam: unrivalled; Riddham: prosperous; Rajyam: dominion/kingdom; Suranaam: over the gods; Api: even; Cha: and; Adhipatyam: lordship.

We are now coming to the end of Arjuna's lamentations. Sri Krishna gave him the freedom to express the inner feelings of guilt. Arjuna feels that even if he wins lordship over the denizens of heaven he would not find the peace or happiness. The grief of slaying so many loved ones would override the happiness of the lordship over the three worlds.

This is a mental and not a physical ailment. No amount of external remedy or wealth would suffice to cure it. The only remedy is "Atma Jnana": the knowledge of one's true Self.

We are going to get that medicine in the subsequent chapters.

सञ्जय उवाच
एवमुक्त्वा हृषीकेशं गुडाकेशः परन्तप|
न योत्स्य इति गोविन्दमुक्त्वा तूष्णीं बभूव ह ||9||

saṃjaya uvāca
evam uktvā hṛṣīkeśaṃ guḍākeśaḥ parantapaḥ |
na yotsya iti govindam uktvā tūṣṇīṃ babhūva ha ||9||

Sanjaya said
Having spoken thus to Hrsikesa, the destroyer of foes said to Krishna "I will not fight" and became silent. ||9||

Evam: thus; Uktva: having spoken; Hrishikesham: to Hrishikesha/ Krishna; Gudakeshaha: to Arjuna/conqueror of sleep; Parantapa: destroyer of foes; Na: not; Yotsya: fight; Iti: thus; Govindam: to Krishna; Uktva: said; Tooshnim: silent; Babhoova ha: became.

Hrishikesha: refer to sloka 10, chapter 1, for its meaning Gudakesha: refer to sloka 24, chapter 1 for its meaning.

Govindam: refers to Krishna. "Gou" in Sanskrit refers to the sacred cow. The cows are considered (symbolically) to be the treasure house of the Upanisads. The milker of the cow, Sri Krishna, extracted the gist of all the Upanisads in the form of milk and gave it to the Arjuna's of the world.

Krishna, as a very young boy, lifted the mountain Govardhana during a heavy downpour of severe rains and gave shelter to all the cows and the cowherds of the village and was bestowed with the title Govinda..

Sanjaya has informed the blind king Dhritarashtra that the mighty Arjuna completed describing in detail his symptoms of grief and then sat down saying, "I will not fight."

Even though physically, Arjuna was a well-trained warrior, he was not trained to fight his own ignorance. The Vedic teaching he received in his younger days did not cover the topic on fighting the ignorance. Sri Krishna now takes up the task of correcting Arjuna's mental state.

तमुवाच हृषीकेशः प्रहसन्निव भारत|
सेनयोरुभयोर्मध्ये विषीदन्तमिदं वचः ||10||

tam uvāca hṛśīkeśaḥ prahasann iva bhārata
senayor ubhayor madhye viṣīidantam idam vacaḥ. ||10 ||

O King, seeing Arjuna lamenting in the middle of the two armies, Hrishikesha, as if smiling, spoke these words. ||10||

tam: to him; uvacha: spoke; hrishikesha: Krishna; prahasanniva: smiling as it were; bharata: o bharata; senayor: of the armies; ubhayor: of both; madhye: in the middle; vishidantam: despondent; idam: thus; vachaha: words.

Sri Krishna, like a good doctor, has listened patiently to the symptoms expressed by Arjuna. The first requirement for a good doctor is to listen patiently to all the symptoms narrated by the patient. The flow of thoughts of the patient should not be disturbed. The patient should not feel that the doctor has no time for him.

At the same time, doctor's facial expression has to bring confidence to the patient. In this instance, Sanjaya has noticed that Sri Krishna has kept a smiling face but was not laughing at the patient's ignorance.

This sloka is depicted as the famous scene of the "Gitopadesham." In the picture of the same, one can see Krishna, the embodiment of dharma, standing in the front of the chariot, with a smiling face holding the whip in his hand depicting the role of the charioteer. Arjuna is seen sitting at the back of the chariot and his face is showing signs of distress.

One can almost say that Krishna is saying to Arjuna "is that all you are crying for?" there is a famous saying from the learned masters: "for an ignorant man, a span of ground appears like an ocean and for the wise man the ocean appears like a small ground"

The ignorant is frightened to cross the small piece of land, while the wise is not perturbed to cross the enormous ground in front of him. There is an ocean of difference between the two.

Krishna, is the embodiment of the "Supreme Knowledge" and Arjuna is the personification of "utter ignorance."

श्री भगवानुवाच
अशोच्यानन्वशोचस्त्वं प्रज्ञावादांश्च भाषसे।
गतासूनगतासूंश्च नानुशोचन्ति पण्डिताः ||11||

śrī-bhagavān uvāca
aśocyān anvaśocas tvaṃ prajñā-vādāṃś ca bhāṣase |
gatāsūn agatāsūṃś ca nānuśocanti paṇḍitāḥ ||11||

The Lord said:
You have grief for whom there should not be any sorrow. Yet, you speak words of wisdom. The wise do not grieve for the dead or the living. ||11||

ashochyan: those who should not be grieved for; anva shochaha: have grieved; tvam: you; prajna vadamscha: and words of wisdom; bhashase': speak; gatasoona: the dead; gatasoonscha: the living; nanu: not; shochanti: grieve; panditaha: the wise.

The entire message of the Gita is "do not grieve" and this is the most important message for all. If we think deeply, the happiness is within each of us but the grief is from external sources.

According to the scholars, this sloka is the beginning of sowing the seed of knowledge in the form of Bhagavad-Gita by the Lord Himself.

It is therefore known as the "Bija Mantra": The seed of the Gita sowed by the Lord is the most potent remedy for overcoming the grief. The sadhaka has to look after the seed and assist in its growth to become a big useful tree for the society.

Arjuna, as we have seen so far was in a state of despair and had requested the master for guidance towards the right action.

The wise do not grieve for the dead or the living: Why?

As we have discussed in the beginning the real us is the "Atman". It does not die at any time. The physical body which covers the atman does die and is born again to fulfill the vasanas stored in its memory bank. Identifying with the physical body and getting attached to it and the surroundings brings out the grief every so often. The ego makes one feel sorry in adverse situations. Knowing this truth makes one a wise man and the wise men do not grieve for the dead.

Why does the Lord say "do not grieve for the living"?

It is only the living beings that experience the grief. The wise are aware of the fact that birth is the beginning of troubles and it goes on till the death. Knowing that it is inevitable after having been born to encounter situations that bring in sorrow, the wise do not grieve for the living. They remain in a perfect state of equanimity of mind and do not succumb to depression.

In the present context, Arjuna, though considered to be wise and powerful has not talked like a wise man. In reality Arjuna is speaking with "half knowledge". "Act like a wise man and not just speak as a wise man" is the advice by Sri Krishna for mankind through the medium of Arjuna.

Each one of us has three limbs/instruments that participate in any one action. They are the "mind, speech and the physical body." In Sanskrit we say: "Trikarana". All the three should work in unison and the sadhaka has to keep all the three pure and clean.

Arjuna spoke words of a wise man but his mind was not acting perfectly. His physical body dropped the bow and he collapsed down unable to hold on to the weapon of action.

The Lord uses the word "Pandita" in the sloka. Really speaking the true Pandita is he who knows his true identity with the Atman and drops his attachment to the physical body and the world around.

The person who has understood the real nature of the Atman is a pandita.

The real nature of the Atman is:

Sat - Truth - the Eternal Truth/Ultimate existence: It was present yesterday in a different form, is present today in the present form and will be present tomorrow in a new form.

Chit - Knowledge: this is the real knowledge of the true identity of the Atman and associating with the Atman and not the physical body.

Ananda - Bliss: knowing the real nature of the Atman who is omniscient, omnipotent and omnipresent gives one the eternal everlasting bliss. The individual does not succumb to the modifications of the physical body.

Roopa: This Atman gets a covering of the five gross elements which becomes the physical body. This undergoes constant changes and experiences, happiness and pain at different periods of life and is prone to death sooner or later.

Naama: The society gives a name to that form for the purpose of identity. This is the "Nama."

So all in all there are five aspects: Sat-chit-Ananda-Nama-roopa. Sat Chit Ananda refers to the atman and nama roopa refers to the physical body.

Lord Krishna is the master of Yoga and called as "Yogeshwara." Yoga is harmony in thought, word and deed. Arjuna wanted to attain Moksha and talked of the Vedas. He did not implement the theory into practice and did not know his true identity of the Atman.

Sri Ramakrishna Paramahamsa says: "do not create conflict between word and deed as nothing good comes out of it.

The purpose of the Gita is to enable the sadhaka to attain the union of the ego with the Atman and lose the body identity.

The first word of advice to Arjuna is "Asochyan: those who should not be grieved for

The last word of advice (sloka 66, chapter 18): maa shuchaha: do not grieve.

These two words summarize the essence of the Gita's teaching. The emphasis is on grief because grief reduces the efficiency of work. The main theme of the Gita is "karma". Not to grieve is the jnana to acquire and this comes from knowing about one's true identity. It is "Atma jnana" and the Sankhya Yoga is about Atma Jnana.

The word "Pandita" is used in the context of the wise who does not grieve for the living or the dead and not as scholar which is the literal meaning. This he has achieved by Atma Jnana. A true pandit is he who has mastered Atma Jnana.

न त्वेवाहं जातु नासं न त्वं नेमे जनाधिपाः।
न चैव न भविष्यामः सर्वे वयमतः परम् ||12||

na tv evāhaṃ jātu nāsaṃ na tvaṃ neme janādhipāḥ |
na caiva na bhaviṣyāmaḥ sarve vayam ataḥ param ||12||

Indeed, it is not that at any time was I not, nor you, nor these rulers of men. Nor shall we ever cease to be hereafter. ||12||

Na: not, tu eva ahaṃ: indeed, also, I; jaatu: at any time; naasam: not was; na tvam: not thou; na ime: not these; janadhipaha: rulers of men; na chaiva: and not also; na bhavishyamaha: not shall be; sarve: all; vayam: we; ataha: from this time; param: after.

Sri Krishna is reiterating the fact that every living being on earth would have had a form before this birth and death of that form paved way for birth in a new form. This new birth depends upon the thoughts entertained in past births. As we have learnt before, we carry a number of unfulfilled desires and hatreds in our mind called vasanas.

At the time of death, the majority of us still retain a number of those vasanas. Depending on the texture of the vasanas, we are given a new form in a new environment. It could be any form of life on earth. The human birth we have now is an opportunity to clear the stored vasanas that is the criterion for retuning back to Him.

Alas, instead of fulfilling or wiping off of those vasanas, we add new vasanas to the existing pile of vasanas. This again leads to a new birth in a new form.

This cycle repeats itself over a period of a number of births and deaths. This in its truest sense is "samsara." The final release is when the mind is free of all vasana imprints. Only rare souls achieve this state of Liberty from future births.

Hence, the Lord states – "it is not at any time you were not, nor you will ever cease to be."

The same principle applies to the Lord. The difference is that He takes incarnation's eon after eon to uproot the evil and protect the righteous. Each time He takes a new form and is given a new name.

He is not born because of the unfulfilled vasanas but incarnates to protect His children.

This knowledge of the true identity with the Atman and negating the physical body is expressed as a Mahavakya by the ancient seers - "Tat Tvam Asi."

It means "Thou Art That." You are the Atman, the masters tell us and advise us not to grieve for modifications and sufferings of the physical body (refer to the introduction).

देहिनोऽस्मिन्यथा देहे कौमारं यौवनं जरा।
तथा देहान्तरप्राप्तिर्धीरस्तत्र न मुह्यति ||13||

dehino 'smin yathā dehe kaumāraṃ yauvanaṃ jarā |
tathā dehāntara-prāptir dhīras tatra na muhyati ||13||

Just as man in this body goes through the various stages of boyhood, youth and old age, likewise, he passes through another body after death. The wise man does not grieve at it. ||13||

dehino: embodied beings; asmin: in this; Yatha: as; dehe': in body; koumaram: childhood; youvanam: youth; jara: old age; tatha: also; dehantara prapti: the attaining of another body; dheeraha: the firm minded/the wise; tatra: thereat; na: not; muhyati: grieves.

Every second of our life is birth of a new life and death of the old. The past is dead and the present is living. We do not realize the subtle changes that happen all along in our lives.

But we do notice gross changes as we grow. From being infants we reach the old age. The changes of infancy, childhood, youth, adult and old age are evident in our external features.

We do not grieve when we move from infancy to childhood and from childhood to adulthood. We do not realize that the past form for all purposes is dead.

Here we must recollect the law of memory. The law states that:

Experiencer and memorizer must be the same entity. I am the only person who can remember my experiences and nobody else can. I am the only one who knows the thoughts I entertained in my earlier days.

मात्रास्पर्शास्तु कौन्तेय शीतोष्णसुखदुःखदाः।
आगमापायिनोऽनित्यास्तांस्तितिक्षस्व भारत॥14॥

mātrā-sparśās tu kaunteya śītoṣṇa-sukha-duḥkhadāḥ |
āgamāpāyino ‹nityās tāṃs titikṣasva bhārata ||14||

The contact of the senses with objects produces heat and cold, pain and pleasure. Those experiences come and go and are impermanent. Endure them, O Arjuna. ||14||

matrasparshaha: contact of senses with objects tu: indeed; kounteya: referring to arjuna; sheetoshna sukha dukhadaha: that which produce feelings of heat, cold, pleasure and pain; agamapayinaha: with a beginning and end or that come and go; anityaha: impermanent; taan: them; titikshasva: withstand/bear with/endure; bharata: addressing to Arjuna.

Matra sparsha: contact of the senses with the objects.

Here, we should remember that the term "senses" is used to mean the Jnanendriyas or the sense organs. We do possess five organs of senses: eyes, ears, nose, tongue and skin. The word "objects" refers to all the objects around us which come in contact with the sense organs.

Each sense organ, we have discussed before, has a specific quality. The ears hear the sound. The eyes see the form of the objects. The nose detects the smell. The tongue experiences the taste. The skin can feel the objects. The five qualities: the sound, the touch, the form, the taste and the smell are collectively termed as "Tanmatras. "All the sense organs send the details of the objects to the centre of activity: the mind.

The mind analyses these details and experiences a reaction. This reaction could be "pain or pleasure", sensation of "heat or cold." Different people react differently to the same object and the same object can produce a different reaction at different times. Some people like coffee and some hate coffee.

The same individual who likes an object will not respond the same way at another time.

The pleasure of having birth of a new baby is wonderful but the experience of death is very painful. There cannot be birth without subsequent death. The more we get attached to the object, greater will be the pain when the time comes to part with that object.

We have therefore to realize that the pains and pleasures, heat and cold are not in the objects. They are the experiences at the mental plane of each individual. It is also a fact that the intensity of these experiences does not remain the same all the time. If we draw these on a graph, the intensity of these reactions increases slowly or rapidly over a period of time and reaches the peak after some time. After remaining in the peak for a varied length of time, the intensity reduces and after some time there is no such experience.

The Lord hence says that these experiences come and go and are not constantly present. The human mind being what it is, likes to keep the sensation of pleasure as long as possible. One does not like the sensation of sorrow and would like it to disappear quickly.

No one can keep the sensation of happiness eternally. Experience of passing exams, getting rank in the exams cannot last forever. After few days one has to come down to the routine life again.

Our duty is to our parents and to the society. We have an obligation to conduct our work in a prescribed way and produce results that are expected from our work. During states of happiness or sorrow, the efficiency of the work is reduced and productivity is affected. It is obligatory on our part that the productivity is not affected.

Hence, Sri.Krishna uses the word "Titikshatva": it means "endure". We must learn the art of not over reacting to any unhappy situations and keep a balanced state of mind at all times. The reaction to the unhappy situations should not distract one from the ordained duties. This can happen only when the mind is steady and calm despite experiencing troubles.

This does not mean we should remain like a stone and not react. We must learn the art of "mind over matter" and control the emotions experienced and divert our mind to the task ahead.

The state of equanimity of mind to the experiences of pairs of opposites is "The Bliss."

He who is in a state of constant peace in himself and does not depend on the pleasures from the outside world is a "Sthita Prajna." We will come across this word towards the end of this chapter.

We must react to the adversities with the attitude of: "this will also pass away". When we can let the mind remain in this frame of mind at all times we are said to be at "Peace" with ourselves.

यं हि न व्यथयन्त्येते पुरुषं पुरुषर्षभ।
समदुःखसुखं धीरं सोऽमृतत्वाय कल्पते ||15||

yaṃ hi na vyathayanty ete puruṣaṃ puruṣarṣabha |
sama-duḥkha-sukhaṃ dhīraṃ so 'mṛtatvāya kalpate ||15||

The firm man who is not affected by pain or pleasure, who remains equal minded, is fit for immortality O Arjuna, chief of mortals. ||15||

yam: whom; hi: surely; na vyathayanti: not afflicted; yete: these; purusham: being; purusharshabha: chief among men; sama dukha sukham: same in pleasures and pain; dheeram: firm/wise; sah: he; amrutatvaya: for immortality; kalpate: is fit.

Immortal: means "no death." We, the life on this earth are physically mortals. After having been born, we have to die sometime or other. Sri Krishna considers that his disciple Arjuna is "chief of mortals." He is using the words of praise to lift him from the state of despondency. Arjuna wanted to abandon the war but had developed sufficient knowledge to request guidance for the "right action".

It is human reaction that words of praise have a wonderful effect on people. The teachers at schools, mums at home will be familiar with this. The students, children like to be praised that they are the best. Krishna, like a good psychoanalyst, uses the tactic of praise to lift Arjuna out of the state of depression.

Dheera: "individual with the firm determination of mind." The determination is related towards the efforts to sustain in fulfilling the goal one is aiming for. I will not let my mind relax till I complete this portion of revision is the determination that makes one a good student.

Our scriptures advise us all to aim for "Liberation". If we have to achieve the goal, we must fulfill all the requirements for the same. The main requirement is "equanimity of mind" at all times and constancy in the discharge of duties at all times. Dheera, in this context refers to he who withstands the pairs of opposite reactions to the impulses from the world around and conducts all his daily duties.

"Immortality." means "no death." Death of what? The answer will be death of the physical body. The scriptures tell us that we are really the "soul" within which keeps the physical body alive. Looking at it this way, the real us, is the "Soul" that is always immortal, it has no death. By wrongly associating with the physical body, we experience the pains and pleasures.

But by a firm control over the mind, with the guidance from the intellect, assisted by the "inner voice of God," we can become immortals.

नासतो विद्यते भावो नाभावो विद्यते सतः|
उभयोरपि दृष्टोऽन्तस्त्वनयोस्तत्त्वदर्शिभिः||**16**||

nāsato vidyate bhāvo nābhāvo vidyate sataḥ |
ubhayor api dṛṣṭo 'ntas tv anayos tattva-darśibhiḥ ||16||

The unreal has no being. The real has no non-being. The final truth of these two has been seen indeed by those who have experienced the essence of things. ||16||

Na: not; asataha: of the unreal; vidyate: is; bhavaha: being; na: not; sataha: of the real; abhava: non being; ubhayorapi: of the two also; drishtaha: seen; antaha: the final (truth); tu: indeed; anayoho: of these: Tatva darshibhihi: by the knowers of the Truth.

It may be difficult to understand this sloka clearly. The two words to note in this sloka are: Sat and Asat.

Sat: Truth. Asat: Untruth.

What is truth and what is untruth?

The Lord says that those who have realized the "Truth in essence" only know the difference.

Who are those that have realized the "Truth in essence"?

We should refer to the previous sloka: The firm/wise man who is not affected by pain and pleasure, who remains equal minded, is fit for immortality.

Truth/Sat is defined as that which remains constant at all the three times: past, present and future.

That which exists in all the three periods of time and extends beyond time is Atman and that is why the Atman is defined as "Sat." It simply means "Absolute Existence." The knowledge of this "Truth" is "Chit" and understanding clearly brings out the "Bliss" (Ananda).

That which does not fit in with this definition cannot be the real truth. Our physical body comparatively is "asat." This is because, I, the named individual was not there before my birth and I am not there after my death.

"Tatva darshinaha"—knowers of the Absolute Truth have realized the "reality of things" and are aware of the impermanent nature of all living beings. "Tatva Darshana" is seeing into the reality of things and "Tatva darshibhihi" are those who have realized the Truth.

"Bhava" or awareness of this truth unaffected by time, space and causation is realized by Tatva darshinaha. Hence the famous mahavakya/mantra "Prajnanam Brahma" meaning the true awareness of "Sat" is Brahma.

Let us look at the five gross elements: the earth, water, fire, air and space. The earth with its geographical boundaries has been here from time immemorial. But it also has a time span of existence. Compared to my life span it has been here for many millions of years. But, it is also a fact that boundaries have changed, water has submerged areas of land and so many geological changes have taken place. The conclusion has to be that it is "asat." It has also a limited existence.

The waters of the rivers and oceans, similarly, are not there constantly. They therefore are also"Asat."

The same applies to "fire." The "sun", ball of fire we associate with, also has limited existence in relation to the life of the universe. So many suns come and go, the physicists tell us.

The "air", using the similar logic is also "asat."

The "space" is the nearest that we can say is "sat" but not really so. The scientists do say that the space also changes. (we associate "space" with the "Sky". The physicists also agree that there is no sky as such.

This leads us to the last one, which is "The Primordial Energy. "This has always been the constant factor.

All the rest undergo changes in course of time.

Our ancient seers analyzed these facts and came to the conclusion that the "Parabrahman", the symbol of "Primordial Energy" is the only "Truth" and everything else is "Untruth."

The body goes through the stages of baby, child, teenager, adult and old age and finally departs this physical world. Each of the stages last few years and we tend to consider each stage as permanent and associate ourselves strongly with the life in that stage.

It is during times of distress that we start questioning about the "creator". Just like the stages in life, the experiences in each stage are only transient and so not real truth. "Titikshatva", the capacity to withstand the problems in life is the hall mark of "Dheera." Dheera is he who is firm in all situations in life and conducts his obligatory duties to the society.

अविनाशि तु तद्विद्धि येन सर्वमिदं ततम्।
विनाशमव्ययस्यास्य न कश्चित् कर्तुमर्हति॥17॥

avināśi tu tad viddhi yena sarvam idaṃ tatam |
vināśam avyayasyāsya na kaścit kartum arhati ||17||

Know that the Atman by which this whole universe is pervaded is indestructible. No one can cause destruction of "That" the imperishable. ||17||

Avinashi: indestructible; tu: indeed; tat: that; viddhi: know; ena: by whom; Sarvam idam: all this; tatam: is pervaded; vinasham: destruction; avyayasya asya: of the imperishable; na: not; kaschit: anyone; kartum: to do; arhati: is able.

It is easy to understand the principle behind the "imperishable Atman" by looking at few examples. We must accept the truth that there is the power of "Atman"(life energy) inside every living creature on earth. There is no exception to this rule. We may give different names to the "soul" but the principle of "divine energy" is the same in all. Similarly, the entire universe is pervaded by the "primordial Energy" and we give different names for it. Electricity is invisible. It can be experienced. It is manifest in different ways like light in bulbs, sound in music system etc. We can destroy the bulbs but we cannot destroy the electricity.

The pots are made up of clay. Pots can be of different varieties but the clay in each of them is same. One can destroy the pots but cannot destroy the clay.

We can destroy great buildings. We can never destroy the space those buildings occupied.

Similarly, we have to understand that the Atman, the energy behind our life is indestructible. The body made up of the five gross elements dies on departure of the Atman inside. All forms of life on this earth get destroyed during deluge, (pralaya). The energy behind its survival will not get destroyed.

We can understand this by looking at the screen in the theatre. So many films are projected on the screen. The scenes change, the films change but the screen is the constant factor. We do not think even for a moment about the screen and get totally absorbed with the events on the screen. Some will be happy events and some will be sad events. Many of us express our emotions in line with the changes. There are very few who do not forget that the events on the screen are only temporary and the screen as such is not affected by the changes.

Similarly, the lesson to learn is that the Atman within us is the constant factor and the body, mind, intellect equipment is ever changing.

अन्तवन्त इमे देहा नित्यस्योक्ताः शरीरिणः।
अनाशिनोऽप्रमेयस्य तस्माद्युध्यस्व भारत॥18॥

antavanta ime dehā nityasyoktāḥ śarīriṇaḥ |
anāśino 'prameyasya tasmād yudhyasva bhārata ||18||

These bodies of the embodied Self, they are subject to destruction. The Self is eternal, indestructible, incomprehensible. Therefore, fight, O Arjuna. ||18||

Antavanta: having an end; ime: these; dehaha: bodies; nityasya: of the everlasting; uktaha: are said; sharerinaha: of the embodied; anashinaha: of the indestructible; aprameyasya: of the immeasurable; tasmaat: therefore; yudhyasva: fight; bharata: O Arjuna.

The Atman, Soul inside each one of us is the Life Principle and is responsible for us being alive. The physical body made up of the five gross elements is brought to life by the power of the Soul within. When the Soul departs, the physical body loses all its qualities and becomes lifeless. The Soul on the other hand departs on death with the subtle mind and intellect to the unknown world. It awaits the command from the Paramatma and His blessings to be born again with the body made up of five gross elements. The Soul never dies. The final destination for it is to merge with the Supreme Soul and this state is known as "Liberation." Thus say the learned elders and Sri Krishna reiterates the fundamental Truth.

Sri Krishna uses the word "incomprehensible." Why? We the humans have the physical body which has three planes of comprehension. They are "Intellect, Mind and Senses."

At each level we have the capacity to partially comprehend any object. But each of these tools has a limited capacity to comprehend. It is impossible to comprehend that which has no form, no qualities: "Nirguna, Nirakara."

The Supreme Soul, as we have learnt so far is without any form or qualities. However much we try, we cannot rise above the planes of the senses, mind and intellect to understand "Him." Here again, we use the word "Him" which is not true.

But, at our level of understanding, i.e.: the intellect, we can partially comprehend the fundamental Truth. The only way out is to merge with the Truth and lose one's sense of identification with the body.

Arjuna is told that all the warriors he is facing have the Atman inside which is indestructible and the physical body which is subject to destruction.

"As you are unable to comprehend the Truth of the Atman,", "as you have taken Me as your Guru", "listen to Me and fight".

This is the message from the learned master to his disciple.

य एनं वेत्ति हन्तारं यश्चैनं मन्यते हतम्।
उभौ तौ न विजानीतो नायं हन्ति न हन्यते ||19||

ya enaṃ vetti hantāraṃ yaś cainaṃ manyate hatam |
ubhau tau na vijānīto nāyaṃ hanti na hanyate ||19||

He who thinks that the Self is the slayer or who thinks that Self is slain; both of these do not know the truth. Self, the Atman does not slay nor is slain. ||19||

Yaha: he/who; enam: this; vetti: knows; hantaram: slayer; yaha: he; cha: and; enam: this; manyate: thinks; hatam: slain; ubhou: both; tou: those; na: not; vijaneetaha: know; na: not; ayam: this; hanti: slays; na: not; hanyate: is slain.

He who thinks that the Self is slayer: Let us not forget that the Self is only a witness to all our thoughts and actions.

The Self is also known as "Sakshi" which means "a witness." From the time we were first born into the world to the present birth, we have accumulated a number of thought imprints in our mind. It is due to the contact of our sense organs with the various forms of life around. The Lord has given the freedom for each individual to learn from the results of his thoughts and actions.

All through the processes of births and deaths, the "Self" is the constant factor and "the physical body" is the changing factor.

Depending upon the type of vasanas, the form we take varies. In the context of the battle of Kurukshetra, where Arjuna is the warrior and facing other warriors, a number of soldiers would be killed by the actions of the warriors.

The Lord is reiterating the fact that the "Atman" is not the slayer of any soldiers. To murder somebody and say that the Lord inside me made me commit the act of murder is not correct. The act of committing the offence solely falls on the individual physical body and not to the Atman. The Atman only gave the body the life and an opportunity to exhaust the vasanas.

He who thinks that the Self is slain: Let us not forget that the death is only to the physical body and not of the "Atman" inside. The warriors who kill the soldiers on the battlefield are only killing the physical body. The subtle bodies of the soldiers, depending upon their vasanas, will have to take new forms of life and come into this world. Not all the soldiers who die on the battlefield get "Liberated."

The innumerable people who die daily on this earth do not attain "Moksha."" Mano nasha" and "Vasana kshaya" are the prerequisites for "Moksha."

Until and unless we clear all the existing vasanas and do not accumulate new vasanas, we are not eligible for "Liberation." Thus says the Lord to Arjuna on the battlefield of Kurukshetra.

न जायते म्रियते वा कदाचि
न्नायं भूत्वा भविता वा न भूयः।
अजो नित्यः शाश्वतोऽयं पुराणो
न हन्यते हन्यमाने शरीरे ||**20**||

na jāyate mriyate vā kadācin
nāyaṃ bhūtvā bhavitā vā na bhūyaḥ |
ajo nityaḥ śāśvato 'yaṃ purāṇo
na hanyate hanyamāne śarīre ||20||

It is not born, nor does it die. After having been, it does not cease to be; unborn, eternal, changeless and ancient. It is not killed when the body is destroyed. ||20||

Na: not; jayate: born; mriyate: die; vaa: or; kadachit: at any time; na ayam: not this (self); bhootva: having been; bhavitaa: will be; vaa: or; bhooyaha: anymore; ajo: without beginning/birth; nityaha: constant/eternal; shashwato: changeless; purano: ancient; na: not; hanyate: is killed; hanyamane: being killed; shareere: in body.

The neutral gender "it" is used to refer to "That" which is not the "physical body. "It" refers to the "Atman" (soul).

Chapter 2, verse 18, Kathopanisad talks of six modifications to the physical body from the time it is born. They are: Jayate: born; Asti: exists; Vardhate: grows; Parinamate: modifies; Apaksiyate: wears; Vinasyati: is destroyed.

In this sloka the Lord is using the two words from that sloka: "Jayate and Mriyate." It means "Birth and death."

At the time of death, the gross body perishes. The subtle body with the mind, intellect and the Atman enters the subtle world of "Moola Prakriti." Parabrahman gives it a new body which goes through all the modifications mentioned above. On death of the gross physical body, again as decided by the Lord, the subtle body enters the "Moola Prakriti" and awaits further births again. All through this process of births and deaths, the Atman inside the subtle body (jivatman) is a constant factor. The gross body is the changing factor.

We attribute birth and death to the physical body and the term does not apply to the Atman. The Atman is encased in the subtle body and will continue to be so till the individual finally realizes the Lord, drops the attachment to the physical body and the world around. This is the "Salvation" (Moksha).There is therefore no birth or death to that jivatman. The changes we notice are only applicable to the physical body. This is all in relation to "past, present and future." This body was not present in the past, is present now and will not be there in the future.

The physical body is therefore said to be "not eternal." Contrary to it, the jivatman inside the subtle body was present in the past, is present in the physical body now and will have a new body tomorrow. This will stop only when one attains "Salvation." Hence, the jivatman is comparatively "eternal." When the physical body goes through the changes from babyhood to old age, the jivatman inside will remain the same and does not change.

Sri Krishna is letting Arjuna know that the physical body of the warriors with a name and form are getting killed in the war but not their subtle bodies.

वेदाविनाशिनं नित्यं य एनमजमव्ययम्।
कथं स पुरुषः पार्थ कं घातयति हन्ति कम् ||21||

vedāvināśinaṃ nityaṃ ya enam ajam avyayam |
kathaṃ sa puruṣaḥ pārtha kaṃ ghātayati hanti kam ||21||

O Arjuna, he who knows that the atman is birthless,
real and imperishable, whom can he slay or cause to be slain?" ||21||

Veda: knows; avinashinam: indestructible; nityam: eternal; ya: who; enam: this; ajam: unborn; avyayam: imperishable; katham: how/then; sa: he; purushaha: man; Partha: Arjuna; kam: whom: ghatayati: causes to be slain; hanti: kills; kam: whom.

"Who am I?" is the question bogging the mind of those in search of the "Eternal Truth".

When awake, we are entrapped by the life around in the material world. Before the "Truth" dawns, alas, we would have developed attachments to those material objects and find it hard to get released from the bondage developed.

When we are asleep, we live in the dream world and experience the sense of attachment to the objects in it.

When we are deep asleep, we lose total body identification and are dead to this world and the world beyond.

Very few are the blessed ones who come to understand that real is the "Atman" and false is the physical body. We are now in "Samkhya Yoga", summary of the Bhagawadgita by Sri.Krishna to His disciple Arjuna, seeker after the "Truth" of one's own identity. The Lord is making it clear that the Atman is birthless, imperishable and eternal. When this is the truth, only the physical bodies of those warriors assembled in the battlefield will get killed. There is going to be a modification in their physical body and their jivatman will take a new body depending upon their thought imprints.

Atman cannot kill others and cannot get killed is the lesson to learn from this sloka. Concerning one's own identification; it is worth recollecting a statement made by Hanuman, the eternal servant of Lord Rama. Once when asked by Lord Rama about his identity Hanuman's reply was:

When I think I am the body, I am your servant,
When I think I am the jiva, I am part of you,
When I think I am Atman, I am you.

वासांसि जीर्णानि यथा विहाय
नवानि गृह्णाति नरोऽपराणि|
तथा शरीराणि विहाय जीर्णा
न्यन्यानि संयाति नवानि देही ||22||

vāsāṃsi jīrṇāni yathā vihāya
navāni gṛhṇāti naro 'parāṇi |
tathā śarīrāṇi vihāya jīrṇāni
anyāni saṃyāti navāni dehī ||22||

Just as a man casts off his worn out clothes
and puts on new ones, so also the Self throws
away its worn out bodies and takes other fresh bodies. ||22||

Vaasamsi: clothes; jeernani: worn out; yatha: as; vihaya: casts away; navani: new; grihnani: wears/takes; nara: man; aparani: others; tatha: so; shareerani: bodies; vihaya: having cast away; jeernani: worn out; anyani: others; samyati: enters; navani: new; dehee: of the embodied.

The example of worn out clothes is very easy to understand and has been used to explain the complicated journey of the Self.

As we have learnt so far, on death of the physical body, the Self loses its physical body (gross body) made up of the five elements. (and so the prayers during burial; "earth to earth, water to water").

The physical body is microcosmic representation of the five gross elements: Bhoomi - the earth; Apo - the water; Anilo - the fire; Vayu - the air; Antarkisha - space.

The subtle body with the mind and the intellect goes to "moola prakriti" and waits for the orders from the Parabrahman to take up a new body depending upon the unfulfilled vasanas. This process goes on till the knowledge dawns and the individual with the blessings of the guru is successful in clearing away all the accumulated vasanas and does not let any new vasana enter his mind.

We are proud on wearing a new suit and look for appreciation from others. The suit in course of time does show signs of wear and tear and we often think of discarding the same.

The wise show the same reaction to the births and deaths of their near and dear ones. They know that this process stops only on attaining "salvation."

Evolution from being a stone man to that of God man is therefore a phenomenon for the physical body and not for the Self. Every new birth is like the new suit and death is the discarding of the worn out suit.

नैनं छिन्दन्ति शस्त्राणि नैनं दहति पावकः|
न चैनं क्लेदयन्त्यापो न शोषयति मारुतः||23||

nainaṃ chindanti śastrāṇi nainaṃ dahati pāvakaḥ |
na cainaṃ kledayanty āpo na śoṣayati mārutaḥ ||23||

Weapons cannot cut, fire cannot burn, water cannot wet, wind cannot dry this Atma. ||23||

Nainam: not this; chindanti: cut; sastrani: weapons; na: not; enam: this; dhahati: burns; pavakam: fire; na: not; enam: this, cha: and; kledayanti: wets: apaha: water; na: not; shoshayati: dries; maarutaha: the wind.

This is one of the most important verses in the sacred text that brings out the nature of the Atman. The examples given point to the Pancha Maha Bhootas - the five great elements.

Weapons - this refers to the element "Earth" which is the constituent of any weapon. Fire - refers to the element "Fire".

Water - refers to the element "Water".

Wind - refers to the element "Air".

None of these can touch the Atman which is so subtle.

The element not brought out here is "Space." (Antarikshaha)

Sri.Ramakrishna gives the following example to understand the subtle meaning in this verse. He says:

Suppose we burn some wood in a room, the smoke that emanates stains the walls of the room but does not affect the space. This is because the space is action less.

When a thing is not seen we tend to explain the same in relation to the seen.

Atman is nirakara/nirguna. (without form and qualities). Hence if we throw water, water cannot wet it, weapons cannot cut it, fire cannot burn and air cannot dry it.

अच्छेद्योऽयमदाह्योऽयमक्लेद्योऽशोष्य एव च|
नित्यः सर्वगतः स्थाणुरचलोऽयं सनातनः||24||

acchedyo 'yam adāhyo 'yam akledyo 'śoṣya eva ca |
nityaḥ sarva-gataḥ sthāṇur acalo 'yaṃ sanātanaḥ ||24||

The Self cannot be cut, nor burnt, nor moistened, nor dried up. It is eternal, all-pervading, stable, immovable and ancient. ||24||

Achedyoyam: this cannot be cut; adahyoyam: cannot be burnt; akledyaha: cannot be wet; ashoshyaha: cannot be dried; eva: also; cha: and; nityaha: eternal; sarvagataha: all pervading; sthanuhu: stable; achalaha: immovable; ayam: this; santanaha: ancient.

This sloka is almost similar to the previous sloka in the meaning it portrays. It reiterates the fact that the Atman is not the five great elements and hence none of the qualities of the elements apply to it. We have to accept the fact that the "Primordial Energy" without a name and form, known as "Parabrahman" decided to play and brought into play the five great elements and the names and forms that evolved from association of the atomic particles of Parabrahman in conjunction with the five great elements.

We cannot trace the origin of "life" or the "maya lila" of the Parabrahman. It is said to be "Eternal and all pervading."

In the same vein we can add that it is immovable and ancient. "Nitya" means "constant." The constant factor in innumerable names and forms is the jivatman who is said to undergo the changes which we call "births and deaths" before attaining reunion with the "Parabrahman." The same Primordial Energy has to be "all pervading". There can be no space in the universe or beyond that has no Primordial energy. The Atman is formless and changeless which is expressed as "Sthanu."

As we have learnt before, this is compared to the "screen" in a theatre. It fails to be registered in the minds of the viewers of any particular picture.

The Self is:

Existence: Truth - Sat.

It is Light: Cit.

It is Bliss: Ananda.

The Truth is: Nityaha: eternal; Sarvagataha: all pervading: Sthanuhu: Firm; Achala: immovable; Sanatanaha: ancient.

These are the adjuncts we find in the sloka with reference to the Atman.

अव्यक्तोऽयमचिन्त्योऽयमविकार्योऽयमुच्यते|
तस्मादेवं विदित्वैनं नानुशोचितुमर्हसि||**25**||

avyakto 'yam acintyo 'yam avikāryo 'yam ucyate |
tasmād evaṃ viditvainaṃ nānuśocitum arhasi ||25||

This Self is unknowable by the senses, unthinkable by the mind and is not subject to any kind of change. Knowing this, you should not grieve. ||25||

Avyakta: unmanifested; ayam: this; achintyaha: unthinkable; ayam: this; avikaryaha: unchangeable; ayam: this; uchyate: is said; tasmaat: therefore; evam: thus; viditya: having known; enam: this; na: not; anushochitam: to grieve; arhasi: should.

"Avyaktoya: unmanifest/unknowable"; "Achintyoyam: unthinkable" "This Self is unknowable and unthinkable" says the Lord.

Anything/object that has a form can be visualized by the eyes; that has a smell can be recognized by the nose; that has taste can be recognized by the tongue, that is tangible can be felt by the skin, that has a sound can be recognized by the ears.

These five are our sense organs. They cannot recognize "That" which has no smell, taste, form and sound to it."That" which is the "Self" within, which is the primordial energy is therefore "unknowable" by us. It is like us incapable of visualizing the mango tree, the imprint (blueprint) of which is inside the mango seed. The sense organs send in the impulses to the mind. The mind receives these impulses from the sense organs and with the help of the intellect analyses the same. With its capacity to store these impulses, the mind can think about the objects around us and can imagine the name and forms of the objects around. It can think easily about what is received from the world outside by the sense organs. The sense organs are not capable of giving information about the "Self" within and the "Self around in all forms of life". Therefore the mind cannot fathom any details of the "Self". Self which has no physical features as such is therefore impossible for the mind to imagine and think about.

The next phrase used is "Avikarya". It means "not subject to any changes." The changes we can perceive start from the birth and go on till the death. Birth, growth, decay, diseases are part and parcel of the physical body. The "Self" does not have any of these properties we can attribute.

The Lord then says "should not grieve." Soka or grief is for that which undergoes changes/lost. Disease, death, parting from the beloved ones etc. bring in the grief. By body identification known as "Dehadrishti" we experience the grief. By raising ourselves to higher intellectual plane, if we can lift ourselves to the level of "Atmadrishti", we will not be subject to the grief. Soka which is the direct consequence of ignorance of our true nature can be overcome by "Atma Jnana". It is knowledge of the Self which can extinguish the grief we get subjected to.

This can be had by the study of the shastras, guidance and blessings of the Sadguru. Arjuna was not illiterate. He had studied shastras. Unfortunately he had not completed the study of the Vedas totally and not understood what he had studied. His mind was not ready to grasp the subtle meaning of the subject taught. Facing the war, imagining the consequences of the act, made him experience the grief. Presence of the Lord who was his own charioteer gave him the once in a life time opportunity to hear the Gita at the appropriate time. Like they say "strike when the iron is hot."

अथ चैनं नित्यजातं नित्यं वा मन्यसे मृतम्।
तथापि त्वं महाबाहो नैवं शोचितुमर्हसि॥26॥

atha cainaṃ nityajātaṃ nityaṃ vā manyase mṛtam |
tathāpi tvaṃ mahābāho naivaṃ śocitum arhasi ||26||

O mighty armed, and even if you think of Him as being constantly born, constantly dying, even then you should not grieve. ||26||

Atha: even; Cha: and; Enam: this (Atman/Self); Nityajatam: constantly born; nityam: constantly; va: or; manyase: think; mrutam: dead; tatha api: even then; tvam: thou; mahabaho: mighty armed; na: not; enam: this; shochitum: to grieve; arhasi: should (be worthy).

Arjuna is referred to as "mighty armed." This could be to encourage or ridicule Arjuna.

Encourage Arjuna by reminding of his physical strength especially in archery.

Or:

Ridicule Arjuna by saying, "what is the use of all your power if you cannot act like a Kshatriya warrior?

Krishna is also reminding Arjuna the truth about the Atman.

Because of its attachment to the mind/intellect/physical body, (can be referred to as the suit), the Atman appears to die one day and be born (with a different body) again another day. It is only the physical body that undergoes the changes.

Wise person, like Arjuna, who had the fortune of spiritual education in early childhood, should have understood the meaning of the immortality of the Atman and mortality of the body. It is the only way not to succumb to grief on parting with the physical body/family and friends.

Grief unfortunately drags one down in the spiritual plane. Let us look at the last word in the sloka - "Arhata."

Arhata means "worthiness", "worthy".

The worthiness of being born as a human is in making proper use of the "intellectual capacity of reasoning." Without the intellect, we are no different to animals. Arjuna was expected to have made use of his intellectual capacity of reasoning but did not do so.

Sri Krishna is advising Arjuna to work according to the job description of a well respected kshatriya warrior of repute. He is reminding Arjuna of his duty by saying "you have no right to be in grief".

We must all learn the art of fulfilling the job description pertaining to our profession.

We have been blessed with birth as humans and the job description according to our shastras is:

"Conduct the work for the society. Do not work for personal gains."

Gains: Moksha is automatically ours if we work diligently and follow the shastras.

जातस्य हि ध्रुवो मृत्युर्ध्रुवं जन्म मृतस्य च।
तस्मादपरिहार्येऽर्थे न त्वं शोचितुमर्हसि॥27॥

jātasya hi dhruvo mṛtyur dhruvaṃ janma mṛtasya ca |
tasmād aparihārye 'rthe na tvaṃ śocitum arhasi ||27||

For certain is death to the born and certain is the birth for the dead. Therefore you should not grieve about the inevitable. ||27||

Jatasya: of the born; hi: for; dhruvo: certain; mrytyur; death; dhruvam: certain: janma: birth; mrutasya: of the dead; cha: and; tasmad: therefore; apariharya: inevitable; arthe: in matter; na: not; tvam: you; shochitum: to grieve; arhasi: should/ought.

This was the statement made 5000 yrs ago and was not anything new even then. Arjuna attended the gurukula ashrama for the basic education. The guru in those days taught the disciples about the Vedas and Upanisads.

It was an accepted fact that majority believed that there was birth after the death. There cannot be any doubt about death for everything that is born.

The youngsters were taught about the Atman, the vasanas (thought imprints on the mind) and the bondage developed as a result of vasanas.

Until and unless the vasanas are exhausted and no new vasanas get stored in the mind, the process of birth and death continues.

It is therefore necessary to develop the mental strength to cope with the problems we face in life including the truth of the inevitable death for everything that is born.

No one advocates one to be like a stone and not grieve.

The lesson to learn from the Gita is the principle of karma and not get bogged down with grief for the consequences actions.

अव्यक्तादीनि भूतानि व्यक्तमध्यानि भारत।
अव्यक्तनिधनान्येव तत्र का परिदेवना ॥28॥

avyaktādīni bhūtāni vyakta-madhyāni bhārata |
avyakta-nidhanāny eva tatra kā paridevanā ||28||

O Arjuna, beings are of unknown origin, known middle and of unknown end. Why then lament for it? ||28||

Avyaktadeeni: unknown origin; bhootani: beings; vyakta: manifest; madhyani: in the middle; bharata: Arjuna; avyaktanidhanani: unmanifest in the end; eva: also; tatra: then; kaa: what; paridevana: grief.

Sri Krishna is reiterating the fact that we all had a past and we have a future. We do not remember the past, we are totally immersed in the present and we are ignorant/unaware of the future. "Vyakta" means "manifest." "Avyakta" means "unmanifest."

The sense organs keep us in touch with the world around. The life revolves round the impulses received from the world around by these sense organs. Their effect is so overpowering that we cannot have recollection of the past births.

Manifest means that which can be seen with the physical eyes and understood using the faculty of the other sense organs.

It is therefore to be understood that we have no idea of the past births we have undergone.

The mind which is a storehouse of thought imprints also cannot recollect the past births. This loss of memory is also a gift from the Lord (chapter 15, sloka 15).

If there was no faculty of forgetting, we will all be mad people running around the streets.

We do not have any recollection of our past and we do not know our future. What births we had in the past and what births we are going to go through in future is not known and cannot be known.

What we need to have is the faith in the statement that we have to undergo innumerable births and deaths to purify our minds contaminated with attachments to the physical world around.

Finally the Lord says "why then lament for it?"

As it is an inevitable occurrence and we have no control over the process, lamenting is not going to be of any benefit.

The word "lamenting" is to be used to mean "grief" that reduces the efficiency of the present actions.

Indirectly we are asked to get on with our day to day duties and fulfill our obligation to the society.

We can understand this by comparison to the bubbles. The bubbles that come from the waves are temporary phenomenon.

They were in unmanifest form in the waters of the waves. They have a short life span. The bubbles burst and the water content joins the water in the waves. They were not recognized in the waves before they manifest and would not be recognized in the waves after they burst. Bubbles keep on coming and going with the force of the waves in the ocean.

आश्चर्यवत्पश्यति कश्चिदेन
माश्चर्यवद्वदति तथैव चान्यः।
आश्चर्यवच्चैनमन्यः श्रृणोति
श्रुत्वाप्येनं वेद न चैव कश्चित्||29||

āścaryavat paśyati kaścid enam
āścaryavad vadati tathaiva cānyaḥ |
āścaryavac cainam anyaḥ śṛṇoti
śrutvāpy enaṃ veda na caiva kaścit ||29||

One sees this as wonder; another one speaks of it as a wonder, another hears it as a wonder, yet having heard, none understand this at all. ||29||

ascharyavat: as a wonder; pasyati: sees; kashcit: someone; enam: this; ascharyavat: as a wonder; vadati: speaks; tatha: so; eva: also; cha: and; anyaha: another; ashcaryavat: as a wonder; enam: this; anyaha: others; shrunoti: hears of; shrutvapi: even having heard; enam: this; veda: knows; na: not; cha: and; eva: also; kaschit: any one/none.

We can see that the three examples quoted here concern the three sense organs: eyes, tongue and ears.

We have learnt so far that the "Parabrahman, the Supreme" is "Nirakara and Nirguna."

He has no form and no qualities and the eyes, tongue and ears cannot recognize Him.

The other two sense organs "nose and skin" cannot also perceive the Supreme. We cannot imagine with our mind and the intellect cannot analyze the same. The Supreme is beyond the sense organs, the mind and the intellect.

Hence, it is impossible to understand the "Parabrahman."

The only way, the saints and scholars help us to reach "That", is via the route of "Transcendental meditation."

We have to learn that we need to drop our physical "I" and dissolve into "It" (meaning Parabrahman).

Reading the great books concerning the "Supreme", going to the temples, listening to the discourses cannot make us reach the "destination in the spiritual path."

After all it is inside each one of us as the "Life Force", "The Atman." The journey in life is to attain "Liberation",

Learning the art of dropping the "I",

Detaching from the attachments to the physical world,

Conducting our ordained duties without expecting the benefits from the fruits of action and finally, prepare to receive the "Prarabdha" which is the results of past actions conducted in ignorance of the "True identity".

One can then ask, "Why go to the temples, listen to the masters, the gurus and read the sacred texts?"

There is a need for constant reminder of the "Supreme" whom none of us can really understand.

The masters who have truly understood the "Supreme", and have dropped the "I", have to teach the ignorant.

This has to be from the primary school level to that of the university education in relation to the spiritual life.

Many a times, we have known that thoughts run faster than words. Words fail to explain the Supreme and so the masters explain the "Supreme" as a wonder to the uninitiated and ignorant. They talk about the Supreme as a wonder, make us realize the same as a wonder and read about the same as a wonder.

This is all because nobody has ever succeeded in defining the Parabrahman in words. It is said that defining him is defiling Him.

It is a fact that in the ecstasy of wonder we forget the surrounding world and merge with the wonder. In a way, he who is truly in wonder has momentarily lost his identity and does not respond to stimuli to attract him back to the present.

देही नित्यमवध्योऽयं देहे सर्वस्य भारत|
तस्मात्सर्वाणि भूतानि न त्वं शोचितुमर्हसि ||30||

dehī nityam avadhyo 'yaṃ dehe sarvasya bhārata |
tasmāt sarvāṇi bhūtāni na tvaṃ śocitum arhasi ||30||

This Self existing in the body of all beings is never killed. You should therefore not grieve for any creatures, O Bharata. ||30||

Dehi: indweller/jivatman; nityam: always; avadhyam: indestructible; ayam: this; dehe': in the body; sarvasya: of all; bharata: Arjuna; tasmat: therefore; sarvani: all; bhutani: creatures; na: not; tvam: you; shochitum: to grieve; arhasi: fit/should.

Dehi: this word refers to the "Jivatman" who is the Atman encased in all the physical bodies of various forms of life on this earth.

The Lord is reminding us again that "He", as the "Atman" is inside all the living forms of life.

As has been reiterated several times, Krishna ascertains again that the "Atman" thus encased does not get killed at any time. Not just killed, but never gets killed, He stresses.

This verse is the summary of Krishna's description about the immortality of the "Atman."

Let us therefore remember to see/recognise "Sat, Chit, Ananda", experience the bliss resulting thereof, and not get attached to "nama and roopa" which is the cause of anger, desire and grief.

स्वधर्ममपि चावेक्ष्य न विकम्पितुमर्हसि|
धर्म्याद्धि युद्धाच्छ्रेयोऽन्यत्क्षत्रियस्य न विद्यते ||31||

sva-dharmam api cāvekṣya na vikampitum arhasi |
dharmyād dhi yuddhāc chreyo 'nyat kṣatriyasya na vidyate ||31||

And moreover, looking at your own duty, you should not waver, for there is nothing higher for a Kshatriya than a righteous war. ||31||

Swadharm: own duty; api: also; cha: and; aveshya: looking at; na: not; vikampitum: to waver; arhasi: should not/ought not; dharmyat: than righteousness; hi: indeed; yuddhat: than war; shreyaha: higher, anyat: other/than; na: not; vidyate: is.

Lord Manu, the progenitor of the human race, postulated what is popularly known as "Manu Dharma Sastra". It is the code of Manu. It consists of a collection of laws based on custom and precedent and the teaching of the Vedas. Basically it defines the law of conduct and its application to all classes of community.

During the period which is over 5000yrs ago, the society was divided into four classes consisting of Brahmana, Kshatriya, Vysya and Sudra. Arjuna belonged to the Kshatriya group. The duty of the Kshatriya was to protect the land and their leaders were the rulers of the region.

Svadharma: it means one's own dharma/duty. The word has a variety of interpretations which we will take up as we proceed with our study. In this context it means the duty of Kshatriya. Arjuna, belonging to the Kshatriya group is reminded by Lord Krishna of his duty.

The present war in which Arjuna was engaged to fight was not an ordinary war. It was the "war of righteousness." Arjuna, who had wholeheartedly given his willingness to fight against the crooked cousins, Kauravas, suddenly, in the middle of the battlefield, loses his mental composure and was ready to abandon the wish to fight for their rights. Letting the cousin Duryodhana rule the land would have harmed the subjects badly. Sri Krishna is reminding Arjuna not to waiver from his ordained duty of a Kshatriya towards the subjects of the land.

"Sreyas" (in the second line of the verse): Sri Krishna says "this righteous war is good for you" (refer to sloka 7 of this chapter). Svadharma, one's own duty fulfilled according to the shastras is a sure way to achieve Moksha.

In a spiritual context, swadharma is in relation to one's own thought imprints: our dharma is that duty which is suited to our temperament which in turn is due to our vasanas which are nothing but our own thought imprints. Until and unless we clear the stored impure vasanas the path to freedom is not clear.

Like a good teacher the Lord is approaching the same subject from different angles and thereby trying to make Arjuna take the right decision to fight the evil Kauravas.

यदृच्छया चोपपन्नं स्वर्गद्वारमपावृतम्।
सुखिनः क्षत्रियाः पार्थ लभन्ते युद्धमीदृशम्॥32॥

yadṛcchayā copapannaṃ svarga-dvāram apāvṛtam |
sukhinaḥ kṣatriyāḥ pārtha labhante yuddham īdṛśam ||32||

For a Kshatriya, O Partha, a righteous war of this type which has come of itself, is the open gateway to heaven. ||32||

Yadrucchaya: of itself; cha: and; upapannam: come; swargadwaram: gateway to heaven; upavritam: opened; sukhinaha: happy; kshatriyaha: Kshatriyas; Partha: Arjuna; labhate: obtain; yuddham: battle; idrusham: such.

Sri Krishna in the process of trying to explain to his disciple Arjuna has now come down from the Aatmic plane to the physical plane. The conclusion is the same. He is reminding Arjuna of the duties of a Kshatriya.

It is interesting to note the words of wisdom from Kunti Devi, the mother of the Pandavas concerning the duties of a Kshatriya. Just before the war she sends a command to her children. She says: "Tell Arjuna and Bhima that the time has come to justify why any Kshatriya mother desires to have sons."

Through these words she is reminding her sons that the duty of a Kshatriya is to defend his land and protect the subjects. The death which is also a possibility in the war should not be the reason not to fight. The women of the household of a Kshatriya, be a mother, wife or sister, has to let the man of the house go to the war zone and fight.

In those days it was an accepted fact that the one who fought in the war and died would go to heaven. Heaven is a place of happiness and comforts. The Kshatriya could enjoy the luxuries on earth by winning or the pleasures in heaven if he dies in the battle. Either way, the pleasure was guaranteed.

In our day to day battle of life, we should fight kama, krodha, the enemies within, be prepared to kill our ego and enjoy the peace emanating from within. This is the duty we owe to our Lord who created us and who is protecting us.

In every walk of life, we come across moments when we have to prove ourselves. We should not shed that responsibility. What we do at the opportune moment will shape our future. We should do the best to our ability, according to dharma and this guarantees sreyas.

अथ चैत्त्वमिमं धर्म्यं संग्रामं न करिष्यसि|
ततः स्वधर्मं कीर्तिं च हित्वा पापमवाप्स्यसि||33||

atha cet tvam imaṃ dharmyaṃ saṃgrāmaṃ na kariṣyasi |
tataḥ sva-dharmaṃ kīrtiṃ ca hitvā pāpam avāpsyasi ||33||

But, if you will not fight this righteous war, then, having abandoned your own duty and fame, you would incur sin. ||33||

Atha chet: but if; tvam: you; imam: this; dharmyam: righteous; sangramam: war; na: not; karishyasi: will fight; tataha: then; swadharmam: own duty; keertim: fame; cha: and; hitva: having abandoned; papam: sin; avapsyasi: incur.

The gist of this sloka which is applicable for each of us is:

If we do not discharge our righteous duties, we would have wasted this precious birth as a human and will be born into lower planes of existence in our future births. Having attained a position in the society, we must discharge the righteous duties pertaining to that position we hold.

Arjuna, in this instance, by abandoning the duty of a Kshatriya, running away from the righteous war, would be subject to ridicule from the seniors, fellow warriors and the subjects of their kingdom. He would have lost his fame as a great and just warrior.

Papa: The word means "Sin". Sin is considered to be an act against the injunction of the sastras. Our sastras do not condemn the sinner but condemn the sinful act.

Let us remember the quote:

Every sinner has a future.

Every saint had a past.

Sage Valmiki, who composed the epic Ramayana, was a hunter in the past but following the advice by sage Narada meditated, cleared all the sinful tendencies in his mind and became the sage who is remembered even today for his epic composition.

We, the so called sinners either by ignorance or immaturity or ego have a birth right to become saints by making changes to our thought imprints and by conducting righteous actions.

We will be able to climb up the spiritual ladder or fall down as a result of our own acts or omission of acts.

Sloka 47 in this chapter will give us more insight into the meaning of this sloka.

अकीर्तिं चापि भूतानि कथयिष्यन्ति तेऽव्ययाम्।
संभावितस्य चाकीर्तिर्मरणादतिरिच्यते ||34||

akīrtiṃ cāpi bhūtāni kathayiṣyanti te 'vyayām |
saṃbhāvitasya cākīrtir maraṇād atiricyate ||34||

People too, will speak of your everlasting dishonor and to one who is honored by his country, dishonor is worse than death. ||34||

Akeertim: dishonor; ca: and; api: also; bhootani: beings; kathayishyanti: tell/speak; te: thy; avyayaam: everlasting; sambhavitasya: of the honored; cha: and; akeertihi: dishonor; maranaat: than death; atiricyate: exceeds. (worse than).

An act of dishonor taints the family's name for generations. It just does not stop at the death of the concerned individual. It is more so for those who achieve great fame and honor from the public in their life.

Disgrace for having committed a dishonorable act, especially for he, who was honored for bravery / social service / contribution to the welfare of the society is like living death. Death is only of the physical body, as we have understood so far. But results of acts that bring dishonor could be called as "immortal". They will remain for centuries in books of history for he who was honored for his services to the society.

History is full of examples of acts by respected elders of the society who brought disgrace for themselves and their country. Those individuals and their acts will remain in the history books for ever.

If Arjuna had decided not to fight, his decision would have tainted the good name of the great Pandu family. It would have been worse than if he had died fighting the righteous war.

भयाद्रणादुपरतं मंस्यन्ते त्वां महारथाः|
येषां च त्वं बहुमतो भूत्वा यास्यसि लाघवम्||35||

bhayād raṇād uparataṃ maṃsyante tvāṃ mahārathāḥ |
yeṣāṃ ca tvaṃ bahumato bhūtvā yāsyasi lāghavam ||35||

Moreover, these great warriors from whom you received honour formerly would think you turned away from the battle out of fear and regard you with little respect. ||35||

Bhayaat: from fear; ranaat: from the battle; uparatam: withdrawn; mamsyate: will think; tvaam: you; maharathaha: the great car-warriors; eshaam: of whom; cha: and; tvam: you; bahumataha: much thought of; bhootwa: having been; yasyasi: will receive; laghavaan: little respect.

Sri Krishna is reminding Arjuna of his position and rank in the society. Arjuna was a very famous and well respected warrior in those days. Arjuna had received a number of honours and was a greatly respected warrior. Unknowingly he had even fought with

Lord Shiva in disguise who presented him the famous bow, the "Pashupathastra".

Abandoning the war and letting his cousins the Kauravas rule the kingdom would have made him and his brothers subject of ridicule not only by the subjects but by all the members of the Kaurava clan. The respect he had earned during all those years would have simply vanished. Arjuna, a Kshatriya by birth, would have found it impossible to face such ridicule.

Sri Krishna by referring to the future consequences of Arjuna's present actions is trying to make him face the present situation boldly and start the war of righteousness.

अवाच्यवादांश्च बहून् वदिष्यन्ति तवाहिताः|
निन्दन्तस्तव सामर्थ्यं ततो दुःखतरं नु किम् ||36||

avācya-vādāṃś ca bahūn vadiṣyanti tavāhitāḥ |
nindantas tava sāmarthyaṃ tato duḥkhataraṃ nu kim ||36||

Your enemies will belittle your ability and in various ways speak words of ill fame. What is more painful than this? ||36||

Avachyavadam: words of ill fame (improper words); cha: and; bahoon: many; vadishyanti: will speak of; tava: thy: ahitaha: enemies; nindantaha: belittling/slandering; tava: your; samarthyam: power; tato: than this; dukhataram: painful; nu: indeed; kim: what.

It is only a continuity of the theme in the preceding verses. Sri Krishna is painting the same picture of acts of cowardice on so many frames so that for an onlooker the impact of the message will be great.

As one climbs up the ladder professionally, including the higher ranks in the army, one is recognized for the acts of bravery. The professional colleagues in that rank develop a high regard to each other. At the same time they do not lose the opportunity to belittle the individual on any mistakes committed. The greatest mistake for a Kshatriya is running away from the battlefield.

Even his wife, children and other members of the family also lose the respect for the individual. (There are many examples of suicide committed by people who faced a life of insults)

हतो वा प्राप्स्यसि स्वर्गं जित्वा वा भोक्ष्यसे महीम्।
तस्मादुत्तिष्ठ कौन्तेय युद्धाय कृतनिश्चयः॥37॥

hato vā prāpsyasi svargaṃ jitvā vā bhokṣyase mahīm |
tasmād uttiṣṭha kaunteya yuddhāya kṛta-niścayaḥ ||37||

O Arjuna, if killed in the battle, you will obtain heaven; if you win, you enjoy the world. Therefore arise, determined to fight. ||37||

Hato: if killed; va: or; prapsyasi: will obtain; swargam: heaven; jitva: having conquered; va: or; bhokshyase: will enjoy; maheem: the world; tasmat: therefore; utthishta: arise; kaunteya: Arjuna; yuddhaya: to fight; krita nishchayaha: resolved.

So far, Sri Krishna has dwelt on the consequences of running away from the battlefield. Now, he is painting the picture of the consequences of facing the battle boldly.

This sloka has to be looked upon by the seekers as a potent mantra.

Arjuna, if killed in the battle would have earned the right to enter the heaven. Kshatriyas are considered as "rajasic", the men of passion. They are on the go constantly trying to fulfill many ambitions.

They were bred to realize that the duty of Kshatriya is to fight the enemy. Death or victory was accepted with grace. They were made to understand that death in the battlefield was an honorable result and they would go to heaven and enjoy the life of luxury.

On the other hand, if they come back successfully after the war, they would be treated as heroes. They would then enjoy the life of luxury on earth.

Arjuna had requested for guidance on the right action to take. On this basis, Krishna is only informing him of the facts of life. He is not giving any commands. If commanded by Krishna, Arjuna would have gladly taken up the bow and arrows and fought bravely. But, he would not have learnt any lessons.

Also, it is a fact that when we analyse the rights and wrongs of any actions and take the decision, our input will be much stronger and the results would be that much stronger. Sri Krishna uses the word "Utthishta." He wants Arjuna to develop the mental strength to stand up and fight.

Spiritually the same rules apply. If successful, we achieve "Moksha.". We must learn to face the problems in life boldly with the sword of knowledge and devotion.

सुखदुःखे समे कृत्वा लाभालाभौ जयाजयौ ।
ततो युद्धाय युज्यस्व नैवं पापमवाप्स्यसि ||38||

sukha-duḥkhe same kṛtvā lābhālābhau jayājayau |
tato yuddhāya yujyasva naivaṃ pāpam avāpsyasi ||38||

Having an equal mind in happiness-sorrow; gain-loss; victory-defeat; engage in battle and thereby you will not incur sin. ||38||

Sukha: happiness; dukha: sorrow; same': equal; kritva: having made; labha: gain; alabhou: loss; jaya: victory; ajaya: defeat; tatho; then; yujyasva: to fight; yuddhaya: for battle; na: not; evam: thus; papam: sin; avapsyasi: shall incur.

This is the secret of Karma Yoga (yoga of action).

Detachment and equanimity are essential weapons for the spiritual seeker.

Work as such does not bind any, but it is the attachment to the results of actions (fruits of action) that binds the individual.

Life is full of waves of happiness and sorrows. Whether we like it or not, whether we want it or not, we are born on to this world and have to face the pains-pleasures; experience happiness-sorrow and victory-defeats as a consequence of our actions.

Learning the art of swimming in the ocean of life is the secret of reaching the shore by the seeker of Truth.

Considering that it is directed to Arjuna in the battlefield:

There were bound to be deaths on both sides in the battlefield of those Arjuna had loved and respected in his life. This would automatically bring in sorrow.

There is bound to be the death of the ones Arjuna wished to be killed because they were the real enemies. By these, we mean the Kaurava brothers, Karna, Shakuni etc. This would bring in happiness.

Arjuna and his brothers would gain the entire kingdom back if victorious or on the other hand lose control of all land and wealth if defeated. This is "gain-loss." Finally, the gain is considered as victory and loss is considered as defeat. It is victory and defeat.

These are the three outcomes of Arjuna's actions on the battlefield.

In our own life, if we consider it as a battle, we will experience these feelings.

The most important word to understand is: "same' kritva." It means "Equanimity in action."

We must continue to discharge our ordained duties irrespective of the expected results of our actions. This way the work automatically becomes an act of worship.

To conduct any work, we need to fulfill the following criterion:

Have a basic education;

qualify for the work undertaken;

follow the job description;

conduct work pertaining to the specialty;

continue to discharge daily household/social duties.

We have to work to the best of our capacity whatever may be the situation in life. Of course there is time for grief and time for elation. But these should not deter one from work. Within a reasonable period one must resume duties.

Every action has a reaction.

Actions towards spiritual progress are "sadhana." (spiritual effort). It is the reaction to the actions that hinder our progress.

The results to be experienced/to be faced could be immediate or delayed. It could also be in later births.

When successful, like passing exams, we feel elated. Waves of elation unbalance the mind.

On facing failure, like failing exams, we get dejected, depressed. Waves of depression unbalance the mind.

It is also a fact that the events in our life with our beloved ones also bring in happiness or sorrow.

When elated, we lose concentration on the work ahead and when depressed we do not have the mood to work.

These apply to social, moral and religious actions.

It is a good idea to consider that success now is not only the result of present actions but also due to the grace of the Lord for presenting us with the results of good actions from the past, including past births. By developing this view, the ego that comes out of success is diminished.

In a similar vein, we should consider that failure now is also the Lord's verdict on results of past actions either in this life or previous lives. We should then say, thank you God, at least one of my bad actions in the past has had its results. I have now paid for that mistake and let me try not to commit mistakes in future.

"papa" means "sin": Sin is an act against the injunction of the sastras. The Lord has said: "you will not incur sin."

He did not say: "you are a sinner."

Our sastras are very clear on this issue: they condemn the sin but not the sinner. They pray to the Lord to bless the sinner and make him not commit such acts again.

एषा तेऽभिहिता सांख्ये बुद्धिर्योगे त्विमां श्रृणु ।
बुद्ध्यायुक्तो यया पार्थ कर्मबन्धं प्रहास्यसि ||39||

eṣā te 'bhihitā sāṃkhye buddhir yoge tv imāṃ śṛṇu |
buddhyā yukto yayā pārtha karmabandhaṃ prahāsyasi ||39||

O Arjuna, this, which has been taught to you, is Samkhya Yoga, about the Atman. Now listen to Karma Yoga, having known which, you shall cast off the bondage to work. ||39||

Yesha: this; te: to you; abhihita: taught; buddhir yoge: yoga of wisdom; tu: indeed; imam: this; shrunu: hear; buddhya: with wisdom; yuktaha: induced; yaya: which; Partha: Arjuna; karmabandham: bondage to karma: prahasyasi: shall cast off.

We have, in the beginning of this chapter, learnt that the word "Samkhya Yoga" means, "complete knowledge." So far in this chapter we are taught about the identity of the "Atman" which is the real entity in us. We must know all about the "Atman" because it is the real "us" and without which we are nonexistent. However just knowing about the Atman is not sufficient. We must know how to live in this world.

In our day to day life in this world, what we learn during our earlier days of education from the teachers at educational institutions is "attaining complete knowledge." With the qualifications achieved, we become eligible to take up work to earn a living.

Life is not just attaining the knowledge (Jnana). The knowledge has to be used to gain wisdom (Vijnana). Wisdom comes from practical application of the theory. We tend to commit mistakes while putting theory into practice and learn from the mistakes.

Perfections in work takes a long time to achieve and rare are those who are totally perfect in all their actions.

In this instance, we are talking about conducting all our daily actions using the knowledge. If the final aim is to attain "Moksha", the actions have to be in the spirit of "no bondage." The basis has to be acquiring the knowledge first and preparing for the practical living in this world. Getting attached to the work and its results will bring "sukha, dukha" which are the causes for bondage. The teaching of the Gita is to learn the art of working and in cutting the bondage to work. Sri Krishna says, the cutting of bondage to work is real "karma yoga." No doubt, when we proceed to study more about the sacred text and learn to read it repeatedly, we will learn the true meaning of the word "karma."

From this sloka we are now taken into the summary of karma yoga.

Practical work, putting the theory into practice is "karma yoga". Sri Krishna has made it abundantly clear in this sloka that we all have to conduct "karma". We all have to do our obligatory duties, whatever stage of life we may be in. There is no escape from "actions." Our duty is to learn the secret of karma yoga which is "non attachment." "Buddhi" is the reasoning capacity that should remind us of this magical word "non attachment." (karma bandham prahasyasi)

Up to sloka 46, we will get the introduction to karma yoga. It is therefore, still theory only and hence it is to be taken as part of "samkhya yoga." From sloka 47 we will get into the doctrine of true karma yoga.

नेहाभिक्रमनाशोऽस्ति प्रत्यवायो न विद्यते ।
स्वल्पमप्यस्य धर्मस्य त्रायते महतो भयात् ||40||

nehābhikrama-nāśo 'sti pratyavāyo na vidyate |
svalpam apy asya dharmasya trāyate mahato bhayāt ||40||

There is no loss of effort in this Karma Yoga. Even if it is stopped in the middle, no harm is produced. Even a little of this knowledge, even a little practice of this Yoga, protects man from great fear. ||40||

Na: not; iha: in this; abhikramanosti: loss of effort; asti: is; pratyavayaha: production of contrary results (harmful results); na: not; Vidyate: is; swalpam: very little; api: even: asya: of this; dharmasya: duty; trayate: protects; mahataha: great; bhayaat: fear.

The two words we must understand in this sloka are:

"iha" and "asya dharmasya".

"iha": it means "in this."

"Asya Dharmasya": it means "of this principle dharma."

Both the words refer to the word "Karma Yoga" referred to in the previous sloka. There we analyzed that the Lord meant "Karma Yoga" as the art of "correct action" which comes from learning about the Atman first. Only actions that follow after "samkhya" (complete knowledge of the Atman) will guarantee the results mentioned in this sloka.

Such of those actions that one conducts after obtaining the theoretical knowledge of the Atman first will protect the individual. It is like saying, "go to the school, the college and complete the educational requirements. Get the degree/qualification for a particular profession and use that knowledge in the field of work you pursue."

We must not forget that the sacred text is all about "Moksha" and "Liberation from the cycle of births and deaths." Lord's promise is concerning this "Moksha."

Every individual who makes an attempt in understanding about the "Atman", one's true identity as the "Atman" (Divinity within) will find the benefit of such understanding in course of time. We must have faith in the principle that "every action has a result and we will experience the result in this birth or future births." We must have Faith in the scripture which is on the principle of " the cycle of births and deaths till one attains absolute purity". This will help in understanding the sacred text.

The sincere attempt in understanding about the "Atman residing in all forms of life" will in the course of time (maybe in this birth or several births later), confer "Liberation."

The Lord promises, "There is no loss of effort." One should not feel that what good he has done is wasted if he does not get the positive results which he/she can experience in this birth. For many, it is not just experiencing in this birth, but the desire to experience immediately on completion of the work.

The beneficial results of any action will come at the time decided by the Lord and we must have a strong and unswerving faith in this.

Finally, the Lord says, "Protects from great fear." What is the great fear?

Fear of inability to continue the sadhana for whatever reason, (death and parting from the near and dear ones) is the great fear of most of us.

Learning about the true identity of "the divine Atman" will vanqish such fear. The true spiritual seeker will then take up the practice with joy and keenness and nothing in this world will distract him/her from such practice. This is true "Karma Yoga."

व्यवसायात्मिका बुद्धिरेकेह कुरुनन्दन ।
बहुशाखा ह्यनन्ताश्च बुद्धयोऽव्यवसायिनाम् ||**41**||

vyavasāyātmikā buddhir ekeha kuru-nandana |
bahu-śākhā hy anantāś ca buddhayo 'vyavasāyinām ||41|

O Arjuna, there is only one faith and thought for those who practice this Karma yoga. The minds of others are divided into various branches and their thoughts are endless. ||41||

Vyavasayatmika: one pointed; buddhi: wisdom; eka: one; iha: here; kurunanadana: of the joy of the Kurus; bahushakhaha: many branched; hi: indeed; anantaha: endless; cha: and; budhayaha: thoughts; avyayasayinaam: of the irresolute (the minds of others).

The important word to understand in this sloka is: Vyavasaya.

One of the meanings for this word is "Agriculture."

The farmer is an agriculturist and he works with single pointed concentration to get the maximum yield for his effort. Let us analyse his work briefly.

Farmer deals with selection of the land and the suitable seeds to sow and the season to sow. To get the best results he conducts the following tasks:

Selects the seed that is suitable to sow in the land. Tills the land and makes it ready to sow the seeds.

Learns about the time to sow the seeds and the preparation of the land for the same. Knows about the average weather pattern for different seasons.

Takes steps to protect the tender shoots in the earlier days from adverse weather conditions.

Clears all the weeds that grow and also takes precautions from other animals that might ruin the crop at any stage of the development.

With all these efforts and with God's grace he gets the yield which feeds him and becomes a source of his income.

To get the final result of getting a good income, he has to wait a long time from the time he sows the seeds. At any one time his thoughts will be on what to do during that period and not day dreaming for the final results.

The knowledge of what to do at each period of the growth, conducting such acts that are needed at that time, hard dedicated

work from morning till evening, each day of the week will contribute to the final successful yield of the crops. Of course, he is aware of the adverse weather condition he might have to face and prays to the Lord to prevent such calamities.
This is true "Karma yoga" put into practice.
This is the faith and thoughts for those who practice karma yoga as enumerated in this sloka.

The sacred text is all about the sowing of the good seeds of thoughts in the human mind. The human mind is to be compared to the land into which the seeds of thoughts are to be sown.

The parents have a duty to get the minds of their children ready ("till" the land) for sowing the seeds of good thoughts.

Early education into good conduct with examples from ancient mythological stories should give children the knowledge thereby sowing the seeds of good thoughts. Carefully guarding the land (mind), the seeds (thoughts maturing to become actions), removal of weeds (impure thoughts) with faith and dedication will guarantee the yield of good citizens of the land that herald peace and prosperity for the region.

This is the "Karma Yoga" or Yoga of action which the Lord is referring to. Majority of us unfortunately do not fit into this category as our minds are filled with endless thoughts of desires and hatreds.

यामिमां पुष्पितां वाचं प्रवदन्त्यविपश्चितः ।
वेदवादरताः पार्थ नान्यदस्तीति वादिनः ||42||

yām imāṃ puṣpitāṃ vācaṃ pravadanty avipaścitaḥ |
veda-vāda-ratāḥ pārtha nānyad astīti vādinaḥ ||42||

O Arjuna, the unwise utter flowery speech. They take pleasure in the eulogizing words of the Vedas. They say "There is nothing else but pleasures." ||42||

Yam: which; imam: this; pushpitaam: flowery; vacham: speech; pravadanti: utter; avipashcitaha: the unwise; vedavada rataha: taking pleasure in eulogizing words of the Vedas; Partha: Arjuna; na: not; anyat: other; asti: is; iti: thus; vadinaha: saying

कामात्मानः स्वर्गपरा जन्मकर्मफलप्रदाम् ।
क्रियाविशेषबहुलां भोगैश्वर्यगतिं प्रति ॥43॥

kāmātmānaḥ svarga-parā janma-karma-phala-pradām |
kriyā-viśeṣa-bahulāṃ bhogaiśvarya-gatiṃ prati ||43||

They are full of desires; their highest goal is heaven, leading to new birth as reward for their actions, and engage themselves in specific works for the purpose of acquiring enjoyments and prosperity. ||43||

Kamatmanaha: full of desires; swargaparaha: heaven as their highest goal; janma karma phala pradaam: leading to new birth as the result of their works; kriya vishesha bahulaam: engage in specific duties; bhogaishwarya gatim prati: for the attainment of pleasures and prosperity.

भोगैश्वर्यप्रसक्तानां तयापहृतचेतसाम् ।
व्यवसायात्मिका बुद्धिः समाधौ न विधीयते ॥44॥

bhogaiśvarya-prasaktānāṃ tayāpahṛta-cetasām |
vyavasāyātmikā buddhiḥ samādhau na vidhīyate ||44||

The minds of such men who are drawn away by attachment to pleasures and wealth cannot be concentrated to remain fixed in divine contemplation and samadhi. ||44||

Bhogaishwarya prasaktanaam: deeply attached to pleasures; taya: by that; apahrutachetasaha: whose minds are drawn away; vyasayatmika: concentrated; buddhi: reasoning capacity; samadhou: in Samadhi; na: not; vidheeyate: is fixed.

We need to take the three slokas together to understand the true import of the words used by the Lord.

To understand clearly the true meaning of the slokas, we should recollect some basic principles of spiritual education.

The subject matter of the ancient method of spiritual teaching was "The Vedas."

The learning of the Vedas was to assist the spiritual seeker in "realizing the Eternal Truth which is nothing but developing the awareness of the Eternal Happiness abiding within each one of us."

The Vedas, as we have discussed in the beginning are broadly divided into three sections. They are:

Karma Kanda, Upasana Kanda. Jnana Kanda

Karma Kanda deals with various rituals and gives the benefits from conduct of such rituals.

Upasana Kanda deals with methods of Sadhana that assist in concentrating on the "Supreme" and controlling the mind from getting distracted to worldly pleasures.

Jnana Kanda is the final section that deals with acquiring the wisdom about the Supreme, dropping the feeling of "me and mine" and uniting back with the Supreme. It is realizing the mahavakya "Tat Tvam Asi" which is popularly known as "Moksha." If we compare this three-tier system of Vedic education to our present day education system, we can understand the implications more clearly.

Before the education, one is considered as "ignorant." The ignorant lives in darkness. He/she is lazy and/or not interested in acquiring knowledge. (tamasic living)

We, the elders in the society have to tempt (bribe) the young kids who are keen to spend their time on playing and enjoying themselves to accept the need for education. To do so, we have to tempt them with rewards like sweets, gifts etc. for showing progress in learning. With the progress in education, the need for giving rewards for success has to get less and less. Instead of rewards as the motive for good work, maturity should bring in the attitude that the knowledge acquired for welfare is the reward for hard work.

The Karma Kanda section of the Vedas deals with various rituals and the benefits one can get by performing them. They offer the promise of "heavenly pleasures" for those who conduct the rituals. This is like inducement to show interest in learning the Vedas.

The Upasana Kanda takes the spiritual seeker a step higher and gets him/her to concentrate more on the end result of acquiring the total knowledge that leads to the path of "Moksha".

Finally, the "Jnana Kanda" is that which takes the seeker away from worldly pleasures and lets them constantly contemplate on the Brahman which gives the end result of "Moksha."

It is important to remember that the Vedic education is to dissuade the seeker from running after the personal pleasures and to live the life of "Peace and Contentment."

They say that "heaven" is an intermediary plane of experiencing higher forms of pleasures. They also teach that the pleasures experienced in heaven are not permanent and are directly proportional to the amount of spiritual effort put in.

It is like spending the money saved by hard work to relax and go for holidays. As soon as the savings are exhausted, we cannot remain in the resort we enjoyed previously and have to start working and saving for next period of holidays. Heaven is to be looked upon as a place of reward for good deeds done on earth.

The one who is looking for pleasures in life, albeit, in an honest way, will experience the heavenly pleasures in relation to the good deeds conducted. As soon as the benefits proportionate to the good deeds are exhausted, he/she has to work again to acquire more spiritual points.

The highest goal for man is to know and realize the Eternal Truth. Every benefit that he/she gets for the efforts which comes short of the final end result should be of no consequence to him/her. Heaven should not be the goal. Those who go after the pleasures of heaven will unfortunately fall down to earth on exhausting good spiritual points acquired by hard work. They have to go through many more cycles of births and deaths before reaching the final goal. This is what the texts refer to as "samsara."

Let us now look at the three slokas in question. "The unwise utter flowery speech."

The wise are those who go for knowledge and learn practically from the knowledge acquired and become wise.

Unwise are those who go for knowledge but do not learn from the lessons in life.

This sloka refers to those who take up the spiritual path and start to learn the Vedas. They do not proceed beyond the "Karma kanda". They are tempted by the heavenly pleasures that come by conducting the various rituals and do not proceed to the next section of "Upasana." They boast about the Vedic knowledge acquired. This is what is meant by "the unwise utter flowery speech."

"They take pleasure in eulogizing words of the Vedas."

It means that they take pleasures in talking about the benefit of the various rituals mentioned in the Karma kanda.

"They say that there is nothing but pleasures."

It refers to the heavenly pleasures that are for the taking for those who conduct the rituals as described in Karma kanda.

"They are full of desires."

They conduct the rituals wishing for the desired results from such rituals. As a consequence they exhaust the merits of good work conducted and fall into the cycle of births and deaths.

"The minds of such men are drawn away by attachments to pleasure and wealth." They concentrate on the beneficial and pleasurable results of the good work conducted. They go for such higher and higher pleasures but stop short of the final pleasure of "Moksha."

They cannot conduct Upasana on the "Eternal Truth." Their minds cannot remain steady on the contemplation of the "Eternal Truth".

Desires distract the mind and they should not go after desires is the Lord's message for the spiritual seekers.

"Vyavasayatmika buddhi samadhou na vidheeyate" (sloka 44):

Refer to sloka 41 for the explanation on "Vyavasayatmika buddhi." "Samadhi" is total single pointed contemplation on the "Supreme" and cutting away totally from worldly distractions. Those who go after the pleasures cannot fix their mind on the Supreme and cannot attain "Samadhi."

त्रैगुण्यविषया वेदा निस्त्रैगुण्यो भवार्जुन ।
निर्द्वन्द्वो नित्यसत्त्वस्थो निर्योगक्षेम आत्मवान् ॥45॥

traiguṇya-viṣayā vedā nistraiguṇyo bhavārjuna |
nirdvandvo nitya-sattva-stho niryoga-kṣema ātmavān ||45||

The Vedas deal with three gunas O Arjuna. Transcend the three gunas, become free from the pairs of opposites. Remain ever in pure satvika state, free from yoga and kshema and be firmly established in Atman. ||45||

Traigunya vishayaa: deal with the three gunas; vedaha: the Vedas; nistraigunyo: without the three gunas; bhava: be: Arjuna; nirdwandvo: free from the pairs of opposites; nityasatvastaha: ever remaining in pure Satva: niryogakshemaha: free from (thoughts of) acquiring and possessing (objects); atmavaan: established in Atman.

Sri Krishna has brought in the subject of "Gunas." Arjuna was already familiar with the word "Gunas".

Let us briefly analyse the meaning of this important word.

We will have more opportunity to learn about it as we proceed further. Chapter 14 is dedicated totally to the subject of "Gunas." (It is also to be found in the introduction section of this book)

"Guna" means "Quality." "Quality" is the outward expression of our inherent nature. This is influenced by the reaction to the impulses brought in by the five sense organs to the mind, the reaction by the mind to such impulses received and the amount of influence the intellect has on the mind. It is not just the impulses received at present but also to the impulses received from the past (and stored).

The gunas are three in number:

Satvic - pure

Rajasic - passionate

Tamasic - lazy, indolent.

Sri Krishna advises Arjuna to transcend the three gunas. Why?

Tamasic guna which is "laziness and indolence" does not assist in the upward progress for the spiritual seeker. On the other hand, it is the cause of downfall of the seeker to lower levels of existence.

Rajasic guna brings in the thirst for more desires. Desires in turn lead to many more actions, subsequent reactions and the cycle goes on and on. This is the cause for innumerable births into this world. Depending upon the quality of desires, the birth could be into one of the many different forms of life.

Satvic guna even though pure in nature has the pitfall of making the seeker feel that he is a pure soul and as a consequence develop the feeling that "I am superior to others." It brings in "ego" which is the cause for rapid and great fall from spiritual heights achieved.

Arjuna had climbed up from tamasic to the rajasic level. Arjuna by birth was a Kshatriya and a man of action. His pure nature by association with revered elders in the family like Bheeshma and with Krishna had lifted him to higher levels of rajas. The next step for him was to lift himself up to satvic level of purity. As a true guru Krishna wanted his sincere disciple not to develop the ego of being "satvic". Hence, his advice "Transcend the three gunas."

"Remain ever pure in Satvika and be established in Atman" is the advice. This state, the learned elders say is "Shuddha Satva."

"Shuddha Satva" is total purity of thoughts. The spiritual seeker having overcome reacting to pairs of opposites like happiness and sorrow; pains and pleasure gets firmly established in the "Atman." He is "Atmavaan".

This state is the same as "Sthitaprajna" which means "Man of steady wisdom." We are going to get an elaborate description of the qualities of "Sthitaprajna" towards the end of this chapter.

Nirdwandwo: free from pairs of opposites.

Heat and cold; pains and pleasures; gain and loss, victory and defeat are the pairs of opposites we encounter in our daily life. These are the reactions to the events that unfold in life. We fall prey to such reactions and forget the spiritual path we are supposed to be walking on. It does not mean free from conduct of the duties but only free from the results of actions we need to conduct to be part of the society we live in.

There is another important word used in this sloka. It is:

Niryogakshema: (we will get a clearer understanding of this word as we progress and in sloka 22, chapter 9 we will discuss in detail.)

Yoga: to acquire

Kshema: to protect/take care of.

On the social plane of living, we are constantly in the process of acquiring objects (from the world around) and trying to safeguard the same. This attachment we develop in turn leads to the pains and sorrows of losing them. So, for spiritual progress, the Lord is advocating us all to develop the quality of "niryoga kshema" (free from acquiring and protecting).

यावानर्थ उदपाने सर्वतः संप्लुतोदके ।
तावान्सर्वेषु वेदेषु ब्राह्मणस्य विजानतः ||46||

yāvān artha udapāne sarvataḥ saṃplutodake |
tāvān sarveṣu vedeṣu brāhmaṇasya vijānataḥ ||46||

To an enlightened person, who has known the Self, all the Vedas are as useful as a reservoir of water in a place where there is a flood everywhere. ||46||

Yavaan: as much; artha: use; udapane: in a reservoir; sarvataha: everywhere; sampludotake: being flooded; tavaan: so much; sarveshu: in all; vedeshu: in the Vedas; brahmanasya: of the Brahmana (enlightened person); vijnanathaha: who knows very well.

This sloka is the continuation on the theme of "Atmavaan" which we discussed in the last sloka. He who is fully established in the Atman has no need of the Vedas. After all the Vedas are the means to understand the nature of the Atman. Once having fully understood the Atman, Paramatman and fully established in Him, the seeker is no more a seeker. He is one with the Atman and is in total bliss with the Atman. Such a person has no need of the Vedas is the meaning implied in this sloka. The example of reservoir and flooding is given to understand the message clearly.

What is the role of a reservoir of water in any town?

The reservoir is meant to store the water and make it simpler to provide water to the needy.

During times of drought and similar situations the water in the reservoir can be directed to the place of the need.

If there is a flood, water is to be seen everywhere. (Let us not get into the argument of health hazards and other problems at this stage. This is only an example and no example can give us a true picture of the Supreme.)

The enlightened person is compared to the place that is flooded. His mind is flooded with the name, form, qualities of the Divine. With faith, bhakti he has understood the Supreme and is fully established in Him. For he, who has understood the Supreme, the Vedas are of no further use. As the Vedas are for understanding the Supreme, the enlightened person need not have to go to classes for understanding the Vedas. There is no need for him to take up the rituals in karma kanda. After all, the karma kanda rituals are for experiencing the heavenly pleasures.

For a post graduate fellow who has mastered the knowledge, there is no need to go back to the university to acquire further knowledge.

Indirectly the message for us all from the Lord is, "Get enlightened, and continue discharging your duty. Do not go for worldly pleasures and do not strive for heaven."

Another important word to note is "vijanataha". "Jnataha" means "who knows." "Vijanataha" means "who knows very well." It is not enough to know the subject well but it is important to know it fully well and understand completely.

This is the prelude for the most important sloka in the sacred text: "Karmanye vadhikarasthe."

The Vedas are for understanding the nature of the Supreme.

The person who has realized the Supreme is said to be enlightened. He has no need to go to the basics to study the Atman. He is flooded with the knowledge of the Supreme.

The reservoir of water mentioned in this sloka refers to the ancillary teaching of the Supreme which includes the Vedas too and which are the highest authority. These are still the avenues for the seeker to get knowledge. But once the knowledge is acquired there is no need to go the study the Vedas (which are only reservoirs of knowledge). Hence the statement "the reservoirs are of no use when there is flooding".

कर्मण्येवाधिकारस्ते मा फलेषु कदाचन ।
मा कर्मफलहेतुर्भूर्मा ते सङ्गोऽस्त्वकर्मणि ||47||

karmaṇy evādhikāras te mā phaleṣu kadācana |
mā karma-phala-hetur bhūr mā te saṅgo 'stv akarmaṇi ||47||

You have the right to work only but never to its fruits. Let not the fruits of action be your motive. Nor let your attachment be to inaction. ||47||

Karmani: in work; eva: only; adhikaraha: right; te': you; maa: not; phaleshu: in fruits; kadachana: at any time; maa: not; karma phala hetuhu bhuh: let the fruits of actions be the motive: te: you; sangaha: attachment; astu: let be; akarmani: inaction.

This sloka has to be divided into four quarters to understand it fully and is one of the most important as it summarizes the entire philosophy of "karma." It demands that the seeker develops the knowledge of "right action." Jnana and Karma have to mingle and together, they take the seeker to higher planes of spiritual enlightenment.

Karmanye vadhikaraste: you have a right to work only
Maa phaleshu kadachana: no right for the fruits thereof.
Maa karma phla-heturbhuh: let not the fruits be your motive.
Maa te sangostv akarmani: let not be attached to inaction.

"Adhikara" (please refer to Tatva Bodha of Sree Adi Shankaracharya to understand the correct meaning of the special word) is the most important word in this sloka and we must understand it clearly. It means "right", "entitlement."

The student who has gained entry into a school, paid the fees is entitled to enter the school and attend the prescribed classes. He has the "adhikara" to be in the school during the classes.

The consultant at a particular hospital, selected by the panel, gets the right to enter the premises and work in the appropriate ward.

The M.P having won the confidence of the electorate has a right to enter the House of Parliament. He has the "adhikara" to do so.

On this basis, due to our past karmas, the Lord has given us the "Adhikara" to live as "humans" on this earth and given us a role to play on the stage of life.

Each one of us, by His blessings, as a result of actions performed both in the past births and in this life, has attained a certain position in family/society we live in.

Let us be clear that it is not just the "right" to work but there is a clause to it. That is: Right to work to fulfill the responsibilities of the job/position allotted.

Like a director of a film/play, "He" has given us different roles to play.

"You have a right to work only" and "no rights for the fruits thereof" has to be understood in this context. We have to work according to the rules of the position we are given. Our sastras call it as "Ashrama dharma". A child has to follow the rules of childhood and the student has to follow the rules of education. We have a duty to fulfill that role.

What we get from our work is to be shared with family/society. Life starts from being in debt from childhood itself.

We are in debt to our parents for the love and affection they put in our upbringing and for the sacrifices they undertake. To the society which provides the basic needs like education, medical care, water supply, electricity etc. during the period of education from kindergarten to university. (Our parent's contribution towards our education is a paltry sum in relation to the contribution by the society.)

When we understand this way, we realize that what we spend from the pay packet we receive when we start working should include a portion for repaying the debt to the society. As a matter of fact, to give a full education for a child till the day of graduation, the amount is so phenomenal that the graduate would have to work without pay for the rest of his/her life to repay this.

So, what we really get from our work as pay/fee cannot be called as "my money".

The second quarter of the sloka "no rights for the fruits thereof" has to be understood on this basis.

The word “adhikara” can be understood as “right of inheritance” also. Unless we are entitled to, we cannot inherit any property from our ancestors.

From our parents, we have inherited the “Divine Soul” with a physical body to conduct the actions as servants of the “Divine.”

Both the Soul and the physical body are precious inheritance and we must look after them carefully. After being born as “humans,” we have a duty to work “humanely.” The results, the Lord says will come on their own accord. But they do depend upon how we conduct the duties.

We must know the “job description” of any job we are selected for and work accordingly. Not conforming to the job description as we know results in losing that job.

As we proceed further and understand the sacred text clearly, we will learn that the results of our actions have to be shared with family/friends/society and not just for personal gains and personal pleasures.

We do get wealth in one form or other from our actions. Students get the wealth of education (jnana) and the employees get a pay packet for their actions. We have to consider that the wealth we get from our actions and what we hold on to, is only as “caretakers” of that wealth and not as the sole owners. Using it for personal gain and pleasures would be equal to committing a crime and we would have to face the consequences of the same.

Maa karma phala hetur bhuhu--”Let not the fruits of actions be your motive”: “Hetur” means “cause for”.

Of course actions do bring in results but the seeker in the path of karma realizes that the results do not come from his actions but there is a divine hand behind the results. With this understanding we have to conduct actions in the spirit of: “let not the fruits of actions be your motive”, which is “Nishkama karma”.

Of course it is a fact that each job has its set standard of pay/ benefits. Having graduated and being appointed as a teacher, the job comes with a pay packet at the end of each month. The pay packet should not be the motive for the job is what we must understand. Working with the thought on the reward at the end of the work automatically reduces the work efficiency. Single pointed concentration on the day to day work will bring in the maximum result in any job undertaken.

The society we are in now has deteriorated so fast that we have started to live not with the money earned yesterday but using the money we hope to get tomorrow. It is the era of "plastic cards, credit cards." We enter into the trap of "Debt" by borrowing the tomorrow's money for today.

Each day's work has to be given its importance and the work fulfilled to one's maximum potential. The pay packet will come on its own accord at the end of the month. Working with the monetary benefit in mind will dilute the efficiency of the work. If the work is not satisfactory, there is a possibility of losing the job also.

Single pointed dedicated work becomes "Divine work." This is "dhyana" in its true sense.

"Nor let your attachment be to inaction":

There may be some, who by not understanding the sloka properly come to think that actions lead automatically to attachment. No one can live without work even for a second. To give up work is a sign of laziness and it becomes "Tamasic." The parents have parental duty towards their children and cannot escape from the same.

The spiritual seeker must know that he has to burn the existing vasanas. By not burning the inherited vasanas, he will not make any progress.

Arjuna wanted to escape from the war and go to the forest to become a sanyasi. He did not want to face the terrible consequences of war. Sri Krishna is categorically warning him not to do so.

For a short while Arjuna might find peace in the forest but soon would get involved in the life of forest and his Kshatriya tendencies would manifest again.

Another explanation for the word "Adhikara": this applies to seekers at higher plane of perfection on the spiritual path.

All the spiritual practices contribute to the purity of the mind. The spiritual seeker in search of "Liberation" has to gain the knowledge. Towards this goal he has to pass through the four gates of entry that finally leads him into the temple of knowledge. These four gates of entry are collectively known as "Sadhana

Chatushtaya." Let us have a brief glimpse into what these four gates are and what do we mean by them.

Sadhana Chatushtaya (four spiritual practices).
Viveka
Vairagya
Shatsampatti
Mumukshatva.

Viveka:

The first gate of entry is "The power of discrimination." This enables the seeker to distinguish between the permanent and impermanent. We mean, between "Eternal Truth (Atman) and non-Eternal Truth (physical body)." The seeker wishing to become one with the Eternal Truth must develop Viveka. It is the first pre requisite for the spiritual seeker.

Vairagya:

Once the philosophy of life that leads to the final goal of moksha is accepted, the seeker has to develop the art of detachment from the lower that bind him and prevent him from moving to higher states of perfection. In other words it is the art of "letting go of the lower to reach the higher." The young child in higher school with the aim of going to the college for higher education has to develop the art of detachment from the attachments in the lower classes. Spiritually it is the absence of all worldly passions and freedom **from all desires except the desire for "Liberation."**

Shatsampatti:

It means six treasures. They are:

Sama:

The mind is fickle by nature. It gets attracted to many objects around this world. The art of controlling this fickle nature of the mind is "Sama."

Dama:

It is control of the sense organs. The horses on a chariot are compared to the sense organs. Unless the charioteer gets the reins and the reins are under the control of the charioteer, they fail to run in the direction desired by the charioteer. They tend to run hither and thither. We should have a strong control over the five sense organs.

Uparathi:

For contemplation on the divine, the seeker not only has to develop Sama and Dama and stop moving towards the desire for worldly objects but also has to learn the art of contemplating on the Atman within. He must practice turning the search light from outer world to the inner world. Uparathi is the art of settling the mind within the heart. Absolute calmness of the mind comes from learning the art of uparathi.

Thithikshatva:

It is the power of endurance. We have discussed this in sloka 14 of this chapter. While progressing in the spiritual path, one is bound to experience trials and tribulations in life. Total freedom from anxiety and mental anguish is essential for progress. Contented life comes when one can master the art of endurance.

Sraddha:

It is absolute faith in the higher. What is the point of studying for a degree in engineering if one does not have faith in the subject and the benefit one gets from the degree? What is the point of spiritual practice if one does not have faith in the higher? Sraddha as we have discussed before acts as a fuel for progress.

Samadhana:

This is the process where there are no more thoughts generating in the mind. It is the state of perfect tranquility.

Mumukshatva:

It is the burning desire for "Moksha" or Liberation from worldly bondage.

The true spiritual seeker who has acquired the wealth of "Sadhana Chatushtaya" is the "Adhikari" to conduct actions as described in this verse and acquire knowledge of the Atman.

योगस्थः कुरु कर्माणि सङ्गं त्यक्त्वा धनञ्जय ।
सिद्ध्यसिद्ध्योः समो भूत्वा समत्वं योग उच्यते ||48||

yogasthaḥ kuru karmāṇi saṅgaṃ tyaktvā dhanaṃjaya |
siddhy-asiddhyoḥ samo bhūtvā samatvaṃ yoga ucyate ||48||

O Arjuna, do your work, be steadfast in Yoga, giving up all attachment, unmindful of success or failure. Such equanimity of the mind is "Yoga." ||48||

Yogasthaha: steadfast in yoga; kuru: perform; karmani: actions (duties);sangam: attachment; tyaktva: giving up; Dhananjaya: Arjuna; siddhi: success; asiddhi: failure; sama: equal; bhootva: having become; samatvam: equanimity; yogam: yoga: uchyate: is said.

In continuation of the theme from the previous sloka, we now are given instructions about the work and the results from the same. After having been told about "Karmanye vadhikarasthe", the Lord says: Yogasthaha kuru karmani:

Do your work, be steadfast in yoga. Yoga in this context refers to "Karma Yoga" or "Yoga of right action."

"Be steadfast in your work and the results will follow the actions." We will succeed in some actions and it makes us feel happy. Some actions do fail and we feel depressed. Balance of mind on facing such results and continuing to fulfill the duties to the family and society is the summary of this sloka.

Whatever action we conduct, must be carried out with total 100% concentration on the same. There should not be any disturbances from the world around. Work has to become an act of worship.

The sense organs are bound to bring in a number of impulses that can easily distract from the work ahead. We do instruct our children to concentrate on the road while walking to the school. We are expected to take care of the traffic around when we are driving a motor vehicle. Failure by the child to take note of oncoming traffic would result in accident. Similarly, failure on our part to concentrate on driving can easily end up in nasty accident.

We not only have to do our work but also do the same with full concentration and not get distracted. This is the message of the first quarter of this sloka.

Sangam tyaktva:

Giving up all attachments.

Attachment to the results of actions,
Attachment to the work itself,
Attachment to the distractions that come during the work,
All should be given up.

This is not easy. If we accept that what we are doing is God's work and as servants of the Lord, it becomes easier.

It is very difficult to accept the statement "do not be attached to the work." Of course it is important that we do perform the various duties in life, both personal and professional. What is needed is that we should not be feeling proud of our position we hold in society and the work we do in relation to it. By God's grace we got to where we are and what we do should be only as His servants. The work then becomes a "duty", an act of worship.

The sense organs and the mind are very powerful. We, the humans are blessed to have got the buddhi which is the reasoning capacity. Even while working, the sense organs will be receiving impulses from the surroundings. Some of those might be strong enough to distract us and take us away from the work in progress. Without our knowledge we get attached to the new impulses received.

Not taking notice of any new impulses,
not getting distracted from work,
not getting attached to them while conducting any work,
conducting the work with total concentration,
all these are conditions to be fulfilled to carry on the obligatory duties is the meaning for the word "Sangam tyaktva."

It is easy to let the mind wander off into its dream world. We must not let the mind get distracted by the impulses brought in by the sense organs but also should not let it go into the treasure house of memories. Attachment easily develops to these impulses/thoughts which reduce the efficiency of work and which could easily cause harm.

Attachment could also be to the fruits of actions. This we have discussed fully in the previous sloka.

Siddhy-asiddhyoh samo' bhootva: Unmindful of success or failure.

Every action ends in a result. We could succeed or fail in the work we conduct. What we need to do is to prepare ourselves fully to the work. Let us also clear all doubts concerning the work.

The student wishing to sit for exams and get a degree has to concentrate on the studies first. He should clarify the doubts that crop up in the mind every so often. With the knowledge gained in the classroom and by the revision work, he has to sit for exams. While writing the answers in the examinations he should not be thinking of success in exams and the benefits from the same. He should also not worry about failure.

As we have discussed before, putting in the best efforts is our job. The results are His grace.

The results depend on two issues: the efforts put in the conduct of the work and the result of actions conducted in the past including past births.

To worry about the results to come is like living in the 'morrow. Let us learn to live in the present and not in the future.

Samatvam Yogam uchyate:

"Samatvam" is equal mindedness under all circumstances. The thought of the results that are going to come or the results that have come (either pleasing or not pleasing), should not reduce the efficiency of the present work.

The end result of union of the Jivatman with the Paramatman is "Yoga."

To achieve this result, first of all the ego has to vanquish. Technically speaking, ego has to lose all its identification and merge with the Atman. This is also "Yoga." Equanimity of mind to achieve this result is also "Yoga."

दूरेण ह्यवरं कर्म बुद्धियोगाद्धनञ्जय ।
बुद्धौ शरणमन्विच्छ कृपणाः फलहेतवः ||49||

dūreṇa hy avaraṃ karma buddhi-yogād dhanaṃjaya |
buddhau śaraṇam anviccha kṛpaṇāḥ phala-hetavaḥ ||49||

O Arjuna, work with attachment is far inferior to nishkama karma. Seek refuge in desireless actions with equanimity of mind. Those who work for fruits are wretched. ||49||

Doorena: by far; hi: indeed: avaram: inferior; karma: action (with motive behind action); buddhiyogat: than the yoga of wisdom (equal minded approach); Dhananjaya: Arjuna; buddhou: in wisdom; saranam: refuge; anviccha: seek; krupanaha: wretched; phalahetavaha: seekers after fruits.

Doorena hyavaram: very inferior indeed.

Karma in the context of the first quarter of the sloka refers to "actions with attachment." (desire fulfilling actions).

The word "Buddhi yogat", in the second quarter of the sloka refers to actions conducted using the reasoning faculty. It is about "Nishkama karma." (desireless actions)

We are told by the Lord that "Desireless actions are far superior to desire prompted actions."

Attitude to work is far more important than the actual value of the work.

When the thought flow is controlled the mind remains serene and calm. Such a mind is called "The intellect". It takes over the reins for the work to be conducted. The experts say that it is "Nischayatmika", which means "clear mind." (intellect)

If the intellect is not brought in to control the thought process generated in the mind or if the intellect is not brought in to control the new impulses received by the mind, agitations develop and the experts say it is "samshayatmika"(the doubting mind).

"Buddhi yoga" is the process wherein the clear intellect reins supreme and the doubting mind is under control.

When one becomes a master over his own mind, like a search light, the mind can be turned away from the external world and diverted towards the Atman inside. We are asked to become masters over our own mind because it leads us to experience the "Eternal Bliss".

Failure to control the mind leads to sorrow and distress. We have to go through many more births and deaths.

"Kripana" means "wretched." Those who conduct desire prompted actions, the Lord says are "Kripanas."

बुद्धियुक्तो जहातीह उभे सुकृतदुष्कृते ।
तस्माद्योगाय युज्यस्व योगः कर्मसु कौशलम् ||50||

buddhi-yukto jahātīha ubhe sukṛta-duṣkṛte |
tasmād yogāya yujyasva yogaḥ karmasu kauśalam ||50||

Endowed with the wisdom of evenness of mind, one releases himself from both good and bad even in this life. Therefore strive for nishkama karma with an equal mind. Skill in action is Yoga. ||50||

Budhiyukto: endowed with wisdom; jahati: casts off (releases himself); ubha: both; sukrute duskrute: good and evil deeds; tasmad: therefore; yogaya: to yoga; yujyaswa: devote thyself (strive); yogaha: yoga; karmasu: in action; koushalam: skill.

The important word in this sloka is "releases himself." We can lift ourselves or ruin ourselves from our actions.

"The evenness of mind born of wisdom": the results of actions, both good and bad, come because of our actions. If we use our wisdom, bring in the reasoning capacity prior to any actions, control the senses and the wandering mind, we will prevent any adverse reactions.

To achieve such state of mind, we should not conduct desire prompted actions. This is the skill in Yoga the Lord is referring to.

The intellect must guide us in the discrimination of good from bad and also give us the determination to carry out the task undertaken properly.

Great souls have conducted acts of welfare to the society on this principle. They had no personal motive from their actions. We see such men/women probably once in a century or so.

Skill in action is Yoga: the capacity to remain detached and equal minded while engaged in any action in the world is the skill Lord is referring to.

We are responsible for our actions.

Our actions bring in results, both good and bad.

The Lord is actually giving us advice on "Preventive medicine."

Pains and pleasures we experience in our life are because of "desires."

When the work is conducted with some desire or other in the mind, the mental balance at the time of work is disturbed. This we have discussed in detail in the preceding slokas.

Lack of concentration on the work ahead is another reason for experiencing painful end results.

The Lord is applying the same rule for "good" also. He says "release from good and bad." As we have studied before, the good brings in a sense of elation and makes us feel proud of ourselves. This is probably the more dangerous enemy in our spiritual path.

कर्मजं बुद्धियुक्ता हि फलं त्यक्त्वा मनीषिणः ।
जन्मबन्धविनिर्मुक्ताः पदं गच्छन्त्यनामयम् ||51||

karmajaṃ buddhi-yuktā hi phalaṃ tyaktvā manīṣiṇaḥ |
janma-bandha-vinirmuktāḥ padaṃ gacchanty anāmayam ||51||

Wise men, possessed of knowledge, having abandoned the fruits of action, go to the abode beyond all sorrow and evil. ||51||

Karmajam: action born; yukta: possessed of; buddhi (equal minded): knowledge; hi: indeed; phalam: fruits; tyaktva: abandoned; maneeshinaha: the wise; janmabandha vinirmuktaha: freed from the bonds of samsara; padam: abode, position; gacchanti: go, hi: indeed; anamayam: free from sorrow and evil.

The word "manishinaam" is addressed to men of wisdom.

The one who knows the true meaning of "Viveka" (refers to sloka 47, meaning of sadhana chatushtaya) is considered to be a wise man. Wise man knows how to differentiate between "Transient and Eternal."

Soon we will be entering into discussion about Sthitaprajna", (man of steady wisdom.)

So far we have discussed about "Karma."

Karma Yoga is about actions that will help us to unite with the "Eternal Truth." He, who has jnana (knowledge) of actions as described by the Lord, is the true wise man and is "Manishi." He is the true karma yogi.

The Lord is saying that the wise men also have to act in this world. They conduct all their duties as an act of worship. They do so with equanimity of mind and do not work for the fruits of actions. But the law of action and reaction says that every action has a result and the wise also do get the results (fruits) for their actions.

As they do not have any worldly desires, their meritorious points for good work are not wasted. The Lord Himself decides on what benefit they should get. "They go to the abode beyond all sorrow and evil", He says. It simply means that they attain "Liberation" and do not have any rebirths into this world of maya.

यदा ते मोहकलिलं बुद्धिर्व्यतितरिष्यति ।
तदा गन्तासि निर्वेदं श्रोतव्यस्य श्रुतस्य च ||52||

yadā te mohakalilaṃ buddhir vyatitariṣyati |
tadā gantāsi nirvedaṃ śrotavyasya śrutasya ca ||52||

When your mind crosses the mire of delusion, you will attain to indifference as to what has been heard and what has to be heard. ||52||

Yada: when; te: your; buddhi: wisdom; mohakalilam: mire of delusion; vyatirishtati: crosses; tadaa: then; srotavyasya: of what has to be heard; srutasya: what has been heard, cha: and. Gamtasi: you will attain.

The mire of delusion for us, the humans, is the "Maya". It is the illusion. Covered by ignorance, as it were, we fail to see the "Truth." This is because of our attachment to the impulses brought in by the sense organs about the world around. These impulses as we have studied so far will give us the experience of happiness or sorrow, both of which are temporary.

It is useful at this juncture if we can recollect one of the guru mantra: "Ajnantimirandasya jnananjana shalakhayaha chakchurum meelitam ena tasmai sri gurave namaha." (salutations to the guru who by giving us the eye of wisdom blesses us to cross the ocean of ignorance).

"Ajnanatimirandhasya" means crossing the ocean of ignorance.

The spiritual seeker has to cross over both the happiness and sorrows in life, develop an indifference to both and will then experience the "Bliss" within.

"Nirvedam" means "indifference."

"Nirvedam shrotavyasa srutasya cha": indifference to what has been heard and what is to be heard.

This sounds confusing and needs to be clarified. We can look at it from two angles.

a) For majority of us, beginners in the spiritual practice:

"What has been heard and what is to be heard" has to be understood as the sum total of all impulses received from the "Jnanendriyas."

"The impulses received from the five sense organs and the impulses to be received in future by the five sense organs" is the true meaning of "what is heard and what is to be heard." "Heard" in this sense refers to all the impulses received from sense organs. We should not confuse it to mean only what is heard by the ears.

When we learn to develop indifference to the impulses received, we will overcome the end result of happiness or sorrow.

b) Another explanation for the expression used (if we consider that the Lord is referring to the Vedas):

To those who have succeeded in their spiritual practice and reached the state of "Sthitaprajna": there is no further need to contemplate on the theory of the scriptures. (refer to sloka 46 in this chapter).

For the rest of us, there is a dire need to continue to hear and think about the Vedas. The only way to cross this mire of delusion is by understanding the correct meaning of "Nishkama karma" and continue to work as described in sloka:

"Karmanyevadhikarasthe" and thereby purify the mind of all existing vasanas.

Sri Madhvacharya, the founder of "Dwaita" philosophy has given a beautiful explanation for the word "Nirvedyam."

He says that that the word means "maximum profit." In the spiritual path, if we can master the art of indifference to the impulses received and to be received, we will reap maximum benefit and experience "The Bliss."

"Maya", the delusion is like electricity. It is not perceptible and acts in a number of different ways. At the intellectual level of perception, maya acts like a film that obstructs the true understanding of the Self within us.

The sastras use the word "Avarana sakti" to express the power of maya over us. (example: imagine a powerful bulb on the ceiling emanating a brilliant glow of light.

Then think of layer after layer of screens covering the light. These coverings can be 30-40 or more.

As the number of layers increase, the brightness emanating decreases and at one point the light is no more to be seen.

The light we are talking of is "Divine Light" within of the Atman. The screens are the layers of thought imprints/vasanas on the mind. The vasanas obscure the glow of light.

When the final layer is taken off, the light glows with its own luminosity. Once experiencing this light of knowledge there is no more delusion and everything is perfectly clear.

Similarly, the "Self", Atman, becomes "Jivatman" by identifying with the physical body and forgets its true identity and when ignorance is cast off it shines with its own luminosity.

श्रुतिविप्रतिपन्ना ते यदा स्थास्यति निश्चला |
समाधावचला बुद्धिस्तदा योगमवाप्स्यसि ||53||

śruti-vipratipannā te yadā sthāsyati niścalā |
samādhāv acalā buddhis tadā yogam avāpsyasi ||53||

When your intellect, though perplexed by what you have heard, becomes steady and immovable in the Self, then you shall attain Self-realization. ||53||

Sruthiv pratipanna: perplexed by what you have heard of the various sastras; te': your; buddhihi: wisdom; yada: when; nischalaha: unshaken; samadhou: in Samadhi; achala: immoveable; sthasyasi: remains fixed; tada: then; yogam: union with the Supreme; avapsyasi: shall attain.

The mind as we have learnt so far, is like a monkey, jumping from one branch of the tree to another. It is difficult to keep it steady and under control. The process of controlling the mind steady is "nischalatvam" (the last word in the first line of this sloka).

To do so, one should hear of Atman, think of Atman and meditate on the Atman. In course of time, the sadhaka/seeker will be able to merge totally in the Atman.

Sri Sankaracharya defines "Samadhi" as the state when the mind is merged into the Atman.

Arjuna had spent his earlier days in the gurukula ashrama and was given the introduction to the Vedas.

The course, if we can call it so, in those days for pupils like Arjuna was the "Karma Kanda" of the Vedas. They were not initiated into the Upasana and Jnana kanda sections of the Vedas.

Karma kanda in a way is hearing about the various rituals, yajnas and the benefit from conduct of the same.

Upasana kanda is thinking and meditating on the Atman and Jnana kanda is final realization and union with the Atman.

Krishna says that karma kanda section of the Vedas when heard is perplexing. But, by meditating on the Atman, analyzing the principle behind all rituals and yajnas, one can steady the mind. His intellect will take over and dictate and control the mind. Only then the sadhaka can remain steady on the thought of the Self.

This is the path to "Self-Realization" and the seeker is on the road to freedom.

Another interpretation to the sloka:

The Jnanendriyas bring in the impulses to the mind. Even though it is the ears that hear, we can say that the mind hears whatever the senses bring in.

Taking this meaning, we can say that "what you have heard" means, all the experiences from the past.

After all, the experiences from the past are responsible for the present. If one uses the intellectual capacity of reasoning and thinks in terms of sanchita karma, one can easily say what is happening now is only "Prarabdha" karma. The seeker then develops the titikshatva for what is happening in his life and concentrates on the task ahead. The task being, "union with the Supreme." (sloka 37, chapter 4)

अर्जुन उवाच
स्थितप्रज्ञस्य का भाषा समाधिस्थस्य केशव ।
स्थितधीः किं प्रभाषेत किमासीत व्रजेत किम्. ||54||

arjuna uvāca
sthita-prajñasya kā bhāṣā samādhi-sthasya keśava |
sthita-dhīḥ kiṃ prabhāṣeta kim āsīta vrajeta kim ||54||

Arjuna said,
O Krishna, what are the characteristics of a man of steady wisdom while he is merged in the "super-conscious state"? How does such a man speak, sit and move? ||54||

Sthitaprajnasya: of the man of steady wisdom; kaa: what; bhasha: description; samadhisthasya: of the man merged with the Supreme (super conscious state); keshava: Krishna; sthitadeehi: the sage of steady wisdom; kim: how; prabhasheta: speaks; kim: how; aseeta: sits; vrajeta: walks.

Sthitaprajna: "Prajna" is "Pure Consciousness".

"Prajnanam Brahma" declares the Rig Veda in Aitareya Upanisad.

Sthita: firm

Pure consciousness is where there are no impurities in the mind. It is united with the antaratma and listens to its voice at all times.

He who has achieved this level of progress in his spiritual path and stays in this state firmly at all times (24/7) is a "Sthita prajna".

He, who is merged in the "Super-conscious state" is said to be in "Samadhi." Samadhi is the last limb of the "Patanjali Ashtanga Yoga", the eight limbed Yoga of Patanjali. (see below)

Samadhi is also the word used to denote "the grave" or "the tomb".

When the Soul departs from the body, there are no more activities left in the body. The jnanendriyas and the mind do not function.

In this sloka, the word is used to denote the state of that individual who is a man of steady-wisdom. His jnanendriyas and the mind are alive but technically speaking they are "dead to the world." The individual is still alive.

The state of "deep meditation" he is in is "Samadhi." Such a seeker who has reached this state is a "Jivanmukta." He is a liberated soul while still alive.

Arjuna asks Krishna for the means of identification of such an individual. He was aware of great souls of his time who had gone to remote corners like the Himalayas and entered into a state of samadhi. He was not sure of any who were living and moving about the world after reaching the pinnacle of sadhana.

He wanted to know such an individual's daily activities and how to recognize him? Wearing of an ochre robe is not the sign of such Jivanmukta.

Truly speaking a man's character is recognizable by the way he speaks and moves about in the society. He is a learned person and knows the sastras. One finds peace, purity and divinity in a Jivanmukta.

We, the rest of us, have not reached such state of perfection. While there are no problems in life, one can express calmness in his actions and speech. As soon as he experiences problems in life or when he has achieved success in his task, he tends to lose the purity and calmness.

We are attached to the material world around us. For the sake of information:

The ashtanga yoga is:

Yama, niyama, asana, pranayama, pratyahara, dharana, dhyana and samadhi. We will discuss these in chapter 4.

Mahatma Gandhi was a strong advocate of the qualities of a "Sthitha Prajna." He used to recite the subsequent slokas 55-72 from this chapter every day. He not only recited them but understood them and practiced them.

श्री भगवानुवाच
प्रजहाति यदा कामान् सर्वान् पार्थ मनोगतान् ।
आत्मन्येवात्मना तुष्टः स्थितप्रज्ञस्तदोच्यते ||55||

śrī-bhagavān uvāca
prajahāti yadā kāmān sarvān pārtha mano-gatān |
ātmany evātmanā tuṣṭaḥ sthita-prajñas tadocyate ||55||

The Lord said:
When a man renounces completely all the desires of the mind, when he is fully satisfied with his mind fixed in Atman, O Partha, he is then declared to be a Sthitaprajna. ||55||

Prajahati: casts off; yadaa: when; kamaan: desires; sarvaan: all; manogataan: of the mind; atmany: in the Self; eva: only; atmanaa: by the Self; tushtaha: satisfied; sthitaprajna: of steady wisdom; uchyate: is called.

He, who has renounced completely all the desires of the mind, and mastered the technique of fixing his mind on the Atman within, is sure to be totally free of all fears and sorrows.

One needs to be associated with such a perfect master to recognize the "perfect blissful state he is living."

This is the first and foremost sign with which one can recognize the "sthitaprajna." "Desire" is the capacity of the mind to see ahead of itself. "Desires" are the root cause for all the ills of life. The store house of all the desires is the mind.

We will, in the subsequent chapters learn about the gunas and their influence on the seeker. Satvic, Rajasic and Tamasic gunas influence the progress of the seeker either to his spiritual heights or towards spiritual decline.

In the earlier stages of sadhana, it is imperative that there should be desires to move from lower tamasic gunas to higher satvic gunas.

Only on reaching the satvic heights of purity, the seeker has to consider his future and abandon all desires.

Sthitaprajna is he who has climbed up the spiritual ladder and reached higher planes. At this early stage of learning, let us not be carried away by the qualities of "Sthitaprajna." As this chapter is the summary of the entire Gita, the qualities of "Sthitaprajna" are brought out in this chapter. We should not, like Sthitaprajna, start abandoning all desires. To start off let us harbor desires to purify our minds of impure thoughts.

The mind is the seat of all activities.

On the one side, it is receiving from the jnanendriyas the impulses from the objective world around. On the other side, it is also receiving the message from the "Antaratma" (the Divine inner voice). Overriding the message from the Antaratma, we give prominence to the impulses from the objective world. The mind analyses these and classifies them as "I like it", "I do not like it", "I hate it" etc. It then sends its army of karmendriyas to get the object of desires.

This process of receiving the impulses and acting accordingly has been going on from birth. Also, as we have studied so far, at birth, the mind is already having a set of stored impulses not acted upon from the previous births. (Of course we need to have belief that we have undergone several births in the past and will have to go through several more births in future)

Every day of our life we receive several impulses from the world around. We cannot react to all the impulses at the same time. Some of them get stored for action at a later date. The mind thus becomes a store house of all the impulses not acted upon. These remain dormant for an indefinite period. Depending upon the strength of the stored impulses or receiving repeatedly the impulses from certain objects, the desire gets stronger and stronger and the mind puts the karmendriyas into action.

Sthitaprajna renounces completely all the desires of the mind". (Prajahati Yada Kamaan Sarvaan Partha Manogataan):

In the pathway of receiving the impulses and acting upon the same, the mind really is not the boss. It cannot consider itself to be the master and do what it pleases. Its rank is below that of the intellect. It has to follow the guidance from the intellect. Only by letting the intellect guide it, the mind can learn the art of purifying itself and thereby renouncing all the desires.

Every desire arising within, before it is put into action, has to be submitted to its high command, the intellect.

The picture of Gitopadesham has to be recollected at this point. (refer to the introduction)

The next lesson to learn for the mind:

The mind has to realize that it has a duty to fix its sight on the Atman inside. Forgetting this rule, makes the mind become the demon "Ego."

He who fulfills these two criterions:

controlling constantly all the desires,

fixing the mind constantly on the Atman.

This makes the individual a "Sthitaprajna."

We see that many a times the devotees flock to the master and ask the question, "Swami, when will I be free from the problems I encounter in this life?"

The true master uses this sloka to give his answer.

He makes it clear that the liberation from the ills of life does not come by magic. The Lord cannot wave His magic wand and say "I clear you of all your past sins and grant you Moksha."

Each one of us has to work for ourselves to come out of the whirlpool called "samsara."

The Gita, the sastras, the masters are all there to guide us.

This can come only from unswerving faith and devotion and by carrying out the spiritual discipline.

The mind has to remain in a constant state of equanimity.

The seeker has to cast off permanently all the desires totally.

Giving up some desires or giving up desires for certain period of time will not suffice.

True knowledge is the capacity of the mind to visualize the dangers/problems ahead and conducting proper actions under the guidance of the pure intellect.

The aim of Vedanta in general and the Gita in particular is to remove the veil of ignorance about the Self within which is the seat of "Eternal and Everlasting Bliss." Practicing renunciation is the first step. It is the sadhana. Experiencing Paramananda is the result. It is "Sadhya."

A Sthitaprajna shows this in his actions.

Atmany evatma tushtaha - contented in Atma only, by the atma.

In this statement, the word "Atma" is used twice and the two have a different meaning.

The first "Atman" refers to the "Self" (Soul) within and is depicted with capital "A". The second "atman" refers to the "mind". It is the "ego", the seat of all desires.

The mind has to accept that the pure intellect is the master and be subordinate to it. The pure intellect should be subservient to the "Antaratma" (inner divine) and the "Atman" inside. In the final stages of spiritual progress, even the intellect gets merged with the "Atman". It then reflects total purity and remains in constant bliss.

दुःखेष्वनुद्विग्नमनाः सुखेषु विगतस्पृहः ।
वीतरागभयक्रोधः स्थितधीर्मुनिरुच्यते ||56||

duḥkheṣv anudvigna-manāḥ sukheṣu vigata-spṛhaḥ |
vīta-rāga-bhaya-krodhaḥ sthita-dhīr munir ucyate ||56||

He whose mind is not troubled by sorrow, who does not go after pleasures, who is free from attachment, fear and hatred is called a sage of steady wisdom. ||56||

Dukheshu: in sorrow; anudwigna manaha: mind untroubled; sukheshu: in pleasures; vigata spruhaha: without going after; veeta raga bhaya krodhaha: free from attachment, fear and anger; sthitadeehi: steady wisdom; munihi: sage; uchyate: is said.

Let us remember that these qualities are that of a perfect master of wisdom. Such knowledge does not come overnight. We, the ordinary mortals cannot avoid but go after pleasures and cannot escape sorrows in life due to the attachments we develop to our own physical body and the objects around the world. As the sastras declare, we have to undergo many births before we can dream of reaching this state of perfect wisdom.

This section of this chapter is not for the seekers in the earlier stages of spiritual sadhana. Like young children, we need to be bribed with sweets so that we like the spiritual science and become seekers after "Eternal Truth."

Three qualities of Sthithaprajna are brought out in this sloka:

1) Dukheshu anudwigna manaha 2) Sukheshu vigata spruhaha 3) Veetaraga bhaya krodhah.

1) Dukheshu anudwigna manaha:

Whose mind does not get troubled by the sorrows in life.

In the context of past, present and future this aspect refers to "Past and present." The mind as we know is like the band master. We are what our minds are.

It is a fact of life that each one of us goes through various experiences in life and some experiences hurt and bring sorrow in our life. There cannot be one individual who can say that he has not experienced sorrow in his/her life.

There is an episode in the life of Buddha worth recollecting at this stage.

When Buddha left his palatial residence he went and meditated under the shelter of the Bodhi tree, enlightenment dawned in course of time. His fame spread far and wide. Once a woman in great distress at the death of her young child came to him and begged him to bring the child back to life.

Buddha agreed to do so but only after she fulfilled one condition. He requested her to get a fistful of rice from a household where there was no death.

The lady went out in great delight. She did not consider this as a great problem. Soon, she realized that there was no household which did not go through death in their family at some time or other.

The moral of the story is: everyone will experience sorrow sometime or other in their life. The period of grief varies from individual to individual depending upon their outlook. If everyone would be in grief indefinitely, the world cannot progress. The sorrow has also a beginning and an end with a peak somewhere along the curve. We all have to put in our input in moving the wheel that makes the society move forwards.

The intellect has to remind the mind that it has to get on with the duties to the body, to the family, friends and the society.

2) Sukheshu vigata spruhaha

Vigata spruha: without hankering.

This aspect refers to the "future." The Lord is advocating the seeker to not hanker after pleasures.

Like sorrow, we do also experience happiness. We have discussed before about the consequences of actions following experience of the pleasures.

The individual experiencing the pleasure will remain in a dream world of his own. His mind automatically will long for more of the same. "Spruhaha" means "longing" for objects of pleasure.

Sthithaprajna is "Vigata spruhaha" - he does not long for such pleasures.

He, a Jivanmukta, lives constantly in the state of "Atmananda." Having united with the "Atman" within, having experienced the "Bliss within," he lives in a constant state of contentment.

He is in a state of constant equilibrium for the results of all past actions, conducts the present actions in the same frame of mind and will remain so in future.

One can compare the intellect to the sun and the mind filled with the vasanas to the clouds. The clouds block the sun only temporarily. The sun will remain as the same bright sun constantly. The clouds do not disturb it in any way.

The troubles that can bring obstacles in the path to realize the Atman can be classified into:

God sent: lightning, thunder etc., (adhi daivika)

Natural catastrophes: fire, flood, landslides etc., (adhibhoutika)

Man made, subjective such as acts due to laziness and other negative tendencies from within. (Adhyatmika)

3) Veetaraga bhaya krodaha: he is free from attachment, fear and anger.

Raga - attachment
Bhaya - fear
Krodha - anger.

Raga is attachment to objects of desire. Attachment can be to one's own modifications of the physical body, to family, friends, material wealth, position in the society etc.

Thought of injury, illness, physical death etc. to one's own body or to the body of loved ones; fear of losing the loved material possessions brings in an element of fear.

When one loses the object of desire or when someone else gets that desired object, it brings out the feeling of anger. Anger in turn could lead to total disaster. (this subject is graphically described in slokas 63 and 64 of this chapter)

As far as he is concerned, the sthitaprajna continues to discharge his duties but does so without the attachment, fear and anger. His actions fit in with the principle of "Karmanye vadhkarasthe". (sloka 47)

When the same Atman is there in everyone where is the question of getting attached to any particular object/individual?

Attachment, fear and anger can come only when there is more than one. Having realized the same Atman in all, having developed the knowledge of seeing that Atman, there is no question of a separate second thing/object/individual as far as the sthitaprajna is concerned. He has no delusion or sorrow.

Sthitadeehi munir uchyate:

Such an individual of steady mind is called "Muni."

"Mounam charati iti munihi" - the one who walks in silence is "Muni."

The Sthitaprajna is engaged in speechless absorption in the Self within, enjoys the Self all around and hence he is a "Muni."

यः सर्वत्रानभिस्नेहस्तत्तत्प्राप्य शुभाशुभम् ।
नाभिनन्दति न द्वेष्टि तस्य प्रज्ञा प्रतिष्ठिता ॥57॥

yaḥ sarvatrānabhisnehas tat tat prāpya śubhāśubham |
nābhinandati na dveṣṭi tasya prajñā pratiṣṭhitā ||57||

He who has no attachment to anything and anywhere, who does not rejoice or hate, his wisdom is fixed. ||57||

Yah: he/who; sarvatra: everywhere; anabhisnehaha: without attachment; tat: that; prapya: having obtained; shubha: good; ashubha: evil; na: not; abhinandati: rejoices; dweshti: hates; tasya: of him; prajna: wisdom; pratishtita: is fixed.

Anabhisneha: without attachment.

Let us not forget that "Sthitaprajna" is he who has achieved in reaching the "Self- state." Whatever qualities we attribute to the "Atman" are to be found in the "Sthitaprajna." Equanimity is his hallmark.

Another point of importance to note is the word "Yaha." It means "who". It implies that the Lord is not referring to any individual in particular. Caste, creed, nationality or sex are not a barrier to learn the sacred text. We should look at such statements as referring to the "Universality" of the message of the Gita.

"Maya" or delusion is the tool of the Lord. He is beyond maya and it has no control over Him. On the other hand, it has a firm control on all of us. To come out of the clutches of maya is possible only when we lose our individual identity and become one with the "Atman."

Sthitaprajna has achieved the state wherein he has no attachment to anything and anywhere. It applies both to the people around him and to the situations he faces in life. He remains as part of the society and not an escapist by nature.

Many a times frustration makes one feel like running away from people/situations. Mere detachment is only a negative existence of escaping from life. Running away is not a sign of true detachment. It is actually a hidden sign of cowardice. Facing the challenges in life and clearing the vasanas from the past is the way forward. Challenges in life should be met with courage, equanimity and the knowledge of the Self.

On the other hand to live in attachment is like being a slave to the pleasures of life. This sloka is in reply to Arjuna's question: "How does a sthitaprajna speak?" Sthitaprajna speaks through his actions. He does not show signs of depression or excessive elation whatever may be the situation he faces.

As we have discussed before both depression and elation reduce the efficiency of work. After having been born on this earth, we have certain duties to conduct and thereby clear the existing vasanas and move forward towards achieving union with the "Parabrahman." This should be our goal in life.

Arjuna wanted to escape from the war and its consequences. He thought that life in the forest would be peaceful.

Explanation for "who does not hate",

Hatred is an extremely strong feeling of dislike:

It is a deep and extreme emotional feeling. It can be directed against individuals and/or groups. It is often associated with feelings of anger, disgust and a disposition towards hostility.

"No hatred" is a very important quality to develop for the spiritual seeker. Instead one must learn the art of forgiving. The Sanskrit word for forgiving is "Kshama." We will have an opportunity to learn more about this in chapter 12 when we will discuss about qualities of a true devotee of the Lord.

यदा संहरते चायं कूर्मोऽङ्गानीव सर्वशः ।
इन्द्रियाणीन्द्रियार्थेभ्यस्तस्य प्रज्ञा प्रतिष्ठिता ||58||

yadā saṃharate cāyaṃ kūrmo 'ṅgānīva sarvaśaḥ |
indriyāṇīndriyārthebhyas tasya prajñā pratiṣṭhitā ||58||

When the Yogi, like the tortoise drawing back its limbs into its own shell, withdraws all the senses from the sense objects, his wisdom is fixed. He is a Sthitaprajna. ||58||

Yada: when; samharate: withdraws; cha: and; ayam: this; kurma: tortoise; angaani: limbs; iva: like; sarvashaha: everywhere;

indriyani: the senses; indriyarthebhyaha: from the sense objects; tasya: of him; prajna: wisdom; pratishtita: is steadied.

The commander in chief of the bodily instruments of cognition is "the intellect." The intellect focusing outwards gets trapped with the life around. The individual whose intellect is pointing inwards and concentrating on the Atman within is said to be a Sthitaprajna.

The concentration achieved by the spiritual seeker who has attained mastery over the multitude of distractions from the objective world is explained using an example in this verse.

The Lord has given the example of the tortoise. We see normally a tortoise with its head and neck and limbs protruding out of its shell and moving about in water where it is living. On encountering any objects, the first reaction by it is the withdrawal of all its limbs into its own shell. Once it does withdraw its limbs, it does not get injured by any objects that it comes in contact with. We can throw a brick at it and the brick does not cause any bodily harm to it.

Technically it is a sthitaprajna. It continues to live in the water but does not get perturbed by the world outside. Let us remember that it is not really a sthitaprajna and it is only an example and no examples can give us the true picture of the Atman. What does a sthitaprajna do?

He continues to live and be part of the society he belongs to. He does not run away into the forest to escape from distractions.

What are the limbs the Lord is referring to?

The limbs of the tortoise are a comparison to the five sense organs and the life around in the pool of water for the tortoise is compared to the objective world. Our senses do get us the contact with the objective world. The reaction to the contact is made by the mind with or without the help of the intellect. These reactions make us feel pain/pleasures.

The sense organs do perceive, the mind does the duty of feeling and the intellect thinks. Withdrawal from the outer world means not to react to the impulses received by the sense organs, not to feel through the mind and not to think using the intellect. His intellect at the same time has changed its mode of action and deals with the "chaitanya" (consciousness) within. It receives the "Ananda" (happiness, peace) from the contact with the chaitanya and lives a life of contentment.

The individual carries on all the worldly duties and takes on the obligatory duties to the family and the society. The results of whatever action he conducts, he offers to the Lord by uttering "Sri Krishnarpanamastu."

Each of the sense organs is like the door to the house. The thief can enter from any door and steal our possessions. The sense organs are the doors for us to receive the impulses that steal our peace.

We can understand by looking at the example of a deaf person. The deaf person does not hear what others are talking about but stays in company of others. The insults thrown at him by some will not register in his mind and he does not get upset. He is not worried about the abuses spoken by others.

For this one needs to develop "Vyavasayatmika buddhi" about which we have already discussed in sloka 41 of this chapter.

Another point to note from this sloka is that withdrawal of the sense organs from the sense objects does not stop the hankering of the mind which is a store house of results of the past actions. We will see how the mind can be controlled in the next sloka.

विषया विनिवर्तन्ते निराहारस्य देहिनः ।
रसवर्जं रसोऽप्यस्य परं दृष्ट्वा निवर्तते ||59||

viṣayā vinivartante nirāhārasya dehinaḥ |
rasa-varjaṃ raso 'py asya paraṃ dṛṣṭvā nivartate ||59||

When a man rejects the sense objects by withdrawing the senses, he becomes free from the sense world only. Even his longing also is removed on intuiting on the Supreme. || 59||

Vishaya: the objects of the senses; vinivartante: turn away; niraharasya: abstinent; dehinaha: of the man; rasavarjasya: longing; rasa: longing (taste); api: even; asya: of his; param: Supreme; drushtwa: having seen; nivartate: turns away.

"Rasavarjam" is rejecting the sense objects as described in the previous verse. The word "rasa" in this sloka refers to the "taste" for the world of objects. Realization of the "Absolute" will remove the taste for the world of objects. Unless one develops sraddha, bhakti on the "Supreme" and learns the art of "meditation" wherein the mind is made to concentrate on the "Supreme" it is impossible to experience "the Bliss."

The mind of the beginner in sadhana has after all experienced the sense world for a long time. Therefore there is a latent longing for the pleasures from the same within the mind. This, the elders say is "Raga". Realization of the Supreme is complete only when the vasanas of the past are burnt out completely. This can be achieved either by:
Gradually making the impact of the vasanas less by:
postponing the desire prompted actions for another day, another day and another day and so on and so forth. This way eventually the strong desires of today get weaker and weaker and finally disappear altogether.

Or

The individual has to concede to the demands of the mind and then experience the results. In the course of time which takes probably many births and deaths, every individual is going to realize the temporary nature of the pleasures and pains. In other words learns from experiences and learns not to repeat the same mistake. There is no fixed time for experiencing this "Bliss" which is the last step in the path towards "immortality."

Destruction of the mind, "Mano nasha" and burning out all vasanas is "Vasana kshaya." These two steps are a must for final success.

"Nirahara" means "no food". In this context the food refers to impulses about all the sense objects of the world brought in by the sense organs.

By constant application of the intellect without looking for the fruits of actions is the means for "Moksha."

"Vishaya" means "the objective world"; "vinivartante" means "recede". Receding from the objective world is equal to reducing the number of desire prompted actions.

What happens when it is not possible to control the mind is taken up in the next few slokas.

It is true that without knowing the "Brahman", one cannot eliminate the attachments. At the same time knowledge of the Brahman cannot arise without the elimination of attachments. Implementing the art of discrimination is the only step to overcome the attachments to the sense objects. This needs constant practice and the method is known as "Dhyana." Keeping the constant memory of the Supreme and continuing to discharge one's duty in course of time brings in success in the spiritual path.

यततो ह्यपि कौन्तेय पुरुषस्य विपश्चितः ।
इन्द्रियाणि प्रमाथीनि हरन्ति प्रसभं मनः ||60||

yatato hy api kaunteya puruṣasya vipaścitaḥ |
indriyāṇi pramāthīni haranti prasabhaṃ manaḥ ||60||

O Arjuna, the turbulent senses do violently carry away the mind of an intelligent man, though he is striving to control them. ||60||

Yatato: of the striving; hi: indeed; api: even; Kounteya: Arjuna; purushasya: of man; vipaschitaha: of the wise; indriyani: of the senses; pramathini: turbulent; haranti: carry away; prasabham: violently; manaha: the mind.

The Lord is warning that the senses are very strong and they do not stop easily. They have such a great influence on the mind that the intellect becomes a weak force and the mind surrenders to the enemy. The enemies in this case are "Kama and krodha".

Sthitaprajna is he who does not fall prey to the enemy (senses). He remembers the strength of the senses and is constantly on vigil.

During turbulence, the wind is so strong that it violently sweeps away many objects.

The impulses received from the sense organs are compared to the wind and sometimes the impulses from one or many of the five sense organs gather great force and become turbulent. The mind in such situations surrenders to this turbulence and does not listen any more to the voice of the intellect.

The seeker therefore has to remember that the first enemy in his path is his own sense organs. The master is he who prepares the proper battle plan and is ready to attack the enemy before the enemy attacks him.

Vipaschitaha: intelligent

The spiritual seeker, an intelligent person, in quest of "Moksha" does try his best to keep on the spiritual path. He knows what he is looking for and works hard at it. He does succeed in making progress because of his determination to achieve the goal. But, the force of habit before taking up the spiritual journey does topple him now and then.

This is because his mind has experienced the pleasures from the material world around him. The sense organs as we know do bring in a barrage of impulses about the objects around. The mind which has experienced the pleasures from some objects is keen to go and get more of those objects that bring in the sensation of happiness. There is a constant battle in the mind of the seeker between the impulse to go after the objects of pleasure and the intellect that warns against such a move. The initial success in controlling the mind does bring in a sense of pride to the seeker. This pride (ego) becomes his weakness and he falls down from the heights achieved by his efforts. His mind gets moved away from being subordinate to the intellect and becomes a slave to the senses.

तानि सर्वाणि संयम्य युक्त आसीत मत्परः ।
वशे हि यस्येन्द्रियाणि तस्य प्रज्ञा प्रतिष्ठिता ||61||

tāni sarvāṇi saṃyamya yukta āsīta mat-paraḥ |
vaśe hi yasyendriyāṇi tasya prajñā pratiṣṭhitā ||61||

Having restrained all the senses, he should sit steadfast intent on Me. His wisdom is steady, whose senses are under control. ||61||

Taani: them (the senses); sarvani: all; samyamya: restrained; yukta: harmonized; aaseetaa: sit; matparaha: intent on Me; vashe: under control; hi: indeed; yasya: whose; Indriyani: senses; tasya: his; prajna: wisdom; pratishtita: steady.

The Lord has given two steps towards attaining perfection in sadhana.

Restraining all the senses.

Sitting steadfast intent on Him.

Restraining all the senses means controlling all the five sense organs, the jnanendriyas. This has been discussed by us in detail already.

We are now advised about the intention of such an act. The wise man is he who remembers why he is carrying out a particular task. In this instance, it is the sadhaka in the process of attaining perfection in the art of total concentration on the Lord and attaining Moksha.

Let us remember about the meaning of the word "Upasana." The Upanisads, Gita being the summary of the Upanisads, are about sitting near the feet of the master, at a lower level than that of the master and keenly listening to his teaching.

The second step given in this sloka refers to the art of upasana. Just sitting in front of the master does not in itself give the final end result. When the Lord says "sit steadfast intent on Me", it means the mind of the seeker has to be diverted towards the thought of the Lord. The mind should not be wandering.

Apart from controlling all the senses, the seeker has to think of the Lord. Keeping the mind blank and controlling the senses does not help in achieving the Moksha. "Sitting steadfast intent on Me" does not mean just sitting down in front of the master. The mind should not dwell on its stored vasanas or recollect events from the past. It should meditate on the various aspects of divinity and enjoy the art of contemplation. The mind should be sitting and not wandering.

"Tasya prajna pratishtita" refers to the seeker's intellect. The intellect, master over the mind has to contemplate on the divinity.

The intellect of the Sthitaprajna, the Lord says, fulfills this criterion and so the Sthitaprajna should be considered as "Jivanmukta." He is a liberated soul while still living in this world.

What we see in the outer world is known as the "objective world." It is "Drishya" (seen).

The "Atman" which the seeker is contemplating on, is the "subjective world." It is the "Drashta" (seer).

Controlling the senses on their own does not make the seeker "a man of knowledge." If it were true, all of us would be "men of knowledge" during our sleep. The mind should not be blank but should, with joy seek the Atman within.

The "shoonya" (voidness) philosophy of the Buddhists is not totally achievable. Apart from the rare few great men, we, the ordinary mortals need a point of concentration.

ध्यायतो विषयान्पुंसः सङ्गस्तेषूपजायते |
सङ्गात् संजायते कामः कामात्क्रोधोऽभिजायते ||62||

dhyāyato viṣayān puṃsaḥ saṅgas teṣūpajāyate |
saṅgāt saṃjāyate kāmaḥ kāmāt krodho 'bhijāyate ||62||

Brooding on the objects of the senses, man develops attachment to them; from attachment comes desire; from desire anger sprouts forth. || 62||

क्रोधाद्भवति संमोहः संमोहात्स्मृतिविभ्रमः |
स्मृतिभ्रंशाद् बुद्धिनाशो बुद्धिनाशात्प्रणश्यति ||63||

krodhād bhavati saṃmohaḥ saṃmohāt smṛti-vibhramaḥ |
smṛti-bhraṃśād buddhi-nāśo buddhi-nāśāt praṇaśyati ||63||

From anger proceeds delusion; from delusion, confused memory; from confused memory the ruin of the reason; due to the ruin of reason, he perishes. ||63||

Dhyayataha: contemplating; vishayaan: objects of the senses; pumsaha: man; teshu: in them; sangaste: attachment in them; upajayate: develops; sangaat: from attachment; sanjayate: comes(is born) ; kamaha: desire; kamaat: from desire; krodha: anger; abhijayate: arises ||**62**||

krodad: from anger; bhavati: arises; sammohaha: delusion; sammohaat: from delusion; smriti vibhramaha: loss of memory; smrtibrhamsaat: from confused memory; buddhi nashaha: ruin of reason; buddhi nashaat: from ruin of reason; pranashyati: perishes. ||**63**||

These two slokas give a graphic description of the fall of the individual who looks for pleasures from the sense objects of the world. They are often quoted by masters while teaching their students/disciples and are considered as two of the best slokas in the entire Hindu philosophy.

The gradual process of self-destruction is portrayed in here with great accuracy. All spiritual aspirants must recollect the meaning of these two slokas every day of their lives. They should always be on guard and look out for the enemy in the guise of desires, entering the house (mind of the seeker), taking over the entire house (seeker's life) and finally destroying the owner (spiritual seeker) of the house.

Dhyanam in its truest sense is continuous contemplation on one object only and that object being "The Supreme Parabrahman." This could be "Nirakara Nirguna Parabrahman (Brahman with no form and qualities) or Sakara Saguna Parabrahman." (Brahman with form and qualities)

In this context the word "dhyayato" has been used with reference to the material world. The object of desire remains as a vasana imprint on the mind of the seeker. The strength of the vasana imprint depends upon the intensity of the thought. Repeated input of the thought imprint from the same object assists in further strengthening of the vasana. This is the meaning of the first quarter of the sloka: "Dhyayato vishayan pumsaha."

This "Brooding on the object of the senses" will involuntarily make the seeker get attached to that thought. The process of attachment is "Sanga." This is the meaning of the second quarter of the sloka: "sangasthe shoopajayate."

The next step in the progress of the thought is the development of desire for the object. Stronger the attachment to a particular thought, more chances of it becoming a strong desire: "Sangat sanjayate kamaha." "Kama" is desire for objects not possessed.

The objects of the senses that end up as desires could be anything from what we see, hear, smell, taste or feel from the world around us as perceived by the five sense organs and transmitted to the mind.

What happens next to these impulses? –

The mind does not take notice of any, or the mind might like particular object/objects, or

It does not like the object / hates the object / is frightened of the object.

The brooding on the objects referred to in these slokas is towards the objects of desire.

Let us now draw a graph of the sequence of events:

Impulses received by the mind from sense organs.

The mind of the seeker likes the impulse (gets attached to that feeling: sanga) and stores the same in its memory bank.

Seeker starts feeling that it would like more of the same and wishing for it. (desire: kama)

He becomes frustrated and angry (krodha) because
does not acquire it or
someone else acquires it or
acquires it but loses it.

Delusion sets in during states of extreme anger. (sammoha)

He loses power of discrimination and forgets his status, the surroundings and shouts abuses not realizing what he is saying and who he is dealing with. (smriti bramsha)

He ends up by being the architect of his own destruction. (pranashyati) This is the graphic description of the path to hell as painted by the Lord.

Kama and krodha are the two eternal comrades of evil. They cannot stay separately.

Frustration in the process of fulfilling the desire, brings in anger that ends up with acts that ruin the individual.

Let us not forget that the desire is not in the object, it is not the defect of the object but it is in the mind of the perceiver.

Mahabharata, the epic, is a beautiful example to understand this sloka. Prince Duryodhana who developed a strong thirst to rule the kingdom did not get his wish fulfilled. He ended up on the battlefield of Kurukshetra, which nearly saw the ruin of the dynasty, massive destruction, the death of soldiers in 18 battalions and finally his own death.

Let us therefore understand that we should "Work for tomorrow but not for pleasures that tomorrow will/can bring. Depending on the work of today and depending upon the actions of the past days (including past births) tomorrow will bring the results automatically."

Sri Ramakrishna says:

"Beware of your thoughts and everything will be all right with you." It simply means that we should analyze the thoughts by making use of our intellectual capacity of reasoning before converting any of them into actions.

In a different way we can say that the contemplation on the "Divine" constantly would help in developing "Desire for the Divine". Contrary to the sensual world, it would bring in a sense of "Peace and tranquility."

रागद्वेषवियुक्तैस्तु विषयानिन्द्रियैश्चरन् ।
आत्मवश्यैर्विधेयात्मा प्रसादमधिगच्छति ||**64**||

rāga-dveṣa-viyuktais tu viṣayān indriyaiś caran |
ātma-vaśyair vidheyātmā prasādam adhigacchati ||64||

But, the self-controlled man, free from objects of attraction and repulsion, with his senses under restraint, though moving among objects, attains Peace. ||64||

Raga: attraction; dwesha: hatred; viyuktais: free from; tu: but; vishayaan: objects; indriyais: with his senses; caran: moving; atma vashair: self-restrained; vidheyatma: self-controlled; prasadam: peace; adhigacchati: attains.

Two words of note in this sloka are: Vidheyatma and Atma vashai.

Vidheyatma refers to the control over the mind, and Atma vashai refers to the restraint over the senses.

"Moving among objects": this is to be understood as moving in the material world. Life is living and about association with people/objects. To live and sustain ourselves in this world we have to associate with the life around. It is all about either attraction or repulsion to the ones we get attached to. "Raga" is attachment and "dwesha" is hatred towards the individual/objects possessed.

The life will be peaceful for he, who does not experience either attraction or repulsion. The sloka is about the method of experiencing the "Peace" while living in this world. Such an individual is a "Sthitaprajna".

How can one honestly have such a control?

We have to look at the regimental life in the army. The army has different cadres from officers of the highest rank to the foot soldiers. There is an order of living among these soldiers. There is peace abiding in the army camp. Members of every cadre carry on their duties and at the same time there is control over each cadre from the ones immediately higher in rank. There is an orderly control over each cadre.

Our body has also the different cadres. We have:

The Atman.

The intellect.

The mind with "Kama, krodha, lobha, moha" in every individual and the sense organs.

Each one has to move from place "a to b" in our lives.

The learned elders say that the final place to reach is where there abides everlasting "Peace."

All the stations in life before the final destination of "Peace" will have a mixture of happiness and sorrow.

The final destination of "Peace" is "Moksha". (salvation) The way to concentrate to achieve this aim will be:

The desire to reach the final destination should be "Kama";

Anger at what prevents us from reaching the destination should be "Krodha";

Greed at wishing to attain salvation should be "Lobha";

Delusion towards the beauty of the final destination should be "Moha."

Love towards the Supreme should direct the chariot towards the goal of one's spiritual life.

These are the four horses on our chariot of life.

In the army, the junior cadre of soldiers obeys the senior cadre officers diligently. They are not allowed to run amok. There will be no order in that camp where the rules of each cadre are not followed.

Similarly, our senses have to be under the control of the mind, the mind under the control of the intellect and the intellect under the control of antaratma.

The sloka refers to the control of the senses: "atma vashai". Restraining the senses by the mind is implicit in this word.

The sloka also refers to control of the mind: "Vidheyatma". The mind has to be obedient to the intellect is implicit in this word.

The self-controlled man free from attraction and repulsion:

The mind receives the impulses from the material world and keeps a store of what it likes and dislikes in its memory bank. It has the capacity to go into this bank and recollect those feelings. When it does so, it loses track of its progress to its destination. By falling prey to either of these two feelings, it fails to experience the "Peace." Where the intellect comes into play and controls the mind from falling prey to the attractions and repulsions, the mind can carry its ordained duties and the seeker will finally experience the Peace.

The charioteer has to hold on to the reins and control the horses.

The individual has to hold on to his tool of action and carry on his duty. The mind is the "individual" and The intellect is the "charioteer."

We can also say "Be a master over yourself." Without such self-mastery, Self- realization is not possible. The Atman should be the guide for the seeker in his daily activities. This is the sure way to success.

प्रसादे सर्वदुःखानां हानिरस्योपजायते ।
प्रसन्नचेतसो ह्याशु बुद्धिः पर्यवतिष्ठते ||65||

prasāde sarva-duḥkhānāṃ hānir asyopajāyate |
prasanna-cetaso hy āśu buddhiḥ paryavatiṣṭhate ||65||

In tranquility, all the sorrow is destroyed. For the intellect of the tranquil minded is soon anchored in equilibrium. ||65||

Prasade': in peace; sarva: all; dukhanaam: sorrows; hani: destruction; asya: of him; upajayate: arises/happens; Prasanna chetasa: of the tranquil minded; hyashu: indeed quickly; buddhir: intellect; paryavatishtati: becomes steady (anchored in equilibrium).

Prasada in this context is to be understood as the tranquil state of the mind.

After all, as we know by now the mind due to its association with the material world around comes to experience happiness and sorrow in various proportions depending upon the karmas of the past.

It is also true that in states of happiness we do not ponder on anything other than the happiness experienced. We are not worried. On the other hand we would like the experience to be everlasting. But, alas, the experience of happiness from the material world can never be eternal. In course of time the happiness is followed by sorrow, it has "a birth, growth, decay and death."

The sloka therefore takes us only to "Sarva dukhanaam". (It does not say "sarva sukhanaam.") It means "during all the sorrows." It is only during times of sorrow that one ponders about why, what, why only me etc. Many a times we do not have an answer for the same. The individual might go to all available sources to get answers to such question and still may not get any satisfaction.

Only in tranquility all the sorrow is destroyed, the Lord says. How?

"The intellect of the tranquil mind is soon anchored in equilibrium" is the Lord's explanation.

The answer to the question "why" will be found by the reasoning capacity: "the intellect". The pure intellect by developing contact with the "antaratman" will have a firm control over the mind. The mind that works as subordinate to the intellect is content to be subservient to its immediate boss. (sloka 38 in this chapter, "Sukha dukhe same' kritva"). It is the meaning of the phrase "tranquil minded is soon anchored in equilibrium."

Keeping the mind tranquil even under all circumstances is the only means to gain purity.

The pure mind does not get troubled by the sorrows in life.

By directing the mind to the intellect, by letting the mind be subservient to the intellect, by the intellect keeping in constant contact with the "Light within of the Atman", no sorrows will hinder the spiritual progress of the aspirant.

The aspirant will have an easy ride on his boat that carries him on the ocean of samsara and reach the shore at the other end. No wave is strong enough to disrupt the passage of the boat. The seeker will be calm and collected in all sorts of adverse weathers that affect his life as he is sure that his Lord will make him reach the destination. It is the "Prasada" by the Lord for the tranquil state of the seeker.

Such an aspirant is "Sthitaprajna."

Let us ponder into the various types of sorrows that we experience in our lives and see what the sastras have to say about the same.

The sastras declare that all sorrows and sufferings can be traced to one of the following three sources.

Adhyatmika b) Adhibhoutika c) Adhidaivika.

The Upanisads teach us to utter the mantra "Shanti" three times at the end of every prayer. They are the blessings by which we request the Lord to help us to overcome the three main problems that hinder our path to attain "Salvation."

Adhyatmika: problems from within oneself: bodily suffering and mental anguish.
Adhibhoutika: problems from all round: refers to the various disturbances from the external world that stem from nature or living beings.
Adhidaivika: troubles faced by the wrath of the divine towards which, one has no control.
Misery caused by the elemental forces like floods and fire fall in this category.
Peace is attained by control of all sense-organs constantly and by constant meditation on the Self. This gives the mind purity. In course of time, such a mind dissolves in the Atman and that is "Liberation".

The first half of the verse says that equanimity in pain and sorrow makes one peaceful.

Happiness is peace. Peace is happiness. This peace of mind is also termed Prasada because it is the grace of God.

All the turbulent rivers lose their turbulence when they merge into the ocean. Similarly, a man who can control the agitations caused by the sense-organs and the mind (by absorbing himself in the contemplation of the Atman) will attain Peace. He is said to have merged himself in the ocean of bliss.

नास्ति बुद्धिरयुक्तस्य न चायुक्तस्य भावना |
न चाभावयतः शान्तिरशान्तस्य कुतः सुखम् ||66||

nāsti buddhir ayuktasya na cāyuktasya bhāvanā |
na cābhāvayataḥ śāntir aśāntasya kutaḥ sukham ||66||

To the unsteady mind there is no knowledge of the Self. To the unsteady mind there is no meditation. To the unmeditative no Peace and to the man without Peace, how can there be happiness? ||66||

Na: not; asti: is; buddhi: knowledge; ayuktasya: of the unsteady; cha: and; bhavana: meditation; cha: and; abhavayataha: of the unmeditative; shanti: peace; ashantasya: of the peace-less; kutaha: how; sukham: happiness.

The Lord is pointing to the positives by bringing in the negative statements.

When we say "Peace" many a times we do not really mean the "Peace" from the spiritual point of view. The word "Peace" is used many a times without actually knowing its true meaning.

Peace could be:

Negative peace;
Positive peace.

Negative peace:

After the passage of experience of deep sorrow which all of us go through in our lives, many a times there is a period when there are no more events that bring in new waves of sorrow. At the same time there are no events that mask the sorrow by bringing in happiness. We tend to say "I am peaceful now". This is "negative peace." Absence of sorrow is wrongly interpreted by many as "Peace." The peace here is conditioned by sorrow.

For examples:

The eerie peace after a major tragedy.

The peace before the storm (like the volcanic eruption - appearance of peace outwardly but boiling up with disturbances within.)

The scenario of cold war. Tragedy: Deep grief followed by a period of no further tragedies - feeling that one is peaceful after the events of that tragedy - through contrast from sorrow, one experiences mental tranquility.

Positive peace:

It is the peace that emanates from within the soul of the seeker and has no bearing with preceding a state of sorrow. The seeker may go through bouts of sorrow or bouts of happiness but is not perturbed by either. He is "at peace with himself" at all times.

Meditating on the world of objects does not bless us with "Positive Peace". The peace experienced is only momentary.

Even for success in the material life, to get the final end result of success, there has to be a long period of education both theoretical and practical. There also, the student has to learn to curb his desires brought in by the senses during the period of study. He needs a steady mind to get the knowledge in the specialty chosen.

To an unsteady mind, (for a student) there is no gain of knowledge towards the specialty of his choice.

Constantly meditating on the subject to study is the pre-requisite for success. The mind can either be towards the world of senses or towards the subject. It cannot be in two places at any one time.

The same rule has to be applied towards the spiritual study for the seeker. His mind has to be in constant meditation towards the Atman within which is a treasure house of "Ananda."

To summarize the same:

Sadhana: effort in life towards fulfilling the objectives both short term and long term. Long term objective: experience of everlasting happiness - "Peace". Positive Peace is a state of experience of everlasting peace.

To experience the Peace we need to gain the knowledge of the Atman. To gain the knowledge of the Atman, need to meditate on the same.

Without meditation and determination, concentration is not possible. Success in meditation is "Yuktaha" Failure to concentrate is "Ayuktaha."

Success is possible by developing "sadbhavana" (good feelings/ thoughts) on the Atman.

At the same time, one should not dwell on happiness from the objects around. Control of the wandering mind from multiple objects around to one single "Atman" is the only means.

Meditating on the "Atman within" gives "Positive Peace." It is everlasting Peace. Hence the last quarter of this sloka: "to the unmeditative no peace, and to the man without peace, how can there be happiness?"

Another interpretation to: "To the unsteady mind there no knowledge of the Self."

The mind will be unsteady in he who has a number of desires. Due to contact with the physical world, it is but natural to get more and more desires. These in turn bring in more desires. We have already discussed the problems about desires.

If the same mind is directed towards the Atman within, the unsteady boat can be made steady. There is less room for disturbing the mind when the object of desire is only one and remains the same constantly.

Those who have fulfilled the desires of the past, wiped off their vasana imprints and do not allow new imprints to be formed in their minds are known as: "Aptakamahas."

The state of perfection will be seen in that sadhaka where they shall be not be a cause of suffering either to himself or to others, either in the outer world or inner world. This state can be achieved only on total annihilation of ignorance. This is a blessing from the Lord when one truly and sincerely requests Him for "Jnana Prasada."

It is no use simply to talk of "Peace" and pray for "Peace". It has to be implemented with actions to bring in Peace.

Such a positive Peace is to be seen in the "Sthitaprajna.". As he has dropped his ego and succeeded in merging the mind with the Atman through the process of steady contemplation, his constant companions will be "Peace and Happiness."

इन्द्रियाणां हि चरतां यन्मनोऽनुविधीयते ।
तदस्य हरति प्रज्ञां वायुर्नावमिवाम्भसि ||67||

indriyāṇāṃ hi caratāṃ yan mano 'nuvidhīyate |
tad asya harati prajñāṃ vāyur nāvam ivāmbhasi ||67||

For, the mind that follows the wandering senses, carries away the discrimination, just as the wind carries away a boat on the waters. ||67||

Indriyanaam: the senses; hi: for; charataam: wandering; yat: which; manaha: mind; anu vidheeyate: follows; tat: that; asya: his; harati: carries away; prajnaam: discrimination; vayur: the wind; navam: the boat; ivambhasi: like in the water.

The boat:

Life that carries us to the destination of our choice is compared to a boat. The destination referred to in the sloka is "Salvation."

The wind: This refers to the gale force/turbulent impulses from the world around sometime or other in the passage of life.

A spiritual aspirant with a good control over the mind will be sailing along the seas smoothly. When the senses send in impulses of choice or when the mind suddenly starts dwelling on the stored memories of the past, the calmness is disturbed. The influence of the results of past actions is responsible for the gale force that sets in. The control over the boat is proportionately reduced. The aspirant will continue to use the oar to navigate in the stormy weathers but the distraction will direct the boat in another direction.

The tug of war between the impulses and control of the mind can lead the aspirant away from the destination or the boat itself might sink. When it sinks the aspirant and anybody who is also carried on the boat will have to swim to the shore. Many a time death or serious injury befalls on such victim/victims.

The mind on one side is exposed to the outer world via the senses. On the opposite side it has the intellect with the Soul within.

Directing the mind constantly towards the Atman within, using the power of intellectual discrimination and controlling the senses firmly and steadily is the secret to success.

The periods of turbulence has to be looked upon as the "test" by the Lord. The master has to test his student not only during the final exams but like the present day education, test is on a "continuous assessment" basis "on the spot tests" without giving any notice.

The highest level of maturity for the aspirant is when instead of feeling sorry for himself during periods of turbulence in his life, with equanimity of mind he should be prepared to face the test and pass the test with merit.

"Govern your mind" is the message from the Lord through this sloka.

तस्माद्यस्य महाबाहो निगृहीतानि सर्वशः |
इन्द्रियाणीन्द्रियार्थेभ्यस्तस्य प्रज्ञा प्रतिष्ठिता ||68||

tasmād yasya mahābāho nigṛhītāni sarvaśaḥ |
indriyāṇīndriyārthebhyas tasya prajñā pratiṣṭhitā ||68||

Therefore, O Arjuna, his knowledge is steady whose senses are completely restrained from the sense-objects. ||68||

Tasmat: therefore; yasya: whose; mahabaho: mighty armed; nigruheetaani: restrained; sarvashaha: completely; indriyaani: the senses; indriyarthebhyaha: from the sense objects; tasya: his; prajna: knowledge; pratishtita: is steady.

Let us note clearly that when the Lord says "restrain the senses", we must know that the senses include both the five sense organs and the mind. (the mind is considered to be the sixth sense).

We are asked clearly "to restrain" the senses, (not to close the senses) and at the same time, direct the thought towards the Atman within.

The Lord has sent us into this world blessed with five working sense organs and the working mind. He is advising us to learn the art to control them, not partial control, but total control.

The senses should not be made defunct. They should be in perfect working order constantly.

We have the "Antarjyothi", the "Inner Light of Wisdom." It is our duty to keep it constantly lit and at the same time steady. It should neither be switched off nor its light be blocked. This is essential for Liberation and to reach the destination safe and sound.

What is good to reach the destination is the lesson to learn for all. At the same time, what is evil and which prevents us from reaching the destination is also the lesson to learn.

The attitude with which the senses are directed towards the sense objects is the deciding factor in achieving success or failure in our mission of life.

The success in our mission of life is achieved when we learn the art of sanctifying the five sense organs and the mind. Thus we can contact only divinity in the world around with our senses.

The Lord is reminding us repeatedly to be vigilant. Control the sense organs and the mind is His constant reminder to the spiritual seeker. These organs take us from preyas to sreyas. (refer sloka 5, chapter 2).

By directing towards the world of objects, we travel in the path to preyas. By directing to the world of divinity, we can travel in the path to sreyas.

Please learn the art of, "What to see, how to see, why to see", is the instruction by the master. The word "Seeing" does not just mean "eyes" only but all the sense organs and the mind.

Step one in the study by the student is to have the light lit within the room, see that the windows are open to let the air in, close the curtains to stop from getting distracted with the scenes outside.

Step two is to see that all his books are at hand and to concentrate on the study.

By following this principle, he is in the right path of understanding the subject under study and mastering the same.

या निशा सर्वभूतानां तस्यां जागर्ति संयमी ।
यस्यां जाग्रति भूतानि सा निशा पश्यतो मुनेः ||69||

yā niśā sarva-bhūtānāṃ tasyāṃ jāgarti saṃyamī |
yasyāṃ jāgrati bhūtāni sā niśā paśyato muneḥ ||69||

That which is night to all beings, in it the sage is awake. Where all beings are awake, that is the night for the sage who sees the Self. ||69||

Yaa: which, nisha: night; sarva: all; bhootanaam: beings; tasyam: in it; jagrati: wakes; samyamee: the self-controlled (sage); yasyaam: in which; jagrati: wake; bhootani: beings; saa: that; nisha: night; pashyataha: seeing; munehe: of the sage.

"Jagat Mithya and Paramatma Satya" is the message from the learned seers to their disciples. It simply means that the only reality is "The Parabrahman who pervades all." The rest is only an illusion. The world as such does not exist from the point of view of "Advaitin" (non dual philosopher) This is the vision of the realized soul.

Majority of us perceive the world as real and are immersed in worldly activities. We are attached to objects of the world and are caught in the net of "Kama, Krodha, Lobha, Moha, Mada and Matsarya."

In this second group, there are a few that are aware of the Parabrahman but are unable to grasp its significance.

There is another group of men that are oblivious to the idea of the God and live the life pursuing the pleasures. We can say that they are "egocentric".

From the point of view of the Advaitin, "Maya" or "Illusion" is ignorance. Ignorance is compared to darkness and knowledge to brightness. On this basis of understanding, the "sage" referred to in this sloka is a man of true knowledge who knows the difference between the real and false. (Nitya and Anitya - Eternal and Impermanent) He is said to be "Awake" as he is living in "light of spiritual knowledge." To the rest who live in world of attachments it is the night as far as the knowledge of the Atman is concerned.

This is the meaning of the first half of the verse.

"Where all beings are awake that is the night for the sage who sees the Self": This refers to the physical day light as compared to the spiritual day light for the sage.

Technically speaking the majority of us are awake during day time. It is the time we are involved in various activities that bind us to the world around us. During the physical daytime, the sage is spiritually living in night because he is not attached to the world around him. He is totally immersed in the "Atman" and does not see the world around him. (living in night)

There are some sages who spend their nights in meditation and sleep for few hours in the daytime. The second half of the sloka refers to these also.

There are some other realized souls, who have mastered the art of withdrawal from the physical world and are still awake during the daytime. They are said to be in the world but not truly living in the world. They are physically awake in daytime but not involved in the affairs of the world. This is the true picture of a "Sthitaprajna."

"Physically awake, spiritually ignorant": this statement applies to majority of us. We are conditioned by the time of the day and immersed in worldly activities and are unaware of the Atman within and all around.

आपूर्यमाणमचलप्रतिष्ठं
समुद्रमापः प्रविशन्ति यद्वत् ।
तद्वत्कामा यं प्रविशन्ति सर्वे
स शान्तिमाप्नोति न कामकामी ||70||

āpūryamāṇam acala-pratiṣṭhaṃ
samudram āpaḥ praviśanti yadvat |
tadvat kāmā yaṃ praviśanti sarve
sa śāntim āpnoti na kāma-kāmī ||70||

He attains Peace into whom all desires enter as waters enter the ocean, which is filled from all sides, and remains unmoved. But not for the man who craves the desires. ||70||

Apooryamanaam: filled from all sides; achalam: motionless: pratishtam: stillness (unmoved); samudram: ocean; apaha: waters; pravishanti: enters; sarve': all; sah: he; shantim: peace; aapnoti: attains; na: not; kama kaminee: desirer of the desires.

The beauty of "Peace" experienced and lived by a man of true wisdom, "Jnani" is explained with reference to a simile of an ocean.

Many a times we hear people using the word "Ocean of Peace." This sloka gives us its explanation.

How do we describe the sea for a young and inquisitive child? The reply should be: The waves, ripples, foam you see now and that which lies beyond your vision around the world, in every seashore, are all in the ocean. You can also see storms and disturbances now and then in the ocean. Apart from these, ocean also has a number of different forms of sea animals in it. Know that these are only on the surface of the ocean. Deep, very deep in the sea, it is all quiet and serene. The sunlight does not penetrate so deep and the storms do not disturb the serenity. Still deeper lie the treasures of the ocean like the rich pearls.

Imagine the vastness of the sea, its deep bed, miles of width, receiving the water from the rivers flowing into it and also from the rainfall. Despite all the waters entering, it seems to be quiet and motionless. One cannot add or subtract the total volume of the ocean. All the waters that enter into it as rivers, do not increase its volume. If the rivers cease to flow, the expansion of the ocean will be the same.

At the same time, the sun absorbs the water from the sea, that is the precursor for the rains. But, the process does not shrink the sea and it still seems to be quiet and motionless.

Compare this to the tanks, small wells and lakes. They overflow and sometimes burst their banks when the flow of water into them is beyond their capacity to withstand. When the heat of the sun is too strong, many a times, they go dry too.

In a Yogi full of peace within himself, like the ocean, despite the bombardment of the sensuous impulses from the world around, there is no disturbance. He is not perturbed. The rivers of desires get absorbed within him but the sea of peace remains ever calm.

But the peace within the majority of us is like the small well or a lake. Our reservoir of peace is too small and shallow. The desirous impulses can make the well of peace within us overflow, the banks can burst and the peace can be shattered.

What we need to understand from this sloka:

Keep the ocean of peace within you full. Let your mind be ever calm. You have the great ocean of peace within you. Do not let the worldly desires and hatreds disturb that peace abiding within you. Let your desires be less and less and let your attitude be "Loka samastha sukhino bhavantu." (Peace for all in this universe.) The noble desires of universal welfare do not make us lose the Peace.

The Lord is advising us not to harbor selfish desires but learn the art of giving joy to others. Selfish desires make us spiritually poor and desires of universal welfare make us spiritually rich.

A Sthitaprajna, the Lord says is constantly in a state of peaceful joy, like the ocean. He is a jnani and he does not seek for worldly pleasures. He absorbs every joy that the life brings to him but absorbs the same in his state of "Brahmananda."

Let us therefore learn the art of the spirit of detachment in attachment to the worldly desires.

विहाय कामान्यः सर्वान्पुमांश्चरति निःस्पृहः।
निर्ममो निरहंकारः स शांतिमधिगच्छति ||71||

vihāya kāmān yaḥ sarvān pumāṃś carati niḥspṛhaḥ |
nirmamo nirahaṃkāraḥ sa śāntim adhigacchati ||71||

That man who, abandoning all desires, lives without longing for them, without the sense of "I" and "mine", attains "Peace." || 71||

Vihaya: abandoning; kamaan: desires; yaha: that; sarvaan: all; puman: man; charati: moves about; nispruhaha: without longing; nirmamaha: without the sense of " mine"; nirahankaraha: without the sense of "I"; sah: he; shantim: peace; adhigachati: attains.

The Lord has given three conditions to be fulfilled for the seeker who is longing for "Peace." They are:

Abandoning of all desires.
No longing for the desires.
Dropping the sense of "I" and "Mine".

Abandoning all desires means: Freeing from the compulsions of desires from past experiences in life and no craving for the new impulses that enter into the mind through the sense organs.

The true goal for the spiritual seeker is "Peace", the "Eternal Peace", while living in this world of objects. So far, from the 55th sloka in this chapter, the Lord has enumerated the qualities of the "Sthitaprajna", the man of steady wisdom.

He lives in constant peace within himself and still is an active member of the society. He has reached such a state of mental maturity wherein he has transcended the desire for "Peace." He has realized that the peace is within him in abundance.

When we say that the true goal for the seeker is "Peace", we must accept that the initial steps have to be taken with a purpose of attaining the peace. There should be a desire for the same.

To experience the peace, the seeker has to get up from the state of tamas and move up to rajas. He should have a yearning to be successful in his quest to find peace. This can be compared to the earlier part of one's education. We start off with a definite motive to take up the study in any selected field.

By making a successful progress, we reach the stage of higher studies. It is like entering from "Ph.D." to "Post Doctorate" level of study. Only a successful student who has reached that stage will understand the meaning of "no further desire to get the Post Doctorate degree." He will be working in his lab like an absent-minded professor, deeply immersed and happy with his work in the laboratory.

When the Lord says," abandoning all desires, living without longing for them, without the sense of "I" and mine", the advice is directed to such sincere seekers who have reached the level of entry into the Post Doctorate Fellowship.

This is in truest sense, "sanyasa" of all the desires. Hence this sloka is considered by the experts as the summary of "Sanyasa Yoga" in this second chapter. This chapter, Samkhya Yoga has summary of all the four main paths of yogas: Karma, Jnana, Bhakti and Dhyana.

Dhyana yoga is also known as Sanyasa yoga.

In our day to day experience, when we are in deep sleep there is no trace of ego left. We do not have any more "I" and "mine" sense in that state. We are dead to the world of objects. We are so peaceful in deep sleep without any trace of happiness or sorrow.

The seeker who would like to experience and live in this state of "eternal peace" has to be constantly asleep to the experiences of the phenomenal world brought in by the senses and stored in the mind.

Only by dropping the longing for the desire to attain peace, the seeker will reach the state of "sthitaprajna." He is truly the man with true wisdom. He is a real jnani. He has no sense of agency and ownership to the objects of the world including his own physical body.

Another important point to note in this sloka: the Lord does not put any condition of caste, sex, religion or creed to experience the "Peace." "Peace" is not the birth right of any one individual or any one group of individuals. It is the universal right for every individual who is born into this world and everyone has a right to long for it and work to attain it.

एषा ब्राह्मी स्थितिः पार्थ नैनां प्राप्य विमुह्यति ।
स्थित्वाऽस्यामन्तकालेऽपि ब्रह्मनिर्वाणमृच्छति ||72||

eṣā brāhmī sthitiḥ pārtha naināṃ prāpya vimuhyati |
sthitvāsyām anta-kāle 'pi brahma-nirvāṇam ṛcchati ||72||

O Arjuna, having obtained this Brahmi state, man is not deluded. Being established in this even at the end of life, man attains oneness with Brahman. ||72||

Yesha: this; brahmee: of Brahman: sthitihi: state; na: not; enam: this; prapya: having obtained; vimuhyati; deluded; sthitva: established; asyaam: in this; antakale: end of life; api: even; brahma nirvana: oneness with Brahman; rucchati: attains.

Brahmi sthithi: state of Brahman. What is Brahman?

It is "Satyam, Jnanam and Anantam" the Vedas declare. It is "Truth, Knowledge and Infinite (without an end)."

Brahman is "Infinite Peace" contrary to the fleeting pleasures of worldly life. Attaining the knowledge of this Eternal Truth and living in "Infinite Peace" abiding within oneself while living life on this earth is "Brahmi Sthithi."

The Lord asserts that establishing the mind in this state is the means to attain oneness with the Brahman - the word used is "Brahma Nirvanam." It is what the Vedas label as "Moksha."

The delusion as we have discussed before is due to the fleeting pleasures and pains from the objective world. When one looks upon an unreal as real it is labeled as delusion. Considering the pleasures from the physical world as permanent happiness is delusion. This delusion disappears on obtaining the "Brahmi sthithi." An individual who thought of himself as a separate entity and has realized that he is none other than an amsha (part) of "Parabrahman", (Tat Tvam Asi) is said to have obtained "Brahmi sthithi."

The second half of the sloka refers to establishing the mind in such a state, even at the end of life. The word "even" is to be noted carefully. It is a well-known fact that the result comes from actions. Actions have to be conducted first and results will come later. Some results come quickly and some take a long time. The result, "Brahma Nirvanam" has to come also from our actions. But, it does take a long time and it is hard work to achieve this result. This knowledge has to dawn on us. It may dawn in this birth or in future births depending upon our past karmas. As soon as it dawns, we are said to be on the path to Liberation. Even when this happens near the end of the present life, man attains Brahma Nirvanam, the Lord reiterates.

This is the message from the Lord to all seekers. He wants us to constantly remember this truth and work at achieving the end result. It does not matter when the result comes. Even if it dawns towards the end of one's life, he is sure to unite with the Parabrahman.

Most of our actions are due to our attachment to our own physical body, family and friends and the objects of the world. By following the Lord's teaching and working on the principle of "Nishkama karma and karma phala tyaga" we can succeed in our mission of life. The struggle to achieve the end result is worthwhile. Freedom from earthly desires and egotism is the recipe to the end result, "Moksha".

There is a Sanskrit word "anubhooti" which means "experience." Brahma Nirvanam is experience of the "Brahman."

All our experiences are due to the inferences at the level of mind and intellect. These are the inferences to the sense objects of the world brought in by the sense organs.

Experience of Brahman through such experiences is termed as "Paroksha anubhooti." It will not give a full picture of Brahman and is not a true experience. There is no such thing as experiencing Brahman. It is only becoming one with the ultimate reality.

To experience the "Brahman" in total we have to transcend the mind and intellect. That experience is known as "Aparoksha anubhooti/direct experience with one's intellectual eyes of wisdom."

He who apparently experiences "Paroksha anubhooti" (experience of others, indirect experience) is the jivatman. He is the Atman attached to the body due to ignorance. The world of objects cannot give a direct experience of the Brahman. (Para—others, aksha—eyes)

He who experiences "Aparoksha anubhooti" is "Jivanmukta", a liberated soul.

The Sthitaprajna, whose qualities are described by the Lord in these slokas is a "Jivanmukta". Through the process of negation from the known to the unknown he has "Aparoksha anubhooti" of the Brahman while living in the world of objects and has discarded all worldly pleasures. ("a" not, Paroksha not others, but direct experience).

Iti Śrīmadbhagavadgītāsūpaniṣatsu brahmavidyāyāṃ yogaśāstre Śrīkṛṣṇārjunasaṃvāde. Samkhya-yogo Nama Dvitiyo 'dhyāyaḥ ||

CHAPTER 3

KARMA–YOGA

INTRODUCTION:

This chapter is given the title of "Karma Yoga" with the word "Karma" to be pronounced with the emphasis on the third letter "r". (For those who are not familiar with the Indian scripture, the pronunciation to include "r" might be difficult but not impossible. Making the "r" silent, what is said sounds like "kama" and gives a totally different meaning. "Kama" is "desire" and "karma is "action.")

The word "Karma" has a number of different meanings and in the context of this chapter we should take it as "action" and "Yoga" to mean " union".

As the sacred text is about union with the Parabrahman, which is "Liberation", we should consider "Karma Yoga" as the actions that assist the seeker towards "Liberation." The conduct of desire-less actions becomes the duty/karma.

Some of the other meanings of the word "karma":

a) Practice of religious duties.

b) Destiny/fate.

c) Moral duties.

d) A ritual.

e) Funeral rites (antya karma)

It is a fact of life that to get something we should be prepared to part with something else.

It is like paying money to buy the goods from the market. We have to earn to get what we want. Nothing in the world is free and there is a price tag attached to it. Without working we cannot get the wages and without wages we cannot buy what we want.

Following this simple logic, "Moksha" does not come from "inaction." It needs input of efforts on our part. The spiritual seeker is he, who puts his efforts towards achieving and is known as "Sadhaka". Karma Yoga gives the path for the sadhaka to attain moksha.

Yajna is "dedicated action". To dedicate the results of actions with total faith and love towards the "Parabrahman" is the sure way to success for the seeker. Actions without faith and love do not get the desired result. Karma according to the instructions by the Lord really is to be considered as "Yajna."

Karma Yoga tells us what our duties are and teaches us the art of properly conducting the same. It tells us that our actions should not bring disruption or sorrow to any forms of life on this earth. This includes the members of the family and friends, members of the society and citizens all over the world (also to include, no harm to other forms of life).

Using the intellectual capacity of reasoning, assisted and blessed by the "consciousness" within, conducting actions towards universal welfare is true "Karma Yoga." This needs control over desire prompted thoughts/speech/actions at the level of mind/speech/body (Mano/vak/kaya) The Lord refers several times in this chapter to "Loka Kalyana" which means "universal welfare".

It is impossible to live without conducting any actions. Our body/mind complex (raga/dwesha) propel us into actions. Human needs are for security and endless entertainment and both cannot be achieved without actions. The results of such actions bind us to further actions and it becomes an endless chain of events. The bondage we thus get trapped into is called "Samsara."

Only positive, joyous, affirmative actions conducted as an offering to the divine will liberate us from bondage. It is necessary for us to be involved in the work we do. After all each one of us have duties to our own body, family and the society.

Commitment to the work without attachment to the results of the work is the art of true karma yoga.

Man is in the transitional stage of evolution. He is in between the stages of animal and divine. Our duty is to evolve spiritually and move onwards to the next stage of evolution. Our actions will take us to divinity or let us fall down to lower levels of life. Karma yoga teaches the path to evolve spiritually.

It is important to note that man is a social animal. We have to live as part of the society and work for the society. From the time of birth till death we are the recipients of benefits in one form or other from the society. We take the same for granted or do not realize the same.

The Lord therefore tells us that it is our duty to offer joyfully the results of our actions to the society. But these actions should not be selfish motivated actions, He stresses. He makes it very clear that selfish actions are the root cause of destruction of a society. Karma yoga teaches us the way to overcome selfish actions.

This chapter teaches us to do so by advising us: "think before acting".

The sastras tell us that what we are experiencing now, whether it is happiness or sorrow, is the result of:

Our own actions of the past which includes actions from the previous births and also the collective acts of the society of which we are also part of (through our actions or inactions).

At any cost we must not neglect our obligatory duties. There is no room for happiness or sorrow to rule over us and to disturb the daily duties.

We must learn to discharge our obligatory duties, whatever stage of life we may be in: childhood, teenage, adulthood or old age, for welfare of:

Our own selves,
Our family, Our society,
The life on this universe, and
finally for The future generations to come.

We have basically two duties:

a) Duties to the Lord who resides within us.

We must keep the body, mind and speech healthy and clean. Neglecting the body is like insulting the Lord within. Through these three instruments we must let the light of knowledge shine through. The "Light of Knowledge" should reflect the "Divinity" within.

We should treat the body like "a temple". The temple has the deity of choice installed in the inner sanctum sanctorum. The priests at the temple conduct the prescribed daily worship to the deity. The rest of the temple premises have to be kept clean and tidy to let the public come in and see the deity within and offer their worship. The temple where there are no prescribed worships of the deity or premises which is not kept clean does not attract the devotees.

Our body should be treated as a temple with the divine Atman within.

b) Duties to the society.

The Lord within is not seen and so not realized as such by many. The same Lord is reflecting in the various people around and all other forms of life. We should learn to recognize this divinity and show respect to all. This should reflect in our actions as individuals/families towards the disabled, the needy and the like. Later on in the Gita, we will learn that every form of life on this earth is the "Vibhuti" or "Glory" of the Lord.

We should not only offer worship to the deity of choice as thanks for what we have received so far but also worship through actions that contribute towards universal welfare. This is a true reflection of the light of knowledge shining inside each one of us.

The actions can be voluntary and involuntary. Respiration and circulation have become involuntary actions and through these we keep the body healthy and alive. Sometime in the life of the unborn child, a light is switched on for involuntary actions which remains on for the rest of our lives.

Similarly, we can make our actions involuntarily divine by keeping His teaching in our memory bank. This is known as "Nidhi dhyasa" one of the three requisites for dhyana/meditation.

"Karma Yoga", as used in the Gita is with reference to our actions in relation to the world we are part of which assist us in the path to Liberation.

These should be actions at all the three levels of "Mind, speech and body."

The root cause of sorrow is not the material world around us but our own ignorance. The scriptures call it "Ajnana." We tend to look for an external source for the sorrow experienced and put the blame on it. It is only a superficial search for the cause of "sorrow." A deeper search will lead us back to our actions that resulted in the experience of sorrow.

The ignorance and the inability to search within delude us and make us experience all types of agitations.

Sri Krishna is trying to teach us through the Gita the way to overcome the delusion. He is giving us the "Jnana" or "knowledge" to trace the cause of all our sorrows.

After the introduction to the Gita and summary of the same in the second chapter, we are taken to the chapter "Karma Yoga." Irrespective of whom the individual is and where he/she hails from, everybody on earth has to "Work." To experience happiness we have to work and to overcome sorrow also we have to work.

"Karma Yoga" is the conduct of right actions that takes us back to experience the happiness that abides within. We are told that the happiness is not in the objects around us but our own perception of the same. The same object which is the source of pleasure for some is the source of sorrow for others.

The knife used in the kitchen to prepare the food, the knife used by a surgeon to operate on the sick, the knife used by a butcher in his profession is a source of happiness.

On the other hand the knife used to kill somebody or the knife that is taken as a tool to play can turn out to be source of sorrow. It is the bhavana /attitude towards the work and the objective of work that makes all the difference.

Karma yoga is to teach the attitude to the work we undertake. Ajnana is the lack of such knowledge in action.

Opposite to the sorrow is the state of happiness.

We will also be told in this chapter that even the happiness can turn out to be source of sorrow.

The happiness we experience from the world around us can be traced back also to ignorance. Happiness from around us has a time span fixed to it. After a while, the peak of happiness fades out and in some cases leads to sorrow also.

Longing for a child after marriage and getting a child within wedlock brings in tremendous happiness. How long does it last?

Birth of a child is not the beginning of eternal happiness but a mixture of happiness/sorrow as the child grows our whole life changes.

If all our actions follow the code as given in the scriptures we find that our entire life is full of happiness without any room for sorrow to creep in. This state of happiness is "Ananda." Karma yoga gives us an insight into our duties and warns us of the consequences of wrong actions.

We, the humans have been given adhikara (sloka 47, chapter 2 for meaning of the word "adhikara") to work in this world. Our duties are simple: They are "Loka Sangraha," (welfare of life on the earth) and "respecting the nature."

Karma yoga is therefore a very important chapter.

We must learn the art of living and working within the space allotted.

According to Sri Ramana Maharshi, Karma Yoga is "purification of the mind." Purification of the mind is avoidance of all thoughts that are egoistic and filing the mind with thoughts on the divine and the divine duties.

अर्जुन उवाच
ज्यायसी चेत्कर्मणस्ते मता बुद्धिर्जनार्दन ।
तत्किं कर्मणि घोरे मां नियोजयसि केशव ||1||

arjuna uvāca:
jyāyasī cet karmaṇas te matā buddhir janārdana
tat kiṃ karmaṇi ghore māṃ niyojayasi keśava ||1||

Arjuna said:
O Keshava, if your belief is that knowledge is superior to action, why do you engage me in (this) dreadful battle? ||1||

Jyayasee: superior; chet: if; karmanaha: than action; te': thee; mata: thought; buddhi: knowledge; tat: then; kim: why; karmani: in action; ghore': terrible; maam: me; niyojayasi: engage.

If we can recollect the second chapter, we will note that both action and knowledge are extolled by the Lord.

An elaborate description of Karma yoga was given through slokas 47-60 and through slokas 11-46 an elaborate description on Jnana yoga.

The Lord ended the Chapter 2 with an elaborate description on the qualities of a "Man of steady wisdom."

We should also recall at this juncture that Arjuna was full of confidence when he went to the battlefield with Sri Krishna as his charioteer. He requested Krishna to take the chariot to the middle of the battlefield so that he could see all the warriors who had assembled to fight for the evil Prince Duryodhana.

Suddenly he developed a serious doubt in his mind about the justification for fighting against the respected elders of his own extended family and his mentors. He lost the nerve and dropped his bow Gandeeva and asked Krishna to guide him on the right path of action.

With this request we can now say that Arjuna moved one step higher in his spiritual plane and saw in Krishna the aspect of a "Guru" and asked for guidance.

The first step taken by Sri Krishna was to go through the four main paths of "Bhakti, Jnana, Karma and Dhyana" in the second Chapter.

Arjuna still had in his heart of hearts no inclination to fight. We seem to get the impression that he would rather give up the kingdom to Duryodhana without a fight and take up "Sanyasa ashrama" (renunciation of duties). That is to be understood by the last quarter of this sloka: "Why do you engage me in this dreadful battle?"

We can also presume that by referring to "Karma and Jnana" he has some doubt about his decision not to fight. It appears that he has a flicker of the light of knowledge that he should act properly and the guide to help him to conduct the right action was

"Krishna." Krishna not as the charioteer but, Sri Krishna, as his master and guru".

This chapter leads us to the right path to take when in doubt and in dilemma.

Bhagawadgita is a jewel in the crown for the entire mankind in general. Let us unfold our mind at the feet of the master and learn the lesson of right action in life with the sole purpose of "Loka Kalyana." (Universal welfare)

व्यामिश्रेणेव वाक्येन बुद्धिं मोहयसीव मे ।
तदेकं वद निश्चित्य येन श्रेयोऽहमाप्नुयाम् ॥2॥

vyāmiśreṇaiva vākyena buddhiṃ mohayasīva me
tad ekaṃ vada niścitya yena śreyo 'ham āpnuyām ||2||

You confuse my intellect as it were with speech which appears paradoxical. Therefore, tell me that "one" path, by which I may for certain attain the highest. ||2||

Vyamishrena: confusing/perplexing; eva: as it were; vakyena: speech; buddhim: intellect; mohayaseeva: confusing as it were (paradoxical); me': my; tad: that; ekam: one' vada: tell; nischitya: for certain; yena: by which; shreyoham: what is best (bliss, the highest); apnuvaam: may attain.

Arjuna wanted to conduct right actions but did not know what that "right action" was".

The important word to note here is "Vyamishrena vaakyena".

He says, "You confuse my intellect as it were with speech which appears Paradoxical."

Arjuna is not saying "you are confusing me," but saying "as it were, confusing me." This is the quality in a genuine seeker who looks upon his teacher as a "Guru."

After all, "Guru" is a "dispeller of darkness." "Ignorance is darkness" is what the experts say. The student must be free to express his doubts with all humility.

Let us see what the confusing words are:

Sloka 31—chapter 2:"For a Kshatriya, a righteous war is the only path to Liberation."

Sloka 45-chapter 2: "go beyond the three gunas."

Sloka 47, chapter 2: you have a right to work,"

Qualities of a "Sthitaprajna."

By listening to "go beyond the three gunas, "Arjuna probably thought that he should not be fighting the enemy. "I should not encourage any type of desires", he thought.

But then Krishna said "you have a right to work". It means that He is implying that Arjuna should be in the war and fighting the enemy.

Finally the description of a "Sthitaprajna" totally confused Arjuna.

Arjuna understood that "Jnana" meant "realizing the Atman within and all around and to move away from the world of senses."

He understood "Karma" as "actions that keep one in the world of senses."

He therefore finally asks, "Tell me what is for my Shreyas?"

The path Arjuna wanted to take was definitely a noble one as it was meant to attain "Moksha." As he was in a hysterical state when the advice was given, the message was not understood clearly. Like a sincere student he is faithfully asking for clarification with all humility.

A true Guru is he who encourages his students to clarify all doubts.

The faith that my Guru will help me to clarify my doubts and help me in achieving the final aim should be the attitude by all sincere seekers. Any doubt based on sincere trust is "Satvic doubt." It is like the child putting forward questions to his/her mother to clear the doubts. The child does so with full of love and faith towards the mother.

Sri Krishna wants Arjuna to develop the true understanding of the words He has used. Proper understanding only comes when the master encourages the students to come forward with any doubts.

श्री भगवानुवाच
लोकेऽस्मिन्द्विविधा निष्ठा पुरा प्रोक्ता मयानघ ।
ज्ञानयोगेन सांख्यानां कर्मयोगेन योगिनाम् ||3||

bhagavān uvāca
loke 'smin dvividhā niṣṭhā purā proktā mayānagha
jñānayogena sāṃkhyānāṃ karmayogena yoginām ||3||

The Lord said
In this world there is a two-fold path, O sinless Arjuna. The path of knowledge of the Samkhyans and the path of action of the Yogins. ||3||

loke'smin: in this world; dvividha: two-fold; nishta: path; pura: formerly; prokta: spoken; maya: by me; anagha: sinless; jnana yogena: by the path of knowledge; sankhyanaam: of the samkhyams: karma yogena: by the path of action; yoginaam: of the yogins;

Anagha: Sinless.

Sri Krishna addresses Arjuna as "sinless." Why?

Krishna had full confidence in the state of mental purity of his disciple. Yes, it is true Arjuna had killed many warriors in the past. He was a Kshatriya and followed the rules of his profession. This could not have been an act of sin. It was the duty of the Kshatriya to "protect."

The soldiers fighting for a country are supposed to be fighting for the country and follow the orders from the seniors. The soldier is fulfilling his role in the society by carrying out the duties of fighting for his country.

Arjuna, one of the top few men in the war, a Pandava, younger brother of Yudhistira was a righteous man and pure by nature. He had decided to fight Duryodhana who was wicked.

Lok'esmin:-- "In this world"

"Loka" in this context refers to the variety of people in the world around. Every individual is conducting "actions" in one form or other.

Dvividha nishta"--"Two fold path":

Sri Krishna refers to two broad categories of people (spiritual seekers) who conduct actions wishing for "Liberation."

"Pura prokta":--Has been said so in the past.

By making this statement, Sri Krishna is referring to the ancient scholars and wise men who gave advice to mankind towards ways of achieving Liberation. Please note that the word "I said so" did not come from the lips of the Lord.

Jnana yogena sankhyanaam karma yogena yoginaam:

The path of Jnana by the men of knowledge and the path of action by the Yogis (Men of action).

Yogena: Yoga is the path that is taken to unite with the "Parabrahman" which is "Liberation."

Both the groups of people have to take a path that leads to Moksha.

We have two main tools given to us by the blessing of the Lord.

The intellect;

The mind with the sense organs and the organs of actions.

Those who make use of the intellect are considered as following the path of "Nivritti".

Others who make use of the mind and the sense organs are considered as following the path of "Pravritti."

Both groups of people are fit to be called "sadhakas" and the steps taken by them are known as "sadhana."

They are in search of "spiritual wealth" which is the meaning of the word "sadhana."

"Samkhya" as we have studied in Chapter 2 is "Complete Knowledge." The word "Sankhya" is to be associated with "Jnana". Jnana Yogis are aware of the pitfalls of associating with the world of objects because the objects bring in a sense of "likes and dislikes" and many a time drag the seeker away from the spiritual path. They stick to their life of the study of the Vedas, Upanishads and sacred texts.

The examples we have are the four eternal youths, the children of Lord Brahma. They are "Sanaka, Sanandana, Sanatana and Sanatkumara." They were asked by the creator Brahma to assist Him in the task of creation but refused to oblige. They are also known as "Antarmukhis": men with the vision of the Atman within.

The other group is those who take the path of action to attain Liberation. They follow the principle of "karma" and conduct actions on the principle of "Nishkama karma and Karma phala tyaga". They follow the rules of the "Ashrama Dharma." (rules of the different stages in life) and assist in sustenance of the universe by their actions. This group of men is considered as "Bahirmukhis". They see and concentrate on the God around in various forms of life and respect the same.

These two are not separate paths and there is no need to enter into an argument as to which is the best.

Somewhere in the middle of evolution, the division between the path of action and the path of knowledge got separated and remained in the minds of many as separate paths.

Sri Krishna is re-iterating the fact that the division is not correct and both are the sadhana paths for spiritual seekers."

Let us understand the Gita in this sense. We have a choice to follow the path that suits our temperament and not argue about which path is best. Try to become sadhakas, work for spiritual wealth, (sadhana) and attain Moksha is the advice by the masters.

न कर्मणामनारम्भान्नैष्कर्म्यं पुरुषोऽश्नुते ।
न च संन्यसनादेव सिद्धिं समधिगच्छति ||4||

na karmaṇām anārambhān naiṣkarmyaṃ puruṣo 'śnute |
na ca saṃnyasanād eva siddhiṃ samadhigacchati ||4||

Man does not reach the action-less state (of Brahman) by non-performance of actions. Man also does not attain perfection by renunciation only. ||4||

Na: not; karmanaam: by actions; anarambham: from non-performance; naishkarmanam: the action-less state (of Brahman); na ashnute: does not reach; na:not; cha: and; sanyasaad: from renunciation; eva: only; siddhim: perfection; na cha samadhigachati: and does not attain.

Let us analyze the first half of the verse:

Man does not reach the action-less state 'by the non-performance of actions: many have a wrong notion that they can reach Parabrahman by non-performance of actions.

Many have a wrong notion that as sin can only result from actions performed, it is best to avoid actions altogether.

They also have a wrong notion that "Brahman is action-less."

If I achieve "Liberation" I do not need to conduct any more actions, they assume.

We are told that all these assumptions are wrong. Why?

Each one of us on this earth is commissioned to live through and exhaust the vasanas from past births. To exhaust all the stored vasanas (vasana kshaya) and achieve the destruction of the so called mind of ours, (Manonasha) we have no choice but to work. Only on achieving the two conditions successfully, i.e.: "vasana kshaya and mano nasha," can we realize the state of "Parabrahman".

Even then, to consider that "Parabrahman is action-less" is also a wrong notion. Parabrahman is constantly at work for the maintenance of the universe He created.

The second half of the verse:

"Man also does not attain perfection by renunciation."

A child gets perfection in walking after several attempts to crawl, to stand up and start learning to walk the first few steps.

We have to live in this world, conduct ordained actions and learn from our mistakes.

Later on we will come to know this as "Jnana and Vijnana". Knowledge by itself cannot make the individual perfect. Actions conducted with the knowledge, learning from the mistakes are necessary to attain perfection. We will be told later on in chapter 7 that one in a million tries to achieve perfection and a rare few among those who try will actually succeed in achieving perfection.

For example, graduation does not give the title of "Professor and Head of the Department." The graduate has to pass through a number of stages of promotion from lecturer to Professor.

Thinking that we know all about actions and the result of actions (good and bad, happiness, sorrow) and deciding to renounce all actions is a foolish assumption.

In continuation of the theme taken up in the previous verse:

Sri Krishna is therefore stressing on the need to conduct actions.

In spiritual evolution we have to climb from being:
Stone man-To Animal man - To Man man - To God man.
The final step is "Liberation."
The higher we climb the spiritual ladder, more responsibility there is on us to conduct actions for the welfare of the universe.

Na karmanaam arambha:
This is the first quarter of the verse. "Arambha" is beginning.
"Na karmanaam" means "not conducting actions."
There is always a beginning and end to any work conducted.
There is no such thing as "not conducting actions." The thought imprints on our mind which we carry as a result of past actions are the beginning for all actions. Sooner or later we have to work to burn all the stored vasanas.
Our philosophy tells us that we have all come from "Parabrahman" and we have to finally go back to Him.

We have to:
Purify our minds of all past thoughts
To obtain Jnana and finally,
To attain Moksha.

Actions performed with this principle are true karma. Such actions then become "Yajna."
The Vedas prescribe various duties to perform by the members of any one given community, to suit the temperament of the individuals. We are part of the community we live in. We have to live in harmony with others. To keep the communities together each member of that community has to take up some form of work. No one in the community has a right not to work.
By asserting that "by not working one does not get liberated", Sri Krishna is giving us the motivation to work for the community.

न हि कश् चत्क्षणमपि जातु तिष्ठत्यकर्मकृत् ।
कार्यते ह्यवशः कर्म सर्वः प्रकृतिजैर्गुणैः ||5||

na hi kaś cit kṣaṇam api jātu tiṣṭhaty akarmakṛt
kāryate hy avaśaḥ karma sarvaḥ prakṛtijair guṇaiḥ ||5||

No one can ever remain, even for a moment, without performing work. Everyone, without his will, is made to do work by the qualities born of Prakriti. ||5||

Na hi: not; kaschit: anyone; kshanamapi: even a moment; jatu: verily; tishtati: remains; akarmakrit: without performance of actions; karyate: is made; hi: for; avashaha: helpless; karma: action; sarvaha: all; prakrutirjair: born of prakriti; gunaih: by the gunas

It is not so difficult to understand the first half of the verse. We cannot remain without performing work even for a moment. The actions we perform are: Voluntary or Involuntary.

From the point of view of our own physical body, we do conduct a number of involuntary actions.

Act of breathing, circulation, digestion are some of the examples of involuntary actions we conduct. We survive because of these involuntary actions.

The act of blinking is another example of involuntary action. It is to protect our eye, a delicate organ and an essential one for survival in this world.

The second half of the verse is a little bit difficult to understand. The Lord says that everyone, without his will is made to work by the qualities born of prakriti. This refers to both voluntary and involuntary actions.

What we are and what we do voluntarily also to a large extent depends upon our "thought imprints" (Vasanas). These are stored in the mind and are the precursors of all our actions. The Hindu philosophy is based on the theory of rebirth after the physical death. We have no control over where we are born next, what form we take and when after death we are born again. The present life is considered to be one of several births and deaths in our life. The life is a sojourn of innumerable births and deaths that ultimately leads one to "Liberation."

The concept of the gunas is based on this theory.

"Prakriti" is nature. The word "nature" refers to one's own nature and also refers to the five gross elements: "earth, water, fire, air and space."

Here, the word refers to our own nature.

The Hindu philosophy classifies the entire population on the basis of these three qualities into the four following categories:

Brahmana, Kshatriya, Vaishya and Shudra.

Brahmana shows predominance of pure thoughts and is recognized by his knowledge of the Self, the scriptures and the like. He is considered to be an evolved soul.

Kshatriya with combination of Pure and Passionate qualities, the pure predominating, is physically strong and conducts duties to protect the innocent and those under his shelter. Arjuna, the warrior belonged to this class.

Vaishyas have a combination of all the three gunas and conduct actions for personal gains. Business class of people belongs to this group.

Shudras show a mixture of rajasic and tamasic qualities, tamas predominating. They are physically strong and conduct duties pertaining to the menial tasks and work needing predominantly physical strength.

The Lord is particularly referring to Arjuna in this instance. If he had absconded from his duties and went away to the forest, his thought imprints would not have changed overnight. He would still carry the gunas of a Kshatriya and his association with life in the forest would have made him conduct actions sooner or later that befit his qualities.

This is the summary of this verse.

By stopping here, one may get a wrong notion that if it is so, that the nature determines all our actions, there is no room for change. We are what we are and we can do what our thought imprints dictate. This is the wrong notion. The human birth is associated with having the "Intellect", the reasoning capacity.

We have an opportunity to change the thought imprints in our mind. This is a slow process and by what we call as "Practice" (Abhyasa) it is possible to change. Starting from the time of birth into this world, there is a latent period before the baby can become a child and then an adult. During this early period of one's life, the immediate family (mother, father etc.) and the society outside the family has an opportunity to bring in a change in the quality of thoughts. It is a slow process but not an impossible task.

The Puranas tell us the story of Prahlada to highlight this point. He was born in a demonic family as the son of the demon Hiranyakashipu. Destiny made his mother, while he was still in the mother's womb, reside in the hermitage of sage Narada. She was given discourses on the leela (acts of play) of Lord Vishnu, the Supreme. This changed Prahlada's thought imprints while he was still in his mother's womb from demonical to those of a saintly nature.

कर्मेन्द्रियाणि संयम्य य आस्ते मनसा स्मरन् |
इन्द्रियार्थान्विमूढात्मा मिथ्याचारः स उच्यते ||6||

karmendriyāṇi saṃyamya ya āste manasā smaran
indriyārthān vimūḍhātmā mithyācāraḥ sa ucyate ||6||

He, the deluded man, who, restraining the organs of action, sits contemplating on the sense objects with mind is called a hypocrite. ||6||

Karmendriyani: organs of action; samyamya: restraining; ya: he; aaste: sits on; manasaa: with mind; smaran: contemplating; indriyarthaan: sense objects; vimoodatma: of deluded understanding; mithyacharaha: hypocrite; iti: thus; uchyate: is called.

The Lord is referring to the two instruments of knowledge: the sense organs and the mind.

Eyes, ears, nose, tongue and the skin are the five sense organs. Their duty is to provide the mind with the details of the objects around.

The mind is to be looked upon as the superior officer to the sense organs. Its role is to analyze the impulses received from the sense organs and act accordingly. It is also a memory bank that keeps a database of all past experiences. It is the most powerful computer and can carry out a number of skillful tasks. We can broadly classify the experiences, as those that are pleasurable and those that are painful and filled with sorrow. The life is a mixture of experiences of both the types. Really speaking our life is a journey towards the abode of the "Supreme" and we say it is the "Spiritual Journey."

The society in general is a mixture of different groups of people. Some are sincere seekers, some are indifferent and some are antisocial. There is still another class of people who are not really seekers of Truth and the Lord uses the word "Hypocrites" to describe them.

The scriptures and the Gita give a description of the correct method of meditation. They tell us to learn the art of controlling the sense organs by the mind, the mind by the intellect and the intellect by the inner conscience. This is a gradual process and takes a long time of sincere effort with the assistance of the learned.

Once there were two friends who decided to go and watch a film in another part of the town. They passed through an arena where there was a spiritual discourse by a master. They decided to go in and listen to the discourse. One of them could not concentrate on the discourse and decided to go to the picture. Both of them agreed to exchange their experiences the next day.

The one who stayed back to listen to the discourse confessed that his mind was not on the discourse but on the movie he had missed. The other one also could not describe the story of the movie and confessed that he felt guilty at not staying back for the discourse.

His mind was thinking of the topic the master was giving in the discourse. The term "Hypocrite" refers to the one who stayed back to listen to the discourse.

The Lord in the form of "consciousness" inside us should be the overall master to control both our mind and the sense organs.

यस्त्विन्द्रियाणि मनसा नियम्यारभतेऽर्जुन ।
कर्मेन्द्रियैः कर्मयोगमसक्तः स विशिष्यते ||7||

yas tvindriyāṇi manasā niyamyārabhate 'rjuna
karmendriyaiḥ karmayogam asaktaḥ sa viśiṣyate ||7||

But O Arjuna, he who controls the senses with his mind and engages his organs of action in karma-yoga, without attachment, is the best. ||7||

Yah: whose; tu: but; indriyani: the senses; manasa: by the mind; niyamya: controls; aarabhate: engaes/starts; karmendriyaihi: by the organs of action; karmayogam: karma yoga; asaktaha: without attachment; sah: he; vishishyate: best.

We have here three steps to be taken by a true Karma Yogi. Such a seeker is considered to be the best by the Lord Himself.

Step 1:

Control of the senses by the mind: The senses are just instruments that carry the impulses from objects around. They do not know if the impulses are good or bad. The mind as the superior master over the senses should control the senses, the Lord says.

If there is a picture which is obscene, the mind should either ask the eyes to shut or not take notice of what is seen. It can direct the eyes to something else which is good.

Step 2:

Engages the organs of action: the mind is the instrument which sends orders to the organs of action to carry out a task. This is "karma" (action). But it is not Karma yoga.

Step 3:

There should not be any attachment to the object and to the results of action and then only it is true "Karma Yoga" and it is the best form of karma, the Lord says.

The Lord has highlighted the need for all the three instruments to be made use of for the conduct of any karma.

The mind

The sense organs

The organs of action.

We know that it is a massive world outside and it has phenomenal number of objects in it. Without the medium of these sense organs we will not have a clue of what is around us. A blind person cannot see the door in front of him and a deaf person cannot enjoy the conversation in a group.

The sense organs help us to be part of the world and to be associated with the world. Making the best use of the instruments given by the Lord, he, who restrains the mind, does not get attached to the objects and commands his organs of action to the path of work (to be part of the world) according to dharma, excels, the Lord says.

नियतं कुरु कर्म त्वं कर्म ज्यायो ह्यकर्मणः ।
शरीरयात्रापि च ते न प्रसिद्ध्येदकर्मणः ||8||

niyatam kuru karma tvaṃ karma jyāyo hy akarmaṇaḥa |
śarīrayātrāpi ca te na prasidhyed akarmaṇaḥ ||8||

Do the obligatory duties as prescribed by the Sastras. It is superior to inaction; By inaction, even the maintenance of the body is not possible for you. ||8||

Niyatam: obligatory; kuru: do/conduct; karma: duty; tvam: you; karma: action; jyaha: superior; hy: for; akarmanaha: than inaction; shareera yatra: maintenance of the body; api: even; cha: and; te: thy; na: not; prasidhyed: would be possible; akarmanaha: by inaction.

The Lord is advocating action and stresses that it is superior to inaction.

He is directing us all towards the "Sastras." The sastras have to be the authority and guide us towards actions or inactions. A learned Guru, who has mastered the sastras and lived the life as enshrined in the sastras is the most apt person to guide the seeker towards understanding the sastras.

Niyatam karma: it means "Obligatory duties" one may then ask: what do we mean by "obligatory duties?"

The duties that are required to be conducted, which are binding on our part and not optional are obligatory duties.

Arjuna wanted to drop all actions and become a sanyasi. He had understood that to be desire-less one must drop actions. That was his fundamental misunderstanding of the sastras.

Each one of us has a duty:

To oneself
To the family
To the society
To the country
And last but not the least, to the universe.

Some scholars say that even the act of "bathing, eating, sleeping" are also obligatory duties. When to bathe, what to eat, when to eat, when to sleep and how long to sleep are all given in the sastras. These are "required duties" to keep the body and mind fit to be a member of the society. They are not "Optional." They are binding duties on our part. By not eating, sleeping or bathing, the maintenance of the body becomes impossible.

As it applies to our own physical body, we do give some importance to these duties. We have to refer to elders/ sastras on how to conduct these actions so that our body and mind are always fit and healthy. Let us not forget that good physical and mental health is required to achieve success in life. Action is the means to keep the body fit.

Let us now look at duties to the society and duties to our own family and friends. One may say that these duties are optional and we will conduct them if we want to. It is up to our choice, they say. This is wrong. It is the main theme of the Gita and specially Chapter 3. The Lord says it is about the need for one and all to act and fulfill their obligatory duties to the society. We should consider our duties to the family and the society also as "Obligatory duties" and bring out the best through those actions.

It is the attitude to work that the Lord is referring to.

A graduate, be it a doctor or any other professional on the day of graduation, comes out with a massive debt to the society. He owes a large debt to the society who contributed to his education and provided the basic needs during his days of study. To work after graduation is therefore "obligatory" to repay the debt.

The attitude to work has to be:

I owe a massive debt to the society. It is my duty to serve the society by applying the skills learnt in the conduct of actions.

Every individual has therefore to conduct his daily duties in the form of offering to all forms of life.

The same law applies to the members of a family in a household. It is the elders in the family who contribute towards the education and look after the needs of the children.

Each member in a household starting from the mother has varied roles towards the other members of the family. The duties by the family members to each other have to be conducted in the same spirit of offering to the family and thereby offering to the society.

We are also told that the "action is superior to inaction."

We have therefore to understand that we cannot drop any of the obligatory duties. Everyone is bound to his/her family and the society. If members in family or in the society fail to fulfill their obligatory duties, the progress in that family and society falters. Instead of experiencing the happiness at the results obtained, there will be sorrow and misery. The failure of the father in his duties to his offspring can be catastrophic.

No one should escape his duties is the firm command from the scriptures and is reiterated by the Lord in this sloka.

By taking up premature sanyasa (retirement) from the worldly duties, the progress in the spiritual path falters. Arjuna was going through this feeling/bhavana in his mind. Luckily, his earlier Vedic education, his respect towards the elders and acceptance of Lord Krishna as his Guru, assisted in guiding him back towards the right path.

"By inaction, even the maintenance of the body is not possible".

This is not difficult to understand. Can we maintain our body and health by not drinking water, by not eating and by not going to sleep?

If we do not fulfill our duties to the family and society, they in turn also in their own way do not look after our needs. The love and respect of the family or the society to he/she who does not fulfill the duties will diminish in proportion and sooner or later the individual who fails to conduct one's duty is going to suffer.

The sastras talk of four types of actions:

Nitya karma
Naimittika karma
Kamya karma.
Nishiddha karma

Nitya karmas and Naimittika karmas refer to the duties for a householder.

Nitya karmas: These are obligatory daily duties.

The Pancha yajnas (five obligatory duties) fall under this category.

Deva Yajna, Rishi Yajna, Pitru Yajna, Nara Yajna and Bhoota Yajna are the five Pancha maha yajnas. They have to be conducted as dedicated acts.

Deva yajna: worship of the deities in the form of daily morning and evening prayers, visiting places of pilgrimage etc. is Deva yajna.

Rishi yajna: worship of the sacred texts, honoring the saints and savants, regular studying the sacred texts are considered as Rishi Yajna.

Pitru Yajna: these are acts to worship the departed souls of the family. As a matter of fact during the annual sraddha for the departed souls, the sastras command that the one who is conducting the Pitru yajna should offer his own points of merit as oblation to 7 generations of departed souls and seven generations of future progeny in that family, thereby assisting the departed souls to receive the points of merit and be able to reach the higher worlds.

Nara Yajna: respecting other humans, ahimsa (non-injury), and assisting those in need in the society is nara yajna.

Bhoota yajna: respect and non-injury to other forms of life is Bhoota yajna. We will learn more about these as we proceed to other chapters.

Naimittika-karmas are those prescribed duties performed on certain special occasions:

Pumsavana (rites to pray for a male child),

seemantonnayana: (rites performed when a woman is pregnant),

Jata karma, (rites to welcome into this world by the father)

namakarana: (rites after the birth of a child and naming the baby),

Karnacedha: (first piercing of the ears for the baby),

Annaprashana: first feeding of rice to the baby,

Akshararambha: teaching the writing of alphabets,

Chooda karma: cutting off the hair on the head,

Upanayanam: rites for wearing of the sacred thread,

Vivaha: wedding ceremony,

Prayers on special occasions like the full moon day or the new moon day,

Duties like "Sraddha" (annual rites to offer for the departed souls).

Kamya karma: desire oriented actions are Kamya karmas. These are to fulfill the desires that are not contradictory to the sastras.

Nishiddha karma: these are acts forbidden by the sastras and the society.

In summary, we can say that every individual on earth must do his/her share of work in his/her field of activity to the best of their capacity.

यज्ञार्थात्कर्मणोऽन्यत्र लोकोऽयं कर्मबन्धनः ।
तदर्थं कर्म कौन्तेय मुक्तसंगः समाचर ||9||

**yajñārthāt karmaṇo 'nyatra loko 'yaṃ karmabandhanaḥ |
tadarthaṃ karma kaunteya muktasaṅgaḥ samācara ||9||**

O Arjuna, work other than those performed for the sake of sacrifice, binds to this world. So perform the work for sacrifice, without attachment. ||9||

Yajnarthat: for the sake of sacrifice; karmano: of action; anyatra: otherwise; lokaha: the world; ayam: this; karma bandhanaha: bound by action; tad artham: for that sake; karma: duty; muktasangaha: free from attachment; samachara: perform.

"Moksha" or "Salvation" is the goal for having taken the birth as humans, says the Hindu philosophy.

The man is known as "Karma jeevi", the one who has to live a life of action. The results of any actions could be:

They take us towards the upward path to Moksha or

They bind us to this world.

Or They take us to the downward path of hell.

Actions that are conducted contrary to the spirit of "Yajna" bind one to this world, He says. He is advocating conduct of actions in the spirit of dedication of the results of actions to the Lord. (it should be acts of Loka Kalyana/welfare of life on this universe)

What is a "Dedicated act?" will be the next question that crops in the mind. Every work is bound to give a result. Good actions give good results.

Only desire-less actions, dedicated to the "Supreme" can be called as "Yajna." All other types of actions, even though good actions are not "Yajnas" in the truest sense.

Any act conducted with an ulterior motive of pleasing someone else and expecting to get something more in return cannot therefore be considered as "Yajna."

The "Supreme Lord", the Parabrahman is without any form (Nirakara) and without any qualities (Nirguna), so says the Vedas. How then, can one dedicate the result of actions to Him?

Without other members of the society and other forms of life on this earth, man cannot survive in this world. He should therefore consider the rest of the society indirectly as an element of the "Supreme" and offer all results of good work back to the society in one form or other. Then only, his work becomes a "Yajna."

Work conducted in this spirit by the citizens of any country will only help the society in that country to prosper.

Arjuna as we know wanted to withdraw from the battlefield. He was in pursuit of Moksha and expressed his desire to Lord Krishna. He certainly did not want to go to hell. His misunderstanding was in thinking that he would incur sin by killing the soldiers in the battlefield.

Krishna is therefore indirectly giving Arjuna a hint to continue fighting and not to think of the consequences. Arjuna had to fight in the war because this would benefit the citizens of Hastinapura, it was also his duty as under the leadership of the evil Duryodhana, the subjects would suffer."

This way, his actions would become "Yajna".

Let our aspirations be "Loka Samastha Sukhino Bhavantu." (Let everyone in the world he happy). Let our work reflect the service towards humanity with no selfish motive. This will certainly lead us upwards in the spiritual path towards "Moksha."

सहयज्ञाः प्रजाः सृष्ट्वा पुरोवाच प्रजापतिः |
अनेन प्रसविष्यध्वमेष वोऽस्त्विष्टकामधुक् ||10||

sahayajñāḥ prajāḥ sṛṣṭvā purovāca prajāpatiḥ |
anena prasaviṣyadhvam eṣa vo 'stv iṣṭakāmadhuk ||10||

The Prajapati, having created mankind in the beginning by Yajna, said, By this shall you prosper. Let this be to you the milk-cow of desires, the wish-fulfilling heavenly cow, Kamadhenu." ||10||

Saha yajna: together with sacrifice; prajaha: mankind; srushtva: having created; purovachaa: in the beginning said; prajapati: Lord of creation; anena: by this; prasavishyadhvam: shall you propagate; esha: this; cha: and; astu: let it be; ishtakamadhuk: milk-cow of desires.

It will be an interesting exercise to learn something about the two words "Prajapati" and Kamadhenu."

Prajapati means "Lord of creation." "Praja" is "mankind" and "pati" is "Lord." It is a late Vedic concept. It is said that Prajapati formed living creatures out of his sacrificial offerings to the Gods.

It is said that there are 7, 8 or 10 or even more, ancient great sages and together they are known as "Prajapatis." These are the "Mind-born" sons of Lord Brahma (Brahma's Manasa Putras).

Lord Brahma, on receiving the command from Lord Vishnu to create life on earth, created the Prajapatis and gave them the command to create the life on earth. These are considered to be the instruments of secondary creation.

"Swayambhu" is an epithet signifying the "self-existent" nature of Brahman. It is considered "unknowable and unfathomable". It is said that Lord Brahma when commanded by Vishnu to create life on earth, converted himself first into two persons, male and a female (see under introduction to Chapter 2) .The male counterpart is "Manu Svayambhuva" and the female "Shatarupa."

Svayambhuva is the name of the first Manu and there are 14 mythological creators who successively rule the 14 eras called "Manvantaras."

Brahma then created the "ten great sages" who became the Lords of all created beings.

These are the progenitors of the various gods, godlings, demons, all species of animals and vegetable life on earth.

"Kamadhenu" is the "wish fulfilling cow of plenty" that emerged from the churning of the ocean by the "Devas and Danavas." It is said to fulfill every desire. Surabhi, Savala are some of its other names by which it is called. It symbolizes the abundance and proliferation of Nature.

The mythological churning of the ocean is popularly known as "Samudra manthana." One could say it is a "secondary" creation myth that regards all things as "existing in potential" in the primordial ocean. Superhuman efforts will be needed to unearth the treasure that would benefit mankind.

The Myth:

The Devas and Danavas are lifelong enemies and are constantly fighting with each other. During one of the fights, the Danavas win over the Devas and occupy the heaven, the abode of the Devas. Lord Vishnu was the only superhuman who could assist in turning the defeat into victory for the Devas and benefit for mankind. The Devas approached Lord Vishnu to help them to regain the "Indraloka" (Amravati.), the capital city of the Devas.

The Devas needed to drink the nectar "Amrita" and become invincible. This immortal nectar, "Amrita" was deep in the ocean and needed to be unearthed. It could not be carried out by the Devas on their own. They needed the physical strength of the Danavas to churn the ocean. Lord Vishnu advices Indra to make peace with the Danavas. On the pretext of getting the nectar out of the ocean, and sharing it with them, the Devas request the Danavas to take part in churning the ocean.

The Devas chose Mount Mandara as a churning rod and coiled the serpent Vasuki around it as a rope to enable them to churn the ocean. The Devas held on to the tail end of the serpent and the Danavas held on to the head end. To prevent the Mount Mandara from getting submerged in the ocean due its heavy weight, Lord

Vishnu took the form of "Tortoise" (Kurma Avatara) and let the Mount Mandara stand on His trunk. Various objects came out of the churning and here is a list of the objects that emerged.

Kamadhenu
Vaaruni, the Goddess of wine
The celestial Parijatha tree
Group of heavenly nymphs (Apsaras)
Cool-rayed Moon
Halahala, poisonous gas,
Dhanvantari, the Physician of the Gods holding on to the vessel of Amrita,
Goddess Sri (Lakshmi),
The elephant Airavata,
Uchraisravas, the white horse.

Majority of us, the humans, take the path of worldly desires and look for worldly objects that bring us pleasure. The needs of humans are plenty and variable. Let us remember that the resources have to come from mother nature. Nature is vast and plenty but not a "bottomless-pit." The process of creation leads to multiplication of life on earth. Our ancestors having understood the rapid multiplication of life on earth in the years to come, realized the need to work in a way that involves respecting nature and its resources.

They came up with the theory of "Yajna." Only by dedicating the results of the work through "selfless acts" could we support nature and make life sustainable for the future generations to come.

The geologists agree that when the world was created, the cosmic forces came into existence first. The creative force of nature is an aspect of the Lord, let us understand this first. The force of nature prepared the field (earth) over thousands of years and made it ready for inhabitation by the life to come in future. It has to be looked upon as a dedicated act.

Man, when he came on to earth, was supposed to use his intellectual capacity of reasoning and work in harmony with the nature. Over the last few hundred years, the greed of man has predominated in all his actions. He is overusing nature's resources and depleting it of the energy. We are destroying the harmony of existence.

By this message through the Gita, the Lord is reminding mankind to check one's desires, work for the society and dedicate his work for the benefit of life on earth. The work, will then, like "Kamadhenu" become a "desire fulfilling tool" that is for the benefit of one and all.

Our prosperity comes from dedicated actions and our ruin by selfish actions. We can lift ourselves or ruin our lives. It is in our own hands.

देवान्भावयतानेन ते देवा भावयन्तु वः ।
परस्परं भावयन्तः श्रेयः परमवाप्स्यथ ||11||

devān bhāvayatānena te devā bhāvayantu vaḥ |
parasparaṃ bhāvayantaḥ śreyaḥ param avāpsyatha ||11||

Cherish the Devas with Yajna. They shall cherish you.
Thus cherishing one another you shall attain the Highest. ||11||

Devaan: the gods; bhavayata: nourish/cherish; anena: with this; te': those; devaha: gods; bhavayantu: may nourish/cherish; vaha: you; parasparam: one another; bhavayantha: cherishing; shreyaha: good; param: Supreme; avapsayathah: shall attain.

The term "Deva" has seven different connotations, (Swamy Chinmayananda)

He who shines, gives light,
He who bestows wealth,
He who blesses with good health,
He who shows the path,
He who makes others shine,
He who sends out music,
He who imparts knowledge and wisdom.
Quote:
Sri Ramakrishna:

"Whatever you offer to the Lord is returned to you magnified and manifold. Take care therefore, that you do not offer anything bad to Him."

There are two sections of people referred to in this sloka. One of them is the Devas and the other one is us, the mankind. It is us who conduct actions either individually or in a group. Our actions can be either selfish or dedicated and the Lord is referring to the dedicated actions by using the word "Yajna."

Devas: the word should be taken as "Illumined ones". The one who is shining because of good deeds is "Deva." Our philosophy considers that the Devas are "Highly evolved souls."

The cosmic forces are also called as "Devas" and this sloka can be understood better if we use the cosmic forces as an example.

In relation to our physical body, the Pancha Maha Bhootas, (Five great elements: the Earth, The Water, The Fire, Air and The Space) are our immediate Devas.

We have already discussed about these five devas and their relationship with the five sense organs (Chapter 2, introduction). Each of one these five is the presiding deity for one of the five sense organs of our body.

The environment has a great influence on our day to day life. Directly or indirectly we need to work to survive in this world. We work in the field of any one of or the combination of these five great elements. The Deva in that particular field of work will confer their blessings on us. We should also remember that there is productivity dormant in any type of work. Any sincere effort has an influence to an extent on the results on the outcome (The philosophy teaches us that some of our past actions also have an influence on our present life).

The farmer working hard will be invoking the Deva, "Mother Earth." The more effort he puts into his work, the more sincere are his efforts, the greater will be the blessings of the Mother Earth.

If at the same time, the results are dedicated to the higher powers, the acts conducted will become "Yajna."

The Lord states that "by cherishing one another you shall attain the highest good." (Param Avapsyatha) what do we understand by this?

We have the freedom to act the way we want. If we use our intellectual capacity of reasoning and conduct our actions, we will be benefitting the society and the society in turn will bless us.

The highest benefit from dedicated actions is "Moksha" which is becoming one with the Supreme. Yajna has the capacity to bring in the union with the Parabrahman.

We can understand the same by looking at the example of "Firewood."

We use the firewood and light it up with fire. What happens to the firewood when it is lit?

The firewood itself becomes the fire and loses its identity as the firewood. The firewood which is fuel in this case, has the capacity to become the fire itself. Similarly, we have the potential to become "one with God only by losing our identity as the "individual" (Ego).

इष्टान्भोगान्हि वो देवा दास्यन्ते यज्ञभाविताः ।
तैर्दत्तानप्रदायैभ्यो यो भुङ्क्ते स्तेन एव सः ||12||

iṣṭān bhogān hi vo devā dāsyante yajñabhāvitāḥ |
tair dattān apradāyaibhyo yo bhuṅkte stena eva saḥ ||12||

Cherished by sacrifice, the devas give you desirable enjoyments. He who enjoys objects given by devas without offering them is verily a thief. ||12||

Ishtaan: desired; bhogaan: objects/enjoyments; hi: so; vah: you; deva: the gods; dasyante: will give; yajna bhavitaha: chesrished by the sacrifice; tair: by them; dattan: given; apradaya: without offering; ebhyaha: to them; yah: who; bhunkte: enjoys; stena: thief; eva: verily; saha: he.

This Sloka affirms the fact that we do get due rewards for conducting the yajna. The Lord has given us further instructions on how to use the benefits conferred by good acts.

It is true that majority think, "I worked hard at it, I sacrificed a lot to receive the benefit, I deserve every penny of what I get and so I would like to enjoy the same."

The scriptures categorically say that it is a wrong attitude. The Lord therefore makes it clear that the benefits received are not just for the individual but have to be shared with others. He not only states that they should be shared but makes it clear who to share them with. He goes to the extent of saying that without offering the results to the Devas, using the benefits for personal enjoyment makes one "a veritable thief."

Let us remember that we are discussing only the results of sacrifices conducted according to the scriptures. We are blessed to be able to conduct the yajnas. Each and every one of our actions has to be in the spirit of "Yajna."

There are those who are unable to conduct the yajna because of poverty, ill health etc. We have to share what benefit we receive from the conduct of any dedicated acts with the needy in the society. Instead of saying "I will enjoy," let us learn to say, "We will share and enjoy."

It is also true to say that the "results reflect the effort put in."

If our actions are true to the meaning of the word "sacrifice", the "Illumined Ones" bless us in return with health, wealth, prosperity.

The sacred text is all about rooting out the evil called "Selfishness." We should remember the meaning of the word "I."

The "I" that limits one to himself only is the most common way of understanding. It is said to be a weak "I".

"I" should include not only myself but those who I love, "I, my extended family and friends,

"I, my extended family, friends, the society, other forms of life"

The "I" should get stronger and stronger by inclusion of others apart from us.

In the Hindu tradition, when we go to the temple, we go along with some form of offering to the deity and hand it over to the priest. The priest recites sacred mantras and offers the same to the deity. He then gives us back the offerings we took. This is the Prasada we get. We then sit for a short while in the temple and share the prasadam. Wherever possible and practicable, we also take some to our house to share with our beloved family and friends.

We feel happy for having gone to the temple and receiving the blessings of the Lord and sharing it with loved ones.

Not only the prasadam obtained at the temple but whatever we earn in our lives (which should be considered as prasadam) by righteous means should also be shared with family, society, for upkeep of temples and religious traditions.

When we receive any form of income, provided it is earned righteously, we should remember this Sloka and share the results with others.

If not we become "Thieves". The thief gets caught sooner or later and has to receive the appropriate punishment. Let us not get caught and suffer the fate of a thief.

One must think of giving something back to the society rather than expecting always to be receiving.

The Lord who has given the entire universe for the life on earth does not expect any returns for Himself. We need to, in His name, offer to the society and it is equivalent to having paid Him back for all His love and mercy.

Any member of the society who does not act as per the directions given in this sloka is said to be acting against the injunction of the sastras. That member will be a liability on the society.

यज्ञशिष्टाशिनः सन्तो मुच्यन्ते सर्वकिल्बिषैः ।
भुञ्जते ते त्वघं पापा ये पचन्त्यात्मकारणात् ||13||

yajñaśiṣṭāśinaḥ santo mucyante sarvakilbiṣaiḥ |
bhuñjate te tv aghaṃ pāpā ye pacanty ātmakāraṇāt ||13||
The righteous that offer food to the Gods in sacrifice and eat the remnants, are freed from all sins. But those who cook the food to satisfy their own needs are sinners and verily eat sin. ||13||

yajna shishtashinaha: who eat the remnants of the sacrifice; santaha: righteous; muchyante: are freed; sarva: all; kilbhishaihi: from sins; bhunjate: eat; te': those; tu: indeed; agham: sin; papaha: sinful ones; ye: who; pachanti: cook; atmakaranat: for their own sake.

This Sloka is a continuation of the last Sloka and elaborates more on the theme of "Sacrifice."

One can say in summary that:

"Share what you have and what you earn by righteous means and survive or be selfish and face the consequences."

Kilbisha: --it means "Sin." What is "Sin"?

"Sin" is defined as "Transgression against the divine law or morality."

"The righteous who offer food to the Gods":

Here, the word food refers to the wealth received/accumulated by actions. As described elaborately in the last verse, the wealth has to be shared. As a matter of fact the sastras have instructions on the way to use one's wealth.

They advise us to divide the wealth into five portions: (as stated in the Puranas and the Bhagavatham)

a) To one's own personal needs. To be part of the society and discharge the obligatory duties, every individual has to look after his/her basic needs. After all, let us not forget that the physical body is the temple with the divine within. We have a basic duty to keep the body (temple) fit and clean at all times. The light of knowledge should illumine the body constantly.

b) For the security of oneself and his/her dependents. When unable to discharge the duties for some reason or other, as far as possible one should try not to be dependent either on the family or society. It is also very important that the dependents do not get into difficulties. Ill health, injury, loss of job, retirements etc. come in this category.

c) To take care of the needs of the dependents and repay the debt to the elders in the family who supported our education when one departs from this world.

d) A portion to the society and especially the disabled therein.

e) Towards upkeep of temples, religious institutions etc. By these acts, every act becomes a worship of the divine, "Yajna" in the truest sense.

Eating the remnants of food: It means that we have the right to use only a portion of our wealth (sections "a, b and c" of the above paragraph) we earn and that too after fulfilling the commands in the sections "d and e" of the above classification.

We must learn to receive the benefits of all dedicated acts in life as "God's grace".

Offering the food to the Gods:

Who is the God we are expected to offer to?

Sections "d and e" in the above classification of sharing the wealth answer this. In this context we must learn to respect both the nature and the society (Nara yajna, Bhoota yajna). We owe a debt to both.

When we do not respect the "Pancha Maha Bhootas," It means, "the environment," sooner or later, we are going to experience the wrath of nature. We hear almost every day of one natural disaster or other where many lose their lives or get hurt. If one can honestly trace the root cause for any of these disasters, we will find that it reflects on the society's actions/inactions of the past. Therefore a portion of our wealth has to be for environmental protection also.

Apart from this, we must endeavor our best not to damage the environment we live in by remembering that our actions of now will reflect on the environment for the future.

The simple prayer for this is: "Sri Krishnarpanamastu." It means that "I offer all, to my beloved Lord Krishna."

Knowingly or unknowingly, we have committed actions that are contrary to the sastras either in this birth or in our previous births. By actions conducted according to the principles of "Karma Yoga" (according to the divine law and morality) we will be able to free ourselves of the results of wrong actions. One single dedicated act of one day cannot wash the sins of our past. Our entire life has to be a "Yajna." Hopefully, by His grace, either in this birth or in one of our future births we can be free of the sins of the past.

"But those who cook food to satisfy their own needs are sinners and verily eat sin."

Let us for a moment look at the damage to our system by eating the wrong foods. What we eat, how we eat and when we eat reflect on our health in future. The medical professions and dieticians also strongly advocate the importance of the right kind of food to one and all.

By not offering the wealth to the society and by being selfish, we are said to eat the sin. Here, eating the sin applies not to the physical body but to our mind." The thoughts generated in our mind as a consequence of wrong actions will have their own repercussions. The effect of eating "Sin" will reflect sooner or later either in this or in the future births.

So, if we want a better tomorrow for ourselves, our family, friends, and the society let us work and use the benefits of our work as per the principles of this Sloka.

One more explanation for Kilbisha:

The sastras direct every individual to perform yajnas every day. They are called as "Nitya karmas." (refer to Sloka 8, Nitya karmas) They are our daily obligatory duties. Any act contrary to it is considered to be a sin. Those who do not conduct the yajnas as directed are deemed to be selfish and are said to eat the sins of their selfish actions.

The verses 10-13 are considered to be the "Arthavada." Arthavada is explaining the reason for any action (artha) to those who argue and put questions like "what, why etc." to whatever action to be performed. It is like the mother/teacher trying to explain the reason for any work they want the child to do.

Arthavada is in four sections. (vada-debate)

Stuti: it means "praise." Trying to give all good points about the work is "stuti." Trying to give the benefits that one can accrue from the action is stuti. In Sloka 10, the word that refers to this aspect of the vada is "vo'stvistakamadhuk." Like Kamadhenu, the wish-fulfilling cow of plenty, you will get the benefit from the work.

Ninda: Pointing out the harmful results from the actions is "Ninda." "You will verily be eating sin" refers to this aspect of the vada.

Prakriti: "It is God's act, ordained in the sacred texts and hence you must do it" is "Prakriti." "Purovacha, Prajapatihi" refers to this aspect of the vada. (Prajapati, the creator said so and I am therefore saying that you should do this work.)

Purakalpa: you will receive the blessings of the respective devas is "Purakalpa." "The devas will bestow on you all your desires". Sloka 12 refers this aspect of the vada.

अन्नाद्भवन्ति भूतानि पर्जन्यादन्नसम्भवः ।
यज्ञाद्भवति पर्जन्यो यज्ञः कर्मसमुद्भवः ||14||

annād bhavanti bhūtāni parjanyād annasaṃbhavaḥ |
yajñād bhavati parjanyo yajñaḥ karmasamudbhavaḥ ||14||

From food, beings are born. Food is produced from rain. Rain comes from sacrifices. Sacrifice is born of action. ||14||

Annad: from food; bhavanti: born; bhootani: beings; parjanyaat: from rain; annasambhavaha: production of food; yajnaat: from yajna; bhavati: arises; parjanyaha: rain; yajnaha: sacrifices; karmasamudhbhavaha: born of action.

कर्म ब्रह्मोद्भवं विद्धि ब्रह्माक्षरसमुद्भवम् ।
तस्मात्सर्वगतं ब्रह्म नित्यं यज्ञे प्रतिष्ठितम् ||15||

karma brahmodbhavaṃ viddhi brahmākṣarasamudbhavam |
tasmāt sarvagataṃ brahma nityaṃ yajñe pratiṣṭhitam ||15||

Know that the actions arise from the Vedas. The Vedas are born from the imperishable Brahman. Therefore, know that the Supreme Being is established in Yajna. ||15||

Karma: action; brahmodhbhavam: arises/born from Brahman; viddhi: know; Brahma Akshara samudhbhavam:arises from the imperishable; tasmaat: therefore; sarvagatam: all pervading; nityam: ever; yajno: in sacrifice; pratishtitam: established.

We need to combine the two verses to understand the significance of the statements there in.

"From food, beings are born."

We are born of food and live on food. Without food we will perish. It is needed for survival and growth of life on earth.

Directly or indirectly, part of the food consumed by man gets converted into the sperm and that consumed by the woman gets converted into the ovum. The union of the sperm and the ovum results in the birth of the foetus. The foetus, nourished by the food consumed by the mother grows to become the baby. This is the meaning behind the sentence in this Sloka which says, "From food beings are born." The same law applies to the birth of all forms of life on earth.

Where does the food come from?

"The food comes from rain"; it is reiterated in the second quarter of the Sloka. The food comes from the soil in the earth. The presence of energy in the soil makes the earth fertile. It is further energized by the rains it receive season after season.

How is rain formed? What is the causal factor behind the production of rain?

The third quarter of the Sloka says: "Rain comes from sacrifice." On the face of it, it does not sound right. We need to analyse the statement in greater depth.

The year is divided into four seasons: spring, summer, autumn and winter. The rain fall is during the rainy season. When man respects nature and conducts actions correctly, the seasons follow in the right order and the rains come in due season. Of late, we have seen that the seasons do not stick to the right schedule and the rains are also not predictable. The experts have accepted that all these are because of lack of respect to the nature and the damage to the environment by our actions. Our actions have all become selfish and we do not care for what happens in other parts of the world by our actions. Individually and as society, we are all becoming more selfish.

If we change our ways, become less selfish, we will be indirectly worshipping the nature and the environment. The actions then are deemed to be in the spirit of "Sacrifice."

We can therefore say that the actions in the spirit of "Sacrifice" will result in the rains that are beneficial to life on earth. Shower of rains by correct actions from all of us individually and as corporate groups will fall on earth by the blessings of the "Higher Powers of Nature."

The "shower of rains" can be interpreted as:

Rains as such that fall at the right time and in right quantity and help in the growth of the crops and also supply the water for drinking for all forms of life.

Rains of "Blessings" from the Higher powers of Nature on us in return for our actions which strictly adhere to the principles of "Dharma" as enshrined in the sastras.

So, the statement "Rains come from sacrifice" is to be considered most appropriate.

"Sacrifice is born of action," says the last quarter of the Sloka. The results of present actions (also, results of actions conducted in the past), determine the future for all of us. The food we get from the earth as a result of the rainfall is therefore essential for new life to come on to this earth and survival of the life already existent on earth. Our individual or collective acts if conducted according to the spirit of righteousness become "Sacrifice." Hence the statement "Sacrifice is born of Action."

How then should we conduct our actions? There should be a guideline and precedent for the way we conduct our actions. Our ancestral seers have gifted us the invaluable treasure, "The Vedas." Our actions must therefore conform to the spirit of the Vedas.

The Vedas being vast and in a language alien to many of the Hindus have been shortened into "Upanisads." Again, the Upanisad language is foreign to many of us.

Lord Krishna, out of compassion to mankind has blessed us with the Srimad Bhagawadgita." It has given us the way to work in the spirit of selfless acts." This is the "Sacrifice in Action."

This is the meaning to understand from "Know that the action arises from the Vedas."

Let the Vedas be our guide to all our actions which have to be in the spirit of Sacrifice. Our actions therefore have to implement the summary of the Vedas. Where does the Vedas stem forth from?

The Vedas arise from the "Imperishable Brahman."

In the beginning, there was no world and no forms of life in the entire universe we know of and the universe beyond. The only entity, if we can say so, was the "Primordial Energy" with no form or qualities. This, our most learned ancestors in their search for origin of life called "Parabrahman."

Parabrahman decided to play a game of creation. This, the seers said was His "Leela." He created the four headed "Brahma" and commanded Him to undertake the task of "Creation."

Brahma after intense "Tapas" created the Vedas which were the precursor to life on earth. He received the gift of these Vedas from the "Imperishable Parabrahman" for His act of intense tapas towards fulfilling His role in the creation of life.

The Vedas contained the essence of "Dharma" and incorporated in them all the details of "Karma." They gave an enumeration of the righteous way of conducting actions for survival of life on earth.

"The Supreme Being is established in Yajna".

The Supreme Purusha, on His part, for having created the life on earth as part of His Leela, therefore has established Himself by His dedicated actions to all forms of life. Through the Vedas, He has given us all directions to work in this world created by Him.

Righteous acts of work performed according to the Vedic injunctions receive shower of blessings from the "Supreme." They become "Yajnas." Brahman is therefore said to reside in the Vedas. Incorporating the principal of the Vedas in our actions is equal to invoking the Brahman and hence the statement "Brahman is established in the Yajnas."

The experts say that what is given in these two slokas constitutes "Dharma Chakra." "Dharma Chakra" means "The wheel of righteousness." The wheel is made up of four sections: the movements along the four sections make it a complete cycle and that is "Dharma Chakra". The dharma is to maintain law and order and it is our duty to take up the Vedas and conduct actions according to dharma.

Brahma—Vedas—Karma—Yajna

Brahma: (The creator who is in constant action for the welfare of life on earth) gave us, the mankind,

The Vedas – Scriptural injunctions.

Karma: (The actions by men/women on earth which when conducted according to the Vedic injunctions would assist in establishing Loka Kalyana/universal welfare)

Yajna: (Dedicated actions.)

एवं प्रवर्तितं चक्रं नानुवर्तयतीह यः |
अघायुरिन्द्रियारामो मोघं पार्थ स जीवति ||16||

evaṃ pravartitaṃ cakraṃ nānuvartayatīha yaḥ |
aghāyur indriyārāmo moghaṃ pārtha sa jīvati ||16||

The man who does not follow the cycle thus set revolving, is a sinner, rejoicing in the senses. He lives in vain, O, Partha. ||16||

Evam: thus; pravartitam: set revolving; chakram: cycle; nanuvartayate: does not follow; iha: hear; yaha: who; aghayur: living in sin; indriyaramo: rejoicing in senses; moghaha: in vain; jeevati: lives.

Here, the Lord has taken the role of advisor/carer and giving the consequence of not following the sastras. The "Dharma Chakra" is to be considered as the "Wheel of Nature" and it is set up by the Lord for nursing, training, disciplining and elevating all beings from "Stone men to God-men" on earth.

In the cycle of "Brahma—Vedas—Karma—Yajna," we, the humans come in at the stage of "Karma and Yajna." The Lord, through Brahma has given us the Vedas ard Upanisads and now, the sacred text, Srimad Bhagawadgita. We have great spiritual masters who can guide us in understanding the sacred texts.

The Vedas are born of Brahman and we are also born of the same Brahman. By offering the fruits of the right actions according to the sacred texts, we are offering the Vedas and ourselves back to the Lord.

"O, Lord, you gave us the instructions for right actions and commanded us to follow the same. We are following those instructions and accordingly offering all the returns from our efforts including ourselves to you and Mother Nature. Please bless the life on this universe with health, happiness and prosperity", has to be the constant prayer to the Divine.

Who are the ones that do not follow the advice?

Those who are ignorant of the Divine.

Those who are immersed in actions only for their personal welfare and are detrimental to the welfare of others.

Let us remember that the Lord commanded us to follow the sastras. Whether knowingly or unknowingly we do not follow His command, either way, we are deemed to have committed a sin and have to face the consequences.

By acting contrary to the advice, in the long run, we will be harming ourselves and our family. Our inaction or wrong actions in a way will set an example for many more and in the course of time the society will come to harm. This is what is meant by the words, "He lives in vain."

"Such people are living in sin, (aghayu), rejoicing in senses, (indriyaramaha), says the Lord. We see many examples in our day to day life wherein we find that the society instead of making progress in the right direction has turned backwards.

Contrary to it, by living according to the injunction of the sastras, we can say that we rejoice in living in Godhood. We then are said to be "Atmaramaha."

He who is an "Antararama" will fulfil his life whereas the "Indriyarama" will destroy his life. "Indriyaramas" one can say have forgotten the God and in a way forgetting God itself is a sin. Forgetting His command is an additional sin. Thus one pays the price for both the sins.

So, let us all know our roles in the society and let the cycle of "Brahman, Vedas, Karma and Yajna," keep on running. The wheel of motion is set by the Lord Himself and let us not be obstacles in the path of the smooth running of the wheel. We will achieve the final union with the Brahman for our role in becoming instruments in fulfilling His desire: "Loka Kalyana." Let it be our solemn duty to keep the cycle constantly in motion and let us not be responsible for bringing it to a halt.

यस्त्वात्मरतिरेव स्यादात्मतृप्तश्च मानवः ।
आत्मन्येव च सन्तुष्टस्तस्य कार्यं न विद्यते ||17||

yas tv ātmaratir eva syād ātmatṛptaś ca mānavaḥ |
ātmany eva ca saṃtuṣṭas tasya kāryaṃ na vidyate ||17||

But the man who rejoices in Atman, who finds satisfaction in Atman, who is contented in Atman, has no work to perform. ||17||

Yah: who; tu: but; atma ratihi: rejoices in the Self; eva: only; syat: may be; atmatruptaha: satisfied in the Self; manavaha: the man; cha: and; atmanyeva: in the Self only; cha: and; santushtaha: contented; tasya: his; karyam: work to be done; na: not; vidyate: is.

After having spoken in detail about "karma" in the sense of "Duty to perform", The Lord has now taken up the topic of the "Liberated Soul" who has directly experienced the Supreme Self and is released from the operation of the "Law of Karma."

Such a realised sage is very hard to find indeed. For the majority of us Karma yoga is the inevitable law of action to perform. We should avoid the dangerous delusion of abandoning karma and taking up life of renunciation.

The realised sage is not deemed a sinner for not performing the actions. But, if he works, he does so for the benefit of mankind. There is no harm whether he works or does not work. Some scholars compare such a soul to a "Paramahamsa." Hamsa" is a mythical swan and is said to be gifted with the unique power of separating milk from water. The realised sage has mastered the art of separating the delusory world from the spiritual land he has come to live in. He is said to be "Atmarati, Atmatripta and Atmasantushta".

Atmarati: He rejoices in the Atman. All the manifold joys from the material world do not tempt him. He finds greater joy from the Atman within and understands that compared to the temporary joys from the material world the perfect joy of the Atman within is matchless.

He is satisfied with the inner joy and does not find any need to go in search of joy. He is therefore described as "Atmatripta." It means "Contented with the Atman."

Atmasantushta: Because of the above two qualities, his life is said to be an ocean of contentment.

In summary, such a Yogi is different from the rest of us. His last activity would have been to establish himself in the Atman, realising and overcoming the momentary happiness and sorrows of the material world. The quality of the Atman within is "Bliss" and the mind that is established in that would automatically be free from innumerable attractions and attachments to the world. Even if he is working, he has not got any trace of attachment to such work or its fruits.

नैव तस्य कृतेनार्थो नाकृतेनेह कश्चन ।
न चास्य सर्वभूतेषु कश्चिदर्थव्यपाश्रयः ||18||

naiva tasya kṛtenārtho nākṛteneha kaś cana |
na cāsya sarvabhūteṣu kaś cid arthavyapāśrayaḥ ||18||

For him, there is in this world, no interest whatsoever by work done or not done. He does not depend upon any being for any object. ||18||

Naiva: not even; tasya: of him; kritena: by action; arthaha: concern; na: not; akritena: non- performance of actions; iha: here; kaschana: any; na: not; asya: of this man; sarva: all; bhooteshu: beings; kashchit; any; artha vyapashrayaha: depending upon any object.

This is a continuation of the theme taken up in the last Sloka.

The majority would like to attain material benefits from work done and pray to the Lord to bless them with Moksha at the end. But the Liberated soul, who is in reality a Jivanmukta does not harbor either of these two desires.

He is a real Jnani and continues to work for the universal welfare wherever there is an opportunity to do so. He has no personal interest either in the work to be done or in the result of the actions performed. His actions will include imparting the knowledge of the sacred texts to those desirous to learn. Overall he sets an example for others to follow.

It is interesting to note that the Lord has not said that the Jnani should abandon work. He has not advised Arjuna to fight or not to fight.

We have the right to fulfil the purpose of human birth. The "right" is not in getting personal material gains but in being a useful member of the society and wishing for the welfare of one and all. Let us therefore learn the sacred text, listen to the masters and conduct actions accordingly.

तस्मादसक्तः सततं कार्यं कर्म समाचर |
असक्तो ह्याचरन्कर्म परमाप्नोति पूरुषः ||19||

tasmād asaktaḥ satataṃ kāryaṃ karma samācara |
asakto hy ācaran karma param āpnoti pūruṣaḥ ||19||

Therefore do the work that has to be done, do it always without attachment. For, by performing action without attachment, you will attain the Supreme. ||19||

Tasmat: therefore; asaktaha: without attachment; satatam: always: karyam: which should be done; karma: action; samacharaha: performance: asaktaha: without attachment; hi: because of; acharan: performing; karma: action; paramam: Supreme; apnoti: attains; poorushaha: the man.

If we skip the word "always" in this Sloka, it would read as:

"Therefore do the work that has to be done, do it without attachment. For by performing action without attachment, you will attain the Supreme."

One can see then that the Lord is advocating Arjuna to fight the righteous battle without actually commanding him to do so. "Forget about the relationship of those assembled here for the battle and do your duty of fighting for upholding righteousness and by this way you will attain Moksha" is the message for Arjunas of the world.

We can say that this is the nearest to a direct command Sri Krishna has given to Arjuna, to pick up the bow and discharge his duty.

As the word "satatam" (always) is included in the Sloka, the message is for the mankind in general.

One of the main prerequisites for Moksha is purity of mind.

The purity comes only in the absence of "Kama". Kama, (desire) is the hurdle towards keeping the mind pure. "Nishkama" (no desires) at all times is the sure means to attain the Supreme. This can be achieved only when there is no attachment to the work and results thereof. The sastras should be used as the authority to differentiate between what to do and what not to do.

Nitya and Naimittika karmas (duties) have to be conducted at all times.

Kamya karma (desire fulfilling actions) will have to be to the fulfillment of those desires that conform to the sastras.

Nishiddha karmas (forbidden actions) are actions prohibited by the sastras and cannot be undertaken at any time. (refer to Sloka 8, Chapter 3)

This is the secret of Karma Yoga.

Moksha, let us not forget is possible only by "total purity of the mind." Mind can only be purified by nishkama karma. This Chapter is all about "Karma" and the means to achieve Moksha through the path of karma. Whatever we do has to be that which pleases the Lord and He will automatically bless us with the due rewards. On our part, we should do so without expecting the benefits and this is "Nishkama Karma."

कर्मणैव हि संसिद्धिमास्थिता जनकादयः|
लोकसंग्रहमेवापि संपश्यन्कर्तुमर्हसि ||20||

karmaṇaiva hi saṃsiddhim āsthitā janakādayaḥ |
lokasaṃgraham evāpi saṃpaśyan kartum arhasi ||20||

King Janaka and others attained perfection by action only. Even with a view of protecting the masses you should perform actions. ||20||

Karmana: by actions; eva: only; hi: verily; samsiddhihi: perfection; asthitaha: attained; Janakadayaha: Jnanaka and others; loka sangraham: welfare of society; evam api: only then; sampasyan: having in view; kartum: to perform; arhasi: should.

King Janaka was a unique individual who was a Kshatriya by birth and considered to be a Brahmin by his power of knowledge. He was the father of Sita. He was noted for his just rule and piety. He showed by his actions that a pious Kshatriya is as fully qualified to perform sacrifices as a member of the priestly class. He was considered as a "Rajarshi" which means he was both a ruler (raja) and a priest (Rishi). It is said that he used to conduct regular discussions on the Vedas in his court and renowned rishis and scholars joined in the discussions. Many a number of rishis also came to learn the meaning of the sacred texts from him. He was a "Jivanmukta", a liberated soul while still living.

Despite the fact that he had mastered the Vedas, he did not disregard his duties as a king.

He protected his subjects with love and affection and at the same time propagated the Vedic teaching. Sita who was well known for her role as a dutiful wife to Lord Rama had learnt the Vedas and conduct of a married woman from her father. He could have renounced the kingdom and gone to the forest to live the life of a mendicant. But, he chose to rule the kingdom and continue to propagate the Vedas.

If all the learned ones decide not to work and pass the knowledge to others, there would not be any progress in the community and no scope for inventions that would benefit the community.

Krishna is reminding Arjuna about the role played by King Janaka who was also a Kshatriya like Arjuna. If Arjuna considered that king Janaka protected the masses, he should also be following the footsteps of that renowned king and protect the subjects. It could be possible only if he continued to be a Kshatriya and assisted his brother Yudhishtira in winning over adharma, propagating dharma and protecting the masses.

Note the word "you should perform actions", by Krishna. Krishna does not say "you must perform actions." It shows that the Lord wanted Arjuna to assimilate what was taught and make up his own mind on the action to take.

यद्यदाचरति श्रेष्ठस्तत्तदेवेतरो जनः ।
स यत्प्रमाणं कुरुते लोकस्तदनुवर्तते ||21||

yad yad ācarati śreṣṭhas tat tad evetaro janaḥ |
sa yat pramāṇaṃ kurute lokas tad anuvartate ||21||

Whatsoever a great man does, that other men do (imitate). Whatever he sets up as the standard, that, the world follows. ||21||

Yadyat: whatsoever; acharati: does; shreshtaha: the best (great); tad: that; eva: only; itaraha: others; janaha: people; sa: he; yat: what; pramanam: standard; kurute: does; lokas: the world; tad: that; anuvartate: follows.

One can say in general that children are copycats and that they tend to imitate what the elders do. The elders therefore have to be very careful in whatever they say or do. It is therefore the duty of the elders in any household to see that they set themselves a high standard of moral living.

The same rule applies to the learned elders in the society. Being eminent and great in virtues is a rare gift from the God. To justify one's actions, many a time we refer to the example of great men. Those who acquire leadership and have a prominent position in the society should therefore be very careful of their speech and actions. It is their social responsibility to the society.

There is an ancient saying, "Yatha Raja, tatha praja." It means, "As the king, so are the subjects." History shows that whenever there was a bad king, there was a band of his followers who followed the king's way of actions and there was anarchy in that kingdom. Arjuna had a duty to follow the rules of living as an eminent leader of a Kshatriya clan and not to corrupt the minds of people. If he took up to sanyasa there would have been a possibility of sowing the seeds of laziness in the minds of the masses.

The elders and the gifted men in any society have a duty to be beacons of that society. They should set a personal standard of life for others to follow. In the present day situation we are unfortunately seeing bad examples set by men in high position in political and sports fields. The younger generation are coming to accept it as the right way of living. It heralds a bleak future for tomorrow to come.

If the masses have to cultivate the faith in God and the law of the sastras, the masters in the spiritual field should set an example of righteous living by following the rules of "Atma Dharma."

In any household if the elders themselves do not know the sastras and do not follow the rules of the society, how can their children learn? What will the society be like when such children grow up and become the leaders of the community?

It is no use talking philosophy without following it in one's daily actions. Krishna is reminding Arjuna of his duty to implement the sastras which he had learnt in gurukula and from the elders in his family.

न मे पार्थास्ति कर्तव्यं त्रिषु लोकेषु किञ्चन ।
नानवाप्तमवाप्तव्यं वर्त एव च कर्मणि ||22||

na me pārthāsti kartavyaṃ triṣu lokeṣu kiṃ cana |
nānavāptam avāptavyaṃ varta eva ca karmaṇi ||22||

There is no duty for Me to do in the entire three worlds, O Partha. There is nothing unattained or to be attained for Me and yet I am also engaged in work. ||22||

Na: not; me': my; asti: is; kartavyam: to be done; trishu: three; lokeshu: worlds; kinchina: anything; na: not; anavaptam: unattained; avaptavyam: to be attained; varte: am; eva: also; cha: and; karmani: in action.

"I am also engaged in action."

Sri Krishna is pointing to His role in the battlefield. He was engaged in action as the charioteer for Arjuna and as the supporter and well-wisher of the Pandavas.

He could have easily destroyed the Kauravas using His divine weapon, "The Sudarshana Chakra" (the disc). He had already demonstrated the power of His chakra when He beheaded the wicked Shishupala during the Rajasuya Yaga conducted by Yudhishtira. Yet, He was engaged in action during the battle as the charioteer. He was (as the story of Mahabharata tells us), engaged in action all through His life.

As a child he had put an end to so many wicked demons and as a young boy had destroyed the wicked Kamsa.

We have to have faith in the fact that He, Lord Vishnu, incarnated as Krishna for the destruction of evil and protection of righteous. As Vishnu He is the master over the three worlds: The Bhooloka, Patala Loka and Swarga Loka (The earth, the netherworld and the heavens). He created the Nature and life on earth as His leela.

As he created the life, He has taken the role of protecting what He created. When He is the master over the three worlds, what else is to be gained by Him? There is really nothing unattained by Him or to be attained by Him. Everything in the three worlds really is His and only His.

Because He created the life, He also has undertaken the role of protector of what He created. He has, given the freedom for us to act and yet He is constantly abiding in each one of us as the Atman. As the Atman, He does not leave us till we attain Moksha.

On death, (we have discussed before), the Atman encased in the subtle body consisting of the mind and intellect, goes to the subtle world (Moola Prakriti) to be reborn again at the appropriate time decided by the Parabrahman.

Even though there is nothing unattained by Him or to be attained by Him, Krishna is constantly trying to protect what He created. He is trying to protect the righteous and the innocent on earth. He is constantly in action and at the same time not attached to actions and the results of actions.

He is setting an example for others to follow the path of Karma Yoga. We have to look at Him as the greatest Karma Yogi on earth.

Let us not forget that He has, through the medium of the Gita given us the Vedas in a format easy to understand and follow.

Let us realise the grace He has bestowed on mankind by giving the guide for right action. It is impossible to describe the role played by Him. His actions speak for themselves. To accept this we need to have sraddha/faith and bhakti/devotion in Him and His teaching.

यदि ह्यहं न वर्तेयं जातु कर्मण्यतन्द्रितः ।
मम वर्त्मानुवर्तन्ते मनुष्याः पार्थ सर्वशः ||23||

yadi hy ahaṃ na varteyaṃ jātu karmaṇy atandritaḥ |
mama vartmānuvartante manuṣyāḥ pārtha sarvaśaḥ ||23||

Surely, if I am not engaged in action relentlessly, without relaxation, men would follow My path in every way, O Arjuna. ||23||

Yadi: if; hy: surely; aham: I, na: not; varteyam: engaged in action; jaatu: ever; karmani: actions; atandritaha: relentlessly; mama: my: vartma: path; anuvartante: follow; manushyaha: men; sarvashaha: in every way.

Sri Krishna through the first half of the verse is confirming the fact that He is engaged in action relentlessly and without relaxation. This statement is in no way to be looked upon as boasting by the Lord about His relentless duty for the universe He created.

If Krishna did really relax for a while and did not engage in actions, there would certainly be quite a few who would use it to offer their own personal excuses for inaction in their lives. They would say, "After all, a great man like Krishna did not do it. There must be some reason for it. It will therefore not be wrong if we do not work also."

Let us admit that we are always good at giving excuses.

We cannot actually say as to how many would actually follow the good example set by great men. On the other hand, it is true when it comes to laziness, inactivity from actions, a momentary indiscretion by great men will remain in the memory of many.

Some people have a divine gift and become great. They have a great responsibility on their shoulders. They should guard themselves against anything they might/might not do or utter/do not utter which might have a bad influence on others.

On a day to day to basis, this law applies to the elders in any family. Excessive relaxation, laziness in actions by elders will leave an impression on the minds of children. It is easy for them to follow such negative actions of their elders.

One of the very important words in this Sloka is: "Atandritaha". It means "without relaxation." We, the sadhakas in spiritual path towards attaining Liberation, should follow this rule of continuous sadhana without relaxation. We should always be alert for the dangers of maya. We can easily be knocked off in our path by the worldly attachments that bring with them the dual enemies of happiness and sorrow (as a result of our desires and hatreds in relation to the world around us).

The sastras warn us by reminding of the truth: "Pramado vai mrityuhu" Which simply means, "Negligence is death."

Negligence/forgetfulness of the awareness of Brahman in the form of Atman within us is "death" says so, Sanatkumara.

उत्सीदेयुरिमे लोका न कुर्यां कर्म चेदहम् ।
सङ्करस्य च कर्ता स्यामुपहन्यामिमाः प्रजाः ||24||

utsīdeyur ime lokā na kuryāṃ karma ced aham |
saṃkarasya ca kartā syām upahanyām imāḥ prajāḥ ||24||

These worlds would perish if I did not perform action. I would be the author of confusion and would destroy these people. ||24||

Utsudeyuhu: would perish; ime: these; lokas: worlds; na: not; kuryam: would do; karma: actions; chet: if; aham: I; samkarasya: confusion of caste; karta; author; syam: would be; upahanyam: would destroy; imaha: these; Prajaha: people.

In continuation of the last verse, Sri Krishna is saying that if He stops work even for a second, the world would perish.

We can understand this if we substitute the word "Krishna" with "All-pervading Energy."

The Primordial Energy, in the form of "Subtle Energy" is pervading the entire world and is un-manifest. It gets converted into various forms of manifest energy that is essential for survival of life on earth. Why, earth, the entire cosmos would perish if there is no energy or there is some disturbance in its working even for a fraction of a second. If there is no manifestation of energy the world would perish and it is the truth we cannot contradict.

The experts all over the world agree that there is orderliness and precision in everything that is happening in our cosmos. The scientists tell us if there is even a minute fraction of change in the speed of revolution of the earth on its own sphere and around the orbit, it would cause unimaginable havoc.

Let us not forget that this movement of the earth is also due to the power of energy. There must be a power somewhere which we are unable to visualize that is silently working constantly and is maintaining the balance on the earth and in the cosmos. Our philosophy attributes it to the "Power of Parabrahman".

Sloka 16 of this chapter talks about the "Dharma chakra." The Lord said that He has set the wheel of righteousness in motion and we have to do our duty too and continue to keep the wheel in motion.

On an individual basis, if I, the elder in the family do not conduct the ordained duties, I would be the author of confusion in my family and my family would perish.

The worth of any man is noticed by the actions he undertakes in his society. What is the difference between the dead and the living?

The one who is living is recognized by his movements and activities.

The society all over the world has different ways of recognizing the righteous acts of welfare by individuals or groups.

On the other hand, the one who acts contrary to the sastras leaves a trail of bad memories behind him and the society would not like to remember his/her name. Sri Krishna, the Purushottama, the eldest of the family of all forms of life created, is telling us that if He did not perform the actions needed, the world He created would perish. The cosmic stability is the result of His karma and He is discharging it most efficiently.

We should understand that He values service to life on earth and He is living the life of constant righteousness.

We should, as the seekers of Truth, do what is most pleasing to our Lord. We are, after all, the representatives of God on earth, as we have been blessed with the physical body and a working intellect over our soul. We should discharge our duties as per the law of karma and make the world a beautiful garden.

Even now, amidst all the chaos and suffering, the world is still in some order and stability and this is due to the righteous actions of a lot of good people in it.

The impersonal attitude to work, "Karma Yoga" in the form of "work is worship" is the most pleasing service we can do to our master.

सक्ताः कर्मण्यविद्वांसो यथा कुर्वन्ति भारत ।
कुर्याद्विद्वांस्तथासक्तश्चिकीर्षुर्लोकसंग्रहम् ||25||

saktāḥ karmaṇy avidvāṃso yathā kurvanti bhārata |
kuryād vidvāṃs tathāsaktaś cikīrṣur lokasaṃgraham ||25||

As the ignorant men act from attachement to action, O Bharata, so, should the wise man act without attachment, wishing the welfare of the world. ||25||

Saktaha: attached; karmani: to action: avidwamso: ignorant; yatha: as; kurvanti: act; kuryad: should act; vidwams: the wise; tatha: so; asaktaha: without attachment; cikirsur: wishing; lokasangraha: universal welfare.

The mind, sense organs and the organs of action are the instruments in our hand. The instruments are the same for both the wise and the ignorant. How one makes use of these depends upon the evolvement of their intellect.

Both the wise and the ignorant work and conduct nitya and naimittika karmas. The wise on his part works without desire for the fruits of actions conducted while the ignorant works with desire for the fruits of action.

Both may work with full zeal. The wise has no sense of doership in his work.

The ignorant think that they are the doers of work and work for their own personal satisfaction.

Because of the attitude of work, the wise are said to be on the path of Liberation. On the other hand, the ignorant are on the path of self-destruction and get caught in the mesh of cycles of birth and death.

It is all because of the attitude to work. So let us use the great instruments of action we are blessed with and work for "Loka Sangraha" (universal welfare) and as a result become eligible for Liberation.

We should all be working, not for personal fulfillment of desires but with nobler thoughts of universal welfare.

The principle of work, the Lord repeatedly reminds Arjuna, is detachment in action.

न बुद्धिभेदं जनयेदज्ञानां कर्मसङ्गिनाम् |
जोषयेत्सर्वकर्माणि विद्वान् युक्तः समाचरन् ||26||

na buddhibhedaṃ janayed ajñānāṃ karmasaṅginām |
joṣayet sarvakarmāṇi vidvān yuktaḥ samācaran ||26||

The wise men should not disturb and confuse the minds of ignorant attached to action. They should perform all actions with yogic equanimity. They should make the ignorant do accordingly. ||26||

Na: not; buddhi bedham: unsettled mind; janayet: should produce; ajnanam: ignorant; karmasanginaam: attached to action; joshayet: should engage; sarva karmani: all actions; vidwan: the wise; yuktaha: balanced; samacharan: performing.

Continuing the theme of advising the wise, Krishna is indirectly hinting that the thought of sanyasa which had cropped in the mind of Arjuna was wrong. Arjuna wanted to run away from the battlefield and take up the life of a mendicant.

The Lord, the wisest among all, by giving us the sacred text, has acted as Jagadguru and He is to be considered as the best teacher in the world.

There are a lot of wise people in the world but most of the wise are not good teachers.

Teaching is a special art. A poor teacher not only fails in giving proper education to his students but might even confuse their minds.

Let not the wise take up the role of teachers and confuse the minds of ignorant is the sincere advice by the Lord.

Majority of people conduct actions but it is mostly an act of "sakama." Sakama is fulfillment of personal desires. They conduct many a rituals as prescribed by the sastras but do so with a prayer to the Lord to fulfill their desires.

The law of karma which advocates actions without the desire for the fruits thereof is very hard for a common man to understand and implement. This philosophy of action is too high for the majority. It is wrong to criticize such people. It gets them more confused. No one should take to life of inaction by abandoning all their attachments and responsibilities.

Between action and inaction, action is far superior. Tamasic life is inferior to rajasic life. In rajasic life there are examples to learn from both good and bad actions. In tamasic life there are no lessons to learn. Indolence makes one a living dead man. The lazy/tamasic man should be roused to ambitions and led to towards actions for pleasures and prosperity (rajasic). In course of further development he will mature to become Satvic.

Krishna wants Arjuna to set an example to the masses by discharging all his dharmic duties and not to run away from the war of righteousness.

Work with yogic equanimity is the advice to Arjuna. What does it mean?

"Yoga" is union of the ego with the "Atman" within and the union of the Atman with the Paramatman.

Equanimity is to conduct actions with a balanced mind which is not perturbed by success or failure. The actions have to be divine with no selfish motive behind and according to the law of karma.

One can say that as a good teacher, Krishna is actually patting the back of Arjuna. "You are a wise man and therefore work wisely" is the "Guhya bhasha" in this Sloka. Mahatma Gandhi set an example for the masses all over the world by not preaching them to learn Gita but showed Gita and the Law of Karma in his actions. That should be the duty and responsibility of the wise that are blessed with the capacity to understand the sastras.

प्रकृतेः क्रियमाणानि गुणैः कर्माणि सर्वशः ।
अहङ्कारविमूढात्मा कर्ताऽहमिति मन्यते ||27||

prakṛteḥ kriyamāṇāni guṇaiḥ karmāṇi sarvaśaḥ |
ahaṃkāravimūḍhātmā kartāham iti manyate ||27||

By the qualities of nature, all actions are performed, in all cases, but one whose mind is deluded by egotism, thinks, "I am the doer." ||27||

Prakriteh: by the qualities of nature; kriyamanani: are performed; guneih: by the qualities; karmani: actions; sarvashaha: all cases; ahamkara: egotism; vimoodatma: deluded mind; karta: doer; aham: I; iti: thus; manyate: thinks.

"By the qualities of nature": The Lord is referring to the three inherent gunas, "Satva, Rajas and Tamas."

We are truly "The Atman", the Vedas declare loudly and clearly. They say "Tat- Tvam-Asi," (Thou Art That.) This is "Tatva shuddhi buddhi", which is buddhi purified by the knowledge of the Atman.

According to this way of understanding, "The Nature" is with reference to our own physical body and the world around us.

As we associate ourselves with the physical body, we consider "The Nature" as the world around us. This is "Dehatma buddhi" which is a wrong understanding as a result of attachment to the physical body.

In this Sloka, the Lord, through His advice to Arjuna, is referring to the nature as the "Mind Intellect equipment" in us.

This will help us to understand clearly His statement, which is: "By the qualities of Nature, all actions are performed."

We have referred to these already as "The Vasanas."

All our actions are the result of the stored imprints in our mind. These have been brought forward from our past, including past births.

Every good/bad thought or impulse is a seed we sow in our subconscious mind which forms into the imprint, Vasana.

When nurtured, vasanas grow into actions. Every act we perform has its rebound effect which we may experience immediately or at a later date and time.

Because of our past actions, we are moulded into the three gunas which are our inherent nature.

We act and react to situations and it becomes our nature.

Without our knowledge, we are drawn into the situation wherein we develop the sense that "we are the doers of actions." As we grow, this feeling matures and we develop "The Ego." It is "The Ahamkara" or "Pride" which takes us into downward path in our spiritual journey.

The second half of the Sloka refers to this "Pride" in Arjuna.

Arjuna, drawn by the powerful Kshatriya vasanas in his subconscious mind has developed a strong sense of "Ahamkara." He has expressed to his master that it would be wrong on his part to kill the respected elders and Gurus in the opposite camp and also be responsible for the death of so many soldiers on both the sides. But, Arjuna was not an ordinary person. He had learnt the Vedas in the Gurukula and Krishna was his companion/mentor in life.

He was supposed to be a wise man.

The duty of the wise man is to analyse his thoughts before they are converted into actions.

Arjuna had to realize that it was a war of righteousness, approved by Sri Krishna and he himself was just an instrument of Lord's leela.

Krishna does not want Arjuna to be deluded by "Ahamkara" but to conduct the duties for the protection of dharma and leave the result to God.

तत्त्ववित्तु महाबाहो गुणकर्मविभागयोः ।
गुणा गुणेषु वर्तन्त इति मत्वा न सज्जते ||28||

tattvavit tu mahābāho guṇakarmavibhāgayoḥ |
guṇā guṇeṣu vartanta iti matvā na sajjate ||28||

But, he, who knows the Truth, understands the divisions of qualities and functions, O mighty armed Arjuna. He knows that the gunas function through the senses amidst sense objects and are not affected by them. Thus knowing, he remains unattached. ||28||

Tatvavit: the knower of Truth; tu: but; mahabaho: mighty armed; guna karma vibhagayoho: division of qualities and functions; guna guneshu: the qualities (senses) amidst the qualities (of objects); vartante: remain; iti: thus; matva: knowing; na: not; sajjate: attached.

Tatvavit: The knower of the Truth. What does Tatvavit know?

Tatvavit knows the difference between the "Seer and the Seen". He knows who the real "Seer" is. He associates himself with the Atman and considers that the physical body and the world around form the "Nature" and are clouded by the qualities of the Nature in the form of the three gunas.

Ignorant is he who does not know this truth. Majority of us are ignorant and in this instance, Arjuna is also ignorant.

Krishna is trying to boost Arjuna's morale by addressing him as "Mahabaho." "Mahabaho" means "mighty armed." Arjuna by his prowess in the art of battle was referred to as "Mahabaho" by those well versed in the art of warfare.

Krishna is referring to Arjuna as a "Mahabaho" but with a totally different meaning attached to it. It is the "Guhya bhasha" in this Sloka. (The word with a secret meaning)

"Mahabaho" is not in comparison to his physical prowess but to his wisdom.

Use your wisdom and fight the ignorance by knowing the divisions of qualities and functions of Nature is Lord's message to Arjuna.

Guna Karma Vibhagayoho: The divisions of qualities and functions of Nature.

Guna vibhaga is division of the gunas. This is the division of the gunas into "Satva, Rajas and Tamas."

Karma vibhaga: The division of functions. We need to understand this statement. At any one time, one of the three gunas predominate and the actions bring out that particular guna into focus.

In the same context, any one individual by the aggregate of the gunas in him, will show the actions that will put him in one of the following four categories:

Brahmana
Kshatriya
Vysya
Sudra.

Arjuna belonged to the Kshatriya clan and his duty was to fight and protect the masses.

Gunas are inherent in the form of "Vasanas" in every individual, including the "Tatvavit." He knows the principal of any action and remains as a witness to all actions by developing the "Atma Buddhi" (knowledge of the Atman).

He understands:

That the gunas are abiding in the mind/intellect equipment,

The jnanendriyas (sense –organs) bring in the impulses of the outer world to the mind,

The mind makes use of the appropriate karmendriyas (organs of action) to take actions as needed concerning the sense objects,

The sense objects are any of the manifold objects animate/ inanimate in the vast world around.

The wise man is not affected by the impulses received from the objective world and remains constantly in a state of "Detachment." He remains uncontaminated by anything physical or material.

Sri Krishna is instructing Arjuna to fight as a Kshatriya and uphold dharma but without the attachment to the results of his action. The "Tatvavit" conducts all his actions with this understanding, is what He says.

Remain as the "Seer" and not be involved with the "Seen" is what we have to understand from this sloka if we want to walk in the spiritual path.

प्रकृतेर्गुणसम्मूढाः सज्जन्ते गुणकर्मसु ।
तानकृत्स्नविदो मन्दान्कृत्स्नविन्न विचालयेत् ||29||

prakṛter guṇasaṃmūḍhāḥ sajjante guṇakarmasu |
tān akṛtsnavido mandān kṛtsnavin na vicālayet ||29||

The man of knowledge should not confuse the minds of those men of imperfect understanding, who, deluded by the gunas of nature, are attached to actions in the material world. ||29||

Prakrutair: of nature; guna: qualities; sammoodaha: deluded; sanjante: are attached; guna karmasu: in the functions of the qualities; tan: those; akritsnavado: of imperfect understanding; mandaan: the deluded; kritsnavat: man of perfect knowledge; na: not; vichalayet: unsettle.

This Sloka is a reiteration of the Sloka 26 in this chapter by the Lord. It is directed to the so called men of knowledge about their role in guiding the ignorant.

Why is the Lord repeating the same message again and again?

We come across in the 701 verses of the Gita many instances where the same message is brought out through different slokas.

One may ask, "why?"

We can understand this by looking at the painting of a picture by an artist. The artist gets an idea and wants to project the same in the minds of the public. He takes up his brush and draws a picture on the canvas.

He then steps back and looks at it from different angles. He goes back and makes a few changes and inspects his work again.

He does so till he is satisfied that he has given the message to the public.

Similarly, Sri Krishna is bringing out the same message in different slokas so that we can get the message well and clear.

The way we understand depends on the plane we are looking from. It depends on the identity of our true self.

The entire Gita and our sastras are to drill into us the "Eternal truth" that we are really "The Atman" and the physical body is like a suit on the Atman.

Those who have realised this and show it in their relation to the material world are "Kritsnavid", (Men of knowledge)

Majority of us associate ourselves with the physical body and the Lord says we are, "Akritsnavid" (of imperfect understanding,) and "Mandaan." (dull witted) We are dull witted because we do not see the truth as such and get attached to the function of the gunas inherent in our mind/intellect equipment.

Generally it is the duty of the learned to teach the ignorant. The teacher is he who knows the art of explaining to the ignorant what is not known or understood.

Unfortunately, not all learned can profess to be teachers. To be a teacher is a special art.

The Lord is "Jagadguru", the teacher for the entire Jagat. He knows how to teach us all.

There are two ways to teach anything:

First method is to know how to be a teacher and then teach.

The second method is to set an example by one's own actions.

The learned are therefore asked by the Lord not to confuse the ignorant by high flown language about the Vedas and Upanisads. He wants the learned to show the true meaning of the sastras by their own actions and thereby set an example for others to follow.

The learned should not advocate abandoning one's duties to the family and society. The learned should help the ignorant to develop sraddha and bhakti in the Lord and give them the necessary knowledge. Like a seed maturing to become a full grown tree, every individual has the opportunity to mature into a learned man but it takes several cycles of births and deaths to achieve the end result.

Saint Purandara Dasa, a great South Indian poet, composer and scholar says in one of his compositions:

"Do not teach Brahma Vidya just because one asked for it. "

To receive the same, the recipient should have the maturity of mind.

मयि सर्वाणि कर्माणि संन्यस्याध्यात्मचेतसा।
निराशीर्निर्ममो भूत्वा युध्यस्व विगतज्वरः ||30||

mayi sarvāṇi karmāṇi saṃnyasyādhyātmacetasā |
nirāśīr nirmamo bhūtvā yudhyasva vigatajvaraḥ ||30||

Surrendering all actions in Me, with the mind fixed in the Self, free from hope and egotism, fight without fever. ||30||

Mayi: in Me; sarvani: all; karmani: actions; sanyasya: surrendering, renouncing; adhyatma chetasa: with the mind fixed on the Self; nirasheer: free from hope; nirmamo: no egotism; bhootva: having become; yudhyasva: fight; vigata jwaraha: without fever.

We are given the path to follow by a sincere spiritual aspirant. The minds of people can broadly be divided into:

Troubled minds and Peaceful minds.

Both are engaged in actions.

The Lord has used the words "hope and ego". Let us look at these two words. "Hope" is for something that is going to come later on. It is for the "future." "Ego" is expression of pride in what is being done/carried out in the "present".

Those who live in hope of the results to come for the work (and planning on the ways of enjoying what is going to come), so confident of themselves of the results to come and express ego are said to be fighting (working) with feverish passion. These are the actions of those with a rajasic temperament.

A true and sincere worker is he who conducts actions without desire for the fruits of actions and is ready to surrender the fruits of actions to the divine. They do not show any sense of ego in what is being done (because they are only agents working for the Lord) and do not live in hope of enjoying the results to come. These are of peaceful mind and there is no feverish passion in their work.

These were rajasic people who have now climbed one step further in their spiritual journey to Satva.

Krishna is asking Arjuna to climb up the spiritual ladder and move from "rajas to Satva" (passion to purity). Arjuna is indirectly asked to fight the war of righteousness and not surrender the kingdom to Kauravas.

This is the nearest Krishna has gone in asking Arjuna to fight. He never commanded Arjuna to fight but is making him realize what his duty is.

We should be able to recognize the symptoms of mental fever and approach the Guru/master for help.

Fight without fever: Arjuna was fighting a righteous war for his brother. He confessed to Krishna his mental state on facing the respected elders on the battlefield. All the symptoms expressed in chapter 1 by Arjuna point to the mental agitations which is an expression of "mental fever."

To get the best out of his Kshatriya potential, Arjuna was asked to fight without the mental agitations, concerning consequences of the war.

Just as one tosses around not knowing what to do when he/she has fever, he whose mind is full of agitations does not know what to do. With proper guidance he should learn to control them, keep the mind calm and take up the ordained duties. For this he needed purity at the levels of his mind, speech and actions which is "Trikarana shuddhi".

Purity of actions: All actions conducted according to the spirit of "Dharma" and surrendering the fruits of the actions at the feet of the Lord is purity of actions.

Arjuna, by deciding to drop his bow and arrows was not expressing purity.

Mind fixed on the Self: one should learn the art of fixing the vision of the God on his/her mind at all times. He/she should not forget that "Atman" is the real "I" and the physical body including the mind is the servant of the "Atman." Purification of the mind is in removing the sense of ego in all the actions performed.

While working as the servant of the Atman, the mind should assert authority over the sense organs and organs of action. We all have a duty to listen to the voice of Antaratma coming from within. It is not wrong to say that we are all guilty of not listening to our Atman before the conduct of any actions.

Arjuna was a renowned warrior, a specialist in using bow and arrow. He knew the art of concentrating on the target and directing the arrow towards the target.

In the present situation, he had to make use of his special art and concentrate his mind on the duty ahead, of protecting dharma. He should concentrate on the task of "Upholding righteousness".

Arjuna showed ignorance about the sastras.

The result of the war would come at the proper time but he had to fulfill the duty as a strong supporting warrior to his brother. There should not be any feeling of either victory or defeat once the decision to fight and enter the battlefield had been taken. There should not be a hope of victory only the simple task of making use of his knowledge in archery. In this instance he had the privilege of listening to the art of conducting the ordained duty by the Lord Himself.

Thinking that he would have done a better job by withdrawing from the battlefield and letting Duryodhana rule shows an element of ego too.

This law applies to all of our actions.

Once having taken the decision to work and got the mind in the mood for work, the concentration should be only on the work and nothing else. There should not be any agitations concerning anything else including the results of actions.

As Swami Vivekananda says: Cause and effect of action:

When there is a cause, the effect will materialize sooner or later.

The effect for which we are working for (future) brings the cause (present) into focus. For this the mind should be focused on the cause (present) only and nothing else (not on future).

Victory over passions like "I", "Mine" in one's battle of life (which disturbs the present action) is true victory.

This is the true spirit of "Karma Yoga."

ये मे मतमिदं नित्यमनुतिष्ठन्ति मानवाः |
श्रद्धावन्तोऽनसूयन्तो मुच्यन्ते तेऽपि कर्मभिः ||31||

ye me matam idaṃ nityam anutiṣṭhanti mānavāḥ |
śraddhāvanto nasūyanto mucyante te pi karmabhiḥ ||31||

Those men who constantly practice, this, My teaching, with faith and free from ill will, are also freed from actions. ||31||

Ye: those; matam: teaching, Me': my; idam: this; nityam: constantly; anutishtanti: practice; manavaha: men; sraddhavantaha: full of faith; anasuyanto: free from ill will; munchyante: freed; te': they; api: also; karmabhihi: from actions.

Those men: it applies to one and all. It is in the spirit of "universal message to all."

Matam Idam: This, My teaching. The Lord is referring to "The Bhagawadgita," His, teaching. It is universal and not the property of any one group of men/religion.

Nityam anutishtanti: Practices constantly. Emphasis is laid on constant practice. Karma Yoga is union with Parabrahman following the path of Karma. Each one of us has varied duties in any set 24hrs of the day. Each of those duties should be conducted in the spirit of "Nishkama Karma and Karma Phala Tyaga." "Anutishtanti" means "puts into practice totally".

Sraddhavaan: with Faith.

What is "Faith"?

Faith is firm belief in the Lord, His teaching on "Dharma and Satya", The Guru who guides the path, the Scriptures and one's own self. Faith helps us to get around the daily routine of programs which are beneficial for our own body, for nature and for society, which includes one's own family and friends. This has to be "Satvic" or "Pure Faith."

Free from ill-will: Animosity/enmity to others is one of the great dangers that can befall on any human being. Ill will comes from deep sense of attachment to oneself, one's possessions and to one's own family and friends. It breeds hatred and in turn results in injury to oneself and others also. Strong sense of "I or Ahamkara" will breed the feeling of ill-will towards others.

Free from bondage: The final destination for the spiritual seeker is "Liberation." Freeing oneself from the attachments in one's life and at the same time following the principles of "Karma Yoga" the aspirant is free to enter the realms of "Moksha."

Repeatedly reading the sacred text "The Bhagawadgita", listening to the experts and reading the explanatory texts available, in course of time, will make the subject easy to grasp. As we continue to study the text repeatedly, we tend to get a clearer and clearer understanding of its essence.

Faith and absence of ill-will are the two requisites to succeed in understanding the philosophy and to attain the goal of life.

ये त्वेतदभ्यसूयन्तो नानुतिष्ठन्ति मे मतम् ।
सर्वज्ञानविमूढांस्तान्विद्धि नष्टानचेतसः ||32||

ye tv etad abhyasūyanto nānutiṣṭhanti me matam |
sarvajñānavimūḍhāṃs tān viddhi naṣṭān acetasaḥ ||32||

But those who carp at my teachings and do not practice, know them as men deluded of knowledge, devoid of discrimination and doomed for destruction. ||32||

Ye: those; tu: but; etad: this (tu+atad: tvetad); abhyasuyanto: carping at; anutishtanto: practice; na: not; me': my; matam: teachings; sarvajnana vimoodhan: deluded of all knowledge; tan: them; viddhi: know; nashtan: ruined; achetasaan: devoid of discrimination.

Let us be clear that the Lord is not talking/boasting of "Krishna philosophy". He has said so many times that what he is saying is only a summary of the Vedas and Upanisads and not a separate philosophy. The Vedas are the most ancient texts (approved and tested) that guide us to action for the welfare of life on earth by following the path of "Truth and Righteousness". It is His strong conviction that the path advocated by the sacred texts is for progress of the individual and the society. Those who do not do so are said to be "doomed for destruction."

The Lord points at two defects that are responsible for the downfall of man in his spiritual path. The spiritual path is in elevating oneself from the state of "Stone man to that of God man on earth."

It is indeed a blessing and good fortune to be born as human. For what good that has been done in the past we are blessed to be born as humans with the intellectual capacity of reasoning. It is the birth right of every individual to make use of this precious birth, progress in the spiritual path and achieve the end goal: Moksha.

To do so one should be able to learn, understand and practice the philosophy incorporated in the sacred texts with sraddha and bhakti. The Bhagawadgita is the summary of the sacred texts given to mankind by the Lord Himself.

Those who criticize His teaching and who do not practice what is taught by the Lord are to be considered as deluded. What is learnt has to be put into practice. It is no use by knowing all the Vedas if one does not understand the same and put them into practice. The learned who do not practice what is learnt are not truly learned. They are also deluded, the Lord says.

He warns that they are doomed for destruction because they are devoid of discrimination between "Eternal and Non-eternal and between Truth and un-truth." They are deluded by the worldly pleasures and laurels they receive for their knowledge.

This takes them down from the plane of man-man on earth to stone man on earth. They have to go through many more series of births and deaths in the cycle of samsara.

सदृशं चेष्टते स्वस्याः प्रकृतेर्ज्ञानवानपि ।
प्रकृतिं यान्ति भूतानि निग्रहः किं करिष्यति ||33||

sadṛśaṃ ceṣṭate svasyāḥ prakṛter jñānavān api |
prakṛtiṃ yānti bhūtāni nigrahaḥ kiṃ kariṣyati ||33||

Even a Jnani acts according to his own nature. Beings will follow nature, what can restraint do? ||33||

Sadrushan: in accordance; chestate: acts; swasyaha: of his own; prakrute: of nature; jnanavan: wise man; api: even; prakrutim: to nature; yanti: follow; bhutani: of beings; nigrahaha: restraint; kim: what; karishyati: will do.

For a clearer understanding of this Sloka it is advisable to read it in conjunction with the next few slokas that follow.

The Lord is emphasizing the power of the tendencies that each one of us is born with. By saying "what can restraint do" he is not trying to discourage the practice of self- restraint. Self-restraint is needed but only on clearer understanding/knowledge of the scriptures. Restraint has to be a slow and steady process.

Let us understand the two words "Jnani and Nature" in this Sloka.

A Jnani is a man of knowledge. Even a man of knowledge has to go through life and experience the result of actions conducted according to his understanding of what he has learnt.

We get theoretical knowledge and get the degree of choice. Even though we do get some practical lessons to get the degree, it is not the same as the practice we take up when we start work. We learn by the results we receive as a result of actions conducted.

In this sense, the Jnani referred to in this Sloka is a man who has learnt the sastras but has only a theoretical knowledge of the same. Mere learning the sastras is not enough. One needs to put it into practice in day to day life. Wisdom, on the other hand comes by experiencing the results of actions. A Jnani in this sense is a man of knowledge but still immature.

We need to recollect the meaning of the word "Nature" referred to in this Sloka.

As we have studied before, each one of us is a combination of two: "Purusha and Prakriti."

Purusha is the divinity/Atman (the subtle energy) within. It is un-manifest but brings the physical body (Prakriti) to life when it comes into contact with the same.

Like Purusha, Prakriti is also un-manifest and comprises of all the Gunas or samskaras (thought imprints from the previous life carried through the subtle body at the time of death) from previous births. It comes to life when it comes into contact with the Purusha.

The Nature referred to in this Sloka is the "samskaras" from the past births in the form of the un-manifest gunas. These have a great influence on our life. Our lives really revolve round the thought imprints of our mind. Every strong thought imprint gets its manifestation sooner or later in our present or future births.

The second half of this sloka:

"Beings will follow nature, what can restraint do?" has to be understood in this context.

We, the ordinary mortals still in the process of intellectual evolution will succumb to our own past unfulfilled desires and hatreds. We are bound to our family, friends and possessions. Attachments rule our lives.

Slow sublimation of their nature (of the ignorant) is the greatest service to mankind the jnanis of the world can give, is one way of interpreting this Sloka.

We can understand this statement by two examples:

The children by nature act on impulse. Every day they do lot of mistakes. It takes a few years for the parents to correct the children and takes several more years for the teachers to put them on the right path. Restraining the children slowly and steadily is the rule to follow in bringing up the children.

A charioteer has to control the horses but does not use the force. Using the reins, he will slowly and steadily control the running of the horses and see that he carries the passengers to the destination safely.

"Restrain by force is more harmful and can be dangerous and the men of knowledge should remember the same is the Lord's advice," is another way of interpreting this Sloka.

Another interpretation of this Sloka:

Jnani refers to a learned man who intellectually understands the principles of religion and philosophy. He has yet to realize "The Truth." A mere intellectual understanding of the scriptures leaves one powerless to control the powerful natural instincts the individual is born with. Even a Jnani will act according to his nature. The Sloka is to remind the Jnani to think before acting and act only according to the scriptures.

"If this is so, how difficult for the ordinary men and women to restrain the instincts is Lord's message to mankind", is yet another interpretation of this Sloka.

If we continue with the next few slokas we will find that the Lord is actually advocating self-restraint as the means for Liberation. Let us not misunderstand this Sloka and be under the false impression that we should not restrain our thoughts and actions.

"What can restraint do?"---it can be both beneficial and harmful. Knowledge or jnana is the means to develop the art of slow and steady restraint. The next chapter to follow is "Jnana Yoga" and it gives us the means to learn the art of self- restraint.

इन्द्रियस्येन्द्रियस्यार्थे रागद्वेषौ व्यवस्थितौ ।
तयोर्न वशमागच्छेत्तौ ह्यस्य परिपन्थिनौ ||34||

indriyasyendriyasyārthe rāgadveṣau vyavasthitau |
tayor na vaśam āgacchet tau hy asya paripanthinau ||34||

In each of the senses abide attraction and repulsion for the object of the senses. One should not come under their sway, for they are man's enemies. ||34||

Indriyasya: in the senses; indriyasyarthe: in the object of the senses; raga: attraction; dwesha: repulsion; vyavasthitou: abides; tayo: of these; na: not; vashamagachet: should come under; tau: these two; hyasya: verily his; paripanthinou: foes.

In the chariot of life, the spiritual seeker is fighting his way through the battlefield of life (Refer to introduction on Gitopadesham).

When we let the intellect come to the forefront in the decisions we take, it is like leading Krishna in front and letting Him be the master over us.

When we let the mind come to the forefront and not take notice of the intellect, it is like letting our ego be the master in our lives.

Raga is when the impulses are pleasing and dwesha when one feels hatred.

These two are some of the reactions that result when the sense organs bring in impulses from the objective world. It is of course the mind that makes this decision of likes and dislikes.

The same object which is pleasing to one may be displeasing to another.

In the same individual, the same object that is pleasing at one time may bring displeasure at a different time.

The mind depending upon raga or dwesha makes use of the organs of action to get the object or to run away from the object or go to the extent of even killing the object. As humans we are supposed to let the intellect guide us in taking the right decisions that benefit us in the spiritual path and benefit the society.

There are four different ways of reacting to the impulses from the world around as brought in by the sense organs.

One can totally close the sense organs and stop totally the impulses entering the mind. By doing so, the common man is not going to survive in the world. After all we have our obligatory duties to the world around. By blocking all the impulses, we are said to be "Tamasic" in our reaction to the world around (Stone man).

One can let the mind/ego decide on the action to take and not make use of the capacity of reasoning. We are then said to be "Rajasic." (Animal man)

We can use the intellectual capacity of reasoning and conduct actions that do not harm the world around. This is "Satvic" reaction. (Man man)

We can use the intellectual capacity of reasoning with the "Antaratma" or "Soul" guiding us, the resulting actions will then become "Divine." (God man)

This is the process of human evolution or decline in the so called journey of life depending on whether we move up or go down this ladder.

As we have discussed before:

"The God Man—The Man Man—the Animal Man—The Stone Man" is about decline of the man. It is spiritual downfall.

The human personality, the Lord is saying, by controlling the raga and dwesha, he can ascend to the divine man from the stage of stone man.

Let our goal in this birth therefore be to mature from subhuman personality to human and from human to that of the divine. Let the senses not become the stumbling blocks in our path. It is in this context the Lord says, "The senses are man's enemies." We need to make the same senses our friends by making use of the Buddhi guided by the Lord within.

The Gita and the scriptures are to change our attitude to life from the base to the noble.

We should refer back to the qualities of "Sthitaprajna", slokas 55-72, chapter 2 to understand this philosophy better.

श्रेयान्स्वधर्मो विगुणः परधर्मात्स्वनुष्ठितात् ।
स्वधर्मे निधनं श्रेयः परधर्मो भयावहः ||35||

śreyān svadharmo viguṇaḥ paradharmāt svanuṣṭhitāt |
svadharme nidhanaṃ śreyaḥ paradharmo bhayāvahaḥ ||35||

Ones own dharma, though devoid of merit, is better than the dharma of another even if well discharged. Better is death in one's own dharma, the dharma of another is fraught with fear. ||35||

Sreyan: better; swadharmaha: one's own duty; vigunaha: devoid of merit; paradharmaat: than the duty of another; swanushtitat: than well discharged; swadharme: in one's own duty; nidhanam: death; sreyaha: better; paradharmaha: another's duty; bhayavahaha: fraught with fear.

In this context, the word "Dharma" has to be understood as "Righteous Action." "Swadharma" is "One's own duty" and "Paradharma" is the duty of others.

Arjuna was trained to act as a warrior. He was a Kshatriya by birth and trained to fight. He was considered to be a great and well respected warrior. In the present situation, he was in the process of discharging his own duty, fighting for his brother and upholding the dharma.

But, he developed a deep rooted fear that his actions were unjust and he should not be fighting some of the well-respected elders in the opposite camp even though they were on the side of "Adharma." He was prepared to surrender the kingdom to his cousin Duryodhana and be willing to live the life of a mendicant.

Even though his intentions of living the life of a mendicant were honorable, he was not ready to enter into the next stage in his life.

To understand this we should briefly look at the "Ashrama Dharmas" according to the Hindu tradition. Ashrama dharma is duties at the four main stages in life. These are:

Brahmacharya - Grihastha - Vanaprastha - Samnyasa.

Arjuna had completed his Brahmacharya ashrama duties by undertaking the prescribed studies. He had entered into Grihastha ashrama. His chosen profession was that of a "Kshatriya." He had matured into a great warrior during the period and was at the peak of Grihastashrama life. He had several more years to fulfill the duties as a warrior and then take up retirement.

It was in order during that period for a retired grihastha to go to the forest and learn to live the life of a mendicant. This would have been the "Vanaprastha" duties. After many years of such duties he would have developed the mental stamina to live the life of a sanyasi and strive for "Moksha."

At this period of the great battle, his swadharma was "Kshatriya dharma" and paradharma was "Vanaprastha" dharma.

Switching over his ashrama dharma and jumping prematurely into the next stage of life would have resulted in the following scenarios.

Duryodhana, the personification of adharma would have become the ruler and the citizens of Hastinapura would have suffered as a consequence. On his part, Arjuna for having absconded from his duty would be considered as having fallen from the spiritual path of progress towards moksha and face the consequences of his sinful action. Instead of heaven, the place for a dutiful warrior, he would have entered hell.

On entering into the forest to live the life of retirement, his body and mind would not have been prepared to such life. His mind would be longing for pleasures of life and his body not prepared to live on roots and vegetables. On encountering those who would have been living in the forest at that time, without his knowledge, he would start working for their welfare as a Kshatriya.

Thus we can see that the vanaprastha dharma he wanted to embrace was fraught with fear. It would have been preferable to fight for dharma and face death in the battlefield rather than abandoning the war.

There is a lot more to study and understand in this Sloka. For those who want an in-depth analysis, here is a detailed explanation.

"Swadharma" is one's own duty. To do so, one must have an answer to the question, "Who am I?" As we have studied so far, each one of us is really the "Atman" within and the physical body is not the real "I". The duty would be therefore that of "divinity" which is the nature of the Atman . The duty of the divine is "Welfare of all."

Swadharma is our actions as humans on earth. It is to use the physical body as the eternal servant of the divine and fulfill the role of expressing the divine. Our swadharma is the law of the Self and is for Self- realization. Fasting, penances, conduct of vratas, and practice of prescribed studies and duties are the swadharma pertaining to Atma dharma.

Thinking that these are futile, that I am not making any progress and abandoning such practices is paradharma. Vacillation or a wavering mind takes the seeker away from sadhana and the knowledge of the Gita helps the seeker to overcome this weakness.

"Paradharma" is duty foreign to one's nature. Actions pertaining to the identification with the physical body and forgetting the divinity within becomes paradharma. Having forgotten that we are the servants of the Atman within and instead of working for the welfare of all, working to fulfill one's own pleasures of life becomes an alien dharma.

Paradharma is the law of the objective world and is for the pleasures of the pluralistic world.

Swadharma would ultimately lead to attainment of Moksha. It is difficult to practice but not impossible.

Paradharma would lead to many more births and re-births into this world and as a consequence having to face the pains and pleasures of life. It is not difficult to practice but it takes us away from the ultimate goal of life which is "Purushartha of attaining Moksha." It is fraught with dangers.

Dharma according to the "Varnashrama". It is the duties pertaining to the four castes, the system evolved in the Hindu tradition. Brahmana, Kshatriya, Vysya and Sudra are the four main castes for the Hindus.

Each of the four castes has specific duties pertaining to that caste.

On that basis, swadharma is duties pertaining to the caste one belongs to and paradharma are conduct of duties pertaining to other castes.

Instead of "caste system" we can use the word "professional duties" which is the present way of the world. The professional duties vary from individual to individual. There are a number of professions and each individual has to take up certain duties and earn a living.

To be eligible to work in any profession one needs a basic training and understanding of the work involved. The learning period is known as the period of education. Usually, it is allocated to the early part of one's life and one expects to complete the basic education between the ages of 16-25yrs.

We all know that it is easy to train the mind of a child when compared to the mind of an adult. Trying to impart education for an adult is not impossible but difficult. Swadharma in this context is duties pertaining to the profession one is trained into and paradharma are duties pertaining to other professions.

Similarly, during education, Swadharma would be studying with dedication for the profession selected whereas paradharma would be diverting to other disciplines mid-course leaving the original choice.

Chaturashrama (ashrama: shelter) Dharma:

The four basic ashramas are: Brahmacharya, Grihastha, Vanaprastha and Samnyasa.

Brahmacharya is the period of education, grihastha is the period of family life and earning a living, vanaprastha is the period of retirement and Samnyasa is the final stage of renunciation from all and preparing to enter into the new world of either moksha or another re-birth.

Swadharma is conduct of duties that befit the period/stage in one's life. Paradharma is to conduct the duties of another stage in life. A student has to learn and not enter into family life. By doing so, he can concentrate on studies to the maximum and get the best out of the education system and come out as a graduate in reasonable time.

In a similar scenario, it is like the adult education system where one tries to learn after the age of 30-35yrs. We all know how difficult it is for adult education both for the teacher and the student. It is not impossible but at the same time, the proficiency of learning will not be as great as when compared to education in the early part of one's life.

Running away from family life and trying to become sanyasi is to be looked upon as paradharma. As a matter of fact, what Arjuna wanted by abandoning the war was paradharma.

अर्जुन उवाच
अथ केन प्रयुक्तोऽयं पापं चरति पूरुषः ।
अनिच्छन्नपि वार्ष्णेय बलादिव नियोजितः ||36||

arjuna uvāca
atha kena prayukto 'yaṃ pāpaṃ carati pūruṣaḥ |
anicchann api vārṣṇeya balād iva niyojitaḥ ||36||

Arjuna said,
O Varshneya, constrained by force as it were, by what does man commit sin even agaisnst his wish? || 36||

Atha: now; kena: by which; prayuktoyam: impelled; papam: sin; charati: does; purushaha: man; anichhan: not wishing; api: even; varshneya: Krishna; baladiva: by force; niyojitaha: constrained.

Krishna is addressed as Varshneya as he comes from the race of Vrishnis.

It is a sincere and pertinent question by Arjuna who is to be considered as a representative of all spiritual seekers.

As a matter of fact one can classify the population into three categories:

Those who are free from evil and sinful acts: The force of maya does not affect them. They are the rare Jivanmuktas on earth. Very few individuals fall under this category.

There are sincere seekers who know some acts and thoughts are sinful and do not wish to do evil. They are aware that there is a mysterious force that makes them do such acts and would like guidance to overcome this force.

Those that do evil knowing it to be evil as such: They are digging the grave for their own destruction and commit the sin of harming others.

Duryodhana, once made a statement on this issue. When asked if he knew what he was doing was wrong, he said: "I know it is bad but I cannot stop it. It is my nature."

We can see that Arjuna has started to look introspectively within himself for the cause of this thought of "sinful act" and sincerely wanted help to fight the same. It is "Swadhyaya" or "self-study". It is the best way forward for the seeker. Having heard the master, he does not hesitate to put forward a question so that he could get the clear-cut answer for the same. He sincerely does not want to commit a sinful act and is desperately seeking guidance from the master.

It is always better to foresee a danger and take steps to avoid the same. Human nature is such that although we know it is wrong to tell a lie, we tell lies. Not only that, we try our best to cover our lies. What could be the mysterious force that makes us do such acts? Let us see what the Lord's reply is for this question.

श्री भगवानुवाच
काम एष क्रोध एष रजोगुणसमुद्भवः ।
महाशनो महापाप्मा विद्ध्येनमिह वैरिणम् ||37||

Śrī Bhagavān uvāca
kāma eṣa krodha eṣa rajoguṇasamudbhavaḥ |
mahāśano mahāpāpmā viddhy enam iha vairiṇam ||37||

The Lord said,
It is desire, it is anger, born of rajoguna. It is all devouring and sinful. Know this as the enemy here. ||37||

Kama: desire; esha: this; krodha: anger; samudhbahvaha: born of; mahasano: all devouring; maha papma: all sinful; vidyenamiha: know this here; vairinam: the enemy.

The soul within each one of us is the divine force and the physical body is composed of matter. The force of energy and the gross matter complement each other and bring out the various forms of life in this universe. The divine force is constantly pure and remains as a witness to the actions of the body at all times. The actions conducted by the physical body on the other hand can vary from being pure satvic to the indolent tamasic.

When rajoguna is predominant, our thoughts and actions demonstrate the will to fulfill a desire. It is "kama" that is referred to in this Sloka. As we have studied before, a number of reasons would bring out "krodha"; (anger) the close associate of kama. (Slokas 62, 63 chapter 2)

The first line of this Sloka highlights the fact that desire and the subsequent angry reactions are the result of predominance of the rajoguna.

Kama/desire is the leader of the devil's team inside us and krodha/anger is its immediate and constant companion. These are followed by the other members of the devil's team in the form of lobha, moha, mada and matsarya. (Greed, delusion, arrogance and enmity) One can say that kama is the cause and krodha is the effect.

Desire is nothing but an agitation arising in the mind of the individual as a result of the impulses received from the objective world. The stronger the agitations, greater are the actions that follow. Someone or something from the objective world comes between the subject and the object of desire. When one does not get what he wants, depending upon the degree of the want, anger stems forth in varying degrees.

Kama has been compared to the fire. We all know the quality of the fire—it keeps on consuming more and more of what is offered to it or what comes in its vicinity.

Its thirst for more cannot be quenched. Hence the adjective used by the Lord, "it is the big devil, (Maha shani)."

How can one conquer this evil? The attempt to satisfy the fire by adding oblations of ghee and oil will make it grow stronger. Let no fuel be added to the fire and it slowly burns itself out. Similarly, we should not make any attempts to satisfy the kama and let it die its natural death. Learning the art of rejecting the desires as soon as they are born is the answer to the problem. Constant inquiry into the nature of the Atman which is Sat, Chit, Ananda itself will eliminate the kama from the mind.

The anger that stems forth dulls the mind and makes it lose its discriminatory property. The consequences of rights and wrongs of any action are not thought of before the start of actions that stem forth due to anger. When such discrimination between dharma and adharma is lost, sinful actions follow. The greater the anger, worst will be the actions that stem forth. Hence the Lord says it is "Maha Papma." (Great sin)

Know this as the enemy here: "Here" refers to this world we are living now and the actions we conduct.

The entire Gita is about bringing awareness of the fact that in everybody's life there was a past that is responsible for the present and it is the past and present that shape the tomorrow to come.

The actions conducted "Now" will shape our future. If we are looking for a healthy and peaceful tomorrow, we need to give great attention to the present. By mastering over the rajoguna traits in us (controlling the desire and anger), we can hope for a better tomorrow in our lives.

It does not mean that we should not have any desires in our lives. Desire is the fuel that moves us in this world. If our path is towards "Liberation" and in contributing to "Universal Peace and Harmony" our desires should be "Satvic". They should fit in with the concept of "Sanatana Dharma" which in turn is the concept of "Purushartha", the goal of life. This is, as we have read before, "Dharma, Artha, kama, and Moksha." Human needs for security are "Artha" and for entertainment is kama. Dharma should be the basis for both. Needs for security (Artha) is to be fulfilled following the path of dharma and only then the dharmic desires are to be entertained.

The first and foremost duty is to know what dharma is and learn the art of instilling it in all our thoughts and actions.

"Artha" is the means for achieving the object or purpose of life. By strictly following the rules of dharma one should work for "Artha."

Only after these two comes the "Kama." Whatever wish we have in life has to be according to the principles of righteousness. We should have the means/capacity to get what we desire. By this we mean the principle of "beg, borrow or steal" should not be the means for fulfilling any desires.

Keeping the final aim of "Moksha" at all times, conducting the dharmic actions that fit in with every stage of life should be the "Satvic desire" in our journey of life.

Rajoguna will act as the enemy in the path to salvation for those who thrive on life of pleasures. Such people are to be considered as ignorant and let us pray for the message of the sacred text to reach as many as possible and lift them up to higher planes of life on this earth.

धूमेनाव्रियते वह्निर्यथाऽऽदर्शो मलेन च |
यथोल्बेनावृतो गर्भस्तथा तेनेदमावृतम् ||38||

dhūmenāvriyate vahnir yathādarśo malena ca |
yatholbenāvṛto garbhas tathā tenedam āvṛtam ||38||

As fire is enveloped by smoke, as a mirror by dust, as the embryo by amnion, so is the knowledge of the Self enveloped by kama and krodha. ||38||

Dhoomena: by fire; avriyate: enveloped; vahni: the fire; yatha: as; adarsho: the mirror; malena: dust; yatha: as; cha: and; albena:

amnion; avrutaha: enveloped; garbhaha: embryo; tatha: so; tena: by it; idam: thus; avritam: enveloped.

Through this verse, the Lord is reiterating the fact that there is "Chit" or the light of the Atman in every individual. We should not forget that the sacred text is universal and the message in it is applicable to one and all. This light of the Atman, ever shining, is the divine knowledge the scriptures talk about.

Each and every individual has the right to realize the true meaning of the maha vakya "Tat Tvam Asi." This aspect is brought out in the words:

Idam Avritam: it means, "This" is enveloped. "This" is a pronoun and in this context is "The knowledge of the Atman"

The smoke, dust and amnion refer to the kama and krodha about which we have discussed in the last verse.

Fanning clears away the smoke that hides the fire within, rubbing the dust off with a clean cloth brings out the shine from the mirror and when the amniotic sac is removed the baby comes out free from the womb. The fire has always been present but the smoke blocked its presence; the reflecting quality of the mirror is its basic quality but is hidden by the dust and the baby is inside the amniotic sac in its own right but hidden by it. The smoke does not extinguish the fire, the dust does not make the mirror lose its original purity and the amnion as such does not harm the baby within.

Kama and krodha are like the smoke, the dust and the amnion. They envelope the Atman within but do not affect the true state of purity of the Atman. The Atman does not get touched or transformed by them. The only result evident by their presence is blocking the brilliant light of the ever effulgent Atman.

If this is so, why is there differentiation between individuals? This question is answered through this verse.

The three examples given refer to the three basic gunas which envelop us all. Through the vasana samskaras we carry in our mind, we demonstrate any one of three qualities at any one time in our day to day life's activities.

As the fire is enveloped by smoke:

This reflects the satvic quality. The smoke that accompanies the fire does disturb the eyes of the seer. It is also true that at the same time it can be pushed away by the simple process of fanning.

The satvic quality has the thin veil of "ego" that hides the purity of the individual. By constant fanning away any thoughts about pride of being satvic, the seeker can reflect the brilliance of the self-effulgent Atman. If he fails to do so, the thin smoke becomes a cloud of thick smoke and hides the true light of knowledge within.

As a mirror is enveloped by dust:

This reflects the rajasic quality. The clean and spotless mirror gives a true reflection of the individual/object. The dust, grease etc. that falls on the mirror, if not cleaned, disrupt the quality of reflection of the object. Clearing this is more difficult and takes a long time.

Similarly, the rajasic quality distorts the light of Atman and it is hard work to clear this quality. It takes a long time to clean and polish off the rajasic quality.

As the embryo by the amnion:

The amniotic fluid and the sack hide the foetus within. The human foetus takes nearly 40 weeks to grow and come out of its covering. The baby finally comes out with the assistance of the tender love and care the mother of the unborn baby gives, during the period of gestation.

The tamasic quality hides the true knowledge. It takes a long time for the spiritual knowledge to emerge out from its sack of ignorance. This can be eliminated by the individual's constant attempts to grow this spiritual knowledge within oneself and assistance by the grace of the guru. Just as it takes nearly 40 weeks for the baby to come out, the seeker needs a long time to express his/her basic divinity.

It is the basic duty of every individual to take off the covering of kama and krodha, realize his/her essential nature and let the divinity of the indwelling glorious Atman shine.

आवृतं ज्ञानमेतेन ज्ञानिनो नित्यवैरिणा।
कामरूपेण कौन्तेय दुष्पूरेणानलेन च ॥**39**॥

āvṛtaṃ jñānam etena jñānino nityavairiṇā |
kāmarūpeṇa kaunteya duṣpūreṇānalena ca ||39||

O Arjuna, knowledge of the Self is covered by this everlasting enemy of the wise in the form of desire, insatiable like fire. ||39||

Avrutam: covered by; jnanam: knowledge; etena: by this; jnanino: of the wise; nitya vairinaha: constant enemy; kamarupena: whose form is desire; kaunteya: Arjuna; dushpoorena: insatiable; analena: by fire; cha: and.

This Sloka clarifies the meaning of the words "mahashana and idam" in the last two slokas.

In Sloka 37, we come across the word "Mahashanaha" which means "all- devouring." The Lord says that the "Desire" is all-devouring. In this Sloka, by using the word "Analena cha" which means "like fire" He is telling us that the desires are like fire and are all-devouring.

In Sloka 38, we come across the word "Idam" as "Tenedam avritam". It means "This is enveloped". What is it the Lord is referring to when he uses the adjective "Idam"?

In this verse He says "Avritam jnanam" which means "Knowledge of the Self is enveloped." Desire envelops and hides the knowledge in every individual is the reply by the Lord to Arjuna's question which we discussed in Sloka 36 of this chapter.

Every movement and expression on the face of the student is noticed by the teacher in such situations. The guru, the expert can read the mind of the student well before he comes out with any questions. After all, "the face is the index of mind" is the proverb we are all familiar with.

The expression on Arjuna's face when Krishna used the words "Mahashana and Idam" in slokas 37 and 38, prompted the teacher Krishna to give a clear explanation for them.

In Sanskrit "Alam" means "enough". "Analam" means "not enough." Fire as we know is never satisfied. It never says "enough". The more one offers oblations like ghee to the fire, it keeps on devouring it. Anala is the Sanskrit word for fire which is never satisfied.

We get a categorical statement by the Lord who says that it is the everlasting enemy of the wise. Who are the wise?

Wise are those who know the rights and wrongs of any of their thoughts and actions. The advanced spiritual seekers who are trying to realize the eternal truth are the wise ones referred to in this Sloka. Even such people succumb to the temptations of desires.

The theme of the sacred text is in guiding the seeker in his spiritual path. It is important that the seeker can anticipate all the different problems that can be encountered in life and learn the means of overcoming them. Among these, "kama" is the worst and the Lord is giving importance to it.

Why are the desires everlasting enemies?

An enemy is considered a hostile foe. In our day to day life, we have instances where an enemy of today actually becomes a friend of tomorrow. One cannot say that the relationship of hostility is permanent. The fire, as an enemy does not belong to this cadre.

For the wise, desires can never be friends but are constant enemies. They are the "Nitya vairies", permanent enemies. Even the desire to become satvic and attain moksha would harm the seeker in the latter stages of his spiritual progress. Hence the adjective "everlasting enemy" is used.

The only solution for the problem is to declare a total war on desires. There should be a constant battle between the seeds of desire brought in by the senses and stored in the mind and seeds of divinity sown by the learned caring elders and the guru.

Quote: Sri Ramakrishna: The indicator on the balance scale moves away from the middle point when there is more weight on one side. The mind of man moves away from the God allured by the weight of lust and greed.

इन्द्रियाणि मनो बुद्धिरस्याधिष्ठानमुच्यते ।
एतैर्विमोहयत्येष ज्ञानमावृत्य देहिनम् ||40||

indriyāṇi mano buddhir asyādhiṣṭhānam ucyate |
etair vimohayaty eṣa jñānam āvṛtya dehinam ||40||

The senses, the mind and the intellect are said to be its seat. By these it deludes the embodied by veiling the wisdom. ||40||

Indriyani: the senses; mano: the mind; buddhi: intellect; adhishtanam: seat; uchyate: is said; etair: by these; vimohayate: deludes; esha: this; jnanam: knowledge; avrutya: enveloped; dehinaam: embodied.

This verse is advice by the Lord to all men with rajasic temperament. Kshatriyas are full of desires and like to accumulate wealth and hold on to power. Arjuna as we know is Kshatriya by birth and Krishna is giving the knowledge to him. He is therefore using explanations to fit in with the nature of Arjuna.

Who is a true warrior?

The following qualities refer to a true warrior. They are:

He wants to know who his enemies are and all the details about them.

How powerful is the enemy?

Where does the enemy reside/hide?

How does the enemy show his presence?

Who are the friends that can help him to fight the enemy?

Kama is the enemy of the seeker and we had elaborate description of the same in the last few slokas. Along with kama come his associates, krodha, lobha, moha, mada and matsarya (anger, greed, delusion, pride and enmity). The six together constitute the "Arishadwargas" which means the group of six (enemies).

Kama resides in the senses, the mind and the intellect, the Lord says.

As the senses bring in the impulses from the outside world to the mind we can accept that the senses and the mind are its seats. We can say that the mind is the house and the senses are its windows. Even in the absence of live impulses, the mind can live on the stored memories in its bank.

But the Lord says that the intellect is also its seat. Why?

This is so because the intellect is not a separate organ as such. It is only the discriminatory aspect of the mind. Strong and powerful desires have the power of blocking its discriminatory capacity.

तस्मात्त्वमिन्द्रियाण्यादौ नियम्य भरतर्षभ ।
पाप्मानं प्रजहि ह्येनं ज्ञानविज्ञाननाशनम् ||41||

tasmāt tvam indriyāṇy ādau niyamya bharatarṣabha |
pāpmānaṃ prajahihy enaṃ jñānavijñānanāśanam ||41||

O best of Bharatas, therefore, control the senses first, kill surely this kama, the sinful destroyer of knowledge and wisdom. (Self-realisation) ||41||

Tasmat: therefore; tvam: you; indriyani: senses; adou: in the beginning; niyamya: having controlled; bharatarshabha: best of Bharatas; paapmanam: the sinful; prajahi: kill; hyenam: surely this; jnana: knowledge; Vijnana nashanam: destroyer of wisdom.

We are now approaching the end of this important chapter in the Gita. We are getting the summary of what has been said so far.

Sri Krishna is reiterating the dangers of succumbing to the dreaded enemy called "Kama" and giving us the means to overcome him.

It is also important to note the word, "sinful destroyer of knowledge." We have to remember that there is already the existence of "Knowledge" within each of us. "Knowledge" is the "Chit" aspect of "Sat, Chit, Ananda." Our true identification has to be with this "Sat, Chit, Ananda" and not to the physical body with name and form. Through the passage of several births, accumulation of vasanas, our karma phala from the past actions has put a veil on the "Chit" and we have forgotten our true identity.

The Vedas boldly declare the maha mantra "Tat Tvam Asi." Forgetfulness of our true identity is referred to in this Sloka as "Destruction of Knowledge". In our spiritual journey, it is a sin to forget our true identity. The destroyer of this knowledge is "Kama" and this has been described as "sinful destroyer of knowledge and wisdom".

The spiritual seekers are those who strive to attain Moksha. The most powerful enemy in their path is "Kama". The objective world is the focus of desires for the ordinary men/women. The world is full of objects/beings that arouse the interest of the individual which progresses to the stage of desire of acquiring the same.

The senses are the first channel of entry into the mind for the impressions of the outer world. It is the duty of the seeker to control the senses.

He who has no discrimination and whose senses are not under control will find that the life's chariot will not lead to the desired destination. In the hands of a good driver, the horses/senses are under control. Similarly, the sacred texts say that the intellect or the reasoning capacity should be the charioteer and have control over the mind and the senses. Only such spiritual seekers who will let the God inside him take control over his mind and the senses will get the blessings of the Lord and realizes the "Eternal Truth" (Sat).

इन्द्रियाणि पराण्याहुरिन्द्रियेभ्यः परं मनः ।
मनसस्तु परा बुद्धिर्यो बुद्धेः परतस्तु सः ||42||

indriyāṇi parāṇy āhur indriyebhyaḥ paraṃ manaḥ |
manasas tu parā buddhir yo buddheḥ paratas tu saḥ ||42||

They say that senses are superior to the body. Superior to the senses is the mind. Superior to the mind is the intellect. One who is superior to the intellect is He. (the Self) ||42||

Indriyani: the senses; parany: superior; ahuh: they say; indriyebhyaha: than the senses; parama: superior; manaha: mind; manasaha: than the mind; tu: but; para: superior; buddhi: intellect; yah: who; buddhe: than the intellect; parataha: greater; tu: but; sah; He.

The Sreemad Bhagawadgita is part of the great epic Mahabharatam which depicts in a story form the power of evil with the support of "Kama and his associates" over good with the support of dharma. It tells us that when the good takes the shelter under the Lord Supreme, the Lord assists in total annihilation of the evil. The finale of this is the scene of the battlefield Kurukshetra with the mighty Kauravas on one side and the Pandavas with the support of Krishna who is the mightiest of all on the other side. The winners at the end are the Pandavas and they did so because of their devotion and total surrender to Krishna.

This Sloka has to be looked upon with the context of life as a battlefield and the fight against the six evils (kama, krodha, lobha, moha, mada/pride and matsarya/enmity) which hinder the path to spiritual progress and final attainment of Moksha.

In this battlefield, we are given a graphic description of the army with soldiers ranging from lower rank to the highest ranking officer.

In our own physical body we have the following instruments in the ascending order of superiority:

The physical body with arms, feet.
The five sense organs.
The mind.
The intellect.
The Atman.

As we ascend from the level of the physical body to that of the Atman, we can see that the preceding organ is subtler than the previous organ. The sense organs are subtler than the gross body and the mind is subtler than the sense organs and so on and so forth.

The law of physics tells us – that which is subtle is always superior to the gross.

Desires lead to attachment to the body, mind and intellect and drag the individual down to the lowest planes of existence. Using the power of the Atman one can fight the evil desires and lift oneself to the plane of the Atman.

In Sloka 41, the Lord advocated sense restraint as the means for spiritual progress. In this Sloka we are given the means to achieve self-restraint. To defeat the enemy one must manage to climb over the enemy and destroy him. To do so, one needs to acquire greater power. This can be done by making use of subtler powers to win over the grosser powers.

To protect the hands and feet, we need to use the sense organs. To protect the sense organs, we need to use the mind. To protect the mind, intellect is needed and finally to protect all of the bodily instruments the power of the Atman is needed. Atman being the subtlest of all is the most powerful instrument we have.

Unfortunately, the mind which is a store house of previous experiences and vasana imprints also can fall prey to the evil enemy desire. The desires enter into the mind and take shelter and in course of time take over the running of the house. The intellect is needed to control the activities of the mind.

The intellect has the "Antaratman" (Atman) on one side and the mind with its store house of imprints on the other side. The antaratman sends in the voice of the divine to the intellect. But the intellect also receives the impulses of the physical world through the mind.

In most cases, in the tug of war between these two forces, intellect falls prey to the enemy "Kama" residing in the mind and refuses to hear the inner voice of the Atman.

The spiritual seeker who knows this truth and strives hard with sraddha and bhakti can, by the use of the Atman, win over the temptations from the outer world. The knowledge of the Self within is the sword that can cut the knot between atma and anatma. (the physical body is anatma)

This chapter, Karma Yoga is all about the advice to Arjunas of the world who are running away from their duty, to uphold dharma and to help them in learning the proper conduct of actions according to the principle of "Nishkama karma and karmaphala tyaga."

The union of the lower self (ego) to the higher Self by the conduct of Nitya Karmas is "Karma Yoga."

The Atman within is the king and the Lord and it is our duty to make use of our physical body to let the glory of the Atman (through divine actions) shine forth for all to see.

एवं बुद्धेः परं बुद्ध्वा संस्तभ्यात्मानमात्मना ।
जहि शत्रुं महाबाहो कामरूपं दुरासदम् ||**43**||

evaṃ buddheḥ paraṃ buddhvā saṃstabhyātmānam ātmanā |
jahi śatruṃ mahābāho kāmarūpaṃ durāsadam ||43||

O Arjuna, mighty armed, thus having known what is greater than the intellect, namely Atman, and restraining the self by the Self, slay the foe in the form of desire which is indeed hard to overcome. ||43||

Evam : thus; buddheh: than the intellect; param: superior; buddhva: having known; samsabhya: restraining; atmanam: the self; atmana: by the Self; jahi: slay; satrum: the enemy; mahabaho: mighty armed; kamaroopam: in the form of desire; durasadam: hard to overcome.

The second quarter of this Sloka (last half of the first line) says "Atmanam Atmana."

We need to understand this clearly,

Atmanam: the self. Atmana: by the Self.

"Atmanam" refers to the senses, body, mind and the intellect. The self-referred to here has the little "s".

"Atmana" refers to the "Atman." The Self-referred to here has the capital "S".

The enemy called desire has to be conquered by the Atman which should control the body, senses, mind and the intellect.

It is important to understand the real from the unreal.

The real is that which is constant in relation to time and space. It is the "Eternal truth" and the scholars say it is "Nitya (constant)". The Atman within is the constant factor in the life of the individual during his sojourn in the form of several births and deaths.

The physical body of the present life goes through the journey of life and takes several names and forms in its course. As it is not permanent, it is said to be unreal and the scholars say it is "Anitya (not constant)".

The real in the form of the Atman is our constant companion in life and He is the real knowledge and bliss. The Atman radiates its power to the bodily instruments and its light of knowledge is reflected on to the intellect. From the intellect it is reflected to the mind and from the mind to the sense organs. From the sense organs it is reflected on to the objects in the material world.

Through our bodily organs we become capable of understanding the objective world. This comes from knowledge which is the subject matter that follows this chapter.

The light that is reflected on to the objects makes the object visible. This light reflects back on to the sense organs which take the information to the mind. This is supposed to be taken from the mind to the intellect and from the intellect to the Atman. Many a time, this process stops at the level of the mind and even the intellect or reasoning capacity is not made use of. When this stops at the level of the mind, it is to be recognized as "ignorance." When it stops at the level of the intellect it has the chance to become "egoistic". Both avidya and ahamkara are dangerous for the spiritual seeker.

In the spiritual journey there is only one enemy and that is "Kama."

To fight the enemy, the warrior has to be mighty armed. Arjuna is addressed by Krishna as "Mahabaho" which means "mighty armed."

The scholars say that the power in the arms represents Indra, the Lord of heaven. Mythologically, Arjuna is the son of Indra. One needs to be as powerful as Arjuna, son of the Lord of heaven to fight the enemy called "desire."

Krishna has used the word "durasadam" in the second half of the Sloka. "Durasadam" means "hard to overcome." The Lord agrees that it is difficult to overcome the enemy but does not say it is impossible. He wants Arjuna to learn to understand the difference between the real and unreal. The knowledge of this difference is the weapon that can cut asunder the knot between "Atma and Anatma." By joining the Atman with the anatman we have temporarily made the Atman into Jivatman. Nishkama karma, karma phala tyaga is the true Karma Yoga and it is possible by acquiring "Jnana" and it is the next chapter that we are taken into now by the Lord.

Iti śrīmadbhagavadgītāsūpaniṣatsu brahmavidyāyāṃ yogaśāstre śrīkṛṣṇārjunasaṃvāde karmayogo nāma tṛtīyo'dhyāyaḥ.

CHAPTER 4

JÑĀNA-YOGA

INTRODUCTION:

"Knowledge is finding association about things." (Swami Vivekananda)

The association of the physical body with the Atman within on an individual basis and the association of the Pancha Maha Bhootas (five great elements-earth, water, fire, air, space) in nature (prakriti) with the divine un-manifest energy is the true essential knowledge.

Jnana—Knowledge.

Ajnana-Ignorance.

The sastras tell us not to go in search of Jnana. The knowledge is compared to "Light". Will anybody go in search of light? When the darkness is cleared, automatically the light shines forth.

The ignorance is compared to darkness and the knowledge to light.

On the basis of the above explanation, when the ignorance is cleared, automatically the knowledge shines forth.

The Atman, ever shining "Light of Knowledge/Jnana" is always within.

What is Ajnana?

Not realising the constant presence of Atman within and succumbing to the feeling of/living the life of -- "Me, Mine" is Ajnana.

It is compared to "Darkness" (Night).

Darkness envelops Night.

The brilliant sunshine clears totally the darkness.

When the ignorance of "me, mine" is cleared, what is left is only "Atman."

Realisation of this truth is "Jnana".

Jnana yoga is the study of this knowledge that leads to ultimate union with the Parabrahman. The subject of "knowledge" is very vast and covers so many different branches. We can broadly divide the subject into:

Spiritual knowledge:

It is the knowledge of the Purusha (the creator) and Prakriti (created). It is the knowledge of the Atman and the physical body composed of the mind, intellect and gross physical body and the knowledge of the constituents of the nature with its working mechanism.

Knowledge of the material world:

The knowledge of the material world has its benefit of bringing success and happiness but only in relation to the material possessions. This, the scholars say is momentary happiness. This is because none of the possessions in one's life are permanent. This knowledge comes from experiences in one's life and by observing the life of others. Without the knowledge of the spiritual science, the success in the material world leads to development of "Ego" which is the main cause of downfall of the individual.

On the other hand, the knowledge of the spirit (Atman) teaches us the art of contentment and the art of detachment in attachment towards the material possessions in life and at the same time guides us towards the ultimate purpose of human birth, namely "Moksha."

To say the same in a different way, we can say that the knowledge in any field gives one a certain amount of power. The power obtained from the knowledge of the material world makes one develop a sense of "Ego."

On the other hand, the knowledge of the spiritual world gives the power to overcome the "ego" and the power to withstand the turbulences in one's life.

Spiritual knowledge assists the individual in conducting actions for the welfare of the society because it teaches the art of realising the presence of Atman in oneself and understanding the presence of the same Atman in all forms of life.

This Jnana is the main gate of entry into the temple of knowledge. The temple with the idol of Atman inside is the living physical body. We block the ever effulgent light of knowledge of the Atman by our ego and Jnana yoga is to assist us in unblocking the ego and letting the light of Atman shine forth.

Our body is like a microcosmic representation of nature. It is constituted of the Atman and the physical body made up of the Pancha Maha Bhootas. (Space, Air, Light, Water and Earth) The nature around us, both the known and unknown parts are the macrocosm, consisting of the un-manifest energy and the five gross elements.

The subject matter of investigation that leads to ultimate understanding of the Supreme Parabrahman is Jnana Yoga.

As we go through the various chapters of the Gita, we will realize that this chapter is only the preliminary or primary course in understanding the Supreme. Detailed explanation on this subject is taught by the Lord later on in the 13th Chapter, Kshetra Kshetrajna Vibhaga Yoga.

Initially the Lord takes Arjuna through the comparison of life in an external battlefield of Kurukshetra with the battle between Kauravas and Pandavas. As He unfolds the entire Gita, we find that He reverts back to the individual human body and makes us realize that the human mind is the true battlefield between divine and un-divine qualities. Victory for the divine qualities with the assistance of the Supreme knowledge over the un-divine qualities leads to Liberation which our scriptures say is "Moksha".

The scriptures talk about "Lighting the light of knowledge." What does it mean? The darkness that has filled a cave for several years can be dispelled within a few seconds by lighting a lamp. Lighting the lamp of knowledge (Jnana) dispels the ignorance (Ajnana). Like in the cave, the ignorance has been within us for a long time and hence the masters say aptly that "Ajnana is beginning-less".

When we go to a temple we see the priest lighting the lamp and offering the light to the deity in the temple. This light is to illumine the God inside the inner sanctum sanctorum. (The old traditional temples in India are built in such a way that the inner sanctum sanctorum is totally dark and the installed deity is not seen. The deity is seen only on lighting the lamp)

Similarly, we are expected to illumine the Atman within and make it visible by lighting the lamp of knowledge. This is possible only by developing the divine virtues, destroying the animal tendencies within and by dropping the "Ego" in all actions. We are expected to understand clearly the "Karma Yoga" and put the same into practice with "Sraddha and Bhakti." Meditation on what has been taught by the Lord not only on what we have read so far but the contents of the subsequent chapters will assist us, the seekers in attaining the Liberation.

Sri Krishna, by incarnating on earth has set an example and shown us the way to act on the principle of true "Karma Yoga" and given us the knowledge to understand the principle of correct actions.

This chapter is to assist the sincere seekers in experiencing the "Ananda/Bliss" and to achieve "Moksha/Liberation". Towards this result actions/karma are essential.

With the knowledge from the last chapter on "Karma" and this chapter one has to work towards the following three results:

Atma hita, Jana hita and Loka hita.

"Hita" means "welfare/what is good".

Atmahita is welfare of the jivatman so that it would unite with the Paramatman at the end.

Janahita is welfare of the men/women of the world and Loka hita is welfare of all forms of life in this world and also acts that do not disturb the balance of nature consisting of the five great elements.

Only on achieving the three aims the spiritual journey is complete in uniting with the "Parabrahman."

श्री भगवानुवाच
इमं विवस्वते योगं प्रोक्तवानहमव्ययम् ।
विवस्वान् मनवे प्राह मनुरिक्ष्वाकवेऽब्रवीत् ||1||

Śrībhagavān uvāca
imaṃ vivasvate yogaṃ proktavān aham avyayam |
vivasvān manave prāha manur ikṣvākave 'bravīt ||1||

The Lord said:
I had taught this everlasting yoga to Vivasvan. Vivasvan taught it to Manu who declared it to Ikshvaku. ||1||

Imam: this; vivasvate: to Vivaswat; yogam: yoga; proktavaan: taught; aham: Me; avyayam: imperishable; vivaswan: vivaswat; manave: to manu; praha: taught; manuh: Manu; ikshwakave: To Ikshwaku; abraveet: taught.

Let us briefly recollect Sloka 15, chapter 3:

Know that the action arises from the Vedas. The Vedas are born from the imperishable Brahman.

Knowledge of the Self is the theme of the Vedas. Vedas are vast and difficult to understand by ordinary mortals. Upanishads/ Vedanta are said to be the final chapters of the Vedas. There are more than 108 Upanishads and still, they are not easy for ordinary mortals to understand in their life time.

Sreemad Bhagawad Gita is the summary of all the Upanishads and the simplest form for all to understand.

This Sloka says that the Vedas are born from the imperishable Brahman and that Krishna taught it to Vivasvan.

We have to understand that Sri Krishna is declaring that He is none other than Brahman.

Vivasvan is the name of "Sun God." "Sun" as we know is the source of light for the entire universe. This light is not for any selected few but to one and all, both animate and inanimate. The scriptures always relate the "Light" to the "Light of Knowledge." Hence, we have to take that "He" has given the light of knowledge to one and all. He has made it the "Universal Knowledge" and not restricted to a selected few. It is important to realize that the Sun god represents actions that follow the principle of "Nishkama karma."

Manu is the first Aryan, progenitor for the entire mankind. He is considered to be the son of Vivasvan, the Sun God. He is said to be the first one to offer oblations to the gods.

The Manu myth gradually expanded and culminated in the appearance as Vaivasvatha, the seventh Manu.

The Light of Knowledge/Vedas was transmitted by Vivasvan/ Sun God, (the source of light to the universe) to Manu.

Manu, it says gave the knowledge to Ikshvaku. It is the name of the king, son of Manu Vaivasvatha who founded the solar dynasty. The role of the kings in ancient India was mainly in upholding dharma and propagating dharma to all its subjects. Hence, the Vedas were taught to the kings for protection of their subjects.

The subsequent information given in brackets is the historical facts that trace the lineage from Ikshvaku to Arjuna.

(The power shifted from the rulers of solar dynasty in course of time to the rulers of lunar dynasty. The first king of lunar dynasty was Pururavas. In the line of Pururavas was born the famous king Yayati.

Another king of fame in the Pururavas lineage was Dushyanta who married Shakuntala and their son was "Bharata". Following his rule, it is said that the Indian sub-continent came to be known as "Bharat".

In the line of Bharata was born a prince named Rantideva. Rantideva was the brother of Kuru, one of the famous kings of lunar dynasty and their lineage came to be known as "Kauravas." Kuru performed tapas in a spot named Kurunjangala. The spot became sanctified and was named Kurukshetra.

The next important king in this lineage was Shantanu who married Ganga.

Shantanu also married Satyavati, daughter of a fisherman. Bheeshma was the son of Ganga and Chitrangada, Vichitraveerya, the sons of Satyavati.

Dhritarashtra was born blind as the son of King Vichitraveerya's widow Ambika. Pandu was born as the son of widow Ambalika. This happened by the grace of Sage Vyasa. The feud for kingdom between the sons of the blind Dhritarashtra and Pandavas led to the battle of Kurukshetra.)

Sri Krishna is now giving the same knowledge to Arjuna, Pandava, son (of the king Pandu).

The Lord uses the adjective, "Imperishable Yoga." Why?

All the results of actions conducted for worldly pleasures are impermanent. They are transitory and last only for a span of time that may last few seconds to several years, whereas the knowledge of yoga of action which is meant to attain Moksha is said to be "Imperishable" (Avyaya). The Yoga of knowledge which follows the Yoga of action is also imperishable. As long as mankind exists in this universe, this law holds good and is the only direct path to Liberation which is the state of "Eternal Happiness or Ananda".

एवं परम्पराप्राप्तमिमं राजर्षयो विदुः ।
स कालेनेह महता योगो नष्टः परन्तप ||2||

evaṃ paraṃparāprāptam imaṃ rājarṣayo viduḥ |
sa kāleneha mahatā yogo naṣṭaḥ paraṃtapa ||2||

This knowledge was handed down in regular succession from generation to generation. The royal sages knew this Yoga. But by long lapse of time it has been lost here, O "scorcher of enemies." ||2||

Evam: thus; parampara praptam: handed down in regular succession; imam: this; rajarshayo: royal sages; viduhu: knew; sa: this; kalena: by lapse of time; iha: here; mahata: by long; yogaha: yoga; nashtaha: destroyed; Parantapa: scorcher of enemies.

"Raja" is "a king." "Rishi" is a "Seer."

The rishis represent the Vedic Aryan current of thought. They are considered as the ideal or the model for others to follow on the path to spiritual development. He who has conquered the mind and senses, practices the art of "Nishkama karma and Karma Phala tyaga" and has attained a vision of the "Supreme" is fit to be called "Rishi."

The post-Vedic mythology classifies the rishis into the following sub-sections.

Maharshi: these are the "saptarshis" (seven rishis) and are said to be the "primal makers of creation". They followed the command by their creator "Brahma" and created the various forms of life on this earth.

Rajarshi: The royal sages are "Rajarshis."

Brahmarshi: Priestly seers are Brahmarshis.

Devarshi: the seers who possessed virtues that merited the title of "Divine virtues" are "Devarshis." (The example is sages Narada and Atri).

The knowledge given by the Lord is to be known as "Brahma Vidya" as it leads to the union with the Brahman. The kings and emperors who learnt, practiced and propagated the Brahma Vidya are given the title "Rajarshi." Such kings possessed both the knowledge of the Vedas and the knowledge to rule the kingdom. King Janaka, father of Sita is the prime example of a Rajarshi. It is said that many great sages went to the Royal assembly in his palace to learn the scriptures.

The practical application of Vedanta to actual life was the contribution by the Rajarshis to mankind.

Let us be clear of the fact that this knowledge is not just the domain of these elite Rajarshis but really for any individual, who has the deep rooted desire to learn "Brahma Vidya", be it a politician, professional, businessman or a laborer.

In olden days, the royal lineage continued from generation to generation and those who practiced Brahma Vidya passed it on to their subsequent generations.

As we have seen in history we do get periods of time when there is a break in the continuity of ancestral teaching and practices. Instead of being true karma yogis, some rajas live as karma bhogis. They lived to enjoy the life. Such selfish and arrogant people fail to follow the good way of living and the practice of spirituality comes to a halt. One can say it is also natural and is like day followed by night.

The same rule applies concerning the revival of good and dharmic way of living. The night has also to be followed by day. Great people and sometimes the Lord Himself incarnate and bring to life the forgotten spirituality and propagation of dharma.

The knowledge can never be lost and the expression by Sri Krishna that it has been lost here is only figurative. In the last Sloka, we have been told clearly that the knowledge is "Avyayam."

The Lord is Eternal and the Dharma He gave to mankind is also "Eternal."

स एवायं मया तेऽद्य योगः प्रोक्तः पुरातनः ।
भक्तोऽसि मे सखा चेति रहस्यं ह्येतदुत्तमम् ||3||

sa evāyaṃ mayā te 'dya yogaḥ proktaḥ purātanaḥ |
bhakto 'si me sakhā ceti rahasyaṃ hy etad uttamam ||3||

This same ancient Yoga has now been taught by Me today to you. For you are My devotee and friend. It is indeed a Supreme secret. ||3||

Sa: that; eva: even: ayam: this; mayaaa: by Me; te: to you; adya: today; yogaha: yoga; proktaha: has been taught; puratana: ancient; bhaktaha: devotee; asi: thou art; Me': my; sakha: friend; cha: and; iti: thus; rahasyam: secret; hi: for; etat: this; uttamam: best.

Sri Krishna is indirectly stating that the yoga taught by Him to Arjuna is nothing new and that He, Krishna, is not just Krishna, cow-herd son of Vasudeva and Devaki, but, the Supreme Parabrahman. He is going to assert this fact in the next Sloka to follow.

Krishna and Arjuna have been friends for several years. Arjuna also had a great respect for Krishna.

Just before the beginning of the Great War, both Duryodhana and Arjuna went to Krishna to ask for his assistance. Krishna had the entire Yadava army behind him. Krishna gave them the choice of either having the Yadava army or Krishna in person on their side. At the same time He said that on His part, He would not take any weapon to fight and would only be the guide. Despite this stipulation, Arjuna opted to have Krishna on his side. He believed Krishna to be an embodiment of dharma.

He accepted Krishna as guru and a guide and surrendered to Him for spiritual guidance.

Krishna is therefore stating that Arjuna is both a friend and devotee.

Later on in the subsequent chapters we find Krishna saying that a true devotee is the best friend of the Lord.

It is surprising to note the point that His advice is said to be a supreme secret. Why?

Popularly, a thing can be said to be a secret for one of the following reasons.

Because one does not want others to know about the same and would like the same to be revealed at a later date. It is like the surprise gifts for special occasions like birth-days, Christmas etc.

One might come across some hidden treasure/wealth and would not like others to get it.

In certain situations, it is imperative for safety reasons to keep some information secret. Nuclear installations, details of war reports are kept secret by the Governments.

These are definitely not the reasons for using the word "Supreme secret "in this context.

What the Lord means is that the knowledge has to be imparted to those seekers (at the right time and right place) who can understand the same and do not use it for personal material gains in life. This way the knowledge is sure to be passed on safely to subsequent generations and benefit mankind, the universe and nature. Those who are not mature to understand the hidden meaning in the slokas, (Guhya bhasha), who understand in a wrong sense or who misrepresent the facts would cause profound confusion in the minds of some. Dharma and Satya (Righteousness and Truth), that are the cornerstones of the philosophy would get misrepresented and lose their true meaning. It is like a diamond that falls into the hands of a monkey.

अर्जुन उवाच
अपरं भवतो जन्म परं जन्म विवस्वतः ।
कथमेतद्विजानीयां त्वमादौ प्रोक्तवानिति ||4||

Arjuna uvāca
aparaṃ bhavato janma paraṃ janma vivasvataḥ |
katham etad vijānīyāṃ tvam ādau proktavān iti ||4||

Arjuna said,
Later was your birth, earlier the birth of Vivasvan. How then am I to understand that you taught him in the beginning? ||4||

Aparam: later; bhavataha: thy; janma: birth; param: prior; janma: birth; vivaswataha: vivaswan; katham: how; etad: this; vijaneeyam: am I to understand; tvam: thou; adou: in the beginning; proktavaan: taught; iti: thus.

This question is to unravel the mystery of who Krishna really is.

It appears Arjuna is questioning the validity of the authority of Krishna's statement. How could the friend he knew for so many years say that He is prior to Vivaswan?

The facial expression on Arjuna must have made Krishna realize that it was a genuine question. The reply from Krishna that comes in the next Sloka makes it clear that Krishna considered it as a question from a genuine seeker in the spiritual path.

If we recollect the story of Mahabharata, we will find that Yudhistira, elder brother of Arjuna conducted Rajasuya Yaga. During the proceedings, Krishna was insulted by the prince Shishupala. Krishna assumes a divine form and uses his discus/ wheel and beheads Shishupala. For some reason, Arjuna did not question who Krishna was at that time. So Arjuna should have known that Krishna is the Lord Supreme of the universe.

We, the humans have an evolved physical body and with that we can have three planes of vision of the world and the objects in it depending upon our spiritual maturity. The three planes from lower level to the highest level of maturity are as follows:

The physical/external plane of vision. With the assistance of the sense organs, we can fathom the form, color, complexion and shape of the object/person. This is external appearance only. This is deha drishti.

Using the mind and intellect, we can look at the character, quality and nature of the object/person. This is mano drishti.

Using the highest spiritual entity, we can visualize the Atman within all forms of life. This is Atma drishti.

The first two are relative truths from the physical and mental plane of vision and the third is Absolute truth from the spiritual plane of vision.

The entire Gita and the Vedic philosophy are to assist the seeker to develop the spiritual plane of vision and see the Absolute Truth of the Atman/Parabrahman in the entire universe.

श्री भगवानुवाच
बहूनि मे व्यतीतानि जन्मानि तव चार्जुन ।
तान्यहं वेद सर्वाणि न त्वं वेत्थ परन्तप ||5||

Śrībhagavān uvāca
bahūni me vyatītāni janmāni tava cārjuna |
tāny ahaṃ veda sarvāṇi na tvaṃ vettha paraṃtapa ||5||

The Lord said:
O Parantapa, many births of mine have passed as well as yours. I know them all, but you know them not. ||5||

Bahooni: many; me': my; vyateetani: have passed away; janmani: births; tava: your; cha: and; taani: them; aham: I; veda: know; sarvani: all; na: not; tvam: you; vetha: know; parantapa: scorcher of enemies.

We need to have Sraddha and Bhakti to accept this statement.

It is the accepted Hindu philosophy that each one of us have had many births and deaths in the past and will have many more of the same in future. The actions we conduct out of ignorance are the root cause for going through so many births and deaths. Not only human births, but our scriptures say that we have gone through births and may go through future births as other forms of life also. It all depends upon the types of actions we conduct/conducted.

By the blessings of the Lord we now are born as humans with the intellectual capacity of reasoning. We have adhikara (the right) in the conduct of our actions and thereby we are responsible for our own destiny.

Why is this so?

One way of answering this is to say that it is all His leela (play). The Lord who created life on earth has given us all the freedom to act the way we want but has also given us the guidance in the form of Vedas as to the right way of conducting actions.

The vast universe with its varied manifestations is full of attraction for each one of us. Forgetting His words of advice or ignorant of His advice we end up conducting actions that bind us to this universe. This is due to "Maya," the experts say.

The illusion makes us forget our true identity as the "Atman" within and also makes us not see the same Atman in all forms of life. We attach importance to name and form and forget the "Sat, Chit and Ananda."

In other words,

We are the slaves to Maya --- Sri Krishna on the other hand is the master over Maya and He wields His power over Maya.

We are born as a result of our actions whereas--- He is born out of His free will.

He has taken several births (Avataras) in the past and He will also take births in future, all out of His own free will. He will also depart from the world out of His own free will.

Whereas we have no control over the time, place and the form of our birth,

He is incarnate.

We are in the cycle of rebirths.

He has full control over the time of his birth and departure from this world ---

We do not have any control over the time of our death.

He remembers all the past, knows the present and is aware of the future of all forms of life. We, on the other hand, do not know our past, do not know the future and think that the life is all about "present." (In the 15th chapter, He tells us that memory and loss of memory are also His blessings to mankind).

अजोऽपि सन्नव्ययात्मा भूतानामीश्वरोऽपि सन् ।
प्रकृतिं स्वामधिष्ठाय संभवाम्यात्ममायया ||6||

ajo 'pi sann avyayātmā bhūtānām īśvaro 'pi san |
prakṛtiṃ svām adhiṣṭhāya saṃbhavāmy ātmamāyayā ||6||

Though I am unborn and eternal in My being, the Lord and controller of all beings, controlling My own nature, I take birth by My own Maya. ||6||

Aja: unborn; api: also; san: being; avyayatma: of imperishable nature; bhootanaam: of beings; iswaraha: the Lord; prakritim: nature; svam: my own; adhishtaya: ruling; sambhavami: come into being (take birth); atmamayaya: by my own maya.

Sri Krishna is saying that He is unborn (aja) and eternal (avyaya). Why?

We, the humans are born into this world and all forms of life are born into this world because of "Karma Phala" (results of actions). Everyone and everything that is born is due to the failure to burn out the existing vasanas in the previous births. The condition for Moksha (Liberation) is "Mano nasha and vasana kshaya" (annihilation of the mind and clearing all vasanas).

Association with the world/nature around resulted in desires and hatreds and the consequent actions are responsible for our repeated births.

But, Sri Krishna's birth is not an ordinary birth like a human. He may have been born as human but not because of any vasanas. He takes birth out of His own free will and we say it is His "Avatara" for the protection of Dharma and uprooting the evil.

On the contrary we are the tools of Maya. Maya enslaves us but the Lord enslaves the Maya.

He, as the Atman resides inside each one of us. He is the Supreme primordial energy. Without the energy we cannot survive. We need energy to live and we need energy to survive. He acts as the energy within and the energy all round us that is resident in nature. Hence He is the Lord.

One other reason for his birth is to set an example for others to follow. We come across several slokas in the Gita that reiterate the fact of His birth is to set an example for mankind.

Let us therefore clearly understand that although apparently He is the son of Devaki and Vasudeva, actually, He, Krishna, is the Supreme Parabrahman.

यदा यदा हि धर्मस्य ग्लानिर्भवति भारत ।
अभ्युत्थानमधर्मस्य तदाऽऽत्मानं सृजाम्यहम् ||7||

yadā yadā hi dharmasya glānir bhavati bhārata |
abhyutthānam adharmasya tadātmānaṃ sṛjāmy aham ||7||

O Bharata, whenever there is decline of righteousness and rise of evil, I manifest Myself. ||7||

Yada yada: whenever; hi: surely; dharmasya: of righteousness; glanirbhavati: declines; abhyuttanam: rise; adharmasya: of evil/ unrighteousness; tada: then; atmanam: myself; srujam: manifest; aham: I.

Two words are of great importance in this Sloka. They are:
Dharma
Srujami'.

We have discussed about dharma several times already. (sloka 1, chapter 1) Dharma is "Righteousness in action. " It is the basic principle of man's existence. It is needed for our existence, peace and happiness.

The Supreme Parabrahman, when He created Brahma, the four-headed Lord for the purpose of creation of life on earth, gave Him the Vedas. The Vedas are the sacred texts for the mankind that teach the humans the art of upholding the dharma.

As individuals, each one of us has to follow the law of dharma, of the Atman within and the dharma of the body. This is to keep the body, which is the temple with the Lord within in good condition during its life on earth. This is for an individual's existence, peace and happiness. If we break this law, as individuals, we have no right of existence and will not experience peace and prosperity.

But we are not just individuals. We are individuals that are part of the society. The universe is not just humans but includes other forms of life and nature in its various manifestations.

As members of society, we are again divided into various nationalities.

There is a need for the existence of each nation and peace and prosperity within each nation. Towards this there is a need for its citizens to follow the law of the land. (Of course, there are defects in the structure of the law in any country and every so often there comes changes in the constitution, supposed to be for the better of its individuals and the nation itself).

Selfishness as we know is one of the root causes of ruin of any society. The Divine Law is needed to supplement the law of the land, to bring stability to the country and assist in its progress. This has to be followed by all its citizens, in order that they experience the maximum benefit in terms of peace and prosperity.

Every so often things happen that bring problems between nations and instability to the global life as a whole. At this time, implementation of the Divine Law is most important to avoid catastrophes.

Dharma which is "the law of the being" and the "principal of man's existence" has to be protected to protect the individual and the universe. The Vedas boldly declare "Dharmo rakshati rakhsitaha." (Dharma protects he who protects dharma.)

As dharma is karma conductive to man's progress, all our actions as individuals and as corporate bodies have to follow the law of dharma.

When the karma becomes "adharma", it impedes the progress of man and the community.

Chapter 3, Karma Yoga when followed with the help of Jnana yoga, (the present chapter) gives the basic rules for conducting duties. This is the command of the scriptures.

The Law of the Divine is for universal existence, peace and prosperity. While continuing to uphold the law of the land, the citizens of any country, the universal citizens have to follow the law of the Divine.

If there is a majority who break the law of the land and/or the law of the divine, anarchy prevails and it destroys the society. It becomes an act of self- destruction. During such times, when there is great danger of anarchy and destruction of society, the Lord says "I Manifest." (Srujami)

We need to understand this word clearly. It means "He" shows His presence. The next question is "which God" comes out and manifests?

There are two ways in which we can approach this issue of "Manifest."

The first one is to see the extraordinary divinity in human form of one who lived or lives the life of a Sthitaprajna/Jivanmukta.

The second one is an actual incarnation of Lord on earth, who takes birth out of His free will.

The sastras clearly state that he who works selflessly and not looking for fruits of action is actually divinity on earth. He who dedicates his life for the welfare of all is said to be God on earth for that period.

During evil times there will arise someone who will reach Godhood by his actions and becomes God Himself and destroys evil. History has many examples of men/women who are considered as Gods by generations that come later on.

What will He do with his incarnation? This is answered in the next Sloka.

परित्राणाय साधूनां विनाशाय च दुष्कृताम् ।
धर्मसंस्थापनार्थाय संभवामि युगे युगे ||8||

paritrāṇāya sādhūnāṃ vināśāya ca duṣkṛtām |
dharmasaṃsthāpanārthāya saṃbhavāmi yuge yuge ||8||

For the protection of the righteous, for the destruction of wicked, and for the establishment of dharma, I am born in every age. ||8||

Paritranaya: for the protection; sadhunaam: of the good; vinashaya: for the destruction, dushkritaam:of the wicked; dharma:righteousness; samsthapanarthaya: for the firm establishment of; sambhavami; I am born; yuge yuge: in every age.

There are three promises by the Lord in this Sloka. It is a promise by the Lord who created the life on earth. As it is He who created the life, He takes full responsibility of its protection. This is His promise for all of us.

We should make a note that He does not bring out the Hindus or the Indians in his statement of protection. Also He has omitted caste, sex, religion, creed of any kind. He has not shown any partiality. We should therefore understand that His promise is for the entire life on earth. Hence, it is one more assertion that the Sreemad Bhagavad-Gita is a universal philosophical message by the Lord of the Universe.

The three promises are:

Protection of the good.

Destruction of the wicked.

Upholding the dharma.

Let us look into the meaning of some of the words used in this verse.

The word "Trana" means "protection." "Pari" means "total, full." The word "Pari" is prefixed to "Trana" to stress the total protection.

Similarly, "Nasha" means destruction". "Vi" means "intensely". "Vinashaya" means "intensely destroying".

Finally, "Sthapana" means "to establish" and "Sam" means "well, very much". "Samsthapana" means "very much protected."

Yuga: it refers to the four periods of time concerning the world's existence according to the Hindu sastras.

These comprise of:

Krita Yuga—duration of 1,728,000 years
Treta yuga-duration 1,296.000 years
Dwapara Yuga—duration 864,000 years
Kali Yuga---duration 432,000 yrs.

The four yugas together represent one "Maha Yuga."

The present eon is Kali Yuga. Starting from the Krita Yuga, the duration is reduced by ¼ at every Yuga. It is supposed to represent a similar quantity of the moral decline in every Yuga.

The Hindu scriptures say that:

In Krita Yuga He manifested as Narasimha and Vamana to destroy demon Hiranyakashipu and the asura Bali. The incarnations were only for protection of the righteous.

Treta Yuga: He manifested as Rama to destroy Ravana. All the three promises in this Sloka apply aptly to incarnation as Rama.

In Dwapara Yuga He manifested as Krishna to destroy Shishupala and Dantavakra and uproot the entire Kaurava clan.

In Kali Yuga, we are told that He will be born as Kalki to uproot evil. They say he will come as a sword wielding warrior on a white horse from the Himalayan region and destroy the evil.

We have already learnt that desire is the seed of action.

We have to stress the fact that His desire for incarnation is only for the protection of the life He has created. For having created the life on earth, He has taken a promise to protect what He has created. It is His "Sankalpa" which is the vow taken by Him before He created the life on earth.

His desire is "Satvic", nay, "Shuddha Satvic." It is a highly pure desire on His part.

The rest of us, in this world, conduct actions which are an admixture of the three basic gunas of "Satva, rajas and Tamas." In general rajas and Tamas predominate during periods of adharma and the Lord in some form or other brings out Satva, to predominate over rajas and Tamas. A balance of power among the three gunas is necessary to protect the social fabric.

Purgation is the law of nature. The cleansing process is a constant cycle on earth. The farmer who sows the seeds, to assist in their growth, has to constantly remove the weeds that hamper the growth of the crops.

The Lord, as a prelude for creation, sowed the seeds of dharma before He created the life. As a good farmer, he has to see that He weeds out "Adharma" which hampers the growth of dharma. This

Sloka is reiterating this task of weeding out adharma undertaken by the Lord.

He says that He incarnates to protect the sadhus. Even though sadhu is generally applied to an ascetic, really it means "righteous person." It is not applicable only to the ascetics.

The Brahmin has to be righteous in protecting the Vedas and scriptures. The Kshatriya has to be righteous in protecting the masses.

The Vaishya has to be righteous in his business transactions and assist the common man to live comfortably. He is not expected to hoard anything for personal gain or bring hardship to the masses.

The Shudra has also to be righteous in conducting his social duties belonging to his profession.

The real sadhu is he, who conducts actions selflessly.

To protect such sadhus, the Lord promises to come down "yuge yuge": in every age. It is not just one incarnation in one Yuga. He is ready to appear any time there is predominance of evil. The divinity in certain special people will show forth its presence in certain regions to uphold dharma in that region. In extreme cases, the Lord incarnates Himself to uproot evil.

He promises to destroy the wicked. There are some who do not like the idea of the Lord punishing, killing wicked people. We have to look at it as a way of clearing the evil from the face of earth. We should understand this aspect of Lord's actions clearly.

In every society, there are authorities to uphold the law of the land and thereby protect the citizens from those who break its law of the land. Also it has a duty to pass sentences to those who break the law.

Similarly, we have to see the Lord as the Universal protector of dharma. After all He is the universal Justice of Law.

To punish the wicked is not to be looked upon as an act of hatred but as an act of mercy by the Lord.

We, the humans have to climb up from being stone-men to the level of God-men on earth.

Most of the criminal acts are by animal men on earth.

We either have to climb up in the spiritual ladder or fall down to lower levels of birth and be born again and again till we develop the intellectual maturity to reach the level of God men on earth. This is the path to Moksha or Liberation.

The Lord is guiding us towards the path of Moksha through the sacred text, the Gita, and he warns us through this Sloka not to fall from the heights of birth as humans.

The sastras say that the birth right of every individual is to attain the final Liberation. The Lord, out of immense love to His creation is only assisting the individual to reach the final goal.

Our enemy is "Arishadwargas." (kama, krodha, lobha, moha, mada, matsarya)

The leader is "Kama", the desire, lustful desire.

If the leader is destroyed, his followers will surrender and peace will be established. The Lord's incarnation is destroying the leaders that bring havoc on earth.

जन्म कर्म च मे दिव्यमेवं यो वेत्ति तत्त्वतः ।
त्यक्त्वा देहं पुनर्जन्म नैति मामेति सोऽर्जुन ||9||

janma karma ca me divyam evaṃ yo vetti tattvataḥ |
tyaktvā dehaṃ punarjanma naiti mām eti so 'rjuna ||9||

O Arjuna, he who thus knows My divine birth and action, having abandoned the body, is not born again, but to Me, he comes. ||9||

Janma: birth; karma: action; cha: and; me': my; divyam: divine; evam: thus; yo: who; vetti: knows; tatvataha: in essence; tyaktva: having abandoned; deham: the body; punarjanma: re-birth; na: not; eti: gets; maam: Me; eti: comes; sah: he.

In the secular world, knowing and becoming are two different entities and we should not apply the same principle in understanding this Sloka.

As a matter of fact this Sloka is really the re-iteration of the Upanishad declaration: Brahmavit Brahmaiva bhavati.

It means the one who knows Brahman, becomes Brahman. Let us try to understand this declaration first.

What the Lord has taught us so far is the fact that each of us has the Atman within which is the true Self. This Self is covered with the outer physical body made up of five elements. We are not the body but the Atman. The Atman is "Brahman."

He who clearly knows this basic spiritual principle of the Hindu philosophy comes to understand and live with the "Eternal Truth."

Such an individual realizes the process of birth and death due to the play of the gunas and maya and soon learns to live with the bliss of "Atma Jnana." Such an individual attains oneness with the Brahman.

This is the Upanishad declaration.

In this Sloka, the attention is drawn to the incarnation of the Brahman as "Krishna." The Gita as we know is incorporated in the epic Mahabharata and it highlights the divinity of Lord Krishna. The Mahabharata is considered as an epic.

The Puranas are a collection of tales of ancient times. In post-Vedic times, the Puranas became the medium for conveying the Vedic teaching to the common man.

In the early Vedic period, there were no forms of God as such. The learned seers who went in search of the life beyond death became convinced of an unknown power behind all the activities on earth. They called the power "the Supreme Brahman." For the sake of description, they said He was Nirguna (no attributes) Nirakara (no form) Brahman. This is the first step in bringing the idea of God to the fellow humans.

Understanding and realizing this idea is very hard for the majority. To make the subject of Brahman easier to understand, the seers took the next step in the description of Nirakara Nirguna Brahman (Brahman with no from and qualities) and brought out the notion of "OM". (refer to the introduction –subject Upanisad)

Those seekers who are mature in spirituality and attain higher levels of Bhakti, known as "Para Bhakti", are able to live unaffected by the changes in the material world. Ultimately, even before casting off their physical bodies they merge into the Supreme.

This Sloka is bringing out the aspect of upasana the"Saguna, Sakara Brahman" (with divine qualities and divine form).

By knowing in detail about the Avatara, accepting the form in which He manifests and developing love, nay, intense love for the same, is the method advocated for the benefit of the common man.

To do so, the seeker has to have faith in the Brahman and belief in the mythological explanations of the Avataras. He/she can select any one of the Avataras (incarnations) to meditate upon.

Meditation is a means of cleansing the mind of impure thoughts. Diverting the attention of the dynamic mind from the material world towards the Atman within needs intense love for the Supreme and concentration on His divinity and divine play. This is the path of Bhakti.

We are expected to realize that Krishna was not just the son of Vasudeva and Devaki but divinity on earth. He has no birth or death. He is immortal and omnipresent.

The seeker has to understand in essence the divinity of Krishna. The word used is "Tatvataha." He who knows the essential principle of Brahman and His manifestations is the real seeker. Knowing in this sense is living the life of divinity and expressing divinity in speech, thoughts and actions.

This implies that the seeker who can see the Lord dwelling in all forms of life, in all aspects of nature, shows love and respect for the same is fit to attain unity with Brahman. Only such a seeker is the real knower. Knowing Brahman is not a theoretical understanding of Brahman. It is the direct experience of the Brahman which is beyond the equipment of body, senses, mind and the intellect. Only such understanding of Brahman is what is meant by "Tatvataha."

An attempt to know Brahman is "Sadhana" and to become one with the Brahman is "Sadhya." Sadhana is practice and Sadhya is the goal to achieve.

वीतरागभयक्रोधा मन्मया मामुपाश्रिताः ।
बहवो ज्ञानतपसा पूता मद्भावमागताः ||**10**||

vītarāgabhayakrodhā manmayā mām upāśritāḥ |
bahavo jñānatapasā pūtā madbhāvam āgatāḥ ||10||

Free from attachment, fear and anger, absorbed in Me, taking refuge in Me, purified by penance in the fire of knowledge, many have attained Me. ||10||

Veetaraga: free from attachment; bhaya: fear; krodha: anger; manmaya: absorbed in Me; mam: Me; upashritaha: taking refuge in; bahavaha: many; jnana tapasa: by the fire of knowledge; poota: purified; madbhavam: My being; agataha: have attained.

This chapter is Jnana Yoga and the Lord is giving the path of Jnana to attain His being which is nothing other than Moksha. He says, "Madbhavam Agataha." It means "attain My being".

Having given the advice, He has also given the means to achieve the same.

He says, "Free from attachment, fear and anger." Conducting karma in the ordinary worldly sense brings in any one of these three consequences. These lead us away from the spiritual path and make us bound to the world of samsara. We have already learnt from the previous chapter that the only way to be free from these three is by "Nishkama karma." We have to carry on conducting all ordained actions to burn our existing vasanas and not accumulate new vasanas in the process.

We are the Atman within and the physical body is covering the same. Attachment which arises out of desires could be either to the body or to the world of objects. Attachment to our desires and attachment to what we want to get from the desires is "Raga."

The fear of not getting the object of desire is "Bhaya". Fear of losing what we get is also Bhaya.

This in turn makes us get angry and this is "krodha."

We have read in the second chapter the consequences of anger. (Slokas 63, 64) We fall down from the path of spirituality and become either animal men or stone men.

This is because the senses and the mind drag us down and move us away from our sadhana.

What should we do?

Our senses including the mind should be directed towards the Divinity within and Divinity all round.

This is what we should understand from the statement "Manmaya Mam upashritaha."

The senses should be absorbed in the Atman (Manmaya). Taking shelter in Him by selfless devotion is "Mam upashritaha".

Karma and Bhakti are the tools in the path of Jnana.

The purification of the mind by knowledge is "Jnana tapas." "Putaha" used in this Sloka refers to the purification of the senses. Understanding the correct way to perform karma and accordingly carrying out the correct actions is "Jnana tapas." Knowing the essential divinity which is one's own nature, seeing the same in all forms of life around and living the life of divinity is real Jnana.

This is the path to Liberation.

We can see that these three paths of Karma, Bhakti and Jnana are not separate entities but are totally intermingled with each other.

The person who sincerely follows Karma Yoga becomes a Jnani.

The Jnani learns to see divinity in its true sense and thereby conducts nishkama karma. The Bhakta is he who sees the divinity in various manifestations and shows his love towards one and all. He has no hatred to anybody.

The experts say that fuel consigned to the fire becomes fire itself.

The fire of the penance, "tapas" which offers the mind and its content of vasanas to the fire of divinity within is "Jnana Tapas."

Quote:

Sri Ramakrishna:

Maya is inherent in Iswara. It is constituted of both Vidya and avidya.

Vidya Maya assisted by the art of discrimination, devotion, detachment and love of beings takes the aspirant Godward. Avidya Maya on the other hand estranges man from God.

Finally the Lord says that this has been achieved by many. He is therefore trying to tell us that it is not as difficult as one imagines. It is possible and this determination is needed in the spiritual path. It gives us the fuel to fly upwards to His abode.

ये यथा मां प्रपद्यन्ते तांस्तथैव भजाम्यहम् ।
मम वर्त्मानुवर्तन्ते मनुष्याः पार्थ सर्वशः ||11||

ye yathā māṃ prapadyante tāṃs tathaiva bhajāmy aham|
mama vartmānuvartante manuṣyāḥ pārtha sarvaśaḥ ||11||

O Partha, in whatever way men approach Me, even so do I reward them, for the path that men take from every side is mine. ||11||

Ye: who; yatha: in whatever way; prapadyante: approach; taan: them; tatha: so; eva: even; bhajami: reward; aham: I; mama: my; vartma: path; anuvartante: follow; manushyaha: men; sarvashaha: in all ways/every side.

So far we have been informed by the Lord that He is not just Krishna, son of Vasudeva and Devaki, but the Omnipresent, Omnipotent, Nirakara, Nirguna Brahman. It is us who have given that power various forms and names and worship the same in different ways.

We have a number of different religious denominations all over the world we know of. In each of those main denominations, there are a variety of different branches. We have come to recognize ourselves as separate entities and our knowledge of the Supreme Power is limited.

We are told that it does not matter how we approach the Supreme, we will get due rewards for our efforts.

The results either in the secular world or spiritual world depend upon our actions, knowledge of the actions and devotion to the actions. The more faith we have in the knowledge we have received, the more faith we have in the scriptures or the texts as the case may be, greater will be our efforts and this in turn gives us the final benefits from the actions.

Every way of living, if aimed at the Divine, will eventually lead us to Him.

Every wish we entertain will remain as a vasana imprint till it is fulfilled or totally wiped off from our mind. The Lord, who stays as the Soul/Atman within does not desert us any time. The Soul never departs. It wears a new suit in the form of a new birth and the same mind and intellect from the previous existence/birth will then have a new body. This is to fulfill the un-manifested vasanas from past birth/births. Depending upon the desires entertained, according to the three basic gunas we either move upward in the spiritual path or fall down from the path.

Every one, at the end, will realize the folly of attachment to worldly pleasures and finally will clear the mind of all vasanas. The mind gets annihilated totally. That state, we have learnt is "Moksha" or Liberation.

This is the message from the Lord through this Sloka to the mankind in general and to every individual being, irrespective of his/her religion, caste, creed sex, social status etc.

All the branches from a tree belong to the same tree. Subsequent branches from the main branch also belong to the same tree. All the flowers and leaves from individual branches belong to the same tree. Finally every fruit belongs to the same tree.

Similarly, all religions, creeds, sects etc. belong to the same tree of samsara of the Lord. We are all His children. We all receive the same love from the Lord. How we reciprocate the love results in the reward we get.

The petrol in cars is the same. The same petrol is needed for all types of cars ranging from simple basic cars to most luxurious modern cars. The petrol is needed to take the car to the destination. The way the car holds on the road depends upon the sophisticated parts in it, the driver who has control over the car, the condition of the road and the weather.

All it means is that different types of persons receive the grace of the Lord in different ways according to their own samskaras. (Actions due to the inherent thought imprints) Those who approach (Prapadyante) Him (with love, faith and conduct appropriate actions) for wealth will get the wealth, those who approach for knowledge will get the knowledge and those who yearn for Liberation will get Liberation. Eventually, as we have discussed, each one of us, will attain Liberation.

If so, can we not see the folly in approaching Him for paltry worldly pleasures? Why should one approach a king for getting a few pennies? Let us learn to approach Him with a desire for Universal welfare and salvation.

Some approach Him for secular prosperity. Even this wish is granted. But the time it takes to mature and get fulfilled depends on various factors like past samskaras, way of approach, types of gunas that are involved in the approach etc. It might even be in future births that one gets the reward. The fact is that we do not remember what we wished for in the past births.

Whatever may be the path the seeker follows, the end result is "Moksha." "Sandhya Vandana" prayers:

Akashat Patitam Toyam Yatha Gacchanti sagaram

Sarva-Deva-Namaskaraha Kesavam Prati Gachati.

It means:

Just as the drops of water from the sky end in the ocean, the salutations to various Gods reach Me.

This Sloka therefore re-iterates the fact that the sacred text is universal with a universal message towards the welfare of all the mankind.

काङ्क्षन्तः कर्मणां सिद्धिं यजन्त इह देवताः ।
क्षिप्रं हि मानुषे लोके सिद्धिर्भवति कर्मजा ||12||

kāṅkṣantaḥ karmaṇāṃ siddhiṃ yajanta iha devatāḥ |
kṣipraṃ hi mānuṣe loke siddhir bhavati karmajā ||12||

They, who long for success from actions in this world, make sacrifices to the Gods, because success is quickly obtained from actions in this world of men. ||12||

Kankshataha: longing for; karmanam: of actions; siddhim: success; yajante: sacrifice; iha: in this world; devataha: gods; kshipram: soon/quickly; hi: because; maanushe: in the human; loke': world; siddhir: success; bhavati: obtained; karmaja: born of actions.

The experts in spiritual science designate the earth as "Karma Bhoomi" (land of action). In this world whatever action performed has a result, albeit good or bad depending upon the type of action.

What are the results of actions?

Our philosophy talks of a total of 14 worlds in total. They are known as “creative worlds”, because they are subject to creation and destruction. They are subjected to changes.

There are seven worlds above and seven worlds below.

On top of all the worlds and separate from all is “Parabrahman”, who is omnipresent, omniscient and omnipotent. His world, if we may say so for the sake of description only, transcends all the 14 worlds. It does not undergo any physical changes and is not subject to any changes.

The sacred text, Sreemad Bhagawatha Purana says that the “Viswaroopa” or “universal form” of the “Parabrahman” consists of and envelops all the 14 worlds. (refer to “samsara and Moksha” in the introduction)

Starting from the earth where we are all living, there are seven worlds upwards up to the abode of Brahman, the creator. These are the abodes of those who have by their good karmas (punya karmas) achieved entry.

The Celestials, Gandharvas, Yakshas, Devas and Sages are to be found in these planes.

Tracing downwards there are seven worlds below the sphere of the earth. Those who by their cruel deeds and actions against the sastras end up in these Lokas.

The first section of the sacred Gayatri mantra:

OM Bhoohu, Bhuvaha, Suvaha, Mahaha, Janaha, Tapaha, Satyam.

This represents the seven worlds that include the earth and higher worlds up to Brahma loka.

The earth is the focal point in as far as the results of actions are taken into account. Good actions take the folk upwards and bad actions take them downwards into one of the nether worlds. As soon as the benefits are used up those who find entry into the higher worlds have to come down to earth and start accumulating meritorious points by their good deeds.

In this sense, the inhabitants of heaven including Indra, the Lord of heaven have a temporary stay in the higher worlds. Each one of those inhabitants in the higher worlds has to come down to earth after exhausting the benefits of punya (results of good deeds). The inhabitants of these worlds have a very long life.

Similarly, those who find entry into nether worlds stay for a length of time depending upon their bad deeds and are born as humans on earth again.

Those who study the scriptures and realize that good actions will take them into higher worlds, will follow the texts that describe various yajnas and sacrifices which please the gods above. The word "gods" used in this sloka refers to the demi gods described in the Hindu texts.

The Hindu religion depicts a number of higher powers that are also benign in nature. (In the sense that they do no harm) They are greater and powerful than the men on earth. They are designated as "Gods." Each one of these powers, if worshipped with sincere faith and devotion bestows grace and fulfills the wishes.

What we have to understand is that the success is quickly obtained by man for the work he does in this world. To do so one must have a sense of devotion and humility and conduct sacrifices that please the higher powers like Indra, Agni, Vayu etc.

Taking the same logic, we can conclude that entry into the lower worlds results from evil actions.

All the other 13 worlds apart from the earth are only places of results of actions conducted on earth either good or evil. We attain hell or heavens depending upon our actions.

The earth is therefore to be considered as the Centre of spiritual realization. We must realize that if we desire fruits of actions we have to be prepared to be born on earth again and again and may be even to fall down into the hellish regions and suffer.

Finally, one in a million realizes the folly of going after the fruits of actions and strives for Moksha. Only a rare few achieve the end result of birth as a human which is "Union with the Parabrahman" with no more re-birth.

चातुर्वर्ण्यं मया सृष्टं गुणकर्मविभागशः ।
तस्य कर्तारमपि मां विद्ध्यकर्तारमव्ययम् ||13||

cāturvarṇyaṃ mayā sṛṣṭaṃ guṇakarmavibhāgaśaḥ |
tasya kartāram api māṃ viddhy akartāram avyayam ||13||

The four-fold caste system has been created by Me according to the differentiation of qualities and actions. Though, I am the author, know Me as non-doer and eternal. ||13||

Chaturvarnyam: the four fold caste system; maya: by Me; srushtam: has been created; gunakarma vibhagashaha: according to the differentiation of guna and karma; tasya: thereof (though); kartaram; the author; api: also; maam: Me; viddhi: know; akartaram: non-doer; avyayam: immutable/eternal.

The caste system as it is practiced in India at present has been a bone of contention amongst many. Even this sloka has been used by many to support their view of the same but unfortunately with incomplete/improper/misguided understanding of its words. It is therefore very important to understand the meaning of the sloka in its totality and not just a part of it.

"The four fold caste system has been created by Me",

Taking this part of the sloka, there are many who, without proceeding further simply say that after all the system has been created by Sri Krishna. They tend to put the blame of the present problems due to the existing method of caste system directly on Krishna.

It is definitely not true and not correct.

As we can see Sri Krishna immediately adds up to the first statement by saying: According to the differentiation of qualities and actions."

We have to understand this section more clearly to remove any misunderstanding. Let us therefore proceed with the analysis of the meaning of the entire sloka.

Chaturvanyam: (the four varnas):

The word "Varna" refers to the color of the person. The word "caste" has been a latter entry into the dictionary of the Hindus. Sri Krishna admits to creating the "Varna" system but does not say "caste system."

When one refers to the "color" of the person, it means "the color of the Centre of Actions." "Color" in this sense is only a poetic description and does not really refer to the physical color of the individual like dark, fair etc. but refers to the color of the gunas inherent within and expressed.

Guna Karma vibhagashu: (divided according to the gunas and actions.) The Centre for all our actions (karma) is "the mind."

The mind is the seat of three basic qualities (gunas) of "Satva, Rajas and Tamas." All the three qualities are inherent in every individual but their proportion expressed outwardly as actions differs from individual to individual. The action expressed according to the gunas is "Guna karma." The division of such actions is "Guna karma Vibhagashu".

Broadly speaking, in any single society, the individuals can be divided into four main groups depending upon their proportion in expressing outwardly the three basic gunas in the form of actions. "Chaturvarna" refers to the four groups of individuals in any society.

We naturally accept that the different parts of the body constitute a single person even though their functions vary. We are expected to use the same logic and accept that the four castes are constituents of one single society and we should act with love and respect towards each of these four groups.

These are: Brahmana, Kshatriya, Vysya and Sudra.

(A description of the qualities of these four classes of people is to be found in chapter 18, slokas 42-44 of the Gita)

A Brahmana is he who has a predominance of Satva and shines forth with the light of knowledge of the sastras. Satva is depicted as pure white in color. Those members in the society who have a true and complete knowledge of the sastras and express the divinity within in all their actions are the brahmanas in the truest sense. The priestly classes of the present are referred to as brahmanas. Their predominant guna expressed in actions is "Purity".

Kshatriya is he who has predominance of rajas and Satva and stands prominently by his physical prowess. He is also a man of knowledge of the sastras. Rajas is depicted as red in color. The ruling classes of people in the days gone by were the Kshatriyas. Passion expressed in action is that of Kshatriyas.

Vysya is he who has a combination of rajas and tamas but with a small portion of satva included. Those members in the society who are businessmen and take part in the trade are the Vysyas. Knack in business, making profit for oneself and at the same time providing material needed for the people in their respective trade/ household needs is that of Vysyas.

Shudra is he who has a predominance of tamas. He is physically strong but has not got the knowledge of the sastras. The labour classes who are physically strong but who do not possess the knowledge of the sastras are considered as Shudras. They undertake the menial tasks that are to be done in the society.

The ancient system was used therefore to classify the people according to their capacity expressed by them. The sacred text tells us that each one of us is born with a set of gunas carried forward from the previous births. By our so called past samskaras (vasanas) each one of us belong to one of these four main groups.

Even though we belong to one of the four categories at birth, we have an opportunity to better ourselves and move upwards. Even the lowest of the low, the Shudra has a right to acquire the knowledge and move up the ladder. The sacred Hindu texts and the Gita clearly state that it is the duty of the Brahmana to impart the knowledge to whoever seeks for the same and assist in his/ her spiritual progress.

Unfortunately somewhere in the middle from the time of creation of the life by Brahman to the present day, this classification was misrepresented and misused.

Child born to a Brahmana was called a Brahmana, to a Kshatriya a Kshatriya and so on and so forth. In course of time this method was accepted as norm and the caste system of the present was born. (The Government of India has used this method for classifying its citizens who are Hindus. This has caused a lot of upheaval in the society and it is not the intention of this author to dwell on such issues).Also it is advisable to refer to "Manu Dharma Sastra".

Sri Krishna, the creator of life on earth says in this sloka that this classification was created by Him only according to the differentiation of qualities and functions of the individual. The entry into the classification is according to the "guna-right and not birthright."

By acquiring the skills needed for any varna system, the individual can progress in life. Sri Krishna says that the "Purushartha" of every individual is to attain "Moksha." If so, this should include all the members of all the four classes mentioned above without any exception. They can attain this final aim only by acquiring the knowledge which the upper class has to impart with love and affection to one and all.

Swami Vivekananda:

It is in the nature of any society to form into groups with each group with certain privileges. Caste system is a natural order with each group member capable of performing certain duties in relation to that caste better than those belonging to the other classes. One can be a governor and other a shoe mender. Governor cannot mend the shoes and shoe mender cannot govern a state. One can be highly knowledgeable when it comes to the scriptures but he cannot look down upon others who do not know the same.

It is not necessary to change the caste system but we must change the way in which it is used. There should be respect and love for each other and no one should consider themselves as superior. Let everyone be taught that the divinity is within each one and the same God is in all. Everyone should be given the opportunity to get the education and work out his own salvation.

"Though I am the author, know me as non-doer and eternal."

What does it mean?

Why does Krishna contradict Himself by saying that He is the author of this system and at the same time describe Himself as the "non-doer and eternal?"

Krishna as such has been depicted as the son of Vasudeva and Devaki and leaving the physical body behind at the end. To dispel any doubt, He has made it clear at the beginning of this chapter that He is Eternal and He is the one who taught the sacred text to Vivaswan.

It is possible that the caste system was probably evident even in Dwapara Yuga and Krishna did not like the practice. He therefore must have used the Gita as an instrument to express His opposition to the system and clarify the rules for the varnashrama.

He admits to being the author of "Varna" system but never says that He is the author of the caste system.

Also, as such, Parabrahman through the medium of the four headed Lord Brahma gave the Vedas to the mankind at the time of creation. Man, in course of time made changes every so often in the system of administration. The caste system is therefore one of such changes that has crept up somewhere in the middle of the cycle of creation and dissolution. It does not befit us to blame Sri Krishna for the misuse of the varnashrama in the name of "caste".

Varnashrama is nothing but choosing one's profession according to the aptitude of the individual. Aptitude in turn brings out the desires and the desires form the basis of vasana. The mind is a store house of vasanas. Predominance of any of the aptitudes makes the individual fall into one of the four varnas.

The Purushasookta says:

The brahmanas were the custodians of the Vedic knowledge and culture and hence the face of the Purusha is associated with "Brahmana."

The Kshatriyas were fighters and kings with military skills and so the arms of the virat symbolize the Kshatriya.

The vysyas were the main segment of the population supporting and sustaining the entire society by their economic activities. As they supported the society, the thighs of the Virat symbolize the Vysyas.

The feet of the Virat represent the Shudra. This is because, without the feet the body cannot stand up. The society cannot stand without the supply of the physical labour. This was the chosen occupation of those who were physically strong but did not have matching brain power.

Diversity is a fact of life and varnashrama is a facet of diversity of nature. Hymn 13 of the Purushasookta:

Brahmanosya Mukhasmaseet: Bahu Rajasya kritaha:
Uru tadesya yad Vaishyaha: Padabhyam Shoodro Ajayata.

His face became the Brahmana, His two arms became the Kshatriya, His two thighs became the Vysya and from His two feet Shudra was born.

Santi Parva of Mahabharata has a similar verse in it recited by the grandsire Bheeshma:

Brahma vaktram bhujau kshatramkrtsnam
urudaram visah Padau vysya stitah sudras
tasmai varnatmane namaha

It means:

My salutations to Varnatma who has Brahmana as His face, shoulders as Kshatriya, stomach and thighs as Vaishya and feet as Shudra.

Herein is a reference to Manu dharma Sastra.

"Manu", first Aryan man, the first to offer oblations to Gods.

Manu dharma Sastra: the Code of Manu. A collection of laws based on custom and precedent and the teaching of the Vedas.

Manusmriti is an outstanding sociological work of ancient India with a comprehensive outlook which has impacted greatly on the Hindu society for all these thousands of years. His influence upon the organization of the society persists till this day. Chapter 4 of Manusmriti deals with his concept of the society. The original concept of social class could be traced back to the Rig-Veda which based the society by recognizing the all-importance of distinct social classes vested with the responsibility for the discharge of strictly specific social duties or obligations. Its concept was that the different social classes are separate and independent of one another and yet they, together, were intended to serve the basic interests of the society as a whole. The so called social classes were only functional divisions of the society. The affiliation of an individual to a certain social class, was his habitual performance of the duties demanded and expected by that social class.

Such a flexibility of the functional role of the individual did not last long and it came to an end in the post-Vedic period, presumably during the period of evolvement of the Dharmasastra of Manu.

The division of the society became a rigid pattern and hardened into the caste system. The differentiation became a birth-right instead of the functional role appropriate to it.

Manu goes on to give a detailed description of the role of Brahmanas and the way they should be treated by the other three classes. He has given importance to the Brahmana and places them at the top of the social order.

He has given the primary and secondary duties of the four classes of people in the society.

न मां कर्माणि लिम्पन्ति न मे कर्मफले स्पृहा |
इति मां योऽभिजानाति कर्मभिर्न स बध्यते ||14||

na māṃ karmāṇi limpanti na me karmaphale spṛhā |
iti māṃ yo 'bhijānāti karmabhir na sa badhyate ||14||

Actions do not taint Me. Nor have I desire for the fruits of actions. He who knows Me thus, is not bound by karma. ||14||

Na: not; maam: Me; karmani: actions; limpanti: taint; Me': My; karmapahale: in the fruits of action; spruha: desire; iti: thus; yaha: who; abhijanati: knows; karmabhih: by actions; na: not; sah: he; badyate: is bound.

Sri Krishna wants Arjuna to realize that He is not just his charioteer, son of Vasudeva and Devaki who showed a number of miracles in His life and destroyed a number of the wicked. He wants us not to give great importance to His leela but to recognize that he is the Supreme Parabrahman incarnating for the protection of Dharma and destruction of evil.

Whenever we conduct any actions we get the feeling like "I did it, I enjoyed it, I feel happy etc." This is because actions/ karma produces modifications of the mind which in turn is due to "Ego." We associate with the physical body and with the present. The Lord does not want us to have the feeling of doership in any of our actions and also not to be attached to the fruits of actions.

Krishna is not just any other individual we come across. He is divine incarnate. He has no vasanas to carry from past births. He has no association with the results of actions and therefore is not bound by the consequences of His actions.

This sloka is reiterating this fact.

His desire if we call it a desire, (really speaking He takes it as His will) is for the welfare of the life He created. Doing it for the sake of duty is His motto. Those who want to tread on the path of spirituality with a desire for Moksha should emulate Him and conduct actions accordingly.

It is important to understand the meaning of the sentence: "He who knows Me thus, is not bound by karma."

"Knowing" is when we put into action what we have learnt.

We should put into action what we have learnt from studying His life, as Krishna of the Mahabharata period in Dwapara Yuga. If our actions also fit in with the principle of Nishkama karma and karma phala tyaga we will be burning the existing vasanas we are carrying and will not get any more new vasanas. Thus we pave the way for our own "annihilation of the mind and Vasana kshaya."

Our learned masters quote the example of the moon when they are trying to explain the principle of His actions.

The moon gets reflected on a clear day in ponds and wells etc. When there is a movement in any one of these containers, the water in turn shakes. This in turn distorts the shape of the reflected moon. The moon above as such does not shake but the reflection shakes.

Our Atman within us is like the reflected moon. Due to our association with the physical body we feel the Atman as ego, we feel reactions due to our desires. Our desires and the consequences of these desires do not affect the Atman but affect the ego. Transcending this feeling is the way to progress on the spiritual path.

By giving Himself as the greatest Karma Yogi to follow, he is leading the mankind towards liberation.

एवं ज्ञात्वा कृतं कर्म पूर्वैरपि मुमुक्षुभिः ।
कुरु कर्मैव तस्मात्त्वं पूर्वैः पूर्वतरं कृतम् ||15||

evaṃ jñātvā kṛtaṃ karma pūrvair api mumukṣubhiḥ |
kuru karmaiva tasmāt tvaṃ pūrvaiḥ pūrvataraṃ kṛtam ||15||

Thus knowing, the ancient spiritual seekers also performed actions. Therefore you shall do the same actions as performed by the ancestors in the olden times. ||15||

Evam : thus; jnatva: knowing; kritam: performed; karma: actions; poorvai: ancient; api: also; mumukshubhihi: spiritual seekers; kuru: do; karma: actions; eva: even; tasmat: therefore; tvam: you; poorvaihi: by ancients; poorvataram: in the olden times; krutam: done.

Mumukshubhihi: those seeking "Moksha" or "Liberation." There were many in the past who followed the spiritual path for attaining the final aim of life: which is "Moksha."

Spiritual seekers were there in the past, are there now and will be there in future.

This principle behind the teaching of the sacred text holds good for all times. What is the benefit from such principle?

The benefit is "Universal welfare" -- "Loka Kalyana." This can be possible only by the conduct of actions.

The actions of the seekers who want Liberation are to be without the sense of "Ego" and without the desire for the fruits of action."

Such actions in turn become the foundation for liberation. This is the process of "Self-realization".

Krishna reminds Arjuna that it is possible only by being part of the society and fulfilling one's role in the society. "Action" or "Karma" associated with the "Jnana (knowledge)" and "Devotion, Faith"" towards the teachings of the Lord is the foundation for success.

Let us understand that this path is open to all of us to understand and implement in our day to day life and will be open for the future generations to come.

Another explanation:

The sacred text Sreemad Bhagawadgita was narrated to Arjuna by the Lord.

Arjuna has to be considered as an example of Rajasic quality. If one can divide the rajasic quality into Satvic Rajas, Rajasic Rajas and Tamasic Rajas, Arjuna would fall in the category of a Satvic Rajasic individual. His actions were on the higher plane of purity.

He was a man of action but his actions were desire oriented.

When he got confused as to the right action to conduct for attainment of Moksha, he received guidance by his guru Sri Krishna on the principle of action.

Arjuna is to be considered as the representative of all those who would like to know the right path to take in their own life.

Hence, on behalf of all those rajasic men desirous of treading the spiritual path, Sri Krishna is giving His opinion. He is saying that for spiritual liberation, one must work and the work has to be like the actions of the ancient spiritual seekers.

Laziness is not the path for liberation.

One may say that there are many rishis and tapaswins who are not really conducting any actions and ask how they will get liberation?

Yes, a categorical yes that they will get liberation. These great souls are conducting tapas for the universal welfare. Their actions are from a higher intellectual plane. Majority of us do not fall in this category because we have not got the will power of conducting such tapas. Karma Yoga is the path for us. Let our actions emulate the learned ancient masters and fit in with the principle of Karma Yoga. Let us understand the same clearly and work for universal welfare.

किं कर्म किमकर्मेति कवयोऽप्यत्र मोहिताः ।
तत्ते कर्म प्रवक्ष्यामि यज्ज्ञात्वा मोक्ष्यसेऽशुभात् ||16||

kiṃ karma kim akarmeti kavayo 'py atra mohitāḥ |
tat te karma pravakṣyāmi yaj jñātvā mokṣyase 'śubhāt ||16||

What is action? What is inaction? In this matter even the wise are deluded. I will teach you that action knowing which; you shall be liberated from the evil. ||16||

Kim: what; karma: action; akarma: inaction; iti: thus; kavayo'pi: sages also; mohitaha: deluded; tat: that; te': to you; pravakshyami:

shall teach; yat: which; jnatva: having known; mokshyase: shall be liberated; ashubhat: from evil.

What is "Ashubha"? Ashubha is "evil". What is evil?

In this context, evil is to be considered as the cycle of births and deaths.

It is the entry into the ocean called "samsara". We have now reached the stage of human birth and we have to swim in this ocean of samsara and reach the shore.

From the spiritual point of view, many do not have a clear idea of what is action and what is inaction. For the sake of clarity, Sri Krishna is informing Arjuna that He will teach the difference between the two.

It is possible that Arjuna's reaction on listening to the last few verses prompted Krishna to explain the intricacies of karma in greater detail. It is no use by simply saying that "I want Liberation and I do not want to fall into the ocean of samsara." We must know clearly all the various aspects of karma and act accordingly. We should become experts in the field so that all the correct actions will become involuntary actions by nature.

For example, breathing and circulation are necessary for survival and we have adopted our central nervous system in such a way that we do not think of these two but still carrying on functioning in these two fields. The actions according to the sastras have to become involuntary actions. They have to become our second nature.

In the next few slokas there will be a clearer view, of this aspect of the philosophy.

कर्मणो ह्यपि बोद्धव्यं बोद्धव्यं च विकर्मणः ।
अकर्मणश्च बोद्धव्यं गहना कर्मणो गतिः ||17||

karmaṇo hy api boddhavyaṃ boddhavyaṃ ca vikarmaṇaḥ |
akarmaṇaś ca boddhavyaṃ gahanā karmaṇo gatiḥ ||17||

The nature of right action, wrong action and also of inaction should be known. Deep and difficult to understand is the path of action. ||17||

Karmano: of action; hi: for; api: also; boddhavyam: should be known; cha: and; vikarmanaha: of forbidden action; akarmanaha: of inaction; gahanaa: deep; karmano: of action; gatihi: the path.

Three words concerning various types of karma have been introduced in this sloka. They are:

Karma, Vikarma and Akarma.

If we understand these three words, we would have gone a long way in understanding the intricacies of action.

First of all we must realize that our physical body owes its existence to the Atman within. The Atman is the energy that keeps us alive and propels us into action. On this principle when we conduct any actions, we must be clear that it is only due to the blessings of the Atman.

Once we understand this truth, the entire process of karma will become crystal clear.

Similarly it is important that we understand that the "Nature" appears active but cannot be alive without the presence of the divine energy.

The Atman/Divine energy is imperishable but the body/nature is perishable.

Let us now precede to analyse the meaning of the three words. Again, it is important to note that we are dealing with the spiritual science and the spiritual path taken by the spiritual seekers. When we use the word "karma", it applies to all actions according to the scriptures.

Vikarma applies to all actions that are contrary to the scriptures.

Akarma has two meanings.

No actions/inaction and "No feeling of doership" in all actions.

It is The "Guhya bhasha" or the hidden/implied meaning. "Inaction."

There is a very big difference between the two.

Karma:

An introduction to this has already been discussed when dealing with sloka 8, chapter 3. Further analysis will give us the following explanation.

These are the following categories of karma:

Varnashrama dharma

Ashrama dharma

Pancha maha yajnas

Kula dharma

Desha dharma

Atma dharma

The actions pertaining to each of the above classifications is "Karma."

Varnashrama dharma has been discussed when dealing with sloka 13 in this chapter.

Ashrama dharma relates to the duties pertaining to the four principal stages in life:

Brahmacharya: first stage in life involves celibacy as a requirement for studies.

Grihastha: second stage in life starting from graduation and entering into married life and professional life.

Vanaprastha: third stage in life starting from the time of retirement from work to the last stage of sanyasa.

Sanyasa is the last stage in life dealing with renunciation of worldly possessions with aspiration for union with the Parabrahman.

Pancha maha yajnas: the duties towards: sloka 8, chapter 3; these five are part of one's daily duties.

Kula dharma: these are duties/custom peculiar to a family/clan.

Desha dharma: we all have a duty to the nation we belong to.

Atma dharma: these are our duties on recognizing that we are the servants of the power within and our actions should be considered as the divine duties of the Atman. Total divinity in all thoughts/actions/speech is Atma dharma.

In the spiritual path that is followed by the seeker, all the above actions become "Karma" only when there is no sense of individuality in relation to the actions and when all the results from the actions are offered to the Lord.

The result of such actions is "Peace".

Vikarma: actions which are contrary to the sastras become "Vikarma."

Actions with a sense of ego and those with a desire for the fruits of actions are considered as Vikarma.

It also includes the forbidden duties known as "Nishiddha karmas" which are actions prohibited by the sastras.

Many of the forbidden duties in spiritual life and secular life are similar. Injury to others, telling a lie, stealing, rape etc. fall in this category.

Whereas some of the duties in the section of "Karma" enumerated above are for a particular sect or groups of people, "Nishiddha karmas" apply to all classes of people in total without exception.

The results of such actions are "Sorrow."

Akarma: the meaning of this word is "No action or inaction." It really refers to actions that do not have "individuality" on the part of the person conducting them.

The true meaning of this word has not been grasped clearly by many. Many believe that it involves no actions on the part of the individual.

He who works with "Jnana" realizes that he cannot escape actions in this life. To burn the existing vasanas he has no other option but to work. However the work has to be without a sense of ego and with no desire for the fruits of action.

Sri Ramanujacharya says that Karma and Jnana are complementary to each other and not two separate entities.

Realizing that we are the servants of the divine who is resident as Atman within and acting for universal welfare is "Akarma" in the truest sense.

Krishna makes it clear that it is difficult to understand the path of karma.

It is important to be aware that laziness is not "akarma" and one needs to dispel this wrong notion.

कर्मण्यकर्म यः पश्येदकर्मणि च कर्म यः ।
स बुद्धिमान् मनुष्येषु स युक्तः कृत्स्नकर्मकृत् ||**18**||

karmaṇy akarma yaḥ paśyed akarmaṇi ca karma yaḥ |
sa buddhimān manuṣyeṣu sa yuktaḥ kṛtsnakarmakṛt ||18||

He who sees actions in inaction, and inaction in action, is the wise man, the yogi, the doer of all actions among men. ||18||

Karmany: in actions; akarmaha: inaction; yaha: who; pasyed: would see; akarmani: in inaction; cha: and; karma: action; yaha: who; sa: he; buddhimaan: wise; manushyeshu: among men; yuktaha: yogi; kritsnakarmakrit: performer of all actions.

What is "seeing action in inaction" and "inaction in action"?

As this is a spiritual discourse, these two sentences refer to the actions of a spiritual seeker.

We have a very good example to understand this, from two events in our day to day lives.

a) Take the example of two trains at a station and we are the passengers on one of those two trains. When the train we are sitting on moves forward, it appears that the other stationary train and the passengers in it is moving in an opposite direction even though that second train is stationary.

Here, motion is attributed wrongly to the motionless. We see action in inaction.

b) Let us imagine that we are on the shore and there is a sailing ship in the waters. From our own viewpoint, it appears that the ship is stationary even though it is in motion.

Here, we attribute inaction to action.

We can see how ignorance covers our vision in these two instances.

In the spiritual journey, as discussed in the previous sloka, we are attributing action in inaction and saying that "I am the doer, I enjoyed the food etc." These actions were made possible only because of the life energy within, which make us feel that we are the doers of actions.

On the contrary, we do not recognize the role of the life energy in all our actions and consider that this energy is static even though it is the real kinetic energy in constant motion to keep the body alive. Herein we mistake "inaction in action."

He who recognizes the role of the Atman within, the role of the divine energy in nature is wise and a Yogi.

Mistaking the self (physical body, inert in the absence of life) as the Self (real doer of actions) is ignorance or egoistic.

"Doer of all actions among men":

This again refers to actions towards achieving "Self-knowledge" which is "Atma Jnana."

As a matter of fact, such a wise man is the doer of actions and is said to have attained the "Brahma Jnana".

A Yogi is he who has no ego or sense of doership in his actions and attributes all to the Atman within. He is said to be in a state of constant bliss and does not succumb to pleasures and pains of day to day life. He is the "Sthitaprajna" and "Jivanmukta."

Let us not therefore desist from our obligatory duties due to laziness or ignorance as it is going to be harmful in the spiritual journey. Let us all diligently conduct all actions in the spirit of "Nishkama karma and karma phala tyaga."

In the words of Swami Vivekananda:

Let not your work produce results for you, and at the same time may you be never without work.

Swami Vivekananda says also:

The perfectly trained alone are at their best both in solitude and society. They are tuned both to action and inaction.

They conduct all their obligatory duties and have no sense of ego.

No action/inaction in action: This is satvika type of action.

Let us take the example of a cinema screen. In the absence of the background screen, the film cannot be projected. It is essential for seeing the film. The screen is not tainted by any actions that take place on it.

The Atman is the screen and the various scenes on the screen are the actions of the body in relation to the secular world. Realizing that I am not the doer of actions and I am the eternal witness for bodily modifications is the way of satvika. There is absolutely no sense of doership.

Action in inaction:

Actions sprout from the thoughts in the mind. Thoughts sprout from the mind. One can be still active without showing any outward actions. As a matter of fact, there is an idiom that says: An idle mind is the devil's workshop.

A wise man is he who can realize and see intense activity in inaction and action in inaction. He looks upon his mind as a bodily instrument which appears not to be in action.

He looks upon the physical body as an instrument with so many activities from morning to night but really not acting on its own at any time. The Atmic energy brings the various bodily actions to the front.

The Lord says such a person is fit for liberation.

यस्य सर्वे समारम्भाः कामसङ्कल्पवर्जिताः ।
ज्ञानाग्निदग्धकर्माणं तमाहुः पण्डितं बुधाः ||19||

yasya sarve samārambhāḥ kāmasaṃkalpavarjitāḥ |
jñānāgnidagdhakarmāṇaṃ tam āhuḥ paṇḍitaṃ budhāḥ ||19||

He whose undertakings are all free from desire and purpose, whose actions have been burnt by the fire of knowledge, him, the wise call a "pandit." ||19||

Yasya: whose; sarve: all; samarambaha: undertakings; kama: desire, samkalpa: purpose; varjitaha: free from; jnanagni: fire of knowledge; daghdha: burnt; karmanaam: actions; tam: him; aahuhu: call; panditam: a sage/pandita; budhaha: the wise.

"Arambha" means "beginning."

"Samarambha" means "beginning of actions or undertaking of actions."

There is usually a purpose and desire behind undertaking important actions in one's life.

For example, the parents decide to send their son to the university they do so with a desire to make him a degree holder who will become eligible to work and stand on his own two feet.

The couple who would like to get married will do so with a desire to enjoy the married life together.

Sankalpa: "mental resolve, volition, purpose, intention."

Usually in the Hindu tradition, before any major undertaking like marriage, building a new house, sending the children to University etc., the concerned persons conduct a "Vrata" (religious observance) to please the Lord and request him to bestow grace. The priest who conducts the Vrata makes the individual repeat some prayers that declare the will/mental resolve to conduct the religious observance.

This intention to conduct the religious observance is "Sankalpa." The purpose behind an undertaking is "Sankalpa."

Kamasamkalpa: if the purpose behind the intention is to fulfill a desire it is called "Kama Sankalpa."

Varjitaha: free from.

Pandit: (also spelt as Pundit): It is a title given to a Hindu scholar. A well learned wise man is a Pandit.

In this sloka Sri Krishna says that a truly wise man who conducts actions in the spirit of nishkama karma (desire-less actions) and with no egoistic feeling is a Pandit. He has understood the principle of "Karma" and knows the intricacies of actions. From this statement we can understand that mere book-learning is not enough to receive the title of "Pandit. " A Pandit should have mastered both the Jnana and karma yogas and should have no personal/selfish desire and purpose behind his actions. He works as the servant of the Lord within. He looks upon his body as "Upadhi" or medium for the Lord to express His actions.

If we can realize that we are "Nimittamatra" (visible agents of actions) we would have understood the philosophy of the Gita.

"Thus says the wise" says the Lord. He does not say "I say so" but brings in the authority of the learned scholars.

The learned scholars compare the knowledge to "Fire." Fire" as we know is a great purifier. The heat from the fire is used in many situations like purifying the gold, sterilizing instruments etc. (water and air are also the purifiers)

The desires are precursors of actions and so our selfish desires have to be burnt out in the fire of knowledge. This comes from "Atma Jnana" or knowledge of the Self.

Our heart beats incessantly and our lungs function constantly without the agency of "I". This is so because they have become "involuntary actions." We do not think of the benefits of breathing and circulation before every breath and heartbeat. There is no "Arambha" for these two acts.

Similarly our actions as members of this universe should be involuntary actions without any desire for actions or for the results of actions.

त्यक्त्वा कर्मफलासङ्गं नित्यतृप्तो निराश्रयः ।
कर्मण्यभिप्रवृत्तोऽपि नैव किञ्चित्करोति सः ||20||

tyaktvā karmaphalāsaṅgaṃ nityatṛpto nirāśrayaḥ |
karmaṇy abhipravṛtto 'pi naiva kiṃ cit karoti saḥ ||20||

He who has given up attachment to the fruits of work, who is ever content, who does not depend upon anything, though engaged in actions, does not verily do anything. ||20||

Tyaktva: given up; karma phala sangam: attachment to the fruits of action; nitya: ever; trupta; content; nirashrayaha: depending on nothing; karmany: in action; abhipravrutta: engaged; api: even; na: not; eva: verily; kinchit: anything; karoti: does; saha: he.

Herein is another description of "Jivanmukta." (Refer to Sthitaprajna—chapter 2, slokas: 55-71)

Who is a Jivanmukta, how does he live and how does one recognize him?

Three characteristics of such a person are given in this sloka.

They are:

Tyaktva karmaphala sangam: abandoning attachment to the fruits of action.

Nitya trupta: ever contented.

Nirashrayaha: does not depend upon anything.

Abandoning the fruits of action is stressed on so many times in the Gita. It is true that every action does bring its results, either good or bad. Whether one wishes for it or not, results will follow every action.

Actions are "present" and results are "future."

One of the principal rules of any action is "live in the present". Living in two planes of "present and future" at the same time reduces the efficiency of the present.

A student studying in the university does so to get a degree and thereby have a source of living. His duty should be to live in the "present" and study. He should be putting 100% concentration on all aspects of study like listening to the teacher, revising what is learnt and preparing for next day's lessons etc. He strives hard to get all his doubts cleared by sheer concentration, assistance of the teachers and study of the concerned texts.

With this effort he completes the necessary exams at the end of the studies.

By the blessings of the Lord (who takes into account the results of actions of the past,) he will get the results.

The next stage is to work and learn to live in self-sufficiency.

The student has no right to be thinking of the life after graduation during his studies. He needs to take into account the life after graduation before deciding on the course of studies. Once having taken a decision to take up a course of studies, the effort has to be totally on the present.

The same rule applies to all the individuals and at all times. The rule is "abandon attachment to the fruits of action".

Everybody is entitled to receive the fruits of action and will get the same on completion of the actions. Even those on the spiritual path are also entitled to get the reward which is "Moksha."

Normally one expects the results immediately at the end of any action. Philosophically speaking this is not possible because it is the grace of the Lord that decides on the time of receiving the result of action. Every action will have a result either now or in the future and the timing of the future is not in our hands.

We have been instructed by the Lord not to be slaves to the desires but do every action as a duty to the Lord.

The next characteristic is "Nitya Trupta." "Trupti" is "contentment."

"Trupta" is he who is content.

"Nitya trupta" is he who is contented at all times.

Contentment applies both during the conduct of actions and also on receiving the results of actions either good or bad. It is important to have aspirations in life but at the same time one has to gracefully accept the end result of actions. One should work for fulfilling the aspirations but be content with the results of such actions. As we discussed before, the results depend upon so many factors.They depend upon our past karmas.

Every karma/action has a result but the time one gets the results varies. This depends totally on the grace of the Lord. The word used in the sastras is "Sanchita Karma". It means accumulated karmas from the past.

Even though the present may have been done with 100% efficiency, because of some of the wrong/bad actions of the past, (the results of which that have been decreed by the Lord,) one may not get the 100% results. We have to accept that knowingly or unknowingly each one of us have done both good and bad actions in the past and have to be prepared to receive the results at any time in our life, either present or in the future.

Similarly, even if the present effort is not total 100% efficient, one may get surprisingly good results, again because of the good/correct actions in the past. (The results of which have been bestowed now on us by His grace.)

He who understands this principle of "Sanchita karma" will learn the art of being content at all times.

The last character of such an individual is "Nirashrayaha." Ashraya means "dependent."

Nirashraya means "not dependent."

In our day to day life, majority of us are dependent upon wealth, family, society and our own physical health. We all cling to something or other in the material world. When we lose the same, when something unpleasant happens to what we are attached to, we lose our sense of balance and get depressed. This reduces the efficiency of actions.

What we have to realize is that none of these are permanent.

He alone who sees the "Sat, Chit, Ananda" and not the "Nama, Roopa" will not depend upon anything from the material world. Happiness and sorrow does not enter the realm of his reactions and his life is constantly experiencing the "Bliss" of the Atman.

The word "Nirashraya" is used in this context. Our shelter has to be "The Lord" and nothing but the Lord.

Such an individual will find his abode of peace in the Atman and never falls down to the level of matter. He does so despite the fact that he is constantly engaged in actions by accepting the fact that he has a role to play in the theatre called "Life."

This is a message for Arjuna to stand up and discharge his duty of protecting the dharma and uprooting the evil by becoming an instrument in the hands of the divine.

Such a discipline is essential for the spiritual seeker.

Sri Ramakrishna quotes this following episode from Sreemad Bhagavatham.

The Gopis were returning home one day and found no ferrymen to carry them across the river Yamuna to Brindavan. Sage Veda Vyasa was at the shore at that time and they explained their plight to him. He tells them not to get worried and that he would lead them back home. "Please give me some food first to appease my hunger" he said. The gopis did oblige and offered him milk, butter etc. After finishing the sumptuous food offered, the sage got up and said "O Yamuna Devi, if it is a fact that I am fasting today, stop flowing and make way for us to go back to Brindavan." To everyone's surprise, the river parted and the party walked back home.

The perplexed gopis asked the sage how after having consumed the food he could say that he was fasting?

The Sage then replied "The ceaseless hankering of my heart for Sri Krishna is my spiritual fasting. The idea I eat, is not allowed to enter my mind. I offered the dishes to the Lord as oblation as He is the presiding deity in my body."

निराशीर्यतचित्तात्मा त्यक्तसर्वपरिग्रहः ।
शारीरं केवलं कर्म कुर्वन्नाप्नोति किल्बिषम् ||**21**||

nirāśīr yatacittātmā tyaktasarvaparigrahaḥ |
śārīraṃ kevalaṃ karma kurvan nāpnoti kilbiṣam ||21||

He who is free from hope, who is self-controlled, who has abandoned all possessions, though working merely with the body, does not incur sin. ||21||

nirasheer: free from hope; yatachittatma: who is self-controlled; tyaktva: abandoned; sarva parigrahaha: all possessions; shareeram: bodily; kevalam: merely; karma: actions; kurvan: doing; na: not; apnoti: obtains; kilbhisham: sin.

Kilbisha means "sin".
Na apno'ti kilbhishaha means "does not incur sin."

We come across the word "sin" fairly often. The dictionary meaning for the word is "transgression against divine or moral law." Any action that results in deviation from the spiritual path is considered as an act of "sin." Actions conducted according to the divine or moral law accumulate points of merit (in the spiritual journey) and actions opposite to it will result in negative points, that take the seeker in a downward path towards self-destruction.

Three further qualifications of a "Jivanmukta" are enumerated in this sloka.

a) Nirasha:

"Asha" is "desire, Hope". "Nirasha" is free from desire, hope.

Let us not forget that "Nishkama karma and karmaphala tyaga" are the two main conditions for any actions we undertake. It is therefore imperative that one should not harbor any desires but conduct all duties as a duty to the divine.

Wishing for "Moksha" is good but it has to be only in the early stages of sadhana. One has to progress from "Tamas to rajas", from "rajas to Satva" and from "Satva to Shuddha Satva." One has to pass through so many cycles of births and deaths before reaching this stage. The true Jivanmukta does not desire to enjoy the pleasures of the material world and at the same time he does not even long to enjoy the bliss of the Atman. By his efforts he does automatically experience the bliss but it is not out of any desire on his part. He does not also look for any fame and credit for himself.

We start off with a desire to pass and that too with distinction in our school and college examinations. This is not wrong. Those who seek to go for Post-doctorate studies do not do so for the degree but for the sake of progress in acquiring the higher knowledge and becoming masters in that specialty. For the dedication they put in this field, they automatically get the title of "Post-Doctorate fellow". This is the nearest one can explain "Moksha".

Let us take another example of mountaineering. The climber fixes the end point firmly and makes sure it is totally secure and can take the total weight of his body in the process of climbing up. He then starts from the bottom end of the rope and starts climbing one step at a time. Even though his final aim is to reach the peak of the mountain, he concentrates on the present and works at climbing one step at a time. To do so, he holds on to the bottom end of the rope firmly with both the hands. With a fine art, he lets go of one hand, moves it upwards to the next step and gets hold of the rope at the next point. At the same time, he lets go totally of the hand which was holding at the bottom end. Adeptly he moves that free hand and takes it up to the next step of progress and holds on firmly at that point. Like that, he makes progress and attempts reaching the top.

In the early steps, there is a strong desire to reach the top but the concentration has to be towards the first step to take. There should be and there will be a need and desire to move to the next step. He aims and works towards the end result but does not live in the dreamland (of reaching the peak) during his journey.

(Let us remember that all these are examples to understand the principle. None of the examples can give a totally true picture of the end result of "Moksha" because it is beyond description)

b) Yata chittatma: self-controlled.

It is the control of the lower self which is the "ego" by the higher Self which is the Atman within.

The ego works through the sense organs, mind and the intellect.

One cannot put any blame on the objective world for the failure to progress. It is our reaction to those sense objects that makes all the difference. The vision we have of the objects has to move from sensual to spiritual. An object of beauty should not become an object of desire. It should become an object of adoration. One should see the hand of the divine in the creation of the object of adoration.

The sense organs should be under the control of the mind.

The mind should be under the control of the intellect.

The intellect should be working hard at listening to the "Inner voice of the divine" (Antaratma) and have a grip on the thoughts that generate in the mind which might distract the seeker.

(Refer to sloka 42, chapter 3)

Eventually such acts of constant self-control will lead to "Atma jnana."

This way, the ego can be subdued and the physical body can be made to work as the servant of the divine Atman within.

Lord Hanuman is said to have the image of His Lord Rama and mother Sita in his heart at all times. He considered himself as the servant of Rama and never as the most powerful vanara (monkey). He lived constantly in self- control.

c) Aparigraha:

The word used in the sloka is "Tyakta sarva parigrahaha."

Parigraha is the concept of possessiveness and greed.

It also refers to the desire for and attachment to material things.

The word comes from the Sanskrit, "Pari", meaning "on all sides," and "Graha", meaning, "to grab." Parigraha is "taking more than one needs."

Aparigraha is non-possessiveness.

Striving for aparigraha, or eliminating parigraha, is one of the Yamas (restraints) that the sage, Patanjali, lists in his Yoga Sutras. Patanjali suggests that parigraha distracts the Yogi from positive motivation. The Yogi should do good because it is the right thing to do, not because of material reward or even a sense of self-satisfaction. Avoiding parigraha is one of the key lessons in the Bhagavad Gita. Sri Krishna advises that a Yogi should give up possessions or attachments that hinder his/her yogic path. Doing so frees the Yogi from dependence on sensual and bodily demands, allowing experience of the true Self at a deeper level. Eliminating parigraha is one of the steps on the road to enlightenment and Moksha (spiritual liberation from cyclical rebirth).

Not receiving any gifts and abandoning all possessions is "Tyakta sarva parigraha." It is the rule of conduct for any spiritual aspirant.

The scriptures declare that he who receives any gift from others automatically receives part of their karma too. Let us understand this clearly.

If the gift is from he who has accumulated bad karma, by accepting gift, the receiver would receive part of the donor's sin.

Using the same logic, if the gift is from he who has accumulated good karma, by accepting the gift, the receiver will get part of the donor's punya.

The accepting of gifts would put the individual under moral obligation and many a times there is an expectation of return of favor.

यदृच्छालाभसन्तुष्टो द्वन्द्वातीतो विमत्सरः ।
समः सिद्धावसिद्धौ च कृत्वापि न निबध्यते ||22||

yadṛcchālābhasaṃtuṣṭo dvaṃdvātīto vimatsaraḥ |
samaḥ siddhāv asiddhau ca kṛtvāpi na nibadhyate ||22||

Content with what he gets without efforts, free from the pairs of opposites, free from malice, balanced in success and failure, though acting, he is not bound. ||22||

Yadruccha labha santushtaha: content with what comes without effort; dwandwateetaha: free from pairs of opposites; vimatsaraha: free from envy; samaha: even minded; siddhou: in success; asiddhou: in failure; cha: and; kritva: acting; api: even, na: not; nibhadyate: is bound.

This is the Jnana yoga, the chapter on knowledge. We are given the knowledge needed to conduct the actions. This Sloka gives a few more characteristics of the Jnani who is also a Jivanmukta.

Every individual has a duty to work for himself, for his family, for the society and for the nature and all these have to be fulfilled in the spirit of "service to the Divine."

The Jnani realizes that he has to work and it is his duty to do so. Karma and Jnana, (work and knowledge) are interdependent.

With this understanding one has to know what is the meaning of the sentence: "Content with what he gets without efforts."

"Effort" according to the dictionary is "putting forth an exertion of strength or power either bodily or mentally". The "Ego" in us makes us feel "I have done it." Putting the 100% effort in what is to be carried out but without the feeling of doership and be happy with what one would get for the work is what is meant by this statement. To do so one must act according to the principle of "Nishkama karma and karma phala tyaga."

Every action has a result either good or bad. We react according to the results received from our actions.

A true Jnani on other hand is aware that he has to face either today or the 'morrow to come, the results of past karmas. He therefore develops the equanimity of mind to face the results of his actions. (sloka 38, chapter 2, Sukha Dukhe Same' Kritva--). He is content in every foreseeable situation.

Vimatsaraha: free from malice. "Matsarya" is malice, jealousy, envious, covetous." Such an individual does not get jealous of others.

He is balanced both in success or failure of his efforts and continues to discharge his ordained duties.

"Does not get bound": Whenever we conduct any action, we feel that we have put our efforts in it. This feeling is the "ego" and the mind feels that "I have carried out the work."

Normally, we are bound to the results of actions we conduct. This is the way we swim in the ocean of samsara. We conduct an action and thereby clear an existing vasana but in the process we get bound to the results and accumulate more vasanas. The entire life becomes an unending process of clearing the vasanas and accumulating new vasanas.

We can stop this vicious cycle only by acting in the true spirit of a "nishkama karma and karma phala tyaga." None of the results of actions conducted in this spirit bring in new vasanas. This is what a true Jnani does spontaneously. By this process of clearing all existing vasanas from the past and emptying the mind of all vasanas, the Jnani does not get bound to this world. This is true "Brahma Jnana."

Normally our actions are related to the three koshas/sheaths: Annamaya kosha, Pranamaya kosha, Manomaya kosha. (The gross physical body, the internal organs and the mind.).

If we can strive to go beyond the level of the mind and intellect, we will find out that the actions were conducted because of the power of the Atman within.

This is what we have to understand by the first quarter of the Sloka "Content with what he gets without efforts."

Because of this attitude he is not affected by success or failure, gain or loss, victory or defeat.

He is free from malice: (ill will, spite) a true karma yogi with the knowledge of Jnana does not bear any ill will to anybody. Despite the failures he may encounter in his work, he does not harbor any personal grudges. He attributes the failures to his past karmas and the fate decreed by the Lord for his past actions.

Such an individual, who has perfected the art of working, does not get bound by the results of his present actions. He will have successfully worked at clearing away the existing vasanas and will not have any more new vasanas entering his mind. He would soon move to the stage of "mano nasha" (destruction of the mind) and attain "Liberation."

The main feature of such an individual who has no sense of ego in his actions is "Trupti." "Trupti" is contentment. He is content knowing that he has put all his efforts in the work and is not interested any more in what he would get out of the work. His actions are always without any Sankalpa.

Quote from Bhajagovindam of Sri Shankaracharya:

Mudha jahihi dhanagamat trishnam
Kuru sadbudhim manasi vitrisnam
Yallabhate nijakarmopattam
Vittam tena vinodaya cittam

O you ignorant, drop your thirst for wealth. Attain that state of the mind which is free from thirst for wealth. Develop the habit of letting your mind be satisfied with what you get from your personal effort.

गतसङ्गस्य मुक्तस्य ज्ञानावस्थितचेतसः ।
यज्ञायाचरतः कर्म समग्रं प्रविलीयते ॥23॥

gatasaṅgasya muktasya jñānāvasthitacetasaḥ |
yajñāyācarataḥ karma samagraṃ pravilīyate ||23||

Of the man who is devoid of attachment, liberated, whose mind is established in knowledge, the whole action performed in the spirit of sacrifice is dissolved. ||23||

gata sangasya: devoid of attachment; muktasya: of the liberated; jnanavasthitachetasaha: mind established in knowledge; yajnaya: for sacrifice; acharataha: acting; karma: action; samagram: whole; pravileeyate: is dissolved.

This Sloka gives us the four essential qualities of a Jnani. They are:

Gatasangasya: devoid of attachment to the world of plurality.
Muktasya: freedom from desires and hatreds.
Jnanavastita chetasaha: mind established in knowledge.
Yajnaaya: conduct of work in the spirit of sacrifice.

Such a person may be conducting/will be conducting thousands of actions but the results of all such actions do not bind him back to the samsara. As we have discussed before this is because with this attitude and understanding of work the present actions do not lead to the accumulation of any further vasanas. He is burning away all his existing vasanas.

Unrestricted mind and senses, desires and hatreds and ego result in accumulation of new vasanas. This leads to subsequent birth into the whirlpool of samsara. Let us be clear therefore that this is the creation of man's own mind and the objective world is only an instrument of his destiny. We have no right to blame the world for what is happening to us. We are the creators of our own destiny.

The perfect sage who has released himself from the enslaving forces of the senses and the mind finds the eternal peace in himself and continues to discharge all his worldly obligations. If the work gets dissolved in the ocean of knowledge, there is no further bondage.

Yajnaaya: Any dedicated work becomes a sacrifice but the dedication has to be to the "Supreme" alone. In the context of the secular world we live in we should consider yajnas as acts of worship of God, acts for the welfare of others and/or any acts conducted to maintain dharma on earth. Only acts that fall in this category do not accumulate any more new vasanas.

The art of living with the feeling of "nothing in the material world is really mine" but fulfilling the duties to the family, society, nature as long as one is living is true "Gatasanga." He gives all his love and affection to those that depend on him but with a sense of detachment in attachment.

Muktasya: because of freedom from attachments he is "Atma nishta and Atmatrupta." (Established in Atman and contented with Atman.)

Sri Madhvacharya:

Gatasangasya: free from friendship to the fruits of actions.

Muktasya: free from bodily attachment and Ahamkara.

Jnanavastita chetasaha: who constantly keeps the mind immersed in the knowledge of the Parabrahman.

ब्रह्मार्पणं ब्रह्महविर्ब्रह्माग्नौ ब्रह्मणा हुतम् ।
ब्रह्मैव तेन गन्तव्यं ब्रह्मकर्मसमाधिना ||24||

brahmārpaṇaṃ brahmahavir brahmāgnau brahmaṇā hutam |
brahmaiva tena gantavyaṃ brahmakarmasamādhinā ||24||

The oblation is Brahman, the offerings (clarified butter) are Brahman, The sacrifice is Brahman (offered by Brahman in the fire of knowledge unto Brahman), and absorption in action is Brahman. ||24||

Brahma: Brahman; arpanam: the oblation; havih: clarified butter; brahmagnou: in the fire of Brahman; brahmana: by brahman; hutam: is offered; eva: only; tena: by him; gantavyam: shall be reached; brahmakarma samadhinaa: by the man who is absorbed in action which is Brahman.

Brahman referred to in this sloka has to be understood as "spiritual or divine energy."Brahman shall be reached by him who cognizes Brahman alone in his action.

This Sloka is with reference to the Yajnas which are ritualistic actions. Yajna represents the spirit in the conduct of all actions in this world.

The traditional yajna was conducted with a building of an altar for sacrificial fire, in which were poured oblations. Sacrifices were offered to invoke and satisfy the deity.

Basically the yajna was a ritualistic act to fulfill a desire knowing that there is always a higher power than the individual and the individual has to show his respect to that power and get his/her grace bestowed on him.

Yajna has four factors incorporated in it:

The deity invoked,

The fire,

The material for oblation,

The individual performing the yajna—karta.

The deity invoked is the higher power whose grace is requested in fulfilling the desire. The highest of the highest power is "Brahman" All other deities we invoke are a part of the Parabrahman.

The fire is symbolic of the "knowledge." "Agni", the fire God is considered as the medium to take the human wishes and oblations to the higher deity.

"Upward" signifying the abode of the higher powers. One has to understand that the fire represents "knowledge". Knowledge as we know is the path to higher aspirations in life.

The Vedas clearly declare that "Knowledge is Brahman."

The materials used in the yajna are the firewood, oil, ghee, naturally occurring herbs and medicinal plants products, food cooked for the yajna, fruits etc. As we know all the articles used for the yajna are a combination of the Pancha Maha bhootas, the five gross elements. Again, from what we have studied so far, the material is not manifest in its form of presentation without the presence of the "energy" within it. 90-95% of the firewood is simply wood. A small but important element is the "energy" within. On burning the firewood, the five elements join back with the five elements of nature and the energy within mixes with the un- manifest "energy" in nature.

Hence the four factors mentioned in the Sloka: "The deity is Brahman, The oblations are Brahman, the offerings are Brahman and the sacrifice is Brahman.

The Sloka reiterates the fact that the main rule for the conduct of any yajna is "total absorption in the act of yajna" and being aware of the fact that the utensils used, materials offered, the performer of yajna, the medium of fire are all expressing "is", meaning they exist because of the presence of Supreme Consciousness in them (they would not be manifest without the presence of energy within).

One of the main activities we conduct every day which is related to our health is eating the food. Using the meal as the example:

The food we eat is the food we have to offer to the Brahman. We are really "The Brahman" residing as the Atman within and the food is symbolically for him. The deity invoked is Brahman.

The different energies that assist in digestion, excretion, circulation, the nervous system are considered to be the fires involved in bodily functions and are to be considered as manifested forms of Brahman.

What we eat is another manifested form of the Brahman. Therefore what we eat, the masters say is also Brahma.

We too, who are eating the food are really the "Brahman" manifest.

It is therefore a very strong tradition to repeat this Sloka before any food is consumed. One can see the similarity with the Christian tradition of saying the "Grace" before consuming the food.

This prayer is to remind us of the "Eternal Truth" and the means to act keeping the Truth in mind constantly.

The sacred texts remind us of the need to keep in mind constantly this verse in the performance of every action we perform in life.

Chandogya Upanishad:
Sarvam khalvidam Brahma: all this is Brahman.

We need to clear the delusion of duality by the process known as "purification of the mind", which is an act of "Tapas" in itself.

The acts conducted with this spirit lose their separate limited quality and their binding power. The binding power that leads one to be born into the whirlpool of samsara is converted into spiritual power that lifts us out of the samsara. Brahman is realized in all that one thinks and acts. Karma melts into Jnana and Jnana melts into karma.

दैवमेवापरे यज्ञं योगिनः पर्युपासते |
ब्रह्माग्नावपरे यज्ञं यज्ञेनैवोपजुह्वति ||25||

daivam evāpare yajñaṃ yoginaḥ paryupāsate |
brahmāgnāv apare yajñaṃ yajñenaivopajuhvati ||25||

Some Yogis perform sacrifice to gods only, while others by the union of the self with the Brahman, offer the self as sacrifice in the fire of Brahman. ||25||

daivam: to devas (gods); eva: only; apare: some; yoginaha: yogis; paryupasate: perform, brahmagnou: in the fire of brahman; apare': others; yajnam: sacrifice; yajnena: by sacrifice; upajuhvati: offer as sacrifice.

We are going to be told in the next seven slokas the different types of yajnas conducted by spiritual seekers. We have two types of yajnas enumerated in this Sloka.

In the first half of the sloka we are informed that some Yogis perform sacrifice to devas only.

We need to understand the meaning of the word "Deva" used here. Depending upon the way we interpret the meaning, we have two explanations for this type of yajna.

Supreme Brahman who is Nirakara, Nirguna is not easy for majority to comprehend. It is very hard to meditate on the formless Brahman with no qualities. By bringing out the same Brahman with a form and attributing divine qualities to that form it becomes easy for the majority to meditate. Our ancestral seers having realized this fundamental truth have therefore brought out the same Brahman in many different forms and attributed divine qualities to each of them. They have thereby given a democratic choice for every individual to worship the form he/she likes/adores. Thus the path of Bhakti/devotion has been encouraged for the simple folks who find the path of knowledge hard to understand and follow.

We have a number of divine forms like Vishnu, Brahma, Shiva, Ganesha, Satyanarayana etc. In the Hindu pantheon of Gods there are so many different types of worship for each of the devas.

Bhaktas/devotees of a particular named God offer worship to that God and meditate on that form with all sincerity and devotion. It helps in their spiritual growth. They are said to conduct yajna in the true spirit by performing all actions to please the deva of their choice.

The other meaning of the word "Deva" is:

The power behind each of the five sense organs, this is also known as "Deva". Sun, space, earth, water and air are the five devas for our sense organs.

The light makes us see. We cannot see in the dark. Hence the light is the power that makes us see.

We associate the sun with the light. Daylight comes from the sun and we are generally awake during the day time.

Hence, sun is considered as the Deva for the eyes. Using this logic of explanation:

Space: Deva for the ears. We can hear only when there is space for the sound to travel.

Earth: Deva for the nose. (smell)

Water: Deva for the tongue. (taste)

Air: Deva for the skin. (touch)

How can one offer sacrifice to these five devas?

By the power of discrimination if we can see what is good for us and do not take notice of what we see which is not good for us this is the yajna for the Deva "Sun." In the fire of knowledge the seekers offer as oblations all the good they see and with the feeling of universal welfare by saying "Sri Krishnarpanamastu, Shivarpanamstu". At the same time they offer as oblations in the fire what is not good for them and the society and thereby burn them away.

The general rule "do not see evil, speak evil and hear evil" is the true act of sacrifice to the devas, the presiding deities of our sense organs.

Others by the union of the self with the Brahman, offer the self as the sacrifice in the fire of Brahman. This is the second type of yajna.

Not all individuals are the same. The world is made up of millions of people and each one in their own sense has a sense of individuality. Among these there are some who have faith in the Vedas and Upanishads and conduct yajna. Amongst those who conduct yajna there are some who with the fire of knowledge realize that they are just instruments in the hands of the divine.

They overcome the barrier of "ego" which acts as a hindrance in the spiritual journey. The "bhavana" (feeling) they conduct any act is simply "I offer the results of all actions to you, "my Lord". They dedicate their entire life to the Lord. Thus they manage to clear away the existing vasanas and do not accumulate any new vasanas. They make their path clear to attain union with the Supreme. They realize that it is the physical body that has to stay alive till death and they make use of their body for the welfare of the society they live in. One can say that these are the true "Jnana Yogis." this is the true knowledge of the Brahman-- "Brahma Jnana".

Sacrifice of the self by the Self means dedicating oneself totally to the Supreme. One can say that it is the surrender of the individual consciousness to the Cosmic Consciousness. This type of yajna makes the apparent man change into the real man, the real man being the "Supreme Parabrahman." (Tat-Tvam-Asi.)

श्रोत्रादीनीन्द्रियाण्यन्ये संयमाग्निषु जुह्वति ।
शब्दादीन्विषयानन्य इन्द्रियाग्निषु जुह्वति ||26||

śrotrādīnīndriyāṇy anye saṃyamāgniṣu juhvati |
śabdādīn viṣayān anya indriyāgniṣu juhvati ||26||

Others sacrifice the senses like the organ of hearing etc., in the fire of sense-restraint. Some others offer sense-objects like the sound etc., in the fire of the senses. ||26||

srotradini indriyani: organs of hearing and other senses; anye: others; samyamagnishu: in the fire of restraint; juhvati: sacrifice; shabdadeen vishayaan: sense-objects such as sound; indriyagnishu: in the fire of the senses.

We have two more types of yajnas described in this Sloka.

The yajnas concern the sense organs and as an example we have the organ of hearing, the ear and its action of hearing.

The same principle applies to all the other four sense organs. The two yajnas are:

Restraining the senses. (Sense control),

and

Rejecting the sense objects. (self-control)

The commentary concerning the "Daivam eva 'pare yajnam," in the last sloka should be used to understand restraint of the sense of hearing. Further analysis of the same subject is undertaken in this sloka.

What is sacrificing the senses in the fire of sense-restraint?

Hearing, seeing, smelling, tasting and feeling (through the sense of touch) are the functions of the ears, eyes, nose, tongue and skin respectively.

Sacrificing these five functions in the fire of restraint is advocated. The total restraint of all the impulses becomes total self-control.

Without sense control it is impossible to control the mind. Without mind control liberation is impossible.

It is like eating for sake of eating and to keep the body fit and healthy. The mind will be able to concentrate on the Atman within.

We have studied already that Moksha is freedom from pains and pleasures arising from the contact with the material world and reveling on the eternal bliss from within. Pleasures and pains are from the objective world and the sense organs are the medium to bring the impression of the objects to the mind. The power of sense restraint can overcome this problem. Sloka 69, chapter 2 on the qualities of "Sthitaprajna" has the same meaning as this verse.

Not taking food certain days in the week, not eating certain types of food, avoiding some foods on certain days, not reading certain types of books, not watching certain types of films etc. are some of the ways prescribed in the sastras to practice "sense-restraint"(sense-control).

In the second type of yajna we are told to reject the sense objects. This is achieved by "self-control" (will power).

It is not total rejection of all sense-objects but there should be a controlled entry. It is impossible to block total entry of all impulses. Having the eyes, one cannot keep them closed at all times, having the ears, one cannot shut the ears all the time. Vigilance is the rule to follow.

It is like the customs control at the port of entry to any country. The customs officer checks the authenticity of entrants into the country and allows a limited entry. The welfare of the country is the criterion for keeping a check on those wishing to enter.

Basically whatever impulses that assist in the adoration of the Almighty should be allowed in. Tamasic and rajasic objects/ impulses should be blocked and Satvic objects/impulses can be allowed to enter.

The way one sees an object can be from so many different angles. It is the way one sees an object that needs to be mastered.

Sensual plane, Physical planes, intellectual plane and finally the highest "spiritual plane" are the planes of visualizing/receiving any object.

In the spiritual plane everything perceived is as a form of the divine.

By letting divine impulses come from all the five senses and blocking the sensual impulses, (which are the root cause of pains and pleasures) the seeker will master the art of self-control.

The mind should make use of the intellectual capacity of reasoning to analyse the impulses coming in. It is like a child who has a large number of toys to play with and one day realizing that she does not need/like certain types of toys and putting them away in a box. In course of time she forgets the existence of those toys which used to give her a lot of pleasure in the past. Once the mind has rejected an object, even when the senses perceive it, it does not get any pleasure out of that object. Such a mind will be able to remain calm in the ocean of samsara.

The sense restraint will make the senses ineffective but self-control makes the same senses more effective.

Sense control is negative discrimination and self-control is positive discrimination.

Sense control is rejecting "bad" and self-control is taking in "the good".

सर्वाणीन्द्रियकर्माणि प्राणकर्माणि चापरे ।
आत्मसंयमयोगाग्नौ जुह्वति ज्ञानदीपिते ||27||

sarvāṇīndriyakarmāṇi prāṇakarmāṇi cāpare |
ātmasaṃyamayogāgnau juhvati jñānadīpite ||27||

Others again sacrifice all the functions of the senses and the functions of breath (vital energy) in the fire of Yoga of self-control, illumined by knowledge. ||27||

sarvani: all; indriyakarmani: functions of the senses; pranakarmani: functions of the breath; cha: and; apare': others; atmasamyamagnou: in the fire of yoga of self- restraint; juhvati: sacrifice; jnana deepite: kindled by knowledge.

The aim of the seeker is Self-realization. What is the barrier to this objective?

What is the tool required to achieve this objective? "The mind" is the answer for both of these questions.

The mind is considered to be the band master in all the bodily actions.

On one side it is bombarded with the information about the material world through the sense organs and has a channel to communicate with the same through the organs of action.

On the other side it has the "Intellect" that assists in the process of Self-realization.

Yoga of self-control: (Atma samyama yoga)

The "self" referred to in this section is the "self" with the small "s". It refers to the ""Ego"."

The seeker is asked to learn the art of controlling the ego/ ahamkara part of the mind.

The fire of yoga of self-control:

The fire as we have discussed before refers to the "Knowledge." Knowledge of one's true identity as the "Atman" will help to overcome the ego. This is the means to control the mind, which has to learn the art of discrimination between "Atman and Un-atman." The ego has to be offered as an oblation in the sacrificial fire to attain spiritual realization. Sri Shankaracharya says in "Atma Bodha" "Nitya Anitya Viveka Vicharana" (analytical discrimination of what is eternal and what is temporary.)

Some experts use the example of a charcoal to understand this Sloka. The charcoal when put in the fire becomes ember and shines brightly. When the fire is extinguished it becomes charcoal again.

When the mind illumined by the knowledge understands its identity with the "Atman" it is like the ember. When it is covered with ahamkara and forgets its true identity it is like the charcoal.

The first step towards this is by sense-control and self-control which we discussed in the last Sloka.

Illumined by knowledge: Jnana (true knowledge of the Self) should keep the fire of knowledge alive and dispel the darkness which is: "Ignorance of the Self."

The mind which is covered with ignorance due to the inherent past samskaras (vasanas) is the barrier to "Self-realization".

To conquer such a mind we need various spiritual disciplines and we have two such disciplines given in this Sloka.

The force of the impulses brought in by the senses and ill regulated health agitate the mind endlessly.

The seeker has to learn the two types of control:

Control of the senses—Indriya nigraha

Control of breath—Pranayama (in answer to the section in this sloka which says: "sacrifice all the functions of breath in the fire of yoga of self-control.)

The fine art of discrimination using the "Jnana" should control the impulses that come in from the senses. This is "Indriya nigraha." This is what is meant by the first quarter of the Sloka which says:

Sacrifice all the functions of the senses (in the fire of yoga of self-control.) Self-control is "Atma-Samyama" the subject matter in the sixth chapter. This needs control of sense organs and organs of action.

Breath control is "Pranayama."

(Herein is a detailed description of the "Pranayama" which the reader may choose to skip.)

Patanjali was an expert grammarian and an author of Yoga sutras, the earliest systematic treatise on Yoga. He advocated the eight limbed practice of Yoga and it has come to be known as the "Ashtanga yoga of Patanjali. (second century B.C)

The eight steps in Yoga are:

Yama: Disciplines/restraints in the spiritual practices.

Ahimsa: non-injury,

Satyam: practicing to speak and follow the truth,

Asteya: not taking other's belongings,

Brahmacharya: celibacy,

Aparigraha: not receiving gifts,

Kshama: capacity to forgive.

Dhriti: firm resolve in the undertaking of any actions. Resolve to fulfill the obligations to one's own body, to family, to the spiritual master, to the society, to other forms of life and to the mother nature in general is "Dhriti."

Daya: compassion to all forms of life, to the ignorant, to the poor, to the disabled etc. is Daya.

Arjavam: it is being straight forward and honest in all dealings socially and spiritually. It requires the capacity to overcome habit of deception.

Mitahara: Moderation in food intake. In this sense "food" includes the impulses received from all the five sense organs.

Niyama-observations needed in the practice of spiritual disciplines like:

Soucham: cleanliness,

Tapas: purification of body, speech and mind.

Swadhyaya: self-study/analysis of one's thoughts and actions.

Iswara poojana: worship of the deity of choice.

Trupti: contentment.

Danam: alms giving.

Astikya: faith in God, spiritual masters and the spiritual texts.

Hri: learning to be remorse by recollecting the faults/errors and make amends for the mistakes.

Vrata: observation of resolves undertaken and the spiritual practices.

Japa: recitation of a mantra like the sacred syllable Om on a regular basis.

Dara: to give liberally without any thought of recognition or reward for the efforts put in.

Asana: It refers to the postures that assist in the practice of meditation. The practice of asana is to develop "body discipline." Various postures like "Padmasana, Virasana, Bhadrasana" are described in the texts. Certain medical conditions or serious illness like a stroke will make it difficult for some to practice asanas. The sastras do give directions for such people also to conduct the yajna.

Pranayama—breath control.

Pratyahara—sense withdrawal. When the mind is totally absorbed in "the task at present" it is said to be in "Pratyahara." In such state the impulses from the surroundings that continue to enter the mind while it is absorbed in a specific task do not divert the mind.

Dharana: constant flow of thoughts on a single task is Dharana.

Dhyana (meditation): This is the constant flow of thoughts on the object of Dharana.

Samadhi: it is act of being absorbed in the union with the Atman achieved by the above methods. There is no more of the objective world in this state for such a seeker.

It is well known fact that there is a clear connection between the consciousness, breath and the body.

The body is kept still by the practice of postures. The breath is controlled through the Pranayama and the mind is kept still through concentration.

If the flow of breath is voluntarily regulated, its effect on the mind is beneficial. On this basis the science of Pranayama evolved in course of time.

It consists of three steps:

Breathing in through the nostril —Puraka
Holding the breathed air in-Kumbhaka
Breathing out—Rechaka.

The Yogi avoids breathing through the mouth. Air taken in /breathed in through the nostril is "Prana" and the air that is breathed out through the nose is "Apana."

Correct practice of Pranayama is said to assist in healing diseases, tones the system, enhances the health and calms the mind.

Is it not true that measured breathing and an attitude of calmness constitute good habits?

The masters recommend the practitioners of Pranayama to learn reciting the holy mantra "Aum" during the procedure.

This method of breath control is considered as a form of sacrifice.

द्रव्ययज्ञास्तपोयज्ञा योगयज्ञास्तथापरे ।
स्वाध्यायज्ञानयज्ञाश्च यतयः संशितव्रताः ||28||

dravyayajñās tapoyajñā yogayajñās tathāpare |
svādhyāyajñānayajñāś ca yatayaḥ saṃśitavratāḥ ||28||

Others offer wealth, austerity and yoga as sacrifice. Some others, the ascetics of self-control and rigid vows, offer study of knowledge as sacrifice. ||28||

dravya yajna: offer of wealth as sacrifice; tapoyajna: austerity as a form of sacrifice; yoga yajna: yoga as a form of sacrifice; tatha: again; apare': others; swadhaya jnana yajna: study and knowledge as a form of sacrifice; cha: and; yatayaha: ascetics; samshitavrataha: persons of rigid vows.

Dravya yajna:

It is the sacrifice by using the wealth as oblations in the fire of knowledge.

The scriptures advocate acquiring the wealth only after learning all about "Dharma". The Purushartha for a Hindu is "Dharma, Artha, Kama and Moksha." "Artha" refers to the wealth one has to acquire in life. Acquiring wealth by righteous means and making use of it to conduct the five "Nitya karmas" is true "Dravya Yajna." (Refer to Karma yoga slokas 8 and 13)

Dana/alms giving is a form of Dravya yajna. The scriptures do give detailed advice/instructions about this type of yajna. Charity comes from giving with love what one has to others who need it. Of course it goes without saying that charity has to be only that which has been acquired lawfully. We will find in the latter chapters of the Gita detailed instructions on the subject of "Danam."

Tapo yajna:

This is the sacrifice wherein the body and the senses are subjected to austerities (tapas) with the sole intention of purification.

We see pictures of sages and those wishing to acquire boons from gods standing in the extreme heat or cold, withstanding the extremes of weather and concentrating on the deity of choice.

The word "Tapas" brings to mind the above picture.

Really speaking "Tapas" is an effort at purification.

A true student working hard in University and coming out with a degree is said to have conducted "Tapas" to acquire the degree by focusing on the subject.

To achieve something higher, one needs to let go of the lower. This is possible by control of the wandering mind and the senses. Any such act conducted to achieve the higher spiritual goal by constant restraint becomes "Tapas."

In chapter 17, slokas 14, 15 and 16 the Lord gives us tapas of the body, speech and mind and that is "Tapas" in the truest sense.

Yoga yajna:

Control of the wandering mind is "Yoga Yajna" and in Sanskrit it is "Chitta Vritti Nirodha".

"Vritti" means "diversions" and "Chitta Vritti" is diversions of the wandering mind. "Nirodha" means "Control."

Constant practice of Raja yoga or Ashtanga yoga constitutes "Yoga Yajna."

Breath control, using the technique of Patanjali's Ashtanga yoga is said to be the way of conducting "Yoga Yajna." (Refer to the last Sloka).

Swadhyaya yajna:

"Swa" means "self" "Adhyaya" means "study."

Learning the scriptures with self-effort and with the help of the guru is "Swadhyaya." "Swadhyaya" also means "self-analysis". Analyzing the events that happen in life and learning lessons from the same is true Swadhyaya.

Study of the sacred texts requires a great deal of self-preparation and this also constitutes Swadhyaya.

When such sacred acts are conducted with a spirit of sacrifice so that the knowledge of the higher dawns, it is known as "Swadhyaya Yajna."

Jnana yajna:

Pursuit of the spiritual knowledge with total purity of the mind, speech and body is true Jnana yajna. This needs the critical analysis of that which is "eternal" and that which is "transitory." Adiguru Shankaracharya calls it as "Nitya Anitya Viveka Vicharana." (Analytical knowledge and understanding of the nature of the Eternal Self and the transient physical world.)

The Jnana yajna is offered as sacrifice by ascetics of rigid vows. (samshrita vrataha)

To become an Olympic runner needs a great amount of discipline and not everybody who undertakes such discipline will win the gold medal. Similarly not all the seekers succeed in attaining the "Moksha" in this life. It needs constant practice of all the above forms of yajnas. Once all the vasanas are cleared, which might take several births into this world; the seeker will be blessed with "Moksha."

With the ultimate aim of achieving salvation, several vows are taken by the different seekers. True Jnana is to make sure that the vows do not become acts of blind rituals.

The Lord used the word "Yatayaha" to describe such seekers. Yati's are those who live the life of asceticism by constantly working to burn their existing vasanas and not acquiring any more new vasanas by their actions.

अपाने जुह्वति प्राण प्राणेऽपानं तथाऽपरे ।
प्राणापानगती रुद्ध्वा प्राणायामपरायणाः ||29||

apāne juhvati prāṇaṃ prāṇe 'pānaṃ tathāpare |
prāṇāpānagatī ruddhvā prāṇāyāmaparāyaṇāḥ ||29||

Others offer as sacrifice the out-going breath in the incoming, and the incoming in the outgoing, restraining the sources of the outgoing and incoming breaths, solely absorbed in the restraint of breath. ||29||

apane': in the outgoing breathe; juhvati: sacrifice; pranam: incoming breathe; prane': in the incoming breathe; apanam: outgoing breathe; tatha: thus; apare': others; pranapana gati: courses of outgoing and incoming breaths; rudhva: restraining; pranapana parayanaha: solely absorbed in the restraint of breathe.

This Sloka is about breath control. It is a specialist subject and the sincere seeker should consult a proper expert in this field. It is my sincere request that the novices should refrain from such practices.

A properly measured breathing technique, according to the medical experts is a tool for healthy living. This technique is "Pranayama."

Normally breathing is an involuntary act. An average adult breathes between 14-16 times per minute. It involves three stages: breathing in, holding the breath and breathing out. We take the oxygen in and breathe out the carbon dioxide.

Depending upon the impulses received from the external world, our breathing pattern changes. Anger, hatred, fear, lust disturb the mind and this in turns alters the breathing pattern. The faster we breath, the greater will be the disturbance on the mind. This is because the brain receives less oxygen and retains more of carbon dioxide. Carbon dioxide dulls the mind whereas oxygen activates the mind.

Rhythmic breathing is seen during states of calmness of the mind. Properly controlled breathing by voluntary methods benefits the mind. The ancient seers of India, the masters in the development of the Hindu culture realized this truth and developed the technique of Pranayama as early as the Vedic period of time.

Prana: the incoming breath. Apana: the outgoing breath.

Repeating the three stages of the cycle of breathing (refer to sloka 27) with correct time for each of three stages, accompanied by the chanting of the sacred syllable "Om" constitutes the technique of Pranayama. Breathing not only regulates the respiratory system but directly or indirectly regulates all other bodily functions which also come under the word "Prana." In a broadest sense, Pranayama is control of all bodily functions.

We are told in this Sloka that even this control of breath should be in the form of a sacrifice.

अपरे नियताहाराः प्राणान्प्राणेषु जुह्वति ।
सर्वेऽप्येते यज्ञविदो यज्ञक्षपितकल्मषाः ||30||

apare niyatāhārāḥ prāṇān prāṇeṣu juhvati |
sarve 'py ete yajñavido yajñakṣapitakalmaṣāḥ ||30||

Others with well-regulated diet, sacrifice life-breaths in the life-breaths. All these are knowers of sacrifice whose sins are destroyed by sacrifice. ||30||

apare': others; niyataharaha: regulated food intake; pranan: life-breaths; praneshu: in the life-breaths; juhvati: sacrifice; sarve: all; api: also; ete: these; yajna vido: knowers of sacrifice; yajna kshapita kalmashaha: whose sins are destroyed by sacrifice.

So far a total of 12 different types of yajnas have been enumerated and of these the last Sloka and the present Sloka deal with control of breath and diet. Breathing and eating are two of the most important actions we conduct and they are for our survival. It is therefore important we understand these clearly.

Well regulated diet:

In chapter 17, verses 8, 9 and 10 we will learn about the foods that are either good or harmful to our body.

Doctors and dieticians stress on the importance of a healthy diet. Basically the food we eat should meet the following requirements:

Pure,

Moderate in quantity,

Fresh,

Earned by righteous means,

Eating at the proper time and place

Offered to God with recitation of prayers

Finally offer to the needy and other forms of life.

By this type of control over the food the mind remains pure and if the mind is pure the seeker will experience the spiritual illumination.

This is because the food we eat is converted into energy and energy is needed for our daily activities including discharge of our spiritual duties.

Unhealthy food and food habits disturb the concentration of the mind needed to conduct all the activities.

The verse says:

Sacrifice life-breaths in life-breaths.

Let us analyze as to what it really means.

It is a fact of life that life lives on life. We should therefore learn to dedicate our life to the service of the cosmic life which is nothing but the various manifestations of life on earth.

Yajnavidaha: It means "the knower's of the 12 types of sacrifices" enumerated so far.

Whose sins are destroyed:

In spiritual practice, sin is applied to that action which hinders the path to Liberation. As we have studied so far, thoughts are precursors of actions. Destruction of the entire vasanas accumulated over so many births by the acquisition of knowledge and conduct of actions according to the knowledge acquired, is the pre requisite for Liberation. "Sins are destroyed" means simply the destruction of all the accumulated vasanas.

The disciplines practiced in the 12 types of yajnas will lead to Self-realization.

यज्ञशिष्टामृतभुजो यान्ति ब्रह्म सनातनम् |
नायं लोकोऽस्त्ययज्ञस्य कुतोऽन्यः कुरुसत्तम ||31||

yajñaśiṣṭāmṛtabhujo yānti brahma sanātanam |
nāyaṃ loko 'sty ayajñasya kuto 'nyaḥ kurusattama ||31||

Those who eat the remnants of sacrifices which is nectar go to the eternal Brahman. To the non-sacrificer, even this world is not, how can he get a higher world? O best of the Kurus. ||31||

yajna shishtamruta bhuja: eaters of the remnants (nectar) of sacrifices; yanti: go; sanatanam: eternal; na: not; ayam: this; loka: world; asty: is; ayajnasya: of the non- sacrificer; kutaha: how; anya: others; kurusattama: O best of kurus.

This Sloka is almost similar to Sloka 13, chapter 3. Yajna shishtashinaha santo': remnants of the sacrifice.

"Prasada" is a word commonly used in the Hindu philosophy. It means the returns one gets after offering his services to the higher power. Yajna shishtamruta bhujo' has to be considered as the returns for the sacrifice and this has to be accepted as the blessings from the higher power.

So far we have had a description of the different types of sacrifices. All the sacrifices have one thing in common and that is "self-denial".

We associate fruits as something we eat and enjoy. Karma Phala is fruit of action performed. In the spiritual sense, eating does not apply only to the food consumed but to the receiving of the results/ fruits of any action conducted.

The Gita is all about actions, fruits of actions and the knowledge about the correct actions. Through the description of the various types of yajnas we are directed towards right actions. Not only we have to conduct right actions but we must also know how to make use of the results achieved.

In brief here is a description of how to make use of the results of actions: (taking an example of the monthly wages received for the work conducted.)

Considering that the body is a temple with the divinity inside it, we all have a sacred duty to look after our body. We have to use a portion of the gains for the welfare of the body. The needs of clothing, shelter, food etc. have to be met depending upon one's social status in the society. Taking care of the bodily needs is not wrong as long as it fits in with the principle of dharma.

One cannot guarantee that he can continue to work all the time. Ill health, injury, retirement etc. reduces the income or completely stops the income. At such times, one should try not to be a burden on others and on the society. Therefore, as a preventive measure, wherever possible one should keep a portion of wealth earned, for needs in such desperate situations.

Everyone will have dependents in life. We cannot say when death approaches us. We should make sure that our death does not make our dependents lose their shelter. We should make provision wherever possible that the dependents are reasonably secure after our death. Part of the wealth is for this type of insurance.

We have a social obligation to the disadvantaged in the society and should contribute towards the society's expenses for the various sections of the community. A portion of the wealth is for this purpose, it is in the form of local taxes and charitable deeds.

Finally we have a duty to contribute towards religious activities like the upkeep of religious institutions, like temples and supporting those who keep our culture alive.

This is the sacrifice or self-denial the Gita talks about.

If we do not follow this basic rule we are considered to be selfish.

Krishna tells us that a selfish person does not really get joy out of this world and whatever joy he gets is limited to a short period of time.

Total destruction of "I" (self) confers the highest reward and that being "merging with the Supreme". This merging is "Liberation". The liberated individual has the abode of the Supreme as His abode and that is "The Nectar" referred to in this Sloka.

If we consider that every individual is a composition of "divinity and man", the task of having been born as human is to express the divinity and annihilate the man element.

एवं बहुविधा यज्ञा वितता ब्रह्मणो मुखे ।
कर्मजान्विद्धि तान्सर्वानेवं ज्ञात्वा विमोक्ष्यसे ||32||

evaṃ bahuvidhā yajñā vitatā brahmaṇo mukhe |
karmajān viddhi tān sarvān evaṃ jñātvā vimokṣyase ||32||

The various forms of sacrifice are spread out in the storehouse of the Vedas (which are the faces of Brahma). Know them all to be born of action. Thus knowing you will be liberated. ||32||

evam: thus; bahuvida: various forms; yajna: sacrifice; vitataa: spread; brahmano: of Brahman mukhe: in the face; karmajaan: born of action; viddhi: know; taan: them; sarvan: all; eva: thus; jnatva: knowing; vimokshyase: will be liberated.

The first half of the Sloka states that all the above mentioned yajnas are not something new brought out by Krishna, the cowherd son of Vasudeva and Devaki but by Brahman.

We should remember the fact that Krishna is the incarnation of the Parabrahman. All these are described in the Vedas which have originated from the Brahman and hence we have the statement that the Vedas are the faces of Brahman.

The various yajnas are from the karma kanda section of the Vedas. The actions as we know are born of desires to achieve the desired objects. The object of desire should be to achieve the Liberation. Actions have to be the means to the end and not an end in themselves. "Jnana" has to be the first step in the path to Liberation. Well planned and well executed actions should become only the means. Individual effort is essential for the performance of yajna. Inaction/inactivity is not the way for majority and is only for the selected few who have already climbed up the spiritual ladder. We must make use of the body, speech and mind to achieve the goal. Any individual who converts karma into yajna in its truest sense is fit for Liberation.

This is another reminder for Arjuna to fight the war of righteousness. He had a duty to fight the enemy in the spirit of "Yajna" and this chapter on Jnana is reiterating the truth to him. Through the medium of Arjuna, we are reminded to do all our karmas in the spirit of yajna. Arjuna expressed his ignorance about the right action but did so to the Supreme Lord Himself and the Gita given by the Lord is to dispel this ignorance.

श्रेयान्द्रव्यमयाद्यज्ञाज्ज्ञानयज्ञः परन्तप |
सर्वं कर्माखिलं पार्थ ज्ञाने परिसमाप्यते ||33||

śreyān dravyamayād yajñāj jñānayajñaḥ paraṃtapa |
sarvaṃ karmākhilaṃ pārtha jñāne parisamāpyate ||33||

O' Parantapa, knowledge-sacrifice is superior to wealth sacrifice. All actions in their entirety, O Arjuna, end in knowledge. ||33||

shreyaan: superior; dravyamayaat: with the objects; yajnat: than sacrifice; jnanayajna: knowledge sacrifice; parantapa: scorcher of enemies; sarvam: all; karma: action; akhilam: in its entirety; jnana: in knowledge; parisamaptate: ends in.

As we go through the Gita we find that in different contexts we hear that particular Sadhana's are superior to others. These should not be taken as contradictory statements. Every method of sadhana that suits the temperament of the seeker is the superior method for that seeker. The end result of any sadhana is acquirement of the "Knowledge."

Which knowledge?

It is as Sri Jagadguru Shankaracharya says "Nitya Anitya Viveka Vicharana" which means a thorough analysis and acquiring the knowledge of realizing that which is eternal and that which is temporary. To know which is "Atma" and which is "Anatma" and realize the "Eternal Truth" and live in contentment with the knowledge acquired, is the real knowledge.

Anything contrary to it is "Ignorance".

"Wealth sacrifice" when not done in the true spirit and done with the purpose of gaining name, fame, reputation will procure only a temporary period of happiness. If it is done with the spirit of "self-denial" and for "acts of welfare", as "nishkama karma and karma phala tyaga" the seeker will experience the "Peace within and Peace all round." The sadhana which uses control of the mind, senses and the prevents the intellect from running towards sense objects whilst diverting the attention to the Atman within and all around, will give the Eternal Peace. The knowledge of discrimination between ego and the Soul is true "Atma Jnana."

In the context of this sloka we have to understand that karma is sadhana (effort) and Jnana is Sadhya (result).

In the second half of this verse Sri Krishna declares that all actions culminate in knowledge.

Let us understand the same by examples.

A child who goes near the fire out of curiosity will realize the pain and suffering after burning the fingers and will not play with the fire any more.

A Student who wastes his time during study term is expected to realize that his failure was because of his lack of attention towards his studies and revision. If he realizes his mistakes and corrects his actions next term it will help in getting better grades.

We all know from our own life's experiences that we suffer due to wrong actions and will sooner or later realize the mistakes and promise not to repeat the same mistakes again. Being what we are, generally we blame others for our failures. There comes a time, according to the scriptures, either in this life or in future births when we do take the blame on ourselves and correct our mistakes. Only then are we said to be on the path of knowledge and become eligible for "Liberation."

Our mind has a covering of ignorance "Avarana" and the thought processes agitate the mind constantly (Vikshepa). By clearing our minds of the "Avarana/covering of ignorance" with the help of knowledge and controlling the "Vikshepa (agitations in the mind)" we will acquire the true spiritual knowledge.

The greatest sacrifice is "Jnana Yajna". It involves two distinct processes:

Pouring the ignorance into the sacrificial fire thus burning away the ignorance,

And pouring the knowledge into the sacrificial fire (for Loka kalyana), thereby working for the welfare of the family, society and the universe.

We have a duty to sacrifice some of our efforts towards the study of the scriptures, satsang etc. and in the process we acquire knowledge.

This acquired knowledge has to be passed on to others and should be used in conducting acts of welfare.

However it should also be used, to prevent the conducting of acts which harm others.

Not harming others is the first step and helping others is the next step in the spiritual sadhana.

Jagadguru Shankaracharya conducted the highest form of Jnana Yajna and blessed the world with the books of knowledge about the scriptures and the Bhagawadgita. Sharing the spiritual wisdom with others is the greatest gift one can give.

The emphasis is on both the need for conduct of karma and excellence of Jnana, these being the tools for final realization.

Sri Ramakrishna:

He is truly a man who has made money his slave. He is not fit to be called a man who does not know how to make use of money.

तद्विद्धि प्रणिपातेन परिप्रश्नेन सेवया ।
उपदेक्ष्यन्ति ते ज्ञानं ज्ञानिनस्तत्त्वदर्शिनः ||34||

tad viddhi praṇipātena paripraśnena sevayā |
upadekṣyanti te jñānaṃ jñāninas tattvadarśinaḥ ||34||

Know that by full prostration, question and service, the sages who have realized the Truth will instruct you in that knowledge. ||34||

tad: that; viddhi: know; pranipatena: by long prostration; pariprashnena: by questions; sevaya: by service; upadekshyanti: will instruct; te': thee; jnanam: knowledge; jnaninaha: the wise; tatva darshinaha: those who have realized the Truth.

The spiritual seeker is in search of spiritual knowledge. He needs instructions/guidance on the ways to understand "The Truth" and approach "The Truth" properly. He has to approach the "Jnani".

This is the meaning of the statement "Upadekshante te' jnaninaha. (The wise will instruct the knowledge)" Who is such a Jnani?

As it is concerning the knowledge of "The Truth", the instructor has to be one who has himself realized "The Truth".

This is the meaning of the word "Tatvadarshinaha." How to approach such an instructor?

"Pranipatena"--By prostration "Pariprashnena"—by repeated questioning. "Sevaya"—by service.

In the Hindu philosophy we use the word "Guru" for the spiritual teacher.

"Guru" is he who dispels the darkness known as "ignorance" whereas ordinary teachers are those who give/assist us with knowledge about the material world.

The way to approach the teacher or guru is similar in certain ways and yet totally different in other ways.

Humility and a desire to learn are common requirements to approach both the guru and the teacher.

In the olden days, thousands of years ago, the science of the material world was taught by the father to son. There were no teaching institutions like what we are familiar with now. As we know in the beginning there were not even the written alphabets with which we are familiar now.

Those belonging to the business and service trades stayed back in the city/town/village of their birth and learnt the trade by observing their father conducting such a trade.

Those belonging to the priestly class and the warrior class needed to go out of their place of birth to a hermitage which was away from the hub of city life. The hermits lived in forests and the place of their residence was known as "ashrama." The word "ashrama" means "shelter." For those seekers of spiritual knowledge these hermitages were a place of shelter which provided boarding/lodging and education. The requirements were, to show the keenness to learn "The Truth" and to be humble.

Along with this the student was encouraged to ask genuine questions to clear the doubts. Only by repeatedly questioning, would the guru come to know the nature of the doubts. He would then find ways to help the student and clear the doubts. As there were no written books, the students had to depend on memory to remember what was taught.

Why the condition of "Pranipatena"? (Repeated prostration)

Pranipata: It is an act to show one's obeisance to the elders.

In this act of prostration, there are two people, the revered/knowledgeable/elder and student/younger person. The student/young one's when they approach the masters/elders take up the following posture:

Standing in front of the elder; join the palms of the two hands together, open them up like the blossoming of a flower and place the head on the palm with an attitude of reverence.

There is another method of prostration which is known popularly as "Sashtanga Pranama". It involves the act of literally falling down at the feet of the master/revered guru/parents/respected elders with eight parts of the body touching the floor.

The eight parts being: "hands, knees, shoulders (two of each), chest and forehead."

This is a sign of respect. The revered ones are representatives, spreading the dharma on earth. The feet are the organs, which they use to move and so thereby spread the dharma. Hence the custom of touching their feet in this show of respect.

This shows the annihilation of ego on the part of the seeker, be he a king/prince/rich member of the society.

This is associated with "Pariprashnena" which means "repeated questioning."

Repeated prostration and questioning is a sign of humility on the part of the seeker who is requesting the seer to guide him in the path of dharma. Unless the doubts are cleared the seeker cannot make progress and the only person to clear the doubts is the seer who is "The Guru". This is by repeatedly questioning on points that are not clear and requesting for forgiveness in slow uptake of the spiritual knowledge.

The questioning is, let me make it clear only to clear the doubts. It is not the fashion of some of the present institutions where one finds the students bombarding the lecturer (with the information collected from sources like internet). This I believe is more in the form of a show off on the part of the student who wants to display his knowledge and test the teacher's knowledge in front of his peers.

Sevaya: By service:

The seeker is also expected to take up some acts of service needed by the guru. The seeker looks after the physical needs of the guru and his ashrama where all the seekers are staying. In return the guru takes care of the spiritual needs of the seeker.

As mentioned already, this system of basic and higher education was unique to the land where there were no universities and educational institutions as we know of today. It was not a business transaction where the student pays a fee and demands returns for the fees paid. In those days the guru did not demand any fees except humility on the part of the student and an interest to learn the Vedas and Upanisads.

When we read some of the Puranas and mythological stories, we come across instances where there was a division of labour on the part of all the students in a particular ashrama.

All students took up the task of going to the forest sometime in the day to bring in "samidha" (barks of certain plants) that were needed for the homa.

Some students went to the river/wells to get water needed for drinking and for washing the clothes/utensils. Others went to collect root vegetables/fruits/flowers and a few cleaned parts of the ashrama. Some took the cattle for grazing, looked after the cowshed and collected the milk from the cows which was also needed for the inhabitants of the ashrama.

Advanced/senior students were allowed to enter into the personal residence of the guru and assist the "Gurupatni" (wife of the preceptor) in all the household chores.

Special students who made exceptional progress were allowed to press the feet of the guru when he was tired and let him gradually doze off to sleep. This has a special significance also. During those moments before going to sleep the guru imparted higher spiritual knowledge to the selected disciple and helped him in making rapid progress in his studies.

Total dedication of the body/mind/speech to the guru is offered via this method of prostration/questioning/seva.

There is no commercial motive on the part of the guru. Let us also make it clear that the guru assists only in expelling the ignorance from the mind of the student. The Hindu philosophy believes that there is inherent knowledge in every individual but it is masked by ignorance in the form the three basic gunas of Satva, Rajas and Tamas.

The Lord ends this sloka with a special word:

Tatva darshinaha: those who have realized the "Eternal Truth."

It refers to the guru who clears all forms of delusion forever from the mind of the seeker and assists him to recognize the Atman in the diversity of manifestations and to realize his own true divine inner nature.

यज्ज्ञात्वा न पुनर्मोहमेवं यास्यसि पाण्डव ।
येन भूतान्यशेषेण द्रक्ष्यस्यात्मन्यथो मयि ||35||

yaj jñātvā na punar moham evaṃ yāsyasi pāṇḍava |
yena bhūtāny aśeṣeṇa drakṣyasy ātmany atho mayi ||35||

O Arjuna, having obtained that knowledge, you will not be deluded again like this. You shall see all beings in yourself and also in Me. ||35||

yat: which; jnatva: having known; na: not; punaha: again; moham: delusion; evam: thus; yasyasi: will get; pandava: Arjuna; ena: by this; bhootany: beings; asheshena: all (not leaving any trace); drakshyasi: see; atmany: in self; atho: also; mayi: in Me.

Having obtained that knowledge: Sri Krishna is referring to the knowledge of the Atman which is the Brahma Jnana.

Arjuna needed urgent therapy for his despondency and received the therapy in the form of "Jnana Yoga".

The second half of the first line of this Sloka: "you will not be deluded again like this."

Arjuna developed mental weakness, the details of which have already been discussed in detail in the first chapter.

Arjuna was not going to become a Satvic person by escaping from the war but would have become a tamasic person. In the situation he was exposed, (in the war of righteousness) he had a duty not to look at the soldiers in the opposite camp in terms of relations but had to see them only as those opposed to dharma.

The spiritual path is to travel in an upward curve from Tamasic to Satvic and not to go down from Satvic to Rajasic or Rajasic to Tamasic.

Arjuna forgot the "Dharma" in this context and hence Krishna gives him the introduction to Jnana and then tells him, "You will not be deluded again like this." Krishna lit the light of knowledge in His disciple and expelled the darkness. With this therapy Krishna says:

You shall see all beings in yourself and also in Me.

When one understands and accepts that the real and eternal in any embodied being is "Atman" then he should see all beings in himself. This is because there is no difference in the "Atman". The only difference is in the external appearance.

Saying the same in another way, the seeker must learn to see "Sat Chit Ananda" in all and not be deluded by "Nama Roopa."

When one can see the divinity in all, there will be no room for hatred, envy, anger, pride or arrogance. These are the root causes for the delusion of attachment to sense objects and to the material world.

Sri Krishna is saying that a perfect Jnani and Himself (incarnation of God) are one and the same. The devotee and the God are one. Only this knowledge gives the true understanding of this sentence which forms the second line of this Sloka.

The entire universe has to be looked upon as one indivisible absolute Reality.

Sri Ramakrishna: "Knowledge leads to unity and ignorance to diversity."

अपि चेदसि पापेभ्यः सर्वेभ्यः पापकृत्तमः ।
सर्वं ज्ञानप्लवेनैव वृजिनं सन्तरिष्यसि ||36||

api ced asi pāpebhyaḥ sarvebhyaḥ pāpakṛttamaḥ |
sarvaṃ jñānaplavenaiva vṛjinaṃ saṃtariṣyasi ||36||

Even if you are the most sinful of all sinners you shall cross over all sins by the raft of knowledge. ||36||

api: even, chet: if: asi: thou art; papebhyaha: than sinners; sarvebhyaha: all; papakruttamaha: most sinful; sarvam: all; jnanaplavena: by the raft of knowledge; eva: alone; vrjinam: sin; samtarishyasi: shall cross.

The emphasis in this Sloka is on "Papa and Papebhyaha" meaning "The sin and those who commit acts of sin."

Hatred, lust, greed, arrogance, enmity, anger etc. make one commit acts of sin. Many a times the root cause for committing the sin is "Ego" which is man's worst enemy in the spiritual progress towards "Liberation."

Attachment to the physical body, one's family, friends, positions acquired in life, prevents progress in the path to Liberation.

We need to have the knowledge that we are in an ocean and that there is a shore at the other side. We have knowingly or unknowingly committed a number of mistakes in the past and that includes past births also.

We should look for the means to get out of the ocean and reach the shore. The means to do this, given by Lord Krishna out of compassion to all, is "Jnana".

The Jnana to dispel the ignorance will then act as 'the raft' for our ' life's' boat and assists us towards having a smooth passage to the shore, overcoming all obstacles in the way.

Swami Vivekananda stresses (refer to the commentary on Sloka 3, chapter 2), that any work which brings out the latent divinity is punya (virtue) and that which makes the body and mind weak and forget divinity is, verily, sin.

Discrimination between "Truth and un-truth" and dispassion to worldly possessions are the keystones of spiritual knowledge, which will assist us in crossing over the ocean of samsara.

यथैधांसि समिद्धोऽग्निर्भस्मसात्कुरुतेऽर्जुन ।
ज्ञानाग्निः सर्वकर्माणि भस्मसात्कुरुते तथा ||37||

yathaidhāṃsi samiddho 'gnir bhasmasāt kurute 'rjuna |
jñānāgniḥ sarvakarmāṇi bhasmasāt kurute tathā ||37||

O Arjuna, just as the blazing fire reduces fuel to ashes, so does the fire of knowledge reduce all actions to ashes. ||37||

yatha: as; edhamsi: fuel; samiddhaha: blazing; bhasmasat: reduced to ashes; kurute': makes; jnanagnihi: fire of knowledge; sarva: all; karmani: actions; tatha: so.

After having compared Jnana to 'the raft' in the last verse, Jnana is compared to "the fire" in this verse.

Any item that is burnt by the fire is considered to be the fuel for the fire.

Firewood is any material made of wood like a chair, table, paper etc. any flammable product can be the fuel. The fuel would have some form of identity before being burnt. After it is burnt, there is no more identity left of the fuel. What is left are only the ashes.

All the actions we conduct, result with the entry of new vasanas on our mind. It is an on-going chain of actions and reactions.

The purpose of the Jnana given by the Lord is to clear the mind of the vasanas and not letting entry to the new vasanas. This is known as "burning of the existing vasanas." The vasanas are technically said to have been burnt to ashes with no more identity left.

Those actions conducted without "the Jnana" (out of ignorance) generally are considered as "sins" because they lead to rebirth into this world of samsara.

Based on this explanation, Jnana is said to burn the sins.

The sastras talk of "Prarabdha, Sanchita and Agami" concerning actions and reactions.

These are:

Sanchita—past

Prarabdha—present

Aagaami—future (not known).

Unfulfilled vasanas from the past (including past births) which have not materialised into actions remain in our mind at the time of physical death as unfulfilled desires/hatreds etc. These are the bundles of vasanas we carry to our next birth, next stage of life. This is "Sanchita karma". It is like the sack we carry on our back as our luggage. No one can carry this bag of vasanas for us and it is solely up to us to carry them. (these are carried in the mind)

In the new birth or the new stage in our life, we will get the fruition of only some of these accumulated vasanas.

Some of the good that we are experiencing now may be the results of good actions in the past. On the other hand, some of the events which bring pain now may be due to the bad actions in the past.

The sastras say this is the "Prarabdha", meaning "The fate". It is the fate decreed by the Supreme for our actions of the past committed knowingly or unknowingly.

What about the future? One may ask. The sastras say "Aagami" meaning "not known".

During "Prarabdha" (present state) we have some of the past vasanas (carried in the sack) fulfilled and we are adding more new vasanas from our present actions. We have to face the results of all of such actions (both good and bad) in the next stage of our life which could also be in the next birth.

Hence the statement by masters "We do not know what the future holds for us for tomorrow, what is to come in our life, either as a new stage in life or in new birth".

The masters say that no one really knows what the future is going to be. By saying "future", they mean tomorrow in one's life or the life in a new birth.

Even though we have no control over the present, due to the results of the past, we, the humans have the chance to have a better tomorrow. This comes by analyzing our thoughts and using the intellectual capacity of reasoning and conducting actions as per the sastras.

The Jnana is to make a better tomorrow not only for us but for the society too.

न हि ज्ञानेन सदृशं पवित्रमिह विद्यते ।
तत्स्वयं योगसंसिद्धः कालेनात्मनि विन्दति ||38||

na hi jñānena sadṛśaṃ pavitram iha vidyate |
tat svayaṃ yogasaṃsiddhaḥ kālenātmani vindati ||38||

Certainly there is nothing as pure as knowledge in this world. He who is himself perfected in Yoga finds it in the Self by himself in due season. ||38||

na: not; hi: verily; jnanena: to wisdom; sadrusham: like; pavitram: pure; iha: here (in this world); vidyate: certainly/indeed; tat: that;

svayam: oneself; yogasamsiddhaha: perfected in yoga; kalena: in time; atmani: in the Self; vindati: finds.

This statement applies to all forms of knowledge, be it spiritual or be it material science but more so in relation to the spiritual knowledge.

The root word for the Vedas is "vid" (to know.) The knowledge of one's own Self, the knowledge of the Eternal Truth is emphasised as the real knowledge in the Vedas. Vedas are the authoritative revealed texts on Hindu philosophy.

The opposite of the knowledge is "ignorance." Ignorance of our true nature, ignorance of our origin has made us fall into this whirlpool called samsara. We are experiencing so much suffering in our life and see suffering all round us because of this ignorance.

The Gita is to remind us of our true nature which is Tat-Tvam-Asi (Thou Art That). What are we doing? What have we done?

We have forgotten this "Maha vakya".We have covered ourselves with ignorance which is the root cause for the development of "ego".

Finds it in the Self:

"The Self" referred to is the Atman/Soul. It is within us and is also is present in all forms of life. It is "Nirakara, Nirguna" (no form, no qualities).

The entire life's journey of every individual is all about this Truth.

We start the spiritual quest with the question "Ko'ham?" "Who am I?" The end for the quest is finding the answer "So' ham". (I am That")

In due course:

The time taken for "Vasana kshaya and mano nasha" (destruction of all vasanas and destruction of the mind) is not in our hands. But, at the end, each one of us will realize the truth and attain Moksha. Moksha is not for selected few but it is the birth right of all.

The Lord does not bestow favors on anybody.

The Lord wants us to develop all the divine qualities (chapter 16)/ qualities of a true Bhakta (chapter 12)/qualities of a true Jnani (chapter 13) / features of Sthitaprajna (chapter 2) or features of a Gunatita (chapter 14). All of these have one thing in common and that is annihilation of "ego" and the need to surrender to Him.

श्रद्धावाँल्लभते ज्ञानं तत्परः संयतेन्द्रियः ।
ज्ञानं लब्ध्वा परां शान्तिमचिरेणाधिगच्छति ||39||

śraddhāvāṃl labhate jñānaṃ tatparaḥ saṃyatendriyaḥ |
jñānaṃ labdhvā parāṃ śāntim acireṇādhigacchati ||39||

The man of faith having knoweldge as his supreme goal, the devoted, having controlled the senses, obtains knoweldge of Atma, and having obtained that, enjoys Peace for ever. ||39||

sraddhaavaan: the man of faith; labhate: obtains; jnanam: knowledge; tatparaha: devoted; samyatendriyaha: who has controlled the senses; labdhva: having obtained; param: Supreme; shantim: peace; achirena: ever; adhigachati: goes.

The three conditions to be met to get the knowledge in any field of activity, either spiritual or worldly, are:
Faith,
Devotion
Control over the senses.

The stronger the determination to acquire the knowledge, the greater is the need to fulfill the above three conditions.

The student who has reached the stage of secondary education and who would like to make substantial progress in the studies has to develop devotion to the subject of his choice and not let the wandering mind get distracted. As he receives the dividends for his efforts, he develops more faith in his plan of action and so makes further progress in his studies.

With this success, he can enjoy the next stage of life because he would be competent and eligible to take the professional duties of his choice and get financial reward for the work conducted. The security of the wealth obtained from the knowledge acquired, should give immense joy in becoming a professional.

We can take the same principle in the study of the spiritual science. Why do we have to undertake such study and austerities?

We should do so to get the knowledge of the Atman that gives the "Bliss". Spiritual studies and spiritual practice are the means to get "The Bliss."

The spiritual seeker is he who is after the knowledge that gives him the Eternal Peace. He has realized that every action has a result and that the result is either happiness or sorrow. Life has taught him the lesson, that both states of happiness and sorrow are temporary and one experience eventually merges into the other. He is on the lookout for that experience which is beyond both sorrow and happiness. The sastras designate this state as "Moksha" which is nothing but "Eternal Peace" (param shantim). It is a process of climbing up the spiritual ladder, the steps of the ladder being the results of life's experiences.

Let us now analyse the three conditions enumerated in this sloka.

Faith:

Unshakeable faith in the scriptures, guru and the masters is the first requisite, along with it one needs to have faith in himself and a strong determination to succeed.

The degree of faith determines the level of success.

The philosophy does not advocate blind faith, even if the teacher is the greatest master.

The Student should make it a point to clear the doubts that crop up in the mind.

Question the master on points you have not understood. Do not blindly follow the guru's teaching.

You can even test the truth of what has been taught.

If you are not convinced, step aside and go the way your intellect guides you.

If and when you face problems in the path you have chosen, think of what was taught by the guru and see if it makes sense.

If you consider what was taught made sense, come back to the guru and continue your sadhana.

What is to be understood is that the sincere seeker should carry out all the instructions according to the sastras he is learning and according to the teacher who taught the subject, with the sincere hope that one day he would experience the best results. This strong conviction assists in making rapid strides towards final success.

The person who believes in the Self, who goes in search of it in a proper manner, will find in every step something or other to prove the statements embedded in the scriptures and the words of his master. The faith never urges one to go contrary to one's judgment.

Doubts never carry one towards progress. The doubts are to be cleared first and the faith has to be established firmly to make the desired progress.

If we look back at our childhood we will find that the faith in our parents made us learn a lot of lessons.

As a rule parents do not want their children to get hurt and so warn them of dangers in day to day life. But many a time, we, the curious children neglect the warning by the parents and sooner or later get hurt.

We should therefore understand and realize that our welfare was their main concern and this protective attitude of the parents should make us feel devoted to them.

Matparaha:

To have the determination to acquire the knowledge that gives "Eternal Peace" should be the spirit of action. After developing the required faith, the devotion to acquire the knowledge becomes the next step to take. Single minded devotion always gets the best results.

The seeker needs to be devoted to his selected subject of the spiritual science. Greater the devotion, stronger will be the enthusiasm to learn and capacity to withstand any adversities that one may encounter.

This devotional attitude should have the harmony of thought, speech and action.

Disharmony between thought, speech and action will never achieve success. There should be total dedication to the acquisition of knowledge.

If one wants to become a rich man, one should first of all have faith in himself that he can become rich one day. He then needs to acquire the knowledge that can make him rich. One cannot become rich just by faith alone. He should be devoted to the acquisition of knowledge that could make him rich.

Samyatendriyaha:

Self-control is essential all through the walk towards the achievement of the final goal. The senses have the knack of taking the individual away towards the sensual world.

There is always something in the world outside that pleases the mind and makes the mind send the organs of action to get it.

The accumulated memory imprints on the mind from the previous experiences in life also make the mind wander towards the sensual world.

What is needed is making use of the capacity of "Intellectual discrimination." There should be a gap between thought and action. The intellectual capacity for discrimination between right and wrong has to be exercised. This is the meaning of "Self-control." It is the control over the ego.

Param Shantim Achirena adhigacchati:

"Soon attains the supreme Peace." The final result of such actions is the experience of the "Eternal Peace." Adverse situations do come in every one's life due to the results of past karmas or due to the actions performed out of ignorance and indiscriminate actions. The beauty is in finding the "Peace" within oneself and this Peace no power in the world can take away.

Actions to get the knowledge of the "Atman" in conjunction with no desire either in actions or in the fruits of actions, will guarantee the success.

Quote: Sri Ramakrishna:

A devotee asked the master once: When will I have the vision of God?

The master took the disciple to the sea shore and held him immersed in water for a while. He then asked the disciple how he felt.

The disciple said, "I thought I would die of want of fresh air." The master said,

You will have the vision of God when you develop the feeling that you will choke unless you have the vision of God. Such a quest for God would reveal Him immediately.

अज्ञश्चाश्रद्दधानश्च संशयात्मा विनश्यति ।
नायं लोकोऽस्ति न परो न सुखं संशयात्मनः ॥40॥

ajñaś cāśraddadhānaś ca saṃśayātmā vinaśyati |
nāyaṃ loko 'sti na paro na sukhaṃ saṃśayātmanaḥ ||40||

The ignorant, faithless, doubting man goes to destruction. For the doubter, there is neither this world nor the other world nor the happiness. ||40||

ajnah: the ignorant; cha: and; ashraddhadanaha: the faithless; samshayatma: the doubting self; vinashyati: goes to destruction; na: not; ayam: this; lokaha: the world; paraha: the next (other); sukham: happiness; samshayatmanaha: the doubting self.

The last sloka gave us the positive aspects of the seeker who moves in the quest of true knowledge with the zeal of total faith.

Three characteristics of the individual who will fail to experience the "Eternal peace" are brought out in this sloka. They are beautifully given in the right order of :

"Ignorance (ajnana),
Lack of faith (ashraddha), and
Doubting nature (samshaya)."

Ajnascha: (Ignorant) The first hurdle in the search for the "Eternal Peace" is ignorance. The ignorant, are those who lack the knowledge of the Atman, they do not understand what dharma is and what constitutes adharma. They do not have the notion that the body is to be looked upon as the eternal servant of the master and they are highly egotistic by nature.

They firmly believe in the material world and in the "present" and they do not believe in the results of past actions. They work for experiencing the pleasures and fortunes of the world and by nature such people are faithless. They do not have faith in the scriptures or the gurus and they consider that whatever they are doing is correct.

Let us pause for a moment and consider the consequences of such beliefs.

If everyone in the world has his own personal idea of what is right and what is wrong, there will be millions of ideas of rights and wrongs and there will be no common consensus.

How can we then teach the future generation about dharma and adharma?

The sastras are the consensus opinion of learned people who had the welfare of the universe forefront as their motive.

The judiciary in any country has fixed views on the correct actions one has to follow in that country. Those who break the law are considered as guilty and receive punishment. The laws act as the sastras in relation to the social life in that country.

Similarly, we are part of life in the universe and our elders have given us the sastras which are the guides for good conduct that result in universal welfare.

We should have faith in such sastras.

The gurus are those who have studied the sastras and experienced the "Truth" encompassed within the scriptures.

The guru should be our guide in spiritual practices.

Faith, practiced sincerely takes one to higher steps in spiritual practice and that much nearer to the "Truth."

Ashradhascha: This sloka is about those who have no such faith and live the life of 'law for themselves.'

The individual should have a desire to understand dharma and approach the sastras and the guru and have no hesitation in approaching them and seeking guidance.

The last of the qualities brought out in this sloka is "Samshaya." Samshaya is "doubting nature."

A person of doubting nature has doubts even about the existence of the "Higher." He doubts the genuine nature of the masters who have the welfare of all as their motto and he does not believe in the scriptures.

One should put in genuine effort to clarify the doubts which will help to overcome the obstacles. Acquisition of "Jnana" is a must to make any true progress.

Sri Ramakrishna quotes beautifully this example:

The mother tells her daughter, "This is your brother." The daughter accepts it with total sincerity and faith. She introduces him to others as "my brother." Where is the proof to give the daughter? The daughter has to simply accept faithfully that her mother's statement is true. If she has no faith in her mother or her words, there is no progress in relationships in that family.

By nature, a doubting person has doubts on everything and everybody. He cannot take one simple step forward towards progress. Because of this nature, he cannot take any positive decisions.

Such people become the failures even in this life. What can one say about their future?

The grace of the Lord comes with such faith and knowledge of the scriptures.

योगसंन्यस्तकर्माणं ज्ञानसंछिन्नसंशयम् ।
आत्मवन्तं न कर्माणि निबध्नन्ति धनञ्जय ||41||

yogasaṃnyastakarmāṇaṃ jñānasaṃchinnasaṃśayam |
ātmavantaṃ na karmāṇi nibadhnanti dhanaṃjaya ||41||

O Arjuna, actions do not bind him who has renounced actions by Yoga, whose doubts are cleared by knowledge and who is established in the Self. || 41||

yoga samnyasta karmanaam: one who has renounced actions by yoga; jnana samchinna samshayam: whose doubts are cleared by knowledge; atmavantam: established in Self; na: not; karmani: actions; nibhadnanti: bind; dhananjaya: Arjuna.

The enlightened man is he who fulfills the following three conditions:

He is constantly established in the Atman. He is aware of his identity with the Atman and considers that the body is the tool to attain perfection in unity with the Supreme.

He continues to discharge all his duties to the society of which he is a part of , thereby burning away all the past samskaras/ vasanas.

He will work in the true spirit of nishkama karma and karma phala tyaga and thereby not accumulate any new vasanas.

This comes by a clearer spiritual knowledge. The knowledge is the tool to clear all doubts and scriptures and gurus are the medium in the attainment of knowledge.

Yoga samnyasta karmanaam: Actions renounced by yoga.

This refers to the present actions. As we have studied before no one can remain free even for a minute without conducting some action or the other. The word "yoga" in this context refers to "Jnana yoga." We should all conduct actions using our knowledge.

The actions have to be in the spirit of "Nishkama karma and karma phala tyaga." There should not be any trace of ego/personal interest in the actions conducted.

Jnana samchinna samshayam: with all doubts cleared totally by the knowledge.

It is true that doubts crop up in some form or other till one reaches the final destination. On reaching the final destination, all doubts will get cleared totally. For this the raft of knowledge is the tool. Sastras and the gurus are the medium to clear the doubts and establish the knowledge.

The seeker has to be established in the Atman always. He should never swerve from the path of "Dharma and Truth."

Only for such an individual, actions do not bind. All his actions automatically become "divine."

तस्मादज्ञानसंभूतं हृत्स्थं ज्ञानासिनाऽऽत्मनः ।
छित्त्वैनं संशयं योगमातिष्ठोत्तिष्ठ भारत ||**42**||

tasmād ajñānasaṃbhūtaṃ hṛtsthaṃ jñānāsinātmanaḥ |
chittvainaṃ saṃśayaṃ yogam ātiṣṭhottiṣṭha bhārata ||42||

Therefore with the sword of knowledge, cut asunder the doubt born of ignorance about the Self, dwelling in the heart, and take refuge in Yoga. Arise O Arjuna. ||42||

tasmat: therefore; ajnana sambhootam: born of ignorance; hrutsnam: residing in the heart; jnanasina: by the sword of knowledge; atmanaha: of the Self; chittva: cut asunder; enam: this; samshayam: doubt; yogam: yoga; aatishta: take refuge; utthishta; arise.

This is the last verse in this chapter on Jnana. We get the summary of what has been said so far. Even though the Gita was taught by Krishna to Arjuna, it is a lesson for all the mankind.

Krishna is stressing on the need to clear all the doubts in the mind of his disciple/friend and indirectly, it is a message for all of us to clear our doubts.

What were Arjuna's doubts?

Could he kill the elders and teachers in the battle?

What right has he got to cause confusion in the society that will lead to anarchy?

Is it not a sin?

Is it not better to take up sanyasa, renounce all and go to the forest?

Taking up sanyasa, surely is it not the path to heaven?

Where are all these doubts?

Doubts as we know are all in the mind. Here, we are told they are in the heart. We should understand this clearly.

The intellect is said to be in the cave of the heart, it is not the 'physical' heart .Lord Krishna is talking of the spiritual heart that shows love and compassion, which is the intellect.

Behind the so called intellect is the "Antaratma" which is the inner voice from the Atman within. It is also the "Antarjyothi" (the light within). This illumines the intellect with the clear light of knowledge. The intellect in turn illumines the mind.

With the light of knowledge beaming on the mind, the doubts will get cleared away.

Between the intellect and mind is said to be the gap that is filled with ego, ignorance and doubts. Because of these, the connection between intellect and the mind is blocked. The light from the intellect does not reflect on the mind and the mind remains in darkness. The mind is then said to work in darkness.

We are told that doubts are due to ignorance. Ignorance of the Atman residing within and which is supposed to be the guiding force in our daily activities is the root cause of misery.

Ignorance is compared to darkness and knowledge is compared to brightness. We can understand this by the analogy of night and day.

As soon as the knowledge dawns, the doubts will get cleared and we can take up our ordained duties.

During the phase of ignorance either we do not use the intellectual capacity properly or we misuse the capacity.

The simile of a sword is used in this sloka. We are asked to cut asunder the knot of ignorance that hinders our progress in spirituality.

The Lord uses the word "Aatishtothishta."

Aatishta: perform.

Uthishta: arise.

"Arise and perform" is the command to Arjuna and Arjuna's of the present world.

Arise from despair born out of ignorance and perform your work is the clear cut message from this sloka.

We are asked to conduct "Yoga."

Yoga in the context is Karma yoga using the knowledge.

It is nothing but "Nishkama karma and karma phala tyaga."

Clearly there is a message for Arjuna that he should not go to the forest and take up sanyasa. Do your duty is the advice and command.

This is the message for all of us. Let us do our duty as per the guidelines given by the scriptures.

We have got the intellect. Let us use this and cut asunder all doubts.

Let us all be fit to fight the battle of life and attain Liberation from sorrows and pains arising from the objective world.

Let us uplift ourselves and in turn let it uplift the society.

Let us be the tools for a happy, prosperous, peaceful world.

If all the people who are blessed with knowledge decide to abandon work as it is a sin and take retirement, what will happen to the world?

Metaphorically speaking, it would come to a halt. This would cause the destruction of life.

WHEN KNOWING AND DOING GO HAND IN HAND, THEN MAN IS AT HIS BEST.

iti srīmadbhagavadgītasūpaniṣatsu brahmavidyāyāṃ yogaśāstre śrīkrsnārjuna samvāde Jñāna yogo nāma caturtho'dhyāyah

CHAPTER 5

KARMA–SAṂNYĀSA–YOGA

Quote: George Washington:

"When I conduct an action I do so with the feeling that everything depends on me. When I complete the work I sit back with the feeling that the result of the work depends totally on His Grace."

INTRODUCTION:

"Karma": "Actions."

Sanyasa: life of renuniciation.

Renunciation of "all desire oriented" actions is "Karma Sanyasa Yoga."

This is in continuation of the fundamentals of action and knowledge described in the previous two chapters under the heading of "Karma Yoga and Jnana Yoga."

As one proceeds to dwell deeper into the subject matter in this spiritual discourse by the Lord, there is going to be some confusion on the meaning of the words "Sanyasa and Tyaga." We do get explanations for these two words every so often during the dialogue and the final explanations are to be found in the 18th chapter.

At this juncture let us understand that:

Sanyasa is "desirelessness" and "Tyaga" is "renunciation of fruits of actions."

In the conduct of any actions sequentially desire, action and result follow in that order.

It is a fact that to get anything in life one should conduct actions.

To get something higher, one should still conduct actions but be prepared to forego the lower pleasures.

Renouncing the lower pleasures to experience "Bliss" is the subject matter of this chapter.

The lower pleasures are concerning the pleasures in this life, in this world of ours — "Bhooloka",

And

The higher pleasures are concerning the pleasures from residence in the higher lokas. These lokas are on higher planes than the earth we live in. These lokas are ruled by devas.

Initially we have to learn to sacrifice more and more pleasures which we get as results of actions in this life of ours to reach the higher planes.

Finally, we should learn to be ready to sacrifice all the pleasures we expect to get from the higher planes of existence to reach the final destination "Moksha."

Apart from the "Moksha" our stay in any of the higher planes is only temporary and has a time span of stay. On completion of enjoyment of stay in those planes, we have to come down to earth and start accumulating points of merit to enjoy pleasures again.

We should conduct actions with the knowledge of what we will achieve as a result of the actions. Once we decide on what we like to achieve, our attention has to be on the actions and no more on the end product. The end product will come on its own in the course of time depending upon our actions. The results of past karmas do have an influence on the results received now. Actions form "the present" and results "the future".

This rule applies to all walks of life and more so for the spiritual seeker aiming to achieve "Moksha."

Mental renunciation in the conduct of actions (absence of "I" ness in actions) and the fruits thereof is "Karma Sanyasa".

The more efforts one puts towards the concentration on the studies, better will be the results and the grades one would get in the final exams. Good grades in turn would help in securing better employment.

It is also important to remember that our efforts/attitude for studies in the earlier years of study before entering the university do influence the results in the final year of exams.

The student who does not concentrate on the present and study as needed and who spends his time enjoying himself would find that the pleasures he experienced are limited.

He would end up by not being able to find a secure means of livelihood and will experience hardship in future life.

The basic rule to follow therefore is: "For the security of tomorrow, sacrifice the pleasures of today."

This is the theme of discussion in this chapter. By giving us the basics of "Karma and Jnana" in chapters 3 and 4, we are now given higher education in spiritual science.

In this chapter we will understand that we need to renounce desire prompted actions that will hinder in the progress towards spiritual maturity.

In this chapter we will learn:

The art of renunciation of sense of agency (ego) in actions and also the art of renouncing the desires and anxiety for results of actions conducted.

अर्जुन उवाच
संन्यासं कर्मणां कृष्ण पुनर्योगं च शंससि ।
यच्छ्रेय एतयोरेकं तन्मे ब्रूहि सुनिश्चितम् ||1||

Arjuna uvāca
saṃnyāsaṃ karmaṇāṃ kṛṣṇa punar yogaṃ ca śaṃsasi
yac chreya etayor ekaṃ tan me brūhi suniścitam ||1||

Arjuna said
O Krishna, you praise renunciation of actions and again yoga of action, of these two which is better? Tell me conclusively. ||1||

sanyasam: renunciation; karmanam: of actions; punar: again; yogam: yoga; cha: and; shamsasi: praise; yat: which; sreyo: better;

yetayor: of these two; ekam: one; tat: that; me': to me; broohi: tell; sunischitam: conclusively.

Arjuna, the disciple who surrendered at the feet of his master Sri Krishna wanted the knowledge that would overcome his ignorance. He was ignorant of which action would be beneficial for him. He was not an ignorant student of the sastras but had not understood the spiritual lessons received earlier. He is now experiencing confusion on whether to stand up and fight or abandon the war.

The last sloka in the previous chapter ended up with the command to stand up and fight from Krishna. Krishna had said "Uthishta."

But, at the same time, some slokas in the previous chapters emphasised on renunciation of actions. Sloka 71, chapter 2, clearly said: "That man who, abandoning all desires, lives without longing for them, without the sense of I and mine, attains Peace."

Arjuna wanted the guidance in the form of a definite statement from Krishna as to which path was the best. He showed the qualities of a sincere student by asking for clarification in what had been taught.

Sloka 34 in the last chapter is all about the approach to the guru in quest of knowledge. (Tad viddhi Pranipatena') By asking for clarification of doubts, Arjuna is following the sastras.

श्री भगवानुवाच
संन्यासः कर्मयोगश्च निःश्रेयसकरावुभौ ।
तयोस्तु कर्मसंन्यासात्कर्मयोगो विशिष्यते ||2||

Śrībhagavān uvāca
saṃnyāsaḥ karmayogaś ca niḥśreyasakarāv ubhau
tayos tu karmasaṃnyāsāt karmayogo viśiṣyate ||2||

The Lord said:
Renunciation of action and yoga of action both lead to the highest bliss. But of these two, yoga of action is superior to the renunciation of action. ||2||

sanyasaha: renunciation; karmayogaha: yoga of action; cha: and; nishreyasakarou: leading to the highest goal (bliss); ubhou: both; tayoh: of these two; tu: but; karma sanyasat: than renunciation of action; karma yoga: yoga of action; vishishyate: is superior.

Nishreyasakarou: without doubt, leading to the highest bliss.

-The word incorporates "Shreyas" in it. We have discussed the meaning of the word in chapter 2, sloka 7.

Shreyas is what is for our welfare.

Sri Krishna is telling Arjuna that both the paths of "Karma and Sanyasa" ultimately lead to the final state of "Bliss."

He then adds the statement that "Yoga of action" is superior. This he says so with reference to the ordinary men and women on this earth. "Yoga of renunciation" is not possible by the majority and hence the preference to the Yoga of action.

Sanyasa is total renunciation of all actions and concentrating totally on the divine. This is a very difficult practice and very few can take up to this method.

We live in the world of a large number of men and women and other forms of life. In our daily life we come across so many different people. As we have learnt before, every individual is a representative of the Lord on this earth. When we learn the art of overcoming the ego and annihilating the same we will be able to express the divinity within. Ultimately, we will, through the path of "Shreyas" attain Moksha.

By following the path of karma, we have an opportunity to come across so many varieties of expression of life. We get an opportunity to develop communication with the Lord's creation. The Lord's wish is "Loka Kalyana", the welfare of life on earth. We, the humans are the medium to fulfill that wish. If each one of us can work for Loka Kalyana, we can make this world a haven of Peace and prosperity.

This is possible by following the path of "karma yoga."

The followers of path of renunciation fail to get an opportunity to fulfill this wish of the Lord.

It is true that by following the path of sanyasa, one can experience quietude and tranquility. There is a need for mental equilibrium and this is fulfilled by following the path of sanyasa. On the other hand actions do bring mental disturbance (sukha, dukha) which disturbs the concentration on acts for Loka Kalyana but it is still possible to develop perfection by practicing the Karma Yoga. We have learnt this by looking at the qualities of a man of steady wisdom in chapter 2.

What we have to understand from this sloka is that:

Jnana resulting in renunciation of ego in all actions and Karma consisting in actions without desires and with no attachment to the fruits of action, both lead to the ultimate Bliss.

If everyone takes to the path of sanyasa, the life on earth will have to come to a standstill and no progress will then be possible. There is a duty to cater for the needs of ordinary men and women and other forms of life. This sloka is directed to such people.

Renunciation should come from ripeness of the mind. This takes a long time and in many cases many births and deaths. Taking the decision to become a sanyasi either out of ignorance or as an act of sudden impulse will make the individual a lost soul on earth.

Instead of taking up the arms and fighting the war of righteousness under the guidance of Sri Krishna, if he had retired to the forest, Arjuna would have become a lost soul in the forest.

This was because Arjuna had not achieved "Mano nasha and vasana kshaya".

We need to burn the existing vasanas (vasana kshaya) and not accumulate any new vasanas (mano nasha). This is possible only by a long life of dedication to actions in the form of "Desire–less actions and no attachment to the fruits of action." (Sloka 47, chapter 2.)

Sri Ramanuja gives a clarification to the word of "Sanyasa" used in this context. He states that "sanyasa" means "Jnana." A true karma yogi while being a part of the society performing nishkama karma attains Jnana of the Atman. This is the later stage of spiritual maturity. Hence, the statement by Sri Krishna that Karma is superior to sanyasa.

ज्ञेयः स नित्यसंन्यासी यो न द्वेष्टि न काङ्क्षति ।
निर्द्वन्द्वो हि महाबाहो सुखं बन्धात्प्रमुच्यते ||3||

jñeyaḥ sa nityasaṃnyāsī yo na dveṣṭi na kāṅkṣati |
nirdvandvo hi mahābāho sukhaṃ bandhāt pramucyate ||3||

O Arjuna, he who neither hates nor desires should be known as a man of eternal renunciation. He who is free from the pairs of opposites is easily set free from bondage. ||3||

jneyaha: should be known; sa: he; nitya sanyasee: eternal renunciation (steady ascetic); yah: who; na: not; kankshati: desires; dweshti: hates; nirdwandvo: free from pairs of opposites; hi: verily; mahabaho: mighty armed; sukham: happiness; bandhat: from bondage; pramuchyate: is set free.

Sri Krishna is making it clear that the act of sanyasa has to be at all the three planes of "Mind, speech and actions." This is known as "Trikarana Shuddhi". (Purity of the mind, speech and actions). Wearing ochre robes and living on the outskirts of town or the forest does not make one a sanyasi. It is not the physical appearance alone that makes one a sanyasi but his mental attitude.

Real sanyasa is not by renouncing what one dislikes and of feeling happy because one escapes from obligatory duties.

Sanyasa is an act of "self–denial". Selfishness cannot make the individual a sanyasi. The act of renunciation should be not just momentary but must be pursued all through the rest of one's life. The Lord uses the word "Nitya Sanyasee." In this context the word means "A steady ascetic" who shows the qualities of a sanyasi in all his thoughts, actions and speech every day of his life.

"He who neither hates nor desires": Desires and hatreds can come only from being a part of and attached to the society and cannot be experienced by he who moves away from the society. This would mean that a sanyasi continues to be living his daily life by being a part of the society and at the same time following the principle of "Nishkama karma and Karma Phala tyaga." Continue to do what you are trained for; continue to conduct "Nitya karmas" as dictated by the sastras is the message by the Lord.

The path to "Moksha" is therefore by being a true "Karma Yogi" and not simply by running away from obligatory duties.

One needs to conduct actions that end in "Mano nasha and vasana kshaya" (Refer to the previous sloka).

The second half of the sloka brings out the theme of "Nirdwandva". One has to be free from the pairs of opposites in life like "happiness, sorrow; pain, pleasure; victory, defeat, heat and cold" and the like. These come from being attached to the physical body and/or attached to the world around and are the reactions of the mind to the impulses received from the sense organs. Developing "equanimity" to the stimuli received, is an essential quality to be developed. This is another requisite for becoming a sanyasi.

If one does not get bound to the world by attachment or aversion, if he gives up selfishness, in course of time he would experience "The Peace within and all around". Such a person can be a householder and perform all his duties.

The starting word of this sloka is "Jneyaha". It means "Should be known." Know what I am going to say is the statement from Sri Krishna.

Bandhat Pramuchyate: "Bandha" is attachment and "Pramuchya" is setting free. "Nitya Sanyasi" is freed from attachment and entitled to experience the "Eternal Peace".

"Raga Dwesha": Desires and hatreds. Renunciation of influences of hatred and desires which bind the individual;

"Dwandva": Pairs of opposites. Abandoning the pairs of opposites;

Such an individual who has managed to burn all the existing vasanas by his actions and not accumulated new vasanas is a true sanyasi.

Let us therefore remember that it is not action but attitudes to actions that can bind or liberate us from this world.

सांख्ययोगौ पृथग्बालाः प्रवदन्ति न पण्डिताः ।
एकमप्यास्थितः सम्यगुभयोर्विन्दते फलम् ||4||

sāṃkhyayogau pṛthag bālāḥ pravadanti na paṇḍitāḥ |
ekam apy āsthitaḥ samyag ubhayor vindate phalam ||4||

Children, not the wise, say that jnana yoga and karma yoga are distinct. He who is truly established in either of them obtains the fruits of both. ||4||

sankhya yogou: jnana and karma yoga; pruthak: distinct; na: not; balaha: children; pravadanti: say; panditaha: the wise; ekam: one; api: even; asthitaha: established; samyak: truly; ubhayor: of both; vindate: obtains; phalam: the fruit.

The Lord uses the word "Panditaha" to denote the wise people. A learned man is many a time called "Pandita." This is not the true meaning of the word. A master in theory may not be a master in practicals. He who knows the scriptures and puts the teaching into practice is a true pandita.

A true Jnani performs his actions with a state of renunciation of ego. He has no feeling of "I'ness."

A true karma yogi on the other hand works with the spirit of "No desire for the fruits of action".

Working in this spirit both Jnani and Karma Yogi will achieve the final result of "Mano nasha and vasana kshaya" which is a pre requisite for Moksha. Both the paths bring out the divinity within the individual.

Not understanding the true meaning of the scriptures, many a grown men/women argue that their path is the best and look down upon the others.

Through this sloka Sri Krishna is only chiding such persons. He is not angry at our faults. On the other hand like a mother to her child, he is telling us that we should not commit such mistakes. He says that only children make such mistakes and not adults. It is a common practice that we excuse the mistakes of the children.

The majority of us are physically grown up but spiritually immature. Those who are spiritually grown up should learn to look upon the rest with compassion and understanding.

Through this sloka we also get a hint of the spirit of "adweshta," (No hatred). He wants religious tolerance. All paths lead to the same goal and one should not hate others who do not follow the same path. We must learn to be tolerant of other faiths, creeds and sects.

"Samyak asthitaha: He who is truly established."

Imperfect understanding leads to differences and quarrels in course of time.

It does not matter if one is following the path of "Jnana or karma". What matters is that he should transcend the feeling of personal doership.

यत्सांख्यैः प्राप्यते स्थानं तद्योगैरपि गम्यते ।
एकं सांख्यं च योगं च यः पश्यति स पश्यति ||5||

yat sāṃkhyaiḥ prāpyate sthānaṃ tad yogair api gamyate |
ekaṃ sāṃkhyaṃ ca yogaṃ ca yaḥ paśyati sa paśyati ||5||

That state which is reached by samkhyas is also reached by yogis. He who sees the oneness of samkhya and yoga really sees. ||5||

yat: that; samkhye: by the samkhyas; prapyate: reached; sthanam: state/place; tad: that; yogai: by yogis; api: also; gamyate: is reached; ekam: one; samkhyam: samkhya knwoledge; cha: and; yogam: yoga; pashyati: sees; sah: he.

Gamya: the final goal; Gamyate: reaches the final goal.

The Lord is to be looked upon as standing at the final goal point and observing the various paths that reach Him. He is seeing two main paths:

The path followed by Samkhyas and the path followed by Yogis.

"Samkhya" as we have discussed in the second chapter means "Uniting with the knowledge." It is all about the knowledge of the "Imperishable Atman" within and all around. He who has fully and clearly understood the "Atman" is a true Jnani. "Samkhyas" in this context is to be understood as "Jnanis".

The word "Yogi" is with reference to "Men of action". A true man of action is a "KarmaYogi."

Chapters 3 and 4 are about attaining the "Moksha" through the medium of "Knowledge and Action."

We have a reiteration of the fact that both the paths are for final union with the "Parabrahman" and experiencing the "Bliss."

The world is full of men with varied temperaments. The various paths are to suit the temperaments of different groups of people.

Men of knowledge should not show partiality to any specific group and be compassionate to all.

The Vedas declare that the knower of Brahman becomes Brahman.

We should read it as "Jnani by action becomes Brahman".

Karma Yoga and Jnana Yoga are just the two sides of the same coin.

A coin has two sides with inscriptions on each side. It is accepted for circulation only when there are inscriptions on both sides. Absence of inscription on either side makes it unfit for circulation.

Similarly, the coin needed to reach the final destination should have inscriptions of karma on one side and Jnana on the other side. The seeker of the final destination should therefore show "Knowledge in actions". The knowing aspect of the knower is "Samkhya" and the becoming aspect is "Yoga".

संन्यासस्तु महाबाहो दुःखमाप्तुमयोगतः ।
योगयुक्तो मुनिर्ब्रह्म नचिरेणाधिगच्छति ||6||

saṃnyāsas tu mahābāho duḥkham āptum ayogataḥ |
yogayukto munir brahma nacireṇādhigacchati ||6||

O Arjuna, but renunciation (sanyasa) is hard to attain (dukham aptum) without the yoga of action. The sage who is harmonised in yoga quickly goes to Brahman. ||6|

sanyasaha: renunciation; tu: but; mahabaho: mighty armed; dukham: hard; aaptum: to attain; ayogataha: without yoga; yogayuktaha: harmonised in yoga; munihi: muni; Brahma: to Brahma; nachirena: quickly; adhigacchati: goes.

Sanyasa is desire–less actions and tyaga is abandoning all fruits of actions. Ego is the centre for desires and hatreds.

Sanyasa is therefore to be understood as renunciation of ego.

When there is no ego, there will not be any trace of desires or hatreds.

Many understand and consider sanyasa as renunciation of all possessions. They decide to leave all the possessions and go to a centre of pilgrimage and start a new life in the vicinity of their beloved God.

There are some who would like to go to an ashrama and spend the rest of their life.

What we should remember is that the most important possession which we must renounce is "The Ego."

Without renouncing ego all other acts of renunciations are of little use.

It is the ego that keeps us attached to all material possessions in this world. But to live in this world we have to conduct actions and work like a karma yogi.

The first step therefore is karma yoga, the second step is Jnana yoga and the third step is Vijnana yoga. "Vijnana" in this context is the maturity that makes the individual develop "Detachment in attachment." (It is true sanyasa) The end result is "Moksha."

The child starts with learning to walk first. Karma yoga in this sense is attempts to learn walking.

In course of time which takes about 2–3 yrs the child becomes competent in walking.

The child develops the full knowledge in the art of walking. This is the beginning of Jnana yoga.

By realizing the benefits/dangers in walking, the child develops wisdom (Vijnana) in relation to walking and this will help her to reach the goal.

Finally the child develops the competence to reach the desired destination. Without walking first, the child would not have reached the final destination. This principle is brought out in this sloka.

Another example many scholars would quote is that of fruits on a tree.

The fruits are not sweet when they are not ripe. They will be sour or bitter. They have to remain on the branches of the tree, expose themselves to all weather conditions, get the nourishment from the environment and finally become ripe. When they are ripe they slowly lose their connection to the branches and fall off to the ground.

What a beautiful example. Falling off to the ground is losing connection with the world and "Moksha" for the fruit. It gets mature only on exposure to the environment and being part of the tree during the process.

Similarly we should be part of the society and sanyasa is after total maturity and natural detachment from all attachments. A Karma Yogi gets nourished by the various modifications of life, becomes a Jnani and finally attains Moksha. He has to develop the knack of working for the welfare of the society. Such self-denial, foresaking personal pleasures for the benefit of society is true sanyasa and the individual is then a true "Karma Yogi."

The majority of us belong to the category of those who have to conduct daily activities.

"Yoga yukto munir Brahma na chirena adhigachati": harmonized muni quickly goes to Brahma.

"Muni" is he who contemplates on the Supreme. "Mounam Charati iti munihi", they say. It means "Muni walks in the path of silence."

He who conducts all his daily duties by silencing the sense organs and preventing them distracting him from his daily duties is both a "Muni" and "Karma Yogi." He is harmonized in Yoga.

Those who would like to consider "Moksha" as the final destination in life's journey should know the art of conducting all actions as prescribed by the sastras. The main focus in the conduct of actions will have to be "Detachment."

"Detachment in attachment" is the key to success.

In the journey of life our only constant companion is "Atman." All the other companions stay for a period of time with us. Either we have to part with them or they have to part with us. We have no say in this matter.

A true sanyasi is he who keeps his sense of balance on parting with his possessions. Mental renunciation of attachments is sanyasa.

योगयुक्तो विशुद्धात्मा विजितात्मा जितेन्द्रियः ।
सर्वभूतात्मभूतात्मा कुर्वन्नपि न लिप्यते ||7||

yogayukto viśuddhātmā vijitātmā jitendriyaḥ |
sarvabhūtātmabhūtātmā kurvann api na lipyate ||7||

He who is devoted to the yoga of action, with heart purified, with mind controlled and senses subdued, who realises his "Self " as the "Self" in all beings, though acting is not tainted. ||7||

yoga yukto: devoted to the path of action; vishuddhatma: heart purified; vijitatma: who has conquered the self; jitendriyaha: subdued senses; sarva bhootatma bhootatma: who realises his Self as the Self in all beings; kurvan: acting; api: even; na: not; lipyate: is tainted.

In general most of us are engaged in actions and find the path of total renunciation almost impossible to practice.

Amongst those who conduct actions there are two types:

Those who work to gratify their senses,

Those who work to please the Atman within and strive for liberation.

This sloka is to assist those who work to gratify their senses. Indicating that by changing the mode in which they work, they can thereby become eligible for salvation.

We have discussed already several times that every action has a reaction. We act because of vasana imprints carried from the past. All the desire or hatred oriented actions in turn bring in more new vasanas. We have to be born again and again to fulfill the new vasanas and accumulate more new vasanas in turn. Thus we go through the endless cycle of births and deaths.

Na Lipyate: This is the last word in the sloka and means "Not tainted"

"Yoga yukto" is the first word and it means "engaged in action."

The knowledge of how to engage in actions and not be tainted, is given in this sloka through four practices:

They are:
Vishuddhatma
Vijitatma
Jitendriyaha
Sarva bhootatma bhootatma.

The above four practices point to the four instruments within us through which we act and we should use all the four instruments in our actions.

Let us look at these four practices:

Vishuddhatma: "Purified heart." The heart referred to is "The Intellect." The intellect which is nearest to the Atman within and which has the capacity to control the mind should be pure. It is the organ for discrimination between right and wrong.

When this instrument gets tainted with impurity the individual expresses "Durbuddhi" ("Buddhi" is intelligence and "Durbuddhi" is perverted intelligence). When this is predominant the actions of the individual become selfish and bring harm to him and also to others.

When this instrument is pure the person expresses "Subuddhi," which means intelligent actions without selfishness. Such actions without any trace of hatred and desires bring tranquility.

Shuddha is purified and Vishuddha is totally purified.

A totally purified intellect is the first of the four points brought about in this sloka. The pure intellect which is powerful can then be the leader and control the mind which is the band master for all bodily actions.

This brings us to the next point in order in this discussion. It is:

Vijitatatma: Self-control over the mind is Jitatma and perfect self-control is "Vijitatma." The mind as we know is a very large memory bank, full of stored imprints from the past. It also receives constantly impulses from the outer world. The sensual impulses from the outside world or the awakening of one of the vasanas (memory bank of thoughts), distracts the mind. It is like a monkey that keeps on jumping from one branch to another. Control of this monkey within us is very important.

By being a charioteer for Arjuna, Krishna has given us a great message. He is saying,

"give Me the control over your mind and let your mind through the organs of action continue to discharge its duties".

A perfectly balanced mind can discharge its duties to the best of its capacity.

(Recollect the significance of the picture of the Gitopadesham—refer to the introduction)

Arjuna is selected by Lord Krishna to be an example of the true karma yogi discharging his duties to protect dharma.

A sincere seeker who is not motivated by personal desires, gradually develops the clarity of understanding needed for the final destination. In the course of time he learns from his own personal mistakes and his vision gets clearer and clearer of the final destination. His actions then become more vigorous, showing a lot of zeal and he develops perfect self-control over his wandering mind.

Jitendriyaha: Indriyais are the senses. Victory over the senses is "Jitendriya."

For any seeker the final destination of "Moksha" is totally obscure in the beginning of his journey and so he has to take the path advocated by the elders and guru.

"Sarva Bhootatma": By developing the qualities of "Vishuddhatma and Jitendriya" he starts getting a vision of Moksha in the latter stages of his spiritual journey. He starts seeing the Atman within himself and in all forms of life, both moveable and non-moveable.

But, all along he should be "Yoga Yukta." He should be devoted in his actions. Perfect devotion to the Supreme, to the guru who guides him in his spiritual path and unswerving faith in the scriptural teaching will give the strength of devotion to his actions.

The knowledge of one cosmic Consciousness apparently appearing as the various forms of creation in this universe is the tool to be perfect Yoga Yukta.

Karma Yoga soon becomes "Karma Sanyasa" which is the title for this chapter.

नैव किंचित्करोमीति युक्तो मन्येत तत्त्ववित् ।
पश्यन् श्रृणवन्स्पृशञ्जिघ्रन्नश्नन्गच्छन्स्वपन् श्वसन् ||8||

naiva kiṃcit karomīti yukto manyeta tatvavit |
paśyañ śṛṇvan spṛśañ jighrann aśnan gacchan svapañ śvasan ||8||

प्रलपन्विसृजन्गृह्णन्नुन्मिषन्निमिषन्नपि ।
इन्द्रियाणीन्द्रियार्थेषु वर्तन्त इति धारयन् ||9||

pralapan visṛjan gṛhṇann unmiṣan nimiṣann api |
indriyāṇīndriyārtheṣu vartanta iti dhārayan ||9||

The harmonised Yogi who knows the truth thinks, I do nothing at all on seeing, thinking, hearing, touching, smelling, eating, moving, sleeping, breathing, speaking, giving, grasping, opening and closing the eyelids. He is convinced that the senses move among the sense objects. ||8-9||

na: not; eva: even; kinchit: anything; karo'mi: I do; iti: thus; yukto: yogi; manyate: thinks; tatvavit: knower of the truth; pashyan: seeing; shrunvan: hearing; sprushan: touching; jighran: smelling; ashnan: eating; gacchan: moving; swapan: sleeping; shvasan: breathing.

Pralapan: speaking; visrujan: letting go; grihnan: seizing/ grasping; unmisan: opening (eyes); nimisan: closing (eyes); api: also; indriyani: the senses; indriyartheshu: among the sense–objects; vartanta: move; iti: thus; dharayan: being convinced.

Herein we get in these two slokas an enumeration of the various voluntary and involuntary actions we conduct in a day. Some of these are essential actions for survival, some to please others, some that give ourselves the pleasures and some as reactions to the impulses received by the sense organs from the surrounding world.

As long as we are alive technically speaking we are "Two in one". We are "The Atman" which is the true eternal entity and "The physical body" which is limited by space, time and causation.

The yogi mentioned in these slokas is he who has understood his true identity as the Atman, attributes his existence to its power and has no feeling of identification with any thoughts or actions of the body. Desire–prompting information from the sense organs do not disturb his balance of mind. He is aware that as long as he is alive he has to work and be a member of the society.

While conducting any of the actions enumerated above, his reaction is "I do nothing, I am not the doer". Purity in word, thought and speech is the hallmark of the Yogi.

example;

our eyes see innumerable things every day. we cannot remember everything seen by them. This is because the mind does not register all that is seen by them. it registers what it likes or makes note of what it does not like.

a perfect yogi is one where desire prompted messages do not get registered.

ब्रह्मण्याधाय कर्माणि सङ्गं त्यक्त्वा करोति यः ।
लिप्यते न स पापेन पद्मपत्रमिवाम्भसा ||10||

brahmaṇy ādhāya karmāṇi saṅgaṃ tyaktvā karoti yaḥ |
lipyate na sa pāpena padmapatram ivāmbhasā ||10||

He, who acts, offering them to Brahman, giving up attachment, is unaffected by (sins) like a lotus leaf by water. ||10||

Brahmana: in Brahman; adhyaya: having placed; karmani: actions; sangam: attachment; tyaktva: gives up; karoti: acts; yah: who; lipyate: is tainted; na: not; sa: he; padma patra: leaf of the flower lotus; iva: like; ambhasa: by water.

This is another poetic picture of the "Doctrine of Karma." The Lord, as an expert artist has drawn so many such pictures like this on "Karma" and will do so many more times in the subsequent chapters to come.

Basically, it is all about "Karma."

We are born into this ocean of samsara because of our past karmas;

We are sustained in the ocean of samsara by our actions.

What about the tomorrow to come?

Will we be born into this world again or can we achieve unity with the Brahman?

The advice on how to work is given along with an example of the lotus leaf.

Those who are familiar with the lotus flower can understand this.

The lotus plant sprouts from the soil at the bottom of the muddy waters in the lake.

One can see the droplets of water on its leaf. The droplets move about with the movement of the wind and the leaf. The leaf has a waxy surface that does not allow the drops to stick to it. The lotus flower that comes out of it has an exquisite beauty.

The plant dies in water at the end of its life span.

It is born in water, stays in water and at the same time its leaves are unaffected by the water on their surface.

Our actions should not be the cause of our rebirth. They should reflect the beauty of divinity within just like the lotus flower that enchants all the lovers of nature with its beauty while it lasts.

By working as the servant of our master, offering the results of all correct actions un–selfishly at His feet, we will be able to exhaust the vasanas we are born with and will not accumulate any new vasanas. This will enable us to act for the welfare of life on earth and finally attain union with Parabrahman.

This means that we must still conduct all our Nitya Karmas:

The Pancha Maha Yajnas—Deva, Rishi, Pitru, Nara and Bhoota yajnas, service to the parents elders and the revered teachers and Yajna, Dana and Tapas.

These should be conducted with devotion, along with prayers to the Lord

The key word is "Brahmany Adhyaya":

It means, "In Brahman, having always placed."

We should read the word "Brahmany adhyaya" as "In Truth, having always placed the intellect in and realizing Absolute Parabrahman in all".

"Live the world of Truth at every moment of your life", is the message.

कायेन मनसा बुद्ध्या केवलैरिन्द्रियैरपि ।
योगिनः कर्म कुर्वन्ति सङ्गं त्यक्त्वाऽऽत्मशुद्धये ||11||

kāyena manasā buddhyā kevalair indriyair api |
yoginaḥ karma kurvanti saṅgaṃ tyaktvātmaśuddhaye ||11||

Yogis, abandoning all attachment, act for the self-purification with body, mind, intellect and also the senses. ||11||

kayena: by the body; manasa: by the mind; buddhya: by the intellect; kevalaihi: only; indriyaih: by the senses; api: also; yoginaha: the yogis; karma: action; kurvanti; perform; sangam: attachment; tyaktva: having abandoned; atma shuddhaye: for purification of the self.

Yoginaha: the yogis: those who are in the path of unity with the divinity within and all around. It refers to all the spiritual seekers who have made good progress in their efforts.

Karma kurvanti: conduct actions;

How?

Sangam tyaktva: abandoning attachments;

Attachment to what?

Attachment to the fruits of actions.

Then why should they conduct actions?

"Atma Shuddhaye': for the purification of the "self".

It refers to the "self" with the little "s". The "Self", with the capital "S" which is the Atman within is ever pure.

The "self" with the little "s" is the physical body (kayena) with the intellect (buddhya), the mind (manasa) and the senses (indriyair).

What is wrong with the "self" and why does it need purification?

In the spiritual sense, we refer to the "vasanas" (thought imprints) as the dirt on the "self".

The purpose of the seeker's journey in life is: To realize that "yesterday" in his life, he was ignorant and had desires, hatreds and had accumulated a number of vasanas.

To also realize that "tomorrow" in his life is the day to "Unite with the Brahman" and he has to conduct actions "today" to fulfill his mission of "Uniting with the Brahman."

This sloka refers to the actions for "Today":

Actions to maintain the body and to be an instrument of the Lord for welfare of life on earth.

They should clear the existing vasanas and there should not be any room for new vasanas.

The new born baby conducts so many actions involuntarily, the baby has no desires but keeps on moving the different parts of the body and many of such movements are needed for the development of the body.

There will be no desires in the actions of the Yogi. This is "Kaya Karma."

During dream state, we move the limbs involuntarily. The dream is at the level of the mind without the involvement of the senses.

The mind of the Yogi will be fixed on the Atman and he has no voluntary involvement with the senses. The senses do carry out the actions to sustain the body and his actions to be an instrument for the welfare of others but his mind is fixed on the "Atman" (Eternal Truth). This is "Manasika Karma."

A drunken man who is inebriated does not know what he is doing. He has no sense of agency in his actions. The Yogi is not a drunken man but he is so totally inebriated with the thought of "Atman" that he does not know what he is doing with the physical body. It is "Indriya Karma."

Thus, a Yogi, by constant union with the Atman, acts: Like a baby, (involuntary actions with no desires),

Like a dreamer– with the mind fixed on the Atman,

And is inebriated with the thought on the Atman.

युक्तः कर्मफलं त्यक्त्वा शान्तिमाप्नोति नैष्ठिकीम् ।
अयुक्तः कामकारेण फले सक्तो निबध्यते ||12||

yuktaḥ karmaphalaṃ tyaktvā śāntim āpnoti naiṣṭhikīm |
ayuktaḥ kāmakāreṇa phale sakto nibadhyate ||12||

The harmonised Yogi, having abandoned the fruits of action attains the Eternal Peace. The non-harmonised, impelled by desire for the fruit of action, is bound. ||12||

yuktaha: harmonized; karma phalam: fruits of action; tyaktva: abandoned; shantim: peace; aapnoti: attains; naishtikeem: final; ayuktaha: non–harmonized; kama karena: impelled by desire; phale: for the fruits (of action); nibhadyate: is bound.

"Conducting actions" is the common factor in both the harmonized and the non– harmonized.

The difference is in their attitude to the work.

Whereas the Yogi works by immersing his mind with the Atman within, the non–harmonized is immersed with the innumerable objects around him.

As there is so much variety in the physical world, the reaction of the mind varies very frequently in the non–harmonized. There is no constancy of purpose in his actions and it is difficult for his mind to settle on any one thing.

However, by fixing the mind on the Atman, there is less of anxiety and worry for the seeker.

Any action impelled by desires for enjoyment leads to bondage.

The only sure way for freedom from bondage is desirelessness.

The only sure way for "Peace" is "non–attachment."

Higher joy in Atman overtakes the lower joys achieved by material possessions.

सर्वकर्माणि मनसा संन्यस्यास्ते सुखं वशी ।
नवद्वारे पुरे देही नैव कुर्वन्न कारयन् ||13||

sarvakarmāṇi manasā saṃnyasyāste sukhaṃ vaśī |
navadvāre pure dehī naiva kurvan na kārayan ||13||

Mentally renouncing all actions and self-controlled, the embodied rests happily in the nine-gated city neither acting nor causing to act. ||13||

sarva karmaani: all actions; manasa; mentally; sanyasya: renounced; aste: rests; sukham: happily; vashee: self–controlled; nava dware: nine–gated; pure': in the city; dehi: the embodied; na: not; eva; even; kurvan: acting; na: not; karayan: causing to act.

What is the embodied doing and what the jiva is doing has to be understood by the seekers.

The jiva is conducting actions pertained to the life on earth and the embodied remains as a witness for the actions of the jiva.

Sarva karmani: all actions

Manasa sanyasaste: mentally renouncing

It means that all actions that are to be performed should be carried out without the sense of "I" ness in them. It applies to both the voluntary and involuntary actions.

As a matter of fact the involuntary actions like breathing, circulation, digestion etc. do not have any sense of "ego". We do not notice acts of breathing, circulation and digestion.

But on the contrary we have a great sense of ego in most of our voluntary actions.

We are told that just as we conduct involuntary actions for the maintenance of our body without ego, our voluntary actions should be carried out in the same manner.

No one can shut himself off totally from the world outside, there should be contact with the world as there is a lot to learn from nature and from the life around. For this we need the senses, the mind and the sense organs. What we need to know is how to make use of them and how to keep them under control.

Vashee: This is the most important word we have to understand in this verse. It means "self–controlled."

The jiva/individual must learn the art of self–control.

What should be controlled is the next question?, one may ask.
We have two basic instruments:
The senses that bring in the impulses and
the mind that analyses the impulses.

The mind stores them and dwells upon them at its own discretion and then uses the organs of actions to fulfill its needs.

We have to control both the senses and the mind. By controlling the mind we should be able to control the organs of action.

Unless we learn to control these two perfectly, we will not experience the "Peace."

Control of the senses: we can understand it better if we recollect the picture of the three monkeys. one closing his mouth, one closing his eyes and the other closing his ears. It simply means to learn not to see evil, not to speak evil and not to hear evil at all times.

Nava Dware Pure': Nine gated city.

It is a beautiful example our scriptures like to put forward to the seekers. The physical body is compared to a city of nine gates.

In the olden days many parts of the world were ruled by emperors, kings and the like.

They usually lived in a large city.These cities would have many gates, The gates had two purposes:

To keep a firm control over the traffic that would come in from outside and to let the residents go out as needed. This would be the responsibility of the guards controlling the entry/exit gates. One can say it is similar to the present customs clearance and security checks found at the ports of entry in any country today.

The security of the king was dependent on making sure that no enemy could come in. As we know the cunning enemy who finds his way in, slowly takes over control and eventually dethrones the king.

2 eyes, 2 ears, 2 nostrils, one mouth, genital and excretory passages are the nine gates referred to as the nine gated city.

Whatever comes into the body has to come through these nine gates. If we can control what comes in and out of these nine gates, we are said to help in keeping our body healthy and this in turn brings in Peace.

The enemy we are talking about in this instance is "The Ego". The ego gets more powerful with every success and soon the individual forgets the Atman within.

Finally, the last quarter of this sloka:

Naiva kurvan na karayan: Neither acting nor causing others to act. This is to reiterate the fact that the Atman is only a witness to all the bodily actions, emotional feelings and mental thoughts. Each one of us are given the freedom to think and act and learn from our own experiences in life. We have to go through the samsara which is a series of cycles of births and deaths.

In the example we have taken, all the residents of the city need to carry out their daily activities, these ensure peace for themselves, their country and prosperity for the society. The monarch remains as a witness without personally interfering in the life of majority.

In relation to the Atman, it is the nearest example we can give.

He who constantly remembers the Atman within and acts as the servant of the divine will experience constant Peace.

On the contrary he who forgets the Atman within and lives for personal pleasures will only experience the transitory nature of pleasures and does not experience "Peace."

न कर्तृत्वं न कर्माणि लोकस्य सृजति प्रभुः ।
न कर्मफलसंयोगं स्वभावस्तु प्रवर्तते ||14||

na kartṛtvaṃ na karmāṇi lokasya sṛjati prabhuḥ |
na karmaphalasaṃyogaṃ svabhāvas tu pravartate ||14||

The Lord does not create agency, nor action, nor union with the fruits of action. But nature leads to action. ||14||

na: not; kartrutvam; agency; na: not; karmani: actions; lokasya: for this world; srujati: creates; prabhuhu: the Lord; na: not; karmaphala samyogam: union with the fruits of action; swabhavaha: nature; tu: but; pravartate: to action.

It is the opinion of many that as God is within every individual, whatever action they conduct is done by the God and God is responsible for his actions. The tendency is that when good things happen we give the credit to ourselves and when bad happens we put the blame on the God. All these notions are wrong, says the Lord.

This sloka is to clear this misapprehension. There is only one reality. We either mis-apprehend "The Truth" or non–apprehend "The Truth". Non apprehension is due to the spiritual ignorance and misapprehension is due to ego. (example: the snake and the rope. Non apprehension of the rope due to ignorance, leads to misapprension that what is seen is a snake with the subsequent reaction of Fear.)

Na kartrutvam: no agency. The feeling of "I" did it is "Kartrutva bhavana". It is a mental attitude. It is due to the ego. The God did not create such agency and it is the individual who creates such a feeling within himself.

Na karamani: no actions. Each one of us conducts a variety of actions. Some are good, some are bad and some are indifferent. The Lord does not make us do any of such actions.

Na karma phala samyoga: No union with the fruits of actions. The Lord does not create union with the fruits of our action. Whatever action is conducted, it will have its own results albeit good or bad and we have to face them.

We should remember that "He" is acting only as a witness to all of our actions.

The word used is that he is "Lokasya Prabhuhu": He is the Lord of this world and as such has taken the role of a judge to the actions conducted by men and women. His role is only that of a witness to all actions (as the Atman within) and passing the appropriate judgment.

In Sanskrit "Loka" means the world created by each individual mind in relation to the sum total of all the impulses received by the sense organs. The mental/intellectual analysis of the impulses received by the sense organs helps each individual create his own world. The loka in which we live in, is that which we refer to as "the world", it is the consensus of the majority formed by the impulses received and analyzed.

In this sense, the creator of our loka will be the ego and not the Lord.

Na Srujati: does not create.

"I did not create any of these" is the definite statement from the Lord.

But what makes us conduct our actions (both good and bad actions)?

"Swabhavastu Pravartate" is the answer.

It means "our nature leads to actions."

It is not the physical world around us but it is our inherent nature.

Our actions are all due to the thought imprints on our minds. The thought imprints imprinted on our mind decide what our nature will be.

If we act at the mental level our actions will be rajasic or tamasic.

On the other hand if we act at the intellectual level the actions are going to be Satvic.

Finally, if we can allow the consciousness to let the light of divine knowledge shine forth, our actions will be Divine and we are said to be on the path of "Union with the Supreme"

and we would be able to experience the "Eternal Bliss."

नादत्ते कस्यचित्पापं न चैव सुकृतं विभुः ।
अज्ञानेनावृतं ज्ञानं तेन मुह्यन्ति जन्तवः ||15||

nādatte kasyacit pāpaṃ na caiva sukṛtaṃ vibhuḥ |
ajñānenāvṛtaṃ jñānaṃ tena muhyanti jantavaḥ ||15||

The Lord does not receive either the bad or the good of any one. Knowledge is enveloped by ignorance and by it beings are deluded. ||15||

na: not; adatte: takes; kasyachit: anyone; papam: demerit; na: not; cha: and; eva: even; sukrutam: merit; vibhuhu: the lord; ajnanena:

by ignorance; aavrutam: enveloped; jnanam: knowledge; tena: by this; muhyanti: are deluded; jantavaha: beings.

Having said that each individual acts on his own and the Lord is just a neutral witness, we now get another firm assertion from Him that He does not receive the good or bad from the results of any one's deeds.

It is a simple statement of fact that good actions result in good results and bad actions result in bad results. We get the results of all the actions conducted by us. The Lord does not receive the results of any actions.

What is then "The knowledge" that is enveloped by ignorance?

The knowledge we should remember is that each one of us is truly "The Atman" within which is part of Parabrahman. Each one of us is "Tat", so says the Mahavakya, "Tat Tvam Asi."

We carry forward the results of a number of actions in our past including the past births. We did not get the results during that birth. The timing of receiving the results are His Grace.

The ignorance is that we do not remember this truth.

Whatever actions we conduct in this life should also bear fruits and these may be sweet fruits or bitter fruits as the case may be.

Some of the so called fruits of action we taste in this life but many results are yet to come. We do not know when such fruits will ripen. We have even forgotten that we have sown the seeds for these fruits with our past actions.

Not only we have forgotten the past but we do not realize that our actions now will give us the fruits at a later date and we have to taste them too.

The ignorance is that we do not know this truth also.

Finally, the ignorance is that we have forgotten our true identity with the "Atman".

The absence of knowledge of these three aspects of our life is "Ignorance". This is referred to in the sloka with the statement "Knowledge is enveloped by ignorance and by it beings are deluded."

The "Ignorance" is referred to as "non–apprehension" of reality which in Sanskrit is "Avarana". This leads to "mis–apprehension" of Reality which in Sanskrit is "Vikshepa."

(refer to sloka 38, chapter 3–the fire is enveloped by smoke, the mirror is covered by dust and the fetus is enveloped by amnion).

ज्ञानेन तु तदज्ञानं येषां नाशितमात्मनः |
तेषामादित्यवज्ज्ञानं प्रकाशयति तत्परम् ||16||

jñānena tu tad ajñānaṃ yeṣāṃ nāśitam ātmanaḥ |
teṣām ādityavaj jñānaṃ prakāśayati tat param ||16||

But to those whose ignorance is destroyed by the knowledge of the Atman, shining like the sun, knowledge reveals the Supreme to them. ||16||

jnanena: by wisdom; tu: but; tad: that; ajnanam: ignorance; esham: whose; nashitam: is destroyed; atmanaha: of the Self; tesham: their; adityavat: like the sun; jnanam: knowledge; prakashayati: reveals; tatparam: that highest.

The journey of life is mixed with happiness and sorrow, it is common for all. But what brings happiness or sorrow differs markedly from individual to individual.

We give more importance to happiness and in that we almost forget the Lord who blessed us with the experience of happiness.

Whereas when we are in sorrow, we start asking questions like "why"?

"Why did I have to suffer"? Why was God so cruel to me"?

And similar questions crop up in our minds.

In the last sloka we understood that "Knowledge is covered by ignorance."

In this sloka we are given the means to clear the ignorance. "Ignorance has to be cleared by the knowledge of the Atman" is the simplest answer from the Lord.

Where is this "Atman"?

Some of my friends from the state of Kerala tell me of a beautiful tradition they follow in their region which brings out the awareness that "The Atman is within all."

On the day of their "New Year", the tradition is:

The members of household or friends ask the question: "Do you want to see God"?

When the answer is affirmative, the individual is asked to close his eyes and is led into a room. Inside the room he is asked to open the eyes. He is made to sit on a chair facing a mirror.

As soon as he opens his eyes, he will see his own reflection.

This is to symbolize the fact that the Lord is within you and by opening your eye of knowledge you can see the Atman within.

The second half of this sloka gives the beautiful example of the sun and the clouds.

The sun is ever shining in the sky during the day time. Many a times, he is not seen because of the dark clouds in the sky blocking him. Even a small cloud can block the view of the sun.

It does not mean the sun is not there but it only means that the cloud blocks the sun and the benefit of sun is not obtained because of the cloud.

As soon as the cloud moves away, the sun shines forth in his brilliance. The sun did not have to move away but the clouds had to disperse.

The sun is to be looked upon as the example of the "Atman", The clouds are compered to the "Ignorance."

The sun, self-luminous will shine forth and The Atman, self–luminous shines forth.

The best example to understand is that of an article made up of radium. Radium as we know is "self–luminous." In a dark room if this article is placed with some item of cloth covering it, the article is not seen. The owner will keep on searching for this article.

As soon as he removes the cloth over the article, even in the dark room, the article shines forth because of its self–luminous property.

"The Atman" within is self–luminous. It is covered by ignorance and is called "Ego". When the mask of ego is removed, the Atman shines forth in its full brilliance.

"Be still and know that I am God" says the Bible.

The important word is "be still". It means "do not move."

It is not physical movement it refers to but refers to the "ego".

The body, mind and the senses have to do their worldly duties without the sense of ego.

This is the perfect state of "Total Intense meditation." In this state, we can see the God within and all around.

तद्बुद्धयस्तदात्मानस्तन्निष्ठास्तत्परायणाः ।
गच्छन्त्यपुनरावृत्तिं ज्ञाननिर्धूतकल्मषाः ||17||

tadbuddhayas tadātmānas tanniṣṭhās tatparāyaṇāḥ |
gacchanty apunarāvṛttiṃ jñānanirdhūtakalmaṣāḥ ||17||

Intellect absorbed in That, Self being That, established in "That", "That" being the Supreme Goal, they go whence there is no return, their sins dispelled by Knowledge. ||17||

tad buddhaya: intellect absorbed in that; tadatmanaha: their self being "that"; tannishtaha: established in "that"; tatparayanaha: "that" being the Supreme Goal; gachyanti: go; apunaravruttim: not returning again; jnana nirdhhoosha kalmashaha: sins dispelled by knowledge.

Tad Buddhaya: buddhi/intellect absorbed in "That.":

Intelligence/intellect is the God's gift and privilege to the mankind. It is important that we learn the art of making proper use of this special gift. For what good we may have done in

the past, we are blessed with the birth as humans. We have to climb up from the plane of "stone man to animal man," from "animal man to man– man", from "man–man to God man". This is possible when our intellect is totally absorbed in "That."

The intellect is the "Reasoning capacity."

The reasoning capacity can be either good or bad. If it is bad it is due to the ego/ahamkara it is then "Durbuddhi" (bad intellect). Selfishness predominates in all such reasoning.

If it is good, it relates to the Atman within. This path will take the seeker on towards the upward path in spiritual progress. Such buddhi which has no ego in it is "Subuddhi" (good buddhi).

"Intellect absorbed in That" refers to "Subuddhi."

It does not mean that we should forget our role in the society. Every act we conduct has to be in the spirit of "Working for our Master." We should continue to discharge our duties to repay the debt to the society and at the same time be humble servants of the Divine Master.

"Intellect absorbed in That" implies remembering this advice from the spiritual masters.

"Tad Atmanaha": their Self being "That":

"self" with the small "s" refers to the "Mind." it is not the Atman but "Jivatma". The Jivatma is the Atman that has developed contact with the outer world and forgotten its true identity. "Tadatmanaha" means the mind has to remember its connection to the Atman, ever pure and in constant bliss. Keeping in memory the true identity of oneself is "Tadatmanaha."

It simply means that one should not have the "Ego" in their thoughts, actions and speech.

"Tan Nishtaha": established in "That":

It refers to the state of the mind in relation to the impulses received from the sense organs. Despite receiving the various impulses from the world around, the mind should never forget the union with the Atman within.

The search light from the mind focused externally through the sense organs should be directed towards the Atman within and the mind at the same time must remember that it should be under the control of the intellect.

Meeting these two conditions is "Tan Nishtaha."

Tat Parayanaha: "That", being the Supreme goal. This refers to the practice of "Meditation".

The sastras advice that "God realization" should be the goal in life. "God realization" means realizing the presence of God in all and respecting the God in all.

Gachyanti Apunaravruttim: They go whence there is no return.

In the material world we live in, absorbed in acquiring material gains we spend our time fulfilling our wishes and dreams.

We have examples of businessmen, industrialists, politicians who have succeeded in their efforts by being totally absorbed in their profession and established in that objective.

The success gained in the material world is related to time, space and causation. The happiness of achieving this success is not permanent.

On the contrary, the "Peace, Bliss" experienced on uniting with the Parabrahman is the end of the spiritual journey. It is union with the "Supreme". When there are no more vasanas stored in the mind and the mind does not register any new vasanas it is said to be the ideal condition to merge with Brahman.

This can happen only when their sins are dispelled by knowledge. The "sins" referred to here are the "vasanas." Clearing the stored vasanas in the mind and not letting new vasanas get registered in the mind comes from "Knowledge". The highest knowledge the sastras would like us to develop, is to understand the Mahavakya "Tat Tvam Asi."

Let us all pause for a moment in our journey, contemplate on what progress we have made so far and on which future actions we would like to undertake, in relation to the goal of life. We must conduct a critical self–analysis of our thoughts and actions only then can we be sure to succeed and experience "Sat Chit Ananda." This takes us all beautifully to the next sloka, which is:

विद्याविनयसंपन्ने ब्राह्मणे गवि हस्तिनि |
शुनि चैव श्वपाके च पण्डिताः समदर्शिनः ||18||

vidyāvinayasaṃpanne brāhmaṇe gavi hastini |
śuni caiva śvapāke ca paṇḍitāḥ samadarśinaḥ ||18||

The sage look with equal eye on a brahmana endowed with knowledge and humility, a cow, an elephant, a dog and an outcaste who feeds on dogs flesh. ||18||

vidya: knowledge; vinaya: humility; sampanne: endowed with; brahamane': on brahmana; gavi: on a cow; hastini: elephant; shuni: dog; cha: and; eva: even; shwapake': an outcaste; panditaha: sages; samadarshinaha: seeing equally.

The sage referred to in this sloka is the seeker who has put into practice the essence of the last verse. He is recognized as a true Pandita. The doctrine of "Universal love" is the hallmark of Gita and is stressed in this verse. It is not only the doctrine of the brotherhood of man but love and compassion to all forms of life.

We learnt from the last sloka that the seekers by such practice would succeed in dispelling their sins by acquiring knowledge.

The highest knowledge to be learnt is "Samatvam". "Equal vision" is "Samatvam." It is seeing the same "Atman" in all. It is the true knowledge and he who puts into practice this philosophy is a Pandita.

The seeker who moves about in the material world would naturally come across a variety of life. The sloka highlights some of the forms of life observed by such a seeker.

The highest social order for Hindus is a Brahmana and the lowest is a Sudra, who is considered as an outcaste. The learned sage sees the same Atman in both and shows his respect to both.

Sri Krishna stresses that Brahmana is not the title received by the right of birth in a Brahmin family but by acquiring knowledge and showing humility.

Brahmana, man of knowledge, well versed in sastras has to put into practice the theory.

One of the main qualities he has to develop is, "Humility." An educated man without humility is an arrogant man. It does not matter which branch of science one takes. Unless one develops humility, the ego will destroy him in course of time. It is a well-known fact that no one will ever know what will happen tomorrow.

It is also important to remember that the knowledge acquired was possible only by the benefits received in various forms from different sections of the society. Respecting the members of the society, being grateful to what is received from the society is stressed in our sastras very strongly.

At the other extreme we have been given the example of an outcaste who is from the lowest order of the social class. Outcaste is he who lives on filthy habits and hence the statement,

"He lives on dog's flesh". (It is only a figure of speech.)

Despite the fact that the sastras declare that "Kshama" (forgiveness) is a divine quality and needs to be put into practice, when it comes to practical life this principle is forgotten.

The pandita who has mastered the sastras remembers to put into practice the principle of forgiveness. He has developed the divine quality of compassion and does not show displeasure or disrespect to any class of people.

(the reader may like to refer to:

Manisha Panchakam, it is a set of five verses (slokas) composed by Shri Adi Shankaracharya, the greatest Hindu philosopher. It is said that in these five verses Shankara brings out the essence of Advaita Vedanta. It is believed that Shankara wrote the Manisha Panchakam at Varanasi (Kashi/Benaras), the ancient sacred city of India. It brings out the true understanding of the scriptures wherein the importance is in recognising and giving true respect to any person who has the correct knoweldge of the Vedas, be he, a Brahmana or a Candala/outcaste.)

As we have discussed before, let us learn to, move from the level of dehadrishti (looking at the level of the physical body) to, Level of manodrishti (looking from the mental plane), to the level of Atmadrishti (spiritual plane) and see the same Atman in all.

The "samatvam" should apply to all forms of life and hence we have the examples of the cow, elephant and a dog.

The cow for a Hindu is the most revered. It feeds on grass and gives the best nourishment for all. "Sarvopanishado gavo doghdha Gopala nandanha" say sage Veda Vyasa.

All the Upanisads are the cows and Sri Krishna is the cowherd, he says. Among animals, the cow takes up the highest order and hence the reference to it.

The elephant though a strict vegetarian animal has to be admired for its massive strength.

Dogs were not the pet animals in the days gone by and they were mainly wild dogs.

The pandita is therefore he who shows the same love and compassion to all classes of people and all varieties of animals.

इहैव तैर्जितः सर्गो येषां साम्ये स्थितं मनः ।
निर्दोषं हि समं ब्रह्म तस्माद्ब्रह्मणि ते स्थिताः ||19||

ihaiva tair jitaḥ sargo yeṣāṃ sāmye sthitaṃ manaḥ |
nirdoṣaṃ hi samaṃ brahma tasmād brahmaṇi te sthitāḥ ||19||

Even here, birth and death are overcome by those whose mind is established in equanimity. Brahman is flawless and is same in all; therefore they are all established in Brahman. ||19||

iha: here; eva: even; tair: by them; jitaha: is conquered; sargo: creation; yesham: of whom; saamye: in equanimity; sthitaha: established; manaha: the mind; nirdosham: flawless; hi: indeed; samam: equal; Brahma: Brahman; tasmaad: therefore; brahmana: in Brahman; te: they; sthitaha: are established.

The way to attain "Moksha" is by uniting the jivatman with the "Atman" within and the "Atman with the Paramatman." Experience of "Ananda" on realizing this "Truth" is the "Jnana". (Sat Chit Ananda)

"Establishing in Brahman" is to be understood as "Uniting permanently with the Atman."

Unless one learns the art of establishing totally in what he/she is doing, it is impossible to get the best results out of such actions. This is true in any aspect of life.

Totally concentrated on every aspect of cooking along with the proper knowledge of cooking will get the best meal ready by the cook. In this example, we have:

Love in cooking—Bhakti

Knowledge of cooking—Jnana

Act of cooking–karma

Concentration on all aspects of cooking—Dhyana.

This sloka is highlighting the fourth aspect of "Concentration on the Supreme."

The first half of the verse says that birth and death are overcome by those whose minds are established in "Equanimity". "Brahman" is referred to as "Equanimity." Let us look into this section first.

The mind is the instrument for either bondage or liberation.

By association with the outer physical world it takes us towards bondage. By association with the Atman within, it takes us towards Liberation.

The waves that come from the physical world should not disturb the balance of the mind.

In our life, the balance in relation to the reactions of "Happiness and sorrow; Victory/defeat; Gains/losses" is the theme of this sloka. Births and deaths of these "dwandvas" (opposites) are inevitable for those who are involved in worldly affairs and have an element of "agency in their actions."

These pairs of opposites tilt the balance and there is no steadiness.

The fall into the cycle of births and deaths which is referred to as "Samsara" by the Scriptures is described as "Evil" in this sloka.

By keeping the "Agency" and living in this world, we are constantly exposed to the evil.

We have to pass through many cycles of physical births and deaths.

The only one who is free from this evil is "Brahman." He has no sense of agency and is in a constant state of "Bliss."

Those seekers who are established in "Atman" can keep the balanced mind and will not go through the cycles of births and deaths. These people are the "Jivanmuktas and the "Sthitaprajnas."

They accept everything as "Lord's Grace" and keep a constant balanced mind. They are established in "Brahman", the Lord declares.

It is a fact of life that like things mix together and unlike things do not mix together. Milk poured on to milk and oil poured in milk is the example we can take.

Milk mixes with milk easily but never with the oil.

The Atman is like the milk and the physical world is like the oil.

To unite with the Atman, the mind, like the milk should develop the qualities of the Atman.

To do so we should develop equanimity and purity.

By learning and the practice of "Atma Dharma" man realizes "Brahman" even in this present life.

न प्रहृष्येत्प्रियं प्राप्य नोद्विजेत्प्राप्य चाप्रियम् ।
स्थिरबुद्धिरसम्मूढो ब्रह्मविद्ब्रह्मणि स्थितः ||20||

na prahṛṣyet priyaṃ prāpya nodvijet prāpya cāpriyam |
sthirabuddhir asaṃmūḍho brahmavid brahmaṇi sthitaḥ ||20||

The man of steady intellect, (sthira buddhi), undeluded, (asammudhaha), knower of Brahman should not be elated having obtained the pleasant and should not be troubled having got the unpleasant. ||20||

na: not; prahyushyet: should rejoice; priyam: the pleasant; prapya: having obtained; na: not; udwijet: should be troubled; prapya: having obtained; cha: and; apriyam: the unpleasant; sthirabuddhir: with steady intellect; asammudaha: undeluded; brahmavit: knower of Brahman; brahmana: in brahman; sthitaha: established.

Perfect Jnani, we have learnt is he who has: A steady intellect, (sthirabuddhi), Un–deluded (asammudaha) and who knows what Brahman is by the practice of spiritual teaching of the scriptures through the medium of Sadguru.

What such a Jnani should be doing during his day to day's activities within the world he is living in, is given in this sloka.

We all know that pleasant and unpleasant situations are part and parcel of one's life.

"You should not be elated on getting the pleasant and depressed on getting the unpleasant" is the message from the Lord to the Jnani.

It is reiterating the fact that the Lord is expecting the Jnani after acquiring the knowledge to continue discharge his duties to the society. Hence this chapter is "Karma Sanyasa Yoga".

Let us also see the subtle hint from the Lord through the Gita to the mankind. He has not said "do not go after pleasures." What He wants us to understand is that when we go after pleasures, we are also going after the pains.

This is the law of nature. Happiness ends in sorrow eventually and sorrow in course of time is superseded by happiness from some source or other. The life is a see–saw of pleasures and pains. If the board of the see–saw is flat and not moving up or down, we get bored in the game. We want to enjoy going up which ends by going down. We work at going up again. We get a thrill at this play.

If we do not want to go after the pain, we should not go after the pleasures.

Rejoice in the success of others and praying for the relief of pain for others, related or not related to you, is the message from the Lord.

This is the philosophy of the Gita that has to be practiced in life.

By establishing in "That" we will be able to live in "Eternal Peace."

बाह्यस्पर्शेष्वसक्तात्मा विन्दत्यात्मनि यत्सुखम् ।
स ब्रह्मयोगयुक्तात्मा सुखमक्षयमश्नुते ||21||

bāḥyasparśeṣv asaktātmā vindaty ātmani yat sukham |
sa brahmayogayuktātmā sukham akṣayam aśnute ||21||

With the Self unattached to the external objects, he finds happiness in the Self. With the "Self" united with Brahman in meditation, he enjoys imperishable happiness. ||21||

bahya sparsheshu: in external contacts; asaktatma: whose mind (self) is unattached; vindati: finds; atmani: in the Self; sukham: happiness; sah: he; brahma yoga yutkatma: united with brahman in meditation; akshayam: imperishable; ashnute: enjoys.

What we have here is the state of mind of the seeker who has progressed in his sadhana in leaps and bounds. This does not come overnight. Spiritual maturity brings this level of acceptance of the "Truth" which is described as "Bliss" in the scriptures.

Everyone has to grow up and learn the lesson of life. Just theory has no place in spiritual progress. Practical experience along with the study of the scriptures, blessings of the Guru and the Lord makes one realize this "Bliss."

The seeker needs to have the two important pre–requisites: "Devotion and Knowledge". With these two as the tools he should conduct actions. The lessons learnt from actions become the guiding stones for the progress.

He would come across experiences in life due to his attachment to objects, which bring happiness but he would learn that the state of happiness is related to the theory of "time, space and causation."The same principle applies also to the experience of pain.

The "self" referred to is the Atman contacting the outer world through the medium of the intellect and the mind. It is the "Jivatma".

By detaching from attachment to the external objects he is free from the pairs of opposites of happiness and sorrow.

The Lord adds that the Jivatma should practice at the same time to divert his attention to unite with his true identity of the Atman which is nothing but a spark of "Parabrahman." This comes only when he masters the practice of seeing the same Atman in every individual and every form of life and gives due respect to all. (Sloka 18—vidya vinaya sampanne)

This state of happiness is the true "Ananda" referred to in the scriptures. It is not just "Ananda" but "Paramananda". (Supreme state of Happiness) Not just that but it is "Imperishable." It is a constant experience of Bliss. It is beyond description. The word used in this sloka is "Sukham Akshayam Asnute." "Akshaya" is referred to something that does not perish.

Love for the sake of love only and not for anything in return is the highest form of love and is true "devotion." Such love of the Lord gives us the experience of "Bliss."

Every experience in life does perish in the course of time. The only experience that does not perish comes from uniting with the Brahman. The greatest source of "Love" is within each one of us, it is inexhaustible and indescribable. The more one taps it, the more will be the experience of "Peace." The next chapter is "Dhyana Yoga" which deals exclusively and in detail on the "Meditation". This is a prelude for the next chapter.

One cannot say it is an experience at all because it only comes on losing one's separate identity. All experiences are short lived and come from keeping the "individuality." We use the phrase "I experienced it" to describe the feelings. In spiritual progress, to realize the "Highest Truth" one has to lose the identity.

The sacred text teaches us the lesson "Sacrifice the less for the greater, the transitory for the Eternal."

ये हि संस्पर्शजा भोगा दुःखयोनय एव ते ।
आद्यन्तवन्तः कौन्तेय न तेषु रमते बुधः ॥22॥

ye hi saṃsparśajā bhogā duḥkhayonaya eva te |
ādyantavantaḥ kaunteya na teṣu ramate budhaḥ ||22||

The enjoyments born of contact with external objects are indeed the source of pain only. They have a beginning and an end. The wise do not rejoice in them, O'Arjuna. ||22||

ye: which; hi: verily; samparshaja: born of contact; bhogaa: enjoyments; dukhayonayaha: source of pain; eva: only; te': they; adyantavantaha: have a beginning and an end; na: not; teshu: in them; ramate': rejoices; budhaha: the wise.

The word to note in this sloka is "Dukha yonaya": It means the womb of pain. "Yoni" means "womb".

Seeds are placed in the womb and they grow into a fully born baby in the course of time. This analogy is brought out in this sloka when the Lord says: "ye hi samsparshaja bhogaa dukha yonaya eva cha." The results of actions conducted, if these are contrary to the sastras, stay like the seeds in the mind of the individual and will sprout forth as painful experiences at a later date.

The pleasures one gets are generally short lived but the painful experiences tend to become the so called painful scars on the mind that remain for a long time.

In the modern world we live in, we come across the problem of dependence on drugs, alcohol and the like. The euphoria of experiencing the pleasure on taking the stimulating drugs lasts only for a short while. The individual without this knowledge finds that the pleasure of taking the drug for the first time was so wonderful and does not like the void he experiences when the effect of the drug wears off. He immediately will go for the second dose and subsequent doses. He forgets the world he lives in and the surroundings. He forgets his duties and responsibilities. Soon he will find himself in a shell in some corner of the house with the drug in his system and totally lost to the world.

In course of time when he develops medical problems he finds that cure for the problem is not easy and the damage done by the habit is irreparable.

A similar situation arises with the smoking of cigarettes. The medical professions describe the effect of smoking as follows:

Nicotine stimulates release of dopamine in brain through receptors and this causes feeling of wellbeing. This lasts for a very brief period and level of dopamine drops rapidly. These make the individual experience low moods and hence the feeling of urge to smoke one more cigarette.

Smoking increases nicotine receptors in brain by 300%.

We all know how smoking brings on innumerable health problems which lead to gross morbidity and high mortality.

So we can see that the pleasures we experience are only drops of water but the sufferings we undergo are like huge rocks of mountains.

The second word to note is "Bhoga." It means "enjoyments." There is great variety of momentary enjoyments one can get in this world. It is important to remember that the happiness is not in the objects themselves as such but it is in the reaction experienced by the individual to the object in question and also related to time and causation. It varies from individual to individual and in the same individual from one time to another period of time. There is a saying that "Bhogi becomes a rogi". (Enjoyer ends up as a patient)

Another word to note is "Rama". (Please note that it is not "Raama" the incarnation of Vishnu who killed demon Ravana) "Rama" literally means "Eternal Joy." We have discussed this Eternal Joy already as the "Ocean of Bliss" which is inherent in every individual.

A Jnani therefore realizes this truth and follows the principle of "Karma Sanyasa" which is the title of this chapter. With this knowledge the life he lives is that of a Jivanmukta (Liberated Soul). He becomes a "Sthitaprajna". He does not hanker for momentary sense pleasures.

शक्नोतीहैव यः सोढुं प्राक्शरीरविमोक्षणात् ।
कामक्रोधोद्भवं वेगं स युक्तः स सुखी नरः ||23||

śaknotīhaiva yaḥ soḍhuṃ prāk śarīravimokṣaṇāt |
kāmakrodhodbhavaṃ vegaṃ sa yuktaḥ sa sukhī naraḥ ||23||

He who is able to resist/endure the impulse born of desire and anger even in this world before the fall of the body, he is a harmonised man and is happy. ||23||

shaknoti: endure/resist; iha: here; eva: even; yaha: who; sodum: to endure; prak: before; shareera vimokshanaat: fall of the body (death); kama: desire; krodha: anger; udbhavam: born of desire; vegam:the impulse; sah: he; yuktaha: united; sukhee: happy; naraha: man. Ihaiva: even here, (in this world, in this birth.)

We are asked to endure the impulses of desire and anger in the world even before the fall of the body.

The word "even" has to be understood clearly. What does it imply?

This takes one to the subject of belief of the average Hindu and the teaching of the sacred texts.

The Hindu believes in the cycle of births and deaths. After physical death the subtle body of ours goes to one of the 14 lokas. The length of stay in the lokas depends upon the points of merit or demerit acquired by our actions in this birth. Paramatma, the Lord Supreme is the judge who decides on where we go and how long we stay in those lokas. (Please look at the topic of Moksha in the introduction for further details of the various lokas)

The point to remember is that the practice of righteous living and acquiring points of merit or acquiring points of demerit by unrighteous living applies only to this life on earth. Hence the earth is called "Karma Bhoomi". We accrue points for every thought and action in this life only and our future birth after death depends upon those points. This sloka is requesting the sincere seekers to resist the impulses of desire and anger in this life. If we miss the boat and succumb to the temptations, we have to undergo future births.

The stay in other lokas is only to experience the results of actions conducted on earth. One does not acquire points of merit to climb up to the higher lokas during their stay in those lokas. At the expiry of stay in those lokas one has to go back to the earth again. This cycle goes on and on till real knowledge dawns. Instead of looking for happiness from our actions we should learn to conduct righteous actions and offer the results of such actions at the feet of the Lord.

It is a fact of life that we look for happiness all through our life. We get happiness from some actions and do not get happiness from other actions. This upsets the balance of the mind and consequently there will be no peace.

In the higher lokas where we will be sent depending upon our points of merit after our death, there will be no actions that result in reactions and the stay is only for reaping the benefits of good actions conducted on earth.

Similarly in the lower lokas where one may have to go, there will be no actions that result in reactions and the stay is only to pay for the wrong actions conducted on earth.

This earth is the only place where the results of actions accrue.

The seeker, who understands this and lives with balance of mind, even if it is before the fall of the body, will experience "The Peace" and he is said to be "a harmonized yogi".

Balance of mind comes from enduring the impulses of desire and anger during the stay in this world, in this life only. There will be no impulses of desire and anger in the other lokas.

Finally, one more point to note in this sloka. It is on the use of the word "Vegam". "Kama krodod bhavam vegam sa yuktaha sa sukhee naraha" it says in the second half of the sloka.

"Vegam" used in this context means "impulse."

Desire and anger make us conduct actions out of impulse. The seeker who by spiritual practice has developed the power to control the impulses arising from desire and anger is a Yogi, the Lord says.

Desire relates to the "future" and anger relates to the "past". Desire is a "want" and so it is the future.

Anger is a reaction to the past.

He who has desire and anger is swaying in between the worlds of past and future.

The Gita is about living in "the present", concentrating on what is to be done and this will therefore be living in "Peace" at all times."

योऽन्तःसुखोऽन्तरारामस्तथान्तर्ज्योतिरेव यः ।
स योगी ब्रह्मनिर्वाणं ब्रह्मभूतोऽधिगच्छति ॥**24**॥

yontaḥsukhontarārāmas tathāntarjyotir eva yaḥ |
sa yogī brahmanirvāṇaṃ brahmabhūtodhigacchati ||24||

He who is happy within, who delights within, who is illumined within also, that Yogi, becoming Brahman attains Moksha. ||24||

yo: who; antah sukhee: happy within; antar arama: delights within; tatha: also; antar jyotir: illumined within; eva: even; cha: and; sa: that; yogi: yogi; brahma nirvana: moksha; brahma bhootaha: becoming brahman; adhigachati: attains.

We are gradually led to the next chapter "Dhyana Yoga" which is all about meditation to attain unity with the Brahman.

We are asked to practice the following three:

Antah sukho: be happy within,

Antar arama: delight/rejoice within,

Antar jyothir: illumined within.

By mastering these three, the seeker, it says: Brahma Bhootaha: becoming Brahman and Brahma Nirvanam: Freedom of Brahman,

Adhi Gachati: attains.

Antaha sukhaha: we should learn to be happy within. After having told us that the impulses from the external world bring in a state of imbalance of the mind, we are asked to look within for happiness. "O, foolish man, do not go out in search of happiness", says the scriptures.

Yes, everyone wants to be happy, but majority go not for real happiness but for transitory happiness that leads to sorrow. We keep on searching for that "Eternal happiness" in the wrong place.

There is a lovely story about an old woman living in a hut. One day she was searching for a pin during daylight outside her house. An ascetic comes to the door and asks her, "Mother, what are you searching for?"

She gives the reply that she was searching for a pin dropped inside the house the previous night.

The ascetic laughs at her and asks her, how could she find the pin outside the house when it was dropped inside the house?

In reply, the old lady puts the ascetic a counter question. She asks, "What are you searching for going from place to place?

The ascetic replies that he was going in search of God. The old lady then laughs back at him and says:

When the Lord is within you, why are you going out like this in search of Him?

The Lord within as the Atman is the source of happiness. The happiness is not in the material objects from the world outside. This is the explanation and meaning for the sentence "Anta sukhee." "Be happy" and not try to "become happy." "Becoming happy" by gaining material possessions is not permanent happiness and "Being happy" with the Eternal source of happiness from within is the way to be happy.

"Antar arama":

"Rejoice from within." Instead of going outside to get something to rejoice with, learn to rejoice being with the "Brahman within" is the message. "Dhyana yoga", the practice of meditation should not be an effort that tires one out but a relaxing experience.

"Antar Jyothir":

"The Light within" is the "Light of Brahman". Whatever we see from our eyes including the sun and the moon, is really a reflected light.

We see objects in day light and not in darkness. We say that we have the light of the rays of sun that helps us to see. We consider that the sun is the source of light. Consider a dead body for a moment. Dead body cannot see any objects. If the sun was illumining everything, the dead body should also be able to see.

Only the living ones can see the sun, the dead body cannot see the sun.

There is something that makes one alive and enables one to see the sun and the objects around.

This something is the "Light of Consciousness within". This power of the "Atman" is so bright that it illumines everything.

In a dark room we say that we can see, only if there is a source of light. Even in broad day light if all the curtains are closed in a house/if all the doors and windows are closed, one cannot see the light outside. The sunshine would still be present outside but we have blocked its entry by closing the windows and doors.

Similarly, we, out of the power of "Maya," which acts as "ignorance", block the vision of the "Atman" within and thereby "live in darkness."

To say it in simple words,

The eye is illumined by the mind, the mind by the intellect and the intellect by the Atman. The Yogi looks for this source of light for the entire world.

We go for "Bahir sukha" which means "external source of happiness and "Bahir Jyothi" which means external source of light.

By the practice of "Vyavasayatmika buddhi" (sloka 41, chapter 2) we can divert the search light of the mind towards one's own Self.

The entire scriptures are for making us realize this "Light of Brahman within and all round" and enjoy the "Bliss" of the same. The "Bliss" they talk about and the "rejoicing" they advocate, is "Brahman" and the Yogi attains this state which is "Brahma Nirvanam."

Once this state is attained, there is no more:

"Enjoyer and enjoyable",

"Subject and object",

"Knower and the knowable".

None of these exists when one unites totally with the "Atman within." There is no more anger for the past or anxiety for the future.

लभन्ते ब्रह्मनिर्वाणमृषयः क्षीणकल्मषाः ।
छिन्नद्वैधा यतात्मानः सर्वभूतहिते रताः ||25||

labhante brahmanirvāṇam ṛṣayaḥ kṣīṇakalmaṣāḥ |
chinnadvaidhā yatātmānaḥ sarvabhūtahite ratāḥ ||25||

Rishis, whose sins are destroyed, whose dualities are cut asunder, who are self-controlled and who rejoice in the well being of others, attain union with Brahman. ||25||

labhante: attains; brahma nirvana: Moksha; rishayaha: rishis; ksheena kalmashaha: sins are destroyed; china dwaidhaha: dualities cut asunder; yatatmanaha: self– controlled; sarva bhoota hite: well– being of others; rataha: rejoice.

Two points are worth noting from this sloka. Who is a "Rishi"?

The word "Rishi" is often used and we need to know the qualities of a Rishi. Four broad qualities of a Rishi are given in this sloka. He who fits in with these four qualities is "Rishi."

How to attain union with Brahman?

"Develop the four qualities, become a true Rishi and you will attain Moksha" is the advice from the Lord to the sincere seekers. The four qualities are:

Whose sins are destroyed: Ksheena Kalmashaha:

As we have discussed several times before, the sins are in the form of the vasanas in the mind. The vasanas are the three basic qualities of satva, rajas and tamas in our thoughts which are stored in the mind. Shifting from the state of laziness to become active and passionate in work, shifting from passionate, to pure acts, and finally shifting from acts for personal salvation (by dropping the ego) to acts for welfare of life on earth, will destroy the sins.

It is "mano nasha and Vasana Kshaya." (destruction of mind/ ego and total annihilation of vasanas)

Chinna dwaidha: whose dualities are torn asunder: There should be no elation towards the pleasant and no depression towards the unpleasant. (sloka 38, chapter 2—sukha dukhe same' krutva)

"Dwaidha" also means–"Uncertainty". Whose uncertainty is torn asunder is "Chinna Dwaidha". By the development of love towards spiritual knowledge, working to get the spiritual knowledge from scriptures and the Guru, this should help in clearing the doubts. When we are certain that what we are doing is correct and it is according to the prescribed/approved texts, we will have no more room for doubts and this will help in making rapid strides towards union with the Brahman. This means there should be no doubt about the "Atman" within and all round and His qualities of "Sat, Chit and Ananda".

Yatatmanaha: who is self–controlled.

There is a strong need to control the "self" which is the "Ego" and bring to prominence the "Self" which is "Divinity."

The senses should be controlled by the mind, the mind by the intellect and the intellect by the inner consciousness. (slokas 42,43 chapter 3)

Sarva Bhoota hite Rataha." Rejoicing in the welfare of others".

It is not enough to just pray for the welfare of others, one should also rejoice in their welfare.

Who are "Others?"

We refer to, in the order of merit:

Ourselves first,

Our nearest families,

Extended family and finally,

Our friends.

Those that do not belong to the above four categories are considered by us as "others."

We also should add animals in the list of others.

It is not "my happiness" but "happiness of others" that is the criteria.

One should not be jealous of others' happiness and should not wish harm for others. To forget oneself in the joy of others, one is fulfilling the role of a human (adhikara) given by the Lord.

When we include these others by "Rejoicing in their welfare", we are fulfilling the criteria set by Sri Krishna and He welcomes us to His abode.

"Rishi" is like a degree that one can get by fulfilling the above four criteria.

It is possible to redirect our lives even in this birth, it is in our own hands.

In another way, the sloka also means that the Rishi of today may have been a sinner of the past, he may have looked for pleasures for himself, had no self-control and been selfish. Yet, by the sadhana of several births he can become a "Rishi".

There is no bar for anyone to become a Rishi and receive the grace of the Lord.

The last quality, "wellbeing of others" implies that the man of knowledge should become a man of action and his actions should contribute towards the welfare of others.

कामक्रोधवियुक्तानां यतीनां यतचेतसाम् ।
अभितो ब्रह्मनिर्वाणं वर्तते विदितात्मनाम् ||26||

kāmakrodhaviyuktānāṃ yatīnāṃ yatacetasām |
abhito brahmanirvāṇaṃ vartate viditātmanām ||26||

To the self-controlled sages who are free from desire and anger, who have controlled their thoughts and who have realised the Self, absolute freedom exists on all sides. ||26||

kama krodha viyuktatma: free from desire and anger; yateenaam: self–controlled sages; yatachetasaam: controlled the thoughts; abhito: on all sides; brahma nirvana: absolute freedom (Moksha); vartate: exists; viditatmanaam: have realised the Self.

Yateenaam: to the self–controlled ascetics.

Yati is the definition of an ascetic who has controlled his passions.

If we revert back to chapter 2 for a moment and look at the qualities of "Sthita Prajna" we will find that:

In sloka 62 we are told that "Brooding over the objects of the senses, man develops attachment to them, from attachment comes desire, from desire anger sprouts forth".

Tracing the history of anger we can see it is the root cause of destruction for individuals, family, and society. We realize that it is desire, attachment and the brooding over the objects of senses, which bring about eventual destruction.

Object of senses: normally one refers to the objective world as being the source of the objects of senses. It is partially correct. By deep analysis we have to understand that if we are truly the "Atman" within, with a physical body, by relating ourselves to the Atman, even the physical body becomes a sense object.

We develop deep rooted attachment to our own body first and with that body, to the objects around us.

Yati is he, who has developed perfect control over his body. What is described in this sloka is a continuation of the previous sloka. We should take it as further qualities of a rishi.

The mind is considered as the band master in our body. It is the centre for all activities. Mind is the centre to the expression of "Ego". We are the "self" with the little "s" and "Atman" within is the "Self" with the capital "S".

Yati, by identifying himself with the Atman, controls the "self".

By controlling the senses which bring in the impulses from the outer world, by being subservient to the intellect which is subservient to the "Antaratma" within, he masters the art of being free from "desire and anger".

This comes from a constant vigil, on the thoughts that generate in the mind. By sincere practice, he has achieved,

"Vasana kshaya"—cleared of all stored vasana in the mind and "Mano nasha"—destroyed the thoughts in his mind which was the "self" with the little "s". It is equivalent to destruction of "ego."

Having achieved the above two, he develops true knowledge of the "Parabrahman" and realizes "Sat–Chit–Ananda". This is what the scriptures describe as "Tatva Jnana". Knowledge of the "Truth" dawns and blossoms in the seeker and he is fit to be addressed as "Yati."

He easily unites with the "Parabrahman" who is within and who is all round and this is "Brahma Nirvanam."

To summarize:

Kama krodha viyuktanaam: free from desire and anger
Yata chetasaam: by controlling the thoughts,
Viditatmaanam: realized the Self,
Brahma nirvana Abhitaha vartate: freedom exists on all sides.

स्पर्शान्कृत्वा बहिर्बाह्यांश्चक्षुश्चैवान्तरे भ्रुवोः ।
प्राणापानौ समौ कृत्वा नासाभ्यन्तरचारिणौ ||27||

sparśān kṛtvā bahir bāhyāṃś cakṣuś caivāntare bhruvoḥ |
prāṇāpānau samau kṛtvā nāsābhyantaracāriṇau ||27||

यतेन्द्रियमनोबुद्धिर्मुनिर्मोक्षपरायणः ।
विगतेच्छाभयक्रोधो यः सदा मुक्त एव सः ||28||

yatendriyamanobuddhirmunir mokṣaparāyaṇaḥ |
vigatecchābhayakrodho yaḥ sadā mukta eva saḥ ||28||

The sage who has shut out all external contacts, fixing the gaze on the centre of the eye-brows, controlling the incoming and outgoing breaths moving in the nostrils, with senses, mind and intellect controlled; free from desire, anger and hatred; liberation as his goal; he enjoys freedom always. ||27,28||

sparshaan: contacts; kritva: having done; bahir bhahyan: outside external; chakshu: gaze; cha: and; eva: even; antare: in the middle (center); bhruvoho: eyebrows; pranapanou: incoming and outgoing breathe; sama: equal; krutva: having made; nasabhyantaracharine': moving in the nostrils.

yatendriyah mano buddhi: senses, mind and intellect controlled; muni: muni; Moksha: liberation; parayanaha: as supreme goal; vigata iccha bhaya krodhaha: free from desire, fear and anger; yaha: who; sadaa: always; muktaha: freedom; eva: verily; saha: he.

These two slokas are the basis for the practice of "Dhyana". "Dhyana" is meditation on a desired object and in the spiritual science it is on "Moksha". We get a detailed explanation on the practice of meditation in the next chapter.

It is practiced by "Moksha Parayanas": those aspiring for Moksha.

The first requisite should be the deep rooted desire/yearning for "Liberation."

As children, we are all told by our parents, elders and teachers that we should be educated. As we grow we understand what they meant by "education." The life for an illiterate in this world is very hard.

We have to undergo basic education first. Towards the latter stages of basic education, we get to know about the various specialties, within the fields of science and the arts. Following this we can decide on a subject in which to specialize and thereby further our studies.

At this stage, we should be developing the deep rooted desire to achieve the objective.

Once we enter deep into the selected subject, as we are nearer to the end of the course, the deep rooted desire has to go. We should be automatically geared by that time to get on with our studies and not get distracted.

The same principle applies to spiritual science. As we grow in our spiritual maturity, we should initially develop the deep rooted yearning for "Moksha". Later on we will learn that we should not entertain any desires including the desire for "Moksha." Depending upon the way we conduct the sadhana, we will be able to drop the desire for Moksha. This may come in this present life or in future births and everything depends upon our vasanas.

What should the seeker who has a yearning for Moksha do?

This question is answered in these two slokas. The first sloka is on control of the physical body and the second sloka is on control of the subtle body.

Bahyan sparshan: impressions coming from the external world,
Bahir krutva: having turned out.

This is the first step. The five sense organs constantly send impulses of the outer world to the mind. We are asked to learn the art of not letting the impulses in. "Turn them out", we are told. What do we mean by this word?

It means that we should act as our own "gate keepers". We must learn the art of letting in what is good and not letting in what is not good.

The field of sense activity is the world around us. Developing the art of controlling entry of impulses from the world is essential. Hence in the "Ashtanga Yoga" of Patanjali, the first two practices are "Yama and Niyama."(slokas 27, 28 chapter 4) Yama is the restraint of senses and Niyama is the regular practice of spiritual rules. This will be the first step towards turning out the impressions coming from the external world.

One can say that the seeker should learn to be deaf and blind to the sensual distractions.

Yatendriya mano buddhir: with senses, mind and the intellect controlled.

Prana panou samou krutva nasabhyantara charinou: having made the outgoing and incoming breaths moving in the nostrils equal.

Having controlled the entry of the impressions of the world, the seeker has to learn the art of controlling the mind and intellect.

Controlling the mind: This aspect refers to:

The reaction by the mind towards the impulses received.

Mind dwelling on the stored impressions from the past. (no day dreaming)

Controlling the intellect:

As we have discussed before, the intellect is the reasoning capacity. The "Ego" does reduce the reasoning capacity of the intellect. The intellect is supposed to act with "Subuddhi" (good intellect) and not with "Durbuddhi". (bad intellect).

When the reaction is good it is Subuddhi and when it is selfish and bad it is Durbuddhi.

Dropping the ego would assist in letting the light of "Antaratma" shine on the intellect and make it react with what is good for the individual in the spiritual sense.

Learning to give a pause between the receiving of impulses and reacting to the impulses received, is a good habit to develop by the seeker. With a pure mind and intellect the reaction should turn out to be good for the seeker and society.

Pranapanou samou krutva:

Regulating the incoming and outgoing breaths through the nostrils.

In the Ashtanga yoga, after Yama and Niyama the third step is "Asana" (correct posture) and the fourth step is "Pranayama."

The spiritual physicians recommend the seeker to control the breathing. The act of breathing is generally an involuntary act and most of the times this is rhythmical and balanced. The entry of oxygen and the exhaling of carbon–dioxide is the role of the respiratory system. There should not be an accumulation of carbon–dioxide in our system as it is harmful. It dulls the brain and reduces its capacity to regulate the bodily actions.

The art of making the respiration rhythmical and balanced is an essential pre requisite in spiritual practice. It is good for health and for the concentration of the mind.

Breathing and the mind are closely interlinked. Controlling one will control the other. To control the mind it is essential to control the breathing.

The next step is:

Chakshuh bhruvor antara eva krutva:

To help in the practice of controlling the senses, mind and the intellect, the masters have recommended that the seeker has to fix his gaze on a spot in the centre between the two eyebrows. It is known technically as "kechari mudra."

If the eyes are fully open, there is chance of too many impulses entering the mind. On the other hand if the eyes are closed, the seeker could easily fall asleep.

Halfway between the two is recommended and to turn the gaze to the centre ,between the two eyebrows.

The spot to concentrate on is known as "Ajna chakra."

There are some who turn the gaze towards the tip of the nose.

Either of the two methods can be followed.

Vigatechha Bhaya krodho:

Free from desire, fear and anger. (refer to sloka 62, 63 chapter 2)

Attachment to the objects of the world brings in desire and this in turn leads to fear and anger. These are the enemies that take away the seeker from his spiritual path. Sri Krishna emphasizes on this all through the Gita several times.

Sada mukta eva saha: freedom always.

He is a true sage who practices these steps and masters the art of self–control. He has no fear of falling down in the spiritual path and lives in constant "Bliss."

He is "Sadananda".

भोक्तारं यज्ञतपसां सर्वलोकमहेश्वरम् |
सुहृदं सर्वभूतानां ज्ञात्वा मां शान्तिमृच्छति ||29||

bhoktāraṃ yajñatapasāṃ sarvalokamaheśvaram |
suhṛdaṃ sarvabhūtānāṃ jñātvā māṃ śāntim ṛcchati ||29||

Knowing Me as the enjoyer of all sacrifices and austerities, The Lord and controller of all the worlds and friend of all beings, man attains Peace. ||29||

bhoktaram: the enjoyer; yajnatapasaam: of sacrifices and austerities; sarva: all; loka: worlds; maheswaram: lord of; suhrudam: friend of; sarva: all; bhootanaam: beings; jnatva: knowing; maam: Me; shantimruchati: attains Peace.

Three aspects of the Lord are brought out by Sri Krishna in this sloka. We should not consider that he is boasting about Himself but giving out the three facets of Himself.

Bhoktaram Yajna Tapasa:

I am the enjoyer of all sacrifices and austerities.

Yajna is a dedicated act and tapas is an act of purification of mind, body and speech.

Both of these bring beneficial results. The Lord says He enjoys the results of these acts. He knows that the result of such actions is for the welfare of life on earth. After all, the entire life is created by Him and who so ever takes care of the life on earth becomes the beloved of the Lord and the Lord does enjoy what they do.

Sarva Loka Maheshwaram:

I am the Lord of all the lokas. We have already discussed on the meaning of the word "Loka." Each sense organ has a designated deity. "The Sun" for the eyes, "Space" for the ears, "Air" for the skin, "Water" for the tongue and "Earth" for the nose. The mind being the headquarter for all the sense organs, is known as the Lord of the sense organs, "Iswara."

Maheshwara" used in the sloka refers to the mind of the individuals. "Sarva Loka Maheshwara" refers to the total minds of all the men/women on earth.

He is not only the Lord, but controller of all the worlds. "The mind rules" in all our daily actions. The mind is alive because of the "Life Force" within.

Suhrudam sarva bhootanaam: Friend of all beings.

After asserting He is the Lord and controller, He immediately says that I am the friend of one and all. Whether he is making us suffer or enjoy he is still our friend.

Whatever we are undergoing is the result of our own karmas and He is helping us to fulfill our desires or hatreds and thereby burn the vasanas stored. By keeping us alive, he is helping us towards achieving "Mano nasha and vasana kshaya."

A true friend is he who does good and does not expect return favors.

Similarly, the Lord does not expect any return favors from us but at the same time stays with us as the individual soul all through our births and deaths till we attain the final union with Parabrahman. He is our best friend.

It is like the mother's love and affection for her child. She is expected to be the child's best friend all through her life, "in childhood, in adolescence and after marriage". The child looks forward to coming to her mother to rest her head on her beloved mum's lap.

The best gift he has given to the mankind in general is the "Gita" to guide us in our life.

Lastly we are told:

Jnatvaa Maam shantimruchati:

Knowing Me as such, man attains Peace.

Each one of us conduct actions, have conducted actions and will continue to conduct actions in future. As a consequence we experience the results. The results either please us or upset us. We get elated or depressed when we receive the results of actions. The results we get are not only of actions that we have done knowingly/unknowingly today but also that which we have done knowingly or unknowingly in the yesterdays of our life. Also it is true that we do not get the results when we want but when the Lord deems fit to grant us the same.

Those who conduct actions in the spirit of "Krishnarpanamastu" and follow the principle of "Karmanye vadhkarasthe" also realize that He is the Lord and controller of all the worlds and a friend of all and thereby live in constant "Peace". They attribute all good results to Him and offer the benefits to Him but take responsibility for the ills of their life on their own head and do not blame the Lord for the same. This is the secret of experiencing the "Peace."

It is not that the seeker gets to see the Lord but experiences "The Peace" which is Nirakara aspect of the Supreme Parabrahman.

Summary:

We will get a good description of sanyasa in chapter 18, slokas 2, 3 and 4.

It is a fact that all our actions/karma, are in the quest of happiness. We all feel that we are the doers of those actions and hence get a feeling of agency behind those actions. As the fruits are the result of actions, if those fruits are sweet we consider ourselves to be the agents to enjoy those fruits. Our spiritual downfall is because of these two notions of "I am the doer and I am the enjoyer."

In an attempt at experiencing the Truth that the we are not the "doers" of actions and it is only a notion of the mind/intellect equipment, some seekers practice "karma" in the true sense but do so in excess and do not believe in any other schools of thought.

There are others who understand the futility of karma and totally renounce it. This chapter is to tell us the futility of both these notions.

Correct spirit of understanding would be:

"Karma is not binding but the motive behind it is binding."

Even by the conduct of good deeds one does not get any merit if the motives and intentions are not pure.

Also, if there is no internal feeling of renunciation, renunciation of karma is not going to be beneficial.

If we consider ourselves as sparks of Paramatman, as the Paramatman is not the doer or enjoyer, we should also be neither the doers nor the enjoyers.

Let us all therefore learn, not to renounce our ordained karmas and also not develop "Abhimana or the feeling of being the doers and enjoyers".

The ego is the root cause of attachment and let us renounce the "ego". This is the true sanyasa to be practiced while continuing to discharge all nitya, naimittika karmas. This is the true jnana which is the result of the annihilation of ignorance gained by the study of the sacred text.

Iti śrīmadbhagavadgītāsūpaniṣatsu brahmavidyāyām yogaśāstre Śrīkṛṣṇārjuna-saṃvāde karma- saṃyāsa-yogo nāma Pañcamo 'dhyāyaḥ.

CHAPTER 6

ĀTMA SAṂYAMA–YOGA

Sri Shankaracharya:
Constant and unbroken thought that flows like oil is Dhyana.

INTRODUCTION

This chapter is also known as "Atma Samyama Yoga". It is the concluding chapter of the "karma Shatka which covers "Tvam" (you) aspect of the Mahavakya "Tat Tvam Asi." The message from this Shatka (group of six chapters) to the sincere seekers is:

"What you are looking for (Tat) is in reality nothing but "You" (tvam). It is not the "you" that relates to the ego but to the Atman within you which is the real you."

It is not to be confused with "Hata Yoga" which is totally different and which deals with severe austerities in control of the "self."

Dhyana is control of the senses. In this context the senses include "sense organs, mind and the intellect", not just control of the senses but concentrating on the Atman within also. One can say that dhyana is developing a perfect state of mind to experience and express the spiritual joy from within.

It is the foundation for spiritual progress for the seeker.

Atma Samyama Yoga means "Yoga of self–control. "Atma" refers to the lower self. The other title for this chapter is "Dhyana Yoga" which means "The Yoga of Meditation."

The method of controlling the senses through the process of meditation is highlighted in this chapter.

One can define dhyana as, "integration of the head (intellect) and heart". When sraddha (faith) and bhakti (devotion) function together it becomes dhyana.

The Atman within, which is the spark of Parabrahman is present in all forms of life. The human life is the most highly evolved among all forms of life. Really speaking there should be an expression of divinity in all the thoughts, actions and speech in every human being.

However, due to the ignorance of the knowledge of the "Self" and deep involvement with the sensual world around, there is a great, almost inexhaustible accumulation of vasanas (thought imprints) in the mind and so the divinity is not expressed by the majority. The vasanas provide the basic nature of individuals and so instead of being "true humans" caring for humanity, the man turns out to be an animal man or a stone man.

The Atman within is the lotus flower within and is a true example of "inaction in action and detachment in attachment." There is a need to unfold this lotus flower, "The Self" within and this can be achieved by "Self–contemplation."

First step in meditation is:

Reduce the quantity of thoughts generated and stored in the mind.

The next step is:

Change the quality of thoughts. Lift from tamasic thoughts to rajasic thoughts, then rajasic to Satvic thoughts.

Finally divert the thoughts on to the Atman within.

This is to say that we should:

Train the mind, transform the thoughts and transcend the thoughts.

This final state is known as "Samadhi" which is "intellectual equanimity."

By a slow and steady process, the seeker has to work towards an inner revolution of character, attitude and values, in order to experience the "Bliss" within, by becoming one with it.

In short, "Dhyana Yoga" is achieved by two means.

Visualizing the Atman within by closing the eyes and by recognizing the Atman all round by keeping the eyes open.

श्री भगवानुवाच
अनाश्रितः कर्मफलं कार्यं कर्म करोति यः ।
स संन्यासी च योगी च न निरग्निर्न चाक्रियः ||1||

Śrībhagavān uvāca:
anāśritaḥ karmaphalaṃ kāryaṃ karma karoti yaḥ |
sa saṃnyāsī ca yogī ca na niragnir na cākriyaḥ ||1||

The Lord said
He who performs his prescribed duties without depending on the fruits of action is a Sanyasi and Yogi, not he who gives up worship of the fire and who remains without action. ||1||

anashritaha: not depending upon; karma phalam: fruits of action; karyam: performing; karma: duties; karoti: performs; yaha: who; saha: he; sanyasi: sanyasi; cha: and; yogee: yogi; na: not; niragnir: without fire; na: not; cha: and; akriyaha: without action.

In general there is a misunderstanding /misconception concerning the meaning of the words "Yogi and Sanyasi".

In general when someone sees a person wearing an ochre robe, he is revered as a "Sanyasi".

Whereas when one sees someone in solitude, in places like a mountain cave or a forest having given up all work, they consider that person to be a "Yogi". Giving up all work is considered to be the way of a Yogi.

Sri Krishna has cleared this misconception.

Just by wearing an ochre robe does not make one a sanyasi and living in solitude in a far off place giving up all, is not a Yogi. They are only external signs, what is needed is inner purification.

What do the spiritual masters say are the hallmarks of a Yogi and a Sanyasi?

True sanyasa is abandonment of ego. It is unfortunately the dearest and also the worst possession which we do not want to give up.

The true purpose of practicing Yoga is about union with the Parabrahman. It is to develop the technique of God realization and union with the form of the Supreme contemplated upon.

Both the Yogi and the Sanyasi are expected to carry on performing all their dharmic duties. Such duties involve conduct of actions and actions in turn do bring results.

Learning the art of neither expecting, nor depending on the fruit of actions, makes one a Yogi and a Sanyasi says the Lord.

We, the mortals, do get attached to the fruits of our actions and get caught in the web called "Samsara."

The first three quarters of the sloka:

anashritaha karma phalam karyam karma karoti saha sa sanyasee cha yogee:

Means:

He who performs his prescribed duties without depending on the fruits of action is a Sanyasi and Yogi."

There are no differences in being a "Sanyasi or Yogi."

Performing of prescribed duties is the first requisite and not depending upon the fruits of action is the second requisite.

The Lord has used the prefix "Prescribed duties." In chapter 3 we have been given the details of "Karma" and chapter 4 gives us the knowledge needed to conduct karma.

Each one of us has to conduct "Nitya Karmas and Naimittika Karmas (refer to sloka 8, chapter 3).

In the earlier stages of sadhana we can conduct "Kamya karmas" to fulfill our wishes.

As we get mature spiritually, our work should be directed towards universal welfare and not to fulfill personal pleasures.

We should never conduct forbidden actions, "Nishiddha karmas."

The expected results from actions, conducted in the different stages/ashramas of our lives should not be the motive for our work.

"Knowing what to do, how to do it and what are the good and bad results of actions" is the Jnana the seekers should develop. To know all about the results of actions before deciding on the action and then doing the action is our duty.

Depending and day dreaming on the fruits of actions, bind us to this world. We fall into the trap of maya that makes us experience sukha or dukha and develop likes and dislikes.

"cha na niragnir na chakriyaha".

Says the last quarter of the sloka.

It means,

"Not he who gives up worship of the fire and who remains without action."

"Worship of the fire": this refers to the lighting the fire of knowledge and conducting the daily prescribed duties which are:

The "Pancha Maha Yajnas":

Deva Yajna, Rishi Yajna, Pitru Yajna, Nara Yajna, Bhoota Yajna. (sloka 13, chapter 3)

We are told not to give up these five sacred duties. We should do these in the spirit of "Yajna" which is "a dedicated act." The results should be in the spirit of dedication to the Lord.

No one should stay without any action, is the Lord's message to mankind. Slokas 48 and 38, chapter 2 give us a better understanding of the word "Yogi".

Who is a Yogi?

He who practices Yoga is a Yogi.

Sloka 48: Yogasthaha kuru karmani—

O Arjuna, do your work, be steadfast in Yoga, giving up attachment, unmindful of success or failure. Such equanimity is Yoga.

It clearly states that the seeker has to do his duties but at the same time fix his concentration on the Supreme and His teachings and work according to His command. He clearly states that the seeker has to be unmindful of success or failure.

Regarding the statement "unmindful of success or failure": Chapter 2 Sloka 38:

Having an equal mind in pain and pleasure, gain and loss, victory and defeat, engage in battle and thereby you will not incur sin.

It is clearly a call for the seeker to fight the battle of life and applies to one and all. Even though Sri Krishna, the Lord himself, was the charioteer and guide for Arjuna, He did not guarantee success to His devotee. It is said that success is the blessings of the Lord and failure is the fault of ours and we should not blame the Lord for failure. We must remember that both are His decisions.

Sri Krishna in the role He played, also experienced failures (apparent only and not real) in His actions several times. But at the end He proved that His was a life of incarnation to establish Dharma. This is to highlight the fact that "Equanimity is Yoga." (Samatvam Yogam uchyate)

He also says "Naivam papam avapsyasi". He who does the work on the principle of "Equanimity of Yoga" gets the chance to burn the existing vasanas and will not accumulate new vasanas.

The successes in life should act as a tonic to develop more faith in The Lord and not to develop the "Ego."

The failures in life should act as a reminder to continue to keep faith in the Lord and fight the battle following the path of righteousness.

This is the method of inner purification which is the true sign of a Yogi/Sanyasi.

यं संन्यासमिति प्राहुर्योगं तं विद्धि पाण्डव ।
न ह्यसंन्यस्तसङ्कल्पो योगी भवति कश्चन ||2||

yaṃ saṃnyāsam iti prāhur yogaṃ taṃ viddhi pāṇḍava |
na hy asaṃnyastasaṃkalpo yogī bhavati kaścana ||2||

O Pandava that which is called samnyasa, know that to be Yoga also. No one becomes a Yogi without giving up desires. ||2||

yam: which; sanyasam: renunciation; iti: thus; prahuhu: call (say); yogam: yoga; tam: that; viddhi: know; na: not; asamnyasta sankalpa: not given up desires; bhavati: becomes; kaschana: anyone (no one).

This is a definitive declaration from the Lord that there is no difference between a Samnyasi and a Yogi.

The fact that Sri Krishna makes it a point to make this statement means that even 5000yrs ago there were many who used the words "Samnyasi, Yogi" and that they considered the two as different. Unfortunately this is still going on and there are a large number who consider that a sanyasi and a yogi are two different types of people. This is the gist of the first half of this sloka.

The word to understand clearly in this sloka is "Asamnyasta Samkalpo": We have to split this into three words:

"A"

"Samnyasta"

"Samkalpo""

"A" is used as negative statement.

"Samnyasta" refers to "acts of renunciation."

"Samkalpa" (resolve): Taking up "samkalpa" is deeply rooted in the minds of many Hindus who undertake auspicious acts like:

"Satyanarayana pooja, Ganesha Pooja, wedding ceremony etc."

Samkalpa is referred to as actions conducted with the desire for fruits of action.

The priest who conducts any religious ceremony goes through the initial steps that include the taking up of samkalpa by the karta (performer of the actions).

The karta is made to repeat the words, "to fulfill my desire —— (by the conduct of such and such an act), I perform this ceremony.

"Samkalpa" brings out the element of desire in the mind of the karta. We should realize that there is an element of selfishness in such acts.

After all we are humans and we have desires. What we learn from the scriptures is that there should be a gradual elimination of desires as we progress in our lives. We will learn as we proceed with the study of the sacred text that we should first of all move up from "Laziness, (Tamas)" to "Passion, (rajas) and from passion to "Pure, (Satva); from selfish actions to unselfish actions.

The seeker in the spiritual path is desirous of "Liberation." As he matures he must learn to conduct actions without even the desire for "Moksha." This chapter is "Dhyana" which is meditation to unite with the Supreme and become one with it. Therefore the advice from the Lord for the mankind is not to have the desire for the fruits of actions.

Samkalpa with a selfish motive behind an action must be absent.

Who becomes a Yogi?

The Lord is making a negative statement by using this phrase "Asamnyasta Samkalpo".

"Samkalpa Samnyasi" is he who has renounced all samkalapas. He has no desires. "Asamkalpa Samnyasi" is he who does not renounce samkalapas.

What we have to do is,

Conduct all actions that are according to the duty of station of life we are in (ashrama dharma).

Do not do so with the desire for the fruits of action,

And finally,

When the fruits do come from the actions, (as it is inevitable), offer the fruits at the feet of the Lord, with the feeling of "Sri Krishnarpanamastu."

By desire–less performance of action which is "Yoga" (could be karma, Jnana, Bhakti or dhyana) one can develop the faculty to renounce the desires for the fruits of action which is "Samnyasa."

With this explanation, we go back to the beginning of this sloka that says Samnyasa and Yoga are one and the same.

The householder who conducts all his actions in this spirit is a true Yogi and a Samnyasi.

One final point to note:

As a matter of fact the priest who conducts the ceremony also includes a sentence which the individual is made to repeat: it is "Idam Na mama". It means whatever I get from this action is not mine but is all the property of the Lord. Many do not realize this but simply repeat what the priest says during the ceremony.

आरुरुक्षोर्मुनेर्योगं कर्म कारणमुच्यते ।
योगारूढस्य तस्यैव शमः कारणमुच्यते ||3||

ārurukṣor muner yogaṃ karma kāraṇam ucyate |
yogārūḍhasya tasyaiva śamaḥ kāraṇam ucyate ||3||

For a muni, who wishes to attain Yoga, action is said to be the means. For the same sage who has attained to "Yoga" inaction is said to be the means. ||3||

arurukshо: wishing to climb; muneh: of a muni; yogam: yoga; karma: action; karanam: the cause; uchyate: is said; yogarudhasya:

who has attained the status (to yoga); tasya: of him; eva: even; shamaha: inaction.

Let us analyze the correct meaning of the words, "Aruruksho, Muni, Yoga, Yogarudha and Shama" used in this sloka.

This chapter is on meditation, (dhyana) and so the word "Yoga" used in this sloka refers to "Dhyana Yoga."

"Aruruksho": aspiring to ascend. He, who would like to climb the spiritual mountain, is "Aruruksha."

Yogarudha is he who has managed to reach the peak of the spiritual mountain.

The mind is like a horse, it is fickle and difficult to control. It needs to be controlled by the intellect. When the intellect (Krishna) firmly controls and becomes master over the mind (by sitting on the back of the horse and controlling it), that state achieved is "Yogarudha".

"Sama" is the perfect control of the mind. There should not be any trace of ego. The mind has to be in a state of tranquility and bliss. This is the state of "inaction." Where there is no ego, there is no action.

The word "Muni" applies to the true spiritual seekers. "Mounam Charati iti Munihi" is the definition of a muni. He who walks in the path of silence is a muni. The spiritual seeker who wants to climb the spiritual mountain has to first of all learn to control his senses and silence the thoughts in his mind. His mind has to be kept silent and not agitated by the sense objects of the world.

The first half of the sloka would then mean:

For a muni—who is a spiritual seeker wishing to climb the spiritual mountain, who wishes to attain yoga—who would like to learn and master the art of "Dhyana",

Action is said to be the means.

The second half of the sloka would mean:

For the muni that is successful in attaining the dhyana, inaction is the means.

The spiritual seeker in quest of the experience of "Eternal Bliss" from within cannot do so in the initial stages by running off to a forest and keeping his eyes closed. He has to go through the high school and graduation courses in spiritual science. Hence, the Lord emphatically states that "Action" is the means to attain to Dhyana Yoga.

"Action is said to be the means": the actions referred to are "Nishkama karma and Karma Phala Tyaga."

This is true Karma Yoga.

Jnana Yoga gives help to conduct actions in this spirit.

To reach to the state of dhyana yoga in chapter 6, one has to have a clearer understanding of the preceding chapters 3, 4 and 5 of the Gita.

This preparation helps to steady the mind and to be free from any further actions. This is "Shama." As a matter of fact, the actions drop off on their own accord in the latter stages of sadhana (spiritual efforts to put in). Through the process of "Sravana, Manana and Nidhi Dhyasa" (Hearing, reflecting and concentrating) the seeker succeeds in experiencing the bliss from within.

Any hasty actions are of little benefit. Every seeker has to manage to bring about "Vasana Kshaya" of all his past vasanas. These have to be burnt out totally to experience the everlasting "Peace".

Perfect purity of the mind is obtained only when there is total destruction of ego. Where there is no ego, there will be no more agitations due to desires, anger, greed, delusion, pride and envy.

Where there are no such agitations, there is constant joy.

When we are full of such spiritual joy, we do not work (no ego) but the Lord works through us.

यदा हि नेन्द्रियार्थेषु न कर्मस्वनुषज्जते ।
सर्वसङ्कल्पसंन्यासी योगारूढस्तदोच्यते ||4||

yadā hi nendriyārtheṣu na karmasv anuṣajjate |
sarvasaṃkalpasaṃnyāsī yogārūḍhas tadocyate ||4||

When a man is not attached to sense objects and actions, having renounced all thoughts, he is said to have attained to Yoga. ||4||

yada: when; hi: verily; na: not; indriyartheshu: in sense–objects; karmasu: in actions; anusajjate: is attached; sarva sankalpa sanyasi: renouncer of all thoughts/resolves; yogarudha: who has attained yoga; uchyate: is said.

We discussed about "Yogarudha" in the last verse. Yogarudha is he who has attained perfection in his sadhana/spiritual efforts.

Three conditions, which are really three steps of a ladder to perfection, are the means to achieve this state.

a) Not attached to sense objects
b) Not attached to actions
c) Renouncing all thoughts.

a) Not attached to sense objects: We live in a world of manifold objects. Those we get attached to become the sense objects for us. It is an individual feeling of attachment and what is liked by one may not be liked by another person.

Yoga is union. Strictly speaking it applies to spiritual life and not to material life. Union in spiritual life is that of our physical body with the Atman within and the Atman with the Paramatman.

When we say our body, in the sense of yoga, it applies to the subtle body of ours which is the mind and the intellect. Contact with the objects can bring about any of the following feelings:

Liking for the objects
Not liking the objects
Not concerned about the objects.
Develop hatred towards the object or
Being frightened of the object.

Depending upon the feeling, the object and the situation, the mind uses the organs of action To: get the object, not to react to the object, or to run away from the object.

b) Not attached to actions is the second stage in progress.

The experience from actions brings about the sensation of happiness, sorrow or fear.

We, the ordinary mortals, like to enjoy the pleasures from the objects and this is the cause for attachment. We are ignorant of the consequences of becoming attached to and subsequently losing the same, which in turn brings sorrow. Consequently, the life becomes a series of actions and reactions resulting in happiness or sorrow.

The first step in spiritual practice is to understand the consequences of attachment to objects and develop the strong will of not getting attached to them. The Lord says "Yada hi nendriyartheshu karmasvanushajjate".

To experience the bliss the mind needs to be diverted towards the Atman within. Whereas the Atman is only one and not seen, (ekam and na drishyam), the objective world is manifold and visible (bahunaam and drishyam). The search light for Atman which is "Bliss absolute" has to be operated by the mind only. Normally the mind operates using the search light for happiness by projecting it outwards.

By the process of self–enquiry and self–analysis which is a slow process, the seeker has to learn non-attachment to the sense objects.

In general most of us are self–oriented and our personal happiness takes the priority in our lives. Without our knowledge many of us are really selfish. We consider ourselves as separate and do not see "unity in diversity." We do not recognize the "Atman" within us which is the same "Atman" in all forms of life.

The perfect Yogarudha has overcome this separateness by developing perfect mastery over his mind. The word "Nirvana" used by Buddhists refers to "Yogarudha".

What is "Meditation"?

It is an art developed by self–study, self–analysis, self–patrol, wherein we learn to lean on to the "Power" within. In our daily transactions we depend upon some object/or other from the material world, be it the spouse, children, house etc. When the support we lean on to weakens or disappears, we get hurt and experience sorrow.

c) Renouncing all thoughts:

The support of the Lord as the only support in life, will help us not to fall and get hurt. As a matter of fact, the more we surrender to the Lord, we will realize that we get everything in life. Dependence on the Lord makes us truly independent.

Sarva Sankalpa sanyasee:

The first step in acquiring anything is "Thinking" about the object of desire. The stronger the thought to acquire the object, the greater will be the effort to acquire it.

"Samkalpa" is the determination to get the desired object. As the life is an endless journey to acquire objects of desire, the only way to find "The Bliss within" is to drop all samkalpas. The process of dropping all the samkalpas is "Sarva Samkalpa Sanyasa." The end result of this sadhana is the emptying of the mind of all stored vasanas.

"Manu Smriti" says that desires are born of "samkalpa." "Yajnas" (dedicated actions) are born of samkalpa. When there are no more desires left, no more vasanas are stored and intense meditation becomes a reality.

The seeker who has reached this state of perfection is a true "Yogarudha." Just because he is thought free, does not mean he is sleeping. (Sloka 69–chapter 2–when the rest of the world is sleeping he is truly awake and when the rest of the world is awake, it appears that he is sleeping.)

उद्धरेदात्मनाऽऽत्मानं नात्मानमवसादयेत् |
आत्मैव ह्यात्मनो बन्धुरात्मैव रिपुरात्मनः ||5||

uddhared ātmanātmānaṃ nātmānam avasādayet |
ātmaiva hy ātmano bandhur ātmaiva ripur ātmanaḥ ||5||

Let a man raise himself by the Self, not let the self go down. For this Self is the friend of the self and the self is the enemy of the Self. ||5||

uddharet: let (him) lift; atmanaa: by the Self; atmanaam: the self; avasadayet: let (him) lower; atma: self; eva: only; hi: verily; atmanaha: of the self; bandhu: friend; atma: of the self; eva: only; ripuhu: enemy; atmanaha: of the self.

It is one of the most important slokas in the Gita and the advice given to mankind by the Lord is full of subtle meanings.

Let the man raise himself by the Self: Uddhared atmanat atmanam:

As we have learnt already, we are two in one. We are the body (constituted of the mind, intellect and the senses which is "The ego") which is referred to as "self" with little "s" and the "Atman" which is referred to as "Self" with the capital "S".

When the divinity in us shines, good actions come forth and we are the friends of the public.

When the selfishness shines forth, our actions make us enemies of the society.

Our mind can be lifted to spiritual heights by:

The grace of the Lord and Grace of the Guru.

But to receive the grace from these two, we have to become true sadhakas and purify ourselves. The reasoning capacity in us (the intellect) has to be the master and the mind has to be subservient to the wishes of the master.

Hence the first quarter of the sloka says: "Let the man raise himself by the Self."

As mind is man, "himself" refers to the mind and the "Self" refers to the Divine Energy within us.

We should lift ourselves by our individual efforts and our sincere actions will be blessed by the grace of Guru and the Lord. "See with your own eyes, walk with your own legs, use your sense organs and mind properly" is His command.

We must feed ourselves to satisfy the hunger. Food eaten by somebody else does not take away the hunger in us.

Nothing comes free in this life. After all we have to pay to get what we want and in the spiritual field also, we have to pay the price of efforts/sadhana to be Liberated and experience the Bliss.

Let us assume that there is a precious diamond at the bottom of the sea. First of all one should know that there is the precious diamond. The next step is to find the means of getting it out. This involves learning deep sea diving and associated actions to lift it up.

The mind (self) is to be compared to the sea. The divinity within us (Atman/Self) is pushed so far down in the ocean and almost forgotten.

One fine day we realize the truth about the presence of this most precious treasure (Atman/Self).

We will then have to find the means to bring the treasure/ divinity out.

We need to dive deep into the bottom of the sea of thoughts to get it out.

For this,

We must know the art of deep sea diving (meditation) and get assistance from various sources.

Study of the scriptures, assistance by the spiritual masters and sacred texts will help us in this effort.

It is important to remember that in the process of recognizing our divinity, we should not develop the pride that we can do it all by ourselves.

In the spiritual path we must learn to wash our mind of all impurities. It must be done regularly because impure thoughts keep on entering the mind. Just as children need the help of learned elders (it is the duty of the elders to do so) to instill the feeling of Sraddha (faith) and Bhakti in the Supreme, as we grow older we have to keep on purifying our mind daily for the rest of our life.

If one is ill, he must know he is ill and get help from the specialists. He must then follow the instructions given by the specialist and take the medications. The medicine may be bitter or the operation to cure may be painful but it is worth the efforts.

We are all mentally sick by the disease known as "selfishness" but we are not aware of it. We must go to our doctors (sastras, guru) and get the medicine.

It all amounts to the fact that we must pay the price to get what we want. The price, in the spiritual context is the effort of purifying our minds of impure thoughts.

The second quarter of the sloka: "Na atmanam avasadayet":

It means "Not let the "Self" go down.

When we forget the divinity within and act without respect to the divinity and the scriptures, it is like letting down the Divinity. Truly speaking the "Self" is ever effulgent and ever pure. There is no such thing as letting it down. By our actions we make the light of divinity get locked within. It is like the servant letting the master down.

The third and the fourth quarters of the sloka:

Atamaiva hyatmano bhandur atmaiva ripuratmanaha:

For this Self is the friend of the self and the self is the enemy of the Self. Two contrasting points are brought out in this section:

The first point is the "Self" alone is the friend of the "self."

We go through the life developing contact with so many people. The life teaches us that none of them are permanent contacts. Either they leave us or we part company with them. It can be due to differences between each other, growing older, developing new contacts or finally the dreaded death. We all need someone to lean on to at times of distress or to experience happiness. We have to shift the supporting pillar from one person to another as we grow older. This is the way of life.

By this way of analyzing we can understand that none of the people from the world including our own close family can be called as our permanent friends.

The Atman within is the only true friend who does not desert us. He is our constant companion from birth to death. He cannot be seen but is always ready to be the pillar for us to lean on to. We keep on running round the pillar of divinity within us but when we are exhausted or tired or distressed we should learn to lean on to Him. He will never say "no".

On the contrary, the last quarter of the sloka asserts that "self is the enemy of the Self." The "self" we have to understand is the "ego" within us. The ego is the enemy in the path of "Self-Realization." It is not actually the enemy of the Atman. Really speaking, the Atman has no enemies and it does not hate anybody. If we lean on to the Atman within and make Him our sarathi (charioteer) in life, he will help us to protect dharma by uprooting our adharma.

The parables from Ramayana and other mythological stories tell us that people like Ravana, Hiranyakashipu hated the Lord and considered him as their worst enemy. But the Lord did not hate them. He loves all His children. He killed the ego in them and took them to His abode. It is His greatness.

So let us remember that we are responsible for the good things in our life and also the bad things in our life. The role of the others in these events is but secondary. The ascent is always hard and descent is easy. But because it is so easy, there is more scope for hurting oneself in the descent. The need for perfection is within us. We are the architects of our destiny.

Every seed by proper care will grow into the tree, to which family the seed belongs. Mango seed grows to become a mango tree and not into a nectarine tree.

Similarly, we have a number of seeds within us. This includes the "God seed." By proper care and nourishment the "God seed" will grow to be "God on earth."

It is better to start practicing the following way of life:

If it is a good act, let me do it now itself.

If it is a bad act, let me postpone it for tomorrow. Tomorrow I may see the action in a different vein and I may not carry out the bad act. It is possible that the thought of a bad deed can be changed to a good deed.

The thought/contemplation on the Atman will help us to bind ourselves to the Atman within. Hence the statement by the Lord:

"For this Self is the friend of the self".

Holding on to the pure thoughts is Japa and it helps us to move towards the divinity.

बन्धुरात्माऽऽत्मनस्तस्य येनात्मैवात्मना जितः ।
अनात्मनस्तु शत्रुत्वे वर्तेतात्मैव शत्रुवत् ||6||

bandhur ātmātmanas tasya yenātmaivātmanā jitaḥ |
anātmanas tu śatrutve vartetātmaiva śatruvat ||6||

The Self is the friend of the self for him who has conquered himself by the self. But to him who has not conquered the self, the self itself is like an enemy. ||6||

bandhuhu: friend; aatma: the Self; atmanaha: of the self; tasya: his; ena: by whom; atma: the self; eva: even; atmana: by the Self; jitaha: conquered; anatmanaha: of unconquered self (not conquered the self); tu: but; shatrutve: in the place of an enemy;

varteta: would remain; atma: self; eva: even; shatruvat: like an enemy.

This sloka is further reiteration of and clarification concerning the message from the previous verse.

The sloka appears as though it is riddled with the word "Atma" so many times. As explained in the previous verse, "Atma" applies both to the "Self" and the "self". The context it is used in should make the point clearer for the student.

Bhandur atma atmanas:

Bhandu: friend.

Atma: the higher Self

Atmanas: the lower self.

The "Self" is the Atman, the divine energy which is specific to each individual. It is a spark of Parabrahman inside us. It is always the friend of the body (mind and intellect) to which it is attached to. It is our constant companion from birth to death. Not just from birth to death but also the companion in the future cycle of births and deaths. It will be the same spark till the individual loses its identity and merges with the Supreme. Therefore it is not wrong to say that the "Self is the friend of the self."

But for who and when is it the friend? The secret word in this sloka is "Tasya".

Tasya means "for him".

The Self is the friend of self for "him".

Who is that "Tasya"?

The second quarter of the sloka makes it clear. It says:

Yenatmaiva atmanaha jitaha.

By him who has conquered himself by the Self.

By him: by the individual

Who has conquered himself: who has conquered his mind (ego)

By the Self: by the Atman within.

It means that each of us have to conquer (the bad thoughts in) our minds by the Atman within. As we have reiterated so many times the Atman within is the real guru for us. It is Sri Krishna, the friend and guru of Arjuna.

If we surrender to Sri Krishna inside us and pray for His guidance, He is surely going to lift us up to the top of spiritual mountain, the Himalayas. We can then experience the "Sat, Chit, Ananda" and live the life of constant Bliss which is "Moksha."

When is the Atman not a friend of the mind?

Anatmanastu shatrutve vartet atmaiva shatruvat:

The spiritual sadhana is all about realising our true identity and to conquer our mind (ego). We should go to war and conquer our mind (ego). This is the meaning of the word "Anatmanastu".

If we have not conquered our mind: Our own mind acts like an enemy.

It harms us at the end by its egotistic way of life. This is the meaning of the word "Shatrutve eva."

The spiritual war between dharmic and adharmic forces is taking place in our own mind. When we do not make use of the divine spark within us (Self), our mind (ego) becomes our enemy and the adharmic forces will destroy us.

The sadhana is to learn the art of making our mind our friend so that it takes the guidance from the intellect (Krishna) within us. This is the "Arjuna" way of life.

On the contrary, if we act like Duryodhana, (the mind not conquered by the Self) who did not get the guidance of Krishna, like Duryodhana we get destroyed.

Let us decide whether we want to be Arjunas or the Duryodhanas of the world and that decision will either take us to Moksha or to our own destruction.

This is the art of dhyana discussed in this chapter. The Sastras, Spiritual texts and the Guru will guide us to understand the Atman within.

जितात्मनः प्रशान्तस्य परमात्मा समाहितः |
शीतोष्णसुखदुःखेषु तथा मानापमानयोः ||7||

jitātmanaḥ praśāntasya paramātmā samāhitaḥ |
śītoṣṇasukhaduḥkheṣu tathā mānāpamānayoḥ ||7||

The man who has subdued his mind is full of Peace. He experiences the supreme Self under all conditions, in heat and cold, pleasure and pain, honour and dishonour. ||7||

jitamanaha: of the self–controlled; prashantasya: of the peaceful; paramatma: supreme Self; samahitaha: balanced/subdued; sheetoshna: in cold and heat; sukha dukheshu: in pleasure and pain; tatha: as also; manopamanayoh: in honour and disgrace

Whether one is a Yogi or a Bhogi (who revels in worldly pleasures), there is bound to be an influx of impulses from the nature and the life around. The Yogi is he who is in search of experiencing the Supreme Self which is "Sat, Chit, Ananda". True "Ananda" is experienced when one learns to live in peace within him and is not perturbed by the influx of impulses.

When we analyze the reactions from the intellectual level, we feel proud when we receive praise and disgraced when we face dishonor. This is "manapamanayo" in the sloka.

At the mental level we feel pleasure when we experience love, kindness etc. and pain when we experience hatred, cruelty and painful situations in life. This is "sukha Dukheshu" in this sloka.

At the physical level we feel heat or cold from the climate around and this is "Sheetoshna" used in this sloka.

What we are asked by the Lord is to develop equanimity in reaction at all the three levels. He says "Samahitaha." Develop the balanced reaction is the advice for a Yogi who is practicing the art of meditation.

What is the result of developing this balanced reaction?

The result is experience of/union with "Sat, Chit, Ananda." The Yogi has to learn to live in Peace in all circumstances to experience the "Ananda."

After all "Sat, Chit, Ananda" is the Supreme Self and "Nama, Roopa" is the individual self.

The Yogi is practicing to break himself from the attachment to "Nama, Roopa". To succeed in this effort, he must develop the equanimity in reaction to the "Dwandvas" (opposites) in life. Once this detachment takes place, attachment to "Sat, Chi, Ananda" is the next step to progress in the sadhana.

This is the lesson for "Dhyana Yoga". Subdue the mind and become a Yogaroodha says the Lord. The first word in this sloka is "Jitatmanaha". It is victory over the mind.

It is the nature of the mind to go through various moods and passions but to overcome this nature of the mind is the training for a Dhyana Yogi.

The intellect of the Yogi who has to succeed in this practice of subduing the mind, should be like a huge mountain. Small or large ripples of waves from the ocean (which is the mind bombarded from the impulses received by the sense organs,) should not shake the huge mountain.

ज्ञानविज्ञानतृप्तात्मा कूटस्थो विजितेन्द्रियः ।
युक्त इत्युच्यते योगी समलोष्टाश्मकाञ्चनः ||8||

jñānavijñānatṛptātmā kūṭastho vijitendriyaḥ |
yukta ity ucyate yogī samaloṣṭāśmakāñcanaḥ ||8||

The Yogi who is satisfied with knowledge and wisdom, who remains immovable, who has conquered his senses, who looks equally on mud, stone and gold, is said to be harmonized. ||8||

jnana vijnana truptatma: satisfied with knowledge and wisdom; kutastho: remains unmoveable; vijitendriyaha: conquered the senses; yuktaha: harmonised; iti: thus; uchyate: is said; yogee: yogi: samaloshtashma kanchanaha: for whom a lump of earth, a stone and gold are the same.

Theoretical knowledge is Jnana and practical knowledge is Vijnana.

In the earlier days of our study we get knowledge and in higher studies we are expected to get wise with the knowledge received.

The student who acquires both the theory and practical knowledge of the specialty subject he/she chooses, becomes a graduate. He will be ready to take up the professional duties and serve the community. Of course, even after taking up professional duties, years of practical experience are needed to make him a specialist in that field of work.

Even in spiritual studies, the seeker must work to get both theoretical and practical knowledge. He should not be satisfied until he acquires practical knowledge. True Vijnana in this sense is perfect "Self-Realization." For a Yogi, this perfect Self-Realization brings in "Trupti"(contentment). Content with the understanding and union with the Atman within is "Truptatma."

This is the meaning of the first quarter of the sloka.

Learn about Truth, dharma and acquire practical knowledge of living the life of Truth and Dharma is the Lord's advice to youngsters in the field of spiritual studies. It does not mean that the wisdom is learnt only by practical experience. It can also be learnt by observation of life around and maturity of wisdom/knowledge.

We are fortunate enough to have so many Puranas and mythological stories, which provide us with examples of Dharma and Adharma carried out in the past and these can help us to live today as useful members of the society.

Kootashta: koota is the iron block used by goldsmith. The goldsmith places the items that need to be modelled on to the block and uses the hammer to get the right shape for the article. All the while the block remains the same and does not undergo any change.

In a similar vein, the perfectly controlled mind should be like the block, says the Lord. Let it receive any number of impulses from the outer world. Use your intellect and hammer those impulses and get them into the shape you want, is his advice.

In a spiritual sense, Kutastha is used to refer to the "Atman." Let the Atman of the seeker, which has become the Jivatma (by association with the world around) become firm and steady. Let the jivatman not get perturbed by the impulses from the sensual world, says the Lord.

What do you get out of this process, one may ask? The answer is "Vijitendriyaha."

Indriyaha is senses, jita is victory and vijita is perfect victory.

Achieve perfect victory over the senses, says the Jagadguru. By making use of our intellect in this way we can climb up the spiritual ladder easily. We can learn by both the good and bad that happens to us or to the society and make corrections in our reactions to the impulses that reach our mind.

Sama loshtashma kanchanaha: looks with equanimity on mud, stone or gold. (See meaning of sloka 24, chapter 14)

This example uses the natural resources of nature.

Depending on the place one lives and depending on ones needs, the value of commodities can vary. Anything that is available freely does not fetch high returns.

For example water fetches a lot of return in Middle East where there is scarcity of water and petrol fetches a lot of return in the western countries where it is not freely available. A millionaire in a desert is ready to give all he has to get a glass of water.

Every object is a combination of five natural elements. The Jnani looks upon mud, stone and gold as natural elements only.

Yukta iti uchyate yogi: yogi is said to be harmonized.

The hallmark of a Yogi is "harmony." A harmonious way of living, assists in bringing about a peaceful society. The seeker who wants to live in harmony in contemplation on the Atman within should live this way of life to experience "Sat, Chit, Ananda."

सुहृन्मित्रार्युदासीनमध्यस्थद्वेष्यबन्धुषु ।
साधुष्वपि च पापेषु समबुद्धिर्विशिष्यते ॥9॥

suhṛnmitrāryudāsīnamadhyasthadveṣyabandhuṣu |
sādhuṣv api ca pāpeṣu samabuddhir viśiṣyate ||9||

He who is equal-minded towards the good-hearted, friends and enemies, the neutrals, arbiters, the hatefuls, relatives, the righteous and unrighteous, he excels. ||9||

suhrut: good hearted; mitra: friend; ari: enemies; udasina: neutrals; madhyastha: arbiters; dweshya: hatefuls; bandhushu: relatives; sadhushu: in the righteous; api: also; cha: and; papeshu: in the unrighteous; sama buddhi: equal minded; vishishyate: excels.

Having given us the instructions on how to react to the world of objects in the last verse, we are now given instructions on how to react to the world of men/women. After all, most of our day to day communication is with fellow human beings.

For survival in this world, we need to depend on the society and the nature. There is a need to learn the art of not only receiving from society and the nature but also of repaying. There are many ways of repaying like giving one's time, knowledge, physical efforts, money, food etc. Most important of all is what one can give and this is "Love." There is an ocean of love within each of us but we tap it only superficially and that too for selfish gains. The Lord within us is an ocean of love. This ocean does not go dry. The more we give, that much more is the multiplication of the stock of love within and it is His Grace.

There is a strong need in today's world for giving love and compassion to fellow humans and other forms of life.

The first word in this sloka is very important and it is "Suhrut". "Suhrut" is that good–hearted person who gives help in need without expecting any return favors. He does not act like a businessman who looks for profits all the time.

Sama buddhir vishishyate: The individual, who excels, according to the Lord, is he, who is a kind–hearted (suhrut) person who shows "Sama Buddhi" (equal mind) towards all the above categories of people. He has equal regard to all types of people he encounters in his daily transactions.

For ordinary mortals it is but natural to show varied reaction at varying levels of social contact and relationship. But here we have the reaction of a "Yogi" who has managed to become "Yogarudha". It is like the view from the top of a mountain. From the peak of a tall mountain, everything at the bottom of the mountain looks the same. He has learnt the art of seeing the same divinity in all. Not only that, he is also aware that the entire life is but a drama staged by the Supreme. For the manager of a stage play, all the actors are the same. He shows the same respect to all the actors because it is the combined action by all the actors that makes the play a successful one. In this life's drama every other person we encounter is another actor and he is playing his role. Expressing the nature of a "Suhrut" towards all is the hallmark of spiritual maturity.

"Drishti" is a Sanskrit word which means "View, vision." Our view varies according to the plane of vision.

Accordingly the vision is classified as:

Dehadrishti —viewed at the physical plane
Mano drishti—viewed at the mental plane

Chittadrishti—view at the intellectual plane
Atmadrishti--view from the level of Atman.

The final step is reached when we have conquered our ego. Living in harmony with nature and the world is "sama buddhi" and this quality is to be developed by practice of "Dhyana". Meditation is not just in simply closing one's eyes and thinking of the Lord but it is learning the art of seeing the same Lord in all. "Please learn to respect all" is the advice by the Jagadguru.

Towards mastering the art of "Self–unfoldment" it is not the conduct of others towards us that is important but it is our conduct towards others.

योगी युञ्जीत सततमात्मानं रहसि स्थितः ।
एकाकी यतचित्तात्मा निराशीरपरिग्रहः ||10||

yogī yuñjīta satatam ātmānaṃ rahasi sthitaḥ |
ekākī yatacittātmā nirāśīr aparigrahaḥ ||10||

The Yogi sitting in a solitary place, alone, self-controlled, without desire, without receiving anything from others, should unite (mind) with the Atma. ||10||

yogi: the yogi; yunjeeta: should unite (mind) with the Atman; rahasi: in a solitary place; atmanam: the mind; ekakee: alone; yatachttatma: self–controlled; nirasheer: without desire; aparigrahaha: without receiving anything from others.

We are now introduced to the method of conducting meditation. This and the following slokas give a detailed description of the method of conducting meditation.

Who should conduct meditation?

The first two words used are "Yogi and yunjeeta". The seeker who wishes to unite with the Atman within and see the Atman in all is a true "Yogi" in context of this sloka. It is also understood that the seeker has progressed in his/her spiritual education wherein he has understood what Jnana is, and what is Karma (chapters 3, 4, 5).

Yunjeeta: merge with the Atman. The seeker should develop the art of meditation so that he/she finally loses his/her ego and merges with the Atman within. It is like salt dissolving in water and losing its identity.

Satatam: "Always." Two ways of understanding the meaning of "always."

One way is, to do so every time one sits for meditation. This applies to the early stages of sadhana.

Every time one sits for meditation he should merge his ego with the Atman.

The other way is to be united with the Atman at all times. This is for the later stages of progress wherein whatever he is doing 24 hours a day, every day in his life, he should be united with the Atman.

What should be united with the Atman?

Atmaanam: here, it means "The mind." the mind of the seeker which is the seat of ego should unite with the Atman.

Rahasi sthitaha: "rahasi" means "a solitary place" and "sthitaha" means "Stationed."

The seeker should be stationed in a solitary place. The Yogi practicing meditation is not to receive any admiration from others but to unite with his own Self. In the early stages of practice, the act of dhyana should be in a solitary place. Let me make it clear at the outset that it does not mean that every seeker of meditation should go to a forest for meditation. To assist in this step our elders have recommended having "a prayer room" in every household.

The solitary place is that where there is no disturbance from the outer world and the sense organs will not get an opportunity to get distracted. As we know our sense organs are unstable and get easily distracted. The mind is fickle and it plays with its memory bank every so often and goes day dreaming on other issues.

Of course it would be great to have the peaceful nature all around for meditation. Hence we hear of many saints and tapaswins living in a forest and conducting meditation under the shelter of a tree or in a cave. The bank of the river is another place for solitude.

In the present world and for the average householder this is not practical. Hence the need for a quiet room in the house, that can be used also as the prayer room. It should be preferable to have the quiet room where there is the least disturbance.

Ekaki: "alone". There should not be any other person during meditation. Where there are a group of people meditating, the practitioners in meditation get distracted by the presence of others. It is hard to stop looking at others who are meditating. In the practice of Bhakti it is recommended to have a group of seekers getting together but for meditation, the seeker has to be alone. (Also to be looked at upon with this view: the mind and the five sense organs-meaning, the mind should be alone contemplating on meditation on the Atman and the senses should not be disturbing the concentration)

What should the seeker be doing in a solitary place and all alone?

"Yata chittatma": self–controlled. Here, the word "self" includes the sense organs, the mind and the intellect. The sense organs should be controlled by the mind, the mind by the intellect and the intellect by the inner conscience. Withdraw constantly from disturbances arising from any of these sense organs is the advice to the seeker.

How should he act and react to the outer world? Two important prerequisites are given. They are:

Nirashee: without desires,

Aparigrahaha: without receiving anything from others.

Nirashee: "Do not have desires" has been repeated so many times and will be repeated many more times. Distraction during any of the four methods of Yoga: Karma, Bhakti, Jnana and Dhyana will drop the seeker from the heights of Yoga achieved. We have learnt also that one should not take the literal meaning of the word "no desires." It all depends upon the spiritual maturity.

A child in kindergarten and primary school education has to be tempted with rewards to make progress. As the student progresses in his educational career he/she should not have the rewards as the temptation to study. The student should do so out of their own volition.

The Post–Doctorate student will not have any desires but works for the sake of work.

Similarly, in spiritual education, whatever may be the path taken, the desire to attain Moksha is the first step. Dhyana yoga can be considered as the last of the four methods of yoga and desire–lessness is an essential prerequisite for this method. The greater the desire to unite with the Supreme by the seeker, the greater are the chances of failing to achieve the objective. This is because, in his eagerness to unite, as soon as he feels he has united with the Supreme, the seeker would immediately open his eyes in elation and comes back to the present world around him.

Aparigrahaha: not receiving anything. Let us be clear at the outset that anything offered for the bare maintenance of the body may be taken. Minimizing the bodily requirements is essential for spiritual progress. The word aparigraha refers to receiving any gifts from others. The seeker who sits in a solitary place in meditation, day after day, will attract the attention of others. Many people passing by, will out of reverence bring items of food, clothing etc. to such an individual. The mind of the seeker is distracted at the sight of these and develops likes and dislikes for what has been brought. Hence, it is stressed that he should not receive anything.

शुचौ देशे प्रतिष्ठाप्य स्थिरमासनमात्मनः ।
नात्युच्छ्रितं नातिनीचं चैलाजिनकुशोत्तरम् ||11||

śucau deśe pratiṣṭhāpya sthiram āsanam ātmanaḥ |
nātyucchritaṃ nātinīcaṃ cailājinakuśottaram ||11||

Having established on a clean spot, a firm seat, which is neither too high nor too low, covered by cloth, (deer) skin and holy grass one over the other. ||11||

तत्रैकाग्रं मनः कृत्वा यतचित्तेन्द्रियक्रियः ।
उपविश्यासने युञ्ज्याद्योगमात्मविशुद्धये ||12||

tatraikāgraṃ manaḥ kṛtvā yatacittendriyakriyaḥ |
upaviśyāsane yuñjyād yogam ātmaviśuddhaye ||12||

There, having made the mind single-pointed, with the actions of the mind and senses controlled, let him practice Yoga for self-purification. ||12||

shuchou: in a clean; deshe: spot; pratishtapya: established; sthiram: firm; asanam: seat; atmanaha: his own; na: not; ati ucchritam: too high; na: not; ati neecham: very low; chailajina kushottaram: a cloth, skin and kusa grass one over the other;

tatra: there; ekagram: single pointed; manah: mind; krutva: having made; yata chittendriya kriyaha: one who has controlled the actions of the mind and the senses; upavishya: being seated; asane: on the seat; yunjyat: let him practice; yogam: yoga; atma vishuddhaye: for the purification of the self.

What is the purpose of conducting dhyana yoga?

Like the other three yogas, Karma, Bhakti and Jnana, dhyana yoga is also for uniting with the Atman within and the Atman with the Parabrahman. It is to experience the Eternal Bliss and be one with it.

Sloka 11 is about the place one has to sit and sloka 12 is about the control over the mind and senses needed for meditation. The first step in meditation is self– purification. "Atma Vishuddhaye" says the Lord. Nothing is attained without purity of the body, mind and speech, "Trikarana Shuddhi", the scriptures declare.

Shuchou deshe: clean spot. The seeker should find a spot which is clean and with clean surroundings. It is to invigorate and elevate the mind to spiritual heights. Siddhah yogis who have mastered the art of meditation can sit and concentrate their mind on meditation in any surroundings.

Pratishtapya: having established (in clean surroundings)

Sthiram asanam atmanaha: established on a firm seat. The seeker should sit comfortably and be established in a suitable posture. We will get the details of the posture to establish in the next sloka.

The time one sits for meditation has to gradually increase from a few minutes to many hours in a day and many days of a week. It is therefore necessary to get established in a firm seat. An unstable seat will distract the mind away from concentration.

Natyucchishtam naati neecham: neither too high nor too low. The seat one takes up should not be too high from the ground nor too low. Sometimes in meditation one may actually nod off to sleep. When this happens there is a possibility of falling down and getting hurt. There is also a danger of falling down and injuring oneself, during intense meditation. Hence the seat has to be not too high from the ground.

At the same time it is possible for creepy crawly insects to get on to the physical body of the seeker in meditation and hurt him. Also, dampness from the ground would cause health problems.

Chailajina kushottaram: (placing) a cloth, skin and kusa grass one over the other. This is to keep the seat clean, firm and levelled. Kusa/holy grass is laid on to the floor first and on top of it is laid the deer/tiger skin and a clean cloth. This is advocated to stop the body's positive energy flowing from the Mooladhara (lower end of the spinal column) towards the negative energy of the ground.

Kusa grass is to keep the seat warm and prevent dampness harming the body.

The kusa grass is rough to sit on and is prickly. It is also uncomfortable to sit on. Therefore a deer/tiger skin is to be placed on top of it. Finally a clean cloth is placed over it. Even though the deer skin is soft, it is possible to get allergic reaction from it. At the same time sitting directly on animal skin makes the body sweat and the seat becomes uncomfortable to sit on.

In the modern day there are many cushions made up of synthetic material that are soft, non-allergic and comfortable to sit on. It is not wrong to sit on them.

We now move on to the next sloka which tells us to have a control over the mind and body.

Taitrakagram manah kritva: make the mind single pointed. The mind is the band master and if the band master makes a mistake the entire concert is a failure. On one side it is exposed to the outer world through the sense organs and on the opposite side it has the Atman within. There are too many objects in the world outside and they are not constant also. Hence it is not possible to develop single pointed concentration. To get an object of desire (kama) there is a need for single pointed concentration but on getting the object we develop attachment. As we studied already attachment leads to anger and this in turn leads to self-destruction. It is comparatively easy to develop single pointed concentration on to the objects of the world but they lead finally to ruin of the individual.

On the contrary, even though it is difficult to concentrate on the Atman it does not lead to destruction but leads to Liberation.

Yata chittendriya kriyaha: controlling the activities of the mind and the senses. The activities of the sense organs are to send the information about the world outside and that of the mind is to analyze these and make a judgment using the intellectual capacity of reasoning.

The mind also is in the habit of recollecting from the stored imprints and acting upon them as needed.

The seeker should withdraw the mind constantly away from attachment to the objects of the world and from the stored vasanas which lead to day dreaming using the memory bank.

The senses should be controlled by the mind. The mind should know what impulses to receive and not to receive from the five sense organs.

The seeker should then proceed to practice the yoga of meditation. The physical body is cleaned by the act of bathing. The mind has to be kept pure by washing off (spiritual bathing) the vasanas and not get distracted by them. (spiritual practices like recitation of the Gita, holy prayers, chanting of mantras are some of the ways to wash the mind)

It is not just enough to wash the mind but it needs feeding also. The food to be provided is the thought on the Parabrahman, His Leela and His divine qualities.

समं कायशिरोग्रीवं धारयन्नचलं स्थिरः ।
संप्रेक्ष्य नासिकाग्रं स्वं दिशश्चानवलोकयन् ||13||

samaṃ kāyaśirogrīvaṃ dhārayann acalaṃ sthiraḥ |
saṃprekṣya nāsikāgraṃ svaṃ diśaś cānavalokayan ||13||

Let him hold the body, head and neck erect and still, gazing at the tip of the nose, without looking around, ||13||

प्रशान्तात्मा विगतभीर्ब्रह्मचारिव्रते स्थितः |
मनः संयम्य मच्चित्तो युक्त आसीत मत्परः ||14||

**praśāntātmā vigatabhīr brahmacārivrate sthitaḥ |
manaḥ saṃyamya maccitto yukta āsīta matparaḥ ||14||**

Let him sit serene-minded, fearless, firm in the vow of celibacy, self-controlled and balanced, thinking of Me, the Supreme Goal. ||14||

samam: erect; kaya: body; shira: head; greeyam: neck; dharayan: holding; achalam: erect; sthiraha: still; samprekshya: gazing at; naasikagram: tip of the nose; svam: one's own; dishaha: directions, cha: and; anavalokayan: not looking; prashantatma: serene–minded; vigatabhir: fearless; brahmacharivrate: in the vow of brahmacharya; sthitaha: firm; manaha: mind; samyamya: having controlled; machitto: thinking of Me; yukta: balanced; aaseeta: let him sit; matparaha: having Me as the Supreme goal.

Samam kaya shirogreeyam : the body, head and neck kept erect;
Dharayan achalam sthiram : holding it still and steady.

When the head, neck and body are kept erect, the spinal cord is vertical and at right angles to the brain stem. It is said that in this posture the bodily energy flows freely through this column. The spiritual energy is stored along the spinal cord in the vertebral column and the brain and the posture aids in the movement of this energy. By doing so the current of flow is free and it moves unobstructed towards the brain centre called the "Sahasrara." It is important to hold the body still and steady in this posture.

This posture is for the physically fit and healthy and has to be practiced from the days of the life as a youth. It is true that there are many who are neither physically fit due to health related problems or develop diseases in the later stages of their life. The rule of holding the body erect does not apply to those. They can meditate in any posture that they feel comfortable in.

The rule of thumb is that the posture should not make the individual all tensed up. It is like the military training. The cadets are asked to stand to attention and then relax. One can see that the way they are standing when relaxed, is also a disciplined standing. The same rule applies in spiritual practice for developing a posture to meditate.

Samprekshya naasikagram: fixing the gaze on the tip of his nose.

Syam dishascan avalokayan: not looking around.

The seeker is asked to practice fixing his gaze on the tip of his nose and to not look around. The two practices go hand in hand simultaneously. One can appreciate this by observing those who are seriously concentrating on reading a book or writing. Their eyes are small and their gaze is focused on to the book. Those who are seriously immersed in their studies do not see what is happening around them, their eyes do not wander freely, looking for something different.

Opposite to these are the children in the classroom who are not seriously listening to the teacher but looking at distractions from their surroundings.

Closing the eyes in meditation could make the seeker fall into a state of sleep rather than concentrate on the Atman. Looking around negates the true purpose of meditation.

The perfect example of one who is in deep meditation and not distracted by surroundings is Lord Shiva. He is depicted as sitting in deep meditation with snakes crawling over his body. There is a lesson to learn from this picture. Shiva is so immersed in deep meditation that he is totally not distracted by anything from the surroundings. Even the crawling snake does not disturb him. (the reference to snakes crawling over the body should be looked upon as follows:

Lord Shiva is in deep meditation. He is not distracted by desires. (The desires are depicted as snakes crawling around)

Sloka 15 is about the attitude of the seeker in meditation.

As the meditation is for attaining union with the Supreme, the seeker should have the following four virtues.

Prashaantatma: Peaceful. It is important to remain peaceful during the period of meditation. All mental agitations have to be brushed aside. Reducing the mental agitations is useful for progress in meditation. Agitation is an expression of ego which is disturbed. The ego has to be totally destroyed for total success in meditation.

Vigata Bheehi: free from fear. "Vigata" is free and "Bheehi" is from fear.

Fear comes from so many quarters and distracts the mind of the seeker. Many are of the opinion that meditation is for sanyasis and not for householders. This is a wrong notion. Meditation is a practice that is a must, in all the four stages of life. Meditation is not just contemplation on the Lord sitting in a quiet room but it is an art of single–pointed contemplation on the work ahead at any time of the day, at any place and to consider work as "worship." Free from the opinion of others on the rights and wrongs of meditation, every individual must practice meditation at least some part of every day.

After all meditation is for Liberation so why fear to take the path that leads to Liberation?

The meditation should not be practiced to achieve a desired wish and approaching the Lord for the same. If it is done with that intention there will be a fear whether God will bless and fulfill the wish.

Then there is the question of whether one can progress in the path for Liberation by the practice of meditation. By having the knowledge of what is Atma and what is Anatma and what are one's duties to their body, family, society and nature, the practice of meditation becomes easier.

Having the guidance and blessings of a guru, the practice becomes simple and there will be no room for fear.

Brahmacharivrate sthitaha: firm in the vow of celibacy.

The one who walks in the path of Brahma is a "Brahmachari." (Brahmam Charati iti Brahmachari)

It also means "enquiry into Brahman and engaging the mind in the thought of Brahman". (Brahma vichara)

Vrata is "resolve"

Sthitaha: firmly established.

It means that there should not be any room for sensual pleasures. Desire to fulfill the sensual pleasures would drag the mind away from the desired objective of uniting with the Atman. The sense organs should not agitate the mind with the thoughts of the outer world and the pleasures from the same.

The mind and body should be pure at all times during meditation. One should be as pure as a baby in thought, word and deed.

Manah samyamya: having controlled the mind.

Machhchittaha: thinking of Me.

Thus, with total control over body, mind and speech, the seeker should be constantly thinking of the Lord. To be successful in meditation there should not be room for any thoughts other than that of the Atman.

Yuktaha: balanced. Everything in life has to have a sense of balance. Moderation in whatever we do is the rule of thumb in actions. Even the act of meditation has to have a balance. Regular practice is the key to success in any field of activity and meditation is no exception.

Aaseeta: let him sit.

Matparaha: having Me as the Supreme Goal.

It is not the physical posture but the posture of the mind that is important. The sincere seeker in dhyana yoga should make his mind sit on the thought of Brahman and not let the senses drag the mind away from reaching the target.

Faith in the Lord, in the scriptures, in the guru and finally faith in oneself are essential for achieving the end result. Success is for he who has total faith (Sraddha) and devotion (Bhakti) in his actions, works at getting the knowledge (jnana) of the same and conducts actions (karma) accordingly.

Concentration on all these aspects is "Dhyana".

युञ्जन्नेवं सदाऽऽत्मानं योगी नियतमानसः ।
शान्तिं निर्वाणपरमां मत्संस्थामधिगच्छति ||15||

yuñjann evaṃ sadātmānaṃ yogī niyatamānasaḥ |
śāntiṃ nirvāṇaparamāṃ matsaṃsthām adhigacchati ||15||

Thus, the self-controlled Yogi, always keeping the mind balanced, attains "Peace" abiding in Me which culminates in the highest bliss of Liberation. ||15||

yunjannevam: thus balancing; sadatmanam: always the self; yogee: yogi; niyatamanasaha:with controlled mind; shantim: nirvana: moksha: paramam: the highest; matsamstham: abiding in Me; adhigachati: attains.

The spiritual seekers are those who are in search of "Liberation." It is not just liberation from the sorrows of this world, it has to be liberation from both joys and sorrows. The mind does not remain in a calm state either in happiness or sorrow.

It is therefore necessary first of all to learn the art of self–control.

"The self" which is the "ego" is always in search of happiness from one source or other. "Ego boosting" has become the way of life for the majority.

By keeping the mind balanced in its reaction to the impulses brought in by the senses and by not letting the mind dwell on the vasanas from the memory bank, there is an opening of the gateway to "Peace."

This has been discussed in the last few verses.

"The Yogi, thus constantly controlling the mind holds it in meditation on the Atman," is the meaning of the first half of the sloka.

Let us not forget the word "Sadaa". It has to be a constant effort. Nay, the effort has to culminate in constant control of the mind. In the beginning it has to be control by determined effort but as one progresses it has to be effortless control. We should not feel sorry or tired of the efforts we are putting in and keep in mind that there is always "light at the end of the tunnel".

The effort is the price we have to pay. "Pay for getting what?"

What do we get by this practice?

Shantim: Peace

Nirvana paramam: the highest bliss of Moksha

Matsamsthaam: of my being

Adhigachati: attains.

We attain Peace, says the Lord.

Where is this Peace? It is not a commodity one gets from this world. It is not a business transaction.

"Peace" is the very nature of the Supreme. He is "Sat, Chit, Ananda" the Vedas declare. Hence the Lord uses the word "Matsamsthaam".

The Peace is "My Being" and the seeker would attain that state by meditation, says the Jagadguru.

Moksha is the highest everlasting Peace and can only be attained by merging with the Atman within and this is what the sincere seekers of dhyana yoga have to strive for.

नात्यश्नतस्तु योगोऽस्ति न चैकान्तमनश्नतः |
न चातिस्वप्नशीलस्य जाग्रतो नैव चार्जुन ||**16**||

nātyaśnatas tu yogosti na caikāntam anaśnataḥ |
na cātisvapnaśīlasya jāgrato naiva cārjuna ||16||

O Arjuna, Yoga is not possible for him who eats too much or who does not eat at all. Nor for him who Sleeps too much or too little. ||16||

na: not; atyashnataha: who eats too much; tu: verily; yoga: yoga; asti: is; na: not; cha: and; ekantam: at all; anashnataha: does not eat; cha: and; atiswapnasheelasya: who sleeps too much; jagrato: who is awake; na: not; eva: even.

This sloka is about moderation in food and sleep.

Why should I show any moderation at all, many would ask?

Moderation in whatever we do has great benefit. Even the modern day physicians ascertain this truth. Preventive medicine is more than 5000yrs old and not something that has started in the last few hundred years or so. This sloka is a proof of it.

Why specifically point out eating and sleeping?

The physical body has to be light and strong to take up meditation as a way of life. Spirituality is closely connected to the state of the body. When one is apparently healthy, he feels confident that he can do anything and achieve anything in life.

When striving for Moksha, a healthy body is essential. We cannot foresee what will be our state of health tomorrow. At least by developing a balanced way of eating from childhood we can prevent some of the future health problems we may have to face that will deter efforts at meditation. An unhealthy body is the greatest obstacle for spiritual practice. It disturbs the concentration of the mind.

Eating too much makes one lethargic and it is not good to be lethargic during meditation.

Also eating too much makes the mind develop likes and dislikes and one starts looking forward for the next meal. Desire for food is not good but need for food to keep a healthy body is not wrong.

Not eating has its problems too. The natural instinct is to make one feel hungry for food. The mind starts thinking of the food and if this habit is continued the body gets weak and a weak body distracts the mind in the sadhana. So, balanced food is essential.

Sick body, by not eating or eating too much the body is subject to pain and suffering which distracts the mind from its track of spirituality.

So, the answer is to take up the middle path and eat what is essential. It is always a good habit, the learned say, to get up from the table before the mind asks for another helping because it is tasty food. When the stomach is half full it is sensible to drink a glass or two of water and make the stomach three quarters full.

Stop craving and develop sensible eating habits is the advice by the medical profession and the spiritual masters too.

Let us now move to the second aspect of sleep.

Sleep is a normal bodily requirement. It is to rejuvenate the bodily organs for the next day. Developing a rhythm of day and night is a good practice.

Sleep as we know is tamasic. But even in tamas there are three types:

Satvic, Rajasic Tamasic.

One of the questions seekers would like to know is "how long should one sleep, how much should one eat, what types of food are to be eaten?"

There is no hard and fast rule for this. It depends upon each individual and his professional duties. A hard manual laborer needs a large quantity of food and a good sleep of nearly 8–9 hours.

Those with not great physical activity, (students) will benefit from sleeping for 6–8 hours a day.

The spiritual seekers should learn to sleep for 4–6 hours a day.

It is always sensible to go to bed early and get up early in morning.

To get up just before sunrise is good for health of the mind and the body.

To be relaxed and spend some time on repeating chants/kirtans before going to bed would prepare the mind for a Satvic sleep.

Too much of sleep would bring inertia and lack of interest in whatever one does.

Too little sleep would make one weak in course of time.

Let us now complete the commentary by taking up an example.

A string instrument needs the string to be in correct tension. The strings should not be too loose nor too tight or the music produced would be of poor quality and also the strings could break too.

The body is a musical instrument of a sort. It also brings out music. To bring the divine music, the strings should be of the correct tension. This is obtained by control in eating and sleeping.

Sri Ramakrishna says that what we eat should not heat our body too much and not excite the mind.

Let us learn not to punish our body and mind by not regulating on food and sleep habits.

युक्ताहारविहारस्य युक्तचेष्टस्य कर्मसु ।
युक्तस्वप्नावबोधस्य योगो भवति दुःखहा ||17||

yuktāhāravihārasya yuktaceṣṭasya karmasu |
yuktasvapnāvabodhasya yogo bhavati duḥkhahā ||17||

For him who is moderate in food and recreation, moderate in exertion in all actions, moderate in sleep and wakefulness, Yoga destroys all pain and suffering. ||17||

yuktahara viharasya: moderate in food and recreation; yukta chestasya karmasu: moderate in exertion in all actions; yukta swapna avabodhasya: moderate in sleep and wakefulness; yogaha: yoga; bhavati: becomes; dukhaha: destroyer of pain and suffering.

Emphasis is placed on "Yukta" which means "Moderation" in this context. In a 24 hour a day we spend our time:

Being awake and spending time on various activities,
on eating and drinking,
on relaxation and professional activities
and the rest of the time in sleeping.

Yuktahara: moderation in food: we have discussed this in the last verse.

Slokas 8, 9 and 10 of chapter 17 is specifically on the food habits. Food is not only for the body but for the mind also. The mind also needs spiritual food for its development. In spiritual practice, mind plays a greater role and it is essential to keep it in right shape.

Yukta viharasya: moderation in recreation.

Recreational activities during day time are also essential. A few moments of recreational activities like taking a stroll in the park, keeping feet up and watching TV or listening to music etc. makes us get back to work with greater zeal.

Yukta chestasya karmasu: moderate in actions. Here, "actions" refer to one's duties in life, be a student, an office worker, a housewife etc.

In the name of efficiency and production, the 21st century has brought in the new ways of making the staff members work in an office for more than 10–12hrs a day. This is along with the incentive of bigger pay packets.

Sooner or later we are going to face a number of problems because of this. Apart from burning out the energy of our young generation this method is stopping the youth of the day from taking up any other activities. Their mental and physical health is going to get affected. Not only that, the hefty pay packet for some, gives more incentive on spending for luxuries which sometime may grow out of proportion. This would also lead to developing habits like drinking, smoking etc.

Yukta swapnavabodhasya: moderation in wakeful state and sleep. "Avabhodasya" is wakefulness and "Swapna" is state of sleep. This has also been discussed in the last verse.

What is the benefit of "Moderation" in all of these activities? "Destroys pain and suffering", is the answer.

"Be moderate and avoid excess" is the command from the Lord. The Yogi has to strive for self–control and thereby let the body and mind function which will be the greatest asset in achieving union with the Parabrahman. As we know union with Parabrahman is "Bliss" and the real blissful state is "no feeling of pain and sorrow".

Excessive zeal in the earlier stages of meditation will burn out the energies both physical and spiritual and many will drop out of the practice within a short period of starting meditation.

It is also a fact that many students who burn the midnight oil out of excessive zeal fail miserably as they cannot continue the practice of keeping awake longer hours daily.

Law of nature is moderation and be a "Yukta" commands the Lord.

The story of "The hare and tortoise" was the example for us in our childhood as an example for moderation. "Slow and steady wins the race" is a well–known proverb. In our younger days when I was in the Boy Scouts, there was a practice called "Komala Pada". For covering a distance of a mile, we were taught to walk a few minutes and run a few minutes and we were made to cover the distance in 20 minutes.

यदा विनियतं चित्तमात्मन्येवावतिष्ठते ।
निःस्पृहः सर्वकामेभ्यो युक्त इत्युच्यते तदा ||18||

yadā viniyataṃ cittam ātmany evāvatiṣṭhate |
niḥspṛhaḥ sarvakāmebhyo yukta ity ucyate tadā ||18||

When the perfectly controlled mind rests in the Self, free from longing for all enjoyments then it is said that the Yogi is united. ||18||

yada: when; viniyatam: perfectly controlled; chittam: mind; atmani: in the Self; eva: only; avatishtate: rests; nispruhaha: free from longing; sarva kamebhyaha: from all desires; yuktaha: yogi; iti: thus; uchyate: is said; tada: then.

After learning the art of moderation as described in the last two verses, we are now given the conditions to be fulfilled to actually unite with the Atman and thereby experience the "Eternal Bliss".

What are the conditions?

"The mind to be totally controlled," is the first condition. We should look at the mind as the warrior sitting in the chariot of life and the horses as his thoughts. The thoughts pull the chariot and the one who knows the art of controlling the horses will be able to reach the final destination.

(refer to the comments on the scene of Gitopadesham in the introduction)

The Mind has to be controlled: Arjuna's of the world need to control their senses which drag them into the world by the four passions of desire, anger, greed and delusion.

Thoughts make us move forward in this world and it is necessary to know which type of thoughts we need to entertain and which ones we should not. Towards this, we need guidance from our intellect which in turn has to be resting on the Atman.

What should such a mind do?

The answer is the second condition to be fulfilled. "Atmany eva avatishtati": rests in the Self.

The mind should surrender to the intellect which should surrender to the Atman within. When the intellect which has become the boss over the mind, rests in the Atman, it is to be understood that the mind also rests in the Atman. As Atman denotes "Bliss" (Peace within) resting in the Atman means "to remain in a constant state of Bliss." This is the "Ananda", the scriptures declare. This is the Eternal Truth declared as "Sat" and the true knowledge of this state is "Chit".

The last condition to be fulfilled is "Nispruhaha sarva kamebhyo".

"Nispruhaha" is free from longing,

"Sarva kamebhyo:" from all desires.

The Lord does not say "Free from desires" but says "Free from longing for desires." For example, it is not wrong to have a desire to become a professional but it is wrong to become a professional to fullfil a number of personal desires that are contrary to dharma.

It is not wrong to have a desire for "Moksha" but it is wrong to be so selfish in the desire and forget the society and one's duty to the society.

Let us not forget the word "Sarva kamebhyo". This is the guhya bhasha (secret word) in the sloka. "Sarva kamebhyo" (all desires) means desires for pleasures in this world and also for the pleasures in the other worlds.

This is true "Tatva Jnana" which is "Knowledge of The Eternal truth." Desirelessness (Nispruhaha) is the tool for Vasana kshaya.

Control of the mind (chittam viniyatam) is mano nasha and Atmany evavatishtati (rests in Atman) is Tatva Jnana.

The mind free from disturbances (both from without and within) can rest in the Atman within and it is true "Dhyana Yoga". (No disturbances from the impulses sent by the sense organs and no disturbances from the stored vasanas)

यथा दीपो निवातस्थो नेङ्गते सोपमा स्मृता ।
योगिनो यतचित्तस्य युञ्जतो योगमात्मनः ||19||

yathā dīpo nivātastho neṅgate sopamā smṛtā |
yogino yatacittasya yuñjato yogam ātmanaḥ ||19||

As a lamp in a windless place does not flicker, is the comparison of the Yogi of controlled mind practicing the Yoga of the Self. ||19||

yatha: as; deepo: lamp; nivatastaha: placed in a windless place; nengata: does not flicker; saa: that; upama: simile; smruta: is thought; yoginaha: of the yogi; yatachittatma: of controlled mind; yunjate: practicing; yogam: the yoga; atmanaha: of the Self.

In the latter stages of dhyana yoga, the mind of the Yogi who has mastered the art remains constantly on the thought of Brahman. His light of knowledge is said to be steady.

This knowledge has been compared to that of a lamp placed in a windless place. When there is no wind such lamp remains steady without any flickering.

Similarly, the mind of the yogi steady in dhyana produces sparks of thoughts on Brahman continuously. There is no room for any other thoughts to enter and contaminate the flow of thoughts. His knowledge is said to be so perfect that the light of knowledge that is shining in him is like the non–flickering lamp. The windows which are the five senses are perfectly controlled and no wind blows from them to disturb the lamp of knowledge.

Slokas 20, 21, 22, 23

What has been explained so far in this chapter has been put together in the following four verses and in verse 23 we get the specific definition of "Yoga".

यत्रोपरमते चित्तं निरुद्धं योगसेवया ।
यत्र चैवात्मनाऽऽत्मानं पश्यन्नात्मनि तुष्यति ||20||

yatroparamate cittaṃ niruddhaṃ yogasevayā |
yatra caivātmanātmānaṃ paśyann ātmani tuṣyati ||20||

When the mind rests, restrained by the practice of Yoga and when seeing the Self by the self is delighted in Self. ||20||

Yatro paramate' should be read as "yatra uparamate":Yatra: where; Uparamate: rests; Chittam: the mind; niruddham: restrained; yoga sevaya: by the practice of yoga; cha: and; eva: only; atmanaa: by the self; atmanam: the Self; pashyan: seeing; atmany: in the Self; tushyati: is delighted.

The first quarter of this verse is "when the mind rests." When does the mind rest?

When the mind is not receiving the impulses from the sense organs and when it is not living in the world of its stored memories.

The answer will be: In deep sleep.

This verse is about the mind when the individual is awake.

One way of not receiving the impulses from the sense organs is to shut them by force. This can be achieved by closing the sense organs. When one does not want to listen to a particular conversation that is taking place, the steps taken are to put the hands over the ears so that the conversation does not enter through the ears. Many a times the mind then immediately goes into a state of day dreaming.

The same pattern applies to the other sense organs.

This is not about the mind resting totally but about the mind resting from its task of receiving impulses from outside. For a Dhyana Yogi, it is the task for experiencing the bliss from associating with the Atman within.

It is like the teacher and the students in the classroom.

The teacher would want the children to have attention on what will be taught. At that time, the students must give a rest to their mind from entering into the world outside the classroom.

The students in the classroom should not nod off to sleep and also not be disturbed by what they see/hear/smell from outside.

Niruddham yoga sevaya:

This is the second quarter of the verse. It should read as, "when the mind is restrained by the practice of yoga".

The task ahead for the seeker is "contemplation on the Atman within." Towards achieving this objective, the seeker has to practice giving rest to the mind from its normal day to day activities.

The practice of yoga that has been described in the last few verses should be undertaken by the seeker.

The horses (they represent the thoughts) should be restrained by two simultaneous actions.

One is by the charioteer taking hold of the reins and restraining them accordingly. The second action is to put the blinkers on the horses so that their vision is straight ahead and not distracted by what is on the sides of the road.

Yatra chaivatmanatmanam pashyati:

"The "self" which is the mind, sees "The Self", the Atman" is the meaning of the third quarter of the sloka.

It is the mind which is the most important organ in the practice of yoga. The Atman by association with the mind and intellect has become the "Jivatma" and perceives the world. It is caught in the web of samsara because of this association.

The task for the seeker is to recognize this truth and dissociate the mind from its attachment to the physical world.

This can be achieved only when the mind starts seeing the "Self" within by the practice of Yoga.

Atmany eva tushyati:

Seeing the Self only from within and is delighted.

The secret word in this sloka is "Eva" which is included in the word: "chaivatmanatmanam".

The delight should come from seeing the Atman alone and not from anything else. The seeker should not experience delight from the external physical world but only from the "Self" within.

सुखमात्यन्तिकं यत्तद्बुद्धिग्राह्यमतीन्द्रियम् ।
वेत्ति यत्र न चैवायं स्थितश्चलति तत्त्वतः ||21||

sukham ātyantikaṃ yat tad buddhigrāhyam atīndriyam |
vetti yatra na caivāyaṃ sthitaś calati tattvataḥ ||21||

Where established, the Yogi knows that bliss which transcends the senses, which is understandable by the purified intellect only and from the experience of the Self does not even move from the reality. ||21||

Sukham atyantikam: bliss infinite; yat tad: which, that; buddhi grahyam: which can be grasped by the reason; ateendriyam: transcending the senses; vetti: Knows; yatra: where; na: not; cha: and; eva; even; ayam: this; sthitaha: established; chalati: moves; tatvataha: from the reality.

"That infinite bliss":

Which bliss?

"The bliss one experiences on seeing the Self within" is the bliss in the context of this quarter of the sloka.

Buddhi grahyam ateendriyam:

"That bliss which can be grasped by the purified intellect and which transcends the senses" is the meaning of the second quarter.

The bliss discussed above can only be grasped by the intellect. It is not possible to do so by the senses. One has to transcend the senses to grasp this bliss.

It is important to note the word "buddhi". "Buddhi" is purified intellect. The intellect can be Satvic, rajasic or tamasic.

Purified intellect is Satvic,

Egoistic selfish intellect is Rajasic

and dull, lazy intellect (clouded by selfishness) is Tamasic.

"Where established he never moves from the Reality." Is the meaning of the second half of the sloka.

Once established in that bliss which is the Reality, (by the purified intellect) he who does not move from this Reality, is the real knower. He has understood the meaning of the statement by the scholars who say "Jagat mithya Brahma Satya" (The world is false and the Brahman is the Truth). He has realized that he is not the "ego".

The first step is to let the ocean of thoughts in the mind remain in a calm state. Towards this the assistance of the intellect is needed. The reasoning capacity should come into operation and the seeker should transcend the thoughts.

Towards this the seeker has to learn the art of bringing out the reasoning capacity, sharpening the same and analyse every thought.

What will he get by this practice?

We get the answer, in the next sloka.

यं लब्ध्वा चापरं लाभं मन्यते नाधिकं ततः ।
यस्मिन्स्थितो न दुःखेन गुरुणापि विचाल्यते ||22||

yaṃ labdhvā cāparaṃ lābhaṃ manyate nādhikaṃ tataḥ |
yasmin sthito na duḥkhena guruṇāpi vicālyate ||22||

Which having obtained, he does not think any other gain superior to it. Wherein established, he is not moved even by great sorrow. ||22||

Yam labdhvaa: which (having) obtained; cha: and; aparam: other; labham: gain; manyate: thinks; na: not; adhikam: greater; tataha: that; yasmin: in which; sthitaha: established; na: not; dukhena: by sorrow; guruna: heavy; api: even; vichalyate: is moved.

"Having obtained the bliss from experiencing the bliss of union with the Atman within" is the meaning of the first section of the sloka.

What will such a seeker do after having obtained the bliss?

The seeker would understand that there is no other experience of happiness which is greater than the bliss he has experienced.

"Tataha" is the guhya bhasha in this sloka. It should be read as "Nothing greater" than "That". The seeker who has started looking for the "Eternal Truth" which is "Sat, Chit, Ananda", by process of elimination (Ne'ti) has come to realize that "Tat" (Eternal reality) is within himself and his body is only the "Upadhi" (vehicle) to experience it.

Yasmin sthitho: in which established

Having the total conviction of the reality, he is firmly established in the union with the Atman within.

What next?

He has to go through the various experiences in life. He looks upon his body as the shadow and not the real Self. Whatever may be the apparent harm done to the shadow does not hurt the real Self.

तं विद्याद् दुःखसंयोगवियोगं योगसंज्ञितम् ।
स निश्चयेन योक्तव्यो योगोऽनिर्विण्णचेतसा ||23||

taṃ vidyād duḥkhasaṃyogaviyogaṃ yogasaṃjñitam |
sa niścayena yoktavyo yogo nirviṇṇacetasā ||23||

Let it be known as Yoga, and that Yoga which is free from sorrow should be attained by the un-despairing and determined mind. ||23||

tam: that; vidyad: let it be known; dukha samyoga viyogam: free from union with sorrow; yoga: union; samnjitam: known as; saha: that; nischayena: determined; yoktavya: should be practiced/ attained; yogo: yoga; anirvinna chetasa: with un– despairing mind.

The practice of meditation with determination to unite with the Self and experience the bliss of the Atman is "Yoga". The end result of union with the Self is also "Yoga".

In this sloka the Lord is talking about the practice and the end result.

The end result is that frame of mind which does not feel any event in life as sorrowful. In a negative way it also includes "any event that produces happiness". This is because the precursor of pain is happiness.

We all know that it is impossible to live without experiencing pain or sorrow in our lives. The reaction to both the past and the present actions give those results.

The seeker may have taken up to meditation and received the guidance for the same from guru and scriptures but he has not cleared the vasanas from the past. The results of these will continue to present themselves at various stages of the sadhana.

The Lord has said:

Sa nischayena: with determination.

Be determined in your efforts and be confident that one day you will achieve the end result, is the advice.

Not just that,

But we are also told:

Yogo'nirvinna chetasaha: (this should be read as yoga anirvinna chetasaha.) anirvinna chetasaha means "with un–despairing mind". During the period of experiencing the pains in life, the seeker should not be despondent. He should not be saying or feeling, "I have been so good in my practice, I have left all attachments in life, why is the Lord still making me experience the painful states in my life?"

With an un–despondent mind and a determined mind the practice of dhyana yoga has to be pursued.

The important word in this sloka is:

Dukha samyoga viyoga:

It means "severance from union with the sorrow." Really speaking the meaning should be read as follows:

"To detach from attachment that produces pain and sorrow".

As we have discussed so many times in the past we should learn to detach from attachment that produces both happiness and sorrow. The detachment should be at the physical, mental and intellectual planes of our existence. "Attach yourself to the Real and learn to bear with the unreal" is the sincere advice to all the seekers. The goal to be achieved by the seeker is to let the mind merge with the Atman, experience Supreme Peace and Bliss and learn to see the Atman all around in all forms of life and in nature. The Atman is not like a material object that is seen by the eyes and heard by the ears, it can only be experienced by intuition. In this context seeing means "experiencing the Atman".

This is the way to practice yoga by the sincere seeker. The message to mankind is:

Be determined in the practice of the yoga of meditation. Do not despair because of upsets in the path of spiritual progress in your life. You are bound to succeed and see the light at the end of the tunnel.

Arjuna had gone into a state of despondency on thinking about the consequences of war. He is asked to practice meditation on what has been said so far. Dhyana is not just sitting in a forest detaching from the world but meditating on the teachings of the Lord and incorporating His advice in daily activities.

सङ्कल्पप्रभवान्कामांस्त्यक्त्वा सर्वानशेषतः |
मनसैवेन्द्रियग्रामं विनियम्य समन्ततः ||24||

saṅkalpaprabhavān kāmāṃs tyaktvā sarvān aśeṣataḥ |
manasaivendriyagrāmaṃ viniyamya samantataḥ ||24||

Abandoning all desires born of sankalpas, completely restraining the entire group of senses with the mind from all sides. ||24||

sankalpa: resolve; prabhavaan: born of; kamaans: desires; sarvaan: all; asheshataha: completely; tyaktvaa: abandoning; manasaa: by the mind; eva: even; indriyagramam: entire group of senses; viniyamya: restraining; samantataha: from all sides.

This and the next sloka elaborate further on the technique of conducting the dhyana yoga.

In this sloka we have been given two techniques to practice.

Abandoning all desires,

Restraining all the senses.

We have discussed several times already about the "desires." Abandoning all the desires is the most important requisite to experience the bliss of the Atman and hence the subject of desires has come up several times and will continue to be repeated in the chapters to come.

Let us recollect the meaning of the word "Moksha":

If one takes it as "having a desire to attain Moksha":

It should be read as:

"The desire at attaining the state of total desire–less–ness".

Desire is, "Longing for the possession of", according to the English dictionary. It is the possession of "that/those" which gives the feeling of happiness. The senses do their duty of bringing in the impulses from the material world to the mind, this is the law of nature and the role of the senses.

The reaction of the mind to what has been brought in, varies from object to object and individual to individual. In the course of time every individual develops his/her own likes and dislikes.

The happiness one experiences from an object, is individual oriented and varies from person to person. It applies to any items like food, jewelry, clothing, partner in life, housing etc.

The mind repeatedly wishing for an object/desired result makes that "the object of desire" for the individual.

In our scriptures we use the word "Sankalpa". "Sankalpa" means "resolve."

"Sankalpa prabhavaan kamaan": desires born of sankalpa.

Tyaktva sarvaan: abandon all. Every seeker who is practicing dhyana yoga is asked to drop all "sankalpas."

Not just abandoning but an adjective is added to it. It is "Aseshataha". "Sesha" means "that which remains." "Asesha" means "nothing remaining."

"Do not have any remains of desires left in you" is the advice for the seeker.

This word "asesha" is the important guhya bhasha to understand. All the desires must be abandoned. Even the desire to attain Moksha must be abandoned. There should not be any trace of likes and dislikes.

In our daily activities we conduct both voluntary and involuntary actions. We cannot survive without conducting actions.

Breathing, circulation, digestion are some of the examples of involuntary actions. We all wish to live and towards this, our autonomic nervous system has been triggered very early in our life and we continue to conduct these actions. They are not desire triggered daily actions anymore.

Similarly towards the task of experiencing the Bliss we should learn to conduct actions as per the Lord's instructions and make these involuntary actions too.

In days gone by they used to say that there should not be any trace of the enemy allowed to survive. They felt that it would give an opportunity for the enemy forces to recoup and get stronger once more.

In the present day context we can say that there should not be any trace of fire left. A spark of fire allowed to remain can turn into great fire and some of the forest fires of recent years can be traced to this cause.

The physicians of today would like to see that there is no trace of any disease left and their patients are totally cured.

Similarly we should practice sincerely, faithfully and with determination so that there should not be any trace of desires left in us. This is because the desires may become the cause for our downfall in the spiritual path.

All desires include both good and bad desires, including the desire to attain Moksha.

The second half of the sloka tells us:

"Restraining the entire group of senses with the mind only from all sides,"

The group of senses: ears, eyes, nose, tongue and the skin are the five sense organs.

On all sides: from every angle of reception for each of the sense organs.

Restraining: the practice of dhyana yoga implies restraint,

This restraint has to be: "entire group of senses" Finally this has to be:

Manasa eva: with the mind only. This is the guhya bhasha in this sloka. All the senses send in the impulses to the mind and this is the organ that should have a total control over all the impulses received from every angle of every sense organ. It is therefore said that one should control the senses by the purity of the mind acquired through discrimination and dispassion.

The question asked by the seekers is "How to control the mind"? This is answered in the next sloka:

> शनैः शनैरुपरमेद् बुद्ध्या धृतिगृहीतया ।
> आत्मसंस्थं मनः कृत्वा न किञ्चिदपि चिन्तयेत् ||25||
>
> **śanaiḥ śanair uparamed buddhyā dhṛtigṛhītayā |**
> **ātmasaṃsthaṃ manaḥ kṛtvā na kiṃcid api cintayet ||25||**
>
> **Slowly and steadily, let him attain quietude by the intellect held firmly, and fixing the mind in Atman, he should not think of anything else. ||25||**
>
> sanaih sanair: slowly and steadily; uparame': attain quietude; buddhaya: with the intellect; dhriti griheetaya: held firmly; atmasamstham: placed in the Self; manaha: the mind; kritva: having made; na: not; kinchid: anything; api: even; chintayet: think of.

The first half of the sloka says,

Slowly and steadily, attain the quietude with the intellect held firmly,

What should be held?

Manaha: of the mind.

The purpose of dhyana is to develop the art of keeping the mind calm. Apart from the time when one is in deep sleep, it is very hard to keep the mind calm. This is because of the input of a number of impulses from the sense organs and the store house of memories within the mind.

Forcible control of the mind is harmful to the body. Its control has to be slow and steady. Regular practice of dhyana over several months/years is needed to achieve the required state of calmness of mind.

A good charioteer is he who uses the reins to gradually slow down the speed of the horses. Any sudden tension on the reins could topple the chariot injuring the passengers.

Similarly, one should not apply the brakes suddenly whilst driving a car, as it could lead to an accident. The Highway Code recommends a safe breaking distance, in relation to the speed of driving. The faster one is driving a car, the longer the time needed to bring it to a halt without any injury to the occupants of the car.

The thoughts in our mind are always running so fast, especially when we want to sit for meditation. The process of controlling the thoughts has to be slow and steady is the advice by the teacher.

The control has to be undertaken by the mind only and the intellect has to guide the mind towards achieving the success. The intellect has to be very firm in its control of the mind.

The perfect example is to be learnt from observing the soldiers in the army. The junior cadets take command from their senior officers and learn to develop perfect discipline. The training makes the cadets good soldiers, who can show the benefit of their disciplined training at times of war.

The second half of the sloka means "let the mind be placed in the Self and not think of anything else".

The seeker is asked to concentrate on the Atman within and nothing else. By constant practice for some part of the day, every day, in course of time he will succeed.

Dhyana as we know is oneness with the object of meditation and dhyana yoga is meditation on the Atman. It is to experience the Peace from within. As the seeker experiences the Peace, he should attempt to keep his mind in that state longer and longer. It should be carried on day after day, every day of his life. Slow and steady wins the race eventually.

Patience is the virtue of a true Dhyana Yogi.

यतो यतो निश्चरति मनश्चञ्चलमस्थिरम् |
ततस्ततो नियम्यैतदात्मन्येव वशं नयेत् ||26||

yato yato niścarati manaś cañcalam asthiram |
tatas tato niyamyaitad ātmany eva vaśaṃ nayet ||26||

Towards whatsoever sense-objects the moving and unsteady mind wanders away, from them all it should be withdrawn and fixed in the Atman. ||26||

yato yato: from whatsoever; nischarati: wanders away; manaha: the mind; chanchalam: restless; asthiram: unsteady; tataha tato: from that; niyamya: having restrained; etad: this; atmany: in the Self; eva: only; vasham: fixed; nayet: bring.

We learnt from the last sloka that the process of controlling the mind has to be slow and steady. There might be some who could misunderstand the sloka and possibly lapse in their practice, thinking that, "it is going to take 'too' longer time to succeed, in experiencing the Peace within. This sloka is to correct such a misunderstanding.

The Lord says,

"From whatever cause the fickle/moving unsteady mind wanders away" (the first half of the sloka):

It is true that the mind is fickle and unsteady. Whenever we try to concentrate on something our mind tends to slip off from concentration by wandering on to some other different object.

What should be done when it wanders away?

The most important thing is to realize that it has wandered away. It should then be restrained from that and should be fixed in the Atman alone.

"Keep a constant vigil on the mind by the intellect and control the same. As soon as it slips off from concentration, bring it back to concentrate on the Atman," we are told. We have to do it again and again and be aware that it would take a long time to bring a perfect control over the mind.

There are two types of people in this world, the ignorant and the non–ignorant. In spiritual terms, the ignorant are those who identify themselves with the mind. Such people do not understand how the mind is wandering away.

The non–ignorant are those who are aware of the instrument of intellect in their body and try to bring it to action at all times. They start questioning their thoughts and learn the art of correcting them. Towards this there is a need for a guide and teacher and a desire to learn.

We can understand this by taking the example of the teacher and students in the class–room.

In the earlier terms and in the earlier years of education, it is natural for the minds of the young students to wander away sometimes, whilst listening to the teacher. Often the teacher uses the word "Attention", sometimes shouting loudly, so as to bring the students attention back to the lesson.

In the latter terms and in senior classes, this is not as necessary, as the students have realized the importance of the lessons and have learnt the art of controlling their wandering minds.

The same law of reasoning applies to those who take up to dhyana yoga.

In the earlier days they should develop the vigil over their mind by the intellect and control it. Once they master the art of concentration their mind does not slip off from the concentration on the Atman. Having realized the fleeting nature of happiness from the objects of the world they move on to experience the everlasting Peace from within.

Control over the mind so that it does not open its "Pandora's box of past memories" is the lesson for the seekers of Dhyana Yoga.

प्रशान्तमनसं ह्येनं योगिनं सुखमुत्तमम् ।
उपैति शान्तरजसं ब्रह्मभूतमकल्मषम् ||27||

praśāntamanasaṃ hy enaṃ yoginaṃ sukham uttamam |
upaiti śāntarajasaṃ brahmabhūtam akalmaṣam ||27||

To this Yogi, whose mind is quiet and peaceful, of subdued rajas, who has become Brahman, free from evil, comes supreme bliss. ||27||

prashanta: tranquil/peaceful; manasa: mind; hy: verily; enam: this; yoginam: yogi; sukham: happiness/bliss; uttamam: supreme; upaiti: comes; shantarajasam: subdued rajas; brahmabhootam: becomes Brahman; akalmasham: free from evil/sin.

The seeker who has practiced the steps enumerated in the last few slokas successfully, will remain peaceful and his mind will be kept quiet.

There are three levels in spiritual progress.

To get up from the state of sleep that includes laziness, indolence etc., one should come out of his tamasic nature. Getting up from the sleep (bed), seeing the beautiful world, the variety in it and becoming active is the first step to take. It is moving from tamas to rajas.

In the process of experiencing the world and enjoying the world, the seeker would go through the pains/sorrows, victory/ defeat and gains/ losses. He experiences happiness and sorrow at different stages in his life. After analyzing the reason for these varied reactions by the study of the sacred texts and from the blessings of the guru, he will need to subdue the rajasic tendency. He has to stop adding more vasanas into his memory bank. (keep mind quiet)

This is the move up to the next stage of satvic rajas.

After moving to higher and higher stages of rajas, he would reach the state of satva (purity).The mind not only remains quiet but is also peaceful.

He is now ready to become one with the object of meditation, i.e.: Brahman. The important word in this sloka is "Akalmasham".

"Kalsmasha" is dirt and "akalmasha" is free from dirt. In this context it refers to the evil tendencies of the six dreaded enemies "desire, anger, greed, delusion, pride/arrogance and enmity."

We can understand it by the following example.

We move into a new house of residence. What do we do first? The house would be dirty to start off.

We, the new owners have to clean the house from top to bottom before moving in.

This makes us happy.

Soon, we would bring in many things that clutter the house and also dirt as such accumulates. If we do not on a regular basis clean the house we would end up by getting health related problems also. This brings unhappiness.

If by constantly keeping in mind this scenario and as recommended by the elders, we maintain regular cleaning habits and do not clutter the house; we would remain peaceful and contented in the house.

Let us now revert back to our body.

It is like the house we moved in to. The jivatman has taken a new body. It will have the previous (Sanchita/past) vasanas. We need to start clearing the mind of the accumulated vasanas.

In the process we should not bring in new vasanas (result of present actions).

If we do not clear the past vasanas and keep on adding more vasanas, our future (Agami/not known) will be painful. But, we will not know our future because of this and hence it is called "Agami" (unknown). We cannot be in peace. We cannot be happy.

If we follow the path of dhyana and keep the mind quiet and peaceful, our tomorrow will be happy and we will be fit to attain union with the Parabrahman. To such a yogi of tranquil mind, of subdued rajas, becoming one with Brahman (by the practice of dhyana yoga), freed from dirt/evil, indeed comes the Supreme Joy.

युञ्जन्नेवं सदाऽऽत्मानं योगी विगतकल्मषः ।
सुखेन ब्रह्मसंस्पर्शमत्यन्तं सुखमश्नुते ||28||

yuñjann evaṃ sadātmānaṃ yogī vigatakalmaṣaḥ |
sukhena brahmasaṃsparśam atyantaṃ sukham aśnute ||28||

Thus, the Yogi free from evil, practicing Yoga, easily attains the highest bliss resulting from contact with Brahman. ||28||

yunjan: practicing yoga; evam: thus; sada: always; atmanam: the self; yogee: yogi; vigata kalmashaha: freed from sin; sukhena: easily; Brahma samsparsham: contact with Brahman; atyantam: infinite; sukham: bliss; ashnute: enjoys/attains.

This sloka is another picture on a new canvas depicting the same scenario but with a few touches added to it with the paint brush.

The seeker should always keep the mind united with the Atman by dhyana yoga and at the same time keep it free from impurity.

The word "sadaa" is the key word in this sloka. In whatever way we are engaged in the day, let us learn to have total concentration on the work and consider the work as dedication to the Lord. After all, every manifestation of life is the Lord in some form or other and so in this spirit every action will become a dedicated act.

After all what is "dedication"? According to the English dictionary, it means, "To give oneself totally to a worthy cause."

Not bringing selfish desires as the motive for work and considering the work as a service to the society/nature, the work becomes a dedicated act. When there is no selfishness in the act, it becomes free from impurity (vigata kalmashaha).

Such a yogi easily realizes Brahman and attains infinite happiness. The practice may feel difficult in the earlier stages and may take several years or even several births to experience the end result. But that yogi who is immersed in the spirit of yoga does not feel it to be a hard practice and enjoys every minute of the dhyana yoga. Brahman is infinite bliss and the yogi practicing thus experiences the bliss. All the experiences of happiness by contact with the objects in the material world have a beginning and an end. The experience of happiness that is ever lasting is "atyantam" and this is only possible by "Brahma samsparsham" which is "Realization of Brahman."

We are given two steps in this sloka to attain Brahman: They are:

The mind has to be:

Free from impurity/selfish thoughts and tendencies and

Brought to dwell in Atman by the practice of dhyana yoga.

Free from evil is purity of mind, body and speech.

Practice of dhyana is "action/karma."

Purity and practice are the two steps to experience and unite with the Supreme.

सर्वभूतस्थमात्मानं सर्वभूतानि चात्मनि ।
ईक्षते योगयुक्तात्मा सर्वत्र समदर्शनः ||29||

sarvabhūtastham ātmānaṃ sarvabhūtāni cātmani |
īkṣate yogayuktātmā sarvatra samadarśanaḥ ||29||

The Yogi harmonised in yoga sees the Self in all beings
and all beings in Me (Self). He sees the same everywhere. ||29||

sarva bhootastham: existing in all beings; Atmanam: the Self; sarva bhootani: all beings; chaatmani: (atmaani cha) and in the Self; ikshate': sees; yoga yuktatma: he, who is harmonised in yoga; sarvatra: everywhere; samadarshanaha: sees the same everywhere.

The purpose of Yoga is to unite with the Supreme. The one who has achieved this unity and remains harmonized with the Supreme at all times is "Yoga yuktatma." What does he see everywhere and how does he perceive the Lord?

This is answered in this sloka.

He sees the Self/Atman in all beings, in all forms of life, in all the varied manifestations of nature.

He sees the entire manifold universe in the Supreme Parabrahman. He sees the Lord in the form of Viswa Roopa."

Let us understand this clearly.

"The Self-referred to here is "Sat, Chit, Ananda" aspect of the Supreme without "Nama, Roopa". It is the Nirakara, Nirguna aspect of the Parabrahman. He does not see the external qualities of the individuals around and does not see them as individuals with name and form. Of course as he has to live in this world, he would be identifying the individuals with names and forms but gives more importance to the Self within them and respects the same. He considers that each individual is a representation of the Divine, for the sole purpose of demonstrating the various qualities, both divine and asuric that are in existence in this world. He will fulfill his role in the stage play, in which he is but an actor with a specific role but he does not let the role get to his head and boost his ego. Even in the animal and plant life, he sees the existence of the divine energy.

His vision of the Lord is that of Viswa Roopa, he sees all forms of life in this universe within the Supreme.

He lives in the total bliss of "Sat, Chit, Ananda".

He recognizes the manifold world as a projection of the Supreme. He only sees the "Eternal Truth" (divine energy) in all.

When one sees the life as man, woman, animal etc. it is called as "Deha Drishti", vision of the external features of the body.

When in the same person he sees father, mother, sister, teacher etc. it is "mano drishti."

Finally by maturity, through the practice of yoga he learns to see the Atman everywhere, it is " Sarva Atma Drishti."

The guhya bhasha in this sloka is "Pashyati". Even though the word means "sees", it is not the seeing with the sense organs but with the intellectual eye of wisdom. He perceives the Supreme and experiences the Supreme everywhere. As the Supreme is bliss, he experiences bliss everywhere. As the Supreme is the "Sat" he sees the "Eternal Truth" everywhere.

To receive the grace of the Lord, we have to acquire the spiritual knowledge, be absolutely pure and develop equal vision.

यो मां पश्यति सर्वत्र सर्वं च मयि पश्यति |
तस्याहं न प्रणश्यामि स च मे न प्रणश्यति ||30||

yo māṃ paśyati sarvatra sarvaṃ ca mayi paśyati |
tasyāhaṃ na praṇaśyāmi sa ca me na praṇaśyati ||30||

He who sees Me everywhere and who sees everything in Me, he never gets separated from Me and I do not get separated from him. ||30||

yo maam: who, Me; pashyati: sees; sarvatra: everywhere; sarvam: everything; cha: and; mayi: in Me; pashyati: sees; tasya: of him; aham: Me, I; na: not; pranashyami: perish/vanish/separated; sa: he; cha: and; Me': Me; na: not; pranashyati: vanishes/ separated/ perishes.

"He who sees Me everywhere and sees everything in Me" is the meaning of the first half of the sloka. It is a reiteration of the meaning of the previous sloka.

Sri Krishna has used the word "Me" three times and "I" once in this sloka. This "Me and I" are different to the "Me, Mine, I and My" used by Arjuna in the first chapter of the Gita. Whereas those words used by Arjuna represented his "ego" in this sloka the words represent "Sat, Chit, Ananda" (Truth, Knowledge and Bliss) of Nirguna, Nirakara Brahman (formless and without qualities) and not Sri Krishna, son of Devaki, Vasudeva, the cow herd boy.

"He" in this context refers to the yogi who has developed the equal vision and sees the Lord everywhere and everything in the Lord.

The guhya bhasha in this sloka is "Pashyati". Literally it means "sees".

In the spiritual context it means "who sees with his intellectual eye of wisdom that transcends the mind and the senses".

When I see a fruit, the difference between a baby who sees the fruit and me is that I know all about that fruit. Similarly when I see a snake I know about it and that its bite may be poisonous and lethal. The difference in the vision of the baby and me is that the baby can see with the physical eye whereas I see it with my understanding of the same.

Likewise, when the individual sees the Lord everywhere in all forms of life and sees all in the Lord he is called a "Yogi" who has succeeded in his efforts to unite with the "Eternal Truth."

What happens to such a yogi is answered in the second half of the sloka.

"He never gets separated from Me and I do not get separated from him" says the Lord in the second half of the sloka.

We have to take it as the Lord's grace on such a yogi. The Lord has no partiality and does not show differentiation due to religion, sex or creed. His grace is bestowed on those who develop such great universal vision and have no trace of "ego" left in their thoughts, actions, and speech.

This vision of "seeing the Lord everywhere and all in the Lord" is known in Vedantic terms as "Sarvatra Sama Drishti" (equal vision in all). Some others say "Sarvam Vishnumayam jagat" (the entire universe is Vishnu and His glory).

Ishavasya Upanisad says "Isavasyam idam sarvam" which means "everything in the universe is pervaded or clothed by the Lord."

The vision is the same in all these statements.

सर्वभूतस्थितं यो मां भजत्येकत्वमास्थितः ।
सर्वथा वर्तमानोऽपि स योगी मयि वर्तते ||31||

sarvabhūtasthitaṃ yo māṃ bhajaty ekatvam āsthitaḥ |
sarvathā vartamānopi sa yogī mayi vartate ||31||

He who worships Me abiding in all beings and who is established in unity, that Yogi abides in Me whatever be his mode of action. ||31||

sarva bhootasthitam: abiding in all beings; yo (read as yah): who; maam: Me; bhajati: worships; ekatvam: in unity; asthitaha: established, sarvatha: in every way; vartamanaha: remaining; api: even; mayi: in Me; vartate: abides.

The first half of the sloka says "He, who worships Me abiding in all beings and who is established in unity."

"He" refers to the yogi who is practicing dhyana yoga, as described so far in this chapter.

He should do so with the clear understanding that the Lord abides in all beings. The Lord has stressed on this point already. We have been told that the seeker has to be established "in unity in diversity." Manifestation of life in the universe is diverse but the essential life principle, "Divine Energy" is the same in all.

The important word in this sloka is "Bhajati". Those who believe in the God principle do conduct worship of the Lord. The method of worship may vary but the act of worship is common to all. The understanding of worship is not clear to many. The majority consider the ritual act of worship as true worship of the deity of their choice.

The act of worship is to please the Lord so that he would bestow His grace on the worshipper. It is impossible to ritually worship the Lord who is abiding in all beings. We can understand by taking the example of our own physical body. The body has so many different parts each doing its specific role to keep the body healthy and they all work in unity. This unity is both in thought and action.

If each of us would conduct the work on this principle the universe would be the happiest place to live and the Lord will be pleased to see that all His creation is happy. This should be the way of worship referred to in this sloka. "Work is worship" and the yogi has to worship the Lord in this spirit.

This point is made clear in the second half of the sloka. "Abides in Me in whatever way he is acting", we are told.

"Bhoota" is past, "Bhavishyat" is future and "Vartamana" is present. "Whatever we are doing now" (present) has to be as per the principle brought out in the first half of the sloka.

We can interpret it as though the reference is to all the four castes of people without differentiation into Brahmana, Kshatriya, Vysya and Sudra. Any one of the four castes of people can take up to meditation in this spirit of "Work is worship" but the work has to be in the spirit of "dedication to the Lord."

Or it would be read also as, "Whatever one is doing now" which refers to "Jnana, Bhakti, Karma, Dhyana". (Study of spiritual science, act of devotion, work and meditation.) Any one of the four ways of yoga are acceptable to the Lord provided one learns to see the Lord in all, strives for universal welfare and does not harm others. "Love all, be kind and friendly to all and such a devotee is the most beloved of Me" says the Lord in chapter 12, which deals specifically on worship.

In this sloka instead he says, "That yogi abides in Me, whatever be his mode of action".

Service to the society is worship of the Lord.

Like the needle in mariner's compass which is always pointing to the north, the mind of the yogi has to be fixed on the Atman (present in all) whatever may be his mode of action at any time in any particular day.

आत्मौपम्येन सर्वत्र समं पश्यति योऽर्जुन ।
सुखं वा यदि वा दुःखं सः योगी परमो मतः ||32||

ātmaupamyena sarvatra samaṃ paśyati yo 'rjuna |
sukhaṃ vā yadi vā duḥkhaṃ sa yogī paramo mataḥ ||32||

He who judges pleasure or pain everywhere by the same standard as he applies to himself, that Yogi is considered to be the highest. ||32||

atmaupanyena: like to his own self; sarvatra: everywhere; samam: equal; pashyanti: sees; yah: who; sukham: pleasure; va: and; yadi: if; dukham: sorrow; sa: he; yogee; yogi; paramo: supreme/highest; mataha: is considered/regarded.

The theory of universal love and compassion is the theme of this sloka.

In this sloka the emphasis is on the reaction of the individual to the events in life. Each one of us goes through so many events every day of our life and experiences the results of those events. Some results/events make us feel happy and others bring sorrow.

How do we react to the pleasure, pains/sorrows of others?

"Others" is a broad word and encompasses the world around. The emphasis of the Lord is on "Universe" as one unit.

Normally we include close family and friends/pets in the circle nearest to us and they become one unit.

Then in order come:

Relatives, colleagues, people in our street, town, district, county, state, country and so on and so forth.

We develop a yard stick in relation to our reaction to pains and pleasures. This yardstick becomes our standard measure. The reaction to the pleasures and pains of our nearest and dearest are almost as near to what we experience ourselves.

He who applies the same yardstick to all the life on earth is the highest, according to the Lord.

He says: "That yogi is the highest, (paramo) it is my opinion. (mataha)".

One can see that the Lord is emphasizing on universal love and affection. This is because the entire universe is His creation. He is both the father and mother of all. As a truly loving parent he feels for all his children.

It is up to us to look upon others in the same way as we look and treat our close family and show the same love and affection to them.

Dhyana yoga is not just meditation but meditation in the form of universal love and affection to one and all. "Let your feeling of the happiness/sorrow of others be the same as your reaction to the results of all events in your life" is the advice to mankind.

The pangs of hunger, bereavement etc. of other people should be of the same nature as his own self. It not only includes humans but other forms of life too. We can say "ahimsa and karuna" (non–injury and compassion) are most dear to our Lord.

"Love others as you love yourself and feel for others as you feel for yourself" and you will be most dear to Me, says the master.

अर्जुन उवाच
योऽयं योगस्त्वया प्रोक्तः साम्येन मधुसूदन ।
एतस्याहं न पश्यामि चञ्चलत्वात् स्थितिं स्थिराम् ||33||

Arjuna uvāca:
yo'yaṃ yogas tvayā proktaḥ sāmyena madhusūdana |
etasyāhaṃ na paśyāmi cañcalatvāt sthitiṃ sthirām ||33||

Arjuna said
O Madhusudhana, this Dhyana Yoga taught by You and attainable by equanimity, I am not able to see any stability on account of unsteadiness of mind. ||33||

yo: which; yam: this; yogas: the yoga; tava: by you; proktam: said; samyena: attainable by equanimity; madhusudhana: slayer of (the demon) madhu; etasya: its; aham: me; na: not; pashyami: see; chanchalatvaat: restlessness/unsteadiness; sthitim: state (of mind); sthiram: steady.

"O slayer of the demon Madhu, which, this yoga taught by you and attainable by the equanimity of the mind": is the meaning of the first half of the sloka.

Arjuna has interrupted the teaching to express a concern of his. His doubt is about the capacity to develop equanimity of the mind.

He is referring to the subject of dhyana taught by Sri Krishna, so elaborately so far. By addressing Krishna as Madhusudhana, Arjuna is indirectly saying, "O Lord, you are an extremely competent warrior and killed the demon Madhu who was so powerful and full of magic tricks. I am sure you will be able to kill my ignorance which like Madhu is playing tricks on my mind and preventing me from clearly understanding what you have taught me so far.

"The subject matter taught by you is not stably retained in the mind because of the nature of my mind which is unstable," Arjuna confesses.

Through this statement, poet sage Veda Vyasa is expressing the concern of the majority of us who have got this weakness inherent in us. Most of our minds are unstable. We get easily distracted. We cannot keep our concentration steadily on any one thing at any one time.

The object of concentration cannot become clear unless the unsteady mind can be retained on the subject in question which is "Meditation on the Atman." But, alas, like monkeys, our mind jumps from one thought to another so fast and dhyana is not an easy option.

Arjuna wants guidance on overcoming this problem and expresses this concern more vividly in the next sloka.

चञ्चलं हि मनः कृष्ण प्रमाथि बलवद्दृढम् |
तस्याहं निग्रहं मन्ये वायोरिव सुदुष्करम् ||34||

cañcalaṃ hi manaḥ kṛṣṇa pramāthi balavad dṛḍham |
tasyāhaṃ nigrahaṃ manye vāyor iva suduṣkaram ||34||

O Krishna, the mind verily is restless, turbulent, strong and unyielding. I think it is as difficult to control as the wind. ||34||

chanchalam: restless; hi: verily; manah: the mind; pramathi: turbulent; balavad: strong; dhruvam: unyielding; tasya: of it; aham: I; nigraham: control; manye: think; vayoh: of the wind; iva: as; sudushkaram: very difficult.

I am not able to understand what you say because of the unsteadiness of my mind, says Arjuna. Control of the mind is as difficult as controlling the force of the wind, he adds.

The subject of dhyana yoga is to teach how to keep the mind firm and steady on the thought of the Atman. By the time one decides to take up this path, he/she would have had a pretty long past. In that process one would have fed the mind with a number of worldly things and made it strong in relation to the association with the objective world. It is difficult to change overnight its path and concentrate on to the Atman within.

The seeker would experience severe restlessness in his attempts to remain in continuous meditation. The stored vasanas are like the objects kept in a large trunk. The trunk is so full and its contents are like springs, trying to spring out at every opportunity. On top of that the input of impulses from sense organs adds to the contents of the trunk which is the store house. It defies all attempts to bring it under control. The interest constantly shifts from one object to the other. Hence, the use of adjectives "chanchalam and dushkaram."

We all know how strong the wind is. Gale force winds are so strong and cause great havoc. All attempts by man to control such forces are futile. Hence the Lord has used the word "Vayo'riva". "Dushkaram" means "difficult" and "sudushkaram" is "extremely difficult." We all know the idiom "The lazy mind is a devil's workshop" and Arjuna's concern brings out the true meaning of this idiom.

Arjuna was an excellent student and hence Krishna selected him to receive the teaching. We can understand it by the words he has used and must learn the ways to react with our teachers.

He says:

Aham Manyate': I think.

He admits to his position of ignorance and so says "I think so". He is getting the upadesha from the master and is on a lower platform to that of the teacher. The humble nature of Arjuna is brought out by this word. Any sincere seeker has to develop this quality if he wants to make any progress in his efforts to take up the study of the sacred text and implement the teachings in his life.

It is interesting to know another meaning of the word "Krishna" which fits in with the title for this chapter "Dhyana Yoga."

"Krish" means, to "Plough and process." "na" means "The Lord of".

The teachings of Krishna are to assist the seeker in taming and controlling the mind. Krishna is the Lord who guides us to plough and process the mind.

श्री भगवानुवाच
असंशयं महाबाहो मनो दुर्निग्रहं चलं ।

अभ्यासेन तु कौन्तेय वैराग्येण च गृह्यते ||35||

Śrībhagavān uvāca:
asañśayaṃ mahābāho mano durnigrahaṃ calam |
abhyāsena tu kaunteya vairāgyeṇa ca gṛhyate ||35||

The Lord said:
O Mahabaho, doubtless the mind is restless and difficult to control. But by practice, O' son of Kunti, and by dispassion it is controlled. ||35||

asamshayam: doubtless; mahabaho: mighty armed; mano: the mind; durnigraham: difficult to control; chalam: restless; abhyasena: by practice; tu: but; Kounteya: son of Kunti; vairagyena: by dispassion; cha: and; gruhyate: is controlled.

Sri Krishna readily agrees with His disciple's statement. He confirms that the mind is restless and difficult to control.

Mahabaho' means "mighty armed." Arjuna was a powerful well trained warrior. Physically he was strong but alas he could not control the forces in his own mind. Krishna wants him to become a mental Mahabahu and fight the army of enemy forces in his own mind that are hindering the spiritual progress.

Nigraham: difficult to control. Nigraha is control and durnigraha is impossible to control.

A true warrior does not run away on seeing the strength of the enemy forces but with the advice from his ministers and commander–in–chief finds ways to combat the enemy forces. The test to find the power of the true warrior is in his capacity to overcome the toughest obstacles in the battle.

Sri Krishna, as a teacher and guide has therefore given the means to overcome the problem. In a nutshell he gives two methods to control the powerful tendencies of the mind.

They are:

Abhyasena: by practice,

Vairagyena: by dispassion.

By these two methods the mind can be:

Gruhyate: is restrained/controlled.

Let us analyze the word "Abhyasa." In simple words it means "Practice." How does it apply to the mind?

The mind is a powerful instrument of ours. The impulses received and analyzed by the mind about the objective world makes the mind develop likes and dislikes. These become the precursors of our actions and indirectly we develop a certain nature. Our nature is nothing but the sum total of our habits. We have given in to the demands of our mind from childhood and developed so many habits, some good and some bad. Abhyasa is an attempt to change our nature.

We can take the example of sportsmen around the world. They are different from others in that they develop a number of good disciplines in their life. As part of their training they change their habits and practice with a strict regime of discipline. Eventually some of them become great sportsmen and win medals in championship games/sports.

By sowing the seeds of good habits and nurturing the seeds sown with love and affection one can gradually change his/her nature. The parents of the child are good examples. Through several years of love and dedication they change the restless mind of their child so that their child can become a good member of the society he/she lives in. A spiritual guide/guru could do miracles in assisting the disciple to change the habits and develop capacity to meditate on the Åtman.

As parents if we can make our children get up early, brush their teeth, wash and pray and develop that into a habit. Later on it should become a way of life for the child when he/she grows up.

Abhyasa/practice by the blessings of learned elders/teachers/guru will undoubtedly help the individual to change for the better.

Why is mind restless?

Because of the likes/dislikes the mind starts running after objects. The stronger the attachment, that much more difficulty there is in weaning off from such attachment. There is a strong need to put down the force of passion and thereby control the mind. Discrimination between right/wrong, good/bad will eventually win the battle and the mind can be made to sit in meditation on the Atman.

Detachment from attachment is "Vairagya." This detachment we have learnt before has to be:

From attachment to the objects around and to the fruits of action.

Do not seek for the illusory painful pleasures and instead go in search of the Eternal Peace is the message from the Lord to sincere seekers.

असंयतात्मना योगो दुष्प्राप इति मे मतिः ।
वश्यात्मना तु यतता शक्योऽवाप्तुमुपायतः ||36||

asaṃyatātmanā yogo duṣprāpa iti me matiḥ |
vaśyātmanā tu yatatā śakyo 'vāptum upāyataḥ ||36||

It is my view that Yoga is not attainable by one whose mind is not controlled. But the self-controlled, striving, can attain it by proper means. ||36||

asamyatatmana: man of uncontrolled mind (self); yogo: yoga; dushprapya: not attainable; iti: thus; me': My; matihi: opinion; vashyatmana: self–controlled; tu: but; yatata: striving; shakyaha: possible; shakyovaptum: possible to obtain; upayataha: by proper means.

In the first half of the sloka we get the reiteration of the fact that union with the Atman is not possible to those whose mind is not controlled.

He uses the word: Me' mataha.

let us understand that the Vedas are the authoritative source and Sri Krishna is the Universal master giving the sacred text to the mankind in a simple language to understand and follow.

How do we control the mind?

In the last verse we have an answer to this question. It is "Abhyasa and Vairagya."

He says:

It is possible to obtain by he who has self–control and is striving to unite with the Atman. This has to be skillful action.

Be skillful in your efforts and strive for attaining the end result which is "union with the Atman" is the message for the earnest seekers.

Let us take the example of two great heroes who climbed the Mount Everest, Edmund Hilary and Ten–Sing. How did they succeed in the mission?

They undertook "Abhyasa" and developed disinterest in everything else. Their aim was to climb the peak of the Mount Everest. They strived several years and put in a hard practice regime to achieve the end result.

They used the skill to combat the adverse weather and altitude problems. Towards it, they got instructions from specialists and collected specialist tools recommended by the masters. With faith, devotion, single minded concentration and guidance from the right sources they reached the peak.

We see in war zones during battle, sometimes the commanders strategically withdraw from the front, regroup and proceed further again. They use all their skills in achieving victory.

This is what we have to understand from this sloka. We should be skillful in controlling the mind and not by authoritative use of the intellect. We must develop techniques to slowly divert the mind from the phenomenal world towards the internal spiritual world.

The mothers skillfully give item "a" to take away item "b" from their children.

The process of transforming an enemy into a friend is not easy but possible. The mind which could be an enemy in our progress spiritually, should be made to become a friend. After all, it is only the mind that can lead us to the Supreme and all other organs are only tools to help in the process.

अयतिः श्रद्धयोपेतो योगाच्चलितमानसः |
अप्राप्य योगसंसिद्धिं कां गतिं कृष्ण गच्छति ||37||

Arjuna uvāca:
ayatiḥ śraddhayopeto yogāc calitamānasaḥ |
aprāpya yogasaṃsiddhiṃ kāṃ gatiṃ kṛṣṇa gacchati ||37||

Arjuna said:
Though possessing faith, yet uncontrolled, what end does the Yogi whose mind falls from Yoga, meet if he departs without attaining perfection in Yoga? ||37||

ayati: uncontrolled; sraddhaya: by faith; upetaha: possessed; yogaat: from yoga; chalita: falls/wanders away: manasaha: the mind; aprapya: not having attained; yogasamsiddhi: perfection in yoga; kaam: which; gatim: end; gachati: meets.

Herein we have a very interesting question from Arjuna. It also applies to those faithful seekers who are practicing yoga, whose minds are still unfortunately strong and mischievous. They slip frequently in their practice and are carried away by worldly desires. Arjuna is asking if such a yogi meets his death before succeeding in his spiritual efforts, where will he go next.

Yati is he who has controlled the mind and "Ayati" is the seeker who has not controlled the mind.

"The seeker practicing yoga with faith and not totally managing to get the mind under control" is the meaning of the first quarter of the sloka.

The purpose of yoga is to get the mind under control and not deviate from the chosen path.

Every seeker has a past and would not know what he did in his past birth/births including the past period in this present birth.

He has developed interest in yoga now, (the present) and faithfully started to practice.

He has a future and he does not know it.

Chalita manasaha: whose mind falls from yoga before attaining perfection. This applies to the yogi practicing yoga with faith, who has not totally managed to get the mind under control.

"Having fallen away" means having failed to keep the mind under control and succumbed to the temptations of the world. This is the meaning of the second quarter of the sloka.

Because he has not attained total perfect control of the mind, the mind succumbs to the impulses received from the world around. Or the memory bank opens up and gives distraction, deviating the concentration from the Atman.

This is the meaning of the third quarter of the sloka.

"O Krishna, what fate does such a person meet?" is the question that is in the last quarter of the sloka.

What will happen to such a yogi? Where does he go next?

Will all his efforts be futile?

Has he to start afresh his spiritual practice all over again?

Everyone wants happiness (Ananda) in life.

Arjuna wanted "Brahmananda" and in the process denied "Dehananda." If he meets death before experiencing "Brahmananda", alas, he never had any happiness in life.

Could this be right?

Arjuna is seeking answers for this question.

"Death is just another event in one's life" is the Hindu philosophy. The Hindus believe in a series of cycles of births and deaths that culminate one fine day in the individual attaining union with the Brahman. Every individual has a birth right to attain salvation. Yesterday is dead and tomorrow is yet to come. Every second we die and every second we are reborn. These are all links in a chain.

Our philosophy says,

"Tomorrow is nothing but a continuation of yesterday but modified by the thoughts and actions of today".

कच्चिन्नोभयविभ्रष्टश्छिन्नाभ्रमिव नश्यति ।
अप्रतिष्ठो महाबाहो विमूढो ब्रह्मणः पथि ।।38।

kacchin nobhayavibhraṣṭaś chinnābhram iva naśyati |
apratiṣṭho mahābāho vimūḍho brahmaṇaḥ pathi ||38||

O Mahabaho, not established in Yoga, and deluded in the path of Brahman, fallen from both, does he not perish like a rent cloud? ||38||

kachit: is it that? na: not; ubhaya vibhrashta: fallen from both; chinna: rent/separated from; abhram: cloud; iva: like; nashyati: perishes; apratishtaha: supportless; vimoodaha: deluded; Brahmanaha: of Brahman; pathi: in the path.

In continuation of the theme of doubt that has cropped up in his mind, Arjuna is now using an example of clouds.

The purpose of the clouds is to shower the rains on earth. A thick, heavy mass of dark clouds foretell a heavy rainfall.

It so happens sometimes, a great gust of wind blows from nowhere and breaks the thick mass of clouds into small clouds which disappear into oblivion soon.

The small clouds that remain after the passing of the wind and which disappear into oblivion are called as "rent clouds." The Sanskrit word for it is "Chinnabhram".

These rent clouds fail to bring the rainfall and on top of that, disappear soon. They lose their distinctiveness as clouds.

An individual takes up to yoga under the spiritual guidance from the masters and the sacred texts. He gathers all his senses under control and concentrates with vigor on the Atman and takes up to the path of meditation.

In the process, he has sacrificed the sense pleasures so that he can experience the "Joy" of the union with the Atman within.

All his thoughts on the Atman are joined together and formed into thick clouds ready to bring in a mass shower of "Joy". But, alas, one of the sense pleasures/vasanas stored in the mind suddenly comes out in gusto and like a gust of strong wind,the thought on the Atman gets shattered.

So, in the present world of strict control and spiritual sadhana, the seeker who repressed all his worldly pleasures for the sake of "Eternal Joy" failed in living the life of pleasures here and failed in experiencing the pleasures hereafter.

He failed in experiencing "Swarga"—heavenly pleasures, and
He failed in attaining "Moksha"—Eternal Joy.

He failed in getting the pleasures from both worlds, the temporary pleasures of the present and the eternal joy of the hereafter.

This is Arjuna's doubt.

Whom should Arjuna approach for an answer?

He addresses this issue to Sri Krishna in the next sloka.

एतन्मे संशयं कृष्ण छेत्तुमर्हस्यशेषतः ।
त्वदन्यः संशयस्यास्य छेत्ता न ह्युपपद्यते ||39||

etan me saṃśayaṃ kṛṣṇa chettum arhasy aśeṣataḥ |
tvadanyaḥ saṃśayasyāsya chettā na hy upapadyate ||39||

O Krishna, you ought to dispel my doubt completely. I cannot indeed get another like you fit enough to clear it. ||39||

yetan me': this, my; samshayam: doubts; chettum: dispel; arhasy: competent; aseshataha: without any trace, (completely); tvat: than thou; anyaha: others; samshayasya: of doubt; asya: of this; chettaha: dispeller; na: not; hi: verily; upapadyate: is fit.

O Krishna, you are the competent person to dispel this, my doubt completely, says Arjuna. He adds another adjunctive in the second half of this sloka.

He says: "To dispel my doubt, there is no other fit like you".

This statement from Arjuna confirms the faith and devotion he had in the guru he had selected to take shelter and guidance from during the peak period of depression when facing the force of the enemy in the battlefield. The depression had made him blind to the reality.

This should be the attitude of the sincere seeker. First of all he should find the competent guru to dispel his ignorance. He should with full faith approach the guru and request for guidance and compassion.

Let us make it clear that there was no selfishness on the part of Arjuna. He was not showering praises to get what he wanted. He had genuine belief that Sri Krishna is the only person to clear his doubts. As we proceed further in the chapters to come, we will find that Arjuna is making the statement to the effect that Krishna is none other than the Supreme Iswara Himself. Who other than the topmost person is competent to answer his questions?

Indirectly, we should understand that pride and arrogance are not to be expressed in front of God, guru and elders.

श्री भगवानुवाच
पार्थ नैवेह नामुत्र विनाशस्तस्य विद्यते ।
नहि कल्याणकृत्कश्चिद्दुर्गतिं तात गच्छति ||40||

Śrībhagavān uvāca:
pārtha naiveha nāmutra vināśas tasya vidyate |
na hi kalyāṇakṛt kaścid durgatiṃ tāta gacchati ||40||

The Lord said,
O Partha, neither in this world, nor in the next world is there destruction for him. O my son, never indeed anyone who does good ever comes to grief. ||40||

Partha: Arjuna; na eva: (naiva) verily not; iha: here; namutra: not in the next world; vinashas: destruction; tasya: of him; vidyate: is; na: not; hi: verily; kalyanakrit: he who does good; kaschid: anyone; durgatim: grief; taata: o my son; gachati: goes.

"O Arjuna, neither here nor in the next world there is destruction of him", is Krishna's answer to Arjuna's questions (sloka 37.38.39).

This sloka reiterates Krishna's assertion that there is life after death. The Vedas declare that the life is a series of births and deaths till the individual attains final union with the Brahman. They also admit that it is not easy and takes several births to achieve final salvation.

He who has been good by taking up to sincere spiritual practice will reap its benefit. He will find the benefit in his future life if by chance he leaves his mortal body in the middle of the spiritual efforts he puts in.

O My son, listen, anyone who does good verily not comes to grief, he adds.

This applies to any individual who is conducting actions of welfare. The Lord is not just referring the seeker following the path of dhyana but all the other three paths of "Karma, Jnana and Bhakti." Conducting duties following any of these paths come under "kalyanakrit".

If you are engaged in good work, if you have failed to achieve perfection in this life, you will not suffer destruction, says Jagadguru. This is the blessings of compassion by the Lord to all sincere seekers.

प्राप्य पुण्यकृतां लोकानुषित्वा शाश्वतीः समाः |
शुचीनां श्रीमतां गेहे योगभ्रष्टोऽभिजायते ||41||

prāpya puṇyakṛtāṃ lokān uṣitvā śāśvatīḥ samāḥ |
śucīnāṃ śrīmatāṃ gehe yogabhraṣṭo 'bhijāyate ||41||

The Yogi who has fallen from Yoga, attains the worlds of the good, and having lived there for many years, is born in the house of the pure and prosperous. ||41||

prapya: having obtained; punya kritaam: attainable by the good; lokaan: the worlds; ushitva: having lived there; sashvateehi: many; samaaha: years; shucheenaam: of the pure; srimataam: of the prosperous; gehe': the house; yogabrashto: one fallen from the yoga; abhijaayate': is born.

The Lord is now tracing for us the path taken by the yogi who dies without attaining perfection in yoga.

The first half of the verse describes the immediate sphere the departed soul (of the yogi) would enter.

The departed soul enters the worlds of good and stays there for many years.

We get the confirmation that there are many higher spheres above the sphere of earth and all these are attainable by the conduct of good actions while one is resident on the earth which is the "Karma Bhoomi" (place for conducting actions).

Depending on the meritorious points accumulated by action conducted on earth, the departed soul enters into any of the higher lokas.

We know that the life span gets longer and longer as one traces the life span from lower to the higher lokas. The life span in Satya loka is the longest and the life on earth is the shortest. Humans live for about 100yrs on earth and in higher lokas for thousands of years. (It is the view of the spiritual seers)

What sort of human birth these yogis get is described in the second half of the sloka.

"Is born in the house of the pure and prosperous."

The Lord is full of compassion, especially on those who do take up acts of "welfare (Kalyana)". The yogi who has conducted acts of welfare after completing the stay in the higher lokas is born in the house of the pure and prosperous.

We can see that the Lord is giving further opportunity to continue the sadhana. This is much easier if the new family in which a yogi is given his next birth, are righteous and live the life of purity. The atmosphere in such family will be congenial for shaping the mind of a young child.

Acts of pure living like getting up early, conducting the daily rituals, partaking in prayers, reading sacred texts, acts of welfare etc. are undertaken in the house of the pure. The newborn is soon guided into that path.

It is interesting to note the Lord uses the words, "Pure and Prosperous". Of these, "pure" is first and "prosperous" is next.

There are different types of prosperity like wealth, health and knowledge. It does not apply to only to the material wealth. One way of understanding the word "prosperity" is where the basic needs of life are met and there is no struggle for survival. It is a well known fact that the priority of a hungry man and a man without shelter are to get food and a place of residence. The immediate priorities of such a person are these two.

By giving the birth in the house of pure and prosperous to the yoga bhrashta, Parabrahman is making sure that the new birth would lead quickly the continuation of the spiritual discipline and the reaching of better heights of progress.

अथवा योगिनामेव कुले भवति धीमताम् |
एतद्धि दुर्लभतरं लोके जन्म यदीदृशम् ||42||

athavā yoginām eva kule bhavati dhīmatām |
etad dhi durlabhataraṃ loke janma yad īdṛśam ||42||

Or, he is even born in the family of the wise Yogis. This kind of birth is indeed very difficult to attain. ||42||

athava: or; yoginaam: of the yogis; eva: even; kule': in the family; bhavati: is born; dheemataam: of the wise; etad: this; hi: verily; durlabhataram: very difficult; loke': in the world; janma: birth; yat: which; eedrusham: like this.

The last sloka is about the spiritual seekers in general who take up to yoga but meet death before making great strides in their efforts.

This sloka is of those yogabhrastas who have already made great strides in their spiritual discipline.

Athava: or—by using this word the Lord is referring to the advanced yogis.

The seeker is born in the house of the wise yogis. The wise as we have learnt before are those who have mastered the art in making use of their intellect which is guided by the Antaratma.

Why? What is the benefit from such a birth?

The wise yogis would act as gurus and guide the yoga bhrashta (in his new birth) from very early in life towards the practice of yoga.

Verily, the birth like this/this kind of birth in this world is very difficult, says the Jagadguru.

Sri Krishna is making it clear that most of the people in this world are orientated towards the physical world in their outlook and very few really take up to serious attempts at uniting with the Parabrahman. But, he admits that such yogis do exist. In His great compassion to the faithful, sincere and devoted seekers, He promises birth in a family of yogis.

It is a fact that great men of spiritual realization are born in the family of those who have conducted great acts of tapas.

We can see that the Lord is giving every opportunity to complete the practice of yoga as quickly as possible for the sincere seekers.

तत्र तं बुद्धिसंयोगं लभते पौर्वदेहिकम् ।
यतते च ततो भूयः संसिद्धौ कुरुनन्दन ||43||

tatra taṃ buddhisaṃyogaṃ labhate paurvadehikam |
yatate ca tato bhūyaḥ saṃsiddhau kurunandana ||43||

O Arjuna, being born in the family of Yogis, he comes to be united with the knowledge acquired in his previous birth, and again strives for perfection in Yoga. ||43||

tatra: there; tam: that; buddhisamyogam: union with knowledge; labhate: obtains; pourva dehikaam: acquired in his former body; yatate: strives; cha: and; tataha: than that; bhuyaha: more; samsiddhou: for perfection; Kurunandana: o son of Kurus

In continuation of the last sloka, Sri Krishna says that the yogabrhashta is not only born in a family of yogis but is going to be blessed with unity with the knowledge acquired in the past birth. We need to expand on this to understand its significance.

Each one of us has a past, present and future. In this sloka we are told about our future after the death of the present body.

It is evident that we do not carry the gross physical body with us to the next birth. Nama and roopa (name and form) will be totally different and we do not remember our past names, forms etc.

At death the subtle body consisting of the mind and intellect with the causal body (Atman) moves to the Moola prakriti awaiting further journey.

What we do in the next birth is influenced by the stored vasanas.

But, inadvertently in the new birth we get so quickly trapped by the new surroundings and instead of trying to empty the stored vasanas we get caught in the web of the new life and its contacts.

The subtle body not only carries the mind but also the intellect. The intellect is next to the divinity/Antaratman. It is constantly talking to us in its own language but we do not take notice of it. The mind is so busy receiving the impulses from the world around that it becomes deaf to its own Antaratma's talk.

The prologue so far is to bring the readers, to the main point of this sloka and understand it clearly.

Tatra: there (in the family of yogis)

The first half of the sloka reads as,

"Being born in the family of the yogis, he gets yogic intellect pertaining to the previous birth."

The important word is "Buddhi samyogam."

The subtle body of the yoga bhrashta carried with it the intellect which had guided the mind in the previous birth towards the path of yoga. The mind of that subtle body was united with the intellect and not to the gross world around in the previous birth. That intellect was in close contact with the "Antaratma" and hence comes to be designated as "Buddhi". (When the intellect gets clouded by ahamkara it is designated as "Durbuddhi" which is perverted intelligence)

The life of the yoga bhrashta in the previous birth was that of yoga and unity with the Atman within. The Lord says that in the new birth the seeker not only is born in the family of yogis but is also united with the intellect from the past which guides him to:

"Strive again for perfection in yoga".

We can understand this by taking examples of students in schools and colleges.

Let us say that Balu was in class 8 and had to move to another city with his parents. If he was a sincere and clever student, the head teacher in the new school would assess his capacity and let him join in class 9. Being a clever student and sincere in his attempts, he would remember what he was taught in the previous school and continue where he left. He would make rapid progress in the new environment.

On the other hand, if he got caught in the city life, new friends etc. his progress might be hindered. He may fail miserably and either stay in the same class the next year or get demoted.

The Balu who would get promoted to the new higher class is he who was blessed to be in a suitable environment and make use of his buddhi, remembered the lessons from the past classes and continued where he had left.

The Balu, who would be demoted or fail would not have used the buddhi, not remembered the past lessons and got caught in the new worldly life.

The same scenario applies to the yogabrhashta. The Lord would bless him to make use of his buddhi and carry on from where he had left his spiritual practice in the previous birth.

What we have to understand from these slokas is that we are the makers of our own destiny. We reap what we sow, so let us therefore sow the seeds of good habits, so that whatever happens to this body, in the next birth we can carry those good seeds and get a better start in life.

Let us also remember that good and bad, knowledge and ignorance follow us from birth to birth. As nothing that is done goes to waste, let us do Japa, tapas, dana, dharma as enshrined in the scriptures and strive for unity with the Parabrahman quickly.

पूर्वाभ्यासेन तेनैव ह्रियते ह्यवशोऽपि सः ।
जिज्ञासुरपि योगस्य शब्दब्रह्मातिवर्तते ||44||

pūrvābhyāsena tenaiva hriyate hy avaśopi saḥ |
jijñāsur api yogasya śabdabrahmātivartate ||44||

By the force of practice in the past births, he is drawn to Yoga without volition. Though desirous only of the knowledge of Yoga, he transcends beyond Shabdabrahma. ||44||

purvabhyasena: former practice; tena: by that; eva: verily; hriyate: is borne; avasho: helpless; api: even; yogasya: of yoga; shabda brahma: word Brahman; ativartate: goes beyond.

The result of past practices is highlighted in this sloka. The stronger the tendencies from the past birth, will mean it is easier to proceed in the path taken before. The yogi who has reached degree levels in his past birth, would find the path easier to proceed. (Like proceeding further to post–graduate studies and to Post–Doctorate studies).

The fish take to water very quickly and the bird takes to air so fast. Similarly for the yogi who has strived hard in the previous births to unite with the Brahman the effort has not been a waste. He would quickly reach higher levels of yogic practice in the new life and be that much nearer to uniting with the Brahman.

"He, by the practice from past births is drawn without volition" says the first part of the sloka.

"Drawn to where" is the question? This is answered in the second half of the sloka. "Even though desirous of knowledge of the Vedas, he transcends the Vedas" says Bhagawan.

We have to understand the word "Shabdabrahma" clearly. "Shabda" means "Sound".

Scripturally speaking, Parabrahman desirous of creating the life on earth first produced the sound, the sound being "OM". This, they say, pervaded the entire space.

Shabdabrahma refers to the Vedas created by the Parabrahman. The Vedas are considered as "Srutis" which means, "those that are heard." They were sounds produced by Parabrahman which were heard by the great rishis during intense meditation in search of the answer for "who am I, where do I come from, where does the body go after death etc."

What does he transcend?

In this context there are two explanations given by the learned scholars.

One school of thought says that "Shabdabrahma" refers to the fruits of actions that are described in karma kanda of the Vedas. According to this explanation, the yogi referred to in these slokas moves straight forward to Upasana Kanda and Jnana Kanda of the Vedas and is that much nearer to uniting with the Parabrahman.

It takes several births to really understand karma kanda and live such a life on earth and the yogi will not go through the births needed to complete the study of karma kanda of the Vedas.

The second school of thought says that "Shabdabrahma" means "Indirect knowledge arising from the study of the scriptures."

Whatever that comes from the study of the texts is still only indirect knowledge. One has to put the theory into practice to proceed further in life. The seeker has to move from Jnana to Vijnana (theory to practice; knowledge to wisdom) which is the theme for the next chapter.

By the sincere and dedicated practice of yoga, the yogi will develop wisdom and soon unites with the Parabrahman, is the explanation from the second school of thought.

Even though initially the seeker started study of the Vedas with a desire to know the Vedas, (Jijnasurapi) by his dedicated practice he proceeds further in his studies and practice but meets death and this is described as yogabhrashta in this chapter. Such a seeker will be given a birth in a family of the pure and prosperous and will reap the benefit given in this sloka.

प्रयत्नाद्यतमानस्तु योगी संशुद्धकिल्बिषः ।
अनेकजन्मसंसिद्धस्ततो याति परां गतिम् ||45||

prayatnād yatamānas tu yogī saṃśuddhakilbiṣaḥ |
anekajanmasaṃsiddhas tato yāti parāṃ gatim ||45||

The yogi who is practicing sincerely and hard, having acquired perfection through many births attains supreme state purified of all sins. ||45||

prayatnaad: with practice; yatamanaha: striving; tu: but; yogee: the yogi; samshuddha kilbhishaha: purified from sins; aneka janma samsidhi: perfected through many births; tataha: then; yaati: reaches; paramam: supreme; gatim: path.

It is true that if we want to acquire something we have to practice sincerely the ways of acquiring the same. For the majority it is not just practicing sincerely but also trying hard to acquire. Of course it goes without saying that one needs knowledge to acquire what one wants. It may take a long time to succeed in our efforts.

The young children who go to school to acquire knowledge have to try hard and sincerely to understand the subject, get good grades in exams, go to higher studies and become graduates. On an average, from kindergarten days to getting a degree it would take about 20 yrs or so.

There is no quick and easy way to success. Success needs planning and determination. With the blessings of the Lord success will come eventually.

Similarly in spiritual studies, to acquire knowledge of the scriptures is the first step and achieving Moksha is the next step. It takes a lot of practice and determination to get the knowledge and takes still longer to achieve salvation.

Because of the vasanas from several births and the input of impulses from the world around that bring happiness or sorrow the process of acquiring spiritual knowledge takes a long time for an average individual. Many of the seekers probably are mature adults but are only beginner students in the path of yoga.

It is therefore not possible for the majority to achieve salvation in the present birth. It takes several births, says the Lord. Clearing all the stored vasanas is to be known as the process of purifying all sins. Not accumulating new vasanas is also a process of purifying the sins.

We should be prepared to wait for several births and not get disappointed if the success does not come in this birth.

Human weakness is that we want the results to be seen and experienced now, in this birth itself.

Just like the example of a student, even a businessman needs to work sincerely and hard for several years to enjoy the benefits of profits.

Hence the sloka says:

But, the yogi striving hard, achieving perfection through several births. The guhya bhasha is "Tu" which means "but".

The yogi may be striving hard but has to develop perfection through several births.

Striving hard and putting all the best efforts is not enough to produce the results now.

It takes several births.

It is not just the physical birth and death the Lord is referring to, but to many births and deaths of experiences in life.

Every experience will either purify or add impurities to it.

Another word of importance is "tataha".

Only then (what was described in the first half)

Purified of all sins, he attains the Supreme State (Salvation).

Let us not forget what the Lord has said in the previous sloka:

He has said that good done in the past does not go to waste. He will see that the seeker would get the proper environment to continue where he left in the previous birth.

Just to summarize, the three conditions to experience freedom from births and deaths (salvation) are:

Sincere striving, continuously practicing and developing Purity.

Let all sincere seekers understand the importance of this statement and implement the advice in their efforts and be assured that they will be rewarded in due course.

तपस्विभ्योऽधिको योगी ज्ञानिभ्योऽपि मतोऽधिकः ।
कर्मिभ्यश्चाधिको योगी तस्माद्योगी भवार्जुन ||46||

tapasvibhyo 'dhiko yogī jñānibhyo 'pi mato 'dhikaḥ |
karmibhyaś cādhiko yogī tasmād yogī bhavārjuna ||46||

The Yogi is thought to be greater than the ascetic, even superior to men of knowledge. He is also superior to men of action. Therefore, strive to be a Yogi, O Arjuna. ||46||

tapaswibhyadiko: superior than ascetics; yogee: yogi; jnanibhyo: than the wise; api: even; mataha: opinion; adhikaha: superior; karmibhyaha: than the men of action; cha: and; adhikaha: superior; tasmaat: therefore; yogee: a yogi; bhava: be; Arjuna: Arjuna.

The aim of spiritual study and life is to unite with the Atman within and realize the presence of Parabrahman in every form of life in this universe. Having achieved the unity it is then imperative that the seeker expresses the divinity within via speech, thoughts and action. Thus comes about the welfare of life on earth. This is the end result of becoming a true yogi mentioned in this sloka. This chapter is "Dhyana yoga" and the emphasis is on "Dhyana."

As a matter of fact the Lord while dealing with specific chapters like Jnana, Karma, Bhakti has stressed in those chapters the superiority of that path in relation to others. Let us not misunderstand this statement. Every path is important and superior in its own way for the people who have that temperament.

It is the temperament of the individual that takes him/her to a particular path.

True dhyana yoga is about total meditation (dhyana) in whatever path one takes. Dhyana/meditation while conducting karma as per the instructions in chapter 3, worshipping as described in chapter 12 and scriptural studies also makes such a seeker a true yogi.

In this sloka we are told the yogi is:

Superior to ascetic: it is commonly understood that an ascetic is one who does intense tapas that involves voluntary mortification of the body. By doing so he is said to please the devas who come down from their celestial abode and grant boons. Certainly the yogi is far superior to such an ascetic who conducts penance for celestial powers and enjoyment.

The Gita tells us that real tapas is all about purification of speech, thoughts and actions.

Superior to men of knowledge: here the knowledge referred to is the study of the Vedas and Upanishads. Just a theoretical knowledge of the Vedas is certainly not superior to the way of life of a yogi. Knowledge acquired from the study of the sastras has to match with efforts to implement the teaching in day to day life.

Superior to man of action: here the reference is to karma kanda of the Vedas. The men of action referred to, are those who study the karma kanda of the Vedas and conduct actions like worship of the fire etc.

Tapswibhy adhiko: superior to ascetic
Jnanibhyo'pi: superior to men of knowledge
Mata: view
Karmibhyascha adhiko: superior to men of action
Finally the Lord says:
Tasmaat yogee bhavarjuna:
Therefore be a yogi, O Arjuna.
Even though it is not a command, the Lord prefers His disciple to be a yogi in its truest sense as described so far in this chapter.
Karma: union between men and entire humanity.
Dhyana: union between the lower self and Higher Self.
Bhakti: union between the individual and his God of Love.
Jnana: union of all existence.

योगिनामपि सर्वेषां मद्गतेनान्तरात्मना |
श्रद्धावान्भजते यो मां स मे युक्ततमो मतः ||47||

yoginām api sarveṣāṃ madgatenāntarātmanā |
śraddhāvān bhajate yo māṃ sa me yuktatamo mataḥ ||47||

Even among all the Yogis, he who worships Me with mind fixed in Me, full of faith, is deemed to be the most devout. ||47||

Yoginaam : among the yogis; Api: even; Sarveshaam: all; madgatena: merged in Me; antaratmana: with inner Self; sraddhavaan: endued with faith; bhajate: worships; yo: who; maam: Me; yuktatamo: most devout; mataha: opinion/is deemed.

"Even among all the yogis".

This is the last verse in this 6th chapter, the Dhyana Yoga.

The first six chapters are considered as "karma Shatka". We had Karma yoga, Jnana yoga and Dhyana yoga in these six chapters.

The yogis referred to in this sloka can belong to any one of the three groups. The Lord is making a final judgment and calls all of them as "yogis" as they are striving to unite with "Him." Each one of them is a sincere spiritual seeker.

The yogis are trying to unite with the inner Self which is "The Lord" himself. The Antaratma is the voice of the Lord from within. The effort of the seekers is to unite with Him. Sri Krishna is saying "Madgatena" which means "fixed in Me." When He is saying "Me" He is pointing that He, Krishna is the manifestation/ avatara of the Supreme with a name and form. He is giving us His true identity.

How should the yogi be conducting the yoga of his choice, be it Karma, Jnana or Dhyana? How would the seeker get His grace?

The yogi should show utter faith in the Supreme and His teaching and also worship Him.

Faith and worship are two prerequisites for receiving His grace.

One can say that this is the view of Krishna, the cowherd, son of Devaki and Vasudeva. But Krishna is the avatara of Supreme Parabrahman and so what is expressed by Krishna is really the summary of the Vedas.

The importance of worship, as an expression of love of the Supreme is stressed by the Lord several times. As a matter of fact, the next six chapters constitute "Bhakti Shatka". The 12th chapter is "Bhakti Yoga". We are now led to the theme of Bhakti which should be an ingredient in all the forms of yoga.

If one considers that the three yogas described in this shatka are the seeds sown in the mind of the seeker, devotion/Bhakti is considered as the water that soaks the seeds, gives the nourishment and assists in the growth of the seeds that culminates in the bearing of fruit. The fruit being "Divine Bliss" which is "Salvation".

It goes without saying that the farmer who is looking for the production of the fruit and sows the seeds has to have complete faith in the Lord. He does not question any decisions of the Lord at any time and accepts life as it comes and puts in his efforts sincerely and with love.

Hence the Lord uses the word "Vyavasayatmika buddhi" (sloka 41, chapter 2). "Vyavasaya" is agriculture and the seeker has to be a farmer in the truest sense who works incessantly for experiencing the "Divine Bliss."

The six chapters that are completed now are all about "Jivatman", the soul expressing as the individual by association with the mind and intellect and using the jnanendriyas and karmendriyas to experience the life around. How this Jivatman can elevate to the level of the Atman within has been described so far.

This is the "Tvam" aspect of "Tat, Tvam, Asi."

"Tvam" means "Thou".

We are now led to the next six chapters which is all about "Parabrahman" and deals with "Tat" (That) aspect of "Tat, Tvam, Asi."

As it needs total devotion to understand the importance of "Tat" the next shatka is considered as "Bhakti Shatka."

Let me recollect what has been said in the introduction to this chapter, Train the mind by dhyana yoga and reduce the thoughts in it.

Next step is: "Transform the thoughts"

And finally transcend the thoughts.

Automatically the seeker can transform himself (through identification and unity with Him) to his real "Self" which is "Brahman."

Iti Śrīmadbhagavadgītāsūpaniṣatsu brahmavidyāyāṃ yogaśāstre Śrīkṛṣṇārjunasaṃvāde Dhyānayogo nāma ṣaṣṭho 'dhyāyaḥ ||

The Gnostics and their remains : ancient and mediaeval

C W. 1818-1888 King

Ceraunia of Green Jade, converted into a Gnostic Talisman.

(See page 197.)

THE GNOSTICS

AND

THEIR REMAINS,

ANCIENT AND MEDIÆVAL.

BY

C. W. KING, M.A.

"Nam veluti pueri trepidant atque omnia cæcis
In tenebris metuunt, sic nos in luce timemus
Interdum nilo quæ sunt metuenda magis quam
Quæ pueri in tenebris pavitant, finguntque futura."

SECOND EDITION.

LONDON:
DAVID NUTT, 270, STRAND.
1887.

LONDON
PRINTED BY WILLIAM CLOWES AND SONS, LIMITED,
STAMFORD STREET AND CHARING CROSS

PREFACE.

WHEN this work first appeared, three-and-twenty years ago, it became at once an object of unmerited abuse, and of equally unmerited praise. Small divines mistaking it for an insidious attempt to overthrow opinions "as by law established," *spurted* at it with pens dipped in the milk of the Gospel, whilst, under the very same hallucination, "Friends of Light" lauded it to the skies—either party equally ignorant both of the subject, and of the purpose of my labours One noted *Zoilus* (whose recollections of Homer would seem to be of the same *deeply-marked* nature as Ensign Blifil's) is disgusted at my citing "Aidoneus" as a title of the God of the Shades, another is astonished at my ignorance in calling Bardanes a *Persian*, whereas he was a native of *Pontus*, not understanding that my argument was equally valid in spite of the mistake—Pontus being originally a province of the empire of Darius, and what is more to the purpose, the actual focus whence Mithraicism diffused itself over the Roman world

A still greater cause of outcry against the book was my presuming to lay presumptuous hands upon the Sacred Ark of Masonry, and openly express my opinion that the "Free and Accepted" of these times have no more real connexion with the ancient *Craft*, out of whose terms and forms, like fig-leaves, they have stitched together *aprons*, wherewith to cover the real nakedness of their pretension, than the Italian *Carbonari* of Murat's day had with the trade of *charcoal burners*, whose baskets were borrowed for the President's throne. King Hiram's skull gnashed his teeth with rage within the *cista mystica*, and one *valiant* young Levite of the course of Abia, proceeds thus logically to confute all my assertions. "Athelstan built a church he could not build without masons, *argal*, Athelstan was the founder of Masonry in England

But enough of this, the same treatment is necessarily in store for the present edition, it must look for

'Verbera, carnifices, robur, pix, lamina, taedae"

The one reviewer of its predecessor who exhibited any acquaintance with the literature of the subject, felt himself (from his position) "in duty bound" to qualify his praise by passing the summary judgment 'that I had displayed in the work more of the spirit of a Gnostic than of a Catholic Christian." This sentence, intended for *condemnatory*, I accept as the highest praise that could be given to my labours—taking γνωστικός in its strict sense of "one addicted to knowledge"; and who therefore studies the history and remains of any opinion for the sole purpose of understanding the truth, and not for the sake of demonstrating the Truth can only exist under *one* defined form

Let me now proceed to state how, in the present edition, I have endeavoured still further to deserve the appellation attached to me by the good-natured *Aristarchus*. My Treatise was the only one upon Gnostic Archaeology (for Dr. Walsh's little book scarce deserves the name) that had appeared since Chiflet's admirable "Apistopistus" (1617),—Matter, in his 'Histoire Critique du Gnosticisme (1827), an excellent analysis of the doctrines of the Gnosis, doing nothing for its monuments, beyond republishing, on a reduced scale, the engravings of the "Apistopistus" The only sources of information accessible to me at the time of writing that edition were the same as those drawn upon by Matter before me, namely the treatises of *Irenaeus* and *Epiphanius* In the interval, I have become acquainted with, and, in order thoroughly to master, have made complete translations of, two recently discovered works that throw much light upon many difficult questions in this investigation. The one is the 'Refutation of all Heresies,' ascribed either to Origen or Hippolytus. its author being intimately acquainted with the doctrines which he holds up for detestation, or for ridicule, and (what makes his criticisms of far higher value to students of the present day) illustrating them by copious extracts from the then so extensive heretical literature, soon to be completely exterminated by the triumph of the "orthodox" Faith.

The other aid is the "Pistis-Sophia," sole survivor of the once numerous family of *Gnostic Gospels*, but fortunately the most important of them all for our purpose, and the very one for whose escape (in its Coptic disguise) the archæologist ought to feel most grateful to the ignorance of the destroyers. For, whereas the other Gnostic teachers appear (as Hippolytus loves to point out) to build up their systems upon the lines of various Grecian philosophies, the "Pistis-Sophia" makes known to us what were the deepest secrets of the so celebrated Egyptian Mysteries, which are identical with those of the Rabbinical Kabbala, the only alteration being that of putting them into the mouth of Scripture personages, in order to adapt them to the prevailing change of ideas This book, therefore, from its very nature supplies a kind of elucidation of contemporary monuments not to be found elsewhere, for the Christian Fathers discuss only the *doctrines* of their adversaries, not condescending to notice their application to the uses of everyday life. It is the latter point that gives such interest to the "Pistis-Sophia"—we gain from it the whole category of *Holy Names*, of such talismanic virtue, the powers and titles of the actual genii, the constitution of the soul, and its state after death. But what is yet more curious, the "Pistis-Sophia" exhibits the leading principles of the Kabbala already established, and applied to the demonstration of the highest truths in exactly the same manner as these principles were used by the heresiarch, Marcus, in the third century. And here it may be remarked parenthetically, that no one really acquainted with the history of religious opinions, can for a moment imagine that Marcus (a born *Jew*, be it remembered) was the first *inventor* of the wondrous machinery which he used in the development of his system, and the 'Manifestation of Truth,'—he did but apply to a new purpose the rules that he found already established as authoritative in the Rabbinical schools For in Religion there is no "new thing"; the same ideas are worked up over and over again; the gold in the *sovereign* of to-day may first have circulated in the new-coined *stater* of Crœsus.

Last, in point of time, but equally valuable with any of the fresh sources that have served me for the completion of this work, must I gratefully acknowledge the oral teachings of Rabbi Dr Schiller-Szinessy—that unchanged representative of the Gamaliels of old—at whose feet I have sat for many years, listening to his exposition of the "Holy Zohar" Whatever may be the date of the *present* form of that transcendental development of the *Torah*—no one but an *inverted* Jew, totally unread in the *Greek* historians of the Gnosis, can fail to perceive that its principles and traditions are the very same as those taught in the schools of Babylon and Tiberias at the time when Simon Magus and Justinus studied there

During the many years that have slipped by since its first publication, I have from time to time re-cast and re-written the entire Treatise, incorporating with the former contents whatever fresh information, reading, or chance, might throw in my way. In the same interval, two other works upon this subject have made their appearance. Dean Mansel's 'Gnostics' is a well-written and accurate summary of all that the Greek Fathers have left us upon the doctrines of the various sects, but, as the book is evidently intended for the use of theological students alone, the author has regarded his subject from a strictly *professional* point of view, totally ignoring the archæological side of the question (with which I am chiefly concerned), as being altogether foreign to the purpose for which he wrote.

On the other hand, Dr. Ginsburg's 'The Kabbala its Doctrines, Development, and Literature,' possesses not only the merit of a lucid exposition of the most abstruse of all *Theosophies*, as contemplated in the shape to which it has been brought by the refining subtlety of successive generations of *Rabbins*—but will be found an invaluable guide to all who attempt the interpretation of talismanic inscriptions For example, the Hebrew *radicals*, which express the Names of the *Sephiroth*, are to be discovered in the strings of Greek consonants, now dumb for want of vowels, which have hitherto baffled the ingenuity of every reader

There seems reason for suspecting that the Sibyl of *Esoteric* Buddhism drew the first notions of her new religion from the analysis of the *Inner Man*, as set forth in my first edition I may therefore promise to myself the gratitude of those "clear spirits" (the Miltonian phrase) who are busying themselves "by searching to find out God," for now making known to them a still more profound theosophy, whose revelations definitely settle hardest problems relating to our mental nature, and the world beyond the grave Investigators of the same order as the *Esoteric Buddhists* will find here a Gospel ready made to their hand—so full of great truths, so original in its conceptions, that it would seem to flow from no human source, and must carry conviction of its divine origin to every mind that shall be adapted by its nature for the reception of the *good seed*

In conclusion, I must express my grateful acknowledgments of the services of my indefatigable friend, Mr S S Lewis, Fellow of Corpus Christi College, but for whose persuasion, and negotiations with the publishers, these pages would never have seen the light Not merely this, but he has enabled me to overcome an apparently insurmountable difficulty in the way of the publication—the failure of my sight, which totally prevented my conducting the work through the press—by taking upon himself the correction of the proofs a laborious and irksome task to any one besides the author, and demanding a sacrifice of time that can only be appreciated by those, who, like myself, know the multifarious nature of the engagements by which every hour of his life is so completely absorbed

Mr Joseph Jacobs has furnished a carefully compiled list of authors quoted in this work, and of the references made to them, which will be found of use to those who wish to pursue the subject still further

C W KING.

TRINITY COLLEGE, CAMBRIDGE,
August 26, 1887

CONTENTS

PART IV

The Figured Monuments of Gnosticism

PART V

Templars, Rosicrucians, Freemasons

INTRODUCTION

THAT nothing upon the subject of Gnosticism should have hitherto been attempted in our language except by Dr Walsh in his very meagre sketch (long since out of print), seemed to me a sufficient excuse for my undertaking the same task upon a more comprehensive scale, as well as upon different principles Dr. Walsh's performance, entitled 'An Essay on Coins, Medals, and Gems, as illustrating the progress of Christianity in the Early Ages,' is little more than an abridgment of some popular Church History for the period comprehended within its scope, illustrated from the very scanty store of monuments at his command, whilst his explanations are, like the source supplying them, based upon grounds altogether fallacious, and, even to the beginner, obviously unsatisfactory

Taking for granted, upon the bare word of their opponents, that the various Teachers of the Gnosis were mere *heretics*, that is, perverters of the regular (!) Christian doctrine which they had at first embraced as a divine revelation, he, like his guides, did not trouble himself any further to investigate the true origin of their systems, but was content with roughly sketching their most prominent features, whilst in explaining their extant productions, he refers all, however diverse in nature, to the same school, and interprets them according to his own preconceived and baseless views of their character.

On such a plan as this, neither the doctrines nor the monuments they have bequeathed to us in such profusion are susceptible of even a plausible explanation, much less of one capable of satisfying an unprejudiced and inquiring mind The method, therefore, of treating the subject which I have followed in the present work is to begin by reviewing the great religious systems of the East, flourishing at the time of the promulgation of Christianity in those regions, with the influence of these systems upon the modes of thought and expression of both the missionaries of the new creed and their opponents, and lastly to establish, upon the testimony of the Apostle to the Gentiles himself, the *previous existence* of the germs of Gnosticism in the cities that were the scene of his most important labours.

In my sketch of these older systems I have done little more than condense Matter's admirable introduction to his 'Histoire Critique du Gnosticisme', but from that point forward have carried on my investigations according to a theory to which that writer once alludes approvingly, although, from some unaccountable reason, he has neglected to follow it out to its legitimate consequences Restricting himself to describing in his lucid and elegant style the speculations of the several heresiarchs, and seeking no further back than the Zendavesta and Kabbala for the storehouses whence they all must have drawn their first principles, he falls into the grave error of representing their doctrines as *novel*, and the pure *inventions* of the persons that preached them

That the seeds of the Gnosis were originally of *Indian* growth, carried so far westward by the influence of that *Buddhistic* movement which had previously overspread all the East, from Thibet to Ceylon, was the great truth faintly discerned by Matter, but which became evident to me upon acquiring even a slight acquaintance with the chief doctrines of Indian theosophy To display this in the most incontrovertible manner, the two systems, each in its highest form of development—that of Valentinus, and that of the Nepalese Buddhists—are described and confronted for the sake of establishing their original identity and throughout these pages innumerable other points of affinity will be found noticed as they present themselves. Actual *historical proof* of the same fact will also be adduced, establishing the important circumstance (but hitherto entirely unnoticed, or disregarded) that Buddhism had already been planted in the dominions of the Seleucidæ and the Ptolemies at least as early as the times of the generation following the establishment of those dynasties, and was provided for in treaties made between those Grecian princes and the great

Hindoo promoter of the religion In the history of the Church it is most certain that almost every notion that was subsequently denounced as *heretical* can be traced up to Indian speculative philosophy as its genuine fountain-head how much that was allowed to pass current for *orthodox* had really flowed from the same source, it is neither expedient nor decorous now to inquire.

In order to obtain a clear view of the principal forms of Gnosticism, as well as to escape relying upon second-hand information (in this case more than elsewhere untrustworthy), I commenced the collecting materials for the present work by carefully perusing the vast 'Panarion' of Epiphanius—a laborious undertaking, but well repaid by the vivid picture he presents of the inner state of society under the Lower Empire, and of the war even at that late period so fiercely waged between Reason and Faith The 'Panarion' is a connected history of the Gnosis in all its developments during the first three centuries—the author quoting Irenæus for the earlier ages, for the later his account is of the highest value, having been derived from personal experience, Epiphanius having in his youth belonged to the Marcosian sect After his days nothing new sprung up in the field of Religious philosophy, before so diversified with the vigorous and more curious flowers (or weeds) of the Gnosis, the civil now combining with the ecclesiastical power to cut down and root out all such daring and irregular growths of the human mind.

Since the first publication of this treatise I have become acquainted with and minutely studied two authorities of the greatest importance for the true understanding of Gnosticism—the one for its philosophy, the other for its tangible remains. 'The Refutation of all Heresies,' of Hippolytus, written two centuries before the 'Panarion,' gives a view of the chief schools of the Gnosis, drawn up with the utmost intelligence united with the most charming candour, qualities sadly to seek in the other ecclesiastical historians. The 'Pistis-Sophia,' the only Gnostic Gospel preserved, throws a light upon the terminology and machinery of the religion that, before its discovery and publication was perfectly unattainable Both these treatises are of recent discovery, and consequently their assistance was lost to the previous historians of Gnosticism I have therefore availed myself largely of these invaluable resources, which will be found doing good service in almost every section of the present work.

After considering the class of speculations that owed their birth to India, next in importance for her contributions to the *opinions*, still more to the *monuments* before us, comes Egypt with her primeval creed, although exhibited in its Romanized and latest phase, and whose productions are too often confounded with the true offspring of the Gnosis These remains are here discriminated, their distinctive characters are pointed out, and they are arranged under several heads, according as their object was religious or medicinal In the consideration of these remains, Bellermann's classification has been chiefly followed, according to which the truly Gnostic are regarded as those only that exhibit the figure of the Pantheus, *Abraxas*, the actual invention of Basilides, and which gives its name to the class The second, *Abraxoids*, includes the types borrowed from different religions by the other Gnostic teachers. The third, *Abraxaster*, consists of such as in their nature are purely astrological, and intended for talismans, deriving their virtues from the stars In the first of these classes much space has been devoted to the ingenious creation of the Alexandrine philosopher, the pantheistic image of the supreme Abraxas; whose title has hitherto been improperly applied to monuments some of which are anterior in date to his embodiment in a visible form, whilst others spring from nations entirely unconnected with his worship. Of this *eidolon* of the *personage* thereby typified, of the meaning of his *name* and titles, much information has been collected, and presented here in a connected form for the benefit of those interested in learning what can on safe grounds be established in elucidation of these abtruse questions

Mithraicism, under whose kindly and congenial shelter so much of Occidental Christianity grew up unmolested, is reviewed in its due order, and the causes explained of an alliance at first sight so inexplicable. With this subject are connected the singular resemblance between the ceremonial of the two, and the transfer of so much that was Mithraic into the practice of the orthodox, and many curious memorials will be found described bearing witness to the reality of this adaptation

After the Mithraic, the religion of *Serapis* comes to be considered, a worship which, besides being the last of the Heathen forms to fall before the power of Christianity, had previously contributed, as largely as the Mithraic, to the constitution of the later Gnosticism It is in truth a great mistake, the confining the name of "Gnostic" (as is commonly done) to the sectaries who, boasting of their "superior lights," declared that they were the only real Christians (as did the Ophites), and that too in virtue of a creed professedly of their own devising Such Gnostics indeed were Christians by their own showing, and regarded all who differed from them as *heretics* but at the same time they based their arguments upon the tenets of Pagan religions, very far from regarding the latter as the empty fabrications of demons, which was the persuasion of the orthodox. But although they accepted these ancient Ethnic legends, it was only because through the help of their "knowledge" they were enabled to discern the truth enveloped within these seemingly profane traditions But the followers of Mithras and of Serapis had in reality, and long before them, a Gnosis of their own, communicated in their *Mysteries* to the initiated few, and they opposed to the predictions of orthodox and Gnostic alike claims and pretensions lofty as their own The Emperor Hadrian, a most diligent inquirer into things above man's nature, got himself initiated into one mystery after another, nevertheless we shall find him writing from Alexandria that the worship of Christ and of Serapis was in that city one and the same, and moreover the sole religion of that immense population Consequently, those initiated into the true secrets of the old religion must have recognised the fact that their deity, whether the Sun or the Soul of the Universe, was nothing but a *type* of the *One*, the Saviour recently revealed to them or else it would appear (which tells equally for our argument) that the new converts, in order to escape persecution, enjoyed their own faith under the covert of the national worship, which was susceptible of a spiritual interpretation quite cognate to their own ideas, and indeed enshrouding the same As for the worshippers of Mithras, their whole elaborate system of sacraments and degrees of initiation had no other object than the securing of spiritual enlightenment and spiritual blessings The foundation being the pure teaching of Zoroaster, its holders were prepared gladly to accept any higher revelation, and to discover that the greater mystery had been foreshadowed in the types and ceremonies of the former one In this way a man might continue a Mithraicist and yet accept all the doctrines of Christianity, as the priests of that religion in their last days assured the incredulous Augustine

After thus pointing out the various elements which the Apostles of the Gnosis worked up so ingeniously into one harmonious whole, incorporating therewith so much of the Christian scheme as fitted to the rest, we come prepared to the examination of the *Symbols* and *Terminology* by which these ideas were communicated to the members of the sect who had attained to the *Arcanum*, the composite *images* or *sigils* "having a voice for the intelligent, which the vulgar crowd heareth not"

Astrology justly claims for her own a large share of the relics popularly called *Gnostic*, for Gnosticism, from the beginning, had linked its own speculations to those of the Magians' national science, and borrowed as a vehicle for its own peculiar ideas the machinery of the latter—its Astral Genii, Decani, and Myriageneses And this truth was seen by the earliest writers upon Gnosticism, for Hippolytus proves conclusively, at much length, that the system of the Peratae (a branch of the Ophites) was nothing more than a barefaced plagiarism from the rules of Astrology. Under this head I have endeavoured to separate the purely Astrological talismans from those to which the *illuminati*, their makers, had given a more spiritual sense. "Astrology, not Christ, is the author of their religion," says Hippolytus of the sects founded by Euphrates and Celbes, and proceeds to give extracts from their writings, held in the highest esteem at the time, which amply bear out his assertion

Next pour in, a multitudinous swarm, the stones covered over with long strings of bare *inscriptions*, genuine offspring of the Kabbala, that betray the handiwork of the idol-hating Jewish dreamers of Alexandria—spells even then ascribed to Solomon, and which secured the favour

> "Of those demons that are found
> In fire, air, flood, or under ground,
> Whose power hath a true consent
> With planet or with element"

One object I have kept steadily in view throughout the whole of this investigation—to show how the productions of the different schools are to be distinguished from each other, and to this particular attention has been given in describing the numerous remains proceeding from the several sources just enumerated, that are collected in the accompanying plates, and thus in some degree to remedy the confusion that reigns at present in the whole department. My predecessor, Matter, busied himself only with the doctrines, making use of the monuments merely in illustration of his remarks, but as my own labours are properly designed to be subsidiary to his invaluable treatise, I refer the reader to him for the more complete elucidation of the *philosophy* of Gnosticism, and give my full attention to its *archæological* side, which he has too cursorily glanced at, and for which nothing has been done of any importance since the publications of Chiflet and Montfaucon

Last to be considered comes the Gnosis in its final and grandest manifestation, the composite religion of *Manes* with its wonderful revival and diffusion over Mediæval Europe, and its supposed connexion with the downfall of the Templars, of which catastrophe the history and causes are here briefly sketched, although to form a satisfactory judgment on the merits of the case is about the hardest problem history can offer With their scandal and their fate is coupled the most singular phenomenon of modern times—the preservation by their *professed* descendants, the *Freemasons*, of so much symbolism that appears to be indisputably Gnostic in its origin. For this, however (unfortunately for the lovers of mystery), a very matter of fact but doubtless sufficient cause can be assigned, and by valid arguments established when the solution of the enigma irresistibly brings to mind Æsop's apologue of the "Fox and the Mask," and his exclamation of disappointment after he had at last mustered up sufficient courage to examine the interior of the awe-inspiring and venerable head This section is illustrated by all the information I have been able to glean from different sources upon the curious subject of *Masons' Marks*—which, yet existing and in common use amongst our own craftsmen and equally so amongst the Hindoos in daily religious observance, can be traced back through Gothic retention, and Gnostic usage, through old Greek and Etruscan art, to their ultimate source, and which attest more convincingly than anything else what region gave birth to the theosophy making such liberal use of the same *siglæ* in Roman times To assist inquirers into this point I have been careful to give references to all the published lists of these Marks that have come to my knowledge, which same rule I have observed as regards other monographs upon the several various questions discussed in the following pages In this way the shortcomings of myself can be supplied by those desirous of fuller information for I am well aware that my own best qualification for attempting an arduous investigation like the present, extending over so many and unconnected branches of learning, lies in a larger practical experience of the monuments themselves, tangible and literary, than was possessed by those who have hitherto attempted it. And as it is a most true adage, "Dans le pays des aveugles le borgne est roi,' there is some probability of my labours proving both novel and interesting to many, who desire to know something authentic upon the much-talked-of but little understood subject of Gnosticism

Related to this religion by their nature are *talismans* and *amulets* in general, for Gnostic symbols and Gnostic formulæ gave their virtue to many of the class being borrowed either directly from the Gnosis, or from the older creeds out of which the latter was constructed. Their employment, and the notions generating them, have been here described, showing the derivation of many of the mediæval examples from the Gnostic class, and by following out the same principle it has been attempted to find a key to their cabalistic legends, which may fit them better than any hitherto offered by their interpreters—*symbols* and *emblems* being with them those conveying the idea of *death*, which last indeed has of all others furnished the richest store of such imagery, for thereby the human mind endeavoured to familiarise itself with the thought of mortality, and by embellishing the idea tried to reconcile itself to the inevitable This being a topic of universal interest, to say nothing of its very important relations to Art, my collections connected therewith have been somewhat extensive, and embrace many particulars neglected by Lessing in his curious essay entitled 'Wie die Alten den Tod gebildet'

With respect to the *illustrations* of this book, many doubtless will be surprised as well as disappointed at finding them derived entirely from monuments of such small apparent importance as *engraved stones*, and, thinking this part incomplete on that account, may accuse the author of negligence in not having had recourse to other evidences of a more public character But the limitation is in truth the necessary result of the nature of the things discussed in this inquiry. Secret Societies, especially the one whose maxim was (as Clemens records) that truly wise one—

"Learn to know all, but keep thyself unknown,"

erect no *monuments* to attract public attention. They deal but in *symbols*, to be privately circulated amongst their members in *passwords* known only to the *illuminati*, or else they embody their doctrines in mystic drawings, like the Ophite "Diagramma", or upon papyri long since committed to the flames The man of taste, but not an antiquary, will certainly exclaim against the rudeness of the drawing in my illustrations, but the truth is that, rude as they look, they in most cases *flatter* their originals, the extreme barbarism of which it was often found impossible to reproduce with any hope of leaving the meaning recognisable Be it remembered that

"Gratia non habitat, non hoc Cyllenius antro"

Pallas no longer, as in the earlier ages of the art, guided the engraver's hand, but Siva and Bhavani (ill-disguised as Hermes and Isis) suggested the designs, or else he was inspired by the Typhonian monsters which imagined the Genii of Astrology. The religion of *Fear*, under its various manifestations, now reigned supreme, having banished the beauteous sensuous machinery of the old Greek Nature-worship, into which nothing that was malignant or hideous was ever suffered to intrude The virtue of the *talisman* lay in the type it carried, and in its own material substance the *manner* of the exhibition of the potent sigil was altogether unregarded. One of the most learned men this University has ever produced once remarked to me that the Gnostic theories reminded him of the visions that float through the brain of a *madman*—not of a *fool.* Circumstances following gave a melancholy *force* to this acute and accurate distinction. Let any imaginative person read my extracts from the "Revelation" of Marcus, with all its crazy ingenuity in deducing the nature of the Deity from the properties of numerals, above all, his exemplification of Infinity by the perpetual multiplication of the letters contained in other letters making up a name—he will speedily find his brain begin to whirl, and be reminded of similar phantoms of numerals recurring in endless series, and the equally endless attempts to sum them up in order to obtain repose, that fill the head when suffering from the first approaches of fever before actual delirium pushes memory from her seat. Or, again, when the febrile disturbance of the brain is yet slighter, one will sometimes awake out of a dream with a fleeting sensation of inexpressible happiness arising from the immediate attainment of Omniscience in virtue of something that has just been revealed to him; but too soon he finds that ineffable *something* has fled for ever, all that is left of it being the faint recollection that it was contained in a *numeral* And one of the most striking points in the revelation of the 'Seherin von Prevorst,' so religiously recorded by Justinus Kerner (and which proves that *all* the wondrous narrative was not imposture), is her declaration that she could see the entire history of each year as it closed, with every event, however trifling, clear and distinct before her mind, all comprehended within the form of a single *numeral*, and her assertion upon these grounds that at the Judgment-Day the whole past life of every man will thus be pictured in a single moment before his mind's eye

About half the number of the drawings for these illustrations were done by myself from the most interesting specimens that came under my notice in the course of several years, so that I am able to vouch for their scrupulous fidelity. Afterwards, when the sudden failure of my sight prevented my carrying on the drawings, the kindness of the then owner of most of the originals came to my assistance and furnished the remainder Most of them in fact were taken from the large and unpublished set contained in the ancient Praun Cabinet (formed three centuries ago), now unfortunately broken up The Gnostic stones, however—73 in number—have been since that time purchased for the British Museum, where they will be found conveniently arranged for consultation, in the Egyptian Room, which contains the works in terra-cotta This my collection of drawings was in truth the occasion of the present work; for after making out a detailed description of each specimen, it became easy to put the mass of materials I had collected for their elucidation into a form available for supporting my explanations by showing the grounds on which they were based and in this way the work has grown up by gradual accretion to its present dimensions The theme offers so boundless a variety of interesting subjects for research, one suggesting another in endless succession, that it can only be compared to Marcus' own exposition of the infinite composition of the Ineffable Name (quoted above), and would alone supply materials for a whole library of distinct treatises upon its various subdivisions

In those few instances where the better style of the original deserved reproduction by a more artistic hand, I have had recourse to the services of Mr. R B Utting, who has executed the woodcuts with a spirit as well as an accuracy that leave nothing to be desired.

PART I

GNOSTICISM AND ITS SOURCES

Τουτοῦ με χάριν πέμψον, Πάτερ,
σφραγῖδας ἔχων καταβησομαι,
Αἰῶνας ὅλους διοδεύσω,
μυστήρια παντα διανοίξω,
μορφὰς δε θεῶν ἐπιδείξω,
καὶ τὰ κεκρυμμένα τῆς ἁγίας ὁδοῦ,
ΓΝΩΣΙΝ καλέσας, παραδώσω
Ophite Hymn, (Hippolytus, v 10)

" Non è puleggio da piccola barca
Quel che fendendo va l' ardita prora,
Nè da nocchier ch' a sè medesmo parca "
(Dante, *Parad* xxiii 68)

THE GNOSTICS AND THEIR REMAINS.

GNOSTICISM AND ITS ORIGIN.

THE general name "Gnostics" is used to designate several widely differing sects, which sprang up in the Eastern provinces of the Roman Empire almost simultaneously with the first planting of Christianity. That is to say, these sects then for the first time assumed a definite form, and ranged themselves under different teachers, by whose names they became known to the world, although in all probability their main doctrines had made their appearance previously in many of the cities of Asia Minor. There, it is probable, these sectaries first came into definite existence under the title of "Mystae," upon the establishment of a direct intercourse with India and her Buddhist philosophers, under the Seleucidae and the Ptolemies.

The term "Gnosticism" is derived from the Greek, *Gnosis*, knowledge—a word specially employed from the first dawn of religious inquiry to designate the science of things divine. Thus Pythagoras, according to Diogenes Laertius, called the transcendental portion of his philosophy, Γνῶσις τῶν ὄντων, "the knowledge of things that *are*." And in later times *Gnosis* was the name given to what Porphyry calls the *Antique* or *Oriental* philosophy, to distinguish it from the Grecian systems. But the term was first used (as Matter on good grounds conjectures) in its ultimate sense of *supernal* and *celestial* knowledge, by the Jewish philosophers belonging to the celebrated school of that nation, flourishing at Alexandria. These teachers, following the example of a noted Rabbi, Aristobulus, surnamed the *Peripatician*, endeavoured to make out that all the wisdom of the Greeks was derived immediately from the Hebrew

Scripture, and by means of their well-known mode of allegorical interpretation, which enabled them to elicit any sense desired out of any given passage of the Old Testament, they sought, and often succeeded, in establishing their theory. In this way they showed that Plato, during his sojourn in Egypt, had been *their own* scholar, and still further to support these pretensions, the indefatigable Aristobulus produced a string of poems in the names of Linus, Orpheus, Homer, and Hesiod—all strongly impregnated with the spirit of Judaism. But *his* Judaism was a very different thing from the simplicity of the Pentateuch A single, but very characteristic, production, of this *Jewish* Gnosis has come down to our times. This is the "Book of Enoch" (v p 18), of which the main object is to *make known* the description of the heavenly bodies and the *true names* of the same, as revealed to the Patriarch by the angel Uriel. This profession betrays, of itself, the Magian source whence its inspiration was derived. Many Jews, nevertheless, accepted it as a divine revelation, even the Apostle Jude scruples not to quote it as of genuine Scriptural authority The "Pistis-Sophia," attributed to the Alexandrian heresiarch Valentinus (so important a guide in the following inquiry), perpetually refers to it as The highest source of knowledge, as being dictated by Christ Himself, "speaking out of the Tree of Life unto IEOT, the Primal Man" Another Jewish-Gnostic Scripture of even greater interest, (inasmuch as it is the "Bible" of the only professed Gnostic sect that has maintained its existence to the present day, the Mandaites of Bassora,) is their textbook, the 'Book of Adam" Its doctrines and singular application of Zoroastrism to Jewish tenets, present frequent analogies to those of the Pistis-Sophia, in its continual reference to the ideas of the "Religion of Light," of which full particulars will be given when the latter remarkable work comes to be considered (see p 14) "Gnosticism," therefore, cannot receive a better definition than in that dictum of the sect first and specially calling itself 'Gnostics," the *Naaseni* (translated by the Greeks into "Ophites"), viz, "the beginning of perfection is the knowledge of man, but absolute perfection is the knowledge of God" And to give a general view of the nature of the entire system, nothing that I can do will serve so well as to transcribe the exact words of a learned and very acute writer upon the subject of Gnosticism ("Christian Remembrancer," for 1866).

"Starting, then, from this point we ask what Gnosticism is, and what it professes to teach What is the peculiar *Gnosis* that it claims to itself? The answer is, the knowledge of God and of Man, of the Being and Providence of the former, and of the creation and destiny of the latter While the ignorant and superstitious were degrading the glory of the incorruptible God into an image made with hands, and were changing 'the truth of God into a lie, and worshipped and served the creature rather than the Creator,' the ancient Gnostics held purer and truer ideas. And when these corrupted and idolatrous forms of religion and worship became established, and were popularly regarded as true and real in themselves, the "Gnostics" held and secretly taught an *esoteric* theology of which the popular creed of multitudes of deities, with its whole ritual of sacrifice and worship, was but the exoteric from Hence all the mysteries which, almost if not all, the heathen religions possessed Those initiated into these mysteries, whilst they carefully maintained and encouraged the gorgeous worship, sacrifices and processions of the national religion, and even openly taught polytheism, and the efficacy of the public rites, yet secretly held something very different—at the first, probably, a purer creed, but in course of time, like the exoteric form, degenerating The progress of declination differed according to race or habit of thought in the East it tended to superstition, in the West (as we learn from the writings of Cicero) to pure atheism, a denial of Providence. This system was adopted likewise by the Jews, but with this great difference, that it was superinduced upon and applied to a pre-existent religion, whereas in the other Oriental religions, the external was added to the esoteric, and developed out of it. In the Oriental systems the external was the sensuous expression of a hidden meaning, in the Jewish, the hidden meaning was drawn out of pre-existing external laws and ritual, in the former the esoteric alone was claimed as divine, in the latter it was the exoteric which was a matter of revelation To repair this seeming defect, the Kabbalists, or teachers of the 'Hidden Doctrine,' invented the existence of a secret tradition, orally handed down from the time of Moses We may, of course, reject this assertion, and affirm that the Jews learnt the idea of a Hidden Wisdom, underlying the Mosaic Law, from their intercourse with the Eastern nations during the Babylonian captivity, and we may further be assured that the origin of this Secret Wisdom is Indian Perhaps we shall be more exact if we say that the Jews learnt from their intercourse with Eastern nations to investigate the external Divine Law, for the purpose of discovering its hidden meaning The heathen Gnostics, in fact, collected a Gnosis from every quarter, accepted all religious systems as partly true, and extracted from each what harmonized with their ideas The Gospel, widely preached, accompanied by miracles, having new doctrines and enunciating new truths, very naturally attracted their attention The Kabbalists, or Jewish Gnostics, like Simon Magus, found a large portion of apostolic teaching in accordance with their own, and easily grafted upon it so much as they liked Again the Divine power of working miracles possessed by the Apostles and their successors naturally attracted the interest of those whose chief mystery was the practice of magic Simon the Magician was considered by the Samaritans to be 'the great Power of God,' he was attracted by the miracles wrought by the Apostles, and no doubt he sincerely 'believed,' that is, after his own fashion His notion of Holy Baptism was probably an initiation into a new mystery with a higher Gnosis than he possessed before, and by which he hoped to be endued with higher powers, and so likewise many of those who were called Gnostic Heretics by the Christian Fathers, were not Christians at all, only they adopted so much of the Christian doctrine as accorded with their system "

The consideration of the local and political circumstances of the grand foci of Gnosticism will serve to explain much that is puzzling in the origin and nature of the system itself *Ephesus* was, after Alexandria, the most important meeting-point of Grecian culture and Oriental speculation In regard to commerce and riches, although she yielded to the Egyptian capital, yet she rivalled Corinth in both, which city in truth she far surpassed in her treasures of religion and science. Her richness in theosophic ideas and rites had from time immemorial been manifested in her possession of Diana, "whom all Asia and the world," worshipped—that pantheistic figure so conformable to the genius of the furthest East, her College of "Essenes" dedicated to the service of that goddess, and her "Megabyzae," whose name sufficiently declares their Magian institution. Hence, also, was supplied the talisman of highest repute in the antique world, the far-famed "Ephesian spell,' those mystic words graven upon the zone and feet of the "image that fell down from Jupiter," and how zealously magic was cultivated by her citizens is apparent from St Luke's incidental notice of the cost of the books belonging to those that used "curious arts" (τὰ περίεργα, the regular names for sorcery and divination) destroyed by their owners in the first transports of conversion to a new faith. Such converts, indeed, after their early zeal had cooled down, were not likely to resist the allurements of the endeavour to reconcile their ancient, far-famed wisdom, with the new revelation, in short, to follow the plan invented not long before by the Alexandrian Jew, in his reconciliation of Plato with Moses and the Prophets. "In Ephesus," says Matter, "the speculations of the Jewish-Egyptian school, and the Semi-Persian speculations of the Kabbala, had then recently come to swell the vast conflux of Grecian and Asiatic doctrines, so there is no wonder that teachers should have sprung up there, who strove to combine the religion newly preached by the Apostle with the ideas so long established in the place. As early as the year A D 58, St Paul, in his First Epistle to Timothy, enjoins him to warn certain persons to abstain from teaching 'strange doctrines,' those myths and interminable genealogies that only breed division. These same 'myths and genealogies' apply, without any doubt, to the theory of the Emanation of the Æons-Sephiroth, and to all the relations between the Good and Bad Angels that the Kabbalists had borrowed from the religion of Zoroaster."

Again, after condemning certain doctrines concerning the

obligation to complete asceticism, adopted literally from the Essenes, the Apostle adds, "keep safe the precious charge entrusted to thee, avoiding profane novelties and the *antitheses* of the *knowledge*, falsely so-called, of which some making profession have gone astray from the faith of Christ" It was assuredly *not* the mere fables by which the new converts sought to enrich and complete the Christian doctrine (such as we still have samples of in the childish, though pious fictions of the Apocryphal Gospels), such things as these were certainly not the "false knowledge," which set itself up against the "true knowledge," that is, Revelation itself, as something superior to that Revelation It must, on the contrary, have been a doctrine professing to make a *science* out of the Christian faith, and that, too, a *science* founding its principles upon *antitheses* Now what are these "antitheses" (or, oppositions) but the teaching of the Zendavesta, concerning the two Empires of Light and Darkness, the two grand classes of Intelligences, the good and the evil spirits, and the perpetual combat going on between them? Now these antitheses, or the principle of Dualism, is that which forms the most conspicuous feature of the Gnostic scheme, and in the Apostle's words we trace one of the most obvious ways in which such doctrines were communicated, and how they insinuated themselves into the infant Church

In fact the ancient commentators, Theodoret and Chrysostom, who were thoroughly conversant with the Gnosticism of their own day, apply this passage of St. Paul to that actual precursor of Gnosticism, his indefatigable rival Simon Magus himself, whose curious tenets had by that time been widely diffused throughout Asia Minor

So deeply rooted were such speculations in the minds of many of the Ephesians, that the Apostle, in his second Epistle to Timothy, written six years later, returns perpetually to the subject, whilst in his Epistle to the Church at Ephesus, he entreats his flock not to be seduced by "vain discourses," or "new-coined appellations," (as one reading has it, and which applies forcibly to the Gnostic nomenclature), nor by human doctrines that have no more solidity in themselves than the wind, whereof no one knows whence it cometh, or whither it goeth. Nay more, he even employs the very terminology of Gnosticism, as when he says, "Ye were dead in error and in sins ye walked according to the *Æon* of this world, according to the *Archon* who has the dominion of the air," that is, the Demiurgus Ildabaoth Here we have the Devs of Zoroaster, whose hosts fill the air, deceive mankind, blind their understandings, and lead them into temptation Again when he adds, "We war not against flesh and blood, but against the *Dominions*, the *Powers*, the *Lords* of the *Darkness*, the malevolence of the *Spirits* in the upper regions"—all these are regular Gnostic epithets, having also their place in the Kabbalistic theology. The later Gnosticism is, in fact, as Chiflet has well expressed it, "the spirit of Asiatic antiquity seeking to assert its empire over the soul of Man by insinuating itself into the Christian Church." The Ophites, even in the early times of Hippolytus, boasted that they of all men were the only real Christians, because they alone *comprehended* the *real* nature of the Saviour At the same time, they diligently attended the celebration of all the ancient Mysteries, notably the Eleusinian and the Phrygian, declaring that through their *knowledge* they had gotten the key to the hidden meaning of the whole ceremonial, which by types and figures foreshadowed the coming of the Christ But indeed, Gnosticism, in its primitive form, had almost supplanted, by spiritualizing it, the beautiful materialism of the early Greek and Latin mythologies. Catholicism, through its unity and greater simplicity, in the end triumphed over the conflicting Gnostic philosophies, which became extinct as a *professed* religion in the sixth century, so far as Europe was concerned, and whose relics in Asia were at the same moment covered over with impenetrable obscurity by the sudden deluge of the Mahommedan conquest Nevertheless, even in the first-named scene of its domination, it was not to be eradicated without leaving behind it deep traces in the writings and symbolisms of the magicians, astrologers, and seekers after the *grand arcanum* throughout the whole course of the Middle Ages Thus there is a passage in Dante (Paradiso, xviii) replete with the profoundest symbolism, and which, of course, our Freemasons claim for their own, and *that* with all possible security, because the very nature of the assumption exempts them from being called upon to publish the interpretation of the mystery. The poet here tells how the *five* times *seven* letters making up the *five* words "Diligite justitiam qui judicatis terram" came forth in the star Jupiter, when the beatified spirits of just princes hovered over the final M, forming their hosts into the figure of an eagle Certainly the importance given to the numerals *five* and *seven* in this revelation savours much of Gnostic phraseology, and reminds one of the thirty letters which make up the quadrisyllabic Name of God, as made known by Truth unto the heresiarch Marcus, the history of which shall be given in the fitting place Dante had before (Canto vi) spoken of the "awe that overcomes him before the B and I C E," evidently the initials of some mighty password, although his commentators most prosaically interpret them as the mere diminutive of the name of his lost love, Beatrice It was to its connection with Gnosticism that primitive Christianity owed the accusation of being a *Magical* system—a superstition not only *nova* but *malefica*. There is a curious passage in Dio Cassius, where, mentioning how the Christian Legion in M Aurelius' Quadian War obtained rain from Heaven through their prayers, he remarks, "the Christians can bring about anything they desire through prayer" In later times the various factions within the Church were fond of retorting upon each other this ancient aspersion of the pagans it was on the charge of magical practices, says Ammianus, that the Arians managed to depose and exile the great Athanasius himself

The history of Gnosticism, written by its contemporaries, still forms a copious library, despite the losses and damages it has sustained through the injuries of time In the carrying out of the chief object of the present work—the elucidation of the *tangible* remains of the Gnosis—no historical record has yielded me by any means so much service as "The Refutation of all Heresies," composed by *Hippolytus*, bishop of Ostia (Portus), early in the third century Many points, hitherto seeming hopelessly enveloped in darkness, have been made clear by the careful perusal of his judicious summaries of the systems of the different gnostic apostles His views of their doctrines are evidently drawn up with equal candour and intelligence, and fully bear out his declaration, "that his design was not to vilify the holders of such doctrines, but merely to make known the sources whence they had really derived their pretended revelation" And he keeps his word throughout, never once indulging, like the later controversialists, in invectives against asserted *practices*, but exhibiting the tenets only of his opponents, and, with much ingenuity, showing up their gross plagiarism from Pagan philosophy His eagerness for discovering the latter source in the fount of every gnostic stream, sometimes leads him to detect relationship that does not actually exist, and still oftener to pronounce a recent *copy* of the other what was in reality drawn directly from the same Oriental prototype—true origin of the old Greek idea with which he identifies it But this invaluable, as well as most interesting, treatise breathes all through that spirit of charity and forbearance that made a writer belonging to a still persecuted religion, happy to be allowed to subsist through the tolerance of its neighbours The abuse and scurrilous tales in which the later Epiphanius revels sufficiently indicate the writer belonging to an established Church, able at length to call in the secular power to assist in convincing all adversaries of their errors by the unanswerable arguments of rack, rope and faggot

Irenaeus, a Gaul by birth, and disciple of Polycarp, himself a disciple of St John, was elected Bishop of Lyon in the year 174 In that city he composed his great treatise generally styled "Five Books against Heresies," written in an easy, and indeed elegant style, although in one place he excuses its rudeness by the fact of his having been forced during so many years to converse "in a barbarous language"—a remark of interest as showing that *Celtic* still remained the vulgar tongue in his diocese. He is supposed to have died soon after the year A D 200, and therefore is somewhat earlier than Hippolytus, who was put to death in A D 222, and whose "Refutation" was clearly written after the death of Irenæus, for he quotes him occasionally by the title ὁ μακάριος, "the deceased", and has incorporated some entire chapters respecting Marcus in his own work

The great *Origen*, another contemporary, has given some important details concerning the religious systems of the Ophites in his celebrated "Reply to Celsus" Two centuries after him comes *Theodoret*, Bishop of Cyrrhus, in Syria, during the second quarter of the fifth century, who has left very full particulars respecting the great Gnostic school flourishing in that region. The other Christian writers who have treated upon the origin and nature of the same doctrines were nothing more than ignorant churchmen, able to discern nothing in any religion beyond its external forms, and which they construed in the darkest possible sense, ever seeking for the worst interpretation of which these external appearances were susceptible At the head of this latter class stands *Epiphanius*, author of the most detailed, and, from its furious partisanship, amusing account of the Gnostic sects that is extant—his vast *Panarion*, "Bread-basket," or rather, "Scrap-basket," a whimsical title intended to express the motly nature of its contents, picked up from all quarters This immense folio (admirably translated into elegant Latin by the learned Petavius) is of the highest interest, full of pictures of the struggles of the human mind to devise for itself a *revelation* that shall plausibly solve all the problems of Man's other nature Its compiler lived as Bishop of Salamis in Cyprus A D. 367-403, and displays great zeal in raking up all manner of scandalous stories against the enemies of his adoptive Church. But there is one thing that gives immense value to his labours, the minute account given of Manichæism—that latest and grandest development of the gnosis, which had come into existence in the interval between Epiphanius and Hippolytus.

The rule observed by all *these later* historians of Gnosticism is to represent it as a mere spurious offshoot and corruption of Christianity, invented, usually out of disappointed ambition, by apostates from the true faith established by the several apostles in the Eastern provinces of the Empire—a mode of representing the system than which nothing can be more unfounded. For in its earliest shape, such as it shows itself in the doctrine of Simon Magus, or of Basilides, the heaven-sent *knowledge* merely added upon the old foundations such articles and terms of the Christian faith as seemed capable of being assimilated to and combined therewith, whilst on the other hand she availed herself of the machinery of the older paganism, to elucidate and prove the mysteries of the new theosophy, and this was conspicuously the character of the systems of Justinus, and of the Peratae, as the very curious extracts given by Hippolytus from their text-books exhibit to the astonishment of the modern reader That sagacious controversialist was right in calling all these heresies nothing better than the old philosophies disguised under new names; his only error lay in not going back far enough to find their ultimate source Basilides, for example, never professed Christianity (in fact, Tertullian calls him a Platonist), but he superadded upon the esoteric doctrines of the Egyptian priesthood the newly-imported notions of Buddhism—that probable source of so much that is strange in the Gnosis The introduction of the religion of Buddha into Egypt and Palestine, a fact only recently discovered, yet substantiated by strong monumental testimony, affords the best solution for innumerable difficulties in the history of religion, but the circumstances relating to this very important question must be reserved for a separate chapter.

As for the actual TEXT-BOOKS of the Gnostics, which in their day formed so immense a library (every founder of a sect being, as if by obligation, a most prolific writer, as Hippolytus shows by the number of works he quotes), hunted up and carefully destroyed by the victorious orthodox, never perpetuated by transcripts after the sectaries became extinct, all have perished, leaving one sole specimen to attest their nature But this survivor is of a character so wild and wondrous, that had fortune left it to our choice we could not have preserved a more characteristic representative of its class This is the *Pistis-Sophia*, "Faith-Wisdom," a work to be perpetually quoted in the following pages, as it throws more light upon the actual monuments of Gnosticism than could hitherto be collected from all the other writers on the subject put together On this account a brief summary of its contents will be the best introduction to our inquiry into the nature of the system.

PISTIS-SOPHIA.

This treatise, ascribed to Valentinus (I know not on what authority) was discovered by Schwartze in a Coptic MS. preserved in the British Museum He transcribed the Coptic text and translated it into Latin ; both texts and version were published by Petermann in the year 1853 The original is copiously interspersed with Greek words and phrases, in fact, the Coptic was evidently so poor a language as to have no terms of its own to express any but the most materialistic ideas The matter of its professed revelation is set forth also with endless repetitions, bespeaking a language destitute of relative pronouns, of conjunctions, and of all the other grammatical refinements necessary for the clear and concise expression of thought *

The authorship of this record is assigned by itself in several places to Philip the Apostle, whom the Saviour bids to sit down and write these things ! This circumstance made me at first conclude it to be the lost Gospel of Philip quoted by Epiphanius, but the particular anecdote adduced by him from that gospel is not to be discovered anywhere in this But as the original is full of wide lacunae, which often fall in very interesting places, as if purposely defaced to escape the eyes of the profane, such an omission is not altogether conclusive against the identity of the two.

The nature of the book may be briefly sketched as follows It professes to be a record of the higher teaching of the Saviour communicated to his disciples during the *eleven* years he passed with them on earth after his crucifixion, and when he had returned from his ascension into Heaven This ascension had been made from the Mount of Olives, where he received from on high two shining vestures inscribed with five mystic words (§ 16), and the names of all the powers whose domains he had to traverse He thus (as he relates to the disciples) passes through the gate of the Firmament, the Sphere of Fate, and the regions

* It is intended to issue an English translation as a supplement to the present work

of the Twelve Great Æons, all of whom in succession are terror-smitten, and fall down before him and sing hymns of praise On arriving at the thirteenth æon, he finds seated below and weeping the excluded Power Pistis-Sophia,* who gives her name to the revelation She, having once caught a glimpse of the Supreme Light was seized with a desire to fly upwards into it but Adamas, the ruler of her proper place, being enraged at this act of rebellion against himself, caused a false light, a veritable *ignis fatuus*, to shine upon the waters of the subjacent chaos which lured down the hapless aspirant, and she was inextricably immersed in the abyss, and beset by the spirits thereof, all eager to deprive her of her native light. This doctrine of the admixture of light, derived from the Treasure of Light, with *matter*, its imprisonment therein, and its extraction and recovery by the appointed "Receivers of the Light" is the pervading idea of this revelation, to a greater extent even than in the Ophite scheme. As part of the same notion comes the frequent allusion to the κέρασμος or chaotic commixture of Light and Matter, to reorganise which is the special object of the Saviour's descent from above.

At least one half of the book is taken up with the account of the successive steps by which she ascends through all the Twelve Æons by the Saviour's aid, and the *confession* she sings at each stage of her deliverance out of chaos Each confession is proposed by Jesus to a disciple for explanation, and is referred to some psalm or other prophecy containing parallel sentiments, this concordance being occasionally made out with considerable ingenuity A remarkable peculiarity is that all throughout Mary Magdalene is the chief speaker, and the most highly commended for her spiritual knowledge, though once she is sharply rebuked by Peter for her presumption in thus perpetually putting herself forward unbidden—and not giving the *men* a chance to speak After Pistis-Sophia has thus regained her lost position, the most valuable portion of the

* This banishment of Sophia from the society of the other Æons is the grand turning-point of the principal Gnostic schemes, although each assigns a different reason for her degradation, as in the system of Valentinus, and also that of the later Ophites

exposition of doctrines commences. The Magdalene asks the great question as to the final cause of Sin (§ 281), to which Jesus returns a long and minute description of the composition of the soul of man, which is fourfold, the divine spark therein (a particle of the Light yet entangled in the κέρασμος) being encased in a three-fold envelope formed out of the *effluvia* of the rebellious Æons, the tendency of which is to keep it in subjection to the passions, and to themselves, so that when separated from the body it may not be able to escape out of their domains, "the regions of mid-space" here represented as places of pain. These Æons are elsewhere identified with the signs of the Zodiac. Next comes a detailed account of the Rulers of the regions of torment (§ 320), of their *authentic* forms, a crocodile, a bear, a cat, a dog, a serpent, a black bull, &c., and of their *authentic* names, these last are not Semitic, but either Coptic or belong, judging from their terminations, to the mystic language generally used upon the Gnostic stones. After this we have the several punishments appointed for the various sins of mankind, and the exact number of years and even of days required for the expiation of each in its proper dungeon (ταμεῖον) These places of torment are all enclosed within the Dragon of Outward Darkness It is worthy of remark that the serpent, whenever introduced, is a thing of evil—a sure indication that the book is under the influence of the Kabbala The same conclusion is deducible from the malignity pervading the entire dispensation which it pictures, and the evident delight it takes in creating and parcelling out the various punishments, of which heretics naturally get the largest share. The philosophic Gnostic schemes have no severer penalty for those who do not listen to them than the want of *Knowledge*, and the subjection to *Matter* After purgation in these prisons the souls are put into new bodies, and begin a new probation upon earth

The judge of souls is the Virgin of Light, attended by her seven hand-maids Certain sins, but few in number, are punished by annihilation, and admit of neither expiation nor atonement. But for all the rest instant remission is procurable, if the friends of the deceased celebrate on his behalf the "Mystery (or, Sacrament) of the Ineffable One." This must be the very earliest notice extant of the belief in the efficacy of the offering up of a *sacrament* for the redemption of souls. There is a singular provision made for the salvation of a perfectly righteous man, but who in his life-time has not enjoyed the opportunity of being converted. The angels take his departed soul, and carry it through all the realms of punishment with the utmost rapidity, and then conduct him before the Virgin of Light, who clothes it in a new body to recommence its earthly career, to obtain there the advantage of the mysteries and so become an heir of Light. The nature of the particular Mystery, so perpetually alluded to in this work, is in no place explained, it is, however, the highest of the Four and Twenty for such is the number of the Mysteries here mentioned, one for each of the grades in its celestial hierarchy, for the *Five Marks*, for the *Seven Vowels*, for the *Five Trees* and for the *Seven Amens* Throughout are interspersed frequent allusions to the seals, and the *numbers* of the Mysteries, courses, and divine personages, borrowed partly from the usages of the Temple, partly from those of the old Egyptian worship They are repeated and involved in a multitudinous, inextricable sequence, that to one not having the key thereto belonging, strongly calls to mind the numerical vagaries that flit before the mind when slightly delirious and which even the plodding German editor confesses, in his preface, often made his brain whirl as he attempted to transcribe them

Lastly comes a long fragment (§ 358), headed "a Portion of the Prayers of Jesus," which tells more directly upon the subject of these researches than anything that has fallen in my way The Saviour, attended by his disciples, standing sometimes on a mountain, sometimes by the sea, and sometimes in mid-air, addresses prayers to the Father, prefaced with long formulae of the same character, and often in the same words, as those covering the more important Gnostic monuments Some of these opening invocations are expounded, and seemingly paraphrased, in the prayers following them, though not in a very satisfactory manner. Also Jesus celebrates, with many singular formalities, a sacrifice of wine and water, which, there is reason to believe, is the grand Mystery or Sacrament so often lauded in the foregoing chapters. The whole closes with a long exposition by him of the influence of the Æons of the Zodiac upon the soul of the infant born under each, and of the fortunate or malign intervention of the planets in such cases Of the latter the *sacred* names are communicated apparently as used by the Magi A few Egyptian deities, *e g* Bubastes and Typhon, are named here, and the Syrian Barbelo is frequently introduced, as a personage of the very highest importance, being no less than the *heavenly* mother of the Saviour himself His earthly Mother is indeed represented as attending at these revelations, but she plays a very secondary part therein to the Magdalene and even to Salome. The last thing to be noticed in this most remarkable fruit of a crazy, mystic imagination—it is hard to say whether more Kabbalist, or Magian, or Christian—is the opposed dualism of many of the Powers introduced as agents in the economy of the universe for example, there is an obedient and a rebellious Adamas (that highest name with the earlier Naaseni), a great and a little Sabaoth, and similar antitheses to be met with also in the later Ophite schemes

THE BOOK OF ENOCH

This most ancient (as it professes) of the Hebrew Scriptures being so frequently referred to as the highest authority by the Æon Pistis-Sophia, a brief summary of its doctrine seems to form the necessary complement to the preceding section The Book of Enoch, though often quoted by the Fathers, had been lost ever since the eighth century (with the exception of a few chapters of a Greek version preserved by Georgius Syncellus), until Bruce brought back three copies of it from Abyssinia. In the canon of that Church it takes its place in the Old Testament immediately before the Book of Job *

* An English translation was made by Dr Lawrence, Bishop of Cashel of which the third edition, with notes, was published in 1837 The best German translation is that of Dillmann, 1857 *Cf* Schodde *Book of Enoch*, 1882

This book is divided into ninety chapters, and begins with the preface "In the Name of God, the merciful and gracious, slow to anger, and of great mercy, and holiness This Book is the Book of Enoch the prophet May blessing and help be with him who loves Him, for ever and ever Amen. Chapter I This word is the blessing of Enoch with which he blessed the chosen and the righteous that were of old And Enoch lifted up his voice and spoke, a holy man of God, while his eyes were open, and he saw a holy vision in the heavens, which the angels revealed to him And I heard from them everything, and I understood what I saw" After this follows the history of the angels, of their having descended from heaven, and produced giants with the daughters of men, of their having instructed them in the arts of war, and peace, and luxury The names of the leading angels are mentioned, which appear to be of Hebrew origin, but corrupted by Greek pronunciation The resolution of God to destroy these is then revealed to Enoch These topics occupy about eighteen chapters From the eighteenth to the fiftieth chapter Enoch is led by the angels Uriel and Raphael through a series of visions not much connected with the preceding He saw the Burning Valley of the fallen angels, the Paradise of the saints, the utmost ends of the earth, the treasuries of the thunder and lightning, winds, rain, dew, and the angels who presided over these He was led into the place of the General Judgment, saw the Ancient of Days on his throne, and all the kings of the earth before him At the fifty-second chapter, Noah is said to have been alarmed at the enormous wickedness of mankind, and, fearing vengeance, to have implored the advice of his great-grandfather Enoch told him that a flood of water should destroy the whole race of man, and a flood of fire punish the angels whom the deluge could not affect In Chapter LIX. the subject of the angels is resumed, Semeiza, Artukaru, Arimeon, Kakabael, Tusael, Ramiel, Damdal, and others to the number of twenty, appear at the head of the fallen spirits, and give fresh instances of their rebellious dispositions At Chapter LXII Enoch gives his son Methuselah a long account of the sun, moon, stars, the year, the months, the winds, and the like physical phenomena This takes up eight chapters, after which the Patriarch makes a recapitulation of the former pages. The remaining twenty chapters are employed on the history of the Deluge, Noah's preparations for it, and the success which attended them. The destruction of all flesh excepting his family, and the execution of divine vengeance on the angels, conclude the work.

FIG. 1.

GNOSTICISM IN ITS BEGINNING.

To begin with the received account of the RISE AND PROGRESS of the Gnostic *philosophy*, for that is its proper appellation, *heresy* being properly restricted to differences of opinion between members of one regularly established community, we find that as early as the year A D 35, the Samaritans were regarding Simon Magus, as "the Great Power of God," and he and his disciple Cerinthus, are represented by the Christian Fathers as the actual founders of Gnosticism, under that accepted name

Of the former, Hippolytus gives a history which there is no reason for not accepting as correct in the main particulars He was a native of Gitteh, in the province of Samaria, and commenced his career, and soon acquired great influence amongst his countrymen, by practising magic after the "Thrasymedian method" (*i e* jugglery, as previously described by Hippolytus), nay more, by working miracles "through the agency of devils" Having fallen in love with a beautiful courtezan at Tyre, he bought her from her owner, and always carried her about with him, declaring that she was the "Intelligence" (Ἔννοια) that of old was imprisoned in the body of the Grecian Helen, then of the Lost Sheep, but now was restored to him for the salvation of the world Even *before* the preaching of Christianity he had set up for a teacher of a new religion, plagiarised from Moses and Heraclitus the "Obscure," based upon the axiom that *Fire* was the First Principle of all things, subordinate to which were the "Six Radicals" a curiously compounded mixture of Judaism and Magism, of which Hippolytus gives a full though not very intelligible summary "This Simon, after he had ransomed Helen, granted salvation unto men by means of his own *knowledge*. For inasmuch as the angels had governed the world ill by reason of their own ambitiousness, he pretended that he was come to set all things right, and having changed his form and made himself like to the Principalities, the Powers, and the

Angels, wherefore it was that he showed himself in the form of man although *not a man* at all, and had suffered the Passion in Judæa, although he had not really suffered it, moreover, that he had manifested himself to the Jews as the Son, in Samaria as the Father, and amongst the Gentiles in other parts as the Holy Ghost, but he submitted to be called by whatsoever name they pleased The Prophets were inspired by the Angels, creators of the world, when they delivered their prophecies, on which account they that believe in Simon and Helen pay no regard to them (the Prophets) even in our times and they do whatever they please, pretending that they are redeemed through *his* grace" "Now this same Simon, when he was by his magic arts deceiving many in Samaria, was confuted by the Apostles, and having been cursed by them, he afterwards fell from his reputation and invented these fables At last, having travelled to Rome, he again ran against the Apostles, and Peter had many encounters with him when he was *seducing multitudes* through his magical practices Finally, having gone into the land of Persia, he took up his abode under a plane-tree, and there preached his doctrine But at last, when he was on the point of being convicted for an impostor, in consequence of his making too long a stay in the same place, he gave out that, if he were buried alive, he would rise again on the third day And in truth, having caused a pit to be dug by his disciples, he commanded himself to be covered over with earth They therefore did what he commanded them, but he never came back unto this day, inasmuch as he was not a Christ Now this is the story told concerning Simon, from whom Valentinus borrowed his first ideas, but called them by different names. For 'Mind,' and 'Truth,' and 'the Word,' and 'Life,' and 'the Church,' and 'Man,' the *Æons* of Valentinus, are confessedly the *Six Radicals* of Simon, namely, 'Mind, Intelligence, Voice, Name, Reason, and Thought'"

But to go on with the series of teachers—this counter-apostolical succession—Simon was followed by Menander, he by Basilides at Alexandria, who, dying about A D 138, was replaced by Valentinus, born of Jewish parentage in the same city This last is styled by Irenæus "Chief of the Gnostics," on account of the importance and wide diffusion of his doctrines even during his own lifetime. In Syria other sects were being founded contemporaneously with these, taking their names from Marcion and Bardesanes, both of whom tradition represents as Persians by origin, and consequently *Magians* by religious training The latter is by some called a native of Pontus, a circumstance, however, making no difference as to the source of his opinions, that region being confessedly the seat of Mithraicism, and ruled over by a line claiming descent from the first Darius, or a satrap of his It is needless to enumerate here the founders of less important sects, until we come to the uprising of Manes, author of the most daring and most permanent theosophy of them all, which fought twice over so long and obstinate a battle with the Catholic faith. This sect, its origin, and tenets, on account of the curiosity of its doctrines, and the immense influence that they exerted over the ancient and mediæval world, will be considered at length in another chapter, as will also the *Ophites* whose name figures so conspicuously in the history of the primitive Church.

What has been mentioned above with respect to the countries producing the founders of all these sects—Egypt, Syria, or Persia—leads us to expect to find one common principle pervading the systems of all, and such is most probably the case The fundamental doctrine held in common by all the chiefs of the Gnosis was, that the whole creation was not the work of the Supreme Deity, but of the Demiurgus, a simple *Emanation*, and several degrees removed from the highest power To the latter, indeed, styled by them the "Unknown Father" (or as Simon first designated him "The Boundless Power," and "The Root of all Things"), they attributed the creation of the *intellectual* world—that is, the Intelligences, the Æons, and the Angels—whilst, to the Demiurgus they referred the creation of the *World of Matter*, subject to imperfection from its very nature. But in order clearly to understand the grand principles underlying these doctrines, it is absolutely necessary to possess the main features of the older systems from which these same doctrines were principally borrowed, these systems being that of the Zendavesta, of the Kabbala (which is little more than a translation of the same), and of the reformed Brahminical religion as taught by the Buddhist missionaries in the dominions of the Syro-Macedonians, or picked up in India by Alexandrian merchants visiting the emporia of Guzerat for the sake of trade.

Although to express their ideas visibly upon their *monuments* (the elucidation of which is the special object of this treatise) the Gnostics largely borrowed the images and symbols of the ancient Egyptian mythology (especially those connected with the Agathodaemon, the Solar god Iao, and the guide of souls, the jackal-headed Anubis), yet these figures were employed in a new sense, unless indeed we suppose (what is probable enough) that their *esoteric* meaning had been from the very beginning similar to that published by the teachers of the new faith This last explanation was in fact the perpetual boast of Valentinus, and runs through every article of his theosophy as we read it in the interesting summary given by Hippolytus, and again, it must never be forgotten, for it is the key to many of the seeming contradictions in the different systems about to be passed in review, that Greek and Jew carried with them their ancient quarrel into the new field of the Gnosis. The former exalts the Bacchic *Serpent*, whilst he makes *Sabaoth* little better than a demon, the latter continues to abominate the Serpent as the impersonation of Satan, but his Sabaoth is the "Great and Good" (as Pistis-Sophia perpetually entitles him), the defender of the believer's soul against the malignant "Æons of the Sphere," and the influence of Judaism radiating from its second focus, the school of Alexandria, was so much more powerful than ordinary readers of history have ever suspected, that a few remarks upon this very curious subject will form a useful introduction to our consideration of its later philosophy.

INFLUENCE OF JUDAISM ON THE ANCIENT WORLD

People in these times are still so influenced by the ideas engendered by the fifteen centuries of ecclesiastical *régime*, during which hatred and contempt for the Jewish race formed an important Christian virtue, that they entirely overlook the influence exercised by Judaism over the minds of the heathen world so long as the Temple stood, and the national worship was celebrated there in all its glory. When the Romans, by their conquest of Syria, and soon after of Egypt, came into direct contact with the Jewish nation, although they disliked them individually, yet they conceived an intense admiration for their ancient, mysterious, and solemn worship. But, in fact, every institution, hallowed by the stamp of antiquity, immediately commanded the respect of the genuine old Roman. The Emperors lost no time in gaining a new patron, of mighty and undefined power, in *Jehovah*, by instituting a daily sacrifice to be ever offered at their own cost on behalf of themselves and empire. The discontinuance of this sacrifice, by the faction of the Zealots which had taken possession of the Temple, is noted by Josephus as the consummating act of the great revolt and attempt to re-establish independence, which brought down final destruction upon Zion. To give a few examples of the hold Judaism had taken upon the imaginations of the highest classes in Rome, whence its vastly magnified power over the minds of the vulgar, may be calculated according to the well-known rule of proportion in such matters. To mark Augustus' freedom from superstition, Suetonius quotes the circumstance of his highly commending the conduct of his grandson Caius, his heir apparent, because—during his visit to Egypt and Palestine—he had forborne to visit Apis in the one and the Temple in the other country. Putting the two religions in this way upon an equality, of itself demonstrates the high place then held by the Jewish in popular estimation, for by that time the Egyptian, as the chapter upon the Serapis-worship will show, had to a great extent superseded the worship of the national deities of Rome. Fuscus Aristius, a friend of Horace's, and therefore to be supposed a person of consequence and of education, makes it his excuse for not attending to a business-matter, that the day happened to be the Sabbath, and that "he was a little superstitious, like many others."

The influence and numbers of the Jews actually residing at Rome under the Republic is strikingly exhibited by some observations of Cicero in his oration in defence of Flaccus. Flaccus, when commanding in Asia, had prohibited the sending of money to Jerusalem. This money can only mean the tribute paid by each adult Jew to the Temple, of half a shekel, or two drachmæ a head. Flaccus seized the money that had been collected for the purpose in defiance of his edict, amounting at Apamea to nearly one hundred pounds weight of gold, at Laodicea to twenty The only gold piece of the age being the *stater*, current for twenty-five drachmæ, and of the weight of fifty to the pound, these collections would give us fifty thousand tribute-payers at the former city, and ten thousand at the other The orator considers this "auri Judaici invidia" so damaging to his cause, that he explains the circumstances in a whisper to the jurymen, in order not to excite the indignation of the Jews amongst his audience He actually declares that Flaccus's enemies had managed that his cause should be tried in that particular court in order to have the aid of the Jews domiciled in that quarter of Rome, to intimidate the jury, and so gain a verdict against him "Sequitur auri illa invidia Judaici Hoc nimirum est illud, quod non longe a gradibus Aureliis hæc causa dicitur Ob hoc crimen hic locus abs te, Laeli, atque illa turba quæsita est Scis quanta sit manus, quanta concordia, quantum valeat in concionibus Submissa voce agam, tantum ut judices audiant Neque enim desunt qui istos in me atque in optimum quemque incitent, quos ego quo id facilius faciant non adjuvabo" (Chapter XXVIII) And what is still more surprising this influence continued to work even after the fall of Jerusalem, and the extinction of the people as a nation Spartianus mentions that Severus in his tour of investigation throughout Asia, when he forbade people to turn Christians, extended the same interdict to the Jewish religion also Again, to show the natural good-heartedness of Caracalla, he instances his indignation on account of the severe flogging which a boy, his playfellow, had received from his father, with the emperor's approbation, on the score of his Judaising The circumstances of the friendship point out that the boy thus made a "confessor" must have belonged to one of the best families of Rome. Such a position yet retained by the religion of Abraham is almost inconceivable at that late period, when it had, besides the vigorous and ever-increasing growth of Christianity, to contend with the varieties of the Gnosis which suited themselves to every taste, and in many instances had sprung immediately out of herself (not out of her hated daughter and rival), and by their union with heathen philosophy, were naturally more attractive to the Gentiles than the original parent. Even at the time when one would have expected the prejudice against anything belonging to that nation to have been the most violent amongst the Romans, we find Vespasian, the actual destroyer of their national existence, erecting a statue in the most honourable of all situations, to an Alexandrian Jew, Tiberius, who had assisted him in his attempt to gain the empire, in some manner not recorded, but possibly in his capacity of the Rothschild of the age by an opportune loan. It is true that Juvenal cannot repress his indignation at all this prostitution to a foreigner of an honour before confined to the most eminent of his countrymen, and hints it to be the duty of every true Roman to express his sense of the injury by committing nuisances under the very nose of the statue.

> "Atque triumphales, inter quos ausus habere
> Nescio quis titulos Ægyptius atque Alabarches,
> Cujus ad effigiem *non tantum* meiere fas est."—I. 130.

In the third century we find the model emperor, Severus Alexander, setting up the image of *Abraham* by the side of Christ and Orpheus, all considered as the divinely-inspired founders of the several schools of mystery (or to go to the probable root of the belief, as so many different *Buddhas*), in the most holy recess of his domestic chapel. A little research amongst the annals of the later emperors would no doubt, furnish many other examples of the hold taken by various particulars of the Jewish creed, in its Babylonian and Alexandrian phases, upon the religious notions of the Romans. The fact is easily accounted for, when men's ideas upon the nature of the soul, of God's Government, and of a future state, are entirely vague, as were those of the educated heathen of those times, when (old traditions being discarded as mere unsatisfying poetical fables) they attempted to build up systems that should explain every difficulty by the help of reason and philosophy alone, although destitute of any solid grounds upon which to lay the first foundation of the fabric. Things being in this state, a religion venerable by its *antiquity* (itself an impenetrable shield against the shafts of infidelity, as even Tacitus concedes "Hi ritus, quoquo modo inducti, antiquitate defenduntur" *Hist.* v. 5), possessing a complete system that solved every problem by a professedly divine revelation, totally setting itself above reason and human experience, but proclaiming unquestioning credence as the most meritorious of virtues, such a religion could not but gain the victory over its disorderly and discordant competitors, which had nothing but arguments deduced from probabilities and analogies wherewith to oppose it The same contest we behold passing under our own eyes, Roman Catholicism with its doctrines overthrown, exploded, rejected by reason, learning, and philosophy, for the space of three centuries, is again rapidly bringing back into her fold her lost sheep, which, having wandered through the tempting ways of Protestantism, and of philosophy or infidelity, however people choose to call it, and unable to discover any reason that will bear the test for standing fast at any ultimate point as the absolute truth, at last return weary and disappointed to whence they started, and find it conducive to peace of mind to accept assertion for demonstration, and the age of a tenet as equivalent to its truth.

There is yet another consideration that is of great importance in the present inquiry, which is the close affinity between the Judaism of this period and Magism, the extent of which will be pointed out in the following sections when we come to speak of the Talmud Remembering how much of the machinery of the one was borrowed from the other, there is little cause for astonishment at discovering that what are generally considered peculiarly Jewish titles of Deity upon relics, may rather be attributed to a Magian source

The three circumstances thus briefly adduced—namely, the direct influence of the religion of Zion as a "mystery" of the most venerable antiquity, vying with those of Egypt and of Babylon, its subsequent indirect influence through its offshoots (which left its visible impress upon things tangible), the virtue of its connection with the creed of the Magi, the secret priesthood, or rather, freemasons of the ancient world, these are the things solving the difficulty that must have struck any inquiring mind when beginning to study the so-called Gnostic remains From the foregoing considerations, at least a plausible reason may be gathered for the fact of the Hebrew names of the Deity, and of his angels, and of the patriarchs, so perpetually being repeated on works presenting the figures of genii and of astral spirits—forms of idol-monsters the most repugnant, one would have thought, to the feelings of the worshippers of those sacred names, profaned by such union, and imagery, from beholding which the true follower of Moses must certainly have recoiled in horror

THE ZENDAVESTA

The Zendavesta, literally "text and comment," is the doctrine of Zoroaster (*Zarathrustra*), comprised in eight parts, written at different periods, but of which the earliest have been assigned to the date of B C 1200–1000 In its present form it was collected by Ardeshir, the founder of the Sassanian dynasty, from oral tradition, at the time when he re-established the ancient religion of Persia

In this revelation the Supreme Being is called "Boundless Time" (*Zarvana Akarana*), because to him no beginning can be assigned, he is so surrounded by his own glory, and so far exalted beyond all human comprehension, that he can only be the object of silent veneration The beginning of creation was made by means of *Emanations* The first emanation of the Eternal One was Light, whence issued Ormuzd (*Ahuramazda*), the King of Light Ormuzd is styled the Firstborn of Boundless Time, and the "Ferouer" of him, or Pre-existing Soul (type or idea in Platonic phrase), had existed from all eternity within the primitive Light By means of his "Word," Ormuzd created the pure world of which he is the preserver and the judge Next, he created in his own image the six *Amshaspands*, who stand about his throne, and are his agents with the lower spirits, and with mankind, whose prayers they offer up to him, and to whom they serve for models of perfection These Amshaspands, of whom Ormuzd is the first, thus making up the mystic number *seven*, are of both sexes, and the Gnostics adopted them, as we shall see further on, into their own systems, with the same distinction of sex. The next series of emanations were the *Izeds*, twenty-eight in number, of whom Mithras is the chief Like the superior order, they watch over the purity and happiness of the world, of which they are the genii and guardians The principal names amongst them are Vohu-mano, Mazda, Asha, Vayu (Ventus), Geusurvi (Soul of the Earth), Sraosha (who exactly answers, in point of duties, to the Grecian Hermes and Jewish Gabriel, for he carries the mandates of Ormuzd, and conveys up to him the souls of the righteous)

The third series, the *Ferouers*, are in number infinite These are the Thoughts or "Ideas" conceived in the mind of Ormuzd before he proceeded to the creation of things They are the protectors of mankind during this mortal life, and will purify their souls on the Day of the Resurrection

The creation of these chiefs, with their angelic hosts, had become necessary Ahriman, the Second-born of the Eternal One—like Ormuzd, an emanation from the Primal Light, and equally pure, but ambitious and full of pride—had become jealous of the Firstborn On this account the Supreme Being condemned him to inhabit for twelve thousand years the space that is illumined by no ray of light—the black empire of Darkness This interval will suffice to decide the struggle between Light and Darkness, between Good and Evil Ahriman, in order to oppose his rival, created in his turn three series of evil spirits, corresponding in number, and antagonistic in office, to each one of the good, and, like them, male and female The first series is that of the *Arch-Devs*, chained each one to his respective planet and of whom the chief is Astomogt, "the two-footed Serpent of lies" These Devs are the authors of all evil, both physical and moral, throughout the universe.

Ormuzd, after a reign of three thousand years, then created

the Animal World in six periods, creating first light—a faint image of the Light celestial—then water, earth, plants, beasts, and lastly, man Ahriman had concurred in the creation of earth and water, for *Darkness* being already inherent in these two elements, Ormuzd was unable to exclude its nature from them

Ormuzd had produced by his *Word* a being the type and source of universal life for all creation, this being was called *Life*, or the *Bull* (the same word in Zend stands for both) This creature Ahriman contrived to destroy, but out of its scattered seed Ormuzd, through the agency of the Amshaspand Saphandomad (*Wisdom*), formed the first human pair, Meschia and Meschiane This couple Ahriman, by a bribe of fruits and milk, succeeded in corrupting, having gained over the female first Then, to all the good animals made by Ormuzd, he opposed, by his own creation, as many mischievous and venomous ones The struggle still goes on, the Power of Darkness often is the superior, but the pure souls are assisted and defended by the good genii, and will ultimately triumph For when things shall seem at their worst, and Evil all-powerful in the creation, three prophets shall appear and restore the lost Light One of these, Sosioch, shall regenerate the world and restore it to its pristine excellence Then comes the general Resurrection, when the good shall immediately enter into this happy abode—the regenerated earth, and Ahriman, together with his angels and the wicked, be purified by immersion in a lake of molten metal, so as to render them fitting members of the new kingdom Thenceforth all will enjoy unchangeable happiness, and, headed by Sosioch, ever sing the praises of the Eternal One.

The religion of Zoroaster was a reformed version of the ancient creed held by the inhabitants of Eritene in Bactria For it is probable that the first gods of the Aryan race before it split into Indian and Zend, were the powers of Nature, *Indra*, thunder, *Mithra*, sunlight, *Vayu*, wind, *Agni*, fire, *Armaiti*, earth, *Soma*, intoxication The worship of the last may have been the source of the Dionysia, introduced from India, as the Greeks themselves always asserted. These powers were called *Ahuras* and *Devas* indifferently, but Zoroaster reduced all these powers to the secondary rank of angels, and used the name *Devas* in a bad sense only. The Zoroastrian was the established religion of the Persians at the time when they conquered Assyria, and to a great extent it superseded the material idolatry of the Babylonians, whose gods Darius and Xerxes melted down without any scruple. But Matter is of opinion that the College of Magi, established long before the Persian conquest of Babylon, accepted the new religion upon the change of masters, retaining nothing of the old besides Astrology and Divination.

It must not be forgotten how large a portion of the Jewish captivity remained permanently in Assyria—only two tribes, Judah and Levi, having been sent back to Jerusalem by Cyrus; and Babylon long continued the seat of a most flourishing Rabbinical school, whilst Judea itself, down to the time of the Macedonian conquest, remained a province of the Persian Empire. How important a part of the Persian population at a much later period were either Jews, or under Jewish influence, appears from the very remarkable assertion of Josephus, "that his nation were encouraged to brave all extremities in their final struggle against the power of Rome by the confident expectation of aid from their brethren beyond the Euphrates." And three centuries later Ammianus notices that Julian's invading army came upon a city entirely inhabited by Jews in the very centre of Persia. After the captivity, the principal literary establishments of the Jews appear to have been seated in central Asia. The schools of Nahardea, of Sora, of Punbiditha, were at least as famous as the schools of Palestine (cf. Jos. Ant. xviii. 12). The latter even appear to have paid a sort of filial deference to these foundations: the Chaldee version of the Pentateuch, made by Onkelos of Babylon, was accepted as the authorised version by all the Jews living in Palestine; and the Rabbi Hillel, coming from that capital to Jerusalem, was received by the doctors of the Holy City as an ornament of the same national school, and this only a few years before the birth of Christ. From all these circumstances it is easy to perceive how much of the Zoroastrian element may have pervaded the Jewish religion at the time of the promulgation of Christianity, when its principal teachers were the Pharisees or "separatists," if, indeed, their doctors did not actually get their appellation from the word *Pharsi*, "Persian"—an etymology that has something to recommend it These doctrines, as then taught, are set forth in the *Kabbala*, or "Traditions," so called from *Kabbal*, "to receive" —the main features of which shall be sketched in the following sections.

THE KABBALA AND THE TALMUD

The origin of the Kabbala is placed by most authors much later than that of Christianity; and, indeed, it is not impossible that its doctrines may have received great developments *after* that epoch,* nevertheless, the elements of them go back to a much more remote antiquity The Book of Daniel bears the most conspicuous traces of this antiquity, and to the attestation of this record are added other proofs no less convincing The idea of *Emanation* is, so to speak, the *soul*, the essential element of the Kabbala, it is likewise, as we have already seen the essential character of Zoroastrism We may therefore consider that it was through their very intimate connection with Persia that the Jews imbibed that idea.

According to the Kabbala, as according to the Zendavesta, all that exists has emanated from the source of the Infinite Light

Before all things existed the Primal Being, the "*Ancient of Days*," the eternal King of Light This King of Light is the *All*, he is the real cause of all existence, he is the Infinite (*En Soph*), he alone is *He*, there is in him no *Thou*, but he cannot be known, "he is a closed Eye"

The universe is the revelation of the King of Light, and only subsists in Him His *qualities* are manifested in it, variously modified and in different degrees, it is therefore his "Holy

* The tradition is that it was first committed to writing by Simon Ben Jochai, who, being proscribed by Titus concealed himself in a cavern for the space of eleven years, the whole of which he devoted to this work, in which he was assisted by the prophet Elias

Splendour"—the *mantle*, as it were, wherewith he must be clothed in silence All is an emanation from this Being; the nearer therefore that any approaches to him, the more perfect is it, and the less so does it become as it recedes from him this idea of *gradation* is eminently Persian Before the creation of the world, the Primal Light filled all, so that there was no void at all, but when the Supreme Being, residing within this Light, resolved to display and manifest his perfection, he retired within himself, and formed around him a void space Into this void he let fall his first emanation—a ray of the Light, which is the cause and principle of all existence, uniting in itself the generative and conceptive forces, being both father and mother in the sublimest sense, pervading all, and without which nothing can for an instant subsist

From this Double Force, designated by the first two letters of the name Jehovah (*Yod, He* *), emanated the First-born of God, the *Tikkun*, or "Universal Type" (Platonic *Idea*), and the general container of all beings, united within himself by means of the Primal Ray He is the creator, preserver, and prime animator of the world He is the "Light of light," possessing the three primitive forces of the Godhead the light, the spirit, and the life Inasmuch as he has *received* what he *gives*, the light and the life, he is considered as equally a generative and conceptive principle as the "Primitive Man," *Adam-Kadmon*, and as man himself is called the "little world," or the microcosm, so this Being, his Type, is properly designated the "great world," or Macrocosm In this then Adam-Kadmon, the principle of light and life, the Kabbalists have united the attributes of the same principles amongst the Persians

Adam-Kadmon has manifested himself in ten emanations, which are not indeed actual beings, but sources of life, vessels of the Almighty Power, types of all the creation Their names are: the Crown, Wisdom, Prudence, Magnificence, Severity, Beauty, Victory, Glory, Foundation, Empire To Wisdom they gave the title *Jah*, to Prudence *Jehovah*, to Magnificence *El*,

* The I H so conspicuously placed on some Gnostic stones probably expresses this name, as being the nearest equivalents the Greek alphabet could furnish for the Hebrew letters

to Seventy *Elohim*, to Victory and Glory *Sabaoth*, to Empire *Adonai*

These are all attributes of the Supreme, as displayed in his works, through which alone it is possible for the human mind to conceive him To the same emanations the Kabbalists give other titles, which constantly present themselves in Gnostic inscriptions For example, the *Crown* (Parmenides also calls the Godhead Στέφανος) has the synonym of *Or*, "Light," (possibly the same with *Om*, the name of a Sabean genius) *Wisdom* is called *Nous* and *Logos*, and is equivalent to the *Sophia* of Gnosticism, she has also the names of *Fear*, *Depth of thought*, *Eden*, according to the several passions that animate her *Prudence* is the "river flowing out of Paradise, the fountain of the oil of unction" *Magnificence* has for symbol a lion's head, *Severity*, a red and black fire, *Beauty*, the colours green and yellow, the symbol of *Beauty* is an illuminating mirror, *Victory* is Jehovah Sabaoth, having for symbol the pillar on the right hand, called *Jachin*, *Glory* has the left pillar *Boaz*, called likewise the "Old Serpent," and sometimes "Cherubim and Seraphim," this principle answers to the genius *Ophis* of the Gnostic systems "Jachin" and "Boaz" signify Strength and Power they figure conspicuously in the symbolism of the secret societies of modern times, and naturally so, for these *illuminati* have borrowed (probably without understanding it) all the terminology of the Valentinians and the Kabbalists "Foundation" becomes the Tree of the knowledge of Good and Evil also Noah, Solomon, and the Messiah—all which titles merely express the eternal alliance existing between the Supreme and all that emanates from him, and in virtue whereof he brings back into himself all the souls that have lost their original purity. "Empire" is the Consuming Fire, the wife of the Church—all three titles being also employed in the Valentinian system.

The relationship of the "Sephiroth," or Æons, to one another the Kabbalists represent by a number of *circles* intersecting in a mysterious manner *ad infinitum;* or again, by the figure of a *Man*, or of a *Tree*, made up of such circles The figure of the Man, *Seir-Anpin*, consists of two hundred and forty-three numbers,

bers, being the numerical value of the letters in the name *Abram*, and signifying the different orders in the celestial hierarchy. The first idea of this type was possibly borrowed from the Hindoo figure of Brahma and the several types typified by the different parts of his body, to which mystical values are still attached by the Hindoos

The ten Sephiroth served as *types* or models for the visible Creation, and from them emanated the Four Worlds, Aziluth, B'riah, Jezirah, and Asiah, each world successively proceeding out of the one above it, and each in succession *enveloping* its superior A theory this, possibly borrowed from Plato's description of the arrangement of the seven spheres, as given in the "Vision of Er," at the end of his "Republic," where he compares them to a set of the hemispherical bowls used by jugglers, fitting into, and moving loosely within, each other (lib x 614B, *seq.*)

These Four Worlds become less pure as they descend in the series, the least pure of all being the *material* world But nothing is entirely *material*, for all subsists through God, the ray of his light penetrating through all creation being the Life of the life, and consequently "all is God" This universal *All* is divided into thirty-two "Gates," the elements or energies out of which all beings are formed

The world *Aziluth* is inhabited by the Parsupham, the purest emanations of the Deity, having nothing material in their composition *B'riah* is possessed by an inferior order, who are the servants of Aziluth, although still immaterial creatures Still lower are the inhabitants of *Jezirah*, to which world belong the Cherubim and Seraphim, the Elohim and the Benê-Elohim But *Asiah* is peopled by gross material existences of both sexes, the Klippoth delighting in evil, whose chief is Belial. These last beings are full of ambition, and ever at war with the pure spirits of the superior worlds, whose empire they unceasingly endeavour to usurp

The three superior orders just described answer to the Amshaspands, Izeds, and Fravashis, of Zoroaster, as do the Klippoth, in their vast numbers and malicious nature, to his Devs. This discord did not exist in the beginning, it was the result of a revolution in heaven, called the "Fall of the Seven Kings," from whom* the Creator, as a punishment, extracted the principle of good and light, and bestowed it upon the inhabitants of the three superior spheres.

This last notion is common to many forms of Gnosticism. The Ophites make Achamoth extract from Ildabaoth and his six sons the inherent ray of Divine Light, in order to bestow it upon Man. Again, the Pistis-Sophia represents two great angels, Melchisedech and Zorocothora (*gatherer of light*) making their annual rounds through the rebellious "Æons of the sphere" (zodiacal signs), and *squeezing* out of them all the rays of Divine Light that are still left in their composition, which having been all extracted, the fulness of time and the kingdom of heaven are come; and so, according to the Kabbala, when the contest shall have endured for the space ordained from the beginning of the world, the Supreme shall deliver the spirits in Asiah from their material envelope, shall strengthen the feeble ray of his light that is within them, and shall establish its pristine harmony throughout all Creation.

The *Human Soul* is composed of all parts borrowed from each of these four worlds. From Asiah it gets the *Nephesh*, or seat of the physical appetites; from Jezirah the *Ruach*, or seat of the passions; from Briah the *Neshamah* or reason, and from Aziluth it obtains the *Chaiah*, or principle of spiritual life. This looks like an adaptation of the Platonic theory of the soul's obtaining its respective faculties from the Planets in its downward progress through their spheres. But the Pistis-Sophia, with its accustomed boldness, puts this theory into a much more poetical

* The author of the Book of Enoch alludes to the same legend. "Over these fountains also I perceived a place which had neither the firmament of heaven above it, nor the solid ground underneath it; neither was there water above it, nor any thing on wing; but the spot was desolate. And then I beheld *seven stars* like great blazing mountains, and like spirits entreating me. Then the Angel said, this place until the consummation of heaven and earth will be the prison of the stars and the host of heaven. The stars which roll over fire are those who transgressed the commandments of God before their time arrived, for they came not in their proper season. Therefore was he offended with them, and bound them until the consummation of their crimes in the secret year."—Chap. xviii.

shape (§ 282) The *Inner Man* is similarly made up of *four* constituents, but these are supplied by the rebellious Æons of the Sphere, being the *Power* (a particle of the Divine light ("Divinæ particula auræ") yet left in themselves), the *Soul* "formed out of the tears of their eyes, and the sweat of their torments", the 'Αντιμῖμον Πνεύματος *Counterfeit of the Spirit* (seemingly answering to our *Conscience*), and lastly the Μοῖρα *Fate*, whose business it is to lead the man to the end appointed for him, "if he hath to die by the fire, to lead him into the fire, if he hath to die by a wild beast, to lead him unto the wild beast, &c" But in truth the entire system of this most wondrous Gospel is a mixture of the Kabbala with the ideas of Magian astrology, clouded under the terminology of the old Egyptian creed, to which belong its "Triple Powers," "Invisible Gods," and "the Proper Forms" assigned by it to the different Æons.

All the human race having sinned in the First Man, that is as regards their *souls*, all which were necessarily *contained within* his soul at the time of the Fall, these souls are exiled hither into prisons of Matter, called bodies, in order to expiate their sin, and to exercise themselves in good during their residence on earth Such as upon quitting the body are not found sufficiently purified for entrance into Aziluth, have to recommence their penance in this world Hence the question of the Disciples whether a man's being *born* blind were the punishment for his *own* sins, which on this supposition must have been committed by him in a *previous* life This penitential transmigration of souls forms a very conspicuous feature in the doctrine set forth in the Pistis-Sophia The wicked, after undergoing torment for periods nicely apportioned to their deserts, in prisons belonging to the several Infernal Powers, are sent into this world again to inhabit human bodies afflicted in different ways—lame, blind, or sunk in abject poverty Similarly the righteous, but *unregenerate*, man is provided with a fresh body wherein to avail himself of the *sacraments* of the new religion; which in his former life he had neglected through ignorance, and not wilfully

The nature of God, and of Man, is therefore the subject of the Kabbala, the Government of the Creation is set forth in the

Talmud, the doctrine of which concerning the *Nature of the Angels* is extremely important for the understanding of much in Gnosticism The whole system in this particular is borrowed from the Zendavesta, and could not have originated *before*, or indeed *without* the Captivity, so opposite is the spirit pervading it to the genius of the Mosaic Law According to it, the government of all things is entrusted to the Angels, of whom there are seventy Princes, watching over each element, nation, and language Thus, Jehuel is the Prince of *Fire*, and has under him seven subordinates Seraphiel, Gabriel, Uriel, Temanael, Shimsael, Hadranael, and Samiel Again, Michael is Prince of *Water*, and similarly attended by seven inferior spirits Moreover, there are an infinity of Angels yet lower in degree, guardians of the various animals, plants, heat, winds, rains, &c There also are others presiding over the passions of the soul, fear, grace, favour, love, and so on Hence it is not to be wondered at, that the Angel who directs the course of the sun should have under him no less than two hundred and ninety-six hosts, whose sum is expressed by the numerical letters in the word *Haaretz* "the earth" The head of them is Metation, the "number of his name" being three hundred and fourteen, and therefore equivalent to that of *Shaddai*, "the Almighty" Metation is the Persian Mithras, the names of the others are all compounded with *El* "God," and contain his titles, or invocations to him * All this celestial roll-call fully explains St Paul's warning to his flock at Colossae against being reduced into a "voluntary (that is, an uncalled for) humility, and the worshipping of Angels," whilst the copious appearance of their names upon talismans strongly testifies to the veneration in which their power was held

This last circumstance was a necessity of the case, for all these monuments proceed from two sources—the two great schools of Magi mentioned by Pliny, the most ancient, the

* The Book of Enoch thus states the names and offices of the "Angels who watch" Uriel presides over clamour and terror, Raphael over the spirits of men, Rugiel inflicts punishment on the world and the luminaries, Michael, who presides over human virtue, commands the nations Sarakiel over the spirits of the children of men who transgress, Gabriel over Ikisat, over Paradise, and over the Cherubim

Chaldean, founded by Zoroaster and Orthanes, the *modern* of his own day, by Moses and Jambres. So Juvenal, after bringing in the proud and pompous Chaldean, the maker of emperors—

> "Cujus amicitia conducendaque tabella
> Magnus civis obit, et formidatus Othoni," (vi 557–8)

makes the poor trembling Jewess fortune-teller steal in with whispers for the lady's private ear—her profession going no further than the interpreting or the vending of dreams—"Qualiacunque voles Judæi somnia vendent." Such nocturnal revelations, we are told, were to be procured by sleeping with the proper talisman put under one's pillow. Thus, a writer on magic quoted by Camillo di Leonardo, lays down that "a woman with her hair hanging down loose, and a man approaching her making a gesture of love, engraved upon a crystal, or jacinth being placed under the head upon going to sleep, will make one see in a dream whatsoever one desires."*

Such being the nature of the case, the existing productions of Gnosticism will be most appropriately investigated in the present Treatise by considering the nature of the various sources from which they emanated. The series commences with the *Mithraic*, as being the most ancient in origin, and in which the Magian and the Jewish Kabbalistic ideas are found the most frequently united. To this class succeed the *Abraxas-gems*, properly so-called, in which the Magian ground-work is modified by the refinements of Basilides, introducing a strong tincture of the primitive Egyptian theology. To Egypt herself more properly belong the *Agathodæmon* talismans bearing the figure of the good serpent, Chnuphis—an emblem which gave its name to that very wide-spreading and clearly defined sect, the *Ophites*. Last of all come the innumerable relics of the

* And again, the "sigil of a man having a long face and beard and eyebrows raised, seated upon a plough, and holding a fox and vulture, with four men lying upon his neck, such a gem being placed under your head when asleep, makes you dream of treasures, and of the right manner of finding them." Also "Cepheus a man girt with a sword, having his hands and legs extended, is held by Aries, and placed in the north. It is of the nature of Saturn and Jupiter, makes the wearer cautious and prudent, and put under the head of a sleeping person makes him see delightful visions."

worship of *Serapis*, that most recent of all the gods in the Egyptian Pantheon, and in which the Brahminical influence is most distinctly to be traced. This last subject, so curious in itself, shall be the subject of the following section, where the numerous facts brought forward may perhaps serve to remove some of the incredulity with which such a thesis will naturally at first be regarded.

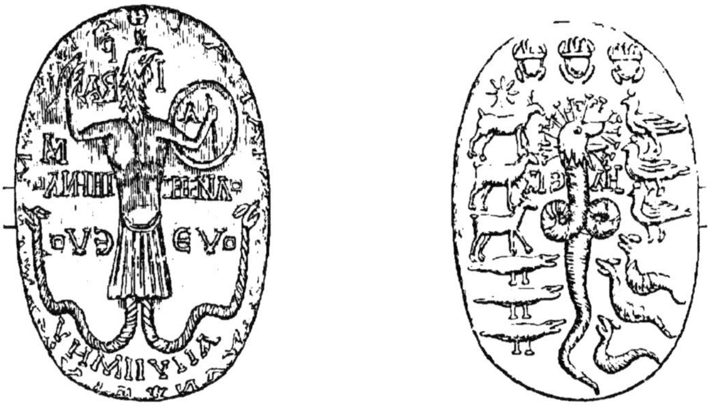

FIG. 2

INDIAN SOURCES OF GNOSTICISM.—Manes.

The *Persian* origin of so considerable a portion of the Gnosis having been set forth in the foregoing pages, it remains to show what portion is due to a purely *Indian* source, and to indicate the channels through which a direct intercourse was carried on between the farthest east and the foci of Gnosticism, Alexandria and Ephesus For the Christian Gnosis was indirectly the daughter of the Hindoo Gnosis, such as it was taught in the various mysteries, possibly in the Eleusinian and the Phrygian For universal tradition made the first founder of mysteries, Bacchus, bring them direct from India and Jove's μῆρος, the fabled birth-place of the god, may have been no other than Mount *Meru*, the Olympus of the Hindoo Pantheon *

Certain Gnostic tenets concerning the duality of the Divine emanations, absorption into the god-head, asceticism, penance, and self-collection, are identical with the Buddhistic teaching upon the same points, of which agreement several remarkable examples will be adduced in their fitting place. But we are not left to mere conjecture on this point, for the actual circumstances of their importation from India are minutely detailed, in one case that doubtless had many parallels, by the laborious Epiphanius in his "Life of Manes," (Hæres lxv) †

This celebrated heresiarch, equally abhorrent to Zoroastrian and Christian orthodoxy, was by birth a Persian, named Cubricus, but who upon commencing his mission assumed the title of *Manes*, signifying in the Babylonian tongue "The Vessel," for the same reason, we may suppose, that Dante gives to St. Paul the epithet "Vas Electionis" This Cubricus had

* The bearer of the phallus (lingam) in the grand Dionysian procession celebrated by Ptolemy Philadelphus was blackened all over with soot, doubtless to indicate the native country of that very equivocal symbol

† The earliest authority, however, (drawn upon by Epiphanius also), is the "Disputation of Archelaus and Manes," held at Charrae in A D 275-9 This book was written in Syriac, but is only extant in a Latin version

been slave, and subsequently sole heir, to a certain wealthy widow who had inherited all the effects belonging to one Terminthus, surnamed in *Assyrian* "Buddas" This Terminthus had similarly been the slave of a rich Saracen merchant, Scythicus, who had studied the Greek language and literature in some place on the borders of Palestine (perhaps the school of Palmyra), and who "had there attained to eminence in the empty learning of this world." By constant journeys between his home and *India*, this Scythicus had amassed a large fortune. With this he settled down in Hypsele in the Thebaid, where he married a beautiful courtezan, whom he had bought and emancipated "Here, out of sheer idleness and licentiousness, he set up to preach new doctrines, not derived from Scripture but from mere human reason"

These doctrines, from the nature of the case, can hardly have been of his own concoction, but, in all probability, things that he had picked up in India, where all the ancient emporia lay on the Guzerat Coast, the seat of the powerful Jaina (Buddhist) monarchy A mere Eastern trader, a common Arab merchant who, after making his fortune by long and dangerous travels in the East, who could afterwards in advanced life set himself down to study, nay more, to attain *proficiency* in the Greek philosophy, must have been a man of no ordinary intellect Assuredly it was not the mere want of anything better to do, (as his malicious biographer asserts), that made him turn preacher of a new religion. His marriage with the enfranchised courtezan looks like a theological addition, added to the portrait for the sake of so completing his resemblance to Simon Magus The nature of the doctrines he was likely to imbibe in the great Indian marts, Baroche, Barcellore, Pultaneh, or in the semi-Grecian cities of Bactria, is attested to this day by the innumerable *Buddhist* temples and topes, with their deposit of relics yet studding the provinces this side of the Indus, and whose contents declare the flourishing state of that religion even when the country had passed under the rule of the Sassanian Kings of Persia.

But to return to Scythicus in his retirement "Taking Pythagoras for guide, he composed four books, namely, 'The

Mysteries,' 'The Summary,' 'The Gospel,' and 'The Treasures'" (Pythagoras was then universally believed to have visited India, and there to have obtained the elements of his philosophy, which has a certain Brahminical character) "After this, Scythicus made a journey to Jerusalem in the very times of the Apostles, and held conferences with the elders of the church upon the Origin of Evil, and such like points But not being satisfied by their explanations, he took to preaching magic, the knowledge of which he had gotten along with his other wares from the *Indians* and *Egyptians* But as he was showing off a miracle upon the roof of his house, he fell down and was killed Upon this, his servant and sole disciple, Terminthus, instead of returning to his mistress at Hypsele, ran off with his money into Persia, where, in order to escape detection, he assumed the name of *Buddas*, which signifies "Wise" (This last fact proves incontestably the nature of the doctrines he and his master had been gathering up in their Indian travels, and the truth lying at the bottom of this story seems to be that he gave himself out for a *fresh incarnation* of Buddha, of which there had been *seven** before his date)

"This Terminthus was himself a man of learning and conversant with his master's four treatises He lodged in the house of a widow, where he used to hold conferences with the priests of Mithras, especially with two, Parcus and Labdacus, upon the Two Principles, and similar subjects. He, too, having been killed by *accident*, like his master, his landlady kept possession of all his baggage, religious books included, and in her turn bequeathed them to her servant Cubricus, the afterwards so celebrated Manes."

It is necessary here to point out a certain violent anachronism in the story as told by Epiphanius. If Scythicus visited Jerusalem at all, he must have done so *before* the year of its destruction, A D 70. His disciple, Terminthus, could therefore not have survived far into the second century. The landlady of the latter could for this reason have hardly had for slave Manes, who flourished about two hundred years later It is,

* The seventh having been that Sakyal who, from Benares, diffused Buddhism all over the peninsula

however, possible that the works plagiarised by Manes had been preserved in her *family* down to the period of his service in it

In this history of Scythicus, however disguised by tradition, we have at one view the complete history of the rise and progress of Gnosticism. We find an Arab merchant of a subtle and inquiring mind, occupying himself during his long and frequent sojourns at the Indian marts in studying the philosophy of these prevailing religionists, the speculations of the Buddhist monks, and equally investigating the secrets of the "wisdom of Egypt," when detained at the other head-quarters of the Eastern trade Then retiring from business, he goes to Palmyra for the purpose of studying Grecian philosophy, as then taught in its school, which philosophy would be no other than Neo-Platonism, thence returning home, he occupies his leisure in reducing to one harmonious system the numerous conflicting theories upon subjects too high for human knowledge, which he had so laboriously collected from the three great fountains of philosophy—India, Egypt, and Athens.

Finally attracted by the fame of a new religion that professed to throw the clearest light upon all things relating to God and Man, being preached at Jerusalem, he immediately starts for the *focus* of this new light, leaving behind him wife and property, only accompanied by one servant, himself an educated man, and his own treasured theological speculations. On his arriving at the Holy City, we find him (as might be expected from his previous training) grievously disappointed in his hopes of at last obtaining the solution of all the problems that had so long occupied his thoughts—for on subjects of that kind the Christian Presbyters could tell no more than what he had learnt already from the *Rabbis* of Alexandria, or the Jaina monks of Guzerat Thus disappointed, he appears to have set up himself for a teacher of a new and higher doctrine, supporting his pretensions (after the customary fashion of the times) by miracle-working, and as a matter of course getting his career speedily cut short, for Jerusalem was not the place where a new religion would be promulgated with impunity by a single individual, and that too an *Arabian.* His disciple, Terminthus, taking warning by his fate, resolves to try another school of profound wisdom, formed from time immemorial, but as yet unvisited by his master, and proceeds to hold discussion with the Wise Men of the East at their head college in Babylon, seeking for the final solution of his difficulties in the doctrine of Zoroaster It is very probable that he, as the result of this study, engrafted upon the system of Scythicus whatever features of the Zendavesta appeared to him the most satisfactory, and consistent best with his preconceived ideas of the truth It would be interesting to know whether he shaped all these fresh acquisitions into conformity with the original Indian groundwork of his master's system As already observed, such appears to have been his course from the title that he assumed, declaring himself an eighth "Buddha," successor to the famous Guatama, founder of the religion, and like him commissioned to teach a new way of salvation Terminthus, like his master, came to an untimely end The Magi were not members of a powerful establishment who would suffer themselves to be puzzled and confuted by an over-wise foreigner, disputing so boldly—

> "Of Providence, foreknowledge, will, and Fate,
> Fixed Fate, freewill, foreknowledge absolute,"

still less to allow him to go off exulting in his victory, as his associated follower Manes likewise found to his cost

Manes himself appears to have belonged to the order of Magi (probably being admitted after gaining his freedom and changing his name), for he is reported to have been famous for his skill in astrology, medicine, magic, and *painting!* This last is curious, it shows that the Magi, like the mediæval monks, monopolised the arts as well as the sciences of their times Whether he conceived the scheme from the accidental acquisition of the writings of Scythicus or not (M Matter supposes him to have got his first inspiration from some Egyptian Basilidan who had found his way into Persia), certain it is that he first gave to these notions a definite shape, and constructed his system with such skill that it spread not merely all over the East but throughout Europe. In the latter region its importance is evinced by the fact (mentioned incidentally by Ammianus) that Constantine himself, before finally changing his religion, following the Apostolical precept "Try all things, hold fast that which is good," carefully studied the Manichæan system under the guidance of the learned Musonianus, whom we must suppose to have been a great doctor of the sect.* Nay more, this religion, after long seeming extinction from the pertinacious persecution of the Byzantine emperors, again blazed forth with extraordinary lustre in the Paulicianism of the Middle Ages.

The grand purpose of the scheme of Manes was the *reconcilement* of the two religions, which had by that time come to dispute the empire of the world—the flourishing, though still unrecognised Christianity of Rome, and the equally vigorous but newly revived Zoroastrism of Sassanian Persia. Calling himself the "Promised Paraclete," Manes accepted the gospel, but only after purifying it from all taint of Judaism, whilst he utterly rejected the Old Testament. But whilst Zoroaster makes all to *begin* in the *harmony*, and to *end* in the mutual reconciliation of the Two Principles, Manes declares these Two Principles immutable and existent from all eternity as they shall continue for ever to exist. His *Good* is Zoroaster's "Lord of Light", but his *Bad* is Satan-Matter, deliverance from whose bondage is to be obtained only through the strictest asceticism. From the Christian Church he borrowed its institution of presbyters and deacons, being sensible how greatly that organisation had conduced to its rapid development, and in his own enterprise it met with almost equal success. Manes was a genuine Pantheist, teaching that God pervaded all things, even plants (of which tenet I subjoin a singular illustration from his once ardent follower, St. Augustine), he also adopted the entire theory of Emanations, exactly

* "Constantinus enim cum limatius superstitionum quæreret sectas, Manichæorum et similium, nec interpres inveniretur idoneus, hunc sibi commendatum ut sufficientem elegit, quem officio functum perite Musonianum voluit appellari ante Strategium dictitatum." Ammianus xv. 6. The sainted Emperor's eulogists have carefully hushed up this trait of an inquiring spirit, anxious to weigh the relative merits of the existing rivals of Catholicism.

as it was defined in the older Gnostic systems St Augustine's words are ('Confessions' iii 10) "And I, not understanding this, used to mock at those holy servants and prophets of thine.* And what was I doing when I mocked at them, except that I myself was mocked at by thee, being seduced gently and by degrees into such absurdities as to believe that the fig weeps when it is plucked, and likewise its parent tree, with tears of milk? Which same fig, however, should any holy man eat, that is to say, after it has been plucked through the *sin* of another, not by his own, he would mingle with his bowels, and breathe out of it *angels*, nay more, particles of God himself, in his sighs and eructations whilst praying, which same particles of the Supreme and True God would have been bound up in that fruit, had they not been set at liberty by the tooth and stomach of the chosen saint; and I, like a wretch, believed that greater compassion ought to be shown unto the fruits of the earth than to man, for whose sake they were created For if any one not a Manichæan, being an hungered, should ask for the same, it would have been thought a crime, worthy of capital punishment, if a single mouthful thereof were given to him" Compare the following rule of the Buddhist priesthood "They will not kill any animal, neither root up nor cut any plant, because they think it has life' ('Ayeen Akbari,' p. 435)

Manes invented a theory of salvation, so very whimsical that it ought to be inserted here, to recreate the wanderer in this dreary and dusky theological labyrinth. "When the Son came into the world to effect the redemption of mankind, he contrived a machine containing twelve bowls (cadi),† which being made to revolve by the motion of the spheres, attracts into itself the souls of the dying These the *Great Luminary* (the sun) takes and purifies with his rays, and then transfers to the moon, and this is the method whereby the *disk*, as we call it, of the moon is replenished" Epiphanius triumphantly refutes this theory

* Alluding to the Manichæan rejection of the Old Testament as a divine revelation

† In the notion of this machine may be traced the influence of the study of Plato in the school of Palmyra, for it is unmistakably borrowed from the eight concentric basins set in motion, one inside the other by the fingers of the Fates, so minutely described in the Vision of Er the Pamphylian

by asking how the moon's disk was replenished during the nine hundred years that elapsed after the Creation before any deaths took place?

But the career of this inventive heresiarch was speedily brought to a close. The Persian king, Varanes I. (about the year 275), alarmed by the rapid spread of these new doctrines, convoked a General Council of the Magi to sit in judgment upon them, by whom the unlucky apostle was pronounced a heretic, and a traitor to his own brethren, and sentenced to be flayed alive.

BUDDHISM.

For the sake of comparison with the above-described systems, all based upon the doctrine of successive *Emanations* from One First Principle, the means of escaping from the bondage of Matter, and the struggles of the souls towards ultimate absorption into its original source, I shall subjoin a very brief sketch of the principal features of the Buddhistic theosophy.* Here also we find a First Buddha in his proper state of eternal repose (the *Indolentia* of Epicurus) corresponding to the Zoroastrian "Boundless Time," and the Valentinian "Bythos." While in this state termed "Nevriti," wishing to create the universe he produced the *Five* divine Buddhas, the makers of the Elements, who in their turn produced the Five Buddhasativas, and by their agency created the material world. The grand aim of this religion is to effect the release of the soul from its connection with *Matter*. All things, according to the Buddhists, exist only in *illusion*, consequently they can only return into non-existence or repose by means of *True Knowledge* (compare the *Gnosis* we

* Buddhism was founded in the fifth century before our era, by Sakya Muni, son of the Raja of Kapila. At the age of twenty-nine he began to study religion, and by force of prayer became the embodiment of the Supreme Deity when thirty-five years old. He chose Benares for the centre of his mission, whence in the space of forty-five years his doctrines were diffused over the fairest districts of the Ganges from the Delta to Agra and Cawnpore. His death is placed by some writers in B.C. 477.

are considering) * "Illusion" is the belief in the reality of the eternal world, the degradation of the soul towards Matter is the effect of a succession of acts, and therefore its release is effected by relinquishing the belief in the reality of external objects

The Buddhists of Nepal, who have preserved the original doctrines of the religion in their greatest purity, teach the following cosmogony Padnapani, one of the original Five Emanations, created Brahma, Vishnu, Siva, or the Principles of Creation, Preservation, and Destruction Adi-Buddha first created thirteen mansions for his own eternal abode, and for the dwelling-place after death of Buddha's followers. Below these are eighteen mansions made by Brahma, lower yet are six made by Vishnu, and lowest of all—three, the work of Siva These three series of abodes receive the souls of the followers of their respective creators.

Below all these lie the mansions of the Planetary gods, Indra and Chandra, and after these there comes the Earth floating upon the face of the waters like a boat Below these waters are the Seven Patala, or regions of Hell, the abode of evil spirits and the damned. This arrangement presents the most striking resemblance to the construction of the Ophite Diagramma (to be given further on), which Origen has described from the original, and which M Matter has reconstructed from Origen's description to illustrate his treatise in his Plate X

The promulgation of these Indian speculations from so remote a source—a difficulty at first sight insurmountable—may nevertheless be readily explained. The spirit of this religion was the spirit of proselytism, the Buddhists from the very beginning sent out their missionaries (some of whose narratives, full of interest, are extant and have been translated from the Chinese) with all the zeal of the old Propaganda. From the

* The Buddhist 'Confession of Faith," regularly set up in the temples, engraven on a stone tablet, runs thus "Of all things proceeding from Cause their causes hath the Tathâgatha explained The Great Sarmana hath likewise explained the causes of the cessation of existence" The essence of the religion therefore is Perfect Knowledge, the object of Virgil's aspiration—

'Felix qui potuit rerum cognoscere causas "

mainland they converted Ceylon, Japan, and the recesses of Tartary, and penetrated into regions where their former presence and tolerated existence are now little dreamed of.* That Buddhism had been actually planted in the dominions of the Seleucidæ and the Ptolemies (Palestine belonging to the former) before the end of the fourth century, at least, before our era is shown by a clause in the Edicts of Asoka. This prince was grandson to Chandragupta (the Sandracottus of the Greeks, contemporary and friend of Seleucus I), who, at the head of an army of 60,000 men, had conquered all India within the Ganges. Asoka, at first a licentious tyrant, had embraced the newly preached doctrines of Buddhism, a Brahminical Protestantism, and propagated them by persuasion and by force through the length and breadth of his immense kingdom, with all the usual zeal of a new convert.

The Edicts referred to are graven on a rock tablet at Girnur in Guzerat. To quote the words of the Indian Archæologist Prinsep, to whom the discovery is due, (article xvii. 'Indian Antiquities'). "I am now about to produce evidence that Asoka's† acquaintance with geography was not limited to Asia, and that his expansive benevolence towards living creatures extended, at least in intention, to another quarter of the globe, that his religious ambition sought to *apostolize Egypt*, and that we must look hereafter for traces of the introduction of Buddhism into the fertile valley of the Nile, so productive of metaphysical discussions from the earliest ages. The line which I allude to is the fifth from the bottom. 'And the Greek King (Yoniraja)‡ besides, by whom the Chapta (Egyptian) Kings, Ptole-

* Two Chinese pilgrims, Fa Hian and Hiouen Thsang, visited Benares at the beginning of the fifth, and at the middle of the seventh centuries of our era. These keen and sagacious observers have left records of their travels in India of the utmost importance to the historian and antiquary. Their narratives are, for the most part, plain matter-of-fact productions, free from the haze and uncertainty of Hindoo writings, and whenever they have been tested by extraneous evidence, have been found to be to a large extent singularly correct. See 'Memoires de Hiouen Thsang,' translated from the Chinese by Stanislas Julien.

† Asoka's zeal was so ardent that he sent his son and daughter, Mahendra and Saugamitra, as missionaries to Ceylon, who in a short time effected the conversion of the island to their new religion.

‡ The Persian envoy in Aristophanes' Acharnians used the same word, 'Ιαόναυ, for the Greek nation.

maios, and Gonkakenos (Antigonus Gonatas) have been induced to allow that both here and in *foreign countries everywhere* the people may follow the doctrine of the religion of Devanipya, wheresoever it reacheth'" The "Essenes," so like to Buddhist Monks in many particulars (for which see the minute description of this ascetic rule as given by Josephus, 'Antiq Jud' xv. 10), had been established on the shores of the Dead Sea for "thousands of ages" before Pliny's time "On the West its shores, so far as they are unhealthy, are shunned by the Esseni, a solitary race, and wonderful beyond all others on the globe, without woman, renouncing all usual enjoyment, without money, associates of the palm-trees, from day to day they are recruited by the flocks of new-comers all those flocking in numerously whom the world drives from itself, all tempest-tossed by the waves of fortune. In this way, incredible to tell, the race wherein no birth ever takes place, has endured for thousands of years, so prolific for them is other people's disgust at the world" (Hist Nat v 15) The great Naturalist's "thousands of years" must be allowed as one of his favourite oratorical tropes, but nevertheless serves for testimony to the belief in the great antiquity of the sect. Perhaps they may have been a continuation of those early ascetic associations known as the "Schools of the Prophets"

The influence of Jewish Essenism upon primitive Christianity (as to rules of life at least) is a thing that will not be disputed by any who have read, with a wish to *learn* the truth, not to *evade it*, the account of it given by Josephus. But over the semi-Christian Gnostics of Syria such long-established authority must have had a still stronger influence. It is easy to discover how the source of the slavish notions about the merits of asceticism, penances, and self-torture (of which Simon Stylites is the most conspicuous illustration), was the same one whence the Indian fakirs drew their practice—for even in their methods they were identical Simon's celebrated life-penance (which gives him his title), undergone upon the summit of a lofty pillar had been practised in the same regions many generations before his time The pseudo-Lucian, in his amusing description of the famous Temple of the "Syrian

Goddess" at Emesa ('De Dea Syria'), particularly notices the phallus or obelisk, 300 feet high, planted in front of the edifice, upon the apex of which the devotee sat without sleep for one and twenty days and nights, keeping himself awake by constantly ringing a handbell. Ideas like these pervade the Christianity of the Lower Empire, nay, they constitute the very essence of the religion. Neither is it difficult to see upon how many points Manes, with his rigid Buddhistic tenets, came into collision with the humane and rational law of Zoroaster (*the brightest system of natural religion ever promulgated*), and what good causes Varanes, with his spiritual advisers, had for condemning his heresy.

In our investigation of this particular subject it must never be forgotten that so long as *philosophy* was cultivated in Greece, (even from the times of the Samian sage, inventor of the name), India was often regarded as the ultimate and purest source of the "True Wisdom," the knowledge of things divine. Even so late as Lucian's time, the middle of the second century, that author concludes his evidently true history of Antiphilus and Demetrius, by making the latter, a cynic philosopher by profession, resign all his property to his friend, and depart for India, there to end his life amongst the Brachmanes, ('Toxaris,' 34). In the same century the well-known pilgrimage of Apollonius of Tyana, and his deep conference with the Indian philosophers, as recorded by his companion Damis, go to prove the same thing, and although the meagre journal of the sage's travelling companion may have been largely supplemented and embellished by the fancy of his editor, Philostratus,* the main features of the narrative are doubtless authentic. The great thaumaturgist's proceedings, as there detailed, show how the apparent difficulty of such a pilgrimage vanishes upon a better knowledge of the circumstances. Apollonius presents himself, first of all, to the Parthian King, Bardanes (a "Philhellene" as he yet boasts himself upon his coinage), and as warm an admirer of Grecian *savants* as any of his Achæmenian pre-

* Who composed his very interesting 'Life of Apollonius' at the request of the Empress Julia, about a century after the death of the philosopher.

decessors, from whom he obtains a *firman* securing to him protection and entertainment, everywhere within the limits of his rule, which extended then, probably, as far as the Indus. Thenceforward his letters of recommendation from the "King of Kings" to the various native princes his allies, secure to the traveller an equally favourable reception A safe and regular communication between the extreme points of the Persian Empire had been from the beginning the great care of its mighty rulers (the first institutors of highways, posting-stages, and post-horses), passing through what was not, as now, a series of deserts infested by robber-tribes, but a populous and well-cultivated country, so favoured, with a passport from the sovereign, the pilgrim would find his journey both expeditious and agreeable

The same facilities were necessarily made use of by the natives of Hindustan It is curious to observe how the occasional "Brachman" who found his way into Greece was received as a model philosopher—like that Zarmanes Chagan, who, coming from Bargose (*Baroche*), finally burnt himself alive upon a pyre at Athens, in the reign of Augustus, of which edifying spectacle Nicolaus Damascenus was eye-witness (Strabo XV) Before him, we have Calanas the "gymnosophist" (a happy Greek expression for *fakir*) in high repute at Alexander's court, and who similarly chose to leave earth in a "chariot of fire" Their example was followed by the "Peregrinus Proteus," so happily ridiculed by Lucian in his book thus entitled, Proteus, to give his apotheosis as much celebrity as possible, chose for its scene the occasion of the Olympic games. This last worthy had been a philosopher, then a Christian teacher, and lastly had started a new religion of his own invention That the sect so celebrated by the ancients under the name of "Brachmanes" was *Buddhistic*, not *Brahminical*, may be inferred from their locality, Bactria, and yet more from a circumstance mentioned by Strabo (Book XV.) He speaks of their devoting thirty years to the study of Theology, living in a community (a *vihar* or monastery), sequestered from the world in the midst of forests in the neighbourhood of the different cities, and totally abstaining from sexual intercourse, and all animal food, on the contrary, the Brahmins hold that to leave children behind them is a most sacred duty, and one upon which their admission into heaven depends. Whether the Buddhists be the true representatives of the primal religion* of their country, or only the *Reformers* of the more ancient Brahminical Church, it is the natural weapon of all dissenters from an established creed, to ridicule and even to pronounce damnable, the favourite tenets of their adversaries Witness Martin Luther with his invectives against vows of virginity, and his well-known motto

"Wer nicht liebt Weib, Wein und Gesang,
Der bleibt ein Narr sein Leben lang"

Similarly we find the Essenes running counter to the ancient prejudices of their nation, and spontaneously embracing what the Mosaic Law had denounced as the greatest of curses—the leaving no offspring behind to keep up their name in Israel

To exemplify the severe discipline maintained in the Brahman communities, Strabo mentions that the mere act of blowing the nose, or spitting, caused the offender to be excluded for that day, as *incontinent*, from the society of his fellow-recluses Similarly Josephus particularises, amongst other Essenian rules, the obligation of abstaining from all natural evacuations upon the Sabbath day But even *their* rigour is surpassed, and in our day too, by a certain sect of Indian Yogis, who profess to have completely emancipated themselves from all such defiling necessities of nature This they effect by living entirely upon milk, which, after retaining a short time in the stomach, they throw up again by swallowing a ball fastened to a string, and maintain the animal expenditure solely through the nutriment imbibed by the system during the continuance of the liquid in the stomach, and which consequently leaves no residuum to descend into the lower bowels. A doctrine this, the finest

* Which of course their theologians claim to be, and treat the Brahmins as corrupters of the true faith For example Hiouen Thsang "They reckon (in the kingdom of Benares) a hundred temples of gods, inhabited by about ten thousand *heretics*, who for the most part are worshippers of Siva" And yet he candidly owns that the Buddhists possessed no more than thirty monasteries, numbering only three thousand members, in the same place

possible *reductio ad absurdam* of the notion of meritorious continence, and exhibiting on the ludicrous side the mischief of being too logical in matters of religion

As for the profundity of the philosophical speculations of the Orientals, even at a very late period, the Byzantine Agathias quotes a very remarkable example Chosroes (better known to us as Nushirwan the Just), besides giving an asylum, as to his brethren, to the last Athenian philosophers, when expelled from their chairs by the stupid bigot Justinian, caused all Plato's works to be translated into Persian, and professed to be himself able to comprehend even the mysteries of the 'Timæus' The Greek sophist is naturally indignant at the impudence of the foreigner who could pretend that "his own barbarous and rustic language" was capable of expressing the divine thoughts of the Athenian sage, for he little suspected that the great King, or at any rate the Magi and "Sufis" about him, were masters of the sources whence Plato may have ultimately drawn his inspiration whilst planning that inscrutable composition The religious instruction of the Persian princes had from the beginning been carefully attended to, and proficiency therein was a matter of pride thus Cyrus the younger puts forward his superior knowledge of Theology (in his manifesto upon claiming the kingdom) as a just cause why he should be preferred to his elder brother

Leaving out of the question the now received theory as to the immigration of the "Indo-Germanic" race into the farthest recesses of Europe, modern history furnishes the example of extensive migration, effected under infinitely greater difficulties, by the hordes of low-caste Hindoos, who, flying from the invasion of Tamerlane, spread themselves all over Europe as Gipsies, still retaining their native language and habits, and to the present day claiming "Sind" or "Sindha" for their national name.

The facts adduced in the foregoing sketch will suffice to indicate the manner in which the germs of the various Gnostic doctrines were imported from the East, how they were engrafted upon previously existing notions, and how vigorously they flourished when transplanted into the kindly soil of Alexandria and Ephesus To complete the general view of the subject, before proceeding to consider the tangible monuments left us by these ideas, it will be necessary to give some account of the forms in which they attained to their fullest development. For this purpose I shall select the three principal systems, represented by historians as the parents of all the rest, those of *Simon Magus*, *Basilides*, and the *Ophites*; the most satisfactory manner of doing which will be to transcribe the exact words of the well-informed and impartial Hippolytus.

SIMONIANISM.

"It is my intention here to exhibit the system of Simon Magus, a native of Gitteh in Samaria, and I will prove that from him all those that come after have derived the elements of their doctrines, and impudently attempted the same things under different appellations. This Simon was skilled in magic and had imposed upon great numbers, partly by practising the art of Thrasymedes after the manner which I have already exposed (in the Book upon 'Magicians'), and partly by miracle-working through the agency of demons. He attempted to set up for a god, being a thorough impostor and altogether unscrupulous and daring; for he was that one whom the Apostles confuted, as is recorded in the Acts.

"Much more wisely therefore and sensibly than Simon did that Apsethus act, when he aimed at being accounted a god, who went to work in Libya; whose story, not being very dissimilar to the scheme of our foolish Simon, it were fitting here to quote, inasmuch as it is quite of a piece with the procedure of the latter.

"Apsethus the Libyan was very desirous of making himself a god, but when, after long labouring, he had failed in his endeavours, he wanted, as the next best thing, to be *supposed* to have made himself a god; and in fact for a considerable time he did enjoy such a reputation. For the simple Libyans used to sacrifice to him as to a Divine Power, in the belief that they were obeying a voice sent forth out of Heaven. He had got together and confined several parrots in one and the same little room, for parrots are plentiful all over Libya, and they distinctly mimic the human voice; and having kept these birds for some time, he taught them to say 'Apsethus is a god.' And when the birds in course of time were taught, and could speak that sentence which he supposed, when spoken, would cause him to pass for a god, then he opened their place of confinement.

and allowed the parrots to escape in different directions And as the birds flew about, the sound was carried all over Libya, and the words travelled as far as the Greek territory (Cyrene), and thus the Libyans, being struck with amazement at the voice of the birds, and not suspecting the trick played them by Apsethus, accounted him a god But one of the Greeks having clearly detected the contrivance of the supposed deity, did, by means of the self-same parrots, not merely confute, but also extinguish that vain-glorious and impudent fellow. This Greek caged several of the same parrots, and taught them to utter a contrary strain, 'Apsethus shut us up, and forced us to say *Apsethus is a god.*' But when the Libyans heard this recantation of the parrots, they all came together with one accord, and burnt Apsethus alive.

"In this light we ought to regard the magician Simon, and compare him to this Libyan, a man who made himself a god in that very expeditious manner, for in truth the comparison holds good in all particulars, and the sorcerer met with a fate not unlike that of Apsethus. I will therefore endeavour to *un-teach Simon's parrots* by showing that Simon was not the Christ 'Who hath stood, standeth, and shall stand,' but a man, mortal, generated from the seed of woman, begotten from blood and carnal concupiscence like the rest of mankind and that such was the fact I shall clearly demonstrate in the course of my narrative. For Simon speaks, when interpreting the Law of Moses, in an impudent and fraudulent fashion, for whenever Moses says 'Our God is a burning and a consuming fire,' Simon, taking what Moses has said in a false sense, maintains that *Fire* is the Principle of all things. He does not perceive the true meaning that God is not 'a fire,' but 'a burning and a consuming fire,' and so not only mutilates the Law of Moses, but plagiarises from Heraclitus, surnamed 'the Obscure' For Simon designates the Principle of all things 'Boundless Power' in the following words 'This is the Book of the Declaration of the Voice, and of the Name, from the inspiration of the Great, the Boundless Power Wherefore the same is sealed, hidden, wrapped up, stored in the dwelling wherein the Root of all things is established.' This *dwelling* he says, signifies *Man* here below, who is born of blood, and also signifies that there dwells within him that 'Boundless Power' which he asserts is the Root of all things But this Boundless Power (or *Fire*, according to Simon) is not a simple substance, in the same way as most people who call the Elements 'simple' account Fire likewise as simple. on the contrary, he maintains that the nature of Fire is, as it were, *double*, and of this double number he terms one part the *Insensible*, the other the *Visible*, asserting that the insensible are contained within the visible parts of the Fire, and that the visible parts are generated by the invisible (This is the same thing that Aristotle expresses by his 'Force' and 'Energy', and Plato by his 'Intelligible' and 'Sensible')

"Again the *Visible* part of Fire contains within itself all things whatsoever one can perceive, or even *fail* to perceive, of things visible. The *Invisible*, on the other hand, is whatsoever one can conceive as an object of thought, but which escapes the sense, or even what one *fails* to comprehend by the thought And to sum up, it may be said that of all things that exist, whether objects of sense or of thought, or, as Simon terms them, Visible and Invisible, the store-house is the Great Fire that is above the heavens 'As it were a great Tree, like to that seen in his dream by Nabuchadonosor, from the which all flesh was fed' And the *Visible* he considers to be the *trunk* of the Tree and the branches, and the leaves, and the bark surrounding the same on the outside All these parts of the great Tree, says he, are kindled from the all-devouring flame of the Fire, and are destroyed But the *Fruit* of the Tree, if it takes a shape and assumes a proper form, is laid up in a storehouse, and not cast into the fire For the fruit is made in order that it may be laid up in the storehouse, but the *husk* that it may be committed to the fire, which same is the trunk, ordained not for the sake of the husk but of the fruit

"And this, according to Simon, is what is written in the Scripture 'The vineyard of the Lord of hosts is the House of Israel, and a man of Judah the well-beloved branch thereof' Now, if a man of Judah be the 'well-beloved branch,' it is a proof that the *wood* can be nothing else than a *man* But as regards the *excretion* and the *dispersion* from the same, the Scripture hath spoken fully and sufficiently for the instruction of all such as be brought to their perfect form according to the saying, 'All flesh is grass, and the glory thereof as the flower of the grass, the grass withereth, the flower thereof fadeth, but the Word of the Lord endureth for ever.' Now this Word of the Lord, says Simon, is the word that is produced in the mouth, that is, Speech, for the place of its birth is nowhere else.

"To be brief therefore, since, according to Simon, the Fire is of the aforesaid nature, and all things that be, both visible and invisible, and vocal and voiceless, and numbered and unnumbered, are this Fire, therefore in his 'Great Revelation' he terms this the Fountain-head of all, the *Great Intellectual*, as constituting each individual of all things in their infinite order, which are capable of being conceived in the mind, and likewise of speaking, of thinking, and of acting. As Empedocles hath it—

"'Through Earth, the Earth perceive, through Water, Water,
Through Air scan Air, through Fire the hidden Fire,
Through Love view Love, through Discord, hateful Discord.'

"For Simon held that all the members of this Fire, both the Visible and the Invisible, possessed *intelligence* and a portion of *mind*. The world that is created, consequently, according to him, comes from the uncreated Fire. The commencement of its creation was in this wise: six 'Radicals' (*lit.* Roots), the First Principles of the beginning of Creation, were taken by the Begotten One out of the Principle of that Fire, for he asserts that these Six Radicals emanated by *pairs* out of the Fire. These Six Radicals he names, 'Mind and Intelligence, Voice and Name, Reason and Thought.' And there exists in these Radicals taken together the whole of the 'Boundless Power,' but existing in *potentiality*, not in *activity*. And this Boundless Power Simon calls 'He who standeth, hath stood, and shall stand,' who, if he shall be *figured* (invested with form) when he is in those Six Powers, shall be in reality, force, power and perfection, the one and the same with the Unbegotten Boundless Power. But if he shall abide in *potentiality* alone in those Six Powers, and not assume a *form*, he vanishes and perishes, as does a grammatical or a geometrical power in a man's mind For potentiality, when it has gotten *art*, becomes the light of things generated, but when it has not gotten art (execution) it remains in inertness and darkness, and exactly as when it did not exist at all, and dies with the man upon his death

"Now of these Six Powers, and of the Seventh which goes along with them, the *First Thought* Simon terms 'Mind and Intellect,' 'Heaven and Earth'; teaching that the one of the male sex looks down upon and takes care of his consort, whilst the Earth below receives from Heaven the 'Intellect,' and fruits of the same nature with the Earth, which are poured down from above. For this cause, says Simon, the Word, often looking down upon the things that spring out of Mind and Intellect, says, 'Hear, O Heavens, and receive with thine ears, O Earth! for the Lord hath spoken I have begotten and brought up sons, but they have despised me' He that saith this is the *Seventh Power*, 'He who standeth, hath stood, and shall stand,' for He is the author of those good things which Moses commended, saying that they were very good.

'Voice and name are the Sun and Moon, 'Reason and Thought' are air and water But with all of these is mingled and combined that Boundless Power, 'He who standeth,' as I have already mentioned.

"Therefore when Moses says, 'In six days the Lord made heaven and earth, and on the seventh day he rested from all his works,' Simon, distorting the passage after the aforesaid fashion, makes himself out to be God When therefore, the Simonians say that there were three days before the Sun and the Moon were made, they understand by it Mind and Intelligence, or Heaven and Earth, and also that 'Boundless Power' of theirs. For these three Powers were made before all the rest. Again, where it is said 'Before all the world he hath begotten me,' these words, as they pretend, refer to the Seventh Power Now this Seventh Power, who was a Power existing *within* the Boundless Power, and who was made before all the world, *this*, as Simon teaches, is that Seventh Power of whom Moses spake.

'And the Spirit of God moved upon the face of the waters,' that is to say, the Spirit containing all things within itself, the Image of the Boundless Power, concerning which Simon saith, 'the *image* is the incorruptible Power governing all things by himself!'

"Now the creation of the world having been after this or a similar fashion, God, says he, made Man out of clay taken from the earth; and he made them not single, but double, both as regards the *image*, and the *likeness* For the *image* is the Spirit moving upon the face of the waters, who, if he be not clothed with form will perish together with the world, inasmuch as he abode merely in potentiality, and was not made *concrete* by activity For this is the meaning of the Scripture 'Lest we be condemned together with the world.' But if it shall take a form, and spring out of an indivisible point, it is what is written in the Revelation 'The little shall become great' This 'Great' shall continue to all eternity, and unchangeable, inasmuch as it is no longer *to be* made (*i.e*, no longer abstract)

"In what way therefore, and after what manner did God form man? In Paradise—for in this point Simon also agreed But this 'paradise' must be the *womb* (according to him), and that such is the true explanation is proved by the Scripture, which saith, 'I am he that formed thee in thy mother's womb,' for so he will have it to be written The womb Moses called Paradise by an allegory, if we choose to listen to the word of God, for if God did form man in his mother's womb, that is, in paradise then 'Paradise' must needs signify the womb. 'Eden' is that same region, and the river going forth out of Eden to water the garden, is the *navel* This navel is divided into four heads, because from each part thereof proceed two arteries running side by side, channels for the breath, and also two veins, channels for the blood When, therefore, this *navel* proceeding out of the region, Eden, is attached to the fœtus at the lower belly which we commonly term the navel . . [Here some words are evidently lost] And the two veins through which the blood flows, and is carried out of the region Eden, through what are called 'the gates of the liver' which nourish the embryo. Again the two tubes which we have spoken of as the channels of the blood, embrace the bladder at each side of the pelvis, and touch the great artery which runs along the same, called the *aorta*, and thus the breath, passing through the veins into the heart, produces the motion of the embryo. For so long as the child is being formed in 'paradise,' it neither takes nourishment through the mouth, nor breathes through the nostrils, for, placed as it is in the midst of fluid, it would be instant death for it, were it to breathe, inasmuch as it would draw a fluid and be destroyed. Moreover, the child is conceived within an envelope, which is called the *amnium*, but it receives nourishment through the navel, and takes in the essence of the breath through the dorsal artery above described. The River, therefore, going forth out of Eden, is divided into four heads, namely, Seeing, Hearing, Smelling, Touching and Tasting, for these are the only senses that the infant formed in Paradise is possessed of.

"This then, according to Simon, is the law which Moses gave and his Four Books are written in accordance with that law, as their own titles do manifest. For the first book is *Genesis*: the very title, he affirms, were sufficient for the understanding of the whole matter. For this 'Genesis' is the *Sight*, into which one section of the River branches off, because the whole outer world is perceived through the sight. Again, the title of the second book is *Exodus*, which signifies that it was necessary for the thing born to pass through the Red Sea (meaning by 'Red Sea,' the blood), and to enter into the wilderness, and to drink of the bitter water (Marah). Now this 'bitter water' which lies beyond the Red Sea, is the path of *knowledge* during life, which leads through places toilsome and unpleasant. But after it hath been changed by Moses, that is, by the Word, that same bitter water becometh *sweet*. And that such is the reality one may learn from everybody who exclaims in the words of the poet:—

> "'Black is the root, the flower as white as milk,
> Named Moly by the gods, full hard to find
> By mortals: but the gods all things can do.'

"Even what is said by the Gentiles is sufficient for the understanding of the whole matter unto him that hath ears to hear He that tasted of the fruit given by Circe* was not only himself not changed into a beast, but by making use of the virtue of the self-same fruit, remodelled, reformed and re called those already transformed by her into their own proper shape For the Faithful Man, and the beloved by that sorceress, is found out by means of that divine and milky potion

"In the like manner Leviticus is the Third Book (or River), which signifies the sense of *smell*, or the *respiration*, for the whole of that Book is concerning *sacrifices* and *oblations* But wheresoever there is sacrifice, there also does a sweet smell of perfume arise up from the sacrifice, concerning which sweet odour the sense of smelling is the approver

"'Numbers,' the Fourth of the Books, signifies the *Taste*, for then the speech is active, inasmuch as it is through the Speech that all objects are designated in *numerical* order

"'Deuteronomy,' Simon makes out, is so named in reference to the child that has been formed for *Touching* For as the Touch doth by feeling *reciprocate* and *confirm* the impressions received by the other senses, proving an object to be either hard, or hot, or slippery—in the like manner the Fifth Book of the Law is a *recapitulation* of the four preceding Books

"All things, therefore (continues he), that are not created exist within us in *potentiality*, not in *activity*, like the science of grammar, or of geometry. In the case therefore where they shall have met with the proper training and instruction, there 'shall the Bitter be turned into Sweet', that is, 'the spears shall be turned into reaping-hooks, and the swords into plough-shares,' they shall be no longer chaff and sticks born for the fire, but the Perfect Fruit, like and equal, as already said, unto the Unbegotten and Boundless Power. But where the Tree shall stand alone, not bearing fruit, there, because it hath not received *form*, it shall be destroyed. 'For now (saith he) the axe is nigh unto the root of the tree Every tree therefore that beareth not good fruit, is hewn down and cast into the fire'

* Simon has here forgotten his "Odyssey", the antidote Moly having been given to Ulysses by Hermes

"According to Simon, therefore, that blessed and inscrutable thing lies *hidden*, and *within* every man, but in potentiality alone, not in activity, the which is 'He who standeth, hath stood, and shall stand', who standeth *above* in the Unbegotten Power, who hath stood *below* in the 'River of Waters' when he was begotten in the *image*, and who shall stand *above* by the side of the Blessed and Boundless Power, provided that he shall have received *form*. For there are three that stand, and unless there be the three Æons that stand, 'the Begotten One is not adorned,' meaning Him, who, according to Simon's teaching, moved upon the face of the waters, who hath been re-created after the image, perfect and heavenly, who likewise is in no degree lower than the Unbegotten Power."

"This is a saying amongst the Simonians, 'I and thou are one; thou before me, I after thee'. '*This* is the One Power, divided into Above and Below, begetting itself, nourishing itself, seeking after itself, finding itself, being its own mother, its own father, its own sister, its own consort, its own daughter, son mother, father, inasmuch as it alone is the Root of all things.'

"That *Fire* is the origin of the generation of all things generated, Simon demonstrates after this fashion. 'Of all things whatsoever that exist, being generated, the final cause of the desire for their generation proceeds out of Fire. For "to be set on fire" is the term used to designate the desire of the act of generation and propagation. Now this "Fire," which is *one*, is changed into *two*. For in the male the blood which is hot and red, like Fire in a visible shape, is converted into seed, in the female this same blood is converted into milk. And this change in the male becomes the generation-faculty itself, whilst the change in the female becomes the instrument (efficient cause), of the thing begotten. This (according to Simon) is the "Flaming Sword," which is brandished to keep the way unto the Tree of Life. For the blood is turned into seed and into milk, and this Power becomes both father and mother, the father of those that be born, and the nutriment of those that be nourished, standing in need of none other, sufficient unto itself. Moreover the Tree of Life, which is guarded by the brandished flaming sword is, as we have said, the Seventh Power, the self-begotten, which comprehends all the others, and which is deposited within the other Six Powers For if that Flaming Sword should not be brandished, then would that beautiful Tree be destroyed and perish, but when it is changed into the seed and the milk, then He that is stored up within them in potentiality, having obtained the necessary Logos (*Reason*) and the fitting place wherein that Logos may be generated, then, beginning as it were from the smallest spark, he shall wax great to perfection, and increase, and become a Power without end, and without change, being equal and like unto the infinite Æon, being no more begotten again to all eternity'

"Now, on the strength of this theory, as all are agreed, Simon made himself out a god unto the ignorant, like that Libyan Apsethus above mentioned, 'being begotten and subject to passion so long as he is in potentiality, but not subject to passion after he shall have been begotten, and have received the image, and having been made perfect shall pass out of the dominion of the first two Powers, that is, of Heaven and Earth' For Simon speaks expressly upon this point in his 'Revelation,' in the following manner 'Unto you therefore I say what I say, and write what I write The Writing is this There are Two stocks of all the Æons put together, having neither beginning nor end, springing out of one Root, the which is *Silence*, invisible, inconceivable, of which Stocks, the one shows itself from above, the which is a great Power, *Mind* of the *all*, pervading all things, and of the *male* sex the other, showing itself from below, is the Great *Intelligence*, and is of the *female* sex, generating all things From thence they correspond with each other, and keep up a partnership, and illuminate the Middle Space lying between them (which is the air), inconceivable, having neither beginning nor end In this Middle Space is the Father, who bears up all things and nourishes the things that have beginning and ending This is "He who standeth, hath stood, and shall stand, being both male and female, a Power after the image of the pre-existing infinite Power, that hath neither beginning nor ending, existing in *Unity*" For the Intelligence in Unity proceeded out of this last and became Twain Now He (the Father) is One, for whilst he contained that

Power within himself he was single, nevertheless he was not the *First*, although he was pre-existent, but when he was manifested to himself out of himself, he became *Second*, and neither was he named the "Father," before that Power called him Father In the like manner therefore as the drawing-forth himself out of himself manifested unto himself his own *Intelligence*, so did this Intelligence also, when manifested, not *create*, but *contemplate* Him, and thereby stood-up the Father within herself, that is to say, the Power. And this Intelligence likewise is both a male and female Power, on which account they answer to one another, for the Power differs not at all from the Intelligence, being one and the same From that which is above, indeed, is formed the Power, from that which is below, the Intelligence. Of the same kind therefore is the *Unity*, which is manifested out of them both, for being *one* it is found to be *Twain*, both male and female, containing within itself the female In this manner the *Mind* exists within the Intelligence, which, when severed from each other, although they are One, are found to be Two'

"Simon, therefore, by publishing these notions, did not merely distort and wrest to his own purpose the sayings of Moses, but equally those of the heathen poets For he makes an allegory out of the Trojan Horse of wood, and the story of Helen with the torch, and much else, which he applies to his own fables concerning himself and his 'Intelligence'* Again he makes out the latter to be the Lost Sheep, which, always taking up her abode in the persons of women, doth cause trouble amongst all earthly Powers by reason of her incomparable beauty, wherefore the Trojan War came to pass because of her For this 'Intelligence'* of his took up her abode in Helen who was born just at that time; and so, when the Powers laid claim to her possession, strife and discord arose amongst all the nations to whom she manifested herself At any rate, it was on this account that Stesichorus, for having reviled her in his verses, was deprived of sight, but afterwards, when he had repented,

* That is his wife Helena By a remarkable, though doubtless undesigned coincidence, Fra Dolcino of Novara also went about accompanied by a similar female "Intelligence"

and written his 'Recantation,' in which he sang her praises, he recovered the use of his eyes. Then, after she had been placed in another body by the Angels and the Powers below (who according to Simon were the creators of the world), she was standing upon a housetop* in Tyre, a city of Phœnicia, where he found her on his landing. For he pretends to have gone thither expressly in quest of her, to deliver her out of bondage, and, after having ransomed her, he always carried her about with him, pretending that this was the Lost Sheep, and he himself was the Power that is over all. But the truth is, the impostor had become enamoured of this harlot, whose real name was Helena, so that he bought and kept her, but out of shame as regards his disciples, he invented the aforesaid fable. Furthermore, nowadays those that be the followers of this deceiver and magician, Simon, imitate his example, asserting that it is right to have intercourse with all women promiscuously, for they say 'All land is land, and it matters not where one sows his seed so long as he does sow it.' Nay more, they pride themselves upon this promiscuous intercourse, affirming that *this* is the 'Perfect Love,' and quote the text 'The Holy of holies shall be made holy.' For they hold that they are bound by no obligation as regards anything usually accounted wicked, inasmuch as they have been *redeemed*. In this way, Simon, after he had ransomed Helena, granted salvation unto men by means of his own *Knowledge* (or the *Gnosis*). For inasmuch as the Angels governed the world badly by reason of their own ambitiousness, Simon pretended that he was come to set all things right, having changed his form, and made himself like to the Principalities, the Powers, and the Angels; wherefore it was that he appeared in man's shape, though not a man at all, and had suffered the Passion in Judæa, although he had not suffered it; moreover that he had manifested himself to the Jews as the *Son*, in Samaria as the *Father*, and amongst the Gentiles elsewhere as the *Holy Ghost*, but that he submitted to be called by whatever name men pleased. The Prophets were inspired by the Angels, creators of the world, when they

* A euphemism for "living in a brothel," such being the mode in which these ladies advertised themselves.

delivered their prophecies, on which account those who believe in Simon and Helena pay no regard to them, even in our times, and they do whatever they please, affirming that they are redeemed through *his* grace For nothing is the cause of damnation, supposing a man to act wickedly, for Evil is evil not through the nature of things but by *convention*. For the Angels who created the world ordained it to be so (as they assert), in order that they might keep in subjection, by means of such fictions, all men who should listen to them Furthermore they explain the dissolution of the world as referring to the redemption of their own sect

"The disciples, therefore, of this Simon, practise magic arts and incantation, and make philtres and seductive spells, they likewise send the so-called 'dream-bringing' demons to trouble whomsoever they choose They likewise practise the rites of the gods named *Paredroi* (the Assessors), they have also an image of Simon in the guise of Jupiter, and likewise one of Helena in the figure of Minerva, and these they worship, calling one the 'Master,' the other the 'Mistress'"*

So much for the system of the renowned Samaritan, in which, it will have been seen, the place of logical reasoning is supplied by quibbles upon words, taken absolutely without any reference to the context—a style of argument, however, for which it must be confessed that he had highly respectable authority In strong contrast to this stands the next system, which displays much of the refinement and sound training (amidst its extravagance) of the Grecian mind

BASILIDES

Hippolytus, in accordance with his theses that all these "heresies" were mere plagiarisms from the more ancient philosophical systems, declares that Basilides stole the entire of his scheme from Aristotle, and proceeds to establish his charge by the following comparative analysis of the two

"Aristotle divides all substance into the *Genus*, the *Species*,

* Here follows the account of his career and end, already extracted (pp 21, 22)

and the *Individual* The Genus is, as it were, a heap composed of many and different seeds, from which heap all the Species are taken, and the genus is the sufficient cause to all things that exist For example, 'Animal' is used absolutely, not signifying any particular animal 'Animal' does not signify a horse, an ox, or a man, but simply 'animal' From this abstract 'animal' all the species of animals universally derive their origin, and this 'animal' without species is the origin of all animals generated according to their species, and not any one thing of things generated Thus, *Man* is an animal, deriving his origin from the 'animal,' and *Horse* is an animal in the same manner Similarly all other animals are derived from that 'animal,' who yet in itself is none of them If therefore that 'animal' is none of these, then, according to Aristotle, the substance of all things that are proceeds out of things that are non-existent, inasmuch as the 'animal,' out of which they all proceed individually, is not one thing (or 'is nothing at all'). And this, being Nothing, is the origin of all that *be*

"Now substance being divided into three classes—the genus, the species, and the individual—we have defined the genus as 'animal,' 'man' as the species picked out of the heap of animals, but as yet undiscriminated, and not separated into the form of a particular being But when I define by a special name, like Socrates, or Diogenes, a man taken from the species the genus, then that being is termed the 'individual' Thus the genus is divided into species, the species into individual, but the individual once being defined by name cannot be divided any further This is what Aristotle calls justly and properly 'Substance,' that which cannot be predicated 'of the subject,' nor 'in the subject' By the term 'of the subject' he means such an idea as 'animal,' which can be predicated of all the subject animals individually—as a horse, an ox, a man—all being called by the same name, 'animal' Hence, what can be predicated 'of the subject' is that which applies to many and different species indiscriminately 'In the subject' means that which cannot be predicated without the previous existence of something else wherein it may exist, as 'white, 'black,' 'just,' 'unjust,' which are the 'accidents' to substance. and therefore called 'qualities,' because expressing *what sort* of thing each thing is But no one quality can exist in itself, there must be something else for it to exist in If, therefore, neither the genus 'animal,' which is predicated *of* all animals existing individually, nor 'accident,' which is only to be found in things that exist, can either of them exist by themselves, and if individuals are made up of these two, namely genus and accident, then it follows that *substance*, which is made up of these three, and nothing besides, is made up of things that are *non-existent*

"If, therefore, what is properly and primarily termed 'substance' (the *Individual*) is made up of these, it is. according to Aristotle, made up of things non-existent

"Besides the terms Genus, Species, Individual, Substance is further designated as 'Matter' and 'Formation' Upon this definition rests the Basilidan theory of the Universe The Universe Basilides divides into several parts That part which extends from the earth up to the moon is destitute of *foresight* and of *conduct*, and is content with its own nature. The part beyond the moon is constituted with foresight, reason, and conduct, up to the surface of heaven This 'surface' is a *fifth* substance, free from all the elements out of which the world was created, this, therefore, is the 'fifth and supra-mundane substance' These three divisions Aristotle has treated of in three separate works his 'Physics,' 'Metaphysics,' and 'On the Fifth Substance' Not merely his ideas, but his words and terminology have been borrowed by Basilides, and applied to the Scriptures How, then, can his disciples, being in reality *heathens*, expect to be benefited by Christ?

"Basilides and his true son and disciple Isidorus, assert that Matthew (the Evangelist) revealed to them certain secret doctrines which had been specially communicated to himself by Christ 'There was a time when there was Nothing, nay, not even that "Nothing" was anything of *being*, but barely and without reserve, and without any sophism, there was altogether *Nothing*. When I use the term "was," I do not mean to imply that this Nothing *was*, but in order to explain what I wish to set forth, I employ the expression "there *was* absolutely

Nothing" Now that which is called "Ineffable" is not absolutely ineffable, for we ourselves give it that name of ineffable, whereas that which is *not even* ineffable is not "ineffable," but infinitely above every name that can be named Even for the Visible world, so multifarious are its divisions that we have not names enough, but we are reduced to conceive many of its properties from the names of the properties already named, these (other) properties being ineffable For an identity of names occasions a disorder and confusion of ideas in the mind of the learner.' (This is a direct plagiarism from Aristotle's discussion of synonyms in his book 'On the Categories')

"When therefore Nothing *was*—no substance, no non-substance, no simple, no compound, no incomprehensible, no sensible, no man, no angel, no God—when there was nothing whatever of what is called by name, perceived by sense, conceived by the mind, but all, and even in a more refined sense than this, being put out of the question—then this No-being God (Aristotle's 'thought of a thought,' which Basilides alters into his 'No-being'), without thought, without purpose, without counsel, without passion, without desire, willed to make the world. I use the word 'willed' merely to express my meaning, it being without thought, without sensation, without will, that this was done, and by 'world' I do not mean that world created afterwards and divided by latitude and longitude, but I understand by it 'the Seed of the World' This 'Seed of the World' contained the *All* within itself, just as the germ of the mustard-seed contains the root, the stalk, the leaves, the grain, the last containing again the rudiments of others innumerable Thus the No-being God created the No-being world out of No-being things, when he deposited the seed containing within itself the complete seeds of the universe And to give an illustration of my meaning the egg of any bird of diversified plumage—the peacock, for example—although itself single, yet includes within itself the many-coloured, multifarious forms of multifarious substances, so, in like manner, did this seed of the world deposited by the No-being God include within itself the multiform, multifarious seeds of the universe

"This seed, then, contained all things that can be named, nay more, all things that can not be named, as yet hidden in futurity, and to come forth after their kind by accretion, and by growth, after the manner in which we see the new-born infant acquire his teeth, his flesh, his father's form, and all his understanding, and all such things that come to the child as it grows up, not apparent in him at the beginning. Now, inasmuch as it is impossible to use the term 'projection' of the No-being God (in fact, Basilides is opposed to all schemes of creation by means of a 'projection'), for we must not suppose *Matter* necessary to his operations in the same way as her threads are to the spider, or as timber and metal to man when he sets about any work, but 'He spake and it was made', and this is what Moses means by his 'Let there be light, and there was light.' Whence, then, was this light? Moses saith not *whence* it was, but that it was from the word of the speaker, but neither He that spoke *was*, neither *was* that which was made. The seed of the world was this word that was spoken, 'Let there be light.' And to this the evangelist refers by his 'And that was the true Light which enlighteneth every man coming into the world.' For man draws his beginning out of that seed, and is illuminated thereby." (This "seed," therefore, divided into infinite other seeds, is nothing else than Aristotle's "genus," which is divided into infinite other "species," as "animal," the genus, itself non-existent, is divided into "species," as ox, horse, man, &c.)

"Having, therefore, got this seed for his starting-point, Basilides goes on thus: 'Whatever I speak of as made after this, there is no need of inquiring *out of what* it was made, seeing that this seed comprehended within itself the principles of the All. Now let us examine what came out of this seed in the first, second, and third place. There was in the seed a *Sonship*, triple, of the same substance with the No-being God, and generated by him. In this triple Sonship one part was subtile, another gross, the third needing purification.* Upon the first *projecting* (emitting) of the seed, the subtile element disengaged itself, ascending aloft "like a feather or a thought,"

* Corresponding to "Immaterial, Material, and Mixed."

and arrived at the No-being One. For Him all Nature desireth, by reason of the super-eminence of his beauty and perfection. The gross part endeavoured to imitate its example, but was weighed down by its coarser nature, and detained within the seed. To assist it, therefore, the Sonship equips it with a *wing*, such as Plato in his "Phaedrus" wings the soul withal Now this wing is the Holy Ghost, which the grosser part putting on, is both advantaged itself, and advantages the other For the wings of a bird are not able to fly if severed from the bird, neither can the soul fly if separated from her wings. Such, then, is the relationship borne by the Sonship to the Holy Ghost, and also by the Holy Ghost to the Sonship Soaring aloft, therefore, upon its wings—that is, upon the Holy Ghost, this Soul Part carried its wings, the Holy Ghost, along with it up to the No-being God, and the Sensible Sonship, but was unable to comprehend the latter, because its own nature is not constituted of the same substance with Him But in the same way as dry and pure air is repugnant to the nature of fishes, so the place, more ineffable than the Ineffable One, and more lofty than all names that can be named, the seat of the No-being God and of the Subtile Part, was contrary to the nature of the Holy Ghost On this account, the Sonship left it *near* to that place which cannot be conceived by mind, nor described by words, though not altogether abandoned by himself, but retaining something of his power (or essence), just as a vessel once filled with a precious perfume ever retains traces of that perfume, however carefully it may have been emptied And this is manifestly like the ointment upon the head "which ran down to Aaron's beard'—that is, the perfume of the Sonship, brought down by the Holy Ghost even into the impurity and degradation of mortality, out of which itself at the beginning had soared aloft, raised by the Sonship, as it were, on eagle's wings, being itself fastened upon his back For all things struggle upwards from that which is below towards that which is above, from the "worse towards the better," whereas nothing of those above in the better place seeks to descend below.'

"The third part of the Sonship—namely, that requiring

purification, remained included within the infinite *head* (or sum) of infinite seeds, both giving and receiving benefit, in the manner hereafter to be explained After the first and second ascensions of the Sonship, the Holy Ghost, which had been left above, became the 'firmament' between the world and the upper world For Basilides divides all things that are into two great classes, the 'world' and the 'upper world', the Spirit, therefore, occupying the interval between the two (namely, the Holy Ghost, which retains the odour of the Sonship) he terms the 'Boundary Spirit' Now after this firmament above the world had been constituted, there broke forth out of the Seed of the World the 'Great Archon,' the Head of the World, or beauty, strength, magnitude indissoluble More ineffable is he than the Ineffable, more powerful than the Powerful, wiser than the Wise, more beautiful than any beauty that can be named. As soon as he was born he soared upwards and reached the firmament, but *that* was the limit of his flight, for he knew not of the existence of anything *beyond* the firmament, and therefore he remained more beautiful, more powerful, more wise than any of the things subjacent, always excepting the Sonship—that is, the Third impurified Person—who still lay enclosed within the immense universal seed Imagining himself, therefore, to be Lord and Ruler and *Intelligent Architect*, he set about the creation of the world In the first place, not wishing to abide alone, he generated unto himself a son out of things subjacent (*mundane elements*), far wiser and more beautiful than himself, for *this* son was in truth the Third Person yet left enclosed within the seed. This thing had been predestinated by the No-being God from the beginning, as soon as he beheld this son he was enamoured of his perfect beauty, and bade him to sit down on his right hand. This they call the 'Ogdoad,' the abode of the Great Archon. The great and wise Demiurgus then made the entire *æthereal* creation, being inspired and empowered thereto by his own son, so far above himself in wisdom" (This idea is copied from Aristotle's "Entelechia" of the natural organic body, the *active soul* in the body being itself wiser, stronger, and better than the body. The theory, therefore, propounded originally by Aristotle concerning the body and the soul, Basilides thus applies to the Great Archon and the Son whom he had created, for as the Archon creates the Son, so does Aristotle make the soul to be the work and effect of the natural organic body) "All things, therefore, are ruled by the providence of the Great Archon" (or rather, by the "Entelechia" of himself and son)—"all things, that is to say, which lie *below* the moon, and *within* the æther—for the moon is the division between the æther and the air

"The creation being finished, there arose out of the seed a 'Second Archon,' but greatly inferior to the first, yet similarly *ineffable* This (Archon) is designated the 'Hebdomad' He proceeded to create all things *below* the æther of which he is the Demiurgus, and he, in his turn, generated a son infinitely superior to himself The intermediate space between the regions Ogdoad and Hebdomad is occupied by the universal seed, the heap of species, the particles whereof are guided by the intelligence implanted in them by the First Creator as to the *times*, the *natures*, and the *changes* in which they have to come forth, and possess no other guide, guardian, or creator

"The whole creation was in this way completed, of the world and of the things above the world, but there was yet left within the seed the 'Third Sonship,' who, in his turn, had to be developed, revealed, and to ascend beyond the Boundary Spirit up to the Subtile Sonship and the No-being One *This* is the interpretation (meaning) of the Scripture 'The whole creation groaneth and is in labour, waiting for the manifestation of the sons of God.' These 'sons' are the *Spiritual Men* left here below to guide and to perfect the souls that from their nature belong to this place 'From Adam unto Moses sin reigned'—that is to say, the Great Archon, who had dominion up to the firmament, and imagined that he alone was God, and that there was none other above him—for all above him was kept in the deepest silence *This* is the 'mystery not revealed unto the Fathers', the Great Archon, the Ogdoad, was, as he supposed, the Lord and Ruler of the universe But of the 'interval,' or middle space, the Hebdomad was the ruler, now the Ogdoad is ineffable, but the Hebomad may be uttered by speech This ruler of the Hebdomad was He who spake unto Moses, saying,

'I am the God of Abraham, Isaac, and Jacob, and the Name of God I have not revealed unto them'—that is, He did not reveal to them the ineffable ruler of the Ogdoad. All the prophets who were before the Saviour's coming spoke through the inspiration of the Second Archon.

"When the time was come for the manifestation of the Sons of God, the Gospel came, penetrating through every power, dominion, and name that can be named, although the Sonship did not come down from his place upon the right hand of the Incomprehensible No-being One. But, like as Indian naphtha kindles at the mere sight of fire a long way off, so do powers fly up out of the seed to the Sonship that is beyond the firmament. The son of the Great Archon of the Ogdoad thus receives, like as naphtha catches the distant flame, the emanations of the Sonship who is beyond the firmament; and this last, the Boundary Spirit, serves for the communication of the thoughts from the one to the other.

"The Gospel thus came to the Great Archon through his own son, and he was converted, and troubled, and became wise, learning his own *ignorance* (or want of knowledge); and this is the interpretation of 'The fear of the Lord is the beginning of *wisdom*.' For the Christ, sitting by him, instructed him concerning the Ineffable No-being One, concerning the Son who is beyond the firmament, and concerning the creation of the universe. The Great Archon being thus instructed, was filled with *fear* and confessed the *sin* he had committed in magnifying himself; and this is the meaning of 'I acknowledge my transgression and I confess my sin.' When, therefore, the Great Archon was enlightened, every creature of the Ogdoad was likewise enlightened, and then came the time for the enlightenment and evangelising of the ruler of the Hebdomad. For this end the son of the Great Archon communicated to the son of the Second Archon the light which he himself had received from above, and *he* communicated his instruction to his Father, who in like manner was convinced of, and confessed *his* sin. By this time every creature of the Hebdomad was enlightened, and had the Gospel preached unto them. For in this division (the region below the æther) also, there is an infinite creation of powers, principalities, and dominions (concerning whom Basilides has a lengthy dissertation, who moreover in this region places the 365 heavens, and their ruler ABRASAX, so called because his name contains that sum, for which reason the year consists also of that number of days)

"After all this it was necessary that the *Unformedness* (ἀμορφία) existing in our region—that is, the Sonship still lying enclosed in the mass like an abortion—should be enlightened in the same manner with those aforementioned The Light therefore passed through the Hebdomad upon the son of the Hebdomad—that is, upon *Jesus*, the son of Mary This is 'the power of the Most High shall overshadow thee,' namely, the power of *unction*, descending from the Supreme through the Demiurgus upon the Son

"The present constitution of things will last until every particle of the Sonship enveloped in the unformed mass shall be attracted into Jesus, shall be disentangled and sublimated by him, and rendered capable of ascending by itself to the first source of Light, to which it bears a natural affinity.

"In this way the Three Persons of the Sonship being all united once more above the firmament, then mercy shall be shown unto the creation, 'which languishes and groans waiting for the manifestation of the sons of God', for all men belonging to the Sonship shall ascend up unto Him When this is accomplished, He will bring upon the world a *deep ignorance*, so that all things here below shall abide in their nature, and desire nothing contrary to their nature By this means the souls appointed to abide here below will be destitute of even the slightest notion of anything existing above them, lest they should be tormented by the fruitless desire of ascending up into the same, like as though a *fish* should desire to pasture with the flocks upon the hills, a wish which, if gratified, would be its destruction. For all things are *eternal* so long as they continue in their natural place, but become *mortal* when they endeavour to escape beyond it The same *ignorance* will envelop the ruler of the Hebdomad, in order that sorrow and grief and confusion may flee away from him, that he may no longer be troubled with the desire of things above him and contrary to his nature This ignorance shall also come over the Great Archon of the Ogdoad, and over all creatures subject unto him, and for the same reason This is the 'restoration of all things', enclosed from the beginning within the seed, and disposed according to its season This is the Saviour's meaning in 'My hour is not yet come', it is also signified by the Magi beholding the star, inasmuch as His coming, proclaimed from the beginning, was subject to the disposition of the stars *

"The Gospel is the *Declaration* of supramundane things, which the Great Archon knew not of But when it was told him of the Sonship, of the Boundary Spirit, and of the No-being God, he rejoiced with an exceeding great joy With respect to the birth of Jesus, all things came to pass as they are written in the Gospels For *He* was the firstfruits of the division of the classes, previously all commingled here below Now, as the world is distributed into the Ogdoad, the head of the universe, whose chief is the Great Archon, and into the Hebdomad, whose chief is the Demiurgus, chief also of our degree where Frailty (liability to error) subsists, it was necessary that this Confusion should be distributed and set in order by Jesus. That part of him, therefore, which was of the 'Unformedness,' namely, his body suffered what it did suffer and returned again into unformedness, that part which belonged to the Hebdomad, namely, his soul, returned again into the Hebdomad after his resurrection, the part belonging to the Ogdoad remained with the Great Archon, and the part belonging to the Boundary Spirit was left there in his ascension. But the third Sonship, thus purified in his passage upwards, was reunited to the Blessed Sonship who is supreme above. (In short, the whole theory of the religion consists in the *Confusion* of the Seed-heap, its *Redistribution* into classes, and the *Restoration* of all things to their natural places This division of the classes was made in the first instance by Jesus, and the sole object of his passion was the restoration of the classes, which were mixed up together, into their proper order And for this reason Jesus himself was

* This may allude to the Rabbinical explanation of the "sign of the coming" of the Messiah as being the conjunction of Saturn and Jupiter in Pisces

distributed as we have shown, amongst the several classes. These then are the things that Basilides fables, who taught in Egypt, and, having learned his wisdom *from the Egyptians* brought forth such fruits as these.)"

This concluding remark of Hippolytus deserves particular notice; it shows that he regarded the Basilidan theory as the mere *adaptation* to present requirements of an ancient esoteric doctrine belonging to the Egyptian priesthood. That it was nothing more than a plagiarism from the Aristotelian philosophy, as the learned Father labours to demonstrate with so much ingenuity, appears to me by no means made out. But the Basilidan theory has one striking feature that distinguishes it from every other form of the Gnosis, in its entirely ignoring the existence of an *Evil Principle*, or of malignity and rebellion against the Supreme God. His two rulers of the upper and lower worlds, the Great Archon of the Ogdoad, and the Demiurgus of the Hebdomad, so far from opposing the Gospel receive it with joy, and humbly acknowledge their inferiority to the sender. The Passion of Jesus is not due to the malice of either of them, but is voluntary, and undertaken as the sole means of restoring confused elements of the All to the *harmony* indispensable for their *eternal* duration. Even the final withdrawing of the Divine Light from the Ogdoad and Hebdomad is done for the same beneficent purpose, in order that both they and their greatness may rest for ever in blissful ignorance, each holding himself supreme in his own creation, and knowing of nothing above it, may no longer be tormented by vain aspirations after a state of perfection for which his nature is not adapted. The benevolent spirit that pervades the whole theory strongly supports the assertion of Hippolytus, and points out for its source the Egyptian mythology, to which the notion of two principles, equal in power but antagonistic in nature, would have been unutterably shocking.

THE OPHITES

The Ophites should hold by right the first place amongst the schools we are considering, for that impartial and acute historian of the Gnosis, Hippolytus, styles them, "The Naaseni who specially call themselves 'Gnostics' But inasmuch as this deception of theirs is multiform and has many heads (a play upon their name of serpent-followers), like the Hydra of fable, if I smite all the heads at once with the wand of Truth, I shall destroy the whole serpent, for all the other sects differ but little from this one in essentials." He therefore commences his history of the Gnostic heresies, properly so called, with a minute account of this one, illustrated with copious extracts from their text-books, on account of their antiquity and importance bestowing much more of his space upon them than upon any other of their offshoots or competitors

Their strange-sounding title "Naaseni"—"Followers of the Naas' (the only way in which the Greek, from its want of aspirate letters, could write the Hebrew Nachash, "Serpent")—was literally rendered by "Ophites," the name which has ever since served to designate them They first assumed a definite existence about the same time as the Basilidans, in the middle of the second century, although the elements of the doctrine are derived from a source much more remote That source was the secret doctrines taught in the various Pagan Mysteries, and likewise certain philosophic theories of the Greeks, although certainly not to the same extent as the learned Hippolytus labours so ingeniously to demonstrate

In support of this statement I shall proceed to quote from the same Father some curious examples of the method in which the Naaseni pretended to recognise their own "knowledge" in the esoteric religions of antiquity After quoting a long passage from Pindar about the conflicting theories as to the creation of the First Man* and the names given to him by different nations, the Ophite text-book continues

* "But the Libyans held that *Iarbas* was the first-born of men, he who, rising up out of their droughty plains, first gathered the sweet dates of Jove And even in our day, the Nile fattening the mud of Egypt,

"This was the Man brought forth by the Earth spontaneously, but he lay without breath, without motion, without stirring, like a statue, being made after the image of their Adamas above, the subject of their hymns, through the agency of several Powers, concerning each one of whom they narrate a long fable. But in order that the Man above might be obtained, 'from whom is every tribe upon the Earth, and likewise in the Heavens,' there was given unto him a *soul*, that through this soul the image of the Man above might suffer and be chastened in bondage. As to the nature and source of this soul sent down to animate this image, the Ophite theory is derived *not from Scripture, but from the doctrine of the Mysteries* 'The Gospel according to the Egyptians' is their text-book on this point. They premise that the nature of the soul is extremely difficult to investigate by reason of its inherent changeableness, never abiding fixedly in the same place, habits, or passion and they adopt in this particular the *notions of the Assyrian mystics* It is a question with them whether the soul comes from the 'Pre-existing,' or from the 'Self-begotten One,' or from the 'Effusion of Chaos' They adopt the *Assyrian* division of the soul as being both one and threefold' For all Nature longs for a soul, the soul is the efficient cause of all things that grow, are nourished and have action For without a soul, growth and nutrition are impossible, even stones have a soul, for they possess the faculty of growth, and this faculty cannot exist without nutrition. All things therefore in Heaven or Earth, and in the Abyss, are eager after a soul This *soul* the Assyrians call 'Adonis,' 'Endymion,' 'Attis', and hence arose the fable of the love of Venus for Adonis, *Venus* signifying *generation* The love of Proserpine for Adonis means that the soul is mortal if separated from Venus, that is, from generation. When the Moon is enamoured of Endymion, it is Nature herself desiring a more sublime soul. When the Mother of the gods emasculates her lover, Attis, it signifies the Power

and giving life to things clothed with flesh, through his moist heat breeds living creatures The Assyrians pretend that the First Man arose in their country, *Oannes*, the eater of fish, but the Chaldeans say he was *Adam*"

above recalling into itself the male energy of the soul. For the Man that is above is of both sexes" [On this account they most vehemently denounce all intercourse with women.] "Attis was deprived of his virility, that is, was divested of his lower, earthly, part, and then translated to the Upper World, 'where is neither male nor female, but a new creature,' the Man above, of two sexes. And to this truth not only Rhea, but all creation, beareth testimony And to this doth Paul refer in Romans (i 20–27) (where they strangely pervert his expression ἀσχημοσύνη, as signifying that heavenly, sublime, felicity, that *absence of all form* which is the real source of every form). These same verses of Paul, according to them, contain the key to their whole system, and to their 'Mystery of Celestial Pleasure' For the promise of 'Washing' applies to none save the man who is introduced into the eternal pleasure, 'being washed with the True Water, and anointed with the Unction that cannot be spoken' The Phrygian Mysteries, equally with the Assyrian, teach the same great truth, when they teach the blessed nature of things past, present, and to come, hidden and yet manifested, the 'true kingdom that is within you' To the same effect they bring forward the *Gospel of Thomas*, which has, 'He that seeketh shall find me amongst children from seven years downwards, for in the fourteenth generation, being hidden, I will manifest myself' [Although in reality this is not a maxim of Christ's, but a maxim of Hippocrates. 'The boy at seven years of age is the half of his father,'—in stature]

"The Egyptians were, after the Phrygians, the most ancient of mankind, and the first establishers of mysteries The Ophites explain as follows the esoteric doctrine concerning Isis, and the genital member of Osiris, lost, sought after, and enveloped by her seven times in a black (or dark blue)* vestment Osiris is the element *Water*, Nature seven times enveloped in an etherial robe, that is, the seven planetary spheres, stands for Generation and Change, or Creation transformed by the ineffable, formless, imageless, incomprehensible Deity The same is implied in the words of Scripture, 'The righteous man shall fall *seven* times, and shall rise again'—his

* Μέλας has both these meanings

all signifying the revolutions of the planets put in motion by the All-mover

"They likewise discourse concerning the essence (or *existence*) of the 'Seed,'* the final cause of all things that exist, although itself none of them, and yet making and generating all things, or, as they themselves express it, 'I become what I will, and am what I am, therefore I say that moving all, I am myself immovable' For it continues what it is, making all things, although itself is made nothing of all that exist To this doctrine the Saviour's words refer, 'Why callest thou me good? One only is good, my Father which is in Heaven, who maketh the sun to shine upon the just and upon the unjust, and sendeth His rain upon the sinners and upon the righteous' And this is the *great and unknown Mystery*, hidden amongst the Egyptians and yet manifested, for Osiris standeth in his temple before Isis, having his secret part exposed and pointed upwards, and crowned with all the fruits of the creation And for this cause, the same member [the Phallus] holds the first position in the most sacred places, being shown forth unto the world, 'like a light set upon a candlestick' it is set up on the house-tops, and in the streets, and for landmarks It is a blessing acknowledged and proclaimed by all, for they call it the 'Bringer of Luck' (ἀγαθηφόρον),—not understanding what they say This mystery the Greeks *got from Egypt*, and observe unto this day For by this symbol they represent Hermes and they entitle that god 'Logicos,' for he is the *interpreter* and Creator of things made, in making, and to be made, and he is represented by this his proper symbol And that *this* is the Hermes, guide, companion, and author of souls, Homer hath perceived, for he saith (Od xxiv 1–2) —

'Cyllenian Hermes summoned forth the souls of the bold suitors,

not meaning those of Penelope's suitors, but of us the awakened and admonished

'From what vast happiness, what height of glory,'

we have fallen, namely, from the Primal Man, the *Adamas*

* The "Seed of the World" in the Basilidan system, as already explained (p 73)

that is above, into this vessel of clay, and become the servants of the Demiurgus, of Ildabaoth, the God of Fire, the *Fourth* in number (for by this name they call the creator of the 'World of Species,' κοσμὸς ἰδικός).

"In his hand his wand Beauteous, all golden, by whose potency the eyes of mortals he at pleasure lulls to sleep, or rouses others from their slumber. For He is the sole author of life and death, therefore is it written, 'Thou shalt rule them with a rod of iron.' But Homer wishing to embellish the incomprehensible reality of the nature of the Logos, has given to him a rod of *gold*, not of iron. Some He casts into slumber, others he awakens, and makes them aware of their condition. 'Awake thou that sleepest, and rise from the dead, and Christ shall give thee light.' For *this* is the Christ that is figured within all the sons of men by the unfigured Logos. *This* is the great and profound mystery of the Eleusinian rites, the cry, YE KYE, *Rain! Conceive!* All things are subject unto Him, for 'their sound is gone forth unto all lands.' And again, *this* is the hidden sense of Homer's

'He waved his wand, they followed with shrill cry.'

That is, the souls in a continuous line, as the poet goes on to express by the simile—

'As in the furthest depths of some vast cave,
Shrill cry the bats when one drops from their chain,
Down from the rock where fast they cling together.'

That is, the souls fallen down from the Rock above, namely from the Adamas. *This* is the Adamas, the chief corner-stone, 'which is made the head of the corner,' because in the head is placed the formative substance, the brain, out of which all generation proceeds. 'I will set the Adamant in the foundations of Zion' is allegorical for setting the figure of the Man (in the soul). And the text, 'This Adamas is firmly held by teeth in the wall,' is the *Inner Man* that is signified, the 'stone cut without hands,' which hath fallen down from the Adamas above into this earthly potter's vessel, this figure of *forgetfulness*.*

* Meaning the *Body*, in which the Inner Man imprisoned has lost all recollection of his primal source.

"The souls follow Hermes, or the Logos.

> 'So moved they, crying, through the darksome paths,
> Hermes their guide, that god devoid of ill'

That is, he leads them to the everlasting places where no ill comes; for whither were they going?

> 'They passed o'er Ocean's wave and Leucas' rock,
> The Sun's bright portals, and the land of dreams'

"This 'Ocean' signifies the generation of gods and the generation of men, ever tossing in a perpetual flow and ebb When it runs *downwards* it is the generation of men, when it tosses itself *upwards* against its boundary,* the rock Leucas, it is the generation of gods 'For this cause,' saith the Wise One, 'I have said ye are gods and the children of the Most Highest, when ye shall make haste to flee out of Egypt, and shall come beyond the Red Sea into the Wilderness', that is, out of this earthly mixture (or confusion) up to the Jerusalem above, which is the mother of the living. 'But if ye return into Egypt (or, into this earthly nature) ye shall die' 'Egypt' being the prison of the body *This* is the mighty Jordan which, flowing downwards, hindered the flight of the Children of Israel, but which Jesus (*i.e.* Joshua) turned, and made to flow upwards"

"Following guides like those just cited, these very strange fellows the Gnostics (observes Hippolytus), the inventors of a new art of grammar (or, criticism), extol beyond all expression their prophet Homer, who hath foreshown these doctrines unto them and, by seducing those ignorant of the Holy Scriptures into such-like fancies, they make fools of them in the manner described."

"Another of their maxims is that 'Whoso saith that the All cometh from *One* is grossly deceived, but he that saith that the All cometh from *Three*, hath the true key to the system of the universe For there is one nature of the Man that is above, Adamas, one mortal here below, one without a king, the generation existing up above, where is Mariam the Sought-After, and Jothor the great and wise, and Sephora, she that

* The Basilidan "Boundary Spirit," or Holy Ghost (p 76)

seeth, and Moses, whose offspring is not in Egypt, for his sons were born unto him in the land of Midian Neither hath this truth escaped Homer, for he sings—

> "All things are parcelled into portions three,
> And to each portion its due honour falls"

For it is necessary that the *Great Ones* (τὰ μεγέθη) should be expressed in words, but in such wise that "hearing men may not hear, and seeing they may not perceive" For if the Great Ones were not uttered, the world could not exist. These three most sublime names are, KAVLACAV, SAVLASAV, ZEESAR *Kavlacav* is the name of the Adamas who is above, *Savlasav* of him who is below, mortal, *Zeesar* of the Jordan that floweth upwards *This* is He that pervades all things, being at once male and female, named by the Greeks Geryon, as having three bodies and flowing out of the Earth whom the Greeks also call "The Moon's celestial horn,' because he has *mixed* and *tempered* all things [a play upon the similar sounding words κέρας and κρᾶσις] "For all things were made through him, and without him nothing was made, and what was made in him is Life" This Life is the life unspeakable, the generation of the Perfect Man, unknown to former ages The "Nothing" that was made without him is the World of Species, for *that* world was made without him by the *Third* and by the *Fourth* One.* *This* is the Cup (*condy*) of Joseph, "out of which the king doth drink and use divination" Of this also do the Greeks (Anacreon) sing in Bacchic frenzy,

> "Bring me boy, the draught divine,
> Bring me water, bring me wine,
> Make me drunk with quaffing deep,
> Lull my charmed soul to sleep,
> For my cup predicts to me
> Of what country I shall be"

Here Anacreon's dumb cup utters the unspeakable mystery, for it tells him to *what country* he shall belong, that is, whether to the *Spiritual* or to the *Carnal* world *This* also is the "Water changed into wine," at the famous wedding at Cana, when Jesus manifested the kingdom of Heaven—that kingdom which is

* Ildabaoth, the God of Fire

hidden within every man, like the leaven sufficient for the *three* measures. Here likewise is the unspeakable secret of the *Samothracian Mysteries*, which none but we the "Perfect" are able to understand, for the Samothracians expressly mention the Adamas who is above—the Primal Man. For in the Temple of the Samothracians stand two naked men, having their hands and their genital members elevated towards heaven,* like the Hermes of Cyllene. These two statues represent the Primal Man, and the Spiritual Man after he is "born again, and made like unto Him every whit."'

"*This* is the true sense of the Saviour's words, 'Unless ye eat my flesh and drink my blood, ye cannot enter into the Kingdom of Heaven', and 'Though ye shall drink of the cup that I drink of, whither I go ye shall not be able to enter.' For He knew the *nature* of His disciples, and that every one must abide in his own nature. For out of the Twelve Tribes he chose the Twelve Disciples, for which cause not all who heard their teaching received or understood the same, for that which is not according to Nature is contrary to Nature. Him (Adamas) do the Phrygians name 'Corybas,' for he descends from the Head (*cory*) who is above, the Supernal Brain, and permeates the All in a manner incomprehensible. And, as the Prophet hath it, 'Ye have heard his voice, but ye have not beheld his form', that is, the *Image* coming down from the Formless One above no one knows, for it is hidden within an earthen vessel. *This* is as the Psalmist hath it 'The God dwelling in the great

* A valuable notice of the type under which the Cabiri were represented in this the most venerated of all the Grecian sanctuaries. It is curiously illustrated by Ficoroni's bronze group, figured in his "Memorie di Labico," and given to the Kircherian Museum. A female, half-draped in a star-spangled robe, rests her hands on the shoulders of twin youths, similarly *arrecti*, with the ears and standing-up hair of fauns, one holds a horn, the other the handle of a vase. The base is inscribed in very archaic letters—

DINDIA MAGOLNIA FIEA DE DIT NOVIOS PLAVTIOS MED ROMAI FECID

where it will be seen that Dindia uses the *matronymic* after the Etruscan fashion. This group, six inches high, served for handle to the lid of a cylindrical pyxis, two palms deep resting on three lion's claws. With it was found a mirror, the back engraved with the combat of Pollux and Amycus, LOSNA with her crescent standing in the middle, the names in regular Etruscan

flood, and crying aloud out of the waters of the sea', that is, He cries aloud out of the multiform *confusion* (or, medley) of things mortal unto the Formless One who is above, 'Save my First-born from the lions' [And in the same sense do they interpret all the similes concerning 'waterfloods,' and the promises of the Deity's never forgetting His chosen people.]

"The Ascension or Regeneration, that is, the conversion of the Carnal Man into the Spiritual, is thus explained by means of a curious perversion of words taken from different Psalms 'Lift up your heads, ye everlasting gates, that the King of Glory may come in. Who is this King of Glory? The very scorn of men, and the outcast of the people, He is the King of Glory, mighty in battle' *Battle* signifies the war in your members ever being waged within this earthly creature made up of conflicting elements. *This* is the *gate* seen by Jacob as he was journeying into Mesopotamia, that is, the young man growing up out of the boy, and *Mesopotamia* signifies the stream of the Great Ocean which flows out of the middle of the Perfect Man The same deity is called by the Phrygians PAPA, because He *appeased* the confusion and chaotic tumult which prevailed before His coming For this name is the unanimous cry παῦε, παῦε,* of all things in Heaven, in Earth, and under the Earth, calling upon Him to *appease* the discord, and to 'send peace to men that were afar off'—that is, to the earthly and mortal—'and to them that were near' that is, to the spiritual and perfect He is likewise called 'dead' by the Phrygians, inasmuch as he is *buried* within the tomb of the body, to which circumstance also apply the words, 'Ye are whited sepulchres, full of dead men's bones and all manner of uncleanness, because the Living Man doth not dwell within you'

"'The dead shall rise from their graves' signifies that the Earthly Man shall be born again spiritual. Unless they pass

* A subsequent thousand years' experience of the blessings of ecclesiastical rule has furnished Walter de Mapes with a more humorous etymology for this title—

"*Papa*, si rem tangimus nomen habet a re,
Quidquid habent alii solus vult pappare
Aut si nomen Gallicum vis apocopare,
Payez, payez dit le mot, si vis impetrare"

through this 'Gate' all continue dead, but him that hath passed through the Phrygians call a *god*, for he becomes a god, having passed through the Gate into Heaven. Paul means the same by his 'being caught up into the third heaven, and hearing unutterable things.' Again, 'the publicans and harlots shall enter into the Kingdom of Heaven before you,' where *publicans* means the Gentiles 'upon whom the *ends* of the world have come',* where 'ends' are the seeds of the universe scattered about by the Formless One, as is set forth by the Saviour, 'He that hath ears to hear, let him hear,' declaring that none but the perfect Gnostics can comprehend this mystery.

"Those beloved by the Formless One are Pearls in this vessel of clay, and to them refers the precept, 'Cast not that which is holy to the dogs, neither throw your pearls before swine,' meaning sexual intercourse with women—an act fit only for dogs and swine. He is also called Αἰπόλος by the Phrygians, not because he really kept flocks, as the profane fancy, but because he is ὁ αἰεὶ πολῶν, 'he that ever turns' the universe in its due revolutions, whence the phrase, the 'poles' of heaven. And Homer (Od. iv. 384–85) says—

> 'Here *turns* about the truthful sea-god old,
> Immortal Proteus by the Egyptians called.'

"He is likewise styled 'Fruitful,' because 'the children of the widow shall be more than those of her that hath a husband,' that is, the *spiritual* who are born again, being immortal, are in number more (though but few of them are born into this life) than the *carnal*, who, in spite of their present multitude, do all perish utterly at last.

"The knowledge of the Perfect Man is very deep, and hard to be attained to. 'The *beginning* of perfection is the knowledge of man, but *absolute* perfection is the knowledge of God.' He (Adamas) is designated by the Phrygians as, 'the Green Wheat-ear cut off', on this account, at the Eleusinian rites, the initiated hold up in silence to the Directors the wondrous mystery, the green ear of wheat. This wheat-ear is the Perfect Son descended from the Adamas above, the Great Giver

* A play upon τελῶναι and τέλη.

of light, like the Hierophant himself This latter is not actually castrated like Attis, but emasculated by the use of hemlock, so that he despises all carnal pleasure, and whilst celebrating the mysteries amidst blazing torches, he cries aloud, 'The holy Brimo hath borne a sacred son, Brimos'—alluding to the Spiritual Birth The rites are therefore named 'Eleusinian' and 'Anactorian,' from the Greek words signifying *Coming* and *Ascending* This is what the initiated themselves declare concerning the mysteries of Proserpine and of the road leading the defunct down to her the poet (Amphis) hath—

> 'But underneath her lies a rugged path,
> Hollow and muddy, yet the best to lead
> Down to the lovely groves of precious Venus.'

"These are the Lesser Mysteries, of *earthly* origin, 'in which men ought to rest themselves for a while, and then proceed to the Greater Mysteries,' that is, to heavenly regeneration

"The Father of the All is furthermore called by the Phrygians 'Amygdalus,' *the Almond Tree*, not meaning the natural tree, but the Pre-existing One, who, having within himself the Perfect Fruit pulsating and moving about in his depths, *tore open* (διήμιξε) his bosom, and brought forth the Invisible Ineffable Son, of whom we are treating * He is moreover denominated the 'Piper,' because that which is born is the harmonious *Spirit* [or, *breath*, the Greek affording no distinction between the two senses of the word] The Spirit is likewise called the Father, and the Son begotten by the Father, for the worship of the Perfect is not carnal, but spiritual therefore, 'Neither in Jerusalem nor in this mountain shall ye worship any more

"*This* is the mystery of the Incomprehensible One, *furnished with innumerable eyes*, whom all Nature longeth after in different ways [Perhaps an allusion to the Brahminical figure of Indra, god of the heavens] This is the 'Word of God,' that is, the

* Some lurking tradition of this mystery may have suggested the machine of the almond (*machina della mandola*) containing the Archangel Gabriel, in the spectacle of the Annunciation constructed by Brunelleschi for the church of Sta Croce See Vasari's detailed account of this remarkable example of a miracle-play

word of the declaration of his great power 'Wherefore it shall be sealed up, and veiled, and hidden, lying in the dwelling-place, where is established the Root of all the Æons, Powers, thoughts [Platonic *Ideas*], gods, angels, spirit-messengers that are, that are not, begotten, unbegotten, comprehensible, incomprehensible, of the years, months, days, hours, moments, whence Time begins to grow and increase by particles For a moment (or geometrical *point*), itself being nothing, made of nothing, indivisible, grows by accretion into a magnitude incomprehensible' This is the Kingdom of Heaven, the grain of mustard seed, the Indivisible Point existing within every one, but only known unto the Spiritual Man

"'There is neither speech nor language, but their voices are heard amongst them,' signifies that whatever men say or do, has all a *spiritual meaning* to the Perfect, even the actors in the theatre utter nothing without the intervention of the Deity For when the audience are seated, and the actor comes upon the stage, clad in a gorgeous robe and twanging his lyre, he sings thus a great mystery without knowing what he says—'Whether thou be the offspring of Saturn, or of blessed Jove, or of the mighty Rhea, hail! *Thee* Assyrians call the thrice-desired *Adamas*, whilst Egypt styles Thee *Osiris*, the Greeks in their wisdom (esoteric knowledge) the *Moon's Holy Horn*, the Samothracians, the venerable *Adamnas*, the Hæmonians, *Corybas*, the Phrygians, at one time, Papa, the *Dead One*, at another, the *God*, or the *Barren One*, or the *Green Wheat-ear* cut off, or him whom the fruitful *Almond Tree* poses the man playing on the pipe' *He* is the multiform *Attis*, whom they thus describe in their hymns 'I will sing of Attis, the favourite of Rhea, with the clashing of cymbals, the bellowing of the Idæan pipe of the Curetes, and will intermingle the sound of Phœbus' lyre Evoe! Evau! Thou that art like unto Pan, unto Bacchus, thou Shepherd of the white stars!'

"For these" (adds Hippolytus) "and other such like reasons, these Ophites frequent the Mysteries of the Great Mother, fancying that by means of what is done there they can see through the whole secret But in reality they have not the least advantage over other people, except that they are not emasculated, and yet they act as though they were For they most strictly forbid all intercourse with women, and in every other respect, as we have fully described, they do the same things as the eunuchs, the regular priests of Rhea"

After giving an account of their worship and glorification of the Serpent (which I shall extract when treating of the Agathodæmon religion) Hippolytus thus continues —"The foregoing is a sample of the insane, absurd, and interminable theories of the sect But to show up, as far as lies in our power, their *unknowing* 'knowledge,' the following hymn* is here inserted, as containing a summary of the whole creed —

"'The generative law of the All was the First Mind,
But the Second was the effused chaos of the First
In the third place the Soul received a law, and began to operate†
Whereupon She (the Soul) enveloped in the figure of a fawn,
Struggles with Death, suffering a probationary penance
At one time, invested with royalty, she beholds the Light,
At another, cast down into misery, she weeps
Now she weeps and rejoices,
Now she weeps and is judged,
Now she is judged and dies
When shall her deliverance be?
The wretched one
Hath entered, as she strayed, into an evil labyrinth
But Jesus said Father, suffer me,
She in quest of evil (or, the chased of evil ones) upon earth
Wandereth about, destitute of Thy Spirit
She seeketh to escape from the bitter chaos,
But knoweth not how to pass through
For this cause send me, O Father!
I will go down holding the Seals,
I will pass through all the Æons,
I will reveal all the mysteries,
I will manifest the forms of the gods,‡
And the hidden secrets of the holy way
I will teach, giving unto them the name of GNOSIS'

"This, therefore, is the system (or pretension) of the Naaseni, who designate themselves 'the Gnostics' But this

* This hymn is written in anapæstic verses, its text is in many places hopelessly corrupted by the transcriber I have therefore often been obliged to conjecture the original sense

† An enunciation of the fundamental doctrine "All is Three," already stated by Hippolytus

‡ That is, will disclose to the faithful the different figures of the Archons of the lower spheres, a promise fulfilled at much length by the author of the Pistis-Sophia

deception of theirs being multiform, and having many heads like the Hydra of fable, if I smite all the heads at a single blow with the wand of Truth, I shall destroy the whole serpent, for all the other sects differ but little from this in essentials."

Hippolytus has not given a connected analysis of the Ophite system, he probably deemed it superfluous labour, as having been already done with much exactness by Irenæus in his great work, to which the former occasionally refers as being then in everybody's hands. To the Bishop of Lugdunum, therefore, we must apply for this information, which will be found given at much length in Chapters xxxi.–xxxiii. of the First Book of his History. He states that the Ophites, like other Gnostics, rejected the Old Testament altogether as the work of a subordinate divinity, and containing nothing of the revelations of their *Sophia*, or Divine Wisdom, whilst they held that the New, although originally of higher authority, had been so corrupted by the interpolations of the Apostles as to have lost all value as a revelation of Divine truth. They drew the chief supports of their tenets out of the various "Testaments" and similar books then current, and ascribed to the Patriarchs and the most ancient Prophets, for example, the book of Enoch.

The primary article of this doctrine was the Emanation of all things from the One Supreme, long utterly unknown to mankind, and at last only revealed to a very small number capable of receiving such enlightenment. Hence he is named *Bythos*, "Profundity," to express his unfathomable, inscrutable nature. Following the Zoroastrian and the Kabbalistic nomenclature they also designated Him as the "Fountain of Light," and "The Primal Man," giving for reason of the latter title that "Man was created after the *image* of God," which proved the nature of the prototype.

The *Beginning* of Creation, that is, the Primal *Idea*, or Emanation, was the "thought," *Ennoia*, of Bythos, who bears also the significant name of *Sige*, "Silence." This *Idea* being the first act of creation of the Primal Man, is therefore properly denominated the "Second Man." Ennoia is the consort (compare the Hindoo *Durga*) of Bythos, and she produced *Pneuma*, "the

Spirit," who, being the source of all created things, is entitled "the Mother of all living," and likewise *Sophia*, the wisdom from on high. As the mother of all living, Sophia is the medium between the intellectual and material worlds. In consequence of this, when Bythos and Ennoia, charmed with her beauty, furnished her with the divine Light, Sophia produced two new Emanations—the one perfect, *Christos*, the other imperfect, *Sophia-Achamoth* (This scheme resembles the Buddhistic, Bythos answering to the First Buddha, Sige, Sophia, Christos, Achamoth, Ildabaoth, to the successive other Five)

Of these emanations Christos was designed for the guide of all who proceed from God, Achamoth, for the guide of all proceeding out of matter, nevertheless the Perfect One was intended to assist and lead upwards his imperfect sister

Furthermore, the Spirit rests upon Chaos, or the *waters of Creation*, which are Matter, Water, Darkness, the Abyss This Chaos was devoid of all *life*, for life proceeds ultimately from the Supreme, who has no connection whatever with Matter. Neither could his purely intellectual daughter, Sophia, act directly upon it, she therefore employed for agent her own emanation, Achamoth, whose mixed imperfect nature fitted her for that office

This First Tetrad, Bythos, Ennoia, Sige, Sophia, were in the meantime creating *Ecclesia*, the Idea of the Holy Church But the imperfect Achamoth upon descending into Chaos, lost her way there, and became ambitious of creating a world entirely for herself She floated about in the Abyss, delighted at imparting life and motion to the inert elements, until she became so hopelessly entangled in Matter as to be unable to extricate herself from its trammels In this condition she produced the creator of the *material* world, the Demiurgus, Ildabaoth

But after this event, Achamoth feeling the intolerable burden of her material part, after long and repeated efforts, at length struggled forth out of Chaos. She had never belonged to the Pleroma, but she attained to the "Middle Space", where she entirely shook off her material part, and determined to erect a barrier between the World of Intelligence and the World of

Matter. Ildabaoth, "Son of Darkness," creator and tyrant of the Lower World, followed the example of Bythos in producing subordinate Emanations. First of all he generated an Angel in his own likeness, this Angel a second, and so on up to the number of six. These are all reflexions one of the other, but they inhabit, with their father, Ildabaoth, seven different regions, to which the Middle Space, dominion of their origin Achamoth, forms the eighth. Their names are Iao, Sabaoth, Adonai, Eloi, Ouraios, Astaphaios. They became the Genii of the seven worlds, or planetary spheres The first four names are the mystic titles of the God of the Jews—degraded thus by the Ophites into appellations of the subordinates of the Creator, the two last signify the forces of Fire and Water

In this degradation of the names most sacred in the Jewish theology, is clearly to be recognised, the very teaching of those "dreamers" reprobated by Jude, v. 8 for despising "Dominion," and speaking evil of "Dignities" For "Dominion" is the "Empire" in the Sephiroth (see page 35) to which the Kabbala assigned the title *Adonai* Now we find here the Ophites making Adonai the *third* son of Ildabaoth, a malevolent Genius, and like his father and brethren, the eternal adversary of the Christ The "Dignities" mean the other personages of the Sephiroth, similarly dishonoured by the new doctrine Jude shows plainly whom he had in view by contrasting in the next verse the audacity of these "blasphemers" with the respect shown by the Archangeod Michael towards his opponent on account of his *angelic nature*, however fallen from his high estate By a most singular coincidence (much too close to have been merely accidental), Jude's censure, nay, his very expressions are repeated by Peter in his second Epistle (ii 10) If either of these Epistles were really written by the Apostles whose names they bear, these passages bring to light the very early existence of this school of Gnosticism, which indeed may have been founded before the promulgation of Christianity But to return to the operations of Ildabaoth. Besides the Spirits above mentioned, he generated Archangels, Angels, Virtues, and Powers presiding over all the details of the creation Ildabaoth was far from being a pure spirit, ambition and pride dominated in his composition. He therefore resolved to break off all connection with his mother, Achamoth, and to create a world entirely for himself Aided by his own Six Spirits, he created Man, intending him for the image of his power, but he failed utterly in his work, his Man proving a vast, soulless monster, crawling upon the earth. The Six Spirits were obliged to bring their work again before their father, to be animated he did so by communicating the ray of Divine Light which he himself had inherited from Achamoth, who by this loss punished him for his pride and self-sufficiency.

Man, thus favoured by Achamoth at the expense of her own son, followed the impulse of the Divine Light that she had transferred to him, collected a further supply out of the creation with which it was intermingled, and began to present not the image of his creator Ildabaoth, but rather that of the Supreme Being, the "Primal Man" At this spectacle the Demiurgus was filled with rage and envy at having produced a being so superior to himself His looks, inspired by his passions, were reflected in the Abyss, as in a mirror, the image became instinct with life, and forth arose "Satan Serpent-formed," *Ophiomorphos*, the embodiment of envy and cunning He is the combination of all that is most base in matter with the hate, envy and craft of Spiritual Intelligence Out of their normal hatred for Judaism, the Ophites gave this being the name of *Michael*, the guardian angel of the Jewish nation according to Daniel (x 21) But they also called him *Samael*, the Hebrew name of the Prince of the Devils.

In consequence of his spite at the creation of Man, Ildabaoth set to work to create the three kingdoms of Nature, the Animal, the Vegetable, and the Mineral, with all the defects and evils they now exhibit Next, in order to regain possession of the best of things, he resolved to confine Man within his own exclusive domain. In order to detach him from his protectress Achamoth, and from the celestial region, he forbade him to eat of the Tree of Knowledge, which could reveal the mysteries and confer on him the graces from above But Achamoth, in order to defeat his scheme, sent her own Genius, Ophis, in the form of a serpent to induce him to transgress the commandment, and so to break the Law of Jealousy Though not so stated, it would appear that the serpent-form was put on by Achamoth's minister in order to escape the vigilance of Ildabaoth, under the disguise of his offspring Satan, Ophiomorphos

Enlightened by eating the forbidden fruit, Man became capable of comprehending heavenly things. Nevertheless Ildabaoth was sufficiently powerful to revenge himself, which he did by shutting up the First Pair in the prison-house of Matter, that is, in the *body*, so unworthy of his nature, wherein Man is still enthralled Achamoth, however, continued to protect him she had extracted from his composition and absorbed into herself the divine Spark of Light, and ceased not to supply him therewith, and defend him in all his trials.

And of this there was full need A new enemy had come into the field against Man, the Genius Ophis whom Ildabaoth had seized, and punished for his share in the affair of the Tree of Knowledge, by casting him down into the Abyss, and who, contaminated by his immersion in Matter, became converted into the exact image of his fellow-prisoner, Ophiomorphos The former was the type, the latter the antitype, and the two are often confounded together Thus we get a third dualism into the scheme Sophia and Sophia-Achamoth, Adam-Kadmon and Adam, Ophis and Ophiomorphos Ophis, at first Man's friend, now began to hate him as the cause (though innocent) of his own degradation With Ildabaoth, and his Sons, he continually seeks to chain him to the body, by inspiring him with all manner of corrupt desires, more especially earthly love and the appetites But Achamoth supplies Man with the divine Light, through which he became sensible of his *Nakedness*, that is, of the misery of his condition of imprisonment in this body of death, where his only consolation is the hope of ultimate release

But the seductions of Ildabaoth and his crew gained over all the offspring of Adam, except Seth, the true type of the Spiritual Man and his posterity kept alive the seed of Light and the knowledge of divine Truth throughout all the generations following When they in the Wilderness received the commandments and institutions of Ildabaoth and his Sons, the Planetary Genii, and afterwards the teaching of the Prophets, inspired from the same source, Achamoth infused into their predictions something higher, comprehended not even by their Lord, and made them preach the advent of the Primal Man, the eternal Æon, the heavenly Christ [The same notion was a favourite one with the Mediæval *Cathari*]

Achamoth was so afflicted at the condition of Man that she never rested until she had prevailed on her mother, the celestial Sophia, to move Bythos into sending down the Christ to the aid of the Spiritual Sons of Seth Ildabaoth himself had been caused to make ready the way for his coming through his own minister, John the Baptist, in the belief that the kingdom Christ came to establish was merely a *temporal* one a supposition fostered in him by the contrivance of Achamoth Besides inducing him to send the Precursor, she made him cause the birth of the *Man* Jesus by the Virgin Mary, because the creation of a *material* person could only be the work of the Demiurgus, not falling within the province of a higher power. As soon as the Man Jesus was born, the Christ, uniting himself with Sophia, descended through the seven planetary regions, assuming in each an analogous form, thus concealing his true nature from their presiding Genii, whilst he attracted into himself the sparks of the divine Light they still retained in their essence [These ' analogous forms " are explained by the fact that the Ophite Diagramma figured Michael as a *lion*, Suriel as a *bull*, Raphael as a *serpent*, Gabriel as an *eagle*, Sabaoth as a *bear*, Erataoth as a *dog*, Ouriel as an *ass*] In this manner the Christ entered into the man Jesus at the moment of his baptism in the Jordan From this time forth Jesus began to work miracles, before that He had been entirely ignorant of his own mission But Ildabaoth at last discovering that he was subverting his own kingdom upon earth, stirred up the Jews against him, and caused him to be put to death When he was on the cross, the Christ and Sophia left his body, and returned to their own place Upon his death the Two took the Man Jesus, abandoned his *Material* body to the earth, and gave him a new one made out of the Æther Thenceforth he consisted merely of soul and spirit, which was the cause why the Disciples did not recognise him after his resurrection. During his sojourn upon earth of *eighteen* months after he had risen, he received from Sophia that perfect knowledge, the true Gnosis, which he communicated to the small portion of the Apostles who were capable of receiving the same. Thence, ascending up into the Middle Space, he sat down upon the right hand of Ildabaoth although unperceived by him, and there he is collecting all souls that have been purified through the knowledge of Christ. When he shall have collected all the Spiritual, all the Light, out of Ildabaoth's empire, Redemption is accomplished and the end of the world arrived, which means nothing else than the reabsorption of all Light into the Pleroma from which it had originally descended.

The sect were divided in their opinions as to the nature of Ophis. Although agreed that this genius was in the beginning the *minister* of Achamoth, the Ophites of Theodoret's time held that he had been converted into the enemy of Man, although by inducing him to break the commandment of Ildabaoth he had proved the final cause of Man's deliverance from his power. But all these nice distinctions, and complicated machinery of Redemption were the invention of the later schools unknown to the sect described by Hippolytus. For the primitive Ophites, retaining the Egyptian veneration for the Agathodæmon, regarded their serpent, The Naas, as identical with either Sophia, or the Christ. That writer says positively "the *Naas* (Hebrew, *Nachash*) is the *only* thing they worship, whence they are denominated *Naaseni*. Even two centuries later when Epiphanius wrote, they employed a living tame serpent to encircle and consecrate the loaves that were to be eaten at the Eucharistic supper. Again Tertullian has (In Præscript.) "Serpentem magnificant in tantum ut etiam Christo præferant"—a passage that suggests that their *ophis* was connected with the antique Solar Genius of the Pharaonic religion. It was a peculiarity of the Egyptians that, like the present Hindoos, they were divided, as it were, into sects, each of which adopted some one deity out of the Pantheon for the exclusive object of worship, paying no regard to all the rest. As in modern Hindooism Vishnu and Siva have engrossed the religion of the country, so in the Egypt of the first Christian century Anubis and Cnuph had become the sole objects of Egyptian veneration, as the monuments hereafter to be reviewed will abundantly evince.

To establish the identity of their Ophis with the Saviour, his followers adduced the words of St. John, "For as Moses lifted up the serpent in the wilderness, even so must the Son of Man be lifted up." All this proves that the section of the Ophites which regarded the serpent as *evil* by its nature, had been led astray from the primitive doctrine of their sect by the prevailing Zoroastrian and Jewish notions upon that subject. The creed of the original Gnostics, the Naaseni, gave a very different view of the nature of the serpent considered merely as a type, a fact which shall be established in the section on the Agathodæmon worship.

Epiphanius gives the following abstract of their doctrine to explain their reverence for the serpent as the true author of divine *knowledge*. "The Supreme Æon having produced other Æons, one of these, a female, named Prunicos (i. e. *Concupiscence*), descended into the waters of the abyss: whence, not being able to extricate herself, she remained suspended in the Middle Space, being too much clogged by matter to return above, and yet not sinking lower where there was nothing cognate to her nature. In this condition she produced Ildabaoth, the God of the Jews, and he in his turn seven Æons or Angels, who created the seven heavens. From these seven Æons Ildabaoth shut up all that was above, lest they should know of anything superior to himself. The seven Æons then created Man in the image of their Father, but prone, and crawling upon earth like a worm. But the Heavenly Mother, Prunicos, wishing to deprive Ildabaoth of the power wherewith she had unadvisedly invested him, infused into Man a celestial spark—the soul. Straightway man rose up on his feet, soared in mind beyond the limits of the eight spheres, and glorified the Supreme Father, Him who is above Ildabaoth. Hence Ildabaoth, full of jealousy, cast down his eyes upon the lower layer of Matter, and begat a Virtue, whom they call his Son. Eve, listening to him as the Son of God, was easily persuaded to eat of the Tree of Knowledge" Such is the brief summary of Ophite tenets, as given by Epiphanius. The details of the elaborate system given in the preceding pages are extracted from Theodoret who flourished half a century later

FIG 1

MACHINERY OF THE GNOSIS

The *doctrines* of the chief schools of Gnosticism having been fully described in the preceding sections, the next step in the natural order of things will be to consider the MACHINERY employed by its teachers to set forth these new doctrines.

The deities of the ancient mythology continued to hold their place in the productions of the great sect whose birth-place was Alexandria, and consequently some insight into the sense in which the novel theosophy adopted them may be obtained by learning what were the powers and attributes of these same gods, when their worship held undisputed possession of the country. On this account, the chief deities of Egypt, and the figures under which they are recognised, must now be briefly described—together with their Coptic titles, so often found on these monuments in strange companionship with the holy names of the Jewish creed, with the Magian Genii, even with the appellatives of Hindoo gods—the very terminology of the religion plainly indicating its remote and multifarious sources

1 The great god of Lower Egypt, Phthas (phonetic, Ptah), is represented in a close-fitting robe, with his feet joined together, and standing upon a base of *four* steps, called the "Four Foundations," and which typified the Four Elements, of which he was the grand artificer—an emblem long afterwards taken in the same acceptation by the Rosicrucians, sometimes he appears as a dwarf and Priapean, sometimes as Phtha-Tore with a beetle forehead His proper attribute is the Cynocephalus baboon His four sons, the Cabiri, are painted as little ugly dwarfs, bearing for badges of office, *a sword, a crocodile, a serpent, a human head* stuck on a hook They become in the hierarchy of the Pistis-Sophia the "Collectors unto Wrath" (ἐριναῖοι), whose office is to accuse souls in the Judgment. The many-armed Genius brandishing similar weapons, often found on Gnostic talismans, probably expresses the same idea in a condensed form

2 Ammon (phonetically, Amen) has a human, and occasionally a ram's, head, from which rises a parti-coloured plume He is modified into "Pan-Mendes," Priapean, and brandishing a whip In the character of "Ammon-Chnubis" he has his feet bound together, and wears the horns of a goat He is often figured as the serpent, called by the Greeks the "Agathodæmon." His symbol is the *vase* "Canopus," for so the Greeks pronounce the name of Chnubis United with the sun, he becomes "Ammon-Ra"

3. The Sun-god, Phre, or Ra, depicted with the head of a hawk, supporting the solar disc entwined with the serpent Uraeus

4 Thoth or Thoyt, ibis-headed, is the "Scribe of the gods" Sometimes he takes the head of a hawk, and becomes the famous "Hermes Trismegistus" His symbol is the winged orb, *Tat*, answering to the *Mu* of the Persians (He is the prophet Enoch's fourth rebellious angel, Penumuc, "who discovered unto the children of men bitterness and sweetness, and pointed out to them every unit of their wisdom He taught men to understand writing, and the use of ink and paper Therefore numerous have been those who have gone astray, from every period of the world even to this day. For men were not born for this, thus with pen and with ink to confirm their faith" [lxviii. 10 13.])

5 Sochos is depicted with the head of a crocodile, and is also symbolised by a crocodile with the tail bent

6. The Moon-god, Pa-Ioh, (*Pa*, being the Coptic definite article) is represented having his feet close together, upon his head is a single lock of hair and the crescent At other times, this deity is figured bi-sexual, and casting gold dust over the heavens, that is, bespangling them with the stars.

7 Osiris is a human figure distinguished by his lofty conical helmet, and holding a crook and a whip. The eye is his symbol

8 Aroeres (Aroi), the Horus of the Greeks, has a single lock of hair upon his head. He is figured as being suckled by Isis and again, as seated upon the lotus, he also occasionally wears the head of a hawk, as being one character of the Solar god

His symbol, the hawk, appears upon the breast of Isis in a torso in the Borgia Collection

9 Anubis (Anbo) is always jackal-headed, and sometimes has also a human one head, springing from a separate neck. His Coptic name, ANBΩ, may often be observed in Gnostic legends

10. Bebon, or Bebys, has the head of a hippopotamus, or a crocodile, and carries a sword a figure which used to be taken for Typhon He stands for the constellation Ursa Major in the Zodiac of Denderah

Of *goddesses* the principal are—

1. Neith expressed by the Vulture, or else by a female with head of a vulture, or lion In the last case she takes the name of Taf-net She symbolizes the vault of Heaven

2 Athor with the head of a cow, or else of a woman covered with the skin of the Royal Vulture. She is denoted hieroglyphically by a hawk placed within a square

3 Isis a female with horns of a cow, between which rests a disk, the lunar circle

4 Sate the Grecian Hera, wearing tall plumes on her head, and sometimes personified with a feather in place of head, stands for "Truth," in which latter quality she appears regularly at the Judgment of the Soul

The Four Genii of the Amenthes, or Hades, are represented with the heads of a man, jackal, baboon, and hawk, respectively, and are often placed together like mummy-shaped figures, forming the Canopic Vases

The *symbols* of the same worship have been to some extent explained by persons writing at a time when they were still a living, though fast expiring, language Of such writers the most valuable is Plutarch, who in his curious treatise 'De Iside et Osiride,' has given the meaning of several of those symbols, and, as it would appear, upon very good authority. According to him, Isis sometimes signifies the Moon, in which sense she is denoted by a *Crescent*, sometimes the Earth as fecundated by the waters of the Nile For this reason water, as the seed of Osiris, was carried in a vase in the processions in honour of this goddess

Osiris is denoted by the picture of an *Eye* and *Sceptre*, his name being compounded of *Os* "many," and *iris* "eye" Upon this point Macrobius states (Sat I 21), "The Egyptians, in order to denote that Osiris means the Sun, whenever they want to express his name in hieroglyphic writing, engrave a Sceptre and on top thereof the figure of an Eye, and by this symbol they express 'Osiris,' signifying this god to be the Sun, riding on high in regal power, and looking down upon all things, because antiquity hath surnamed the Sun the 'Eye of Jupiter.'"

The *Fig-leaf* stands for "King", and also for the "South."

The *Lizard*, which was believed to conceive through the ear, and to bring forth through the mouth, is the type of the generation of the Word, that is, the *Logos*, or Divine Wisdom (This belief explains the appearance of a lizard upon the breast of certain figures of Minerva) *

The *Scarabeus*, in its making spherical receptacles for its eggs, and by its retrograde motion, imitates the action and movement of the Sun. This insect had no female, according to the popular belief of the Egyptians

The *Asp* expresses a planet, for like that luminary, it moves rapidly, though without any visible organ of locomotion.

The *Ibis* stands for the Moon the legs of the bird, when extended, making an equilateral triangle (It is hard to discern any analogy between the Moon and this figure of geometry, but yet the Pythagoreans denoted Athene by the same sign But that Plutarch is here correct is proved by many gems which show a triangle set upon an altar and adored by the baboon, Luna's favourite beast.) How the later Egyptians symbolised the Sun and Moon is well expressed upon a jasper (Waterton) where Horus, seated on the lotus, is adored by the baboon, in the field are the sun-star and the crescent attached to their respective figures, and also the *Triangle* very conspicuously placed

Horus—Plutarch remarks—wears a crown of the branches of the Persea, because its fruit resembles in shape the *heart*, its leaves, the *tongue* The legend goes that the tree (*Cordia myxa*, or Sebestene plum) was first planted at Memphis by the hero *Perseus*, whence its name. In memory of his mythic ancestor,

* Of which a fine example, an intaglio, is figured in the Museum Odescalchum

Alexander ordered that a garland of Persea leaves should form the prize at the games he instituted at his new Capital The tree never wants a succession of flowers and fruit, the latter Pliny compares to a red plum, adding that it will not grow in Europe

We next come to a professed treatise upon this recondite subject, Horapollo's 'Interpretation of the Sacred Animals' Unfortunately, this work bears upon its face clear evidence of having been excogitated by some pragmatical Alexandrian Greek, totally ignorant of what he was writing about, but impudently passing off his own stupid *conjectures* as to the meaning of the figures on the ancient works surrounding him, as though they were interpretations handed down to him by antique authority He must have written under the Lower Empire, when the art of reading hieroglyphics was entirely lost, for we know that it still existed in the first century, Tacitus particularly notes that an *aged* priest read to Germanicus upon his visit to Thebes the contents of the historical tablets on the edifices of that city. "Mox visit veterum Thebarum magna vestigia, et manebant structis molibus literæ Ægyptiæ priscam opulentiam complexæ, jussusque e senioribus sacerdotum patrium sermonem interpretari" (Ann II 60) This happened A D 19 It would appear that the knowledge of hieroglyphics was fast dying out, and only preserved by members of the previous generation *

It is only in a few instances that Horapollo has preserved some genuine tradition of the meaning of those symbols which were the most generally used, and therefore the last to be forgotten Of these explanations the most important are what follow

"The *Cynocephalus* baboon denotes the Moon, because that beast has a certain sympathy with the luminary, and during her dark quarter sits without eating, his eyes fixed upon the

* But the Demotic writing must have lingered much longer in use, for Capitolinus, cap 34, mentions the "Egyptian" as one of the current alphabets of the third century "The soldiers raised a tomb to Gordian at Circeium Castrum, on the confines of Persia, placing upon this edifice (*moles*) an epitaph in Greek Latin, Persian, Jewish, and *Egyptian* letters, so that it might be read by everybody "Divo Gordiano, victori Persarum, victori Gothorum, victori Sarmatarum, depulsori Romanarum seditionum, victori Germanorum, sed non victori Philippiorum"

ground as though mourning for her loss. He moreover denotes the *priestly order*, because he is naturally circumcised, and abhors fish and fishermen. Erect and with uplifted paws and a basilisk (asp) upon his head, he symbolises the New Moon, whose first appearance he hails after this fashion By his voiding his urine at fixed and regular intervals, he first suggested to observers the regular division of the day into hours, and furnished the first idea of the invention of the *Clepsydra*, or water-clock

"The *Dog* (Jackal) represents the sacred scribe because that functionary ought to be always studying, and likewise should *bark at*, and make himself disagreeable to, everybody. In another sense he expresses a Prophet, from his habit of staring fixedly at the statues of the gods

"The *Hawk* means 'God,' or 'Sun.'

"The *Lion*, from the resemblance of his *round* face to the solar orb, is placed beneath the throne of *Horus*, the Egyptian title of the Sun

"The Rising of the Nile, called in Coptic *Nou* or *Nei*, is denoted by three large vases, and also by a lion, because it attains its full height when the Sun is in that sign of the Zodiac, for which same cause the spouts of the sacred lavers are made in the shape of lions' heads

"By the *Ibis* is signified the *heart*, because the bird belongs to Hermes, who presides over the heart and all reason The Ibis also, by its own shape, resembles the form of the heart, concerning which matter there is a very long legend current amongst the Egyptians"

But the most graphic account of the symbols and ceremonies employed in the worship of Isis, whilst yet in its full glory (the middle of the second century), is to be obtained from the description of her Procession which Apuleius (himself one of the initiated) has penned in the eleventh Book of his "Golden Ass" "Next flow on the crowds of people initiated into the divine mysteries, men and women of every rank, and all ages, shining in the pure whiteness of linen robes, the latter having their dripping hair enveloped in a transparent covering the former with their heads shaven clean, and the crowns thereof shining white—these earthly stars of the nocturnal ceremony, raising as they went a shrill tinkling with *sistra* of bronze, silver, and even of gold. But the chief performers in the rites were those nobles, who, clad in a tight-fitting robe of linen descending from the waist down to the heels, carried in the procession the glorious symbols of the most potent deities.

"The first held out at arm's length a *lamp*, diffusing before him a brilliant light, not by any means resembling in form the lamps in common use for illuminating our evening meals, but a golden bowl supporting a more ample blaze in the midst of its broad expanse The second, similarly robed, held up with both hands the *Altar* that derives its name from the beneficent *Providence* of the supreme goddess The third marched along bearing aloft a *palm branch* with leaves formed of thin gold, and also the *Caduceus* of Hermes The fourth displayed the symbol of Justice, the figure of the *left hand* with the palm open, which, on account of its natural inactivity, and its being endowed with neither skill nor cunning, has been deemed a more fitting emblem of Justice than the right hand The same minister likewise carried a small golden vestibule made in a round form like an *udder*, out of which he poured libations of milk. The fifth carried a *winnowing fan* piled up with golden sprigs The last of all bore a huge *wine jar*.

"Immediately after these came the Deities, condescending to walk upon human feet, the foremost among them rearing terrifically on high his dog's head and neck—that messenger between heaven and hell displaying alternately a face black as night, and golden as the day, in his left the caduceus, in his right waving aloft the green palm branch His steps were closely followed by a cow, raised into an upright posture—the cow being the fruitful emblem of the Universal Parent, the goddess herself, which one of the happy train carried with majestic steps, supported on his shoulders By another was borne the coffin containing the sacred things, and closely concealing the deep secrets of the holy religion. Another carried in his happy bosom the awful figure of the Supreme Deity, not represented in the image of a beast either tame or wild, nor of a bird, nor even in that of man, but *ingeniously devised* and inspiring awe by its very strangeness, that ineffable symbol of the deepest mystery, and ever to be shrouded in the profoundest silence. But next came, carried precisely in the same manner, a small vessel made of burnished gold, and most skilfully wrought out into a hemispherical bottom, embossed externally with strange Egyptian figures. Its mouth, but slightly raised, was extended into a spout, and projected considerably beyond the body of the bowl, whilst on the opposite side, widening as it receded into a capacious opening, it was affixed to the handle, upon which was seated an asp wreathed into a knot, and rearing up on high its streaked, swollen and scaly neck."

These images and symbols require a few remarks in elucidation suggested by the notices of ancient writers, or by the representations of these very objects upon extant monuments of the same religion. The "udder-shaped" vessel exactly describes the one so frequently placed upon the Gnostic gems, and which Matter so strangely interprets as the "Vase of Sins" of the deceased—an unlikely subject to be selected for a talisman intended to secure the *benevolence* of heaven. Much more to the purpose is Kohler's conjecture that it is one of the earthen pots used to be tied round the circumference of the irrigating wheel, still employed for raising the water of the Nile to fertilise the adjacent fields, "fecundating Isis with the seed of Osiris" in ancient phrase, and certainly the *string* fastened about its top favours such an explanation; in fact, we have an example of similar veneration for a vessel in the case of the Canopus, the pot that held the same water when purified for drinking. The "winnow-fan" is also often represented, placed over this hemispherical vase; the same instrument played an important part in the marriage ceremony of the Greeks. When piled with fruit of all kinds, it was placed on the head of the bride; the same significant article, a broad, shallow basket, was the cradle of the infant Bacchus—the "mystica vannus Iacchi." The golden "Bowl," serving for lamp, often figures amongst the various emblems adorning our talismans. The "Sistrum" got its peculiar outline from the Indian *Yoni* (emblem of the female sex), and it was on account of its similar shape the almond, *luz*, was also held sacred in Egypt, which seems the true origin of the "vesica piscis," serving as the inclosure for divine figures The British Museum possesses a Hindoo altar in hardstone, neatly polished, having its flat top formed into the shape of the *lingam-yoni*, at each corner of the square a little idol is squatted This Indian figure, signifying the Active and Passive Powers of Nature in conjunction for the work of Creation, is sculptured like a round shallow basin, with long projecting lips tapering to a twist, with an obtuse cone rising out of its middle Now this is the exact shape of a large brown lamp from Herculaneum (Caylus, vii pl 33), only that from its centre, instead of a cone, springs a bent fore-finger, *digitus obscœnus* (with the same meaning as the lingam) serving for handle to carry it by, whilst from the sides project the three arms of the Egyptian *Tau* This vessel must have belonged to the Isis-worship in that town, no doubt as popular there as it is known to have been at the neighbouring Pompeii As for the office of "Anubis-bearer," it is related that when Commodus discharged that duty in the procession, he gratified the insane cruelty of his nature by cracking the shaven skulls of all within reach with the weighty head of the idol, and it seems to follow as a matter of course that the Anubis of Apuleius, in order to display *alternately* an ebon and a golden visage, must have possessed a *pair* of heads, human and canine, just as he is figured, holding the caduceus and palm upon certain Basilidan gems Lastly, the mysterious image, too awful to be described, but whose nature is darkly hinted at as neither of *bird*, *beast*, nor *man* These very expressions would tempt me to believe a compound of all three, in a word, the veritable figure of the Abraxas god. And be it remembered that this image was the "Supreme God," and he, we know, was the IAO of Egypt. This idol must have been of *small* dimensions, for it was carried in the *bosom* of the devotee's robe, and my suspicion is strongly confirmed by the existence in the late Mertens-Schaffhausen Collection of a bronze statuette, five inches in height, found in the south of France, and thus described in the Catalogue. "No 2002 Statuette of Iao standing, armed with cuirass, shield and whip, his head in the form of a cock's, his legs terminating in serpents"

PART II.

THE WORSHIP OF MITHRAS AND SERAPIS.

"O voi ch' avete gl' intelletti sani,
Mirate la dottrina che s' asconde
Sotto il velame degli versi strani."

"Salve vera Deûm facies, vultusque paterne,
Octo et sexcentis numeris cui litera trina
Conformat sacrum nomen, cognomen et
Omen. (Mart. Capella Hymn. ad Sol.)

ΦΡΗ = ΤΗϹ = 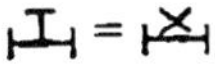

THE WORSHIP OF MITHRAS.

1. ORIGIN OF MITHRAICISM.

The innumerable monuments of every kind bequeathed to us by the widely-spread worship of the deity styled *Mithras*, serve, at the same time, copiously to illustrate the important contributions of Zoroastrian doctrine towards the composition of Gnosticism. The Mithraic religion, according to Plutarch, first made its appearance in Italy upon Pompey's reduction of the Cilician Pirates, of whom it was the national worship,* and who, when broken up into colonists and slaves all over Italy, propagated it amongst their conquerors. In the new soil the novel religion flourished so rapidly as, in the space of two centuries, to supersede (coupled with the earlier introduced Serapis worship) the primitive Hellenic and Etruscan deities. In fact, long before this final triumph over the sceptical, Pliny appears disposed to accept Mithraicism, in its essential principle, as the only religion capable of satisfying a rational inquirer, as may be deduced from this noble passage (ii. 4): "Eorum medius Sol fervidus, amplissima magnitudine, nec temporum modo terrarumque sed siderum etiam ipsorum cœlique Rector. Hanc esse mundi totius animam ac planius mentem, nunc principale Naturæ regimen ac *Numen* credere decet, opera ejus æstimantes. Hic lumen rebus ministrat, aufertque tenebras, hic reliqua

* This deity, under other titles, had ever been the great god of Pontus. As patron of Sinope he appears under the form of Helios-Dionysos, upon the medallion of Pharnaces II. In his proper name he was the patron of Trebizond, being worshipped on the Mount Mithras overhanging that most ancient of Grecian colonies. For destroying his statue, the fanatic Eugenius, justly punished by Diocletian, was adopted, in the succeeding times of superstition, for the tutelary saint of the Byzantine Empire of Trebizond.

sidera occultat, illustrat, hic vices temporum annumque semper renascentem ex usu Naturæ temperat, hic cœli tristitiam discutit, atque etiam humani nubila animi serenat hic suum lumen cæteris quoque sideribus fœnerat; præclarus, eximius, omnia intuens, omnia etiam exaudiens, at principi literarum Homero placuisse in uno eo video. Quapropter effigiem Dei formamque quærere imbecillitatis humanæ reor Quisquis est Deus, *si modo est alius*, et quacunque in parte, totus est sensus, totus visus, totus auditus, totus animæ, totus animi, totus sui" Thus, during the second and third centuries of the Roman Empire, Mithras and Serapis had come almost to engross the popular worship even to the remotest limits of the known world For Mithraicism was originally the religion taught by Zoroaster, although somewhat changed and materialized so as better to assimilate itself to the previously established Nature Worship of the West. Under this grosser form it took its name from *Mithras*, who in the Zendavesta is not the Supreme Being (Ormuzd), but the Chief of the subordinate Powers, the Seven Amshaspands Mithra is the Zend name for the sun, the proper *mansion* of this Spirit, but not the Spirit himself. Hence the great oath of Artaxerxes Mnemon was, "By the light of Mithras,' a counterpart of the tremendous adjuration of our William the Conqueror, "By the Splendour of God!" But the materialistic Greeks at once identified the Persian Spirit with their own substantial Phœbus and Hyperion Thus Ovid has,

"Placat equo Persis radiis Hyperiona cinctum" (Fasti I 335)

In this view of his nature Mithras was identified with other types of the Sun-god, such as the "Phanaces" of Asia Minor, and the "Dionysos" of Greece, and thereby soon usurped the place of the latter in the long established Mysteries, the ancient Dionysia The importance into which the Mithraica had grown by the middle of the second century may be estimated from a fact mentioned by Lampridius, that the emperor himself (Commodus) condescended to be initiated into them Nay more, with their penances, and tests of the courage of the neophyte, they may be said to have been maintained by unbroken tradition through the secret societies of the Middle Ages, then by the Rosicrucians, down to that faint reflex of the latter, the Freemasonry of our own times. But this curious point must be reserved for the last Section of this Treatise investigating the nature of the last named societies. My present object is to point out the gradations by which the Mithraic principle passed into the Egyptian and semi-Christian forms of Gnosticism.

The mystic name *Abraxas* (asserted to have been the coinage of the Alexandrian Basilides) is said to mean either in actual Coptic "Holy Name" (as Bellermann will have it), or, as seems equally probable, is merely the Hebrew *Ha-Brachah* "Blessing," Græcised, in the same sense. That the symbolic figure embodying the idea of the Abraxas god has a reference to the sun in all its components is yet more evident, as shall be shown hereafter; similarly, the Brahmins apply their Ineffable Name *Aum* to the "fierce and all-pervading Sun"; and Macrobius devotes much curious learning to prove that all the great gods of antiquity, whatever their names and figures, were no more than various attempts at personifying the One Deity, whose residence is the sun. It must here be remembered that Basilides was by no means a *Christian heretic*, as the later Fathers found it expedient to represent him, but rather as his contemporary Clemens, relates, a philosopher devoted to the study of divine things, and thus possibly imbued with such Buddhistic notions as the intercourse between Alexandria and the cities of Guzerat (then ruled over by the Jaina kings) may have naturalized both in Egypt and in Palestine. This metropolis, as the grand emporium for foreign doctrines as well as foreign wares, supplies the reason for the frequent union of Mithras with Abraxas in the same stone, proceeding from the Alexandrian talisman-factory. A curious exemplification is a green jasper (Marlborough), bearing on one side the normal Zoroastrian device, Mithras slaughtering the Bull; on the other, the well-known Gnostic Pantheus. A truly Indian syncretism, which converts all deities from separate beings into mere deified attributes of one and the same God, and (for the initiated few, that is) reduces that seemingly unlimited polytheism into the acknowledgment of the existence of the Supreme Creator.

That model of a perfect prince, Severus Alexander, must have imbibed a strong tinge of the Gnosis (as indeed might have been expected from his birthplace and style of education), for although upon every *seventh day* he went up to worship in the Capitol, and also regularly visited the temples of the other Roman gods, he nevertheless "was intending to build a temple unto Christ, and to rank Him in the number of the gods Which thing Hadrian also is said to have thought of, and actually to have ordered temples *without images* to be built in all the chief cities of the Empire which same temples, because they contain no gods, are now called temples raised to Hadrian himself, although in reality he is reported to have prepared them for the purpose above-named. But he was prevented from carrying out his design by those who consulted the oracles (*sacra*), and discovered that, if it should be carried out, everybody would turn Christian, and thereby the other temples would be all deserted" (Lampridius i 43). Indeed, there is every reason to believe that, as in the East, the worship of Serapis was at first combined with Christianity, and gradually merged into it with an entire change of name, though not of substance, carrying along with it many of its proper ideas and rites, so in the West the Mithras-worship produced a similar effect upon the character of the religion that took its place Seel, in his admirable treatise upon Mithraicism ('Mithra,' p 287) is of opinion that "as long as the Roman dominion lasted in Germany, we find traces there of the Mosaic law and in the same way as there were single Jewish families, so were there single Christians existing amongst the heathen The latter, however, for the most part, ostensibly paid worship to the Roman gods in order to escape persecution, holding secretly in their hearts the religion of Christ It is by no means improbable that, under the permitted symbols of Mithras, they worshipped the Son of God, and the mysteries of Christianity In this point of view, the Mithraic monuments, so frequent in Germany, are evidences to the faith of the early Christian Romans" This same supremacy of the Mithras-worship in his own times makes the grand scheme of Heliogabalus prove less insane than it strikes the modern reader at the first impression. He was intending (according to report) to permit no other worship at Rome than that of his own god and namesake, the Emesene aerolite, apt emblem of the Sun, "bringing together in his temple the Fire of Vesta, the Palladium, the Ancilia, and all the other most venerated relics, and moreover the *religion* of the Jews and Samaritans, and the *devotion** of the Christians" (Lampridius 3). To such a heterogeneous union that numerous section of the Roman public who shared Macrobius' sentiments on the nature of all ancient gods, could have found no possible objection so far as the *principle* was concerned

That such a relationship to Christianity was actually alleged by the partisans of Mithraicism (when in its decline) is proved by the remarkable declaration of Augustine himself (John I. Dis 7) "I remember that the priests of the *fellow in the cap* (*illius pileati*) used at one time to say, 'Our Capped One is himself a Christian'" In this asserted affinity probably lay the motive that induced Constantine to adopt for the commonest type of his coinage (the sole currency of the Western provinces), and retain long after his conversion, the figure of Sol himself, with the legend "To the Invincible Sun, my companion (or guardian)" A type capable of a double interpretation, meaning equally the ancient Phœbus and the new Sun of Righteousness, and thereby unobjectionable to Gentile and Christian alike of the equally divided population amongst whom it circulated Nay more, this Emperor when avowedly Christian, selected for the grandest ornament of his new Capital, a colossal Apollo, mounted upon a lofty column, which retained its place until cast down by an earthquake in the reign of Alexius Comnenus.

Through a similar interchange, the old festival held on the 25th day of December in honour of the "Birth-day of the Invincible One," and celebrated by the Great Games of the Circus (as marked in the Kalendar "VIII KAL IAN. N INVICTI. C. M xxiv†) was afterwards transferred to the commemoration of the Birth of Christ, of which the real day was, as the Fathers

* This curious distinction between "religio" and "devotio," is meant to mark the difference between a national and established creed and one held by individuals, without any public sanction

† Signifying that twenty-four consecutive races of chariots were exhibited on that occasion in the Circus Maximus

confess, totally unknown. Chrysostom, for example, declares (Hom. xxxi.) that the Birthday of Christ had then *lately* been fixed at Rome upon that day, in order that whilst the heathen were busied with their own profane ceremonies, the Christians might perform their holy rites without molestation.

And Mithras was the more readily admitted as the type of Christ, Creator and Maintainer of the Universe, inasmuch as the Zendavesta declares him to be the First Emanation of Ormuzd, the Good Principle, and the Manifestation of Himself unto the world. Now it was from this very creed that the Jews, during their long captivity in the Persian Empire (of which when restored to Palestine they formed but a province), derived all the angelology of their religion, even to its minutest details, such as we find it flourishing in the times of the Second Kingdom. Not until then are they discovered to possess the belief in a future state; of rewards and punishments, the latter carried on in a fiery lake; the existence of a complete hierarchy of good and evil angels, taken almost verbatim from the lists given by the Zendavesta; the soul's immortality, and the Last Judgment—all of them essential parts of the Zoroastrian scheme, and recognised by Josephus as the fundamental doctrines of the Judaism of his own times.

To all these ideas Moses in the Law makes not the slightest allusion; his promises and threatenings are all of the earth, earthy; he preaches a religion of *Secularists*, and such a religion was, down to the latest days of Jerusalem, still maintained by the Sadducees. Now these Sadducees were the most ancient and respectable families of the nation, who boasted of keeping the law of Moses pure, and uncontaminated from the admixture of foreign notions imbibed by the commonalty during their long sojourn amongst the Gentiles. Nay more, there is some reason to accept Matter's etymology of the name of their opponents, the Pharisees, as actually signifying "Persians," being a term of contempt for the holders of the new-fangled doctrines picked up from their conquerors. And this etymology is a much more rational one, and more consistent with the actual elements of the word, than the common one making it to mean "Separatists"—an epithet by no means applicable to a party constituting the immense *majority* of the race. It is only necessary now to allude to the ingenious theory of Bishop Warburton, set forth in his 'Divine Legation of Moses,' who converts the absence of all spiritualism from his teaching into the strongest argument for its being directly inspired from Heaven.

But from whatever source derived, how closely does the Zoroastrian idea of the nature and office of Mithras coincide with the definition of those of Christ as given by the author of the Epistle to the Hebrews, that profound Jewish theologian, who styles Him the "Brightness (or *reflection*) of his glory, the express *image** of his person, upholding all things by the word of his power," and again, "being made so much better than the angels as he hath by inheritance obtained a more excellent *Name* than they," and here it may be observed that the *Reflection* of the *Invisible* Supreme in his First Emanation is a distinguishing feature in most of the Gnostic systems Mithras used to be invoked *together* with the Sun, and thus, being confounded with that luminary, became the object of a separate worship, which ultimately superseded that of Ormuzd himself and this was the only one propagated by the Pontic colonists and their converts amongst the nations of the West Secondary deities often usurp the places of those of the first rank, so Vishnu and Siva have entirely eclipsed Brahma Serapis had played the same part with the Pharaonic gods of Egypt, and yet more striking analogies from modern creeds are too obvious to require quotation Through this relationship of ideas Mithraic symbolism found its way into early Christian art in many of its particulars The bas-relief over the portal of the Baptistery at Parma (a work of the 12th century). has all the aspect of a Mithraic monument, and certainly its design would be very difficult to understand from a Scriptural point of view

* Ἀπαύγασμα—χαρακτὴρ, the latter word literally "impression of a seal," is the exact counterpart of the Hebrew title, "Tikkan," the Primal Emanation

II. THE MITHRAIC SACRAMENTS.

The principal rites of the worship of Mithras bore a very curious resemblance to those subsequently established in the Catholic church; they likewise furnished a model for the initiatory ceremonies observed by the secret societies of the Middle Ages, and by their professed descendants in modern times. The Neophytes were admitted by the rite of *Baptism*; the initiated at their assemblies solemnly celebrated a species of *Eucharist*: whilst the courage and endurance of the candidate for admission into the sect were tested by *twelve* consecutive trials, called "The Tortures," undergone within a cave constructed for the purpose; all which "tortures" had to be completely passed through before participation in the Mysteries was granted to the aspirant.

The two distinguishing Rites, or "Sacraments" (to use the technical term) are thus alluded to by Justin Martyr (*Apol.* II.) in the earliest description which has been left us of their character. "The Apostles in the Commentaries written by themselves, which we call *Gospels*, have delivered down to us that Jesus thus commanded them: He having taken bread, after that He had given *thanks*,* said: Do this in commemoration of me; this is my body. Also having taken a cup and returned thanks, He said: This is my blood, and delivered it unto them alone. Which things indeed the evil spirits have taught to be done, out of memory, in the Mysteries and Initiations of Mithras. For in these likewise a cup of water, and bread, are set out, with the addition of certain words, in the sacrifice or act of worship of the person about to be initiated: a thing which Ye either know by personal experience or may learn by inquiry." Again, Tertullian, writing in the following century, has in the same connection: "The Devil, whose business it is to pervert the truth, *mimicks the exact circumstances* of the Divine Sacraments, in the Mysteries of idols. He himself *baptises* some that is to say, his believers and followers; he promises forgive-

* This expression seems to prove that the notion of *blessing*, or consecrating, the elements, had not then (the second century) crept into the Christian practice.

ness of sins from the *Sacred Fount*, and thereby initiates them into the religion of Mithras thus he *marks on the forehead* his own soldiers there he celebrates the *oblation of bread* · he brings in the symbol of the Resurrection, and wins the crown with the sword." By the "symbol of the Resurrection" Tertullian clearly means that "simulation of death" mentioned by Lampridius (of which more hereafter), and which is typified on so many talismans by the corpse bestridden by the Solar Lion The final ceremony he has himself explained in another passage "Blush, my Roman fellow-soldiers, even though ye be not to be judged by Christ, but by any 'Soldier of Mithras,' who when he is undergoing initiation in the *Cave*, in the very Camp of the Powers of Darkness, when the *crown* (garland, rather) is offered to him (a sword being placed between, as though in semblance of martyrdom), and about to be set upon his head, is instructed to put forth his hand, and push the crown away, transferring it perchance, to his shoulder, saying at the same time My crown is Mithras And from that time forth he never wears a crown (garland), and this he has for the badge of his initiation, for he is immediately known to be a 'soldier of Mithras,' if he rejects a garland when offered to him, saying that his crown is his god Let us therefore acknowledge the craftiness of the Devil, who copies certain things of those that be Divine, in order that he may confound and judge us by the faithfulness of his own followers." As to the ceremony here mentioned, unimportant as it may seem to the modern reader, it may be remarked that as the wearing a garland was indispensable among the ancients on all festive occasions, the refusal of one upon such occasions would be a most conspicuous mark of singularity, and of unflinching profession of faith But every dispassionate observer will perceive that these over-zealous Fathers proceed to beg the question when they assume that the Mithraic rites were devised as *counterfeits* of the Christian Sacraments inasmuch as the former were in existence long before the first promulgation of Christianity, unless indeed to *imitate* by anticipation be considered as merely another proof of the mischievous sagacity of its diabolical opponent On the other hand, there is good reason to suspect that the simple commemorative, or distinctive, ceremonies, instituted by the first founder of Christianity, were gradually invested with those mystic and supernatural virtues which later ages insisted upon as articles of faith, by the teaching of unscrupulous missionaries, anxious to outbid the attractions of long-established rites of an apparently cognate character. By this assimilation they offered to their converts through the performance of, as it were, certain magical practices, all those spiritual blessings of which the rites themselves were, at their institution, the *symbols* only, not the instruments. A very instructive illustration of such union of Mithraicism and Christianity, in the celebration of the Eucharist, is afforded by the Pistis-Sophia's description of the great one celebrated by the Saviour himself upon the shore of the Sea of Galilee, which will be found given at length in its proper place. And lastly, it deserves to be mentioned that "eating the flesh and drinking the blood" of a human sacrifice was far from being a mere figure of speech in certain of these mystic celebrations. Pliny gives high praise to Claudius for having suppressed the worship of the Druids (whom he considers as identical in their religion with the Magi), in whose rites "it was esteemed the highest act of religion to slaughter a man, and the most salutary of proceedings to eat the flesh of the same." And in this notion, which necessarily became attached by suspicion to the proceedings of all secret societies, lay most probably the root of the belief so widely diffused amongst the Roman vulgar, that the real Eucharist of the first Christians at their nocturnal meetings was the sacrifice, and the feasting upon, a new-born child, concealed within a vessel of flour, into which the catechumen was directed by his sponsors to plunge a knife.

In the particulars preserved to us of the Mithraic Sacrament, certain very curious analogies to those of the Christian rite cannot fail to arrest our attention. The "Bread therein used was a round cake," emblem of the solar disk, and called *Mizd*. In this name Seel discovers the origin of *Missa*, as designating the Bloodless Sacrifice of the Mass, assuming that this Mizd was the prototype of the Host (*hostia*), which is of precisely the same form and dimensions.

It is not out of place to notice here the various etymologies which have been proposed for the word *Missa* The most popular one, which moreover has the sanction of Ducange, derives it from the words "Ite, missa est," with which the priest dismissed the *non-communicant* part of the congregation, before proceeding to the actual consecration of the Eucharist The translation of the phrase by the vulgar into "Depart, it is the Missa," would certainly be obvious enough. But, according to the rule in all such cases, the *object* sacrificed gives its name to the ceremony, rather than a phrase from the ceremonial itself, and this object had from time immemorial gone by the name of *hostia*, or "victim" The early Christians were quite as partial as the Gnostics to the naturalizing of the Hebrew terms belonging to the Mosaic ordinances, and applying the same to their own practices. Thus the old Covenant went amongst them by the name of *Phase*, for example —

> "In hoc festo novi Regis,
> Novum *Pascha* novæ legis
> Vetus *Phase* terminat"

The Rabbins have possibly preserved a tradition that explains the true origin of the water. Alphonsus de Spina, in his "Fortalitium Fidei" (II 2), asserts that its circular form is a symbol of the sun, and that it is in reality offered in sacrifice, at the celebration of the Mass, to the genius of that luminary! For the Kabbalists hold that Moses and the prophets were inspired by the genius of Saturn, a good and pure spirit, whereas Jesus was by that of Mercury, a malevolent one, and the Christian religion was the work of Mercury, Jupiter and the Sun, all combining together for that purpose. There is yet another curious analogy to be noticed, when it is remembered that the Mass symbolises the *death* of its first institutor A *round* cake (the *chupatty* of such evil notoriety at the commencement of the Sepoy Mutiny) is, amongst the Hindoos, the established offering to the Manes of their ancestors. The Christian "breaking of bread," besides symbolising the great sacrifice once offered, seems, from the account of the Manifestation at Emmaus, to have been done in some peculiar way which should serve for a *masonic* token, or means of mutual recognition amongst the brethren

The sacramental Cup, or *chalice*, is often represented as set upon the Mithraic altar, or rather, *table*, and a curious piece of jugglery connected with its employment (though not amongst the Mithraicists), is described by Epiphanius (Hæres xxxiv). The followers of Marcus, in their celebrating the Eucharist, employed *three* vases made of the clearest glass These were filled with wine which, during the progress of the ceremony, changed into a blood-red, purple, and blue colour, respectively "Thereupon the officiating minister, or more properly speaking, *magician*, hands one of these vessels to some lady of the congregation, and requests her to bless it Which done, he pours this into another vase of much greater capacity, with the prayer, "May the grace of God, which is above all, inconceivable, inexplicable, fill thine inner man, and increase the knowledge of Himself within thee, sowing the grain of mustard-seed in good ground!" Whereupon the liquid in the larger vase swells and swells until it runs over the brim

The worship of Mithras long kept its ground under the Christian emperors in the capital itself, and doubtless survived its overthrow there for many generations longer in the remote and then semi-independent provinces At the very close of the fourth century, Jerome, writing to Læta, says, "A *few* years ago, did not your kinsman Gracchus, a name the very echo of patrician nobility, when holding the office of Prefect of the City, break down and burn the Cave of Mithras, with all the monstrous images which pervade the initiatory rites, as Corax, Niphus, the Soldier, the Lion, the Persian, Helios, and Father Bromius?"

In the imagery here alluded to, it is easy to recognise figures that perpetually occur upon the still extant representations of the Mithras worship. In *Corax*, the Raven, in *Niphus*, Cneph the serpent, the *armed man;* the *Lion* bestriding the human victim, the youth in *Persian* garb, the *Sun*, expressed either by Phœbus in his car, or by the star with eight rays, and *Bromius* "the Roarer," appropriate title of the Grecian Dionysos, who also appears as the Asiatic *Phanaces*, a youth holding a torch in each hand, one elevated and one depressed to signify his rising and setting Chiflet's gem (Fig. 62) may on good grounds be taken for a picture of the Mithraic ritual, and upon it all the forementioned figures and symbols are easily to be discovered Two erect serpents form a kind of frame to the whole tableau; at the top of which are seen the heads of Sol and Luna confronted, between them stands an eagle with outspread wings, at the back of each, a raven. In the field are two naked, crowned men on horseback, trampling upon as many dead bodies, between them a kneeling figure in supplicatory attitude, over whose head are two stars Behind each horseman stand two soldiers. In the exergue is set out a table supporting a loaf, a fawn (sacred to Bacchus), a chalice, and something indistinct, but probably meant for the *crown* Tertullian speaks of The reverse presents a more simple design two crested serpents (*dracones*), twined about wands, and looking into a cup; two stars over a table resting upon a larger vase, and on each side a bow, the ends of which finish in serpents' heads

In this composition we probably see portrayed certain amongst the tests of the neophyte's courage, which, according to Suidas, were termed the "Twelve Degrees" or "Tortures" These corresponded in nature, although of vastly more severe reality, with those trials of courage to which our Masonic Lodges subject the "apprentice" who seeks admission amongst them During the Mithraic probation, which lasted *forty* days,* the candidate was tested by the Four Elements, he lay naked a certain number of nights upon the snow, and afterwards was scourged for the space of two days These Twelve Tortures are sculptured upon the border of the famous Mithraic tablets preserved in the Innsbruck Museum, and a brief account of their several stages will serve to elucidate much of what remains to be discussed I. Man standing and about to plunge a dagger into the throat of a kneeling figure, who holds up his hands in supplication. (This scene appears analogous to the one in the modern ceremonial, when the candidate, ordered to remove the bandage from his eyes, beholds many swords pointed in the

* Perhaps the origin of the Lenten term of self-inflicted punishment

most threatening manner at his naked breast.) II. Naked man lying on the earth, his head resting on his hand, in the posture of repose. (Probably the penance of the bed of snow.) III. The same figure, standing with hands uplifted in a huge crescent (perhaps an *ark*, and representing the trial by water. To this last, Plato is reported to have been subjected during his initiation in Egypt, and to have but narrowly escaped drowning). IV. The same, but now with the *pileus*, cap of liberty, upon his head, rushing boldly into a great fire (the trial by fire). V. He is now seen struggling through a deep stream, and endeavouring to grasp a rock. VI. Bull walking to the left.

On the other side come the remaining stages. VII. Four guests reclining at a horseshoe table (*sigma*), upon which is set a boar roasted whole. VIII. Youth guided up a flight of interminable steps by an aged man. IX. Youth kneeling before a man in a long robe, whose hand he grasps in prayer. X. The same figures, but their positions are interchanged. XI. Seated man, before whom kneels a naked, crowned, youth, escorted by one in a long robe. XII. Naked man holding up the hind legs of a cow, so as to receive in his face the stream still regarded by the Hindoos as the most efficient laver of regeneration, and consequently always administered to persons at their last gasp. The same sacred fluid (as I am informed by a Parsee) is used in the sacramental cups drunk by every male upon his first admission into that religion, which takes place on his completing his seventh year. Nay more, such is the belief in its cleansing virtue, that scrupulous Parsees always carry a bottle thereof in their pocket, wherewith to purify their hands after any unavoidable contact with unbelievers.[1]

Very similar ceremonies to these were practised in the secret societies of the Middle Ages, if we choose to accept Von Hammer's interpretation of certain mysterious sculptures, still to be seen in the Templar-churches of Germany, and which he has copiously illustrated in his 'Mysterium Baphometis revelatum.' In the intaglio already described, the kneeling neophyte is encompassed by all the terrific and mysterious host of Mithras, so remorselessly destroyed by the zealous Gracchus.

And again, the corpses trampled on by the crowned horsemen clearly refer to that recorded test of the candidate's fortitude—the apparent approach of death—for Lampridius puts down amongst the other mad freaks of Commodus, that during the Mithraic ceremonies, "when a certain thing had to be done for the purpose of inspiring terror, he polluted the rites by a *real murder*." an expression clearly showing that a scenic representation of such an act did really form a part of the proceedings The *Raven* properly takes its place here, as being the attribute of the Solar god in the Hellenic creed, on which account it is often depicted standing upon Apollo's lyre

Many other gems express the spiritual benefits conferred by the Mithraic initiation upon believers A frequent device of the kind, is a man, with hands bound behind his back, seated at the foot of a pillar supporting a gryphon with paw on wheel, that special emblem of the solar god, often accompanied with the legend ΔΙΚΑΙΩΣ, "I have deserved it" Another (Blacas) displays an unusual richness of symbolism the same gryphon's tail ends in a scorpion, whilst the wheel squeezes out of its chrysalis a tiny human soul that stretches forth its hands in jubilation, in front stands Thoth's ibis, holding in its beak the balance, perhaps the horoscope of the patient This talisman too, unites the Egyptian with the Magian creed, for the benefit of the carrier, for the reverse displays Isis, but in the character of Hygieia, standing upon her crocodile, the field being occupied by strangely complicated monograms, of sense intelligible to the initiated alone, and doubtless communicated to the recipient of the talisman, who found in them "a New Name written, that no man knoweth, save he that receiveth the same" But both doctrines and ceremonial of this religion are best understood through the examination of extant representations displaying them either directly or allegorically, which in their turn are illustrated by the practice of the faithful few who still keep alive the Sacred Fire, namely the Parsees of Guzerat The series therefore will be most fittingly opened by the following curious description of a cave of Mithras, as discovered in its original and unprofaned condition, written by that eminent antiquary, Flaminius Vacca (No 117)

III A ROMAN MITHRAS IN HIS CAVE

"I remember there was found in the vineyard of Sig. Orazio Muti (where the treasure was discovered), opposite S. Vitale, an idol in marble about 5 palms high ($3\frac{3}{4}$ ft.), standing erect upon a pedestal in an empty chamber, which had the door walled up. This idol had the head of a lion but the body that of a man. Under the feet was a globe, whence sprung a serpent which encompassed all the idol, and its head entered into the lion's mouth. He had his hands crossed upon the breast, with a key in each; four wings fastened upon the shoulders, two pointing upwards, two downwards. I do not consider it a very antique work, being done in a rude manner, or else indeed it was so ancient that at the time when it was made the good style was not yet known. Sig. Orazio, however, told me that a theologian, a Jesuit Father, explained its meaning by saying it signified the Devil, who in the times of heathenism, ruled over the world: hence the *globe* under his feet, the *serpent* which begirt his body and entered into his mouth, signified his foretelling the future with ambiguous responses; the *keys* in his hands, his sovereignty over the world; the *lion's head*, his being the ruler of all beasts; the *wings*, his presence everywhere. Such was the interpretation given by the Father aforesaid. I have done everything to see the idol, but Sig. Orazio being now dead, his heirs do not know what has become of it. It is not, however, unlikely that by the advice of the same theologian, Sig. Orazio may have sent it to some *limekiln to cure its dampness*, for it had been buried many and many a year." Thus was this most interesting monument destroyed through the conceited ignorance of a wretched ecclesiastic, himself more truly a worshipper of the Evil Principle, than was the ancient votary of the beneficent Lord of Light who carved that wondrous image. Vacca adds, "I remember, there was found in the same place, after the above-mentioned idol, another, only in bas-relief, also having a lion's head but the rest of the body human, with the arms extended, in each hand a torch, with two wings pointing upwards, two downwards, from between which issued a serpent

At his right stood an altar with fire, from the idol's mouth proceeded a ribbon or scroll extending over the fire."

This *lion*-headed deity can be no other than Jerome's "Pater Bromius," a Grecian title of Bacchus, and he, we are told, distinguished himself under that disguise in the famous war of the giants—

> "Tu cum Parentis regna per arduum
> Cohors Gigantum scanderet impia,
> Rhœtum retorsisti *leonis*
> Unguibus horribilique mala."
> (Horace, Od. II. xix. 21-24.)

And, tracing back this composite figure to the real source of such iconology, it is found to be the very one under which "Nri-singha-avatar" is depicted. It was assumed by the deity in order to destroy the tyrant Hiransyakaçipu, who had obtained the gift of invulnerability against all *known* beasts, either by day or night.

A Mithraic cave, with the contiguous buildings, was discovered at Spoleto in 1878. In the end wall were the usual three niches for the god and his torch-bearers. In front of them an altar inscribed "Soli invicto Mithræ sacrum." Close to the altar, a tall phallic stone, perforated with a square hole near the top—perhaps the "stone symbolizing the Birth of Mithras" mentioned by Firmicus. The cave, with the ground plan of the whole edifice is given in the 'Archæologia,' vol. 47, p. 205.

IV. MITHRAIC TALISMANS.

Mithraic gems are, for the most part, earlier in date than those emanating from the Gnosticism of Alexandria, with whose doctrines they had no connection whatever in their first origin. Little difficulty will be found on inspection in separating the two classes, the former being pointed out by the superiority of their style, and yet more so by the absence of the Egyptian symbols, and long Coptic legends that generally accompany the latter. Indeed many of them belong to the best period of Roman art—the age of Hadrian, and it is easy to perceive how the worship of Apollo gradually merged into that of his more spiritual oriental representative, in the times when religious ideas of Indian origin began to get the upper hand throughout the Roman world—a religion essentially speculative, and dealing with matters pertaining to another life and the Invisible, utterly different in nature from the old Grecian creed, so materialistic, so active, so entirely busying itself with the Present and the Visible.

In accordance with the rule that prescribed the proper *material* for talismans, the Jasper (Pliny's *Molochites*), green, mottled, or yellow, is almost exclusively employed for intagli embodying Mithraic ideas and which take the place of Phœbus and his attributes amongst the glyptic remains of the second and third centuries. To judge from their fine execution, certain examples of the class may even date from the age of the first Cæsars, and thus form as it were the advanced guard of that countless host of regular Gnostic works, amidst whose terrific barbarism ancient art ultimately expires. In their beginning these Mithraic works were the fruit of the modified Zoroastrian doctrines so widely disseminated over the Empire after the conquest of Pontus—doctrines whose grand feature was the exclusive worship of the Solar god as the fountain of all life—a notion philosophically true, if indeed the vital principle be, as some scientists assert, nothing more than electricity. As will be shown hereafter ("Serapis"), the later Platonists, like Macrobius, laboured hard to demonstrate that the multitudinous divinities of the old faiths wheresoever established, were no other than various epithets and expressions for the same god in his different phases. The aim of all the school was to accommodate the old faith to the influence of the Buddhistic theosophy, the very essence of which was that the innumerable gods of the Hindoo mythology were but *names* for the *Energies* of the First Triad in its successive *Avatars*, or manifestations unto man.

To come now to the actual types setting forth these ideas, prominent amongst them is the figure of the *Lion* (he being in astrological parlance the "House of the Sun"), usually surrounded with stars, and carrying in his jaws a bull's head, emblem of earth subjected to his power. Sometimes he tramples on the serpent, which in this connection no longer typifies wisdom, but the Principle of Evil For in all religions emanating from the East, where deadly poisonousness is the most conspicuous character of the snake-tribe, the reptile has been adopted as the most speaking type of the *Destroyer*. In the West, on the other hand, where the same species is for the most part innocuous, and a mere object of wonder, it has always symbolized wisdom, and likewise eternity, from the popular belief in the yearly removal of its youth through casting the slough, on this account the serpent was made the companion of Apollo and Aesculapius, and furthermore plays so important a part in Scandinavian mythology, holding the whole universe together in its perpetual embrace.

Mithras himself often makes his appearance, figured as a youthful Persian, plunging the national weapon, "Medus acinaces," into the throat of a prostrate bull (which expresses the same doctrine as the type last mentioned), whilst overhead are the sun and moon, the group standing in the centre of the Zodiac But the completest assembly of Mithraic figures and symbols that has come under my notice, is the intaglio published by Caylus ('Recueil d'Antiquités,' vi pl 84). It is engraved upon a very fine agate, 2 × 1½ inches in measurement In the centre is the usual type of Mithras slaughtering the Bull, the tail of which terminates in three wheat-ears, and between the hind legs hangs a huge scorpion, below is the Lion strangling the Serpent—emblem of darkness and of death On each side stands a fir-tree, admitted into this system because its spiry form imitates a flame, for which same reason its cone was taken for the symbol of the element fire, and therefore borne in the hands of deities in the most ancient Syrian sculptures Against these fir-trees are affixed torches, one pointing upwards, the other downwards, which clearly stand for the rising and setting of the Sun At the side of one is a scorpion, of the other, a bull's head Above each tree again is a torch, each pointing in an opposite direction The principal group is flanked by Phœbus in his four-horse, Luna in her two-horse car Above the whole stand two winged figures entwined with serpents and leaning upon long sceptres, between whom rise up three flames, besides four more at the side of the right-hand figure, making up the mystic number seven—perhaps representing the seven Amshaspands or Archangels. A naked female, surrounded with stars, kneels before the angel on the left—doubtless the soul for whose benefit the talisman was composed—soliciting his patronage.

Could this elaborate composition be interpreted, it would certainly be found to contain a summary of the Mithraic creed as it was received by the nations of the West. As it is, however, some portions of the tableau are explained by certain legends to be found in the Parsee sacred books; whilst others derive light from comparison with the larger monuments of the same worship. Thus, the termination of the bull's tail in ears of wheat allude to the fifty life-giving plants which sprang from the tail of the Primæval *Bull* (or *Life*, the same word in Zend) after he had been slain by Ahriman. Of the same animal the seed was carried up by the Izeds (genii) to the Moon, where, purified in her beams, it was moulded by Ormuzd into a new pair, the parents of all that exists in earth, air and water. The scorpion is appended to the part of the body, properly under the influence of the sign so called for as Manilius teaches, "The fiery scorpion in the *groin* delights." In this particular situation it expresses Autumn, as the serpent underneath does Winter; and with good reason takes the place of the bull's genitals, for, as the same poet sings (iv. 217.)

> "With fiery tail when Scorpio threatens war,
> As through the stars he drives the solar car,
> He searches earth with penetrating rays
> And the mixed seed deep in her furrows lays."

The torches raised and lowered signify the East and West. In the circular altar of the Villa Borghese (Winckelmann Mon. Ined. No. 21) the bust of Luna appears resting on a crescent over an aged head in front face with crabs' claws springing out of his forehead—a speaking type of Oceanus. The bust of the *rising* sun, with his customary badge, the eight-rayed star, in point, rests upon an erect flambeau, whilst that of the *setting* luminary looking downwards, is placed upon another lowered towards earth. Again, the serpent winding *four* times about the figures may signify the sun's annual revolution; an explanation rendered the more plausible by the torso of Mithras at Arles, in which the Zodiacal Signs occupy the intervals between the coils of the same serpent. The lion and raven stand for the attendant priests, for in these mysteries the higher officials were denominated *Lions*, the lower *Ravens*; whence the rites themselves got the name of "Leontica," and "Coracica."

The fires, the planets and the genii presiding over them are in number *seven*—a numeral the most sacred of all amongst the Persians. But of these seven Fires, *three* are ever depicted in a special manner as those most worthy to be held in reverence. These three are the "Fire of the Stars," that is of the planet Venus, named *Anahid*, the "Fire of the Sun," or the Fire *Mihr*; and the "Fire of Lightning," or the Fire *Bersiov*, that is, the planet Jupiter. The *Mihr* is the winged orb, so common in all Assyrian sculpture—an emblem which serves to explain the Prophet's simile, "the *Sun* of Righteousness with healing in his *wings*."

The worship of the Fire Gushtasp (or that of Anahid) figures on the Zend sculptures as a very ancient worship, and also in the "Shah Nameh," just as that of the goddess Anaitis does in many Greek authors from Herodotus downwards. This historian observes (I. 131) that *at first* the Persians worshipped only the sun, moon, and elements, until they learnt from the Assyrians the worship of Venus Urania, whom they called *Mitra*, the same being the Mylitta of the Babylonians, the Alata or Alilat of the Arabians. Now Mitra (feminine of Mithras) and Anahid, are one and the same goddess, that is to say, the Morning Star, a female Genius, presiding over love, giving light, and directing the harmonious movement of the other planets by the sound of her lyre, the strings whereof are the solar rays—"Apollo's lyre strung with his golden hair." (Creuzer, Kal. de l'Antiq. ii. 731). In this doctrine we discover the reason for the *separation* of the Fires upon Caylus' gem into *two* groups, the principal group consisting of the three most anciently adored, the subsidiary one of the remaining four.

Other Mithraic symbols are of a very speaking character, and almost explain their own meaning at first sight. Thus Mithras *piercing* the bull's throat with his dagger signifies the *penetration* of the solar ray into the bosom of the earth, by whose action all Nature is nourished; as is further expressed by the *Dog's* licking up the blood that pours from the wound. The sign Capricorn frequently introduced into the same group, declares the necessity of *moisture* to co-operate with the Sun's influence in bringing about the germination of the seed sown; whilst the *scorpion*, in the significant position above noticed, expresses the generative *heat*. The union of two diverse religions, already mentioned, is curiously exemplified by those stones that show the Mithraic group surrounded by sets of the sacred animals of *Egypt*, arranged by threes—crocodiles, goats, calves, vultures, hawks, ibises—standing around in attitudes of adoration, and gazing upon the great work of their supreme lord, Mithras (see page 41, fig. 2).

Mithraic bas-reliefs cut upon the smoothed faces of rocks, or upon tablets of stone still abound throughout the former western provinces of the Roman Empire; many exist in Germany; still more in France; others in this island, along the line of the Picts' Wall, and a remarkably fine example at York, the station of the Sixth Legion. The famous "Arthur's Oon" (destroyed in the last century) upon the Carron, a hemispherical vaulted building of immense blocks of stone, was unmistakably a *Specus Mithraicum*—the same in design as Chosroes' magnificent Fire temple at Gazaca. Inasmuch as the sun-god was the chief deity* of the Druids, it is easy to imagine what ready acceptance the worship of his more refined Persian equivalent would find amongst the Celtic Aborigines, when once introduced by the Roman troops and colonists, many of whom were Orientals. To the last circumstance a curious testimony is incidentally borne by Lampridius, when he remarks that the entire military force employed by Maximinus in his great in-

* As "Belenus" he continued to the last the patron god of Aquileia, that Gallic metropolis of Cisalpine Gaul, and to his power was ascribed the death of Maximin when besieging that city. The acclamations of the senate on the receipt of the news of their deliverance from the tyrant, prove that Belenus was held to be another name for Apollo. A *shoe* of the giant emperor, a convincing testimony, literally an "ex pede Herculem," to his incredible stature, was yet to be seen in the days of Lampridius, nailed to a tree in the *sacred grove* at the place of his fall.

vasion of Germany, was the same that had been raised by Severus Alexander, and which had accompanied him to the scene of his murder, "either the North of Gaul or *Britain*," which same army the historian describes as "potentissimus quidem per *Armenios* et *Osrhoenos*, et *Parthos*, et omnis generis hominum." For this sagacious emperor had appointed to subordinate commands in his own army all the prisoners of royal or noble birth whom he had taken in his preceding Persian campaign.

Although the modern Parsees, like their Achæmenian ancestry in the days of Herodotus, abominate idols and all visible representations of things divine, yet do they still piously cherish the ideas embodied on the sculptures just passed under review. Amongst these, most conspicuous is their veneration for the *Dog* which they yet esteem the most holy of animals. Tavernier (I. 493) was on this account greatly scandalised by the Guebres of Surat, "They have another strange custom—when a person is on the point of death, to take a little dog, and place it upon his breast. When they perceive that he is at his last gasp, they apply the dog's muzzle to the dying man's mouth, and make it bark twice when in this position, as if they meant to make the person's soul enter into the dog,* which they pretend will deliver it unto the angel appointed to receive the same. Moreover if a dog happens to die, they carry it out of the town, and pray to God in behalf of that piece of carrion, as though the brute's soul could derive any advantage from their prayers after its death." Following up this analogy, the sculptured dog licking up the bull's blood may actually be intended for such a vehicle of departing life. In these times the Parsees expose their dead, upon gratings laid on the summit of the "Tower of silence," to be consumed by the birds alone; but under the Sassanian monarchy it was the inviolable rule to lay out all corpses in the open fields to be devoured by the dogs. This was no more than carrying out to the full a very ancient principle of the Zoroastrian religion. Herodotus (I. 140) states from his own knowledge that the corpse of a Magus was not allowed to be buried before it had been *attacked* by a bird or

* My Parsee informant assures me this ceremony is now modified into the merely bringing a dog into the dying man's chamber.

dog, adding that the same was *reported* of the other Persians. The Magi regarded the killing of a dog equally criminal with that of a human being. This primitive style of obsequies the Sassanians strove hard to enforce upon all nations subjected to their sway, viewing as a great sacrilege the placing of dead bodies in the bosom of the earth, a still greater, the consuming them by the sacred element, *Fire*. This practice above all others scandalised the narrow-minded Byzantines, the historian Agathias expressing his horror at the casting the dead to the dogs, whatever their rank or dignity in life, as in the case of the great Satrap Mermeroes, whom he *saw* thus exposed naked in the fields to be so devoured. When the last seven sages of Greece, expelled from their professional chairs at Athens by the stupid bigotry of Justinian, sought refuge in the ostentatious hospitality of Nushirwan the Just, even they (despite their philosophy) found themselves obliged, by their disgust at the sight of this practice,* to return home with sad loss of dignity, and submit to the spirit of the times. If the dogs refused to touch the carcase, this was looked on by the friends of the deceased as the very worst of indications as to the ultimate destination of his soul. The Parsees, who, with more decency, constitute the raven† (or equally sacred creature) sexton and sepulchre in one, derive a similar augury from observing which eye is first attacked by the bird, the preference for the right one being the token of salvation, for the left, of the reverse.

A very curious portion of the initiatory ceremony in the

* To which they would have been forced to conform had they continued under the protection of the Sassanian king.

† The same practice prevails in Thibet with the motive thus assigned. "Several bodies exposed on the banks of the stream were being devoured by crows and buzzards, which soon leave nothing but the skeletons, which are washed away by the summer rise of the stream. The Thibetians believe that as each buzzard, gorged with its foul repast, soars into the heavens, a portion of the spirit of the deceased is taken up into heaven. In the case of rich people Lamas are employed to divide the body into small pieces and carry it up to the top of a hill where the vulture and buzzard soon dispose of it. Interment of the dead is also practised, but only among the poorer people, who cannot afford to pay Lamas to perform the ceremony of exposing the body."—Cooper's 'Travels of a Pioneer of Commerce,' p. 270.

ancient Mysteries was the giving of the "Mark of Mithras." After successfully undergoing each stage of the ordeal, the accepted candidate was *marked* in a certain indelible manner, but the exact nature of this marking cannot now be ascertained. The expressions used by St. Augustine (in Johan. i. dis. 7) lead us to conclude two things: firstly, that the *engraved stones*, the object of our consideration, were given to the candidate at the end of his probation, for a token of admission into the fraternity, and for a medium of recognition between members: and secondly, that every one, upon admission, was stamped with a *secret Mark*, indelibly imprinted in his flesh. "Something of the sort has been copied by a certain Spirit, in that he will have his *own image* to be purchased with *blood*, forasmuch as he was aware that mankind were some day or another to be redeemed by the shedding of blood." This last expression shows that this Mark was not *burnt in*, but *incised* or tattooed; and the same conclusion may be deduced from St. John's using the term χάραγμα, *engraving*, not στίγμη, *branding*, for that badge of servitude which all the subjects of the Second Beast, "having horns like a lamb's, and speaking like a dragon," were forced to receive, either *in* their right hands (i.e., upon the palm) or upon their foreheads, and he caused all, both small and great, rich and poor, free and bond, to receive a Mark in their right hand, or in their foreheads: "and that no man might buy or sell, save he that had the Mark, or the Name of the Beast, or the Number of his Name" (Rev. xiii. 17). These words contain a compendious account of the different kinds of "Stigmata" then in use to distinguish those devoting themselves to any particular deity. The *Mark* was the figure of the special symbol or attribute of that deity (exactly answering to the caste-marks of the modern Hindoos): the *Name* was his own, written at full length in some sacred language: the *Number* was the more recondite way of expressing that name, either by a single numeral in the primitive Chaldæan fashion, or by other letters taken numerically, and yielding the same sum. The author of the Apocalypse very probably had the Mithraicists in view when penning this allegory; yet we may be certain that the members of a *secret* society did not receive the mark of member-slip upon any *conspicuous* part of their persons. The same necessity meets us here, as in every other branch of this inquiry, for placing the origin of all such sectarian bodily Marks in India—the true fountainhead, directly or indirectly, of so many Gnostic practices. *There*, the votaries of the several deities are still distinguished, each by the proper symbol of his patron-god impressed upon his *forehead*, but by a milder process than of old, being traced, not in his own blood, but with the ashes of cow-dung, the powder of sandal-wood, or coloured earths, daily renewed. Inasmuch as amongst them the symbol of Fire (Bramah) is an equilateral Triangle, with the apex pointing upwards, it may be *conjectured* that the Mithraic χάραγμα was the same simple figure, by which indeed Horapollo informs us the Egyptians symbolised the Moon, and Plutarch that Pythagoras expressed the goddess Athene.* Clarkson, however, asserts positively that the Mark of Mithras was the "Tau mysticum," but whence he derived this knowledge I have never been able to ascertain.†

The *Seven Stars*, so conspicuous upon these talismans, doubtless stand for something higher than the mere planets; in all likelihood they denote the Seven Amshaspands, the First Order of Angels in the Zoroastrian hierarchy, and who became the "Seven Spirits of God" to the later Jews, and thence by gradual transition give the epithet "Septiformis munere" to the Spiritus Sanctus of Christianity. Of these Amshaspands the names and offices are: Ormuzd, source of life and creation; Bahman, king of the world; Ardibehest, giver of fire; Shahrivar, of the metals; Çpandarmat (the Gnostic Sophia), queen of the earth; Khordad, presiding over time and the seasons; Amerdad, over trees and plants. Of these the highest in place are (after Ormuzd) the four named next in gradation. Below this order stand the Izeds, twenty-seven in number, ruled over by Mithras; they govern the heavenly bodies and the elements

* Herself the lunar deity according to an old tradition preserved by Aristotle.

† There is very good reason to discover a Mithraic mark in the "Phanaces" or, Sun between two Crescents, the regular badge of the kings of Pontus, and as such put upon the staters of Athens bearing the names of Mithridates and Aristion. (In the Duc de Luynes Collection.)

Against each Amshaspand and Ized is arrayed a corresponding Angel of Darkness, to thwart all his operations, namely, the Seven Arch-Devs, and the Twenty-Seven Devs

V GNOSTIC SACRAMENTS AND INITIATIONS AS CONNECTED WITH THE MITHRAIC

In my account of Mithraicism notice has been taken of the very prominent part that sacraments for the remission of sin play in the ceremonial of that religion, the following extracts from the grand Gnostic text-book will serve to show how the same notions (and probably, forms) were transferred to the service of Gnosticism

Baptism, Remitting Sins —(Pistis-Sophia) (298) Then came forth Mary and said Lord, under what form do *Baptisms* remit sins? I have heard thee saying that the Ministers of Contentions (ἐριδαῖοι)* follow after the soul, bearing witness against it of all the sins that it hath committed, so that they may convict it in the judgments Now, therefore, Lord, do the mysteries of Baptism blot out the sins that be in the hands of the Receivers of Contention, so that they shall utterly forget the same? Now, therefore, Lord, tell us in what form they remit sins, for we desire to know them thoroughly Then the Saviour answered and said Thou hast well spoken of truth those Ministers are they that testify against all sins, for they abide constantly in the places of judgment, laying hold upon the souls, convicting all the souls of sinners who have not received the mystery, and they keep them fast in chaos tormenting them But these contentious ones cannot pass over chaos so as to enter into the courses that be above chaos, in order to convict the souls therefore receiving the mysteries, it is not lawful for them to force so as to drag them down into chaos, where the Contentious Receivers may convict them But the souls of such as have not received the mysteries, these do they desire and hail into chaos whereas the souls that have received

* The Cabiri, "punishers," of the ancient mythology, performing their former duties under the new dispensation

the mysteries, they have no means of convicting, seeing that they cannot get out of their own place, and even if they did come forth, they could not stop those souls, neither shut them up in their chaos Hearken, therefore, I will declare to you in truth in what form the mystery of Baptism remitteth sins. If the souls when yet living in the world have been sinful, the Contentious Receivers verily do come, that they may bear witness of all the sins they have committed, but they can by no means come forth out of the regions of chaos, so as to convict the soul in the places of judgment that be beyond chaos But the counterfeit of the spirit* testifies against all the sins of the soul, in order to convict it in the places of judgment that be beyond chaos, not only doth it testify, but also sets a *seal* upon all the sins of the soul, so as to print them firmly upon the soul, that all the Rulers of the judgment place of the sinners may know that it is the soul of a sinner and likewise know the *number* of sins which it hath committed from the seals that the counterfeit of the spirit hath imprinted upon it, so that they may punish the soul according to the number of its sins this is the manner in which they treat the soul of a sinner (300) Now therefore if any one hath received the mysteries of Baptism, *those mysteries become a great fire*,† exceeding strong, and wise, so as to burn up all the sins and the Fire entereth into the soul secretly, so that it may consume within it all the sins which the counterfeit of the spirit hath printed there Likewise it entereth into the body secretly, that it may pursue all its pursuers, and divide them into parts—for it pursueth within the body, the counterfeit of the spirit, and Fate—so that it may divide them apart from the Power and the Soul, and place them in one part of the body—so that the fire separates the counterfeit of the spirit, Fate, and the Body into one portion, and the Soul and the Power ‡ into another portion The mystery of Baptism remaineth in the middle of them, so that it may perpetually separate them, so that it may purge and cleanse them in order

* Ἀντιμῖμον Πνεύματος, one of the four component parts of the soul equivalent apparently to our "Conscience"

† A clear allusion to the Mithraic "torture of the fire"

‡ The particle of the Godhead mixed up in the quadruple composite of the Inner Man

that they may not be polluted by *Matter* Now therefore, Mary, this is the manner whereby the mystery of Baptism remitteth sins and all transgressions

(301) And when the Saviour had thus spoken, he said to his disciples Do ye understand in what manner I speak with you? Then came forth Mary, saying Of a truth, Lord, I perceive in reality all the things that thou hast said Touching this matter of the Remission of Sins, thou speaketh aforetime to us in a parable, saying I am come to bring *fire* upon the earth, nay, more, let it burn as much as I please And, again thou hast set it forth openly, saying I have a baptism wherewith I will baptise and how shall I endure until it be accomplished? Ye think that I am come to bring peace upon the earth? By no means so, but dissension, which I am come to bring For from this time forth there shall be five in one house, three shall be divided against two, and two against three This, Lord, is the word that thou speakest openly But concerning the word that thou spakest I am come to bring fire upon the earth, and let it burn so much as I please in this thou hast spoken of the mystery of Baptism in the world, and let it burn as much as thou pleasest for to consume all the sins of the soul, that it may purge them away And again thou hast shewn the same forth openly, saying I have a baptism wherewith I will baptise, and how shall I endure until it be accomplished? The which is this, Thou wilt not tarry in the world until the baptisms be accomplished to purify all the perfect souls. And again what thou spakest unto us aforetime "Do ye suppose I am come to bring peace upon earth," &c (302) This signifieth the mystery of Baptism which thou hast brought into the world, because it hath brought about dissension in the body of the world, because it hath divided the Counterfeit of the spirit, the Body, and the Fate thereof, into one party, and the Soul and the Power into the other party The same is, "There shall be three against two and two against three" And when Mary had spoken these things the Saviour said Well done, thou Spiritual One in the pure light, this is the interpretation of my saying

Then Mary went on and said Bear with me, Lord whilst I yet inquire of thee Lo! we know now fully after what form

Baptism remitteth sin Now therefore declare unto us the mystery of the Three Courts, and the mystery of the First Mystery, and likewise the mystery of the Ineffable One, in what form do these also remit sin? Do they remit sin in the *form of baptism* or not? (303) The Saviour answered again By no means, but all the mysteries of the Three Courts remit in the soul, and in all the regions of the Rulers, all the sins that the soul hath committed even from the beginning They remit also the sins that the soul shall have committed afterwards up to the time that each one of the mysteries taketh unto itself, the time whereof I will declare unto you hereafter Moreover the mystery of the First Mystery, and the mystery of the Ineffable One, remit unto the soul in all the regions of the Rulers all the sins and transgressions that it hath committed And not only do they remit, but they do not *impute sin** to the soul, from henceforth for ever by reason of the free-grace of the mystery and the exceeding glory of the same Then said the Saviour Do ye understand all that I have said unto you? Then Mary answered Lord, I have caught up all the words thou hast spoken Now therefore as to the saying that all the mysteries of the Three Courts remit sins, and blot out iniquities Concerning this same matter hath David the prophet spoken, saying "Blessed are they whose sins they have remitted, and whose iniquities they have covered," and as to thy saying that the mystery of the First Mystery, and the mystery of the Ineffable One, do not only remit all sin unto the soul for ever, but also do not suffer sin to be *imputed* unto the same for ever and ever, by reason of the free-gift of the great mystery, and the exceeding glory thereof, concerning this same matter David the prophet foretold, saying "Blessed are they unto whom the Lord will not impute sin," which signifieth they will not impute sin from henceforth unto those that receive the mystery of the First Mystery and the mystery of the Ineffable One Then answered the Saviour Well done, thou Spiritual One, this is the interpretation of my word.

(305) Then Mary continued, saying Lord, if a man shall

* This is the doctrine that "knowledge" renders all actions free from sinfulness—as held by the Simonians

have received the mystery in the mystery of the First Mystery, and afterwards shall turn back and sin, and again shall repent and pray in his own mystery, shall his sin be remitted to him or not? Then answered the Saviour, Whosoever after receiving the mystery shall again sin twelve times, and again repent twelve times, and then shall pray in his own mystery, his sin shall be remitted unto him But and if, after these twelve times, he shall turn again and transgress, then of a truth his sin shall never more be remitted, so that he may turn again unto his own mystery whatsoever it be For such an one there is no repentance, unless indeed he hath received the mystery of the Ineffable One that remitteth all sins, and shall remit them at every time.

Then said Mary Lord, those who have received the mystery of the First Mystery, and then have turned back and sinned, if such without having repented shall depart out of the body, shall they inherit the kingdom or not, forasmuch as they have received the free gift of that mystery? (306) The Saviour answered Of such the judgment shall be the most merciful amongst all the judgments, for their dwelling is in the Middle Gate* of the Dragon of Outer Darkness, and at the end† of all those that be in torment, because such an one hath received the free gift of the mystery, and hath not remained steadfast therein Then said Mary Such as have received the mystery of the Ineffable One and then shall turn back and sin, but afterwards shall repent in their lifetime, how many times shall their sin be remitted unto *them?* Then answered the Saviour To such an one, not only if he turn back and sin once, and then repent, shall his sin be remitted, but even if he doth so continually, so long as he shall repent whilst yet alive, not being in hypocrisy, and shall pray according to his own mystery, because those mysteries are merciful and remit sin at every time (307) Then asked Mary But if such an one shall depart out of the body before he hath repented, what then shall happen unto him? (307) Then answered the Saviour Of such an one the judgment shall be worse than of any other, and

* This term is borrowed from the ancient Gates of the Amenti

† The lost place, answering to the Limbo of the mediaeval Hell

exceeding great, for even if those souls be *new ones*,* they shall not return unto the changes of the earthly bodies, neither shall they do any work, but they shall be cast out into the uttermost parts of the Outer Darkness, and shall be consumed so that they shall not exist for ever and ever

(308) To this declaration Mary refers the saying "Salt is good, but if the salt hath lost its savour," &c

The following extracts, from the same high authority, will much elucidate the *pass-words* communicated to the dying believer, which form so important a feature of the Gnostic system

Benefits of Initiation —I will declare unto you that mystery, which is this Whosoever shall have received that *One Word*, when he shall depart out of the body of the Matter of the Rulers, there shall come the Contentious Receivers to loosen him out of that body, which same Receivers loosen every one departing out of the body And when they shall have loosened the soul that hath received that mystery which I have declared unto you, in that very moment wherein he is set loose, he becometh a great *flood of light* in the midst of them And the Receivers shall fear the light of that soul, and shall tremble, and shall cease through their fear of the great light which they behold And that soul shall fly up aloft, and the Receivers shall not lay hold upon him, neither shall they discern by what way he is gone, inasmuch as he is become a great *Ray of Light*, and flieth up aloft, neither is there any Power that can overtake him, nor ever come nigh unto him at all (228) But he passes through all the regions of the Rulers, and also the regions of the offspring of the Light, neither doth he give in a declaration in any region, nor yet a defence of himself,† nor yet the pass-word (or symbol). Neither can any Power of them all draw near him, but all the regions of the Rulers and of the offspring of the Light shall

* That is, have occupied the body for the first time, not souls that after punishment for their sins in this life, have been placed again in bodies to undergo a second probation upon earth

† All this is borrowed from the Egyptian "Ritual of the Dead," concerning the soul's passage on its way to the palace of Osiris Socharis, "the Occidental," through the One-and-twenty *Gates*, each guarded by its own Genius, and each requiring a separate address

sing hymns, each one in his own place, fearing the flood of light that clotheth that soul, until he shall come into the place of the heirs of the mystery that he hath received, and become conjoined with the members of the same Verily, I say unto you, he shall be in all the regions in the time that a man can shoot an arrow. Again I say unto you, whosoever shall receive that mystery and make himself perfect in all the types and figures thereof, that man is in the world, but he is more excellent than the angels, and shall be before them all, he is a man in the world, but he is better than the archangels and shall be before them all (229), he is higher than all the tyrants, and all the lords, and all the gods, and all the luminaries, and all the pure ones, and all the triple powers, and all the Primal Fathers, and all the Unseen Ones, he is a man in the world, but he is more excellent than the great unseen Primal Father, and shall be more exalted than he, and above all those pertaining to the Middle-space, and above all the emanations of the Treasury of Light, and above all the confusion,* and above every region of the Treasure of Light, he is a man in the world, but he shall reign with me (230) in my kingdom, he is a man in the world, but he shall be a king in the Light, he is a man in the world, but he is not of the world, and verily I say unto you, that man is *I*, and I am *that man;* and in the dissolution of the world, when the universe shall be raised up, and all the number of perfect souls shall be raised up, and I am made king over all the offspring of the Light, and when I am made king over the seven AMHN,† and the Five Trees, and the Three AMHN, and the Nine Keepers, and when I am king over the Boy of the boy which be the Twin Saviours, and over the Twelve Saviours, and over all the number of perfect souls which have received the mystery of Light, then whosoever shall have received the mystery of the Ineffable One, they shall be joint kings with me and shall sit upon my right hand and upon my left hand in my kingdom Verily I say unto you, those men are I, and I am

* The Creation of the Demiurgus, in which the Particle of the Godhead is *mixed up* and lost in the heap of Matter

† Title probably borrowed from the former *Amenti*, the four sons of Osiris, and keepers of Elysium

those men For this cause have I said to you formerly, ye shall sit upon your thrones on my right hand and on my left in my kingdom, and ye shall reign together with me (231). Therefore I did not refrain, neither was I abashed to call you my brethren and my fellows, inasmuch as ye shall be joint kings with me in my kingdom These things therefore I said unto you, knowing that I was about to give unto you the mystery of the Ineffable One, because that mystery is I, and I am that mystery. Now therefore not only ye shall reign with me, but also whatsoever men shall have received that mystery they shall be joint kings with me in my kingdom; and I am they, and they are I. But my throne shall be more exalted than theirs, and inasmuch as ye shall receive sorrows in this world beyond all other men whilst ye are preaching the words that I declare unto you, therefore your thrones shall be next to my throne in my kingdom For this cause I said of old time, in the place where I shall be, my twelve ministers shall be also, but Mary Magdalene, and John the Virgin, shall be the most excellent amongst my disciples And all men that shall have received the mystery of the Ineffable One shall be upon my right hand and upon my left, for I am they and they are I, and they shall be equal with you in every thing, but your thrones shall be more exalted than theirs, and my throne shall be more exalted than yours (232) And all men that shall find out the *Word* of the Ineffable One, verily I say unto you all the men that shall know that *Word*, the same shall understand also the knowledge of all the words that I have spoken unto you, both in their depth and in their height, in their length and in their breadth. And what things I have not told you those I will tell you in their place and in their order in the emanation of the universe Verily I say unto you, they shall know how the world is established, and after what form those that pertain unto the height (highest place) be made, and for what end the universe was created

And when the Saviour had said these things, Mary Magdalene came forward and said Lord, be not wroth with me if I seek out everything with diligence Whether is the Word of the mystery of the Ineffable One, one thing, and the Word of the Knowledge of All, another? Then the Saviour answered, and said. The Word of the mystery of the Ineffable is one thing, and the Word of the Knowledge of All is another Then said Mary. Suffer me, Lord, to ask thee yet again one thing Unless when we are living we understand the knowledge of the whole Word of the Ineffable One, we shall not inherit the kingdom of Light? (233) Then the Saviour answered, and said. Of a truth, whosoever shall have received the mystery of the kingdom of Light, the same shall go to inherit it into that place the mystery whereof he hath received But he shall not obtain the knowledge of the All, wherefore all things were made, except he shall have known that One Word of the Ineffable, the which is the knowledge of all And again, there is no way of knowing that One Word of knowledge, except a man shall have first received the mystery of the Ineffable One, but every man shall go to inherit that place the mystery whereof he hath received. For which cause I said to you formerly "He that believeth a prophet shall receive a prophet's reward, and he that believeth a righteous man shall receive a righteous man's reward," which is this of whatsoever place each hath received the mystery, into that same place shall he go He that hath received a humble mystery, the same shall inherit a humble place. He that hath received an excellent mystery, the same shall inherit an exalted place, and every one shall abide in his own place in the light of my kingdom, and every one shall have authority over the Course that is below him, but over that which is above himself he shall not have authority, but shall abide in his inheritance of the light of my kingdom, dwelling in a great light unto which there is no measure, next to the gods and to the Unseen Ones, and he shall be in great joy and gladness (234)

Now therefore I will speak with you touching the glory of those also that shall receive the mystery of the First Mystery He that hath received the same, at the time when he shall depart out of this body of Matter, the Contentious Receiver shall come that they may take his soul out of the body, and that soul shall become a great Ray of light and shall fly aloft through the midst of them, and shall pass through all the regions and shall not give-in any declaration, or defence, or symbol, token (pass-word), but shall pass through all, that he may come and reign over all the places belonging to the First Saviour. In the like manner he that hath received the Second Mystery and the Third and Fourth up to the Twelfth* (235), that soul likewise shall pass through all the regions without giving in his defence, or token, and shall come and reign over all the places belonging to the Twelve Saviours. And in like manner those receiving the second mystery shall reign over the places of the Second Saviour amongst the heirs of light. In like manner those receiving the third and the fourth up to the twelfth, shall reign over the regions of that Saviour whose mystery each hath received. But they shall not be equal with those that have received the mystery of the Ineffable One, but shall abide in the Courses of the Twelve Saviours.

Then Mary answered, saying: Lord, suffer me yet again. How is it that the First Mystery hath twelve mysteries, whereas the Ineffable hath but one? Jesus answered: Of a truth He hath but One, but that mystery maketh *three* others; the mystery is indeed *one*, but to each of them there is a different form, and moreover it maketh *five* mysteries.

As for the First Mystery, when thou hast performed it well in all the forms thereof, when thou departest out of thy body thou shalt forthwith become a great Ray of light, and it shall traverse all the regions of the Rulers and all the regions of Light, all being afraid of that light of the soul, until it shall come into its own kingdom. As for the Second Mystery, he that shall perform the same rightly in all the forms thereof, if he speak it over the head of a man departing out of the body, and *into his two ears*, that man departing out of the body when he hath received the mystery a second time, and been made partaker of the *Word of Truth*,† that man's soul shall become, when it leaveth the body, a great flood of light, so as to traverse all the regions until it cometh into the kingdom of that mystery. But and if

* This gradation seems borrowed from the twelve degrees in the Mithraic initiation.

† This is what Epiphanius relates of the practice of the Heracleonites of communicating the pass-word to the ear of the dying man.

that man hath not received that mystery, neither hath been made partaker of the words of truth, if he that hath performed that mystery shall speak the same into the ears of him who is departing out of the body, verily I say unto you, the soul of that man, although he hath not received the mystery of Light nor partaken of the words of truth, shall not be judged in the places of the Rulers, neither shall it be punished in any place, neither shall the fire touch it, by reason of the mystery of the Ineffable which goeth along with it And they shall hasten to deliver that soul one to the other, and shall guide it Course after Course, and place (239) after place, until they bring it before the Virgin of Light for all the regions shall fear the mystery and the *Mark** of the kingdom of the Ineffable One that is with it

And when they have brought the soul unto the Virgin of Light, she shall see the Mark of the mystery of the kingdom of the Ineffable One which is with it And the Virgin of Light marvelleth thereat, and she judgeth that soul, but suffereth him not to be brought unto the light until he hath accomplished the ministry of the light of that mystery, which be these the purification of the renouncing of the world and of all the *Matter* that therein is And the Virgin of Light sealeth him with a special seal, which is this in the same month in which he hath departed out of the body, she will cause him to be placed in another body that shall be righteous, and shall obtain the divinity of truth and the high mystery, so that he may inherit the same, and also inherit the Light for ever and ever. This is the grace of the Second Mystery of the Ineffable One

As touching the Third Mystery the man that hath performed the same duly in all the forms thereof and shall *name* that mystery over the head of one departing out of the body whether he be living or *dead, or abiding in the midst of the torments of the Rulers*,† and their different fires, they shall make haste to release

* It has the impression of the royal seal stamped upon it

† Here we have the first hint of masses performed for the dead A similar idea is involved in the practice mentioned by St Paul of being "baptized for the sake of deceased persons" A singular Italian usage alluded to by Dante in his 'Vendetta di Dio non Teme Suppe,' refers to something of the sort done to appease the manes A homicide who had eaten sops in wine upon the grave of the slain man was thereby freed from the *vendetta* of the family —(Purgat xxxiii 35)

that man out of them all, and shall bring him before the Virgin of Light, who shall place him in a righteous body that shall inherit the light.

(243) Moreover in the dissolution of the Universe, that is, when the number of perfect souls is made up, and the mystery is accomplished on account of which the Universe has been created, then I will spend a thousand years, according to the years of light, ruling over the offspring of the light, and over the number of the perfect souls which have received all the mysteries Then Mary said, Lord, how many years in the years of this world is one year of light? Jesus answered, One day of light is one thousand years of this world, wherefore thirty and six myriads and a half of the years of the world make one year of light I shall therefore reign a thousand years of light, being king in the middle of the last *Parastates*,* being king over all the offspring of light, and over all the number of perfect souls that have received the mysteries of light And ye, my disciples, and each one that hath received the mysteries of the Ineffable One, shall be upon my right hand and upon my left, being kings together with me in my kingdom And those likewise that receive the three mysteries of the five mysteries of the Ineffable shall be kings together with you in the kingdom of light But they shall not be equal with you, and with those receiving the mystery of the Ineffable One, for they shall continue kings behind you And those receiving the five mysteries of the Ineffable shall remain behind the three mysteries being kings also Likewise those receiving the twelve mysteries of the First Mystery, they too shall abide as kings behind the five mysteries of the Ineffable One And they also are kings each one of them according to his course, and all receiving in the mysteries in all the places of the Court of the Ineffable One, so that they shall be kings also, but come after such as have received the mystery of the First Mystery, being sent forth according to the glory of each, so that those receiving high mysteries shall dwell in high places, but those receiving humble mysteries shall abide in humble places

* The deity whose place is next to the Supreme Light, to judge from the primary sense of the word

These are the *Three Lots* of the Kingdom of Light, and the mysteries of these Three Lots of Light are exceeding great Ye will find them in the great Second Book of IEV, but I will give unto you and declare unto you the mysteries of each lot, which be more exalted than any other place (246), and are chief both as to place and as to order the which also lead all mankind within, into lofty places, according to the count belonging to their inheritance, so that ye have no need of any of the *lower mysteries*, but ye will find them in the Second Book of IEV which Enoch wrote when I spoke with him out of the Tree of Knowledge and out of the Tree of Life in the Paradise of Adam

Now therefore after I shall have declared unto you all Emanation, I will give and I will tell unto you the Three Lots of my Kingdom which be the chief of all

Inasmuch as *Ordeals* and *Meritorious Penances* held so important a place in the Mithraic ceremonial, it will not be irrelevant here to adduce for comparison a series of the kind as excogitated by the extravagant imagination of the Brahmins The penances of the *demon* Taraka, the Tapa-asura, by means whereof he constrained Brahma to grant him whatever he chose to demand, are thus enumerated, each stage being of one century's duration. 1. He stood on one foot, holding up the other with both hands towards heaven, his eyes fixed immovably upon the sun 2. He stood on one great toe 3 He took for sustenance nothing but water 4 He lived similarly upon air 5 He remained immersed in the water 6 He was buried in the earth, continuing, as during the last penance, in continued adoration. 7 He performed the same act in the fire. 8 He stood on his head with his feet upwards 9 He stood resting on one hand 10 He hung by his hands from a tree. 11 He hung on a tree by his feet, with his head downwards (The twelfth degree Moor has, for some reason, omitted)

By means like these, termed the *Yog*, the ascetic *Yogī* is enabled to obtain nine several gifts, that set him above all the laws of Nature For example, he may expand or contract his body to any size he pleases, he may float in the air upon a sunbeam, he may exert all his sense at an infinite distance from the objects of them, with other capabilities of like kind

And with respect to the sixth penance of Taraka, this, incredible as it appears, is still performed. To be buried alive in a small vault covered deep with earth until a crop of grain, sown over him at the time of inhumation, shall be ripe for cutting, is yet esteemed the most efficacious of good works for extorting from heaven the blessing most desired by the patient or his *employer* (the doctrine of *vicarious* atonement being most thoroughly Hindoo) The English Resident at Runjeet Singh's court has minutely described all the preparation made by the royal proxy, (whose regular trade it was thus to die for others), and the successful completion of his penance, which occupied the space of six weeks The Resident assisted at the closing and the opening of the vault, and was certain that no deception could possibly have been practised by the Yogi The blessing aimed at was the gift of fecundity for a favourite queen of Runjeet's

The "Taurobolia," or *Baptism of Blood*, during the later ages of the Western Empire, held the foremost place, as the means of purification from sin, however atrocious Prudentius has left a minute description of this horrid rite, in which the person to be regenerated, being stripped of his clothing, descended into a pit, which was covered with planks pierced full of holes, a bull was slaughtered upon them, whose hot blood, streaming down through these apertures (after the fashion of a shower-bath), thoroughly drenched the recipient below The selection of the particular victim proves this ceremony in connection with the Mithraica, which latter, as Justin says, had a "Baptism for the remission of Sins", and the Bull being in that religion the recognised emblem of *life*, his blood necessarily constituted the most effectual laver of regeneration. No more conclusive evidence of the value then attached to the Taurobolia can be adduced, than the fact mentioned by Lampridius that the priest-emperor Heliogabalus thought it necessary to submit to its performance, and a pit, constructed for the purpose as late as the fourth century, has lately been discovered within the sacred precincts of the Temple at Eleusis, the most holy spot in all Greece

The subject will find its most appropriate conclusion in the list of "Degrees" to be taken in the Mysteries, as laid down by M Lajard, in his elaborate treatise, 'Le Culte de Mithra,'* These degrees were divided into four stages, Terrestrial, Aerial, Igneous, and Divine, each consisting of three The Terrestrial comprised the Soldier, the Lion, the Bull The Aerial, the Vulture, the Ostrich, the Raven. The Igneous, the Gryphon, the Horse, the Sun. The Divine, the Eagle, the Sparrow-Hawk, the Father of fathers Lajard's theory is best elucidated by quoting his way of expounding a very frequent cylinder-subject He finds the admission to the degree of "The Soldier," in the group where a man is seen standing before a "hierophant," or priest, who stands on the back of a bull *couchant* on a platform The hierophant, wearing a cap tipped by a crescent, holds out to the neophyte a curved sword, symbol of admission into the Order. A priestess stands apart, separated from him by the horn, or Tree of Life, over which soars the emblem of the Assyrian Triad Her cap is tipped by the Sun-star, but she also wears the crescent, to show the hermaphrodite nature of Mylitta!

* Lajard discovers upon the Babylonian cylinders representations of admission to the several degrees, of which they were given, as certificate to the initiated and accounts for their enormous extant numbers by the supposition that every one, upon proceeding to a higher degree, threw away the cylinder marking the preceding one But the complicated system of the Mithraici was evidently the creation of much later times, and of a religion vainly struggling for life

Fig. 5

ST AUGUSTINE ON GNOSTICISM

The transition from orthodoxy to Gnosticism, in its last and most elaborate phase is well pointed out by the following reminiscences of St. Augustine, describing his own experiences. In his eighteenth or nineteenth year he had begun to study the Scriptures, to satisfy himself as to the truth of the religion in which he had been brought up "Consequently I set to work to study the Holy Scriptures, in order that I might discover what was their true character And lo! I behold a thing not discovered unto the proud, nor revealed unto babes, but humble in gait, lofty in issue, and veiled in mysteries, and I was not such a one as could enter therein, neither to bow down my neck unto the steps thereof For I did not think then, as I speak *now*, when I was studying Scripture, but it seemed to me unworthy to be compared with the sublimity of Cicero's eloquence. Nevertheless that Scripture was such as should grow up together with babes, but I disdained to be a babe, and being puffed up with pride I fancied myself a grown-up man So it came to pass that I fell in with men full of pride, dotards, too carnal, and great talkers, in whose mouth is a snare of the Devil, and bird-lime made up with a mixture of the syllables of Thy Name, and of our Lord Jesus Christ, and of the Paraclete's, our Comforter the Holy Ghost All these names did not proceed out of their mouth except as far as the sound and echo of the tongue go, but their heart was utterly void of truth And they used to repeat 'Truth and Truth,' and so did they repeat her name to me, but she was nowhere amongst them, but they spoke false things, not only concerning thee who art the Truth in truth, but even concerning the elements of this world of ours, thy creation, concerning which even the philosophers, who declared what is true, I ought to have slighted for the love of Thee, O my Father, the Supreme Good, the Beauty of all things beautiful. O Truth! Truth! how inwardly did the marrow of my soul sigh after thee even then, whilst *they* were perpetually dinning thy name into my ears, and after various fashions with the mere voice, and with *many and huge books* of theirs. And these were the dishes upon which were served up to me who was hungering after thee, nothing but the *Sun and the Moon*, thy fair works indeed, but not thyself, and not even the *first* amongst thy works. For thy spiritual works are before those corporeal works, however splendid and heavenly they may be. But even for those, thy higher works, I hungered and thirsted not, but for thee only, O Truth! wherein there is no change, neither shadow of turning. And again there were set before me, in those same dishes, splendid phantoms, than which it were even better to love the Sun himself, for *he* was true as far as regards one's eyes, rather than to love those fictions whereby the soul was deceived through the eyes. And yet because I believed them to be Thee, I ate thereof though not greedily, because Thou didst not taste in my mouth as thou really art, for thou wert not those empty fictions; neither was I nourished thereby, but rather weakened. Food in dreams is like to the food of one awake, yet the sleepers are not fed by the same, for they sleep on: but those dishes were not in any wise like unto Thee as thou *now* hast spoken to me, &c."

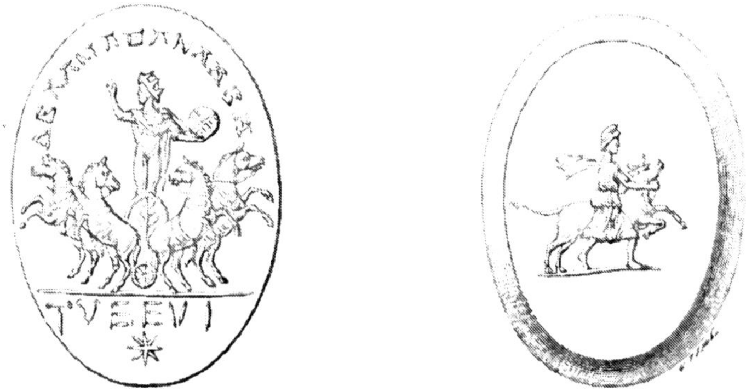

Fig. 6.

THE WORSHIP OF SERAPIS.

I. The Figured Representations of Serapis

The next great series of monuments to be considered are those emanating from the worship of Serapis, that mysterious deity, who, under his varying forms, had, during the second and third centuries of our era, completely usurped the sovereignty of his brother Jupiter, and reduced him to the rank of a mere planetary Genius. Unlike the generality of the deities who figure upon the Gnostic stones, the *Alexandrian* Serapis does not belong to the primitive mythology of Egypt.* His worship may be said to be only coeval with the rise of Alexandria, into which city it was introduced from Sinope by the first Ptolemy, in consequence of the command (and repeated threats, in case of neglect) of a vision which had appeared to him. After three years of ineffectual negotiation, Ptolemy at last obtained the god from Scythotherius, king of Sinope; but when the citizens still refused to part with their idol, a report was spread, that it had spontaneously found its way from the temple down to the Egyptian ships lying in the harbour.

The prevalent opinion amongst the Greeks was that the figure represented Jupiter *Dis* (Aidoneus) and the one by his side, *Proserpine*. This latter the envoys were ordered by the same divine messenger, to leave in its native shrine. Another story, also mentioned by Tacitus,† made the statue to have been brought from Seleucia by Ptolemy III, but this rested on slighter authority. It is, however, a curious confirmation of this last tradition that Serapis is named by Plutarch ("Alexander,") as the chief deity of *Babylon* (Seleucia in later times) at the date of the Macedonian Conquest—a proof that

* The difference between him and the ancient Theban Serapis (as the Greeks translated his title "Osor-Api"), shall be pointed out futher on.

† Who narrates the whole affair at great length—a proof of the influence of the religion in his day—in his History, iv. 84.

he at least regarded that god as identical with *Belus* Now, it is a remarkable coincidence that *Ana*, the First Person in the primitive Chaldean Triad, is likewise "King of the Lower World," and that his symbol, the vertical wedge, stands also for the numeral 60, which last is often used to express hieroglyphically the name Ana

It was Timotheus, an Athenian Eumolpid, and, in virtue of his descent, Diviner to the king, who indicated Pontus as the residence of the unknown god, whose apparition had so disquieted the monarch by commanding himself to be sent for without declaring whence. The figure, seen in the vision, was that of a *youth*, a circumstance that tallies ill with the mature majesty of the great god of Alexandria * But the Helios Dionysos, a veritable Chrishna, who graces the reverse of the gold medallion of Pharnaces II, coined at Sinope in the following century, agrees much more exactly with this description of the nocturnal visitor.

Speedily did Serapis become the sole lord of his new home, and speculations as to his true nature employed the ingenuity of the philosophers at Alexandria, down to the times when they were superseded by the discussions on the doctrine of the Trinity, waged with equal zeal but infinitely worse temper. Every conflicting religion strove to claim him as the grand representative of their own doctrine Macrobius has preserved one of the most ingenious of these interpretations, as made by the 'Rationalists,' a party so strong amongst the later Greeks (I 20) "The City of Alexandria pays an almost frantic worship to Serapis and Isis, nevertheless they show that all this veneration is merely offered to the *Sun* under that name, both by their placing the corn-measure upon his head, and by accompanying his statue with the figure of an animal having three heads, of these heads, the middle and the largest one is a

* The great god of Assyria, Adad, "The One," the oracle-giving Jupiter of Heliopolis, was thus figured in his *golden* statue as a beardless youth, brandishing aloft a whip and holding in his left hand the thunderbolt and wheat-ears The rays crowning his head pointed downwards to signify their influence upon the earth, who stood before him in the figure of *Atergatis*, the rays in her crown pointing upwards, to express the *springing up* of her gifts She was supported, like Cybele, upon the backs of lions

lion's, that which rises on the right is a dog's in a peaceable and fawning attitude, whilst the left part of the neck terminates in that of a ravening wolf. All these bestial forms are connected together by the wreathed body of a serpent, which raises its head up towards the god's right hand, on which side the monster is placed. The *lion's* head typifies the Present, because its condition between the Past and the Future is strong and fervent. The Past is signified by the *wolf's* head, because the memory of all things past is scratched away from us and utterly consumed. The emblem of the fawning *dog* represents the Future, the domain of inconstant and flattering hope. But whom should Past, Present and Future serve except their Authors? His head crowned with the *calathus* typifies the *height* of the planet above us, also his all-powerful *capaciousness*, since unto him all things earthly do return, being drawn up by the heat he emits. Moreover when Nicocreon, tyrant of Cyprus, consulted Serapis as to which of the gods he ought to be accounted, he received the following response:—

"'A god I am, such as I show to thee,
The starry heavens my head, my trunk the sea,
Earth forms my feet, mine ears the air supplies,
The sun's far-darting, brilliant rays mine eyes.'"*

From all this it is evident that the nature of Serapis and the Sun is one and indivisible. Again, Isis is universally worshipped as the type of earth, or Nature in subjection to the Sun. For this cause the body of the goddess is covered with continuous rows of *udders*, to declare that the universe is maintained by the perpetual nourishing of the Earth or Nature." This last curious remark shows that Macrobius regarded the Alexandrian Isis as the same with the Ephesian Diana, for the ancient Isis of Egypt had only the usual complement of breasts. This philosopher had started with the axiom (I. 17), "Omnes deos referri ad Solem," and begins by demonstrating from the various epithets

* I cannot help suspecting that this description supplied Basilides with the idea of his celebrated *Pantheus* the Abraxas-figure. The head of the *bird* was the fittest emblem of the air, the *serpent*, according to Herodotus, was the offspring of earth, the *breast* of man was the Homeric attribute of Neptune.

of Apollo, that *he* was the same god with the one styled the Sun. He then proceeds to prove the same of Bacchus, Hermes, Aesculapius, and Hercules. His ingenious explanation of the serpent-entwined rod of Hermes, and club of Aesculapius, will be found applied further on to the elucidation of the remarkable symbol on the reverse of all the Chnuphis amulets. After this, Macrobius passes in review the attributes and legends of Adonis and Atys, also of Osiris and Horus, and comes to the same conclusion concerning the real nature of all these personages, adding parenthetically a very fanciful exposition of the Signs of the Zodiac, as being merely so many emblems of the solar influence in the several regions of creation Nemesis, Paris, Saturn, Jupiter, and finally the Assyrian Adad, are all reduced by him to the same signification

This brings us to that most wondrous identification of all, which Hadrian mentions in a letter to his brother-in-law Servianus, preserved by the historian Vopiscus in his Life of the Tyrant Saturninus "Those who worship Serapis are likewise Christians, even those who style themselves the bishops of Christ are devoted to Serapis The very Patriarch himself,* when he comes to Egypt, is forced by some to adore Serapis, by others to worship Christ. There is but one God for them all, Him do the Christians, Him do the Jews, Him do the Gentiles, all alike worship" Severus Alexander, too, who daily paid his devotions to Christ and Abraham, did none the less expend large sums in decorating the temples of Serapis and Isis "with statues, *couches*, and all things pertaining to their Mysteries,"† whilst he left the other gods of Rome to take care of themselves

And as connected with the same subject, it may be here observed that the conventional portrait of the Saviour is in all probability borrowed from the head of Serapis, so full of grave and pensive majesty. Of the first converts, the Jewish foredilections were so powerful that we may be sure that no attempt was made to portray His countenance until many generations

* The Patriarch of Tiberias, head of the Jewish religion, after the destruction of Jerusalem

† A very favourite representation of Isis upon our talismans shows her reclining upon a couch

after all who had beheld it on earth had passed away.* Nevertheless, the importance so long attached to the pretended letter of Lentulus to the emperor, Tiberius, describing Christ's personal appearance, demands a notice in this place Its monkish Latinity and style betray it, at first sight, for the authorship of some mediæval divine Yet, incredible as it may seem, even a learned man like Grynæus has been so besotted through his pious longing for the *reality* of such a record, as to persuade himself that Lentulus, a Roman Senator and an eminent historian, could have written in the exact phrase of a mendicant friar "There has appeared in our times, and still lives, a Man of great virtue, named Christ Jesus, who is called by the Gentiles a Prophet of Truth, but whom his own disciples called the Son of God, raising the dead, and healing diseases A man indeed of lofty stature, handsome, having a venerable countenance, which the beholders can both love and fear His hair verily somewhat wavy and curling, somewhat brightish and resplendent in colour, flowing down upon his shoulders, having a parting in the middle of the head after the fashion of the Nazarenes, &c" (Grynæus, 'Orthodoxia' I p 2) This forgery reminds one of Pliny's remark, "Pariunt desideria non traditos vultus, sicut in Homero evenit." The wish is father to the image of the venerated object; and the conception is too joyfully accepted by the loving soul for it to trouble itself overmuch in scrutinizing the legitimacy of the same. for, as Martial exclaims with full truth "quis enim damnet sua vota libenter?"

But to return to the Egypt of the times of Gnosticism In the very focus of that theosophy, Alexandria, the syncretistic sects which sprang up so rankly there during the three first centuries of the Roman empire, had good grounds for making out Serapis a prototype of Christ, considered as Lord and Maker of all, and Judge of the quick and the dead For the response given to Nicocreon, above quoted, evinces that the philosophers at least saw in Serapis nothing more than the emblem of the 'Anima

* What proves the want of any real authority for the portraits of the Saviour is the fact that the earliest monuments in sculpture or painting, represent him as *youthful* and *beardless*

Mundi,' the *Spirit* of whom Nature universal is the *body*, for they held the doctrine of

> " the one harmonious whole,
> Whose body Nature is, and God the soul"

So that by an easy transition Serapis came to be worshipped as the embodiment of the One Supreme, whose representative on earth was Christ

The very *construction* of the grand Colossus of Serapis ingeniously set forth these ideas of his character It was formed out of plates of *all the metals*, artfully joined together, to typify the harmonious union of different elements in the fabric of the universe, the "moles et machina mundi" This statue was placed upon the summit of an artificial hill (whose vast interior was divided into vaulted halls, containing the famous library), ascended by a flight of a hundred steps—a style of building totally diverse from the native Egyptian and the Grecian model, but exactly following the Indian usage, as may be seen by the grand pagoda of Siva at Tanjore, and by the *topes* and *dagobas* of the Buddhists.

The remarkable construction of this Colossus may reasonably be supposed to have suggested to the Alexandrian Jew, who *completed* the Book of Daniel, the notion of the similarly compacted *Image* which figures in Nebuchadnezzar's Dream That his description of the latter was penned long after the coming of Serapis into that city is manifest from the minute details this *prophet* gives concerning the constant squabbles going on between Antiochus Epiphanes and Ptolemy Philometor, his nephew, together with the final intervention of the Roman Senate The popular belief of the Alexandrians (Christian as well as pagan) was that the profanation of this statue would be the signal for heaven and earth to collapse at once into pristine chaos—a notion bearing clear testimony to the grand idea embodied by the figure At last, however, although his worship, thus defended by deep-rooted fear, had been tolerated by the Christian government long after the other gods of Egypt had been swept away, this wonderful Colossus was broken down by "that perpetual enemy of peace and virtue" the

Patriarch Theophilus, in the reign of Theodosius, and its mutilated trunk, dragged triumphantly through the streets by the mob of rejoicing fanatics, was ultimately buried in the Hippodrome.

Like that of Mithras, the worship of Serapis was widely diffused over the West. A very curious exemplification of this is to be found in Ammianus' notice that Mederich, king of the Alemanni, had, when detained as a hostage in Gaul, been taught certain Greek Mysteries, and for that reason changed the name of his son Agenerich into *Serapion.* But Serapis had a natural claim to the adoration of the Gauls, who, as Cæsar tells us, actually boasted of descent from *Dis Pater.*

The new-comer from Sinope does not seem to have brought his name with him When Ptolemy consulted his own priesthood upon this important point, Manetho boldly identified the Pontic god with their own Osor-Apis, chiefly on the score of his attribute Cerberus, which he considered the counterpart of the hippopotamus-headed Typhon who attends Osor-Apis in his character of sovereign of the Lower World This deity is no other than the Bull Apis, who, after death, assumes the figure of Osiris, the regular form of Egyptian apotheosis, and so frequently seen applied to deceased kings Osor-Apis, as he now becomes, is depicted as a man with the head of a bull, and carrying the ensigns by which we usually recognize Osiris The god of Alexandria therefore differs in form as widely as in origin from the original patron of Thebes, with whom he has no other affinity than in name, and *that* rests only on the arbitrary interpretation of the Egyptian priests, so successful in persuading the Greeks that the mythology of the whole world was but a plagiarism from their own.

M Mariette in 1860 excavated the Theban Serapeum, as it was called in Roman times, with its long avenue of sphinxes, he also discovered the catacombs where the Apis Bulls were deposited after death, and found there no fewer than sixty, two of their mummies yet reposing undisturbed It is amusing to notice how neatly the Greeks turned the Coptic Osor-Apis into the more euphonious ὁ Σάραπις.

II. The Probable Origin of Serapis.

The ancient speculations cited in the preceding chapter are all baseless theories, due to the ingenious refinements of the Alexandrian literati, and springing out of the system of allegorical interpretation in which the New Platonists so much delighted. It is evident that upon his *first introduction* into Egypt, Serapis was regarded by the Alexandrians as identical with Aidoneus, or Dis, the Lord of the Lower World. Now, all his attributes suggest him to have been of *Indian* origin, and no other than *Yama*, "Lord of Hell," attended by his dog "Çarbara," *the spotted*, who has the epithet "Triçira," *three-headed*, and by his serpent "Çesha," called "Regent of Hades;" in fact, some have discovered in the name Serapis* but the Grecian form of Yama's epithet, "Sraddha-deva," *Lord of the obsequies*, that is, of the funeral sacrifices offered to the *Pitris* or *Manes*. Yama also is styled "Lord of souls," and "Judge of the dead;" another office assimilating him to Serapis in the character under which the latter came to be specially regarded —a point, moreover, which at a later date afforded stronger reasons for identifying him with Christ. A plausible etymology of the name Serapis may be found in another of Yama's epithets, "Asrik-pa" the *Blood-drinker*. This explanation is confirmed to some extent by the ancient tradition, of which Homer makes such fine use when he describes Ulysses' mode of evoking the ghosts, and their eagerness to lap up the life-blood of the victim (Od. xi. 35) —

"Seizing the victim sheep I pierced their throats,
Flowed the black blood, and filled the hollow trench;
Then from the abyss, eager their thirst to slake,
Came swarming up the spirits of the dead."

And connected with the same notion was the practice of strewing *roses* over the graves of departed friends—

"Purpureos spargam flores et fungar inani munere,"

for (as Servius explains it) the *red* colour of the flower

* It is not improbable that the name under which the god was worshipped at *Sinope* had something of this sound, and which suggested to Manetho the idea of identifying him with his own Osor-Api.

represented *blood*, and thereby served as a substitute for the living victim.*

This analogy between Yama and Serapis may be further extended by the consideration of certain other points connected with the office of the former deity. For example, unto the souls of the righteous he appears as "Dharma-rāja," and has a servant "Karma-la" (the Hermes Psychopompos of the Greeks), who brings them into his presence upon a self-moving car. But unto the wicked he is "Yama," and has for *them* another minister, "Kash-Mala," who drags them before him with halters round their necks, over rough and stony places. Other titles of Yama are "Kritānta" and "Mrityu." The connection of the latter with *Mors* is evident enough, making it a fitting appellation for *Dis* (*Ditis*), in which again unmistakably lies the root of our name *Death*, applied to the same Principle of Destruction.

Yama as "Sraddha-deva," monarch of "Pātāla" (the infernal regions), has for consort Bhavani, who hence takes the title of "Patala-devi," as upon Earth she is "Bhu-devi," in heaven, "Swardevi." Her lord owns besides Çarbara, another dog named "Çyama," the *Black One* (now we see wherefore the mediæval familiar spirits like Cornelius Agrippa's black spaniel, and Faustus' "pudel" chose that particular figure), whom he employs as the minister of his vengeance. As Judge of Souls he displays two faces, the one benign, the other terrific. Another of his titles is "Kalantika," *Time as the Destroyer*: it can hardly be a mere accidental coincidence that such was the exact name given to the head-dress worn by the Egyptian priests when officiating—in later times a purple cloth covering the head, and falling down upon the neck, surmounted by two plumes.

* One of the most frequented places of pilgrimage at Benares is the 'Gyan Bapi,' "Well of Knowledge," in the depths whereof Siva himself resides. It was dug by the genius Rishi, with that god's own trident, to relieve the world after a twelve years' drought. The pilgrims throw into it offerings of all kinds, flowers included. Another well in the same city of supreme efficacy for the washing away of all sin, is the *Manikarnika*, so called from the ear-ring of Mahadeva, which fell into it. Vishnu had dug this well with his *changra*, quoit, and filled it with the luminous sweat of his body.

"Kali-Bhavani," the Destructive Female Principle is represented* in this character with a visage exactly identical with the most ancient type of the Grecian Gorgon—such as we still behold it guarding the Etruscan sepulchres, and lowering horrifically upon the sacrilegious intruder, as in that notable example in the tomb of the Volumni at Perugia, where it forms the centrepiece of the ceiling of the grand hall. Formed of a Tiger's head in its first conception by the excited fancy of Hindoo superstition, the Etruscan demon still exhibits the same protruded tongue, huge tusks, glaring eyes, wings in the hair, and serpents twining about the throat. Of such aspect was doubtless that "Gorgon's Head, the work of the Cyclops," which was shown to Pausanias as the most notable object in the Argive Acropolis—a proof that the earliest essays of Pelasgic art had been made in realising this idea. Again, in that most ancient monument of Grecian art, the Coffer of Cypselus (made before B.C. 600), the same traveller states (v. 19.), "Behind Polynices stands a female figure, having tusks as savage as those of a wild beast, and the nails of her fingers like unto talons: the inscription above her, *they tell you* means Κῆρ (Fate)." This name therefore must have been a *foreign* word, translated to Pausanias by the Custodian of the Temple. Plutarch (Life of Aratus) supplies another singular illustration of the Worship of these terrific idols of the olden time in the most polished ages of Greece. The Artemis of Pellene was of so dreadful an aspect that none dared to look upon her: and when carried in procession, her sight blasted the very tree and crops as she passed. When the Ætolians were actually in possession of and plundering the town, her priestess, by bringing this image out from the shrine, struck them with such terror that they made a precipitate retreat. This Artemis consequently must have been a veritable Hecate, a true Queen of Hell, an idol moreover of *wood*, ξόανον (like her of Ephesus), otherwise the priestess had not been able to wield it so effectually to scare away the marauders. Again, the recorded dream of Cimon, which presaged his death, was that a black bitch bayed

* Roth, 'Zeitschrift der Morgenlandischen Gesellschaft,' iv. p. 425, and Muir in Royal Asiatic Society's Journal, i. p. 287.

at him in a half-human voice, "Come to me, I and my whelps will receive thee gladly." The Hellenic gods, now and then shew themselves under an aspect strangely at variance with their usual benevolent and *jovial* character. A true Siva was that "Dionysos Omestes" (The Cannibal), unto whom Themistocles, forced by the Diviners, sacrificed the three sons of Sandauce, own sister to Xerxes, when taken prisoners on the eve of the Battle of Salamis. It must be remembered that tradition made Perseus bring back the Gorgon's Head, trophy of his success, from Ethiopia, a synonym at first for the remotest East—it being only in Roman times that "Ethiopia" was restricted to a single province of Africa The *harpe* too, the weapon lent to the hero by Hermes, is from its form no other than the ankuṣa, elephant-hook, which is carried for attribute by so many of the Hindoo Deities * Sufficient explanation this why Persephone (*Destroying-slayer*) was assigned by the earliest Greeks as Consort to Aidoneus, and also why Ulysses, on his visit to her realms, should have been alarmed,

> "Lest from deep Hell Persephone the dread
> Should send the terror of the Gorgon's Head"

From the influence of this terror upon the otherwise undaunted wanderer, these same two lines came to be considered as endued with a wonderfully strong repellent power, for Marcellus Empiricus prescribes them to be whispered into the ear of any one choking from a bone or other matter sticking in his throat; or else to write them out on a paper to be tied around his throat, "Which will be equally effectual"

Lucian remarks ('Philopatris,') that the reason why the ancient warriors bore the Gorgon's Head upon their shields was because it served for an amulet against dangers of every sort, on the same account, in all likelihood, was it put for device on many archaic coinages, Populonia, Paros, &c For

* The Gorgon of the gems ('Ant Gems,' Pl XX, 4), and of the coin of Neapolis is regularly to be seen to this day, sculptured in relief upon the pillar set up on each side of the gates of Hindoo temples, as I am informed by our great oriental archæologist, Col Pearse She goes by the name of "Keeper of the Gate" Now we see why her head decorated the pediments of temples in Greece and Rome, and formed the keystone of triumphal arches even in the time of Constantine, as the lately-discovered entrance to his "Forum of Taurus" convincingly attests

what could be more effective for the purpose of scaring away all evil spirits than the visible countenance of the Queen of Hell? Timomachus the painter (contemporary with the first Cæsar) made his reputation by such a subject, "præcipue tamen ars ei favisse in Gorgone visa est," are the words of Pliny, which masterpiece is supposed the original of the horrific fresco discovered at Pompeii, the finest example of the art that has reached our times Many centuries after the fall of Paganism did this image retain its power, Munter figures ('Sinnbilder der Christen') a Gorgon's Head surrounded by the phonetic legend, +VOMEΛΛAINHMEΛΛAINOMENAOCOΦICHΛHЄC ЄKЄOCΛЄONBPVXHCЄIKЄOCAPNOCKVMHCH, intended for — Υἱὸς Θεοῦ Μελαίνη μελαινομένη, ὡς ὄφις εἴλει ἡσυχῇ, ὡς λέων βρυχήσει, καὶ ὡς ἄρνος κοιμήσει "Black, blackened one, as a serpént thou coilest thyself quietly, thou shalt roar like a lion, thou shalt go to sleep like a lamb!" The same inscription, but so barbarously spelt as to be unintelligible, probably forms the legend upon the famous Seal of St. Servatius, preserved in Maestricht Cathedral. The seal is a large disc of green jasper, engraved on both sides, and is attached to a small slab of porphyry, traditionally passing for the Saint's portable altar. Servatius died A.D 389, but the workmanship of his seal betokens the tenth or eleventh century for its origin. An important evidence of the veneration of the Christian Byzantines for their guardian demon is afforded by the exhumation (Spring of 1869) in the Ahmedan, Constantinople, of the Colossal Gorgonion, six feet high from chin to brow, carved in almost full relief on each side of an immense marble block, which once formed the keystone of the gateway to the Forum of Constantine Though the execution betrays the paralysis of the Decline, yet the general effect still remains grandiose and awe-inspiring

Having thus traced Bhavani in her progress from Archaic Greek to Byzantine times, let us observe the part she plays in the superstitions of Imperial Rome. The idea, full of novel horrors, was gladly seized by the extravagant genius of Lucan*

* Who had in all probability learnt them at some of the Mysteries, all of Asiatic origin, so popular in his times with all persons making pretensions to the title of philosophers

to animate the exorcisms of his Thessalian sorceress Erictho (Pharsalia, vi 695)

"And Chaos, ever seeking to enfold
Unnumbered worlds in thy confusion old
And Earth's dull god, who pining still beneath
Life's lingering burthen, pinest for tardy death
* * * * *
Tisiphone, and Thou her sister fell,
Megaera, thus regardless of my spell,
Why haste ye not with sounding scourge to chase
The soul accursed through hell's void formless space?
Say, must I call you by the names your right,
And drag the hell-hounds forth to th' upper light?
Midst death I'll dog your steps at every turn,
Chase from each tomb, and drive from every urn
And *thou*, still wont with visage not thine own,
To join the gods round the celestial throne,
Though yet thy pallor doth the truth betray,
And hint the horrors of thy gloomy
Thee, Hecate, in thy *true* form I'll show,
Nor let thee change the face thou wearest below
I'll tell what feasts thy lingering steps detain
In earth's deep centre, and thy will enchain,
Tell what the pleasures that thee so delight,
And what tie binds thee to the King of Night,
And by what union wert thou so defiled,
Thy very mother would not claim her child,
—I'll burst thy caves, the world's most evil Lord,
And pour the sun upon thy realms abhorred,
Striking thee lifeless by the sudden day,
If still reluctant my behests to obey
Or must I call *Him* at whose whispered *Name*
Earth trembles awestruck through her inmost frame?
Who views the Gorgon's face without a veil,
And with her own scourge makes Erinnys quail
To whom the abyss, unseen by you, is given
To which your regions are the upper heaven,
Who dares the oath that binds all gods to break,
And marks the sanction of the Stygian lake?

All these personifications are in a spirit quite foreign to that of Grecian mythology, but thoroughly imbued with that of India Lucan's Chaos is the Hindoo Destroyer, the Negro giant, "Maha-Pralaya," swallowing up the gods themselves in his wide-gaping jaws His "Rector terrae" pining for the promised annihilation that is so long in coming, finds no parallel in classical religions,* and his character remains to me utterly inexplicable. His Furies "hunting souls to make them fly," instead of being like the old awful Eumenides, the impartial avengers of guilt, are mere demons, or churchyard ghouls But his Hecate is manifestly Bhavani herself, her "facies Erebi" being the Gorgonian aspect which the latter was when reigning in "Yama-putri," but which she puts off when presiding on earth, or in heaven, whilst the "infernal banquets" that so enchant her are the human sacrifices regularly offered up by Bhavani's special votaries, the Thugs. In the first, or *infernal* aspect, a true "facies Erebi," she is depicted wearing a necklace of human skulls and grasping in each hand a naked victim ready to be devoured. She probably still shows us in what shape the Artemis of Pallene appeared to scare away the Ætolian plunderers The title of her lord "pessimus mundi arbiter" is far more applicable to the Destroyer Siva than to the inoffensive Pluto of the Greeks Unless indeed the Neronean poet may have heard something of the Demiurgus Ildabaoth, "Son of Darkness, or Erebus," existing under a different name in some ancient theogony The Gnostics did not invent—they merely borrowed and applied

Bhavani, in her character of "Kali," is sculptured as a terminal figure, the exact counterpart in outline of the Ephesian Diana Even the stags, those remarkable adjuncts to the *shoulders* of the latter, are seen in a similar position springing from Kali's *hands* The multiplied breasts of the Ephesian statue were also given to the Alexandrian Isis, who is allowed by Creuzer and the rest to be the Hindoo goddess in her character of "Parvati" Now this remark applies only to her statue in the Serapeum, not to those belonging to the ancient Pharaonic religion, and Macrobius's expressions show that her real character *there* was as much a matter of dispute as that of her companion, Serapis Again, Diana as *Hecate* or Proserpine, belongs to the infernal world over which she rules with the same authority as Bhavani over Yama-Putri. The Ephesian

* Unless, perhaps, obscurely shadowed forth by Hesiod, from whom Milton drew his grand picture of Chaos, on whom wait—

'Orcus and Hades and the *dreaded Name*
Of Demogorgon"

image, made of cypress wood, had "fallen down from heaven," which only means, had come from some very remote and unknown source.

III Monuments of the Serapis Worship.

Innumerable are the statues, bas-reliefs, and gems, many of them in the best syle of Roman art, emanating from the worship of Serapis, a thing not to be wondered at in the case of a divinity whose idea involved the two strongest principles that actuate the conduct of mankind—the love of riches and the fear of death For the god of the subterranean world was necessarily lord also of its treasures, a truth expressed by the dedication to Serapis of an altar as "Iovi custodi et genio thesaurorum" (Winckelmann, 'Pierres Gravées de Stosch,' p 83) And similarly the older Roman Pluto takes the title of "Jupiter Stygius," but the comprehensiveness of the idea as expanded by the monotheistic tendency of later times is most fully manifested by the invocation (Raspe, No 1490) ЄIC ZЄYC CAPAΠIC AΓION ONOMA CABAꞶ ΦꞶC ANATOΛH XΘꞶN "One Jupiter, Serapis, Holy Name, Sabaoth, the Light, the Day-spring, the Earth!"

Talismanic gems very commonly bear the full length figure, or the bust of Serapis, with the legend ЄIC ΘЄOC CAPAΠIC (often abbreviated into Є Θ C), "There is but one God, and he is Serapis" ЄIC ZꞶN ΘЄOC, "The One Living God." Sometimes the purpose of the amulet is distinctly expressed by the inscription, NIKAO CAPAΠIC TON ΦΘONON, "Baffle the Evil-eye, O Serapis" or in the curious example published by Caylus, where the god stands between Venus and Horus, and the legend KATA XPHMATICMON intimates that the gem had been "so" engraved in consequence of a vision or other divine intimation. Around his bust on a jasper (Praun) appears the invocation, convincing proof of his supposed supremacy, ΦYΛACCЄ ΔIA, "Protect Jupiter," the ancient king of heaven being now degraded to the rank of an astral genius and benignant horoscope. Invocations like the above bear the unmistakable stamp of the age when the old, liberal, mythology of the West, which had pictured Heaven as a well-ordered monarchy peopled by innumerable deities, each one having his own proper and undisputed position therein, was fast giving place to the gloomy superstitions of Syria, which made the tutelary divinity of each nation or sect the sole god of Heaven, condemning those of all other races as mere deceivers and evil spirits.

There are, however, many gems, fine both as to material and workmanship, which give us, besides Serapis, the primitive Egyptian gods exactly as they appear in the most ancient monuments, but engraved in the unmistakable style of Roman art. Most of these are to be referred to the efforts of Hadrian to resuscitate the *forms* of that old religion whose *life* had long before passed away in this equally with the grander department of sculpture. Under his zealous patronage, the religion of the Pharaohs blazed up for a moment with a brilliant but factitious lustre, a phenomenon often observed to precede the extinction of a long established system.* To this period belongs a beautiful sard of my own, which represents Serapis enthroned exactly as Macrobius describes him, whilst in front *stands* Isis, holding in one hand the sistrum, in the other a wheatsheaf, with the legend, HKYPIAEICIC AΓNH† "Immaculate is our Lady Isis!" This address is couched in the exact words applied later to the personage who succeeded to the form, titles, symbols and ceremonies of Isis with even less variation than marked the other interchange alluded to above. The "Black Virgins" so highly venerated in certain French Cathedrals during the long night of the Middle Ages, proved when at last examined by antiquarian eyes to be basalt statues of the Egyptian goddess, which having merely changed the name, continued to receive more than pristine adoration. Her devotees carried into the new priesthood the ancient badges of their profession, "the obligation to celibacy," the tonsure, the

* Shering, in his 'Benares,' observes that the Hindoos are now building and restoring temples everywhere with greater zeal and cost than at any time since the final overthrow of Buddhism, and yet the religion itself is utterly worn out.

† In inscriptions of this period the long I is usually written EI.

bell, and the surplice—omitting unfortunately the frequent and complete ablutions enjoined by the older ritual. The holy image still moves in procession as when Juvenal laughed at it (vi 530), "Escorted by the tonsured, surpliced, train" Even her proper title "Domina," exact translation of the Sanscrit *Isi*, survives with slight change, in the modern "Madonna" (Mater-Domina) By a singular permutation of meaning the flower borne in the hand of each, the lotus, former symbol of *perfection* (because in leaf, flower, fruit, it gave the figure of the Circle, as Jamblichus explains it), and therefore of fecundity, is now interpreted as signifying the opposite to the last—virginity itself The tinkling *sistrum*, so well pleasing to Egyptian ears, has unluckily found a substitute in that most hideous of all noise-makers, the clangorous bell But this latter instrument came directly from the Buddhistic ritual in which it forms as essential a part of the religion as it did in Celtic Christianity, where the Holy Bell was the actual *object* of worship to the new converts. The bell in its present form was unknown to the Greeks and Romans its normal shape is Indian, and the first true bell-founders were the Buddhist Chinese Again *relic-worship* became, after the third century, the chief form of Christianity throughout the world, which finds its parallel in the fact that a fragment of a bone of a Buddha (that is, holy man in whom the deity had dwelt during his life) is actually indispensable for the consecration of a *dagobah*, or temple of that religion, equally as a similar particle of saintliness is a *sine quâ non* for the setting-up of a Roman-Catholic altar

Very curious and interesting would it be to pursue the subject, and trace how much of Egyptian, and second-hand Indian, symbolism has passed over into the possession of a church that would be beyond measure indignant at any reclamation on the part of the rightful owners The high cap and hooked staff of the Pharaonic god become the mitre and crosier of the bishop, the very term, *Nun*, is Coptic, and with its present meaning the erected oval symbol of productive Nature, christened into the *Vesica piscis*, becomes the proper framework for pictures of the Divinity the *Crux ansata*, that very expressive emblem of the union of the Male and Female

Principles, whence comes all Life, and therefore placed as the symbol of Life in the hands of gods, now, by simple inversion, changes into the orb and cross, the recognised distinction of sovereignty.

But to give a last glance at Serapis and his attributes: his bust on gems is often accompanied by a figure resembling a short truncheon from the top of which spring three leaves, or spikes. Can it be some plant sacred to the god, or else some instrument of power?—certain it is that Iva, Assyrian god of Thunder, carries in his hand a *fulmen* of somewhat similar form in the Ninivitish sculptures. A dwarf column, supporting a globe, a corded bale, the letter M,* are all frequently to be seen in the same companionship. Another symbol is of such mighty import in the domains of the Lord of Souls, that its discussion may fairly claim to itself the space of the following section.

* Perhaps the Greek numeral = 40, which was the number sacred to the Assyrian Hoa, god of Water. A conjecture, therefore, may be hazarded that these figures symbolise The Four Elements under the protection of the supreme Lord, Serapis.

FIG. 7.

THE *CADUCEUS*, AND ITS SYMBOLISM.

Macrobius seems to afford us some clue for solving this enigma by his remarks upon the true universality of the sun-worship under different names (Sat i. 19). "That under the form of Mercury the *Sun* is really worshipped is evident also from the *Caduceus* which the Egyptians have fashioned in the shape of two dragons (asps), male and female joined together, and consecrated to Mercury These serpents in the middle parts of their volume are tied together in the knot called the 'Knot of Hercules,' whilst their upper parts bending backwards in a circle, by pressing their mouths together as if kissing complete the circumference of the circle, and their tails are carried back to touch the staff of the Caduceus, and adorn the latter with wings springing out of the same part of the staff The meaning of the Caduceus with reference to the nativity of man, technically termed his *genesis* (or horoscope), is thus explained by the Egyptians they teach that *four deities* preside and attend at man's birth—the Daimon (his genius), Fortune, Love, and Necessity. By the two first of these they hold that the Sun and the Moon are meant, because the Sun, as the author of spirit, heat, and light, is the producer and guardian of human life, and therefore is esteemed the *Daimon* that is the *god* of the person born. The Moon is the *Fortune*, because she is the president over our bodies which are the sport of a variety of accidents *Love* is signified by the kissing of the serpents, *Necessity*, by the knot in which they are tied. The reason for adding the *wings* has been fully discussed above For a symbol of this nature the convolution of the serpents has been selected in preference to anything else, because of the *flexuosity* of the course of both these luminaries From this cause it comes, that the serpent is attached to the figures both of Aesculapius and of Hygiea, because these deities are explained as expressing the nature of the Sun and the Moon For Aesculapius is the health-giving influence proceeding out of the substance of the

Sun, that benefits the souls and bodies of mortals * Hygieia again is the influence of the nature of the Moon, by which the bodies of things animated are holpen, being strengthened by her health-giving sway For this reason, therefore, the figure of the serpent is attached to the statues of both deities, because they bring it about that our bodies strip off, as it were, the slough of their maladies, and are restored to their pristine vigour, just as serpents renew their youth every year, by casting off the slough of old age And the figure of the serpent is explained as an emblem of the Sun himself for the reason that the Sun is perpetually returning out of, as it were, the old age of his lowest setting, up to his full meridian height as if to the vigour of youth Moreover, that the dragon is one of the chiefest emblems of the Sun, is manifest from the derivation of the name, it being so called from δέρκειν, 'to see' For they teach that this serpent, by his extremely acute and never-sleeping sight, typifies the nature of the luminary, and on this account the guardianship of temples, shrines, oracles, and treasures is assigned to dragons That Aesculapius is the same with Apollo is further proved by this fact, not merely that he is reputed the son of the latter, but because he also is invested with the privilege of divination For Apollodorus, in his Treatise on Theology, lays down that Aesculapius presides over augury and oracles And no wonder, seeing that the sciences of medicine and of divination are cognate sciences for medicine predicts the changes for good or ill about to succeed in the human body. As Hippocrates hath it, the physician should be competent to predicate of his patient 'both his present, his past and future condition,' which is the same thing as divination which foreknows, as Homer says,

'The things that be, that shall be, and that were "

It has been already stated how, in the Mithraic worship, the image, surrounded from foot to head by the spiral convolutions of the serpent, had become the established emblem of the deity himself The incidental remark in the above citation, that the

* Or in modern scientific phrase, *Aesculapius* is but another name for *electricity*

flexuous motion of the reptile represented to the Egyptians, the annual course of the sun, affords the sufficient reason why his image should be thus encircled by so significant an attribute. Taking therefore into account the fact that the disputed symbol we are considering was by its nature primarily confined to talismans designed for medical agents, there is at once sufficient reason to suppose it connected with the worship of Aesculapius; and secondly, as it always appears in such cases in company with the Agathodæmon, the undoubted emblem of the Solar god, it may be inferred to be either a symbol or a hieroglyphical representation in little of the same type. In other words, the *figure* signifies nothing more than a serpent-entwined wand, and its *sense* only contains an allusion to the principal visible manifestation of the nature of the Sun. But this point must be left for fuller examination in its connexion with the hitherto unexplained Sigil which invariably makes its appearance on the reverse of the Chnuphis talismans, and which therefore must have been regarded as an essential element in their potency.

FIG. 8.

DEATH, AS DEPICTED IN ANCIENT ART

The King of the Shades has formed the subject of the preceding investigation. The natural sequence of ideas requires us to consider by what visible form ancient imagination expressed the direct agency of his power, and represented to the eye the unwelcome apparition of the "Satelles Orci."

Mingling among the Cupids, whether sculptured or glyptic, and easy to be mistaken for one of the sportive group by the casual observer, comes the most popular antique embodiment of what to our notions is the most discordant of all ideas. He can only be distinguished from the God of Love by observing his pensive attitude, his action of extinguishing his torch either by striking the blazing end against the ground or by trampling it out with the foot; otherwise he leans upon it inverted, with folded wings, and arms and legs crossed in the attitude of profound repose. At other times he is divested of wings, to typify the end of all movement, and whilst he quenches his torch with one hand, he holds *behind* him with the other the large hoop, *annus* (which the Grecian Ἐνίαυτος carries *before* him), to signify that for his victim no more shall the year roll on.

To understand how so charming a type came to be appropriated to such a signification, it is necessary to cast off modern associations, and to recollect that to the ancient mind, arguing merely from the analogy of Nature, death presented itself as merely the necessary converse of birth, and consequently carried no terror in the thought—"nullique ea tristis imago," as Statius happily words it. For it implied nothing worse than the return to the state of unconsciousness, such as was before Being commenced; or, as Pliny clearly puts the case, "Unto all the state of being after the *last* day as the same as it was before the *first* day of life; neither is there any more sensation in either body or soul after death than there was before life." On this account the mere return, as Byron hath it—

> "To be the nothing that I was,
> Ere born to life and living woe,"

inspired no fears beyond those springing from the natural instinct of self-preservation. Many carried this indifference to the opposite extreme—exemplified in the trite story of the Thracians lamenting on the occasion of a birth, and rejoicing on that of a death in the family. Pliny boldly declares that the greatest favour Nature has bestowed on man is the shortness of his span of life, whilst the later Platonists, as seen in that curious chapter of Macrobius, "On the descent of the Soul," termed the being born into this world "spiritual death," and dying, "spiritual birth." But after the ancient order of ideas had been totally revolutionised—when the death of the body came to be looked upon as the punishment of Original Sin, and as the *infraction*, not the *fulfilment* of a natural law—the notion necessarily assumed a more horrific aspect, which again was exaggerated to the utmost of their power by the new teachers, for it supplied them with the most potent of all engines for the subjugation of the human soul—"Æternas quoniam pœnas in morte timendum." The ancient type, therefore, which implied nothing but peace and unbroken repose was therefore at once discarded, as totally inconsistent with the altered view of the reality. Add to this the fact that everything in the shape of Cupid had been forcibly enrolled amongst the Cherubim and Seraphim, and had thereby received a character yet more foreign to that of the newly-created King of Terrors.

Hence the Christians were driven to seek in the ancient iconology for a more fitting representation of the offspring and avenger of transgression—something that should be equally ghastly and terror-inspiring—and such a representative they found made to their hand in the former way of picturing a *Larva*, or bad man's ghost. This had always been depicted as a *skeleton*, and such a figure was recommended by old association to their minds in the times when (as Bottiger phrases it) "the Christians creeping forth out of their catacombs substituted for the Genius with inverted torch, the skulls and mouldering bones of their own martyrs." And that the *larva* was popularly imagined in a skeleton form, appears, amongst the rest, from Ovid's line in his 'Ibis'—

> "Insequar atque oculos ossea larva tuos."
> "Where'er thou turn'st my injured shade shall rise,
> And flit, a fleshless ghost before thine eyes."

Seneca also laughs at the vulgar notion of "larva-forms, frames of bare bones hanging together," and Trimalchio, at his famous dinner, in order to promote conviviality, throws down upon the table a silver larva, so ingeniously made as to bound about on the board with every limb quivering, whilst the host hiccups out the admonition—

> "Heu, Heu, nos miseros, quam totus homuncio nil est,
> Sic erimus cuncti, postquam nos auferet Orcus.
> Ergo vivamus dum licet esse bene."

Such a larva sometimes makes his appearance on the gem, introduced there for the same purpose—to remind his wearer of the shortness of life, and the wisdom of making the best use of the portion allotted to him—speaking, mutely, the words of Virgil's 'Copa Syrisca'—

> "Pone merum et talos, pereat qui crastina curat!
> Mors aurem vellens, Vivite, ait, venio."

Thus upon one gem we behold him holding forth in his bony hand the *lecythus* (long, pointed vase of oil), that regularly accompanied every Greek interment, whilst he leans with his elbow against a huge *amphora* of wine, as though recommending the enjoyment of its contents whilst yet in one's power.* Another, a more fanciful composition, depicts Cupid casting the light of his torch into the depths of an immense Corinthian *crater* out of which a skeleton is throwing himself headlong, as though scared away by the hateful glare—a design whose abstruse meaning may perhaps be interpreted by the foregoing

* Exactly the same lesson is taught by a drinking-cup in the Orleans Museum, the decoration of which is a dance of skeletons. (Mem. Soc. Antiq. de France, vol. xxxi.)

remarks ('Impronte Gemmarie,' ii 10, 11)* A skeleton, likewise, was often painted on the wall of tombs, for example, in that pathetic scene at Pompeii, where a mother is represented laying a mortuary fillet over the bones of her child. In all these cases the form is merely intended to symbolise the *condition* of death by placing before the eye the body as deserted by life, reduced to the state most expressive of mortality and decay, and which cannot be mistaken for one of sleep But it is easy to perceive how ready was the transition from the hieroglyph of mortality regarded as a *state* (especially when to the popular mind the figure also represented a restless and malignant spiritual being) to the adoption of the same inauspicious shape for the embodiment of the idea of the actual principle of destruction

But to return to antique imagery of the same sense. The idea of death is ingeniously and curiously expressed in a fresco decorating the lately discovered vault of Vincentius and Vibia, in the Catacombs of Praetextatus, Rome In the scene labelled "abreptio Vibie et Discensio," the messenger of Fate, "Mercurius," appears placing one foot and leading the way into a huge *orca* laid sideways on the ground The allusion to *Orcus* in the name of such a vessel, *orca*, is sufficiently obvious, and in fact both may spring from the same root, ἕρκος, *inclosure, prison* But the most common type, perpetually repeated on sarcophagi and tablets, is the *Horse*, significant of departure, looking in through the window upon a party carousing—life's festive scene Yet more forcibly is the same notion carried out in an Etruscan sculpture (figured in the Revue Archeologique, 1844), where the angel of death, *Charun*, armed as usual with his ponderous mall, actually leads this horse upon which sits the deceased with head muffled up, "capite obnupto"—the established form in sentencing a criminal to execution The same reason, probably, made the horse's head

* Such a larva also points the moral of the scene embossed upon a lamp, published by De Witte (Mem Soc Antiq de France 1871), where a philosopher seated, and grasping a scroll, is apostrophising a skeleton standing before him, at his feet lies an infant in swaddling-clothes These adjuncts declare the subject of the philosopher's meditations—the destiny of Man from birth to death

so popular a subject for signet-gems; it served there for a *memento-mori*, like the death's heads so much in vogue amongst the jewels of the Cinque-cento time, although the antique symbol carried with it a widely different admonition. The same notion may possibly lie at the bottom of that immemorial custom in South Wales of the mummers carrying the skull of a horse in their Christmas merry-makings.

Cognate to this is that most ancient representation of the conveyance of the departed soul to the realms of bliss—imagined as some happy island in the far West—upon a fantastic hippocampus, in figure like a winged sea-serpent, and who later became the Roman Capricornus, "Ruler of the Hesperian Wave"—

"Thou, for thy rule, O Capricorn! hast won
All that extends beneath the setting sun,"

as Manilius defines the authority of that amphibious sign. But the original conception is often engraved upon Phœnician scarabei, and no doubt can remain as to its intention, since Caylus has published an Etruscan vase (i. pl. 32) where this same monster is painted joyously careering over the sea, whilst on its other side stands the mourner, *præfica*, chaunting the funeral hymn over the corpse laid out upon its bier of bronze.

To continue within the earliest portion of the subject, it must be observed that in the most ancient monument of Greek sculpture whereof any account remains—the Coffer of Cypselus (executed earlier than 600 B.C.)—*Night* was represented carrying in her arms two children, alike in all respects save colour, the one white, the other black, having their *legs crossed* * their names being inscribed over them—*Sleep* and *Death*—for their mother was hastening to the aid of the expiring Memnon. Thus it is manifest that from the very dawn of pictorial art the *crossed legs* were the accepted emblem of the most profound repose, whilst the sluggard's wish for "a little more folding of

* διεστραμμένους τοὺς πόδας. The very obvious meaning of these words critics have contrived to misunderstand and to render as "distorted!" Nor is this all, entirely upon the authority of this blunder, Propertius' "somnia *vana*" have been turned into "somnia *vara*," and ever since the whole tribe of Dreams are believed to walk *bandy-legged*.

the hands in slumber" bears the same testimony to the import of the *crossed arms* of the Roman Genius who leans on his inverted torch. In that master-piece of Roman chasing, the Pompeian *discus*, "The Death of Cleopatra," the object of the design is indicated with equal truth and pathos by the placing of the beauteous infant genius at the knee of the dying queen, on which he rests his elbow to form a support for his head as though dropping off into a gentle slumber. The traditional attitude* retained its significancy well understood far down into the Middle Ages: witness so many cross-legged effigies of warriors resting from their toils—who for that sole reason popularly pass for crusaders.

But in the whole long catalogue of emblems, not one expressed the *abstract* idea so definitely as that most frequently employed in such sense—the Gorgon's Head. Accepting the explanation already offered (p. 167), that at its origin this terrific visage was designed for the "vera effigies" of the Queen of the dead, it was the most speaking emblem of her office that could possibly be chosen. In the Heroic ages it was universally *painted*, or embossed upon the warrior's shield; and with the progress of art, cut in cameo, became the regular decoration of the imperial breastplate;† in which post it served, as Lucian remarks ('Philopatris'), "both to terrify enemies and to avert all danger from the wearer," conveying to all beholders the menace of death exactly as now by an undesigned coincidence does the death's head and cross-bones painted upon the pirate's flag. The Byzantines, in the true spirit of their gloomy superstition, discarded the Præ-Italian type for whose beauty they had lost all feeling, and reverted to the image invented by the horror-loving genius of Pelasgic barbarism. They saw in it the most faithful representation of their Μοῖρα, the destroying demon or *ghoul*, still believed by the Greek peasant to haunt

* The child's skeleton in the Pompeian painting above quoted, similarly folds his feet.

† Accipe belligeræ crudum thoraca Minervæ,
Ipsa Medusææ quam timet ira comæ.
Dum vacat hæc Cæsar, poterit lorica vocari,
Pectore cum sacro sederit, Ægis erit.

Mart. vii. 1.

ruins and desolate places That the figure was received in such a sense into Byzantine symbolism, the examples of amulets already quoted convincingly declare From Byzantine the Gorgon passed into Gothic art, which ever revelling in grotesque horror, its inspiring genius being the *skeleton* which intrudes his ghastliness into every mode of ornamentation, even of a mirror-frame (Lucrezia Borgia's for example) contrived to render the image yet more terrible by converting the face into a fleshless skull, and substituting for the hawk's wings lent by Hermes, which previously impelled its flight, the skinny pinions of her own congenial and much-loved fowl, the sepulchre-haunting *bat*

But of all these emblems, not one is so full of poetry and truth as the device of the *Winged Foot* crushing the Butterfly, Life. The Foot, chosen probably for the same reason as the Horse, as conveying most speakingly the notion of *departure*, was equally accepted as the emblem of death Horace's simile must occur to every reader —

> "Pallida Mors æquo pulsat *pede* pauperum tabernas
> Regumque turres"

On this account the Foot became the peculiar attribute of the infernal deities, and the figure of one carved in stone was often dedicated in the temple of Serapis *—apparently as an *ex voto* commemorating the donor's escape from the very threshold of his dark domain. Singularly related to this custom is what Moor notices of the pairs of feet carved in stone commonly seen in the vicinity of Hindoo temples, traditionally said to be memorials of *suttees*, marking the spot whence the devoted widow stepped from earth upon the funeral pile, that is into the Gate of Heaven

It has long been a question how the Grecian *Hades* ("The Invisible One") and the Roman *Pluto* were depicted in a bodily form as they were originally conceived—for their *Egyptian* equivalent, Serapis, figures much more frequently in

* A colossal example of the finest workmanship was exhumed at Alexandria a few years ago It may have been contemporary with the coin of Commodus from that mint, which has for reverse a head of Serapis placed upon a foot for pedestal, with the date of his seventh year

monuments of Imperial date than either of his brethren, Jove or Neptune In the latter style he is regularly sculptured as *Plutus*, "Lord of Riches," seated on a throne, holding a cornucopia, and extending with his right hand a cluster of earth's choicest gifts But under what form the primitive Greeks had imagined their Aidoneus, God of the Shades, before Serapis was introduced into their mythology, is a question that has never been satisfactorily answered We should have found him on the scarabeus of the Etruscans and early Italiotes, had not a long-enduring respect for things divine (expressly enjoined by Pythagoras) prevented their placing in their signets, used for everyday purposes, the actual figures of the gods, whose absence they supplied by their well-known attributes For this reason a popular Etruscan seal-device is Cerberus, represented sometimes as a man with three heads of a dog, but more commonly in the shape so familiar to us from later arts But the Egyptians had contrived to make their Guardian of the Shades much more formidable in aspect by equipping him with the heads of a lion, crocodile, and hippopotamus We are also certified in what shape the Etruscans imaged their god of the lower world, *Mantus*, for he is painted with serpent legs, like Typhon, wielding a huge butcher's cleaver, and attended by Cerberus, enthroned upon the court placed below the niche of interment, *loculus*, in the Campana tomb, Cerveti

The "Helmet of Hades" is named by Homer (v 845), which Pallas puts on in order to render herself invisible to Ares, which *helmet* the scholiast explains by "cloud and invisibility"—whence it seems but natural to infer that, as this deity was rendered *invisible* by his very attribute, no attempt would be made to depict his personal appearance A figure of a god in long flowing robes, and wielding a trident wanting one of its prongs, sometimes painted on the Nolan vases, has been taken for an Aidoneus, but on no sufficient grounds, there being better reason to consider him a Poseidon in the archaic style The epithet "Renowned for horses" is given to the same god elsewhere by Homer (v 445), allusive doubtless to the *swiftness* of the Destroyer and in the same title may, perchance, lie the motive which made the Greeks adopt the *horse*, as above noticed, for the commonest symbol of his power. If we could meet with any genuine antique and *early* representation of the Rape of Proserpine it would at once decide the question by portraying the grim Ravisher himself, but the inauspicious nature of the subject (so conspicuously set forth in Suetonius' anecdote of the ring with the story presented by Sporus to Nero for a New Year's gift) has completely excluded it from the artist's repertory, so far as anything now remaining informs us. Stosch's Collection, amongst its immense variety of mythological designs, contains nothing of the sort, whilst Raspe gives for its representative only a single antique paste (and that, too, of very dubious attribution) where a god with quiver on shoulder is carrying off a Nymph in a car drawn by two swans—attributes properly bespeaking an Apollo, and if really given here to Pluto, proving the work to belong to those latter times of Paganism when Hades, Serapis, Phœbus, were equally interpreted as mere titles of the Solar god.

As for the Roman Pluto, or, to give him his native name, *Dis* (*ditis* from the same root as *death*), there was the best of reasons for excluding him from the province of art which admitted nought that was hideous or of evil augury. For there can be no doubt, that, to the popular imagination, he still continued the *Charun* * whom we still behold lording it over the sepulchres of their Etruscan teachers in the arts, a giant of horrid aspect with pointed ears, and tusky grinning jaws, winged buskins on legs, extending with one hand a hissing serpent, with the other wielding a monstrous mall. It was probably the traditional influence of the idea that caused the same instrument, *mazza*, to be retained at Rome for the execution of peculiarly atrocious criminals down to the recent introduction of the guillotine.

That Pluto was really so personified in the shows of the Amphitheatre, as late as the third century, may be gathered from the remark of Tertullian (Apol. xv.), that, "amongst the other scenic cruelties of the afternoon, the spectators laughed at the sight of Mercury raising the dead with his *red-hot* wand [applied doubtless to the feet of the slaughtered gladiators to

* As Etruria was the only school of art for Rome until very late times, she supplied the *figures* equally with the *names* of all the Roman deities.

ascertain if life still lingered within them], whilst the 'Brother of Jupiter,' armed with his *mall*, escorted the dead bodies of the combatant" [for the purpose clearly of giving them the *coup de grâce*] The primitive Etruscan image passed down into the belief of their mediæval descendants, for Dante brings on the stage —

"Charon, demonio con occhi di bragia"
"*Charon, a devil with live-coals for eyes*"

It is time now to dismiss the Lord of the Shades, and to consider by what *Emblem* ancient art sought to express the *Shade* itself, the disembodied spirit The Greeks of early times appropriately painted it in the shape of a *bird* with a human head, as on that beautiful vase, "The Death of Procris" (British Museum), where such a fowl is conspicuously seen winging its flight from the mouth of the wounded Nymph The celebrated Orléans (now Russian) scarabeus, engraved with the "Death of Achilles," has its back carved into the same creature, tearing her breast in an agony of despair This expressive type was not, however, the birth of Grecian genius, but adopted, without alteration, from the most ancient symbolism of Egypt In the "Judgment of the body and soul," regularly painted on the mummy-cases, the former, depicted as a mummy, stands before Osiris, "Lord of the West," to answer for its *actions*, whilst the soul, in shape of a hawk, with human head and wings uplifted, is brought before the same god under another form, to give an account of its *thoughts* And the same soul, purified, and admitted amongst the gods, appears as before, but tranquilly standing with a golden disk, "a crown of glory," set upon her head figures of the last kind in bronze frequently occurring amongst Egyptian remains, complimentary mementoes of deceased friends Again, this same bird is often found painted on the mummy-case right over the *heart* (named in Coptic, "the abode of the soul"), a plain proof of what it signifies there, although Father Kircher, with his wonted extravagance, chose to explain it as figuring the *iynx*, the bird so renowned in the magical operations of the Greeks Again, the same notion is expressed by the simple figure of a bird flying away, as often is done in Etruscan works, where the subject represented is the death of a hero. Latest of all, this somewhat grotesque Egyptian conception was modified by Grecian culture into the graceful girl with butterfly wings—the well-known Psyche—and such a form is seen seated upon the summit of Achilles' tomb, before which the sacrifice of Polyxena is about to be offered. This ancient human-headed Bird, by a natural transition of ideas, came ultimately to be applied to express a widely different meaning. Instead of the *dead*, it was made to stand for the *destroyer*, and the Syrens are always painted in this shape whenever their interview with Ulysses becomes the theme of ancient art, or when they engage in their unlucky contest with the Muses. But here, for the sake of more grace, in the conformation of the monster, the whole of the female bust is adapted to the body of the fowl. Despite their beauty and melodiousness, the Syrens were considered as the most malignant and destructive of beings, for which reason the *Harpies* likewise were depicted in precisely the same figure. Although identical at first, the more refining art of Roman times introduced a distinction between them by giving to the Syrens the complete *bust*, to the Harpies the *head* only of the woman. Inasmuch as the name signifies "Snatcher-away," the Harpy was understood to embody the abstract idea of death, which acceptation explains why she is often represented armed with a sword, or carrying on her shoulder the funeral *lecythus*, and torch. For the same reason the Harpy holds a conspicuous place in the decorations of many ancient tombs, unlesss, indeed, the emblem may have been used there in its Egyptian sense.

In what shape Death was personified by Euripides, in his Alcestis, cannot be made out from the insufficiency of data afforded by the lines relating to his appearance on the stage. It is, however, plain that the poet brought forward Θάνατος in a bodily form, perhaps considering him the same with Aidoneus, for he styles him "King of the Dead," and Macrobius, speaking of the same event, uses for his name the Roman equivalent, "Orcus." All that can be gathered from the incidental allusions of the other *dramatis personæ* to this apparition, is that he was robed in *black*, and carried a *sword*, wherewith to sever a lock from the head of his destined victim, and so devote it to the subterranean gods. It is, however, possible that Euripides brought on this Θάνατος in that harpy shape which sometimes is found in antique art where the bust is that of a grim aged man, in place of the smiling female's, and who, as badge of office, carries a naked *sword*. In such a form the Destroyer must have flitted before the eyes of Statius, when about to make prey of the young and beautiful Glaucius:—

> "Subitas inimica levavit
> Parca manus, quo diva feros gravis exuis *ungues*?"

This last word can apply to nothing but the Harpy, of whom *claws* were the distinctive attribute:—

> "*Unguibus* ære parat nummos raptura Celæno." *

Nevertheless, a representation like this had in it nothing grotesque or offensive to the Athenian eye. Far different was the Pelasgic Κῆρ, likewise *robed in black* (according to Homer's normal epithet for her), in the form which the archaic sculptor had given her upon the Coffer of Cypselus, "having tusks as fierce as those of any wild beast." Such a conception was eagerly embraced by the gloomy genius of the Etruscans, ever delighting in the monstrous and the horrible. She therefore figures on their signets in a form to be described in the very words of Pausanias, having a huge Gorgonian head, grinning jaws, arms wreathed with serpents, impelled by quadruple wings, like an Assyrian deity, and her action that of furious haste. So, doubtless, appeared the Furies, brought on the stage by Æschylus, when the horror of their strange aspect struck the Athenian audience with such deadly fright. For his purpose he must have revived a very ancient and *forgotten* type of the idea: for the paintings on the vases of his epoch exhibit the Eumenides, who persecute Orestes, under a no more terrific form than as shadowy old women brandishing serpents and torches, as they chase their victim from shrine to shrine.

* The same picture must have been in Horace's mind when he uses the figure

> "Mors atris circumvolat alis."

TOMB-TREASURES.

Serapis, in his double character of God of Death and God of Riches, has been the subject of preceding chapters, the present one shall be devoted to the consideration of the most striking method by which human superstition sought to turn to account the two ideas To propitiate the *Manes* by placing his most valuable or beloved effects in the sepulchre of the defunct, dates probably from the very institution of interment, but the account now to be cited is the most interesting of any on record, owing to the circumstances of the time, person, and place It is literally translated from the description of an eye witness, the earliest of Italian antiquaries, M L Fauno, given in his 'Antichita de Roma,' p 154, published 1553

"In February, 1544, in the Chapel of the King of France, which is now being built in St Peter's, after the plan of Julius II, the workmen, in excavating, came upon a marble coffin, which, from the things found therein, was clearly known to be the tomb of Maria, wife of the Emperor Honorius Of the body, indeed, there was nothing left, except the teeth, the hair, and the two leg-bones From the robes which were interwoven with gold, and from the head-tire, which was cloth of silk and gold, there was extracted by smelting more than *forty* pounds weight of the purest gold" [Suecius says *thirty-six*, but makes the total of all the gold found to amount to the above weight when they were melted down by order of Paul III., to be applied to the building fund of the Cathedral]

"Within the coffin lay a silver box, one and a half foot long by eight inches deep with many articles inside, the which we shall proceed particularly to describe There were vases and different things in rock crystal, thirty in all, big and little, amongst which were two cups, as it were, not very large, the one round, the other oval shaped, with most beautiful figures in intaglio of middling depth (*mezzo-cavo*), and a *snail-shell* (nautilus), likewise in crystal, fitted up for a lamp in fine gold, with which in the first place the mouth of the shell is overlaid, there being only left a hole for pouring in the oil, by the side of which hole is fixed a *fly* of gold upon a pivot, turning backwards and forwards, for the purpose of closing the orifice In the same way is also made a nozzle with beak (*zippio*) for holding the wick, drawn out long and sharpened with the greatest elegance, and so fastened to the crystal that it appears all one piece naturally The cover also is equally well made. The shape of the shell is that of a great sea-shell, encompassed all round with its points, which in this vessel are polished and very smooth, so excellently wrought is the crystal There were also vases and various articles in agate, with certain little animals, eight in all, and amongst them two very beautiful vases, one like the glass *ampullae*, made big and squat for holding oil and such like liquids, so worked, so beautiful, and thin that it is a wonder to behold The other is in the shape of those ladles with long handles used at Rome for baling water out of cisterns, and is supposed to be a vessel used by the ancients in their sacrifices [a *ligula* for the purpose of ladling the wine out of the great standing *crater*] Next came four little vessels in gold of different kinds, and another little vessel of gold with a cover set round with jewels A little gold heart that had been a pendant with jewels set in it, a buckle of gold with six gems of different kinds set in it, also twenty-four other buckles of gold of various patterns with little gems set in them, furthermore, forty-eight rings and *hoops** of gold of different shapes, one of them in red bone, and various gems A mouse in "chelidonia," a reddish quartz, is also specified by Suecius [which must be the next item], also three little animals in *red bone*, also two ear-drops in emerald or plasma with two jacinths, four small crosses with red and green stones, a pendant in the form of a bunch of grapes, made of purple stones, eight other little gold pendants of different sorts with gems set in them The remains of a string of *crepundia*, the usual decoration of little children. [Maria had died at the age of *four*, being thus early betrothed to Honorius by his father the all-powerful Stilicho] Three little gold crosses set with emeralds, a piece of a small fine necklace with certain green

* *Verghe* 'verga,' like the French verge, signifies a plain gold wire forming a ring having no head

stones strung upon it Another little gold necklace with twenty-four beads of plasma Another necklace with twelve heads of sapphire cut almond shape Another little necklace of gold wire folded up (*raccolto*), but broken into four pieces Two small buttons in gold, fourteen little gold-wire rings like those of a coat of mail, three more crosses with some emeralds, and a round gold plate like an Agnus Dei,* with these words upon it, STILICHO VIVAT Two bracelets (*maniche*) of gold, set with certain red and green stones Two large pins or *stiletti* for the hair, one in gold nearly a palm (nine inches) long inscribed with these words, DOMINVS HONORIVS DOMINA MARIA the other in silver without inscription There were likewise many fragments of enamels and other stones Also silver nails [their heads] partly flat, partly in relief, which had fastened down a cover of silver upon a little coffer Also a small plate of gold with these words written or rather *scratched* in Greek, MICHAEL GABRIEL RAPHAEL VRIEL" [Laurentius Surius makes out *forty* gold rings set with precious stones, besides an emerald set in gold, engraved with a head supposed to be that of Honorius, which was valued at five hundred gold ducats] We have particularly described all the above-named objects because Claudian, a poet of those times, declares that to the Empress Maria were sent similar rare presents from her betrothed, which perhaps may have formed the greatest part of these things The words of the poet are—

"Jam munera nuptæ
Præparat, et pulchros Mariæ sed luce minores
Elicit ornatus quidquid venerabilis olim
Livia, divorumque nurus gessere superbe" (v 10-13)

This account enables us to form some notion of the treasures deposited to a greater or less degree in all the tombs of important personages, but more especially in those sumptuous structures raised to the memory of the dead throughout Asia Minor The same fact sufficiently accounts for the furious onslaught made upon the tombs all over the Roman world, so soon as the change of religion had extinguished the old veneration for the *Manes* and the things consecrated to them—a profanation, and a

* A disk of stamped wax about three inches in diameter

destruction of works of art, which Gregorius Theologus, inspired by a taste and good feeling very surprising in a Byzantine saint, has attacked in one hundred and eighty-two very interesting and often poetical epigrams.

The same custom was kept up (although we can hardly suppose with any lingering belief in its ancient efficiency) by the Merovingian and Carlovingian successors to the wealth of the Western Empire. The learned Canon Chiflet has left in his interesting book, 'Anastasis Childerici Regis,' a complete history of tomb-treasures, serving to illustrate his account of that of Childeric the Frank, accidentally found in the precincts of Tournay Cathedral, May 1654. The deposit, as far it could be recovered from the first finders, consisted of the arms of the king, the trappings of his horse (buried with him), all of gold encrusted with garnets, his gold tablets and writing-stylus, abundance of golden-bees originally stretched over his mantle (which gave that curious idea to Napoleon I.), a bull's head for a pendant (the primitive Frankish badge of sovereignty), and lastly, a *viaticum* in the shape of one hundred Byzantine *solidi* of contemporary emperors, and as many denarii of several and much earlier Cæsars. The canon, by zealous perquisitions, succeeded in recovering all these articles, including the most important of all, the royal signet ring of massy gold, engraved with the image and superscription of Childeric, for his patron the Archduke Leopold, then governor of the Low Countries. At some subsequent period the most important of these relics passed into the collection of the Bibliothèque Impériale, where they continued in all due honour until the disastrous robbery of 1808, when it is supposed, with too much probability, that they were melted down along with the rest of the booty!

FIG. 9.

GNOSTIC CONNECTION WITH SUPERSTITIOUS PRACTICES

1 THE EVIL EYE

Serapis we have seen, in one of his representations lately noticed, specially invoked to defend his votary against the *Evil Eye* under its abstract title of φθόνος. A glance therefore at this most ancient superstition (which still flourishes in full vigour in the same countries that gave it birth) will form a fitting prelude to the coming section, which takes for subject talismans and amulets of every class

The belief in the power for mischief of the eye of an envious or malignant person (to counteract which was the principal object of so many of the amulets that have come down to us) was universal amongst all ancient nations It is needless to bring forward classic writers to support this statement, such as Apollonius Rhodius, where he skilfully avails himself of the notion, and makes Medea by her basilisk glance alone work the death of Talas, the Brazen Man, guardian of the Cretan shores, for even St. Paul (Rom i 29) sets down this action of the soul working through the eye in the list of sins of the deepest dye But the actual *manner* of operation upon the sufferer I have nowhere found explained except in the following passage from Heliodorus ('Æthiopica,' iii. 8), and which therefore deserves to be inserted at length in this prelude to the subject "Tell me, my good Calasiris, what is the malady that has attacked your daughter?" "You ought not to be surprised,' I replied, "if at the time when she was heading the procession in the sight of so vast an assemblage of people, she had drawn upon herself some *envious eye*" Whereupon, smiling ironically, "Do you then," asked he, "like the vulgar in general, believe in the reality of such fascination?" "As much as I do in any other fact," I replied, "and the thing is this the air which surrounds us passing through the eyes, as it were through a strainer, and also through the mouth, the teeth and the other passages, into the inward parts, whilst its external properties make their way in together with it—whatever be its quality as it flows in, of the same nature is the effect it disseminates in the recipient, so that when any one looks upon beauty with envy, he fills the circumambient air with a malignant property, and diffuses upon his neighbour the breath issuing from himself, all impregnated with bitterness, and *this*, being as it is of a most subtile nature, penetrates through into the very bone and marrow. Hence envy has frequently turned itself into a regular disease, and has received the distinctive appellation of *fascination* (βασκανία) Consider also, my Charicles, how many people have been infected with ophthalmia, how many with other pestilential diseases, not from any contact with those so affected, or from sharing the same bed or same table, but merely from breathing the same air Let also (and above all the rest), the origin of love be a support to my argument, for *that* owes its first origin to the sight which shoots like arrows the passion into the soul And for this there is very good reason, for of all the senses and passages of the body, the sight is the most easily excited, and the most inflammable, and consequently the most susceptible with regard to external emanation, in consequence of its own natural fiery essence, attracting to itself the visits of love. And if you wish for a proof drawn from Natural History, recorded likewise in the Sacred Books, the bird, the yellow-hammer, cures the jaundice, and if a person so affected shall but look at that bird, the latter at once tries to escape and shuts its eyes, not as some think, because it begrudges the benefit to the sick man, but because, if looked upon by men, it is forced by its nature to attract his disease into its own body, like an exhalation, and therefore shuns the glance as much as a blow And amongst serpents, the basilisk, doth not he, as you may have heard, kill and blast whatever comes in his way by means of his eyes and his breath alone? And if some give the stroke of the Evil Eye even to those they love and are well disposed towards, you must not be surprised, for people of an envious disposition act not as they *wish*, but as their Nature *compels* them to do"

II On a Ceraunia of Jade Converted into a Gnostic Talisman.

Few relics of antiquity combine in one so many and so widely differing points of interest, with respect to the material, the strangely dissimilar uses to which the same object has been applied in two opposite phases of the history of Man, and, above all, the curious superstitions engendered by its peculiar form, as does the stone brought under the notice of the Archæological Institute by General Lefroy, now in the Woolwich Repository. The kindness of that gentleman having afforded me full opportunity for the careful examination of this interesting monument, I proceed to embody, in as succinct a form as their multifarious nature will permit, the observations suggested to me by that examination

The subject, therefore, of this section is a small stone celt of the common pattern, but of very uncommon material (in the *antique* class), being made, not of flint, but of dark-green jade or nephrite, 2 in by 1½ in in length and greatest width, and brought, there is reason to believe, from Egypt many years ago, by Colonel Milner, aide-de-camp to Lord J Bathurst during the English occupation of Sicily in 1812 Each of its two faces is occupied by a Gnostic formula, engraved with much neatness, considering the excessive hardness of the material, in the somewhat debased Greek character that was current at Alexandria during the third and fourth centuries of our era

The most important of these two formulæ has been ingeniously forced to take the outline of a wreath composed of broad leaves, in number *fourteen* (or the sacred *seven* duplicated), and doubtless intended for those of the "Five Trees" that figure so conspicuously in Gnostic symbolism, the ends being tied together with four broad ribbons. This is a design of which no other example has ever come to my knowledge amongst the innumerable and wondrously varied devices excogitated by the prolific fancy of this religion of mysteries. Upon the four ties are engraved in very minute letters different combinations of the seven Greek vowels, whilst each of the leaves is emblazoned with some "Holy Name," of which many can be easily recognised as constantly recurring in charms of this class, others are disguised by a novel orthography, whilst a few, from the uncertain forms of the lettering, defy all attempts at interpretation.

To the first series belong ΑΒΡΑϹΑ, "Abraxas," properly an epithet of the sun, but designating here the Supreme Deity; ΙΑѠΟΥΙΕ, "Iao, Jehovah," ΑΒΛΑΝΑ, "Thou art our Father!" ΓΑΜΒΡΙΗΛ, a curious mode of spelling "Gabriel," that testifies to the difficulty ever felt by the Greeks of expressing the sound of our B, ΑΚΤΝΟΝΒѠ, which contains the Coptic form of Anubis, ΔΑΜΝΑΜΕΝΕΥϹ, the sun's name in the famous "Ephesian Spell," and, most interesting of all, ΠϹΑΝΤΑΡΕΟϹ, who can be no other than the ΙΨΑΝΤΑ of the *Pistis-Sophia*—one of the great Τριδυνάμεις, a Power from whom is enthroned in the planet *Mars*. To the uncertain belong ϹΟΥΜΑ, probably for ϹΟΥΜΑΡΤΑ a name occurring elsewhere, and perhaps cognate to the Hindoo *Sumitri*, ΧѠΝΟΝΙΧΑΡ which may be intended for ΧΑΡ-ΧΝΟΥΜΙϹ, a common epithet of the Agathodæmon Serpent, ΑΕΙѠΕΗΑΑΝΗϹ, ΝΕΙΧΑΡΟΠΛΗϹ, the two last, spells unexplained but very uncommon, ΜΟΝΑΡΧΟϹ, whilst ΑΧΑΡϹΙϹ and the rest appear here for the first time, if correctly so read.

The other face is covered with an inscription, cut in much larger letters, and in *eight* lines. This number was certainly not the result of chance, but of deep design, for it was mystic in the highest degree, representing—so taught the profoundest doctor of the Gnosis, Marcus—the divine Ogdoad, which was the daughter of the Pythagorean Tetrad, the mother of all creation.* The lines 2, 4, 5, consist of Greek letters used as *numerals*, intermixed with *sigla*, which, from their constant occurrence upon monuments of a like nature, are supposed, with good reason, to be symbols of the planets. The numerals, on their part, probably denote various deities, for the Alexandrian Gnosis was the true daughter of Magism, and in the old theology of Chaldea every god and astral genius had a *number* of his own, and which often stands instead of his proper

* St Hippolytus, Refut Om Hæres vi 50

name in dedicatory inscriptions * Thus, the number of Hoa (Neptune), was 40, of Ana (Pluto), 60, of Bel (Jupiter), 50, of the Sun, 20, of the moon, 30, of the Air, 10, of Nergal (Mars), 12, &c

A fragment of the *Pistis-Sophia*† supplied the "spiritual man" with a key to the right interpretation of similar stenography in his own creed "These be the *Names* which I will give unto thee, even from the Infinite One downwards Write the same with a sign (cypher), so that the sons of God may manifest (understand?) them out of this place This is the name of the Immortal One, ΑΑΑ ωωω ‡ And this is the name of the Voice whereby the Perfect Man is moved, ΙΙΙ These likewise be the interpretations of the names of the Mysteries The first is ΑΑΑ, and the interpretation thereof is ΦΦΦ The second, which is ΜΜΜ, or which is ωωω, the interpretation thereof is ΑΑΑ The third is ΨΨΨ, the interpretation thereof is ΟΟΟ The forth is ΦΦΦ, the interpretation thereof is ΝΝΝ The fifth ΔΔΔ, the interpretation thereof is ΑΑΑ, the which is above the throne of ΑΑΑ This is the interpretation of the second ΑΑΑΑ, namely, ΑΑΑΑΑΑΑ, the same is the interpretation of the whole Name"

Lines 7, 8, are made up of vowels, variously combined, and shrouding from profane eyes the *Ineffable Name* ΙΑΩ which, as we are informed by many authorities (the most ancient and trustworthy being Diodorus Siculus),§ was the name of the God of the Jews, meaning thereby their mode of writing "Jehovah" in Greek characters

Line 3 consists of the seven vowels placed in their natural order. This was the most potent of all the spells in the Gnostic repertory, and its importance may justify the extensiveness of the following extract from the grand text-book of this theosophy, which sets forth its hidden sense and wondrous efficacy. The primary idea, however, was far from abstruse, if we accept the statement of the writer "On Interpre-

* On this curious subject, see Rawlinson's 'Ancient Monarchies,' iii p 466

† Cap 125

‡ That is, 1000 and 800 tripled The next numbers are 10,000 tripled, and so on

§ 'Bibliotheca Historica,' i 94

tations," that the Egyptians expressed the name of the Supreme God by the seven vowels thus arranged—ΙΕΗΩΟΥΑ.* But this single mystery was soon refined upon, and made the basis of other and infinitely deeper mysteries. In an inscription found at Miletus (published by Montfaucon), the Holy ΙΕΟΥ-ΑΗΩΑΕΙΟΥΩ is besought "to protect the city of Miletus and all the inhabitants of the same," a plain proof that this interminable combination only expressed the name of some *one* divine being. Again, the *Pistis-Sophia* perpetually brings in ΙΕΟΥ invariably accompanied with the epithet of 'the Primal Man,' *i.e.*, He after whose image or *type* man was first created. But in the fulness of time the semi-Pythagorean, Marcus, had it revealed unto him that the seven heavens in their revelation sounded each one vowel which, all combined together, formed a single doxology, "the sound whereof being carried down to earth becomes the creator and parent of all things that be on earth."†

The Greek language has but one word for *vowel* and *voice*; when therefore, "the seven thunders uttered their voices," the seven vowels, it is meant, echoed through the vault of heaven, and composed that mystic utterance which the sainted seer was forbidden to reveal unto mortals. "Seal up those things which the seven thunders uttered, and write them not."‡ With the best reason, then, is the formula inscribed on a talisman of the first class. For hear what the *Pistis-Sophia* delivers touching its potency.§ "After these things his disciples said again unto him, Rabbi, reveal unto us the mysteries of the Light of thy Father, forasmuch as we have heard thee saying that there is another baptism of smoke, and another baptism of the Spirit of Holy Light, and moreover an unction of the Spirit, all which shall bring our souls into the treasurehouse of Light. Declare therefore unto us the mysteries of these things, so that we also may inherit the kingdom of thy Father. Jesus said unto them, Do ye seek after these mysteries? No mystery is more excellent

* This is in fact a very correct representation, if we give each vowel its true Greek sound, of the Hebrew pronunciation of the word Jehovah.

† Hippolytus, vi. 48.

‡ Rev. x. 4.

§ Pistis-Sophia, cap. 378.

than they, which shall bring your souls unto the Light of Lights, unto the place of Truth and Goodness, unto the place of the Holy of holies, unto the place where is neither male nor female, neither form in that place but Light, everlasting, not to be uttered Nothing therefore is more excellent than the mysteries which ye seek after, saving only the *mystery of the Seven Vowels and their forty and nine Powers*, and the numbers thereof. And no name is more excellent than all these (Vowels),* a Name wherein be contained all Names and all Lights and all Powers Knowing therefore this Name, if a man shall have departed out of this body of Matter, no smoke (of the bottomless pit), neither any darkness, nor Ruler of the Sphere of Fate,† nor Angel, nor Power, shall be able to hold back the soul that knoweth that Name. But and if, after he shall have departed out of this world, he shall utter that Name unto the fire, it shall be quenched, and the darkness shall flee away. And if he shall utter that Name unto the devils of the Outer Darkness, and to the Powers thereof, they shall all faint away, and their flame shall blaze up, so that they shall cry aloud 'Thou art holy, thou art holy, O Holy One of all holies!' And if he shall utter that Name unto the Takers-away for condemnation, and their Authorities, and all their Powers, nay, even unto Barbelo,‡ and the Invisible God, and the three Triple-powered Gods, so soon as he shall have uttered that Name in those places, they shall all be shaken and thrown one upon the other, so that they shall be ready to melt away and perish, and shall cry aloud, 'O Light of all lights that art in the Boundless Light! remember us also, and purify us!'" After such a revelation as this, we need seek no further for the reason of the frequent occurrence of this formula upon talismans intended, when they had done their duty in this world, to accompany their owner into the tomb, continuing to exert there a protective influence of a yet higher order than in life

For the student of the mineralogy of the ancients this celt

* Evidently alluding to the collocation of the vowels on our talisman

† The twelve Æons of the Zodiac, the creators of the human soul, which they eagerly seek to catch when released from the body in which they have imprisoned it

‡ The divine mother of the Saviour, and one of the three 'Invisible Gods," cap 359

has very great interest in point of *material*, as being the only specimen of true jade, bearing indisputable marks of either Greek or Roman workmanship, that, so far as my knowledge extends, has ever yet been brought to light This ancient neglect of the material is truly difficult to explain, if the statement of a very good authority, Corsi, be indeed correct, that the sort showing the deepest green is found in Egypt The known predilection of the Romans for gems of that colour, would, one should naturally expect, have led them in that case to employ the stone largely in ornamentation, after the constant fashion of the Chinese, and to value it as a harder species of the *Smaragdus* The circumstances under which this relic was brought to England render it more than probable that Egypt was the place where it was found, a supposition corroborated by the fine quality of the stone exactly agreeing with what Corsi remarks of the Egyptian kind. That *Alexandria* was the place where the inscription was added upon its surface can admit of little question, the lettering being precisely that seen upon innumerable other monuments which can with certainty be assigned to the same grand focus of Gnosticism In addition to this, it is very doubtful whether in the third or fourth centuries a lapidary could have been found elsewhere throughout the whole Roman Empire capable of engraving with such skill as the minute characters within the wreath evince, upon a material of this, almost insuperable, obduracy From the times of the Ptolemies down to the Arab conquest, and even later, Alexandria was the seat of the manufacture of vases in rock crystal This trade served to keep alive the expiring Glyptic art for the only purpose for which its productions continued to be demanded—the manufacture of talismans, consignments of which must have been regularly shipped, together with the crystal-ware,* to Rome, and equally to the other important cities of the empire

The primitive Egyptians, like the early Chaldeans, used stone in the place of metal for their cutting instruments, and continued its use for making particular articles down into historic times Herodotus mentions the regular employment of

* "Dum tibi Niliacus portat crystalla cataplus"—Mart xii 72

the "Ethiopian stone" sharpened, for a dissecting-knife* in the process of embalming, and similarly for pointing the arrows† carried by the contingent of the same nation in the army of Xerxes. The Alexandrian citizen, half-Jew half-Greek, who had the good fortune to pick up this primæval implement, doubtless rejoiced in the belief that he had gotten a "stone of virtue," most potent alike from substance, figure, and nature and therefore proceeded to do his prize due honour by making it the *medium* of his most accredited spells—nay, more, by inventing a new formula of unusual complication and profundity whereby to animate its inherent powers. As regards its *substance*, the stone probably passed then for a *smaragdus* of exceptional magnitude, and that gem, as Pliny records,‡ was recommended by the magi as the proper material for a talisman of prodigious efficacy, which, duly engraved, should baffle witchcraft, give success at court, avert hailstorms, and much more of like nature. The *smaragdus* of the ancients was little more than a generic designation for all stones of a *green* colour, and the entire Gnostic series strikingly demonstrates that this hue was deemed a primary requisite in a talismanic gem—the almost exclusive material of the class being the green jasper and the plasma.

Again, as regards *figure*, this celt offered in its *triangular* outline, that most sacred of all emblems, the mystic Delta, the form that signified maternity, and was the hieroglyph of the moon. This belief is mentioned by Plutarch,§ and explains why the triangle so often accompanies the figure of the sacred baboon, Luna's special attribute, on monuments, where also it is sometimes displayed elevated upon a column with that animal standing before it in the attitude of adoration.

Lastly, the supposed *nature* of this gift of Fortune was not of Earth, inasmuch as it then passed for a holy thing that "had fallen down from Jupiter," being, in fact, nothing less than one of that god's own thunderbolts. A notion this which will

* ii. 86.

† vii. 69.

‡ xxxvii. 10.

§ 'De Iside et Osiride,' cap. 75. He adds that the Pythagoreans called the equilateral triangle "Athene"—a curious confirmation of the tradition quoted by Aristotle, that the Attic goddess was one and the same with the Moon.

doubtless strike the modern mind as so strange, or rather as so preposterous, that it necessitates my giving at full length my reasons for making such an assertion. And in truth the subject is well worth the trouble of investigation, seeing that the same superstition will be found to extend from an early period of antiquity down into the popular belief of our own times throughout a large extent of Europe.

It is in accordance with this notion that I have designated this celt a "ceraunia" (thunderbolt-stone), and it therefore remains for me to adduce my reasons for giving it what must appear to most people so unaccountable and highly inappropriate an appellation. *Sotacus*, who is quoted elsewhere by Pliny "as one of the most ancient writers on mineralogy," is cited by him* "as making two other kinds of the ceraunia, the black and the red, resembling *axe-heads* in shape. Of these, such as be black and round are sacred things; towns and fleets can be captured by their instrumentality. The latter are called *Bætyli*, whilst the oblong sort are the *Ceraunia*. Some make out another kind, in mighty request in the practices of the magi, inasmuch as it is only to be found in places that have been struck by lightning." One would have been utterly at a loss to understand what the old Greek had been speaking about in the chapter thus confusedly condensed by the later Roman naturalist, or to discover any resemblance in form between the lightning-flash and an axe-head, had it not been for the popular superstition that has prevailed in Germany from time immemorial to the present day, and of which full particulars are given by Anselmus Boetius in his invaluable repertory of mediæval lore upon all such matters, written at the beginning of the seventeenth century.†

Under the popular names of "Strahl-hammer," "Donner-pfeil," "Donner-keil," "Strahl-pfeil," "Strahl-keil" (lightning-hammer, thunder-arrow or club, lightning-arrow, &c.), and the Italian "Sagitta,"‡ he figures stone celts and hammers of five

* xxxvii. 51.

† 'Gem. et Lapid. Hist.' ii. cap. 261.

‡ 'Saetta" (a vulgar Italian execration), is now restricted to the lightning-missile, the archer's shaft being expressed by the Teutonic "freccia," in accordance with the genius of the language which reserves the old Latin terms for the things

different, but all common, types, remarking that so firm was the belief in these things being the "actual arrow of the lightning" (ipsa fulminis sagitta), that should any one attempt to controvert it he would be taken for a madman. He however confesses with amusing simplicity that the substance of these thunderbolts is exceedingly like the common flint used for striking fire with, nay, more, he boldly declares he should agree with those few *rationalists* who, on the strength of their resemblance in shape to the tools in common use, pronounced these objects to be merely ordinary iron implements that had got *petrified* by long continuance in the earth, had it not been for the testimony of the most respectable witnesses as to the fact of their being discovered in places just seen to be struck with lightning. Besides quoting some fully detailed instances from Gesner, he adds that several persons had assured him of having themselves seen these stones dug up in places where the lightning had fallen. The natural philosophers of the day accounted for the creation of such substances in the atmosphere by supposing the existence of a vapour charged with sulphureous and metallic particles, which rising above a certain height became condensed through the extreme heat of the sun, and assumed a wedge-like form in consequence of the escape of their moisture, and the gravitation of the heavier particles towards their lower end! Notwithstanding this celestial origin, the virtue of the production was not then esteemed of a proportionally sublime order, extending no further than to the prevention or the cure of ruptures in children, if placed upon their cradles, and also to the procuring of sleep in the case of adults. In our own times Justinus Kerner mentions* the same names for stone celts as universally popular amongst the German boors; but they are now chiefly valued for their efficacy in preserving cattle from the murrain, and consequently the finders can seldom be induced to part with them

not of this world,—using those of the *lingua militaris* for every-day purposes The flint arrow-heads found in the *terra marna* of the primæval Umbrian towns, are believed by the peasantry to have this celestial origin, and are highly valued as portable "light-conductors"

* In his little treatise on Amulets.

It must not, however, be supposed that Sotacus picked up this strange notion from the Teutones of his own age, whose very existence was probably unknown to him, his informants were unquestionably those magi cited at the conclusion of Pliny's extract. The Greek mineralogist had lived "apud Regem," that is, at the court of the King of Persia, very probably in the capacity of royal physician, like his countrymen Democedes and Ctesias. In that region he had ample opportunities of seeing stone celts, for Rawlinson observes* that flint axes and other implements, exactly identical with the European in workmanship, are *common* in all the most ancient mounds of Chaldæa, those sites of primæval cities. Such elevations above the dead level of those interminable plains were necessarily the most liable to be lightning-struck, and hence probably arose the idea that these weird-looking stones (all tradition of whose proper destination had long since died out amongst the iron-using Persians) were the actual fiery bolts which had been seen to bury themselves in the clay. And again, to revert to the German belief, it must be remembered that Thor, the Northern Jupiter, is pictured as armed with a huge hammer in the place of the classical thunderbolt. The type of the god had been conceived in the far-remote ages when the stone hammer was as yet the most effective and formidable of weapons, and was preserved unchanged out of deference to antiquity, after the true meaning of the attribute was entirely forgotten. Nevertheless, his worshippers, accustomed to behold the hammer in the hand of the god of thunder,—ὑψιβρεμέτης Ζεύς,—very naturally concluded that these strange objects, of unknown use, found from time to time deep buried in the earth, were the actual missiles which that deity had discharged. It is a remarkable proof of the wide diffusion of the same belief, that the late owner of the relic under consideration, habitually spoke of it as a "thunderstone,"—a name he could only have learnt from the Arabs from whom it was procured, seeing that no such notion with respect to *celts* has ever been current in this country. But every one whose memory reaches back forty years or more may recollect, that wheresoever in England the

* 'Ancient Monarchies,' i. p. 120.

fossil *Belemnite* is to be found, it was implicitly received by all, except the few pioneers of Geology (a word then almost synonymous with Atheism), as the veritable thunderbolt shot from the clouds, and by that appellation was it universally known. I, for one, can recollect stories, quite as respectably attested as those Boetius quotes concerning the *Ceraunix*, told respecting the discovery of new fallen belemnites under precisely the same circumstances, and, in truth, the same author does in the preceding chapter treat at length of the *Belemnites*, and his cuts show that the name meant then what it does at present, but he assigns to the missile an infernal instead of a celestial source, giving the vulgar title for it as "Alpschoss," (elfin-shot,) which he classically renders into "dart of the Incubus," stating further that it was esteemed (on the good old principle, "similia similibus curantur") of mighty efficacy to guard the sleeper from the visits of that much dreaded nocturnal demon The Prussian, Saxon, and Spanish physicians employed it, powdered, as equally efficacious with the *lapis Judaicus*, in the treatment of the calculus It was also believed a specific for the pleurisy in virtue of its *pointed* figure, which was analogous to the *sharp* pains of that disease, for so taught the universally accepted "Doctrine of Signatures"

The *Ceraunix* of Sotacus, however, comprised, besides these primitive manufactures of man, other substances, it is hard to say whether meteorites or fossils, the nature of which remains to be discussed. Photius,* after quoting the paragraph, "I beheld the *Bætylus* moving through the air, and sometimes wrapped up in vestments, sometimes carried in the hands of the ministers," proceeds to give a summary of the wondrous tale told by the discoverer of the prodigy—one Eusebius of Emesa. He related how that, being seized one night with a sudden and unaccountable desire to visit a very ancient temple of Minerva, situated upon a mountain at some distance from the city, he started off, and arriving at the foot, sat down to rest himself. Suddenly he beheld a globe of fire fall down from heaven, and a monstrous lion standing by the same, but who

* 'Bibliotheca,' 1063, R

immediately vanished Running to pick it up as soon as the fire was extinguished, he found this self-same *Bætylus*. Inquiring of it to what god it belonged, the thing made answer that he came from the Noble One (so was called a figure of a lion standing in the temple at Heliopolis) Eusebius thereupon ran home with his prize, a distance of 210 stadia (26 miles), without once stopping, being quite unable to control the *impetus* of the stone! He described it as "of a whitish colour, a perfect sphere, a span in diameter, but sometimes assuming a purple* shade, and also expanding and contracting its dimensions, and having letters painted on it in cinnabar, of which he gave the interpretation The stone, likewise, if struck against the wall, returned answers to consultors in a low whistling voice" The grain of truth in this huge heap of lies is obviously enough the fact that Eusebius, having had the good fortune to witness the descent of a meteorite, and to get possession of the same, told all these fables about it in order to increase the credit of the oracular stone (which doubtless brought him in many fees) amongst his credulous townsfolk Damascius† (whose Life of Isidorus Photius is here being epitomised) adds, that this philosopher was of opinion that the stone was the abode of a spirit, though not one of the mischievous or unclean sort, nor yet one of a perfectly immaterial nature He furthermore states that other *bætyli* were known, dedicated to Saturn, Jupiter, and the Sun, and moreover that Isidorus and himself saw many of such *bætyli* or *bætylia* upon Mount Libanus, near Heliopolis in Syria

As for the derivation of *bætylus*, the one proposed by the Byzantine Hesychius, who makes it come from *bæte*, the goat-skin mantle, wherein Rhea wrapped up the stone she gave old Saturn to swallow, instead of the new-born Jove, cannot be considered much more satisfactory than Bochart's, who, like a sound divine, discovers in it a reminiscence of the stone pillar which Jacob set up at Bethel, and piously endeavours to force Sanconiathon, who speaks of the "living" stones, the bæthylia,‡

* The Greek purple included every shade from crimson to violet

† A stoic philosopher under Justinian

‡ "Moreover the god Uranus devised *bæthylia*, contriving stones that moved as having life"

to confirm his interpretation by correcting his text into "anointed"

But this last *bætylus* is beyond all question the same thing with that described by the Pseudo-Orpheus,* under the names of *Siderites*, and the *animated Orites*, "round, black, ponderous, and surrounded with deeply-graven furrows" In the first of these epithets may easily be recognized the *ferruginous* character common to all meteorites (*siderites* being also applied to the loadstone), whilst the second (*Orites*) seems to indicate the locality where they most abounded, viz, Mount Lebanon

Sotacus' notice, indeed, of the efficacy of the *bætylus* in procuring success in seafights and sieges, is copiously illustrated by the succeeding verses of the same mystic poet, who, it must be remembered, can claim a very high antiquity, there being sufficient grounds for identifying him with Onomacritus, a contemporary of Pisistratus, in the sixth century before our era The diviner Helenus, according to him, had received this oracular stone from Apollo, and he describes the rites, with great minuteness, for the guidance of all subsequent possessors of such a treasure, by means of which the Trojan woke up the spirit within the "vocal sphere" This was effected by dint of thrice seven days' fasting and continence, by incantations and sacrifices offered to the stone, and by bathing, clothing, and nursing it like an infant. Through its aid, when at length rendered instinct with life, the traitorous seer declared to the Atridæ the coming downfall of Troy, the stone uttering its responses in a voice resembling the feeble wail of an infant desiring the breast. It is more than probable that Orphesius in describing the Orites, had in view the *Sālagrāma*, or sacred stone of Vishnu, still employed by the Brahmins in all propitiatory rites, especially in those performed at the death-bed. Sonnerat describes it as "a kind of ammonite, round or oval in shape, black, and very ponderous" The *furrows* covering its surface were traced by Vishnu's own finger ; but when found of a violet colour, it is looked upon with horror, as representing a vindictive avatār of the god. The possessor keeps it wrapped up in linen garment like a child, and often bathes

* Λιθικά, 355.

and perfumes it—precisely the rites prescribed by our poet for the due consultation of the oracle of the Siderites

From all this it may safely be deduced that the "stone of power," whether *bætylus* or *orites*, was in most cases nothing more than a fossil, either a ferruginous nodule, or an echinus filled with iron pyrites Their being found in abundance in one particular locality, precludes the idea of these at least being meteorites, which latter, besides, never assume any regular form, but look like mere fragments of iron slag This explanation is strongly supported by the drawings Boetius gives* of what was then called the "Donner-stein," or "Wetter-stein," (thunder, or storm-stone,) and which he very plausibly identifies with Pliny's *Brontias* "that got into the head of the tortoise during thunder-storms," and which is described in another place as the "eye of the Indian tortoise" that conferred the gift of prophecy. His carefully drawn figure of this Donner-stein (which also passed for the "grosser Kroten-stein," bigger toad-stone), shows it to be only a fossil echinus of a more *oblate* form than the common sort The regular toadstone, plentifully to be seen in mediæval rings, was, on the other hand, the small hollow hemisphere, the fossil tooth of an extinct fish, found in the greensand formation In that age the Donner-stein was held to possess all the many virtues of the Toadstone, Belemnite, and Ovum Anguinum, in counteracting poison, giving success in all enterprises, procuring sleep, and protection against danger of lightning. But the old physician, so much in advance of his times, cannot help winding up the list of its virtues with the hint, "Fides sæpe veritate major"

The axe-heads and hammer-heads of stone, known to us by the general designation of celts, have, until recent explorations, been regarded as comparatively of rare occurrence amongst ancient relics obtained from Eastern lands and from some other continental countries Our information, however, in regard to objects of this class has become greatly extended Mr. James Yates published, in the Archæological Journal, examples of stone celts from Java, an interesting specimen obtained at Sardis is figured, vol xv. p 178, and some others

* ii cap 264

were found by Mr Layard at Nineveh. The occurrence of any ornament or inscription upon such objects is very rare, but amongst numerous stone implements obtained in Greece one is noticed by M de Mortillet (Matériaux pour l'Histoire primitive de l'Homme, Jan 1868, p. 9), of which he had received from Athens a drawing and an *estampage*, it is described as "une hache en pierre serpentineuse, sur une des faces de laquelle on a gravé trois personnages et une inscription en caractères grecs L'ancien outil a évidemment été, beaucoup plus tard, quand on a eu complétement oublié son usage primitif, transformé en talisman ou pierre cabalistique"

At the annual meeting of the Antiquaries of the North, on March 21st, 1853, under the presidency of the late King of Denmark, several recent acquisitions were exhibited, obtained for his private collection at Frederiksborg Amongst these there was an axe-head of stone (length about 6½ inches), perforated with a hole for the handle, and remarkable as bearing on one of its sides four Runic characters, that appear to have been cut upon the stone at some period more recent than the original use of the implement It has been figured in the Memoirs of the Society, 1850–1860, p 28, see also Antiquarisk Tidsskrift, 1852-1854, pp 258–260 I am indebted to a friend well skilled in Runes and Scandinavian archæology, Dr. Charlton, formerly secretary of the Society of Antiquaries of Newcastle, for the following observations on this interesting relic

"The first letter is L, and, if we accept the idea that these were Runes of Victory, it may stand for the initial of Loki, the second is Th, and may stand for Thor, the third O for Odin, the fourth, Belgthor, with a T above it, may refer to Belgthor's friendship and alliance with Thor, and the T stands for Tyr We may imagine the names of the Northern gods to have been cut on this stone axe to give it victory in battle, just as the old Germans and Saxons cut mystic Runes on their swords, a practice noticed by Haigh in his 'Conquest of Britain by the Saxons,' p. 28, pl. 1, where he has figured amongst various examples of the *futhorc*, or alphabet of Runic characters, one inlaid on a sword or knife found in the Thames, and now in the British Museum. At p 51, *ibid* pl iii. fig 20, he has cited also the Runic inscription on the silver pommel of a sword found at Gilton, Kent, formerly in the collection of the late Mr Rolfe, of Sandwich, and subsequently in the possession of Mr Joseph Mayer This relic is now in the precious museum bestowed by his generous encouragement of archæological science on the town of Liverpool The interpretation given in the latter instance is as follows,—Eke victory to great deeds *

"There was another explanation given of the characters on the Danish stone axe It was read—LUTHFR O—Ludr owns namely, the weapon thus inscribed"

In the ancient Sagas, as remarked in Nilsson's 'Primitive Inhabitants of Scandinavia' (translation by Sir John Lubbock, Bart, p 214), mention occurs of amulets designated life-stones, victory-stones, &c, which warriors carried about with them in battle to secure victory A curious relation is cited from one of the Sagas, that King Nidung, when about to engage in conflict, perceived that he had neglected to bring a precious heir-loom, a stone that possessed the virtue of ensuring victory He offered the hand of his daughter, with a third part of his kingdom, to him who should bring this talisman before the fight commenced, and, having received it, he won the battle In another narrative, the daughter of a Scanian warrior steals during his slumbers the stone that was hung on his neck, and gave it to her lover, who thus became the victor Nilsson observes that stones are found in museums, for instance a hammer-stone with a loop, that appear to have been worn thus as talismans in war

It is perhaps scarcely necessary to advert to certain axe-heads of stone, in their general form similar to those with which we are familiar as found in Europe, upon these implements are engraved rude designs, such as the human visage, &c These objects, of which an example preserved in a museum at Douai has been much cited, may be "victory-stones" of an ancient and primitive people, but they are now recognised as of Carib origin, and not European

* 'Archæologia,' vol xxxii p 321 A spear-head inscribed with Runes is noticed, Journ Brit Arch Ass,' vol xxiii p 387 There exist certain massive rings of metal inscribed with Runes, that may have been, as some antiquaries suggest appended to sword-hilts as charms One of these rings, lately found at Carlisle, is in possession of Mr Robert Ferguson, of Morton, near that city

PART III

ABRAXAS, ABRAXASTER, AND ABRAXOID GEMS.

THE AGATHODÆMON WORSHIP

"THERE was a time" (says M. Matter with much force) "when it was from Judaism, especially from the Kabbala, and the system of Philo, that people sought to derive the great transition of the human mind from the ancient into the modern world—a revolution in which so important a part is played by *Gnosticism*. So far as regards the explanation of the writings and the understanding of the views given by Origen, Irenæus, and the other Fathers upon Gnosticism, the Jewish element still retains its ancient pre-eminence; but in the case of the *tangible* monuments come down to us from the Gnostics themselves, we ought henceforth to be fully convinced that it is in the *antiquities of Egypt* we must look for our chief information: and if the ideas, terminology, and symbols of Judaism (that is, of the Kabbala) have lent certain doctrines to this system, yet it is *Egyptian* art that has furnished it with the greatest part of its symbols."

This grand development of the old Wisdom of Egypt in a new phase is the most conspicuously exhibited in that very numerous class of engraved gems popularly and indiscriminately called *Abraxas*, *Basilidan*, and *Gnostic* stones, almost the sole production of the expiring Glyptic Art during the last two centuries of the Western Empire. But, contrary to the generally received notion concerning their nature, a careful study of their numerous subdivisions has fully convinced me that only a very small minority amidst their multitude present any traces of the influence of Christian doctrines; being for the most part the fruit of religious ideas which had flourished long before the first dawn of Christianity. An important portion, indeed, originating in the primitive Egyptian Mythology, have more connexion with Magic and Medicine than with any religious object; and their employment as talismans establishes for them a higher antiquity than belongs to the real "Abraxas" gems, the date of whose origin is historically ascertained. The subject therefore will be more conveniently approached by considering in the first place the Agathodæmon, Chnuphis, or Chneph figures, often named "Dracontia," and erroneously attributed to the Ophites and such-like semi-Christian sects, as their actual *inventors*.

It cannot however be denied, that although these last-named sectaries did not *invent* this emblem, yet that they generally adopted it for their distinguishing badge or, to use their technical word, "seal." And this circumstance leads to a remark which, applying to all talismans alike, may aptly serve for preface to the following dissertation upon their several classes. In the primitive Nature-worship of the Old World all religion consisted in the deification of the great visible Powers of the Universe. The Supreme Beings therefore belonged to the present World, consequently all the blessings they could confer were limited to this life. The means, of whatever kind, supposed to secure the goodwill of these Powers had for object tangible blessings alone—wealth, peace, long life, posterity—in fact all those rewards promised by Moses to the obedient Israelites. The engraved stones under consideration, being legacies of this older religion, were designed to secure temporal not spiritual benefits to the wearers. The latter were not even dreamed of by people holding the belief "mors ultima linea rerum est." This fact explains why so many of the Gnostic gems are in reality no more than medicinal agents, and prescribed by physicians, Heathen and Christian alike, in their regular practice, from Nechepsos down to Alexander Trallianus. On the other hand the true Gnostics, whose sole profession was the knowledge of the other world, when they applied to the doctrines of the ancient religion the same method of interpretation that the Kabbalists had used for Moses and the Prophets (of which the *Pistis-Sophia* has left us such ingenious specimens), subjected all the productions of the former creed to the same Procrustean torture, and consequently availed themselves of these same symbols—nay, more, continued to manufacture them in their own sense of their import.

The *Agathodæmon*—"Good Genius"—whose very name furnishes the reason why he should be chosen to figure on an ornament intended to defend its wearer from all disease and mischance, is depicted as a huge *serpent* having the head of a *lion*, surrounded by a crown of *seven* or *twelve* rays—components conspicuously announcing that he is the embodiment of the idea of the Sun-god. This figure is usually accompanied, either on obverse or reverse, with its proper title, written variously ΧΝΟΥΒΙΣ, ΧΝΟΥΦΙΣ, and ΧΝΟΥΜΙΣ, accordingly as the engraver fancied he could best master that difficulty to the Greek mouth, the true sound of our letter B. This name Salmasius* considers as a rendering of the Coptic ΧΝΟΥΒ, *gold*, and hence explains another title which sometimes takes its place, ΧΟΛΧΝ-ΟΥΒΙΣ, as "All-golden." Jablonsky, however, derives the word more plausibly from ΧΝΟΥΜ, *good*, and ΙΣ, *spirit*, and thus makes "Agothodæmon" to be the literal translation of the name.†

This last had become in the third century the popular name for the hooded snake of Egypt. Lampridius has "Heliogabalus Ægyptios dracunculos Romæ habuit, quos illi *Agathodæmonas* vocant." This kind was the Uraeus, to be seen commonly on Egyptian monuments, where it is the badge of royalty placed upon the head of the sovereign. It is the *hadji hasher* of the modern Arabs, the cobra di capello of the Hindoos. I have met with a large sard engraved in the late Roman-Egyptian style, with two imperial busts *regardant*, reverse, the Chnuphis Serpent, with the legend in *Roman* letters AGATHODAEMON, the sole instance known to me of such an amulet with a *Latin* inscription, but which goes far to confirm Jablonsky's interpretation of the Coptic title. In classical Greek the original Chneph becomes *Canopus;* hence the Canopic vase often appears between two serpents for heraldic supporters. But in those lower times, so fruitful in the Chnuphis talismans, no more Canopic vases appear on gems.

* He has treated the subject at some length in that learned miscellany of his, the treatise 'De Anno Climacterico.'

† The prototype appears to have been that ancient figure of Amon (the Sun) designated as HFE 'The Serpent" *par éminence*, and which was a winged serpent having human arms and feet. He is thus painted on mummy-cases as guardian of the inmate.

The ancient Agathodæmon, in the form of his congener the Cobra, still haunts the precincts of the Hindoo temples, as of old the shrines of Isis, and issues from his hole at the sound of a fife to accept the oblation of milk from the attendant priest As with the ancients so with the Hindoos, he is the special keeper of concealed treasure, and when a zemindar deposits his hoard in the prepared hiding-place, he, to make assurance doubly sure, builds up a serpent therewith, to watch over the gold Suetonius records that Tiberius had a most appropriate pet in a "serpens draco", but having found it one day devoured by a swarm of ants, the suspicious Cæsar took warning from its fate to beware of the force of a multitude of feeble individuals, and consequently secured his person against all danger of popular outbreak by shutting himself up in the inaccessible fastness of Capri

But to return to the type of the Agathodæmon upon our gems Over the seven rays of the lion's crown, and corresponding to their points, stand often the seven vowels of the Greek alphabet, ΑΕΗΙΟΥΩ, testifying the Seven Heavens, a mystery whereof notice shall be taken in the fitting place The reverse of such gems is invariably occupied by a special symbol resembling the letter S, or Z, thrice repeated, or the convolutions of a spiral cord, and traversed by a straight rod through their middle, a symbol for which many and the most whimsical explanations have been proposed Of these the most ingenious, but also the most fanciful, makes it represent the spinal marrow traversing the spine—certainly an apt device for a medicinal talisman But whatever its primary meaning it was probably imported in its present shape from India (that true fountain-head of Gnostic iconography) It is to be seen in two varieties, upon series 16 and 17 in Plate VII. of E Thomas' admirable Essay on the Primitive Coinage of India, amongst the punch-marks

The Chnuphis Serpent

A Limoges enamelled plaque of the twelfth century (in the collection of Mr Octavius Morgan) represents on its one half "Moyses" lifting up the Brazen Serpent to the "Filii Israel" On the other half, "similis Aaron" is seen inscribing with a reed pen the mystic Tau Cross upon the foreheads of the elect. The first of these tableaux offers the most extraordinary feature in its representation of the serpent, depicted here with *lion's head and mane:* the veritable Agathodæmon Chnuphis of our Alexandrian talismans The preservation of this form to so late a period fills one with surprise it indicates a traditionary belief that the symbol was the giver of life and health The belief must have come down from the times when the Egyptian talisman was commonly worn, in the way Galen mentions, as a protection to the chest The Brazen Serpent of Moses and the Plasma Agathodæmon of King Nechepsos had in all probability one and the same origin, giving currency to those little ingots which formed the sole money of the Hindoos before the establishment of the Macedonians in Bactria But the most probable solution of the question is that the symbol stealthily represents the serpent-entwined club of Aesculapius (itself so hard to account for), or the wand similarly encircled, which was the badge of Egyptian priesthood And what renders this conjecture of mine almost a certainty is an *as* of the gens Acilia, bearing for obverse the head of Aesculapius, for reverse a *wand* (not the usual club) placed vertically and encircled by his serpent in *three* convolutions. This type, if slightly defaced by wear, would become identical in appearance with the Chnuphis symbol The spiral frequently takes the form of the letters S S S disconnected, traversed by a straight line The curative virtue ascribed to the sigil, again, tends to indicate its derivation from the proper badge of the god of the healing art. For the eminent physician Marcellus Empiricus (who flourished at Bordeaux in Theodosius' reign) promises wonderful effects in the cure of pleurisy from the wearing of this very figure engraved upon a cerulean Scythian jasper Whether this promise be true or not, marvellous has been the vitality of the symbol itself, for reduced to a double S S upon a bar, it became a favourite device in the times of chivalry, being taken as the rebus upon the word *Fermesse** (SS *fermées*) and the emblem of constancy Hence comes it that this ancient Egyptian symbol now adorns

* This sigla in its simplest form, Ϟ, makes its appearance in profusion over all the buildings of Henri IV., where it is popularly ex-

the Collar of the Garter, formerly known as the "Collars of SS" Meyrick's derivation of the name from the initial of "SouveraYne," motto of Henry IV. when Earl of Derby (and on whose effigy the Collar first appears), is of little weight, for that king was long posterior to the institution of the Order and its insignia Even more preposterous is Camden's idea that the name originated in the initials of Sanctus Simo Simplicius, a famous Roman lawyer, and therefore was taken for badge by his profession—a theory which assuredly does not account for Henry's queen, Joan of Navarre, being similarly decorated with her husband upon their monument

That the Agathodæmon sigil was not only pre-Christian, but ascended to the remotest antiquity in its use as a talisman, plainly appears from Galen's notice thereof (De Simp Med 6 ix) "Some indeed assert that a virtue of this kind is inherent in certain stones, such as *it is certain* is possessed by the green jasper, which benefits the chest and mouth of the stomach, when tied upon them Some indeed set the stone in a ring, and engrave upon it a serpent with head crowned with rays, according to the directions of King Nechepsos in his thirteenth book Of this material I have had much experience, having made a necklace out of stones of the kind, and hung it about the patient's neck, descending low enough to touch the mouth of the stomach, and they proved to be of no less benefit than if they had been engraved in the manner laid down by King Nechepsos" This treatise by Nechepsos must have been a regular Manual for the use of Magicians, for Ausonius mentions its author as

"Quique magos docuit mysteria vana Nechepsi
"Nechepsos, teacher of vain Magic's lore"

plained as relating to Gabrielle d'Estrees, a rebus in its sound, 'S percé d'un *trait*' But Longpérier has shown that the same figure is to be found on the medals of Henri's mother and sister, and even upon articles made for Anne of Austria, and he acquiesces in the explanation given in the text, which is taken from an old book, 'Les Bigarrures,' chap "Des Rebus de la Picardie," by Etienne Tabouret, Sieur des Accords—('Revue Numismatique' for 1856, p 276)

'*Fermesse*, dont l'Amour peint un Chiffre d amour
Commune en l'ecriture, mais rare dans le cœur,
Mais ainsi que la forme est d'un arc mis en deux
Le desir inconstant froisse et brise tes nœuds,
Ce pendant que les mains ta *fermesse* figurent"
Lovs Papon,' 16th century

The book, perhaps the foundation of the pretended Evax, was the first source of the notions concerning the virtues of sigils and gems preserved to us in the mediæval "Lapidaria." Pliny (vii. 50) quotes him along with his countryman Petosiris as an astrological authority, according to whose rule of the "Tetarto-morion" (or law deduced from the position of three signs, *Trine*) the possible duration of human life in the region of Italy extended to 124 years. And before dismissing Nechepsos and his book it may be as well to add here—for the fact will be of service in a further stage of this inquiry—that Pliny mentions (xxx. 2) a second school of Magic, "but more recent by many thousand years" than Zoroaster's, and founded by the *Jews*, Moses, Iannes and Jotapes. The first of the trio may be the Talmudist to whose "secret volume" Juvenal alludes—

"Tradidit arcano quaecumque volumine Moses."

Although the Apostle couples Iannes along with Lambres amongst the Egyptian opponents of the Hebrew legislator, Juvenal also informs us that the nation retained even in his times their ancient fame of veracious interpreters of dreams; nay, more, grown "wiser than Daniel," they even *produced* them to order—

"Qualiacunque voles Judæi somnia mittunt."

"The Jew, for money, sends what dreams you choose."

Hippolytus in the following century remarks that the "Samaritans, or "Simonians," founded by the first preacher of the Gnosis, Simon Magus himself, availed themselves of this power in order to plague their adversaries, "sending the *dream-producing* demons to trouble whomsoever they please." The mediæval name for engraved gems regarded as talismans, viz., "Pierres d'Israel," is better founded than is generally supposed. The obvious difficulty that graven figures—nay, more, idols—could not have been the work of Jews, is answered by the Rabbinical gloss upon the Second Commandment, which allows the wearing of any sort of design cut in *intaglio*, though prohibiting anything of the sort in relief.

The choice of the green *jasper* (now called *plasma**) for the Agathodæmon sigils was probably dictated by the resemblance of its colour to that of the sacred Asp—green banded with brown As for the figure itself, a very ancient testimony as to its nature and signification is afforded by the tradition Eusebius has preserved (I 7) "The serpent, unless injured by violence, never dies naturally, for which reason the Phœnicians have given it the name of the 'Good Genius,' *Agathodæmon.* For the same cause the Egyptians have called it 'Cneph,' and given to it the head of a hawk, because of the especial swiftness of that bird" The priest of Epeae, entitled "Head-interpreter of sacred things and Scribe," had expounded the allegory thus "The most divine Nature of all was one Serpent having the face of a hawk, and most delightful in aspect, for when he opened his eyes he filled all the places of his native region with light, but when he closed them, darkness immediately ensued" The serpent on our gems, however, does not appear invested with a hawk's head, but with a *lion's*, for which reason this legend applies better to the Abraxas-god, occasionally equipped with a hawk's or lion's head, in place of his proper one, that of a cock But the idea is certainly embodied in that common design upon the Mithraic gems, a man grasping a serpent, of which the radiated head points at his eyes and seems to supply them with light Furthermore, the meaning of the figure of the Agathodæmon is clearly denoted by the Chaldee legend frequently accompanying it CEMECEIΛAM, "The Everlasting Sun," which is sometimes followed by ΨE, probably used as sacred numerals, for they have the power in Greek arithmetic of 705. This same legend is attached to a *classical* figure of Phœbus (such as he appears on the coins with the legend SOLI INVICTO COMITI) engraved upon a yellow jasper in the Marlborough Cabinet—a fact sufficiently attesting the accuracy of the interpretation here given to the Chaldee inscription

Astrology likewise lent its aid to accrediting the virtues of the

* The green *jasper* of the moderns was the molochites or molochas of the ancients, for Pliny describes it as *opaque*, dark-green, and specially used for amulets

sigil. That great authority Hephaestion (quoted by Salmasius, *i e*) observes that XNOYMIC is the name of one of the *Decani*, or three chief stars in Cancer, whilst another astrologer laid down that the star so called was set in the breast of Leo, and *for that reason* was efficacious for the cure of all diseases in the chest of man And in fact we find this latter dictum confirmed by the prayer ΦΥΛΑССЄ ΥΓΙΗ СТОМАХОN ΠΡΟΚΛΟΥ, "Keep in good health the chest of Proclus," engraved upon the back of one of these very Chnuphis gems Others of the same kind are again surrounded by a long Coptic legend often arranged in the outline of a serpent, varying in words, but always terminating in the epithet ΓΙΓΑΝΤΟΡΗΚΤΑ or ΠΑΙΚΤΑ, "Breaker" or "Mocker" of the Giants—that is, of the evil and rebellious Angels, for the Grecian fable of the War of the Giants against Jove had then revived, a Zoroastrian interpretation being applied to the rebellion of Ahriman and his demons against Ormuzd and the Ministers of Good

The method of employing a talisman is thus prescribed in the Magic Papyrus, § 9 —"A Spell of Alleius Craeonius, spoken to the Lamp," "*Ωχμαρμαχω τοννουραι χρη μιλλον δερκυων να Ιαο σοιμψηφισον σοιμψηνις σωσια σιαωι*, Thou that shakest the world! Enter, and deliver an oracle concerning such and such a matter *Θοιο κοτοθ φθουφνουν νονεβουη επτασπαχατωι* The engraved stone (λ γ) Serapis seated in front, having the Egyptian crown (*βασιλήïον*) ξξ, and upon his sceptre an ibis, on the back of the stone the Name, and lock it up and keep it for use. Hold in thy left hand the ring, and in thy right a branch of olive and of bay-tree, waving them over the lamp, repeating all the while the spells seven times And having drawn the ring upon the proper finger of thy left hand, facing and being inwards (the engraving), stick the gem against thy left ear, and go to sleep, without returning answer to any one" The object of this charm was (although not so stated) to procure prophetic dreams, which are actually enumerated amongst the effects to follow from the use of the one that stands next in the MS

Although the original intention of these Chnuphis sigils was unquestionably the one pointed out in the preceding pages, yet there is every probability from the nature of the case that the same were adopted and interpreted in a *spiritual* sense by the numerous and influential sect that first assumed the title of "Gnostics." They had an all-sufficient reason for so doing, in the fundamental doctrine of their creed. The well-informed and temperate Hippolytus, writing at the most flourishing period of these transitional theosophies, thus opens his actual 'Refutation of all Heresies' and his Fifth Book with the description "of that sect which hath dared to boast the *Serpent* as the author of their religion, as they prove by certain arguments wherewith *he* hath inspired them. On this account the apostles and priests of this creed have been styled 'Naaseni,' from 'Naas,' the Hebrew word for *serpent*: but subsequently they entitled themselves 'The Gnostics,' because they alone understood the deep things of religion. Out of this sect sprung many other teachers, who by diversifying the original doctrines through inventions of their own became the founders of new systems." Further on he has a passage bearing immediately upon this subject. "This *Naas* is the *only thing* they worship, for which reason they are called 'Naaseni' (*i.e.* *Ophites*, or Serpent-worshippers). From this same word *Naas* they pretend that all the temples (*ναοί*) under Heaven derive the name. And unto this Naas are dedicated every rite, ceremony, mystery, that is, in short, not one rite can be found under Heaven into which this Naas doth not enter. For they say the Serpent signifies the element Water, and with Thales of Miletus contend that nothing in the Universe can subsist without it, whether of things mortal or immortal, animate or inanimate. All things are subject unto him; and he is good, and hath all good things within himself as in the horn of a unicorn, so that he imparts beauty and perfection unto all that is, inasmuch as he pervades all things, as flowing out of Eden, and divided into four heads. . . . This Naas is the 'water above the firmament,' and likewise the 'living water' spoken of by the Saviour. Unto this *Water* all Nature is drawn, and attracts out of the same whatever is analogous to its own nature, each thing after its own kind, with more avidity than the loadstone draws the iron, the ray of the sea-hawk gold, or amber straws. Then they go on to boast We are the *Spiritual*, who have drawn our own portion out of the living water of the Euphrates that flows through the midst of Babylon, and who have entered in through the True Gate, the which is Jesus the Blessed And we of all men are the *only Christians*, in the Third Gate celebrating the Mystery, being anointed with the ineffable ointment out of the *horn* like David, not out of the *earthen vessel* like Saul who conversed with the Evil Spirit of carnal concupiscence "

Euphrates, a more recent teacher of the sect, who founded the branch calling themselves "Peratai," or Fatalists, has a passage that indicates the sense in which his followers may have accepted these Chnuphis gems "To them therefore of the Children of Israel who were bitten in the Wilderness Moses showed the *True and Perfect Serpent*, in whom whosoever trusteth he shall not be bitten by the serpents of the Wilderness, that is, shall not be hurt by the *Powers* No one therefore is able to heal and to save them that be gone forth out of Egypt, that is, out of the body and out of the world, save that Perfect, Full of all fulness, Serpent In Him whosoever putteth his trust, that man perisheth not by the serpents of the Wilderness, that is, by the gods of the nativity."

These last Powers, whom Euphrates (a pure astrologer) in another place calls the "gods of death," are the stars of the horoscope, "which impose upon all that be born the fatal yoke of the changeful nativity," that is, the necessity of *death*, the necessary consequence of *birth*, a doctrine that clearly leads to the efficacy of the Serpent sigil as a talisman to protect the wearer against the malign influence of the astral genii The Ophites, in fact, were the legitimate descendants of the Bacchic Mystae, whose religion during the two centuries preceding our era must have been the predominant one in the great cities of Asia Minor. An argument derived from Numismatics establishes the common fact—the coinage of the chief cities Ephesus, Apamea, Pergamus, was issued chiefly in the form of *Cistophori*, having for obverse the Bacchic Serpent raising himself out of the sacred coffer, for reverse, two serpents entwined round torches.

THE ABRAXAS.

I. Abraxaster, or Borrowed Types

Bellermann in his lucid little treatise, 'Drei Programmen uber die Abraxas-gemmen,'* has divided his subject into three parts—the true *Abraxas*, all of which bear the Pantheos commonly so entitled, whose creation is assigned to Basilides himself, the *Abraxaster*, or types borrowed from the old religions, but adapted by the Gnostic semi-Christians to the expression of their own new ideas, and *Abraxoid*, which, though vulgarly accounted Basilidan gems, have no connection at all with Basilides' own doctrines, but owe their origin entirely to the astrologers of *his* or anterior times.

The *Abraxaster* gems, therefore, on account of this priority of their first creation, have by right the first claim to be considered, and this mode of treating the subject possesses the additional advantage of elucidating the sources of many ideas that strike us as so extraordinary in the Gnostic creed.

The strangely heterogeneous mixture of creeds that prevailed over the Roman Empire during the two centuries between the reigns of Trojan and Constantine is exemplified by numerous allusions in the 'Historia Augusta,' equally with their tangible monuments, which are the subject of this inquiry. What vast encouragement (little enough needed, of a truth) must have been given to the talisman-makers by the accession to imperial power of the Syrian priest Heliogabalus! "He used to sacrifice *human victims*, selecting for the purpose, throughout all Italy, boys of noble birth and conspicuous beauty, having both parents living, in order that both parties might feel the keener anguish. In fact *Magicians* of every sort attended upon him and practised their arts every day, whilst he gave them every encouragement, and returned thanks to the gods for his having met with their especial favourites, at the same time that he was prying into the entrails of the sacrificed children, and torturing the victims to death, after the rules of his national religion." – (*Lampridius*.) And yet the same amusing chronicler puts it

* Berlin, 1820.

down amongst the *accomplishments* of his model Emperor, Severus Alexander, cousin-german to the monster he has previously portrayed—"that he was a great proficient in Judicial Astrology (*mathesis*), so that he gave permission to astrologers to profess and teach that science publicly at Rome. He was moreover very well skilled in divination by victims (*haruspicina*); also an excellent diviner by birds (*ornithoscopos*), so far as even to surpass the Augurs of Spain and Pannonia" This same "every way accomplished gentleman' (to use the Elizabethan phrase) set up the statues of Abraham and Christ side by side with Orpheus and Alexander in his private chapel (*Sacrarium*), whilst his mad predecessor had conceived the grand notion of founding one universal syncretistic religion, for having conveyed to Rome his Emesene god (the *aerolite*), he built for him a temple on the Palatine, whither he transferred the Palladium, Vesta's fire, the Ancilia, the Cybele—in short, whatever object of worship was most sacred to the Romans Nay, more—he talked of drawing into the same centre the "*religions* of the Jews and Samaritans and the *devotion* of the Christians, in order that his deity, Elagabal, might possess the mystery of every other creed."—(*Heliogabalus*, 3)

Of the Abraxaster class the figures are for the most part drawn from the ancient iconography of the Egyptian religion, but they were adopted in a more spiritual sense by the newly-arisen sects, holding the doctrines of Christianity strangely amalgamated with the old teachings of the Mysteries *

Of all these borrowed types the most frequent and most important is the Jackal-headed *Anubis* (sometimes double-headed, the human being superadded to his own), and bearing the caduceus of Hermes to denote his office of conducting souls, not as of yore through the shades of the lower world,† but along the planetary path to their final rest in the Pleroma. Thus the Gnostic

* Many of the actual *types*—the mummified erect Osiris, the reclining Isis, the Nile, the Horus on the lotus-flower, the Anubis, &c—occur on the contemporary Alexandrian coins they therefore can only be accounted Gnostic productions when their Hebrew inscriptions certify their authorship

† In the paintings on the mummy-case of Petemenopt (or Ammonius), Osiris the Occidental, invoked in the papyrus ritual inclosed with the corpse, is seen seated on his throne,

Gospel, "Pistis-Sophia" (§ 20), describing the Saviour after receiving his luminous vestment, inscribed with the Five words of power and with the names of all the Domination to be encountered in his Ascension, makes him come first to the Gate of the firmament, then to the God of the sphere, then to the Sphere of Fate, and lastly to the Twelve great Æons all which Powers when they beheld their own *names* written upon his vesture were smitten with fear and began to sing hymns unto him

This Anubis-Hermes appears sometimes waving a palm-branch, to proclaim his victory over the Powers of Evil, or presiding at the *psychostasia* "weighing of the soul," the scene commonly pictured in the Egyptian Ritual of the Dead In the latter character he stands here for Christ, the Judge of the quick and the dead, but his successor in mediæval art is the Archangel Michael, who holds the scales. In the old Greek gems Hermes is often represented as bending forward, caduceus in hand, and by its mystic virtue assisting a soul to emerge from the depths of the earth—a strange coincidence in form, probably too in origin, with the mediæval picture of the Saviour lifting souls out of Purgatory The Zoroastrian Hell, a burning lake of molten metal, into which, on the Judgment-Day, Ahriman with his followers were to be cast, had for object the ultimate *purification* and restoration to their pristine state of the condemned—a merciful doctrine, held by Origen, and partly allowed by Jerome

Hermes in this particular character of *Psychopompos* was made great use of by the Naaseni (Ophites) as the prophetic representative of the Saviour in his grandest office They interpreted Hermes' leading souls through darkness into Elysium as Christ's guiding the minds of the *enlightened* out of *Ignorance* into *Knowledge*, in their special sense of the words. As may well be supposed, they descanted largely upon that

at his side, his wife and sister, Isis In front stands an altar, loaded with flowers, fruits, and libations Anubis, recognisable by his jackal's head crowned with the *pschent* (tall cap), because, like the Hermes of the Greeks, he discharges important functions equally in the supernal and infernal regions (the place of the Four Amenti), presents to his sire the defunct Petemenopt, swathed in his sepulchral bandages, and holding up his hands in the attitude of supplication

peculiar symbol, under which form Hermes, surnamed Cyllenius, was worshipped. Amongst their mystical expositions of the object one curious fact appears, that its popular name was *ἀγαθοφόρον*, "bringer of good luck," for which cause it was set up at cross-roads, and upon house-tops But as regards the ancient religion, since it is thus made out that this attribute, later modified into a Pillar, stood for Cyllenius, guide of departed souls (exactly as the same figure, *lingam*, represents Siva, Lord of the dead in modern Hinduism), the reason becomes obvious why its sculptured representations should have been the earliest form of monument placed over the departed. The monuments secured for the dweller in the grave the perpetual protection of the Guide and Shepherd of souls, a colossal phallus crowns to this day the summit of the oldest tomb, the date of which is historically certain, the tumulus of the Lydia king, Alyattes The Asiatic colonists carried with them into Italy the same belief in the protective virtues of the symbol, carved in stone it regularly surmounted the door of the sepulchre One lately came into my possession, inscribed around with the name and patronymic of the deceased Etruscan, whose repose it had so long guarded, SVSES FELVS FENTV, "Suses, son of Phintas"

This double character of Anubis is very curiously expressed by the figure upon a sard belonging to myself, which to the casual observer presents that most orthodox of types, the Good Shepherd, carrying a lamb upon his shoulders, leaning upon his staff, his loins bound with a girdle having long and waving ends But upon closer examination this so innocent personage resolves himself into the double-headed god of Egypt, the lamb's head doing duty for the jackal's, springing from the same shoulders with that of the man, whilst the floating end of the girdle is turned into the bushy tail of the wolfish beast, and the "latrator Anubis" bursts upon our astonished eyes This identification of character in Anubis and Christ enables us rightly to understand that drawing, the discovery of which created such a sensation at Rome a few years back, scratched (*graffito*) roughly on the plaster of a room in a house buried (in ancient times) under the extended buildings of the Palatine

It represents this same jackal-headed man holding in front of him a Latin Cross with his outstretched hands, and standing on a pedestal, in front of his worshipper, who makes the customary form of *adoration* by raising his hand to his lips, and who has expressed the object of his handiwork by the inscription ΑΛΕΞΑΜΕΝΟϹ ϹЄΒЄΤЄ ΘΈΟΝ In reality the production of some devout, but illiterate Gnostic, it is construed by its present owners* into a shocking heathen blasphemy, and a jibe upon the good Christian Alexamenos, because they mistake the jackal's head for that of an ass, and consequently imagine an intentional caricature of their own Crucifix.

The discovery of this picture clearly illustrates a passage of Tertullian (Apol xvi) where he says to his opponents "Like many others you have dreamed that an *Ass's Head* is our god. But a new version of our god has lately been made public at Rome, ever since a certain hireling convict of a bullfighter put forth a picture with some such inscription as this, 'the god of the Christians ΟΝΟΚΟΙΗΤΗΣ ' He was depicted thus—with the ears of an ass, and with one of his feet hoofed, holding in his hand a book, and clothed in the toga." An exact description this of the Anubis figured by Matter (Pl. ii c No 1.), save that instead of a book the god carries a cadceus and palm-branch. The same calumny was somewhat later transferred by the Christians themselves to the account of the Gnostics Not being acquainted with the Egyptian beast, they mistook (perhaps intentionally) the head of the jackal for that of the ass, which in truth it strongly resembles in the rude drawing of our gems Thus we find, at the close of the fourth century, Epiphanius asserting "that the Gnostic Sabaoth has, according to some, the face of an *Ass*, according to others, that of a Hog, on which latter account He hath forbidden the Jews to eat swine's flesh" This second notion was a very ancient one, being alluded to by Petronius in 'Judæus licet et *porcinum* numen adoret" Now *Sabaoth* being held by the Gnostics as the national god of the Jews, it seems probable that this same confusion of one beast with the other was the real source of

* Having been cut from the wall and deposited in the museum of the Collegio Romano

the opinion so prevalent amongst the ancients, and quoted by Tacitus (Hist v. 4) "The sacred object so zealously guarded from profane eyes within the Sanctuary at Jerusalem was the figure of the *wild ass* by whose guidance they had relieved their thirst and their distress, Moses having, through the observation of the movements of a troop of these animals, discovered the spring, the waters of which saved his followers from perishing in the desert." This legend was furthermore connected with the belief that the real god of the Jews was Bacchus, for the ass was sacred to the god of wine. For this dedication Pliny finds a singular reason in the fact that the ass was fond of fennel, a deadly poison to all other quadrupeds, but a plant specially consecrated to Bacchus (xxxv 1) Again, the spurious gospel 'The Genealogy of Mary' assigns for the cause of the death of Zacharias, son of Barachias, that once entering the Temple he beheld standing within the Sanctuary a man with the face of an ass, and when he was rushing out to cry unto the people, Woe unto you! Whom do ye worship? he was smitten with dumbness by the apparition. But afterwards, when he had recovered his speech, and revealed what he had seen unto the Jews, they slew him for a blasphemer And this they gave as a reason wherefore the High Priest had bells fastened around the hem of his garment, in order that this monstrous deity might by their tinkling be warned of the approach of man, and so have the time to conceal himself. This wild story is preserved by Epiphanius alone, for the original work is entirely lost It was ascribed to St Matthew, and was taken for their special textbook by the Collyridians, who got their name from their custom of sacrificing cakes to the Virgin Mary, whom they pretended was also born of a virgin Faustus, bishop of Riez, cites this same gospel concerning the parentage of Mary. But the apocryphal gospel, 'The Birth of Mary,' still extant, is of a totally different character, being a mere monkish invention of the most orthodox stupidity, and which, coupled with the 'Protevangelion,' became the source of all the mediæval pictures and sculptures that set forth the history of the Madonna

To the same Egyptian family likewise belongs the boy *Harpocrates* or *Horus* (the vernal Sun), having the symbol of fecundity monstrously exaggerated and seated upon the lotus, which expressed the same idea by its abundant seeds, and also *Perfection* because for its flower, fruit, bulb, all exhibit the form of the *circle*, as Iamblichus observes. Macrobius too remarks that *Horus* is the Egyptian equivalent for Apollo, who gave his name to the twenty-four *hours* of day and night and this acceptation of his character is recorded by the Alexandrian plasma (Vienna Cabinet, I 39) which identifies him with the Grecian Sun god ΜΕΓΑϹ ѠΡΟϹ ΑΠΟΛΛѠΝ ΑΡΠΟΚΡΑΤΗϹ ЄΤΙΛΑΤΟϹ ΤѠ ΦΟΡΟΤΝΤΙ He often appears accompanied by Anubis in the character of his messenger Again, Horus is seen adored by the kneeling Cynocephalus baboon, the animal consecrated to Luna This last curious animal also belonged to Thoth, scribe of the gods, and makes a favourite Gnostic device performing his devotions before a pillar covered all over with inscriptions and supporting a *triangle*, symbol of the Moon whose influence was supposed singularly to affect his constitution. This *pillar* clearly enough denotes those "Pillars of Hermes," by means of which Iamblichus solved all the questions propounded to him by Porphyrius (*Jam De Mysteriis*, II).

To make the allusion more certain, these beings are even designated in the spells by their proper name of "Titans." Ficoroni has given in his *Formæ* No. 4 a mould for casting the reverse of a medalet, of the 3 B size, bearing the Dioscuri facing each other, holding their spears point downwards, in token of amity, in their left hands each a *situla* Behind, vertically CABAѠT in two lines in the exergue TITAN, space not admitting the remainder of the title—too well-known besides to require more than such a reminiscence

Horus is often figured sailing through the heavens in the sacred boat, the *Baris* steered by two hawks, solar emblems, with sun and moon overhead, and taking the same titles ΙΑΩ, ΑΒΛΑΝΑΘΑΝΑΛΒΑ, &c, as the great Abraxas-god himself, and with reason, the same idea being couched in the two personifications. *Horus*, as Heliodorus records (Æth. ix 22), was also applied to the Nile, whose Greek name Νεῖλος also contained the mystic solar number 365, this voyager in the *baris* is analogous to the Hindoo Neryana, the child floating in his argah leaf upon the face of the waters having his whole body coloured *blue* (nila). To complete the resemblance the *situla* regularly carried from a cord in the hand of Anubis is the very *lotah*, brass drinking cup, of the modern Brahmins. Those common emblems, the baris and the coiled serpent, have their Gnostic meaning fully explained by a remarkable passage in the Pistis-Sophia (§ 359). "And the disk of the sun was a *Great Dragon* whose tail was in his mouth, who went up into the Seven Powers on the left hand, being drawn by four Powers having the similitude of white horses. But the going of the Moon was in the shape of a *boat*, the rudder whereof showed a male and female dragon with two white cows drawing the same, and the figure of a child on the stern guiding the dragons, who drew away the light from the *Rulers* (the regular synonym in the book for the rebellious Æons, lords of the Zodiac), and in front of the child was the similitude of a cat."

The *Regeneration* of the "Spiritual Man" occasionally decorates these talismans, being symbolised in the most materialistic manner by the Solar Lion impregnating a naked woman, the recognised emblem of the soul, who "quadrupedum ritu," submits with joy to the vivifying operation. And the spiritual man thus regenerate is again depicted under the form of a human outline holding up by the neck a huge serpent, both of them entirely filled up with inscribed letters, amongst which the mystic Seven Vowels largely predominate.

Scaliger however, as cited by Salmasius in the above-quoted work, takes this figure to be the representative of the combined 365 Æons, all whose names are *supposed* to be condensed within his outline—in short he is the emblem of the Pleroma, and stands for the "Adam-Kadmon" of the Kabbalists, the Primal Man, the Ophite *Adamas*, after whose image the second Adam was made. Or again, this same combination may have been intended to display the Seven Vowels, with their forty and nine Powers, the virtues whereof are so wondrously exalted by the inspired writer of the Pistis-Sophia (§ 378), whose words are cited in another place.* But as the fact bears directly upon the

* Goodwin's 'Magic Papyrus,' gives, at the end of a spell (No. 1) terminating in several vowel-combinations, these directions for pro-

sigil before us, it may be mentioned here that the same gospel (358) makes the Saviour open his "Prayer" with the ejaculation, ΑΕΗΙΟΥΩΙΑΩΩΑ ΙωΙΑ, which, as enveloping the mystic Name of God, were the most obvious spell to be selected to fill up so important a talisman. Neither is it out of place to conclude this inquiry with the notice that the motto of the mediæval House of Hapsburgh was the *Latin* vowels A E I O V These enigmatical letters were interpreted by the arrogance of succeeding generations, puffed up with imperial dignity, into the initials of the prophecy "Austriae est imperare orbi universo." But I more than suspect that the *five* Latin letters were adopted by some *illuminato* amongst the ancient Dukes (perhaps acquired during his alchemical studies) as containing the same transcendental virtues with the Gnostic *seven* of the Greek alphabet

The *winged* goddesses Athor and Sate, representing the Roman Venus and Juno, sometimes are found accompanied with such legends as makes it evident they too had been pressed into the Gnostic service, as representatives of certain amongst the *feminine* Æons * But another shape repeatedly presents his monstrosity to our astonished gaze, whose true character almost sets conjecture at defiance, but evidently the offspring of very diverse ideas most strangely commingled. He is an aged man, Priapean, four-winged, with four hands grasping as many sceptres, he has likewise the spreading tail of the vulture and stands in the *baris*, or upon the coiled serpent, or on a tree-trunk, horizontal, whence project *five* lopped off branches. Some potent saviour must he be, for he is addressed, like Abraxas himself, by the title ΑΒΛΑΝΑΘΑΝΑΛΒΑ¹ But the most prominent symbol in the monstrous collocation suggests an explanation of its hidden meaning, supplied by the following

nouncing each—

"A, with the mouth opened, rolled about like a wave

O, in a short manner for spiritual threatenings

A Ω, unto Earth, Air, Heaven

E, after the fashion of the cynocephalus

O, in the same manner as above said

H, with gentleness aspirated

T, unto the Shepherd (Hermes), as if it were long"

* Valentinus made his Æons in pairs, male and female.

exposition of Justinus, that wildest teacher in all the Gnosis. "For this cause said he unto *Eden*, Mother, behold thy son! meaning his animal and carnal body. He himself, however, having commended his spirit into the Father's hands, ascended up unto the Good One. Now this Good One is *Priapus*, He that *created before* anything existed. On this account he is called Priapus because he *first made* all things (ἐπριαπύισε) * For this reason is he set up in every temple, being honoured by all Nature, and likewise in the roadways, having the fruits of Autumn hung about him, that is, the fruits of the Creation whereof he is the author, inasmuch as he first made the Creation which before was not."

That very frequent type, a mummy swathed in the coils of a vast serpent, is easily explained as an allusion to the protection in the next world of the ancient agatho-demon,† or the spiritual Naas of the more recent Ophites. The same belief also generated that more graceful allegory, the woman enthroned on the back of the same reptile, like the Atergatis of Phœnicia.

Interesting above the rest for the part it played in mediæval superstition is the *Osiris*, or *old man*, with radiated head, a terminal figure always shown in front face with arms crossed on the breast, the true *Baphomet* of the Templars. Sometimes he is borne aloft upon the heads of four Angels, upon whom two streams pour forth from his sides. This group has been explained as Ormuzd borne up by the Four Elements, although it may possibly refer to the notion the prophet Enoch mentions (xviii. 3) "I also beheld the *Four Winds* which bear up the earth and the firmament of heaven." The idea in truth has rather an Assyrian than Egyptian cast, for in Assyrian works Athor (Mylitta) often appears pouring out from her extended arms the Waters of Life, and again the Persian female *Ized* Arduisher is by interpretation "The giver of living water."‡

A curious specimen of ancient form, borrowed in a more

* That is, the proper symbol of Priapus, either the phallus or the Egyptian Tau.

† The HFE painted on the mummy cases in that very capacity.

‡ At Tarsus (1863) was discovered in company with aurei of Sev. Alexander and Gordian III., a talisman thus described by Longperier: "Amulet formed of lapis-lazuli, set

spiritual sense, is furnished by a pretty sard, found in the Punjab (Major Pearse), engraved with two figures of the Roman Providentia facing each other, in the field between them, the heads of Sol and Luna, and below XAIA, the Hebrew for *Life*.

The common figure ⊙ may be explained by Eusebius's description of the Egyptian hieroglyph for the world, as a circle coloured sky-blue and besprinkled with flames, in the centre an extended serpent, the whole being carelessly imitated by the letter ⊙ in the Diagramma of the Ophites.

An armed man, the Mithraic *soldier*, one of the figures regularly set up in the mystic Cave of the Solar god, often decorates a talisman, holding a spear tipped with the head of a cock, a mark of honour granted by the Persian kings to distinguished valour (as by Artaxerxes to the Carian who slew Cyrus the Younger), or else grasping a serpent in each hand. A sect that sprung up in Egypt, the Phibionites, took the title "Militant," Στρατιωτικοί. Another figure, the three-headed, three-bodied god, who, standing like Priapus, grasped with one hand the symbols of fecundity, with the other, asps and scorpions, must be the visible embodiment of the Great Τριδύναμεις, who figure so prominently in the celestial hierarchy of the Pistis Sophia. The *Trees* sometimes enlisted in the Talismanic corps may find their motive in the "Almond-tree" of the Phrygian Mysteries, in which the Naaseni discovered the name of the Great Creator of All, or else to the "Mystery of the Five Trees," mentioned in that oft-quoted revelation, on whose true nature light is thrown by Justinus' exposition making out

---

in a gold frame of rude workmanship, with a ring for suspension. The two faces are engraved in intaglio, and represent an Æon with four wings and bird's tail, holding two spears, and with a Venus and the inscription (not reversed) APΩPI ΦPACIC, some letters of which are concealed by the setting. Length, 0 0034, weight 5 20 grammes (= 95 grs troy)." The same legend accompanies a Venus Anadyomene upon a large hæmatite (Praun) now in the British Museum. Montfaucon, pl. clxi. has a Venus unveiling inscribed APΩPI OPACIC, "The Vision of Arori," and another with APPΩPIΦ IACIC and on the field CANKTA for the owner's name. It was under such a form as this that the Supreme Tetrad brought down Truth from Heaven to display her beauty to Marcus as he describes in his Revelation' (see p. 218).

the *Trees* of Paradise to be the *Angels* generated between the Demiurgus Elohim and his daughter Eden.*

There is a sigil of this class, that from its frequency must have been considered of peculiar virtue. It represents a fish with immense head and shoulders, but diminutive body, as if seen from above; the reverse of the stone thus inscribed—

XΘCHΘ
MBϘY

One of the three sacred fish of the Nile must figure here, and in this talismanic character passed, with an appropriate mystic interpretation, into the symbolism of the Alexandrine Christians.

II. Abraxoids, or Gems confounded with the true Gnostic

Our invaluable and most charming guide, Hippolytus, when describing the *Astrotheoscopi*, "Seekers of God in the stars," begins with a simile more apposite than complimentary to the fashion which then prevailed for combining astrology with every species of religion. He compares these inquirers to that silly fowl the bustard, which suffers itself to be caught by the following device. "When a man discovers a flock he begins to dance and make grimaces in front of them. The birds stand motionless, staring at him in wonderment until his confederate steals up to them from behind and knocks them on the head. In the same way (adds the good Saint, evidently much refreshed by his joke) do the people seduced by such teachers stare up at the stars, until at last they find themselves hopelessly caught in the snare of the heresy." As an example of this most curious system of theology it will suffice to quote their exposition of the doctrine conveyed by one constellation out of many. "Ophiuchus represents with his stars a man on his knees, in appearance oppressed with

* An authentic description of the Tree of Knowledge will doubtless be acceptable to my readers. "The Tree of Knowledge also was there, of which if any eats he becomes endowed with great wisdom. It was like a species of the tamarind-tree, bearing fruit which resembled grapes extremely fine, and its fragrance extended to a considerable distance. I exclaimed, 'How beautiful is this tree, and how delightful is its appearance!'"—(Book of Enoch, xxxi. 3-4.)

fatigue, a posture for which that great authority in Astrology, Aratas, is at a loss to account But rightly understood, he is *Adam* engaged in watching the Dragon's head underneath him, which is biting his heel Over his head are seen the Lyre, and the Crown. The *Lyre* was the invention of the infant Hermes, who is in reality the Word of God their position therefore announces that whosoever gives heed unto the Word, he shall obtain the Crown; but if he refuses to hearken unto the Word, he shall be cast down below with the Dragon" In another place Hippolytus observes "The doctrine of the Chaldæans concerning trines, quadrates, benignant and malign stars, Euphrates the Peratist applies to Christianity, by changing the concord and discord of the stars into the constitution of the Æons, the transition of Good Powers into Evil ones, and the harmony of their respective particles From the same source he gets his "Toparchs" and "Presidents," and all the other imagery of the astrologers"

Such being the nature of the actual foundations of Gnosticism, no wonder that it should so frequently be impossible to decide whether a talismanic sigil be the expression of some semi-Christian tenet, or merely the imagined similitude of some astral Power whose influence was thus secured for the wearer's protection For the gods of Magianism, the religion that has so deeply tinged all Gnostic doctrines, were no other than these starry Powers The Agathodæmon himself gave his name to one of the three Decani of Cancer, as Hephaestion hath already informed us The very title, "Decanus," Salmasius with some reason derives from the Chaldee *Dekan*, "inspector," and thereby makes it equivalent to the Greek "Horoscopos," "The god that looks down upon the nativity." The common Latin derivation, in its military sense of "sergeant," Salmasius rejects as foreign to the idea conveyed. Again, Charchnumis is named as the First Decanus in Leo, and this title actually appears around a serpent with human and radiated head, figured by Salmasius in the same chapter This name is sometimes written ΧΟΛΧΝΟΤΒΙΣ, which the same authority explains as "The All-golden One"

A Greek astrologer quoted without name by Salmasius gives

this curious piece of information "There are appointed in each one of the Signs, three Decani of different forms; one *holding an axe*, the others represented variously These figures engraved in rings are amulets against all mischance" As Teucer asserts, with other great astrologers of his times. "This, alas! too scanty notice of their attributes shows at least one of their number to be the old Babylonian god described by the prophet Baruch (*Epistle* 13, 14)—'He hath a sceptre in his hand like a man, like a judge of the kingdom—he hath in his hand a sword and an *axe*'" But not merely the Decani of the Signs were thus worn in rings, but equally so the signs themselves, and the stars rising together with them, technically called οἱ παρατέλλοντες. Such images were termed στοιχεῖα, whence those who made a business of engraving them got the name στοιχειωματικοί They performed their work with many ceremonies, and always under the *inspection* of the particular Decanus, or star, whose sigil they were embodying, On this account Epiphanius speaks of the sun, moon, and planets as στοιχεῖα, terming μορφώσεις the figures of the constellations formed by the imaginary collocation of the stars The same writer uses the expression, "The stars that be vainly imagined in the shape of figures, which are called Signs of the Zodiac" As Diodorus distinguishes between *planets* and στοιχεῖα, it follows that the term was equivalent to our "constellation" All this evinces that the Arabian writers were correct in translating στοιχειωματικοί by "talisman-makers." How these later astrologers thought proper to portray the Ascendants of each Sign in their "Table of the Myriogeneses" will be described in my chapter upon Talismans

A curious Praun gem represents Mercury enthroned and bearing the attributes of Jupiter, with the strange legend ΕΠΠΤΑ (*sic*) ΧΡΤΣΟΣ, which has been absurdly interpreted as referring to his *seven*-stringed lyre. More probably was the gem the signet of some "Hebdomadarian" or votary of the Number Seven, a sect of sufficient importance to get from Hippolytus a separate section for themselves in his great work The identification of Hermes with the Christian *Logos* was one grand feature in the doctrine of the Naaseni, so lucidly set forth by that learned

Father He was of opinion that this Hebdomadarian doctrine (derived from ancient Egyptian philosophy) was the true source of every form of Gnosticism This potent Numeral is illustrated by another device of frequent occurrence in cameo, the Delphic Є crowned with a fillet, and below, the legend ΧΡΤΣΟΤ This can be no other than that most holy of Numerals the Delphic Ἐι, or *Five*, on the mystery whereof Plutarch has left a very curious dissertation, and it represents the *golden* figure of that same numeral dedicated by Livia Augusta at the shrine of her husband's peculiar patron. And similarly the gem above referred to exhibits Hermes invested with supreme dominion, and accompanied by his own special *number*, "testudo resonare *septem** callida nervis"—the Magian method for symbolizing the different Powers of Heaven, which shall be explained in its due place, when we come to treat of the "Seven Voices"

The oldest adaptations of the imagery of the old religions mark the earliest preaching of the Gnosis Its first apostle, Simon Magus, who passed himself off upon the Samaritans as the *third* manifestation of the Christ, was worshipped as late as Hippolytus' times, in statues made in the form of Jupiter His famous concubine Helena (in whom Simon has discovered the Lost Sheep of the parable whilst carrying on her profession in a brothel at Tyre) was similarly adored under the forms of Minerva and the Moon (Hipp vi 19) The main doctrines of the Naaseni were supported by ingenious applications of the symbolism employed in the Eleusinian, Phrygian, and Samothracian Mysteries, of which Hyppolytus has given a full and very interesting account

Phœnicia, again, furnished our talisman-makers with a copious repertory in the exaggerated symbolism of the figures whereby their priesthood had expressed their notions of the Divine Power. "Taut, the great god of the Phœnicians" (says Samoniathon), "in order to express the character of Kronos, made his image with four eyes—two in front, two behind, open and closed, also with four wings—two expanded upwards, two folded downwards The eyes denoted that the godhead sees

* The compound Ἑπτάχρυσος is made after the same rule as the Ἑπτάχαλκος, the place in the wall of Athens where Sulla took the city

when sleeping, and sleeps when waking, the attitude of his wings, that he flies in resting, and rests in flying Upon his head are two wings, denoting Reason and the Senses" It is very provoking that Diodorus (xx 10) should have given no further description of the famous Kronos, *Melcarth*, of Carthage than the brief remark that it held the hands open, palm upwards, but sloping downwards, so that the child sacrificed, when laid upon them, should roll off into a pit of fire at the foot * When Agathocles was pressing hard the siege, and hope was almost lost, no fewer that three hundred children of the nobles were offered to Melcarth at one and the same time.

Inasmuch as the genius of the planet Saturn, or Kronos, was held by the Talmudists to be good and pure, contrary to those of the other planets, the Four-winged image, so common upon Gnostic gems, may reasonably be considered as a copy from the ancient original, devised by Taut Saturn, the sole inspirer of the Law and the Prophets, had special claims to the veneration of the Alexandrine Kabbalists And this belief explains wherefore Valentinus fixed upon this planet for the abode of Ildabaoth, the Giver of the Law to the Children of Israel in the Wilderness

It sounds like a paradox to assert that our "Gnostic" gems are not the work of the Gnostics, but taking that appellation in its strictest sense, the thing is perfectly true The talismans we are considering never exhibit any traces of that admixture of Christian and Pagan doctrines which properly constitutes the Gnosis, that subject of the descriptions and the attacks of the Fathers of the Church. Their elements are drawn from the ancient religions of Babylon and Egypt, mixed at times with the formulæ of the Jewish Kabbala The "Gnostic" stones are in reality the paraphernalia of magicians and dealers in charms (charm-doctors in modern phrase), and only belong to the Ophites, Valentinians, and other subdivisions of the Christian Gnosis, in so far as those theosophists were especially given to

* This tradition was verified by N Davis, who in excavating the ruins of the temple found, at a great depth, a thick layer of ashes mingled with burnt human bones The discovery is well described in his section "Moloch and his Victims"

the cultivation of the Black Art, as the notices above cited abundantly declare. This delusive study prevailed at the period of the grand development of Gnosticism to an extent which no one can credit who has not studied the historians of the Later Empire The accusation of "magical practices" proved a ready weapon for destroying an obnoxious individual against whom no tangible crime could be charged what stronger proof of this than its being effectually employed (as Ammian tells us) to expel that pattern of orthodoxy, the great Athanasius, from the patriarchal throne of Alexandria? The same historian notices that under the timid Valens it sufficed to establish this capital charge if the suspected person had been seen walking at night-time in the neighbourhood of any cemetery, where he might possibly have gone to hold conference with the demons of the dead

But to exhibit the true source and nature of these "Gnostic" inscriptions I shall transcribe a spell from the "Magic Papyrus," to which I shall have occasion frequently to refer The author of this wondrous Manual of Necromancy was unmistakably of the old unmixed Egyptian religion, and very probably a priest of Isis Nevertheless, he not merely employs the very words found on our talismans, but even the same peculiar arrangement of them Any one desirous of preserving so valuable a charm in a more durable material than papyrus or lead, had only to order a lapidary to copy it for him upon a jasper, and a regular "Gnostic" monument would have been bequeathed to our times The maker having carefully specified the virtues of composition, gives us to understand the value of similar forms still existing on stones VII "Take a sheet of hieratic paper, or a leaden plate, and an iron link of a chain (κρίκος), and place the link upon the paper, and mark both inside and out with a pen the form of the link Then having described the circular outline of the link, write upon the same outline, inscribing upon the paper the name and the characters on the outside, and inside the thing which you wish *not* to happen, or that a man's mind may be bound so as not to do such and such a thing Then placing the link upon its outline which you have made, and taking up the parts outside the outline, sew up the link with thread so as to completely conceal it, piercing through the characters with the pen; and when you wish to bend, say—'I bend such a one not to speak to such a one, let him not resist, let him not contradict, let him not be able to look me into the face, or to answer me, but let him be subject unto me so long as this link is buried. And again I bind his mind, his senses, his desires, his actions, that he may be sluggish towards all men, in case (a certain woman) marries such a one,' or else, 'in order that she may *not* marry such and such a one.' Common (*i.e.*, to be said in Greek.)

"Then taking it to the grave of one untimely deceased, dig four fingers deep, and put it in and say—'O departed Spirit, whosoever thou art, thou art *this*, I deliver unto thee such a one, that he may not do such and such a thing. Then cover it up and depart. And you will do this best when the moon is on the wane. The words to be written within the circle are these: ΑΡΟΑΜΑΘΡΑΕΡΕϹ ΚΙΓΑΛΑΧ ЄΖΑΝΤΑ ΙΑΡΟΥΝΗ ΑΚΗ ΙΑⲰ ΔΑΡΥΝΚⲰ ΜΑΝΙΗΛ ΜΗ ΠΡΑΧΘΗΤⲰ ΤΟ Δ (δεῖνα) ΠΡΑΓΜΑ ЄΦ' ΟϹΟΝ ΧΡΟΝΟΝ ΚЄΧⲰϹΤΑΙ Ο ΚΡΙΚΟϹ ΟΥΤΟϹ ('*Let not such and such a thing be done for so long a time as this link is buried.*') Bind it with knots, making a twist of them, and so deposit it. The link may also be cast into a disused well, or into the grave of one dead before his time. And after the characters, write also these words below the link as a plinth (or a *square*): ΑΡΧΟΟΛ ΛΑΙΑΑΜ ϹЄΜЄϹΙΛΑΜΦ ΑΜΜΟΦΟΡΙⲰΝ ΙⲰΑΗ ΦΘΟΥΘ ЄⲰΦΡΗ Ο MELICTOC ΔΑΙΜⲰΝ ΙΑⲰ ϹΑΒΑⲰΘ ΑΡΒΑΘ ΙΑⲰ ΛΑΙΛΑΜ ΟϹΟΡΝΟΦΡΙ ЄΜΦΡΗ ΦΡΗ ΦΘΑ ΧΡⲰΙⲰ ΙΑⲰ ΒΑΒ ΟΥΡΗ ΘΙΜΑΜЄΝ ΦΡΗ ΒЄ ΝΟΥϹΙ ϹΑΒΑⲰΘ ΒΑΡΒΑΘΙΑⲰ ΘΑΧΡΑ ΟΥΧЄЄΘ ЄϹΟΡΝⲰΦΡΙ, and the inscription at the top of the page, which also you must place within it.

ΙΑЄⲰΒΑΦΡЄΝЄΜΟΥΝΟΘΙΛΑΡΙΚΡΙΦΙΑЄΥЄΑΡΙΦΙΚΡΑᾹΙΘΟΝΦΥΟ ΜЄΝΡΦΑΒΑⲰЄΑΙ

(This spell is repeated at the foot of the page, inscribed in one continuous circle, to show that it reads either way. It occurs also on a gem (Brit. Mus.) followed by ΔΟΥΑΙ ΧΑΡΙΝ ΙЄΡⲰΝΙΜΑ ΠΡΟϹ ΠΑΝΤΑϹ, "Give to Hieronima favour in the sight of all men;" and also on another, figured by Montfaucon, II. pl. 164—a proof of the importance attached to it at the time.)

"And the same arrangement may be written upon a leaden plate, and having put the link within it, fold it over and seal with gypsum, and afterwards the base beneath, upon which ΙΑΕΩ as before directed, and also these words ΒΑΚΑΞΤΧΤΧ ΜΕΝΕΒΑ ΙΧΤΧ ΑΒΡΑCΑΞ ΑΤ, "Prevent such and such a thing" But in the *original* the Names are found as follows ΑΜΦΟΟΛ ΛΑΙΛΑΜ CΕΜΕCΙΛΑΜ ΙΑΕΩ ΛΟΒΑΚΑΞΙΧΤΧ ΑΡΑCΑΞΑΤ ΑΡΧΩΜ ΕΛΑΧ ΜΕΝΕCΙΛΑΜ ΙΑΕΩ ΟΤΩ ΒΑΚΑΞΙΧΤΧ ΑΡΑCΑΞΩΤ, "Prevent such and such a thing."

ΚΙⅭΝVΒ
ΒΙΕΝVΒ□ϷΗΓ□Ϸ□□ϷΗΙΧΝ□VΒΙⅭΝΑΑΒ

ΔΑϷΗ □Ϸ□ΜΑ

On the reverse of a Chnuphis plasma (Lewis Collection), ΚΙCΝVΘ and ΝΑΒΙC (*prophet*) occur, as also on the Bosanquet gem The last words may be corrupt Greek, "Restore the sight", the object of the talisman

FIG 10

III. The True Abraxas Gems

Having in the preceding sections cleared the ground of the innumerable usurpers of the title "Abraxas gems," we can conveniently proceed to consider the wondrous Sigil, the invention whereof is universally ascribed to Basilides himself. And for this asumption there are very good grounds, for it is certain that such a Sigil never occurs executed in a style that bespeaks a date anterior to the grand heresiarch's, the first years of the second century.

This figure, which has given its name to the whole family, is designed to represent the god "Abraxas," for so his name is written invariably on the gems, although the Latin Fathers to suit the genius of their own language have transposed the final letters. The etymology and *value* of the name require a whole section to themselves, so deep are the mysteries that they contain.

The purpose of the composition was to express visibly, and at once, the 365 Æons, emanations from the First Cause, whose number was probably first suggested by its own numerical signification, and consequently the figure may be taken as a speaking type of the *Pleroma*, the *one* embracing *all* within itself, an idea fittingly embodied in a name containing the sum of all its component powers. To shadow forth therefore this grand doctrine, the image in question is a "Pantheus," or combination of many discordant attributes expressing the amalgamation of many different ideas in one and the same figure. Hence he is depicted with the head of a *cock*, sacred to Phœbus, or else of a *Lion*, symbol of Mithras and Belus: his body, *human* and clad in armour, indicates his guardian power, for he is a Virtue Militant "putting on the whole armour of God"; his legs are the sacred *asps*, types of the Agathodæmon, likewise indicating *swiftness*, for in this way, says Pausanias, was Boreas pictured upon the Coffer of Cypselus: in his right hand he brandishes a *scourge*, the Egyptian badge of sovereignty; on his left arm a *shield*, usually emblazoned with some word of power, declaring his perpetual warfare against the rebellious Angels, the "Gods of death." Bellermann has proposed with much ingenuity an interpretation of this Pantheus in the more spiritual sense better consonant with the esoteric teaching of its inventor. According to him, the whole represents the Supreme Being, with his Five great Emanations, each one pointed out by means of an expressive emblem. Thus, from the human body, the usual form assigned to the Deity, forasmuch as it is written that God created man in his own image, issue the two supporters, *Nous* and *Logos*, symbols of the inner sense and the quickening understanding, as typified by the serpents, for the same reason that had induced the old Greeks to assign this reptile for an attribute to Pallas. His head—a cock's—represents *Phronesis*, the fowl being emblematical of foresight and vigilance. His two hands bear the badges of *Sophia* and *Dynamis*, the shield of Wisdom, and the scourge of Power.

This Pantheus is invariably inscribed with his proper name, ΙΑΩ, and his epithets, ΑΒΡΑΣΑΞ and ΣΑΒΑΩΘ, and often accompanied with invocations such as, ΣΕΜΕΣ ΕΙΛΑΜ, "The Eternal Sun", ΑΒΛΑΝΑΘΑΝΑΛΒΑ, "Thou art our Father" (sometimes curtailed, but generally so arranged as to read the same both ways), or ΑΔΟΝΑΙ "The Lord."*

In all this a further relationship to the ancient idea of the Sun-god is readily to be discovered. Phœbus, as the god of day, is similarly furnished with a *whip*, and the *serpent*, according to the Egyptians, hieroglyphically expressed his tortuous course through the Zodiac. "Adonai" was the Syrian title of the Sun, whence *Adonis* or *Thammuz* denoted that luminary at the winter solstice. Moreover, the Gnostic epithets above are the very words composing that "short prayer," from the use of which at all sacrifices Macrobius (I. 23) makes out that the influence of the Sun is the Power supreme over all. "O Sun, Father of All, Spirit of the world, Strength of the world, Light of the world!" But the God adored under the name of

* Besides these regular titles others are occasionally used, of unknown import. Thus a well-engraved Abraxas figure (John Evans) has over his head BICTYC, below his feet EICIT.

"Abrasax" is clearly shown by the Bosanquet jasper (more particularly described elsewhere), exhibiting the Pantheus in the very car, and attitude of Phœbus, and by the Alexandrian coin of Hadrian presenting Serapis similarly engaged That the latter was the Solar deity, all mythologists were agreed, and this identity of action would lead one to suspect that "Abrasax" was no more than the *mystic* name of the tutelary god of Alexandria

The older Chnuphis was occasionally (though rarely) erected with Abraxas on the same talisman, an example of which is offered in one of the most remarkable of the class ever brought under my notice It was brought from Bombay by a Jew (1874), and sold to M Gaston Feuardent, whence it came into the possession of the Rev S S Lewis

Red jasper of fine quality, $1\frac{1}{4} \times 1\frac{1}{4}$ inch, with figure of Abraxas, holding whip and shield, engraved in unusually good style upon the convex face Round the edge, beginning over the head, runs continuously,

ⴲANΛ✡ƆΛ ΛVΛΛIⴲ
Λ⊠VAV✡ΛVIAHAI

at the back of the head, P, under beak, I, over right shoulder, BA (probably *nexus* of ABΛAN), across the field, each side of waist,

□ΛИHHI IHHNΛ□

Again, across field on a level with his loins, on each side,

□VЭ ЄV□

(perhaps *Eoia*, "The Serpent," in Syriac)

Between the serpent legs,

AIIVIIMHV

On the other side, which is almost flat, is the Chnuphis Serpent, erect, with the Seven Vowels inserted between the rays of his head Across the middle of the field,

HΛ ЄIX ("Thy God")

Over his head, three scarabei in a row, to the right, three goats, and three crocodiles above each other, to the left, as many ibises and serpents so arranged

GNOSTIC PLAQUE

The most remarkable specimen of the class known to me was obtained (Jan. 1876) from Sambon, a noted *antiquario* at Naples It is a circular bronze disc, $2\frac{3}{4}$ inches (the ancient *palmus*) in diameter, with a small projection to top, perforated for suspension. The surface of the obverse bears a genuine patina, and the characters of the legend have the true antique formation, but, for reasons hereafter to be stated, the reverse strikes me as an addition of later times—not, indeed, a forgery to entrap the antiquarian, but something intended in all good faith to augment the virtues of the original talisman

The Abraxas-god, advancing to the right, with arms extended crucifix fashion, holding sword and shield, above his head and arms,

ΙΑΘ ΙΑω ΑΛωΝ
ωΗ

On each side of figure—

Ηω ΜΑ Μω ωΝ ΒΑΑ ΟΛ ΒΑΛ✡ CΘ ЄΡ C	CЄ ✡ ΦVΛΑΖΟΝ ΖωCΙΜ ΟΝ

The whole inclosed within a coiled serpent

Reverse King with hand on breast, seated on throne, seen in front-face Over his head,

CΦΡΑΓΙC CΑΛΟΜωΝΟC

On each side of the figure—

ЄΠΗΝΑ CVΜΑΗΑ ΟCΑΛΛΑΜ ΑΣΑΒΑ ΜЄΑΖΑ Χ ΟΥC	ΑΒΟ VΑC ΜΟΤΗΕ ΝЄΤЄ ΚЄΝЄ ΗΗЄ ΑΑΒ Λ

Under the footstool, similarly surrounded by the coiled serpent,

Ƶ Ƶ Ƶ

This Solomon is a truly mediæval piece of drawing, the lettering, too, evidently differs from that of the obverse, and as the surface of the plate is fresher on this side, it is probable that the whole has been added upon the empty back of the original plate

Some legends, following the rule of the famous ΑΒΛΑΘΑΝΑΛΒΑ, read indifferently from either end A good example occurs on the reverse of a serapis, carried in the *baris* between Sol and Luna

ΑCW
ΒΑΦΡΕΜΕ
ΜΟΥΝΟΘΙΑΡ
ΙΚΡΟΙΦΙΑЄVЄΑΙ
ΦЄΡΚΙΡΑΝΘΟΝ
ΥΟΜЄΝЄΡΦΑ
ΒΟЄΑΙΙ

(Sard, from collection of Mr Webb Ware, Cork)

Horus seated in the *baris*, on prow and poop are perched the sacred birds, neatly engraved on dark-green jasper (Pliny's Molochites) On the reverse—

ΧΑΒΡΑΧ
ΦΝЄCΧΗΡ
ΦΙΧΝΟΦΝVΡΝ
ΦΜΧΜΕΜΧ

Amongst the various contents of a tomb at Saintes, discovered in 1885, was a *metal* ring set with a heliotrope engraved with the Agathodæmon, furnished with a human trunk, standing On the reverse a novel formula—

ΧΛΧΧΑ
ΧΙΟVΧΙΡΟ
VΧΑΗΑ

Ruchael, "Spirit of God," is known as the name of an angel, but the other words defy interpretation

The best executed of such talismans known to me, belongs to Mr Webb Ware, of Cork. It is an elliptical sard, about $1\frac{1}{4}$ inches long and wide, engraved very neatly, with Serapis seated on the Baris, busts of Osiris and Isis on prow and poop, above, ΑΛΔΑ, below, ΒΑΙΝ On the reverse, finely cut—

ΑЄω
ΒΑΦΡЄΝЄ
ΜΟΥΝΟΘΙΛΑΡ
ΙΚΡΙΟΦΙΑЄΒЄΑΙ
ΦΙΡΚΙΡΑΝΘΟΝ
ΥΟΜЄΝЄΡΦΑ
ΚΟЄΑΙ

There is no distinction between Α and Λ in the original, but I have made it where clearly required The ΑΛΔΑ is a novelty, but many words in the long formula are of common occurrence in other gems

IV The God Abraxas as described by the Christian Fathers

That the Pantheus upon our gems was really intended to picture forth the deity styled "Abraxas" can be established by the indirect evidence of many contemporary writers Irenæus remarks of the Basilidans, that "they use *images*, incantations, and all other things pertaining unto Magic" Further on (xxiii) he adds their custom of giving names to their *images* of pretended angels And, what bears more directly on the subject, Tertullian (*Apol* xvi), after laughing at the god of the heretics as "biforme numen" (evidently in reference to the serpent legs, "biformes" being the classical synonym for the Giants similarly equipped), then goes on to say, "They have taken unto themselves gods with wings, or with heads of dogs or lions, or else *serpents from the legs downwards*" Here we have unmistakeable reference to the Magian, Egyptian, and Mithraic idols so common upon these talismans, and in the last words to the serpent-legged and veritable Abraxas-god

Lastly, Epiphanius, after stating that Basilides had taught that the Supreme Being—out of whom proceeded Mind, Intelligence, Providence, Strength, and Wisdom—was named Abraxas, proceeds to describe in what manner the idea was embodied by the heresiarch "Having taken their vain speculations, he and his followers have converted them into a *peculiar and definite form*, as a foundation for their own erroneous *idolatrous* and fictitious doctrines." Further on he adds "With respect to their 'Kavlacav,' what person with any understanding would not laugh at their converting a Hebrew word into a *bodily shape* in order to represent their idol, at their personified Principalities, in a word, at their fondness for *images*, whilst through these fancies they sow error in the minds of the ignorant for the furtherance of their disgraceful and lying trade?" Then proceeding, it would appear, to the analysis of the figure itself, he exclaims "It is a Spirit of deceit, which, like the playing upon a pipe, leads the ignorant into many sins against the Truth Yea, even his *legs* are an *imitation of the Serpent* through whom the Evil One spake and deceived Eve For after the pattern of that figure hath the flute been invented for the deceiving of mankind Observe the figure that the player makes in blowing his flute Doth he not bend himself up and down to the right and to the left, like unto it (the serpent)? These forms hath the Devil used to support his blasphemy against heavenly things, to destroy with destruction things upon earth, to encompass the whole world, taking captive right and left all such as lend an ear to his seductions"

V "ABRAXAS"—ETYMOLOGY OF

Of this "Great Name," many etymologies have been proposed Of all these the most satisfactory is perhaps the one offered by Rabbi Abraham Geiger, making it the Grecised form of *Ha-Brachah*, "The Blessing" For there is good reason for believing that the Ξ had the sound of SH, which explains the strange metamorphosis of the Persian "Artashir" into "Artaxerxes" By the same rule the Rabbi interprets the talismanic ΕΛΞΑΙ as representing *El-Chai*, "The Living God" The same interpretation is again confirmed by the true solution (so long sought in vain, and now suggested by Mr. W A Wright) of the mighty spell *abracadabra*, which receives a most fitting sense when rendered by *Ha-Brachah-dabarah,* "Pronounce the Blessing," where "Blessing" stands for the name of the Blessed One, that most potent of exorcisms

Another derivation, extremely acute, but probably untenable, had been previously offered by Bellermann in the Coptic compound signifying "The Blessed Name," made of the word *ab* or *of*, "let it be," *Rah*, "adore," and *Sax* for *Sadsh*, "name" This formula would agree in a remarkable manner with the regular Jewish synonym for the Ineffable Name Jehovah, viz., *shem Hamephorash*, "The Holy Word", which the Rabbins compress into "The Name" or "The Word" It is, besides, a singular coincidence that the Egyptian word *Abrak* should be used by Moses (Gen xli 43), where Pharaoh commands that Joseph shall ride in his own chariot, and that they shall cry before him *Abrak*, "kneel down!" where the Coptic word is actually retained in the Hebrew text, and not rendered by an equivalent in that language * A precedent for expressing a sacred title in an unknown tongue is furnished by St John (Rev xix 12). "His eyes were as a flame of fire, and upon his head were many crowns, and he had a *name* written (upon them) that *no man knew* but himself and he was clothed in a vesture dipped in blood, and his name was called The Word of God" And again (iii 12) "He that overcometh will I make a pillar in the Temple of my God, and he shall go no more out, and I will write upon him the *name* of my God, and the *name* of the City of my God"

All this supplies a reason for the occurrence of the word *abra* in so many sacred titles A very remarkable instance is to be seen in the wall-painting of the tomb of Vincentius and Vibia, in the Catacomb of Prætextatus at Rome. Now this Vincentius is described in his epitaph as priest of *Sabazius*, a title connected with the Iao-worship, and the name *Abracura* is inscribed over the head of the consort of *Dispater*, the two Rulers of the Shades into whose presence Vibia's soul is ushered by Hermes In the first title, *cura* is plainly the Latinised κούρη *Virgin*,

* Sharpe, however, makes *Abrasax* a pure Egyptian phrase, signifying "Hurt me not," as addressed to the deity represented on the gem — ('Egypt Mythol' p xii)

the regular synonym for Proserpine, whilst *Abra* seems to have the same deeper meaning in which it was employed by the talisman-makers.

The efficacy of a Mystic Name is set forth in the Book of Enoch (lxviii 19) "This is the Number of the Kesbal, the principal part of the oath which the Most High dwelling in glory revealed unto the holy ones Its name is Beka He spoke to holy Michael to deliver to them the *Secret Name*, that they might understand that secret name and thus remember the oath, and that those who pointed out every secret thing to the children of men might tremble at that Name and oath This is the power of that oath, for powerful is it and strong And he established the oath of Abrac by the instrumentality of the holy Michael These are the secrets of this oath, and by it were they confirmed Heaven was suspended by it before the world was made for ever By it has the earth been framed upon the flood, whilst from the concealed parts of the hills the agitated waters proceed forth from the creation unto the end of the world By this oath the sea has been formed and the foundation of it By this oath the sun and moon complete their progress, never swerving from the command given to them for ever and ever By this oath the stars complete their progress And when their names are called they return an answer for ever and ever . . And with them he establishes this oath by which their paths are preserved, nor does their progress perish Great was their joy"

VI. Abraxas—its Numerical Force.

To find out some deep mystery expressed by the *numerical* value of the letters in a name is the grand foundation of the famous science of the Kabbala Although the Jewish Talmudists now engross all the honour of the discovery, it is but consistent with the known character of that very uninventive race to suspect that they borrowed the first notion from a foreign source—Chaldæa, the real fountain-head of all their spiritual knowledge The earliest instance that can be quoted of this way of expressing a name is St. John's so much discussed "Number of the Beast," employed to screen from vulgar curiosity some dangerous secret. What though its analysis has supplied good Protestants like Bishop Newton with a deadly weapon (in their own eyes) against the Pope, after the sum total has been reduced into its integrals Λατεινὸς; yet a prosaic non-controversialist will be more inclined to suspect that the Kabbalistic number shrouds the name of some potentate of the times who had happened to make himself especially formidable to the beholder of the Vision.* But the titles *Jao*, *Abraxas*, and the like, instead of being recent Gnostic *inventions*, were in all likelihood recognised "Holy Names," and borrowed from the most ancient religions of the East. Pliny must be alluding to something of the sort when he mentions with a sneer the miraculous powers ascribed by the Magi to amethysts engraved with the *names of the Sun and Moon*—names certainly from the nationality of his authorities not inscribed in either the Greek or the Latin tongue. In the "Shemesh Eilam," "Adonai," "Abraxas" of these talismans we may reasonably recognise the words of power referred to by the great naturalist.

The Alexandrine Greeks, proceeding upon the axiom that "things equal to the same thing are equal to one another," spied out the sacred number 365 in many Holy Names, and thus proved the identity of the several personages, so denominated, with one another. To give a few examples: the same sum is obtained by adding up the numerals in Μειθρας and in Αβρασαξ, and whether we interpret the latter as "Blessing" or "Holy Word," both are equally applicable to the Persian god. Again, the Egyptians, says Heliodorus (Æth. ix. 22), discovered the same value in Νειλος, appellation of that earliest god and father of their land, entitled in their hymns *Horus* also, properly the name of the Sun.† In the new-coined religions of Egypt, other and stranger mysteries were extracted out of

* Who expressly tells us that "his number is the number of a man;" that is, the sum of the numerical letters in the name of a certain person. The Hebrew characters representing "Cæsar Nero" produce by addition the required sum.

† Amongst the many points of

sacred names by following the old process Kircher publishes a gem inscribed XNOYMIΣ PI, and supposes, with much apparent reason, the last syllable to be added in order to make up a sum equivalent to χριστὸς = 1480 That most ingenious of the Gnostics, Marcus, based his whole system upon these numerical deductions According to him, the Saviour calls himself A and Ω, because these letters stand for 801, which is the sum of those in περιστερὰ, the Dove, assumed in virtue thereof for the vehicle of the Holy Ghost But the profoundest mystery that rewarded his researches is the fact, certainly a very curious coincidence, that all the 24 letters of the Greek alphabet added together yield the exact "number of the Name" Ἰησοῦς = 888 But his own words well deserve to be quoted (Hip vi 50) "Now Jesus had this ineffable origin From the Mother of all things the First Tetrad, proceeded another Tetrad, and there *was* an Ogdoad, whence proceeded the Decad, so there were Eighteen" The Decad therefore having come together with the Ogdoad, after that it had decoupled the same, produced the number Eighty And again after that it had decoupled the Eighty it begot the number which is Eight hundred, so that the whole number of the letters proceeding from the Ogdoad according to the Decad is eight hundred and eighty and eight—the same is Jesus For the Name Ἰησοῦς by the value of its letters is the number 888 And, verily, the alphabet of the Greeks has eight monads, and eight decads, and eight hundreds, producing the number 888, which is made up by all the numbers, the same is Jesus For this cause doth He call himself A and Ω, to set forth his generation from the All." At first sight it will strike the reader, accustomed only to *Arabic* numerals, as a work of incredible laboriousness to discover numerical values, so aptly tallying in different words, of totally different components But the difficulty was in truth much less than it appears The Greek, accustomed perpetually to use the letters of his alphabet

close connexion between Hindoo and Egyptian Mythology is the name of the sacred river, so nearly resembling the Sanscrit *nil*, "blue," referring to the remarkable colour of its waters "In Nilo cujus aqua *mari* similis," observes Pliny (xxxv. 36), speaking of a picture by Nealces of a naval battle upon that river The Arabs still distinguish its upper confluents as the *Blue* and the *White* Nile

indifferently as symbols of *number* and of *sounds*, perceived the two forces at the same glance in every word that caught his eye, and easily estimated the total value of each proper name, more especially when he made it his business to attend to such coincidences. The same operation would be equally familiar to ourselves were our "Arabic" numerals exchanged for the first ten letters of the Roman alphabet, instead of being what they are, the ancient Palmyrene somewhat modified by the wear of ages and a long course of travel.

The use of the *Numerical Value* of Names is remarkably exemplified by a *Midrash*, which makes the 318 men of Abraham's household, with whom he defeated the Five Kings, to be no more than his *one* servant, Eliezer, the numeral letters in whose name exactly make up that sum—a coincidence, though accidental, truly astonishing!

That genuine Gnostic, Dante, employs with great effect this numerical expression of a Name in that most mystical prophecy with which his 'Purgatorio' closes:—

> "Ch'io veggio certamente, e però il narro,
> A darne tempo già stelle propinque,
> Sicuro d'ogni intoppo e d'ogni sbarro,
> Nel qual un Cinquecento-dieci-e-cinque,
> Messo di Dio, anciderà la fuia,
> E quel gigante che con lei delinque."
>
> (Canto xxxiii. 40–45.)

The interpretation whereof is found in the word DVX formed out of the Roman letters, and applying to the "General" of the Ghibelline League, from whom such great things were expected by the poet for the chastisement of the Papacy and the restoration of the Imperial power.

FIG. 11.

THE ABRAXAS RELIGION.

That most philosophic of the Fathers, Hippolytus, commences his account of the systems of Basilides and his successors with this ingenious and appropriate simile "It behoves all their hearers, as they see that the doctrines of these heretics are like unto a sea tossed into waves by the fury of the winds, to sail by them without heeding them, and to look out for the tranquil harbour for themselves For that sea of theirs is both full of monsters, and difficult to traverse, and may be likened unto the Sicilian wherein are the fabled Cyclops, Charybdis and Scylla . and the rock of the Syrens which the Grecian poets tell how Ulysses sailed it past when he craftily baffled the cruelty of those inhospitable monsters For the Syrens singing clear and musically used to beguile all sailing by, through the sweetness of their voice seducing them to come to land Ulysses learning this is said to have stopped with wax the ears of his crew, and having tied himself fast to the mast in this way sailed past the Syrens and overheard all their song Which same thing it is my advice that all who fall in with these seducers should do, and either to stop his ears, on account of his own weakness, so to sail by unheeded the doctrines of heresies, without even listening to things too easily capable of seducing him by their sweetness, like the melodious Syrens' song, or else faithfully binding himself fast to the Tree of Christ to listen to them without being shaken, putting his trust in that whereunto he hath been tied, and stand fast without wavering"

The Abraxas Deity, his titles, nature and form already having been discussed, it remains now to give a sketch of his great Apostle and his doctrines To begin with the earliest notice of them—

Clemens Alexandrinus lived in the same city, and in the same century, with *Basilides*, the reputed founder of the Abraxas religion During some years of that period they were contemporaries, and it is more than probable that Clemens was personally acquainted with Basilides—he being a very remarkable personage of his times On this account Clemens' testimony to the character of the Basilidan doctrine deserves infinitely more reliance than the statements of the later Fathers, whilst at the same time he passes a more judicious, and also a more favourable judgment upon its nature. He describes the system as consisting in a constant attention to the soul, and intercourse with the Deity considered as the fountain of universal Love In his own words, "The Basilidan doctrine consists of *two* parts, the first part busies itself with divine things, and considers what is the First Cause *through* which all, and *without* which nothing is made, of what constitution are the things that pervade, or include, each other the forces which exist in Nature, and unto what they tend The other part relates to things human as to what is Man, what things be consistent or inconsistent with his Nature, what he has to do and to suffer In this department Basilides includes Virtue and Vice, what is Good, what is Evil, and what is Indifferent" In short we are here reminded of a description of a Buddhist missionary The amiable but fanciful Clemens, whose own Christianity was no more than a graft upon the congenial stock of his original Platonism, could see very little to blame in the transcendental speculations of Basilides In his eyes the latter was not a *heretic* that is, an innovator upon the accepted doctrines of the Catholic Church, but only a theosophic speculator who sought to express old truths by new formulæ, and perhaps to combine the same with the new faith, the divine authority of which he was able to admit without renouncing his own creed—precisely as is the case with the learned Hindoos of our own day

But far different is the picture of Basilides, as drawn by the pen of bigoted orthodoxy in the two next centuries, after his doctrines had been taken up and carried out to monstrous precision by the swarms of semi-Christian sects that sprung up in the very bosom of the Church These notices are subjoined in chronological order, for they give in a few words the grand features of the perfected system Hippolytus has left an excellent analysis of the Basilidan doctrine, well deserving of careful study, although it is hard to see how it bears out the assertion at the opening, that this *heretic* took his entire system ready made from Aristotle, with his *genus, species* and *individual,* but pretended to have received the same from St Matthew, who had communicated to him the esoteric doctrines which he alone had received from Christ when on earth The philosophic Bishop, however, is mild in censure, nay, seems rather captivated by the ingenuity of the Alexandrine mystic But Tertullian, with no sense of the beauty of a clever piece of sophistry, launches out like a true African barrister "After this, Basilides the heretic broke loose He asserted that there was a Supreme God named Abraxas, by whom was created Mind whom the Greeks call *Nous* From Mind proceeded the Word, from the Word, Providence from Providence, Virtue and Wisdom, from these two again, Virtues, Principalities and Powers were made, from these infinite productions and emissions of Angels By these Angels the 365 heavens were created Amongst the lowest Angels, indeed, and those who made this world, he sets last of all the god of the Jews, whom he denies to be God, affirming that he is one of the Angels' Similarly the still later Jerome has (*Amos III*) "So Basilides, who called Almighty God by the portentous name of *Abraxas,* saying that the same word according to Greek numeration, and the sum of his annual revolution, are contained in the circle of the Sun, whom the heathen taking the same amount but expressed in different numerical letters call *Mithras*, him whom the simple Iberians worship under the names of *Balsamus* (*Baal-samen,* "Lord of heaven") and *Barbelus* ("Son of Baal") And that this wondrous title *Abraxas* had long before been applied to the Sun-god in the formulæ of The Mysteries may be inferred from various incidental allusions of ancient writers Thus Theosebius the philosopher (says Photius, in his 'Life of Isidorus') drove a devil out of a woman by merely invoking over her "the *Rays of the Sun,* and the Name of the God of the Hebrews" The same explanation is much supported by the words of Augustine. "Basilides asserted the number of heavens to be 365, the number of the days in the year. For this reason he used to glorify a *Holy Name,* as it were, that is the word Abraxas, the letters in which, taken according to the Greek method of computation, make up this number"

The Basilidan doctrine of "Emanation" was greatly refined upon by Valentinus, whose muster-roll of the celestial hierarchy shall be given in its proper place. Suffice it here to observe that the entire theory resembles the Brahminical; for in that theogony each Manifestation of the One Supreme Being, regarded by the vulgar as a separate self-existing deity, has a *female partner* the exact counterpart of himself, *through* whom, as through an instrument, he exerts his power—to express which doctrine this other half is styled his *Durga*, "Active Virtue." This last name, "Virtue," actually figures in all the Gnostic lists of Emanations; and the great Æon, Pistis Sophia, in her second "Confession" perpetually upbraids herself for having quitted her male Σύζυγος, *partner*, in her proper habitation, to go in quest of the Supernal Light: whilst she equally reproaches *him* for not descending into Chaos to her aid. The system of Dualism, in fact, pervades the whole of that wondrous revelation.

Brahminical inspiration is possible in many other points of the doctrine of Basilides, as will appear by the following extracts from Irenæus—whose judgment was not warped, like that of Hippolytus, by the mania for deriving his system from the Aristotelian. Basilides (according to him) lived at Alexandria under Trajan and Hadrian (the first half of the second century), and commenced life as a student of the *Oriental Gnosis*—an epithet sufficiently indicating the source of that philosophy. Being converted to Christianity he attempted, like many others, to combine his new faith with his old, for the explanation of things both spiritual and natural. To do this he invented a terminology and symbolism of his own. In the promulgation of his peculiar notions concerning God and the Divine attributes—the Word, the Creation, the Emanation of spirits and worlds, the Architect of the universe, and the multifarious forces of Nature—he took the same road with his contemporary Saturninus in Syria. His system was a combination of Christian, Jewish, Persian and Egyptian notions, but the entire composition was moulded by the spirit of the Oriental Gnosis. These tenets their author zealously promulgated. For many years he taught in the school of Alexandria; he was also a most prolific writer. Clemens says he published twenty-four volumes of "Interpretations upon the Gospels," besides "Odes" and "Spiritual Songs", all of which have perished The doctrines he thus disseminated his contemporary Irenæus represents in the following manner —

"Basilides in order to invent something more refined and plausible in the Gnostic speculative philosophy pushed his investigations even into the Infinite He asserted that God, the uncreated eternal Father, first brought forth *Nous* or Mind, and Mind, the *Logos*, Word, this in turn, *Phronesis*, Intelligence, whence came forth *Sophia*, Wisdom, and *Dynamis*, Strength" Irenæus understands Basilides as making a Quinternion of Beings or Personal Intelligences *external* to the Godhead but Bellermann with more reason takes them as signifying personified *attributes* of the Supreme *forms* of his working internally and externally According to this explanation Basilides would only have borrowed his system from the Kabbala it is however equally likely that he drew the whole from a much more distant source, and that his "Uncreated" and "Quinternion" stand in truth for the *First* Buddha and the successive *Five*

"When the uncreated eternal Father beheld the corruption of mankind, he sent his Firstborn, Nous, into the world in the form of Christ, for the redeeming of all that believe in him out of the power of those who fabricated the world—namely, the Demiurgus and his Six sons, the planetary Genii Nous appeared amongst men as the Man Jesus, and wrought miracles This Christ did not die in person, but Simon the Cyrenian to whom he lent his bodily form, suffered in his stead, inasmuch as the Divine Power, the Nous of the Eternal Father, is not corporeal, and therefore cannot *die* Whoso therefore maintains that Christ has died is still the bondman of *Ignorance*, but whoso denies the same, he is a freeman, and hath *understood* the purpose of the Father" From this tenet the Basilidans got the opprobrious title of "Docetae" (*Illusionists*) Similarly the pious Brahmins explain away all such of their legends as are inconsistent with our notions of divine dignity by making them all "Maya" (*illusion*) The same is also the doctrine of the Koran (Cap. iv) upon this point "And for that they have not believed upon Jesus, and have spoken against Mary a grievous calumny, and have said, Verily we have slain Christ Jesus, the Son of Mary, the apostle of God, yet they slew him not, neither crucified him, but he was represented by one in his likeness, and verily they were disagreed concerning him, were in a doubt as to this matter, and had no true knowledge thereof, but followed only an uncertain opinion They did not really kill him, but God took him up unto himself, and God is mighty and wise"

The system just described coincides to a remarkable degree with the Brahminical, where the First Principle produces in succession the Five Powers—Mahasiva, Sadasiva, Rudra, Vishnu and Brahma—who are held by some for mere *attributes* of the Godhead, by others are taken in a materialistic sense for Æther, Air, Fire, Water, Earth But possibly, as Mosheim so long ago maintained, the whole Gnostic system is derived, not from the Kabbala, nor from the Greek philosophy, but from the theosophy of the Brahmins.

Another circumstance in the Basilidan practice, mentioned by Irenaeus, will receive abundant illustration from the study of these talismans "Furthermore the sect have invented *proper names* for these Angels, and class them under the *first, second, third* heavens, and so on Besides this, they endeavour to explain the names, origin, powers, and Æons of their pretended 365 heavens—similarly they give its own name to the terrestrial sphere, which they say the saviour (whom they call *Kaulacav*) has visited and then abandoned Who understands this rightly and knows the Æons with their respective names, the same shall be *invisible* unto, and beyond the power of, those Æons, in the same manner as the Saviour Kavlacav himself was As the Son of God remained unknown in the World, so must also the disciple of Basilides remain unknown to the rest of mankind, as they know all this, and nevertheless must live amongst strangers, therefore must they conduct themselves towards the rest of the world as beings invisible and unknown Hence their motto, 'Learn to know all, but keep thyself unknown,'—and for this cause they are accustomed to deny the fact of their being Basilidans Neither can they be detected as Christian heretics, because they assimilate themselves to all sects Their secret constitution however is known to but a few, perhaps to one in a thousand or two in ten thousand The local situation of their 365 heavens they parcel out just like land-surveyors Their doctrine is contained in a sacred book, and likewise in *Symbolic Figures* The Supreme Lord, the Head of all things, they call *Abrasax*, which name contains the number 365"

So much virtue being involved in a perfect knowledge of the names of the Æons, it would be unpardonable not to subjoin them, as far as they can possibly be procured at present and, the following may be taken for their most authoritative roll-call, having been drawn up by Valentinus himself, the profoundest doctor of the Gnosis, and who had elaborated to the highest degree the system first sketched out by Basilides He arranges them in pairs, male and female, in the order of their successive emanation from Bythos, the pre-existing, eternal Principle The number of pairs is *fifteen*, or the sacred number Five three times repeated Their names, it will be seen, are Hebrew words, the *va* preceding some of the female powers being merely the copulative "and" Matter supposes Valentinus to have been of Jewish origin, although born at Alexandria Tertullian states that he was first of all a Platonist, then a convert to Christianity, but having been disappointed in his aspirations to a bishopric he founded a religion of his own

1 Ampsiu, Ouraan = Depth, Silence
2 Bucua, Thartun = Mind, Truth
3 Ubucua, Thardedia = Reason, Life
4 Metaxas, Artababa = Man, Church
5 { Udua, Casten / Udu, Vacastene } = Comforter, Faith
6 Amphian, Essumen = Fatherly, Hope
7 Vannanin, Lamer = Motherly, Charity
8 Tarde, Athames = Eternal, Intelligence
9 Susua, Allora = Light, Beatitude
10 Bucidia, Damadarah = Eucharistic, Wisdom
11 Allora, Dammo = Profundity, Mixture
12 Oren, Lamaspechs = Unfading, Union
13 Amphiphuls, Emphsboshbaud = Self-born, Temperance
14 Assiouache, Belin = Only begotten, Unity
15 Dexariche, Massemo = Immovable, Pleasure

Epiphanius has evidently copied one pair (5) twice over,

misled by a slight difference of spelling, and thus adds one pair to the proper fifteen

It will be very instructive to compare this Valentinian system of Emanation, which makes all to proceed in pairs, male and female, out of the First Cause, with that Indian theosophy which this very feature indicates as its real source, in the latter, every Principle is divided into a male and female Energy, each exactly alike the other—"the same, distinguished by their sex alone." Each deity exerts his power through the agency of his female Principle or *Sacti*, which in turn possesses a *Váhan* "vehicle," that is an instrument or attribute, which is fixed and represented in a material form Of the Persons in the Supreme Triad the Sactis and their Váhans* are —

1 Of Brahma, Saraswati, goddess of harmony and the arts (the Jewish *Wisdom*), her váhan is a swan, or goose (Hence Juno's Capitoline bird, afterwards explained by an historical fiction)

2 Of Vishnu, Lakshmí, goddess of Prosperity, she has the title of Kamala, "lotus-bearer," her váhan is Garuda, the man-eagle Vishnu in one Avatar takes the name "Varáha," and his consort 'Varáhi," in which case her váhan is a buffalo

3 Of Siva, the Changer or Destroyer, the Sacti is Bhaváni, goddess of *fecundity*, and consequently of *death*, for the first implies the second "Nascentes morimur, finisque ab origine pendet"

Nothing perishes, things only take a new form called by the *ignorant* Death (Compare the title 'Gods of death," which the Ophites were so fond of giving to the "Gods of the Nativity," the astral genii ruling the horoscope) Bhaváni's appropriate vehicles are the Bull, emblem of generation, and the Tiger, of destruction

And before going further I cannot resist observing how these names and symbols manifest the far-spreading influence of the nations they embody The Sassanian queens in their gem

* It might even be suggested that Indian influence shines through the whole Apocalypse The Four Beasts (borrowed it is true from the First Vision of Ezekiel) are these Vahans, ministers of the Divine Will Later times assigned each to an evangelist The Four-and-twenty Elders had their prototypes in the Saints to the same number of the Buddhist theology, the "sea of glass or crystal" is the vast crystal block suspended in the highest heaven, the shrine of the Supreme Being, absorption into whom is the true object of the believer

portraits generally bear the lotus in the hand,* "Varanes" is a common name for the kings of that line, and the Brahminic Bull, the commonest of all signet devices with their subjects. But as the dominions of the later Persian kings extended as far as the Indus, Hindoo princesses doubtless entered their harems and communicated their own religion to their children.

Again, many of these Sanscrit titles bear a resemblance, certainly not accidental, to words frequently occurring in the Gnostic inscriptions. Thus, "Sumitri," wife of Vishnu in his seventh Avatar, may explain Σουμαρτα, and "Natha," a title of Vishnu and Crishna, the equally common Ναυτιτα. "Isa," lord, feminine, "Isi," *lady*, is perhaps even the origin of *Isis*; and "Nila," *dark-blue*, and epithet of Parvati, is more appropriately transferred to Father Nilus. Vishnu in infancy as Narayana floating in his "Vat," leaf boat over the face of the waters, and coloured all over *blue*, may be compared to the child Horus wafted in the *baris*. The most ancient of all creeds having, as above shown, made the lotus the symbol of Plenty, the reason becomes obvious for the introduction of its seed-vessels, always mistaken for poppyheads, amongst the wheatears in the cornucopia of Ceres.

The above quoted Σουμαρτα seems to have been applied by the Gnostics to the Sun-god, for Montfaucon gives (Pl. 157) a figure of Sol so inscribed, with χερουβι on the reverse, a manifest invocation to all the angelic host. And as the protection of this celestial hierarchy is so perpetually sought by our talisman-makers in their "voluntary humility and worshipping of angels," I subjoin the names of the Hindoo Guardians of the "Jehabs," quarters of the world, which may perhaps lurk in their Grecised form amongst these interminable strings of titles.

E.	Indra	N.W.	Váyu
S.E.	Agni	N.	Kuvera
S.	Yama	N.E.	Isana
S.W.	Nirriti	Above	Brahma
W.	Varuna	Below	Nága

Of the centre, Rudra.

* In the character of Kamalá, as the later Greek, and the Roman ladies in that of Isis.

THE INEFFABLE NAME IN THE HINDOO FORM

We have already seen how important a part the notion of an "Ineffable Name," denoting the inconceivable Supreme, plays in the machinery of the Gnosis, and here again the original idea is to be found fully developed in the practice of the Brahmins. This awful name emblazoned in *three* Sanscrit letters within a cartouche formed by a coiled serpent (that normal inclosure for a Holy Name in Gnostic art)* is fittingly borne up by the elephant headed Ganesa, god of *Wisdom*. The word being triliteral is rather AUM than OM, as usually written in English. It is never to be uttered aloud, but only mentally by the devout. Of the characters, A signifies the Creator, U the Preserver, M the Destroyer, that is, the Triad Brahma-Vishnu-Siva. "If pronounced aloud, the sound much resembles *Amen* as drawled out by a country parish clerk. In fact it is used for "Angiekai," *So be it!* in token of approbation ("Moor, Hindoo Pantheon) † And here a very curious analogy is to be pointed out in the assertion of the Talmudists that the word *Amen* if shouted aloud is of power to open the gates of Heaven. In the Pistis-Sophia the "Three Amen," and again the "Four Amen," are repeatedly mentioned amongst the other Mysteries revealed by the Saviour in his esoteric teaching. On this account the word may be

* As the Pistis-Sophia informs us, "the disk of the sun was a great dragon having his tail in his mouth," the meaning of this figure whereon the sacred word is emblazoned becomes sufficiently obvious.

† OM MANI PADHVM "Glorification of the Deity," is the Thibetian Confession of Faith, engraved on stone tablets set up everywhere over the country, and everlastingly chanted by the Lamas as they tell their beads. (Cooper's 'Travels of a Pioneer,' p. 208) Huc mentions that the Lamas assert that the doctrine contained in these words is immense, and that the whole life of man is not sufficient to measure its depth and extent. Knox ('Overland through Asia') describes the ruined "Monastery of Eternal Repose," built at the junction of the Augoon with the Amoor by an emperor of the Yuen dynasty to commemorate his visit to that region. On the summit of the cliff are three columns, 5 to 8 feet high of marble granite, and porphyry and granite, bearing inscriptions commemorating this foundation, and also this formula in Chinese, Mongolian and Thibetan.

suspected to have some connexion with the Hindoo Sacred Name, unless indeed Valentinus had got it nearer home, from the four "Amenti," guardians of the dead, and sons of Osiris. The common explanation that "Amen" signifies *Truth* in some Eastern dialect, does not seem to rest on good foundation. The Kabbalist Marcus discovered a great mystery in *Αμην*, taken numerically, the number Ninety-nine became formed by the union of the Eleven and the Nine and *therefore* set forth by the parables of the piece of silver, and the ninety and nine sheep, "which is the reason why we use 'amen' in prayers."

Other Hindoo titles of the Deity are "Tat" and "Sat" = Virtue. These are recognisable in the Egyptian gods Tat or Hermes, and Sate, Truths. It is likewise more than probable that the mighty AUM itself often lies enshrouded amidst the lines of vowels filling our talismans. Certainly the Praun calcedony (No. 517) bearing on one side the Delphic Apollo in a good style of art, on the other (by a later hand) a man dancing with his apron filled with fruits, presents in its legend *πιρσπαιοω αουμ ολει*, the Sanscrit triliteral in the only form in which Greek characters could express the sound.

The origin of this Ineffable Name is thus related ('Inst. Menu' ii. 370). Brahma milked out as it were from the three Vedas the letter A, the letter U, and the letter M, together with the three mysterious words "Bhur," "Bhavah," "Swar" or Earth, Sky and Heaven. From the three Vedas also the Lord of Creation, incomprehensibly exalted successively milked out the three Treasures of the ineffable text, beginning with the word "Tat," and entitled the "Savatri," or Gayatri. A priest who shall know the Veda, and pronounce to himself both morning and evening that syllable and that holy text preceded by the Three words shall attain that sanctity which the Veda confers: and a "*twice born*" man who shall a thousand times repeat those Three apart from the multitude, shall be released in a month even from a great offence, as a snake from its slough. The Three great immutable words preceded by the Triliteral syllable and followed by the Gáyatri which consists of three measures, must be considered as the *mouth*, or principal part of the Veda." In this doctrine lies the very origin of all talismanic inscriptions, for their essence is the stringing together of sacred names Nay more, the actual Three words, disguised by Coptic pronunciation, or purposely sealed from profane eyes by a duplication of vowels, very probably exist in the midst of certain Gnostic formulæ. In the spell of Battus, hereafter to be quoted, words of the same sense as the Hindoo Three do in reality occur

The Gáyatrí or holiest verse of the Vedas is "Let us adore the supremacy of the Divine Sun, the Godhead, who illuminates all, who recreates all, from whom all proceed, unto whom all must return, whom we invoke to direct our progress aright in our progress towards the Holy Seat" Another is, "Earth, Sky, Heaven, Let us meditate upon that most excellent Light and Power, of that most generous, sportive, and resplendent Sun, that it may guide our intellects" In all this there is something that irresistibly reveals the Gnostic invocations whenever they can be interpreted, and the 'Divine Sun' finds its counterpart in the 'Shemesh Eilam' so perpetually repeated

This Gáyatrí is contained in the confession of faith of the Brahmin "This new and excellent praise of thee O, splendid playful Sun (*Pushan*) is offered by us to thee. Be gratified by this my speech approach this craving mind as a fond man seeks a woman May that Sun who contemplates and looks into all worlds be our Protector! Let us meditate on the adorable light of the Divine Ruler (*Savitri*), may it guide our intellects Desirous of food we solicit the gift of the splendid Sun, who should be studiously worshipped Venerable men, guided by the understanding, salute thee, Divine Sun, with oblations and praise"

Moor hereupon makes the very pertinent remark 'It is difficult to conjecture why this text should be so studiously kept secret, for its exposition, unconnected with any idea of mystery, and affectation of profundity, does not appear likely to have the effect so dreaded by all priests of guiding the intellect of mankind to the discovery of Truth"

As already remarked our Gnostic formulae when expressed in Greek have a spirit and a rhythm that strikes the ear as the echo of these primitive invocations, witness the legend upon the plasma described by Creuzer (Archeol. iii. last plate) Within the serpent-formed cartouche is an inscription of many lines, the first half an undecypherable medley of letters, which like Marcus' thirty syllabic appellation of the Supreme Tetrad, must express the name of the Unknown God, who in the following portion is invoked as "The Primal Father, incorporeal, pervading all things, self-existing, the seal of Solomon" then come more mystic epithets ending with "lion-headed," evidently the Mithraic figure of that kind The declaration that the unknown legend is the "Seal of Solomon" is extremely interesting, as showing the early date of the celebrity attained by that most famous of talismans, which, be it remembered, was reported to derive its virtue from the mighty throne of God engraven on the gem

Many further analogies between the two theosophies may be detected in the Hindoo forms of worship published by Moor Of the Persons in the Supreme Triad, Brahma represents the Creator, Vishnu the Preserver, and Siva the Destroyer But the last is more truly the Changer, all *death* being only *change* Siva therefore in one of his characters becomes identified with Yama, god of the Shades Now, seeing that the first two Persons are symbolised by the elements Fire and Water, the analogy of the Hellenic Triad, Zeus, Poseidon, Hades, becomes at once apparent Here also we find the originals of the "Great Τριδυνάμεις," who hold so high a place in the hierarchy of the Pistis-Sophia.

The famous Inscription of Buddha-Gaya, Bengal, dated the year 1005 of the era of Vikramaditya (B C 57) contains this remarkable passage "Amaradiva [son of Sandracottus] having heard this voice caused an image of the Supreme Spirit, Buddha, to be made, and he worshipped it, according to the law, with perfumes, incense, and the like, and he thus admired [magnified] the Name of that Supreme Being, an Incarnation of a portion of Vishnu Reverence be unto thee in the form of Buddha, reverence be unto thee, Lord of the Earth! Reverence be unto thee an Incarnation of the Deity, and the Eternal One. Reverence be unto thee O God, in the form of the God of Mercy the Dispeller of pain and trouble, the Lord of all things, the

Deity who overcomes the sins of the *Kali yug* (Iron Age), the Guardian of the universe, the emblem of Mercy towards all them that sue thee—OM, the Possessor of all things in vital form, Thou art Brahma, Vishnu, and Mahesa (Siva); Thou art the Lord of the universe, Thou art the proper *form* of all things,* moveable and immoveable, the Possessor of the whole And thus I adore thee Reverence be unto thee the Bestower of Salvation, Reverence be unto thee the Destroyer of the Evil Spirit Kesi, † O Damadara shew me favour! Thou art he who resteth upon the face of the Milky Ocean, and who lieth upon the serpent Sesha. Thou art Trivikrama, who at three strides encompasseth the earth, I adore thee, who art celebrated by a thousand names, and under various *forms*, in the shape of Buddha, the God of Mercy, be propitious, O thou Most High! Having thus worshipped the Guardian of mankind, he became like one of the just He joyfully caused a holy temple to be built of a wonderful construction, and therein were set up the *Divine Feet* of Vishnu, for ever Purifier of the sins of mankind, the images of the Pandus, and the *Descents* of Vishnu (Avatars) and in like manner of Brahma and the rest of the divinities" (Hind Panth p 223)

It may here be observed how extensively this symbol of the *Divine Foot* has pervaded the religions of the West Feet either in relief or *in cavo*, cut in stone, are common about Hindoo temples according to tradition they are memorials of suttees, the self-sacrificing widow having mounted from that stone upon the pyre This usage supplies the connection of the symbol with Serapis, the translated Yama, god of Hades Compare the colossal Foot dedicated to the Serapis of Alexandria, as his special attribute, and recently exhumed from the ruins of his temple ‡ It is richly sandalled, and on the top sits enthroned the god himself, with his attendants Cerberus and the Serpent, *Tricasa*

* Meaning the pre-existing Type, the Platonic *Idea*, the Persian Ferouher the Rabbinical Adam-Kadmon—all springing from this source

† This explains the title of the deity so often put on our talismans, Γιγαντορήκτης

‡ The religious importance of the symbol is attested by an Alexandrian coin of Commodus, having for reverse this same Foot, with the bust of Serapis placed on the section of the leg (Feuardent, 'Egypte Ancienne' pl xxvii)

and *Sesha* in Grecian disguise The same Foot, winged and girt with the Serpent placed between two seated lions, is cut on the altar inscribed "Deo Sarapi M Vibius Onesimus ex visu" (Montfaucon, pl 122) The same idea produced in Ceylon the print of Adam's foot upon the summit of the Peak, bearing his name, whence he had ascended to his Creator, and equally in the very metropolis of Christianity, that of Christ himself stamped in the basalt paving-stone of the Via Appia, still worshipped in the church and entitled, "Domine quo vadis?"

An ancient silver plate, found in a pit at Islamabad, at the northern end of the Bay of Bengal, records the hallowing of the site of a projected temple there in the deposit in that pit of 120 small bronze images called "Tahmudas," twenty of larger size, "Languda," one large in stone, "Langudagari," and a brass vessel containing two of the bones of "Thacur" This last title, "Noble,"* is the regular style of a god, or a deified mortal In mediaeval ecclesiastical usage (which probably still continues) it was indispensable for the consecration of any altar in a church that a relic (bone) of some Saint should have been deposited under its base The same silver plate contains this account of the birth and infancy of Buddha This coincidence, if accidental is very curious "When Buddha Avatar descended from the region of souls, and entered the body of Mahamaya, the wife of Soontala Danna, Raja of Kailas, her womb suddenly assumed the appearance of clear transparent crystal in which Buddha appeared, beautiful as a flower, kneeling, and reclining on his hands When born he had on his head two *feet*, and on his hands the marks of wheels Brahma attending at the birth received the infant in a golden vessel, and delivered him unto Indra."

This intimate connection of the theosophies of India and Greece was originally (before the period of direct commerce) kept up through the medium of the Persian Magi, as the classical writers themselves show by casual but trustworthy allusions. Their notices were till lately reckoned amongst the other fictions of "Graecia Mendax," but better acquaintance with Sanscrit and Pehlevi records have revealed their truth

* Exactly answering to the ancient *Divus*, the Catholic *Saint*

For it is now accepted as certainly proved by the oldest portions of the Zendavesta (the "Gathas," or hymns) that the primitive religion of the whole Aryan race, previous to the great division, was a simple worship of the Powers of Nature. This religion was reformed by Zoroaster, who retained the old names for his Angels, but superadded the idea of the One Supreme

Ammian in his account of Julian's Persian expedition, gives the following curious, though oddly blundered, details upon this subject (xxiii. 6) "In these tracts are situated the fertile lands of the *Magi* [in Media], concerning whose profession and pursuits, since we have come upon them, it will be fitting to give here some brief information Plato, that greatest authority upon celebrated doctrines, states that the Magian religion, known by this mystic name of 'Machagestia,' is the most uncorrupted form of worship in things divine To the philosophy of this religion, Zoroastres, a Bactrian, in primitive times, made many additions drawn from the Mysteries of the Chaldæans, as did still later Hystaspes, a very learned prince, father of Darius This King Hystaspes, when he was boldly penetrating into the unknown regions of *Upper India*, had come upon a certain wooded solitude, the tranquil silence of which is occupied by those incomparable sages, the Brachmans Instructed by their teaching in the science of the motions of the world and heavenly bodies, and also in *pure religious rites* as far as he was able to gather them—of the notions thus acquired he transfused a certain proportion into the creed of the Magi The latter coupling these doctrines with their own peculiar science of foretelling the future, have handed down the whole through their descendants to succeeding ages Thenceforth, in the course of many generations to the present time, a multitude, sprung from one and the same stock, dedicates itself to sacred offices It is said they preserve unextinguished the Sacred Fire which first of all fell down from heaven, a portion whereof used always to be carried before the kings of Asia as a good omen The number of persons so descended was at the first but small, and they were exclusively employed by the Persian kings for the performance of religious services It was considered a great offence to approach the altar, or to touch the sacrifice, before a Magus, after reciting the appointed prayers, had poured upon it the preliminary libation. But through gradual increase they are grown into the name and dimensions of a distinct people, and inhabit villages unprotected by walls, being allowed to follow their own laws, being respected on account of their religious character. It was from this race of men that the seven, as ancient history records, usurped the Persian throne upon the death of Cambyses, and were crushed by the conspiracy of that Darius who gained the kingdom through the neighing of his horse." The worthy, but pedantic old soldier, in his anxiety to show off his historical reading, has committed certain very ludicrous blunders in this account. The father of Darius was no "ancient king of Persia," but merely governor of that *province* (ἔπαρχος) under Cambyses (Her. iii. 70). His name, derived from "Gushtasp," the planet Venus, was doubtless common enough wherever Magism was the established religion. And yet more ludicrously does Ammian convert the *one* Magian usurper, Smerdis, into *seven*, the actual number of the Persian nobles who put him down. Nevertheless, the tradition has great value, as proving the previous existence of the Magi in a community of diviners and seers (like the ancient Jewish fraternities, "Sons of the Prophets,") and the subsequent modification of their doctrines by the importation of Brahminical ideas, following upon the conquest of Indian provinces. Such being the case, one need not be surprised at finding *Sassanian* kings named after Hindoo deities, like the numerous *Varanes* (from "Varani," Vishnu's title) just as others of their line assume that of the proper Persian god, Ormuzd, in the form of that favourite royal appellation, Hormisdas (Ahoromasdi).

ABRAXAS-GEMS, THEIR MATERIALS, WORKMANSHIP, AND NATURE.

Following the axiom, "that the body is more than the raiment," the foregoing chapters have been devoted to the consideration of the notions which our talismans have *invested* with visible form. These visible forms, therefore, their materials, and manufacture, now come before us for explanation —a wide field for curious research, and extending into many diverse regions of Archæology.

The *genuine* Abraxas-gems, that yet fill our cabinets, came originally for the most part out of Egypt; others, as their differing style shows, from Asia; others again from Syria, where many Basilidans had established themselves at an early period. Amongst these philosophising semi-Christian sects the figure of Abraxas was held in high esteem. "They used it (says Bellermann) as a *Teacher* in doctrine, in obedience to whom they directed their transcendental researches and mystic instruction; as a *Token* and a *Password* amongst the initiated, to show that they belonged to the same fraternity; as an *Amulet* and a *Talisman*, and lastly as a *Seal* to their documents."

Gnostic intagli are almost the sole productions of the Glyptic Art, during the time it was dying out, all through the last two centuries of the Western Empire, if we except a few rude figures of the goddess Roma, Victories, and Eagles made for legionary rings. As may easily be supposed the art displayed in these designs is at its lowest ebb, being itself a degenerate successor to the debased Egyptian school of Alexandria.* The

* Their barbarism, however, is often in advance of that of their real period. A convincing example is the one found in the great treasure-trove of Tarsus where the latest coins went no later than Gordian III. It was a black hematite, with a four-winged, sceptre-holding Æon, reverse Venus Anadyomene, with her usual title ΑΡΩΡΙΦΡΑCΙC, scratched in so rude a style that one would have placed its execution three centuries later, but for the company in which it was found. Another point of interest was its retaining the original setting—a cable-mounted frame, with loop, of massy gold—proof of the value placed upon its potency. (Franks Collection.)

engraving seems to have been entirely executed by means of a coarse *wheel*, like that characterising the Sassanian stamp, then commonly used in Persia, a country which, by the bye, was the source of many of the ideas expressed in these figures and inscriptions. The choice Indian Sards, Nicoli, and Amethysts which embellished earlier periods, are replaced by coarser materials, the native productions of the countries which had engendered the new creed, the Jasper of Egypt dark green, or sometimes mottled with yellow and red, the Plasma, usually of bad quality, passing from a dirty olive-green into common Calcedony, and quite as abundantly the fibrous Hæmatite more or less magnetic. Indeed the opaque Jasper and the Loadstone, those special materials for signets at the fountains of the Magic Art, Egypt and Assyria, had, from time immemorial, engrossed the reputation of the most fitting vehicles for talismanic figures. The former was Pliny's *Molochites*, "opaque, and of the colour of a mallow leaf, of innate power as an amulet to protect children;" its black variety was his *Antipathes*, "recommended by the Magi as a sure defence against witchcraft of every kind;" whilst the Hæmatite is the Persian *Kamhaken*, perhaps the true etymology of *cameo*, a word that came into Europe in the ages when every engraved stone passed for a talisman.

So constant is this rule of unmitigated barbarism that Gnostic types when found well executed and in fine stones, as sometimes is the case, will on examination always prove to emanate from the Cinquecento school, a period when anything pertaining to Astrology or the Kabala was reproduced in vast abundance under the impulse of the revived spirit of mystic speculation. To this and the following century, must be referred the authorship of those large jaspers, not unfrequent in Collections, presenting the terminal figure of Osiris, the field occupied with astrological cyphers and *modern* Hebrew letters. Of these imitations, betraying themselves by their own excellence, the most conspicuous was a large Amethyst, obtained by me at Florence, engraved with an erect figure of the hawk-headed Phre, Priapean, holding the Cynophalus upon his hand, and standing on the coiled serpent, an intaglio in the best Roman manner, that no era of Gnosticism had been capable of producing.*

Antique pastes with subjects do not exist, and for a very sufficient reason. The *material* of a talisman being quite as essential to its virtue as the *sigil* engraved upon it, the mystery whereof the profound Camillo di Leonardo shall hereafter declare in his own words. Again, the genuine stones were in themselves so cheap, and the work upon them produced so expeditiously and with so little care, as to leave small temptation for counterfeiting them in a baser substance. The only exception that has come under my notice to the inferior quality of the stones employed by the Gnostic engravers is the singular Garnet tablet of the Hertz Cabinet, of which a description will be given in its proper place, when we come to treat of inscriptions.

The *Lettering* of the legends† upon these talismans has a peculiarity of execution that of itself serves to identify almost every stone belonging to the Gnostic series. The letters are all formed by *straight* lines, the Θ, O, and Σ, being quite square, either from the rudeness of the instrument employed to cut them or because want of skill prevented the engraver from attempting curvilinear characters, to do which neatly requires the utmost dexterity and long practice, being in fact the most difficult task that can be demanded from the *wheel*. For it was with this newly-invented instrument, as the equality of their lines demonstrates, that these ill-shaped characters were faintly

* I had long suspected that the Cinquecento period produced much Gnostic work in the ruder style, and at length have obtained proof demonstrative of the truth of this suspicion. Amongst a large lot of coarsely-cut Gnostic jaspers of very recent work, my attention was caught by one (an inscription of several lines) *cut* upon a tablet of that streaky agaet paste so popular at that period but quite unknown to the ancients. The piece had been highly polished and then engraved with the wheel, the design probably copied from a genuine stone.

† Stiechel explains the inscription upon the shield borne by an Abraxas figure, written thus, XVX IAXV as no more than the customary form in that position, the Name Iao with the Sign of the Cross thrice repeated (to make up the mystic number, Seven). He quotes in support of this acute explanation a gem published by Matter, bearing ΧΦΕΝΕCΧΗΡΦΙΧ, expressing the sound of the Hebrew *Pene zets rpua* = "His face—this—healed."

traced upon the stone In all likelihood the same artists were the Alexandrian glass-workers, famed long before for their engraved vases, Martial's "tepido toreumata Nili," for Pliny uses the significant expression, "vitrum, aliud torno teritur, aliud argenti more caelatur," "some glass vessels are cut out by means of the drill, others carved in relief in the same manner as silver plate" The Ξ in these inscriptions is invariably formed by drawing a short line across the diagonal of a Z, so that in rude work, it cannot be distinguished from the latter character

These inscriptions are often found *superadded* upon the backs of gems of much earlier date, evidently for the purpose of converting them into talismans Of such conversions the most remarkable known to me are, a fine cameo (Marlborough Cabinet) a bust of Commodus, on the reverse of which has been rudely cut the Abraxas-god surrounded by a legend, unintelligible though sounding like Greek words

ΔΟΥΓΕΝΝΑΙΟΔΕΜΕΝΑΙΒΑΣΙΛΙΣΚΟΣ

Another cameo (Royal Cabinet) with the helmeted heads regardant of Constantine's two elder sons, has received the very unorthodox addition of Anubis, also surrounded by a long legend in huge characters, so barbarous as to defy transcription A third (Devonshire Parure, No 79), a fine head of Hercules, lapis lazuli, has received the Gnostic baptism by the addition on the back of a scarabeus with expanded wings (recognised emblem of the Creator), and the word of power ΑΒΡΑΣΑΞ The extremely debased style of all such additions plainly indicates a period long posterior to that of the originals, whilst the position they occupy, necessarily concealed when in use, proves that the whole object of such *improvements* was the supernatural protection of the wearer

The finest example of Gnostic conversion is an onyx cameo (Vienna Cabinet), representing some young Cæsar under the form of Jupiter Axur, standing in front face with the thunderbolt in his left hand, his right resting on the sceptre, the ægis hangs down his back for paludamentum, at his feet the eagle on one side a trophy with seated captive, hands tied behind, all in a good style in low relief The talisman-maker has cut a line of square characters, resembling Palmyrene, down each leg from hip to foot, a nimbus of the same round his head, others on the field and, to make all sure, has covered the back of the gem with 16 lines in the same abstruse lettering. It is carefully figured in Arneth's 'Cameen des K. K. Cabinettes,' (Pl. xviii. 2), who suggests Julian for its subject, without considering that the 'Philosopher" wore a long beard during the period when such a representation of him as *this* was permissible. Besides, for the two centuries before Julian's times, Serapis was the only type under which the reigning emperor was allowed to be complimented, the old Latin 'Jovis Axur' having grown obsolete. The hero of this apotheosis is much more probably Titus, or even his brother. The cameo is of respectable dimensions, being $2\frac{3}{4}$ inches high by $2\frac{1}{2}$ wide.

As regards the history of Glyptics these inscribed gems have a value of their own, as fixing the date when the *wheel* came generally into use in the engraver's *atelier*, for the minute and elegant lettering of earlier times will be found, when examined with the microscope, to have been *incised* in the gem with the diamond point, whence its perfect regularity and freedom.

Of these Gnostic inscriptions in general, Raspe (Catalogue of Tassie's Pastes, p. 38) has given accurate transcripts, from an immense collection belonging to every shape and period of Gnosticism. Chabouillet has more recently done the same for the very large series in the French Cabinet, in his valuable 'Catalogue des Camées de la Bib. Imp.' p. 282. In the 'Gorlæ Dactyliotheca,' (3rd ed. 1695), Nos. 326–486 are entirely Gnostic and astrological designs, and include the greater part of those first published by Chiflet in his 'Macarii Abraxas-Proteus,' ed. 1610 whose plates were re-engraved for the purpose on a reduced scale but with large additions, apparently made by the learned editor of the work, Gronovius. But the most extensive series of actual representations of the whole class are the plates to the Section 'Les Abraxas' of Montfaucon's grand work 'L'Antiquité expliquée.' Many of his examples were drawn from the fine Cabinet of gems belonging to the Library of St. Geneviève, besides others, and very interesting specimens, from a previous work by Capello.* Though roughly engraved, they seem to have been copied with laudable attention to accuracy

* Who professes to copy originals in the ancient Cassel Cabinet, although many of his types are so unparalleled in modern collections that Matter suspects them mere creations of his own fancy But examples of some of the strangest amongst them have lately come under my own notice, apparently mediæval Arabic talismans, which Capello, very pardonably, mistook for remains of the ancient Gnostics

FIG. 12

LEGENDS AND FORMULÆ

Foremost in the rank of Words of Power stands the "Mystery of the Seven Vowels," so important as to demand a separate section for its discussion with befitting reverence. Though inferior to these, great no doubt was the virtue of those interminable strings of letters that fill both faces of many a Gnostic stone—later refinements upon the celebrated Ἐφέσια Γράμματα, as Clemens aptly remarks. Amongst these interminable formulæ lurk, no doubt, those potent spells composed by Solomon himself, by repeating which and at the same time applying to the sufferer's nose his ring (under whose gem was placed the herb prescribed by the same oracle of wisdom) the Jew Eleazar drew out through their nostrils the devils possessing many people, in the presence of Vespasian, his tribunes and chief officers. The sapient Josephus adds, that to make sure of the exit of the diabolical occupant, the exorcist commanded him to overturn in his flight a basin of water placed at a considerable distance, which was forthwith done, to the consternation and conviction of all the heathen spectators. The Ephesian Spell, the mystic words graven on the zone of the Great Diana, were commonly used by the Magi of Plutarch's times for the same purpose.

And there can be no doubt that such invocations were often efficacious. Demoniacal possession was nothing more than epilepsy (its very name, signifying *possession*, being derived from that same belief), for Galen, after rationally discussing the natural causes of the malady, remarks that the vulgar universally attributed it to the agency of devils. Now our experience of Mesmerism (so far as there is any reality in that pet science of charlatans) clearly shows what inexplicable effects can be produced upon persons labouring under nervous derangement by words of command authoritatively pronounced. How much greater the effect of those words in old times, when uttered in an unknown tongue by a person of imposing presence and over patients already filled with the belief of his power to relieve them! Hence the Casting-out of devils became the grand staple of their trade with all the Thaumaturgists, both old and new, of the ages with which we are dealing. That the cure should be permanent was a thing perfectly immaterial, it sufficed the exorcist's purpose if the manifestation of his power should be successful for the moment, to the edification of the awestruck crowd of believers, and to the confusion of the few *Rationalistic* doubters amongst the crowd.

Such spells gave power likewise over demons ranging about unconfined in fleshly prison. Eucrates, in Lucian's amusing 'Philopseudes,' boasts that he is so accustomed to meet thousands of them roving about, that he has come not to mind them at all, more especially since "The Arabian has given me a ring made out of the nail from a cross, and taught me the spell composed of many *Names*." The last remark is valuable for our purpose: it proves that the legends in an unknown tongue on our talismans are sometimes to be explained from the Arabic,* and also may consist of strings of titles of the one deity invoked. Virgil's—

> "Crines effusa sacerdos
> Ter centum tonat ore deos, Erebumque, Chaosque,
> Tergeminamque Hecaten, tria virginis ora Dianæ,"
> (Æn. iv. 510)—

distinctly refers to the same superstition, for Servius explains these "three hundred gods" in the spells of Dido's Massylian sorceress, as not meaning so many *different* deities, but only so many *epithets* of *Hecate* herself, whose very names he, for the same reason, fancifully derives from the numeral ἑκατόν. The same idea yet survives in the religious exercise of the devout Moslem, the mental repetition and reflection upon the Ninety-and-nine Arabic epithets of the One Almighty.

* In fact, the "unknown characters" sometimes occurring in the field of these talismans are unmistakeably Himyaritic letters belonging to that primitive alphabet of Arabia. Osander and Levy have published gems bearing intagli, of good execution of Persian deities (therefore long anterior to Gnostic times), and neatly engraved Himyaritic legends. This character is perfectly vertical, handsome and well defined in its differences; it is a modification of the Palmyrene, and the parent of the modern Ethiopic.

The great object of these adjurations was to address the Deity by the names under which he was known to all the nations of Earth, in this way making sure of addressing him by the appellation wherein he most delighted. This is the fundamental principle of, and sufficient explanation of, the entire class of these talismanic legends; and of their syncretism. No. 10 of the 'Magic Papyrus' affords a most valuable illustration. "I call upon thee that didst create the Earth, and bones, and all flesh, and all spirit, that didst establish the Sea, and that shakest the Heavens, that didst divide the Light from the Darkness, Thou, the Great, Directing Mind, that disposest all things, Eye of the world! Genius of genii (δαίμων δαιμονίων), God of gods, the Lord of spirits, ΙΑΩ ΟΥΗΙ, hearken unto my voice! I call upon Thee, the Master of the gods, O loud thundering Zeus, O sovereign Zeus, Adonai! Lord ΙΑΩ ΟΥΗΕ! I am he that calleth upon thee in the Syrian tongue, the great God Ζααλαηρ Ιφ φου, and do not thou disregard my voice in the Hebrew language, Αβλαναθαναλβα Αβρασιλωα. For I am σιλθωχωουχ λαιλαμ βλασαλωθ Ιαω Ιαω νεβουθ σαβιοθαρ βωθ αρβαθ Ιαω Ιαωθ σαβαωθ παγουρη ραγουρη βαρουχ Αδωναι Ελωαι ιαβρααμ βαρβαραυω ναυ σιφ. O lofty-minded, ever-living Crown of the world, containing all, Σιετησακτι ετη βιων = σφη = νουοι = σιεθυ = χθεθωι ηρυγχ ΩΗΑΗΗΩΑΙ Α ΩΗΙΑΩ ασιαλ σααπηαλσω εθμουρησινι σεμ λαυ λου λουριγχ. (This spell) looses fetters, causes blindness (i.e. makes one invisible), procures dreams, gives favour, for whatsoever purpose thou wishest."

One circumstance, very unaccountable, connected with these Inscriptions is wherefore the *Pehlevi* character, the national writing of the Magi in those times, should never be used in formulæ so often embodying the doctrines of that profession. Neither are any complete legends to be found written in *Punic*, although that character with the last mentioned was at the time universally employed, in various modifications, all over Asia and Africa. In the latter country Punic was not superseded by Latin until a very late period of the Empire, for in the second century Apuleius ('Apology') wishing to prove the neglect of his stepson's education by the boy's uncle who had taken charge of him (the family belonged to the large city Madaura in

Numidia), declares that though arrived at the age of sixteen he could speak nothing but Punic and the little Greek he had picked up from his mother, "praeter Punicè, et siquid adhuc a matre Græcissat" "And some years later, the emperor Severus, a descendant of Hannibal's, had to blush for his sister when she came from his native place Leptis to Court, "vix Latine loquens." It is true the characters which are often scattered over the field of these gems have much the look of Punic, others again of Palmyrene Syriac, whilst some are obviously the same with the strange Nubian characters to be seen in abundance graven on the rocks at Silsilis, upon the upper Nile As for the square (modern) Hebrew, all works presenting them are mere fabrications of the astrologers and Rosicrucians of the 16th and 17th centuries. *Hieroglyphical* writing, though naturally to be looked for in the manufacture of Alexandria, hardly occurs at all, it is probable that even its modification the Demotic had long before been superseded (in that capital at least) by the Greek alphabet The only exception known to me is the agate published by Caylus ('Rec d'Ant. viii pl 8), presenting the common four-winged Priapic genius in the sacred boat, the reverse bearing a long vertical line of neatly cut genuine hieroglyphics. The Arabic "Kamar" *Moon*, sometimes found in these formulæ, illustrates Pliny's remark, that the Magi ordered the Name of the *Sun* or *Moon* to be engraved on emeralds or amethysts, in order to convert them into amulets against witchcraft, and giving success at Court An emerald (Praun) of very bad quality, however, inscribed ΙΑΩ ΣΑΒΑΩΘ ΑΒΡΑΣΑΞ, may represent the very kind of amulet alluded to But that Alexandria was the grand *fabrique* of talismans is equally apparent to the mineralogist from the *materials*, as to the archæologist from the *lettering* employed in their construction Nevertheless it still remains unexplained why the Magi should not have written their own spells in the character then solely current in the vast dominions of the Sassanian kings

The *language* of these inscriptions is never Latin, rarely Greek, frequently Syriac, but most commonly corrupt Hebrew For this choice the sufficient reason is given by Iamblichus in a letter to Porphyrius, where he expressly states that, "The gods are well pleased with prayers addressed unto them in the *Egyptian* or *Assyrian* tongues, as being ancient and cognate languages to *their own*, and moreover those in which prayer was first made unto them; and therefore they have stamped as sacred the entire speech of those holy nations." It is a singular coincidence that Justinus Kerner, in his extraordinary work, 'Die Seherin von Prevorst' (in reading which one continually fluctuates between the conviction of its being an impudent fiction, and the uncomfortable suspicion that it may be a revelation of the profoundest truth), assigns a similar reason for the writing used by the visitant from the spirit-world so greatly resembling Arabic, "because *that* had the best claim to be considered the primitive language of mankind." This "Seer" was a peasant girl, worn out by long sickness to that degree as to belong more to the next world than to this. Consequently she had become sensible of the presence of spiritual visitors, and acted as a medium of communication between them and those in the flesh. Kerner, a physician, took her into his own house the better to observe these singular phenomena, and kept a regular diary of her health and of her disclosures during several months until her death, with a minuteness of which only a German is capable. He writes evidently in all good faith, and, amidst heaps of nonsense, puts down some startling occurrences beyond the flights of forgery and confirmed by one's own experience.

But as concerns the "Language of the other world," in every country "Omne ignotum pro magnifico" has ever been the maxim of priestcraft, the soundness of which has been demonstrated by the experience of all time. More particularly does this apply to forms of prayer. Thus Orpheus:

"Then whilst the cauldron bubbles o'er the flame,
Address each godhead by his mystic name;
Full well th' immortals all are pleased to hear
Their *mystic names* rise in the muttered prayer."

Of such mystic invocations it will be advisable to adduce examples from writers contemporary with their use, before proceeding to the consideration of actual remains of similar nature. Of the numerous specimens cited, the following are the most noteworthy. The 'Pistis-Sophia' (§ 358) makes the Saviour "standing upon the shore of the sea, the ocean, call upon God with this prayer, saying, Hear me, O Father, thou Father of all fatherships, Infinite Light, *Αεηιουω Ιαω Αωι ωια ψινωθερ θερινωψ νωψιθερ ζαγνουρη παγουρη μεθμομαωθ νεψιομαωθ μαραχαχθα θωβαρραβαθ θαρναχαχαν ροροκοθορα Ιεου Σαβαωθ*." And again (§ 375) in this valuable description of the Gnostic Sacrament: "Then said Jesus, bring me fire and vine-branches. And they brought them unto him, and he, placing upon them an offering, set two vessels of wine, the one on the right, the other on the left of the offering. He set before them the offering: he put also a cup of water before the vessel of wine which was on the right hand, and he set a cup of wine before the vessel of wine that was on the left, and he set loaves of bread, according to the number of his disciples in the middle between the cups. He set likewise a cup of water behind the loaves. And Jesus, standing before the offering, made all the disciples to stand behind him, being all clothed in linen garments, having all of them in their *hands the number* of the Name* of the Father of the Treasury of Light. And he cried aloud, saying, Hear me, O Father, Father of all fatherships, Boundless Light, *Ιαω Ιουω Ιαω αωι ωια ψινωθερ θερινωψ νωψιθερ νεφθομαραχθα ιηαιαμεναμαν αμανηι* of heaven! *Ισραι αμην αμην σουβαι βαι αππααη αμην αμην δερρα αραι απαοι αμην αμην σασαρσαρτου αμην αμην κουκιαμην μαι αμην αμην ιαι ιαι τουαπ αμην αμην μαινμαρι μαριη μαρει αμην αμην αμην*." Again Irenæus copies out a formula "couched in Hebrew words, to inspire greater awe into the Gallic neophyte (at Lugdunum)," as used by certain Gnostics there in administering baptism: *βασσεμα χαμοσσε βα αιανομα ματαδια ρουαδα κουστα βαβαφορ καλαχθαι*, "I invoke Thee, Supreme over every virtue, the Light of the Father by name, the Good Spirit, the Life, because thou hast reigned in the body." Another of their formulæ was—*Μεσσια ου φαρεγ ναμεμψαιμεν χαλδαιαν μοσεμεδια ακφραναι ψαοια Ιησου Ναζαρια*. "I do not separate the Spirit, the Head, and the Supercelestial

* Meaning, perhaps, having their fingers arranged so as to express this number; for Pliny mentions a very *old* statue of Janus displaying the fingers in such manner as to indicate his own *numeral*, that of the days in the year.

Virtue, the Merciful One May I prosper in thy name, O Saviour of Truth "

But as regards the expression of divine mysteries by means of letters of the alphabet, Marcus stands pre-eminently first amongst the Gnostics, as the following extracts from his "Revelation" will conclusively attest. "The supreme Tetrad came down unto me from that region which cannot be seen nor named, in a female form because the world would have been unable to bear their appearing in a male figure, and revealed to me the generation of the universe, untold before either to gods or men. When first the Father, the Inconceivable, Beingless,* sexless, began to be in labour he desired that his Ineffable should be born, and his invisible should be clothed with form He therefore opened his mouth and uttered the Word like unto himself This word standing before him showed that he was manifesting himself as the form or type of the Invisible One Now the uttering of the Name came to pass in this wise He (the Supreme) spake the first word of his name, the which is a syllable of *four* letters He then added the second syllable, also of *four* letters Then the third, composed of *ten* letters Finally the fourth, made up of twelve letters Thus the utterance of the whole name consists of *thirty letters*, and of *four syllables* Each letter has a form-pronunciation and writing of its own, but neither understands nor beholds that of the whole Name, nay, not even the power of the letter standing next to itself Now these sounds united make up the Beingless unbegotten Æon, and *these* are the *Angels* that always behold the face of the Father Thus the Father knowing himself to be incomprehensible gives unto each of the letters, called Æons, its own proper sound, mas-

* The Kabbalistic "En-Soph" In this *boundlessness*, or as the En-Soph, God cannot be *comprehended* by the intellect, nor described by words for there is nothing that can grasp or define Him to us, and as such He is a certain sense *non-existent*, in because as far as our minds are concerned that which is perfectly incomprehensible does not exist To make this existence perceptible, and to render himself comprehensible, the En-Soph had to become active and creative But the En-Soph cannot be the direct Creator, for he has neither will, intention, desire, thought language, nor action, as these properly imply *limit*, and belong to finite beings, whereas the En-Soph is Boundless "

much as none of them singly is competent to utter the entire Name."*

The substance of the revelation brought down to Marcus by Truth is to be found in the Kabbala, which makes the mystic names of God to consist of four, twelve, forty-two and seventy-two letters respectively. The Kabbalists go so far as to assert that the forty-two victims offered by Balaam in order to obtain a favourable response, were consecrated to one of these great names. If indeed Moses was learned in all the wisdom of the Egyptians, the magic virtues of numerals would have formed an essential part of his learning, as we see from the doctrine of Pythagoras, confessedly derived from Egypt. It looks very much like as if the framers of the genealogy of Jesus had the same object in view, when they forced the generations to the required number by omitting *three* of the kings in the second division, being able to deal with the *third* in whatever manner they pleased. On counting the number of the vowels that evidently have some deep purpose in occurring without consonants on so many talismans of the age of Marcus, we should, I expect, often find it tally with that of one or the other of these Holy Names.†

A subsequent revelation of the same Tetrad to Marcus, serves to account for the frequent appearance of the naked woman, the Venus Anadyomene of earlier times, upon Gnostic monuments. "After having declared these things, the Tetrad added: I will shew unto thee *Truth*, whom I have brought

* This is a regular Talmudic notion, as the Rabbins propound. "At first the Name of *twelve letters* was communicated to every one, but when the profane multiplied it was only communicated to the most pious of the priests, and these pre-eminently pious priests absorbed it from their fellow-priests in the chant. It is recorded that Rabbi Tarphon said: I once went up the orchestra in the Temple after my maternal uncle, and bending forward my ear to a priest I heard how he absorbed it from his fellow-priests in the chant. R. Jehudah said in the time of Rab the divine name of *forty-two letters* is only communicated to such as are pious, not easily provoked, not given to drinking, and are not self-opinionated. He who knows that name and preserves it in purity, is beloved above, cherished below, respected by every creature, and is heir to both worlds."—(Babylon. Mid. 71 a.)

† This explains the Σενγα βαρφαραγγες, 'those who stand before the Mount," so commonly following angelic names upon our talismans, where also the long strings of letters may be designed to express their Æon unbegotten.

down from the celestial mansions that thou shouldest behold her naked, acknowledge her beauty, hear her speaking, and be astonished at her wisdom. Look up therefore at her head A and Ω, at her neck B and Ψ, at her shoulders with her hands Γ and X, at her breasts Δ and Φ, at her chest E and Υ, at her back Z and T, at her belly H and Σ, at her thighs Θ and P, at her knees I and Π, at her legs K and O, at her ankles Λ and Ξ at her feet M and N This is the body of Truth, this the form of the letters, this the character of the writing. Whereupon Truth looked upon me (Marcus) and opened her mouth, and uttered a word, and that word became a Name, a name which we know and speak—Christ Jesus and having named him she held her peace."*

This "figure of Truth" is made up, it will be perceived, by taking successive *pairs* of letters from each extremity of the alphabet, perhaps, thereby constituting them male and female, and thus making them types of so many Æons All this suggests a rational question, whether the primary application of the name "Logos" to the Divine Emanation, was not at first a mere interpretation of the Rabbinical Synonym "Name, or Word," the respectful substitute for the ineffable Name Jehovah, the *Shem Hak Kodesh*, and that later, the secondary meaning of *Logos*, "Reason" suggested to the Platonising Jews of Alexandria its analogy to their own Sophia-Achamoth, the first-born of the Supreme Cause And finally, the composition of this Holy Name, extending to *thirty* letters, illustrates the purport of that interminable polysyllabic title which runs either in one unbroken circle, or sometimes in the outline of an erect serpent, around the margin of so many Gnostic gems, and circumscribes the mystic device engraved in the centre In the latter arrangement of the inscription, one is tempted to recognise that "Good and Perfect Serpent" of the

* Similarly in the Kabbalistic diagram of the Sephiroth, the *Crown* is the head, Wisdom, the brain, Intelligence the heart, Love the right arm, Gentleness the left arm, Beauty, the chest, Firmness, the right leg, Splendour, the left leg, Foundation, the genitals, Kingdom, or Shekinah, the union of the whole body The Venus Anadyomene so often seen on our talismans was probably adopted by the Gnostics in this spiritualised sense, and thereby still continues to personify the virtue, *Truth*

Naaseni—that Messias whose visible type in the heavens their eyes, sharpened by faith, discovered and adored in the Constellation *Draco*

To come now to the actual remains of Gnostic manufacture, which preserve to us formulæ of the nature just considered, the most important, to judge from its frequent occurrence, and the evident care bestowed upon its engraving, is the one here transcribed My copy is taken from an example formerly in the State collection, probaby the finest talisman known It is a thick plaque, somewhat heart-shaped, of dark garnet, $2\frac{3}{4} \times 1\frac{1}{2}$ inches in its greatest dimensions, bearing on the one side 14 lines, on the other 11, neatly cut in the Greek character in the third century but making no distinction between the A and the Λ

Obverse

ΑΤΩϹΛϹΛΩΛΛΩΝЄ
ϹЄΜЄϹЄΙΛΛΜΛΒΡΛϹΛΖ
Ϲ3ΖΥΡΡΛΤΗΛΚΡΛΜΜΛ
ΚΡΛΜΜΛΚΛΝΛΡΙϹϹϹЄ
ΓΓЄΝΒΛΛΦΛΡΛΝΓΗϹ
ΛϹΝΙΛΜΒΩΝΛΡΟΥ
ΛΝΤΛΜΙΥΠΗΛΝ
ΜΟΡΛΡΛΧϹΙΔ
ΛΛЄЄΤϹΜΛΙ *

Reverse.

ΟΙΓΙϹΩΡΟΥΑΡ
ΙΛΩΡЄΩΗΛΦΟΝ
ΑΙΩΛΙΗΤΟϹ
ΩΛΙΗΜΛΟΗΛΩ
ЄΩΛЄΥΩЄΥΗ
ΩΛΙЄΥЄΙΗΙЄ
ΛΗЄЄЄΥΩ
ΗΛΩΛЄΥЄΩ
ΓΗЄЄΩΛЄЄ
ΩΗΛΩΗΝΗΦΙ
ΗΛΩΥΗΝЄΨ
ЄΜΗΛΙΛΟΛ
ΑΗΩΩΩ
ЄΩΩ

Amongst the titles on the obverse several familiar names may be detected, such as *Alon*, *Shemesh Eilam*, *Abrasax* The long style filling the fourth line is clearly the correct spelling of the abbreviated *Agrammacamereg* addressed in another part of the "Prayers of the Saviour," as the first of the "Invisible Gods" The next line *Shemgensalpharanges*, "they who stand before the mount of Paradise," can be no other than the Æons just described by Marcus as the "Angels who always behold the Father's face". whilst in this Jewish hierarchy of heaven the old god of Egypt, Anubis, oddly intrudes himself under his Coptic title of *Ambo*.

* Probably meant ἀλεξετέ με "Defend me!"—of exactly similar sound in the spoken language

Both inscriptions agree literally with those upon the large oval calcedony figured by Chiflet (fig 69) except the addition in the letter of a few words inclosed within a coiled serpent placed at the top of the obverse. Out of these inscriptions his friend Wendelin, by taking the language as good Greek, had contrived to elicit a most orthodox invocation to the Trinity, which however was evidently far from satisfactory to the sceptical and more sagacious Canon. Amongst the Townley gems is a large sard, agreeing in all except a few letters with Chiflet's specimen—convincing attestation to the supposed virtue of the formula. For the purpose of comparison I insert another, lately discovered, engraved on a much more minute scale than any of the preceding (Whelan's copy.)

ZZZ
TRYЄ
✡ ✡
ΑΓωЄΑCΑωΑΑωΝC
COMЄCЄΙΑΑΜΑΒΡΑC
CӠZYΡΡΑΗΑΚΡΑΜΜΑ
ΚΡΑΜΜΑΚΑΜΑΡΙCCCЄ
ΓΓΟΝΒΑΑ♆ΑΒΑΝΓΗC
ΙΜЄCCΙΑΑΜωΒΗΑΜ
ЄΝΙΑΜΒωΝΑΡΟΥ
ΝΤΑΜΙΧΑΗΑΑ
ΜΟΡΑΧЄΙ♆Υ
ΡΑΒЄΤЄΜΑΙ
ΑΝω

ΟΜЄCωΤΟΥΑΡ
ΙΑωΡЄΟΗΛΦΟΝ
ΑЄΟΑΙΗΤΟC
ωΑΙΜΑωΗΑΟ
ΙωΑΟΥωΟVΗ
ωΑΙΥΗΑΗΙC
ΑΗЄЄЄΙΥωΥ
ΗΑωΑЄΥCωL
ΤΗЄCωΙΑCC
ωΗΑωΗΝΙΙ∇Ι
ΗΑωΥΗΑΑЄΥ
CΜΗΑΙΑΟΑΥ
ΙΗΗωωωΥΗ
ΙωωΗΗ

Dark red agate, 1 × 7/9 in. sent me by Mr Whelan, Nov 25, 1881

Doubtless such immense and overcharged pieces of mystery served in their time the purpose of pocket prayer books, out of which the owner recited the due invocations at the sacred rites. To some such *manual* of devotion, the pseudo-Orpheus possibly alludes by

> "Pray, with the flowered *Petraces* in thy hand,
> When hecatombs before the altar stand"

The Orientalist desirous of exercising his ingenuity upon the decyphering of these, for the most part unexplained monuments will find an immense collection of them in Raspe (Nos 433–633) copied with scrupulous accuracy. The reason he there gives for the attention he has paid to a class previously so neglected is a very sound one. "All these sects have evidently borrowed their *symbols*, and probably also their respective explanations, from the iconology and mysteries of the Egyptians and other nations of the East. If as regards the meaning of hieroglyphics and symbols they had no better information, the Gnostics of Egypt and Syria had at least national tradition to depend upon—a point assuredly of some weight. If therefore the more recent sects of Gnostics with their symbolical learning have established new opinions and fresh modifications of religion upon the basis of the old, we are not therefore to conclude that they knew nothing about, and wantonly gave a new meaning to, the symbols which they thus misapplied. This is the only rational point of view in which these amulets and engravings ought to be studied."

Raspe's collection I shall now proceed to supplement by copies of several unpublished examples—the most interesting that have come under my notice in a long course of study, and such as serve best to illustrate the theories proposed in the foregoing pages. And to show the curious and puzzling nature of the whole class, they often present the critical examiner with signs and *siglæ*, now supposed the exclusive property of national religions, the most diverse from one another, as they were remote from the recognised metropolis of Gnosticism. Intermingled with the regular Greek characters appear strange signs analogous in form, often identical with, the Caste-marks of the Hindoos, and which in their turn became the parents of those used by the mediæval alchemists and Rosicrucians, and (during the same ages) of the true professors of Masonry. The consideration of these *Sigla*, of which I have collected a large series belonging to all ages and countries, has proved sufficiently fruitful to supply materials for a separate and important subdivision of this Treatise. One example, described under "talismans and amulets," presents unmistakeable evidence of the use of *Runes* in the Alexandrine studio, whilst another, shortly to be noticed, demonstrates that the Gnosis may dispute with Hibernia her supposed peculiar invention of the mysterious *Oghams*.

A tablet of aquamarine (?) communicated to me by the

Rev Greville Chester, bears the inscriptions in well-formed characters—

Obverse.

ΙΕΡΚΡ
ΒΔΩΡΓΟΛΕΟΡΟ
ΑΛΧΑΜΧΑΒΡΑC
ΗΤΑΔΩΝΑΙCΑ
ΑΩΘΑΓΙΑΔΥΝΑ
ΜΙCΒΟΗΘΕΙΜ

Reverse

CΑΒΑΩΘΩΥΕΑΗΩ
ΡΜΑΡCΑΒΑΟΥΦΕΙ
ΟΡΘΟΘΑΥΜΑΘΙΜ
ΥΧΡΩCΕΜΕΝΟΧ
ΑΠΕΡΚΡΗΦΤΑΩ

Extremity

ΘΑΩΘΟΥ

A string of titles ending with "Lord of hosts! defend me"

ΙΛΕΩΒΛΦΡΕ
ΝΕΜΟΝΟΘΙΛΑΡ
ΙΚΡΙΦΙΕΥΕΛΛΙΦΙΡΚ
ΙΡΑΛΙΝΥΟΜΕΝΕΡΦΑ
ΒΩΕΑΙΑΝΑΕΙΑΥΕΕΑ
ΩΕΙΩΙΑΙΑΙΑΝΙΝ
ΝΙƆΛΖΧΙΦVΛΑ
ΖΟΝ

Sapphirine calcedony, the size of a pigeon's egg —(Forman Collection)

The concluding word φύλαξον, "Do thou protect," clearly evinces that this elegantly engraved invocation was addressed to some *one* deity rejoicing in many titles, and styled "propitious" by its opening ἰλέω.

ΜΙΕΙΧΑΗΛ
ΓΑΒΡΙΗΑVΑΦ
ΑΗΛΕΕΕΕΕΝΓΕ
ΝΒΑΡΑΝΓΗ
ΝΙΑW

A very thick stone of sapphirine calcedony This is purely Jewish, perhaps the ware of some "Magna sacerdos arboris" sold to the Roman ladies, for it puts the buyer under the protection of the Archangels "Michael, Gabriel, Raphael, who stand before the Mount of Paradise of Jehovah."

A remarkable exemplification of the mixture of two opposing creeds is found in the ΟΡΩΡΙΟΥΘ, "Light of lights," accompanying the figure of a globose vase with bands hanging from the neck. This is evidently "the small golden vessel shaped like a cow's udder, containing the libations of milk" mentioned by Apuleius as carried in the Isiac procession by the same official who bore aloft the Hand of Justice. The *gridiron*-like object often laid upon it, is the regular Egyptian door-key, made of wood. In one example figured by Mattei (Pl. vi. 6), the key is shown of the regular *Roman* form in the same position, which places the meaning of the more usual figure entirely out of doubt. This shows the reason for κλειδοῦχος, "the keybearer," being a priestly title.

Other types purely Egyptian, offer some curious improvements upon the old "qualia demens Ægyptus portenta colat." For example, one (Praun) exhibits Anubis, but now equipped, with two heads and four hands holding torches and daggers, styled on the reverse ΠΕΡΑ—ΑΜΒΟ—ΥΒΑΚΑ—ΚΞΙΚ—ΥΚ. In another (Nelthropp) the Cat-headed goddess, Taf-Neith stands lotus-crowned, and is addressed as ΚΥΧΒΑ—ΚΥΧΒΑ*—ΚΑΧΥΑ—ΒΑΖΑΚΑΧ—ΚΧ. Again Anubis with the superadded heads of Pan (*Mendes*) and a cock (*Phre*), with arms outstretched in the form of a cross, his body supported upon the legs of an ibis, has over the heads respectively written the initials Θ, Π, Χ. On the reverse ΑΙΗΒ-ΩΠCΧ—CΥΝΟ—ΧΡΑ. But the most curious composition of this nature known to me is presented by a large elliptical mottled jasper, measuring $1\frac{1}{8}+\frac{3}{4}$ inch, very boldly cut, and better drawn than usual—apparently a Solar talisman (Mr. Topham, Rome). The obverse shows a *gryllas* in the outline of a cock having the head of Pan, scorpions for tail-feathers, and the whip of Sol stuck in his rump to complete that appendage, standing upon a serpent—overhead are the sun-star and crescent, on his back rests a tailed globe (a comet?) in front Α, in the field below the astral *siglæ*. On the reverse, ΟΓ (73?) over

* *Chaldee*, "The Star, the Star."

the Agathodæmon serpent uncoiled, and crawling, a star and A Below the serpent, ΕΔΩΓ ΗΙΗΩ, the letters inverted, then another line ΗΙVΟΜϹΟΙ Below this again the triple S on the bar that always accompanies the Agathodæmon, ΙΑΗΙΕΩ–ΙΕΟVΩΗ, reading thus in the impression In the last word ' the Great Ιεου "—special title of the Supreme Being in the Pistis-Sophia may easily be detected, whilst the triple-headed deity previously described, very probably expresses the conception of those mighty Τριδυνάμεις θεοὶ, who play so important a part in the theology of the same book of wonder

The following examples are the more genuine offspring of the Kabbala, consisting of letters alone, uncontaminated by the presence of the idols of Misraim First for beauty of material and engraving stands a large *citrine* (occidental topaz) formerly in the Praun cabinet, now in the Gnostic Series, British Museum

On one side is an oval enclosing ΗΙ (perhaps denoting the Ogdoad and Decad, the base of Marcus scheme, *see* Hep vi 52), an eye, emblem of Osiris, a square bisected, and Δ, which last letter may also numerically represent the Tetrad of the same Doctor

The other face of the gem presents,

ΑΜΑΡΥϹΜΗΡΙΑЄΜΙΟΥΩ
ΡΟΔΑϹΝΑΒΑΡЄЄΗΙΟΥΩ
ΝΑΒΑΡΝЄΗΙΟΥΩ
ЄΡЄΘΡΑΥΜΟΥΩ
ΖΑΓΕϹΟΨΙΟΥΩ
ΟΡΘΡΟΧΟΡϹЄΥΩ
ΑΧΑΗΜΑΡЄΩ

The next is a legend which, with trivial variations, frequently occurs Caylus (VI Pl 11) gives it very rudely added, upon the reverse of a female portrait The present copy is from a large calcedony, somewhat coarsely executed, having on its other face the triple S and bar (Praun) —

ϹΤΟΧΒΑΘΑ
ΗΜΑΛΑΧΙϹΘΟΜ
ΜΑΚΟΧΨΟΧ
ΑΒΡΑΜΜΑΩΘΗ
ΑΒΡΑΜΜΗΛ

The Hebrew Patriarch figures in this legend, and in many more of the same kind, as the divinely inspired founder of a

Gnosis, a reputation he enjoyed even amongst the heathen, who put him in the same category with Orpheus, first institutor of Mysteries "Sev Alexander in larario suo—omnes sanctiores in quibus Apollonium, et (quantum scriptor horum temporum dicit) Christum, *Abraham*, et Orpheum, et ejusmodi cæteros habebat." (Lampridius 29)

To the same family belongs a yellow jasper (Maskelyne) displaying a *perforated* quatrefoil over the name ΙΑω, then the mystic vowels ΑΕΙΗΟΥωΑΙ, then ΓΑΒΑωΘ (*sic*) and on reverse ✲ ΜΙΧΑΗΛ ✲ The quatrefoil is originally the symbol of Sitala, the Tenth Tirthakoor, or deified Jaina saint, whence it found its way along with the other Buddhistic machinery, into Mediæval symbolism, in which it resembles an *angel* *

Very remarkable on account of its adjuncts, is a green jasper (Praun) bearing a long neatly-cut legend, the central portion of which is circumscribed by two lines, cut by short strokes at different angles, exactly after the fashion of the Irish Oghams In the latter, as is well known, all the letters of the Roman alphabet are represented by the different positions of very short lines in relation to one continuous line in the middle, and it is impossible to imagine any other purpose subserved by the similar contrivance on our talisman The Ogham is *supposed* to be an invention of the first missionaries to Ireland, it was used as late as the Civil War by Lord Glamorgan in his correspondence with Charles I It is, however, very possible that the monks carried this simple stenography from Rome to their Celtic mission †

ΠΥΡΟϹΟΧ
ΚΡΗΦΟ
ΥΜΑΡΤΑ
ΑΡΦΟΥ
ΥΘЄΡ
ΦΟΥΘΑΙ

ΧΟΥΒΥ
ΛΑΙΛΑΜ
ΘΑΛΘΑΛ
ΨΥΘΑΘΟ
ΡΟϹΙω

ΑΝΟΧ
ΜΟΥΙ
ΥΑΛΑΛ

Ιω
ΛΥЄΠΙΘΙΑΑΚΥΘω
ϹΥΠΙΝЄΙΨΙΑ

* One of the heaviest charges against the mediæval Manichæans was the adoration of an *Octagon*, as the figure of God

† The talisman-makers loved to press into their service all the strange characters that came to their knowledge Even the Runic of the farthest north added its virtue to the Praun hepatic amulet to be fully noticed in its proper section

A minute figure of Abraxas, green jasper (Praun) takes a new title "Abrachars" in the invocation ΑΒΡΑΧΑΡϹ—ΑΓΡΑѠΑ—ѠΑΡΙѠΝΙΕ

Thoth's caduceus within a wreath, is accompanied by the legend on the reverse ΑΚΡΙѠΦΙ' on a brown calcedony in my collection

Of all Agathodæmon talismans, no more elegant specimen has come to my knowledge than a large emerald-like plasma (Bosanquet) displaying the serpent "the Good and Perfect One" erect above his invariable concomitant sigla, and whom the reverse propitiates by the beautifully cut address ΟϹΟΡ—ΜΕΡΦ—ΦΕΡΓΑΜΑΡΑ—ΦΡΙΔΥΡΙϹ—ΧΝΟΥΦΙϹ—ΝΑΒΙϹ—ΚΙϹΝΥΘ True green jade, very convex on back (Rev. S S Lewis) In the field, each side of serpent ΙѠΙ $\frac{MN}{V}$ - ΙΘΙ "With me, with me!" in pure Chaldee Reverse in two lines, round the usual symbol

ΧΝΟΥΜΙϹИΑΑΒΕΙϹΒΕΙΝΥΘΕΕΕ
ϹΟΡΟΟΡΜΕΡΦΕΡΓΑΓΒΑΡΜΑΦΡΙ□ΥΙΡΙΡΙΓΞ

All cut with unusual precision and neatness of work The legend has many words in common with Mr Bosanquet's plasma

Jerome's "Pater Bromius" of the Mithraic Cave has probably some share in the title "Sabbaoth," so often coupled with "Adonai," for Bacchus rejoiced in the epithet "Sabazius," derived from the shout "Sabbaoi" raised by the celebrants of his Orgies—a word identical with the Hebrew "Sabi" *glory!* Certain sectaries of our own day who bellow out the same word at their "Revivals," are little aware what an ancient and congenial authority they have for their vociferation

"Adonai," *our Lord*, is converted by the Greek into Adoneus, a synonym for Pluto, and Orpheus, as already quoted, points out the identity of Bacchus, Pluto, and Sol This is the foundation for the ancient exposition of the Syrian rite, the Mourning for Adonis ("The women weeping for Thammuz") as really applying to the sun's loss of power at the winter quarter. *Adoneus* or *Aidoneus*, becoming interpreted according to Greek etymology, was supposed to signify him "that walketh unseen," whence spring the "helmet of Adoneus," that rendered the wearer invisible, and Catullus's application of the title to the intrigue-loving Cæsar

> "Perambulabit omnium cubilia
> Ut albulas columbas aut *Adoneus*"

The same Adonis had the name "Sal-Anbo" (which often occurs in Gnostic legends) as appears from the statement in Lampridius, "that Heliogabalus exhibited *Salanbo* with all the lamentation and tossing of head proper to the *Syrian* ceremony,"—whereby he gave the omen of his own impending fate.

The Delphic E has already been noticed—but its importance demands further particulars of its history, which have been preserved by Plutarch in his curious treatise upon the subject. The Greeks with their usual fondness for explaining all mysteries *rationistically*, considered the letter as the simple numeral, *Five*, set up in the Temple to denote the original and proper number of the far-famed "Wise Men," but which in later times had been raised to *seven*, by the addition of two more who had small claims to the honour The legend went that these Five Wise Men, to commemorate the accidental meeting of them all in Delphi at the same festival, had dedicated the numeral carved in wood, which, decaying through age, the Corinthians replaced by a facsimile in bronze, which last was finally transmuted by Livia Augusta into another of *gold*, as more consistent with the dignity of the god of the place, whose son her husband claimed to be, and whose received image he represented in his features.

Others, more profoundly, interpreted the letter as representing by its proper sound in the Greek alphabet the declaration ΕΙ, "Thou art" as addressed to the Godhead—thus making it equivalent to the title ὁ ὤν, "the living God," so frequently given to Jehovah

But it is much more consistent with the simplicity of antique times, to understand the figure as merely standing for the number *Five*, a number sacred for *itself*, not for its reference to the fabled sages of a later period The idea of its virtue may have come from an Indian source, where it is the cause of the five-headed shape assigned to Brahma. From India it would find its way to

Delphi in company with the Gorgon-heads, themselves masks of Bhavana the Destroyer, which guarded the actual oracle—a singular connexion, noticed by Euripides in his 'Ion.' But it should be remembered that the Hyperboreans, reputed founders of the Oracle, were placed between the Caspian and the frontiers of India. The *Omphalos* itself "shaded with garlands, and encompassed with Gorgons" was no other than the Brahminical *Lingam*, as its figure demonstrates, whether as repictured in the early vase paintings when embraced by Orestes seeking sanctuary there from the pursuing Eumenides, or with Apollo seated thereon, stamped on the money of the Seleucidae—direct descendants of the god. In form reduced to an obtuse cone, the emblem had nothing obscene in appearance, its hidden meaning being a matter of revelation to the initiated few. The same conically-shaped stone was the sole representative of Venus in her most ancient temples—Paphos for example. Again that earliest of all statues of Apollo, the Amyclæan, described by Pausanias was a veritable Hindoo *Lat*—a bronze column 30 cubits high, to which later art had added a head, hands holding bow and spear, and *toes* (ἄκροι πόδες). But his throne, in the middle of which the idol *stood* erect, was an after-thought of the best times of Greece, covered with elaborate figures and reliefs, the work of Bathycles, or of Myron, with his scholars.

And in truth this very lunar-shaped ϵ seems to belong to the same class of Indian importations, and to have been originally a mere Caste-mark—indeed, if placed horizontally ω, it becomes at once the badge of the sectaries of Vishnu. What strongly confirms this explanation is the fact, that this symbol had been consecrated at Delphi many centuries before that shape of the *letter* came into the Greek alphabet—a change only dating from the age of Antony and Cleopatra, upon whose medals, struck in Asia Minor, the lunar-shaped ϵ is first observable.

In the earliest dawn of Grecian philosophy we find Pythagoras* building his whole system upon the mystic properties of

* Who is constantly affirmed to have visited India, Apuleius stating of him, 'Sed nec his artibus animi expletum mox Chaldæos, inde Brachmanas, eorum ergo Brachmanum Gymnosophistas adiisse."—('Florida.')

Numbers, and declared by tradition to have been taught the science in Egypt; nay more, Plato himself has penned in his Republic a certain section in the same line, worthy of any Alexandrian Kabbalist. In our own day, with the Sikhs to hold a "Punch," or council of Five, was the formal mode of deliberating upon all matters of State. And inasmuch as the most serious things have a ludicrous side, this sacred Numeral only preserves its reputation amongst ourselves from having given the name to the well-known beverage, by reason of the *five* ingredients that go to its concoction—perhaps too, because its brewing was the inevitable result of the coming together of the same number of Englishmen in the times when our language was enriched by so many loans from the Hindostanee.*

A remarkable feature in the theogony of Valentinus is curiously illustrated by a Praun Calcedony elegantly engraved, and mounted in a gold frame by some later Oriental owner, who justly deemed the gem a talisman of uncommon power. "The Father at last sent forth a mighty Æon, called the *Cross*, and who contained within himself all the other thirty Æons. The same was likewise denominated *Terminus*, inasmuch as he served for *Boundary* between the Fulness (*Pleroma*) and the Deficiency (*Hysteroma*)." Our gem presents the Egyptian Tau, as a Deus Terminus, topped with a human head, and surrounded by a continuous legend composed of vowels interspersed with rare consonants, probably expressing the thirty Æons contained within the sigil's self. On the base of the Terminus is the legend ΝΙΧΑΡΟΠΛΗϹ, often occurring on talismans. The same words are found at the foot of a cruciform trophy, above which is the Christian X upon a stone in the French Cabinet (No. 2222) also followed by ΙΩΑ upon the back of a gem (*silex*) published in the 'Gottingische Anzeiger,' Nos. 35 *a*, *b*, which clearly emanates from Mithraic notions, for it represents the usual lion-headed, serpent-girt man, a torch in one hand, in the other a sword, serpent, and crown of victory, soaring aloft from the back of a lion, under which lies a prostrate corpse.

* For example *caste* and *dam*. The latter is the probable source of the common English expression that emphasises the small value of a thing, which ignorance softens into *curse*. Similarly used is *rap*, the smallest of the Swiss money.

A very curious instance of the employment of Gnostic figures in the art of Medicine is offered by the stone which Matter has published (Pl. II., C. 4) The obverse displays the Agathodæmon serpent placed between Phre (Sol) and a female in the act of adoration. Overhead are the mystic Vowels, below the undershaped vase, already noticed, placed upon a low altar, the whole encompassed by a legend in some unknown tongue But the other side explains in lucid Greek the object of the composition. TACCON THN MHTPAN THC ΔЄINA ЄIC TON IΔION TOΠONOTON KYKΛON TOY HΛIOY, "Place the womb of such or such a one into its proper region, O, the circle of the sun" Matter, in his explanation, has fallen into a ludicrous mistake, by interpreting *μητρὰν* as *μητέρα* he converts the words into a prayer for the soul of the mother of a certain Dina! But the real translation shows that the gem was made for *any* purchaser, to be worn as a preservative against the "prolapsus uteri," a female complaint very common in ancient times, owing to the abuse of the hot bath, so relaxing to the internal muscles, and also to the general employment of "abortiva," whenever thought desirable In fact the very definite expression of the object, MHPIKON, *uterine*, is found on other gems, and places the correctness of the attribution of the former one quite out of doubt

The "circle of the sun" means the *navel*, which marks the natural position of the organ concerned, for the navel in the microcosm was supposed to concide with the sun in the universe. This idea produced the far-famed hallucination of the Byzantine anchorites, respecting the mystical Light of Tabor, which shone upon the devotee in virtue of long-continued fasting, and unintermitted fixing of the eyes upon the region of the navel, whence at length it streamed forth, as from a focus, the "true creation of an empty brain and an empty stomach."*

* A neatly engraved ring stone, hæmatite, lately communicated to me, has a line of several of the common *siglae*, followed by two more containing IAω APIHA BIKTO-PINA, "Jehovah Lion of God (protect) Victorina!" When proper names can be deciphered on these talismans they are always those of women A Praun gem, similarly opening with a line of *siglae* and the names Iao and Gabriel, was made for a certain Sabinia Quinta

Another circumstance bearing upon this employment of the sigil is that Isis, the peculiar goddess of maternity, is often figured in Roman sculpture, holding up in her hand a conical object, pouch shaped, exhibiting a triangular orifice This object some have taken for the Persia plum, much more probably does it represent the organ in question, the most natural and expressive symbol of that divinity's peculiar function In her mystic coffer were carried the distinctive marks of both sexes, the *lingam* and *yoni* of the Hindoos Their Isis, Parvati, who in this character takes the name of *Deva* "the goddess" pre-eminently, bears in her hand for distinctive badge the yoni, or bhaga, often a precious stone carved into that shape Similarly her consort, Siva, carries the lingan or phallus For example, the Nizam's diamond, the largest stone of its kind known *certainly* to exist, exhibits evident traces of the native lapidary's clumsy endeavours to reduce the native crystal to the proper shape for the hand of the great goddess Ugly omen to happen under a female reign, this diamond was accidentally broken in two just before the outbreak of the Sepoy revolt

Deva's Mark, as borne upon their foreheads by Parvati's sectaries, is formed by three strokes, the two outside white or yellow, the centre always red. It is interpreted as representing the womb, *methra*, of Bhavani (another of Parvati's names) out of which proceeded all that exists The close relationship between the Egyptian and Hindoo goddesses cannot fail to strike the observer, Isis carries the very same attributes with Parvati—the kid and cobras—upon the talisman—published by Caylus (IV, Pl 16) But the Egyptian goddess, having but one pair of hands, is forced to clasp in each the several attributes borne singly by her many-handed Indian prototype.

A singular union of two contrary deities in one body, is presented by a hematite (Praun), representing Anubis, who, besides his proper jackal's head, is equipped with another, maned on the neck, and unmistakably that of an ass, as Typhon,* the evil one, was depicted, moreover, one of the feet,

* The ass was sacred to Typhon Plutarch (De Iside, 31) quotes an Egyptian legend that this deity fled from the "Battle of the Gods" upon

too, of the figure is clearly *hoofed*, so as to leave no doubt as to the ownership of the second head The same discordance of characters is still further set forth by what he bears in his hands, the two of Anubis holding up *torches*, the two of the malignant Typhon, *swords*. This odd combination probably expressed the same idea as did the Anubis seen by Apuleius, who exhibited at one time a face black as the night, at another golden as the day, in order to express his functions exercised both in heaven and in hell The reverse bears an inscription containing the Coptic name of the god, ΠΕΡΑ—ΑΜΒѠ—ΥΒΑΙΑ—ΚΞΙΚ—Λ

the back of an ass for over seven days' space without stopping, until he came into Judæa where he begat two sons, Hierosolymus and Palæstinus Sir G Wilkinson has met (although but rarely) with the figure of an ass-headed deity, or demon, in Egyptian sculptures

FIG. 13

PART IV.

THE FIGURED MONUMENTS OF GNOSTICISM

ΤΩΙ ΝΙΚΩΝΤΙ ΔΩΣΩ ΑΥΤΩΙ ΦΑΓΕΙΝ
ΑΠΟ ΤΟΥ ΜΑΝΝΑ ΤΟΥ ΚΕΚΡΥΜΜΕΝΟΥ ΚΑΙ
ΔΩΣΩ ΑΥΤΩ ΨΗΦΟΝ ΛΕΥΚΗΝ ΚΑΙ ΕΠΙ
ΤΗΝ ΨΗΦΟΝ ΟΝΟΜΑ ΚΑΙΝΟΝ ΓΕΓΡΑΜΜΕΝ
Ο ΟΥΔΕΙΣ ΕΓΝΩ ΕΙ ΜΗ Ο ΛΑΜΒΑΝΩΝ

THE FIGURED MONUMENTS OF GNOSTICISM

GNOSTIC SIGLÆ, SYMBOLS, LEGENDS EXPLAINED

THE inscriptions in Greek characters upon Gnostic talismans are frequently interspersed with mystic figures, formed out of straight lines set at right angles to each other, and intermingled with dots. These lines Bellermann plausibly enough supposes to represent the "sacred lots," of the same nature as the celebrated *sortes Antiates*, held in the hands of the much-consulted Fortuna of Antium. In their usual form these lots were only little sticks and balls, taken up by the handful from an urn, and thrown at random on the ground. The diviner examined the patterns thus produced by their casual collocation, and predicted the future from them according to the rules of his art. Bellermann goes on to suppose that the figures on our talismans represent certain configurations of the lots, regarded as peculiarly lucky to the consulter. This explanation is supported by the Geomancy of the modern Arabs,* where lines drawn at haphazard on the sand by a stick held between the fingers are interpreted by persons professing that method of divination. Our own divination, by means of tea-grounds, is carried on upon the same principle, the fortuitous arrangement of the

* ('Each tribe either found or introduced in the Caaba their domestic worship, the temple was adorned or defiled with 360 idols of men, eagles, lions, and antelopes, and most conspicuous was the statue of Hebal, of *red agate*, holding in his hand seven arrows, without heads or feathers, the instruments and symbols of profane divination."—Gibbon, chap. 12.)

particles producing to the experienced eye definite pictures and letters of the alphabet.

These Siglæ, however, may possibly have had another origin. The regular badge of the *Magus*, as prescribed in the Vendidad, is a bundle of divining-rods—three, seven, or nine in number. Hence the rebuke of Hosea: "My people ask counsel of *sticks*, and their *staff* declareth it unto them." These same divining-rods placed upon the altar are commonly represented upon the Magian signets, bearing for official type the Mobed at his devotions, and may therefore be supposed to have passed down to the talisman-makers of later times.*

That others amongst these angular forms are numerals is certain from the nature of the case, and from Horapollo's express declaration that the Egyptians represented 10 by the figure ┌ and 100 by the same four times repeated in the form of a square, thus □. *Ten* being the "perfect number" of the Valentinian creed (whose fountain-head was Alexandria), its frequent appearance amongst the religious formulæ of the sect is naturally to be looked for. The primitive Egyptian numerals were of the simplest kind, but their abbreviated combinations ultimately became distinct symbols for the different days of the month, and out of these the Arab astrologers concocted their own system. This circumstance affords reason for another solution—that some of these siglæ indicate the particular days connected with the astrological intention of the talisman.†

And besides all these, there is every probability that these siglæ include actual cuneiform letters, belonging to the Assyrian alphabet, but their forms somewhat corrupted by the semi-

* The ancient Teutons practised the same method of divining future events. A shoot of a fruit tree was cut into pieces, each being distinguished by certain marks, *notis quibusdam*, probably meaning "Runes." The consulter threw them down at random on a white cloth, with eyes turned to heaven he took up three separately, and interpreted the response from the inscriptions upon them.—(Tacitus, Germ. x.)

† Some of these siglæ may be recognised in the inscriptions in an unknown character, cut in the hard sandstone rock, and very numerous about Silsilis, Upper Nubia, where they accompany figures of elephants, giraffes, and ostriches—all animals long since extinct in that country. Specimens were published by Greville Chester in the 'Archæological Journal' for 1864, p. 274.

Greek wizard, who employed them in ignorance of their true nature The Assyrian language being considered as late as the times of Iamblichus peculiarly grateful to the heavenly Powers, what more reasonable than that some at least of these invocations should continue to be couched in their original cyphers? Be it remembered, the cuneiform character was the national one of the whole Persian empire down to the Macedonian conquest, and must have been preserved in religious usages long after that event by the Magi They, at least, were a very unlikely class to trouble themselves about the Greek alphabet or Greek literature, professing, like the Talmudists, a pious horror for both This is well exemplified on the restoration of the native dynasty under the Sassanians, Greek, employed for four centuries by the Parthian line, is at once expelled from the coins by the Pehlevi character, true daughter of the primitive cuneiform There is moreover one all sufficient reason for seeking the origin of these inexplicable siglæ at Babylon they constituted a religious stenography The Babylonians "attached to each god a certain *numeral*, which may be used in the place of his proper *emblem*, and may even stand for his *name* in an inscription " (Rawlinson, 'Anc Monarchies, iii, 466) To give those of the principal deities

First Triad Anu = 60, Bel = 50, Hoa = 40
Second Triad Moon = 30, Sun = 20, Air = 10
Beltis, or Mylitta = 15, Nergal, or Mars = 12, Nin, or Saturn = 10

Of the other planets the numerals have not been discovered, but their names are, Nebo, Mercury Merodach, Jupiter, Ishtar, Venus

The great gods are Anu, *Pluto*, Bel, *Jupiter*, Hoa, *Neptune* Their consorts are, respectively, Anat, Beltis, Davkana The minor gods are, Sin, or Hurke, answering to the later Lunus Deus, San, the Sun, Vul, the Æther Their respective consorts are, "The Great Lady", Gula, or Anahit, Tula, or Shula The Pythagoreans had a symbolism of the same nature, denoting Minerva by an *equilateral triangle*, Apollo by *unity* Strife, by the numeral *two*, Justice, by *three*, and the Supreme Being by *four* (Plat De Is. et Os 75) * I find a very strong confirmation

* In the Egyptian Ritual papyrus, Hermes by is *mystic name* of the Thoth is addressed as "the second god A"

of my belief that the Gnostic *Powers* were similarly designated by their numerals, in Raspe's gem, No 601, where CENΓEN is inscribed in the exergue under a serpent coiled into a cartouche containing several of the siglæ under consideration Now this legend (to be explained farther on) is, when written in full, always followed by the names of the Archangels, whence it may justly be inferred the same names are still here, but represented in their mystic form *

"The Great Names" constitute the very essence of every Gnostic spell. To begin, therefore, with their consideration is obviously the most appropriate and propitious mode of approaching this part of our work—pandere res alta terra et caligine mersas There are three titles perpetually occurring, and consequently to be supposed denoting beings of the highest importance in the Gnostic hierarchy of heaven Their meaning was unknown until the fortunate discovery of the grand Valentinian gospels The Pistis-Sophia informed us (§ 361) that they are the holy Names of the Three Τριδύναμεις, who are IΨANTAX-AINXEOTX, a Power emanating from whom resides in the planet Mars, BAINXWWX † in Mercury and ΠICTIC COΦIA in Venus Above this Triad is one still higher, the "Three Unseen Gods," AΓPAMMAXAMAPEΓ, BAPBHΛW (the Heavenly Mother of Jesus), and BΔEΛΛH (§ 359)

The "Five Words" written upon the shining vesture sent down to Jesus at His glorification (§ 16) were ZAMA

* The Turks represent the Great Name *Allah* by an oval crossed with intersecting lines, which is often seen stamped on their old armour, for an amulet Now this very mark occurs in the Gnostic set, and it is more than probable that its true meaning is preserved in the Turkish tradition

† In Goodwin's 'Magic Papyrus' the Serapean Divination (No 1) names this Power "Appear and give heed unto him who was manifested before Fire and Snow, Βαινχωωχ, for Thou art he that did make manifest Light and Snow, Terrible-eyed-thundering-and-lightning-swift-footed-one" This papyrus, now in the British Museum, was bought of Atanasi, Swedish Consul at Alexandria who sold several others of the same nature to the Leyden Library All are supposed to have been found together in a catacomb at Thebes, and to have formed the stock of some magician of the second century of our era, as the handwriting leads us to infer Goodwin edited the Brit Museum specimen for the Cambridge Antiquarian Society in 1852, and enriched it with notes giving invaluable assistance to all who study Gnostic remains

ΖΑΜΑ ωΖΖΑ ΡΑΧΑΜΑ ωΖΑΙ—"The robe, the glorious robe of my strength." The same revelation furthermore imparts to the faithful the mystic names of the planets. "Hearken now, I will tell unto you the Incorruptible Names of the Planets, which be ωΡΙΜΟΤΘ, Saturn, ΜΟΤΝΙΧΟΤΑΦωΡ, Mars, ΤΑΡΠΕΤΑΝΟΤΦ, Mercury, ΧωΣΙ, Venus, ΧωΝΒΑΛ, Jupiter These be the incorruptible names of the same" (§ 362) Of these, the names from each Triad are to be recognised upon talismans, ΒΑΙΝΧωωωΧ most commonly of all, but no example of these planetary appellations has hitherto come to my knowledge.

The Naaseni (says Hippolytus) taught that the universe could not hold together unless the names of the Great Ones (τὰ μεγέθη) were uttered These were ΚΑΤΑΚΑΤ ΣΑΤΑΑΣΑΤ, ΖΕΗΣΑΡ "The first is the name of the *Adamas* who is above; the second, of him who is below, the third of the Jordan that floweth upwards" "Above are Mariamne the Sought-after, and Jothor the great and wise, and Sephora she that seeth, and Moses" According to the text-book of another sect, the Peratæ, ΧωΖΖΑΡ is the Power whom the ignorant and profane call Neptune ΚΑΡΦΑΚΟΣΗΜΟΧΕΡ is the Steward of the East ΕΚΚΑΒΑΚΑΡΑ of the West, called by the vulgar the Curetes ΑΡΙΒΑ is the Ruler of the Winds, ΣωΚ-ΛΑΜ, or Osiris, rules the twelve hours of the night, ΕΝΤω, or Isis, those of the day her sign is the Dog-star ΒΗΝΑ is Ceres, or the Left-hand Power of God, presiding over nutrition, ΜΗΝ is the Right-hand Power that presides over the fruits of the earth In the same doctrine, *chozzar*, called by the ignorant Neptune, "who converts into a sphere the dodecagonal pyramid, and paints with many colours the gate of that pyramid," has Five Ministers, ΑΟΤ, ΑΟΑΙ, ΟΤΩ, ΟΤΩΑΒ, the name of the fifth being lost Hence it is probable that the strings of vowels, so often found on these stones, may contain the names of elementary genii similarly expressed

Origen (viii 58) quotes Celsus to the effect, that the Egyptians made six-and-thirty (or more) dæmons or ætherial powers preside over the several parts of the body, giving some of their names, Chumis, Chuachumes, Knat, Sichat, Bou, Erou, Eribiou,

Romanor, and Reianoor "Whoever therefore prefers being in health to sickness, and happiness to trouble, ought to pay all possible honour to these Powers" Origen therefore accuses Celsus of attempting to divert men from the worship of the one God to that of six-and-thirty dæmons, only known to Egyptian magicians, because he cannot understand how "the Name of Jesus, pronounced by the truly faithful," can cure the sick and those possessed by devils, the evidence for which is far stronger than that of the effect of the names of Chnumis, Sichat, and the rest of the Egyptian catalogue In another place (i 22) he shows it was not Moses only that knew the name of Abraham and his friendship with God, for that others (pagans) use the words "the God of Abraham" when they are driving out devils And again the Egyptians use in their rites, from which they promise wonderful effects, the names of Abraham, Isaac, Jacob, and Israel Also (iv 33) Origen mentions the use of the form "The God of Abraham, the God of Isaac, the God of Jacob" in incantations, and that the same is often to be met with in books of Magic He adds that the formula "The God of Abraham, the God of Isaac, who didst overwhelm the Egyptians and the King of the Egyptians in the Red Sea," was in common use against demons and the Powers of Evil All this goes to prove that the talismans inscribed with the name of Chnumis and the other thirty-five dæmons named (who now by this assistance may be hereafter recognised) were of a *medicinal* character, whereas those with "Abraham," equally common, were more properly of the nature of talismans

In the Book of Enoch the Archangel Uriel gives us the mystic names of the two great luminaries "The names of the Sun are these, one Aryares, the other Tomas The Moon hath *four* names the first, Asonga, the second, Ebla, the third, Benase, and the fourth, Erae"

The Pistis-Sophia (§ 125) furnishes the adept with the key to the most important of the numerical cyphers "These be the Names that I will give unto thee, even from the Infinite One downwards. Write them with a sign (cypher?) that the sons of God may manifest (understand?) them out of this place. This is the Name of the Immortal One, $\overline{AAA}$ $\overline{\omega\omega\omega}$ And this ıs the name of the Voice through whose means the Perfect Man is moved, ĪĪĪ These likewise are the *interpretations* of the names of the Mysteries The first is AAA, the interpretation thereof ΦΦΦ The second which is MMM, or which is ωωω; the interpretation whereof is ΛΛΛ The third is ΨΨΨ, the interpretation whereof is OOO The fourth is ΦΦΦ, the interpretation whereof ıs NNN The fifth is ΔΔΔ, the interpretation whereof ıs AAA, the which is over the throne AAA This is the interpretation of the second AAAA, which is AAAAAAAA, and the same is the interpretation of the whole Name."

To pass from the cyphers, where all is guess work, to the actual inscriptions, engraved legibly enough in the Greek character, but presenting us with what *Jerome* aptly terms more "tormenta verborum." Many of the more common formulæ, Bellermann, by the aid of Hebrew, Coptic, and Syriac,* has satisfactorily explained, of others his interpretations are manifestly absurd. AMAPΓEA seems to be the Chaldee *Amarchel*, a president. ANOX XOΛ XNOTBIC, "I am All the Good Spirit, or the Universal genius of good" AIN ΘAPPAI, "The eye shall behold" AΔONAI ΛANTAΛA, "Lord! Thou art the Lamb"† XωCA MIΛAωΘ exactly represents the Hebrew words signifying "He hath seen the Pleroma"

> AMΛAXƆ
> AMAƟAZ
> LZAI

ıs rendered by Stiechel "Salama zebaam jatzael" = "Peace unto the army of these" (of the celestial Æons)! This agrees with

---

* Prof Stiechel, in his essay 'De Gemma Abraxea nondum edita,' Jenae, 1848, has acutely and satisfactorily elucidated some very important formulæ, giving a key to the whole class The necessity for employing Oriental languages in spells is curiously illustrated by Hippolytus' statement, that the magicians of his time used to write the answers to the questions proposed to their demons partly in *Hebrew*, partly in Greek letters

† AP ωPI, followed by the Greek

words ΦPACIC, ΦACIC, IACIC, "Declaration," "Manifestation," "Healing," is always attached to a figure of Venus Anadyomene, and admits of the translation 'Mountain of Light" The Venus therefore seems adopted here for the "Virgin of Light," who holds so high a place in the celestial hierarchy of the Pistis-Sophia At any rate the sense of APωPI, "Mountain of Light," strongly favours this acceptation

the benediction pronounced by the Marcosians in administering the holy unction, "Peace be unto all upon whom this holy Name rests!"

Some of these inscriptions display an evident affectation of obscurity by their transposition of parts of the same word from one line to another, the only key to which is the observing the different sizes of the characters employed, and taking those of the same size as belonging to the "disjecta membra" of the same word. A most instructive example of this artifice is supplied by the legend cut on the reverse of a magnificent Serapis head (Wood), which reads thus:

IABATAOP
ΘΟΝΑΤΗCΛΑΙ
ΑΡΒΑΘΙ
ΛΑΜ
ΑѠ

This will only be translatable if transposed as follows: IABATAOP ΘΟΝΑΤΗC ΛΑΙΛΑΜ ΑΡΒΑΘ ΙΑѠ 'Jehovah, the Pure Æther, the Fire,* for ever, the Four, Iao," where "the Four" signifies the *Tetrad*, so conspicuous in the Theogony of Marcus. This legend seems much of the same nature as the Greek one cut on a piece of copper (communicated to me by Prof. Ch. Babington) ὁ διὰ πάντων Νοῦς, αἰθὴρ, πῦρ, πνεῦμα, ἐλωεὶν ἐλωεὶν (Elohim). The only word in the first legend not reducible to Hebrew is Θονατ, but it seems to correspond to the 'Æther' of the copper piece, ΑΡΛΑΝΑ ΘΑΜΑΚΑ ΣΑΛΒΑΝΑ ΧΑΜΚΙΜ, "Our Light, let thy goodness grant unto us a full lap" whence the object of such a talisman would seem to be the procuring of fecundity.†

ΑΝΑΚΛΑ ΑΚΔΑΑΘѠΙѠΙ, "Pursue then (my foes) unto destruction, O Lord," is found very appropriately engraven on the reverse of a sphinx, the recognised emblem of power and slaughter.

* ΑΒΡΑΜ, which often occurs in these legends, may perhaps refer to the Rabbinical "Sen-Anpen" the Primitive Man, made up of 213 numbers the numerical value of the *Hebrew* letters in the name.

† HC represents the Hebrew word for "Fire" and this explanation is confirmed by the ΤΟ ΦѠC ΠΥΡ ΦΛΟΞ accompanying a figure of Phre on a gem elucidated by Froehner in his 'Byrsa,' part i.

ΒΑΡΙΑ ΖΑΣΤΑ ΙΑω, "Jehovah the Creator, the Destroyer" Chaldee slightly corrupted

ΙΑΘΑΙ, "The providence of God"

ΜΑΘΑΗΕ, "The honour of God"

ΡΕΟΤΗΛΕ, "The will of God."

ΧωΜΙ, "The power of God"

ΣΒω "Wisdom"

These Coptic words thus designate the Five Emanations from the Godhead—viz, Phronesis, Logos, Nous, Dynamis, Sophia

כאיר עיני

"enlightening mine eye,'

or

כאירני — n

"enlightening me,"

Menenі M'ueni

If ΗΝΑΜΕΡω and ΜΑΡωΗΝΙ are really the same, it will be conclusive against n, where the *en* is an *affix* The form then might be

עיני מאיר

enimen

Query what of the ω?

ΙΘΙ placed on each side of the Chnuphis serpent engraved in green jade (S S Lewis) is correct Hebrew for "With me," which gives an appropriate sense if understood as a prayer for the constant presence of the protecting Spirit.

ΜΕΣ ΧΑΝΑΛω,* "The Messiah be propitious unto me"

ΜΑΡωΗΝΙ,* "Enlighten mine eyes"

ΚΑΤΛΑΚΑΤ The Basilidan name for the Saviour is written by Epiphanius ΚΑΤΛΑΚΑΤΧ, who ridicules it as an expression taken from Isaiah (xxviii 10) without any regard to the

* The Syrian Alexander Severus expresses his indignation at the sight of a certain notorious rogue, Arabianus, coming to Court, by exclaiming "O Marna, O Jupiter," &c, where his native "Our Lord" he renders by "Jupiter," for the benefit of his Roman hearers This word the monkish transcribers very naturally converted into "Maria" ΗΝΑΜΕΡω, which often accompanies the figure of the Cynocephalus, seems to be equivalent to the phrase in the text and as that beast belongs to Thoth, god of *knowledge*, this interpretation has at least appropriateness in its favour

real meaning of the words Bellermann, however, thinks he has found a more sensible derivation for the title in Arabic, signifying "Strength upon strength," that is, the "All-powerful", or else in the Coptic KAB, "a lamp," and so implying "The burning and the shining Light."

MOTΘ, "Mother," Plutarch informs us (De Is. et Os.), was a title given to Isis This word contains a plain allusion to the earth, "lutum Prometheum," whence Man was taken MOTΘ and IEOTΔ are translated by Sanconiathon as "Hades" and "Only-begotten," the offspring of the Phœnician Cronos

NOOT for the Coptic NOTT, "God"

MAI MTM TXΛTM ωI, "Being, Fount, Salvation, Food, Iao" implying that Iao is the source, food, life, and salvation of the soul

OPωPIOTΘ, 'Light of Light"*

TAΛA APAIω ωAPAOPO NTOKO NBAI, "Protector, Creator, rule, speak, O Lord," is a very common formula

ΣΕΣΕΜΕΝ ΒΑΡΑΝΓΗΝ ΙΑω, written with many variations, and followed by the names of the great Angels, has been ingeniously deciphered by a learned Hebraist (Rev R Sinker) as representing the sound of "Shengab hor anje Jehevoh," "They that stand before the Mountain of God," that is, the Angels of the Presence †

XAIA, "Life,' is seen on a field of the Roman gem bearing two figures of *Providentia*, with the Sun and Moon on the field overhead (Major Pearse)

Three Greek characters often occur in juxtaposition—viz, the E set on its back, a vertical line crossed by two horizontal strokes, and Z. They stand for the numerals 5, 3, and 7, the Triad, Pentad, Heptad—lucky and sacred numbers in the religious notions of the East. For the same reason the inscriptions on our gems will be found to be arranged for the most part in either three, five, or seven lines. This also accounts for the name Iao being often written with its elements repeated

* This legend always goes with the udder-shaped vase of the Isiac rites

† Γαβριηλ, Μιχαηλ, Ραφαηλ σεν-γε(ν)β αραγνηη Ιαω

ג׳ מ׳ ר׳ שְׁנגב הַר ענגין יְיָ

σεγεν βαρ ἑνχε

שנגב הר ענג

ΩΑΙΑΩ,* for the sake of obtaining the venerated numeral, five. And, again, by introducing another vowel, Η, the Holy Name is repeated under five different forms, ΗΑΙ ΑΙΗ ΗΙΩ ΑΙΩ ΙΑΩ.

The *Priest* officiating, commonly figured in these designs, wears upon his head the "calantica," a square of purple cloth whence spring two flamingo feathers, a badge which made πτεροφορος a synonym for the Egyptian priesthood. The staff in his hand, emblem of his office, has the serpent coiled *five* times about it. This "sceptrum sacerdotale" furnishes the true explanation of the meaning of many ancient insignia, beginning with Moses' wand, then the club of Æsculapius, and closing with its derivative the rod in the spiral of SSS that so constantly goes with the Agathodæmon serpent upon the Chnuphis gems.

As for the *geometrical figures* so often introduced, they may be supposed to have had much the same import here as in the formulæ of the Rosicrucians, who obtained these with other Gnostic paraphernalia probably by tradition from the Arabs, for their pretended founder, the Great Unknown A. S., is declared to have acquired his small learning at the College of Damascus. In their system the Square stands for the Four Elements, the Triangle for the body, the spirit, and the life, and also for Sun, Moon, and Mercury. The last Triad Paracelsus interprets by *salt, sulphur, quicksilver*—the three radical forces of Nature according to his system. The *Rhombus* represents the Orphic Egg, out of which issued the whole Creation.

Phœnician Numerals may, from the very nature of the case, be looked for amongst the marks that cannot be referred to the Greek alphabet. The notation was simplicity itself: *one* to *nine* being expressed by vertical strokes, so many times repeated; *ten* by a horizontal one, *twenty* by two such parallel to each other, sometimes slightly curving together. In the

* Stiechel has a very ingenious explanation of this permutation of vowels, he makes it express different tenses of the Hebrew verb *to exist*, thus—

ΙΕΩΑΙΗ = vivit existens
ΑΙΩΟΥΕΥ = isque est Iao
ΑΙΗΑΗΙΩΗ = existens vivit
ΩΑΙΗΟΥΕ = isque Iao

Palmyrene notation *five* has a special cypher, a sloping line upon which in the middle stands another at right angles.

It was to be expected that Samaritan characters should make their appearance upon the productions of a religion of which the reputed founder was a Samaritan, whose professed followers also formed an important sect as late as the times of Hippolytus. Stiechel interprets the reverse legend on his above-quoted gem as having its commencing words written in this alphabet thus—

ΔV Z	=	qui tenet
VI	=	signum sit
PAΦAω	=	ejus sanat
PPΓVΦω	=	exorcistæ corpus
TABPII	=	facultates
IHIAII	=	et vitam
IIII	=	fiat! fiat!

He also points out that the important word "Auth" = *sign* or *token*, is written in these legends in four different ways: ΘVO, EVO, EIW, VIE.

It is possible that in certain legends the letters, taken in an order known to one having the key, would give a definite meaning, and this suspicion is supported by the reversing of some of the characters. Certain it is that the Donatists adopted such a device in order to disguise their proscribed war-cry from the victorious Catholics. A door-lintel at Tebessa exhibits the well-known formula thus—

VDES ☧ DICA
EOLAY SVM
G

to be read by the brethren "Deo laudes dicamus." A second lintel bears the same in monogram.

The most famous spell of all, ABRACADABRA, is first mentioned by Serenus Sammonicus, the most learned Roman of his times, and physician to Caracalla, to whom he dedicated his poetical 'Guide to Health,' entitled 'De Medicina præcepta saluberrima.' This work, remarks Spartian, was the favourite study of the unfortunate Cæsar, Geta, for attachment to whose cause this true son of Apollo was afterwards put to death by the imperial fratricide. Severus Alexander also, "who had known and loved Serenus," greatly admired his poetry, putting him on a level with Horace, as Lampridius' expressions seem to intimate This high authority orders the word to be written out in the form of an inverted cone, and declares it of virtue against all diseases

"Thou shalt on paper write the spell divine,
Abracadabra called, in many a line,
Each under each in even order place,
But the last letter in each line efface
As by degrees the elements grow few
Still take away, but fix the residue,
Till at the last one letter stands alone
And the whole dwindles to a tapering cone
Tie this about the neck with flaxen string,
Mighty the good 'twill to the patient bring
Its wondrous potency shall guard his head—
And drive disease and death far from his bed"

The belief in the virtue of this recipe flourished through the Middle Ages It seems alluded to in the 'Dialogue on Masonry,' ascribed by Leland to Henry VI for amongst 'the things that Masons conceal" is "the winnynge of the facultye of *Abrac*" perhaps signifying the possession of this mystical arrangement of letters unless, indeed, one chooses to suspect in this "facultye" a deeper sense, some traditionary knowledge of the ancient Abraxas religion Again, De Foe mentions how people commonly wore the word written in the manner above prescribed, as a safeguard against infection during the Great Plague of London

As for the etymology of the word, the most satisfactory yet offered is the compound of the Hebrew *Ha-Brachah*, "blessing," and Dobara, "speak", meaning the "Blessing of the Mystic Name"—that is, utter the Tetragrammaton, invoke the Holy Name of Jehovah, itself the mightiest of charms *

It is very remarkable, considering its high repute, that no Gnostic stone bearing such an inscription should be known to exist On the other hand that normal address to Iao, ΑΒΛΑΝΘΑΛΑΒΑ, "Thou art our Father!" is so found on talismanic jaspers arranged in the exact pattern recommended by

* By the mere utterance whereof the philosopher Theosebius though unacquainted with magic, was able to cast out devils from all who applied to him for aid

Serenus for the paper spell, and probably so done in compliance with his directions. One is strongly tempted to discover in this same *Ha-Brachah* the real origin of the equally famous title "Abraxas." The Greek letters, constantly in use for numerals, at once presented their numeric value in every word to the practised eye of the Kabalist.

The celebrated letter of Christ to Abgarus was (according to Cedrenus) sealed with the initials of the seven Hebrew words, whose Greek interpretation was Θεὸς Θεόθεν θαῦμα θεῖον At the mere sight of the seal the king was healed of his gout and of his *black* leprosy, all but a slight trace upon the face remaining to be cleansed by the waters of baptism Cedrenus' Greek reads like a popular formula, and may serve to explain the legend on the reverse of an Abraxas gem in my possession, ΙΧΘΕΘΩΗΙΑΙΑΩ, as to be read Ἰησοῦς Χριστὸς Θεὸς ἐκ Θεοῦ Ἰαῶ, "Jesus Christ, God of God, Jehovah" This inscription encloses the letters ΙΗ placed conspicuously in the centre, and which probably represent, as nearly as the two discordant alphabets allow, the Hebrew letters *Jod*, *He*, the Kabalistic name of the *Tikkun*, "Express Image," or First Emanation of the Godhead

The Crescent and Seven Stars, amongst which are scattered the mystical Seven Vowels, has for reverse this formula —

IΦOIꟼXA
ᒣAΓIXƎꟼƎ
ƆIΓTOBƎN
ΘHΛATO

Its first line, but written ΑΧΘΙΩΦΙ, is cut in beautiful characters on the reverse of a caduceus within a wreath Sinker reads it as עקר יפי, *Essence*, *Beauty* probably the rest are names of virtues It is inconceivable that the Sephiroth—mightiest spell of all—should be omitted in these gems It is made up of the *Ten* attributes of Jehovah—viz, The Crown, Wisdom, Prudence, Security, Magnificence, Goodness, Glory, Victory, Fortitude, Kingdom. There is consequently a probability that these Names often lurk in the phonetic Hebrew, enveloping all in darkness We have for guide the analogy of the present Arab talismans, consisting of the ninety-nine epithets of Allah written on a scroll.

THE NAME ΙΑΩ

Diodorus Siculus, when enumerating the different legislators of antiquity, says, "Amongst the Jews Moses pretended that the god surnamed *Iao* gave him his laws" (i. 94). And this is elucidated by the remark of Clemens Alexandrinus, that the Hebrew *Tetragrammaton*, or Mystic Name, is pronounced ΙΑΟΥ and signifies "He that is and shall be." Theodoret states that the same four letters were pronounced by the Samaritans as ΙΑΒΕ (*Jave*), by the Jews as ΙΑΩ. Jerome (upon Psalm viii.) says, "The Name of the Lord" amongst the Hebrews is of four letters, *Iod, He, Vau, He*, which is properly the Name of God, and may be read as ΙΑΗΟ (*Iaho*) (that is in *Latin* characters) which is held by the Jews for unutterable. The author of the 'Treatise on Interpretations' says, "The Egyptians express the name of the Supreme Being by the seven Greek vowels ΙΕΗΩΟΥΑ." * which sufficiently explains the mighty potency ascribed to this formula by the inspired author of the 'Pistis-Sophia,' and equally so its frequent appearance upon the talismans now under consideration.

Rabbi Tarphon (Tryphon), who could remember the Second Temple, noticed that the Ineffable Name, though occurring a hundred times in the course of the daily service, was "rather

* According to the Talmud, the Name of God, which was communicated only to the most pious of the priesthood was composed of *twelve* letters. And upon our talismans the vowels inclosing ΙΑΩ are often found repeated so as to make up that number, whence it may be inferred that their union represents the same ineffable sound. In the same passage mention is made of another Name of God, consisting of forty-two letters, which in its turn may serve to account for the lines of often-repeated vowels similarly to be met with.

Dante alludes to a curious tradition that the name of God, revealed to Adam, was I, which succeeding times changed into *El*:—

'Pria ch' io scendessi all' infernale ambascia
I s'appellava in terra il sommo Bene,
Onde vien la letizia che mi fascia.
ELI si chiamò, poi, e ciò conviene,
Chè l'uso dei mortali è come fronda,
In ramo, che sen va, ed altra viene."
(Parad.' xxvi. 133)

warbled than *pronounced*" A precious hint this, as indicating how the Gnostic strings of boneless vowels give an approximation to the audible and yet unuttered sound Since the destruction of the Temple, the Name has never been heard in prayer, or pronounced aloud It is communicated, indeed, to every Rabbi, after his ordination, but not in full One half of it is told, the rest he is left to make out for himself

The first idea of an "Ineffable Name," and all its inherent virtues, evidently came to the Egyptians (from whom the Jews borrowed it) from the Hindoo doctrine respecting the title AUM,—itself, like the AIΩ trilateral—representing the Triad, Brahma-Vishnu-Siva A standing for the Creator, U for the Preserver, M for the Destroyer The connection between Indian and Egyptian mythology is certain, however difficult to account for, the names of the principal deities in the latter having the appearance of pure Sanscrit Thus Isis signifies in that tongue the *Mistress*, Tat and Sat, *Virtue* and *Power*, Serapis, Sripa, the *Blood-drinker*, Nila, *Blue-water*, &c The original identity of the two religious systems no one can doubt who has *intelligently* studied the monuments of each but which country instructed the other?

The balance of probabilities is strongly in favour of India, the confinement of the peculiar system within the narrow limits of Egypt betokening an importation by a *colony* from some very remote source Traces of a very ancient intercourse between the two countries are discernible, though very dimly, in history The Periplus of the Red Sea mentions that as late as Caesar's time the town Endæmon on that coast was the entrepôt where the Indian and Egyptian traders used annually to meet. In prehistoric times therefore it is conceivable that Brahminical missionaries may have laboured amongst the aborigines of the Valley of the Nile This religious analogy manifests itself in the meanest details, in the sacred titles as well as attributes For example, as the Brahmins teach that each of the letters A, U, M envelops a great mystery, so does the *Pistis-Sophia* ('Prayers of the Saviour,' § 358) interpret the I, A, Ω, as the summary of the Gnostic, or Valentinian, creed "I signifies *All goeth out*, A, *All returneth within*, Ω, *There shall be an end of* *ends*" thus expressing the grand doctrines of the *Emanation*, the *Return*, and the *Annihilation*, or rather reabsorption, of the Universe *

To turn now to Greece—in the same way as *Abraxas* is no other than a numerical title of the Solar god, so does *Iao* actually make its appearance as an epithet of the same divinity. Macrobius (Sat i 18), whilst labouring to prove that the Sun-worship was in truth the sole religion of Paganism, under whatever name it was disguised, gives a notice very much to our purpose The Apollo of Claros, when consulted as to the true nature of the god called Ἰαὼς, gave the following response —

"The sacred things ye learn, to none disclose,
A little falsehood much discretion shows,
Regard *Iaos* as supreme above,
In winter Pluto, in spring's opening Jove,
Phœbus through blazing summer rules the day,
Whilst autumn owns the mild *Iaos'* † sway "

Here we find Iao expressly recognised as the title of the Supreme God whose physical representative is the Sun Again we have Dionysos or Bacchus added to the list by Orpheus, who sings

"Jove, Pluto, Phœbus, Bacchus, all are One "

A distinct recognition this of the grand principle of Brahminism—that all the different deities are but representations of the different attributes of the One The same truth is curiously expressed upon a talisman (Hertz collection) which at the same time sets forth the triune nature of the Supreme Being whose visible type is the Sun. It is a *heart-shaped* piece of basalt engraved with seated figures of Ammon and Ra (the Zeus and Helios of the Greeks), with the sacred Asp erect between them. The reverse bears the invocation neatly cut in characters of the third century—

ΕΙС ΒΑΙΤ ΕΙС ΑΘΩΡ ΜΙΑ ΤΩΝ ΒΙΑ ΕΙС ΔΕ ΑΧΩΡΙ
ΧΑΙΡΕ ΠΑΤΕΡ ΚΟϹΜΟΤ ΧΑΙΡΕ ΤΡΙΜΟΡΦΕ ΘΕΟϹ

* This has a remarkable analogy with the Brahminical definition of God as 'the Self-existing, Eternal, Supreme Being who is the Cause of everything, and into whom everything is finally absorbed"?

† ἁβρὸν Ἰαὼ where the epithet seems suggested by the name Abraxas so generally coupled with it

"There is One Bait, One Athor, their power is one and the same, there is One Achori Hail Father of the universe, hail God under three forms!" Concerning the three figures a word is necessary in explanation of their titles As for the hawk-head Ra, Horapollo gives for reason of the type "The *hawk* stands for the Supreme Mind, and for the intelligent soul The hawk is called in the Egyptian language '*Baieth*,' from *bai* soul, and *eth* heart, which organ they consider the seat or inclosure of the soul" A sufficient explanation this for the shape in which the talisman is formed *Achoreus*, the virtuous priest-councillor of the last of the Ptolemies (see Lucan), derives his name from the sacred serpent here invoked

That *Iaos* was recognised by the Greeks as an epithet for the Sun in the autumnal quarter has been shown from Macrobius The philosophical interpreters of the ancient mythology discovered in *Dionysos* also a mere type of the same luminary "One is Zeus, Hades, Helios, and Dionysos" And Serapis is substituted for the last in an oracle quoted by Julian nor must it be forgotten that the main object of Macrobius in the above-quoted dissertation is to prove, that Serapis is a representative of the various powers of the Solar deity all combined in one figure Again, to the same effect, comes Virgil's famous apostrophe—

> "Vos, O clarissima mundi,
> Lumina labentem qui cœlo ducitis annum,
> Liber et alma Ceres!"

where "Bacchus" and "Ceres" do no more than interpret Osiris and Isis, the Sun and Moon. Here lies the reason for equipping Bacchus with *horns* in some of his statues

"Accedant capiti cornua *Bacchus* eris," says Sappho to Phaon For in Hebrew a *radiated* and a *horned* head is expressed by the same word. When Moses came down from the Mount, "cornuta erat facies ejus," according to the version of the Vulgate, and on the strength of this mistranslation Christian art hath ever graced the Jewish lawgiver with these appendages

In this very title *Iao* undoubtedly lies the origin of the universal persuasion of the ancients that the Jehovah of the

Jews—whose name was thus expressed in Greek letters—was no other than the Egyptian Bacchus For this notion they found strong support in the Golden Vine which formed the sole visible decoration of the Temple, in the "blowing the trumpets at the New Moon," and the custom of keeping the Feast of Tabernacles in huts made of leafy boughs, accompanied with many of the ceremonies used at the Grecian Dionysia "Quia sacerdotes eorum tibia tympanis concinebant, hedera vinciebantur, vitisque aurea templo reperta" (Tacit. Hist v 5) This opinion as to the real nature of the Jewish worship Tacitus quotes as the one generally held by the learned of his own times, although he cannot bring himself to accept it as satisfactory—although merely on the grounds that the gloomy and unsocial character of the religion seemed to disprove its relationship to the merry worship of the "god of wine," the only character in which the Romans recognised Bacchus Nevertheless this ancient theory has found supporters in modern times, notably in the overlearned Dr Stanley, rector of St George the Martyr, who (without giving much scandal to his own easy-going generation) advocated this heterodox opinion in an elaborate treatise which puts to shame the boldest flights of the 'Essays and Reviews,' or even the interpretations of our indiscreet apostle to the Zulus Ludicrously enough, the German Jews still celebrate the Feast of Purim, and the Fall of Haman, by getting as royally drunk as their means afford, and thus to the present day do their best to perpetuate the old Roman aspersion Amongst the later Gnostics, indeed, some rites were unmistakably borrowed from the Bacchanalia, singularly modified by Christian doctrine Epiphanius relates (Hæres xxxvii) how that "they kept a tame serpent in a chest or *sacred ark*, and piled loaves upon a table before the same, and then called upon the serpent to come forth. Whereupon, opening of himself the ark, he would come forth, mount upon the table, and twine about the loaves, which they broke in pieces, and distributed amongst the worshippers, calling this their 'Perfect Sacrifice' and their 'Eucharist'"

Another explanation as to the true character of the god

named Iao must not be passed over in silence, however little foundation it may have in truth, seeing that it is supported by the authority of the learned historian of Gnosticism, Jacques Matter. The Moon to the Egyptians, as to the Orientals of to-day, was of the *masculine* gender, and was designated by the phonetic name *Aah* or *Ioh*. Thoth was sometimes identified with this deity; and therefore Thoth's emblem, the ibis, accompanied with the crescent, bears the legend *Ioh*, "because (says Plutarch) Mercury attends the Moon in her journey round the earth in the same way as Hercules doth the Sun." When Thoth, *Tat*, appears as Mercury he has the head of an ibis, but in his character of the Moon-god, or *Deus Lunus*, he shows the face of a man supporting the lunar crescent enclosing the sun's disk and surmounted by a double plume.

Hence came the notion mentioned by Plutarch, that "the Egyptians call the Moon the Mother of Creation, and say it is of both sexes;" and to the same effect Spartian (Caracalla, vii.) explains that the Egyptians in the mysteries (*mystice*) call the Moon a male, though designating it a female in ordinary speech. He adds that the people of Carrhal (famed for its great temple of Deus Lunus) hold that "whatsoever man thinks the moon should be called of the feminine gender shall pass his life a slave unto women, whereas he that holds it to be a male deity shall rule over his wife and be secured against all female treachery." A very sufficient reason this for the fondness of Spartian's contemporaries for wearing in their signet rings the *vera effigies* of the Carrhene god, a youth in a Phrygian cap, his bust supported on the crescent that gives his name. This elegant effeminate lunar genius is in truth no other than the modernized and tasteful version of the grim old Assyrian "Sin," pictured in the Ninevitish monuments as an aged man leaning on his staff as he floats through the heavens on the crescent, presenting a ludicrous resemblance to our popular idea of the "Man in the Moon." A blue calcedony in my possession fully illustrates Plutarch's title of "Mother of Creation." It exhibits a perfect hermaphrodite figure wearing the Egyptian head-dress, and squatting down so as more clearly to display its bisexual nature; below creeps a snail surmounted by a butterfly, the well-understood emblems of lasciviousness and life, the fount of propagation

All this brings us to Matter's theory (based on a statement of Origen's), that *Iao, Adonai, Sabaoth* signified the genii of the Moon, the Sun, and the Planets—being far inferior in power and even antagonistic to *Abraxas*, who is the actual representative of the Supreme Source of Light Matter therefore explains the warlike attitude in which the Abraxas-god is regularly depicted as declaring his office of scaring away the Adversary, or *demon, Iao*, who is expressed by his *name* alone, placed in the lowest part of the scene, to denote his inferiority But the authority of the monuments themselves is more than sufficient to upset such an interpretation of the meaning given to them by the actual manufacturers The doctrine mentioned by Origen was, it cannot be denied, that of the more recent sect, which set itself above all old Egyptian or Hebrew tradition but it most assuredly was not of the immense body of primitive Kabbalistic Gnostics who excogitated and put their trust in the *sigils* that they have bequeathed to us in such fantastical profusion These talisman-makers evidently held *Thoth* and *Moses* in equal reverence they had nothing to do with the Valentinians, who had an obvious motive for exalting their newly-invented invisible *Tetrad*, by so immeasurably degrading below it the most venerated names of the old religion The Valentinians were Greeks by education, really drawing their inspiration from Pythagoras and Plato, and only too well pleased with the opportunity of venting their natural spite upon the most cherished ideas of the Alexandrine Kabbalists, the grand fabricants of our talismans, those veritable "Pierres d'Israel."

The *Pistis-Sophia* continually introduces, as a most important actor in its scenes of the judgment and purification of the soul, "the great and good Iao, ruler of the Middle Sphere," who when he looks down into the places of torment causes the souls therein imprisoned to be set at liberty The very collocation of the words on our talismans clearly denotes that *Adonai, Sabaoth*, are equally with *Abraxas* the titles of Iao, who is the god actually represented by the symbolical figure these words accompany What else would be the motive for their collocation in a prayer like this (on a gem published by Matter himself)—"Iao, Abraxas, Adonai, Holy Name, Holy Powers,* defend Vibia Paulina from every evil spirit"? And, again, these same names perpetually occur united together, and followed by the address ΑΒΛΑΝΑΘΑΝΑΛΒΑ, "Thou art our Father", CEMEC ΕΙΛΑΜ, "Eternal Sun", a mode of adoration that could not possibly have been applied to beings of a discordant, much less of an antagonistic, nature to each other Besides, if Abraxas were the opponent and ultimate destroyer of Iao, it would have been absurd to put the names of the two in such close union, the latter even taking precedence, each, too, being equally invoked in the accompanying prayer, and honoured with the same epithets of majesty Moreover the composite figure, or Pantheus, which, as all writers agree, represents the actual god Abraxas, is much more frequently inscribed with the name ΙΑω than with ΑΒΡΑCΑΞ, and nevertheless, though the former name stands alone, it is followed by the same glorification, "Thou art our Father," &c, as when the two names are engraved in juxtaposition It is moreover quite opposed to all the rules of symbolism to represent the one actor in a scene by his proper figure or emblem, and to indicate the other by the simple letters of his name and equally repugnant to common sense to depict the figure of the god with the *name* of his adversary placed in the most conspicuous portion of the tableau The absurdity is as great as though in Christian art one should paint a Crucifix with *Satan's* name in the place of the holy I N R I, and give for explanation the hostility of the two personages. And lastly, it has been already shown that the numerical or Kabbalistic value of the name Abraxas directly refers to the Persian title of the god, "Mithras," Ruler of the year, worshipped from the earliest times under the apellation of Iao Matter himself

* A parallel to this form still exists in the Turkish amulet composed of the ninety-and-nine epithets of Allah written on a paper, and believed to possess wondrous protective power The spirit of all Oriental religions is to glorify the one object of adoration by heaping upon him a multitude of honorific titles expressive of his various attributes Amulets of this and various other kinds are regularly sold at the mosques

publishes (Pl. iii. 2) a gem that should have convinced him of his error, had he not overlooked the force of its legend. The type is Horus seated on the lotus, inscribed ΑΒΡΑCΑΞ ΙΑѠ—an address exactly parallel to the so frequent ΕΙC ΖΕΥC CΑΡΑΠΙ on the contemporary Heathen gems, and therefore only to be translated by "Abraxas is the One Jehovah."

The "Great Name" with its normal titles is often to be observed interpolated by a Gnostic hand upon works of a better period and creed, but whose subjects were fancied analogous to the ideas conveyed by the Iao Pantheus: such as Phœbus in his car, the Lion—House of the Sun, the Sphinx emblem of royalty, and the Gorgon's Head of the Destructive Force, or of Providence.* But the most interesting of such *adopted* types that has come to my knowledge, as unmistakably pointing out the deity really understood by the name Abraxas, is a work discovered by myself amongst the miscellanea of a small private collection (Bosanquet). In this we behold the familiar Pantheus with head of cock, cuirassed body, and serpent-legs brandishing the whip and driving the car of Sol,† in the exact attitude of its proper occupant, Phœbus. In the exergue is the salutation CΑΒΑѠ, "Glory unto thee;" on the reverse, in a cartouche formed by a coiled asp—precisely as the Hindoos write the Ineffable Name AUM—are engraved the titles ΙΑѠ ΑΒΡΑCΑΞ, attesting that one deity alone is meant, and that one to be the Ruler of the Sun.

* The holy name has often been added to intagli of a foreign nature merely for the sake of turning them into talismans: for example, on the reverse of a heliotrope with Victory, inscribing a shield (R. S. Williams, Utica, U.S.)

† Exactly as Serapis (also a type of the Sun-god) makes his appearance upon an Alexandrian coin of Hadrian's, which has been already cited (section 'Abraxas gems'). The god is giving the benediction with his right hand, and holds a sceptre in his left. Upon another coin of the same emperor and mint he is seated on the Ram, clearly meaning the Sun in that sign, and perhaps having no deeper meaning than the date of the month when coined.

ABRAXAS, NEW TYPE OF.

A most singular variation upon the normal type of the Abraxas pantheus gives him the head of Serapis for that of the usual cock. In the field between the serpents are the genital organs, of disproportionate size, represented in a state of rest, not as the *fascinum* properly appear on amulets; and unmistakably displaying the seal of circumcision. This circumstance is another proof to be added to all those previously observed, that the fabricators of this class of talismans were the Egyptian Jews. As the distinguishing principle of the Gnosis in all its forms was the reprobation of the "doing the work of the Demiurgus"—that is, the propagation of the species—it is evident that the object of this symbolism was not of a religious kind. It is probable that the idea was to produce a talisman of medicinal use, perhaps for the cure of impotence or other affections of the parts represented. Of medicinal talismans, expressing their purpose by the legends they bear, numerous examples have been already published. The one now described was made known to me through an impression brought by the Rev. S. S. Lewis of a jasper in the Bourgignon collection at Rome. Another very uncommon subject in the same collection is a skeleton seated on a throne, holding a lance, or perhaps sceptre. Although perfectly corresponding with the mediaeval representation of Death, yet the spirited though rude extension of the intaglio is that of the earlier Gnostic period, and the idea intended was that of a *larva*, not that of the Destroying Power. In the Stosch Cabinet is a similar figure borne along in a car by steeds as fleshless as himself, like the Wild Hunter of the German legend.

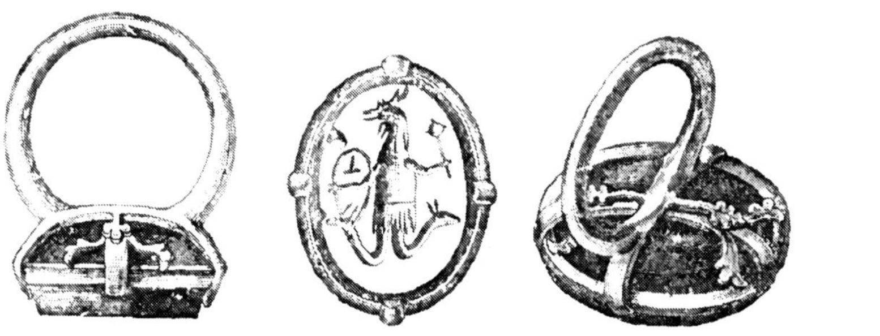

FIG. 14.

ORIGINAL PURPOSE OF THESE FORMULÆ

The *interpretation* of Gnostic legends and the nature of the deity to whom they were addressed have been thus far the subjects of our inquiry the next step is to search contemporary writers for information as to the *special purpose* for which the talismans so enriched were originally manufactured The motive for placing in the coffin of the defunct *illuminato* these "words of power" graven on scrolls of lead, plates of bronze, the gems we are considering, and doubtless to an infinitely greater extent on more perishable materials, derives much light from the description Epiphanius gives (Hær xxxvi) of the ceremony whereby the Heracleonitæ prepared their dying brother for the next world They sprinkled his head with water mingled with oil and opobalsamum, repeating at the same time the form of words used by the Marcosians in baptism, in order that his *Inner Man*, thus provided, might escape the vigilance of the Principalities and Powers whose domains he was about to traverse, and mount up unseen by any to the Pleroma from which he had originally descended Their priests therefore instructed the dying man that as he came before these Powers he was to address them in the following words "I, the son from the Father, the Father pre-existing but the son in the present time, am come to behold all things both of others and of my own and things not altogether of others but belonging unto Achamoth (*Wisdom*), who is feminine and hath created them for herself But I declare my own origin from the Pre-existing One, and I am going back unto my own from which I have descended" By the virtue of these words he will elude the Powers, and arrive at the Demiurgus in the eighth sphere, whom again he must thus address "I am a precious vessel, superior to the female power who made thee, inasmuch as thy mother knoweth not her own origin, whereas I know myself, and I know whence I am; and I invoke the Incorruptible Wisdom who is in the father and in the mother of your mother that hath no father, nay, not even a male consort, but being a female sprung from a female that created thee, though she herself knows not her mother, but believes herself to exist alone. But I invoke the mother." At this address the Demiurgus is struck with confusion (as well he might be), and forced to acknowledge the baseness of his origin whereupon the inner man of the Gnostic casts off his bondage as well as his own *angel*, or soul, which remains with the Demiurgus for further use, and ascends still higher into his proper place. For every man is made up of *body*, *soul*, and *inner man*, this last being the more spiritual nature. This same belief was the popular one of the Jews, as appears from Rhoda's exclamation at the unhoped-for reappearance of Peter, whom she supposed already put to death.

The Achamoth here mentioned is the Sephandomad of Zoroaster, the Wisdom of the later Jews—so fully described by the pseudo-Solomon under that title (vii. 25). "She is the Spirit of the virtue of God, the pure emanation of the brightness of the Almighty, the brightness of the eternal Light, the mirror without spot of his majesty, the image of his goodness." "Wisdom hath made her house upon seven pillars." The *naked woman*, or Venus Anadyomene, so often seen on these gems, is the same idea expressed by the ancient Greek type. One given by Caylus ('Rec. d'Ant.' vi. Pl. 21) explains its destination in terms sufficiently clear, despite their corrupt Byzantine orthography. ΙΑΩ ΣΑΒΑΩ ΑΔΟΝΑΙ ΗΚΑΙ ΕΛΛΑΞΕΙΩΝ ΤΟΤ ΤΑΡΤΑΡΟΤ ΣΚΟΤΙΝ, "Jehovah, Sabaoth, Lord, come and deliver me from the darkness of Hell!"

Could the long legends covering so many of these jasper tablets be interpreted, most probably their purport would be found of the same nature with the just-cited Heracleonitan passport for the Pleroma: it were but a natural precaution on his friends' part to supply the deceased brother with a correct copy of such long-winded involved professions of faith, and which otherwise would be extremely apt to escape his memory; the more especially as being only confided to him by his spiritual guides when he was already at the last gasp.

Of the practice itself, the origin undoubtedly lay in the very ancient Egyptian rule of placing in the mummy cases those elaborate "Litanies of the Dead" of which so many have come down to our times * papyrus scrolls containing the prayers to be addressed by the soul to each god whose "gate" it has to traverse on its way to final rest To prevent mistakes, the portrait of each deity is prefixed to the column of prayers due to him, and this same arrangement is found in the leaden scrolls belonging to the heterogeneous doctrine of the Gnostics

The same custom yet holds its ground in India, probably its pristine source Tavernier notices that the Brahmins placed on the breast of the corpse seven pieces of paper, inscribed with the prayers to be uttered by the soul as soon as released from its corporeal envelope by the flames of the funeral pile †

The gem-talismans that remain in such varied abundance are themselves recognised in the few surviving writings of the Gnostic teachers The *Pistis-Sophia* is full of allusions to the *Seals* and *Numbers* of the different Æons and the other Powers,‡ and with the repeated promise of the Saviour to reveal these all unto his hearers, a promise which, unfortunately, is not fulfilled in the book as it has come down to us Nevertheless the very allusion sufficiently declares the sense in which we are to understand the CΦPAΓIC so frequently to be seen on the talismans The motive for providing the defunct believer

* "Papyri, it is well known, were frequently kept in readiness, with blank spaces for the names and occupation of the deceased the papyrus in fact formed part of the regular funeral appliances They were of three classes namely *Ritual*, *Books of Transmigrations, and Solar Litanies*, or descriptions of the passage of the soul through the earth in the solar boat These highly curious MSS contain minute descriptions of all the regions through which the soul was supposed to pass after death"—C W Goodwin A MS of this kind, written in the fourth century before our era, was found by the Prince of Wales when excavating in Egypt, and has been published with facsimile But the finest example known is the one preserved in the Soane Museum, hitherto unpublished

† The Lord Taraka, if duly propitiated will breathe into the dying man's ear a *mantra* or charm of such power as will secure him a safe passage to heaven

‡ "Then they bring the soul before the *Virgin of Light*, and it showeth unto the Virgin her own *seal*, her own form of defence, &c" This very illustrative portion of the teaching of Valentinus is found in the Pistis-Sophia

with a good supply of these imperishable credentials is sufficiently explained by the "Scheme of the Ophites" (published by Origen), which details the prayers to be addressed to the Seven Planetary Powers by the released soul, in its upward flight.

The prayer to Ildabaoth contains this indication: "O principal Spirit of the Pure Intelligence, Perfect Work in the eyes of the Father and of the Son, in presenting unto thee in this *seal* the sign of Life open the gates closed by thy power unto the world, and freely traverse thy domain."

Again, in saluting Iao (here taken from the Lunar Genius): "Thou that presidest over the Mysteries of the Father and of the Son, who shinest in the night-time, holding the second rank, the first Lord of Death! in presenting thee with this thine own *symbol* swiftly pass through thy dominions."

To Sabaoth: "Receive me, on beholding this pure symbol against which thy Genius cannot prevail; it is made after the *image* of the type; it is the body delivered by the Pentad."

To Orai (Venus): "Let me pass, for thou seest the symbol of thy power annihilated by the sign of the Tree of Life." (Is this *sign* the Cross, as Matter supposes, or the actual tree occasionally to be found on Gnostic gems?) And it must be remembered that the primary meaning of *symbolum* is the impression of a signet, which makes it more probable that such is the sense in which the word is used in all these passages. It may further be conjectured that in this conversion of the *symbolum* into a passport to heaven originated the theological use of the word to signify a creed or summary of the articles of Faith.

This same service of talismans in the next world is clearly recognised in the Pistis-Sophia (§ 293), where Mary Magdalene gives this curious version of the business of the tribute penny: "Thou hast said that the soul giveth an account of itself, and likewise a *seal* unto all the Rulers that be in the regions of King Adamas, and giveth the account the honour and the glory of all the *seals* belonging unto them, and also the hymns of the kingdom of Light. This therefore is the word which thou spakest when the *stater* was brought unto thee, and thou sawest that it was of silver and likewise of copper * Thereupon thou didst ask, Whose is this image? and they answered, Of the King Then when thou sawest that it was of silver and also of copper, thou saidest Give the part which is the King's unto the King, and the part which is God's unto God. The which meaneth this After that the soul hath received the Mystery it giveth an account of itself unto all the Rulers and unto the dominion of King Adamas, and also giveth the glory unto those that pertain to the Light And thy saying that it shone, when thou sawest it, of silver and copper, it is the image and likeness of the soul The power of the Light which is therein, the same is the fine silver but the *Counterfeit of the Spirit* (Conscience) is the *material* copper "

The grand doctrine of Gnosticism was this The soul on being released from the body (its prison-house and place of torment) has to pass through the regions of the Seven Powers, which it cannot do unless impregnated beforehand with *knowledge* otherwise it is seized upon and swallowed by the dragon-formed Ruler of this world, Satan Ophiomorphos, and voided forth through his tail upon earth again, where it animates a swine or some such beast, and repeats its career once more But should it be filled with *knowledge*, it eludes the Seven Powers, and tramples upon the head of Sabaoth ("of whom they say he hath the hair of a woman") and mounts up unto the eighth heaven, the abode of Barbelo, the Universal Mother, and who according to the Pistis-Sophia is the celestial Mother of the Saviour Epiphanius quotes from the Gospel of Philip another formula, intended to extort a free passage from the same Planetary Genii "The Lord hath revealed unto me what words the soul must use as it ascendeth up into heaven, and how it must make answer unto each one of the Celestial Virtues 'I have known myself, I have *collected* myself from all parts, neither have I begotten sons unto the Ruler of this world, but I have plucked up the roots, and gathered together the scattered members I know thee who thou art, for I am

* A curious remark, pointing clearly to Alexandria as the place where this Gospel was written its tetradrachm of imperial times being very base silver indeed

one from above' But if convicted of having left any offspring upon earth, the soul is detained there until it shall have collected all and attracted these into itself"

This "Self-Collection" was only to be effected through the observance of perpetual chastity, or rather (inevitable compromise) the practice of the various unnatural vices that regularly spring from such an article of faith If however a woman of the congregation should through want of precaution allow herself to become pregnant, the Elders produced abortion, took the fœtus and pounded it up in a mortar along with honey, pepper, and other spices and perfumery Then this "congregation of swine and dogs" assembled, and every one dipping his finger into the mess tasted thereof. This they called their Perfect Passover, saying 'We have not been deceived by the Ruler of concupiscence, but have gathered up again the backsliding of our brother" The very plain-spoken Epiphanius gives exact particulars, not to be put into a modern tongue of the mode in which the faithful observed in one sense their vow of perpetual chastity, without renouncing the joys of Venus This he illustrates by the singular explanation then current of the ancient myth of Saturn's devouring his own offspring, against which interpretation and the practice thereon founded, even Clemens had found it needful to warn the orthodox two centuries before

To exemplify the punishment ordained for having done the work of the Demiurgus by leaving offspring upon earth, the Ophites told a wild legend how that Elias himself was turned back from the gates of heaven, although to his own conscience a pure virgin, because a female demon had gathered up of his seed during his sleep, and formed infants therewith, which to his unutterable confusion she then and there produced in testimony of his sin Hence springs the mediæval notion of the *Succubæ*, nocturnal temptresses of the continent, although these were supposed to do the work of their father the Devil in a different way, by procuring him the needful supplies for his amours with the witches, to whom he stood in the ex-officio relation of paramour

All this is in strict accordance with what is found in the

fragments of the "Gospel to the Egyptians", for Clemens (Stromata iii) quotes therefrom this dictum of the Saviour's "When Salome asked the Lord how long shall Death prevail? He answered unto her, So long as ye women do bring forth children Wherefore she said, Then I have done well in not bearing children, seeing that there is no necessity for generation To which the Lord answered, Feed upon every herb, but that which hath bitterness, eat thou not Again when Salome asked when the things should be known concerning which she inquired, the Lord answered, When ye shall not need a covering for your nakedness, when the two shall become one, the male with the female, neither male nor female" It is to these overstrained rules of morality that St Paul alludes when he expostulates with the Colossians (ii 20) asking them, "Why are ye subject to ordinances (or rather, make laws for yourselves without any warrant), namely, touch not (women), taste not (flesh), handle not (things unclean)"

From the consideration of the value and use of these Gnostic Symbols in the world to come, we are naturally led to inquire in what manner they were employed by their owners in *this* The meaning of the word itself has gone through many transitions "Symbolism" properly signified the contribution of each member towards the expenses of a Greek drinking-party For this purpose each pledged his signet-ring to the caterer and afterwards redeemed it by paying his quota of the bill For this reason Plautus transfers the name of symbolum to the ring itself. The signet being considered the most trustworthy of all credentials, the word came to signify any token serving for the purpose of a credential For example, Caylus figures (Rec V. pl 55), a bronze right-hand, the natural size, inscribed on the palm ΣΤΜΒΟΛΟΝ ΠΡΟΣ ΟΤΕΛΛΤΝΙΟΤΣ, "Credentials to the Velaunii" (a Gallic tribe whose seat was round Antibes) * The wrist at the section is closed, forming a base,

* The best, as well as the most interesting example of a symbolism extant, is the one figured by Caylus, without any conception of its value (Pl 87, 1) It is an ivory disk, two inches in diameter, engraved with two fishes, placed side by side, with a palm-branch between them, the reverse is inscribed

I
ΑΔΕΛΦΟΤ
X

The well known emblems show this

so that the hand could stand upright of itself A pair of clasped hands, symbol of faith (still called in Italy *fede*), was the common present from one nation or army to another on making alliance "Miserat civitas Lingonum veteri instituto dono legionibus *dextras* hospitii insigne" (Tac Hist. i 54). From the nature of the case such presents must have been made in the precious metals, and consequently none have been preserved This connexion of ideas shows plainly why in ecclesiastical language symbolum stands for a profession of *faith*, a creed, i e. gr "Symbolum Apostolicum" And so by degrees the word degenerated into its present sense of any *token* denoting an idea, more especially a religious one.

Emblem again has passed through equal vicissitudes At first, a little silver chasing, intended for letting into plate as an embellishment of the surface—which the term ἔμβλημα neatly expresses—the designs being always mythological, its name remained, after the fashion had expired, to denote any representation of that nature. There is, however, a distinction in the real meaning of *emblem* and symbol, the former expressing by actual representation, the latter by hieroglyphs, the idea they convey Thus the *emblem* of Victory is a winged female holding a palm, the *symbol* of Victory is the palm by itself

The BAMBINO—the favourite idol of the women of Rome—bears, in its type and decoration, the most convincing of all testimony as to the real source of the religion in whose pantheon it plays so prominent a part It is a wooden figure, about two feet high, now passing for the *vera effigies* of the Infant Jesus, but to any eye acquainted with Indian art, an unmistakable copy of the Infant Buddha. The figure, in almost full relief, stands in front face, with arms crossed on the breast, and holding the lotus flower in the one hand, in the regular attitude of the Hindoo god. But the most striking feature in the design is the shape of the background, which has no prototype in Roman art, but is cut into the so-called "pine-

---

ticket to have been the pass of some "Brother in Christ Jesus," in the primitive ages of the Church, serving as his introduction to the faithful in whatever part he might require their help

apple" outline, which invariably accompanies the sacred images of India On the head is a crown, in the Oriental style, and the close-fitting garment, reaching from neck to ankle, and now passing for the swaddling-clothes of the baby, is profusely studded with precious stones—the offerings of a later time The very tradition as to its place of manufacture supplies an inkling of the truth, for it is said to be the work of a monk at Jerusalem, and carved out of one of the sacred olive-trees. The pious artist must have been inspired by the sight of the Indian prototype, for the resemblance is far too close to be accidental, if indeed, the whole affair be not another instance of a "christened Jove"

The very nature of things renders it a necessity for the members of every secret society to possess means for mutual recognition that shall escape the observation of the outer world The partakers of the Eleusinian Mysteries, appear, from certain allusions in the classics, to have been furnished by their sponsors with something of the kind The refusal to wear a garland at a feast was accepted as the sign of a Mithraic brother Certain it is that our popular notion about the "Masonic Grip" was equally current as applied to the Gnostics in the times of Epiphanius "On the arrival of any stranger belonging to the same sect, they have a *sign* given by the man to the woman, and *vice versa* In holding out the hand under pretence of saluting each other, they feel and tickle it in a particular manner, underneath the palm, and by that means discover whether the new-comer belongs to the same society Upon this, however poor they may be, they serve up to him a sumptuous feast, with abundance of meats and wine And after they are well filled the host rises, leaving his wife behind, bidding her, 'Show thy charity unto this our brother,'" &c, carrying out his hospitality to an extent that in our selfish times no one can expect to meet with unless amongst the Esquimaux

As may well be supposed, these *symbola* are widely diffused, for Gnosticism was more than co-extensive with the empire of Rome, and long survived her fall Besides our gems, plates of bronze and lead (and even of gold in the remarkable example found near Carnarvon), and rude copper medallions, engraved with similar devices, are constantly disinterred from ancient cemeteries, where they had so long protected the repose of their original possessors. Of that rarer class, the medallions, the most interesting known to me, was found in Provence (Praun Cabinet). It shows in *intaglio* the Abraxas god, for reverse, the triple Hecate, executed with considerable spirit: types well illustrating the syncretistic nature of the creed by this union of an ancient and a newly-devised type. The sepulchre of Maria, wife of the most orthodox Honorius, contained, amongst a variety of amuletic figures (or perhaps toys—little animals, mice, &c.), carved in crystal and agate, a gold plate inscribed with the names of the "Angels of the Presence." On account of the great interest of this discovery, I have inserted a complete translation of Fauno's account, the only description ever penned of the rifling of an imperial tomb. And when Bishop Seffred's coffin (deceased 1159) was opened in Chichester Cathedral, upon his bony finger still lay the episcopal ring, set with an Abraxas jasper, no doubt recommended to him in life and death by the numerous virtues so particularly set forth by Camillus Leonardi. When did the belief in the virtue of these talismans really expire? The Young Pretender, with the superstition inherent in his family, had sought to enlist in his service the mighty Abraxas himself for his ill-starred expedition. In his baggage captured at Culloden by General Belfort, was found a bloodstone, set in silver as a pendant, engraved with the well-known Pantheus and for reverse the naked Venus, *Achamoth*, legend ATITA. (Figured by Walsh, pl. 7.)

Provence is yet a fruitful source of these interesting memorials of the wide-spread theosophy. Gnosticism from the beginning took root and flourished in Southern Gaul, as the elaborate treatise of Irenæus attacking it, as no newly-invented thing, very clearly demonstrates. Its success was probably due to the close affinity of its leading doctrines to the Mithraic and original Druidical systems previously reigning there. Later still, in the middle of the fourth century, a new form of Gnosticism, broached by Priscillian, Bishop of Avila, who was put to death for his pains by the British emperor Magnus Maximus. Gibbon's note upon the unlucky heresiarch is so characteristic of his style that I cannot forbear quoting it "The bishopric of Avila (in Old Castile) is now worth 20,000 ducats a year, and is therefore much less likely to produce the author of a new heresy" That Spain also had, long before Priscillian's preaching, received and warmly embraced that of Basilides, although so far removed from its fountain-head, is apparent from a passage in Jerome's 29th letter to Theodora "Our friend Licinius, when that most foul heresy of Basilides was raging throughout Spain, and like a pestilence and murrain was devastating all the province between the Pyrenees and the Ocean, held fast the purity of the Christian faith, far from receiving Amargel, Barbelo, Abraxas, Balsamus, the ridiculous Leusiboras, and the other such-like monstrosities"

That Britain had to some extent received the same doctrines, the Carnarvon gold plaque is sufficient evidence And its existence throws light upon the singular fact mentioned by Matthew Paris, that when Eadred, in collecting building materials for his conventual church, was pulling up the Roman foundations of Verulamium, he came upon a little cupboard, "armariolum," in the thickness of an immense wall containing scrolls in an unknown tongue At last a very aged monk, Unwona by name, made them out to be written in the ancient British language, and containing invocations to the gods formerly worshipped in the place But Verulamium was so entirely Roman, as far as its public edifices were concerned, that the use of the native language in any documents accompanying the foundation of a temple is in the highest degree improbable, the regular Gnostic Greek would be equally puzzling to the old Saxon monk, and his explanation was a safe cloak for his ignorance. The late period of the Roman occupation, when Gnosticism most flourished, will account for the preservation of "scrolls" (parchment no doubt) through the few centuries intervening before the abbotship of Eadred

It is more than probable that such doctrines lurked unnoticed amongst the native Gallo-Romans, during the times of the Arian Gothic kings, and did no more than revive into the flourishing Manicheism of the Albigenses in the twelfth century The fact of these sectaries having received the same share of persecution from Catholics as the Waldenses themselves is not alone sufficient to prove them equally good Protestants with the latter, though *that* is now taken for granted, especially by expounders of the Apocalypse, when hard put to it to find the required "Two Witnesses" against the Scarlet Lady

Gnosticism has left traces of itself, whether by direct or indirect descent amongst those mysterious sects of the Libanus, the Druses and Anseyrets As late as Justinian's reign, according to Procopius, no fewer than a million Polytheists, Manicheans and *Samaritans* (the last also a sect of Gnostics)* were exterminated in Syria alone, during the systematic persecution, so long carried on by this pedantic bigot As that region soon afterwards fell under the more tolerant Caliphs, who never troubled themselves about the religion of their subjects, provided their tribute were punctually paid, these doctrines may very well have come down in some sort to our days, considering the secluded position of the people holding them, and the tenacity of life possessed by every well-defined system of religious ideas

* And the most ancient of all for they claimed Simon Magus for their founder

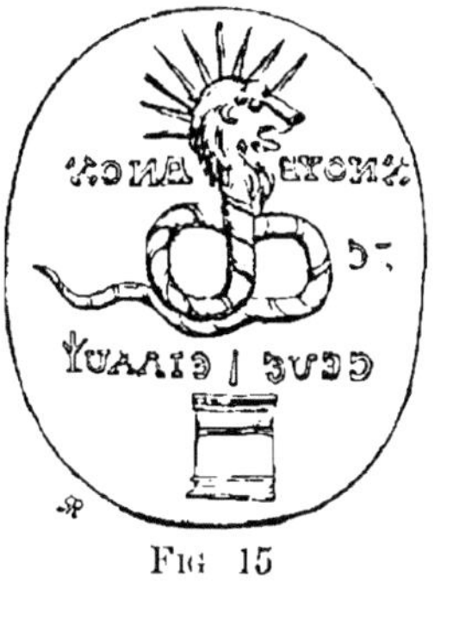

FIG 15

GNOSTIC THEOGONY

The several grades in the Gnostic Theogony, through all of which the soul had to pass before it could attain to supreme perfection, are briefly set before us in this passage of the Pistis Sophia (247) —

"And when the Saviour had said all these things unto His disciples, Andrew came forward and spoke 'Lord, be not wroth with me, but have compassion upon me and reveal the mystery of the word which I will ask Thee, otherwise it is a hard thing in my sight and I understand it *not*' Then the Saviour answered and said unto him 'Inquire what thou wouldst inquire and I will declare the same unto thee, face to face, and without a parable' Then Andrew answered and said 'Lord, I wonder and marvel greatly how men that be in this world, when they are departed from out of this body of *Matter*, and have gone out of the world, how shall they pass through these firmanents, and all these rulers, and lords, and gods, and all these Great Invisible Ones, and all these that belong to the Middle-space, and those that belong to the place of them upon the right hand, and all the great emanations of the same, so that they may come within (beyond) them all, so that they may inherit the kingdom of Light? This business, therefore, Lord, is full of trouble in my sight' When Andrew had thus spoken, the spirit of the Saviour was moved within Him, and he cried out and said · 'How long shall I bear with you, how long shall I suffer you! Do you then not understand at all, and are ye still ignorant? Know ye not and do ye not understand that ye are all angels, and archangels, and rulers, and lords, and gods, and the other Powers, and the glory thereof, you *from* yourselves and *in* yourselves in turn, proceeding out of one mass, and one matter, and one being, and all proceeding out of one *confusion* *

* Κερασμὸς i e the mixture of the Light Divine with brute Matter which it was the object of the Saviour's coming to rectify

And by the commandment of the First Mystery this confusion must needs be, until the great emanations of Light and the glory of the same shall have cleansed it, and they shall cleanse it not of themselves, but through the compulsion of the Great Ineffable One. And they have not received torments, neither have they changed their places at all, neither have they despoiled themselves, nor transformed themselves into various figures, neither have they been in the last affliction For this cause chiefly ye are the dregs of the Treasury-house, and ye are the dregs of them that pertain to the right hand, and ye are the dregs of the great Invisible Ones and of all the Rulers, and in a word ye are the dregs of them all And ye were in great sorrows, and afflictions, and transformations, and in sundry shapes of this world, and by reason of these sorrows, ye were in agony and fought with this world and all the Matter that is therein, and ye did not slacken your hands in fighting against it until ye had found out the mysteries of the kingdom of Light, which rendered you, who fought, a pure Light, and ye were made the pure Light'"

All which implies the grand idea that Man, although made of inferior, though cognate stuff, to the Angelic Powers, is susceptible, through the attainment of *knowledge*, of a perfection superior to theirs

THE SCHEME OF THE OPHITES

Gnostic symbols, with their uses in this life and in that to come have thus far been the subject of our investigation, which naturally leads us to consider the ideas that their devisers entertained of the constitution of the next world and of the nature of the soul itself. As to the former of these deeply interesting questions, the Gnosis specially laboured to afford the exactest information to its disciples, and in this class the one preserved by Origen (in Celsum vi.), leaves nothing to be desired in point of fulness, and may confidently be accepted as the most authoritative of all such celestial *cartes de route*

This learned Father had, by some means or other, become possessed of a parchment chart on which were depicted the successive stages of the soul's heavenward journey, with the several *Powers* * it must encounter in its flight, and the proper invocations (specimens of which I have already given) whereby it should extort permission to traverse their dominions. This chart was known to the faithful as the "Schema, or Diagramma, of the Ophites." Amongst these invocations the one addressed to Iao, genius of the moon, is peculiarly important as illustrating the use of the most numerous class of the talismans we are considering. "O thou that presidest over the mysteries of the Father and of the Son, Iao who shinest in the night, who holdest the second place, the First Lord of Death, who makest part of that which is without God! In presenting to thee thine own *memorial* (or likeness) as a token (or passport) I swiftly traverse thy domain after having conquered through the Word of Life that which was born of Thee." The MSS. read τὸν ἴδιον ὑπὸ νοῦν σύμβολον, which has no meaning, but can only be the corruption of τὴν ἰδίαν ὑπόνοιαν, a word often used by Plutarch in the sense of symbol. Now what else could this "memorial" of Iao be but his own image engraved in gems? This deity is styled "Lord of Death," because the moon (Isis) presides over the birth, development and change, of which death is the necessary consequence, of things terrestrial.

* This was merely an adaptation to the new notions of the sect of the old Egyptian ritual always placed, entire or in part, within the mummy-case, and entitled, "The Book of the Gates, concerning the manifestation unto the Light." These *Gates*, leading to the palace of Osiris, were one-and-twenty in number, and were guarded each by its particular deity, to be duly addressed in his turn. The papyrus of Petamenoph, otherwise Ammonius (d. under Hadrian), has been admirably explained and translated by Champollion, and published in Cailliaud's 'Voyage à Meroé,' iv. p. 22. Or the belief may have had a Chaldæan origin, even more ancient than the Egyptian. Lane-Fox and others have translated a tablet giving an account of the descent of the goddess Ishtar into Hades, "the Land of no Return." The Lord of Earth gives her a green bough of the Life tree, and she passes successively through the Seven Gates, surrendering at each in order, her crown, ear-rings, head-jewels, frontlets, finger and toe-rings, and necklace. The Lord of Hades gives her a cup of the Water of Life, and she returns, receiving back her jewels in the same order in which she gave them up.

Of the theory therein embodied, much was evidently derived from the same source as the Neo-Platonic doctrine concerning the *planetary* origin of the soul's faculties, which shall be related further on The chart itself was founded on that essential doctrine of Gnosticism, that the soul, released from the body, mounted upwards, eager for absorption into the Infinite God-head, or "Boundless Light," that *summum bonum* of Oriental aspiration (the Buddhist Nirwana "perfect Repose, the Epicurean *Indolentia*"), but on its way was obliged to traverse the successive regions of the planets, each ruled by its presiding genius These genii were of a nature somewhat *material*, and therefore malignant, and in this respect corresponding to the Seven Devs, Ahriman's ministers, who according to Zoroaster are chained each to his own planet. To obtain the indispensable permission of transit, a different adjuration to each Power was required, all which have been already given from Origen's copy of the Chart Their *names* were put down therein, as Adonai, genius of the Sun, Iao of the Moon, Eloi of Jupiter Sabao of Mars, Orai of Venus, Astaphai of Mercury, and Ildabaoth of Saturn *

All these names are to be read, more or less commonly, upon our talismans, although probably used there in a different sense from that accepted by the author of the Diagramma The Jewish angels Michael, Gabriel, Surid, Raphael, Thantabaoth, and Erataoth, were likewise inscribed as names of the genii presiding over the constellations, the Bear, Serpent, Eagle, Lion, Dog, Bull These notions are manifestly of Magian root, acquired by the Jews during the long period that their country was a province of the Persian Empire, and had grown into an essential article of religion

St Paul found it needful to warn his flock against the "worshipping of Angels" nevertheless, the adoration and the multiplication of their names went on augmenting to that pitch, that a Council held under Pope Zachary reduced them, as objects of worship to three only, Michael, Gabriel, Raphael.

* The Ritual above cited contains regularly *eight* invocations addressed to Thoth, recommending the soul of the defunct to the guardians of the same number of regions over whom he is the president

This retrenchment of the heavenly host was endorsed by a capitulary of Charlemagne's issued from Aix-la-Chapelle In the Diagram under consideration, Michael was typified by a lion, Suriel by an ox, Raphael by a serpent, Gabriel by an eagle, Thantabaoth by a bear, Onioth or Zartaoth by an ass

The reward promised to the Angel of the Church at Thyatira (Rev ii 28), "And I will give him the Morning Star," seems to be connected with the same belief in the Planetary Presidents Dante, in his Paradiso, going doubtless upon old tradition, makes Mercury the abode of spirits moved to glorious deeds in life by the love of fame, Venus, of true lovers, Luna, of theologians, Mars, of martyrs for the Faith, Jupiter of good princes, Saturn of such as have led a contemplative and recluse life

The above-quoted names of the Planetary Genii were in the Jewish religion either titles and attributes of the Most High, or else of his chief ministering spirits, but in the Gnostic *Scheme* they had been degraded from their high estate, and reduced into secondary deities of a mixed nature, partaking of good as well as of evil, yet all equally anxious to win souls from Abraxas, the proper lord and creator of the universe The only explanation for such a misapplication of the sacred titles is a very brief one, these semi-Buddhist philosophers who found the root of all evil in Matter, and consequently in the *material* creation, employed these old hallowed names to denote the agents of the Creator, who on account of this their office were regarded as mere demons, and by an exactly similar process they are found misappropriating the most sacred names of the Christian revelation But of this blasphemous perversion and wanton desecration of the ancient terminology no trace is to be discovered upon our talismans, their makers belonging to the Kabbalistic School of Alexandria, which reconciling Moses with Zoroaster, continued to employ these appellations in their primary time-honoured sense

The source of this notion concerning the Planetary Rulers can be traced very far back The power of Ildabaoth, or Saturn, and his sons over the soul, as well as the astrological notion about the influence of the stars over man's destiny, are clearly part and parcel of what the Alexandrian Platonists had taught concerning the planetary origin of the soul and its faculties, thus expounded by Macrobius (Som. Scip i 12). "The soul on its descent from the One and Indivisible source of its being in order to be united to the body, passes through the Milky Way into the Zodiac at their intersection in Cancer and Capricorn, called the Gates of the Sun, because the two solstices are placed in these signs Through Cancer, the 'Gate of Man,' the soul descends upon Earth, the which is *spiritual death* Through Capricorn, the 'Gate of the Gods,' it reascends up into heaven, its new birth taking place upon its release from the body So soon as the soul has left Cancer and the Milky Way, it begins to lose its divine nature, and arriving at Leo enters upon the first phase of its future condition here below During its downward progress, the soul, at first a *sphere* in form, is elongated into a *cone*, and now begins to feel the influence of Matter, so that on joining the body it is intoxicated and stupefied by the novel draught This condition is typified by the Crater of Bacchus placed in the heavens between Cancer and Leo

"The soul thus descending, as it passes through each sphere receives successive *coatings*, as it were, of a luminous body, and is furnished at the same time with the several faculties it has to exercise during its probation upon Earth Accordingly, in Saturn, it is supplied with reason and intelligence, in Jupiter, with the power of action, in Mars, with the irascible principle, in the Sun, with sensation and speculation, in Venus, with the appetites, in Mercury, with the means of declaring and expressing thoughts, in the Moon, with the faculty of generating and augmenting the body" Hence, as the Planets contain all the elements that, so to speak, make up the Inner Man, the genii, their rulers ("Lords of Death," as Valentinus calls them), exercise their tyranny over the soul through the medium of these faculties, so long as the soul is *encrusted* with their contributions during its imprisonment in the body

It is curious to compare with this Grecian theory the "Doctrine of the Servants of Saturn," dwellers in the farthest North (unmistakably a fragment of Druidical lore), preserved to us by Plutarch in his treatise 'On the Face in the Moon' They taught that in the generation of man, the Earth supplied the *body*, the Moon the ψυχή, the Sun the νοῦς What the ψυχή is to the body, the same is the νοῦς to the ψυχή This composite nature undergoes a double death In the first, Demeter, whose companion is the Earthly, or Supernal, Hermes, forcibly separates the ψυχή (animal soul) from the body This soul, after a certain penance in the Middle Sphere, in order to purify it from the pollution of the flesh, is caught up into the Moon, and passes through the Earth's shadow during an eclipse, after a probation proportionate in length of time unto its deserts, whereas, the wicked, if they try to enter before their purification be completed, are scared away by the terrific *Face* The good abide in the Moon, in the enjoyment of perfect tranquillity, and becoming δαίμονες or *genii*, busy themselves with the regulation of human affairs upon earth, rendering oracles and similar services to mankind But should these beatified spirits misconduct themselves, they are put again into a human body, and sent down to Earth (This is the very doctrine of Manes, who made the light of the Moon to depend upon the brightness of the blessed one therein resident a theory which Epiphanius triumphantly overthrows by asking how the luminary was supplied during the eight centuries that elapsed between the Creation and the death of Adam ?)

But after a certain time, the νοῦς aspires to reascend to its fountain head the Sun, whereupon Persephone, with her colleague the Celestial Hermes, separates it with gentleness and by slow degrees from the grosser ψυχή This is the Second Death the νοῦς flying up to the Sun, but the ψυχή remaining in the Moon in a dreamy sort of existence, until gradually absorbed into her substance, exactly as the Earth gradually absorbs into herself the remains of the body Calm and philosophic souls are easily absorbed, but active, passionate, erotic natures with great difficulty, they wander about in midspace, divested of the νοῦς, becoming *Tityi* and *Typhones*,* throwing confusion

* Names of the chief giants who warred against Jupiter The legend clearly comes from the same source as that in the Book of Enoch "And the Giants who were born of the spirit and of flesh shall be called

into oracles, as the so-called Typhon does at Delphi, until in the end they likewise are drawn back and attracted into the substance of the Moon

Justinus Kerner, in his treatise 'Die Seherin von Prevorst,' improving upon the old notion, most ingeniously anatomises the Inner Man, and makes him to consist of three members, *Seele, Nerven-Geist, Geist* The Nerven-Geist, or nervous energy, being of a grosser nature, continues united with the Seele after its separation from the body, rendering it capable of becoming *visible* to the living in the form of an apparition, and enabling it in other ways to affect material objects, to make noises, move about articles of furniture, in short, to commit the various annoyances comprehended under the term "es spukt" And here be it observed the commonness of such visitations in Germany is amusingly exemplified by the necessity of having an impersonal verb to express them, just as we say "it rains," "it blows," so do the more sensitive Germans say "it ghosts" According to its previous training in life, this composite being requires more or less time to dissolve, the Seele alone being immortal, and consequently the Teutonic spectres assume a more and more diminutive form as their time of probation wears away Analogous to this is Plato's explanation of the *acknowledged facts* of spirits haunting tombs having been immersed during her union with the body in gross sensual pleasures, the soul becomes equally unable and unwilling to abandon her old companion and dwelling-house before the same be totally consumed.

To the above-quoted theories explaining the nature of the soul, and its final destination, the recent discovery of that precious monument of Gnosticism, the Pistis-Sophia enables us to add a third, infinitely more complete in all its details. This last

---

evil spirits upon earth and on earth shall be their habitation Evil spirits shall proceed from their flesh because they were created from above, from the holy watchers was their beginning and primary foundation Evil spirits shall they be upon earth, and the spirits of the wicked shall they be called The habitation of the spirits of heaven shall be in heaven, but upon earth shall be the habitation of terrestrial spirits who are born on earth The spirits of the giants shall be like clouds which shall oppress, corrupt, fall contend, and bruise upon earth"—(xv 8)

revelation improves upon the Neo-Platonic doctrine by making the astral genii "the Rulers of the Sphere" (Zodiac) *create* the soul from their own substance "out of the tears of their eyes and the sweat of their torment," animated with a spark of that Divine Light which has not yet been totally extracted from their fuller nature. For these Zodiacal Lords evidently answer to the rebellious Angels of the Jews, and the Seven Devs of the Magi, in fact the whole treatise represents the religious ideas of the latter, more closely than of any other system.

THE CAUSE OF SIN

(Pist.-Soph. 282) "And when the Saviour had spoken these things, he continuing in his discourse said unto Mary: Now, therefore Mary, hear concerning the thing whereof thou askest of me, Who is it that constraineth man to commit sin?" Now therefore when (the parents) have begotten the child, when there exists in him a small *power*, and a small soul, and a small "counterfeit of the spirit" (conscience) * in a word, all the three in him being small together. No one of them understandeth anything at all, whether it be good or evil, by reason of the weight of the heavy oblivion (of the former life) that holdeth them, the body likewise being small. And the child eateth of the meats of the world of the Rulers. And the soul gathereth to itself out of the portion of the soul that is concealed in these meats, and the Counterfeit of the spirit gathereth to itself out of the portion of evil that resideth in the meats and in the lusts thereof, the body, likewise, gathereth the insensible *Matter* that is in the meats. But the *Fate* herself taketh not out of the meats, inasmuch as she is not mixed up with them, but in what shape she came into the world, in the same she continueth. And little by little, the power, the soul, and the counterpart of the spirit grow to their full stature, and each one thereof is sensible after its own kind.† The power is sensible to seek after the Light above, the soul is sensible to seek after the place of Righteousness of the mixture, which same is the place of

* 'Αντίμιμον πνεύματος.

† I.e. adapted by its constitution.

confusion, the counterfeit of the spirit also seeketh after all wickedness and lusts and sins; and the body is sensible to nothing save how it may draw strength out of Matter, thus the three are forthwith sensible, each one according to its own nature, and the contentious ones (ἐριδαῖοι) also send ministers who shall follow them in order to bear witness against all the sins that they may commit, to regulate the manner in which they shall punish them when they come up for judgment, the counterfeit of the spirit also thinks upon and is sensible to all the sins and the evils that come near to that soul, which proceedeth from the Rulers of the Great Fate, and bringeth them into the soul.* But the inner power seeketh after the Place of Light, and all the godhead, whilst the counterfeit of the spirit turneth the soul awry, and constraineth it to work all its own unlawful deeds, and all its passions, and all its wickedness continually, and it abideth a different creature from the soul, and is an enemy to the soul, and causeth it to commit all these sins and wickednesses, and also stirreth up the ministers of contention, to bear witness against the sins that it is about to cause the soul to commit. And it cometh to pass that it resteth not day or night, and it troubleth the soul in dreams and in the lusts of this world, and maketh it to lust after all the things of this world; in a word, it urgeth the soul to do all the things that the Rulers have laid before it, and it is at war with the soul, continuing that it shall do the things it would not. Now therefore *this* is the enemy of the soul and constraineth it to do all kinds of sins, and when it comes to pass that the time of that man is accomplished, then cometh his Fate, which driveth that man unto the death appointed him by the Rulers, and by means of the bonds wherewith men are tied by Destiny. Then come the contentious Receivers to conduct that soul out of the body, and after that these Receivers go about with the soul through all the regions shewing unto it the Æons of the world,† whilst the counterfeit of the spirit and fate follow after that soul but the *power*

* The Platonic "divinæ particula auræ", the extrication of which from the *confusion*, μίγμα, was the real object of Christ's descent on earth according to Valentinus

† The sense seems to require the translation, "exhibit the *soul* unto the Æons"

that was in it goes up unto the Virgin of Light And after those three days the Receivers lead that soul down from above into the hell of Chaos, they deliver it unto the tormentors (and the Receivers return again into their own places), who punish the same according to the measure of its sins as ordained by the Archons for the discharge of souls And the counterfeit of the spirit becomes the guard over the soul, appointed over it, convicting it, in one place of punishment after the other, of the sins which it hath committed, and it leadeth the soul into the region of the Archons of the Middle space And when it hath arrived in their presence, they lead it unto the Mysteries of Fate, and if they find them not (sealed upon the soul), they seek after their own share, and those Archons punish the soul according to its sins, according to its deserts, of those punishments I will declare the form unto you in the 'Emanation of the Universe' But after it has come to pass that the time of the soul's different punishments is accomplished in the prisons of the Archons of the Middle-space, then the counterfeit of the spirit leadeth the soul upwards out of all their regions, and bringeth it before the light of the Sun, according to the commandment of the *Primal Man** IEOT, and bringeth it before the judge, the Virgin of Light And she trieth that soul, and in case she shall find it to be sinful, she planteth within the same (a particle of) the power of her own light, according unto its station in life, its body, and its share of sensibility. Then the Virgin of Light putteth her seal upon that soul and delivereth it unto one of her Receivers, who will see that it be placed in a body befitting the sins that it hath committed (in a former life) And verily I say unto you she shall not let the soul be released from the changes of its bodies (various metempsychoses), until it shall have accomplished its uttermost cycle in the shapes whereof it may be deserving, of all which I will tell you the form, and likewise the form of the several bodies into which they shall place the souls, according to the sins of each

"But if it be a soul that hath not obeyed the counterfeit of the spirit in all its doings, but is righteous, and hath received the mysteries of Light that be in the First Court, or those that be in the

* The Seir Anpin of the Rabbis

Second Court, or those in the Third which is the innermost part (*adytum*)—when the time of that soul in the body is accomplished, and when the counterfeit of the spirit followeth after that soul, together with fate, whilst the soul is on the road that leadeth on high, and before it is far distant therefrom, it uttereth the mystery for the breaking * of all the *seals* and all the bonds of the counterfeit of the spirit wherewith the Archons have bound it unto the soul. And it having uttered those words, the bonds of the counterfeit of the spirit are loosed so that it ceaseth to persecute that soul, and lets it go according to the commandment given unto it by the Archons of the Great Fate, who said unto it, Let not that soul go free, unless it shall utter unto thee the mystery for the breaking of the bonds wherewith we have bound thee unto it. Thereupon the soul, thus set free, leaves fate behind unto the Archons of the way of the Middle-space, and destroys the counterfeit of the spirit leaving it for the Archons in the place wherein they had bound it (at first) unto the soul, and in that moment it becometh a great flood of light, shining exceedingly; and the Receivers who had fetched it out of the body are afraid of that light, so that they fall down upon their faces, and the soul is made as it were *a wing* † *of light*, and passeth through all the regions of the Archons, and through all the courses of the Light, until it entereth into the place of its own kingdom for which it hath received the mystery.

"But if it be a soul that hath received the mystery in the First Court, which is the outer part, and after receiving and performing the mystery and being converted shall again have sinned, and when its time in the body is accomplished, and the Receivers come to fetch it, and the counterfeit of the spirit and fate pursue it by reason of the seals and bonds wherewith it hath been bound together with them by the Archons—then if the soul whilst yet in the way of its pursuers should utter the mystery that breaketh those seals and bonds, forthwith they are all loosed and the counterfeit of the spirit ceases to follow after the

* I.e. the formula, perhaps the "mystery of the seven vowels," so highly lauded elsewhere.

† I.e. a winged thing, referring perhaps to the ancient emblem of the human-headed bird used in the same sense.

soul And the soul leaves its pursuers behind, for none of them have their own power, but the soul keeps its own power Then the Receivers that belong to the mystery which the soul hath received come and snatch it away from the contentious Receivers, and these return to do the business of the Archons in the occupation of fetching away souls. But the Receivers of the soul, who pertain to the Light, themselves become a wing of light to that soul, and a vesture of light unto it And they lead it not into Chaos, because it is not lawful to lead a soul, that hath obtained the mysteries, into Chaos, but they bring it into the road of the Archons of the Middle-space And when they are come before the Archons of the Middle-space, the Archons depart out of the way of that soul, being in great fear, and in cruel burning, and in divers shapes, in a word being in great fear unto which there is no measure And in that moment the soul utters the mystery of its defence before them, and they fall upon their faces out of fear of the mystery and of the defence which it hath uttered And the soul leaves with them their *fate*,* saying unto them Take to yourselves your fate, I am not coming into your place from henceforth, I am made a stranger unto you for ever, I am coming into the place of my own inheritance And after the soul hath said this, the Receivers of the Light fly away with it on high, and bring it before the Æons of Destiny, giving it the proper speech of defence for the place and the *seals* thereof, and the soul shews to them the counterfeit of the spirit and utters the mystery that sundereth the bonds wherewith they had bound them both together, saying to them Take to yourselves your counterfeit of the spirit, henceforth I come not in your place, I am made a stranger unto you for ever And it shews them the *seal* of each and the form of defence Then the Receivers fly away with the soul and bring it through all the Æons, shewing the seal, and the defence, in all the regions of King Adamas, and of all the Rulers of the places of the left hand (which defences and seals I will declare to you when I explain to you the emanation of the mystery) Then they bring the soul before the Virgin of Light, and it giveth to the Virgin her own seal, defence, and

* Viz, the separate portion of its composition implanted in it by these Archons at its birth

the glory of hymns, and the Virgin of Light with the seven other Virgins examine that soul—all of them, that they may all find their own marks, their own seals, their own baptisms, and their own unctions upon it (292) Then the Virgin of Light sealeth that soul, and the Receivers of Light baptize the same and give unto it the spiritual unction And each of the Virgins of Light sealeth it with her own seal Furthermore the Receivers deliver it over to the great Sabaoth, the Good One, who is hard by the gate of Life in the region of those pertaining unto the right hand, whom they call 'the Father', and the soul rendereth unto him the glory of his hymns, of his seals, and of his justification Then the great good Sabaoth sealeth it with his own seals, and the soul rendereth the knowledge, and the glory of hymns, and the seals belonging to the whole region of those that pertain unto the right hand These also all seal it with their own seal, and Melchisedek, the great gatherer of Light—who is in the region of those pertaining to the right hand—also sealeth that soul Then Melchisedek's gatherers also seal it and lead it into the Treasury of Light, and the soul rendereth glory and honour and their proper seals in all the regions of Light Then those pertaining to all the regions of the Treasury of Light seal it with their own seals, and so it entereth into the place of its inheritance."

STATE AFTER DEATH OF THE UNINITIATED

(261) "Then stood forth Mary and said, Lord, as concerning just men and perfect in all righteousness, such a man in whom there is no sin at all, shall they torment him with all these judgments and punishments, or shall they not? Or shall they carry such a man into the kingdom of heaven or not?

"The Saviour answered and said unto Mary, The just man perfect in all righteousness, that hath never committed sin, but yet hath never obtained any one mystery of Light, when his time cometh for departing out of the body, straightway there shall come for him the Gatherers belonging to that one of the great Triple Powers who is the greatest amongst them, in order that they may take away that soul from the Contentious Gatherers, and during three days they shall go about with that soul amongst all the creatures of the world (i.e. throughout all creation) After the three days they shall lead him down into Chaos, so that they may deliver him out of * all the punishments therein, and out of the judgments, and they shall bring him unto all the judgment-places, but no flame of Chaos shall afflict him greatly, (262) nevertheless they shall in some wise afflict him for a little space, but speedily shall they have compassion upon him, and draw him up out of Chaos so as to take him out of the Road of the Middle-space, and from all the Rulers thereof And these shall not punish him with their cruel torments, but the flame of their regions shall afflict him in some measure, and after they have brought him into the unmerciful place ΑΧΘΑΝΑΒΑΣ they shall not torment him with the cruel torments therein, but they shall keep him there a little while, and afflict him in some measure with the heat of the torments of that place But they shall quickly have compassion upon him, and bring him forth out of all those places, neither shall they lead him by the way that goeth from out of the Æons, for fear lest the Rulers of the Æons should hold him too firmly, but they shall conduct him by the path of the Sun's light, in order to bring him before the Virgin of Light And she doth try that soul that she may find it free from sin, and she ordereth it not to be carried unto the Light because the *mark of the Kingdom of Light* is not upon it, but she sealeth it with a special seal, and takes care that it be put into a body of righteousness belonging to the Æons (263) This man will be good, so that he will obtain the seals of the mysteries of the Light, and inherit the kingdom for ever and ever

"But if he shall have sinned once, twice, or thrice, they shall reject that soul, sending it back again into the world according to the *form of the sins that* it may have committed, the form whereof I will declare unto you hereafter But verily, verily I say unto you, that even the righteous man that hath committed no sin at all cannot be brought into the Kingdom of Light, forasmuch the seal of the mysteries of that kingdom is not found

* Protect him against any suffering from

upon him Once for all, I say unto you, a soul cannot be brought into the kingdom, if it be without the mysteries of the Kingdom of Light '

FUTURE PUNISHMENTS

The Gnostics did not fail, after the example of their orthodox rivals, to employ the strongest stimulants of terror in order to gain converts, as is forcibly manifested by this picture of the varied torments of the world to come, the appointed heritage of all who obtained not the Gnosis which they preached ('Pistis-Sophia,' 255) —

"And Jesus continuing in his discourse said unto the disciples, When I shall have returned into the Light, preach ye unto the whole world Say unto them, Slacken not by day and night to seek until ye shall find the mysteries of the Kingdom of Light, that shall cleanse you, and render you a pure light, and shall bring you into the Kingdom of Light Say unto them, Renounce the world and all the *Matter* which is therein, and all the cares and the sins thereof—in a word, all the conversation that therein is—that ye may be worthy of the mysteries of Light, that ye may be saved from all the punishments that are in the judgment-places Say unto them, Renounce murmuring, that ye may be worthy of the mysteries of Light that ye may be saved from the burning of the Figure of the *Dog* Say unto them Renounce obedience (to the world), that ye may be saved from the judgments of the Figure of the *Dog* Say unto them, Renounce invocation (of idols), that ye may be worthy of the mysteries of Light, that ye may be saved from the torments of *Ariel* Renounce a lying tongue, that ye may be saved from the burning rivers of the Figure of the Dog-shaped one Renounce false witnessing, that ye may be set free, that ye may be saved from the same rivers Renounce boastings and pride, that ye may be saved from the burning pits of Ariel. Renounce self-love, that ye may be saved from the judgments of *Orcus* * Renounce talkativeness, that

* These regions and the shapes of their Rulers seem to have been suggested to our author by the Egyptian mummy-case paintings of the *Gates*

ye may be saved from the fires of Orcus Renounce unjust judgments, that ye may be saved from the torments that be in Orcus Renounce covetousness that ye may be saved from the rivers of smoke of the Dog-shaped Renounce the love of this world, that ye may be saved from the pitched-coats burning of the Dog-shaped Renounce robbery, that ye may be saved from the rivers of deceit of Ariel. Renounce evil speaking, that ye may be saved from the torments of the river of smoke Renounce wickedness, that ye may be saved from the burning seas of Ariel. Renounce unmercifulness, that ye may be saved from the judgments of the *Dragon-shapes* Renounce anger, that ye may be saved from the rivers of smoke of the Dragon-shapes Renounce reviling, that ye may be saved from the burning seas of the Dragon-shapes Renounce robbery, that ye may be saved from the boiling seas of the same Renounce thieving, that ye may be saved from *Ildabaoth* Renounce backbiting, that ye may be saved from the burning rivers of the *Lion-shaped* one Renounce fighting and quarrelling, that ye may be saved from the boiling rivers of Ildabaoth Renounce stubbornness, that ye may be saved from the ministers of Ildabaoth and his burning seas Renounce evil deeds, that ye may be saved from all the devils of Ildabaoth and from all his punishments Renounce desperateness, that ye may be saved from the seas of boiling pitch of Ildabaoth Renounce adultery, that ye may be saved from the seas of brimstone and pitch of the Lion-shaped Renounce murders, that ye may be saved from the Ruler of crocodiles, which is the first creature in the ice that is in the Outer Darkness Renounce cruelty and ungodliness, that ye may be saved from the Rulers of the Outer Darkness Renounce impiety, that ye may be saved from weeping and the gnashing of teeth Renounce witchcraft, that ye may be saved from the mighty frost and hail of the Outer Darkness Renounce blasphemy, that ye may be saved from the great dragon of the Outer Darkness. Renounce

---

in which are seated so many genii with heads of hawk, baboon, man, crocodile, lion, jackal, vulture, winnowing-fan, and serpent, all armed with swords These were the Gates passage through which on his way to the judgment seat Anubis is prayed to procure for the defunct in the papyrus-ritual buried with him

false doctrines, that ye may be saved from all the torments of the great dragon of the Outer Darkness.

"Say unto them that teach false doctrines, and unto every one that is taught by them, Woe unto you, for, unless ye repent and leave your error, ye shall fall into the torments of the great dragon of the Outer Darkness, exceeding cruel, and they in the world shall not redeem you out of them for ever and ever, but ye shall be utterly destroyed unto the end. Say unto them that slight the doctrine of truth of the First Mystery, Woe unto you, for your punishment shall be evil beyond that of all men: ye shall abide in the great frost, ice, and hail in the middle of the dragon, and in the Outer Darkness, and they in this world shall not redeem you from this hour forth for ever, but ye shall be in that place, and in the dissolution of the universe ye shall be consumed, so that ye shall be destroyed for ever."

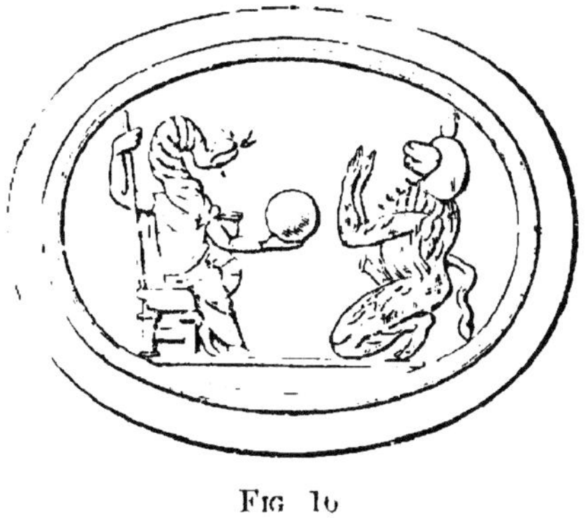

FIG. 16

TALISMANIC LEADEN SCROLLS

The only classical notice of the employment of these engines for moving the invisible world (not, however, for good, but for evil) is to be found in the Annals of Tacitus (ii. 69), who thus enumerates them amongst the means, real or imaginary, whereby Livia's agent, Piso, occasioned, or aggravated, the final illness of the too popular Germanicus. "The severity of the attack (a fever) was heightened by the suspicion of poison on the part of Piso; and in fact there were discovered, hidden in the house-walls, fragments of human corpses, spells and curses and the name of Germanicus engraved upon plates of lead, also ashes half-burnt and soaked in blood, and other pieces of witchcraft by means whereof it is believed that souls are made over unto the Infernal Gods." A very remarkable example of the practice of this malevolent superstition has been published by Visconti (Op. Var. iii. 256). It is a sheet of lead found, folded up, within a tomb opened at the Hippotade Gate of Athens, and a copy of which he had received from M. Fauvel. The inscription, full of blunders both in spelling and grammar, is arranged in ten lines, seemingly meant for trochaic tetrameters, and may be read thus:

1 Ἑρμὴς χθόνιος, Γῆ κατοχύς
2 καὶ προς τὴν Φερσεφονην
3 Φερσεφυνη καταδῶ Δεξιαν
4 πρὸς τούτους ἅπαντας
5 καὶ Κλεοφραδὲς
6 καταδῶ πρὸς τοὺς αὔτοις ἴοσι
7 και Ναυβάτην καταδῶ πρὸς τοὺς αὔτους
8 Τληπόλεμον καταδῶ
9 καὶ τοὺς μετὰ Κτησίου ἅπαντας
10 καταδῶ *

"Infernal Hermes, imprisoning Earth, and also Persephone! I lay a spell upon Dexias before all these deities, also upon Cleophiades, Naubates, Ctesias with all his family."

* *κατάδεσις κατάδεσμος* are used by Plato for witchcraft and the Hebrew 'Chabar," *to bewitch*, properly signifies *to bind*.

The defunct Athenian must assuredly have departed this life full of charity towards all his neighbours to have taken such pains to carry with him a memorandum so expressive of his wishes on their behalf. It reminds one of the old Monmouthshire farmer, who (as tradition tells), dying of a broken heart, ordered the bitterest verses of the "Cursing Psalm" to be engraved upon his tombstone for the benefit of his enemy, as it may yet be seen at Christchurch, near Caerleon, Monmouthshire The Verulamium scrolls (p 339) contained invocations of the opposite character, for the benefit of the parties named therein Yet another variety are the leaden scrolls found numerously in the lately discovered Demetrium of Cnidus Some evidently belong to a kind of ordeal—the accused party asking to be ill-treated by Persephone in the next world, if guilty of such or such a charge, others contain similar ill wishes against individuals therein specified who have injured the writers. By far the most curious of these relics is the leaden plate, found at Bath (1880), engraved with four lines of words placed in their proper order, but spelt backwards for the sake of disguise, and about four inches square It is thus read by Zangemeister

"Qui mihi mantilium involavit
Sic liquat com aqua olla ta
Si qui eam salvavit vinna vel
Exsupersus Verianus Servianus
Itianus Sagarbalis Cubus
Minianus cum Sovina
Ceramanilli"

This reading is not satisfactory in many places The lost object is written MATHV, MATEHV, to be read backwards, like all the rest, and therefore bears no resemblance to "mantelium"

The malignity of the Greek character is exemplified in nothing more strongly than in the open toleration of the use of such engines of spite In the great Temple of Demeter at Cnidus, Mr. Newton found many of these leaden scrolls invoking the vengeance of the goddess of the place, her daughter, and the other infernal gods, upon individuals specified by name It will be remarked that this "dira detestatio" was not contingent upon the refusal of a just demand, as in the case of the worthy

Silurian hereafter to be mentioned; but were the means of revenge resorted to by persons too cowardly to use those supplied by nature, or probably for the mere sake of gratifying spite.

As a Roman *pendant* to this Athenian legacy of curses, I copy the leaden scroll found, many years ago, in the garden of the Villa Manenti, upon the Via Latina. De Rossi, who first published it in the 'Bullettino del Instit. Arch. Rom.' for 1852, is of opinion that orthography and characters indicate the date of the last century of the Republic. "Quomodo mortuos qui istic sepultus est nec loqui nec sermonari potest, seic Rhodine apud M. Licinium Faustum mortua sit, nec loqui nec sermonari possit. Ita ut mortuos nec ad Deos nec ad homines acceptus est, ita Rhodine apud M. Licinium accepta sit, et tantum valeat quantum ille mortuos quei istic sepultus est, Dite Pater! Rhodinen tibi commendo ut semper odio sit M. Licinio Fausto, item M. Hedium Amphionem, item C. Popillium Apollonium, item Vennonia Hermiona, item Sergia Glycinna." It is easy to construct a history out of these lines, the despairing lover dying from the perfidy of the fair Rhodine, who has jilted him for the noble Licinius. Faustus prays the God of Hell to make her distasteful to her possessor, and also to punish her aiders and abettors, whose Greek cognomens show them to be of the condition of freedmen.

In the same strain we have the commination, sounding to us so jocular, but doubtless in its own time intended for something very serious, addressed to Nodens, discovered amidst the ruins of his not much frequented temple in Lydney Park, Gloucestershire. 'Devo Nodenti Silvianus anilum perdedit, demediam (sic) partem donavit Nodenti inter quibus nomen Seniciani nollis permittas sanitatem donec perferat usque Templum Nodentis.' Whereby the half-civilized Silurian, as his name betrays, in artless grammar and orthography, beseeches the local deity never to allow Senicianus or any of his family to enjoy health, until he brings back the ring, the loss of which Silvianus ascribes to him, and restores it to the rightful owner at the temple of Nodens; in which case one half its value is promised to the god for his assistance in recovering the stolen property.

These thank-offerings to "Neddyn diw" (perhaps identical with the Etruscan "Nethunos") were made in coppers, the very "stipes" out of which the tesselated pavement of his temple was paid for, as the inscription thereon yet testifies They were found plentifully strewed over the floor, of every date down to Honorius, then some sudden raid of barbarians gave the whole establishment to the flames

The idea of "binding" is practically carried out in Spell VII of Atanasi's 'Mag Papyrus,' which directs you to lay the link of a chain (κρίκος) upon a leaden plate, and having traced its outline, to write thereon, round the circumference, the common Gnostic legend (reading both ways) continuously

ΙΑΕΩΒΑΦΡΕΝΕΜΟΥΝΟΘΙΛΑΡΙΚΡΙΦΙ
ΑΕΥΕΑΡΙΦΙΚΡΑΛΙΘΟΝΥΟΜΕΝΕΡΦΑΒΑΩΕΑΙ

Within the circle must be written the nature of the thing it is desired to prevent The operation is entitled the "Ring of Hermes"

The link was then to be folded up on the leaden plate, and thrown into the grave of one dead before his time, or else into a disused well After the formula above given was to follow, in Greek, "Prevent thou such and such a person from doing such and such a thing"—a proof that the long string of epithets all referred to the same Power

We now come to relics of the same sort, but of diverse intention, being those passports to eternal bliss, so frequently mentioned in the course of the preceding dissertation Of these the most complete example is the Leaden Book formerly belonging to the celebrated Father Kircher, in whose collection it first made its appearance, but concerning the *provenance* of which nothing is known, although Matter *suspects* it to be the same that Montfaucon gave to Cardinal Bouillon, who died at Rome in 1715 But this identification is entirely ungrounded, as shall presently be shown The same writer has given facsimiles, in his 'Excursion Gnostique,' of the seven pages composing the book, now deposited in the Museum Kircherianum. These leaves are of lead, 3 × 4 inches square, engraved on each side, with a religious composition for heading, under which are, in every case, *five* lines of inscription, that mystic number having doubtless been purposely adopted by the spell-maker. These lines are written in large Greek capitals, square-shaped, and resembling the character commonly used on Gnostic gems. Intermixed are other forms, some resembling the hieroglyphs still current for the Signs and Planets, others Egyptian Demotic and Pehlevi letters. The language does not appear to be Coptic, but rather some Semitic tongue, many words being composed entirely of *consonants*, showing that the vowels were to be supplied by the reader. The chief interest, however, of the relic lies in the designs heading each page, in which we recognise the usual figures of Gnostic iconology, together with others of a novel character, all touched in with a free and bold graver with the fewest possible strokes. The purport of the writing underneath may be conjectured, on the authority of the 'Litany of the Dead'* and the 'Diagramma of the Ophites,' to be the prayers addressed by the ascending soul to these particular deities, each in his turn. The very number of the pages, *seven* in all, comes to support this explanation. The Astral Presidents to be propitiated in the heavenward journey are represented in the following manner:—

1. A nude female figure, in which the navel (the "circle of the Sun") is strongly defined: she makes a gesture of adoration to a genius in a conical cap and short tunic, armed with a trident, Siva's proper weapon, and consequently appropriated afterwards by the mediæval Ruler of Tartarus.

Reverse. Palm within a circle or garland, and a large Caduceus.

2. Female in flowing robes, addressing a gigantic fowl, much too squat apparently, in its proportions for the ibis of Thoth: perhaps intended for the yet more divine bird, the phœnix.

* In the pictures to which the disembodied spirit "before his journey addresses his prayers to the various gods and then enters upon his labours. He attacks with spear in hand the crocodiles, lizards, scorpions and snakes which beset his path, and passing through these dark regions he at length reaches the land of the Amenti, whose goddess is a hawk standing upon a perch. Here the sun's rays cheer his steps, and he meets amongst other wonders the head of Horus rising out of a lotus-flower, the god Pthah, the phœnix, his own soul in the form of a bird with a human head, and the goddess Isis as a serpent of goodness. The soul then returns to the mummy and puts life into its mouth."—(Sharpe, 'Egypt. Mythol.,' p. 65.)

Reverse. Nude female adoring a certain undefined monster, furnished with large ears, and placed upon a low altar The first line of the accompanying prayer seems to begin with the Pehlevi letters equivalent to S, P, V

3 Horus, leaning upon an instrument of unknown use, regarding a huge tortoise, better drawn than the rest, which is crawling towards him

Reverse Female in long flowing robes, holding up her hands to a naked child (Horus ?) who is in the act of leaping down to her from a lofty pedestal

4 Anubis attired in a short mantle (reminding one of Mephistopheles) attentively contemplating a lofty hill, the apex whereof has the form of an eagle's head

Reverse Female in rags leaning on a staff advancing towards another richly clothed and crowned, who lifts up her hands as though terrified at the apparition

5 Abraxas in his proper form, looking towards a female fully draped who offers him some indistinct symbol, much resembling an E turned upside down The prayer below opens with the word ΙΑΩ, whence it may be fairly *conjectured* that the first characters in each of the other pages give the name of the deity pictured above

Reverse Frog and serpent facing each other · ancient emblems of Spring, but probably used here in their mediæval sense as types of the Resurrection of the body

6 A headless man with rays issuing from his shoulders, and holding out a torch, appears falling backwards with affright on the approach of a winged dragon

Reverse A squat personage with radiated crown stands in front face in the attitude of the Egyptian Typhon On the other side stands a very indistinct figure, resembling a Cupid, having square-cut wings, his back turned to the spectator

7 Female with robe flying in an arch over her head, as Iris is commonly pictured, extends her hand to an approaching bull the drawing of the latter being vastly superior to any of the other figures One is led to discover in this group Venus and her tutelary sign, Taurus

Reverse Female reclining on the ground, towards whom advances a large bird, seemingly meant for a pigeon

In the sacred animals figuring in these successive scenes it is impossible to avoid discovering an allusion to the forms the Gnostics gave to the planetary Rulers A legend of theirs related how the Saviour in his descent to this lower world escaped the vigilance of these Powers by assuming their *own form* as he traversed the sphere of each, whence a conjecture may be hazarded that similar metamorphoses of the illumined soul are hinted at in these inexplicable pictures

We now come to the consideration of a second relic of the same kind, known as "Card Bouillon's Leaden Book" How Matter could have supposed this to be the same with Kircher's (supposing him ever to have compared his own facsimiles with Montfaucon's) is a thing totally beyond my comprehension For Montfaucon, in his Plate 187, has given every leaf of the former, apparently copied with sufficient fidelity the pictures on which I shall proceed to describe for the purpose of comparison with those in the Kircherian volume, for the general analogy in the designs attests the similar destination of both monuments, whilst at the same time the variation in details proves the existence of *two* distinct specimens of this interesting class.

The leaves within the two covers, connected by rings secured by a rod passed through them, are only *six* in number, whilst the inscriptions, though in much the same lettering as the Kircherian copy, fill only *four* lines on a page, and only *four* pages in all the other eight pages having pictures alone

Now to describe these pictures, which seem in better drawing than those of the former set * Page 1 Man, nude, standing up 2 Female fully draped, walking 3. The same figure, extending one hand. 4 Anubis in a short mantle 5 The usual figure of the Abraxas god. 6 Bird-headed man surrounded with rays (Phre ?). 7. Bust of Serapis 8 Female reclining 9 Terminal figure in the form of a cross 10 Frog. 11 Ibis, or Phœnix 12 Female holding above her head a star-spangled veil

* The improvement is probably only due to the French copyist

Montfaucon supposes all these figures represent the genii who preside over the *hours* of the day—the first being expressive of *rising*, the last of *night*, and calls attention to the fact that the *seventh* page is assigned to Serapis, who sometimes receives the title of ἑπταγράμματος θεός. But in his Plate 188, Montfaucon copies from Bononi's 'Museum Kircherianum' another leaden book "found in a sepulchre," which actually has seven pages, and two figures heading each, in the specimen pages: and this may possibly be the one since published in its entirety by Matter, although at present the leaves are separate, not connected into a book, which may be the result of accident during the century and a half that has elapsed since it was first noticed.

Another discovery of the same nature has been made in our own times and investigated with the greatest care. In the year 1852, whilst excavating the ruins of a tomb in the Vigna Marini, near the Porta Pia, a marble sarcophagus was brought to light, ornamented with a bas-relief representing either the Adoration of the Magi, or else the prototype of that scene, the "Birth of the New Sun." The floor of the tomb was paved with a mosaic equally ambiguous in subject, whether a Madonna and Child, or, what the concomitants render more probable, Isis suckling the infant Harpocrates. Several minor sarcophagi in terra-cotta surrounded the larger one, and in these were found many leaden plates, rolled up into scrolls, not bound-up like books. Eleven of these can still be deciphered. Matter publishes facsimiles of three of the best preserved, but none of them present any legends like the examples above described.

On the first is seen Anubis wearing a long tunic and buskins, and holding out a scroll; at his feet are two female busts: below all are two serpents entwined about the same object as in the second scroll, where also the same busts appear, viz. a corpse swathed up like a mummy. In the second scroll these busts are set on each side of the Anubis, a large figure much mutilated, but attired as above, and holding out a cross, the "Sign of Life." Under his feet lies the corpse, encircled in the numerous folds of a huge serpent, the Agathodæmon, guardian of the deceased. And this last type supplies the motive for so frequently placing upon gems the serpent-girt mummy. In the olden creed the serpent watched over tombs as well as over buried treasure. When Æneas is offering sacrifice at his father's grave (v. 84)—

"Dixerat haec, adytis cum lubricus anguis ab imis
Septem ingens gyros, septena volumina, traxit,
Amplexus placide tumulum, lapsusque per aras,
Coeruleae cui terga notae, maculosus et auro
Squamam incendebat fulgor, ceu nubibus arcus
Mille jacit varios adverso sole colores.
Obstupuit visu Æneas. Ille agmine longo
Tandem inter pateras, et levia pocula serpens,
Libavitque dapes, rursusque innoxius imo
Successit tumulo, et depasta altaria liquit.
Hoc magis inceptos genitori instaurat honores,
Incertus geniumne loci famulumve parentis
Esse putet."

In the third scroll, the most valuable of all, the same Anubis bears on his arm an oblong object, perhaps the Roman *scutum*, held so as to convert the outline of the figure into a complete Latin cross. Across this shield and the field run a number of Gnostic symbols, conspicuous amongst which is the sigil prescribed by Alexander Trallianus as a cure for the colic. 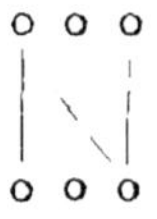 Others resemble some ordinary Masons' Marks. For example, an eight-armed cross, a circle, and a square cut by horizontal and vertical lines: at the god's foot is a rhomboid, the Egyptian 'Egg of the World,' towards which crawls a serpent coiled into a circle. A remarkable addition is the inscription carved over the tunic in semi-cursive letters:

KЄBNƬ	ЄKBΛ
ΦKTK	KCI
BKЄ	A
NΦ	Θ
✡	

Under the pairs of busts in the other scrolls is the letter ω, repeated *seven* times in a line: reminding one of the "Names," the interpretation whereof has been already given from the *Pistis-Sophia* (p. 16). Very remarkable also is the line of characters, apparently Palmyrene, upon the legs of the first Anubis. As for the figure of the *scrpent*, supposing these talismans to emanate not from the Isiac but the newer Ophite creed, it may well stand for that "True and perfect Serpent" who "leads forth the souls of all that put their trust in him out of the Egypt of the body, and through the Red Sea of Death into the Land of Promise, saving them on their way from the serpents of the Wilderness, that is, from the Rulers of the stars"

As for the symbols so largely used here and in other Gnostic monuments, their frequent construction out of lines terminated by dots or heads irresistibly suggests a theory for their origin In this respect, and in general form, they strikingly resemble certain characters in the *oldest* Babylonian alphabet This alphabet, simple in construction, long preceding the elaborate *nailhead*, is allowed to have been pictorial, i e hieroglyphic, in its nature It is very conceivable that, revered for antiquity, this primitive character was preserved in sacred usages long after it had grown obsolete in common life The cuneiform continued the national alphabet of Persia down to the Macedonian conquest, and doubtless was the one generally employed by the natives (very few of whom probably learnt the language of the new masters) until it was replaced by its last modification the early Pehlevi And as for the primitive hieroglyphic letters, it was natural that certain of them forms, expressing peculiarly sacred ideas (as the ✡ signifying "God"), should retain a mystic, perhaps thaumaturgic, value in the practice of the Magi long after their original meaning was forgotten And these very Magi were the teachers of the talisman-makers of Gnostic times.* This explanation is strongly supported by the recent discovery, that in the Assyrian inscriptions every deity has a certain *numeral* assigned him, which said numeral frequently stands in the place of his full name For example, the numeral for *Anu* (Pluto) is 60, for *Baal* (Jupiter) 50, for *Hoa* (Neptune) 40 the same

* This conjecture of mine has at last been verified by that high authority in Assyrian literature, Professor Sayce He finds in the assemblage of siglæ on the back of the Mithraic gem (Pl LI 1) the regular cuneiform characters, somewhat depraved, for *God*, and *Heaven* for BI and RI Besides these he recognises at least three out of the Cypriote syllabary, some of the rest remind him of the cypher alphabets of the East as given by that old author Ibn Wahaby, of which Von Hammer has made a translation

rule holding good for the sun, moon, and planets. Hence is it more than probable that our Gnostic talismans exhibit to us those very "numeri Babylonii" which Horace dissuades the fair Leuconoe from consulting in her unadvised desire to learn the Future. Such relics of old Chaldean lore would, it may well be supposed, never cease to be reproduced as they were originally shapen; the current Pehlevi would have carried on its face too recent a stamp to impose upon superstition.

All numerals were at first letters of an alphabet. Some amongst the unknown characters and "Masons' Marks" found on talismans cannot but be *numerals*, considering the essential part the properties of numbers play in several divisions of the Gnostic family. This notion is strongly supported by what Hippolytus (*Egyptian Theology*) says of a certain numeral, lost in the text, but from a subsequent passage clearly the Ten. "Which is a *sacred Number*, and which is written down and tied about the necks of sick people as a means of cure. In like manner a certain plant which terminates in the same number (of leaves) being similarly hung around the patient produces the same effect, in consequence of the *virtue* of that Number. Moreover a physician cures his patients when they amount to that particular number, but when the number of them is against him he does so with great difficulty. The Egyptians attend much to such numerals, and calculate all similar matters according to this rule; some reckoning by the vowels alone, others by all the letters in the Word." The plant meant may have been the *Agnus castus*, still regarded by the Turks as a potent amulet, and called *Kef Maryam*, "the hand of Mary," on account of its digitate form. The same *hand* made of blue glass is tied round children's necks, or on the part of the body to be protected against the stroke of the Evil-eye. Again, that important sect the Marcosians are shown by Hippolytus to teach no better doctrine than "a mere patchwork of scraps, stolen from the notions of Astrology, and from the Pythagorean art of *numbers*." In their theosophy the sacred numerals were the 30, the sum of the letters constituting the Ineffable Name, and the constituents of the same viz. 8, 10, 12, expressed in Greek by Η, Ι, ΙΑ or, again, by an intricate combination of these numerals giving the sum 99, written in Greek ρ. In another place (iv. 51) Hippolytus observes that "almost every heresy is indebted to the science of arithmetic for its *invention* of the Hebdomads, and its emanation of the Æons; although the different teachers divide them variously, and change their names, doing in reality nothing more: in all which way of proceeding Pythagoras is their true master, he who first brought with him out of *Egypt the use of numbers in such matters.*"

The so-called "Pythagorean Numerals" of unknown antiquity, whether or not due to the Samian sage, are said to be preserved to us by Boethius, "the last of the Romans," in his treatise on Arithmetic. That they would be the true parents of our *Arabic* numerals is at once apparent by inverting the figures standing for 1, 2, 5, 7, 9, 0. Then forms look like certain Palmyrene letters slightly modified. The Palmyrene is a very ancient Syriac alphabet, totally different in origin from either Punic or Pehlevi. The ancient importance of this character is apparent from what Epiphanius notices (Hær. lxvi.): "Manes divided his work into 22 books, being the number of the letters in the Syriac alphabet. For most of the Persians use the Syriac character as well as the Persian, just as with us many nations, although having a national alphabet of their own, yet employ the Greek. Others again pride themselves upon using the most cultivated dialect, viz. that current in Palmyra, both the dialect itself and its letters, and these are 22 in number."

In this affectation of the learned in Persia, a sufficient reason presents itself for the occasional appearance of Palmyrene letters in spells composed and sold by the Magi or their semi-Grecian disciples under the Roman Empire. The practice went back far beyond the epoch of the great heresiarch, for many Babylonian cylinders are known inscribed, instead of the cumbrous cuneiform, with a Semitic lettering, sometimes more resembling the Palmyrene than the Punic. And even when the Pehlevi had become the national alphabet of Persia there was very good reason why the cultivators of polite literature should prefer the Palmyrene alphabet for its superior copiousness, their own possessing no more than fifteen distinct characters. And, lastly, the remark of Epiphanius deserves attention as to certain

Western nations then possessing alphabets of their own for it proves, contrary to the received opinion, that as late as A D 400 they had not all been superseded by the Greek or the Latin letters throughout the whole extent of the Roman world

The curious question of these Numerals, and the deep ideas involved therein, has led us far away from the proper object of this chapter—sepulchral scrolls Their use was carried on by the Christians down to comparatively recent times Fauno describes amongst the innumerable *bijoux* of all kinds deposited in the coffin* of the infant imperial bride Maria Honorii " a small plate of gold on which were written, or rather scratched, the words, in Greek, Michael, Gabriel, Raphael, Uriel " And the Abbé Cochet has figured in his very interesting researches † in the old Norman cemeteries many leaden plates, cross-shaped, inscribed with prayers, placed regularly upon the breast of the buried body. Out of four examples found in the old cemetery of Bouteilles, Dieppe, the most complete formula, written in a character that cannot be later than the thirteenth century, runs as follows " Dñs IHC XPC qui dixit discipulis suis quodcunque ligaveritis super terram erit ligatum et in celis quodcunque solveritis super terram erit solutum et in celis de quorum numero licet nos indignos nos esse voluit ipse te absolvet per ministerium nostrum quodcunque fecisti cogitatione locutione negligenter atque necibus omnibus absolutum perducere dignetur in regnum celorum qui vivit et regnat Deus per secula saeculorum amen. Omnipotens Deus misereatur animo Mesaline condonet peccata tibi preterita presentia et futura liberet te ab omni malo conservet et confirmet itinere bono et perducat te Christus filius Dei ad vitam eternam et ad sanctorum consortium absolutione et remissione penitentia tribuat tibi Masaline omnipotens pius et misericors IHC Amen " The Abbé states that it is still the custom in the Russian Church for the *popa* at a funeral, after reading the form of absolution, to place the paper in the hand of the corpse to accompany him into the grave.

The remarkable properties of Numerals captivated the fancy

* Discovered Feb, 1544, in digging the foundations of the Chapel of the Kings of France, in St Peter's, Rome, and fully described by M L Fauno in his 'Antichita di Roma,' p 154 published 1553

† 'Sepultures Gauloises,' chap xiii

of Man as soon as the science of arithmetic was invented. From their powers of infinite multiplication the ancients gave them sexes: making the odd the males, the even the females of the species. This assumption plays a great part in the theosophy of Marcus. From this idea, the next step was a very easy one—the attribution of mystic virtues to certain combinations of numerals that produced curious results by their addition. Of such, the most striking example is the Magic Square; the grand mediæval charm against the plague, and therefore conspicuous in Albert Durer's picture of 'Melancholy,' where the dull goddess sits in gloomy abstraction, surrounded by the emblems of all the arts and sciences. This, which however

4	14	15	1
9	7	6	12
5	11	10	8
16	2	3	13

added, gives the same result, viz., 34.

The celebrated Caireen magician of forty years ago, employed a diagram constructed on the same principle, but with different numerals, into the middle of which, traced on a sheet

4	9	2
3	5	7
8	1	6

of paper, he poured the little pool of ink which served for mirror to exhibit the spectres of the persons called for by his dupes. And, to conclude this subject in an appropriate manner, a fifteenth century MS. in the library of this college, amongst a number of charms, gave this "for procuring favour with all men;" always carry about you written down—

A . X . H . B . X . U . Y . III . K . O

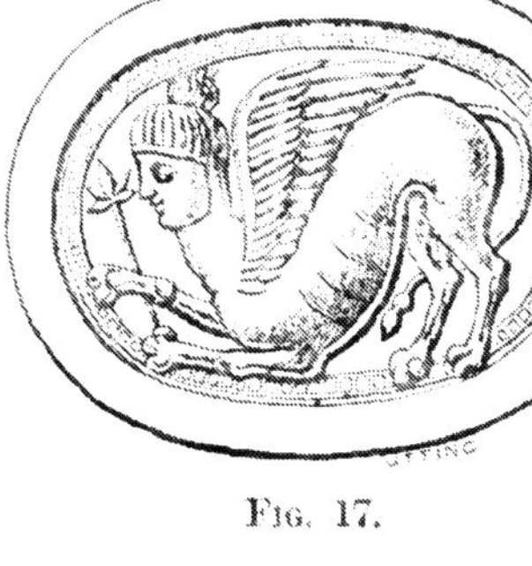

Fig. 17.

PART V.

TEMPLARS, ROSICRUCIANS, FREE-MASONS

"*Inscriptiones* propter quas vadimonium deseri possit at cum intraveris, Di Deaeque! quam nihil in medio invenies" (Plin. H N Praef)

TEMPLARS, ROSICRUCIANS, FREE-MASONS.

PRESERVATION OF GNOSTIC SYMBOLS AMONGST THE FREEMASONS

At the first sight it is absolutely startling to recognise so many Gnostic (primarily Indian) symbols, figuring so conspicuously amongst the insignia and illustrated formulæ of our Freemasons, and that, too, apparently in their original sense as exponents of the deepest mysteries, human and divine—a circumstance of itself lending a specious colour to the pretensions of the Order to the most venerable antiquity "Inscriptiones propter quas vadimonia deseri possint Sed ubi intraveris, Dii Deæque! quam nihil in medio invenies," to quote old Pliny's words in speaking of the charlatans of his day For the pleasing illusion vanishes when we come to investigate the line of their descent; and the Fraternity, though claiming them as its own legitimate inheritance, turns out at the end a mere daw in borrowed plumes

To begin by stating these claims, as recently put forward by one of their most zealous and pugnacious defenders "The mere *title* may be comparatively modern, for the society in antediluvian (!) and prehistorical times most undoubtedly was not called Freemasonry But the *thing* was in existence, and has descended to our own day" "On the arrival of the Romans in Britain, we find Cæsar and several of the Roman generals who succeeded him in the government of the island becoming patrons and protectors of the craft, but there is no information to be found in regard to the usages and customs prevalent among them at that time. Their lodges and conventions were regularly held, but were open only to the initiated fellows There is enough however to show that the same society which now flourishes everywhere was then in existence, holding lodges and conventions and having its initiated fellows. I may add, that a regular list of Grand Masters can be produced quite as genuine and reliable as that of the Archbishops of Canterbury, or of the Kings of England If that in itself is not valid evidence enough of the continued existence of the same society in England from the earliest historical period down to the present date, I don't know what *would* be admitted as sufficient evidence" "Going back to A D 300 we find the Emperor Carausius supporting it, and appointing Albanus, his Steward, Grand Master This was none other than the famous St Alban, the first British martyr, who was born at Verulam, now St Albans, in Hertfordshire"*

The above is an unusually brilliant specimen of the logic of the Brotherhood, that assumes in every notice of *building* and *builders* to be found in antiquity a recognition of the then existence of their own society exactly as at present constituted. The old guild of *working-masons* seems to have made pretensions of the same nature (if we allow the genuineness of the *supposed* Bodleian MS copied by Locke), for their great patron Henry VI informs his scholar that "the Mystery was first brought into England by Peter Gower" (Pythagoras)—a corruption of the name, by the way, plainly betraying that he had obtained this piece of information from a *French mouth*, probably from some one in the suite of his queen. It is not unlikely that this connexion of the Father of Mathematics with the building trade arose from the study of that science by the Greek and Roman architects for upon the vital importance of a knowledge of Mathematics to his own profession Vitruvius repeatedly and strongly insists But this very king, whom our Freemasons claim as their chief resuscitator, furnishes the most conclusive evidence against the reality of their modern pretensions By the advice of the Bishop of Winchester, better known as Cardinal Beaufort, he passed an Act, in his third year, forbidding

* From a letter published in the 'Cork Constitution,' Jan 15 1866, by John Milner, B A, Chaplain to H M S Hector

Masons to hold lodges or any meetings whatsoever, which protection is clearly directed against no higher things than mere "trade-union" proceedings. But at a later period he showed the Masons more favour, and even attended their meetings, as did his contemporary James I. of Scotland. But the question is set at rest by the language of the Act.* "First, Whereas by the assembling congregations and confederacies made by the Masons in their grand chapters and assemblies the good cause and effect of the *Statute of Labourers* be openly violated and broken, in subversion of the law and to the great damage of all the commons, our said Lord the King willing in this case to provide remedy by the advice and assent aforesaid, and at the special request of the said commons, hath ordered and established, that such chapiters and congregations shall not be hereafter made, they that cause such chapiters and congregations to be assembled and holden, if they thereof be convict, shall be judged for felons. And that all the other masons that come to such chapiters and congregations, be punished by imprisonment of their bodies, and make fine and ransom at the king's will."

The language of this Act is sufficiently conclusive, but for accumulation of proofs, I shall proceed to establish the same position by giving a summary of the *oldest*, and only *genuine* document extant on the subject of Masonry. This document is a MS. Bib. Reg. 17. A. I. ff. 32, written in a hand that cannot be *later* than the close of the 13th century, and of which a copy has been published by J. O. Halliwell. It commences with a history of Architecture from the beginning, and of the introduction of the art into England, and then proceeds to give, in rhyme, the Rules of the Craft, conceived in precisely the same business-like spirit as those of a Trades-Union. The preamble is "Hic incipiunt Constitutiones Artis Geometricae secundum Euclydem."† Once upon a time a certain king and his nobles had such large families as to be unable to maintain them decently, and taking counsel together devised they should be

* 'Statutes at Large,' ed. Keble, 1695. 3 Hen. VI. cap. 1.

† What follows is a much condensed summary of the sense of the old Mason's rhymes.

taught some trade whereby to live. A great clerk Euclyde proposed teaching them geometry, called *Masonry*, the most honest craft of all He ordered that the most advanced of his scholars should be styled Master by the rest, but that he should call none of his inferiors either *subject* or *servant*, but always *my dear brother*

> "In this manner by good wit and Geometry,
> Began first the Craft of Masonry"

Euclyde invented and taught the same in Egypt many years afterwards it was brought into England in King Athelstan's time This good king loved the Craft and built many towers, halls, bowers, and temples. But finding out many defects in the Craft he determined to reform the same and summoned an *Assembly* of all the masons in England together with all his lords and commons, and,

> "Fifteen Articles there they brought,
> And Fifteen Points there they wrote"

Art I The master must be just and true, and pay his fellows according to the price of provisions neither exact more from his employer than he pays his men, nor take bribes from either side.

II Every master-mason must attend the general congregation or *Assembly*, wherever it shall be held, unless hindered by sickness, else shall he be accounted disobedient to the Craft and full of falseness

III No prentice to be taken for less than seven years, for in less time he cannot learn his business either to his employer's profit or to his own

IV. No bondsman may be taken for prentice Otherwise it might so happen that his lord might take him out of the *lodge* itself, and so occasion great tumult, for all the masons would stand together by their fellow The prentice must therefore be taken of the master's own degree, but of old times it was ordained he should be of gentle blood, and even great lords' sons took to this geometry.

V The prentice must be of lawful birth, and sound both in mind and body

> "For an imperfect man of such blood,
> Should do the Craft but little good
> A maimed man he hath no might,
> Ye may it knowen long ere night"

VI The master must not take from his employer the same pay for the prentice as for the perfect workman. Nevertheless, before the prentice's time is out, as he increases in knowledge, so may his wages be proportionably raised.

VII The master must neither for love nor money clothe, feed, or harbour a thief, nor a homicide, nor one of bad fame, all which would bring the Craft to shame

VIII. If the master finds any of his men incompetent he must turn him off, and take another in his place, "as such a hand would do the Craft short worship'

IX The master must undertake no job that he is unable to finish, and must see that he lays the foundation so that it will neither give nor crack

X No master-mason must supplant another under penalty of ten pounds unless where the work has tumbled down through the incompetence of the first builder In all points of this "curious Craft" masons must live together like brethren

XI. No mason is to work by night unless for the sake of trying experiments for amending errors

XII. No mason must disparage the work of another, but rather must praise the same, and if wrong, privately advise him how to aright it

XIII The prentice must be taught every branch of the business, and be put upon work suitable to his ability

XIV. The master must take no prentices, unless he have divers jobs in hand, in order to teach them the trade

XV The prentice must be a friend to his master, never deceive him for the sake of another, neither stand by his fellows in a wrong cause, nor take a false oath

These *Fifteen Points* were likewise ordained at the aforesaid Assembly —

I The mason must love God, Holy Church, and his fellow-masons, wheresoever he may go

II. The mason must work as truly as he can upon the work-day, and so deserve his pay upon the holy day.

III The prentice is on no account to divulge any trade secrets

> "This Third Point it must be special,
> Let the prentice know it well,
> His master's counsel he keep and close,
> And his fellows', by good purpose,
> The secrets of the *chamber* he tell to none,
> Nor in the *lodge* whatever is done
> Whatever thou seest or hearest them do,
> Tell it no man wherever thou go
> The counsel of hall and eke of bower,
> Keep it well in great honour,
> Lest it should bring thyself to blame,
> And bring the Craft into great shame"

IV That no mason be false to the Craft nor maintain his cause against it. neither do prejudice to master nor fellow, and that the prentice stand in awe

V. The master must take his wages, whatever ordained him, without disputing The master, if unable to find them work as before, to give them warning in the forenoon.

VI If any dispute or quarrel arise amongst the masons, the master must make them put off the settlement thereof until the next holy day, and not allow it to be settled upon a work-day, lest it should hinder the work in hand

VII Not to lie with thy master's or fellow's wife or concubine under penalty of serving another seven years of prenticeship

VIII If thou hast taken any job under thy master, be a faithful middleman between thy master and thy fellows.

IX When the fellows have a *common chamber* then they must take the stewardship in turns, week by week. All victuals to be paid for as received, and regular accounts to be kept of the common expenses

> "Of thy fellows' goods that thou hast spent,
> When, and how, and to what end,
> Such accounts thou must come to
> When thy fellows would thou do"

X. If a mason lives amiss and is false to his work, he must, without favour, be convened before the Assembly, and punished according to the law of old ordained or, in case he refuses to appear, he must forswear the profession.

XI. If a skilled mason observe his fellow cutting a stone and likely to spoil it through his own ignorance, he must advise him in fair words, and teach him how to amend it, not to bring shame upon the whole work

XII That whatever shall be ordained in the Assembly, being present the master and fellows, nobles, burghers, and the sheriff of the county, and the mayor of the town, *that* thou shall maintain against all thy fellows, if disposed to dispute the same

XIII. The mason must swear never to be a thief himself, nor for any fee or reward to abet one that is

XIV. Before the Assembly breaks up, each must be sworn unto his master and fellows, to the king, and to all these present Also they must seek out every one that hath contravened any one law thereof, and bring them up before the Assembly

XV. And if found guilty, they must forswear the Craft

> "And so mason s craft they must refuse,
> And swear it never more to use,"

unless they consent to make amends. If refractory, the sheriff is to cast them into prison during the king's good pleasure, and take their goods and chattels for the king s use The Assembly must be held every year, or at least every third year Unto the same must come every man of the Craft, and all the great nobles, to amend all infractions, and to swear obedience to the Constitutions of King Athelstan, and especially to make bold petition to the king that he stand by the masons everywhere and enforce the same statutes

Next follows 'Ars Quattuor Coronatorum,' a manual of religious and moral duties, and also of good manners in company.

> "The Four Masters—
> Who were as good Masons as on earth could go,
> Gravers and image-makers they were also,"

were commanded by the Emperor to make an idol to be worshipped On their refusal he first imprisoned and tortured them, and at last put them to death These be the "Quattuori

Coronati," and their festival falls on the eighth day after All Saints Many years after Noah's Flood, was begun the Tower of Babylon. It was built up to the height of seven miles, by order of Nebuchadnezzar, for a refuge in case of another deluge But an angel, in order to punish his pride, smote all the builders with confusion of tongues After this Euclid taught geometry, and gave his scholars the following rules

Behaviour in Church—To use the holy-water on going in to kneel down, never sit nor stand, make no noise nor talk, but pray all the time, saying certain prayers given in the text. To attend mass daily, but if at work to repeat a certain prayer upon hearing the mass-bell.

In Company—On coming before a lord, to doff cap or hood nor put in on again until bid, make two or three bows with the right leg, hold up thy chin, look him sweetly in the face, do not scrape the foot, nor spit or blow thy nose On entering a hall amongst the *gentelles*, be not presumptuous on account of thy birth or skill

> "In hall or chamber where thou dost gan,
> Good manners make the man"

When sitting down to meat, see thy hands be clean and knife sharp cut the bread and meat ready for eating If sitting by a worshipful man, suffer him to help himself first. Keep thy hands clean, smudge not the napkin, on which thou must not blow thy nose nor pick thy teeth at table, neither drink with anything in the mouth, nor dip thy chin too deep in the cup, nor talk to thy neighbour when drinking

> "In chamber among the ladies bright,
> Spare thy tongue, and spend thy sight"

Talk not of thine own matters, neither for mirth nor for mede Play only with thine equals On meeting a man of worship be sure to cap him, walk a little way behind him, never interrupt his speech, be brief and fair in thy replies, &c

> "Christ then, of his grace,
> Give you both the wit and space
> Well this book to con and read,
> Heaven to have for your mede
> Amen! Amen! So mote it bee!
> So say we all *par charite*"

Any reader of common intelligence will perceive that the good priest, author of this the oldest extant document upon Masonry, had not the remotest idea of the same as being the possession of a *secret society*, established for some hidden end, whether religious or political The very rules which he professes to transcribe from the Constitutions of Athelstan, are as plain-spoken, matter-of-fact as those of a modern Trades-Union, differing only from the latter in the larger admixture of common sense and honesty that they display, the whole winding up with directions for behaviour in good society, as laid down by some anticipatory Chesterfield. The "secrets of the lodge" are manifestly nothing more than matters pertaining to the trade discussed amongst the masons at their lodgings after work, and very inexpedient for them to be divulged to outsiders And to come to the most essential point of the question which these Constitutions fully establish, "the Assembly" is, so far from being a secret chapter, held by the Free and Accepted Brethren only, that it *must* actually be presided over by the sheriff of the county, and the mayor of the town where it is held ! for the purpose of settling all matters connected with the building-trade, being in fact nothing more than what was called in those times an "Assize of Labour"

An interesting feature in the treatise is the fact of its ascribing these same "Constitutions" to King Athelstan. There is very good reason for accepting this statement as founded upon trustworthy tradition The Saxon Prince was the first British sovereign who possessed either wealth or inclination for decorative architecture or building of any sort His father, Edward the Elder, and his aunt Ethelfleda "the Lady of Mercia," are recorded as the first of the Saxon line who built fortifications of stone about their chief cities Before this the Saxons, like all other Teutons, had no other idea of building than of constructions in wood, all stone-masons had to be brought over from France when wanted (as numerous references, unnecessary here to quote, conclusively evince), in which country architecture had kept up a feeble existence after the fall of the Empire, its preservation being due to the patronage of the Church, which kept growing in wealth and power in proportion as the Roman authority died away. The simplicity of the Constitutions in prescribing the convening of mere *craftsmen* under the presidency of the sheriff and mayor, betokens a truly Saxon state of society, and moreover a time when these masons were actually working-men. Under the Normans, regular architects (in one sense) first appear as the "Masters," who were almost invariably churchmen. Furthermore, the prohibition against taking a "*bondman*" for prentice unmistakably betokens the same early period, when domestic slavery, not mere *villanage*, was recognised by law: the Norman legislation makes no such distinction of bond and free.

Aubrey indeed quotes the authority of Dugdale that "the Fraternity of Adopted Masons," having *signs* and *passwords* for the purpose of mutual recognition, owed its origin to a company of Italian masons, who in Henry III.'s time obtained a patent from the Pope to go about Europe, building churches. But the absurdity of this statement is manifested by a single fact: when the Italians of that period wished to erect any important edifice, so far from being competent to do so for other nations, they were forced to call in architects from Germany and France. To give a few decisive examples, as regards the wealthiest and most polished states of that country:—Pisa employed Guglielmo il *Tedesco* to plan her celebrated Campanile; Florence, Lapo, *alias* Jacopo il *Tedesco*, father of Arnolfo (who had already gained high reputation by the triple church he had built at Assisi for the Franciscans), to construct their bridge "Alla Carraia," the Bargello or Townhall, several churches, and to drain the Piazza Grande. Even a century later the Visconti were obliged to employ German architects to design the Duomo at Milan. It is true Henry III. had in his pay one Peter "civis Romanus," but only in the capacity of a decorative artist, for the mosaic work at the Westminster Shrine. But in truth, during the entire Gothic period, architecture, as a national art, may be said to have been extinct in Italy, the grand centre of the art then being established in the very middle of France.

All this evidence goes to show that our Freemasons have no

relationship, either actual or traditional, with the mediæval guilds bearing the same appellation, a pretence they so zealously maintain. The latter were corporations of real workmen, in which each person, after serving a regular apprenticeship, and, according to the custom still kept up in some counties, producing a *trial-piece* to prove his competency, was admitted "free" of the Guild, and "accepted" amongst the members of the same. The compotations accompanying the ceremony are in truth the sole point of resemblance between the ancient and the modern Freemasons.

The 'Bulletin Monumental' for 1884, p 34, contains a memoir, "Les signes de Tacherons sur les remparts d'Avignon," which gives the fullest collection (six pages) of these marks that has ever been published. They can be here traced from Roman times where they appear as single letters or as Trionian shorthand, down to the actual Masons' Marks of mediæval and modern times. Many clearly represent the tools used in building Some of these marks, and more of those from Avignon, are to be recognised upon Lichfield's "Baphometic Tablet," which may, after all, be no modern forgery, but a genuine register of such segli of the seventeenth century *

The mediæval guild of Masons, as we have seen, was no more a *secret society* than were the guilds of Carpenters, Cordwainers or Tailors Every man indeed belonging to the first-named (and this is the only thing belonging to the Craft, that really carries with it an air of mysterious antiquity) had, upon admission, a *mark* (or cypher) assigned him, which he was bound to put upon every stone he dressed (a rule still observed) in order to distinguish his work from that of his fellows, against the time when the materials should be examined by the master-mason, who paid him for those approved, but stopped his wages for those spoiled through his fault Similarly every "Merchant of the Staple" joined with his initials upon his seal, or trade mark, the *mark* of the staple-town to which he belonged This latter, though

* Most interesting of all, on account of their early date, are the Masons' Marks at Westminster Hall, lately published by Dr Freshfield, in the Archæologia, Vol 50, Part I

much alike in outline, was variously modified so as to indicate each of the fifteen towns in England, Ireland, and Wales, appointed by Edward III In all mediæval documents relating to building, the name "Freemason" signifies merely the worker in hewn stone, the inferior workman who ran up the body of the wall in rubble or ragstone being called the "Rough-waller" Lastly, a very puzzling question presents itself—if our Freemasons be the legitimate successors in an unbroken line of the ancient lodges and guilds, how came it that all the principles of Gothic architecture were utterly lost within less than a century?

But to return to the marks themselves, of which many collections have been published gathered from regions the most widely separated. Their history is indeed full of interest but likewise of obscurity, "res alta nocte et caligine mersae" Many of them are traditional, and go back to the highest antiquity, being found on Phœnician* and Greek buildings (as well as on vases and coins of the earliest times), and in still larger abundance and variety in all mediæval architecture These marks were in the beginning religious symbols, many of them being identical with the *caste-marks*, whereby to this day the followers of the respective Hindoo gods are distinguished from one another This religious significance explains also their occurrence on Celtic monuments, as on the Stonehenge lintel, and the Newton Stone, Aberdeen, and so numerously on the Gallic coins, but they have for centuries, further back than can be traced, degenerated into the mere signatures of illiterate mechanics.† To illustrate this curious point, I shall adduce a

* A most interesting example is the stone in the second course of the Temple Wall, S E Jerusalem, discovered Jan 1869 It bears two marks, deeply cut, ᚼH and H Other marks in *red paint* resemble Phœnician letters Deutsch observed many such on the walls of the old Castle of Sidon, built from ancient materials He considers them numeral, unity to 9 being represented by vertical lines, 10 by a horizontal, 20 by two parallels, &c It is, however ridiculous to attribute the foundation of the Temple Wall to Solomon's architects, the fact of its being cut through ten feet of rubbish thrown from above proves it to have been done long *after* the city was inhabited, and therefore the work of Agrippa

† Who have introduced a refinement upon the old system, viz, the necessity of every mark terminating in an odd number of *ends*

few of the most remarkable examples of lapidary symbolism,* giving, as in duty bound, precedence to the late discovery at Stonehenge. The mark is cut upon the fallen impost lying across the supposed altar. It is nine inches long and clearly defined, and may be described as a semicircle of which the diameter being produced, its own length terminates in a second semicircle reversed and open, combined with the Roman letters, L, V; having in fact much the appearance of a *sigla* or *nota scriptoria*. The mark has therefore something in its look that suggests the signature LVCIUS Had the sagacious Stukeley discovered this inscription he would unquestionably upon the strength thereof have ascribed the whole fabric to the British Lucius so renowned in fable It must not however be concealed that our fashionable scepticism has impugned the reality of even this most venerable "handwriting on the wall" Dr. Thurman has hunted up three credible witnesses ready to make affidavit that they saw with their own eyes a certain stranger cut the sigil † But inasmuch as it would be equally facile, by means of *leading questions* dexterously put, to obtain the testimony of the same number of "bucolical juveniles" that they were present at the erection of Stonehenge itself, the genuineness of the mark (so *un*modern in configuration) seems to me in no measure disproved Symbolic figures, spirals and interesting circles are found on the stones in Newton Grange, Drogheda Cave, Routh Linn, Old Berwick, Doddington Moor, Northumberland, Long Meg, Cumberland The latter have been published in the Archæological Journal.

But to proceed to actual Caste-marks We find a casual allusion to their use in ancient writers, who state that the badges distinguishing the three orders of the Egyptian priest-

xix p 78 ‡

* Regular Masons' marks are visible upon the great hewn stones of the Buddhist buildings at Sarnath, which are known to have been erected before the sixth century, and more of the same kind are found on the ruined buildings of the same religion still to be traced incorporated into the Brahminical edifices within the neighbouring Benares Sherring, 'Sacred City of the Hindus'

† It must be remembered the stone is so hardened by weathering as to turn the best chisel!

‡ Lists of Masons' marks have been published in the following works 'Archæologia' (1845), for Scotland, by Prof Chalmers, Marks

hood were the ⊖ signifying the *sun*, the ⊤ *eternal life*, and the △ *pleasure.* With the Hindoos, the equilateral Triangle symbolises Mahadeva, or Siva, that is, the element Fire personified The same figure *inverted* stands for Vishnu, Water

The two, intersecting each other, form the *Sherkun* or six-points, that is, the two elements in conjunction

The five-pointed figure, made by bisecting the sides of an equilateral triangle by a line as long as one side, and drawing lines from each extremity of the said line to each foot of the triangle, symbol of Siva and Brahma (the latter god having *five* heads) became, later, the famous "Solomon's Seal" This appellation it must have got in early times, as in virtue thereof it is sculptured along with the seven-branched candlestick upon Jewish tombs dating from the Lower Empire * The Hindoos still venerate the figure as replete with virtue Similarly the *Sherkun* is engraved on a large scale upon each side of the gate of the Fort at Agra, although the building is of Mohammedan work

A point, *Puru* is the Deity, self existing A circle, *Brahm*, eternity Hence a triangle within a circle is the emblem of Trinity in Unity, and the circle inscribed within a triangle the converse

Worshippers of *Sacti*, the Female Principle, mark their sacred vase with a right angle bisected by a line, and similarly the worshippers of Isis used so to mark the vessel necessary at her rites. But the Vishnaivas have for the same object a symbol of wondrous vitality and diffusion for it is seen equally on Greek coins and vases, on the Newton Stone, Aberdeen, in ecclesiastical sculpture, where it takes the name "Tetragam-

at Brechin, and signatures to St Ninian's Roll, coming down to the date 1814 Ditto, for 1844 contains a memoir by G Godwin, with five plates of marks from England (Gloucester, Tewkesbury) France, Germany (Koln) 'Annales Archeologiques' (1844–5) 'Signes Lapidaires,' from Coucy, Avignon Palais de Justice, Paris, Vincennes Rheims, Strasburgh Most curious of all are those given by Ouseley ('Travels,' pl 82), as "characters of some unknown alphabet," found by him on the stones of the Old Palace (a Mohammedan building) of Saaditalat, near Ispahan, which nevertheless have a striking resemblance to the European class.

* Numerous examples may be seen in their catacomb at Rome, lately discovered

maton," being ignorantly supposed the compounds of the letter Γ four times repeated, and its sound and power confounded with those of the sacred "Tetragrammaton," or the Hebrew quadriliteral name Jehovah This mark is properly the symbol of Sitala, the seventh incarnation, entitled "Trithalesor," a title exactly translated by the alchemical *Trismegistus* its name is the *Suastika*, an emblem of Resignation, so that the figure may have passed into Byzantine art with some recommendation from a knowledge of its real meaning. In Gothic nomenclature this mark becomes the equally renowned "Fylfot," as to whose etymology the following conjecture may be hazarded The Swastika signified at first the arms crossed over the breast, the regular Indian gesture of submission, and also the legs similarly folded as the statues of Buddha are usually represented The symbol is evidently nothing more than the rough outline of the arms and legs thus disposed May not therefore the Gothic name *Fylfot*, applied to the same hieroglyph, bear through some remote tradition a reference to its real meaning, and imply the sense of *Fold-foot*? In the same way the old Greeks appear to have recognised its true sense, when they changed its simple form into the three conjoined legs that so aptly allude to the name Trinacria In all probability the great popularity of the symbol, wheresoever the Indo-Germanic race penetrated, was due to the same feeling that renders it still so respected in the land of its origin, its power as a talisman to protect all places where the figure is painted up The exclamation "Swastika" the Hindoos still employ as a mode of assent, synonymous with "Amen," "So be it" * As the symbol of Resignation the Mark forms the distinctive badge of an ascetic When a man desires to become a *Bandya* (Buddhist monk) the rites required for his initiation occupy three days, foremost amongst which the Swastika is solemnly set up upon an altar of unbaked bricks, the neophyte being seated on the ground with his legs disposed after the same fashion In China the Mark is the badge of the *Pon*, the strictest sect of Buddhists, who attribute its invention to Buddha himself, about six centuries before our era This

* Or, to speak masonically, "So mote it be!"

fact may explain how "denying oneself and taking up the cross" came to signify the embracing an ascetic life, for so evident are the traces of Buddhist influence over the institutions of the Essenes, that it is probable enough the symbol retained its pristine acceptation amongst the sect.

The Swastika occurs amongst the signet-devices of the old Jaina kings of Guzerat (belonging to the far-removed epoch of Buddhist supremacy in Hindostan), in company with that intricate square figure which when appearing on Greek works is denominated a *Labyrinth*. Other sectarian Marks are three parallel lines placed horizontally, or vertically, to denote their respective deities: others of truly Masonic aspect, are the wheel, crescent, heart, *vesica piscis*, all variously modified to express ritualistic differences. That the Gnostics borrowed many of these symbols directly from Buddhism,* adding them to their old stock of Egyptian devices, is apparent upon the inspection of any large collection of Abraxas gems. The lingering influence of this importation continually peep out where least to be expected. In the finest known MS of the Apocalypse, the work of a French illuminator about the middle of the thirteenth century (in the library of Trinity College, Cambridge), the most elaborate of all its decorations is the heading to chapter xiv, filling half a page. It represents "The Lamb standing upon Mount Zion," surrounded by the saints; above, is the Godhead, typified by an immense golden *Quatrefoil*, encompassed by the Four Beasts which bear the names of the Evangelists; at each side and below are the Four-and-twenty Elders, arranged in groups of six, eight, and ten. Within the Quatrefoil is seen an empty throne covered with a cloth crossed by diagonal blue lines, in each diagonal so formed is painted in red a circle containing a point. This *geometrical* expression of the idea of the Deity, so opposed to the characteristic anthropomorphism of regular Gothic art, may perhaps have been inspired by the Manicheist spirit that still actuated the Southern French. But to go back to the source—in the

* Scythicus, the preceptor of Manes, is actually declared by Epiphanius to have picked up his novel ideas during his visits to India as a trader from Alexandria.

Chinese system, *Yang*, the Male, Active, Principle has for his own possession, the Sun, Fire, and all the higher phenomena of Nature to him belong the uneven numbers *Yn*, the Female, Passive, Principle, possesses the Earth, Moon, and the even numbers. The same notion as to the sexes of Numbers was taught by Pythagoras, and by the Gnostic Marcus, after him *Yang* is represented by the circle, *Yn* by the square, the two Forces combined, by two interlaced circles, ⚭, the actual badge of the Mediæval Vehm-Gerichte

Having thus briefly noticed our Masonic Symbols, let us proceed to consider the society itself, and here a circumstance of the utmost importance to this inquiry must always be kept in view the Freemasons, as at present organised into a mystic fraternity, derive their name from nothing but an *accidental* circumstance belonging to their first establishment It was in the Common Hall of the London Guild of the Freemasons (the trade) that their first meetings were held, under Christopher Wren for president, in the time of the Commonwealth * Their real object was political—the restoration of Monarchy—hence the exclusion of the public, and the oath of secrecy enjoined upon the members The pretence of promoting the study of architecture, and the choice of the place where to hold their meetings, suggested by the profession of their president, were no more than blinds to deceive the existing government. There is a curious analogy to all this in the history of another famous society, the Neapolitan *Carbonari*, which similarly derived its name, terminology and insignia from the accidental circumstances under which it was created. Like Wren's associates, the first Carbonari were defeated Royalists and fanatical Republicans joined in unnatural union by one common hatred of the powers that be—the old Bourbonists equally with the chimerical founders of the shortlived "Parthenopean Republic," equally forced to flee for their lives to the mountains, the former to escape the well-deserved vengeance of the French under Murat, the latter so fiercely persecuted by Cardinal

* In April, 1646, when Ashmole was admitted member Others named as present on that occasion were Lilly the astrologer, Dr Pearson, the two Whartons, Hewitt, and Oughtred the mathematician

Ruffo upon the first restoration of royalty at Naples. These desperate men, lurking about in the Abruzzi forests, were forced to assume the disguise of the only inhabitants of these wild regions, the *carbonari*, charcoal-burners, as the best means of eluding pursuit. After their forces had grown to a regular confederation, the disguise, so suggestive and terror inspiring, was retained for a *uniform*, a charcoal-sack was the badge of membership, a charcoal-measure the throne of the President, and their conclaves were held by rule in the midnight forest When Ferdinand, "the Well-beloved," was firmly seated on his ancient throne, for the third and last time, his diligent eradication of his former friends, the Constitutionals, folks almost equally crazed with the original "Parthenopean" patriots, sent thousands of exiles to swell the ranks of the Carbonari. Soon the society was able to establish ramifications all over Italy, thanks to the paternal government of the Austrians and their *protégés*, the various restored princes of the Bourbon and Este lines, and thus in our own times *Carbonaro* and *Liberal* came to mean pretty nearly the same thing, and the Italian "Carbonaro" to know no more about charcoal-burning than the English "Mason" does about building.

But although this Society of Freemasons was convoked in London, and established branches all over England, furnishing also the members with the means for secret recognition, and all for a political end, yet in its true origin Freemasonry had nothing political in its nature, neither was the aforesaid convocation in London the real commencement of its existence This final organisation was only the adaptation to a special end of another society, then in fullest bloom, the *Rosicrucian* If we reflect how rankly both astrology and alchemy were flourishing at that time in England,* and that the Rosicrucian sect was essentially of *Protestant* growth, we may on good grounds conclude that this sect already numbered many English members from amongst the educated classes and the philosophers of the

* Oxford produced the two great lights of the Hermetic philosophy, Robert de Fluctibus (Fludd) and his contemporary Eugenius Philalethes (Thos Vaughan) The latter, born in 1612, is said by a writer of the year 1749 to be then living at Nuremberg, as the president of the *illuminated* throughout the world

day These last were for the most part ardent Royalists, hating the established order of things, joined with many fanatical Republicans equally impatient of the new despotism of Cromwell. In the Rosicrucian system Religion and Philosophy, the latter meaning little more than astrology and alchemy,* were strangely interwoven, and the terminology of the one was borrowed to express the ideas and aspirations of the other This hypothesis is strongly recommended from its adoption by the acute De Quincey in his essay entitled "Freemasons and Rosicrucians" ('London Magazine,' 1824), where he shows how the Rosicrucians, when driven by persecution out of Germany, re-appeared in England as Freemasons, taking that name from the place of meeting, and from nothing else Under the new appellation the sect was re-imported into the Continent as an *English* institution De Quincey, however, makes their object to have been purely religious without any admixture of politics, and so far differs from Nicolai, whose views have been adopted by myself in what precedes, and who, being himself an *illuminato* of the first water, ought certainly to be regarded as the higher authority of the two

The latter writer has given in his 'Tempel-Herren' what appears to be the best supported account of the rise† and progress of Rosicrucianism He points out for its founder a Lutheran mystic, J V. Andreæ,‡ almoner to the Duke of

* The position of the latter science in this century cannot be more strongly exemplified than by the actual existence of current coins declaring themselves to be made out of Hermetic metal by the symbols for mercury and lead (☿ ♄) stamped on their reverse Examples are three ducats of Gustavus Adolphus (Paris Cabinet), thalers of Wilhelm, Landgrave of Hesse, and contemporary coins of the city of Erfurt This subject has been well handled by Martin Reg in his memoir, "Anciennes Pièces Hermétiques," 'Revue Numismatique' for 1867

† 'The Rosicrucians their Rites and Mysteries, with Chapters on the ancient Fire-and-Serpent Worshippers, and explanations of the Mystic Symbols represented in the Monuments and Talismans of the Primæval Philosophers' By Hargrave Jennings, London, 1870 A truly 'Masonic' production, without "method in its madness," but valuable for giving many Rosicrucian (or rather Kabbalistic) expositions of symbols, extracted from Fludd's writings The compiler has moreover, laid my 'Gnostics' largely under contribution, and even reproduced my engravings with sundry fanciful improvements that wonderfully heighten their mystic value

‡ Solomon Sember, however, in

Wurtemberg early in the seventeenth century. At least, the writings of this divine, wherein the *Rosy Cross* prominently figures were the first indications that made the existence of the fraternity known to the outer world. But Andreæ appears to have done no more than borrow the symbols and occult means of communication already existing from time immemorial amongst the astrologers and alchemists (in other words the wealthy and the learned of the age, when the Emperor Rudolf II was the greatest patron of the "curious arts" ever recorded in history) in order to employ them on the furtherance of a visionary scheme of his own. This scheme was the fusion of all Christian sects * into one universal brotherhood, and the projector wisely commenced his apostleship by attempting to bring over to his side the most eminent of the mass by the utilization of such ancient and venerated machinery. The well-meaning enthusiast had evidently disregarded the remark of the sagacious Julian (Am. Mar. xxi. 5), confirmed as it is by the experience of every succeeding generation, owes as much as any, "Nullas infestas hominibus bestias ut sunt sibi ferales plerique Christianorum." As a matter of course, his scheme of universal brotherhood dissolved in smoke as soon as established, but the older philosophy, whose garb he had adopted, bloomed with fresh vigour under the new organisation and euphonious name.

But before going any further, let us for diversion's sake hear the Rosicrucians' own story, and examine some of their doctrines and insignia, which have an important bearing upon the subject of our inquiry. The Rosicrucians, says Boyle, make their founder to have been a certain German, only known as A. C., who having gone to Damascus in the year 1387, was instructed in their mysteries by the *College of Arabian Sages* †

his 'Collections for the History of Rosicrucianism,' assigns a fabulous antiquity to the sect.

* Exactly the same scheme, based upon Judaism, is the crime that now keeps in perpetual imprisonment Nicholas Ilyin, the far-famed 'Convent Spectre" of Solovetsk in the Frozen Sea, universally believed in Russia to be the lost Grand Duke Constantine.—(Dixon's 'Free Russia.')

† This tradition may have some truth in it, allowing for an error of locality. At *Cairo* the Fatemite sultans (Ismaelites be it remembered) had three centuries before this date

there established. Returning home he communicated his knowledge to a small number of chosen associates, dying in 1484. It is a matter of importance to notice that in this legend Syria is made the fountain head of the new philosophy. The Rosicrucian Creed, according to the 'Essay on Spirits' (dedicated to Mr Locke, 1647), contains, amongst others, this palpable adoption of the Pythagorean system:—

> "Ante omnia Punctum extitit non mathematicum, sed diffusivum extrinsecæ Monados, intrinsecæ Myriados, omnia et nihil, Est et Non.
>
> Haec Monas commovebat se in Dyadas, et per Triadas egressæ sunt facies luminis secundi.
>
> Hic respiciens superiorem et inferiorem Parentem iisdem deinde protulit Vultum Triformem."

In the second paragraph Clarkson* discovers an allusion to the Vesica Piscis, which is in truth a figure generated by two circles intersecting at their respective centres, and for the same reason, the secret sign of the Brethren of the Vehme-Gerichte was the two annular links of a chain. The Egg formed by *three* intersecting circles, contains in its upper section seven triangles, and as many in its lower section, which are the opposing genii of Light and Darkness. This was the *idol* which the Manichæans were accused of worshipping on the charges brought against them by the Popes (Clarkson, p. 20). Still more does the "Vultus Triformis" of this Creed arrest our attention as bearing a more than accidental affinity to the triple-faced idol, the adoration whereof was so persistently laid to the charge of the Templars—the real meaning of which accusa-

founded the far-famed lodge, entitled 'the House of Wisdom." Here the student passed through *nine degrees*, beginning with Obedience, Mysticism, Philosophy, Doubt, &c., up to Absolute Incredulity. William of Tyre (xix. 17) tells a wonderful story, how Hugo of Cæsarea and Geffroi of the Temple, envoys to Cairo on business of the Order, were led by the Soldan himself to the palace Kashef, and conducted through numerous courts of the richest architecture, full of strange birds and beasts, to the inmost hall, where the Soldan having first adored the unseen 'Master," the curtains of gold and pearl were suddenly drawn back, and that dignitary appeared seated in unspeakable glory on a golden throne, attended by his chief officials.

* 'The Symbolical Evidence of the Temple Church. Were the Templars Gnostics?'

tion shall be investigated in its proper place This same "tête d'un homme monstrueuse," image of "le Dieu qui ne meurt pas" so often mentioned in the confessions of the Knights, may be recognised beyond all mistake in the hideous head with flaring hair and beard, and eyes wide open, as if just severed from the body, placed upon a box inscribed X P S, which repeatedly occurs amongst the Rosicrucian pictures in the Diary of Hosea Lux. This MS, the most remarkable of the kind extant, or ever composed, written between the years 1568 and 1612, is full of mystic drawings, beautifully done in pen and ink, which may be either prophetic hieroglyphs, or else enshroud the *arcana* of some seeker after the Elixir of Life the latter it would rather seem, to judge from the perpetual introduction of certain *very significant* emblems The author must have belonged (as an actual Mason assures me) to a Lodge of Templars, as is proved by his use of the "hand in hand" and "foot to foot" insignia As exhibiting the whole list of the present Masonic signs, but employed for Rosicrucian purposes, at so early a date, this Diary is of the utmost value to the history of the Order * To quote a few of the most important embellishments of these mystic pages the same "Baphometic" Head appears in another place set on a box inscribed with "Solomon's Seal," containing a retort over the head is a disk, set all round dial fashion but with hearts instead of numerals, in the field is written the opposite motto "Timore et tremore" Another is picture presents the Head hovering above the Ark of the Covenant, all enclosed within the outline of a *heart* out of whose aorta issues a naked boy bearing a flaming star and crescent conjoined. Yet more mysterious is the heart containing T over a bell resting upon a star above all, for a crest is set Solomon's Seal, for supporters to the shield, his pillars Jachin and Boaz, flanked on the right by that King seated, on the left by a naked man standing, who pierces the heart with a long rod. Singular, too, is the man with uplifted hands, having instead of a face Solomon's Seal enclosing a retort Other symbols

* Through the kindness of the present owner, Mr J F Hodgkin, F S A I have had opportunity to make a minute examination of the MS

frequently occurring on these pictures are the naked boy extended on the spokes of a wheel, or again placed upon an egg set in a candlestick the king's bust crowned with the winged crescent (on which the merest novice in alchemy can discern the allusion to *regulus* of antimony and *quicksilver*) the egg containing a circle whence issue rays of light, probably typifying the *crucible*, for another heading shows the same figure within a furnace with the infant *metal* springing rapturously from its womb, the five links of a chain interlaced all these being Rosicrucian emblems now embalmed in the repertory of the Freemasons These drawings, besides their artistic value with respect to their fertile invention and incredibly minute finish (Lux being a copper-plate engraver of some eminence), are highly interesting as pictorial exponents of the Hermetic philosophy still so flourishing at the time of their execution Of such designs, nothing can surpass in elaborate execution and impenetrable mystery the large drawing of the naked female standing upon musical notes, holding in her right a torch tipped with a beautiful face whence issue flames, an owl perched upon her extended left hand, on her breast for brooch Sol's head in a crescent Upon a pedestal is set a tall long-necked alembic containing the most obvious emblem of the generative power, emitting upwards the stream of Life, which is caught into the mouth of a cherub whose hair forms a bunch of flowers supporting the before-mentioned disk of hearts, whilst his hand holds forth a wheatsheaf In the field lies a crown over a marshal's bâton shaped like a phallas Another drawing full of interest is the portrait of a man in a fur cap with plume, wearing round his neck a pendant inscribed like the jewel of the G A, from which again is hung a human foot, with his right hand he points to a crescent divided into three parts enclosing X A P, his left rests on the head of a mighty hammer De Quincey, in the above quoted essay, describes a manuscript work by Simon Stadion, of Wurtemberg, written in the year 1604, under the title, "Naometria, seu nuda et prima Libri intus et foris scripti Expositio, et Prognosticticus" It is a series of dreams and prophecies based upon the Apocalypse in which he speaks of "Stellæ matutinæ ductu anno 1572 conspectæ"; and constantly brings in the Rose and Cross, on which account he is generally supposed to have been a Rosicrucian Martin Luther also took for his seal the Rose and Cross; some deep religious significance, at the time well understood, must have recommended the device to the choice of the "Tertius Elias"

Besides these obligations to the Rosicrucians, the London Freemasons also borrowed much of their phraseology from Lord Bacon's work, still fresh in men's minds, in which, adopting the idea of the "House of Wisdom," a technical term with the Arab astrologers, he proposed the foundation of a "Solomon's House," or learned community dedicated to the cultivation of experimental philosophy and the advancement of science These philosophic and royalist plotters, in order to cloak the true nature of their proceedings, conducted their conclaves according to the rules prescribed by Bacon and the same ceremonial and nomenclature they carefully maintain to the present day

A final and demonstrative proof of the recent and *English* origin of Freemasonry is afforded by the dates of institution of the various Foreign Lodges, which are by their own profession branches of the parent Society in London The Parisian was not founded until the year 1725, the Madrid in 1728, and the Florentine in 1733. And yet France and Italy had been the birthplace of the actual *art* of masonry, and the scene of the full glory of its revival

Another important fact remains to be noticed, the *Rosicrucians* still subsist amongst the Parisian Freemasons as the designation for their highest degree (to be conferred upon distinguished English visitors), although all disclaim those mystics as being the parent stock, inasmuch as that truth, if allowed, were utterly incompatible with their own claim to immemorial antiquity Nevertheless, they loudly profess to trace their descent through the line of the Templars down from that splendidly fabulous origin they arrogate to themselves

But to return to Andreæ, and the honour Nicolai assigns him as the creator of the immediate parent of modern Freemasonry, certain it is that his far-famed Rosy Cross had been ages before the regular badge of the Knights Templars Considering how widely the Order had spread its branches, obtained possession and affiliated to itself multitudes both male and female amongst the laity all over Europe, it would be a mere absurdity to believe that all its traditions were swept away at one stroke by the suppression of the Templars in the year 1307.* In fact, the Parisian *Templiers*, as the most important division of the French Freemasons still style themselves, pretend to have kept up the succession of Grand Masters unbroken, nay more, to have preserved the archives of the Order ever since that date. François I is even reported to have burnt alive, with a contrivance of refined cruelty in "The fiery bath," four unfortunate gentlemen convicted of being Templars,† which, if true, suffices to prove the existence of that fraternity down to a period but little removed from the public manifestation of the Rosicrucians. Truly was he by such proceedings "semina odii in longum jaciens," to borrow the forcible simile of Tacitus, if we are to believe Barruel's express declaration that Spartacus Weishaupt's *Jacobins* did no more than pay to royalty the so long deferred legacy of revenge handed down to them by generation after generation of secret societies—fulfilling the last Templar's solemn vow of vengeance against Philippe le Bel, and all future kings in his person By order of the same François I, his general Almeida, extirpated with a cruelty unusual even in those times the remnant of the Albigenses still lurking in the villages of Provence, a sect, it should be remembered, of genuine Manichæans, transplanted thither from the East at a comparatively recent date As Manichæans, they would naturally have preserved the symbols, and tokens for mutual recognition so much in vogue, as history and existing monuments attest,

* Even the sceptical Michelet allows "il est possible que les Templiers qui echappèrent se soient fondus en societes secrètes En Écosse ils disparaissent tous excepte deux Or, on a remarqué que les plus secrets mystères dans la Franc-maçonnerie sont reputes emaner d'Écosse, et que les hauts grades y sont nommes Écossais V Grouvelle et les ecrivains qu'il a suivis'—('Hist de France,' iii p 129)

† Communicated to me by a 'Brother', the historical authority I cannot discover

amongst all followers of the Gnosis And such machinery and grown yet more into articles of necessity, after continued persecution had transformed their congregations into regular secret societies

But dismissing all such speculations, we are under no necessity for connecting the Rosicrucians with the ancient Brethren of the Temple, in order to account for their display of the Gnostic symbols which figure so conspicuously in Andreae's plates, and which have since been so diligently illustrated (though often with erroneous ingenuity) by Von Hammer in his 'Mystery of Baphomet Revealed,' yet even his *misinterpreted* examples go to prove the same truth, and his 'Baphometic Idols,' whose adoration should have been the heaviest count in the charges against the Templars (though unmistakably of Cinque-cento design and workmanship), are astrological and cabbalistic sigils breathing a purely *Rosicrucian* spirit in their syncretism of symbolic forms. For there is one point in these sculptures alone sufficient to upset all Von Hammer's elaborate structure—the Arabic legends, being cut in current Neshki characters, betray their modern manufacture, for had they been contemporary with the flourishing times of the Templars, the primitive Cufic must, as a matter of course, have been employed Yet, at the same time, these same legends indicate clearly enough the fountain-head of the doctrines held in common by all similar fraternities

But before considering this last and so important point, the subject will be more conveniently approached by our first considering the principal arguments set forth by the learned Orientalist in support of his theory His object in truth is sufficiently declared by the title of his treatise, 'Mysterium Baphometis Revelatum seu Fratres militiæ Templi quà Gnostici et quidem Ophiani, apostasiæ, idololatriæ, et quidem impuritatis convicti per ipsa eorum monumenta" (published in the *Mines de l'Orient*, vol vi) The treatise is copiously illustrated with fine copper plates of magical statuettes, architectural ornaments, mystical inscriptions, vases, and coins As regards *historical* evidence, the main foundation of his hypothesis rests upon certain heads in the Articles of Accusation against the

Templars, despatched by Pope Clement V. to all archbishops, &c These are—

"*Art* 42 Item, quod ipsi per singulas provincias habeant Idola, videlicet *capita*,* quorum aliqua habebant *tres facies*, et alia unam, et aliqua *cranium* humanum habebant

"*Art* 54. Item, quod aliquod caput illorum cingebant seu tangebant chordulis quibus si ipsos cingebant, circa camiciam seu carnem.

"*Art* 55 Quod in hac receptione, singulis fratribus prædictæ chordulæ tradebantur, vel aliæ longitudinis earum"

In this girding with a consecrated string there is a striking analogy to the *Kosti* † prescribed by the Zoroastrian religion, still assumed by every Parsee upon his initiation (which takes place upon his completing his *seventh* year), and thenceforth constantly worn over the shirt This distinctive badge was the most likely of all to be retained by Manes (himself a Magian) in his Christianised modification of the Persian creed Other articles, unnecessary to quote, allege the permission and even the obligation of unnatural practices But, from the very beginning, this last accusation, so needless to be proved, because so readily believed, has been brought against the members of all secret societies, as Ovid shows by the popular tradition respecting Orpheus, the acknowledged founder of the Grecian mysteries

"Ille etiam Thracum populis fuit auctor amorem
In teneros transferre mares, citraque juventam,
Ætatis breve ver et primos carpere flores "‡ (Metam x 83–85)

Clarkson has more recently discussed the same question in his very ingenious essay 'Upon the Symbolical Evidence of the Temple Church. Were the Templars Gnostic Idolaters as

* Such a head of silver was actually seized in the Parisian Chapter-house, but the Templars passed it off for a reliquary containing the skull of one of the 11 000 virgins, in spite of the long beard with which it was furnished (Rayn p 299) Another is said to have been found elsewhere bearing the numeral LIII These damning evidences would naturally have been made away with by the Templars upon the first alarm of the inquiry.

† Woven out of *seven* threads by the wife of the *Mobed* or fire-priest

‡ 'Dum erat juvenis sæcularis, omnes pueri clamabant publice et vulgariter unus ad alterum, Custodiatis vobis ab osculo Templariorum' Wilkins, *Conc Britann* ii p 360)

alleged?' He endeavours to prove their Manicheism by means of *architectural* evidence, deduced from the members of the edifice and the geometrical relations discoverable in the ground plan But, dispassionately considered, such arguments are of little weight, inasmuch as they could be found, if looked for (under a similar prepossession), in many other buildings, both mediæval and modern, having no connection whatsoever with the Brethren of the Temple. Again, a fatal objection to his theory is the fact, that all such "Round Churches" are acknowledged copies of the Holy Sepulchre at Jerusalem, which, whether Helena's original building, or merely a Gothic reconstruction by the Frankish kings (the more probable explanation), was certainly not subjected to Templar influence in the laying out of its plan The circular, domical shape had been given by Helena to her church simply because that form, according to the Roman notion handed down from Etruscan antiquity, was regarded as most appropriate for a *tomb* Hence, to go no further back, it was adopted for Helena's own sepulchre (*Torre pignatara*), and for that of her grandchild, Constantia In illustration of his hypothesis Clarkson adduces the statement of Clemens Alexandrinus about the "Primary Elements" of the old Egyptians, and *supposes* them to have been the *square*, the *angle*, the *semicircle*, the *circle*, the *oval*, the *line*, the *waved line*, *triangular*, and *the cross*. These would represent the seven primary consonants, of which the invention was attributed to Memnon, viz, the letters with their equivalent sounds, B, C, D, L, M, N, S Should this theory have any truth in it, the frequent introduction of such figures into talismanic inscriptions obtains a satisfactory explanation.

But it is now full time to return to Von Hammer's Baphometic Idols, and his profound interpretations of their figures and inscriptions It is obvious at the first glance that the idea of most of them was suggested by the Roman Jupiter Hercules, or Silenus (classical types, by the way, entirely unknown to the art of the 12th and 13th centuries), their heads, or rather their faces, are *triple*, eyes and ears are plenteously distributed all over the body, which is moreover adorned with planetary signs. Our author sets them down without hesitation as the actual figures of the "Old Man" adored by the Knights, described so persistently by the witnesses against them as "une ydole avec *trois faces*."* The same statuettes are for the most part girded with serpents, whose heads they hold in their mouths, or in various distorted attitudes, amply sufficient grounds for Von Hammer to connect them with the Ophite mysteries. But this very attribute, together with the numerous eyes studding the body, would rather seem to betray an acquaintance in the sculptor with similar Hindoo creations—Indra, the eye-bespangled god of the firmament, for example. Similar fancies had found their way even into the Cinque-cento dress; Queen Elizabeth is painted in a gown thus embellished. Some, again, of these figures carry the Egyptian Tau (*marculus*, Masonic *Knocker*) conspicuously suspended from the neck. But, as already hinted, the artistic composition of these well-executed monstrosities, and the classical *motives* everywhere peeping out in their outlines, seem altogether foreign to the quaint simplicity of early mediæval art.

The three "Baptismal Vases," or *Fonts*, on which he lays so much stress, are nothing but little stone cups six inches high at the utmost, covered with bas-reliefs, the phallic character whereof would seem to point to their employment in the brewing of the Elixir of Life from its most obvious ingredients. The second of these reliefs, explained as denoting the "Baptism of Fire," does in truth recall to our recollection the "Twelve Tortures" of the Mithraic rock-tablets; for it exhibits a naked boy holding various instruments—the axe, lyre, bucket of Anubis—whilst another, blowing a horn, feeds the fire in a furnace. Of the third vase, however, the decoration savours strongly of Judaism, representing the lifting up of the Brazen Serpent, though the female reclining below appears rather to

* "Car tantôt après ils alloient adorer une *Idole*, et pour certain icelle idole etait une vielle peau, ainsi comme toute embaumée et comme toile polie; et illecques certès le Templier mettoit sa très vile foy et croyance et en lui tres fermement croyoient. Et en icelle avoit ès fosses des yeux escarboncles reluisants comme clarté du ciel; et pour certain toute leur esperance etoit en icelle, et etoit leur Dieu souverain, et mêmement se affioit en lui de bon cœur." (Art. 3. Vie de Philippe le Bel, chap. 66. 'Chronique de S. Denys.')

caress the living reptile that encircles her, than to be alarmed at its embrace, whilst the Candlestick of the Tabernacle, which the second female is quenching from a vase at the bidding of Von Hammer's "Mete," personified as a regular Dutch Solomon, but with uplifted hands whence drop off chains, all betray the same source of inspiration Bacchic and sidereal symbols, amongst which the phallus of course predominates, are plentifully strewn over the field But the Arabic legends in the *modern* lettering, in this case, equally with the classical air of the design in the second, suffice to convince the sober archæologist that all three vases are nothing more than a portion of the paraphernalia of those Rosicrucian or alchemical quacks, who fattened upon the credulity of that arch-virtuoso, Rudolf II, ever since whose reign these "fonts" have been treasured up in the Imperial Cabinet A sufficient notion of Von Hammer's mode of explaining these monuments is afforded by his interpretation of the Arabic inscription upon the scroll displayed in the hands of his "Mete" (according to him the Ophite *Sophia*), a female yet bearded figure whose sex is ostentatiously revealed to view. "Exaltatur Mete germinans, stirps nostra Ego et Septem fuere Tu es unus Renegantium Reditus πρωκτὸς fit"

The Baphometic idol, that "Head of the Old Man," which makes so fearful a figure in the Articles of Accusation, reminds one of the crowned Osiris seen in front face, otherwise that terminal figure often to be found cut on certain large green jaspers, which differ widely in style from the true Gnostic talismans dating from the Lower Empire, but rather have something about them bespeaking a mediæval and Arabian origin. For example, Raspe* gives a gem (No 588) with "God the Father" crowned with five stars, and several barbarous characters Reverse, a square, a sphere, a pentagon of Pythagoras, and several astrological and geometrical figures Such a talisman was lately found in the tomb of a *Knight Templar* which was opened in Germany And here it may be parenthetically observed, that our Freemasons, in order to give a better colour to their pretence of descent from the Templars, perpetually talk of them as the greatest *builders* of their times,

* 'Descriptive Catalogue of Engraved Gems'

and as the best patrons of the *subordinate* body of working masons. Nothing can be more baseless than this assertion. The Order invested its wealth in a far more profitable manner than in stone and mortar, and really did nothing in the way of architecture, if compared with the great monastic Orders of the same period. In proof of this, notwithstanding its enormous possessions in England, no more than *four* churches were built for "Temples."

Von Hammer, amongst the numerous examples he has so indefatigably collected, presents many of a nature seemingly quite antagonistic to Catholic art, and of truly Gnostic and Oriental character. Conspicuous amongst them are the Three Vases, already described, in which he discovers examples of the true "Sangraal," that mystic cup which shines so brightly forth in the early romances of chivalry, the quest thereof being the highest adventure proposed in the *Morte d'Arthur*, perfect chastity being the indispensable condition for attaining unto the sight of the miraculous vessel. And in truth the decoration of these mystic fonts, used in the "Baptism of *Mete*" (the Gnostic Wisdom), whence their title "Baphometic," furnishes a very plausible foundation for the charges our author brings against their *supposed* inventors. But as for the obscene sculptures taken from the Templar churches, which he refers to the rites of the *Venus Mascula* celebrated therein, these are to be found in equal abundance and shamelessness amongst the carvings of other churches totally unconnected with the Order, for example, notably at Arcueil, near Paris. Such sculptures either contain a moral grossly expressed, according to the taste of their barbarous age, the censure of some particular vice, or may be no more than the ebullition of the brutal humour of the beery artist. But the gravest error into which this too sagacious interpreter has fallen is the attempt to identify the heresy of the Templar with the *Ophite*—that primitive form of the Gnosis, swallowed up so many ages before the foundation of the Order, in the overwhelming flood of Manicheism; a flood indeed that may, even at its source, Syria, have carried away as many inquiring spirits amongst the Knights, as it was simultaneously intoxicating in Italy and Provence. A great absurdity, too, is the building up his grand hypothesis upon the inexplicable "Mete," which he finds out for himself in these unintelligible legends, seeing that the Archaic Μῆτις was never used in Gnostic times as synonymous with Σοφία, *Achamoth*, an identity nevertheless taken for granted in his argument. And by the same rules does Von Hammer explain the Masons' marks that he has collected, although they in no wise differ from others found in mediæval buildings of every conceivable destination and origin

Before quitting this part of the subject, a word must be said upon other etymologies that have been proposed for the mighty word "Baphomet" One, equally consistent with Von Hammer's views, and much more so with the genius of the Byzantine language, would be βαφὴ Μητρός, "Baptism of the *Mother*," that special designation of Barbelo in the Valentinian theology.* Such Greek technical phrases *may* have been perpetuated in the Manichean ritual, wherever, and however late, it was introduced into France.

Another explanation makes Baphomet the corruption of *Behemoth*, meaning the golden calves Opis and Mnevis, whose bones were exhibited to their worshippers, set out upon the lid of the coffin So in later times were the bones of Manes displayed for the adoration of his followers; and those of the G M Hiram,† according to report, at the initiation of a Templar. Hence came the *Death's Head* and *Coffin*, that figure so conspicuously at the Carbonari Conclaves, and the cognate engine of terror at our Masonic receptions, when the candidate for admission "being brought to the G P receives that sudden and awful impression on his mind that cannot fail to have the desired effect a part of the ceremony that ought to be well attended to, as well for the *honour* and *safety* of the new-made brother, as of the Fraternity at large " But to return to etymology. Visconti is probably in the right after all, in considering "Baphometa" no deeper mystery that the French corruption of the name "Mahomet," as repeated by the ignorant witnesses for the prosecution.

* Which made her the *heavenly* mother of the Saviour

† Being set upon a coffin containing a corpse, elevated upon a catafalque of five steps (Clarkson)

But although the fanciful Orientalist has pushed this theory to an unwarrantable and even ludicrous extent, yet proved facts, coupled with probabilities, will induce the unprejudiced inquirer to acquiesce in the conclusions of the judicious Raspe "The Gnosis of Basilides was an *occult science* which, according to his tenets, should be known only and communicated to one in thousands, and to two in ten thousands, and that if the Knights Templars were guilty of any offence at the time of their extermination, it was that of having adopted the doctrines of the Gnostics, and consequently of having renounced the established doctrine of the Church on the human nature of Christ, and on the Trinity in the place of which they, with the Gnostics, professed one Supreme Being, Father and Creator of all the Powers which, emanating from him, have created and do govern this world At their reception or initiation into the *highest degree* of the Order they received βαφὴ μήτους, or μήτιος—that is to say, the *Baptism* or *Tincture* of *Wisdom*; they were presented with a sign or *symbol* of their baptism, which was the Pentagon of Pythagoras, and they worshipped a kind of *image* or *idol*, that like the Abraxas on this gem was the figure of a Bearded Old Man, or rather the representation of the only Supreme Being that they admitted and professed." The gem referred to is a jasper (Townley) presenting "Abraxas, the Sun, or God-Father, or Demiurgus according to the Gnostics and necromancers This head is crowned, the beard long, the hands crossed upon the breast for the rest, he is formed as a Term, or a mummy In the field are eight stars, probably an allusion to the eight Powers, or heavens, that are subordinate to them, according to Epiphanius. In the field are two Hebrew letters, תה

"Reverse. The same God the Father, or Abraxas, in the same attitude, standing above four angels placed upon a sphere and receiving his emanations, in the field are three, on the sphere are five stars There are besides in the field two Hebrew letters, three lines of inscription, &c."

Figures of unquestionably mediæval workmanship do, however, exist, which would have stood Von Hammer (had he known of them) in far better stead than the easily recognisable legacies of Rudolf II and his Rosicrucian quacks Such is the brass statuette published by Caylus (Rec d'antiq. v Pl., 32) representing a man in tight jerkin and hose (as worn under armour), but head covered with a jester's horned hood. Upon his belly is emblazoned a blazing sun, he is girt with the broad knightly belt, engraved all round with planetary signs, and regular Masons' Marks, which also run round the edge of the tripod upon which he stands The figure, about five and a half inches high, extends both hands with the palms uppermost, and these are pierced with holes for the reception of the supports of some vessel, probably a magician's lamp Amongst other devices engraved on the trunk, most conspicuous are the eagle, serpent, and crucible supporting a retort Caylus places his drawing of it amongst his Egyptian monuments, but reasonably enough distrusting such an origin for the inscriptions, suggests, with no better reason, that the work belongs to Persia

Manicheism has been so repeatedly referred to in the foregoing pages, as to make it necessary to give a brief explanation of the way, in which that strange creed may possibly have affected the religion of the Templars And here, all is either assertion of enemies, or modern theory, hardly any monuments remaining that can be with certitude attributed to the Manicheans, though so numerous in their time, for they had drawn within their own circle every older form of Gnosticism in the interval between Constantine and Justinian. This deficiency is partly due to the fast increasing barbarism of those ages, which produced nothing in the way of art, however degraded. Their sole religious monuments were sacred books, prayers, spells, committed to perishable materials, parchment, papyrus, diligently sought out and destroyed by every persecutor. The extirpation of Gnosticism was vigorously prosecuted by the later emperors of the West, and by those of the East, Arian equally with Catholic. In this pious career the first step was made by Magnus Maximus, the British usurper under Gratian, by putting to death Priscillian, bishop of Avila, and his chief adherents, in spite of the very *unsaintly* remonstrances of the good Martin of Tours. The usurper's punisher, Theodosius, also made Manicheism (Priscillian's crime) a capital offence, his edict being the first *statutable* infraction of the old Roman principle of universal religious toleration In the reign of his son, Epiphanius boasts of having brought about the exile of seventy women, some noble, through whose seductions he had himself at one time been drawn into joining the Marcosians Such a vaunt leads to the suspicion that the renegade had saved himself by turning evidence against his fellow sectarians at the opening of the persecution Or again, this absence of Manichean relics may be accounted for by the rigid character of the creed itself, the offspring of Magism, therefore regarding all imagery as idolatrous and sinful, a tenet latterly carried out to the fullest extent by the iconoclastic Albigenses

To come now to the *second* diffusion of Manicheism over Europe. In the middle of the seventh century, under Constans II, Constantinus Sylvanus, a native of Samosata, broached that last and most far-spreading heresy, the *Paulician* The name arose from his combination of the doctrine of St Paul with that of Zoroaster, but he had intermingled a larger proportion of the former ingredient than his precursor Manes had thought fit to do in his original theosophy The new teacher easily united into one church the remnants of the old Gnostics, especially the Manicheans of Armenia, and the still unconverted Zoroastrians of Pontus and Cappadocia Incessantly persecuted by the Byzantine powers, their chief Carbeas founded a new capital for his sect, the impregnable Tephrice, in the mountains near Trebizond, but which was ultimately destroyed by Basil the Macedonian about the year A D 880 But in the middle of the preceding century, the irreligious Constantine Copronymus had transplanted a large colony of these Armenian Paulicians into the depopulated Thrace, where their numbers were largely augmented in the tenth century by a fresh reinforcement drawn from the Chalybian Hills and planted in the valleys of Mount Haemus by John Zimisces Here their missionaries converted the neighbouring pagans, the Bulgarians, whence the sect derived a new and more odious appellation, one which in course of time from denoting heresy in religion was fixed to the branding of heresy in love War-like and fearless of death, we find these Paulicians serving in the Byzantine armies, notably in those of Alexius Comnenus in his wars with the Normans of Sicily. From this island as a focus they diffused their doctrines over Italy, they gained numerous converts even at Rome and Milan, but spread with still more astonishing rapidity through the South of France. Persons even whose interests were diametrically opposed to the progress of the sect, joined it with inexplicable fervour, twelve canons of the Cathedral of Orléans were burnt alive at one time for embracing Paulicianism These few facts, selected from the wide range of their history, will suffice to illustrate the diffusion of Manichean notions during the period when the Templars were at the height of their prosperity and power.

But Gnosticism in one shape or other, was still surviving in the very head-quarters of the Order, amongst their closest allies or enemies, the mountaineers of Syria The Templar Order had been modelled after an original, the last to be looked for according to modern views, for Von Hammer has here been successful in demonstrating that its constitution is a servile copy of that of the detested "Assassins" The statutes of the latter prove the fact beyond all gainsaying, they were found upon the captives of their capital, Alamoot, by the Mogul, Halakoo, in the year 1335, when by a most singular coincidence, Caliph and Pope were busied in exterminating the model and the copy in the East and West, at one and the same time From these documents were verified the "Eight Degrees" of initiation as established by Hassan, the first Grand Master or "Prince of the Mountain' These degrees, probably suggested by the ancient Mithraic tests, were —

I The Trial of knowledge.

II. The Trial of Persuasiveness, i e, the talent for proselytism

III. Denial of the truth of the Koran, and of all other sacred scriptures

IV The Trial of silent and perfect obedience.

V The Disclosure of the names of the Great Brothers of the Order, royal, sacerdotal and patrician, *in all parts of the world*

VI The Confirmation of all the preceding steps of knowledge.

VII The Allegorical interpretation of the Koran, and of all

other scriptures. In this lodge the divinity of all founders of religious systems was alike denied. Religion was shown to be a mere step to *knowledge*, its narratives to be merely allegorical and exhibiting the progress of civil society thus, *Man's Fall* signified political slavery, *Redemption* his restoration to liberty and equality.

VIII That all actions were indifferent, provided only they were done for the good of the Order, * there being no such thing, absolutely, as vice or virtue

It will be seen that the principle running through these "Degrees" is identical with that pervading the main counts in the Articles of Accusation brought against the Templars

The same author (*History of the Assassins*) shows that the organization of the Templars was exactly modelled upon that of the Assassins, and thus confronts the several degrees in each of the two orders

Of the Assassins

I The Grand Master, or Prince of the Mountain

II The Dais-al-Kabir, or three great viceroys under him.

III. The Dais, or provincial masters.

IV. The Refek, or chaplains.

V. The Lazik, or military body

VI The Fedavee, or death-devoted.

VII. The Batinee, or secret brethren, *i e*, those affiliated to the order

Of the Templars

I The Grand Master

II The three Grand Priors

III The Provincial Prior

IV The Chaplains

V. The Knights.

VI The Esquires.

VII The Serving-brethren

VIII The Donati and Oblati

IX. The Affiliati †

* The maxim of the Jesuits "that implicit obedience includes the commission of a *mortal* sin"

† The benefits of affiliation were obtained at the small annual fee of two or three *deniers* One of the

The "Donati" and Oblati" were sworn, in return for the protection afforded to them by the Order, to leave to it all their property at their deaths, and consequently to refrain from having offspring, or even to stand sponsors to the children of others. If married at the time of joining the Order, they were bound to put away their wives. Infraction of the vow was punished by perpetual imprisonment. The "Affiliati" had, probably, nothing to do with the secrets of the Order; they merely, in return for a certain sum paid down, received their daily maintenance (their *commons*) out of the corporate fund; such an arrangement being a simple anticipation of the principle of life annuities, and admirably suited to the requirements of those barbarous times.

It is not a matter for surprise that the grand elements of ancient Gnosticism should have thus been discovered lurking in the secret rules of the Order of Assassins; when the origin of that order is investigated, it proves to be only a branch of the Ismaelites, or those Persians who supported the cause of the descendants of Ali. But Abdallah, himself a *Magian*, had from the beginning founded in the midst of these Ismaelites, a secret society composed of those Persians who had, through Arab compulsion, embraced Mohammedanism only in name. By inculcating those vital dogmas of the old Gnosis, that *knowledge* was the real end of Religion, and that in all scriptures the *allegorical* interpretation was the only true one, Abdallah united under his teaching the remnants of all the older religions that still lurked in Persia; in fact he did in Persia under the Caliph, what the new Manichean Chrysocheir was doing at Tephrice under the Byzantine emperor. The Ismaelites having gradually become absorbed into the new sect, succeeded, in the tenth century, in placing a prince of Ali's line upon the throne of Cairo, thus founding the Fatimite dynasty. After this, Hassan, who had served with distinction under the Seljuk Sultans, aided by his brethren to when he had returned, having captured the hill fortress of Alamoot or 'The Vultures' Nest' (1090 A.D.), set himself up there as an independent prince, and established

chief causes of Philippe le Bel's hatred against the order was their refusal, in the early part of his reign to admit him into this class.

his community as a *political body*, under the constitution already described In a short time these bold sectaries made themselves masters of all the strong places of Lebanon, thereby securing their independence of the Egyptian Caliph The Druses are only the modern representatives of the suppressed Assassins Like them, they are Ismaelites, their ostensible founder being Hakim, a Fatemite Caliph of Cairo, who professed himself the new incarnation of the Godhead Their notion that the present seat of their ever absent Grand Master is *Europe*, tallies curiously enough with Von Hammer's theory about the close relationship that existed between the Templars and the actual progenitors of the Druses These same Druses may also possibly represent the 'polytheists and Samaritans' who flourished so vigorously in the Lebanon as late as the times of Justinian, to whose persecuting zeal Procopius ascribes the extermination of a *million* inhabitants of that district alone Of their present creed, preserved in unviolated secrecy, nothing authentic has ever come to light, popular belief amongst their neighbours makes them adorers of an idol in the form of a calf, and to celebrate their nocturnal assemblies, orgies like those laid to the charge of the Ophites in Roman, of the Templars in mediæval, and of the Freemasons (continental) in modern times. Their notion of their Head residing in *Scotland* has an odd resemblance to the German appellation "Scottish Brethren," given to our Masons Some such association of ideas seems to have led the Lessing to maintain that "Freemason" in German *Masson*, has nothing whatever to do with the English meaning of the word, but comes from *mass* only, the proper name for a Templar lodge, called also a "Round Table" For this derivation he cites Agricola, an authority removed by no more than 150 years from the date of the suppression of the Order. On this account, he adds, the old Templar buildings in Bologna and Milan still retain the title "de la magione," that is, "of the *masson*," although a less acute critic would, most assuredly, only be able to discover here nothing deeper than an Italian corruption of the French *maison* in its common sense

The influence of the Crusades and their results upon the mind and life of mediæval Europe cannot possibly be exaggerated

The true masters of the Western barbarians in philosophy, science, and many of the arts, were the Arabs, firstly, those of Syria, later, of Spain. Together with their learning they communicated other ideas, far different from those originally contemplated by their pupils. Nevertheless, the connection between their science and their secret creed was so intimate that, in reality, no other result was to be looked for. So much of primitive Gnosticism, before its admixture with Christianity, was based upon Magism, that is, upon astrological ideas, as to make it often difficult to determine whether a Gnostic monument involves a religious notion, or is merely a sidereal talisman. For example, the Decani of the Signs, whose figures, according to Teucer, were commonly worn as amulets, are often to be seen bearing the names inscribed of Michael and other Jewish angels. In the flourishing times of Mahommedanism, before the spread of universal ignorance had established everywhere the dull reign of uninquiring orthodoxy, there existed at its very heart (probably originating in Persia) an esoteric body, styling themselves *Sufi*, a title evidently derived from the Greek Σοφοί, their predecessors. Now this title appears assumed as equivalent to the previous Γνωστικοί, although with far more arrogance, since these "wise" men claimed the *possession* of that knowledge of things divine which the Gnostics by their own designation were only "*desirous of knowing*." Meantime, the tenets they held were precisely those of the old *Antitactae*, "ordinance-haters," as to the indifference of all things pertaining to the body, and the invalidity of the Jewish moral law (the mere appointment of the Demiurgus), as regarded the regulation of the life of the "Spiritual Man." Just as it is a constant charge of the Fathers against the primitive Gnostics that they outwardly conformed without scruple, in order to escape all annoyance, to the established religion of whatever place they chanced to inhabit, it is equally probable that the Manicheans and other sectaries of Asia, persecuted with like zeal by orthodox Byzantine and Zoroastrian Persian, would gladly shelter themselves under the easy cloak of the true religion of their Arab conquerors, during the two centuries following Justinian's reign, and either save their liberty by *professing* Mahommedanism, or else continue, as tributaries, in the unmolested exercise of their old faith, being confounded by the uninquisitive conqueror under the general name of *Infidels* * "The sects of Egypt and Syria," says Gibbon, "enjoyed a free toleration under the shadow of the Arabian Caliphs," and therefore may reasonably be supposed to have maintained their peculiar notions and observances down to the time of the Crusades Of such protracted existence we have the most convincing proof at the present day in the numerous sect, the Mandaites, or Nazarenes of the Shat-el-Arab, and Bassora, veritable Gnostics, holding a creed, the true image of that of Manes, in their 'Book of Adam,' and detested by their Christian and Moslem neighbours alike.

Now, inasmuch as these Sufi were composed exclusively of the learned amongst the Persians and Syrians at a time when *learning* signified little else than proficiency in medicine and astrology (the two points that brought the Eastern sages into amicable contact with their barbarous invaders from the West), it is easy to see how the latter may have imbibed the *esoteric* doctrines simultaneously with the other teaching of those who were their sole instructors in all matters pertaining to science and art. Now the Sufi doctrine was based on that grand idea —one universal creed that could be secretly held under the outward profession of any established religion—taking, in fact, virtually the same view of all religious systems as that in which the philosophers of old had regarded them. Such too had been a striking feature in the Gnostic teaching the *Naaseni*, or Ophites, says Hippolytus, boasted in language truly Masonic, "We of all men are the only Christians, standing in the *third gate*, and anointed with the ineffable unction out of the *horn* like David, not out of the *earthen vessel* like Saul, who consorted with the evil spirit of carnal concupiscence" These same *genuine* Christians at the same time zealously celebrated all the Mysteries of Paganism, affirming that in their higher *knowledge* they possessed the only key to the one truth locked up under those superstitious ceremonies And in our day the acknow-

* The semi-Magian Abdallah and his new Ismaelites have a strong family resemblance to Weishaupt and his illuminati in the last century

ledgment of one universal religion by the Freemasons, as expressed by their requiring from the candidate for admission nothing more than the declaration of his belief in one God, is denounced with pious horror by the bigots of every variety of the Christian scheme

This recognition of one universal religion in fact pervades all the works of the lights of Mohammedan literature. In the *Makamat* of Hariri the sermons preached by his hero the Dervish are full of a sentiment more sublime when touching upon things pertaining unto God—a sentiment harmonising infinitely more closely with those of enlightened religious men of our times upon the same subject—in a word, these sermons breathe a spirit in every respect more *Christian* (to use the modern phrase) than characterises any writings of the actual Christian divines, the contemporaries of the author * But this is necessarily so, Hariri and Mohammedans like him being guided by the traditions of the old philosophy still secretly maintained amongst them, whilst the spirit of modern Christianity is strongly, though unconsciously, directed by precisely the same influence revived, though under a different name, and professedly contemning its real source

Again, the greatest of all Mohammedan sovereigns, the Mogul Akbar, was a true *Sufi*, equally so was his prime minister and historian, Abul Farez It would be difficult to find in a modern Christian prayer-book, much less in any one composed in his age, an address to the Deity so sublime, so consonant with our present notions, as the invocation opening his *Ayeen-Akbari* In all such outpourings of Oriental adoration no allusion whatever to their special lawgiver is to be detected, nothing to betray any distinctive sectarian prejudice, the reader, if unacquainted with the history of the author, would admire, but know not to what creed to adjudge the composition. Akbar, according to his vizier, "made a point of never ridiculing or condemning any form of religion " He had thus, perhaps without knowing it, reverted to the grand and distinguishing feature of the religion of Greece and Rome in their best times that discerned the same great truth, the real basis of universal

* He flourished in the ninth century

toleration, that all religious systems were but expressions of the same idea,

"By saint, by savage or by sage"

Wherever, in ancient times, the principle of toleration was apparently violated, it was in cases where the rites, by their corruption, had become prejudicial to public welfare, as when the Senate put down the Bacchanalia, or Claudius the Druids in Gaul, on account of their human sacrifices, exactly as Hiero of Syracuse had made it an article in his treaty with the vanquished Carthaginians, that they should discontinue their burnt-offerings of young children to Melcarth. Hesiod's maxim, Μὴ ἀρρητοῖς μωμεύειν, was that of his race, as well as of the Roman, and the same was the guiding principle of Akbar. From a hint dropped by his panegyrist it would almost appear that the Emperor had imbibed some slight tinge of Zoroastrian doctrine, for he remarks his particular veneration for the element of fire, and again the significant circumstance of his regulating his frequent daily prayers by the position of the sun in the heavens, and, what bears directly upon our subject, his favourite occupation was to converse with the *Sufi* and the learned of all nations and religions. It sounds also very odd to hear a Mohammedan grandee, like this writer, declaring that amongst the Brahmins were to be found "the most virtuous men upon earth," those very religionists in whom Akbar's successors, like Aurungzeb, could (quite according to our own ideas of what necessarily should have been his feeling) discern nothing but devil-worshippers, whom it was his bounden duty either to convert or exterminate.

The constant intercourse between Syria and Europe, maintained first by the flocks of pilgrims perpetually crowding to Jerusalem, then by the Crusades, and lastly by the establishment of the Frankish kingdom in Palestine, and of the different principalities upon the coast, produced vast effects, both apparent and concealed, upon the nations of Europe, more especially those seated upon the Mediterranean. Arabian influence brightly manifests itself in the poetry of the Troubadours, half-amatory, half-mystical like its model, of a spirit differing as widely from the materialism of classic elegiacs, as does the pointed "Saracenic" architecture, with all its forms suggested by the tentpole and curtain from the massive Romanesque which it so rapidly displaced. Of poetry and architecture alike the germs had been carried into France by the causes already noticed, and kept in full vigour by the permanent establishment of the two great military orders having their headquarters in Jerusalem, but looking principally to France for recruits and resources. For the Crusades were eminently a French *idée*, and both leaders and soldiers in the most important of them, were either actual Frenchmen or princes holding territories in France—our Norman kings for example. How many arts, the most admired in those ages, are direct importations from Syria or Egypt! Glass-working in all its processes connected with the manufacture of ornamental and coloured vessels, and painted windows, enamelling, majolica, damascening on steel, the coinage of gold, the cultivation of the silkworm. The Italian language has preserved this history in the terms, purely Arabic, still designating things pertaining to all such processes, as *zecca*, *tazza*, *cameo*, *mantece*, *rocca*, *gala*, *patacca*, *ricamare*, &c. Italian Gothic, particularly its civil branch, as exemplified in the buildings of the great maritime cities on the Mediterranean (those on the Adriatic continued faithful to the Byzantine taste), such as Genoa, Pisa, Florence, is a mere transcript of Cairo and Rosetta: to the latest days of the style bearing no resemblance to the Gothic then flourishing beyond the Alps.

This diffusion of Oriental ideas over Europe has a very important bearing upon the present inquiry, for it explains the readiness with which Manicheism was embraced in France during the two centuries preceding the fall of the Templars. These very Templars are found during their residence in Palestine exhibiting a tolerant spirit, utterly inconsistent with the ostensible object of their institution, making alliances with any of the neighbouring Emirs able to assist them in holding their own against the common enemy, the Soldan of Egypt: amongst whom figures conspicuously that arch-Gnostic, the redoubtable "Old Man of the Mountain." *

* His practice of intoxicating the neophyte with *hashish* (extract of hemp) before admission into his terrestrial paradise, gave the sect the name, afterwards accepted by the Italians in its present opprobrious sense.

A distinguishing feature of Gnosticism was the profession of continence, at least as far as regards the propagation of the human species, which was denounced to the "spiritual" as the doing in the highest measure the will of the Demiurgus, and the perpetuating the reign of Matter The strange means they adopted to preserve their vow inviolate may be learnt by referring to Clemens, where he quotes their interpretation of the ancient fable about Saturn's devouring his own children, or to Epiphanius when he describes the rites of the Ophite eucharist In no other doctrine of the Gnosis is the Buddhistic influence more clearly traceable than in this, for any intrinsic merit in similar asceticism (as practised purely for its own sake) was never dreamed of by the Grecian philosophy, that offspring of reason in her brightest and most uncorrupted development This self same affectation of purity contributed, even more than the proclaimed liberty of conscience, to promote the spread of Gnostic tenets in every age of their development, from Valentinus down to the grand apostle of Languedoc, Nicetas of Constantinople His Manichæan bishops owed their success in great measure to their black robes and professed abstinence from, nay, more, pious horror of, all the pleasures of sense For any preaching is certain to obtain flocks of converts that shall make besides the promise of fully explaining things too high for man's understanding, an outward and noisy profession of asceticism, and proclaim the exaltation of the poor and the certain damnation of the rich as a capital article of its creed For the vulgar mind ever admires what is difficult merely *because* it is difficult, however useless in itself may be the result, or even pernicious to society in its consequence, if logically carried out, and inasmuch as the abstinence from sensual pleasures is to them the hardest of all tests, so much the more is the ostentation of similar self-denial the most effectual method for gaining ascendency over brutish intelligences, utterly incapable of distinguishing the means from the end Moreover, such doctrines find powerful allies, ready existing for them, in the natural enviousness and greed of common souls The actually poor being ever the vast majority in the land, such hearers joyfully receive the teaching that promises the punishment of their betters in the next world, purely as a counterbalance to their superior happiness in *this*: whilst as scarcely any one considers himself as a truly *rich* man, but is constantly climbing upwards towards a point that constantly recedes before him at every successive stage of his ascent, even the wealthy convert is enabled to hold the comfortable assurance that he himself continues in the category of the poor, and that the anathema is only launched against the one immediately above himself on the social ladder. In this feeling lies the true secret of the amazing success of Manicheism, its rapid absorption into itself of the earlier Gnostic forms, and above all, of the facility with which it got possession of those very regions where the Catholic Church was the most richly endowed, and where her clergy, particularly the *Regular*, were attracting the greatest envy by their wealth and ostentation.

The Templars began their course in actual poverty, leading a doubly hard laborious life—that of monk and soldier combined. To express this poverty the original device or common seal, of the Order, bore two knights mounted upon the same horse, the most striking exemplification of humility that could be imagined in those days of chivalry. Becoming ashamed of such a badge as they grew in power, they altered it into the somewhat similar outline of a *Pegasus*—such at least is the old tradition. The Winged Horse, however, may from the first have involved a more spiritual meaning, allusive to the heavenward aspirations of those initiated into the Order. And when their career was drawing to a close, amidst the wealth and luxury that drew down upon them so cruel a destruction, the brethren, no doubt through some ingenious mode of self-deception, still flattered themselves that their vows were as faithfully observed as in the very springtide of their institution.

The strange and obscene* ceremonies observed on the admission of neophytes into the various secret societies that

* "*Art.* 26. Item, quod in receptione Fratrum hujus Ordinis, vel circa, interdum recipiens et receptus aliquando se deosculabantur in ore, vel in umbilico seu in ventre nudo, vel in ano seu in spina dorsi."

"*Art.* 29. Item, aliquando in virga virili."

"*Art.* 30. Item, quod in receptione sua illa faciebant juxta eos quos recipiebant quod Ordinem non exierunt."

flourished under the Lower Empire and in the Middle Ages are all of them no more than faint traditions of the penances, or "Twelve Tortures" that purchased admission into the Cave of Mithras. How widely diffused were these *Mithraici*, especially in the West, is attested by the innumerable tablets, altars, and inscriptions still remaining in Germany, France, and this country. The religion of Mithras was so readily embraced and flourished so extensively amongst all the Celtic races, in consequence of its analogy to the previously dominant Druidical religion.

This affinity had struck with astonishment that sagacious observer, the elder Pliny, who must have had ample opportunity for forming a correct judgment during his protracted military service upon the Rhine. He declares (Nat. Hist. xxx. 4) "Gallias utique possedit (*Magica*) et quidem ad nostram memoriam, namque Tiberii Cæsaris principatus sustulit Druidas eorum et hoc genus vatum medicorumque per senatus consultum. Quid ego hæc commemorem in arte Oceanum quoque transgressa, et ad Naturæ inane pervecta? *Britannia* hodieque celebrat, tantis ceremoniis ut *dedisse Persis* videri possit, adeo ista toto mundo consensere quamquam discordi et sibi ignoto. Nec satis æstimari potest quantum Romanis debeatur, qui sustulere monstra in quibus hominem occidere religiosissimum erat, *mandi* verò etiam saluberrimum." A hundred years before, Cæsar (Bell. Gall. vi. 13) had stated "Disciplina Druidica in Britannia *reperta* atque inde in Galliam translata esse æstimatur, et nunc qui diligentius eam rem cognoscere volunt plerumque eò discendi causâ proficiscuntur." The subjects of study in the Druidical school were literally those of the Magian Gnosis, "Multa præterea de sideribus eorumque motu, de mundi ac terrarum magnitudine, de rerum natura, de *deorum immortalium vi ac potestate* disputant." For Pliny by his "Magica" understands the rites instituted by Zoroaster, and first promulgated by Osthanes to the outer world, this Osthanes having been "military chaplain" to Xerxes during his expedition into Greece. And this judgment of the Romans is fully borne out by native evidence, for Druidism (such as it appeared in its final struggle with Christianity during the short-lived independence of Britain after the withdrawal of the legions) is a religion agreeing most wonderfully in many important points with the doctrine of Zoroaster. Thus, it expressly teaches the eternal existence and antagonism of the Two Principles, the final triumph of Good, and the Renovation of all things. A most valuable fragment of early Druidical teaching Plutarch has preserved to us in his strange essay "On the Face in the Moon," by the title of the "Doctrine of the Sons of Saturn," which is full of Gnostic ideas, those of Manes for instance, and even of Gnostic expressions.

Now Manes himself started as a Zoroastrian priest, and framed his new creed (according to Epiphanius) by engrafting upon the original the transcendental Buddhistic notions picked up by his true master, Scythicus, during his travels in India. Is there not then a possibility that some sparks of the ancient Mithraic doctrine may have lingered unnoticed in the West* until made to blaze up anew by the congenial breath of the Paulician Apostles? Indeed, one may even now discern the awful antique ceremonial as parodied to the minutest particular in the procedure of the modern convivial *hetæria*, for Jerome's *Miles*, the lowest grade in the Cave of Mithras, the Templars' "watchman placed on the roof of the house or church wherein the Chapter is held" (Art. 101), have their exact representative in the armed man, the "Tiler," lowest official, who stands sentinel at the door of the Freemasons secret conclave.

The Druidical temple, always circular in ground-plan, whether formed out of native rocks, or built with Gallo-Roman masonry as in its latest example at Lantef in Bretagne (figured by Caylus, vi. pl. 124), consisting of two concentric enclosures pierced with numerous arches, bears in this point a remarkable analogy to all other structures dedicated to the element of fire. Such is the plan of the temple of Moloch (uncovered at Carthage by Davis), the Roman Vesta's temple, the Guebre fire temples at Balkh, to this day circular towers, and the great Sassanian temple at Gazacas destroyed by Heraclius in his

* Similarly there is every reason to believe that the mediæval Witches' *Sabbat* preserved uninterrupted the ceremonial of the ancient rural *orgia*, the only change being in the *name* of the presiding deity. Michelet is of this opinion in describing the immense *Sabbats* of the 17th century.

invasion. The spherical edifice within the palace containing the abominable idol of Chosroes, the image of himself, enthroned as in heaven, and all round him the sun, moon, and stars, which the superstitious king worshipped as gods; angels also had he placed standing about him like sceptre-bearers. Moreover, this enemy of God had so contrived by means of certain mechanism that drops of water should fall from the ceiling to imitate rain, and that sounds of thunder should reverberate therefrom. Our Verulamium also boasted a Mithraic temple commensurate to the importance of the place, until destroyed by the superstitious barbarian, Ealdred, eighth Abbot of St. Albans, for to no other purpose could have served "the very deep grotto, covered with an unbroken hill of earth, and approached by a subterraneous passage," the ruins of which were yet visible when Matthew Paris wrote: "*Specus* quoque profundissimum monte continuo circumseptum, cum *spelunca* subterranea quam quondam Draco ingens fecerat et inhabitavit, in loco qui *Wurmenhert* dicitur, in quantum potuit explanavit, vestigia tamen æterna habitationis serpentinae derelinquens."*

The foregoing considerations seem to furnish a reasonable solution of the problem set to the archæologist in the continued existence of genuine Gnostic symbols (whether in their pristine significancy or as mere dead forms, is for the Masons themselves to judge) still paraded before us as things holy and full of meaning. Treasured up amongst the Sufis of Persia, and the dark sectaries of the Lebanon, thence transmitted to the Templars, and handed over by them to their legitimate heirs the Brethren of the Rosy Cross, these signs maintain a perpetual vitality. The famous *Pentacle* (Solomon's seal) of the Templars was, thinks Nicolai with good reason, the powerful symbol, prescribed in the Diagramma of the Ophites to be offered by the ascending soul to the Genius of each sphere, to extort from them free passage to the supernal Light. "O First and Seventh One (Ildabaoth, æon of Saturn), born to rule with power, chief Word of the pure Intelligence! Perfect Work in the sight of the Father and the Son, by presenting unto thee in this seal the *sign of life*, I open the gate which thy power hath closed to

* *Gesta Abbatum S. Albani*, ed. H. T. Riley, vol. i, page 25.

the world, and freely traverse thy domains" A sufficient reason this for the constant appearance of this particular sigil upon tombstones of every date. The reverence with which the Hindoos still regard the same figure has been already noticed In its *five points* lies concealed the same expression of the virtues of that numeral as was conveyed to the Grecian philosopher by the Delphic ϵ, interpreted in the same sense as by Plutarch, in the Middle Ages the Pentacle was held a sure protection against all danger of fire—though found unavailing, alas! for its knightly wearers, Beranger's dictum being too well verified,

> "Les heretiques n'ont pas trouvé
> Onguent pour la brûlure,"

and was therefore regularly painted up in buildings that from their destination were particularly liable to such risk, brew-houses amongst the rest This last custom explains how the pentacle came at last to indicate the places where fermented liquors were on sale

As for the transmission of these symbols, the question would be at once settled should we accept the bold declaration of Lessing, for which, however, we have only his own authority (*Fortsetzung des Ernst* p 53) "The Lodges of the Templars were in the very highest repute during the 12th and 13th centuries, and out of such a Templars' Lodge which had been *continually kept up* in the heart of London, was the Society of Freemasons established in the 17th century by Sir Christopher Wren" But this venerable tradition is directly contravened by the testimony of the most unimpeachable of all witnesses, the grand *illuminato*, Spartacus Weishaupt himself At Munich, in the St Theodosius Lodge (in 1777), he received the first Masonic degrees, but was inexpressibly disappointed on finding in Masonry nothing beyond "les jeux d'une fraternité innocente!" Nevertheless he suspected that something deeper yet remained, and soon his expectations were fulfilled. That same winter his friend, Cato Zwack, had an interview at Augsburg with a certain Abbé Marotti, who conferred upon him the highest degrees, even those of the *Scottish* Lodges, and expounded to him all the mysteries, founded, according to the

Abbé, upon the religion and history of the Church Zwack lost no time in communicating his acquisitions to Weishaupt, who replies "The important discovery you have made at *Nicomedia*, in your interviews with Marotti, gives me extreme pleasure, let us profit by the circumstance, and extract from it all the advantages possible." Weishaupt had therefore been anticipated by his explanation of their symbolism, which he himself adopted in the new Mysteries he founded Barruel adds (*Jacobinisme*, iv 81) that the charge of *illuminatism* does not apply to the first three degrees of Masonry, neither to such as hold that these three degrees alone belong to the real, ancient, fraternity This would intimate that the "Rosicrucian" had been later grafted upon the original number of gradations in the Masonic hierarchy

For the sake of comparison I shall give Barruel's account of the degrees amongst the Illuminati, the predecessors of the Jacobins, viz,

I Novices
II Brethren of Minerva
III Minor Illuminate
IV. Major Illuminate, or Scottish Novices
V Scottish Knights.
VI The Lesser Mysteries Epoptæ, or Illuminati Priests
VII. The Regent or Illuminato Prince
VIII. The Greater Mysteries, the Magus or King-Man

Like the Rosicrucians, each novice upon admission received his *characteristic*, or mystic name, taken from Roman history he then studied the geography of the Order which classicised modern places after a similar fashion then he acquired the *cypher*, of which the simple set was this

12	11	10	9	8	7	6	5	4	3	2	1
a	*b*	*c*	*d*	*e*	*f*	*g*	*h*	*i*	*k*	*l*	*m*

The other, more abstruse, cypher consisted of *particular symbols* The Noviciate lasted from two three years, according to the age of the Candidate. One of the things most strictly prohibited was to ever write the *name* of either Order or Lodge, they must be expressed by ʘ and ⊓ respectively *

In the admission to his degrees Weishaupt adopted all the Masonic ceremonial. For example, in making the "Scottish Knight," the "secret conclave" was hung with green, the Prefect, booted and spurred, wearing St Andrew's Cross by a green ribbon tied *en saltire*, sat under a green canopy, and received the candidate similarly equipped, holding a mallet for sceptre There was also the triple Benediction, and the sacrament, to conclude, administered by the Chaplain At the making of the *Epoptas*, he was taken, blindfolded, by his sponsor in a perfectly closed coach, by a circuitous route, into the hall now hung with *red*, on a table covered with scarlet were laid the crown and sceptre, heaps of gold mingled with chains On a cushion lay a white robe and girdle The novice was told to choose if he took the gold, he received a severe reprimand, phrased with a lot of *humanitarian* cant too tedious to copy here, and unnecessary besides—seeing that the same is perpetually dinned into our ears at the present day †

At the end, the Hierophant delivered a long address upon natural liberty and equality, and all the rest thereto pertaining Weishaupt, a professional *Atheist*, was both astonished and diverted at finding eminent Protestant divines, after their initiation, declaring that all these notions were the genuine doctrines of the Gospel which was certainly a very awkward truth to be held by the friends of the established order of civilised society It is not, however, less a truth, if the same

* "'Brother A B, *Write* upon this MS of the R S of this Degree' In his *attempt* to do this he receives a severe and prudent C by the J D placed behind him for that purpose, by the C F united to his F &c"—*Masonic Ceremonial*

† The popular notion of the brand-mark received by Masons on initiation is derived from the *stigmata* impressed upon the ancient mystæ at their admission A remarkable example is that of Ptolemy Auletes, who was thus marked in several parts of the body with the lotus, the colocynth-flower, and the timbrel of Cybele (Plutarch, 'De dignoscendo adulatore') The marking of the Mithraici has been noticed in the section devoted to that worship (pp 139, 140) Hence came the mediæval belief in the secret mark impressed by the Devil at the *Sabbat* upon those who swore allegiance to him, and which mark could be recognised by the witch-finders from its insensibility to pain

doctrines be carried out to their logical consequences, instead of being employed in defending ideas deduced in reality from a totally different source But Barruel, the refugee, who had just seen the doctrines of liberty, equality and fraternity practically and naturally expounded by means of the guillotine, reasonably enough puts down this declaration of Weishaupt's as the most conclusive proof of his audacious impiety

The symbols, forming the proper subject of the present enquiry, embodied in their origin the deepest mysteries of Brahminical theosophy, they were eagerly accepted by the subtile genius of the Alexandrine school and applied to the hidden wisdom of Egypt, and lastly, in their captivating and illusory promise of enlightenment, the few bright spirits of the Middle Ages sought for something better than the childish fables, engendered by monkery upon the primal Buddhistic stock, which then constituted the Faith and these holy figurations still continue to flourish, but only as the insignia and mummery of what, at best a mere charitable, is perhaps only a convivial association In the same way Apollo's golden Pentagon, which of yore blazed on high above the Delphic shrine, in the Middle Ages the badge of the proudest Order of Chivalry and a sure defence from peril of lightning and fire, has come at last to be degraded into the mere sign of a German pothouse!

A Master-Mason of the very highest degree lately informed me that he had detected the *Signs* now in use, engraved amongst the sculptures in the Cave-temples of Elephanta, and, what is still more important, that, although the Brahmins are Masons, yet if a European makes the *Sign* to them, they immediately put their hands up before their eyes, as if to shut out the sight of the profanation of things holy. But this curious fact can be explained with the utmost certainty The Dionysiac Mysteries, the most popular of all in Greece, were believed to have been introduced direct from Syria, and necessarily brought along with them all the signs and rites of their birth-place. The painted vases of the period of the *Decadence*, of the fourth and third centuries before our æra, take for their favourite subject scenes from the celebration of these Mysteries, and in these pictures, mystic

Siglæ perpetually recur, amongst which the *Fylfot* shines conspicuous But in truth, all the ancient Mysteries came from the East, as their names, the *Phrygian*, the *Mithraic*, the *Iliac*, declare, and these Mysteries existed publicly almost to the close of the Roman Empire, and how much further down into mediæval times they existed as secret and prohibited things, it is impossible to decide

From the very nature of things we may be certain that their signs and symbols, after the esoteric doctrines were forgotten, passed into the repertory of all "who used curious arts," the alchymists, astrologers, and wizards of the Dark Ages, and then became the property of Rosicrucians, who truly were the parent *stock*, and not a recent brand (as is now pretended) of the present Freemasons *

A most important contribution to the history of Masons' marks has (1877) been obtained through the researches of Sig. Arnoaldi Veli amongst the Gallic cemeteries around Bologna Many of the vases there exhumed bear *Siglæ* upon their bases, more rarely upon their sides, which are unmistakably of the same nature, and, what is more curious, are constructed on the same principle as those used by the regular stone-mason at this very day

Those in Class A (see Veli's *Scavi presso Bologna*) may be considered as of the highest authority, because they are the actual stamps of the potter, impressed upon the clay before baking. That they distinguished individuals, and were not merely religious symbols, but stood for the *proper* names of people unacquainted with writing may be inferred not only from the established custom of antiquity in this respect, but from the much more frequent occurrence of the class, of which he gives examples in list B These are scratched upon the bases *after* baking, and therefore must have been added by the

* The Jews have a tradition that the boards of the Tabernacle were marked with Hebrew letters, as a guide for their adjustment in the setting up of that migratory Temple Writing, therefore, becomes one of the thirty-two works interdicted to every religious Jew upon the Sabbath day It is a singular coincidence that the stones of the Wall of Servius Tullius at Rome are inscribed with Mason's marks that much resemble Phœnician letters

buyers, not by the makers The great variety in the forms of these latter siglæ sufficiently proves that they were the "marks" of private persons, not of clans or tribes Class C, of similar "marks" engraved upon articles of metal, lead irresistibly to the same conclusion It must, however, be observed that although these characters cannot be distinguished at first sight from the modern Masons' Marks of which I have given specimens in the large Plate, it appears upon examination that no care has been taken to make them end in an *odd* number of points—the guiding rule with the modern craft

To come from the Cisalpine to the Western Gauls, some evidence of the same practice is deducible from their coins The large billon pieces, evident copies of Alexander's tetradrachms, found so plentifully in the Channel Islands, often bear a figure, upon the cheek of the Hercules' head, and repeated in the field of the reverse What can these symbols, placed so prominently to catch the eye, have been intended for, but to inform the world what particular tribe of the confederation using one national type had issued the coin thus distinguished? There is some analogy to this in the Greek series, where distant cities use the type of Athens, or Corinth, but make it their own by placing some appropriate symbol in the field We need not however, carry out this theory to the same fanciful length as does the Baron Donop, who, struck by the evident resemblance of these figures to the Hindoo Caste marks, builds upon it a complete history of the migration of the Aryans into Jersey, and points out the Puranic deities to whom each of such symbols is to be referred. Of these figures, again, a great variety, and much better executed, are to be seen in the field of the pretty hemi-drachms of Solimara, which, as well as those above mentioned, belong to the times immediately preceding Cæsar's conquest of Gaul—a date clearly ascertained from that of the Roman denarii often forming part of the same deposits. Of the continued use of these "Marks" under the Roman rule in Gaul some vestiges are still to be discovered. The "Pile Cinq-Mars" which cuts so ludicrous a figure in Rabelais' description of Garagantua's horse, is a lofty quadrangular column, ending in a point, in the most compact and skilfully executed brickwork, apparently built within the first century of the Empire. Upon each face, towards the top, are wrought in bricks of different colour from the main structure various devices of the same sort as those of the coins. These can be nothing else than the "armorial bearings," of the several cities or tribes that had combined together for the erection of so costly a monument, which we may safely suppose intended for one of those 'plurima simulacra" of Mercury which Cæsar noticed in Gaul, and which forms the intermediate link between the upright stones (*menhirs*) roughly cut into a phallic shape at top, of the uncivilised aborigines; and the grand Colossus of Zenodorus, to which native taste had advanced by the time of Nero.

A lucky accident has thrown in my way another, and much more curious proof of the use of these "marks" by the more barbarous part of the Celts at a much later period. That the decoration of the skin which gave the name to the "Picts" consisted in *stigmata* in the literal sense of the word, and not in mere dyeing with woad (like the early Britons) is made out by Claudian's definite expression,

> " *ferroque* notatas
> Perlegit exanimes Picto moriente figuras."—*De Bello Getico*, xxvi. 417-18.

"The Book of Kells" is a MS., written some time in the ninth century. In one of the facsimiles of its pages published by the Palæographical Society, amongst the ornamentation of one vast initial letter, the most conspicuous is the figure of a naked man, writhing himself amongst its most intricate convolutions. This man's body is entirely covered with "marks" of various forms, and from the circumstances under which the drawing was made we can safely assume that we have here preserved to us the portrait of a true Pict, taken from the life. The four centuries that had elapsed since Claudian wrote were not likely to have changed the customs of a country so remote, and in which the small amount of civilisation derivable from its Romanised neighbours must have gone backwards in proportion as they relapsed into their pristine barbarism. This pictured Pict may also lead us to conclude that the sigil seen upon the cheek of the Jersey Hercules was actually tattooed upon that of the Gaul who issued the coin.

Out of deference to the popular belief in the Masonic *Brand mark*, I shall wind up this section with a few observations upon that most time-honoured method of distinguishing those initiated into any mystic community. To give precedence to the Patron Saint of Freemasons, St. John the Divine, his making the followers of the Beast receive his *Mark* "upon the forehead and the palm of the hand," is a clear allusion to the Mithraical practice, of which Augustine (as already quoted) speaks, in mentioning "a certain Demon, that will have his own image purchased with *blood*." Ptolemy Philopator, whom Plutarch describes as "passing his *sober* hours in the celebration of Mysteries, and in beating a tambourine about the palace," submitted also to receive the Dionysiac brand-marks; which were, no doubt, those symbols so plentifully introduced into the vase-paintings of Bacchanalian rites. "Brand-marks," however, is an incorrect name for such *insignia*, for they were imprinted on the skin, not by fire, but by the milder process of *Tattooing*, as we learn incidentally from Vegetius (I. cap. 8), and also that it was the regular practice in the Roman army, in his day, the close of the fourth century. He advises that the recruit be not tattooed with the devices of the standards (*Punctis signorum inscribendus est*) until he has been proved by exercises as to whether he be strong enough for the service. That these tattoo marks were the distinctive badges painted on the shields of the different legions, may be inferred from their insertion in the epitaphs of individuals of each corps.

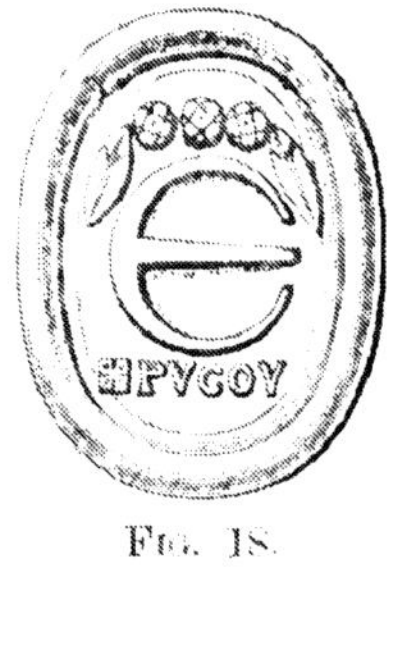

FIG. 18.

WOODCUTS IN THE TEXT

Frontispiece Ceraunia of green jade, converted into a Gnostic talisman described at p 197 Presented to the Repository, Woolwich, by General Lefroy

Title-page The Ophite version of the "Good Shepherd," described at p 230 Sard (New York)

Agathodæmon Serpent, inscribed ΙΘΙ *With Me* [thou shalt be safe] Remarkable mineralogically, as being cut in a piece of true jade (Nephrite) (Lewis Collection) P xii

No 1 The Gnostic Gorgon, a late Byzantine amulet The legend, full of blunders and contractions, is ΑΓΙΟCΑΓΙΟC ΚΤΡΙΟC CΑΒΑΩΘ ΕΝ ΤΟΙC ΤΨΙCΤΟΙC ΕΤΛΟΓΗΜΕΝΟC, "Holy, holy, Lord of hosts, in the highest, Blessed!" Drawn to the actual size, from a cast, sent to me many years ago by the late Mr Albert Way But by a singular chance, the gem itself (a green jasper) two years back, came into the hands of Mr W Talbot Ready who supplied me with a drawing of it, from which it appears that its other face represents Saint Anne, with the Infant Madonna in her arms, and her name and title in the field, the legend around being ΤCΤΕΡΑ ΜΕΛΑΙΝΗ ΜΕΛΑΙΝΟΜΕΝΗ ΩC ΘΑΛΑΤΤΑΝ ΓΑΛΗΝΗ CΑΙΝΕΙ, "O, womb, black, blackening, as the calm soothes the sea [be thou quiet] The gem is therefore a talisman for the protection of women during pregnancy, a fact accounting for its frequent occurrence, Chiflet figures another (the Gorgon side only) in his "Apistopistus," No 70 P 20

No 2 The Abraxas-god, as he is usually represented, with shield and whip to scare away all evil spirits The reverse exhibits the Agathodæmon Serpent, surrounded by triplets of the sacred animals of Egypt, all paying him adoration The legend in the field ΕVΙΑ, is Syriac for "Serpent," the rest remains unexplained Drawn to the actual size, from a red jasper, discovered at Bombay, to which place it had probably been carried by the Persian refugees of the seventh century (Lewis Collection) P 11

No 3 A circular green jasper (of the size of the drawing) preserved from time immemorial in Maestricht Cathedral, where it passes for the "Seal of Saint Servatius," although in reality many centuries posterior to his date, being a late mediæval work The obverse represents the bust of some saint, the reverse, the Gnostic Gorgon, around both rims a most barbarous attempt at a common Byzantine spell, that is, of a few of the first words only The spell, in full, may be translated thus, "Death, (Μοῖρα) black, blackening, as a serpent dost thou writhe, as a lion dost thou roar, but as a lamb shalt thou lie down!" P 57.

No 4. The Abraxas-god mounted in the chariot of the Sun This design is unique in its kind, and of great value, as proving the original identity of the Basilidan deity with the Solar Power He has, however, been adopted into the new religion by the legend of the reverse, the "Great Names," *Iao* and *Abraxas* placed within a coiled serpent, emblem of Eternity Green-jasper (Bosanquet.) P 103

No 5. Horus, the Vernal Sun, seated on the lotus, type of the world, and reviewing the adoration of the Baboon, attribute of the moon Jasper (New York.) P. 155

No 6. The Sun in his car, in his hand the orb, he is saluted in the legend as "Thou art our Father!" and the word in the exergue Trallianus tells us is one of his titles, and enters into a spell against gout The reverse exhibits Luna guiding her milk-white heifer, the Grecian substitute for the silver *antelope* of the Hindoo Chandra Hæmatite (New York) P 157

No 7 Isis, one lotus on her brow, holding a sceptre Sardonyx (Muirhead) P. 175

No 8 Caduceus, within a myrtle wreath On the reverse is beautifully engraved ΑΡΙΚΩΦΙ, which is the exact transliteration of the Hebrew charm against the special demon of the *latrina*, and which is found in the Talmud, being consequently more ancient that the fourth century The meaning is "Upon the head of a lion" Sard. (New York) P. 178

No 9 The Abraxas god, engraved in so superior a style that the work must date from the earliest period of the sect Green jasper (New York) P 194

No 10 The Abraxas god, with the title "Ioa, Son of the Universe!" This is a truer version of the Hebrew than the "Eternal Son," proposed by Matter Hæmatite. (New York) P 244

No 11 Talisman against the Evil Eye The much-dreaded organ is shown encompassed by the symbols of the deities presiding over the days of the week, as the *Lion* for the Sun, the *Stag* for the Moon, the *Wolf* for Mars, &c, all combining to baffle the force of the stroke This attribution of days came from the Chaldæan astrologers: it is represented in a painting at Herculaneum, but the earliest use of it to mark a date is found in Dio Cassius, who observes that Jerusalem was taken "on Saturn's Day" Sard. (New York) P 256

No 12 Drawing rudely scratched on the plaster of the wall of a guard-room, or the Palatine, representing a man of the lower class *touncatus popellus*, or a slave, making a gesture of adoration to a biform diety elevated upon steps, with the explanatory inscription "Alexamenos, worships (or is worshipping) God." It is disputed whether this be a *bona fide* adoration of the jackal-headed Anubis, or the caricature by some heathen scoffer of the convert, Alexamenos and his newly-found god, depicted here in the shape described by Tertullian See remarks at page 230 P 279

No 13. Bust of Apollo, in the Greek style, interpolated by a later hand with a talismanic legend, that would have defied all interpretation but for the existence of another of the same nature, yet rather more explicit This is a portrait of Pescennius Niger (Paris), inscribed with an invocation to the "Holy King, Apollo," to preserve the health of that Emperor, expressed like the present one, chiefly by the initial letters. Ours, therefore, must be read Βασιλεὺς Ἀπόλλων Ἱερὸς Σεου(ηοον) [σῶζε] and, in the same way, calls upon the God of Health to show this favour to Pescennius' rival, Severus Sard (New York) P 302

No 14 Talismanic Ring of Bishop Seffrid, found in his tomb, now preserved in the Cathedral Library, Chichester. P 328

No 15 The Agathodæmon, declaring by the legend "I am Chnumis, Sun of the Universe, 700" The Greek numeral must be the Number of a Name," just as 888 is that of *Jesus*, but what that name was, I leave to deeper Kabbalists than myself to discover. Calcedony (British Museum) P. 340

No 16 Serapis and Agathodæmon combined in one body, enthroned and holding the Orb, as being Lord of the Universe He receives the adoration of the Cynocephalus, attribute of the moon, whence, perhaps, it may be inferred that Serapis is to be understood now in the more restricted sense of the Solar Power Green jasper (New York) P. 358

No 17 SPHINX, emblem of mystery, sporting with a *narthex*, the wand carried by the candidates for initiation into the Dionysia Campanian style, engraved upon the base of a Sard Scarabeus (New York) P 372

No 18 The *golden* Delphic E, surmounted by a fillet of roses For the explanation of the symbol, see p 297 Cameo in agate-onyx (New York) P 431

No 19 Vase, the lower part modelled as a triple face of the boy Atys, at the base lie the pastoral staff and pipes Atys, in the Phrygian Mysteries, is invoked as the "Shepherd of the white stars, and guiding them by the sound of his piping," which Tatian (Hymn to the Mother of the Gods) explains by identifying him with the power that governs the motions of the heavens Red jasper (New York) P. 466.

DESCRIPTION OF THE PLATES.

The drawings were, for the most part, made from gems in the Praun Cabinet, now transferred to the British Museum, some few from my own collection, now in the Museum of Art, New York The materials are either dark green and yellow jaspers, or calcedonies varying in colour from olive green to light yellow All designs are drawn to double the actual size

Plate A

VARIOUS TYPES OF THE GOD ABRAXAS

1 Abraxas brandishing a whip, to scare away malignant influences, his shield emblazoned with some word of power Reverse, the usual Greek transliteration of the Hebrew name of God

2 Abraxas, armed with a sword, the exceptionally neat execution of the intaglio bespeaks the first days of the religion

3 Abraxas, wielding a *mace*, a Persian weapon that betrays the Asiatic origin of this particular design, the *thunderbolt* in the field identifies this Power with the classic Jupiter The reverse exhibits the Triple Hecate, Queen of Hell, brandishing various weapons for the same prophylactic purpose as the god himself A unique combination of ideas, engraved upon a circular copper plaque, found in the south of France

4 The Agathodæmon Serpent, with radiated head, identified by the legend with the god Abraxas One of the few types that can with confidence be attributed to the sect of Ophites

5. Abraxas, of very debased and late execution The title "*Sabaoth*" on the reverse, properly signifying "of hosts," was mistaken by the ignorant Hellenists for the actual *name* of a Power, by translating "Lord of Hosts" as "the Lord Sabaoth " Under this title he figures largely in the sigillum of the "Pistis-Sophia"

Plate B

1. Abraxas, represented here with the head of an *ass*, and thereby identified with Typhon, a singular perversion of ancient ideas. This gem is valuable as distinctly declaring its purpose by the legend on the

reverse, ΦΥΛ(φύλασσε), "Defend me," addressed to the Power depicted upon it, and thus putting out of doubt the destruction of all the other specimens of its class

2 Abraxas, of neat work and early date, not later than the fourth century.

3 The Giant Typhoeus defying Jove his *serpent*-legs denote that he is the son of Mother Earth This beautiful intaglio, which is of Italo-Greek workmanship, and found at Cumæ, is introduced here merely to show the source whence the sectaries of the Decline borrowed the idea of similar combinations of discordant natures (Burnt sard New York)

4 Abraxas, with whip and shield, combining his influence with *Horus*, seated on the lotus, the regular personification of the Vernal Sun The meaning of the type is set forth in the legend, which is the Greek transliteration of the Hebrew *Shemesh Ilam*, "Sun of the Universe" The union of the two types indicates that Abraxas is here to be understood in his original sense, the simple personification of the Solar Power.

Plate C

1 Terminal figure, perhaps allusive by its form to Justinus' Æon, "The Cross" The interminable legend surrounding it yields no intelligible words, but the title below the Herme, ΝΙΧΑΡΟΠΛΗC occurs also on a talisman in the French Cabinet The reverse gives the Seven Vowels (or "Voices") that shroud the Ineffable Name, which has never been uttered aloud since the day of the destruction of the Temple, but is communicated only in half-whispers to every Rabbi upon his ordination It is a remarkable fact that a Talmudist, who remembered the Second Temple, observes that this Holy Name was "*warbled* rather than pronounced" in the course of the service, hence we may suspect the *possibility* of imitating its sound by the permutation of vowels that form so important an element in the construction of our talismans

2 Father Nile, reclining and holding forth a cornucopia, emblematic of amity * As the "number of his Greek name," 365, is equivalent to that of Abraxas, it is probable that, according to Kabbalistic rules, he here represents that god This explanation is supported by the type of the reverse, Horus, seated on the lotus, addressed by the Greek transliteration of the Hebrew *Ablanathanalba*, "Thou art our Father!"

3 Horus seated in the *baris*, or sacred boat, the prow and poop whereof terminate in the hawk's head of Phre, and the ox-head of Apis. He is here addressed by the Ineffable Name

4 The same deity, addressed as before by the salutation *Ablanathanalba*, followed by an unintelligible word. The unskilful gem-engraver, unable to form curves in the lettering, has given to his B the form of K, and increased the difficulty of deciphering this legend

5. The same, but now seated upon the scarabæ, type of the Creator,

* The type also of an Alexandrian coin of Hadrian

enclosed within the coiled serpent, emblem of Eternity With these purely Pharaonic sigils the reverse combines the name of the Jewish angel Michael, and the Seven Vowels of the Ineffable Name, thus presenting an instructive example of that reconciliation of, apparently, the most antagonistic creeds which is the very foundation of Gnosticism

PLATE D

SIGILS OF THE CNUPHIS SERPENT.

This class of figures has no connection with Gnosticism considered as a development of Christianity, being nothing more than talismans for the protection of the chest, as I have already shown from Galen It is true indeed that the Kabbalists of Alexandria sought to heighten the *medicinal* efficiency of the ancient Pharaonic sigil by adding to it formulæ of their own fashion, embodying the all-powerful Name, but this did not endow the gem with any *spiritual* sense The appellation "Kabbalist" I shall always employ in this treatise in its strictest acceptation, and the present is as good a place as any for stating my reasons for doing so It is the rule nowadays to treat the Kabbala as the pure production of the Middle Ages, and such it probably is, in the form under which it is now presented to us I will not, indeed, go as far as the most learned Rabbi of our times, and boldly assert that Moses himself was a profound Kabbalist, although "the Wisdom of the Egyptians," in which Holy Writ declares he was a proficient, was beyond a doubt something of very much the same nature Whatever unprejudiced person will carefully read what I have adduced of the doctrines of Sastri and of Marcus (themselves "converted" Jews) will find there the regular system of the Kabbala fully developed, and its earliest and Egyptian rudiments in the "Pistis Sophia" of Valentinus No person really acquainted with the history of religions can suppose that these theosophists *invented* these rules of interpretation they merely transferred principles sanctioned by antiquity from the explanation of the Old Testament to that of the New

To return to our *Chnuphis*, *Chubis*, or *Chuphis* (for thus the Greeks transliterated the Coptic *Kneph*) it is probable that the veneration in which this sigil of the Pharaoh Nechepsi was held, was the true source of the legend concerning Moses's elevation of the Brazen Serpent At all events, I know of an enamel picture of the scene (date, thirteenth century) in which the Serpent, lifted up on the Cross, is figured with the radiated lion's head, really as he is seen on these talismans This particular sigil is generally engraved on calcedony, varying in colour from olive-green to waxy-white The best executed have for material the plasena traversed by an opaque white line (Pliny's *Iaspis Grammatias*), the estimation of which as an amulet by the Orientals he particularly mentions

1 The reverse of this gem reads *Chumis*, accompanied by a row of vowels that appear to contain the word IEH, which is, according to Kabbala, an *inferior* title of God.

2 The Serpent elevated above the *thymele*, Bacchic altar—a combination betraying the influence of the Dionysiac Mysteries. He declares in phonetic Hebrew, "I, I am the Good Spirit." The reverse of this gem had been covered with a long invocation in minute characters, now almost entirely lost by the fracture of the material in the fire to which it had accompanied its owner (New York)

3 This Chnuphis, of exceptionally fine work and yet finer material, has each of the *seven* rays of the crown tipped by one of the seven vowels that make up the Ineffable Name The reverse exhibits the serpent-entwined wand, (badge of the Egyptian priesthood) which generally goes with this sigil, and doubtless added to its power. Moses's rod and Aesculapius's club hence took their origin

4 Another Chnuphis, in the ordinary style It is noticeable how the gem-cutter has endeavoured to give variety to the endless repetition of the same sigil, by altering the arrangement of the serpentine folds

Plate E

MONUMENTS OF THE SERAPIS WORSHIP

1 Serapis, viewed as the Sun-god, enthroned, at his feet, the triple-headed monster described by Macrobius Before him stands Isis, or Mother Earth, holding a bunch of wheat-ears and poppy-heads, to mark her character The legend is the invocation "Immaculate is Our Lady, Isis!" A fine specimen of Alexandrian art, in a beautiful sard (New York)

2 Venus, arranging her hair at a mirror, held up to her by a Cupid, two Loves, hovering in the air, hold a myrtle-crown over her head The inscription "The Manifestation of Aroriph," occurs in a similar connection upon a gem in the Paris Cabinet It is hard to determine whether she be the "nuda veritas," whose Kabbalistic revelation to Marcus is given in my text, or merely a talisman for engendering love towards the wearer, the material, magnetic hæmatite, supports the latter acceptation. The reverse exhibits Horus, seated on the lotus, planted upon the *baris*, which is constructed out of long papyrus-stalks lashed together He here takes the title of *Abraxas*, and is surrounded by adoring triplets of all the animals held sacred by the Egyptians. The symbol of the Sun is seen at his right

3 Bust of Serapis, very curious for the prayer surrounding it, "Protect Jupiter!" a proof that Serapis is here regarded as the Supreme Being, and the ancient Jupiter reduced to the rank of an astral Power, as, indeed he was occasionally so understood in better times Thus Persius —"Saturnumque gravem nostro *Iove* fregimus una" (v 50)

4 Isis, veiled, with the *tubulus* on her head, and leaning on a tall sceptre, in the pose of the Roman Juno, for whom she might be mistaken but for the invocation on the other side, "Baffle, Serapis, the Evil Eye!" which declares the object of this talisman

5 Serapis, enthroned, seen in front face Inscribed "Hermes," followed by three letters, the initials of some then well-known address to that god Or if merely a private signature (Martial mentions a physician of the name) the initials refer to his business The God of the Shades was a very fit patron for a professional who had doubtless done his best to swell the ranks of his subjects Red jasper (New York)

PLATE F

ANCIENT EGYPTIAN TYPES ADAPTED TO GNOSTIC IDEAS.

It is in this class that the influence of Judaism is more strongly marked than in any other family of these monuments These gems were designed as amulets against the power of demons, either considered specially, or as manifested in the diseases of which they were the final cause to mankind But before proceeding further, it will tend much to the elucidation of this curious subject briefly to sketch the *orthodox* Jewish doctrine upon this point There is no such thing in existence as a spirit *naturally* evil, inasmuch as God, being all goodness, was absolutely incapable of creating evil Satan is himself an angel, like the others, and has his own place in the Court of Heaven, but he is deputed to test, by temptation, the strength of Man's virtue, since without a *struggle* there can be no *crown* The Babylonian Rabbi, Philemon,* having demonstrated this grand truth to the satisfaction of his numerous school, was surprised the next day by a visit from this *Ange mal entendu*, in a bodily shape, who tendered him public thanks† for the pains he had taken to set his character in a true light But, unfortunately, the Demiurgus had commenced his work by creating so vast a number of spirits, that the Sabbath-even came upon him before he had made bodies enough for half of them. These poor houseless beings are not naturally malignant, but are jealous of their more fortunate brethren, for the same reason that "the man who has no coat to his back hates the man that has" They therefore roam up and down the world, ever striving to force their way into bodies already occupied, where their struggles with the rightful owner give birth to all the maladies that flesh is heir to It is remarkable that the latter belief is universal among primitive races, however widely separated—the Samoiedes, the Hindoos, the Red Indians Something similar, too, may be found in Plutarch's curious disquisitions on the nature of demons, contained in his two Treatises upon Oracles

It is the fashion of our days to believe that the Jews borrowed all their metaphysical theories from the Platonists of Alexandria, but whoever has gone deeply into the subject sees good reason to suspect that both Jews and Greeks had gone, independently of each other, to a much more ancient source for such traditions

* Or "Polemo," as the Hebrew may equally well be read

† "Kissed his knees" is the expression in the Talmud

1. The Agathodæmon Serpent, mounted upon a pair of human legs. A unique variety of the class—the same idea being more usually embodied in a human figure with head and neck of a serpent, or in a serpent with the head of Serapis The long invocation on the field evidently begins with the name of "Abraxas"

2 The jackal-headed Anubis, an *Egyptian* sceptre in each hand, advancing between the Sun and the Moon, the regular emblems of Eternity A remarkable specimen of religious syncretism, for the power of the Pharaonic god is doubled by adding, on the reverse, the name of Michael, guardian-angel of the Jewish race, between four stars, which certainly stand for the letters of the Great *Tetragrammaton*

3 Mummy, enveloped in the folds of the guardian Agathodæmon The detached letters around (often so found in these gems) seem to cloak the word "Initia" If so, this may have been a token (*symbolum*) given to the neophyte upon his initiation into certain mysteries a custom to which St John alludes, mentioning the "white stone" with the New Name graven thereon, to be given to him that overcometh

4 A Power equipped with double arms and wings, bearing sceptres to mark his dignity, and carrying on his head the sacramental Table The tree-trunk below, with its *Five* lopped-off branches, had doubtless a deep mystic meaning, probably the *degree* of the person who carried the talisman Of the most barbarous execution, but valuable for the name "Baincho" on the reverse · the astral Power, according to the "Pistis-Sophia," resident in the planet Mercury

5 Anubis, in one hand the sceptre, in the other the lustral vase, standing above the open left hand, which Apuleius informs us was the type of *Justice* At his side is the goddess of Truth, her head formed out of a bunch of ostrich-feathers under her feet the udder-shaped vessel carried in the Isiac procession One deity is invoked by "Thou art our Father!" the other is "Sun of the Universe!" The letters in the middle seem to make up the owner's name, "Pia . "

6 Anubis, advancing with the sceptre and *situla* the legend on the reverse is unexplained

7 A talisman, certainly meant to be of mighty efficacy, for it combines the influences of Anubis, Cnuphis, and Horus with that of the God of the Jews, rudely cut upon the four sides of a cube of steaschist

PLATE G.

EGYPTIAN TYPES (*continued*)

1. In this composition an element from a little-used source is introduced The Grecian Apollo, distinguished by his proper attribute, the bay-branch, is seen caressing the Ibis, sacred to Thoth, scribe of the gods. The latter deity being identified with Hermes, his bird carries the caduceus, it also bears upon its head the corn-measure, typical of abundance

2 The Ass-headed Typhon, or the Principle of Evil, with quadruple

wings and one foot hoofed, carries by the tail two monstrous scorpions: over his head a scarabæus flying. Of no esoteric meaning, but simply an amulet against the bite of the reptile, made after the rule in such cases prescribed. The most convincing proof of the practice is the early Greek gem published by Gen. Cesnola ('Cyprus' pl. xl. 17), representing two asps, with the explanation EXK, and to this day the Arabs always draw upon their amulets the figure of the thing against which it ought to guard the wearer.

3. A *Dual* Power, who combines the jackal's head of Anubis with the ass's head of Typhon, whence one of his feet is hoofed, brandishes in his four hands swords and torches, wherewith to scare away the evil spirits. The legend on the reverse, ΠΕΡΑΑΜΒΑ VΒΑΚΑ ΚΞΙΚ Λ, has not been read, but contains the Coptic name of Anubis.

4. The Sun-god, Phre, with radiated head, *adoring* the seated Thoth, ibis-headed, and using the invocation (cut on the reverse) "Thou art our Father!" Inasmuch as the Neo-Platonists made Hermes to be the Power that regulates the motion of the heavens (for which reason Julian addressed his morning prayer to *him*), there is evident reason why the god of Day should thus do homage to Thoth as his superior and director.

5. A very popular *Gryllus*, its components being the emblems of the elements—the *Bird* standing for air, the *Lion* for Fire, the *Ram's head* for Earth, and the *Bacchic* mark for water. This Pagan talisman has been Gnosticised by Thoth's ibis, with the Holy Names, "Abraxas" and "Iao," but the work on both sides is evidently from the same hand, and in the style of the fourth century. The material is a rarely-used stone—*obsidian*.

PLATE II

EGYPTIAN TYPES (*continued*)

1. Tortoise lying upon the lotus, which springs out of the back of a crocodile. The unexplained legend of the reverse occurs again in connection with an analogous design—a vulture-headed winged Genius, seated on the back of a double-headed crocodile, published by Walsh (No. 13) in his 'Coins, Gems, &c., illustrating the Progress of Christianity.'

2. The Ark of the Covenant, apparently copied from the "Altar of Lyons," that so common device of the brass coins of Tiberius. The engraver of this late Roman gem had not studied the minute description of the Ark, given in the Law. There is a Rabbinical tradition (although savouring too much of Alexandrian philosophy to demand any credit) that the Cherubim placed over it were represented as male and female, in the act of copulation, in order to express the grand doctrine of the essence of *Form* and *Matter*, the two principles of all things. When the Chaldeans broke into the Sanctuary, and beheld this most astounding emblem, they naturally enough exclaimed "Is this your God, of whom you boast, that He is such a lover of purity!"

On the side is a blundered attempt at the mystic word, *Tetragrammaton*, i e the Name of Four Letters,' *viz.*—*Jod*, *He*, *Vau*, *He*. For the Names of God, according to the Kabbala, are made up respectively, of *Four*, *Forty-two*, and *Seventy-four* letters. The second explains the motive for the number of sacrifices offered up by Balaam in his fruitless attempt to propitiate the God of the Hebrews, and perhaps may have induced the composers of the Genealogy of Jesus (though working independently of each other) to bring out the same mystic number by curtailing the second series of *three* of its kings

3 A doubly-winged and doubly-armed Power, holding four Egyptian sceptres, and standing on a coiled serpent, enclosing a Holy Name. The legend is a transliteration of the Hebrew for "Light of Lights" Another form of such transliteration is given by Caylus ('Recueil d'Antiquites,' vi. Pl 21), σρωοριονσ, reading from the end backwards, cut for reverse to a coiled serpent enclosing various *sigla*

4 Thoth's baboon, bearing on his head the Solar disk, in the attitude of adoration The reverse bears HNA-MEPω, sometimes written MAPω-HNI, "Enlighten my eyes!" whence we may suspect this very common type to be no more than an amulet against ophthalmia

5 This gem is given here as a good specimen of a type of which great numbers are to be met with, although its whole conception, and the vague symbols in the field—the Solomon's Seal, celestial globe, etc entirely out of the antique taste, refer its creation to the fancy of mediæval quacks and astrologers Was the figure suggested by the idol "in the shape of an *Old Man*," with whose worship the Templars were so persistently charged? The present example, belonging as it does to the original Praun Cabinet, must have been executed before the beginning of the seventeenth century

6 The outline of the human figure filled up with "Holy Names," and thereby representing *Adam Kadmon*, "the Primitive Man" of the Kabala The finest example of this curious design, and in which the letters are the most clearly defined, is the one Caylus gives (l c pl 22), which has been cut by a later hand on the reverse of a Lion *passant*, in the Persian style

7 The Baboon adoring a *Triangle*, Egyptian symbol of the Moon, elevated upon a column bearing an inscription The fact that the Pythagoreans (who avowedly got their whole system from Egypt) symbolised Athene by the triangle, lends strength to the idea that the Attic goddess was in her origin merely the expression of the Lunar Power

Plate J

SUBJECTS CONNECTED WITH THE MITHRAIC MYSTERIES

1 This pretty design may be tersely described in a line of Manilius —

"Quadrijugis et Phœbus equis et Delia bigis"

Sol and Luna in their appropriate equipages a heathenish device enough, but the same hand has backed their influence by the invocation, "Iao

Sabaoth, Abraxas," He, i.e. the living God, protect Aparastathe, the bearer of this talisman. Similar formulæ, always attached to *women's* names, very frequently occur.

2. The Zoroastrian *Dog*, of whom and whose office so much has been said in the text. The ill-cut *Bird* is intended for the *Raven*, the usual Mithraic attribute.

3. The *Lion* of Baal, the Syrian Sun-god, below, the Scarabæus typifying the Creative Power. The Phœnician inscription *Osan ēl*, "God gives strength," is the name of the owner of the signet. Lévy quotes an agate scarabæus at the British Museum exactly similar to this gem (a fine sard), a proof of the popularity of both type and name.

4. A unique talismanic device, converting a male Sphinx into a novel bird, by the addition of the legs of a crane and the tail of a scorpion. It is engraved in the Persian style: my motive for admitting it into the present class.

5. The Zodiacal Lion, guided by its astral Genius in its course through the seven planets.

6. The Sun-god, with radiated head, mounted upon a camel, typifying the East. Below is set the fire-altar of Mithraic worship. He is followed by Chanticleer, attribute of the god of Day, preceded by the Horse—his peculiar sacrifice, as Ovid tells us:—

> "Placat *equo* Persis radiis Hyperiona cinctum,
> Ne detur Celeri victima tarda deo." (Fasti I. 305–86.)

PLATE K.

MITHRAIC (*continued*).

1. Circular copper plate, of the same size as the drawing, bearing the name of *Aurelius Furellius*, the person for whose benefit the talisman was devised. It represents a female figure, standing in the attitude of adoration, legend, "The Birth of Salvation." On the reverse is seen the Solar Lion bestriding a corpse, a type so frequent in this class that it may reasonably be referred to the entrance-rite of initiation, the "simulation of death" alluded to by Spartianus.

2. The most elegant of these mystic designs that has ever come to my knowledge. Two Cranes, one with the head of a Ram, the other of a Bull, stand guardians over the Mithraic sacramental table, under which lies crouched the Solar Lion, "the House of the Sun." Upon the table are set the sacred vessels, above it is the Delphic E, badge of Apollo, between two Palmyrene (?) letters, and over all the Seven Planets, engraved with an accuracy worthy of its elegance in a very fine sard.

3. A talisman of uncommon potency, to judge from the profusion of symbolism with which its two faces are overloaded. A four-winged, four-armed Power, standing like the Babylonian Belus in the air, is involved with a multiplicity of legends, amongst which the usual formulæ "Thou art our Father," "Sun of the Universe," "Michael," "Adonai,' can clearly

be read The reverse shows a female figure standing and adoring the Deity, who guides the Solar light In the legends we can distinguish "Abraxas," "Michael," and "Michalo."

4. This type only differs from the last by the addition of the prostrate man under the Lion's feet, and that nothing definite can be made out of the disjointed inscription The reverse merely bears the *Great Name* "Iao, Sabaoth," and the Seven Vowels The potency of such words is still an article of faith with all *true* Jews. In the year 1835–6, the Rabbi of Neutra, in Hungary, actually stood his trial for murder on the charge of having cursed, by the "Ineffable Name" an *enlightened* lady whom he had ordered to leave the synagogue on the Sabbath-day, because she had ventured to make her appearance there with her *hair in sight*, and who had died suddenly on the very same day The Rabbi only escaped conviction by publicly and solemnly disclaiming the possession of any such power, to the inexpressible disgust of his whole congregation, who looked upon him as a wretch that had denied his God in order to save his life!

PLATE L

MITHRAIC (*continued*)

1 The Mithraic Lion, moving through the stars of heaven The reverse exhibits a complete assemblage of the *Siglæ* that are found, dispersed, upon so many talismans That they stand for the names of deities and astral Powers may be guessed from the fact that Mohammedans still express *Allah* by a circle filled up with diagonal lines

2 Lion-headed Man, doubtless a *Leonticus* (one of the grades in the Mithraic Mysteries), uttering, with uplifted hand, the inexplicable adjuration, "O, Centaur of God, Thou match for a hundred [demons]!" Here ἑκατοντομάχος is formed after the analogy of μονομάχος, "a match for one"

3 A *Mobed* (Zoroastrian priest or *Magus*) performing his nocturnal devotions before an altar, on which are set up various *sacra*, amongst which may be recognised the regular insignia of his profession, the Sword and the Divining-rods Engraved upon the base of a calcedony cone, an early form of the signet in Assyria

4 Horus, the Vernal Sun-god, making the gesture of adoration, his whip resting upon his left arm He is seated upon the seed-vessel of the lotus, that aptest symbol of the Universe, in virtue of its innumerable contents In the long, clearly-cut legend that fills the exergue, no hitherto-explained formulæ are to be recognised.

PLATE M.

GENERAL TALISMANS

1 Zodiacal Monster, compounded of Scorpio and Capricornus, carrying a legionary standard. Bearing in mind that the former *Sign* is under the patronage of Mars, according to Manilius—"Pugnax Mavorti Scorpius haeret"—and the latter a badge of the second Augustan Legion, we may

reasonably suppose this gem to have been engraved for the benefit of some member of that corps Sard (New York Museum)

2 Three lines of the usual Gnostic *siglae*, in a cartouche formed by a coiled serpent, precisely in the same way that the Brahmins still write the Great Name AUM— a sure evidence of the meaning of these mystic characters Sard., set in an iron ring, of which only fragments remain

3 Fortuna, with rudder and horn of plenty, standing The word *Feliciter*, in scattered letters, the usual acclamation of the crowd, and the *palm-branch* prove this gem a present to some favourite *auriga* Its purport is the same as that of the monogram so often found enclosed in the field of the Antoniate medal, also accompanied with a palm, which has at last been made out to contain the elements of *Palma Feliciter*!

4 Masks of Silenus and of Bacchus, combined into the outline of an elephant's head, bearing a caduceus in his trunk. The typical beast of *India* is an allusion to the *Indian* origin of the god, and the conceit was a favourite with the Romans, to judge from the number of such compositions that they have bequeathed us Red jasper (New York)

5 Astrological *Trine*, or figure produced by dividing the circle of the Zodiac into equilateral triangles Here, Virgo (Astræa) at the apex of a triangle, is borne up by Taurus and Capricorn This was the horoscope of Pescennius Niger, who placed it on the reverse of a coin, on account of its appropriateness to his surname of *Justus*, of which virtue Astræa was the emblem

6 The Gorgon's Head · the type explains itself by the legend, "I protect Rhoromandares"—some Greco-Persian, to judge from his Oriental name. The younger Lucian tells us in his 'Philopatris' that the Gorgon was placed upon the shields of the Heroes as being "a thing that wards off all dangers" Red jasper (New York)

7. Mars, grounding arms, in the costume of a soldier of the times of Constantine The legend declares the virtue of the *sigil*. "Mars hath cut off the disease of the liver' But a most interesting point in the amulet has been discovered by Prof Stephens, viz, that the four characters behind the head of Mars are the Runes for ABLE, *Help* Under Constantine and his sons, the Franks (as Ammian observes) were paramount in the army It is easy to conceive how some officer of that nation has thought to augment the great virtue of this important talisman by the addition of one of his national spells Engraved in a slight manner, upon hæmatite

8 Naked Warrior, upon a prancing steed, brandishing a *mace*, that specially Oriental weapon, legend, "The Seal of God" Curious for the material—a turquoise, to the present day the Persians firmly believe in the protective virtue of this gem, to which they give the name of *Phiruz*—"The Victor"

Plate N.

GENERAL TALISMANS (*continued*)

1 Universal Nature, symbolised in a highly poetic manner, combining all her forces for the protection of the bearer The *Eagle* of Jupiter (Air), the *Dolphins* of Neptune (Water), the *Lion* of Sol (Fire), are moulded into the mask of Pan, whose semi-bestial nature is of the *Earth*, earthy

Winckelmann, in describing an intaglio of the Stosch Cabinet (No 1232) Pan, playing upon his syrinx, seated in the centre of the Zodiac, observes that the ancients considered this god as the "Type of the Universe", and saw in his horns and shaggy hairs mystic allusions to the solar rays For the same reason Apollo shared his Gryphon with Pan, and Orpheus sings of him as "Attuning the harmony of the world with his sportive music" Onyx cameo (Rollin and Feuardent)

2 Isis, standing, with the *Asp*, badge of royalty, rising from her forehead The Coptic legend opens with the name of *Osiris* The characters in the inner circle seem to be Demotic—they are *not* Palmyrene I have published this gem, as being the finest example of the class that has ever come to my knowledge, by the kind permission of its owner, Mr J C Robinson Dark jasper (On the reverse, a later hand has inscribed the "Great Name," and the Seven Vowels, to adapt the talisman to the new creed)

Nos 3 and 6 are very frequent forms, made up entirely of *siglae* and *Numerals*, on which latter subject more shall be said further on

4. This spell, "Great is the *Name* of the One God," is the Jewish defiance to its rival, "Great is the *Name* of Serapis, —of which Caylus publishes a beautiful example, in *relief*, of antique paste—a material that indicates a large manufacture of the same article to meet a constant demand

5 Certain astral Powers, represented by their then well-known symbols, are enlisted, by this engraving, in the service of a lady, *Sabinia Quinta* A popular kind of talisman this another very similar is known to me, made for the benefit of one *Victorina*

Pythagoras is perpetually referred to by Hippolytus as the real master of the Gnostics in the application of *Numerals* to the expression of things divine He is known to have learned his system in Egypt, and necessarily brought away with him the cyphers which he found employed for the same purpose amongst his teachers The primitive Egyptian numerals were of the simplest nature, but their *abbreviations* ultimately became distinct symbolical cyphers for the several days of the months, and out of these cyphers the Arabs composed their own system of notation. Hence it follows that many of the Gnostic *siglæ* may be no more than numerals connected with the astrological use of the charm on which they occur. In fact, Porphyry says of Pythagoras (in his 'Life') that his famous 'Numbers' were merely hieroglyphs, whereby he expressed ideas connected with his own philosophy The so-called "Pythagorean Numerals" are shown in the MSS of Boethius's Geometry, composed in the sixth century And that the "Numbers" of Pythagoras were *Ten*, appears from the remark of Aristotle (Met xii 8) "that some philosophers maintained that ideas and numbers were of the same nature, and amount to *Ten* in all"

That the Numerals as written down by "the last of the Romans," were Egyptian demotic characters in their origin is a very probable conjecture, but it is a curious fact, and remarkably confirms what has been said above, that several of them when viewed upside down assume the exact form of our present Arabic cyphers.

Plate O

HINDOO SYMBOLS AND CASTE-MARKS

I *No* 1 Type of Mahadeva or Siva Fire personified

No 2. Type of Vishnu Water

No 3 The *Sherkun* symbol of the union of the two Elements

No 4 The five-pointed figure representing the conjunction of Brahma (*Creator*) with Siva (*Destroyer*) becomes the famous "Solomon's Seal," the badge of the Jewish nation, and therefore engraved upon their tombs in the Roman Catacombs

The equilateral Triangle, *Trikun*, symbolises Triune Co-equality A Point (mathematical) the self-existing Deity The circle expresses Brahma, or Eternity The Triangle inscribed in the Circle, Trinity in Unity The Circle within the Triangle, Unity in Trinity

The worshippers of a *Sacti* (Female Power) mark their sacred jars with the very expressive symbol, *No* 5, those of Vishnu with *No* 6, and those of Siva with *No* 8, which signifies the copulation of Siva with Durga

Amongst the signatures of the ancient *Jaina* (Buddhist) kings, occur the symbols 8 and 9; and also the so called "Maeander," that frequent decoration of Greek Coins

The six following symbols are various *Caste-marks*, which religious Hindoos put upon their foreheads every morning, with ashes of cowdung, or coloured earths, and powdered sandalwood, producing a great variety in them by the employment of different colours Those figured here designate the followers of Vishnu

II These marks distinguish the votaries of Siva and his wife, Parvati The most obvious symbol of the Passive Principle of Nature, the mystic *Yoni*, (and with which Sesostris branded the nations that had submitted to his arms without resistance) is decorously repressed in the general form of these marks, the two Deities being those that preside over propagation and change which the vulgar call by the name of *Death*

III Other caste-marks, denoting minor differences in the sects that bear them they are given here because they include in their number some that appear to have been the originals of certain Mediæval *siglæ*

IV Characters cut upon the rock in the sandstone quarries of Silsilis in Upper Egypt That they are *alphabetical* may be inferred from the fact of their accompanying the figures of various animals, they are of great interest to us, being identical with those so often found upon our talisman.

V Palmyrene characters from a finely-cut inscription now in the Louvre

VI *Siglæ*, exactly of the nature of Masons' Marks, and of very ancient date, for they are found on the pottery deposited in the Gallic tombs around Bologna Some are stamped in the clay *before* baking, and therefore must have indicated the maker's name, but the greater number have been scratched on the surface at some later time, probably when placed in the sepulchre, to carry down to posterity the memory of the deceased Those here given are selected from the list figured by the Conte Gozzalini in his very instructive memoir 'Gli Scavi presso Bologna,' 1877

VII Masons' Marks, cut on the ashlar of the old Palace of Sadilat, near Ispahan, whence they were copied by Ouseley, in the belief that they were inscriptions in some unknown tongue

VIII Masons' Marks from the "Drawing-room" of Raglan Castle, an Elizabethan building They will suffice for specimens of the notation, all the mediæval, early or late, being of the same nature, though infinitely varied in minor details Many lists of these have been published from time to time, the most recent, of the Marks in Duffield Church, a Norman building, published in the Journal of the Derbyshire Arch Soc, ix p 168

IX Every genuine Free Mason (*not* Rosicrucian *recoctus* Freemason) after serving his apprenticeship, and being made "free and accepted" of the Craft, receives his own "Mark," which he must thenceforth cut upon every stone that he dresses, in order to identify his own work when pay-day comes The essential principle in the Mark is that it must have an *odd* number of terminations The Marks here set down were in use with the masons employed in the construction of the South Wales Railway. The most convincing proof of the emptiness of the lofty pretensions of our so-called Freemasons, is that they actually are entirely ignorant that this most ancient rule of the Craft, to which they pretend to belong, is still regularly followed

BIBLIOGRAPHICAL APPENDIX

BY

JOSEPH JACOBS, B A

PART I — GNOSTICISM AND ITS SOURCES, pp 1–112

THE Gnostic heresies play so important a part in the Christianity of the first three centuries that they naturally come up for treatment in all the Church histories for that period, such as those of Gieseler, Neander, Hase, and Schaff, as well as in the histories of Christian doctrine (Hagenbach, F K Meier, F C Baur, A Neander, L Noack, &c), and even in the histories of philosophy of Ueberweg, Zeller, &c But the monographic treatment of the subject from the theological standpoint—the Gnostic gems attracted early attention—may be said to have begun with

A Neander — *Die genetische Entwickelung der vornehmsten gnostischen Systeme* Berl 1818 [Sober and clear]

C A Lewald — *De Doctrina Gnostica* 1818

J Matter — *Histoire critique du gnosticisme et de son influence sur les autres sectes religieuses et philosophiques pendant les six premiers siècles* Paris, 2 tomes, 1828 [Second and best edition, Strasbourg, 3 tomes, 1843 Somewhat superficial and viewy, but still useful, giving outlines of whole subject, including iconography]

E Burton — *Inquiry into the Heresies of the Apostolic Age* Oxford, 1830 [Bampton lectures for 1829, uncritical superseded for English readers by Mansel]

J A Moehler — *Versuch uber d Ursprung des Gnosticismus* Tub 1831

F C Baur — *Die Christliche Gnosis* Tubingen, 1835 [The place of publication indicates the tendency of this publication Baur's views are read to best advantage in his *Das Christenthum der 3 ersten Jahrhunderte*]

Norton — *History of the Gnostics* 1845

H Rossel — *Geschichte der Untersuchungen uber d Gnosticismus* in his *Theologische Nachlass* Berl 1847

R A Lipsius — *Gnosticismus* in Ersch and Gruber Bnd 71 1860 [The starting-point of new lines of inquiry rendered necessary by the publication by Miller of the *Philosophumena* attributed to Hippolytus (Clar Press, 1851)]

W Moller — *Geschichte der Cosmologie der griechischen Kirche bis an Origenes* Leipzig, 1862

H L Mansel —*The Gnostic Heresies of the First and Second Centuries* London, 1875 [Posthumous Edited by J B Lightfoot Best English work, clear, fair, mainly founded on Lipsius, classification of sects geographical His arrangement is *Notices of Gnosticism in New Test* (iv v)—*Precursors, Simon Magus and Menander* (vi)—*The Ophite Sects* (vii)—*Cerinthus, Carpocrates, Nazarenes and Ebionites* (viii)—*Syrian Sects, Saturninus, Tatian, Bardesanes* (ix)—*Egyptian, Basilides* (x)—*Valentinus and Valentinians* (xi xii)—*Asiatic Gnosticism, Marcion* (xiii)—*Judaising Reaction, Clementines, Elkesaites* (xiv)]

A Hilgenfeld —*Die Ketzergeschichte des Urchristenthums* Leipzig, 1884 [Ill-arranged, but at present the work round which discussion on Gnosticism centres]

These are the chief monographs on the whole subject. Besides these, several articles in theological reviews may be mentioned, many of them reaching the length of monographs They were mostly occasioned by the various publications mentioned above, as can be seen by their dates F R Lucke in *Berliner theol Zeitsch* 1819, J C L Gieseler in *Hall. lit Zeit* 1823, and in *Studien u Kritiken*, 1830, F C Baur *ibid*, 1837, H T Cheever in *Amer Bibl Repos* 1840, R Baxmann, *Deutsche Ztst* 1861 [translated *Amer Theol Rev* 1862], Hilgenfeld in *Ztst f wiss theol* Bd xiii. Articles in encyclopedias often show original research, or present useful summaries besides the epoch-making one of Lipsius in Ersch and Gruber, reference may be made to the same writer's article "Gnosis in Schenkel's *Bibel-Lexikon* (1868), C P Wing in McClintock and Strong, vol iii 1873 [useful bibliography], W L Alexander in last edition of Kitto and J. L. Jacobi in Herzog-Plitt

The SOURCES are scanty and scattered, at any rate as regards independent works by Gnostics In addition to scattered fragments in Grabe's *Spicilegium*, there have been published—

Munter —*Odæ gnosticæ* Kopenh 1812

Norberg —*Codex Nazareus vel Liber Adami* Leiden, 1815

[The so-called Bible of Gnosticism, i e of the Mendaites, on whom see *Christian Review*, Jan 1855, and Petermann in Herzog]

A Hahn — *Bardesanes Gnosticus Syrorum primus hymnologus* Leipz 1819

A Hahn —*Antitheses Marcionis Gnostici.* Leipz 1823

M G Schwartze —*Pistis Sophia, opus gnosticum a codice manuscripto Coptus Londini descripsit et Latine vertit M G Schwartze*, edidit J H Petermann Berl 1851–3

[Now considered to be a production of the later Ophite schools, see R Kostlin, *Die gnostische System des Buches Pistis Sophia* in *Theol Jahrb* for 1854]

But the real sources of our knowledge of Gnosticism are to be found in the earliest heresiologists, Irenæus (*Adv hæreses*), Epiphanius (*Adv hæreses*), and Hippolytus (*Elenchus* and *Philosophumena*), on the trustworthiness of these a considerable literature exists

G Volkmar—*Die Quellen der Ketzergeschichte* I Bnd 1855
R A Lipsius—*Zur Quellenkritik des Epiphanios* 1865
„ *Die Quellen der altesten Ketzergeschichte* 1875
A Harnack.—*Zur Quellenkritik d Gesch des Gnosticismus* 1873
, „ in *Zt f lut Theol* 1874, pp 143–226

Hilgenfeld's *Ketzergeschichte* goes thoroughly into these sources

---

P 3—*Aristobulus* Valckaener's monograph *De Aristobulo Judæo*, 1806, is still the fullest and best.

P 4, vide p 18, note on Enoch
"Book of Adam"—*Codex Nasareus Liber Adami appellatus, syriace transcriptus, latineque redditus a M Norberg* Berlin, 1815

P 7—Of the large literature on Ephesus it is sufficient to refer to Guhl, *Ephesiaca*, Berl 1843, Falkener, *Ephesus and the Temple of Diana* 1862

P 8—On traces of Gnosticism in the Gospels C C Tittmann, *De vestigiis Gnosticorum in Novo Testamento frustra quæsitis*, Leip 1773, translated *Contributions to Foreign Literature* New York, 1827 On Pre-Christian Gnosis, Lightfoot *Colossians*, pp 80 seq

P 14—Title given above, also Kostlin's monograph

P 24—Jews in ancient world form the subject of Prof Mayor's elaborate notes on Juvenal xiv 96–106, running over twelve closely printed pages and preceded *more suo* by an elaborate bibliography of previous treatment. The only thing of importance since is a paper of Heyd's *Les juifs devant l'opinion romaine* in *Rev des etudes juives* 1884 The relations of Gnosticism and Judaism formed the subject of the historian Graetz's first work, *Gnosticismus und Judenthum* Krotoschin, 1846

P 29—The Zendavesta is now translated in *Sacred Books of the East*, vols iv xxiii and xxxi For literature see Tiele, *Outlines of the History of Religion*, § 100 Chief work, Haug, *Essays on the Parsis* in Trubner's Oriental Series On Persian influences on Jewish angelology, Kohut, *Angelologie des Talmuds* 1868

P 33—Dr. Ginsburg collected in small compass the modern views on the Kabbala in his monograph *The Kabbala* 1866 It has attracted little attention from Jewish scholars since that date. All scientific inquirers place the origin of Kabbala in the twelfth century, though mysticism akin to it appears as early as Bible times On the great influence of the Kabbala in Middle Ages cf Stockl, *Gesch d Philos im Mittelalter* Bnd ii On the Talmud at the time of writing three monographs are about to appear—Prof Strack separately, Dr Ginsburg in Smith-Wace, *Dict of*

Christ Biog, and Dr Schiller-Szinessy in *Ency Brit* Hamburger's *Real-Encyclopadie*, though unequal, is useful and at present the easiest means of getting second-hand information about Talmudical topics

P 40 —Camillo Leonardi, *Speculum Lapidum* Ven 1502

P 42 —The earliest monograph dealing with the relations of Gnosticism to the East is J J Schmidt, *Verwandschaft d gnostischen Lehre mit den Religionssystemen d Orients* Leip 1828 On Manes and Manichaeism the great work is still Beausobre, *Histoire critique du Manichéisme* 1731 But important additions to our knowledge have come from Oriental sources, which are given in somewhat haphazard fashion but with excellent index in Flugel, *Mani, seine Lehre und seine Schriften* Leip 1862 Early works on Mani are given in Fabricius, *Bibl graec* t vii p 310 seq, ed Harles See also Kessler, *Untersuchungen z Genesis d manichaisch Religionssystem* 1876

P 49 —For bibliography of Buddhism see Tiele, *Outlines* § 82 A good short account by T Rhys Davids (S P C K) The best recent books are Oldenburg, *Buddha, his Life and Doctrines*, 1885, and H Kern, *Der Buddhismus u seine Geschichte in Indien* Leipz 1885

P 51 *n* —See *Buddhist Records of the Western World*, translated by S Beal 2 vols 1885

P 52 —The best account of the Essenes is in the appendices to Lightfoot's *Colossians*, strangely neglected by German inquirers as Lucius

P. 58 —The special literature on Simon Magus is rather large

Mosheim – *De uno Simone Mago* in his *Dissert ad hist eccl pert* 2nd ed vol ii Alton 1767

A Simson —*Leben und Lehre Simon Magiers* in *Zt f. hist Theol* 1841

F Huelsen —*Simonis Magi vita doctrinaque* Berl 1868 [Progr]

A Hilgenfeld —*Der Magier Simon* in *Zt f wiss Theol* 1868, pp 357–96.

R A Lipsius —*Die Quellen d romischen Petrussage* Kiel, 1872

W Moller in Herzog-Plitt, 1884, t xii pp 246–56

On the alleged statue of Simon see A van Dale, *De statua Simonis Magi* Amst 1700, and *Corp Ins Lat* vi 1

P 70 —On Basilides besides the Disputatio in Zacagni, *Collect monument veter* see

Uhlhorn —*System des Basilides* 1855

Baur in his *Theol Jahrb* 1856

Hofstede de Groot —*Basilides als erste Zeuge f neutestament Schriften* [translated from Dutch] 1868

J L Jacobi —*Ueber d ursprungl Basilid System* in *Zt f. Kirchengesch* 1877 p 493 ff

P 82 —Besides the Ophite Textbook 'Pistis Sophia' mentioned above, the special treatments are to be found in

Mosheim —*Gesch d Schlangenbruder* Helmst 1746–8
A Fuldner —*De Ophitis* Rint 1831
Lipsius —*Ueber de ophit System* in *Zt f wiss Theol.* 1863–4
F. Giraud —*Ophitæ, dissertatio historico-theologica de eorum origine placitis ac fatis* Paris, 1884 [best modern work]

P 101 —On the Egyptian Pantheon see Lipsius, *Der Gotterkreis d alten Aegypter* Berlin Academy, 1851, and Tiele *l c*, § 29 Their representation in art best given in Perrot-Chipiez, *Histoire de l'Art dans l'Antiquite—Egypte* (also English translation, 1884) Maspero, *Archeologie égyptienne* 1887

Part II —Worship of Mithras and Serapis, pp 115 *seq*

The interesting problems that have collected about the worship of Mithras have been dealt with in the following special works —

Sainte-Croix —*Recherches critiques sur les mystères du paganisme* Paris, 1817.
Seel —*Die Mithras Geheimnisse* 1823
Hammer —*Mithriaka* Vienna, 1834
Creuzer —*Das Mithreum* Heidelb 1838
Lajard —*Recherches sur le culte public et les mystères de Mithra* Paris, 1847–8
Windischmann —*Mithra* 1857

Shrines of Mithras are described by J Hodgson in *Ælena Archeologia* i 274–320, who gives the earlier literature, and by Stark, *Zwei Mithræen d grossherzogl Alterthumersammlung in Karlsruhe* 1861

P 116 —On the Persian relations of Mithraicism see Burnouf, *Sur le Yaçna*

P 117 —For another etymology see G Barzilai, *Gli Abraxas, studeo archeologico* Trieste, 1873

P 119 —This view of the origin of Christmas was first enunciated by Wernsdorf, *De origine solemnium Natalis Christi ex festivitate Natalis Invicti*, Wittenb 1757, he is followed by Jablonsky in his *Opuscula*, Amst 1809, vol iii p 351 seq, who argues that the Basilidians caused the adoption (p 361)

P 120 —The latest monograph on the Sadducees and Pharisees is that of E Montet, *Essai sur les origines des partis saducéens et pharisééns* Paris, 1883 A full bibliography at end of Seiffert's article *Sadducaer* in Herzog-Plitt

P 129 —Flam Vacca in Nordini, *Roma Antiqua*, pt iv 1771

P 137 —On contemporary Parsees, T D F Karaka, *History of the Parsis*, 2 vols 1885

P 139 —Caste-marks of modern Hindoos are given in Sir G Birdwood's *Industrial Arts of India* 1880 (plate M)

P 153 —On penances in general, the exhaustive work of F W H

Wasserschleben, *Die Bussordnungen der abendländischen Kirche.* Halle, 1851. On those of the Brahmins, Sir M. Williams, *Modern India*

PP 158 seq —See bibliog note on p 104

P 174 —The mitre is unknown in the Eastern Church, v Hefele, *Beiträge z Kirchengeschichte*, t ii

P 179 —Reference may be made here to Lessing's well-known essay

P 195 —The latest study of the *jettatura* is, I am informed by Mr. Nutt, a series of articles, *La Fascination*, by Tuchmann in *Melusine* 1885–7

Part III —The Agathodæmon Worship and the Abraxas Gems, pp 215 seq

P 217 —On serpent worship comp introductory essay to Fergusson, *Tree and Serpent Worship*, second ed 1873 Among Semites, Baudissin, *Studien zur semit Religionsgeschichte* I § iv.

P 226 —J Bellermann, *Ueber die Gemmen der Alten mit dem Abraxasbilde* Stück 1–3 Berl 1818, 19, 20

P 230 —This formed the subject of a monograph by F X Kraus, *Das Spottcrucifix* Freib 1872 V cut on p 279 here

P. 251 —Vide Barzilai's tract quoted in bibliog note on p 117

P 254 —On the age of this "Gematria" see J Gow, *Hist of Greek Mathematics*, p 44

P 259 —For bibliography of Basilides see note on p 70

P 263 —On Valentinus, G Heinrici, *Die Valentinische Gnosis und die Heilige Schrift* Berl 1871

P 279 —On the fig see monograph referred to in bibliog note on p 230

P. 281 —The 99 epithets of God in Islam form the subject of E Arnold's poem, *Pearls of the Faith* 1882

P 281 *n* —Levy, *Gemmen und Siegel* 1869, p 47–9 and Taf iii

P 284 —*Die Seherin von Prevorst* was published 1866, and translated into almost all European languages

Part IV —The Figured Monuments of Gnosticism, pp 305 seq.

Gnostic gems have long attracted the attention of antiquarians, their separate investigation beginning with

Macarius —[Heureux] *Abraxas seu Apistopistus* Ant 1657, with appendix by Chifflet [Plates included in Gorlæus, *Dactyliotheca*, 3rd edit Leyd 1695]

Kirchmann —*De annulis* 1657, c xxi

Montfaucon —*L'Antiquité expliquée* Paris, 1722, vol ii livre iii. Les Abraxas, pp 353 seq Supp vol ii 1724, pp 209 seq

Gori.—*Thesaurus gemmarum astriferarum* Florence, 1750, fol. [includes essay by Passeri, *De gemmis Basilidianis*]

Marrette.—*Traité des pierres gravées* 1750 II 68–73

F Munter.—*Versuch uber d Kirchlichen Alterthumer der Gnostiker* 1790

Bellerman.—Vide bibliog note to p 226 [only vignettes on title pages]

Kopp.—*Palæographia critica.* 1819–29, 4 vols [third and fourth on Abraxas]

Matter.—*Histoire du gnosticisme* 1828 [2nd edition, 1843]

Hammer.—*Deux coffrets gnostiques du moyen âge.* 1832

Stickel.—*De gemma Abraxea nondum edita* 1842.

Matter.—*Voyage gnostique en Italie* 1852

King.—*The Gnostics and their remains, ancient and mediæval* London, 1864 [First edition of present work including all the gems in the preceding and more also 13 plates and 27 woodcuts]

No collection of consequence has been made or published since 1864 till the present volume

P 309.—On ΙΑΩ see Graf v Baudissin's elaborate essay "*Der Ursprung des Gottesnamens* Ἰάω" in his *Studien zur semitischen Religionsgeschichte*, 1876, pp 181–254 On the name itself cf S R Driver, *Recent Theories on the Origin and Nature of the Tetragrammaton* in *Studia Biblica* 1885, pp 1–20

P 370.—On the *apices* of Boethius considerable discussion has arisen Woepcke, in *Jour Asiat* 1863, p 54, traces them from India, T H Martin, *Annali di matem* 1863, p 350, from Egypt, while Friedlein, *Zahlzeichen*, pp 15–19, &c, and Weissenborn in *Zt Math Phys*, 1879, declare the passage in Boethius to be a forgery See Gow, *Hist Greek Math*, p 38

P. 372.—On magic squares treated mathematically, see De Morgan in *English Cyclopædia*, *sub voce* sect *Arts and Sciences*, vol v col 415.

PART V.—TEMPLARS, ROSICRUCIANS, FREEMASONS

ON the TEMPLARS the most complete history is still that of Dupin, *Histoire de l'ordre militaire des Templiers* Bruxelles, 1751 On their mysteries, Loiseleur, *La doctrine secrète des Templiers* Orleans, 1872 And the trials, Michelet, *Procès des Templiers* 1871 The statutes contained in Merzdorf, *Geheimstatuten des Ordens der Tempelherren*, Halle, 1877, have been shown to be fictitious by H G Prutz, *Geheimlehre und Geheimstatuten des Tempelherren Ordens* Berl 1879 See also F Schottmuller, Der Untergang des Templer-Ordens, mit urkundlichen Beitragen 2 vols 1887

On the ROSICRUCIANS the earlier literature is given in W v Murr, *Ueber d wahren Ursprung d Rosenkreuzer* See also Buhle, *Ursprung und vornehmste Schicksale d Orden d Freimaurer und Rosenkreuzer*, 1810, and Klupfel, *sub voc.* in Herzog-Plitt On the origin of Freemasonry, full references in R. F. Gould's huge and uncritical *History of Freemasonry*, vol. i. 1884.

P. 393*n*.—A third edition in two vols. appeared in 1887.

P. 409.—On the influence of these Manichæan sects in spreading Eastern folklore through Europe, see M. Gaster, *Greeko-Slavonic Literature*, 1887.

P. 416.—*Assemblies of Al Hariri*, translated by T. Chenery, vol. i. 1867, and Rückert's remarkable translation, *Der Verwandlungen des Abu Seid*.

INDEX

FIG. 19.

LONDON: PRINTED BY WILLIAM CLOWES AND SONS, LIMITED, STAMFORD STREET AND CHARING CROSS.

PLATE A

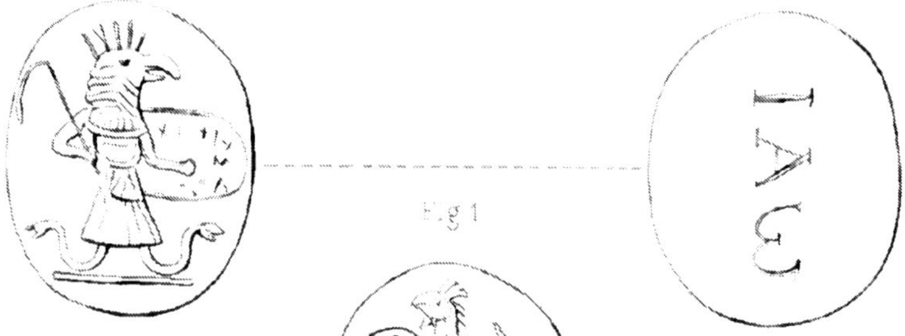

Fig. 1

Fig. 2

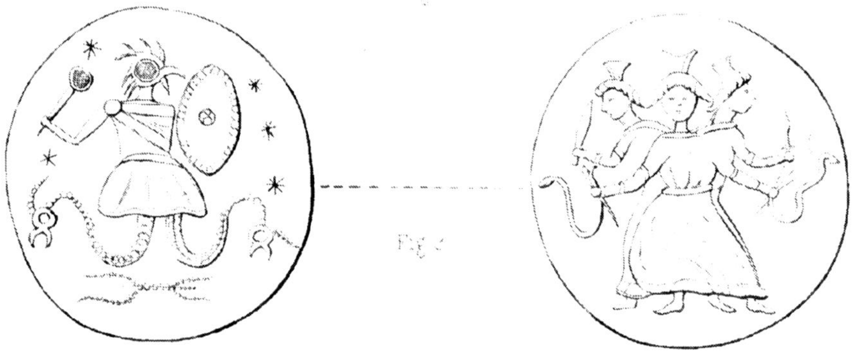

Fig. 3

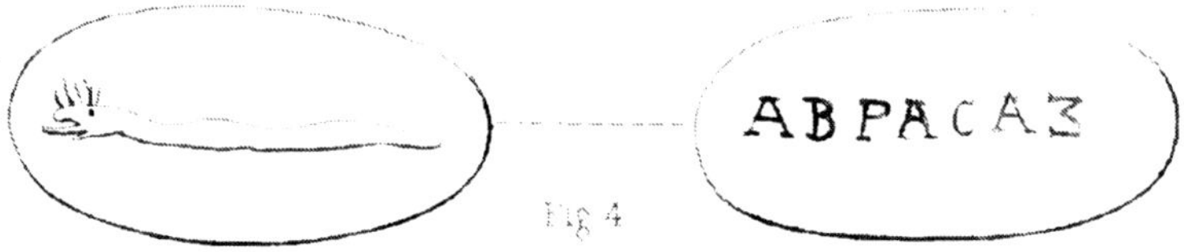

Fig. 4

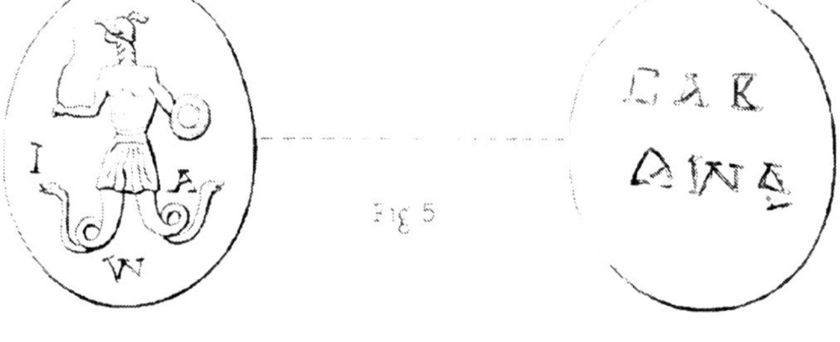

Fig. 5

ΛΥΦ
1
2
3
ΙΑ
ΑΒΡΑCΑΝ
4

ΙΑΩ

ΧΝΟΥΜΙϹ

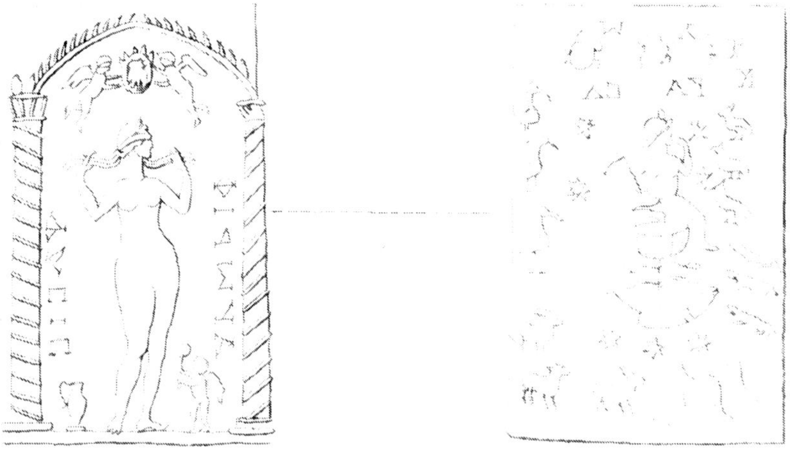

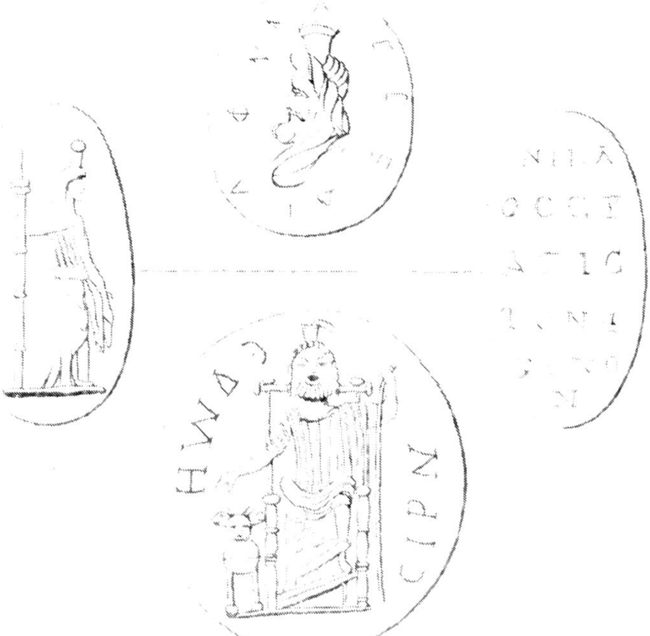

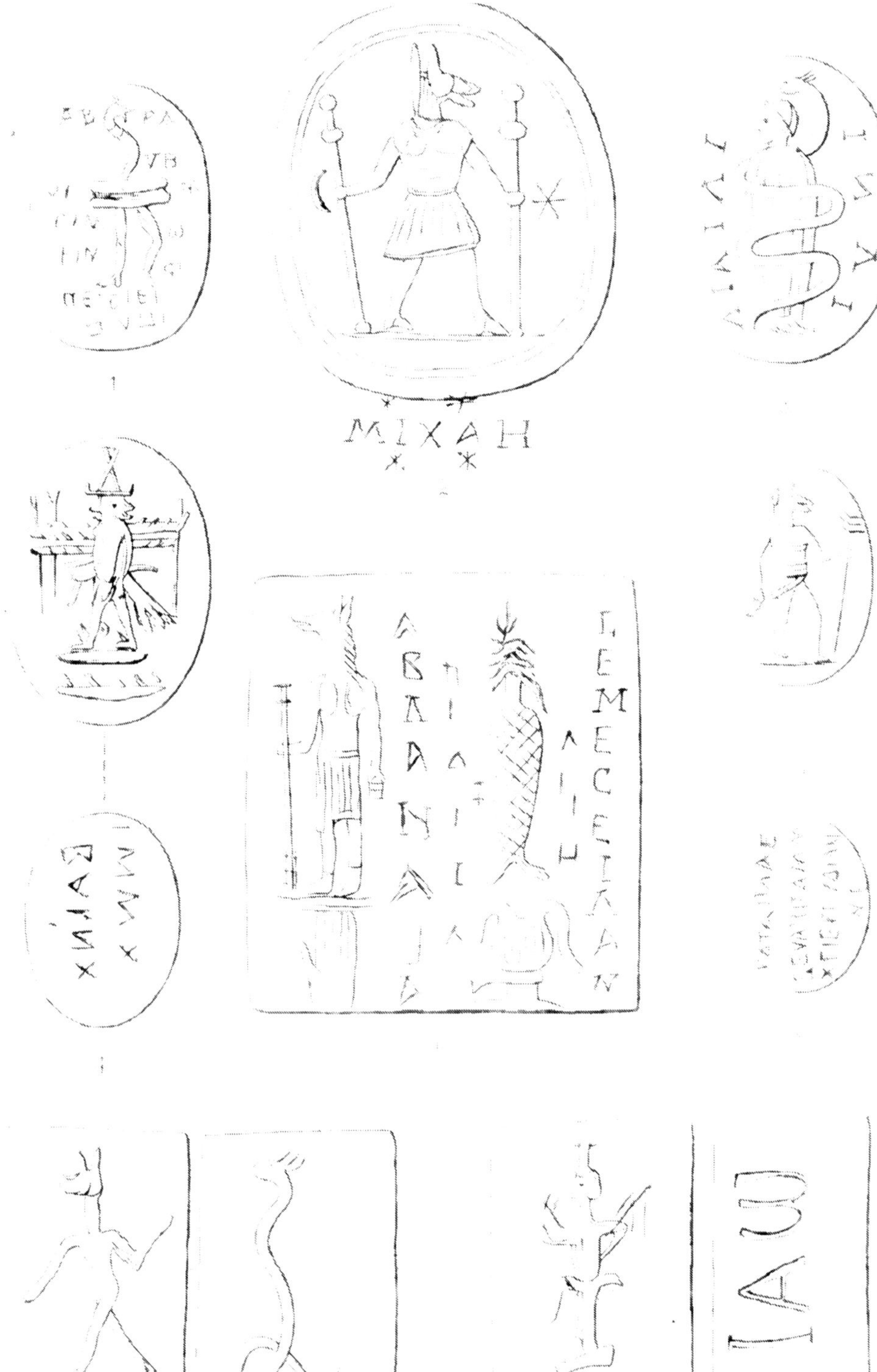
ΙΑω

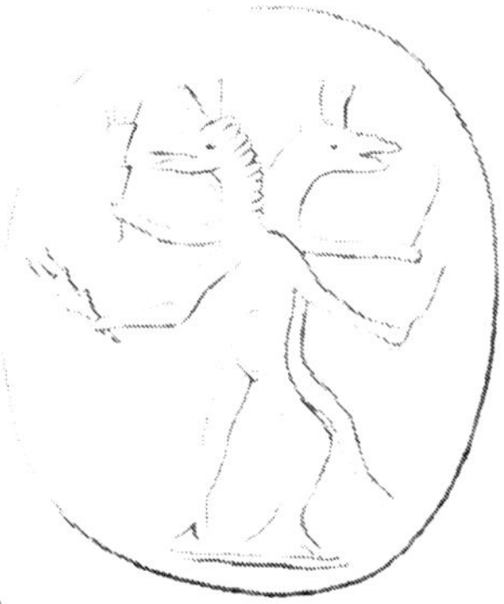

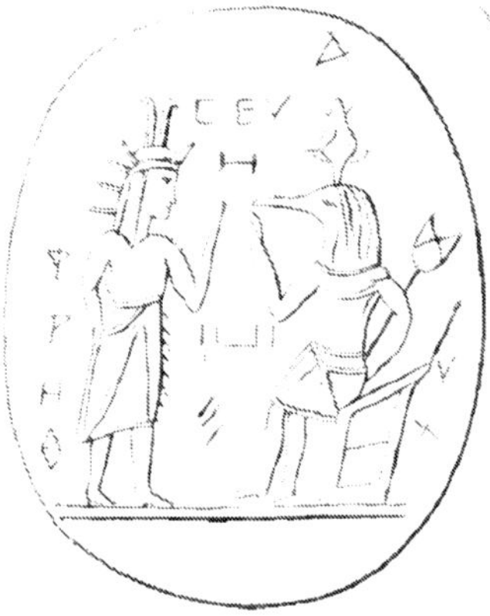

IAW

ΙΑΡΒΑΘΑ
ΓΡΑΜΝΗΦ
ΙΒΛΩΧΝ
ΗΜΕΩ

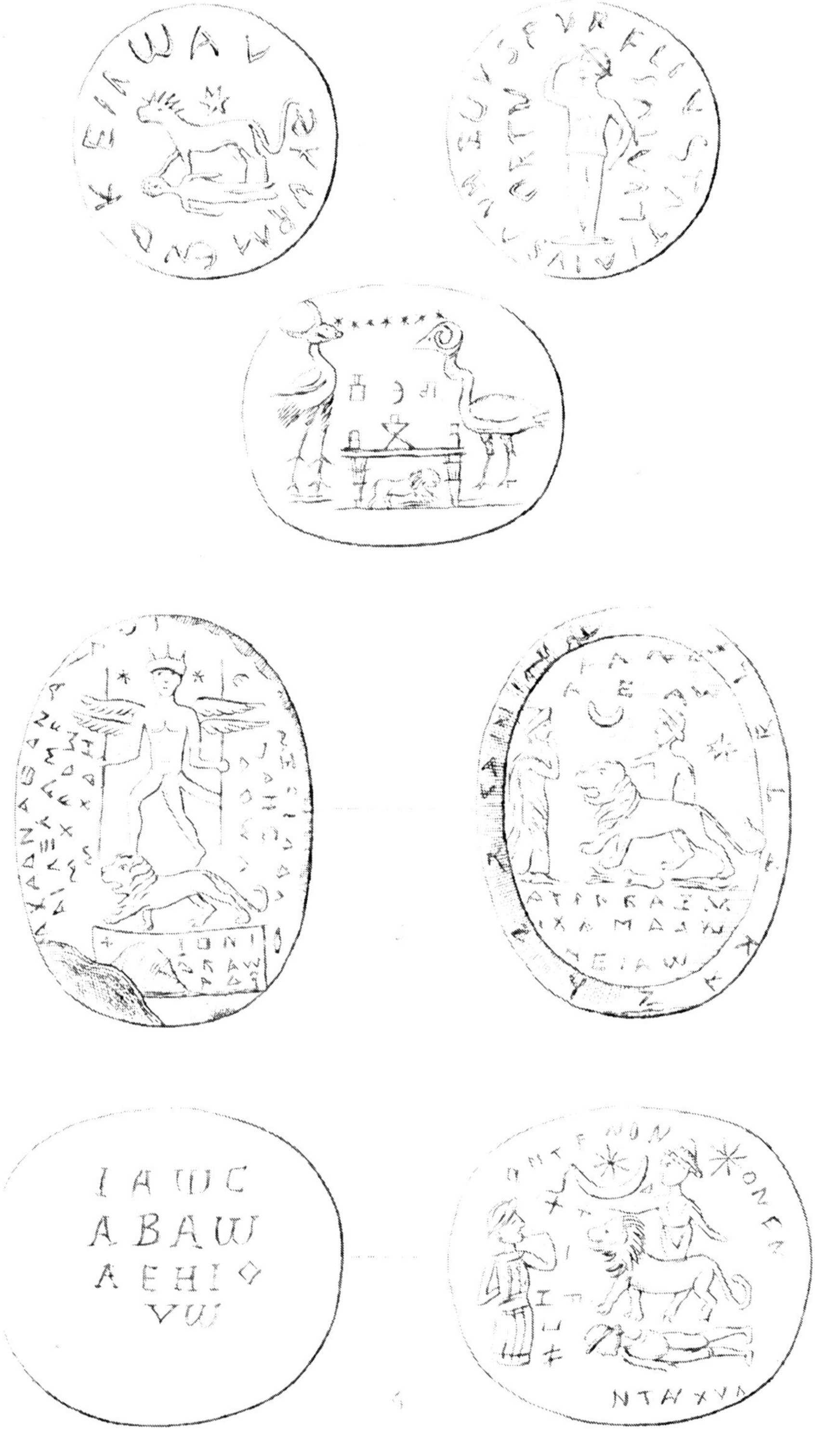
IAWC
ABAW
AEHI
VW

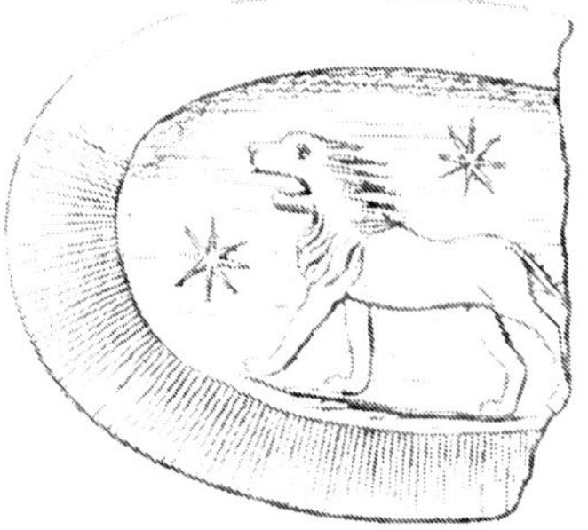

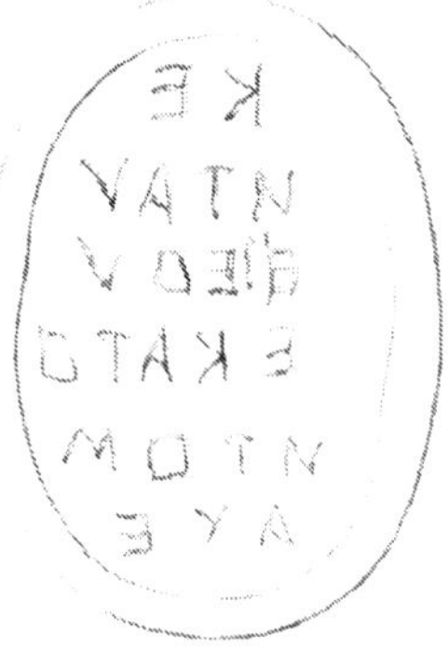

4

6

8

PLATE II

3

4

1

2

5

6

THE CAMBRIDGE SCIENTIFIC INSTRUMENT COMPANY

CPSIA information can be obtained at www.ICGtesting.com
Printed in the USA
LVOW112309070113

314712LV00012B/821/P

9 781176 649521